Demographic Analysis

Demographic Analysis

SELECTED READINGS

Edited by

JOSEPH J. SPENGLER Duke University

and

OTIS DUDLEY DUNCAN University of Chicago

THE FREE PRESS, GLENCOE, ILLINOIS

Library of Congress Catalog Card No. 56-10585

Contents

V

Acknowledgments

The editors and The Free Press acknowledge, with thanks, the permissions granted by publishers and copyright holders to reprint papers included in this volume. Specifically, acknowledgment is due the following:

The American Academy of Political and Social Science, publishers of *The Annals of the American Academy of Political and Social Science*, for permission to reprint the following articles: "Trends in Longevity," by Louis I. Dublin and Alfred J. Lotka, vol. 237 (January 1945), pp. 123-133; "Statistical Perspective on Marriage and Divorce," by Kingsley Davis, vol. 272 (November 1950), pp. 9-21; "Cultural Pluralism," by Clyde V. Kiser, vol. 262 (March 1949), pp. 117-130; "Age and Sex in Population Analysis," by Robert E. Chaddock, vol. 188 (November 1936), pp. 185-193; "Puerto Rico: A Crowded Island," by Kingsley Davis, vol. 285 (January 1953), pp. 116-122.

The American Association for the Advancement of Science, for permission to reprint "Selective Internal Migration: Some Implications for Mental Hygiene," by Dorothy Swaine Thomas, in Publication No. 9 (1939), pp. 256-262.

The American Eugenics Society, for permission to reprint "Possible Effects of Differential Fertility on Genetic Endowment," by Frederick Osborn, *Eugenical News*, vol. 37 (September 1952), pp. 47-54.

The American Geographical Society of New York, publishers of *Geographical Review*, for permission to reprint "The History of Population and Settlement in Eurasia," by Abbott Payson Usher, vol. 20 (January 1930), pp. 110-132; and "Empirical Mathematical Rules Concerning the Distribution and Equilibrium of Population," by John Q. Stewart, vol. 37 (July 1947), pp. 461-485.

The American Journal of Economics and Sociology, Inc., for permission to reprint "Population Pressure and Economic Development in Indonesia," by Justus M. van der Kroef, *American Journal of Economics and Sociology*, vol. 12 (July 1953), pp. 355-371.

The American Philosophical Society, for permission to reprint "Some Demographic Aspects of Aging," by Frank W. Notestein, *Proceedings of the American Philosophical Society*, vol. 98 (February 1954), pp. 38-45.

The American Public Health Association, for permission to reprint "Uses of the Life Table in Vital Statistics," by Louis I. Dublin and Alfred J. Lotka, *American Journal of Public Health*, vol. 27 (May 1937), pp. 481-491.

The American Sociological Society, publishers of the *American Sociological Review*, for permission to reprint the following articles: "Overseas Migration from Europe Since World War II," by Dudley Kirk and Earl Huyck, vol. 19 (August 1954), pp. 447-455; "Internal Migration in Sweden and Intervening Opportunities," by Eleanor Collins Isbell, vol. 9 (December 1944), pp. 627-639; "Negro Intelligence and Selective Migration: A Philadelphia Test of the Klineberg Hypothesis," by Everett S. Lee, vol. 16 (April 1951), pp. 227-233; "Cultural Pluralism and Linguistic Equilibrium in Switzerland," by Kurt Mayer, vol. 16 (April 1951), pp. 157-163; "The Labor Force as a Field of Interest for the Sociologist," by Philip M. Hauser, vol. 16 (August 1951), pp. 530-538; "Demographic Factors in Labor Force Growth," by S. L. Wolfbein and A. J. Jaffe, vol. 11 (August 1946), pp. 392-396; "Is the Intelligence of the General Population Declining?" by Otis Dudley Duncan, vol. 17 (August 1952), pp. 401-407.

The American Statistical Association, publishers of the *Journal of the Ameri-*

can Statistical Association, for permission to reprint the following articles: "The Population of the World in the Year 2000," by Frank W. Notestein, vol. 45 (September 1950), pp. 335-345; "Pitfalls in Population Forecasts and Projections," by Harold F. Dorn, vol. 45 (September 1950), pp. 311-334; "Fertility Trends and Differentials in the United States," by Clyde V. Kiser, vol. 47 (March 1952), pp. 25-48; "Birth Rates and the Interwar Business Cycles," by Virginia L. Galbraith and Dorothy S. Thomas, vol. 36 (December 1941), pp. 465-484; "Redistribution of Population, 1940 to 1950," by Henry S. Shryock, Jr., vol. 46 (December 1951), pp. 417-437.

The Biometrics Society, for permission to reprint "Time-Specific Life Tables Contrasted with Observed Survivorship," by Margaret Merrell, *Biometrics Bulletin,* vol. 3 (September 1947), pp. 129-136.

The Committee on Publication and Documentation of the Eighth Pacific Science Congress, for permission to reprint "Population Growth in Southeast Asia," by Irene B. Taeuber, which is appearing in the proceedings of this Congress.

The Duke University Law School, for permission to reprint "Economic Aspects of Immigration into the United States," by Joseph J. Spengler, *Law and Contemporary Problems,* vol. 21 (Spring 1956), pp. 236-255 (Copyright 1956 by Duke University).

The International Statistical Institute, publishers of the *Bulletin of the International Statistical Institute,* for permission to reprint "The World Distribution of Urbanization," by Kingsley Davis and Hilda Hertz, vol. 33 (No. 4, 1954), pp. 227-243; and "Dynamic Aspects of the Relation of Population to Economic Development," by Frank Lorimer, vol. 33 (No. 4, 1954), pp. 243-254.

The Metropolitan Life Insurance Company, publishers of *Statistical Bulletin,* for permission to reprint "A Century of Progress in Longevity," vol. 30 (October 1949), pp. 1-3.

The Middle States Association of Colleges and Secondary Schools, for permission to reprint "The Size and Quality of Future School and College Enrollments," by Dael Wolfle, *Proceedings of the 66th Annual Convention* (1952), pp. 41-47.

The Milbank Memorial Fund, for permission to reprint the following articles: "The Relation of Employment Levels to Births in Germany," by Dudley Kirk, *Milbank Memorial Fund Quarterly,* vol. 20 (April 1942), pp. 126-138; "Utilization of Human Resources through Industrialization," by Wilbert E. Moore, *Milbank Memorial Fund Quarterly,* vol. 28 (January 1950), pp. 52-67; "A Statement of General Principles and Concepts of Population Genetics," by Laurence H. Snyder, *Milbank Memorial Fund Quarterly,* vol. 25 (October 1947), pp. 367-372, and vol. 26 (July 1948), pp. 328-329; "Present Knowledge Concerning the Effects of Differential Fertility," by Harold F. Dorn, *Milbank Memorial Fund Quarterly,* vol. 25 (October 1947), pp. 359-366; "Population and Wealth in Egypt," by Charles Issawi, *Milbank Memorial Fund Quarterly,* vol. 27 (January 1949), pp. 99-113; "Demographic Glimpses into Burma, 1952," by Philip M. Hauser and Evelyn M. Kitagawa, in *The Interrelations of Demographic, Economic, and Social Problems in Selected Underdeveloped Areas* (New York, 1954), pp. 103-129; "Population Increase and Manpower Utilization in Imperial Japan," by Irene B. Taeuber, *Milbank Memorial Fund Quarterly,* vol. 28 (July 1950), pp. 273-293.

The National Council on Family Relations, publishers of *Marriage and Family Living,* for permission to reprint "The Life Cycle of the Family," by Paul C. Glick, vol. 17 (February 1955), pp. 3-9.

The New York State Joint Legislative Committee on Problems of the Aging, for permission to reprint "The Economic Effects of Changes in Age Composition," by J. J. Spengler, in *Birthdays Don't Count,* Legislative Document (1948)

No. 61, pp. 102-122 (Albany, New York).

The New York University Press, publishers of the *Journal of Economic History*, for permission to reprint "Notes on France's Response to Her Declining Rate of Population Growth," by Joseph J. Spengler, vol. 11 (Fall 1951), pp. 403-416.

The Office of Population Research, Princeton University, publishers of *Population Index*, for permission to reprint the following articles: "Recent International Differences and Trends in Expectation of Life," by George J. Stolnitz, vol. 19 (January 1953), pp. 2-10; "Recent Discussion of the Net Reproduction Rate," by George J. Stolnitz and Norman B. Ryder, vol. 15 (April 1949), pp. 114-128; "The Marriage Boom," by John Hajnal, vol. 18 (April 1953), pp. 80-101; "Preliminary Analysis of Recent Demographic Trends in Italy," by Bernardo Colombo, vol. 18 (October 1952), pp. 103-129; "The Demography of War: Germany," unsigned article, vol. 14 (October 1948), pp. 291-308.

The Population Investigation Committee, London School of Economics, publishers of *Population Studies*, for permission to reprint the following articles: "Demographic Pattern in History," by Josiah Cox Russell, vol. 1 (March 1948), pp. 388-404; "Résumé of the Indianapolis Study of Social and Psychological Factors Affecting Fertility," by Clyde V. Kiser and P. K. Whelpton, vol. 7 (November 1953), pp. 95-110; "The Development and Structure of Brazil's Population," by Giorgio Mortara, vol. 8 (November 1954), pp. 121-139; "Population Distribution and Growth in Africa," by L. T. Badenhorst, vol. 5 (July 1951), pp. 23-34.

The Rural Sociological Society, for permission to reprint "Literacy and Social Change in Underdeveloped Countries," by Hilda Hertz Golden, *Rural Sociology*, vol. 20 (March 1955), pp. 1-7.

The United Nations, for permission to reprint the following papers presented at the World Population Conference, Rome, 1954: "The Past and Future Population of the World and Its Continents," by the Population Division of the United Nations; and "Population Growth and Economic Development in the U.S.S.R.," by Warren W. Eason.

The U. S. Bureau of the Census, for permission to reprint "The Population of Communist China: 1953," *International Population Reports*, Series P-90, No. 6, March 4, 1955.

The U. S. Bureau of Labor Statistics, for permission to reprint "Changes in Working Life of Men, 1900 to 2000," by Stuart Garfinkle, *Monthly Labor Review*, vol. 78 (March 1955), pp. 297-300.

The U. S. Public Health Service, for permission to reprint "Social Class Variations in Mortality," by W. P. D. Logan, *Public Health Reports*, vol. 69 (December 1954), pp. 1217-1223.

The University of Chicago Press, publishers of the *American Journal of Sociology*, for permission to reprint "The Impact of War on Population and Vital Phenomena," by Philip M. Hauser, vol. 48 (November 1942), pp. 309-322.

The University of North Carolina Press and The Williams & Wilkins Company, publishers of *Social Forces*, for permission to reprint the following articles: "The Process of Urbanization," by Hope Tisdale (Eldridge), vol. 20 (March 1942), pp. 311-316; "Population Pressure and Other Factors Affecting Net Rural-Urban Migration," by C. Horace Hamilton, vol. 30 (December 1951), pp. 209-215; "The Field of Population Quality," by Julian L. Woodward, vol. 17 (May 1939), pp. 468-477.

The University of Toronto Press, publishers of *Canadian Journal of Economics and Political Science*, for permission to publish an excerpt from "Some Aspects of Population History," by K. W. Taylor, vol. 16 (August 1950), pp. 301-313.

The Wayne University Press, for permission to reprint "Notes on the Rate of Growth of the Chinese Population," by A. J. Jaffe, *Human Biology*, vol. 19 (February 1947), pp. 1-11.

Introduction

As construed in this volume, the term "demographic analysis" comprehends not only the statistical manipulation of population data, but more important, the study of such data as a method of solving empirical problems. The point of view differs from that of the companion volume of readings, *Population Theory and Policy,* in that, in the latter, the results of demographic analyses are more or less assumed and these results are examined for their implications for socio-economic structure and change. In the present volume the readings exemplify the work of the research demographer dealing with delimited concrete problems. Only a few of the selections are primarily methodological, though many contain points of methodological interest. To have laid primary emphasis on technique would have been to duplicate needlessly the several excellent treatises on methods of population research already published or about to appear.

The editors have not attempted to write a textbook of demographic analysis, but have supplied brief introductions to the several chapters. These provide a framework for the selected readings and, in some instances, cover important points which have not received sufficient attention in those readings.

It is contemplated that the volume may be used by itself as a relatively self-contained basis for a course in demographic analysis, in combination with the companion volume for a course emphasizing both theory and research, or as a sourcebook of outside readings in conjunction with one of the standard texts on population problems or methods of demographic research. The large number of reading selections and the diversity of the sources from which they are drawn permit the instructor a good deal of latitude in adapting the material to his own course outline. Since no single volume can cover the entire field exhaustively, supplementary bibliographies have been included. These may be useful to instructors who wish to develop a given topic more intensively, to students working on individual projects or reports, and generally to the reader who wishes to gain an overview of current research on population. The bibliography is limited largely to recent (post-World War II) literature in periodicals and symposia; it is assumed that book-length monographs and treatises are better known and more accessible than the fugitive journal literature. In the bibliography of regional analyses, however, books are listed as well, because of the limited number of journal articles which cover a given region adequately.

We want to express our thanks to the authors who generously gave permission to reprint their papers, and to absolve them of responsibility for any erroneous impressions of their work that may be conveyed by our remarks in chapter introductions. We also gratefully acknowledge the permissions to republish these selections granted by the original publishers and copyright holders.

February, 1956

Joseph J. Spengler
Otis Dudley Duncan

Demographic Analysis

Chapter I

PAST AND PROSPECTIVE GROWTH AND DISTRIBUTION OF WORLD POPULATION

The selections comprising this chapter review the past and the prospective spread of world population. Usher's paper describes the growth and spread of population in Europe and Asia between Roman and modern times. The paper by the United Nations experts summarizes the growth of world population since the seventeenth century and reveals that five principal growth patterns are to be found in the world today; it also provides estimates of future growth, while the paper by Notestein treats of the factors expected to determine future population growth. Taylor's paper contributes to our understanding of the population growth process and lends support to Malthus' interpretations. Russell's paper throws light upon a variety of medieval population movements. Dorn's paper indicates why population forecasts may go wrong and implies that a population projection should be looked upon as a growth model rather than as a predictive instrument. The role of migration in population growth is treated in Chapters IV and V.

The rate of world population growth has trended upwards through time and now is higher than ever before. As the United Nations experts suggest, information concerning the quantitative aspects of population is quite meager for pre-nineteenth century times. In Roman times the population of the world supposedly ranged between 200 and 250 millions, something like half this number perhaps having been cumulated since the period of the Trojan War. By 1000 A.D. this number had risen, perhaps to 275 millions, M. K. Bennett's estimates suggest. During the next three hundred years numbers increased somewhat less than 1/8 per cent per year to 384 millions, with Europe, where the frontier was being pushed back, experiencing an increase of somewhat over 1/6 per cent per year. The century succeeding 1300 witnessed a slight decline in world population, principally because of a reduction of one-third or more in the population of Europe occasioned by recurring visitations of the plague. During the next two centuries the population of the world and Asia, respectively, increased about 1/8 per cent per year; that of Europe, about 1/3 per cent per year. As a result of the inroads of the white man, the population of the Americas may have declined by three-fourths in 1500-1650. Since 1650 the average annual rate of growth of the world's population has gradually risen, moving from 0.29 per cent in 1650-1750 to 0.75 per cent in 1900-40 and to about 1.2 per cent at present.

This account indicates that, contrary to popular impression, population often has decreased rather than increased, and that until quite recently man's numbers have increased very slowly when they increased at all. To the decimating effect of epidemics, of which some notice has been taken, might be added the decimation effect of war, of which no notice has been taken; for on occasion war has resulted in the permanent destruction of agricultural resources on which millions have depended for livelihood. Witness what happened in once populous sectors of the Middle East and the Fertile Crescent, in northern Ceylon, and in other areas dependent on complicated irrigation and drainage systems. It is only in recent times that high rates of growth have become possible, and yet, so high or so sustained have been these rates of growth, that in many a country population already is in excess of the number compatible with the maintenance of as high a level of per capita income as might have been maintained had the population been smaller.

Concerning the mechanisms regulating population growth and the sources of increase and decrease information is limited. An increase may be brought about by an increase in natality or by a decrease in mortality; and conversely for a decrease. Prior to the present century mortality was much more volatile than natality, particularly at times when plague and famine could make tremendous inroads into populations. Variations in mortality must have been primarily responsible, therefore, for variations in the rate of population growth, the diminution of peak plague and other epidemic mortality after 1400 probably having contributed notably to the growth of Europe's population between 1400 and the eighteenth century. Such increase in the rate of population growth as took place in the eighteenth century was occasioned principally by declines in mortality. It was the continuing decline of mortality, moreover, which made possible continuation of high rates of population growth in the nineteenth century, especially in the second half when the tendency of natality to decline became more and more widespread.

In the future the course of a nation's population growth will depend largely upon its stage of demographic evolution. If a nation's population remains in that stage in which mortality is still relatively high, its growth will probably be governed by the course of mortality, since in these circumstances natality will probably trend downward. If, on the contrary, mortality is quite low already, variations in natality will dominate the rate of population growth.

Until relatively recently both mortality and natality, when they began to decline, would decline very slowly. In recent years, however, the rate at which mortality can decline in a country characterized by high mortality has proved to be high by nineteenth century standards. In some instances also the rate at which natality has declined in recent years has been above that observed before World War I. Presumably, it is now possible for the rate at which natality declines to be raised appreciably above the pre-1914 level. Whether this possibility will be realized, however, remains to be seen.

THE HISTORY OF POPULATION AND

SETTLEMENT IN EURASIA

By Abbott Payson Usher

THE study of economic geography, which has made such rapid advances in recent years, presents many questions closely related to the history of population and settlement. Vidal de la Blache was keenly aware of these contacts with history, and his last work, "Principles of Human Geography," contained much historical material. The full appreciation of certain problems of economic geography requires, however, a systematic study of the process of settlement, because the nature of social adaptations to resources must ultimately be treated as a concrete problem in the history of settlement. Many writers have believed that there were no data sufficiently trustworthy to admit of even the most general sketch of the history of settlement in Eurasia, but important work has been brought out latterly, and the larger aspects of the process of settlement can now be established. Many details are wanting; the. conclusions must be interpreted with care.: but suggestive and important results are now attainable.

Of the categories that may be applied to the process of settlement only one is a common use, "frontier," a well known term though of ill defined content. We commonly associate the term with low densities of population, irrespective of the relation of the condition of the region to a process of settlement. Semiarid steppe is incapable of supporting more than a thin nomadic or seminomadic population. Such regions are "fully" settled even when the absolute density is low. Should the term "frontier" refer to absolutely low densities or should it apply exclusively to early stages in the process of settlement? The latter use of the term seems likely to be the more significant. The other aspect of the problem is adequately met by setting up a separate classification—maturely settled regions with low densities.

In a region in process of settlement, there is a stage intermediate between anything that can be legitimately termed "frontier" settlement and the complete occupation of the country that we may describe as mature settlement. Many of the economic problems of the intermediate stage of settlement are dominated by the presence of "free," or unoccupied, land; but it would seem desirable to distinguish between frontier conditions and such intermediate problems at the stage in settlement when agriculture begins to achieve sufficient

3

adaptation to the character of the region to produce, in some portions of the settled area, well defined methods and types. The intermediate stage is concerned with the diffusion of these characteristic types over the whole area, just as the frontier stage is concerned with the development of the primary types of culture appropriate to the region.

These categories of settlement can scarcely be identified with specific density intervals, because the potentialities of different regions vary enormously. There are considerable differences in the north temperate countries of Europe and America, but still wider range in India and China. Obviously, the density of population under mature settlement is profoundly influenced by all the characteristics of the region. In so far as it is possible to establish regional types, density intervals can be given that are roughly significant in discriminating between mature and intermediate settlement. It is doubtful if any density figures for large regions can be of much significance in distinguishing the transition between frontier conditions and intermediate conditions of settlement.

Frontiers are of two types, border frontiers and included frontiers. The first of these types is most familiar today and by far the most explicit. In such regions there is a well defined boundary line between the occupied and unoccupied land and between the areas of tentative and incomplete occupation and the forms of settled agriculture characteristic of intermediate stages of settlement. This type has dominated the history of the newer countries of the nineteenth century in the United States, Canada, Australia, and some of the South American countries.

In the history of Eurasia since the beginning of the Christian era frontiers have never been of such a type. At the dawn of history there were inhabitants in practically the entire area, pursuing methods of agriculture that were not negligible. Population was sparse, agricultural technique rudimentary, and much of the best land uncleared or unoccupied. Settlement was localized for various reasons—political, military, and economic. The frontier character of settlement lay in the distances between the occupied localities and in the extensive type of exploitation predominant. Conditions in Gaul in Caesar's time are fairly representative of this phase, which probably is the typical form of the frontier throughout the history of Eurasia. The distinction between such a frontier and early stages of intermediate settlement is not sufficiently explicit to be defined with rigor. The distinction must needs be based upon the technique of agriculture rather than upon any map of settlement or any specific density figure, whether absolute or relative to the presumed density of population in the region when maturely settled. It would be tempting, for instance, to say that the transition from the frontier condition takes place when the density first exceeds one-fourth or one-third of the mature density. This would be, however, a rather arbitrary solution of a problem that does not require so specific an answer.

Maturity of settlement is indicated by stabilization of population and complete occupation of the area capable of exploitation. At this point the pressure of subsistence upon population begins to manifest itself most clearly. No further growth of population is possible under the established type of culture. The attainment of this stage, however, does not preclude further growth if technical advance signally increases the resources that may effectively be exploited. Thus, the changes occurring in Europe between 1750 and 1850 opened up new potentialities in the utilization of minerals and reorganized the mechanisms of marine and land transport upon so commanding a scale that the relation of resources to economic activity was completely transformed. Before these changes the resources effectively exploited were predominantly agricultural; forests and grazing areas constituted important adjuncts, subject to somewhat similar conditions of limitation. The utilization of minerals was restricted within a narrow field. The development of massive utilization of minerals and mineral products was revolutionary in its effect. The change is of such importance historically that one must use the term "mature settlement" in somewhat different meanings before and after it.

In India and China, at the present time, considerable areas may be properly described as maturely settled, although the full development of mineral resources would probably make possible further growth of population. Consideration of these phases of mature settlement thus shows that in this instance also the attempt to identify such a stage with specific densities of population is likely to be misleading. Although mature settlement is commonly associated with stabilization, it is not a "static" condition. The history of China, too, suggests that relative stabilization may take place during some intermediate stage in settlement.

MATERIALS FOR POPULATION STUDY

The comprehensive enumerations of population characteristic of modern statistical procedure were systematically begun only in the middle of the eighteenth century and were not general even among the principal European countries until the early part of the nineteenth century. Some enumerations of individuals were made in some of the Italian states during the sixteenth century and perhaps elsewhere in Europe, but they were confined to the bare enumeration of the population without the details of age and marital condition that distinguish the series begun in Sweden in the middle of the eighteenth century. Experience has shown the difficulty of securing high standards of accuracy even when the purpose of the enumeration is freed from all elements of political and economic bias, and it is thus with good reason that early materials on population have been treated with suspicion and even disdain.

All the early materials suffer from the elements of error that are most dreaded by the modern statistician: the enumerations include only a portion of the population, and thus the absolute figure can be computed only by using some more or less arbitrary coefficient; the enumeration, such as it is, suffers too from the undoubtedly serious intrusion of administrative interests and popular apprehension. Whether the records were to be used as a basis for military levy or as a basis of taxation, both the officials and the objects of their solicitude had interests in various kinds of inaccuracies and omissions. It must be admitted, therefore, that no early records relating to population can be regarded as an adequate basis for judgments of the absolute population. But it does not necessarily follow that these records are without importance. The broader problems in the history of population do not require minute accuracy in respect of the absolute population; we need some knowledge of the relative population of different areas, and we need some knowledge of the secular trend of the growth of population over long periods of time. Changes in the mass of population are relatively slow over long periods of time when conditions are stabilized, but profound changes may take place within a century or two during periods of active growth. Small fluctuations in population are thus of little significance during periods of stabilization, and the fact of growth is too conspicuous to be obscured even by rough approximations when notable growth occurs.

It is possible, too, to exercise no little control over early estimates of population. Figures for large areas not available in much detail can frequently be checked by details available for a portion of the area. It is thus possible to discover whether the more general figures are in fact based upon an actual enumeration of some kind or whether they are mere unsupported guesses by a person without comprehension of the meaning of numbers. Quintanilla's figures for Spain in the late fifteenth century can thus be excluded from serious consideration.[1] Many statements about population in antiquity can similarly be shown to have no serious statistical value. More important, however, are the presumptions that can be formed about densities of population upon the area in question through knowledge of well ascertained densities in areas of similar economic condition. The characteristics of irrigated regions are quite specific, and no less so the features of settlement in Mediterranean countries and in northwestern Europe. There are certain norms of expectation which constitute a rough basis for the control and interpretation of results.

---

[1] Konrad Häbler: Die wirtschaftliche Blüte Spaniens im 16. Jahrhundert und ihr Verfall. Berlin, 1888.

The elements of error in early data lead towards an estimate that is unduly low rather than towards an excessively high figure. We have, thus, partial enumerations of several classes: "families," in the sense of the members of a household; the male population of military age; the entire "adult" population; lastly, various kinds of enumerations of taxable persons. The computation of the total population from any of these partial enumerations involves evident uncertainties. The coefficients used, if chosen conservatively, will probably be too small, especially if we attempt to use the proportions of the age groups derived from modern figures. Heavy mortality in the lower age groups more than offsets the lower expectations of life among the adults. The magnitude of probable error from these sources would scarcely exceed ten per cent. The computation from the number of "families" is most uncertain, but the absolute population would scarcely be less than four nor more than five times the number of families: the use of the mean coefficient 4.5 thus leaves a possible error of ten per cent.

The probable error from omissions of persons presumed to be enumerated is of course utterly incalculable. Careful study of the full detail of the series of figures commonly throws some light on the question. Comparison of enumerations with each other is even more illuminating. When details are available it is usually possible to detect serious omissions and thus to select from the mass of material the portion which is most trustworthy. Even the best figures will inevitably contain some omissions, so that, for purpose of modern comparisons, as much as twenty per cent is frequently added to the results of direct computation from the contemporary records. Over fairly large areas the estimates from carefully selected materials will probably be, at best, within ten per cent of the absolute population.

The merits of such partial enumerations are shown best perhaps by the computations of the population of England since the Elizabethan period by John Rickman.[2] Reports of total births, deaths, and marriages were secured from the parish registers, so that the enumeration was modern though the original records were contemporary. Estimates were made upon each basis, and an average was taken of the results. The final figures constitute a series that connects with the actual census returns in 1801, with an error of about three per cent. Unless one assumes an extraordinary degree of chance in the distribution of probable errors, this series for England from 1570 to 1800 must exhibit the primary features of the trend of population in England and Wales both for the area as a whole and for the counties. For

[2] Census of Population: Great Britain, 1841. Introduction. Estimated Population of England and Wales, 1570-1750. Commons Papers, Session of 1843, Vol. 22.

There are earlier studies for the eighteenth century available in the census reports for 1811 and 1831.

relatively long periods of time such a series is of genuine value, but figures obtained by such methods would obviously be of little value for any study of the changes of population from year to year.

One of the serious hazards in the study of early materials on population is the question of the extent of the area enumerated. Whether the computation is made for some modern political area or for the contemporary area, some bridge must be found between modern surveys and the contemporary political divisions. In England and in China the older administrative divisions have survived without significant change. In France the areas of the administrative divisions of the old régime were computed when the modern statistical surveys were made in the nineteenth century under the supervision of Moreau de Jonnes. Careful study of the sixteenth century enumerations in Spain shows that the modern provinces correspond to the older administrative divisions except in old and new Castile, so that modern figures for areas can be used for a large portion of the country. The areas capable of settlement in Egypt and Mesopotamia have been computed by modern engineers. The areas of the older political divisions in other regions can be computed only by some one of the various planimetric methods. With large maps and substantial care in the demarcation of the areas to be measured, the errors would not be serious, though the figures obtained would be approximations only.

Study of population has much to gain from direct reduction of all estimates to density figures in terms of the contemporary political divisions. If the known results are then marked on the map, as much has been done as is wise. If the returns do not cover the entire area it is safer to leave blank spaces on the map or in the table than to attempt to estimate the population of the unrecorded areas by pure inference. The dangers of the latter course are illustrated in the data at hand for Italy and Spain, which disclose important displacements of population within the larger regions even when there are no significant changes in the total population. Beloch took an important step forward in recognizing the necessity of careful computation of areas, but in his work on the Middle Ages and early modern period he still remained under the influence of the older notion that a statement for the modern political divisions must be the ultimate end of such statistical studies.

Europe and the Near East at the Time of Augustus

Although some data are available for Greece and parts of Italy before the establishment of the Roman Empire it is scarcely necessary to review those materials in the present essay. The figures disclose rather notably the facts that are clearly implicit in the general history of the period. There was a steady drift of population westward, culminating in the migrations from peninsular Greece after the age of Pericles. Apart from the trading colonies in Egypt and the Levant, these migrations were the outcome of the opportunities for frontier colonization in Italy and the western Mediterranean. The settlement

TABLE I—POPULATION OF THE ROMAN EMPIRE AT DEATH OF AUGUSTUS, 14 A. D.

COUNTRY	POPULATION (In millions)	AREA (In thousands of square kilometers)	DENSITY	
			Per sq. km.	Per sq. m.
EUROPE	23	2,231	10	26
Italy	6	250	24	62.2
Sicily	0.6	26	23	59.5
Sardinia and Corsica .	0.5	33	15	39
Narbonensis	1.5	100	15	39
Three Gauls	3.4	535	6.3	16.3
Danube	2.0	430	4.7	12.2
Greece	3.0	267	11	28.6
Spain	6.	590	10	26
ASIA	19.5	665.5	30	77.5
Province of Asia . . .	6	135	44	114
Rest of Asia Minor .	7	412	17	44
Syria	6	109	55	143
Cyprus	.5	9.5	52	135
CONTINENTAL AFRICA .	11.5	443	26	67.5
Egypt	5.0	28	179	465.0
Cyrenaica	.5	15	33	85.5
Africa (Province) . .	6.0	400	15	39.0
TOTAL ROMAN EMPIRE .	54.0	3,339.5	16	41.5

of the Mediterranean littoral was not completed much before the establishment of the Roman Empire.[3] Caesar's expeditions into Gaul constitute the natural line of demarcation between the completion of an important stage in the history of the settlement of the west and the opening of a new frontier whose mature settlement was destined to occupy the next 1500 years. The computations of the population of the Empire at the death of Augustus thus afford a rough index of conditions at one of the most important periods in the history of the settlement of the western world.

　　The earlier estimates of Beloch are given in Table I.[4] The estimate

　　[3] Julius Beloch: Die Bevölkerung der griechisch-römischen Welt, Leipzig, 1886, pp. 161–222, 506.
　　[4] Beloch, op.cit., p. 507. See also his articles: Die Bevölkerung im Altertum, Zeitschr. für Social-wiss., Vol. 2, 1899, pp. 505–514; Die Bevölkerung Italiens im Altertum, Klio, Vol. 3, 1903, pp. 471–490. Seeck's criticisms and Beloch's replies appear in Jahrbücher für Nationalökonomie und Statistik, Vol. 68, 1897, pp. 161–176 and 321–343.

for Italy has been somewhat increased in a later discussion of the problem by Beloch, and some new data have become available for small areas in the Near East. In general, however, the table stands as the best estimate now possible to make. The materials used in the preparation of the table are far from being homogeneous, so that full critical discussion runs to great length. The importance of the problem would warrant a comprehensive revision of the entire table, but until that large task is completed the work of Beloch is our safest guide. The figures are doubtless the lowest that could be justified from the sources; nearly all of them could be increased without reaching results that would be at all improbable.

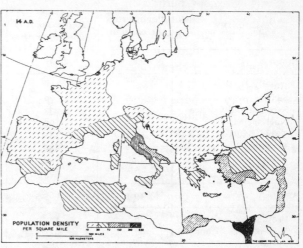

FIG. I—Population density in the Roman Empire at the beginning of the Christian era (death of Augustus, 14 A. D.).

The geographical aspects of the materials will be most readily perceived in Figure 1, which, except for Italy and Greece, is based directly upon the data presented in the table. Upon the basis of the enumeration of towns and villages for the twelve regions of Italy, an attempt has been made to distinguish between the gradations of density in the peninsula. The results are sufficiently consistent with earlier returns to be highly probable, and it is important to recognize that the settlement of the Po Valley had not proceeded very far. Population was still massed in central Italy in Latium and Campania, which were undoubtedly more densely peopled than in the early modern period. Such high densities of settlement upon really small areas probably account for the gross exaggerations of the total population of the ancient world common at one time. Similarly, a figure for peninsular Greece has been computed in order to correct the impression that would be derived from the table, which combines peninsular Greece with extensive frontier regions in Macedonia and Epirus.

The general aspect of the map shows that the major portions of the eastern and central Mediterranean littoral were maturely settled. There were important exceptions in the western Mediterranean in what is now Morocco, Spain, southern France, and the Po Valley;

also in Macedonia and Thessaly. Extensive regions were thus open to settlement both in essentially Mediterranean regions and in northwestern Europe. These opportunities resulted in notable changes in the massing of the population of the Empire during the next three centuries, and it is much to be regretted that we have no adequate study of conditions in Roman Gaul for any date in the later Empire.

The figures for the eastern provinces of the Empire present serious difficulties except perhaps in Egypt, for which a fairly good figure is available.[5] It seems clear that the Near East was at least as densely settled as at the close of the nineteenth century; but it is doubtful that the total population of the Near East, as some writers believe, was much greater then than in modern times. Probably the beginning of the Christian era was a period of medium prosperity for the region, and we may perhaps assume that the mass of population was neither the maximum achieved at any time since nor the minimum. In that event there is much essential truth in the conclusion that the population of the Near East and also the Middle East had already become stabilized—ceasing to show any clear growth, though fluctuating somewhat widely around a mean. Such a notion of conditions must obviously not preclude considerable redistributions within the area; notably in Mesopotamia, Persia, and what is now Russian Turkestan and Bukhara.

Western Europe in the Fourteenth Century

After the death of Augustus we find no material for a general study of population in Europe until the first half of the fourteenth century. There are local figures which afford a thin basis for some inferences, but at present there is no material of outstanding significance. For the period immediately preceding the Black Death, in the midcentury, there is fairly good material for England and France.[6] We have a good figure for Brabant in 1374.[7] The other figures are not very adequately supported, though important sections of Italy are well represented. The returns indicate that France had reached a density of population about equal to the modern density. The population in 1340 must have been closely comparable to the population of 1800; and, as growth has been slow during the nineteenth century, the differences are not large even at the present time. The Po Valley had also reached a substantial density of population, though

---

[5] Beloch's work is notably supplemented by Eugène Cavaignac: Population et capital dans le monde Méditerranéen antique (Publs. Faculté des Lettres de l'Univ. de Strasbourg, fasc. 18), Paris, 1923.

[6] A. P. Usher: An Introduction to the Industrial History of England, Boston, 1920, pp. 92–97.
A. J. C. A. Dureau de la Malle: L'État des paroisses et feux des baillages et sénéchaussées de France (1328), Bibliothèque de l'École des Chartes, Vol. 2, 1840–41, p. 170.
Pierre Émile Levasseur: La population française (3 vols., Paris, 1889–1892), Vol. 1, pp. 152–175.
[7] Joseph Cuvelier: Les dénombrements de foyers en Brabant (XIVe–XVIe siècle), Brussels, 1912, pp. ix–xcii.

considerable growth continued to take place in that region. England and Germany were still thinly settled; and, despite vicissitudes, growth was continuing in both areas.

The most important single figure for this date is therefore the figure for France, which definitely marks the completion of a notable stage in the settlement of Europe. Fortunately, this is one of the best documented figures for the period. The material used is an

TABLE II—POPULATION OF WESTERN EUROPE, 1340

COUNTRY	COMPUTED POPULATION	DENSITY PER SQUARE MILE
England	[2,225,000]	43
Germany	. . . .	[43]
Brabant (1374)	. . . .	91
France	21,000,000	103
Spain	[6,000,000]	[25]
Catalonia (1378)	450,000	32
Aragon (1404)	250,000	13
Italy	[10,500,000]	. . .
March of Ancona (c. 1325)	. . . .	151
Romagna (1378)	. . . .	78
Tuscany (1338)	. . . .	220
Naples (1447)	. . . .	52

enumeration of about one-third the area of France in connection with the organization of the expedition against Flanders. These materials were first published in detail by Moreau de Jonnes. Levasseur went over the entire problem with great care, and his judgment was subsequently confirmed by corroborative evidence discovered by Boislisle. Although the material is not a desirable basis for an estimate of the absolute population, the general statement that the density was closely comparable to that of 1800 is hardly open to doubt. We may say, therefore, that the mean density of population in France in 1340 was *about* 100 per square mile. For the broad purposes of a general sketch of the history of population such a statement is wholly adequate.

The figures for Brabant, Aragon, Catalonia, and parts of Italy are for the close of the fourteenth century. It is commonly supposed that the ravages of the Black Death were not offset before the close of the century, so that it is fairly conservative to assume that there was not a large difference between the population of these districts at the two dates. Many writers hold that population was greater in most parts of Europe before the Black Death than at any date thereafter during that century, but this seems to be a rather extreme proposition. Study of the subsidy rolls in England indicates that population was probably smaller in 1340 than in 1377. In countries

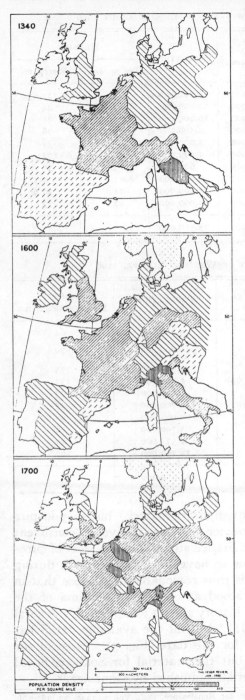

that were more maturely settled the recovery from losses may not have been as rapid. The inferences drawn by Beloch from available material are given in Table II,[8] as well as the details for portions of Spain and Italy. The relative densities are also shown on Figure 2.

It is unfortunate that the material for Italy is so scanty. Beloch feels fairly certain that the central portions were more densely settled than either the Po Valley or the southern portions of the peninsula. Although the figure for Ancona is almost exactly on the border line between two grades of shading, the map has been shaded on the basis of its inclusion in the upper group. The impression given by the map is probably correct, but this undoubtedly important section is not very adequately documented.

SEVENTEENTH AND EIGHTEENTH CENTURY FIGURES FOR WESTERN EUROPE

At the close of the seventeenth century material is more abundant and better in quality. That for England, Italy, Spain, the low countries, and portions of Germany is very good indeed. The figure for France is hardly more than an unsupported contemporary estimate upon an ultraconservative basis. Estimates of a more opti-

---

[8] Julius Beloch: Die Bevölkerung Europas im Mittelalter, *Zeitschr. für Socialwiss.*, Vol. 3, 1900, pp. 405–423.

TABLE III—POPULATION OF WESTERN EUROPE ABOUT 1600

COUNTRY	AREA (In sq. km.)	POPULATION	DENSITY	
			Per sq. km.	Per sq. m.
Italy	295,000	13,000,000	44	114
Spain and Portugal	585,000	10,000,000	17	44
France	470,000	16,000,000	34	88
England and Wales	150,000	4,500,000	30	78
Scotland and Ireland	160,000	2,000,000	12.5	32
Netherlands . . . . : .	75,000	3,000,000	40	104
Denmark	40,000	600,000	15	39
Sweden, Norway, Finland . .	1,080,000	1,400,000	1.3	2.5
Poland and Prussia	210,000	3,000,000	14	36.9
Germany	720,000	20,000,000	28	73
Total	3,785,000	73,500,000		

TABLE IV—POPULATION OF WESTERN EUROPE, 1700

COUNTRY	MODERN AREA (In sq. m.)	POPULATION	DENSITY PER SQUARE MILE
United Kingdom . . .	121,600	7,700,000	64
Austria	115,882	{ 16,800,000	70
Hungary	125,609		
Germany	208,054	15,500,000	75
Belgium	11,373	1,550,000	137
Holland	12,648	1,175,000	98
Denmark	15,582	700,000	45
France	207,054	20,000,000	95
Spain	194,783	5,700,000	29
Portugal	35,490	1,575,000	45
Italy	110,550	11,250,000	102
	1,158,625	81,950,000	

mistic type are encountered in contemporary material, but they inspire no confidence. The figure of Froumenteau that is given is consistent with the general impression that France stood at a low level of prosperity at that date. There seems to have been some growth during the seventeenth century, and it is thus reasonable to suppose that in 1600 the population of France stood at one of the minima of the fluctuations that characterize its history since 1300. Beloch's general conclusions are given in Table III,[9] but all the available detail has been used in preparing the map for this date (Fig. 3). Most of the material is taken from Beloch, but the material for Spain is based upon a special study of the materials published by Gonzalez.[10]

[9] *Idem:* Die Bevölkerung Europas zur Zeit der Renaissance, *ibid.*, Vol. 3, 1900, pp. 765–786; reference on p. 783.
[10] [Tomas Gonzalez]: Censo de población de las provincias y partidos de la corona de Castilla en el siglo XVI, Madrid, 1829.

For 1700 the studies of Beloch are supplemented by the work of Dieterici, which is especially important for central Europe.[11] Table IV gives the best estimate that can be made for the larger political areas, but Figure 4 has been prepared from somewhat more detailed statistics for all the primary countries. For Spain no details are available until 1768. It is especially important to note the relative uniformity of the density of population despite the fact that returns have been computed for counties in England, for generalities in France, and for the more important independent states and provinces of Germany and Italy. Before the massive development of mineral resources that characterizes the Industrial Revolution the tendency was clearly towards a relatively uniform density of population over wide areas. The areas of significant concentration were small, and the areas of low density are obviously regions ill adapted to agriculture by reason of one or more deficiencies.

POPULATION FIGURES FOR CHINA

Materials for the study of the population of China are more abundant than for Europe or any single European country, and the difficulties of interpretation are not greater. There are problems which for many years led people to presume that the figures were utterly unreliable, but recent studies have provided solutions with adequate documentation. The returns were used as a basis for taxation, and the unit of enumeration has commonly been presumed to be the family. But some enumeration of individuals (mouths) was made as part of the return, and at some periods the return of "mouths" is held to be more trustworthy than that of families. The bias likely to develop from the system of taxation is minimized by the return of both taxable and nontaxable persons. The periods of greatest difficulty are the Sung and early Tsing dynasties (Table V). In the Sung period, the basis of enumeration of "mouths" was changed, and males alone were included.[12] In the early reigns of the Tsing Dynasty only males of military age (16–60) were recorded.[13] When adjustments have been made for these divergences of practice, the series of returns becomes essentially self-consistent and conforms to the expectations created by the history of the country.

---

[11] K. F. W. Dieterici: Über die Vermehrung der Bevölkerung in Europa seit dem Ende oder der Mitte des siebenzehnten Jahrhunderts, *Abhandl. Königl. Akad. der Wiss. zu Berlin*, 1850, Phil.-hist. Kl., pp. 73–115.

Häbler, *op. cit.*, Exkurs I.

Julius Beloch: La popolazione d'Italia, nei secoli XVI, XVII e XVIII, *Bull. Inst. Internatl. de Statistique*, Vol. 3, Part I, 1888, pp. 1–42.

[12] Lionel Giles: A Census of Tun-Huang, *T'oung Pao*, Vol. 16, 1915, pp. 468–488.

[13] Chang-heng Chen: Changes in the Growth of China's Population in the Last 182 Years, *Chinese Econ. Journ.*, Vol. 1, 1927, pp. 59–69.

Han Liang Huang: The Land Tax in China, New York, 1918 (Columbia Univ. Studies in Hist., Econ., and Public Law, Vol. 80, No. 3), pp. 96–97.

TABLE V—POPULATION OF CHINA

YEAR	DYNASTY	NUMBERS OF PERSONS (in millions)	
		RETURNED IN CENSUS	PROBABLE TOTAL
2	Han	59.5	71.0‖
156	Han	50.0	60.0
606	Lang	46.0	55.0
733	Lang	45.4	54.0
754	Lang	52.9	63.5
1080	Sung	33.3*	79.0
1260	Yuen	53.6	65.0
1290	Yuen	58.8	70.5
1381	Ming	60.5	72.5
1393	Ming	58.6	70.1
1491	Ming	56.0	66.0
1578	Ming	63.5	75.0
1661	Tsing	21.0†	105.0
1690	Tsing	20.3	101.5
1710	Tsing	23.3	116.5
1749	Tsing	177.4	177.4
1780	Tsing	276.6	276.6
1812	Tsing	360.4	360.4
1842	Tsing	413.0	413.0
1860	Tsing	260.0‡	?
1885	Tsing	377.6§	377.6
1923	Tsing	414.0	414.0

*" Mouths " in Sung enumerations refers to males only.
†" Mouths " in early Tsing enumerations refers to males between 16 and 60.
‡This low figure is commonly attributed to the devastations of the Tai Ping rebellion, but the enumeration is probably seriously defective.
§The province of Kansu is included for the first time.
‖Increased by 20 per cent to allow for omissions.

These enumerations include the area that is now comprised in seventeen of the eighteen provinces of China proper. The border province of Kansu was under Chinese control for most of the period, but until the close of the nineteenth century it was administered as part of the dependent territory of Chinese Turkestan, and there are clearly some errors in the figures attributed to this area in the tables.

The record is notable for the relative stability of population at a figure that for this region is really low. Without analysis of details and in the light of the economic history of the times, it would be rash to hazard any conjecture as to the basis of this relative stabilization at less than one-fifth the population capable of being supported in the area without any conspicuous change in the technique of agriculture and industry. It is equally difficult to explain the timing

TABLE VI—ESTIMATED POPULATION OF THE PROVINCES OF CHINA*

(*In thousands*)

PROVINCE	AREA (In thousands of sq. m.)	1393	1491	1578	1749	1780	1812	1842	1885	1923
Chili	115.8	....	[4,130]†	[5,100]	13,933	21,529	27,990	36,879	17,900	34,186
Shansi	81.8	4,890	5,230	6,370	9,509	12,864	14,440	17,056	10,800	11,080
Shantung	55.9	6,330	8,100	6,800	24,011	21,763	28,958	29,529	36,500	30,803
Honan	67.9	2,299	5,230	6,200	12,847	20,275	23,037	29,069	22,100	30,831
Hunen { Hu-	83.3	5,640	4,500	5,250	8,672	15,423	18,652	20,048	21,000	28,443
Hupeh { Kuang	71.4				7,527	16,021	27,370	28,584	33,600	27,167
Shensi	75.2	2,795	4,680	5,410	6,734	8,237	10,207	10,309	3,300	9,465
Szechwan	218.5‖	1,730	3,103	3,720	2,506	7,947	21,435	22,256	71,000	49,782
Kansu‡	125.4	....	....	......	5,709	[15,136]	[15,354]	[19,512]	5,400	5,927
Kiang Su§	38.6	[12,900]	[9,560]	[12,520]	20,972	29,495	37,843	39,646	21,300	33,786
Anhwei§	54.8				21,567	28,085	34,165	36,596	20,600	19,832
Chekiang	36.6	12,520	6,370	6,200	11,877	20,494	26,256	30,437	11,700	22,043
Kiangsi	69.4	10,780	7,820	6,930	8,428	18,049	23,046	26,513	24,500	24,446
Kweichou	67.1	....	309	348	3,075	5,081	5,288	5,679	7,700	11,114
Fukien	46.3	4,700	3,720	2,062	7,620	11,980	14,779	25,799	23,500	13,157
Kwangtung	100.0	3,602	2,180	6,040	6,460	15,211	19,174	21,152	29,700	37,167
Kwangsi	77.2	1,770	2,020	1,420	3,687	5,749	7,313	8,121	5,100	12,258
Yunnan	146.7	310	150	1,740	1,946	3,201	5,561	5,823	11,700	9,839
Total 17 Provinces**	1,407.0	[70,266]	[67,102]	[76,110]	171,371	261,440	345,514	393,486	372,000	405,399
Total 18 Provinces	1,532.4				177,080	276,576	360,868	413,008	377,400	411,326

*The figures for 1393, 1491, 1578 represent the recorded persons plus 20 per cent; thereafter the recorded persons.
†Part only. Metropolitan district and some outlying areas.
‡Until 1882, part of Sinkiang (Chinese Turkestan). Figures in brackets are probably for the entire province.
§Boundaries somewhat variable.
‖Includes late addition from Tibet.
**Excluding Kansu.

of the rapid growth from the beginning of the Tsing Dynasty, which is in fact closely comparable with the growth of population in England during the period 1750–1900. Relative stabilization since 1840 and the difficulties of interpreting the early Tsing records have obscured the primary features of this notable period of expansion.

TABLE VII—DENSITY OF POPULATION OF THE PROVINCES OF CHINA

(*Per square mile*)

PROVINCE	1393	1578	1749	1780	1812	1842	1923
Chili	..	..	120	187	244	318	295
Shansi	60	78	117	158	177	210	134
Shantung	114	121	435	390	520	530	552
Honan	34	92	188	300	342	430	454
Hunan { Hu-	36	34	104	185	223	241	341
Hupeh { Kuang . .			106	225	387	400	380
Shensi	36	72	89	112	136	137	125
Szechwan*	7.9	17	11	37	98	102	228
Kansu†	..	..	45	[120]	[122]	[156]	47
Kiangsu	..	..	545	765	980	1002	875
Anhwei	[240 +]	[230 +]	392	513	621	670	362
Chekiang	344	170	324	562	715	830	601
Kiangsi	156	100	121	261	334	383	352
Kweichow	...	5	46	76	78	84	167
Fukien	102	44	165	258	318	555	284
Kwangtung . . .	36	60	64	152	191	211	372
Kwangsi	22	18	47	73	95	105	159
Yunnan	2.1	11	13	22	38	40	67
17 Provinces‡ . . .	[50]	[54]	122	185	246	274	390

*The Ch'engtu plain, of about 2100 square miles, contains one-tenth of the modern population.
†Until 1882, part of Sinkiang (Chinese Turkestan). Figures in brackets are probably for the entire province.
‡Excluding Kansu.

The growth of this period is as difficult to understand as the earlier stabilization, though various factors may readily be suggested. Miss Lee's study of Chinese agriculture[14] discloses a great increase in the cultivated area during the period of rapid growth in the eighteenth century. Table V gives returns for selected years since the full achievement of power by the Han Dynasty, but this represents only a small fraction of the material available in Chinese.[15]

Returns for the provinces are available in European languages from the beginnings of the Ming Dynasty, and, as the administrative geography of China offers serious problems before that date, these

[14] Mabel Ping-hua Lee: The Economic History of China (Columbia Univ. Studies in Hist., Econ. and Public Law, Vol. 99, No. 1), New York, 1921, Table at p. 436.
[15] T. Sacharoff (Zakharov): The Numerical Relations of the Population of China . . . or The Rise and Fall of the Chinese Population, transl. by W. Lobscheid, Hongkong, 1864, pp. 53–54. Many of these data are also given by Miss Lee, *op. cit.* Data for the recent period are taken from The China Year Book, 1926–1927, pp. 2–3.

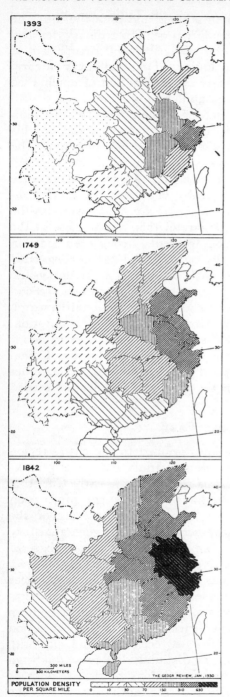

FIGS. 5 to 7—Population density of China by provinces in 1393, 1749, and 1842 respectively. Compare Tables VI and VII.

returns afford whatever data are easily available at present, irrespective of linguistic problems. The statistical material is given in Tables VI and VII.[16] The significance of the data, however, will be most readily seen in the series of maps (Figs. 5, 6, 7). The provinces of the southwest present many palpable elements of frontier conditions, though in part at least they had long been settled. The general densities of the great central plain are also surprisingly low, so low that one must presume the existence of substantial areas that were not taken effectively into cultivation. The areas of the provinces are relatively large, and few of them are really homogeneous. The provincial figures are therefore scarcely adequate to afford a complete description of the characteristic features of settlement. Have we to do with localized concentrations at relatively high densities or a widely diffused population at the low densities indicated for the total area of each province? One is inclined to believe that the former type of settlement is the more common; but there is really no certainty. It is evident from travelers' accounts and from modern studies that general provincial figures are hardly significant for the large province of Szechwan on the frontier of

[16] W. W. Rockhill: An Inquiry into the Population of China, *Ann. Rept. Smithsonian Instn. for 1904*, p. 662.

T. Sacharoff, *op. cit.*, p. 55.

The China Year Book 1926–1927, p. 3.

Some additions have been made to the earlier figures.

Tibet.   Part of the province is mountainous and unfertile, but the Ch'eng-tu plain carries today a population of extraordinary density. We may be certain that the character of agricultural occupation of this great plain is of considerable antiquity.   Followed out with care, the case of this province might lead to an explanation of much that is now obscure in the history of the population of China.

The uncertainties present in estimates of the population of China since 1885 illustrate perfectly the inadequacy of material of this character for studies of population over short periods of time.   The probable error exceeds by a large measure any possible increase per year or even per decade, so that for such purposes the returns cease to have any serious value.   We are really unable to feel much conviction about details after 1842.   The figure for that year may be too large, but census work was more careful than at the close of the century.   Professor Walter F. Willcox presents strong arguments in favor of the position that the population of China has not exceeded 320,000,000, either in the midnineteenth century or in recent years. His most recent discussion of the problem will appear in the second volume of Migration Statistics to be issued by the National Research Council.[17]   It is not intended to call these conclusions in question, but in view of the uncertainties of the data it seemed best to adopt the maximum possible estimate throughout the tables for China. In the present article only the general trend is emphasized together with the broader contrasts between the more and less densely settled provinces.

THE MIDDLE EAST

The term Middle East is sometimes applied to the entire region east of Syria and Armenia to the borders of India and eastern Turkestan.   Despite the importance of this region in the early Christian era and during the Middle Ages, we have no statistical information about the population.   Conditions in the Middle East are of the utmost importance in any concepts we may form of the general history of settlement, and consequently before entering upon that phase of our subject some attention must be given to the problems of this area.

The vagueness of information has given rise to wide divergences of opinion extending down to the present time, because no enumerations have been made in the area even in recent years.   We know from historical sources that the latter nineteenth century was not a period of great prosperity: for various reasons, economic and political, general conditions must be regarded as distinctly less favorable than at various times in the past.   The descriptions in the writings of the Arab geographers indicate clearly that the tenth century was the

---

[17] See also his paper "The Population of China in 1910," *Bull. Inst. Internatl. de Statistique*, Vol. 23, Part II, 1928, pp. 347–361, and *Journ. Amer. Statist. Assn.*, Vol. 23, 1928, pp. 18–30.

period of greatest prosperity during the Caliphate, and later historians indicate the sixteenth and seventeenth centuries as periods of prosperity in Persia.

We have also the means of establishing the dates of the primary changes in the rivers and irrigation works in Mesopotamia. The first break with the hydrographic system of antiquity occurred as the result of floods in the fifth century of the Christian era. The Tigris overflowed its banks in its lower course and joined the Euphrates in forming a swamp above Basra. This damage was partially repaired, but greater floods in 629 A. D. opened up the new channel again, and the Great Swamp became a permanent feature of the basin. Its extent was perhaps somewhat diminished when the Tigris returned to its older course early in the sixteenth century. These changes reduced the cultivated area of the lower basin both by the enforced abandonment of the land on the old course of the Tigris and by the flooding of a considerable area between Basra and Kufa. At the close of the twelfth century there were further losses through the silting up of the Nahrawan canal, east of Baghdad.[18] This great irrigation work became a complete ruin in the course of the next century, partly through neglect, partly because of changes in the régime of the river that increased the difficulty of maintaining the works. In Mesopotamia economic conditions must have been relatively less favorable after the seventh century; but these local difficulties did not prevent the region as a whole from attaining notable prosperity in the tenth century.

The general features of the economic development of these regions of the Middle East were fixed at an early date. Settled agriculture was restricted to the river valleys, and the larger areas were dependent upon some measure of irrigation. Rainfall was supplemented by using the underground seepage from the mountains.[19] The outstanding features of this general system were definitely established long before the beginning of the Christian era, but we have no means of knowing the area to which this technique was applied. Some writers assume that Persia had a population of fifty millions in the time of Darius; even if we disregard the question of numbers, this is certainly the earliest date that can be given for a full settlement of the region, and it would be more conservative to assume that the full settlement of the region did not take place until later, either under the Selucid Dynasty (311–129 B. C.), or at the latest under the Sassanid Dynasty (229–628 A. D.). We may assume, then, that while there have been fluctuations there has been no real growth of population in this area since the early part of the Christian era or perhaps earlier.

The Middle East undoubtedly presents special features in respect

---

[18] Guy Le Strange: The Lands of the Eastern Caliphate, Cambridge, 1905, pp. 25–30.
[19] Compare "Irrigation Systems of Persia," by C. B. Fisher, Geogr. Rev., Vol. 18, 1928, pp. 302–306.

to the distribution of the population over the total area. The major portion is concentrated in relatively large towns, surrounded by villages of considerable size. The village population lives under conditions sensibly different from the dispersed rural population of the north temperate zone, and the proportion of the population living under positively urban conditions is high. According to General A. H. Schindler the population of Persia in 1884 was distributed as follows:[20]

	PERSONS	PER CENT
99 towns	1,963,800	25.6
Villages	3,780,000	49.5
Nomads	1,909,800	24.9
	7,653,600	100.0

These totals are possibly somewhat low, but the proportions are suggestive of the profound differences in the type of settlement. Such a proportion of urban population was not achieved in Europe until the railroad had exerted a significant influence upon the distribution of the population. The town was the basic feature of social life in the Near and Middle East. The characteristic features may be studied in the large-scale maps of Bukhara and Samarkand. The general appearance of these districts must be much as it was in the tenth century when described by the Arab geographers. These high concentrations on relatively small areas are likely to lead us to overestimate the total population. It would probably be possible to prepare significant maps of settlement for the period of the Caliphate as the habitable areas can be tolerably well identified in the Arabic sources.

THE PROBLEM IN INDIA

India presents a very difficult problem, but recent studies by W. H. Moreland[21] throw much light upon conditions during the sixteenth century. Analysis of the military forces put in the field in the south in 1522 leads to the conclusion that the south contained about one-half the population of 1911—in all about 30 millions. For the important region of the valley of the Ganges no means exists for a direct estimate of numbers of persons, but during the reign of Akbar accounts of the cultivated area were gathered which yield important results to careful study. In the northwestern portion of the United Provinces and in the eastern section of the Punjab the cultivated area amounted to about three-fourths the standard of 1911. This stretch extended from Lahore to Agra, including especially the region between the Ganges and the Jumna. Easterly from Agra

---

[20] George N. Curzon: Persia and the Persian Question (2 vols., London, 1892), Vol. 2, p. 493.
[21] W. H. Moreland: India at the Death of Akbar: An Economic Study, London, 1920, pp. 16–22.

the standard of cultivation declined steadily until at Allahabad the proportion fell to about one-fifth the standard of 1911. This low standard of cultivation continued thence down the valley almost through Bihar. Bengal is known to have been populous, but we have no record of the relative density; and lack of data makes it similarly impossible to form any estimate for Gujarat. These inferences are expressed in graphic form in Figure 8. The practical identity of agricultural methods makes it possible to draw inferences about population from these records of the cultivated area. Moreland concludes:

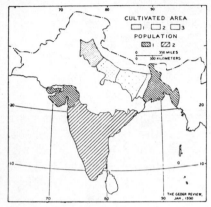

FIG. 8—India in the sixteenth century. Stipple shows extent of area cultivated in 1600 in relation to modern area: 1, over 75 per cent; 2, 20 to 75 per cent; 3, less than 20 per cent. Ruling shows: 1, populous areas of unknown density; 2, area with 50 per cent of population of 1911.

If now we apply these conclusions to the figures of the last census, we shall find that the population of the northern plains from Multan to Monghyr must have been well over 30 millions and probably little less than 40 millions at the period to which the statistics relate. We have thus a total of at any rate more than 60 millions in sight for the northern and southern areas taken together, but without allowing anything for two populous regions, Bengal and Gugarat, or for any part of the more sparsely populated but extensive intervening area; and, when we bring these excluded tracts into account, we are justified in concluding that there must have been at the least somewhere about 100 millions of people in India in order to carry on the activities disclosed by contemporary authorities. The number is absolutely very great and would have appeared almost incredible to European observers of the period, but it is only one-third of what the same area contained in the year 1911; various arguments could be adduced for a higher figure, but the nature of the data compels us to be content with indefinite estimates, and it appears to me that we shall run no risk of serious error if we take 100 millions as indicating a total, not indeed attained by careful enumeration but rendered probable by a consideration of all the relevant facts which are available.

MAPS OF SETTLEMENT STAGES

Although many problems demand further investigation and more extended critical discussion than is possible in this paper, it has seemed desirable to prepare a series of maps which represent concretely a conservative view of the stages of settlement at the three critical dates 14 A. D., 1340, and 1600 (Figs. 9–11).

The general features of these maps are obvious. None of the centers of massive modern population was maturely settled at the beginning of the Christian era. Northwestern Europe may be confidently classed as a frontier. India and China were in early phases

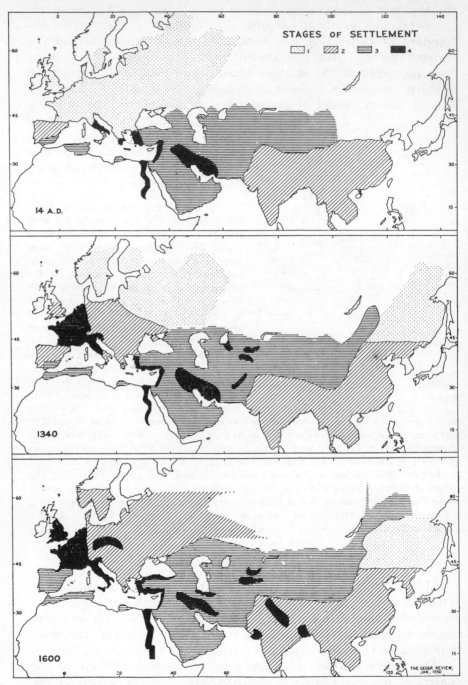

FIGS.·9 to 11—Stages of settlement in Eurasia about the beginning of the Christian era, the mid-
fourteenth century, and the beginning of the seventeenth century respectively. The numbers have
reference: 1, frontier regions; 2, regions at intermediate stage of settlement; 3, maturely settled
regions with low densities of population; 4, maturely settled regions with high densities of population.

of the intermediate stage of settlement. In the Near and Middle East settlement was mature, but the absolute mass of the population was not large, because the areas capable of significant settlement were small. Shading of the map involves, almost inevitably, some exaggeration of the actual areas. By the fourteenth century the progress of settlement in Europe was notable, and growth continued throughout the fifteenth and sixteenth centuries. At the close of the sixteenth century India was still incompletely settled, though portions of the Ganges Valley were beyond doubt maturely settled. China was only on the verge of the period of notable development that established the modern patterns in her density map. Thus we may say that the Mediterranean region achieved substantial maturity of settlement by the beginning of the Christian era. Northwestern Europe achieved maturity of settlement, with some areas excepted, by the close of the sixteenth century. India and China did not achieve full maturity of settlement until the early part of the nineteenth century.

THE PAST AND FUTURE POPULATION OF THE

WORLD AND ITS CONTINENTS

By the Population Division, United Nations

Population statistics adequate for a detailed review of world population growth have not existed long enough to permit a search—however interesting that might be—into the remote past. For recent decades, statistics are sufficient for a general comparison of rates of population growth in various parts of the world, but for some major areas even the current size and rate of increase of the population is not accurately known. Speculations about future population are possible only on the basis of assumptions which, while perhaps plausible in the light of available knowledge, can only be of limited validity.

1. World population during the past 300 years

Despite the dubious nature of the historical evidence, the careful estimates made by scholars for recent centuries provide an interesting starting point for a discussion of past population trends and their probable implications for the future. The figures presented in Table I, for the years 1650 to 1900, are based on the research of Walter Willcox[1] and modified only by

Table I. Estimates of World Population by Continental Divisions, 1650-1950

Continent	ESTIMATED POPULATION (MILLIONS)				
	1650	1750	1850	1900	1950
World total	470	694	1,094	1,550	2,454
Africa	100	100	100	120	198
America	8	11	59	144	330
Northern America[a]	(1)	(1)	(26)	(81)	(168)
Latin America[b]	(7)	(10)	(33)	(63)	(162)
Asia[c]	257	437	656	857	1,320
Europe[d]	103	144	274	423	593
Oceania	2	2	2	6	13

a. i.e. America North of Mexico.
b. i.e. America South of the United States.
c. excluding the Asiatic part of the U.S.S.R.
d. including the Asiatic part of the U.S.S.R.

subsidiary estimates with respect to the Asiatic part of the U.S.S.R.[2] Estimates for 1950 have been prepared by the United Nations Population Division, on the basis of official estimates for various countries, with additions and corrections as needed.

These estimates indicate a rapid multiplication of the world's inhabitants,

---

1. Willcox, Walter F., *Studies in American Demography*, Ithaca, N.Y. (U.S.A.), 1940.
2. Based mainly on Volkhov, Dinamika naseleniya SSSR, Moscow, 1930.

the total for 1950 being more than five times that of 1650. The growth of world population, moreover, has been accelerating: humanity more than doubled in the 200 years from 1650 to 1850; the same relative increase occurred again in only 100 years from 1850 to 1950. Increase from 1900 to 1950 was also more rapid than the growth of the preceding half-century.

In the perspective of the thousands of centuries of man's previous existence on earth, the modern era must appear as one of unusually prolonged and unusually rapid growth. In earlier epochs, there probably were also periods of growth, alternating with periods of stagnation or even decline, but it is highly improbable that there has ever been an era of sustained world-wide growth such as that of the past 300 years, or a period of such rapid growth as occurred during the past 50 years. For, had mankind's numbers been continuously increasing as rapidly as they did from 1900 to 1950, the whole present world population could have descended from one human couple in only 24 centuries. Nevertheless, it is known that human beings have peopled the earth for thousands of centuries before recorded history began.

The trends of growth have not been the same in all parts of the world. It will be noted that the population of Asia has probably grown most steadily though never at a very rapid rate. The population of Europe grew most rapidly in the latter half of the nineteenth century, but somewhat less rapidly in more recent times. Whether the population of Africa before 1850 was increasing or not cannot now be known, but it is most probable that substantial growth has begun only in recent times. The growth of the combined population of the Americas during the past 200 years has been prodigious but whereas Northern American population grew most rapidly between 1750 and 1900, its rate of growth has more recently been surpassed by that of Latin America. Rapid population growth in Oceania began relatively recently with the arrival of European settlers in Australia and New Zealand; the trends in the more remote past are, however, unknown.

Immigration has made a major contribution to population growth in Northern America and Oceania whose earlier populations were scant. Since the populations of these continents have now attained more considerable sizes, the relative importance of immigration has declined. Migration can still be an important factor of growth in certain areas for brief periods of time (e.g., immigration to Australia in recent years has been considerable), but the current and future growth of most major regions of the world are now predominantly determined by the balance of births and deaths.

Birth and death statistics unfortunately do not exist for any considerable historical period except for a few countries of Northern and Western Europe and, for shorter periods, the remainder of Europe, Northern America, parts of Latin America, Japan and Oceania. Although we lack the detailed statistics to substantiate this view, there is general agreement that the acceleration of world population growth, in the modern era, is the result of a fall in death rates and not of a rise in birth rates.

2. Population changes during the past 30 years

Population estimates, for all countries of the world within their present boundaries, for the years 1920, 1930, 1940, and 1950, have been compiled by the Population Division of the United Nations with additions and corrections wherever needed. The resulting totals for continents are shown in Table II. It should be noted that many of these estimates are subject to various errors and that even the resulting continental totals are not entirely trustworthy. In particular, it is not possible now to make any firm estimate for that fifth of mankind which inhabits the Chinese mainland.[3] Therefore, it has been possible only to estimate the 1950 population of the Chinese mainland at the rounded figure of 500 million. Earlier estimates for the population of China were derived by assuming, in agreement with the findings of several students of Chinese population, that the rate of increase was 0.5 per cent per annum. It is obvious that these estimates for China may contain very large errors.

Table II. Estimates of Population of Continents, 1920-1950[a]

Continent	1920	1930	1940	1950
World	1,830	2,019	2,235	2,454
Africa	139	154	172	198
America	207	244	277	330
Northern America[b]	(117)	(135)	(146)	(168)
Latin America[c]	(90)	(109)	(131)	(162)
Asia[d]	990	1,080	1,199	1,320
Europe[e]	486	531	576	593
Oceania	8.8	10.4	11.3	13.0

a. Estimates for Asia and world totals may err considerably because of inaccurate knowledge of the population of China.
b. i.e. America North of Mexico.
c. i.e. America South of the United States.
d. excluding the Asiatic part of the U.S.S.R.
e. including the Asiatic part of the U.S.S.R.

By comparing the figures in Table II for successive ten-year intervals, we can estimate the decennial population increases for each continent. These increases, together with the average annual rates of increase, are shown in Table III. From these figures, acceleration of population growth can be noted in the cases of Africa and Latin America. The population of Asia would probably also have grown at an increasing pace had it not been for great hardships suffered in the areas under temporary Japanese occupation, and other setbacks connected with post-war readjustments, in the 1940-1950 period.

3. The latest official estimate, supplied by the Nationalist Government of China for the year 1948, gave the population of the country as 463 million; this estimate was admittedly not up-to-date for various parts of the country. On the other hand, it has been officially reported that the population count taken in 1953 by the Communist authorities on the mainland resulted in a total which "greatly exceeds" all figures used previously (prior to the count of 1953, the Communist authorities usually quoted an earlier figure of 475 million).

Table III. Absolute and Relative Increases of Population of Continents[a]

Continent	POPULATION INCREASE (MILLIONS)			AVERAGE ANNUAL RATE OF INCREASE (PER CENT)		
	1920-30	1930-40	1940-50	1920-30	1930-40	1940-50
World	189	216	219	1.0	1.0	0.9
Africa	15	18	26	1.0	1.1	1.4
America	37	33	53	1.7	1.3	1.8
Northern America[b]	(18)	(11)	(22)	(1.4)	(0.8)	(1.4)
Latin America[c]	(19)	(22)	(31)	(1.9)	(1.9)	(2.1)
Asia[d]	90	119	121	0.9	1.1	1.0
Europe[e]	45	45	17	0.9	0.8	0.3
Oceania	1.6	0.9	1.7	1.7	0.8	1.4

a. On the assumption that the population of China increased, in every decade, at the rate of 0.5 per cent per annum. Estimated absolute and relative increases for Asia and the world total may consequently be in error.
b. i.e. America North of Mexico.
c. i.e. America South of the United States.
d. excluding the Asiatic part of the U.S.S.R.
e. including the Asiatic part of the U.S.S.R.

In Northern America and Oceania, the increase of population has fluctuated, being relatively large in the 1920's and 1940's, but small in the 1930's: the economic depression which characterized this latter period resulted at the same time in unusually low birth rates and a cessation of immigration, whereas in other periods of relative prosperity the opposite tendencies can be observed. Falling or low birth rates also reduced the rates of population growth in Europe (including the Soviet Union) in the 1930's; the small numerical increase for the 1940's, however, is due in large measure to heavy loss of lives caused by World War II.

In the three decades, from 1920 to 1950, world population grew apparently at an almost constant rate of very nearly 1 per cent per annum. It is rather surprising that this rate was nearly the same for all three decades, from 1920 to 1950. The economic depression of 1930 and subsequent years slowed down considerably the growth of perhaps one-fourth of mankind where birth rates fell to abnormally low levels. Military and civilian losses as well as birth deficits associated with World War II affected large areas of East and Southeast Asia, the Soviet Union and various parts of Europe. If, despite these disturbances, world population continued to increase at more or less the same rate, then, in the absence of those intervening factors, world population growth would probably have accelerated, and would have appreciably exceeded 1 per cent per annum in the most recent decade. Therefore, despite temporary setbacks, it appears that the epoch of accelerating world population growth, which can be traced back for 300 years, has not yet reached its climax.

3. The current situation

Many students of world population have distinguished three broad types of demographic situations by which the various regions of the world can be characterized, namely: a) regions of high mortality and fertility, b) regions of declining mortality and high or declining fertility, and c) regions of low mortality and fertility.[4] In a more recent United Nations study,[5] however, it was found convenient, for the purpose of evaluating potentialities of future population growth, to further subdivide types a) and b) above and hence to distinguish five types of demographic situations. These five types are defined by the following characteristics: 1) High birth rates and high death rates, 2) High birth rates and declining (though still rather high) death rates, 3) High birth rates and fairly low death rates, 4) Declining birth rates and fairly low death rates, and 5) Low or fluctuating birth rates and low death rates. In this study, the world was divided into 25 regions, 24 of which were identified with one of the five types.

Type 1, high birth rates and high death rates, was found to apply to the middle part of Africa, this being the only major region in the world for which there is still no evidence of a tendency towards a systematic decline of death rates. The statistics of this region are not very trustworthy. The current rate of population growth was estimated as approximately 1 per cent per annum.

Several regions were found to conform to Type 2, having high birth rates and declining (though still rather high) death rates. These regions were: Northern Africa, Southwest Asia, Central South Asia, and Southeast Asia (Mainland and Islands). Rates of population growth, for the 1940-1950 period, in these areas varied from 1.25 per cent per annum (Central South Asia) to 1.60 per cent per annum (Mainland Southeast Asia). In the absence of reliable statistics for Indonesia, the current growth rate for the Southeast Asian Islands was estimated at 1.50 per cent per annum.

Mainland East Asia was also regarded as a region essentially belonging to Type 2, but no firm estimate of its current rate of growth could be made. In the past, the population of China was believed to be increasing at a rate of approximately 0.5 per cent per annum. Views about current conditions on the Chinese mainland differ widely, some believing that they are favourable to population growth and others believing that they are not. Hence, any rate of increase between zero and one per cent per annum was considered possible for this region.

Populations of Type 3 were found in Southern Africa, the Central American Mainland, the Antilles, and Tropical South America. In all of these areas, birth rates are high and death rates fairly low, with consequently very rapid population growth. Current growth rates for Southern Africa and Central America were found, according to statistics, to equal 2.15 and 2.87 per cent per annum, respectively. In the Antilles and Tropical South America, where vital statistics are less adequate, growth rates were estimated from the 1940-1950 period and found to be 1.82 and 2.23 per cent per annum.

4. See, e.g., United Nations, *The determinants and consequences of population trends,* New York, 1954, Chapter IX, "Future Population Trends". These three demographic types were also distinguished in an article prepared by the United Nations Population Division on "The past and future growth of world population . . ." *Population Bulletin,* no. 1, December 1951, New York.

5. United Nations. Population Division. *Framework for future population estimates, 1950-1980, by world regions* (mimeographed document), New York, 1954.

Populations with declining birth rates and fairly low death rates, as defined by Type 4, were found in Temperate South America, Japan, the Balkan peninsula, and the Soviet Union. The current growth rate for Temperate South America, 2.37 per cent per annum, was considered abnormally high owing to large numbers of recent immigrants; the rate observed for the 1940-1950 period, which was 1.76 per cent, was regarded as a better estimate of increase under ordinary conditions. Current growth rates, according to available statistics, were found to be 1.80 per cent per annum for Japan, and 1.25 for the Balkan peninsula. For the Soviet Union, an estimated rate of 1.5 per cent was used.

Populations of Type 5, with low or fluctuating birth rates and low death rates, were found in Northern America, all parts of Europe except the Balkan peninsula and the Soviet Union, and in Australia and New Zealand. Current growth rates for Northern America, Australia and New Zealand were found abnormally high because of unusually high birth rates and unusually large numbers of immigrants; it was estimated that under ordinary conditions the populations of these two areas would increase at the rates observed during the 1940-1950 period, which were 1.39 and 1.52 per cent per annum, respectively. East-Central Europe, with an estimated rate of 1.31 per cent per annum, was found to be another area of Type 5 where current growth is relatively rapid. In the remaining parts of Europe, current rates of growth were less than 1 per cent per annum, the lowest being that of the British Isles, with 0.50 per cent per annum.

The only region of the world which could not be assigned to any one of the five types is that of the Pacific island territories (other than Australia and New Zealand). The current rate of population growth for this heterogeneous group of areas was estimated as approximately 1 per cent per annum.

By combining the various estimated growth rates representing "normal" current conditions, "normal" current rates of population growth, by continent, may be estimated as follows:

Africa .... 1.2 per cent per annum
America .... 1.8 per cent per annum
   Northern America (1.4)
   Latin America   (2.2)
Asia[a] .... 1.0 per cent per annum
Europe[b] .... 1.1 per cent per annum
Oceania .... 1.4 per cent per annum
World[c] .... 1.2 per cent per annum

     a. Excluding Asiatic part of the U.S.S.R. Assuming a current rate of
       growth of 0.5 per cent per annum for the population of China.
     b. Including Asiatic part of the U.S.S.R.
     c. Assuming a current rate of growth of 0.5 per cent per annum for China.

These rates are identical with the 1940-1950 rates shown in Table III in the cases of Northern America, Asia (assuming the population of China to grow at 0.5 per cent per annum), and Oceania. A lower rate was obtained in the case of Africa only because a different method of estimating was used, many of the estimates referring to the middle part of Africa being subject to considerable errors. For Latin America, a further recent acceleration of population growth is noted, as compared with that observed for 1940-1950. The current rate of population growth in Europe (including the Soviet Union) is still appreciable, though it had been very small in the period comprising World War II. Assuming a rate of 0.5 per cent for the population of China, and "normal" conditions in all other parts of the world, the current rate of world population growth should be of the order of 1.2 per cent per annum. This estimate may, however, have to be revised if it becomes known that the population of China is growing at a different rate.

4. Future population of the world and its continents

In the recent United Nations study referred to,[6] separate assumptions, believed to be plausible, have been made concerning possible future changes in rates of growth for populations of each of the five demographic types. In general, it was assumed that the growth rates of populations under a given demographic type will change in the direction of the current average growth rate of the subsequent type. Because it cannot be foreseen how rapidly some of these changes will occur, three alternative assumptions were made in each instance, representing "high", "medium", and "low" expectations, respectively. Barring disastrous events, such as wars or major break-downs in social organization, it is believed improbable that future population will either exceed the "high", or fall short of the "low", expectation. Future population will probably fall somewhere within the range of these extreme estimates.

Detailed results of these various computations, for five-year intervals from 1950 to 1980, are presented in that study, including also some rather tentative estimates of future population for all countries of the world. The totals obtained for continents are summarized in Table IV below.

While it is possible for population growth in some regions to be unex-

Table IV. Estimates of Population of Continents for 1950 and for 1980, According to "High", "Medium", and "Low" Expectations

Continent	1950	ESTIMATED POPULATION (MILLIONS) 1980		
		"High"	"Medium"	"Low"
World	2,454	3,990	3,628	3,295
Africa	198	327	289	255
America	330	577	535	487
Northern America[a]	(168)	(240)	(223)	(207)
Latin America[b]	(162)	(337)	(312)	(280)
Asia[c]	1,320	2,227	2,011	1,816
Europe[d]	593	840	776	721
Oceania	13.0	19.2	17.5	16.1

a. i.e. America North of Mexico.
b. i.e. America South of the United States.
c. excluding the Asiatic part of the U.S.S.R.
d. including the Asiatic part of the U.S.S.R.

6. United Nations. Population Division. *Framework for future population estimates, 1950-1980, by world regions* (mimeographed document), New York, 1954.

pectedly rapid and in others to be unexpectedly slow, there is some likelihood that some of the resulting errors of prediction will compensate. This makes it more probable for the world as a whole than for any particular region that actual future population will be contained within the limits of the "high" and "low" expectations. Barring events of an unforeseeable nature, it is unlikely that the population of the world in 1980 will be greater than 4.0, or less than 3.3, billion. These estimates may have to be modified if it becomes known that the current size and rate of growth of the population of China has been severely misjudged.

Future growth will not be equal among the various parts of the world. Thus, on the "medium" assumption the population of Africa would increase by 46 per cent, that of Northern America by 33 per cent, that of Latin America by 92 per cent, that of Asia by 52 per cent, that of Europe by 31 per cent, and that of Oceania by 35 per cent. For particular regions within these continents, future increases of population will also vary. For the Central American Mainland, the region of highest current population growth, the "medium" assumption foresees an increase by 116 per cent. For the British Isles, where current growth is slowest, the "medium" projection allows for an increase by 16 per cent only.

Owing to probably different future rates of growth, the proportions of mankind's numbers contained in each continent will change considerably, as shown in Table V. The relative importance of Latin America and Asia will rise, while that of Northern America and Europe declines.

Table V. Proportions of World Population Contained in Each Continent, According to Population Estimates for 1920, 1950, and 1980, on the "Medium" Assumption of Future Growth

Continent	PER CENT OF WORLD POPULATION		
	1920	1950	1980 ("medium" estimate)
World	100.0	100.0	100.0
Africa	7.6	8.1	8.0
America	11.3	13.4	14.7
Northern America[a]	(6.4)	(6.8)	(6.1)
Latin America[b]	(4.9)	(6.6)	(8.6)
Asia[c]	54.1	53.8	55.4
Europe[d]	26.6	24.2	21.4
Oceania	0.5	0.5	0.4

a. i.e. America North of Mexico.
b. i.e. America South of the United States.
c. excluding the Asiatic part of the U.S.S.R.
d. including the Asiatic part of the U.S.S.R.

THE POPULATION OF THE WORLD

IN THE YEAR 2000

By Frank W. Notestein

THIS PAPER is devoted to variations on two themes, neither of which is profound but both of which are too often neglected. The first theme is that the population of the world in the year 2000 will depend very much on events between the present and that date. The second is that the size of the population by the end of the century is much less important than the process by which the population of that date is reached. Neither of these themes denies, of course, that the population of the future depends also on events already past. To come to grips with our problem we must, therefore, first consider the demographic situation and the nature of the processes of change. We can then discuss the ways in which the events of the future may modify the situation. It is only fair to warn the reader that he will not discover here, or elsewhere, how large the population is going to be by the end of the century. The only way I know of finding the answer to that question is to keep alive until that date.

There is little point in discussing the population of the world as a whole. The situation is far too heterogeneous to make it useful to do so, and the problems, although of world-wide importance, are the problems of particular peoples and particular areas. For our purposes it is more useful to consider each of the three types of demographic development first proposed by Warren S. Thompson, for which, however, I prefer the descriptive titles: (1) Incipient Decline, (2) Transitional Growth, and (3) High Growth Potential.[1]

REGIONS OF INCIPIENT POPULATION DECLINE

The populations in the stage of incipient decline are those that have virtually completed their demographic transition from high fertility and mortality to low fertility and mortality. Their net reproduction rates have been near or below the levels that, if maintained, would ultimately produce a stationary population. Fertility is in large meas-

---

[1] Thompson discussed these types under different names in his book *Plenty of People,* published in 1944. (First edition, Lancaster, Pa., The Jacques Cattell Press; second edition, New York, The Ronald Press Co., 1948.) In fact he used essentially the same types in a paper I had until recently overlooked, which was published in 1929. "Population," *American Journal of Sociology,* XXXIV (6): 959–975. May, 1929.

ure under rational control, and mortality prior to the end of the child-bearing period is very low. The falling death rates and birth rates of the past have resulted in populations with high average ages. This type includes the populations of Northern, Western, and Central Europe, the United States, Australia, and New Zealand, and more doubtfully those of Canada and Southern Europe. In ordinary course, these populations will grow for a time because their present age distributions tend to support birth rates and to depress death rates. They are properly designated as populations of incipient decline, however, because any perpetuation of the prewar trends in fertility and mortality would lead to decline. In fact they may grow indefinitely, become stationary, or possibly decline. Without immigration, however, they will decline unless the downward trend of the birth rate is permanently checked.

Prior to the war most demographers, and the writer among them, felt that, in the absence of strong positive measures to encourage child-bearing, further declines in the birth rates could be expected. There were three main reasons for this expectation. In the first place, the downward trend got under way in a differential fashion, spreading from the upper urban classes of the population down through the social-economic structure and outward from the city to the rural regions. By the end of the interwar period the highest rates were the ones that were declining most rapidly, the lowest were declining least rapidly, and no evidence of a real up-turn was in sight. In the second place, the differences in fertility were closely correlated with differences in the prevalence and effectiveness of contraceptive practice, and there was every indication that contraceptive materials were becoming more abundant, and that the knowledge of their use was spreading. In the third place, the middle class standards, which had been such a strong factor in the motivation for small families, appeared to be spreading throughout the mass of the population. Thus the nature of the trends, the means by which they were brought about, and the nature of the pressures and incentives motivating restrictionist practices all suggested a pattern of decline that had not run its course. On such evidence most of us predicted continued decline unless strong pro-natalist policies were brought to bear.

Instead of further declines, a baby boom got under way with the economic revival in the late 'thirties. The number of births was amazingly sustained during the war, and shot up in the postwar period. We are now in the position of speaking of a secular decline in fertility in spite of a fifteen-year period of generally rising birth rates. Our critics are asking how many years it takes to make a trend, and implying that demographers form an elite corps of double-distilled false prophets—that is, prophets who, being proved wrong, insist on staying that way.

It is evident that the magnitude of the increase in births throughout the Western world has surprised most of us, and that the implications of the rise in births for future population change are not entirely clear. Meanwhile, however, some useful information is at hand. Recent evidence for Great Britain[2] suggests that two technical faults led to some exaggeration of the downward trend of marital fertility during the interwar years.[3] One was the failure, in which I participated, to recognize that the shortage of males caused by the casualties of the First World War and by emigration, was only a temporary depressant of female fertility. The other was the possibility that the swings of depression and recovery, war and its aftermath, may have concealed an essential stability in the size of families of couples marrying since 1927. Our earlier work may therefore have exaggerated somewhat the decline in fertility during the interwar period.

The technical difficulties, however, are relatively minor. Their correction would have resulted only in projections showing slower declines in the birth rates. In fact, there has been a spectacular and unforeseen rise in birth rates throughout the Western world, and the increase has altered the growth characteristics of the population for decades to come. The birth boom has clearly pushed back the date at which a population decline might appear. It is much less certain, however, how large the net addition to births will be when the whole story is in, or that the rise in births represents the launching of an upward trend in family size. All available evidence suggests that the primary source of the additional births was a sharp decline in the age of marriage. When marriage age is dropping, new families are being formed at a faster rate than the population can permanently sustain. After marriage age stabilizes, other things equal, the births will decline. If marriage age should rise the decrease in births would be sharp. The work of the Royal Commission,[4] of Whelpton,[5] and of others, all indicate that the rise came very largely from increases in first and second children. Meanwhile, the specific risks of birth in the very high orders have clearly continued to decline. We cannot be at all certain that there has been any upward trend in family size. Although the possibility of such a trend resulting from early marriage cannot be ruled out, there is no evidence of the re-emergence of the large family. Perhaps the best generalization is that the trend toward decline in family size has been at least temporarily checked.

If the decline in family size has been checked, or perhaps reversed, to what may the check be attributed, and are these factors likely to continue in effect? It seems to me clear that many of the normal peacetime pressures on family size were virtually removed during the war and postwar period. First we had the prewar revival after a deep de-

---

[2] *Report of the Royal Commission on Population.* London, H. M. Stationery Office, 1949.

[3] Hereafter I shall refer to marital fertility, or the average number of children born to married women, as the size of family.

[4] *Super cit.*

[5] Whelpton, P. K., "The Meaning of the 1947 Baby Boom." *Vital Statistics—Special Reports,* 33 (1): 1–10. Oct. 7, 1948.

pression; then, particularly in Europe, the wartime and postwar economic controls; finally in the United States we had the postwar prosperity, and in Europe an extension of child allowance systems. In general money was abundant,. goods were scarce, but rationed and subsidized in ways that favored children. In some countries, moreover, military service was less likely for men with children, and maternity and child allowances were common. For the most part governmental policies probably were not intended to sustain births. It may be doubted, however, that there has been a time when child rearing was as heavily subsidized. One also is inclined to wonder whether it will be possible in peacetime to devise an explicit policy for the encouragement of childbearing that is as powerful as the various controls and subsidies of the wartime period proved in fact to be.

One matter in this analysis disturbs me. In retrospect the forces that encouraged births during the war are clear, but this is after-the-fact analysis. Before the fact I, for one, did not think it possible that any policy, however strong, would over-ride the terrors of the wartime experience in Britain. The moral presumably is that having been wrong in the past, I must be prepared to be wrong again, and perhaps am so in the present instance.

So far as the future growth of population of this type is concerned, it seems to me that the following points can be made on the basis of present evidence.

1. The high level of births of the 'forties has definitely postponed the date at which maximum populations could be anticipated in any realistic terms. It is much less clear that the birth boom will have added very much to the population that otherwise might have been expected by the end of the century. Whether it has will depend largely on whether it involves a change in family size or merely a change in the ages at which mothers bear children.

2. In this type of population, in which there is a large measure of rational control of fertility, the annual increments to the population are likely to be irregularly distributed through time because childbearing is sensitive to the swings of the political, social, and economic climates. Such swings produce irregularities in the age distribution that bring complicated problems of social-economic adjustment.

3. Public policy can have a great effect on the birth rate. The prewar analysts recognized this fact, projected future declines without reference to it, and then expressed the belief that an awareness of the trend toward slowing growth would stimulate pro-natalist policies that would modify the trends projected. Because of the war, such policies have come sooner and have been stronger than was anticipated. They have done much more to impair the relevance than the validity of the prewar demographic work.

4. Turning now to prospects for future change, we must first note one contingency that is all too real, yet cannot be usefully taken into

account. It is possible that there will be a war of such destructive and disorganizing nature that the growth characteristics of the population will be sharply changed. If so, about the last thing to worry about will be our mistaken estimates of future population. This possibility, therefore, is not taken into account in the present discussion.

Between now and the end of the century, it seems to me that we may expect sharply fluctuating, but rather low, average rates of increase among the populations of this first type. On the one hand, many of the forces tending toward a reduction of family size are likely to continue in effect. On the other hand, we have yet to see a nation approaching a stationary population that did not launch strong measures to stimulate childbearing. I expect that efforts to increase births will be one of the major preoccupations of those concerned with social legislation in the Western world. Indeed, it has already become so in a few nations. Personally, I think it likely that during the next fifty years the growth of this type of population will average less than half of one per cent per year, and that these populations will represent a substantially smaller part of the world's total by the end of the century than they do today. The important fact, however, is not the size, or the proportion, or the speed of growth. The important fact is that populations of this type can check their growth any time it becomes desirable to do so by means of reducing fertility rather than by that of increasing mortality. I doubt that the provision of an adequate standard of living for the growth that will come in this group presents grave technical or social problems. The greatest danger, it seems to me, is that concern about slowing growth may drive societies to a renewed emphasis on the obligations of the individual to reproduce for the benefit of the state, church, party, or other extra-personal unit. There is danger that the emotional reaction to slowing growth will lead us to seek people for society, rather than to enrich society for the people.

REGIONS OF TRANSITIONAL GROWTH

The next earlier stage of demographic evolution is that of transitional growth. It is given the name because the processes of modernization have already begun to reduce fertility and mortality in ways that are very likely to bring rapid growth. The regions in this stage include Eastern Europe, the Soviet Union, Japan, and parts of Latin America. The populations are heavily dependent on agriculture, but are in the process of urbanization and industrialization. Education and the technological skills are poor but improving. The agrarian family, and the attitudes toward childbearing that accompany it, are still important, but are being modified by the encroachments of an increasingly urban and secularly minded community. Under the influence of such developments, death rates have been declining for a considerable time. The essential characteristic, however, is that even the birth rates, which respond much more slowly than death rates to changes in the social setting, have a well-established downward trend. With death rates leading the birth rates in the decline, there is a substantial margin of growth which may be expected to continue for some time. This stage is one of almost automatic growth, such as that through which Western Europe and the United States were moving in the latter part of the nineteenth and early part of the twentieth centuries. Unquestionably, public policy can shorten or lengthen the transitional period and modify its rate of increase, but it seems unlikely that anything but severe political disorganization could check growth.

Between now and the end of the century, it seems likely that growth will exceed an average of one per cent per year for this population type. In the case of Japan, it seems very doubtful that such growth will, or could, occur, at least in the home islands. Her population, like that of England, is far beyond the size that can be supported by a self-contained economy. The development of foreign markets and sources of food and raw materials before heavy American subsidies are withdrawn, coupled with emigration and a sharp decline in the birth rate, would seem the only way of avoiding stark tragedy. Otherwise the areas of this type apparently have the resources required to provide better living for more people, as skills and equipment improve. These populations, therefore, represent another sector of the human race that has a reasonably good chance of absorbing its growth long enough to permit the transition to efficient population replacement based on low birth and death rates.

REGIONS OF HIGH GROWTH POTENTIAL

The third of our population types is that of high growth potential. It is the least homogeneous of all, having as its only essential characteristic the fact that the birth rates have thus far given no clear indication of a downward trend. Its death rates in general are high, but some of them are declining rapidly, others little, and it is possible that some are rising. Some of the populations are growing rapidly, others slowly, and, for all we know, some may be declining. The populations are designated as those of high growth potential because, without exception, the birth rates are very high and sufficiently resistant to change to guarantee rapid and sustained population growth any time it becomes possible to achieve something less than extremely high mortality. More than half of the world's population falls into this class, which includes virtually all of the Far East except Japan, most of Africa north of the Union, much of Latin America, and most of the Middle East. Some of the populations are densely settled on the land, others are rather sparsely settled. We may consider the less densely settled regions of this type first.

In much of South America, Borneo, Sumatra, New Guinea, Africa, and the Middle East population densities are low, and unused resources are relatively abundant. If large amounts of capital were available and would be used for development, the regions could carry much larger populations than they do at present, and provide much higher levels of living than exist today. In a period of rapid economic development, the populations would grow very fast indeed, for development would require the control of many diseases now ravaging the people. Moreover, development would cut the death rate long before the slower processes of social reorientation would begin to put pressures on the birth rate. Under these conditions growth might very well exceed two per cent per year. Such growth would not complicate world problems of food supply, however, for if it were to come it would do so because of the expanding productivity of the regions themselves. In one sense the Middle East is in a particularly favorable position. The presence of oil goes far to solve the immediate problems of available funds with which agriculture can be rehabilitated, industries started, and education, health, and skills improved.

Whether the population of these more sparsely settled regions will grow rapidly is another matter. They will if there is economic development. The difficulties in the future, just as in the past, seem less those of resources than of social, economic, and political organization. Given the solutions to these problems, the processes of population growth should not become major obstacles to an escape from the stable equilibrium of poverty and early death.

It is the people living in the densely settled areas of high growth potential who present the most serious problem. These areas include Egypt, India, China, Korea, Formosa, Java, and most of the Caribbean. The populations are mainly agrarian, have very low levels of living, and are crowded on relatively undeveloped and inadequate resource bases. In these circumstances it is difficult to see how productivity can be increased sufficiently to support rapidly rising levels of living during a period of population growth such as that through which Europe and Japan have moved.

There is no reason to suppose that the average birth rate for the population of this type is as low as 40 per thousand, official reports to the contrary notwithstanding. Nor is there reason to expect that birth rates will decline rapidly. The social organizations, customs, and beliefs governing reproduction remain today those that throughout the centuries have elicited the births necessary for survival in the presence of uncontrolled mortality. These institutions, customs, and beliefs change only gradually, as the experience of the Western world and that of Japan have shown. Unless new elements enter the situation, we may expect birth rates to be little changed for several decades and to remain relatively high during the period with which we are concerned.

Birth rates of 40 per thousand do not guarantee a growing population. They guarantee only the alternative of growth or excessively high death rates. With a birth rate of 40, a population will grow at a substantial rate even if the expectation of life at birth is only one-half that of the present white population of the United States. Something of the potentiality of the situation may be appreciated if we remember that under Japanese rule the population of Formosa increased by 93 per cent in the thirty-five years from 1905 to 1940. Its average annual rate of growth was nearly two per cent. Under Japanese rule, birth rates remained effectively unchanged, but stable government and economic development, with the protection of health that these entail, stimulated rapid growth. Whenever similar improvements in mortality are possible we may expect similar growth among the populations of this type. Fertility is high enough to maintain increases up to two per cent per year any time death rates can be reduced to levels that the modern nations of the Western world would consider scandalously high for their own people.

If we deal with expectations rather than hopes, I doubt that we should predict rapid population growth at least for the next two decades. The reason for such pessimism—that is the expectation that death rates will be high—lies essentially in the problems of social and political organization that these populations face under difficult economic conditions. The economies must expand substantially just to take care of their increased populations unless death rates are to rise. Resources are not abundant, and capital is very scarce and difficult to accumulate under conditions in which only a little tightening of the belt makes the difference between life and death. Meanwhile, the masses of the population are becoming aware that other people have an easier lot, and are beginning to aspire to higher standards. There is, moreover, a new political consciousness among the people, and new loyalties are replacing old ones. Tight economic conditions, mounting popular aspirations, and divided loyalties make an explosive mixture. There may be a considerable period of disorganization as the populations pass from one regime to another. If so, the danger of catastrophes is very real, as the losses through starvation and epidemics of the past decade show. The margins of life are simply too narrow to permit great retrenchment without mounting death rates. It is by no means impossible that the population growth will be heavily checked by catastrophic losses from time to time and from place to place, and that widespread disorganization could hold growth to an average rate as low as half of one per cent. It should always be remembered that this condition will come only if the world's worst death rates rise spectacularly and hundreds of millions of people die for lack of life's simplest essentials.

There are, of course, other possibilities. One is that strong and wise indigenous governments will provide political stability and, with the assistance of the world, develop agriculture, transportation, and industry at a rapid pace. If this should happen, death rates would drop as a result both of the growing abundance of the means of subsistence and of the public health measures that such changes would require and make possible. It goes without saying that in order to bring about the improved living conditions which such growth implies, the multipliers for annual economic production would have to be very large. For example, doubled incomes for doubled populations would require a higher multiplier than four in economic production to provide the capital that such economic expansion entails.

Even under relatively favorable conditions, two somewhat different risks seem to me to threaten sustained advances in living levels and health. One risk is that economic production cannot be expanded rapidly enough. Resources are not abundant, and the populations are huge, illiterate, and technologically untrained. Yet, unless economic production can be expanded very rapidly, additions to the population will absorb most of the additions to production. In this case, by the end of the century, our successors will point out, as we, looking at the past, do today that the fruits of development have been mainly more people instead of higher levels of living and health.

The other risk is that by the end of the century the potentiality for further population growth will still be very large. Doubling per capita income for a doubled population in fifty years is one thing. Being prepared to continue the process is quite another. Yet, if we are to judge by the experience of Japan and the Western world the risk is a very real one. It is real if, in the future as in the past, reliance for the reduction of birth rates is placed on the slow and somewhat automatic processes of social change incident to economic development. Birth rates decline under the impact of urban industrial development, rising levels of living, education, and health; but they do so only gradually. Hitherto, the process has involved multipliers for the population of more than threefold, and the circumstances have been much less difficult than those found among the billion people now under consideration. It seems to me that there is grave danger that mounting numbers will be a major obstacle to sustained improvements in health and living levels unless special measures are taken to speed the reduction of the birth rates among the masses of the peasant populations. This task is far from easy. There seems to be no general realization of its importance among the world's leaders. We have little knowledge of the means by which the small family ideal can be efficiently transmitted to agrarian populations, and given the wish for smaller families among such populations, we have at present no sufficiently cheap, effective, and acceptable birth control methods to meet their needs. Between now and the end of the century, the experience of these populations probably will be varied. Some catastrophes are probable, and some successful transitions to efficient replacement are possible. The important fact is that unless growth considerably exceeds one per cent per year, it is unlikely that living levels will have risen or that birth rates will have fallen very much. If lack of production limits population growth, then little change may be expected either in living levels, or in the social conditions that produce high fertility.

As observed at the outset of this paper, we cannot know what the future population will be, and its size is less important than its modes of change. It seems likely that growth will be rather slow among the populations that have already achieved low mortality and adopted the small family system. The important thing, however, is that these populations can control their growth by modifying their fertility instead of their mortality. Most of the populations in the stage of transition to the small family system may be expected to grow rapidly; but these populations seem likely to achieve their transitions to efficient replacement. Among the sparsely settled populations with high growth potentials, there is room for large expansion. Growth will be rapid if the political and economic obstacles it developed are overcome. It is only in the densely settled populations of high growth potential that growth itself is likely to be a major obstacle to sustained advances in health and material welfare. These populations, however, include more than half of the human race, and their situations are extremely difficult. We do not know that they will grow; we know only that they will grow unless death rates mount, and that growth will be rapid if death rates decline. For them the essential problem is not the size of the population by the end of the century. The crucial problem is whether the intervening processes of social, economic, and political evolution will permit the ultimate termination of growth by means of falling birth rates rather than by means of rising death rates.

Whatever the course of population growth, I doubt that the technological problem of food production will provide the major difficulty. From a technological point of view, man already knows how to produce much more than he is at all likely to produce. The most difficult problems are those in the fields of social science and social engineering. They are the inter-related processes of social, economic, and political change which come to a focus in the problems of population growth. These problems of change should lie at the heart of the social disciplines. Unfortunately, the social sciences, including demography, have little to contribute. We know very little of the processes of change, and are not trying very hard to learn. Yet, it is on the more adequate knowledge of the processes of change in demographic, social, economic, and political fields that the chances for sustained advances in health and material welfare of half the human race may well depend.

SOME ASPECTS OF POPULATION HISTORY

By K. W. Taylor

Statistical evidence regarding populations is very scanty prior to the open-ing of the nineteenth century, but there is a great deal of indirect evidence from which approximate population levels can reasonably be inferred. I propose to deal briefly with three countries: France, England and China.

Population estimates for pre-literate periods of history have to be derived from anthropology and archaeology and the light they cast on the carrying capacity of a territory, having regard to resources of soil, flora and fauna, and to the state of the industrial arts at any given time. Rätzel, for example, has inferred that pure "collectional economies," that is hunting and fishing, in the Europe of 2,500 years ago would probably support from 3 to 6 persons per 100 square miles; that hunting plus some primitive agriculture would support from 0.5 to 2 per square mile; pastoral economies up to 5 per square mile; and settled but primitive agriculture from 5 to 15 per square mile.

On the basis of this kind of evidence and inference we may hazard an estimate that the present area of France had a population of about 4 or 5 million in the period just before the Roman Conquest. The Roman occupation, with its peace, order, and good government, its roads, its military and ad-ministrative centres, and its organization of agriculture and industry, made possible a fairly rapid increase in population; and it has been estimated that at the height of the Roman period of civilization (*circa* 300 A.D.) it had increased to about 12 to 15 million. In other words, the population trebled during a period of about 300 years.

The disintegration and eventual collapse of Roman civilization in France, the incursions of the barbarians, the disappearance of any effective central government, and the general disorders that accompanied the retreat into the dark ages put the economy of France back almost to the stage of primitive subsistence farming, and by the middle of the eighth century the population appears to have reverted to a level not much above the pre-Roman period, that is, probably somewhere between 6 and 8 million. The restoration of order and the development of an effective feudal system came with and followed Charlemagne, and population began to recover slowly but steadily. The twelfth and thirteenth centuries saw further improvements in trade and com-munications, in government and administration, and in the technique of agriculture.[9] Based on some detailed administrative records which have survived it is possible to make a reasonably sure estimate of 21 million as the

[9]See K. F. Helleiner, "Population Movement and Agrarian Depression in the Later Middle Ages" (*Canadian Journal of Economics and Political Science*, vol. XV, no. 3, Aug., 1949, pp. 368-77).

population of France in 1340, or a trebling of the population from its low point 600 years earlier.

At this level the increase in population appears to have ceased, and all the available evidence indicates a population for France between 20 and 22 million for the next 400 years. A moderate rate of increase was resumed in the eighteenth century, accelerated in the first half of the nineteenth, slowing down again after 1850. A figure of about 40 million was reached in 1910, and the French population has been relatively stable at that point for the past forty years.

In summary, France appears to have had a population "ceiling" of about 5 million under primitive agriculture, of about 20 million under pre-industrial European civilization, and a ceiling of about 40 million in the environment of the recent past.

The population history of England illustrates some further interesting factors affecting population growth. In the period before the Roman Conquest the available evidence suggests a population a little below 1 million. At the height of the period of Roman occupation, when England was a prosperous province of the Roman Empire and a large exporter of grain to the Roman armies of the Rhine, the population of the present area of England was probably about 4 or 5 million, a figure never again reached until the Elizabethan age. As in France, the collapse of Roman power, the marauding invasions from the north and from across the sea, and the reversion to a harassed and primitive agriculture indicate a probable population of about 1 million in, say, the eighth century.

The records of the Domesday Book, compiled in 1086, give a reasonably assured estimate of 1.8 million for that year. With the unification under the Normans, the growth of a village economy and the feudal system, population increased slowly. By 1485 it was about 2.7 million, an increase of 50 per cent in 400 years. Most of this increase appears to have taken place in the thirteenth century during which the feudal village economy matured and a town economy developed in the area south and east of a line from Southampton to the Wash, based upon a developing trade with France and the Low Countries.

The sixteenth century of the Tudors and Elizabeth produced a revolutionary change in the English position. Between the date of the early voyages of discovery around the Cape and across the Atlantic and the close of the Elizabethan age, a period of just over 100 years, the population of England was almost doubled. This rapid increase was the result of two sets of causes. There were great internal improvements—a century of domestic peace and strong efficient government, the first great enclosure movement which in spite of its short-run social problems greatly increased the efficiency of agriculture, and the economic results of ecclesiastical reform. But most important was the major revolution in environment consequent upon the discovery of America and the sea route to India. These sea-borne discoveries shifted the economic centre of gravity of Europe from the Mediterranean and the northern Italian cities to the Atlantic coast line. Cadiz, Lisbon, London, and Antwerp in due course grew up to and surpassed Venice and Genoa in wealth and importance. Prior to 1485 England was a frontier state on the outer fringe of the world; its economy was oriented toward Europe; its population and its modest wealth were heavily concentrated in the south and east; and its trade flowed through the small harbours at the eastern end of the Channel and the Thames estuary. Suddenly it found itself strategically set down at the very gateway to Europe. The profits of overseas trade poured in and found employment in new overseas ventures, in trade and shipping, and in textile and other manufactures which spread up through the Midlands and into Yorkshire, with accompanying improvements in internal communications. Before the end of the century Bristol came to rank second only to London in wealth and commercial importance. Like a potted plant, long left undisturbed on a window-sill, and then transferred to an open garden, the economy of England threw out new leaves and branches. By 1625 the lop-sided concentration of population in the south and east disappeared, as the west, the midlands, and the north responded to the effects of the new geography.[10]

After crossing the 5 million mark the population of England levelled out again as it approached the new ceiling made possible by the new environment. Further increase was slow, averaging about 1 per cent per decade during the next 100 years. Then came the Industrial Revolution with an extraordinary five-fold increase in 150 years, but the history of this period is too well-known to require comment.

To summarize, the population of England appears to have had a ceiling of about 1 million under conditions of primitive agriculture, a little over 2.5 million as a frontier province of fifteenth-century Europe, close to 6 million as a pre-industrial trading power, and about 40 to 45 million under the culture and conditions of the recent past.

The history of population in China is a fascinating topic, but on this occasion I shall discipline my enthusiasm and restrict my account to a brief and rather dogmatic sketch of the last 2,000 years. There is a great wealth of material on this subject, scattered through many thousands of volumes of Chinese dynastic annals and the commentaries of Chinese scholars.[11] Most of

[10]See a particularly interesting series of population maps in A. P. Usher, *An Introduction to the Industrial History of England* (Boston, 1920).

[11]For the average non-Chinese scholar the material appears almost as confusing as it is large; and even for those who have some familiarity with Chinese history and with the idiom of Chinese thought, the subject presents serious difficulties of reconciliation and interpretation. The official dynastic histories of China total well over 3,000 "volumes"; in addition there are many thousands of volumes of annals, and innumerable works by private scholars. Materials on population and related topics are scattered through all these classes of works. There are, however, a great many works devoted primarily to tax rolls, census reports, land distribution, etc. So far as I am aware no European and no modern Chinese scholar has made any systematic examination of all the available material. Among the best summaries of the basic raw materials on population in a European language is Edouard Biot, "Sur la population de la Chine et ses variations, depuis l'an 2400 avant J.C. jusqu'au XIIIe siècle de nôtre ère" (*Journal Asiatique*, ser. 3, vol. I, 1836, pp. 369-94, 448-74). In ser. 3, vol. II, 1836, pp. 74-8, he abstracts the principal figures for the fifteenth and sixteenth centuries; and in ser. 3, vol. V, 1838, pp. 305-31, he examines the problem of interpreting various technical terms used in the census records. These articles by Biot are chiefly a summary and examination of the section on population in the celebrated encyclopedia *Wen Hsien Tung Kao* compiled by Ma Tuan-lin early in the fourteenth century, and expanded by later scholars. E. H. Parker in "A Note on Some Statistics

the population records thus available are usually referred to as census records, but they are not properly such. They are primarily a part of the records relating to taxes, to military service, or to water-control or irrigation projects, and hence involve all the familiar problems that such records present.

Data relating to the earliest historical periods of Chinese history (800 B.C. *et seq.*) cannot be regarded as very satisfactory but could justify an estimate of something in the neighbourhood of 15 to 18 million during the Confucian period (*circa* 500 B.C.) for an area covering about 30 per cent of modern China (roughly the north-eastern quadrant). As the Chou dynasty disintegrated in the third century B.C., prolonged disorders, civil wars, and banditry spread death and destruction, and by the time Kao Ti the founder of the great Han dynasty had destroyed his rivals and reconstituted an effective central government the population appears to have been reduced by perhaps as much as 50 per cent.[12]

The Han dynasty (205 B.C.-221 A.D.) was one of the golden ages of Chinese history. Chinese are still proud to call themselves "the sons of Han." For 400 years domestic peace was not seriously interrupted; active programmes of flood-control and irrigation were developed; and the frontiers of settlement were pushed south and west. It is from the middle of the Han dynasty that we begin to get regular and useful population data. By the early part of the first century A.D. the population of China had reached about 60 million, and it remained not far from this level for the next 200 years. The area covered by this population was about two-thirds of the area of modern China, reaching westward to the lower ranges of the mountains bordering Tibet, and to the south it included the small but rich alluvial plains south of the middle reaches of the Yangtze (in the northern parts of the modern Hunan and Kiangsi).[13]

In due course the Han dynasty fell into decay and collapsed. With prolonged periods of violent disorder the country broke up into quarrelling rival Kingdoms, and for 400 years there was no central government. Fragmentary data for this period suggest a population of about 25 million at the close of the fifth century. At last in 618 China was reunited under the Tang dynasty which ruled for 300 years. Conditions of peace and the restoration of water-control works produced a recovery of population and by 750 it stood at about 65 million (that is, back at the former ceiling). Another cycle of dynastic collapse

Relating to China" (*Journal of the Royal Statistical Society*, vol. LXII, 1899, pp. 150 ff.), prints a table giving the officially recorded population for each year from 1651 to 1860, with a few brief explanations and comments. See also Bielenstein, "The Census of China during the Period 2-742 A.D." (*Museum of Far Eastern Antiquities*, Bulletin 19, 1947, pp. 125-63), and Liu Nan-ming, *Contributions à l'étude de la population chinoise* (Geneva, 1935).

[12]An ancient Chinese chronicler, describing the fifty years, 255-205 B.C., wrote, "Tsin in conquering the other six nations destroyed one-third of the population. In building the Great Wall 400,000 perished; in the mountain campaigns of the southern frontier 500,000 were lost; and in Korea 700,000 perished. For thirty years dead bodies filled the roads. Tsin's successor destroyed 200,000 in the trenches before Sian. Han, who finally conquered Tsin, destroyed several millions more." Quoted in the *Indo-Chinese Gleaner*, no. 6, Oct., 1818, p. 190.

[13]In this, and in the later expansions of their effectively occupied area the Chinese absorbed very little foreign population, but pressed the primitive aboriginal tribes back into the hill country, southward and westward.

and heavy mortality occurred in the tenth century, to be followed by a new and brilliant flowering of Chinese life and culture under the Sungs. In addition to reaching great heights in poetry and philosophy, in painting and in ceramics, the Sung administration followed a vigorous policy of improving and expanding water-controls and the encouragement of agriculture and new agricultural settlement, which carried the population up to 100 million at the end of the eleventh century.[14] Recurring dynastic disorders and the Mongol and Manchu invasions from time to time reduced this figure, but for 600 years with each returning era of peace the population pressed back toward this new ceiling.

In 1700 the population of China was about 110 million, and for 1850 the recorded figure had advanced to 420 million. It has been the fashion among recent Western demographic scholars to take little more than a look at these figures and promptly dismiss them as incredible, and along with them cast doubt upon all official Chinese population records. I shall argue that these records, properly interpreted, are substantially correct and consistent with the known history of this period.

In the first place the sustained rate of increase is not extraordinary.[15] It averages less than 10 per cent per decade. This was a century and a half of unbroken peace, strong and enlightened government, and a period of considerable improvement in all the agricultural and industrial arts and crafts. It also appears to have been a period which, in comparison with earlier centuries and with the succeeding century, was relatively free of disastrous floods, droughts, and famines.

Secondly, it was a period during which the mature settlement of much of the area of the rich provinces south of the Yangtze was accomplished. This mature settlement of a predominantly hilly country, extraordinarily well served by major and minor rivers, was made possible by great improvements in the art and skill of rice-growing, particularly in the careful and laborious terracing and irrigation of the steep hillsides. The significance of this steady southward expansion is shown by an examination of the provincial population totals for the years 1743 and 1842. In 1743 the nine southern provinces had a population of 33.7 million, in 1842 141.7 million, or an increase of 320 per cent. The nine northern provinces in the same years increased from 124.8 million to

[14]The importance of water-controls in the maintenance of Chinese agriculture and the expansion of settlement deserves special notice. Especially in rice-growing areas, a controlled water-supply is essential. Chi Chao-ting in *Key Economic Areas in Chinese History* (London, 1936), gives a good account of the significance of public works related to water-control, including an interesting regional-chronological analysis of the undertakings which throws much light on the direction and timing of the expansion of settlement. Li Chi in *The Formation of the Chinese People* (Cambridge, 1928) gives a regional-chronological analysis of city wall-building which helps to illumine obscure periods of Chinese population history. See also Yao Shan-yu, "The Geographical Distribution of Floods and Droughts in Chinese History" (*Far Eastern Quarterly*, vol. II, 1943, pp. 357-78).

[15]By way of comparison the population of Egypt which was about 5 million in the Augustan age, was only about 2½ million in 1800, rose to 11 million by 1907, and is now about 20 million. The population of India-Pakistan in 1600 was about 100 million, in 1850 about 200 million, by 1900 it was 280 million, in 1920 305 million, in 1940 385 million, and the estimate for 1950 is 420 million.

261.3 million, or by 110 per cent. The north doubled its population, but the south more than quadrupled. In 1743 the south contained 20 per cent of the total population, and in 1842, 35 per cent. In other words, it was only in the eighteenth and first half of the nineteenth centuries that the Chinese completed the occupation and settlement of their own country.

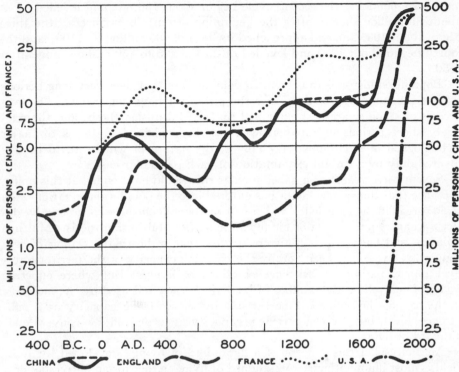

APPROXIMATE SMOOTHED CURVES OF LONG-TERM TRENDS IN POPULATION
(semi-logarithmic scale)

In the third place the Columbian discovery of America provided China with important new crops yielding high food values per acre. During the sixteenth and seventeenth centuries the cultivation of maize, sweet potatoes and peanuts spread around the world from America to China and in due course the Chinese became the largest producers in the world of sweet potatoes and peanuts and ranked second in the production of maize. During the latter part of the sixteenth century the Spaniards opened direct trade across the Pacific between South America and Asia, trading their pieces-of-eight for silks, porcelains and other manufactures. This trans-Pacific trade grew rapidly in importance and contributed to the development of manufactures and the increase in population of the coastal provinces of South China.[16]

Since 1850 the population of China appears to have come up against a new ceiling in the neighbourhood of 425 to 450 million. Current estimates put it

[16]During the seventeenth and eighteenth centuries, as a result of this trade, Spanish pieces-of-eight supplanted domestic Chinese coins as the principal currency of these southern provinces. I am indebted to Dr. L. C. Goodrich, Professor of Chinese at Columbia University, New York, for directing my attention to these and other points.

at 450 to 460 million (including Manchuria, the population of which is now overwhelmingly Chinese), which would indicate a maximum increase of only about 8 per cent in 100 years.

To summarize, the history of population in China can be represented by four successive sigmoid curves. The first approached its limit of about 18 million by 500 B.C.; the second cycle began about 150 B.C. and levelled off at about 60 million shortly after the beginning of our Christian era; the third began about 1000 A.D. and approached its limit of 100 million by 1100; and the fourth began about 1700 and levelled off in the 425 to 450 million range after 1850.

Population histories thus seem to demonstrate that over very long periods of time the curve of growth follows the pattern I have suggested. The long periods of stability are best explained by the Malthusian thesis, and the relatively short periods of rapid growth can be explained in terms of major technological or environmental changes, the nature of which are to be discovered only by a careful examination of each particular case.[17]

Seventy-five years ago a paper such as this would have ended at this point, but since that time a new factor has entered into the population equation—the rapid spread in the knowledge and use of reasonably effective contraceptive devices. This requires a major modification in the Malthusian thesis. Malthus believed, and I think history demonstrates, that hitherto the ceiling of any population cycle had been set by the carrying capacity of the territory at a level approximating a subsistence standard of living. But where effective means of controlling the number of births is known and used by the majority of the people, the ceiling will be set not by the carrying capacity at a subsistence level, but by the carrying capacity at a desired or conventional standard of living.

An analysis of this concept of a "standard of living" developed by J. A. Field is most illuminating.[18] A standard of living, either for an individual or a group or class, consists in the number and character of the desires which take effective precedence over the desire to marry or to increase the size of one's family. Malthus had recognized that a desire to maintain or improve one's standard of living was a part of the prudential checks to population, but he did not believe that prudential checks could operate effectively except on a very small fraction of the people; hence they could not save the population as a whole from a subsistence level. The relatively recent extension of birth-control practice to the masses of the people in Western European countries and in most parts of North America tends more and more to make procreation an alternative form of economic consumption. Parents can now consciously choose between maintained or improved levels of consumption and a larger family.

This popularization of voluntary control and planning of the size of families has developed a new set of worries for social demographers, as evidenced by the large volume of literature that has appeared during the last thirty years

---

[17]It should be noted that ceilings can be lowered as well as raised. In addition to the examples cited in this paper, reference may be made to Mongolia and Turkistan where a major climatic change seems to have set in 800 or 900 years ago and turned what was once a populous pastoral country into a desert.

[18]*Essays on Population by James A. Field, passim*, but especially at pp. 385-99.

centring around the rapid fall in the birth-rate, the invention of the reproductive index and its decline below replacement level, and the refinement of
population projections into the future. The recency of the introduction of this
new element into our North Atlantic culture precludes confident views as to
its longer-run implications. It has created possibilities of rapidly rising and
sustained standards of living for the masses of people; it has also made
possible a "twilight of parenthood." It is this second possibility that has been
worrying a great many people.

The behaviour of birth-rates in many countries during the past decade,
and especially during the past three years, has posted a warning that some of
these alarms may prove to have been premature. Whatever the reasons (and
they are various) the numbers of births during the war years were much greater
than anticipated, and the expected post-war peak in births has unexpectedly
continued for a further three full years. Undoubtedly many of these births
constitute the making up of a gap created by the war. Prosperity plus social
security have also had their effects. People are marrying at a younger age, and
there are some indications that the fashion in parenthood is toward having the
numbers of children desired at fairly short intervals, instead of spreading the
same number of births over twice as many years. Clearly such a change in
fashion does not alter the true rate of growth.[19] Some years must elapse before
safe conclusions can be drawn regarding the meaning of the current upsurge
in births; for it is not the birth-rates of a year or even a decade that count, but
the ultimate size of completed families. We shall have to await the evidence
of the size of the completed families of the current generation of parents before
the meaning of the statistics of the past ten years becomes clear.[20]

If the world can escape a cataclysmic war, the prospects for a great increase
in the productivity of human labour during the next fifty years seem assured.
The benefits of this increased capacity to produce can be taken up in various
ways: in more consumer goods and services, in more defence, in more leisure,
and in more people, or in any combination of these. Modern communities, by
varying the climate of opinion as well as by more positive measures, can
exercise a limited freedom of choice in deciding how they will enjoy these fruits
of progress. Unlike our forefathers we are no longer obliged to put almost all
of them into the cradle and then prematurely into the grave.

[19]Except for later "accidental" births which in the United Kingdom are estimated to be
about 10 per cent of all births to families who plan their births. *Report of the Royal Commission
on Population* (1949), p. 77.

[20]This widespread unpredicted upsurge of births has already produced a 1950 population
for the United States equal to the 1960 population as projected by the United States Bureau
of Census as recently as 1946. Until quite recently, the trend of births and deaths in the United
States indicated a probable population in 2000 of 150 to 175 million. Reasonable projections
could now be made for 200 to 240 million. (See J. S. Davis, *The Population Upsurge in the
United States*, Food Research Institute, 1949, and his article in *Foreign Affairs* of Apr., 1950.)
Projections made for Canada a few years ago indicated 14 to 15 million for 1971. We are almost
at 14 million now, and close to 18 million seems like a probable 1971 estimate. The projection
of 50 million more Americans, enjoying a still higher standard of living, has interesting implications for Canadian trade, investment, and the balance of payments.

DEMOGRAPHIC PATTERN IN HISTORY

By Josiah Cox Russell

'There are certain strategic advantages in taking Malthus as the starting-point for a study of population theory.... His true claim to fame rests upon the fact that people listened to what he said.'[1] Listening to him, both the public and the historians learned that population was determined largely by subsistence and other environmental factors and was therefore a product of historical forces rather than a cause of historical action. No one could accuse Malthus of being a demographic determinist. Very largely as a result of his views historians and others have tended to accept population as a fact to be taken for granted. In encyclopaedia articles, population usually appeared as a separate topic, much like *flora* and *fauna*, but well outside of the long section devoted to history. Placed in this inconspicuous and innocuous position, population has not received much attention from historians.

Further, demography has often been sponsored by mathematically minded persons who fail to stir the historians' enthusiasm: census officials, life insurance and other statisticians, sociologists, biologists, birth control and anti-birth control protagonists and ultra-nationalists. The interest of the census officials and life insurance specialists is written off as professional. Statistics is too often a kind of untouchable subject whose mention invokes a well-worn comparison which is supposed to be humorous. With this, unfortunately, sociology is infected and even economics (though far less so). The interest of the biologists tends to confirm the historian in his belief that population is naturally alien to real history. The topic is the subject of controversy among many whose bias is obvious in religion or nationalism: they are dangerous companions for any who value their reputation for impartiality. So while the historian finds 'population' next to 'popularity' in the card index, he regards it as popular with all of the wrong people. This short prefatory statement is designed to answer the question certain to rise upon further reading of the present paper, namely, 'If population is so important, why has it not been more carefully studied by historians?'

In view of the historian's attitude towards demography it is not surprising that population has not taken any particular form in the historical mind. Demography, like many other subjects, often embraces a wide variety of topics, but to-day the field is usually limited to a fairly well integrated body of knowledge involving total population and the factors which modify it. These considerations include size of

---

[1] J. A. Field, *Essays on Population*, ed. H. F. Hohman (Chicago, 1931), pp. 249–50. On Malthus, see especially J. J. Spengler, 'Malthus' total population theory: a restatement and reappraisal', *The Canadian Journal of Economics and Political Science*, II (1945), pp. 83–110, 234–64, especially the conclusion on pp. 262–4.

communities, birth-, marriage- and mortality-rates, age structure, and migration.[1] Such a body of closely related phenomena involving humanity might be expected to have interesting interrelationships and patterns of development which would preserve their essential characteristics over the centuries. Moreover, such factors as birth, death, migration and propinquity of residence are among the most pervasive influences upon human thought. The attitude of civilization toward them should help shape our culture. And in turn these demographic developments should be expected to affect human thought and action.

In the present article the pattern of demographic factors which help to cause human physical type to persist in given localities is considered first (§ 1). Then comes (§ 2) the study of human efforts, in the form of social control, to maintain population within the limits of subsistence. Thirdly, there is a consideration of conditions in which population breaks away from such control, to produce either a decline or an increase without relation to subsistence. § 4 is devoted to a discussion of migration. In the last two sections the major trends of population history are considered (§ 5) and the possibilities of the influence of population upon historical development (§ 6) assessed.

1. *Persistence of physical type*

A key problem of historical interest has been the question of persistence of physical type. It has been, indeed, an axiom of the physical anthropologists who see a continuation of prehistorical physical types even in present-day individuals. Other scholars have in many cases been inclined to question or to ignore this persistence of type, assuming that migration and conquest in the past must have blurred physical distinctions until racial continuation was largely destroyed. Upon this fundamental question the historical demographer is in a strategic position to shed light.[2] Its solution demands a study of processes of population change and function, many of which have been worked out for the present time. If the pattern of population structure and change of to-day can be projected far into the past, some explanation of the persistence of physical type may be reached.

One factor in this phenomenon of persistence is the size of human settlements. The largest communities are few in number and are usually well scattered. Clusters of great cities are often really great metropolitan areas. The smaller the size the more numerous the communities usually are, although in times when nearly everyone lived in villages this was not true. Recent study has shown that there is a definite

---

[1] The general outline of demographic study can be seen in the subject headings of *Population Index*, the quarterly bibliography (also containing occasional articles upon phases of population study) published jointly by Princeton University and the American Population Association. There are several books on the subject, among which the following may be mentioned: R. Benini, *Principii di demografia* (Florence, 1901); P. Mombert, *Bevölkerungslehre* (Jena, 1929); Otto Most, *Bevölkerungswissenschaft*; A. M. Carr-Saunders, *World Population* (Oxford, 1936). An attempt to apply the general outline to medieval history appears in my 'Late medieval population patterns', *Speculum*, XX (1945), pp. 157–71.

[2] Such an attempt is made in my 'Short, Dark Folk of England', *Social Forces*, XXIV (1946), pp. 340–7.

relationship between size and numbers of places within areas.[1] As yet the significance of this relationship does not appear great for history. Much more significant is the relationship between the size of community and such demographic factors as sex ratio, marriage-rate, and birth-rate: these relationships go far, as we shall see, to explain the persistence of type.

Let us begin with the sex ratio, usually given as the number of men per 1000 women in the population. The figures for England of 1377 show clearly that as places increase in size the sex ratio declines markedly.[2] The same holds true for modern population except for a few cities and areas where special conditions of employment attract great numbers of one sex. Industrial cities or frontier areas have in the past drawn more men than women, while a governmental city like Washington has more than the average of women.

The relative numbers of men and women might be expected to affect the attitude of the sexes to each other. The shortage of women in the frontier states of the United States was probably responsible for early adoption of women suffrage as well as for the granting of other rights and privileges to women. The numerical preponderance of women in England after the First World War was undoubtedly a major factor in setting the voting age for women at 30 and in postponing the 'flapper act' until 1928.

The sex ratio also parallels the percentage of persons who marry in a particular area. The greater the number of women, the smaller the percentage of married persons in the population.[3] Since marriage is usually the result of a choice by men, it would seem that a surplus of women leads men to wait, relying upon the excess of women to assure themselves of eventual marriage. There is, however, another factor in the situation. The family is usually not so effective a unit in the economic life of the city as it is in the smaller communities or upon the farm. In the latter place every member of the family can participate in the economic activities of the homestead while in the city the economic opportunities for the family are either limited or interfere with care of the children.

In a city environment of fewer men, fewer marriages, and fewer economic opportunities for wives and children, it is not surprising that there should be fewer children than in the smaller places. Further, the original advantage of the smaller places in birth-rate is increased by the higher death-rate among children in the larger places.[4] To some extent the normal inferiority of the cities in birth-rate is

---

[1] H. W. Singer, 'The "Courbe des populations", a parallel to Pareto's law', *Economic Journal*, XLVI (1936), pp. 254–64 and literature cited on pp. 258–63. The census enumeration of cities by size groups which have no mathematical relationship to each other provides one difficulty in these studies. Another difficulty is caused by the tendency to record population by such areas as townships rather than by communities. The differences between legal and actual communities is another problem.

[2] These data derive from poll tax returns of 1377 which have the names of the inhabitants upon the back of the returns. More detailed information upon these returns which, unfortunately, are only a fraction of the total number of returns, will be given in my *Medieval British Population* (to be published in 1948 by the University of New Mexico Press).

[3] Ibid. See also Eliz. R. Kramm and Dorothy S. Thomas, 'Rural and urban marriage in relation to the sex ratio', *Rural Sociology*, VII (1942), pp. 33–9.

[4] Even to-day this is generally true although the public health programme of some of the larger places and the decline of mortality from children's diseases have lessened the difference in mortality, for which originally the greater probability of infection in the larger places was apparently responsible.

offset by the selective emigration of persons of childbearing age to them, but this merely obscures the inability of the populations of the larger places to reproduce themselves.

The natural result of the differential in survival between the smaller and the larger places is a migration from the former to the latter. And since the smaller places have a high sex ratio (that is, more men) it is obvious that more women than men must have migrated from them to the cities. What kind of women would migrate? We might expect that these would be the persons to whom marriage came late or not at all. Since men tend to marry women of similar physical and mental characteristics[1] the women who differ from the norm in the community should leave in disproportionate numbers.

The atypical persons, particularly the women, have pressure upon them to leave the small places for the melting-pot of the larger communities. Here they enter a dwindling demographic current which causes nearly all groups that join it to decline in numbers.[2] On the other hand, the smaller places not only preserve their physical types[3] but tend to define them more accurately with succeeding generations as the atypical are forced out. Thus, unless disturbed by mass migration, such as has occurred in some of the New England towns, these places preserve their type for centuries.

The chances are, indeed, that the various regions and even smaller areas within the United States will develop more marked physical types as time moves on. The process is already at work, but as yet it is the geographical and climatic factors rather than the effects of selective mating and migration which have produced the situation. This is, of course, contrary to the idea that our processes of integration and levelling in this country are producing a typical American and destroying the individuality of the inhabitants of the various parts of the country.[4]

Such conditions explain why the anthropologists are probably correct in their assumption of the persistence of physical types throughout the centuries. This persistence of human types has other historical implications. If type persists, then other phases of local life should also persist. Folk-lore, provincial customs and other phases of local activities have a presumption of continuity which is hardly possible if there have been notable and general interruptions of physical continuity. Doubt about such continuity indicates that it is not the product of conscious human effort and policy.

---

[1] Burgess and Walter, 'Homogamy in social characteristics', *American Journal of Sociology*, XLIX (1943), pp. 109ff.; C. A. Anderson, 'Our present knowledge of assortative mating', *Rural Sociology*, III (1938), pp. 296–302.

[2] This disappearance of the Irish in the U.S. is a phenomenon which is already being commented upon. The Jews have lived in the cities for so many centuries that they are better suited to urban environment than other groups. This is reflected in their expectation of life.

[3] The persistence of regional intellectual characteristics has been commented upon by P. Bonfante, 'La persistenza dei caratteri fisici e psichici nella popolazione dello stesso territorio, I', *Proceedings of the International Congress for Studies in Population*, vol. III, pp. 163–6; also in *Genus*, I (1934), pp. 3–6.

[4] There is, of course, the possibility of production of both a general American type and quite distinctive regional and local types. Even within communities distinctive types may be defined and preserved. The 'railway tracks' and racial groupings help to maintain these.

2. *Social control of population*

More elemental than persistence of type is the survival of mankind within the limits of its subsistence. Humanity has been very conscious of this problem, the problem of having enough children for survival but not sufficient to produce overpopulation. This has been difficult since both the human and the subsistence factors are variables. Civilized society has sought the answer in large part in the formula that marriage should follow the attainment of suitable means of support.[1] The wealthy have not needed to consider this matter, while the very poor have often been rather irresponsible about it. The middle-class have been most concerned, and for that reason marriage has sometimes been regarded as peculiarly bourgeois. The medieval guild and manor kept this idea in the forefront of their thought, and it is a fairly general policy in our world to-day.

The existence of such a principle of dependence of marriage upon jobs makes for an interesting pattern of population by age. In general, marriage ought to be open to persons within the twenties and, if possible, by the age of 25. Roman men seem to have married at about 26 on the average.[2] Medieval figures are not easy to secure, but the age of marriage for women was not so low as many have assumed.[3] Modern figures are, of course, easier to obtain. Thus it seems that, even in the pre-modern world, the population could normally be maintained if men married in their midtwenties and women a little earlier. But since they could marry earlier, the possibility was always present of a situation in which more children might be born and a rapid increase of population might occur.

Another factor in the demographic problem is the age-distribution of the population. This may be presented in the form of a life table; and a comparison of life tables of various eras shows a remarkable consistency among pre-modern figures. The life table for men born in the years 1426–50 in England is a good example of data concerning conditions before the development of modern medicine.[4]

If we know the average age of marriage and have a life table available we can estimate the size of the average family, assuming the population to be practically stationary at the time. The number of men above the average age of marriage should equal the number of families, except for a small number of families headed by (usually) widows. Since the life table represents the age grouping of a stationary population, the number of men above the average age of marriage may be divided into twice the total number of males to get the average number of persons to the

---

[1] Other methods are used, but this seems to be the most efficient and general method employed since Christianity frowned upon infanticide and abortion.

[2] A. G. Harkness, 'Age of marriage and at death in the Roman Empire', *Transactions of the American Philological Association*, XXVI (1896), pp. 35–72.

[3] See my *Medieval British Population*, ch. VII.

[4] See Appendix. The percentage of persons in each age group may be secured by dividing the total (in the life table), 32,965 into the numbers in the column L_x. This is true if (a) the population is not changing rapidly and (b) the population has not been much affected by migration. The pattern of life expectancy is similar to the pattern called 'Oriental' by W. F. Willcox, 'Length of Life in the early Roman Empire', *Congrès International de la Population*, Paris, II (1937), pp. 14–22.

family.[1] For pre-modern times the number is usually about 3·5 persons.[2] This figure is lower than the five which is often assigned as that of the household.

To-day it requires about 2·7 children to a marriage to keep up the population; earlier times, with their heavier child mortality, must have required about twice as many in even the most favourable circumstances prevailing then.[3]

Even if we must correct the estimate by an allowance for more and earlier marriages the figure can hardly be reduced below six children to a family. The United States is not much more than replacing itself now, and other countries are already below the replacement level in births: some of the latter have been and are making efforts to increase their birth-rate.[4]

The hingeing of marriage upon means of support has provided a partially automatic control of population. In times of expanding economic opportunity men get jobs easily and marry earlier. These men usually have more children than those who marry later. Furthermore, the time between the generations is shortened, and this also tends to increase population. Conversely in bad times men marry later or not at all, which slows down the rate of population increase or actually reduces the number of people. By and large the population of the world has restricted itself in a reasonably satisfactory fashion most of the time.[5]

3. *Failure of social control*

Refusal to adjust human policies and institutions to the maintenance of population within the limits of subsistence has led to failure of social control of population. It may have resulted from the substitution of some other ideal than such adjustment or from extraordinary environmental conditions which more than offset the flexibility of normal social control. The substitution of other ideals has produced both increase and decrease of population in the past: whereas extraordinary environmental conditions have usually resulted in a decline. An instance of the latter is the Black

---

[1] The number is doubled to include females who approximately equal the number of males.

[2] Only in times of rapid population increase is this apt to be larger. The size of the household is important in estimating total population from evidence of fiscal and other data—the hearth tax of the later Middle Ages, for instant. These units sometimes vary considerably from normal household size. For the U.S. to-day see P. C. Glick, 'Types of families: an analysis of census data', *American Sociological Review*, VI (1941), p. 830.

[3] If the medieval life table is compared with a modern one (Dublin and Lotka, *Twenty-five years of Health and Progress*, New York, 1937, p. 34, for instance), one finds that of an original cohort of 1000 about 803 survived to age 45 in 1935 whereas in the medieval period only about 326 reached that age. Thus, allowing the assumptions of stationary age grouping and no migration, it required 2·46 times the modern 2·7 children to a family to maintain population: this would be about 6·6 children. However, the medieval table is based upon figures which are not too certain for infant mortality. The number of children actually required may easily have been seven or nine rather than eight.

[4] D. V. Glass, *Population Policies and Movements in Europe* (Oxford, 1940), especially ch. II, pp. 86–98.

[5] Other methods are given in A. M. Carr-Saunders, *Population* (London, 1925), pp. 15–17. Perhaps the most gruesome method is discussed by S. F. Cook, 'Human Sacrifice and Warfare as Factors in the Demography of pre-colonial Mexico', *Human Biology*, XVIII (1946), pp. 81–102. For a study of the relationship of marriage and tenure of land see G. C. Homans, *English Villagers of the Thirteenth Century* (Cambridge, Mass., 1941), ch. x.

Death of 1348 and succeeding decades. As we have seen, the number of children necessary to maintain the population in pre-modern vital conditions was quite large. Even then, under favourable auspices, population could increase, but it is equally clear that the margin of surplus was small and might be wiped out by any serious demographic disturbance.

This kind of situation occurred during the period of the Black Death. The original epidemic of 1348–50 probably carried off about a fifth of the people: the larger figures which are usually offered have been based upon estimates which failed to consider the age-specific mortality of the disease.[1] The bubonic plague killed the older persons in much larger numbers than the younger, so that data based upon older persons, notably the clergy, give too high a figure. The plague remained in endemic and occasional epidemic form until about 1430. During this period an average of at least ten or eleven children[2] to the family must have been required to replace the population: it is not surprising that the English population, and probably the European, was not much more than half its pre-plague size by 1400.

Plague, indeed, was probably responsible for the greatest single impetus in the decline of the Roman Empire: the attack of A.D. 166 must have been of serious proportions. Since recovery did not follow as in the fifteenth century much else must have been wrong. Many causes of Rome's fall have been suggested: political despotism, heavy taxation, ossification of the economic structure, soil erosion, slavery, malaria, and even depopulation. To these tuberculosis might be added as another contributory factor.[3] The extensive urbanization of the Empire would probably have been sufficient to have precipitated the decline, given the other unfavourable conditions listed above. Once a pattern of human action, such as that leading to depopulation, has been established it often continues under its own momentum, long after the original cause has ceased to operate.

While society for the most part is intensely interested in adjustment of population to subsistence, it occasionally sets up some other ideal. In India and China the religious duty of maintaining the family and ancestor worship have supplanted this

[1] On English population see my *Medieval British Population*, ch. IX.

[2] The life table for persons born 1376–1400 shows that on a comparative basis with modern population it would take about 14·5 children to keep up the population. The estimate of ten or eleven is based upon the greater proportion of persons married in the period and upon earlier marriage as a result of economic opportunities opened by the plague. The disturbed conditions could hardly have permitted even eleven on the average. H. P. Fairchild, *People* (New York, pp. 44–5), estimates that at best an average of fifteen to a family would be the top limit.

[3] The heavy death-rate of the Romans aged 20–30 years would seem to indicate heavy incidence of tuberculosis. See article by Willcox cited in n. 4, p. 392. Other factors are discussed in K. S. Gapp, 'The universal Famine under Claudius', *Harvard Theological Review*, XXVIII (1935), pp. 258–65; T. Frank, 'Race mixture in the Roman Empire', *A.H.R.* XXI (1916), pp. 689ff. criticized by E. Cicotti, 'Motivi demografici e biologici nella rovina della civiltà antica', *Nuova Rivista Storica*, XIV (1930), pp. 29ff; A. Landry, 'Quelques aperçus concernant la dépopulation dans l'antiquité gréco-romaine', *Revue Historique*, CLXXVII (1936), pp. 1–33; V. H. Simkhovitch, 'Hay and history', *Political Science Quarterly*, XXVIII (1913), pp. 385–403; E. Huntingdon, 'Climatic change and agricultural exhaustion as elements in the fall of Rome', *Quarterly Journal of Economics*, XXXI (1917), p. 173; J. Bourdon, 'Les méthodes de la démographie historique', *Bulletin of the International Congress of Historical Sciences*, 1936; literature cited under 'malaria' in the *Enciclopedia Italiana*.

demographic ideal.[1] Children are married early and are kept within their father's or even their grandfather's house. The result has been an increase in population out of all proportion to the means of subsistence, producing a state of society almost like that envisaged by Malthus. In good years a considerable part of the people lives but little above the starvation line; in bad years famine destroys much of the marginal group. If humanity refuses to solve its demographic problem intelligently, nature does it ruthlessly with a certain contempt for human dignity.

For a time the Industrial and Medical Revolutions threatened to produce as serious an overpopulation in Europe as Oriental religious ideas do in Asia. As time went on, the old check on population increase, the linking of marriage to jobs, was largely lost because of the extensive economic opportunities opened up for men, women, and children. Simultaneously, the decline in mortality allowed millions to live who would otherwise have died early. Population in Europe and America rose with amazing rapidity throughout the nineteenth and early twentieth centuries.[2] England and Wales, for instance, had less than nine millions of people at its first census of 1801 but, by the end of the century, had passed the thirty million mark. Other countries had the same experience. It is not surprising that thoughtful persons the world over were disturbed by the prospect of untold millions of people.

In the long run developments occurred which counteracted this demographic upturn. Society raised the minimum age for employment and concentrated more in larger cities where birth-rates were low. The spread of education has both postponed marriage and set up higher standards of living. These in turn have been conducive to a greater employment of methods of birth control.[3] There followed a radical reduction of the birth-rate in countries as a whole.

The rate of increase in the past has differed by countries and regions. Nearly every country has experienced a period of expansion of its people: these periods have usually been characterized by territorial expansion and aggressiveness. Some periods of expansion have left little impression. The Hundred Years War was one of the worst failures: England's war against a much larger France failed to leave much evidence demographically. On the other hand, the Spanish era of expansion in the sixteenth century was channelled into the New World with a most economical use of demographic opportunities. Certainly it saved Spain from a long and bitter fight against the Berbers of North Africa.

Society does, then, occasionally lose demographic control and exhibit startling losses and gains in population. Usually an adjustment of some kind is made with reference to subsistence, although the present situation in India and China is a grim one, while the possibility of a population race between Russia and the rest of the Western world is now in prospect.

---

[1] Kingsley Davis, 'Human fertility in India', *The American Journal of Sociology*, LII (1946), pp. 243–54; Ta Chen, 'Population in modern China', ibid, pt. II, pp. 1–126 and literature cited there.

[2] R. R. Kuczynski, *Population Movements* (Oxford, 1936), pp. 23–30; and others believe that the decline of mortality was primarily responsible for the great increase.

[3] N. E. Himes, *Medical History of Contraception* (Baltimore, 1936). See also W. S. Thompson, *Plenty of People* (Lancaster, Pa., 1944), ch. III for underlying principles.

4. *Migration*

Migration is, of course, one of the great factors in population movement. But its occasionally spectacular character has given mass movement too great a prominence among historical influences. Even the consistent operation of ordinary demographic forces of an exceedingly unspectacular character produces certain movements of people which fall under the head of migration. In general, these movements are probably more important than the better heralded developments. In spite of the attention given to the subject the relations of the migrants to those already in the territories concerned are not well studied and are still open to misunderstandings.

As we have seen in the first section the failure of the larger communities to replace their own population leads naturally to a migration from the smaller places to fill the vacuum. The existence of greater numbers of women than men in the cities indicates a larger number of women as migrants, since as a whole the numbers of the sexes are approximately equal. The probability of the migration of atypical women has been mentioned: the same is probably true to less extent of the men. For both sexes certain types of occupational appeal must also have drawn persons to the cities. Little has been done to isolate the effectiveness of this particular appeal to migration.

The effect of distance upon migration in the distant past is not very well known. Some late medieval evidence would show that in England at that time the amount of migration varied inversely with distance.[1] This would be a natural assumption. It would be modified by unusual opportunities or by unusual geographical configuration. The crusades provide interesting cases of long-distance migration: the colonization of the New World does likewise. The wealth of the migrants is another factor. The United States would have had a quite different migration history if, in the mid-nineteenth century, the Irish had had more money and the Germans less.

Some of the most spectacular demographic movements have been associated with possibilities of sudden wealth: 'Pike's Peak or Bust' is paralleled by other rushes, to California, South Africa, the Yukon, or Australia. These migrations have drawn, for the most part, the ambitious, the strong, the healthy, and the young, who faced the hardships incident to the struggle in the hope of magnificent rewards. Of a quite different character are the migrations of the sick, the aged or the feeble towards the climates which promise warmth and health. Even in death there is migration to the home cemetery. Many migrations, however, are seasonal in type: harvest workers moving north to ripening crops or pastoral people moving up the valleys to the summer pasture. In the case of the medieval Mesta, these journeys covered several hundred miles a year from southern Spain to the higher country.[2]

The most impressive migrations are usually those of ruling classes, normally fighting groups, such as the great German invasions of the first half of the Middle

---

[1] By a study of the origin of the freemen of York. See my *Medieval British Population*, ch. XI. See also *Science*, N.S. XCIII (1941), pp. 89–90. On this phase of migration as well as other problems in the topic see D. S. Thomas, *Research Memorandum on Migration Differentials* (New York, 1938).

[2] For this migration see J. Klein, *The Mesta* (Cambridge, Mass., 1920).

Ages. Yet they frequently involved only a fraction of the population. After the Norman Conquest, the Anglo-Saxon nobility was largely displaced, many of them migrating as far east as the Byzantine Empire,[1] while their places were taken by William's followers. Yet the few thousand families involved in this exchange hardly disturbed the million or more people who merely submitted to the new lords as they had acquiesced in subordination to the old. The change probably made little difference: within a few generations they called their children William, John, or Henry instead of Ethelred, Egbert, or Alfred. The relative indifference of the subject classes to change of rulers is illustrated by a recent article showing that Odoacer was probably a Hun rather than a German.[2] The inhabitants of Italy were evidently not much interested in Odoacer's origin, and his reign probably did not differ materially from that of Theodoric or Ricimer. Like the Huns of Odoacer or even the Ostrogoths of Theodoric, ruling classes often disappear, leaving scarcely a trace of their physical type upon the demographic pattern of the area, however profound their effect upon the administrative history of the country.[3]

Frequently the story of the destruction of the ruling class is cast in such general terms that the destruction has been interpreted as applying to most of the population. But armies in ancient days were seldom large enough to damage great areas in a short time. Only in our time, and occasionally before, has there been a wholesale displacement or destruction of peoples. To-day patriotism, levelling social classes into a unified citizenry, with intense hatred of national enemies, has caused the removal and the destruction of masses of people on a scale never attempted before. Even Cato's 'Carthage must be destroyed' was mild compared to the devastation of the last decade.

In a sense the Romans were a super ruling class who imposed themselves upon the whole of the existing structure and in many cases hardly disturbed the preceding ruling classes. The Romans naturally restricted the warlike and predatory activities of their predecessors, but often allowed them to enjoy a considerable part of their previous income and powers. The revival of the Celts in England after the Romans left was probably made possible by the persistence of elements of the older organization modified by conformity to Roman principles of imperial administration. In most of the provinces the process of cultural assimilation very markedly changed the original pattern until a thorough Romanization resulted, but it was not a well directed and intentional process on the part of.the Empire.

A conquering group accompanied by a considerable body of settlers creates a real problem in the matter of adjustment of the existing people to the migrants. Here the study of maps or plots of farming settlements often suggests the pattern which obtained.[4] The allocation of land made at the time of the original settlement is often

---

[1] F. M. Stenton, 'English families and the Norman Conquest', *Transactions of the Royal Historical Society*, 4th series, XXVI (1944), pp. 1–12, especially pp. 4, 5.

[2] R. L. Reynolds and R. S. Lopez, 'Odoacer: German or Hun', *American Historical Review*, LII (1946–7), pp. 36–53, 836–45.

[3] The round-headed people who once held sway in England are a case in point. Few of the descendants of this gifted race seem to be left in the island.

[4] This has been attempted in my article, 'The Short Dark Folk of England', *Social Forces*, XXIV (1946), pp. 343–4.

preserved in outline with considerable fidelity. The pushing aside of one group by another normally follows only if the original group is very primitive. The North American hunting Indian lost badly because his way of life demanded so much land: Europeans were not willing to reserve territory for nomadic purposes. The ideas of the pueblo-Indians about ownership and use of land are more easily understood: those Indians have been relatively secure in their lands.

Migration varies also by social class, wealth and education. During the Middle Ages the educated clerks had a common language, Latin, which permitted them to move freely in clerical circles throughout the cultural area of western Europe. Arabic enabled, and to some extent still enables, its masters to circulate throughout the Mohammedan world.[1] To a less extent this freedom of movement was enjoyed by feudal lords and by merchants because of their money and common interests. In modern times there has been a kind of international society of wealth and power which has transcended national lines and languages.

Thus migration is the product of a series of forces. The unequal replacement of population to be found in places differing in size induces local migrations. Economic opportunities or quests for health and comfort produce constant social movement. Mighty mass migrations have brought about relatively permanent demographic changes while the spectacular ruling class conquests have often had quite ephemeral results. Mankind thus moves in great restless currents which often, like rivers, retain a pattern of motion over the centuries, though occasionally the demographic pattern is altered within a short time.

5. *Trends of population and trends of history*

Despite efforts to regulate population and to maintain stability of subsistence the western world has seen three long trends in numbers, two upward and one downward. These trends seem fairly clear[2] although the data available for estimating population are not as satisfactory as might be wished. Until the eighteenth century the idea of a census for determining the total number in a population was almost unknown.[3] Even such a well-known achievement as the Roman census is open to a wide variety of interpretations.[4] The demographer has, for the most part, to use data secured for purposes of taxation. The figures thus obtained must be corrected

---

[1.] Emphasized recently by P. H. Hitti, 'America and the Arab Heritage', *The Arabic Heritage* (Princeton, 1944), p. 32. For medieval clerical migration see C. H. Haskins, 'The Spread of Ideas in the Middle Ages', *Speculum*, I (1926), pp. 19–30.

[2] This article deals primarily with western data but the trends of Asiatic population appear to have been similar, at least in recent centuries. A. P. Usher, 'The history of population and settlement in Eurasia', *Geogr. Rev.*, XX (1930), pp. 110–32. Beloch has written most upon the long trends of early population: *Die Bevölkerung der Griechisch-Römischen Welt* (Leipzig, 1886); and three articles upon ancient, medieval, and Renaissance population in *Zeitschrift für Social Wissenschaft*, II (1899), pp. 505–14; III (1900), pp. 405–23 and 765–86. For other bibliography see *Enciclopedia Italiana* article on 'Popolazione'.

[3] Early and good data from Sweden are given in D. S. Thomas, *Social and Economic Aspects of Swedish Population Movements*, 1750–1933 (New York, 1941).

[4] Tenney Frank, *Classical Philology*, XIX (1924), pp. 304 ff. On ancient population problems see T. Waleck-Czernecki, 'Sur les méthodes de la statistique des populations anciennes', *La Pologne au VIIe Congrès International des Sciences Historiques* (Warsaw, 1933); Cicotti, *Indirizzi e metodi negli studi di demografia antica*.

for omitted areas, exempt classes of persons and other inadequacies. Even then one has frequently only the number of houses or of heads of families, which must be multiplied by some appropriate number to secure an estimate of the total population. Once this is achieved for a large area at a definite time, the trends of total population may be estimated by a sampling process, using fragmentary data of other periods. The process is interesting but taxes our ingenuity.

Fortunately, as more information is secured about population more answers are available to difficult questions. For instance, evidence emerges which shows a definite relationship between the metropolitan centre or centres and the smaller places within a geographical area. If considerable numbers of the larger cities can be shown to be declining in a given period, the normal condition of most of the lesser places, as well as of the total population, is likely to be one of decline. Since the trend of population in the cities is often easier to follow than that of country places this demographic relationship between metropolitan areas and smaller places is a valuable axiom. It naturally works the other way also. Thus a population estimate for London at the time of the Domesday Book can be made upon the basis of trends for both Middlesex and the whole country.

In general, there have been three major movements of population in the Mediterranean and European world since about 1000 B.C. The first was a long period of increasing population which continued until the dawn of the Christian era. Its highest point was reached in succession by the several countries in the area until about the end of the third century A.D. The highest total population was probably during the second century. The constant urbanization was but one phase of the great expansion of peoples in the area. While the city of Rome may have had its population sustained by migration from the entire Empire after the beginning of the decline of Italian population, the other cities of the peninsula probably followed the general trend. In recent years even distant England is considered to have reached the limits of its expansion in the third century.

The second great phase of demographic history was the decline which occurred in the Mediterranean-northern European area from about A.D. 200 to A.D. 700. This decline was probably not so sharp in the area north of the Alps as it was in the Mediterranean area, where urbanization had gone the farthest. Indeed, it may well be doubted if any depopulation occurred in the area east and north of the old Roman frontier. It probably did not affect the territory in which Mohammedanism took hold at all.[1] The very evident contraction of the cities is the best evidence of the extent and depth of the decline.

Whatever caused and maintained the great decline, its effects ran out about A.D. 700–1000. From about the latter date to the present time population has increased in the European world and its extensions in newly discovered lands. The first phase was a fairly rapid increase which was ended abruptly by the Black Death.[2]

---

[1] The expansion of Islam was in part a riding of the demographic current of the time.
[2] Some evidence in my *Medieval British Population* would seem to indicate that medieval population was levelling off in England by 1348 and that, without the intervention of the plague, it would have stabilized at 4–5 million persons.

The plague continued as a factor until about 1430 and probably reduced the total population to a little above one-half of the pre-plague figure. From 1430 until near the end of the eighteenth century the increase resembled the medieval rise but it has not been determined satisfactorily. The last century and a half has seen a stupendous increase in numbers induced largely by the Industrial Revolution, but the present indications of lowering birth-rate foretell a levelling off of the population of most peoples by the end of the present century. The chronological pattern of the declining birth-rate is much the same throughout the world except that different countries are at different stages. Thus France has increased but little in the last two generations, England's birth-rate has been declining rapidly, while Russia's high birth-rate probably has a gradual decrease.

Against these trends of population may be set the general trends of history. The Roman Empire persisted some centuries beyond the beginning of the decline of its population. If this decline became general by A.D. 200, it preceded the end of the Empire in the west by perhaps 300 years, depending upon which of several dates is chosen as its terminus. The decline preceded the triumph of Christianity by only a hundred years. Christianity was an Oriental religion and developed in those parts of the Empire which had probably begun their demographic decline earlier than the total decline of the area as a whole. There is a change in history beginning about 1000 which parallels but follows by a century or so the upturn of population. The typical developments of this period got well under way only in the twelfth century. The second half of the Middle Ages is markedly different from the first half.

The Black Death turned the population trend downward for only about eighty years. From then on there was a gradual increase until about 1800 and a very rapid increase thereafter. The great break in religion and in other phases of life occurred not in 1348 nor in 1430, but, again, a century later. Similarly, the more striking changes of the modern world are the products of the last hundred years rather than of the first generation of the Industrial Revolution.

If, then, we correlate the changes in trend of population with those of the major turns of history we find that the population changes occur a century or more before the changes in history. Precedence then goes to population change rather than to historical changes. If population change does always underlie historical change, the discovery of such a relationship raises the question as to the extent and kind of influence which demographic changes produce upon the general course of human development.

6. *Demographic influence upon history*

Little has been written upon the possibility of demographic influence upon the broader trends of history, although the effect of certain shorter trends, such as the consequences induced by decreasing population, has received attention.[1] The

---

[1] Some instances of such population studies are: A. Lösch, 'Population cycles as a cause of economic cycles', *Quarterly Journal of Economics*, LI (1937), pp. 649ff.; H. P. Fairchild, 'When the population levels off', *Harper's*, 1056 (1938), pp. 596–602; Frank Lorimer, 'The significance of imminent population changes in the United States', *Milbank Memorial Fund Quarterly*, XV (1937), pp. 207–18; J. M. Keynes, 'Some economic consequences of a declining population', *Eugen. Rev.* XXIX (1937), pp. 37–47; Stewart, 'Measure of influence of population', *Sociometry*, V (1942), pp. 63ff.

subject presents all the difficulties of any field in which there are few criteria to help in giving an answer acceptable to the learned world. One can, however, begin with the time correlation between demographic and historical data and consider whether the types of demographic change could have been the cause of the historical trends. For other types of demographic influence the same procedure may be followed. If sufficient evidence of this type is available, the presumption in favour of demographic influence increases. Demographic influence, or any other influence, should be detected in the interests of an era.

The problem of analysing such interests is important for establishing principles of historical determinism. The deepest interests of any age must be sought in the ideals of the men whom that age regards as beyond human criticism, in the beliefs so abhorrent to that age that its holders are not protected by normal judicial processes, and in the pattern of life that institutions of the age are designed to protect. Society is intolerant of that which it holds dear and tolerant of those areas of thought which it values less. Further, each age rationalizes its own conditions in terms of its chief interests; that is, it tends to exalt the existing situation.

The problem of determining the influence of population change is complicated by the fact that such change apparently sets up economic forces which are themselves powerful influences. Thus the separation of the economic and demographic forces is difficult since their integration is so close. However, the direct influence as it appears in rationalizations may be separated profitably.

The two types of demographic trends show different rationalizations. The people of the era of increasing population should naturally be interested in the family as the institution of its increase. That is true of both the classical and modern periods. The Roman emperors did their best to encourage population increase: they were representative of the demographic trends of the time of the establishment of the Empire. The spirit of celibacy was strong in the early medieval period, forcing the clergy to adopt it even against their own will.[1] This again is what might be expected of an age of declining population. The large family was the ideal of a century ago. To-day the two-child family is usually pictured as the ideal: it is consonant with our practically balanced population. The appearance of polygamy among the Mormons is precisely what might have been expected of the rapidly growing West. These rationalizations are significant in that they were outside of, and often somewhat antagonistic to, the very general human desire to stabilize population.[2]

As mentioned above, the influence of population change is probably felt most on the economic life of a people. The effect of population increase is known to be an increasing prosperity if it occurs within the limits of subsistence.[3] We all know how prosperous boom-towns are with their striking development of property values,

---

[1] H. R. Bitterman, 'The beginning of the struggle between the regular and secular clergy', *Medieval and Historiographical Essays in Honor of J. W. Thompson*, ed. Cate and Anderson (Chicago, 1938), p. 25. The emperors were forced by public opinion to abolish laws against celibacy. Cf. Cicotti in *Metron*, IX, pp. 150–1.

[2] This probably explains the two types of demographic ideas of the Middle Ages: celibacy for the clergy and marriage for the laity. Even for the latter there was a feeling against second marriages.

[3] R. R. Kuczynski, *Population Movements*, pp. 61–79; J. R. Marriott, 'Population and prosperity', *Nineteenth Century*, CXXI (1937), pp. 636–79.

their optimistic attitudes, and their enthusiastic citizenry. On the other hand, the depression of the declining city is also known, with its low rents, its conservative attitudes, and its general air of hopelessness.[1] Is this true of long periods of history as well as of modern cities?

In general, the two periods of increasing population, classical and modern, have been eras of prosperity of varying quality. Certainly the late Roman-early medieval period was as depressed as one would expect of an epoch of declining population.[2] The general characteristics of the two types of historical periods thus do conform to the expected under the population influence thesis given above. It might be questioned whether the variation in prosperity was not the cause of the population changes except that the population change preceded the economic change.

The most prominent result of the combination of population-economic conditions has been in the attitude toward life on earth. In times of long-continued prosperity and population increase, this life has been regarded as a good life, while in adverse conditions the opposite has been true; the people have longed for the next world and its heavenly possibilities. This has had a profound effect upon heroic ideals, institutions, and loyalties. In general, the secular state has represented this world, and the Church, the next world.

We tolerate a variety of loyalties only where we are not intensely interested. The era of declining population and depression permitted only one church: it was evidently interested in religion in a primary way. The political loyalties of that period were often surprisingly complicated. The Roman Empire of the West and the barbarian kingdoms which succeeded it all succumbed in these centuries. Even a political papal state arose, the bishops and abbots had a large amount of secular power, and the Church penetrated deeply into the lives and habits of its communicants. Both classical and modern times have seen the state elevated to a similar position: we may accept any one of several religions, but we must have only one patriotism.

The sinners and saints reflect the same alinement. The great sinner of the medieval periods was the heretic, while the saint was usually celibate and poor. The saint was associated with the divine to the extent that he could perform miracles: such was the faith that existed in the supernatural in that period. The classical age deified some of the Roman emperors, but felt little need of the supernatural. This world was satisfactory to them. To-day our heroes are apt to be national leaders, and our confidence in humanity is illustrated by the belief of at least one modern religion that its lay leaders can accomplish miracles of healing.

To this reconstruction of history certain objections at once appear. Why, for instance, should monasticism have increased so rapidly and have reached its height in the age of population growth following 1100? Ought not this age to have been primarily one of secularization?

---

[1] See n. 1, p. 400. Also M. M. Rosen, 'Population growth, investment and economic recovery', *American Economic Review*, XXXII (1942), pp. 122–5 and the literature cited there.

[2] For a study of this age see my 'The Ecclesiastical Age: a demographic interpretation of the period A.D. 200–900', *Review of Religion*, V (1941), pp. 137–47.

The explanation is probably one of cultural lag. The new prosperity of the period found expression in the ways of the preceding period, in the endowment and building of great churches and monasteries. Yet it will be noticed that even within the great ecclesiastical expansion, a secular trend set in after the height of enthusiasm for austerity had been reached in the Cistercian and Carthusian movements of the twelfth century. The Austin canons of the same century, the mendicant friars of the thirteenth, and the collegiate churches of the fourteenth century indicate an increasingly secular interest. During these centuries lay brothers almost disappeared from the religious houses. In the fifteenth century the decline of monastic libraries and increasing evidences of boredom on the part of the monks show a continuation of the secular trend, illustrated even more by the extensive construction of parish churches and widespread enthusiasm for preaching and theology.

In even the early stages of the shift from increasing to declining population some psychological effects are apparent. In this stage Rome established its fortified frontier as monumental evidence of the relaxation of Roman aggressiveness. The Maginot Line was a symbol of France's lessening demographic expansion, while the reluctance of Great Britain to fight an offensive war on the continent was another sign of the same state of mind.

The very nature of population change defines its possibilities as an influence upon history. With rare exceptions it is a slow, ponderous force. Major diversions in population trend exert influence so slowly that their results are apparent only one or more centuries later as they induce alterations in economic life and intellectual currents which oppose, modify and sometimes overcome the inertia of the last great demographic movement. Thus the very tardiness of the change would allow its causes to escape attention. Population change acts somewhat as a geological disturbance which tilts the land into a different plane. The movement of population, like that of water forced in a new direction, still follows as far as possible the old watercourses and only reluctantly creates another pattern by erosion. Yet even then the outlines of the older system remain, adding complexity and variety to the pattern.

APPENDIX

Generation life table of males born 1426–1450 in England

The data for this table are drawn from the manuscript inquisitions post-mortem in the Public Record Office in London for ages over four. These inquisitions give the date of death of the deceased and the ages of the heir or heirs. The demographic data for each person thus come from two inquisitions: (1) the inquisition giving his age when he enters upon his inheritance, and (2) the inquisition upon his death. The accuracy of the date of death is high, since the actual day of death is usually given. The years given for the age of heirs average within one of the correct number for heirs up to the age of 23 and within 3 years between 23 and 35. Since most of the heirs are under 35, the data are very satisfactory.

The data available for children under 5 are very few. Since the expectation of life for India a generation ago was very close to that of this period of English history for almost the whole of the ages 5–80, I have assumed that the Indian expectation, particularly of the more agricultural parts, would resemble the medieval English expectation and have substituted it. A more detailed discussion of these data will appear in my *Medieval British Population* (to be published by the University of New Mexico Press in 1948). Another and earlier life table appeared in *Speculum*, xx (1945), p. 160.

Generation life table of males born 1426–1450 in England

Age interval	Mortality rate for interval	Probability of surviving the interval	Number surviving to age x of 1000 born	Number of years lived in age interval	Years of life remaining at age x	Expectation of life at age x	Age at death
x to $x+n$	q_x	p_x	l_x	L_x	T_x	e_x^0	
0	14·00	86·00	1000	907	32,965	32·96	32·96
1–4	10·00	90·00	860	3512	31,858	37·04	38·04
5–9	7·69	92·31	774	3720	28,346	36·62	41·62
10–4	4·26	95·74	714	3495	24,626	34·49	44·49
15–9	6·02	93·98	684	3318	21,131	30·89	45·89
20–4	10·18	89·82	643	3052	17,813	27·70	47·70
25–9	13·48	86·52	578	2695	14,761	25·54	50·54
30–4	10·56	89·44	500	2368	12,066	24·13	54·13
35–9	16·35	83·65	447	2052	9,698	21·70	56·70
40–4	12·95	87·05	374	1750	7,646	20·44	60·44
45–9	17·37	82·63	326	1488	5,896	18·09	63·09
50–4	16·48	83·52	269	1235	4,408	16·39	66·39
55–9	28·57	71·43	225	965	3,173	14·10	69·10
60–4	24·19	75·81	161	708	2,208	13·71	73·71
65–9	24·47	75·53	122	535	1,500	12·30	77·30
70–4	28·17	71·83	92	395	965	10·49	80·49
75–9	41·18	58·82	66	262	570	8·64	83·64
80–4	33·33	66·67	39	162	308	7·90	87·90
85–9	50·00	50·00	26	98	146	5·62	90·62
90–4	80·00	20·00	13	40	48	3·69	93·69
95–9	100·00	0	3	7·5	7·5	2·50	97·50

PITFALLS IN POPULATION FORECASTS

AND PROJECTIONS

By Harold F. Dorn

E XPERTS ON population have projected their curves into the future
and the outlook is startling. Manufacturers who try to estimate
future markets have been expecting a population of 140 million by
1940, but the calculations of our contributors . . . show . . . that hardly
more than 132 or 133 million are to be expected by 1940." . . .

"As our statisticians look further into the future, they see possibilities
of still greater declines in growth with the probability of a stationary
population. They show that we shall probably attain a population between 145 and 190 million during the present century with the probability that the actual population will be nearer the lower figure than the
higher. Such a prospect is radically different from that predicted a
generation or even a decade ago" [1].

These words written by President Hoover's Research Committee on
Social Trends in 1933 marked the beginning of a new era in the development of demography. Population forecasts were not new in the United
States. Since the earliest days of the nation, geologists, business men,
writers, economists, statesmen and even presidents had published predictions concerning the growth of the population of the United States.
But no single group of these forecasters ever had been generally recognized as having special competence to prognosticate demographic
changes. As a result, persons from all walks of life felt free to peer into
the crystal ball of the future and to chart the growth of the nation's
population.

The words of President Hoover's Research Committee on Social
Trends recognized a particular group, called demographers, and gave
endorsement to their special ability to forecast population changes.
This endorsement was widely accepted by the public, by business men,
by governmental agencies and by fellow scholars and scientists.

It was an auspicious beginning. Seven years later the Director of the
Bureau of the Census announced that the population of the United
States on April 1, 1940 numbered 131,669,275 persons. Allowing for
underenumeration, officially recognized by the Bureau of the Census,
demographers nearly a decade prior to this date had predicted the total
population more accurately than the Bureau of the Census had been
able to count the actual population! In the words of Irene Taeuber in

an article reprinted with approval by the editors of *Population Index*, "With improved data, new techniques, and the precise measurement of the demographic transition that was occurring, demography tended to become science rather than literature" [2].

Confidence in the reliability of estimates of future population became widespread. O. E. Baker undoubtedly expressed the opinion held by many demographers and non-demographers alike when he said, "The population of the United States ten, twenty, even fifty years hence, can be predicted with a greater degree of assurance than any other economic or social fact, provided the immigration laws are unchanged" [3].

This belief gained wide acceptance in spite of the fact that estimates frequently were prefaced with disavowals of predictive accuracy. The following statement by Thompson and Whelpton is typical:

"Some care must be exercised in the use and interpretation of these estimates. It is to be emphasized that they are not predictions of future population size, nor are they to be assumed to indicate the probable sex and age structure. They are, strictly speaking, merely statements of what the size and the sex, age, color and nativity composition of the population would be at specified future times if birth rates, death rates, and immigration were to follow certain specified trends.

While it is true that the fertility and mortality assumptions have been chosen with regard to the indicated trends of vital rates, the purpose of the estimates is to show the approximate range within which future populations would fall under the influence of current trends, rather than to arrive at a single most probable figure" [4].

But most readers obviously assumed that these sentences were merely a polite bow to scientific caution and did not take them very seriously. Nor can they hardly be blamed. For why should demographers be continually revising population forecasts with ever increasingly elaborate assumptions if they themselves did not believe that the forecasts had some validity? And were not demographers writing papers and making speeches which either implicitly or explicitly accepted the validity of the forecasts? It seemed incredible that demographers were merely doing sums in arithmetic for self entertainment; they must be serious and really believe that the projected population estimates were in fact reasonable forecasts or predictions of the future.

So overwhelming was this belief that economists, governmental officials and business men accepted the projections as being substantially correct. This acceptance was buttressed by the developments of population change during the decade of the 1930's.

On January 31, 1941 the Bureau of the Census reported, "If the 1930 birth and death rates had continued, the population of the country would more than reproduce its numbers by about 11 per cent per generation. . . . In 1940, however, as a result of changes in fertility and mortality during the decade, the population was no longer maintaining its numbers. As a matter of fact, if the 1940 birth and death rates continue, the population would in the long run fail to reproduce itself by about 4 per cent per generation" [5].

But, as a matter of historical fact, the 1940 birth and death rates did not continue unchanged. The men and women who bear children refused to have their personal relationships regulated by governmental press releases. By 1942 the birth rate had increased 20 per cent since 1939. Concerning this increase, the Metropolitan Life Insurance Company stated, " . . . the conditions of 1942, continued unchanged into the future, would lead us to a population eventually increasing at the rate of 18 per cent per generation" [6]. Did this really mean that the hypothetical John Q. Public, who in January 1941 was doomed to become an ancestor without progeny, now could look forward to a long, if not numerous, line of descendants?

In my analysis of this change in the birth rate in September 1942 I pointed out that the increase had resulted principally from a larger number of first and second births and concluded, "It is not possible to permanently maintain a population by an increase in the number of first and second births alone, especially when the number of births of the fourth order and higher is decreasing. For this reason the computation of net reproduction rates based on the number of births registered during one year not only is unwise but may also be misleading. . . . "

"The apparent increase in the birth rate since 1933 is the result of an increase in the number of first and second births and, consequently, does not represent an increase in the lifetime fertility of the women of childbearing ages. It is doubtful that this increase will continue beyond 1942. After that date a decline seems inevitable, at least for the duration of the war. If such is the case, the potential decrease of the population, somewhat prematurely announced by the Bureau of the Census in 1941, will become a reality" [7].

After increasing slightly during 1943, the birth rate started declining but by the end of 1945 still was about 13 per cent higher than in 1939. Beginning in 1946 the trend was abruptly reversed; the 1947 birth rate exceeded the 1939 rate by nearly 50 per cent. This was the highest birth rate since possibly 1920. Concerning this, Whelpton said in a report of the National Office of Vital Statistics dated October 7, 1948, "It is just as improbable that the high rate of 1947 will remain in effect as it was that the low rates of 1933 would do so. Both were the results of unusual conditions—the great depression of the early 1930's and the demobilization and high prosperity following World War II" [8].

During 1948 the birth rate declined about 4 per cent. By now some demographers were becoming uneasy. The April 1949 issue of *Population Index* stated, "Until recently the course of population development in Western nations was generally believed to be well charted and understood. This is now a matter of some doubt" [9].

The disquietude of consumers of population forecasts was vigorously expressed by Joseph S. Davis of the Food Research Institute at Stanford University before the American and Western Farm Economics Association in Laramie, Wyoming on August 20, 1949. With all the righteous indignation of a trusting wife who has just discovered the activity of a philandering husband, Professor Davis charged, "I am ashamed that, like most of my fellow social scientists, I have so long accepted the conclusions of the population specialists with naïve faith. . . it is disheartening to have to assert that the best population forecasts deserve little credence even for 5 years ahead, and none at all for 20–50 years ahead. . . . Population forecasting is *not* a simple matter. Available techniques do *not* permit reliable prediction to be made for 5, 10, 20 or 50 years ahead. The best may be *far* wrong. Our net reproduction rate is *not* near unity, but has been well above it ever since 1940. It is *not* reliable as a basis for prediction. There is *no* assurance of any peak population at any future date. The age structure of the population does *not* 'inherently' point to cessation of growth and eventual population decline. Our major population problems are not prevention of such decline. There is no adequate basis for expecting the fertility rate, or the crude birth rate, to drop to or below the level of the early 1930's and to remain at that low level . . . planning for food, agriculture, industry, schools, et cetera, can *not* be safely done on the basis of supposedly expert population forecasts . . . . If we continue to build on the crumbling foundations I have described, we shall have no excuse for consequent errors in our own work" [10].

With this devastating indictment Professor Davis arraigned demographers before the bar of judgment not only of fellow social scientists but of the entire nation. Are they guilty or not guilty? Before rendering final judgment let us first look at the development of demography, and more especially population forecasting, in historical perspective and then examine briefly the current demographic situation.

EARLY FORECASTS

As I pointed out previously, forecasting the future population of the United States is not a recent development. Benjamin Franklin, as early as 1751, estimated that the population of the colonies was doubling about every 20 years due to natural increase alone [11]. The early forecasters had almost no basic demographic data beyond the total size of the population available as a guide and even these meager data covered only a very few years. It is not surprising then that forecasts prepared during the early years of the nineteenth century assumed an indefinite increase in population at a geometric rate. Several presidents, including Thomas Jefferson and Abraham Lincoln, in the days when presidents undoubtedly prepared their own papers, advised Congress that the population of the nation would continue to increase at a rapid rate. In his second message to Congress, Lincoln thought that the total population very likely might be as large as 102 million in 1900 and 217 million around 1925 [12].

By the middle of the nineteenth century the belief that population could continue to increase according to the Malthusian Law, $P = Ce^{rt}$, was being questioned. The Compendium of the United States Census for 1850 summarized the projections of various forecasters and presented a number of new estimates based on a decrease in the rate of growth.

Several of these early predictions proved to be surprisingly accurate for relatively long periods of time. The estimates of Bonynge published in 1852 did not deviate from subsequent census enumerations by as much as 3 per cent until 60 years later in 1910 when his estimate exceeded the census enumeration by 5 per cent [13]. His estimates for later dates, however, have considerably exceeded census enumerations and the estimate of 703 million for 2000, seems likely to be at least 3 to 4 times the possible population on that date.

Another remarkably accurate series of predictions were those prepared by Gannett for the National Conservation Commission in 1909 [14]. These deviated by not more than 3 per cent from the census enumerations from 1910 through 1940; his estimate for 1950, 150 million, will miss the census count probably by less than one per cent. The estimate of 249 million for 2000 undoubtedly is considered by most demographers as at least 25 per cent too high. But as will be pointed out later it is viewed as being exceedingly probable or even somewhat too low by some economists. It should be remembered though that the year, 2000, is nearly a century after the preparation of the original estimate.

But as Gannett so aptly remarked, "Several predictions of our population have been made at various times by different and more or less complicated and elaborate methods. One or two of these predictions have by accident hit very near the truth, as made known by later censuses, but all have been finally wide of the mark" [15]. Moreover these estimates were all wide of the mark because they assumed a much larger increase in population than actually took place. Evidence is abundant to demonstrate that the slower than expected increase of population did not result from population increase outrunning means of subsistence. Something had happened to the Malthusian Law.

By the end of the nineteenth century, some persons trained in the more rigorous disciplines of mathematics and the natural sciences began to question the value of qualitative wisdom or the mechanical extrapolation of trend curves such as the Malthusian Law as methods of prediction. One of the first of these was Pritchett writing in the

Quarterly Publications of the American Statistical Association in 1891 and again in the *Popular Science Monthly* in 1900 [16, 17]. He observed that the Malthusian Law could not accurately describe the growth of population in the United States and that, in general, the Law was irrational since with indefinite increase in time population also would increase without limit, which is manifestly impossible.

. Pritchett restated the general law of population growth as follows: When not disturbed by war, famine, immigration, etc., population increase goes on at a constantly decreasing rate. It should be possible to express this law by means of some rational mathematical function. "And it does not in the least diminish the value of such a mathematical formula, for the purpose of prediction, that it is based upon no knowledge of the real causes of the phenomena which it connects together" [17].

Examining the growth of population from 1790 to 1880 Pritchett observed that it could be reproduced very closely by a third degree power series, $P = A + Bt + Ct^2 + Dt^3$. The fact that this function had no upper asymptote and that if extrapolated backward in time P would become zero or even negative apparently did not seriously disturb Pritchett. So firm was his faith in the ability of rational mathematical functions to describe demographic phenomena that he prepared estimates for ten centuries in advance.

His faith brought little credit to the American Statistical Association which published his forecasts nor did it positively advance knowledge of how to forecast population growth. The estimate for 1910 was only 3 per cent too high but the error increased rapidly thereafter. The estimate for 1950, 191 million, will be about 27 per cent in excess of the census enumeration. The estimates of 386 million for 2000 and of 41 billion for 2900, do not appear realistic at this time.

LOGISTIC CURVE

Attempts to predict population growth by means of some rational mathematical function involving population and time reached their zenith in 1920 in the publication by Pearl and Reed of a paper in which they derived an empirical curve which conformed to certain reasonable postulates concerning the growth of populations [18]. This was an independent discovery of a function which much earlier in 1838 had been suggested by the Belgian mathematician, Verhulst, but which had remained unnoticed undoubtedly due to the absence of sufficient reliable demographic data by which its validity could be tested [19]. This curve, $P = K(1 + e^{a+bt})^{-1}$ now known as the logistic was placed on a firm rational basis by Lotka shortly after the publication of the paper by Pearl and Reed [20].

I do not believe it essential for the purposes of this discussion to develop the rational basis of the logistic. It will be sufficient to state that

TABLE I

ENUMERATED AND ESTIMATED POPULATION OF THE UNITED STATES
(in millions)

Year	Census[1]	Pearl[2]-Reed[2] I	Pearl[2]-Reed[2] II	Dublin[3] 1931 High	Dublin[3] 1931 Low	Scripps[4] 1928 (Jan. 1)	Scripps[5] 1931 (Jan. 1)	Scripps 1933[6] High	Scripps 1933[6] Low	Scripps 1935[7] High	Scripps 1935[7] Medium (April 1)	Scripps 1935[7] Low	Scripps 1943[8] High	Scripps 1943[8] Medium	Scripps 1943[8] Low	Scripps 1947[9] High	Scripps 1947[9] Medium (July 1)	Scripps 1947[9] Low	Census[10] 1949 (July)
1900	76.0																		
1910	92.0		91.4																
1920	105.7	107.4	106.1			123.6													
1930	122.8	122.4	120.1	131.0	131.0	138.3	132.5	134.5	132.5	132.6	132.0	131.2							
1940	131.7	136.3	132.8							139.2	137.0	134.1	138.7	138.5	138.3				
1941	133.2																		
1942	133.7																		
1943	134.7																		
1944	136.5																		
1945	138.1																140.8		
1946	139.6																142.2		
1947	141.2																143.3		
1948	144.0																144.5		
1949	146.6																		
1950	149.2	148.7	143.8	139.0	139.0	151.6	139.8	148.5	140.5	146.1	141.6	136.2	145.0	144.4	143.0	148.0	146.0	144.9	
1960		159.2	153.0	147.0	146.0	162.7	143.9		146.0	159.5	149.4	137.1	156.5	153.4	147.7	162.0	155.1	149.8	144.0
1970		167.9	160.4	151.0	148.0	171.5	144.6	190.0	145.0	172.8	155.0	134.0	167.9	160.5	148.7	177.1	162.0	151.6	146.2
1980		174.9	166.3	154.0	145.0		142.9			185.8	158.3	127.6	179.4	165.4	145.8	increase thereafter	increase until about 2000 then decline	decline thereafter	148.2
1990		180.4	170.8	154.0	140.0		declines thereafter		declines thereafter		declines thereafter	declines thereafter	189.4	167.1	138.9				149.9
2000		184.7	174.3	152.0		186.0							198.7	166.6	129.1				160.0
ultimate		ultimate 197.3	ultimate 184.0											decline	decline				

[1] Enumerated population, 1900–1940; calculated as of July 1, 1941–1949.
[2] Science, 92, 486–488, 1940.
[3] Problems of Population, 1932, pp. 115–125.
[4] The Am. J. Sociol., 34, 253–270, 1928.
[5] Problems of Population, 1932, pp. 77–86.
[6] Recent Social Trends, p. 48.
[7] J. Am. Stat. Ass., 31, 457–473, 1936. (High is based on high fertility, low mortality, 200,000 net immigrants annually beginning 1940; medium is based on medium fertility and mortality with 100,000 net immigrants annually beginning 1940; low is based on low fertility, high mortality, no net immigration.)
[8] National Resources Planning Board, 1943, p. 29. (High is based on high fertility, low mortality, 100,000 net immigrants annually beginning 1945; medium is based on medium fertility and mortality, 100,000 net immigrants annually beginning 1945; low is based on low fertility, high mortality, no net immigration.)
[9] Bureau of the Census, 1947. (High is based on high fertility, low mortality, 200,000 net immigrants annually beginning 1950; medium is based on medium fertility and mortality, 100,000 net immigrants annually beginning 1950; low is based on low fertility, high mortality, no net immigration.)
[10] Bureau of the Census, Series P-25, No. 18, 1949.

it is in harmony with our rational ideas about population growth. Moreover, there can be no doubt concerning the theoretical validity of the logistic as a description of many diverse types of growth phenomena. But the question confronting us is, does the logistic represent the past growth of the population of the United States with such reliability that it can, with confidence, be used to predict the future?

Pearl and Reed fitted their first logistic to the population of the United States from 1790 to 1910 before the results of the 1920 census were available. They forecast the 1920 and 1930 populations with an error of less than one per cent. The forecast overestimated the 1940 population by 3.5 per cent and it will underestimate the 1950 population by about one per cent. (These forecasts, together with others discussed below, are presented in Table I.) The projections are accurate enough to satisfy all except the most captious critics and set an example of forecasting ability which might well be the envy of other social scientists.

But was this accuracy really due to the discovery of the natural law of population growth and the superior ability of demographers to foresee the future or was it merely a fortuitous historical event such as the earlier forecasts prepared during the nineteenth century which were mentioned above?

As soon as a preliminary count of the 1940 census enumeration was announced Pearl and Reed published a comparison of this count with the estimate by Logistic I [21]. Even though the estimate exceeded the census count only by about 3.5 per cent Pearl and Reed did not have the courage of their convictions. Apparently they agreed in part at least with Thompson and Whelpton who earlier had written, "An S shaped curve has been fitted to the past population of the United States by Pearl and Reed, and prolonged to indicate the future population. To the authors, it seems probable that these estimates will prove too high due to restricted immigration and lowered birth rates" [22].

Pearl and Reed were prepared for this contingency. Their earlier investigations of the ability of the logistic to describe the growth of a great variety of populations had led to the enunciation of the principle, that any population can be expected to continue to follow, in its later growth, the same logistic curve it has followed in its earlier growth, only if no serious changes have occurred in conditions governing previous growth. If changes do occur, a new logistic should be computed.

In spite of the fact that the 1940 forecast met rigid mathematical tests for a good forecast in that it deviated from the census enumeration by less than twice the standard error of forecast, Pearl and Reed decided to compute Logistic II from census data for the entire period 1790–1940. The fit to past growth was remarkably close and resulted in an estimated 1940 population less than one per cent greater than the census count. Pearl and Reed did not express a clear choice for either

Logistic I or Logistic II but suggested that the relative merits should be decided by future events. However, they seemed to have a slight preference for the fledgling Logistic II over the time tested Logistic I which had remained tried and true for 30 years.

Alas, their faith was ill rewarded. In 1950, Logistic I will underestimate the census count by about one per cent but the newer Logistic II will fail in its first test since it will underestimate the census count by about 4 per cent. This may not appear large when compared with predictive errors of many other social, economic and biological phenomena but it fails to meet the mathematical requirements for a good forecast since it will deviate by about twice the standard error of forecast from the census count and what is worse this error will become progressively greater in the future. No, here was not a mathematical law which could mysteriously, within its parameters, contain the forces governing past population growth in such a manner that, following the demographer's touch, the future would be accurately portrayed. Just as for the Malthusian Law, something had happened to the logistic law.

USE OF NET REPRODUCTIVE RATES

A method of analysis of population growth, different in conception from those discussed so far in this paper, had gained widespread acceptance by the early 1930's. In 1911, Sharpe and Lotka had shown that a population continuously subject to a fixed set of fertility rates for women of each age and a fixed set of mortality rates for each age, in the absence of migration, ultimately would assume a stable age distribution [23]. The ultimate birth rate, death rate and rate of natural increase, therefore, could be computed and compared with those prevailing at any time prior to stabilization. These ultimate rates were called true birth and death rates and their difference, the true rate of natural increase.

These concepts were extended by Lotka in subsequent papers, but were first brought forceably to the attention of demographers by the publication of a paper by Dublin and Lotka in the *Journal of the American Statistical Association* in 1925 in which these concepts were applied to the analysis of population growth in the United States [24]. They pointed out that as a result of high fertility and mortality rates in the past, the current age distribution of the population was unusually favorable to a high crude rate of natural increase. However, if the existing fertility and mortality rates should continue unaltered, in the absence of migration the age distribution of the population would change in such a manner that the annual rate of natural increase would be reduced about 50 per cent, from 11.1 to 5.5 per 1,000.

Lotka also showed how to compute the ratio of total births in two generations. This had been first shown by Böckh in 1884, but had been subsequently overlooked [25]. This ratio, now known as the net reproduction rate, was given wide publicity by the publications of Kuczynski beginning in 1928 [26].

Net reproduction rates for all possible segments of the population were computed and published. When the requisite birth and death statistics were lacking, demographers invented ingenious substitutes for the net reproduction rate. Never before had the procreative effort of a population been so closely studied.

As demographers kept a sensitive finger on the fluttering demographic pulse of the population, their regular bulletins pointed more and more to the possibility that the population of the United States was but a withering branch of a decaying ancestral tree. Not only was the true or potential rate of population growth rapidly declining to a level which would eventually result in a decrease in the size of the total population but also the actual excess of births over deaths was becoming smaller and smaller. In 1939 I pointed out that during 1935 and 1936, the first two years for which vital statistics then were available on a residence basis, 5 of the 93 cities of 100,000 or more population and 14 cities of 50,000–99,999 population actually had more registered deaths than births [27].

It is not surprising that population forecasts based on the true rate of natural increase reflected the pessimism of the time. In 1931, Dublin presented two projections of the population of the United States before the General Assembly of the International Union for the Scientific Investigation of Population Problems in London [28].

The most optimistic forecast assumed that the birth rate would continue to fall until it reached a level which would support a stationary population under the best mortality conditions foreseeable. An expectation of life at birth of 70 years by 1970 seemed the maximum possible. Accordingly, Dublin assumed that the true birth rate and death rate would be equal and stabilized at 14.3 by 1970 and that they would continue at that level until 2100.

With these assumptions the population of the United States faced a dismal future. In the absence of migration, it would reach a maximum of 154 million between 1980 and 1990 and then decline to 140 million by 2100. Even so Dublin reported, "the supposition on which this first estimate is based seems altogether too optimistic."

His second "more reasonable" estimate assumed that the true birth rate would fall to a level of 13 per 1,000 by 1970 and then gradually decline until it reached a level of 10 per 1,000 by 2100. With the same mortality assumption as before and in the absence of migration, a maximum population of 148 million would be reached by 1970 followed by a decline to 140 million by 2000 and to 76 million by 2100.

These predictions are remarkable not so much for their specific numerical values as for the fact that a prominent American demographer had stated publically that the population of the United States almost certainly would decline in the very near future. The most pessimistic of previous forecasters had assumed merely that the rate of increase would approach zero at some distant time. Moreover, Dublin expressed the opinion that "my extreme prediction for 2100 may turn out to be conservative after all."

It is hardly necessary to ask, how have these forecasts stood the test of time? The census enumeration in April 1950 will report a population larger than the maximum resulting from Dublin's second forecast and within 3 or 4 million of the maximum forecast by his first optimistic projection. No, the true rate of natural increase and the net reproduction rate, in spite of their theoretical importance, did not hold the key to the future. In fact they seemed to obscure the future. Just as with the Malthusian Law and the logistic curve, something was wrong with the net reproduction rate.

ESTIMATES OF SCRIPPS' FOUNDATION

The most authoritative and widely accepted series of population estimates have been those flowing from the tireless industry of Whelpton of the Scripps Foundation. His procedure which he terms the analytical method, "consists of (1) analyzing mortality, fertility, and migration trends in different population segments, (2) framing hypotheses regarding the future trends of these factors by observing their previous behaviour and appraising the influence of changing industrial, social, and legal conditions, and (3) building up successive hypothetical populations, beginning with the last actual population, by applying hypothetical factors to different population segments. The results thus show the composition as well as the size of the indicated future population" [29].

The first of these predictions was published in 1928 [30]. I shall call the numerical results of Whelpton's computations, predictions or forecasts for convenience in discussion. However, he has steadfastly maintained that he was not predicting the size of the population at some future date. "No claim is made that the Scripps Foundation estimates represent a law of population growth. They are simply the results of an empirical process. . . . These estimates represent simply what will happen under certain conditions of immigration, birth-rates, and death-rates, conditions that are believed to be reasonable, based on the experience of recent years" [31].

I shall not digress to discuss whether a rose is a rose. Regardless of Whelpton's protestations, the results of his computations have been widely regarded and used as forecasts of future population change not only by fellow demographers but by other social scientists and by governmental officials and businessmen.

The 1928 projection missed the 1930 enumerated population by less than one per cent but overestimated the 1940 census enumeration by about 7 million or somewhat more than 5 per cent. In 1950 though, it will again be within one per cent of the census population. The population would continue to increase at a decreasing rate, reaching 186 million by 2000. Although prepared by an entirely different method, these estimates were closely similar both in trend and absolute size to those resulting from Logistic I prepared by Pearl and Reed.

Concerning these estimates Whelpton said, "It is true that striking medical discoveries may cause the population to vary upward from these predictions. More likely, however, wars or a greater practice of of birth control may cause a variation downward" [32].

Additional study apparently convinced Whelpton that the last sentence was true, for three years later before the same sessions of the International Population Union at which Dublin presented the estimates mentioned above, he read a paper which made the pessimistic Dublin appear relatively optimistic [33]. The population of the United States now was scheduled to reach a maximum of 144.6 million by 1970 and to decline rapidly thereafter.

Whelpton explained this radical change in point of view as follows: "The fact that the present estimates indicate a population for 1975, which is about 31,000,000 below that indicated by the estimates prepared four years ago, serves to illustrate the cumulative effect during a 45 year period of the acceleration in the decline in the birth-rate from 1927 to 1931, since the same method of estimating was followed in both cases and little change was made in the trends of death-rates and immigration. Perhaps the actual course of population growth will lie between the two extremes, although at present it appears as though the lower estimates are the more probable, and that the maximum during the century will not exceed 150,000,000, even though surpassing the 142,600,000 mark resulting from our present calculations" [34].

The population projections of the Scripps Foundation were given an aura of authority with their acceptance by President Hoover's Research Committee on Social Trends. Here was the stamp of approval of fellow social scientists who presumably would be expected to be most critical. Moreover, the Committee had at least quasi-official standing.

The report of the Committee published in 1933 contained two alternative forecasts of population prepared by the Scripps Foundation [35]. The low estimate did not differ materially from the forecast presented by Whelpton before the International Population Union in 1931. The high estimate was somewhat less than Whelpton's 1928 forecast up until 1950 but after that date it assumed a less rapid decline in the rate of growth so that the population would number 190 million by 1980.

The authors placed very little confidence in the high estimate. Concerning it, Thompson and Whelpton said, "It is believed by the authors, however, that the actual population will be considerably nearer the minimum than the maximum figure, especially by 1980" [36]. They preferred a forecast obtained as a weighted average of the two estimates, but giving increasingly greater weight to the lower up to 75 per cent for 1980. On this basis the future population would be about 143 million in 1950, increasing slowly thereafter to about 157 million by 1980. The future still looked dark.

The interest and concern of various governmental agencies about the effects of the gloomy population outlook upon the nation found expression in a report, *The Problems of a Changing Population*, published by the National Resources Committee in 1938 [37]. Revised estimates of future population changes, prepared by the Scripps Foundation, were included in this report and strongly influenced the Committee's recommendations.

The estimates prepared for this report represented a full-blown shot gun approach to population forecasting. All possible combinations of the various assumptions concerning the trend of fertility, mortality and migration gave 18 series of possible future population change. This wide variety of projections emphasized the position Whelpton always had maintained but which few people really believed, namely that his projections were not forecasts of actual populations but were intended to show the inevitable consequences of the continuation of certain assumed trends in fertility, mortality and migration. Only three series will be mentioned, here, those selected by Whelpton to represent high, medium and low estimates.

The low series was more pessimistic than any previously published. The population would reach a maximum of about 137 million between 1955 and 1960 and thereafter decline rapidly [38]. The high series resulted in forecasts slightly lower than the high estimates prepared for the President's Research Committee on Social Trends. The total population would continue to increase, though at a decreasing rate, and by 1980 would number about 186 million. Whelpton did not consider either of these very probable for he said, "At the present time it seems to us that the medium series will be closer to what happens than the high or low, though probably somewhat too high. According to this series, the population will reach its maximum of about 160,000,000 soon after 1980, and then begin to dwindle numerically" [39].

This opinion was shared even more strongly by the Committee on Population Problems for it did not even include the high estimate in the body of its report. The highest estimate shown in detail by the Committee was Whelpton's medium series which assumed medium fertility, medium mortality and net immigration of 100,000 annually after 1940. As pointed out above these assumptions would result in a declining population before the end of the century. The possibility that the population of the United States, before the end of the century, would reach a maximum from which it would decline was becoming almost a truism. Even a governmental agency could endorse this belief without criticism. A slight modification of the medium estimate (assuming no net immigration) was republished, with apparent approval, by the Bureau of the Census in 1941 [40].

The onset of the war, a somewhat more rapid decline in mortality than had been anticipated and the continuation of the upward turn in the birth rate which had started in the middle 1930's led the National Resources Planning Board to request the Scripps Foundation to revise the 1937 forecasts. The revised estimates published in 1943 were higher than the 1937 figures but under most combinations of assumptions concerning the trend of fertility and mortality, a gradual slowing down and an eventual cessation of population growth was projected [41]. As Thompson and Whelpton said, "the outlook for the population of the United States remained much the same."

In spite of war casualties, the population continued to increase so rapidly that by 1945, it exceeded the highest estimate made only 3 years previously. Although the Scripps Foundation saw no reason for materially altering its long range projections of fertility and mortality trends, it was apparent that the "baby boom" had made obsolete the base population on which future projections rested. Accordingly, a set of revised estimates were prepared and published in 1947 under the sponsorship of the Bureau of the Census [42].

Whelpton summarized these by saying, "The outlook after 1950 is for a continuation of the long time decline in population growth, both in absolute number and rate. Moreover, there is a strong possibility that within a few decades the population will reach its maximum size and will begin to decrease unless heavy immigration is resumed" [43]. This view also must have been shared by the Bureau of the Census for it had selected the forecasts based on medium fertility and mortality and no net immigration for publication in advance of the complete report [44]. According to this set of assumptions, a maximum population of some 165 million would be reached about 1990 after which a decline would occur.

Because of the interest in such figures, the report contained a series of annual forecasts for 1946–1949. By the time the report was published in the latter half of 1947, the actual population at that time, as subsequently calculated by the Bureau of the Census, exceeded the number forecast in the report by nearly two million.

With population increase outstripping the speed of governmental printing presses, heroic action clearly was called for. On February 14, 1949 the Bureau of the Census issued revised forecasts of population for July 1, 1948 to 1955 [45]. The forecast for July 1, 1950, was nearly 2 million greater than the highest and five million greater than the lowest 1947 forecast for that date. As of December, 1949, it is likely that this revised "revised" estimate may be nearly two million too low.

REASONS FOR PAST FAILURES

Demography, is it science or literature? It is no answer to the record I have just sketched to say as did the editors of *Population Index* in their review of the 1947 forecasts prepared by the Scripps Foundation and the Bureau of the Census, "the revised estimates are not predictions. They are projections . . . " [46]. Predictions, estimates, projections, forecasts; the fine academic distinction among these terms is lost upon the user of demographic statistics. So long as numbers which purport to be possible future populations are published they will be regarded as forecasts or predictions irrespective of what they are called by the demographers who prepare them.

What is wrong with the methods of forecasting population I have just described? Must they be discarded as unsound and should demographers as Professor Davis suggests, return to qualitative wisdom as a forecasting method? [47]

It is hardly necessary to mention why the Malthusian Law failed. It is inherently irrational since it assumes that population will increase indefinitely with indefinite increase in time. But what of the logistic curve, popularly known as the law of population growth?

So far as I have been able to judge neither Pearl nor Reed, at least as soon as the first flushes of parental pride had subsided, maintained that the logistic was anything more than an empirical curve which described exceptionally well the past growth of the population of the United States. Its standing as a law of population growth was critically examined by Wilson and Puffer in 1933 in a publication apparently little known to demographers with the conclusion, "If . . . the statement that the logistic . . . affords a rational law to such an extent as to permit the extrapolation of the curve for forecasting purposes and the interpretation of the constants as constants of nature, we are forced to take serious exception to it . . . " [48].

The use of the logistic as an empirical curve to describe population growth implies that the parameters average the factors which produced the observations. When the curve is extrapolated for predictive purposes, this implication is absurd unless the growth of population actually has an inherent stability. At first thought, it may seem preposterous to assume that there can be any inherent stability in population growth. But observations on many human populations in the past reveal that there has been amazing stability over long periods of time in population growth.

Furthermore in forecasting we are interested, from the statistical point of view, primarily in the trend line. For any given year in the future, the observed point may fall above or below the projected trend line; except in unusual instances, it will not fall exactly on the curve.

But granting all this, it seems unlikely that the logistic will be used extensively for forecasting population growth in the United States.

I have already pointed out that Logistic I projected from 1910 has predicted the subsequent population with remarkable accuracy. However, Logistic II projected from 1940 probably will run well below the growth of population for at least 20 to 30 years and possibly longer. In other words, it will depart systematically from the probable growth of population. Even though the general trend may be roughly correct, the projected curve is biased. But by what criteria shall we determine that the logistic should be projected from 1900, 1910, 1920 or some other date?

The logistic does not explicitly reveal the relative influence of the elementary demographic factors, births, deaths and migration upon population change. Instead it conceals their separate effects within its parameters. For the analysis of current demographic changes, this is a serious defect. On the other hand, the work of Lotka has demonstrated that the use of mathematical functions, of which the logistic is one, illuminates many fundamental theoretical problems in demography [49]. Interestingly enough, however, this virtue, as will be pointed out below, is one of the reasons for the failure of certain population forecasts in the past.

There are many statistical difficulties with the logistic such as the fact that a population must be past the point of inflection of the curve before future growth can be described with even rough accuracy and the fact that the curve is not linear in its parameters so that projections of components of the total population present knotty theoretical and practical problems, but these were exhaustively discussed by Wilson and Puffer so that I shall not mention them further here.

There is another, perhaps more important, reason for the failure of the logistic as a predictive curve during the present stage of demographic development of the population of the United States, even though the logistic may be the method of choice for forecasting the future of populations in a different stage of demographic development. This reason I wish to discuss in connection with the explanation for the failure of the true rate of natural increase and the net reproduction rate as methods of forecasting population.

By 1920 some, if not all demographers, realized that the change in the total size of the population was not a reliable guide to the future growth of the population of the United States. As annual statistics of births and deaths became more generally available, population change was analyzed in terms of the crude rate of natural increase and migration.

By 1925, due largely to the work of Lotka, the crude rate of natural increase as a measure of the inherent capacity of a population to replace itself was abandoned in favor of the true rate of natural increase and its correlative, the net reproduction rate. This resulted from the realization that the crude rate of natural increase was affected so strongly by the existing age composition that it was a misleading index of the inherent capacity of the population to replace itself. The net reproduction rate, being independent of the existing age structure, became the measure par excellence, of the inherent replacement power of the population.

A series of annual net reproduction rates were computed. Strangely enough, it did not appear inconsistent to demographers that the inherent replacement capacity of the population should fluctuate from one year to another just as the crude rate of natural increase. No one seriously questioned the practice of using the fertility and mortality rates of a single year as a measure of long time prospects of population growth; whatever doubts may have arisen were quieted by using the average for several years.

Demographers acted as if hypnotized by the logical power of the theoretical analysis of demographic changes in a stable population and ignored a fact which they knew full well, that the population of the United States was not stable. Actually, except for the temporary age structure of the population, the age-specific fertility rates which are the basis of the net reproduction rate are affected by all the other factors which produce annual fluctuations in the crude birth rate, a rate which had been abandoned as a measure of the inherent capacity for replacement. The sex ratio, variations in the marriage rate both currently and in the past, changes in child spacing, the number of children previously born to a family, response to changes in economic conditions, these and many other factors determine the net reproduction rate of a given year.

As Hajnal so aptly remarked, "the question, 'To what extent is the population replacing itself according to the rates of *this* year?' is a futile question. In however refined a way we analyze the fertility rates of a given year they will still reflect temporary fluctuations" [50]. Whelpton graphically illustrated this fact when he calculated that if the first birth rates derived from the fertility experience of 1942 were to continue unchanged, 1,000 women living through the childbearing ages would produce 1,084 first births, a feat of demographic prowess which undoubtedly would have aroused the envy even of the goddess Diana [51].

Until it was forcefully impressed upon them by the changes in fertility before, during and after World War II, demographers did not appreciate the full implications of a fact which they had been pointing out for several years, the extent to which the number of births during a given interval of time is the result of planned control of fertility. The failure to evaluate correctly the role of voluntary control of fertility operating either through the postponement of marriage or through the deliberate spacing of children after marriage is a major factor in the failure of demographers to foresee with precision the trend of future population growth. The measurement of this factor requires different methods of analysis than those hitherto available or used.

This explanation of the failure of the net reproduction rate to project reliably the future trend of fertility applies equally well to the extrapolation of age-specific fertility rates, for these are but the basic elements of the reproduction rate.

With the widespread adoption of methods of controlling fertility the decision of a couple to have or not to have a child in a given year is strongly influenced by the number of children already in the family and by prevailing economic conditions. This means that not only the number of births but also the average size of existing incompleted families may fluctuate irregularly from year to year. Moreover, family limitation may be exercised before the desired size of family is reached. Thus even though the ultimate number of children is fixed, the spacing of births over the reproductive period may vary widely from time to time.

The only way to form a correct judgment of long time population growth is to analyze carefully the trend in the marriage rate and the number of children per marriage. Except for changes in migration and in mortality, which at the present time exert a relatively minor influence compared with fertility, the principal factor in the long time trend of population growth is the trend in the size of completed families.

Fortunately recent studies indicate that the size of completed families, although declining for at least a century, has showed remarkable stability compared with indexes of current fertility [52, 53]. It may be a matter of doubt as to whether this size ever has dropped below the level necessary to permanently replace the population but if it has, it certainly is not as far below as indicated by the net reproduction rates.

RECAPITULATION

You have heard the charge; I have reviewed the evidence. What is the verdict? I find demographers guilty of

1. Giving the impression that projected populations were relatively inevitable and certain.

2. Underestimating the effects of scientific developments on lowering mortality rates.

3. Believing that the demographic development of a theoretical stable population must inherently characterize current demographic developments in an actual unstable population.

4. Assuming that the observed fertility and mortality of a single year or short period of years is a reliable guide to future trends.

5. Giving undue weight to recent downward cyclical fluctuations in fertility while making long range population projections.

6. Assuming that because birth rates have declined for several generations they must inevitably continue to decline.

7. Forgetting that the voluntary control of fertility can cause the birth rate to rise as well as to fall.

8. Consistently overestimating the rate of decrease in the growth of the population of the United States.

9. Being too uncritical of the work of fellow demographers.

How does this analysis affect the outlook for future population growth? Does it imply that most of the assumptions of demographers concerning the trend of population should be discarded? Does it mean that we should reject, as Professor Davis believes, the view "that growth of the United States population, so rapid as to double in 50–100 years is certainly over"?

Professor Davis' answer to these questions is an unequivocal, categorical yes. "There is now strong reason *not* to expect, within this century, *any* peak followed by levelling off and decline. . . . Barring extreme catastrophes, my own guess is that the population in 2000 will be between 200 and 300 million. But this is only a guess. The range between these projections for the year 2000 is extremely wide; and I believe that no one can yet appraise the factors that will be at work with sufficient accuracy to make a dependable forecast within a range of 50 million. It is often important to realize what we cannot know."

"Furthermore, I make bold to challenge the view—held by almost all demographers of all schools—that our population must, later if not sooner, reach a peak of any size, at any time, from which a decline is probable if not inevitable" [54].

The principal explanation of the fluctuations in the birth rate since 1930 may be found in fluctuations in the marriage rate and in the spacing of children during the reproductive period of family life. As yet there is no conclusive evidence that the size of completed families has increased permanently. However, it is too early to tell whether the high birth rate of the present decade represents merely a "catching up" of postponed births together with some drawing on the future or a real increase in the eventual size of families formed during this period. As of now, the former conclusion appears more likely, although it would not be surprising, if economic conditions remain favorable, for the size of families completed during 1960 to 1965 to be somewhat greater than the size of families being completed at the present time. Any large increase though would represent a major demographic revolution.

In summary, the belief that the rate of population growth in the United States is slowing down remains substantially correct. However, the rate at which it is slowing down and the date on which the total size of the population may become essentially stationary now appear quite different than before the war. The possibility of a decline in total numbers before the end of the century seems unlikely, although we should not forget that the birth rate can decline just as rapidly as it can rise.

A preliminary assessment of the possibility of a continuation of the large numerical natural increase of the 1940's through the decade 1950 to 1960 should be possible within the next two years. The total number of registered births during the first 10 months of 1949 was about one per cent larger than the number registered during the corresponding period of 1948. However, the provisional marriage rate based on marriage licenses issued during the first nine months of 1949 is about 14 per cent below the figure for 1948. The number of marriage licenses issued in cities of 100,000 or more, January–October 1949, is lower than the number issued for the same period during any year since 1941 with the exception of 1944. Normally, a drop of this magnitude should be reflected in a drop in the number of births during 1950 and 1951. Whether or not this will be true, only time will tell.

The estimation of population for periods as short as even five years in the future probably will become increasingly difficult unless economic conditions remain stabilized. If the present analysis is correct, the widespread adoption of voluntary methods of birth control make probable a sharp response of fertility to marked fluctuations in economic conditions. This may be true even though the long time trend in population change continues to be well charted. It remains to be seen, however whether a continuation of the present or even a rising standard of living will result in a permanent rise in the average size of completed families. If it does, it will be a new experience in the demographic history of the United States. At present the odds seem to be against such an event happening. It is well to remember, though, that past experience shows future events have little respect for the opinions of demographers and economists alike.

REFERENCES

[1] *Recent Social Trends in the United States.* Report of the President's Research Committee on Social Trends, 1933, Vol. 1, p. xx.

[2] Taeuber, Irene, "Population Studies in the United States," *Population Index,* 12, 254, 1946.

[3] Baker, O. E., "Population Trends in Relation to Land Utilization", *Proc. Second International Conference of Agricultural Economists,* 1930, p. 284.

[4] Thompson, Warren S. and Whelpton, P. K., *Estimates of Future Population of the United States 1940-2000.* National Resources Planning Board, 1943, pp. 3-4.

[5] Bureau of the Census, Series P-5, No. 2, January 31, 1941.

[6] *Statistical Bulletin,* Metropolitan Life Insurance Company, August 1943.

[7] Dorn, Harold F., "The Potential Rate of Increase of the Population of the United States," *The American Journal of Sociology,* 58, 185–187, 1942.

[8] Whelpton, P. K., "The Meaning of the 1947 Baby Boom." *Vital Statistics, Special Reports,* 33, 7, 1948. (National Office of Vital Statistics.)

[9] *Population Index* 15, 123, 1949.

[10] Davis, Joseph S., "Our Amazing Population Upsurge," *Journal of Farm Economics* (Proceedings Number), November 1949.

[11] Spengler, Joseph J., "Population Predictions in Nineteenth Century America," *American Sociological Review,* 1, 905–921, 1936.

[12] Spengler, Joseph J. *op. cit.*, p. 911.

[13] Bonynge, Francis, *The Future Wealth of America*, 1852.

[14] Gannett, Henry, "Estimates of Future Population," *Report of the National Conservation Commission*, Vol. 2, pp. 7–9, 1909.

[15] Gannett, Henry, *op. cit.*, p. 8.

[16] Pritchett, H. S., "A Formula for Predicting the Population of the United States," *Quarterly Publication American Statistical Association*, 2, 278–286, 1891.

[17] Pritchett, H. S., "The Population of the United States during the Next Ten Decades," *Popular Science Monthly*, 58, 49–53, 1900.

[18] Pearl, Raymond and Reed, Lowell J., "On the Rate of Growth of the Population of the United States since 1790 and its Mathematical Representation," *Proceedings National Academy of Science*, 6, 275–288, 1920.

[19] Verhulst, P. F., "Notice sur la loi que la Population suit dans son accroisissement," *Correspondance Mathématique et physique publiée par A. Quetelet* x, 113–121, 1838.

[20] Lotka, Alfred J., *Elements of Physical Biology*, 1925.

[21] Pearl, Raymond, Reed, Lowell J. and Kish, Joseph F., "The Logistic Curve and the Census Count of 1940," *Science*, 92, 486–488, 1940.

[22] Thompson, Warren S. and Whelpton, P. K., "The Population of the Nation," *Recent Social Trends in the United States*, Vol. I, Chapt. I, p. 46, 1933.

[23] Sharpe, F. R. and Lotka, A. J., "A Problem in Age-Distribution," *Philosophical Magazine*, 21, 435–438, 1911.

[24] Dublin, Louis I. and Lotka, Alfred J., "On the True Rate of Natural Increase," *Journal of the American Statistical Association*, 20, 305–399, 1925.

[25] Böckh, R., *Statistisches Jahrbuch der Stadt Berlin*, 1884, p. 30.

[26] Kuczynski, Robert R., *The Balance of Births and Deaths*, 1928.

[27] Dorn, Harold F., "The Natural Decrease of Population in Certain American Communities," *Journal of the American Statistical Association*, 34, 106–109, 1939.

[28] Dublin, Louis I., "The Outlook for the American Birth Rate," *Problems of Population*, edited by G. H. L. F. Pitt-Rivers, 1932, pp. 115–125.

[29] Whelpton, P. K., *Needed Population Research*, 1938, pp. 6, 7.

[30] Whelpton, P. K., "Population of the United States, 1925 to 1975," *The American Journal of Sociology*, 34, 253–270, 1928.

[31] Whelpton, *ibid.*, pp. 267, 270.

[32] Whelpton, *ibid.*, p. 270.

[33] Whelpton, P. K., "The Future Growth of the Population of the United States," *Problems of Population*, edited by G. H. L. F. Pitt-Rivers, 1932, pp. 77–86.

[34] Whelpton, *ibid.*

[35] *Recent Social Trends in the United States*. Report of the President's Research Committee on Social Trends, 1933, Vol. I, pp. 48–49.

[36] *Recent Social Trends, ibid.*, p. 48.

[37] *The Problems of a Changing Population*, National Resources Committee, 1938.

[38] Whelpton, P. K., "An Empirical Method of Calculating Future Population," *Journal of the American Statistical Association*, 31, 457–473, 1936.

[39] Whelpton, *ibid.*, pp. 470–471.

[40] Bureau of the Census, Series P-3, No. 15, July 23, 1941.

[41] *Estimates of Future Population of the United States 1940–2000*, National Resources Planning Board, 1943.

[42] *Forecasts of the Population of the United States, 1945–1975*, Bureau of the Census, 1947.

[43] *Ibid.*, p. 39.

[44] Bureau of the Census, Series P-46, No. 7, Sept. 15, 1946.

[45] Bureau of the Census, Series P-25, No. 18, Feb. 1949.

[46] *Population Index* 14, 195, 1948.

[47] Davis, Joseph S., *The Population Upsurge in the United States*, War and Peace Pamphlets No. 12, 1949—Food Research Institute, Stanford University.

[48] Wilson, Edwin B. and Puffer, Ruth R., "Least Squares and Laws of Population Growth," *Proc. Am. Acad. Arts and Sciences*, 68, 287–382, 1933.

[49] Lotka, Alfred J., "*Analyse demographique avec application particuliere l'espèce humaine*," Paris 1939.

[50] Hajnal, J., "The Analysis of Birth Statistics in the Light of the Recent International Recovery of the Birth-Rate," *Population Studies* 1, 137–164, 1947.

[51] Whelpton, P. K., "Reproduction Rates Adjusted for Age, Parity, Fecundity, and Marriage," *Journal of the American Statistical Association*, 41, 501–516, 1946.

[52] Woofter, T. J., "Completed Generation Reproduction Rates," *Human Biology* 19, Sept. 1947.

[53] Whelpton, P. K., "Cohort Analysis of Fertility," *American Sociological Review*, 14, Dec. 1949.

[54] Davis, Joseph S., (ref. 47).

The readings in this chapter exemplify the techniques by which demographers study mortality and bring out the major sources of variation in mortality that have been discovered.

Statements about the level, trend, or variation in mortality can be expressed in a number of ways, according to the purpose and convenience of the investigator and the availability of relevant data. The "crude death rate," or number of deaths in a year per 1,000 of the average population of that year, indicates the rate at which the population is losing numbers by death. It is not, however, a reliable indicator of health conditions or longevity, because it is greatly affected by the age composition of the population. "Age-specific death rates," or their weighted average, the "age-standardized death rate," may be used to make mortality comparisons freed of the influence of age composition. Alternatively, it is possible to compute by actuarial methods the probability of dying at each age (often called the "mortality rate" as distinguished from the "death rate"), and then develop the schedule of mortality rates into a "life table." When life table values are available for a country, or group, expectation of life at birth, or 1,000 divided by this value (the "life table death rate"), may be used to indicate mortality conditions. The first paper by Dublin and Lotka explains the anatomy of the life table and indicates certain applications of life table techniques in vital statistics. There are many other kinds of application of these techniques, among them the tables of working life developed in the Bureau of Labor Statistics, described in Garfinkle's paper. A so-called "multiple-decrement" table, the table of working life deals simultaneously with changes in the size of the labor force due to mortality and to entrance into and departure from the labor force. A similar approach may be used to describe the attrition of the single population through death and marriage. In fact, life tables can be constructed for any kind of "population," including, for example, such physical aggregates as telephone poles or aircraft engines.

A "conventional life table" takes a cross-section of mortality experience by age at a given point in time, and regards it as the record of survivorship of a hypothetical cohort of persons living out their life span from birth until the death of the last member of the cohort. The "generation life table" is similarly constructed, but is based on the mortality experience of an actual cohort of persons observed over a period of time. (See Merrell's paper.) When carefully interpreted, both types of life table have important uses, though they do not give the same picture of mortality conditions, since they take different "slices" of experience. Because the complete record of an actual cohort is difficult to obtain, most studies employ the conventional, rather than the generation, life table; or else they rely on death rates (crude, specific, or standardized) which, like the conventional life table, are based on cross-sectional rather than longitudinal data.

Study of a large number of life tables and other mortality indexes has shown that human longevity is a function of the constitutional or hereditary capacity of the organism, together with the modifications produced therein by the diverse and powerful environmental influences which are incident upon the organism. Apparently, a certain (small) proportion of infants is physiologically incapable of surviving birth for more than a few hours, while the survivors remain exceedingly vulnerable to environmental hazards for some time. Accordingly, the age curve of mortality is universally high at the beginning of life, then drops to a low point in the later childhood or early adolescent years. From this point onward the probability of dying increases with each increment of age. The almost universal finding that female mortality rates are more favorable than those of males, age for age, probably is to be explained, likewise, as reflecting constitutional factors. (From the standpoint of mortality, women are not the "weaker sex".) Yet the fact that the size of the sex differential and the proportion of persons surviving into old age vary greatly from time to time and from place to place indicates that environmental influences may modify considerably the expression of constitutional tendencies.

While it has often been observed that isolated local populations are highly vulnerable to introduced diseases, and may suffer extreme mortality until they can develop a degree of immunity, it is doubtful that the heterogeneous aggregates called "races" differ genetically in capacity for survival, at any rate to an extent that is demographically significant. American Negroes, for example, have responded with better mortality records to improvements in their social and economic circumstances, and now have a life expectancy at birth similar to that recorded for whites just 20 years ago, as is shown by the figures in the article, "A Century of Progress in Longevity." There is thus every reason to believe that given equally favorable circumstances Negroes could duplicate the current mortality experience of whites.

The remarks just made about races doubtlessly apply, *mutatis mutandis,* to regional and temporal variations in mortality. Mortality specialists are inclined to attribute the striking improvements in mortality in Western countries over the last couple of centuries to increases in the level of living, generally, or more specifically to advances in nutrition, sanitation, medical technique, and the like. (See Dublin and Lotka's paper on mortality trends.) Likewise, the interregional differences in mortality levels documented in Stolnitz's paper are attributable to the combined impact of cultural, economic, and ecological factors, rather than to hereditary differences.

A clue to the factors accounting for differences and changes in mortality levels is found in the study of causes of death. High mortality rates are generally associated with a heavy incidence of infectious and contagious diseases, low rates with a relatively greater toll of the so-called degenerative diseases. Research in public health has shown clearly the responsiveness of the former to changes in environmental factors and medical control, while the latter, though doubtlessly affected by environmental factors, have historically been more resistant to both environmental improvement and medical progress.

The impact of socio-economic circumstances on mortality is suggested by the social class differences in mortality revealed in Logan's study, the findings of which are corroborated directly and indirectly by a considerable body of research. Such differences reflect both specific occupational hazards and the general influence of class differences in the level of living on factors determining mortality; but the latter is the more important influence, as has been shown by the fact that the mortality of females classified by the occupations of their husbands varies according to socio-economic level in much the same way as that of males classified by their own occupations.

USES OF THE LIFE TABLE IN VITAL STATISTICS

By Louis I. Dublin and Alfred J. Lotka

FOR the benefit of those readers who may not be acquainted with the detailed structure of the life table, a brief description of its principal columns will first be given, using, by way of illustration the life table for white males in the United States in 1934, as computed in the Statistical Bureau of the Metropolitan Life Insurance Company. This table is reproduced as Table I.

Column 1 of this table gives the age of life from birth to age 104. The second column shows the survivors to each age of life out of 100,000, starting out at birth (age 0), and diminishing from age to age in accordance with the mortality of 1934. The figures in this column are generally denoted by the symbol l_x. The third column indicates the corresponding deaths in each year of life, the figures in this column, usually denoted by d_x, being simply the differences between two adjacent figures in the second column. The fourth column gives the death rate in each year of life, or, to be more exact, the probability at a given age of dying within 1 year, this being denoted by the symbol q_x. So, for example, the death rate at age 10 is obtained by dividing the deaths in this year of life, namely 123, by the number of persons entering this age, namely 91,625. This quotient, expressed in parts of a thousand, is 1.34.

The fifth and sixth columns are auxiliary columns employed in computing the seventh column, which gives the expectation of life at each year of age. The fifth column gives the average number of persons living in each year of life; for instance, in the first line opposite age 0, we find 97,090 which is the average of 100,000 and 94,179. The figures in this column may also be interpreted as the number of years of life lived within a given age of life; so, for instance, the figure 97,090 is the number of years lived by the survivors of the original 100,000 in passing through the first year of their life.

Column 6 is obtained by cumulating the figures in column 5 beginning at the end; for example, the figure 31 in column 6 opposite age 100 is the sum of $2+4+8+17$, the figures appearing on the same line and the lines below in column 5.

Lastly, column 7, as already noted, gives the expectation of life or the average after-lifetime at each year of life. It is obtained as the quotient of the figures in column 6 and the corresponding figures in column 2, for this gives a total number of years lived by survivors of a cohort after a given age, divided by the number of persons entering that age.

A table such as this, it is seen at once, contains a great deal of detailed information and is a source from which many problems in population study must be answered.* Incidentally, it should be remarked that life tables, as generally constructed, represent a fixed mortality of a particular calendar year or period. Such a table tells us what *would* be the number of survivors to

---

* The details of the computation of a life table are rather highly technical. For a detailed description of two alternative methods that have been employed for this purpose the reader may be referred to *Length of Life—A Study of the Life Table*, by Louis I. Dublin and Alfred J. Lotka, Ronald Press, 1936, p. 307, Chapter XIV.

TABLE I

Life Table for White Males in the United States, 1934

1	2	3	4	5	6	7
	Of 100,000 Born Alive		Rate of Mortality per 1,000 Number Dying Between Ages x and x+1 Among 1,000 Living at Age x	Number of Years Lived by the Cohort Between Ages x and x+1	Total Number of Years Lived by the Cohort from Age x on, Until All Have Died	Complete Expectation of Life or Mean After-Lifetime; Average Number of Years Lived After Age x per Person Surviving to Exact Age x
Age	Number Surviving to Exact Age x	Number Dying Between Ages x and x+1				
x	l_x	d_x	$1,000q_x$	L_x	T_x	$\overset{o}{e}_x$
0	100,000	5,821	58.21	97,090	6,023,954	60.24
1	94,179	840	8.92	93,759	5,926,864	62.93
2	93,339	413	4.43	93,133	5,833,105	62.49
3	92,926	287	3.09	92,783	5,739,972	61.77
4	92,639	226	2.44	92,526	5,647,189	60.96
5	92,413	191	2.07	92,318	5,554,663	60.11
6	92,222	172	1.87	92,136	5,462,345	59.23
7	92,050	158	1.72	91,971	5,370,209	58.34
8	91,892	139	1.51	91,823	5,278,238	57.44
9	91,753	128	1.39	91,689	5,186,415	56.53
10	91,625	123	1.34	91,564	5,094,726	55.60
11	91,502	124	1.35	91,440	5,003,162	54.68
12	91,378	129	1.41	91,314	4,911,722	53.75
13	91,249	139	1.52	91,180	4,820,408	52.83
14	91,110	150	1.65	91,035	4,729,228	51.91
15	90,960	165	1.81	90,878	4,638,193	50.99
16	90,795	181	1.99	90,705	4,547,315	50.08
17	90,614	196	2.16	90,516	4,456,610	49.18
18	90,418	212	2.34	90,312	4,366,094	48.29
19	90,206	226	2.51	90,093	4,275,782	47.40
20	89,980	239	2.66	89,861	4,185,689	46.52
21	89,741	251	2.80	89,616	4,095,828	45.64
22	89,490	260	2.91	89,360	4,006,212	44.77
23	89,230	268	3.00	89,096	3,916,852	43.90
24	88,962	273	3.07	88,826	3,827,756	43 03
25	88,689	278	3.14	88,550	3,738,930	42.16
26	88,411	283	3.20	88,270	3,650,380	41.29
27	88,128	289	3.28	87,984	3,562,110	40.42
28	87,839	297	3.38	87,691	3,474,126	39.55
29	87,542	307	3.51	87,389	3,386,435	38.68
30	87,235	318	3.65	87,076	3,299,046	37.82
31	86,917	332	3.82	86,751	3,211,970	36.95
32	86,585	347	4.01	86,412	3,125,219	36.09
33	86,238	365	4.23	86,056	3,038,807	35.24
34	85,873	383	4.46	85,682	2,952,751	34.38
35	85,490	403	4.71	85,289	2,867,069	33.54

TABLE I (Cont.)

Life Table for White Males in the United States, 1934

1	2	3	4	5	6	7
			Rate of Mortality per 1,000			Complete Expectation of Life or Mean After-Lifetime; Average Number of
	Of 100,000 Born Alive		*Number Dying Between Ages x and x+1 Among 1,000 Living at Age x*	*Number of Years Lived by the Cohort Between Ages x and x+1*	*Total Number of Years Lived by the Cohort from Age x on, Until All Have Died*	*Years Lived After Age x per Person Surviving to Exact Age x*
	Number Surviving to Exact	*Number Dying Between Ages x*				
Age	*Age x*	*and x+1*				
x	l_x	d_x	$1,000q_x$	L_x	T_x	e_x
36	85,087	424	4.98	84,875	2,781,780	32.69
37	84,663	445	5.26	84,441	2,696,905	31.85
38	84,218	467	5.55	83,985	2,612,464	31.02
39	83,751	492	5.87	83,505	2,528,479	30.19
40	83,259	518	6.22	83,000	2,444,974	29.37
41	82,741	548	6.62	82,467	2,361,974	28.55
42	82,193	581	7.07	81,903	2,279,507	27.73
43	81,612	620	7.60	81,302	2,197,604	26.93
44	80,992	663	8.19	80,661	2,116,302	26.13
45	80,329	709	8.83	79,975	2,035,641	25.34
46	79,620	759	9.53	79,241	1,955,666	24.56
47	78,861	809	10.26	78,457	1,876,425	23.79
48	78,052	861	11.03	77,622	1,797,968	23.04
49	77,191	914	11.84	76,734	1,720,346	22.29
50	76,277	968	12.69	75,793	1,643,612	21.55
51	75,309	1,022	13.57	74,798	1,567,819	20.82
52	74,287	1,077	14.50	73,749	1,493,021	20 10
53	73,210	1,133	15.47	72,644	1,419,272	19.39
54	72,077	1,191	16.53	71,482	1,346,628	18.68
55	70,886	1,255	17.70	70,259	1,275,146	17.99
56	69,631	1,326	19.04	68,968	1,204,887	17.30
57	68,305	1,406	20.59	67,602	1,135,919	16 63
58	66,899	1,496	22.36	66,151	1,068,317	15.97
59	65,403	1,591	24.33	64,608	1,002,166	15 32
60	63,812	1,688	26.46	62,968	937,558	14.69
61	62,124	1,783	28.70	61,233	874,590	14.08
62	60,341	1,872	31.02	59,405	813,357	13.48
63	58,469	1,952	33.39	57,493	753,952	12.89
64	56,517	2,028	35.89	55,503	696,459	12.32
65	54,489	2,103	38.60	53,438	640,956	11.76
66	52,386	2,181	41.64	51,296	587,518	11.21
67	50,205	2,264	45.09	49,073	536,222	10:68
68	47,941	2,350	49.02	46,766	487,149	10.16
69	45,591	2,435	53.41	44,374	440,383	9.66

TABLE I (Cont.)

Life Table for White Males in the United States, 1934

1	2	3	4	5	6	7
						Complete Expectation of Life or Mean After-Lifetime; Average
	Of 100,000 Born Alive		*Number Dying Between Ages x and x+1 Among 1,000 Living at Age x*	*Number of Years Lived by the Cohort Between Ages x and x+1*	*Total Number of Years Lived by the Cohort from Age x on, Until All Have Died*	*Number of Years Lived After Age x per Person Surviving to Exact Age x*
	Number Surviving to Exact Age x	*Number Dying Between Ages x and x+1*	*Rate of Mortality per 1,000*			
Age x	l_x	d_x	$1,000 q_x$	L_x	T_x	$\overset{\circ}{e}_x$
70	43,156	2,511	58.19	41,901	396,009	9.18
71	40,645	2,573	63.30	39,359	354,108	8.71
72	38,072	2,616	68.70	36,764	314,749	8.27
73	35,456	2,636	74.34	34,138	277,985	7.84
74	32,820	2,634	80.27	31,503	243,847	7.43
75	30,186	2,613	86.55	28,880	212,344	7.03
76	27,573	2,571	93.25	26,288	183,464	6.65
77	25,002	2,511	100.42	23,747	157,176	6.29
78	22,491	2,432	108.15	21,275	133,429	5.93
79	20,059	2,337	116.51	18,891	112,154	5.59
80	17,722	2,226	125.63	16,609	93,263	5.26
81	15,496	2,101	135.59	14,446	76,654	4.95
82	13,395	1,962	146.49	12,414	62,208	4.64
83	11,433	1,811	158.42	10,528	49,794	4.35
84	9,622	1,649	171.36	8,798	39,266	4.08
85	7,973	1,477	185.28	7,235	30,468	3.82
86	6,496	1,300	200.15	5,846	23,233	3.58
87	5,196	1,122	215.95	4,635	17,387	3.35
88	4,074	948	232.64	3,600	12,752	3.13
89	3,126	782	250.21	2,735	9,152	2.93
90	2,344	630	268.65	2,029	6,417	2.74
91	1,714	494	287.95	1,467	4,388	2.56
92	1,220	376	308.10	1,032	2,921	2.39
93	844	278	329.13	705	1,889	2.23
94	566	199	351.22	467	1,184	2.09
95	367	137	374.62	299	717	1.94
96	230	92	399.54	184	418	1.81
97	138	59	426.23	109	234	1.68
98	79	36	454.89	61	125	1.56
99	43	21	485.63	33	64	1.44
100	22	11	518.53	17	31	1.33
101	11	6	553.68	8	14	1.23
102	5	3	591.16	4	6	1.13
103	2	1	631.06	2	2	1.03
104	1	1	673.49	..	..	.94

age 10, 20, etc., *if the mortality at each age remained constant as of the calendar year or period for which it is constructed.*

APPLICATIONS OF THE LIFE TABLE

It is significant that two seemingly opposed designations have been applied to the same thing; " Mortality Table " or the " Life Table." Quite in accord with this dual character of the life table, its applications may be broadly classed in two categories—-applications relating primarily to mortality and death rates, and applications relating primarily to survivals. In the field of life insurance we find a corresponding duality of interests related to these two aspects of the life table: insurance for the benefit of others in the event of death of the insured; and insurance in the form of endowments or annuities for the benefit of the insured himself in the case of his survival.

Application to problems of mortality —On this occasion we are concerned with applications to general demographic problems. In the first category, applications relating more particularly to mortality, we have, first of all, the direct use of the life table as a gauge or measure of the mortality in a given population or group of persons. The crude death rate, for well known reasons, is not a good measure, because it is quite seriously affected by differences in age composition. Standardized death rates, on the other hand, have the disadvantage that they depend on an arbitrarily selected standard population. The life table is free from this arbitrary feature, and, of course, with its several columns, exhibiting, for a " cohort " or " generation " traced from birth through life, the number of survivors, the number of deaths, the death rate, and the expectation of life at each age, such a table gives much more detailed information than a general death rate, whether crude or standardized.

There is, however, necessarily a relation between the picture presented by the life table and the corresponding general death rate. This is exhibited in Figure I in which there have been plotted, as abscissae, the values of the standardized death rates for white males in each of the states of the Union as of 1929–1931, against the corresponding values of the expectation of life at birth, as ordinates. It will be seen that the scatter of points thus shown clusters very closely about a straight line. In point of fact, the coefficient of correlation is almost unity, its exact value being $r = -.992 \pm .002$. This suggests that the expectation of life could be gauged *approximately* for any one of these states, if the standardized death rate and the regression equation were given. This equation in the present example takes the form

$$e_0 = 78.337 - .0174 \, d$$

where d is the standardized death rate per 100,000. In Table II the values of the expectation of life thus computed for each state from the regression equation is shown, together with the difference between the value thus computed and that obtained by the more accurate process of computing the life table. It will be seen that in all but two instances the error is less than one year, and in all but seven it is less than one half year. Incidentally, it is of interest to compute the correlation coefficient using the crude death rates. The correlation in that case is considerably less close, namely $r = -.752 \pm .063$. Figure II illustrates the much wider scatter of the values of the crude death rate and the expectation of life at birth. The correcting effect of standardizing the death rate shows itself in these results.

Historical study of past longevity— The expectation of life at birth, which we thus recognize as a more efficient measure for purposes of comparison than the simple death rate, gives us an

TABLE II

Expectation of Life at Birth and Standardized * *Death Rates per 100,000 for Each State of the United States, Except Texas, 1929–1931—White Males ‡ All Ages*

State	Expectation of Life at Birth $\overset{\circ}{e}_0$	Standardized Death Rate	$\overset{\circ}{e}_0$ Computed from Stand. D.R. by Regression Equation $\overset{\circ}{e}_0$	Col. (4)–Col. (2)
(1)	(2)	(3)	(4)	(5)
South Dakota †	64.38	828.0	63.95	—.43
Kansas	63.24	885.8	62.94	—.30
North Dakota	63.24	855.1	63.47	+.23
Iowa	63.04	896.3	62.76	—.28
Nebraska	62.92	895.5	62.77	—.15
Oklahoma	62.72	900.3	62.69	—.03
Minnesota	61.97	947.9	61.86	—.11
Wisconsin	61.51	975.5	61.38	—.13
Idaho	61.44	962.5	61.61	+.17
Washington	61.37	990.2	61.13	—.24
Oregon	61.17	995.5	61.03	—.14
Arkansas	60.43	1,013.2	60.73	+.30
Mississippi	60.34	1,035.1	60.35	+.01
New Hampshire	60.24	1,042.0	60.23	—.01
Indiana	60.04	1,057.9	59.95	—.09
Vermont	59.97	1,040.7	60.25	+.28
Michigan	59.80	1,083.3	59.51	—.29
Ohio	59.78	1,079.5	59.57	—.21
Wyoming	59.78	1,050.7	60.08	+.30
Connecticut	59.77	1,081.8	59.53	—.24
Missouri	59.76	1,068.4	59.77	+.01
Montana	59.40	1,080.7	59.55	+.15
Alabama	59.37	1,088.4	59.42	+.05
Kentucky	59.37	1,054.1	60.02	+.65
United States §	59.31	1,103.7		
Massachusetts	59.29	1,104.5	59.14	—.15
Illinois	59.02	1,115.9	58.94	—.08
Florida	58.99	1,098.1	59.25	+.26
New Jersey	58.96	1,146.7	58.41	—.55
North Carolina	58.95	1,116.5	58.93	—.02
Georgia	58.92	1,130.6	58.69	—.23
Tennessee	58.76	1,087.7	59.43	+.67
Maine	58.70	1,112.3	59.00	+.30
Virginia	58.69	1,128.6	58.72	+.03
California	58.56	1,139.6	58.53	—.03
Louisiana	58.42	1,145.4	58.43	+.01
Utah	58.42	1,124.2	58.80	+.38
Delaware	58.25	1,145.1	58.43	+.18
West Virginia	58.14	1,102.4	59.18	+1.04
Rhode Island	58.06	1,187.9	57.69	—.37
New York	57.84	1,219.5	57.14	—.70
Maryland	57.72	1,206.2	57.37	—.35
Pennsylvania	57.68	1,207.1	57.36	—.32
South Carolina	57.64	1,198.2	57.51	—.13
Nevada	55.77	1,334.8	55.14	—.63
Colorado	55.40	1,254.4	56.54	+1.14
New Mexico	49.46	1,650.5	49.65	+.19
Arizona	48.08	1,750.4	47.91	—.17

* Standardized on the basis of " Standard Million " of England and Wales. 1901.
‡ White Males include Mexicans
† Based on deaths for 1930 only.
§ Exclusive of Texas and South Dakota.

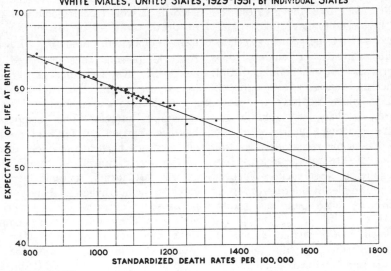

FIGURE I

CORRELATION DIAGRAM
EXPECTATION OF LIFE AT BIRTH AND <u>STANDARDIZED</u> DEATH RATES
WHITE MALES, UNITED STATES, 1929-1931, BY INDIVIDUAL STATES*

*EXCEPT TEXAS

interesting index by which to establish a historical survey of longevity at different periods.

Naturally, data for the remote past are scant and unreliable. Estimates based on tombstone inscriptions in ancient times, indicate that in certain Roman provinces of Africa, the expectation of life at birth may have been about 35 years. In the city of Rome itself, possibly conditions were less favorable, and we may broadly surmise that the expectation of life at birth there was somewhere between 20 and 30 years.

For the long stretch of years from the time of the Roman Empire to the latter part of the 17th century, we have not the basis for even the roughest of estimates. About the end of the 17th century, judging by a somewhat crude table prepared by Halley on the basis of mortality in the German city of Breslau, the expectation of life at birth was about 33½ years. From the early 18th century on, life table construction became more systematic, and indications are that, at the beginning and up to about the middle of the 19th century, an average length of life of 35 or 40 years may have been common in various localities among civilized people. By the beginning of the present century, the figure had risen to about 49 years. Thus there was a gain of about 9 years in the second half of the 19th century, far outstripping, in proportion, the gain of about 7 years in the preceding 150 years. Since 1900, the improvement has been even faster. At the time of the last census, 1930, our expectation of life at birth here in the United States was just about 60 years, and according to our life table for the year 1933 we had definitely reached 61 years. But we still have 5 more years to gain in expectation of life at birth before we equal the world record which today is held by New Zealand, namely 66 years.

The life table gives the expectation of life not only at birth, but at each year of life, and the question arises how persons of different ages have shared in the gain in expectation of life. Without going into detail, we may recall the familiar fact that the greatest reductions in mortality have taken place in infancy, so that the gain in expectation of life is greatest at birth. However, there are gains in childhood and adolescence and maturity, although one of the facts which we have to record with regret, is that, from midlife on, gains have in recent years been but slight, and in some recent decades the expectation of life at these ages has actually suffered a setback. This is shown, for example, in the case of white males, in the accompanying graph, Figure III.

Curtailment of life due to individual causes of death—The life table is capable of more refined applications than its gross use in connection with the general mortality from all causes combined. As ordinarily constructed, the table makes no distinction of deaths according to cause. But it is a relatively simple matter so to modify the computation, as to obtain a life table representing, for example, the mortality such as it would be if some one cause of death, or a group of such causes, were eliminated, assuming, however, that the persons thus preserved from death by the particular causes eliminated, were subject to and ultimately succumbed to the mortality from the remaining causes. This computation has been carried out for 8 of the principal causes of death, namely diseases of the heart; cancer, all forms; tuberculosis, all forms; chronic nephritis; cerebral hemorrhage; diabetes; angina pectoris; accidental and unspecified violence. The results of these computations are shown in Table III. The table is so arranged as to show the years of life that would be gained if the specified cause of death could be completely eliminated. So it is seen that the expectation of life at birth would be increased by nearly 2½ years if heart

FIGURE II

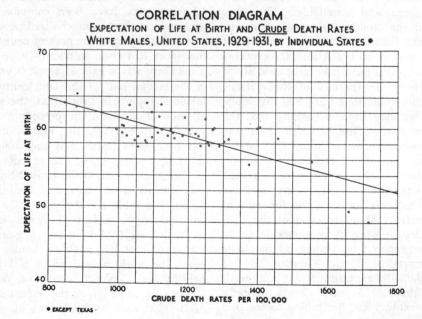

CORRELATION DIAGRAM
EXPECTATION OF LIFE AT BIRTH AND CRUDE DEATH RATES
WHITE MALES, UNITED STATES, 1929-1931, BY INDIVIDUAL STATES •

* EXCEPT TEXAS ·

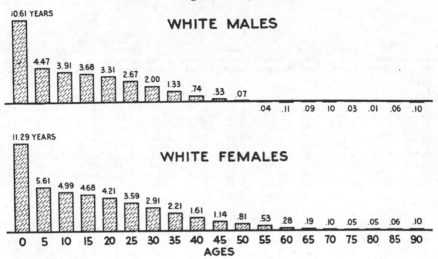

FIGURE III

IMPROVEMENT IN EXPECTATION OF LIFE
1929-31 COMPARED WITH 1901
United States Original Registration States

WHITE MALES

10.61 YEARS
4.47 3.91 3.68 3.31 2.67 2.00 1.33 .74 .33 .07
.04 .11 .09 10 .03 .01 .06 .10

WHITE FEMALES

11.29 YEARS
5.61 4.99 4.68 4.21 3.59 2.91 2.21 1.61 1.14 .81 .53 .28 .19 .10 .05 .05 .06 .10

0   5   10   15   20   25   30   35   40   45   50   55   60   65   70   75   80   85   90
AGES

disease could be eliminated. Accidents and unspecified violence also represent a large item in the case of males, accounting for 2 years of life. In the case of females, this is a less serious item, namely 0.80 year. Another large item is cancer, especially in the case of females, 1.79 years. In surveying these figures, it must be borne in mind that, other things equal, a cause of death which operates early in life, or through the whole range of life, naturally produces a greater loss of years than a cause which operates later in life.

An interesting point brought out by Table III, is that the effect of eliminating two or more causes of death together is cumulative. Thus, in column 10 is shown the sum of the individual years of life, that would be gained by eliminating each of 8 causes *separately*. Column 11, on the other hand, shows the number of years of life that would be gained if all these 8 causes were eliminated *simultaneously*. It will be

seen that the effect of jointly eliminating these 8 causes ranges from 52 to 81 per cent, according to the age and sex considered, in excess of the sum of the separate effects for each cause. This is a fortunate situation, for it means that our combined efforts to reduce the mortality from various causes result in more than merely the summation of the individual effects that would arise from the elimination of each of such causes separately. In other words, our gains in this field of work are cumulative. The reason for this is that if, for example, tuberculosis is eliminated at the same time as heart disease, not only those persons would be restored to life who ordinarily would have died from tuberculosis, but also a further number, namely those who, having been saved from heart disease, would subsequently have succumbed to tuberculosis if heart disease alone had been eliminated; and a similar statement holds with regard to those who, having been saved from

TABLE III

Years of Life That Would be Gained by the Elimination, Singly and Jointly, of 8 Causes of Death—White Males and White Females, United States Registration States of 1920 in 1930

Years Gained by the Elimination of Single Cause

Sex and Age	Diseases of Heart	Cancer, All Forms	Tuber-culosis, All Forms	Chronic Nephritis	Cerebral Hemor-rhage	Diabetes Mellitus	Angina Pectoris	Accidental and Un-specified Violence	Sum of Individual Effects of Each Cause of Death	Cumu-lative Effect of 8 Causes Combined	Per Cent Excess of Col. (11) Over Col. (10)
(1)	(2)	(3)	(4)	(5)	(6)	(7)	(8)	(9)	(10)	(11)	(12)
Males											
0	2.41	1.12	1.10	.97	0.81	0.19	0.27	2.05	8.92	13.57	52.13
12	2.61	1.22	1.11	1.07	0.90	0.21	0.30	1.84	9.26	14.17	53.02
22	2.60	1.23	1.01	1.07	0.92	0.20	0.31	1.48	8.82	13.69	55.22
32	2.62	1.24	0.76	1.07	0.95	0.19	0.31	1.08	8.22	13.01	58.27
42	2.62	1.22	0.51	1.05	0.97	0.18	0.31	0.79	7.65	12.38	61.83
52	2.52	1.12	0.29	1.01	0.96	0.17	0.27	0.53	6.87	11 44	66.52
62	2.26	0.88	0.15	0.91	0.89	0.14	0.21	0.34	5.78	9.89	71.11
72	1.84	0.53	0.06	0.74	0.70	0.08	0.12	0.21	4.28	7.52	75.70
82	1.27	0.23	0.02	0.48	0.42	0.03	0.05	0.15	2.65	4.58	72.83
Females											
0	2.58	1.79	1.09	1.10	1.04	0.37	0.14	0.80	8.91	13.74	54.21
12	2.73	1.90	1.06	1.17	1.11	0.38	0.15	0.58	9.08	14.25	56.94
22	2.70	1.93	0.85	1.16	1.13	0.37	0.15	0.49	8.78	13.95	58.88
32	2.70	1.94	0.51	1.16	1.16	0.37	0.16	0.43	8.43	13.55	60.74
42	2.69	1.82	0.32	1.13	1.18	0.38	0.16	0.39	8.07	13.13	62.70
52	2.58	1.49	0.19	1.03	1.13	0.35	0.15	0.34	7.26	12.22	68.32
62	2.38	1.04	0.12	0.90	1.03	0.26	0.14	0.31	6.18	10.65	72.33
72	1.98	0.59	0.06	0.69	0.82	0.12	0.09	0.28	4.63	8.26	78.40
82	1.38	0.25	0.01	0.42	0.51	0.03	0.04	0.24	2.88	5.21	80.90

tuberculosis would subsequently have died from heart disease, if tuberculosis alone had been eliminated.

Application of the life table to problems of survival—In the second category, applications of the life table to problems related more directly to survival, are such problems of great practical importance as the forecasting of the future population, and the making of estimates of the population classified by sex and age during post-censal current years.

Both these problems require for their solution the construction of a population, classified by age, at some subsequent time, as the survivors, at that time, of two groups of persons, namely first, those living at a given earlier period, and second, those that are born in the interim. The number of these survivors is determined by means of a life table, or a succession of life tables, applicable to the period of time considered. The number of births, so far as forecasts are concerned, can only be estimated on some reasonable hypothesis. In the case of estimates of post-censal current population, we stand on more secure ground in this respect, since we have available statistics of births registered in the years elapsed since the last census.

Application of life table to measure the capacity for growth of a population—An application which has very important bearings on population policy is the computation of the true rate of natural increase, that is, the measure of the excess of fertility over mortality, such as it appears when the influence of temporary features of the age distribution is eliminated. As is by this time well known from our previous publications * the mere excess of the birth rate over the death rate does not give a true measure of this feature. Our low death rate of about 11 per 1,000 gives us a very incorrect idea of the intrinsic mortality in our population. This is evident from the mere fact that in the long run a death rate of 10 per 1,000, after the population had become stationary, would correspond to a mean length of life of 91 years. We all know perfectly well that the average length of life among us today attains no such figure as this. It is only a little over 60 years.

Similarly, our birth rate figure is deceptive. Low as it is, 17.1 per 1,000 (1934), it is still bolstered up by the influence of past high birth rates in giving us a higher proportion of persons within the reproductive ages today than we should have on the basis of our current fertility. If proper allowance is made for this feature, we find for the latest date available a true birth rate of 15.2 per 1,000, a true death rate of 15.8 per 1,000, and, as is now a familiar fact, we find ourselves definitely in the red as regards the balance of fertility over mortality, with a negative true rate of natural increase, namely —.6 per 1,000. The curve of the birth rate, which formerly was above that for the death rate, crossed the latter about 1930 or very soon after.

CONCLUSION

Only a few applications of the life table to problems in vital statistics have been presented by way of example. The list might be extended to include such topics as the probability of dying from specified causes; the age distribution of deaths from specified causes in a generation of persons traced from birth to the extinction of the entire generation; the proportion of widows and of orphans in the population, and the related problem recently discussed by P. Luzzatto-Fegiz in his article The Occupational Evolution of a Generation *; or, to mention one more example, the extinction of a line of descent—a problem which is of interest not only in human vital statistics but also in relation to certain problems in genetics.†

The fact is that possibilities of such applications are legion. It has not been the purpose of this brief paper to attempt even a summary of this subject, but only by a few landmarks here and there to give some idea of the scope and nature of the field. It is the less necessary to attempt here an exhaustive presentation, as we have recently published a volume of some 400 pages dealing, in some detail, with these matters, under the title " Length of Life— A Study of the Life Table." To this volume we must, therefore, refer for further details.

---

* To these the reader must be referred for details of method of computation. He will find them described in the *Journal of the American Statistical Association*, 1925, pp. 305–339; also, though with less detail in *Length of Life*, by Louis I. Dublin and Alfred J. Lotka, Ronald Press, 1936, pp. 244 *et seq.*

---

* *Population, J. International Union for the Scientific Investigation of Population Problems*, 1935, Vol. 2, p. 37.
† Lotka, A. J. The Extinction of Families. *J. Washington Academy of Sciences*, 1931, Vol. 21, pp. 377, 453.

CHANGES IN WORKING LIFE OF MEN,

1900 TO 2000

By Stuart Garfinkle

No RECORD OF PROGRESS in the 20th century would be complete without reference to the dramatic increase in the average length of life, which, for men in the United States, rose from about 50 years in 1900 to about 65 years at midcentury. Equally important in terms of economic well-being, but perhaps not as well known, is the increase in the average length of *working* life for men, which rose from 32 to 42 years in the first half of the century. On the basis of recent trends, the average life expectancy may rise to 73 years in the year 2000 and working life may increase to 45 years.

These facts come from tables of working life for men which have been developed by the Bureau of Labor Statistics. The first tables were prepared for 1940 and 1947 and presented in 1949.[1] This article presents the tables of working life for 1950.

These tables are very similar to standard life tables, which summarize the mortality experience of a population for some particular period of time. The life table starts with a hypothetical group of persons—usually 100,000—born alive and follows it through successive ages as it experiences the attrition caused by death, using the mortality experience for each age group as of the base period. A number of significant measures can be obtained from such a table, the most familiar of which is the "life expectancy"—the average number of years of life remaining after each specified age. Similarly, the tables of working life follow through successive ages the experience of an initial cohort of 100,000 at birth. But in addition to showing attrition caused by mortality, these tables show the number who may be expected to work or seek work over their life span, the rates at which persons enter and exit from the labor force, and "work-life expectancy"—the average years of labor force activity remaining after each specified age. For any group of workers whose ages are known—as, for example, the

workers in an industry or an occupation—the tables provide a means for estimating prospective losses resulting from both death and retirement from the labor force.

Patterns of Working Life, 1900–1950

The tremendous strides made in the last half century in the control of contagious diseases and other afflictions that killed off many children—particularly in the first year of life—have profoundly affected the pattern of working life. In 1900, of 500,000 boy babies born alive, only about 386,000 young men would reach age 15–19.[2] (See chart.) By 1950, 475,000 would reach this age group, the proportion dying having decreased from about 25 percent to a remarkably low figure of 5 percent. The decline in the mortality rates in the middle and older age groups has been substantial but much slower than for younger groups. These changes in death rates from 1900 to 1950 brought about dramatic increases throughout the entire economically active age range (20–65) of from 25 to 55 percent in the numbers of men alive out of the initial 100,000. (See chart.) Since virtually all men from 20 to 65 normally work, the labor force potential increases almost as much as the population through reduced mortality.

The chart also points up two other major differences in the patterns of working life in 1900 and 1950. One is the much earlier age of labor force entry in 1900. Despite the much smaller popula-

---

[1] The 1940 tables, by Seymour L. Wolfbein, were published in "The Length of Working Life" in Population Studies, December 1949 (printed in Great Britain). Both the 1940 and the 1947 tables and a detailed exposition of the substance and techniques of this work were presented in BLS Bull. 1001, Tables of Working Life, from which some of the descriptive materials here are taken. See also a series of five articles on the tables in the Monthly Labor Review: August 1950 (p. 193), September 1950 (p. 323), October 1950 (p. 438), and November 1950 (pp. 560 and 589).

[2] The population and labor force figures used in the chart are based upon data from the National Office of Vital Statistics of the Department of Health, Education and Welfare and from the Bureau of the Census of the Department of Commerce.

Stationary Population and Labor Force, Males, 1900* and 1950

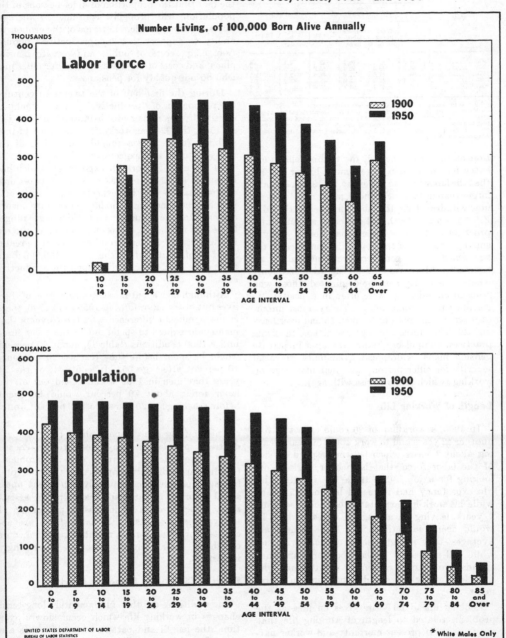

Number Living, of 100,000 Born Alive Annually

UNITED STATES DEPARTMENT OF LABOR
BUREAU OF LABOR STATISTICS

* White Males Only

TABLE 1.—*Average life and work-life expectancy for men, 1900–2000*

Year	At birth			At age 20		
	Average number of years—			Average number of years—		
	Life expectancy	Work-life expectancy	Outside labor force	Life expectancy	Work-life expectancy	In retirement
1900 [1]	48.2	32.1	16.1	42.2	39.4	2.8
1940	61.2	38.3	22.9	46.8	41.3	5.5
1947	64.2	41.6	22.6	48.0	42.8	5.2
1950	65.5	41.9	23.6	48.9	43.2	5.7
2000 [2]	73.2	45.1	28.1	53.8	45.1	8.7

[1] For white males in 11 original death registration States.
[2] Estimated by assuming continuation of labor force participation rates by males as they prevailed in the spring of 1954 except for drop of 10 percentage points among men 65 and over; assumes continuation of mortality trends which have prevailed from 1920 to 1950 (cf. Social Security Administration Actuarial Study No. 33).

tion at the earlier period, the rate of labor force entry for young men was so much higher in 1900 that the labor force in age group 15–19 was actually larger than in 1950. Secondly, many older workers now withdraw from the labor force before they die. Fifty years ago death and disability accounted for practically all labor force separations.[3] Only a small proportion of the population survived to the age which is now considered conventional for retirement. Moreover, in an agrarian economy where self-employment predominated, those who reached an older age were often in a position to continue to do some work. Today, most important among the reasons for men 55 and over leaving the labor force are: age restrictions in hiring practices, compulsory retirement ages in private pension plans, widespread availability of social security for older persons, and inability to go on working (which tends to rise with age).

Length of Working Life

In 1900, a workman of 20 could expect to live another 42 years and to work about 39 years, leaving about 3 years which he would spend outside of the labor force, that is, neither working nor looking for a job. (See table 1.) By 1950, his life expectancy had increased by about 7 years, while his work-life expectancy had increased only 4 years, leaving an average of 6 years which he would spend in retirement. These figures are averages: they include the young man who dies while still a member of the labor force and thus spends zero years in retirement and the man who lives long enough to spend a long time in retirement.

Looking ahead 50 years gives an idea of the problems related to length of working life that may arise. If present mortality and worker par-

ticipation trends continue to 2000, the retirement period will lengthen to about 9 years or 3 times what it was in 1900. (See table 1.) This plus the fact that the proportion of older persons in the population will probably continue to increase raises a serious problem in terms of the economy's ability to support this "nonproductive" population, e. g., costs of public and private pension plans, and costs of old-age assistance for older men who do not qualify for pensions.

During the first half of the twentieth century, the proportion of "productive" years to "nonproductive" years remained substantially unchanged. In 1900, the 32-year work-life expectancy of men at birth (table 1) was roughly two-thirds of the average total life expectancy of 48 years. In 1950, the average work-life expectancy, which had increased to 42 years, was still about two-thirds of the total 65-year life expectancy, in spite of a younger retirement age and later entry into a work career. In the younger and older age ranges there was no change in working years and the entire increase of 10 years resulted from the greater number of men, out of the initial 100,000 born alive each year, who lived through the productive ages.

Although men spent the same proportion of their lives out of the labor force in 1950 as in 1900, there is one significant difference. Of the 16 years that men could expect to spend out of the labor force under 1900 conditions (table 1), about 80 percent would be spent before they reached 20 and only 10 percent after age 65. In contrast, of the 24 years that men in 1950 would spend out of the labor force, about 70 percent would be spent before reaching age 20 and almost 20 percent would occur after age 65.

This shifting age composition of the "nonproductive" population tends to create a social problem. Children are ordinarily supported by their parents, but aged persons are frequently dependent upon social security, private pensions, or public assistance. Therefore, as an increasing proportion of the years spent outside the labor force are accounted for by older men, maintaining the income of these older persons becomes increasingly important.

Effect of Changes in Economic Activity

In addition to the fundamental long-term changes in working life which occur slowly over time, the length and pattern of working life are also affected by short-run economic factors. The experience of the 1940's shows that the ebb and flow of working life in the shorter run corresponds closely with fluctuations in economic activity,

[3] Separations due to "retirement" as shown in the tables include all exits from the labor force for reasons other than death, e. g., because of old age, disability, eligibility for pension, or long-duration unemployment.

especially changing employment opportunities. (See table 2.)

After a decade of severe dislocation of economic activity and reduced employment opportunity, 1940 labor force participation rates at both ends of the age scale were low in comparison with the corresponding rates in the more prosperous year of 1950, which followed a decade of high employment levels. The rate for the age group 15–19 years was about 45 percent in 1940, and over 8 percentage points higher in 1950. In 1940, inexperienced young men were at a disadvantage in job competition, and very few (about 6 percent) who went to school had part-time employment. In contrast, many young people held full-time jobs in 1950, and almost one-third of the students had jobs.

Sharp changes also took place in the separation patterns between 1940 and 1950. Declining death rates during the decade reduced the number of men who would have left the labor force because of death. A shift in the retirement pattern apparently was brought about by the generally higher level of job opportunities in the postwar period. Many older men who would have left the labor force in the depressed 1930's continued to work both during the war period and the prosperous postwar years and thereby actually reversed the long-term trend toward an earlier age of retirement.

Even under sharply improved economic conditions in 1950, however, the long-term trend toward an increasing number of expected years outside the labor force continued, although at a sharply reduced rate (table 1). Total life expectancy rose 4.3 years, while work-life expectancy rose only 3.6 years, thus increasing the period outside the labor force by more than a half year during the decade.

TABLE 2.—*Abridged table of working life, males, 1940 [1] and 1950*

Age interval	Number living of 100,000 born alive—			Accessions to the labor force (per 1,000 in population)	Separations from the labor force (per 1,000 in labor force)—			Average number of remaining years of—	
	In population	In labor force			Due to all causes	Due to death	Due to retirement	Life	Labor force participation
		Number	Percent of population						
	(Within age interval)				(Between successive age intervals)			(At beginning of age interval)	
1940									
10–14	461,865	6,196	(2)	431.0	8.2	8.2		51.3	45.8
15–19	458,100	205,229	44.8	441.6	12.0	12.0		46.8	41.3
20–24	452,589	405,067	89.5	68.0	14.9	14.9		42.4	36.8
25–29	445,845	429,795	96.4	7.9	17.6	17.6		38.0	32.3
30–34	438,014	425,750	97.2		28.0	21.9	6.1	33.7	28.0
35–39	428,373	413,808	96.6		37.8	29.7	8.1	29.6	23.8
40–44	415,611	398,155	95.8		53.3	42.1	11.2	25.5	19.8
45–49	398,028	376,933	94.7		80.2	60.8	19.4	21.8	16.0
50–54	373,582	346,684	92.8		117.8	85.9	31.9	18.3	12.4
55–59	340,970	305,850	89.7		211.6	115.7	95.9	15.1	9.2
60–64	299,545	241,134	80.5		376.7	148.9	227.8	12.2	6.8
65–69	248,456	150,316	60.5		495.5	191.8	303.7	9.6	5.6
70–74	189,583	75,833	40.0		576.4	262.4	314.0		
75 and over	232,278	44,830	19.3						
1950									
10–14	477,806	21,000	(2)	483.5	5.3	5.3		53.6	47.9
15–19	475,282	251,899	53.0	354.0	8.5	8.5		48.9	43.2
20–24	471,255	418,003	88.7	73.3	9.8	9.8		44.4	38.6
25–29	466,652	448,453	96.1	6.0	10.7	10.7		39.8	34.0
30–34	461,671	446,436	96.7		15.1	14.1	1.0	35.2	29.3
35–39	455,169	439,693	96.6		23.3	21.3	2.0	30.8	24.9
40–44	445,488	429,450	96.4		42.6	33.4	9.2	26.6	20.6
45–49	430,539	411,165	95.5		70.9	51.5	19.4	22.6	16.6
50–54	408,140	382,019	93.6		116.3	77.4	38.9	19.0	13.0
55–59	375,956	337,608	89.8		195.5	109.7	85.8	15.7	9.7
60–64	332,858	271,612	81.6		337.2	142.3	194.9	12.7	7.2
65–69	279,537	180,022	64.4		485.9	180.1	305.8	10.1	5.9
70–74	417,261	92,553	42.6		558.6	247.5	311.1		
75 and over	287,742	61,289	21.3						

[1] Labor force data for 1940 have been adjusted to allow for a revision in Census Bureau enumeration procedures introduced in July 1945.
[2] In accordance with current Census definitions, only persons 14 years of age or over are enumerated in the labor force. No meaningful percentage of the population in the labor force could therefore be computed for the age interval 10–14 years.

TIME-SPECIFIC LIFE TABLES CONTRASTED

WITH OBSERVED SURVIVORSHIP

By Margaret Merrell

In obtaining life tables for any group of individuals, biological or physical, there are two basically different types of observation which are commonly used. One of these consists in the classification of individuals at a fixed time into separate age groups and then in the recording of deaths for all the various ages simultaneously. The life table derived from this evidence is a time-specific or static life table because the deaths for all the ages are recorded at the same time. The second type of observations consists in following a group of individuals born at approximately the same time, from birth to the death of the longest-lived member of the group. In this case the survivorship curve is determined by direct observation. It has been called a generation or cohort or fluent life table [1]. The life tables resulting from these two different types of evidence on longevity will, except under unusual circumstances, be different in form, and in any case will be quite different in meaning.

To consider an example of the two life tables, suppose we wish to study the present day survival of Ford automobiles. We may ask two different questions: what is the longevity of Fords at the current rates of survival, or what is the survival of the current model of Ford? That is, in one case we ask about current rates of cars existing at the *present time* and in the other about the *present model* and its future rates. To answer the first question we might get the date of manufacture (that is the age) of all the Fords registered on January 1, 1947, and during the following year get, by date of manufacture, the number of these cars irrevocably eliminated from service, that is, the deaths. Death in this case would be due to accidents, old age, or perhaps disease and malformations. From the age-specific death rates we could construct a survivorship curve for Fords for the year 1947. It would give us the way in which a group of Fords would survive if the 1947 rates pertained throughout their careers. The other life table could be obtained by following the 1947 models throughout their future existence to determine the number finally retired from service up to successive dates. This would give us the survivorship curve for the 1947 models, by direct subtraction. These two survivorship curves would be quite different and in this familiar problem everyone will think of a number of reasons why this is so. The cars registered on January 1, 1947 will be residues of different lots of cars, each remnant having its own peculiar ability to survive 1947 conditions, depending on age, basic quality, damage due to past experience, and nature of repair. The common element for all of them is that their experience is being studied for the year 1947. On the other hand the dynamic life table for the 1947 models will have the experience of successive years of time but the survivorship curve will be that of cars manufactured in the same year, and therefore will have a certain homogeneity which the fixed-time life table does not possess.

All of the factors that I have mentioned as contributing to the difference in the two life tables for Fords have their direct counterpart in biological life tables. Inherent capacity, environmental hazards, methods of preventing and repairing damage, are continually shifting to a greater or less degree in the biological as well as in the physical world. The individuals existing at any time are survivors out of different lots of individuals and a single survivorship curve determined by putting together their experience in a given period will be different from the survivorship of a given lot of individuals followed through their lives. Thus for biological species also, the static and the dynamic life tables will be different in both form and meaning.

Yet frequently the choice of life table in this field is made solely on the issue of convenience. For long-lived forms, like man, it is not convenient to follow a group of individuals from birth to death, so for this reason alone we sometimes employ the static life table. For short-lived forms, like the beetle or fruit-fly, it is often more convenient to start with a given brood and follow it through life than to keep track of the ages and deaths among different broods. The question of convenience has sometimes led to the error of comparing a specified-time life table for man with a generation life table for some other biological form. The scientific question at issue is the important point in these problems and that life table should be set up which is relevant to the scientific question.

If we turn to human life tables we can see the effect of determining survivorship on a fixed-time basis as compared with a generation basis.

Figure 1 gives the survivorship of males in Massachusetts for fixed times approximately 10 years apart from 1890 to 1940. The 1890 life table, for example, shows how a hypothetical group would survive if it died off according to the 1890 age specific rates. We can see from this graph the improvement in the rates from 1890 to 1940.

But the graph also shows the other type of life table in giving the survivorship for males born in 1890. This was constructed in the following way. The people born in 1890 were infants in that year, 1 year olds in 1891, 2 year olds in 1892, etc. The rates of dying at these ages in these calendar years are therefore the rates pertaining to this group[1]

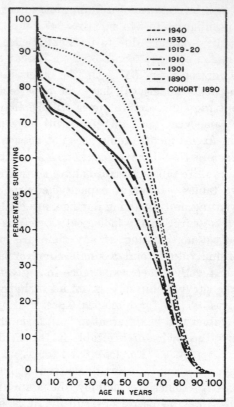

Figure 1. *Percentage surviving from birth to successive ages, Massachusetts males.*

as they pass through life. It is possible in terms of these rates to construct a survivorship curve for the 1890 cohort from birth to their present age of 56 years. I have carried this curve only to 50 years since the last life table I was able to construct on a known population distribution was for the census year of 1940. It is seen that the people born in 1890 had a survivorship curve unlike that of any of the years through which they lived. Conversely the survivorship based on the rates of a given calendar year would not be the survivorship of any group followed throughout life.

Which of these curves do we want? If we want to compare the risks of dying in different calendar years we probably want the fixed-time life table. Whatever the multiplicity of factors in this year and

---

[1] Although migration effects keep the composition of this group from remaining exactly the same in the sense of a laboratory experiment or an ideal follow-up, in a practical sense the same group is being followed.

in the past which produced the death rates of the calendar year, these rates were the actual current situation and the survivorship curve based on them helps us to see the implications of those rates. Certain aspects of the improvement in mortality with time, and the comparison of the mortality of different places at the same time are well shown by such curves. On the other hand, for certain prognosis problems, such as have been considered by Lotka [2] on the future age structure of our population, chances of orphanhood, and so on, the dynamic problem must certainly be considered.

If we consider the description of survivorship for other biological forms, the same issues arise. The question has been raised of getting the life table for a forest. In this case it is clear that the two forms of life table need to be very sharply distinguished since they would be widely different. The fixed-time life table would show the effect on survivorship of a current program of selective cutting, along with the natural mortality of the trees. The generation life table would show the survivorship of the same generation of trees from seedlings to final death influenced by all the time changes in forest preservation or destruction which would accompany their life span; this would give us the information we would need in evaluating a large scale reforestation program. The two life tables would therefore supplement each other in providing knowledge on which to plan a sound program.

If we consider the shorter-lived forms which are studied frequently in the laboratory, the contrast in the two types of life table is also great. The very fact of short life means that brief fluctuations in the environmental conditions may be very profound in their effect, and chance or deliberate alterations in environment will be different if they pertain to a single generation at some stage in its life span or if they affect a population composed of all ages.

I have been discussing a life table primarily in terms of a survivorship curve. I should like now to turn to a consideration of the age specific rates which are behind the survivorship curve and see how time is involved here. We study these age specific rates for their scientific meaning but the biological interpretation of the risk for a given calendar year is very dependent on how the rates for successive generations have been changing.

I want to illustrate this by a study on tuberculosis, made by Dr. Wade Frost [3].

Figure 2 shows the age-specific rates for males of Massachusetts for deaths from all forms of tuberculosis at certain fixed periods of time from 1880 to 1940. It had been noted by students of the subject that this curve had undergone a drastic change in shape. Back in 1880 the peak of mortality was in the 20's and at successive periods of time the peak became later and later in age until in 1940 it was in

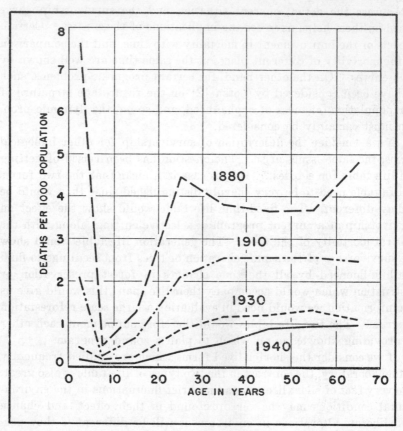

Figure 2. *Age-specific death rates from tuberculosis for different calendar years, Massachusetts males.*

the 60's. Prior to Dr. Frost's work on this, the interpretation had generally been that tuberculosis was changing in its relation to man, that at earlier times it was most devastating to young adults, but in recent years, either the disease or the resistance of people had changed so that the effects of the disease had become more serious later in life. In other words, tuberculosis had become an old age disease.

In order to test this explanation Dr. Frost examined the death rates for successive cohorts of people.

The columns given in Table I are the age-specific death rates in successive time periods which we have just seen. If now we consider the people who were under 10 in 1880 as one group, (called the 1880 cohort), their death rates are in the 1880 column; they were 10 to 20 in 1890, and their death rate is in the 1890 column; 20 to 30 in 1900, and so on. The diagonal stepped lines indicate the death rates for

TABLE I

AGE SPECIFIC DEATH RATES PER 100,000 FROM TUBERCULOSIS FOR MASSACHUSETTS
MALES, 1880 TO 1940, WITH RATES FOR COHORT OF 1880 INDICATED

Age	1880	1890	1900	1910	1920	1930	1940
0 - 4	760	578	309	209	108	41	11
5 - 9	43	49	31	21	24	11	2
10 - 19	126	115	90	63	49	21	4
20 - 29	444	361	288	207	149	81	35
30 - 39	378	368	296	253	164	115	51
40 - 49	364	336	253	253	175	118	86
50 - 59	366	325	267	252	171	127	92
60 - 69	475	346	304	246	172	95	109
70 +	672	396	343	163	127	95	79

this group as they pass through life. Similarly the 1890 cohort may be followed through to age 50–59; the 1900 cohort to age 40–49, and so on.

Now if we look at these cohort curves shown in Figure 3 we find that they all have their peak in the 20's, that they are all approximately the same shape, that there is no evidence at all that tuberculosis is becoming an old age disease. Each successive generation has its greatest toll taken in the 20's. What then is the explanation for the apparent shift in the risks seen in Figure 2? It lies in the fact that in successive generations the rates have come down at all ages, the form of curve remaining the same. When we get the rates at a particular time, say 1940, we cut across the rates for all the various cohorts, at different points on the age scale. We have the 30-year-old rate from the 1910 cohort, the 40-year-old rate from the 1900 cohort, etc. The older rates pertain to earlier cohorts when *all* the rates were higher. Thus our 1940 curve does not represent the way tuberculosis is affecting any single group of people in passing through their lives, but rather shows that the old people have come through such heavy exposure to the disease in their youth that there is more tuberculosis among them than among even our 20-year-olds today. It would not do to anticipate that our present 20-year-olds would show a higher rate in old age than they have now. Tuberculosis is still primarily a young person's disease.

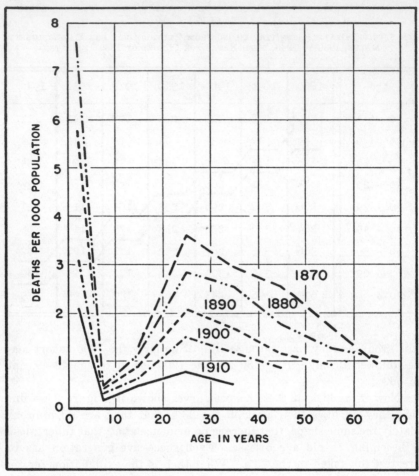

Figure 3. *Age-specific death rates from tuberculosis for successive 10-year cohorts, Massachusetts males.*

It is the fact that age changes *in a person* are perfectly correlated with time changes that leads us to think of any age difference as representing a time flow. But age differences at a fixed time cannot be so interpreted. The very form in which the life table is put, that of survivorship, tempts us still further to think of the curve as giving us a flow of people through their lives. We must therefore distinguish clearly between the case where it does really represent the survivorship of a group and the case where it represents in very picturesque form, a static set of age-specific rates.

REFERENCES

[1] Dublin, Louis I, and Mortimer Spiegelman, "Current versus generation life tables," *Human Biology,* vol. 13, pp. 439–459, 1941.

[2] Lotka, A. J., "The structure of a growing population," *Human Biology,* vol. 3, pp. 459–493, 1931.

[3] Frost, W. H., "The age selection of mortality from tuberculosis in successive decades," *American Journal of Hygiene,* vol. 30, no. 3, sec. A, pp. 91–96, 1939.

A CENTURY OF PROGRESS IN LONGEVITY

By the Metropolitan Life Insurance Company

The scientific, social, and economic progress made in our country in the past century probably has no counterpart in all human history. Every branch of the medical and sanitary sciences has shared in this advance, with the result that the death rate has been greatly reduced and many diseases which once were rampant are now either under control or well on their way toward control. Compared with a century ago, we now enjoy a vastly higher standard of living—more abundant and better food, shelter, clothing, educational and recreational facilities. Perhaps the best single index that can satisfactorily measure this progress over the last 100 years is the increase in the expectation of life at birth.

In 1850, conditions were such that the expectation of life at birth in the United States was only about 40 years. By 1952, according to the National Office of Vital Statistics, this figure had risen to 68.6 years. In other words, within four generations the expectation of life had risen by about 28 years, or by two thirds. Further details, by sex and age, are given in the accompanying table.

The table clearly illustrates several salient points with respect to the trend of longevity in our country.[1] In the first place, most of the gain in expectation of life has been made under age 50 for white males and under age 60 for white females. Furthermore, these gains increase both absolutely and relatively as one traces the figures from these higher ages back to birth. Thus, a white boy baby born in 1952 had an expectation of life at birth of 66.4 years, or 28 years more than the baby of 1850. For white females, the corresponding figure for 1952 was 72.7 years, just 32 years greater than that for 1850. These facts illustrate a second point, namely, the greater increase in longevity among females than males, thus widening the difference between the sexes. Since 1910, white females have been experiencing an increase of about one half year per annum in their expectation of life.

The third point worth noting is that the gain in longevity was at a much more rapid rate during the second half of the century under review than in the first half. For example, the gain of 28 years for white males is made up of a 10-year gain from 1850 to 1900, and of an 18-year gain since then. In the case of white females, the 30-year gain within the last century is divided into 10½ years up to 1900, and 21½ years in the subsequent period.

Reliable figures for expectation of life for colored persons are available

---

1. The discussion which follows is summarized from *Length of Life* by Louis I. Dublin, Alfred J. Lotka, and Mortimer Spiegelman (Ronald Press, N. Y., 1949).

From *Statistical Bulletin*, Metropolitan Life Insurance Company, 30 (October 1949), 1-3. The table and figures in the text pertaining to 1952 have been taken from "Gains in Longevity Since 1850," *Statistical Bulletin*, 36 (February 1955), 5-8; in all other respects the text of the 1949 article is unchanged.

only since 1900; these are shown in the lower tier of the accompanying table. The record here is also one of marked gain. In 1900, colored persons had an expectation of life about 16 years less than their white contemporaries, and even five years less than white persons of a half century earlier. By 1952, the difference in longevity between the colored and the white was reduced to 5⅓ years, but the colored were still only on a par with the white population of 1929-1931.

The medical and public health leaders of a generation ago could hardly have expected such gain in longevity as has been achieved; those of two generations ago could not even have imagined it. With these solid accomplishments behind us, there is still room for optimism in looking toward the future. The medical and sanitary sciences are advancing at a fast pace; our standards of living are still improving rapidly; and our people have become alert to their stake in sound public health and medical care. With the expectation of life of the American people now near the Biblical three-score-and-ten mark, there is good reason to expect an average of 75 years within the next generation.

EXPECTATION OF LIFE IN THE UNITED STATES, 1850 TO 1952

CALENDAR PERIOD	AGE								
	0	10	20	30	40	50	60	70	80
WHITE MALES									
1850*	38.3	48.0	40.1	34.0	27.9	21.6	15.6	10.2	5.9
1890*	42.50	48.45	40.66	34.05	27.37	20.72	14.73	9.35	5.40
1900-1902†	48.23	50.59	42.19	34.88	27.74	20.76	14.35	9.03	5.10
1901-1910†	49.32	50.86	42.39	34.80	27.55	20.59	14.17	8.96	5.07
1909-1911†	50.23	51.32	42.71	34.87	27.43	20.39	13.98	8.83	5.09
1919-1921‡	56.34	54.15	45.60	37.65	29.86	22.22	15.25	9.51	5.47
1920-1929‡	57.85	54.65	45.84·	37.51	29.35	21.65	14.75	9.17	5.26
1929-1931	59.12	54.96	46.02	37.54	29.22	21.51	14.72	9.20	5.26
1930-1939	60.62	55.86	46.77	38.06	29.57	21.71	14.86	9.29	5.30
1930-1941	62.81	57.03	47.76	38.80	30.03	21.96	15.05	9.42	5.38
1949-1951	66.31	58.98	49.52	40.29·	31.17	22.83	15.76	10.07	5.88
1952	66.64	59.17	49.73	40.54	31.39	23.01	15.95	10.34	6.15
WHITE FEMALES									
1850*	40.5	47.2	40.2	35.4	29.8	23.5	17.0	11.3	6.4
1890*	44.46	49.62	42.03	35.36	28.76	22.09	15.70	10.15	5.75
1900-1902†	51.08	52.15	43.77	36.42	29.17	21.89	15.23	9.59	5.50
1901-1910†	52.54	52.89	44.39	36.75	29.28	21.86	15.09	9.52	5.43
1909-1911†	53.62	53.57	44.88	36.96	29.26	21.74	14.92	9.38	5.35
1919-1921‡	58.53	55.17	46.46	38.72	30.94	23.12	15.93	9.94	5.70
1920-1929‡	60.62	56.41	47.46	39.20	30.97	22.97	15.70	9.71	5.46
1929-1931	62.67	57.65	48.52	39.99	31.52	23.41	16.05	9.98	5.63
1930-1939	64.52	58.98	49.71	40.90	32.24	23.96	16.44	10.19	5.76
1939-1941	67.29	60.85	51.38	42.21	33.25	24.72	17.00	10.50	5.88
1949-1951	72.03	64.26	54.56	45.00	35.64	26.76	18.64	11.68	6.59
1952	72.65	64.79	55.11	45.52	36.12	27.19	19.00	12.00	6.81
NONWHITE MALES¶									
1900-1902†	32.54	41.90	35.11	29.25	23.12	17.34	12.62	8.33	5.12
1901-1910†	32.57	40.73	33.78	27.97	22.23	16.64	11.87	8.29	5.43
1909-1911†	34.05·	40.65	33.46	27.33	21.57	16.21	11.67	8.00	5.53
1919-1921‡	47.14	45.99	38.36	32.51	26.53	20.47	14.74	9.58	5.83
1920-1929‡	46.90	44.86	36.76	30.65	24.55	18.83	13.66	9.12	5.54
1929-1931	47.55	44.27	35.95	29.45	23.36	17.92	13.15	8.78	5.42
1930-1939	50.06 ~	46.56	38.05	31.11	24.65	18.98	14.13	9.53	6.01
1939-1941	52.26	48.34	39.52	32.05	25.06	19.06	14.37	10.11	6.58
1949-1951	58.91	52.96	43.73	35.31	27.29	20.25	14.91	10.74	7.07
1952	59.13	53.27	44.00	35.57	27.54	20.38	14.99	11.14	8.04
NONWHITE FEMALES¶									
1900-1902†	35.04	43.02	36.89	30.70	24.37	18.67	13.60	9.62	6.48
1901-1910†	35.65	42.52	36.17	30.09	23.81	18.08	13.17	9.52	6.50
1909-1911†	37.67	42.84	36.14	29.61	23.34	17.65	12.78	9.22	6.05
1919-1921‡	46.92	44.54	37.15	31.48	25.60	19.76	14.69	10.25	6.58
1920-1929‡	47.95	44.86	36.98	30.93	24.67	18.85	14.01	10.01	6.49
1929-1931	49.51	45.33	37.22	30.87	24.30	18.60	14.22	10.38	6.90
1930-1939	52.62	48.29	39.90	32.88	26.11	20.09	15.28	10.88	7.18
1939-1941	55.56	50.75	42.04	34.40	27.19	20.95	16.10	11.82	8.02
1949-1951	62.70	56.17	46.77	38.92	29.82	22.67	16.95	12.29	8.15
1952	63.72	57.28	47.57	38.89	30.63	23.23	17.38	12.94	9.15

*Massachusetts only; white and nonwhite combined, the latter being about one percent of the total. Longevity in Massachusetts considered to be indicative of that in the country as a whole at that time.
†Original Death Registration States.
‡Death Registration States of 1920.
¶Data for periods 1900-1902 to 1929-1931 and 1939-1941 relate to Negroes only.
Source—Various publications of the National Office of Vital Statistics and the Bureau of the Census.

TRENDS IN LONGEVITY

By Louis I. Dublin and Alfred J. Lotka

LIVING conditions as we know them here today imply, among other things, a high standard of public health. But as we look back over the centuries, or look abroad over some of the more remote parts of the earth, we find a wide range of circumstances, for not all peoples have shared equally in the advancement of science and the technical arts. Some have been held back by adverse climatic conditions, as in the extreme north; others are handicapped by outmoded traditions or by sheer superstitions; and still others have lagged in following the lead of the most progressive nations. And so, as contemporaries on this same globe, we find the white population of New Zealand enjoying an average length of life of about 67 years and, by way of contrast, the people of India and China living on an average a bare 30 years, corresponding perhaps to the conditions among the Romans in classic times. These divergences are not due to basic differences in human stock. The upper limit of life—the span of life as it is called—for those who do survive is much the same for most of these inhabitants of the earth today, and has undoubtedly been much the same throughout historic time. There have been a few centenarians in various eras and various nations, but the century mark has never been greatly exceeded by anyone.

AVERAGE LENGTH OF LIFE

A general survey of the situation as it stands today can be gathered from Table 1, which at the same time gives some indications of the historical developments.[1] In discussing this table we shall for the sake of simplicity refer to the figures for males. The figures for females in practically all instances run more or less parallel, but at a somewhat higher level.

A very good starting point in studying this table is the long series for Sweden, which extends back to the middle of the eighteenth century. At that time males had an expectation of life of 33.2 years. This early figure for Sweden is appreciably above that for India in 1931, and no doubt even today. The opening of the nineteenth century apparently saw some improvement in Sweden, for the figure rose to a level of about 40 years, which was maintained essentially unchanged until towards the last quarter of the century. From about that time on, the series of figures shows a continued and definite upward trend, culminating in a level of 63.2 years for the period 1931–35, not far from double the figure at the beginning of the series. The other Scandinavian countries, as well as the Netherlands, in recent years, have shown high figures not unlike those of Sweden. This group of countries ranks second only to the record performance of New Zealand.

On a somewhat lower level are the figures for Germany (59.9 years in

[1] For more complete details see Louis I. Dublin and Alfred J. Lotka, *Length of Life* (New York: Ronald Press, 1936), 400 pp.; also *Population Index*, published quarterly by the Population Association of America at Princeton, N. J.

TABLE 1—Expectation of Life at Birth and at Age 40 in
Principal Countries at Various Epochs

| Country and Period | Expectation of Life | | | | Country and Period | Expectation of Life | | | |
| | At Birth | | At Age 40 | | | At Birth | | At Age 40 | |
	Males	Females	Males	Females		Males	Females	Males	Females
Australia					Russia (Europe)				
1881–90.......	47.20	50.84	26.50	29.08	1926–27........	41.93	46.79	28.02	32.12
1932–34.......	63.48	67.14	31.11	34.04	Sweden				
England and					1755–76.......	33.20	35.70	23.75	25.21
Wales					1816–40.......	39.50	43.56	23.66	26.41
1841.........	40.19	42.18	26.56	27.72	1861–70.......	42.80	46.40	26.30	28.70
1937.........	60.18	64.40	29.57	32.78	1871–80.......	45.30	48.60	27.80	30.10
France					1881–90.......	48.55	51.47	29.27	31.28
1817–32.......	38.33	40.83	27.00	26.58	1891–00.......	50.94	53.63	29.90	31.75
1928–33.......	54.30	59.02	27.62	31.37	1901–10.......	54.55	57.00	30.77	32.54
Germany					1911–20.......	55.60	58.38	31.07	32.61
1871–80.......	35.58	38.45	24.46	26.32	1921–25.......	60.72	62.95	32.39	33.43
1932–34.......	59.86	62.81	30.83	32.33	1926–30.......	61.19	63.33	32.16	33.25
India					1931–35.......	63.22	65.33	32.50	33.54
1881.........	23.67	25.58	18.90	20.03	United States				
1931.........	26.91	26.56	18.60	18.23	(white)				
Italy					1789 (Mass.,				
1876–87.......	35.08	35.40	26.25	26.67	N. H.).......	35.47	*a*	26.04	*a*
1930–32.......	53.76	56.00	30.39	32.14	1850 (Md.).....	41.8	44.9	25.8	29.5
1935–37.......	—	57.49	—	32.30	1900–02.......	48.23	51.08	27.74	29.17
Japan					1901–10.......	49.32	52.54	27.55	29.28
1908–13.......	44.25	44.73	26.82	29.03	1909–11.......	50.23	53.62	27.43	29.26
1935–36.......	46.92	49.63	26.22	29.65	1919–21.......	56.34	58.53	29.86	30.94
New Zealand					1920–29.......	57.85	60.62	29.35	30.97
1891–95.......	55.29	58.09	—	—	1929–31.......	59.12	62.67	29.22	31.52
1934–38......	65.46	68.45	32.03	34.05	1930–39.......	60.62	64.52	29.57	32.24
					1939–41.......	62.81	67.29	30.03	33.25
					1942.........	63.65	68.61	30.27	33.86

a The figures on this line relate to total persons.

1932–34), France (54.3 years in 1928–33), and Italy (53.8 years in 1930–32). Of the Balkan and neighboring countries, Hungary had an expectation of life at birth of 48.3 for males in 1930–31 and Bulgaria 45.9 in 1925–28. It might be observed that these figures show a downward tendency as we move geographically from the northwest corner of Europe to the south and east. Somewhat in line with this observation is the fact that the latest figure available for Russia (1926–27) is 41.9, the level reached in Sweden, for example, even before the middle of the last century.

Special interest for us in the United States naturally attaches to the figures for England and Wales, whose habits and customs are closest to our own. Here we note, for example, in 1937 England and Wales had an expectation of life of 60.2 as compared with 60.6 in the United States in 1930–39, the nearest comparable dates for which both figures are available.

In our own United States, early indications based on fragmentary data show that the average length of life about the time of the Revolution was probably about 35½ years. By the middle of the nineteenth century this had increased close on to 42 years. From about 1900 forward, a more fully representative set of life tables is available. These show continued rise up to the latest life table for 1942, which has an average length of life of 63.7 years for males and 68.6 years for females. The average length of life for white males has increased by no less than 15½ years since the beginning of the present century, while the gain for white females is even more, namely, 17½ years. This means that the average length of life has been increased by practically one-third in four decades, a result which would have seemed fantastic if anyone had suggested it as a forecast in 1900.

EXPECTATION OF LIFE AT AGE 40

Much less spectacular than the gains in the average length of life, or, as it is termed alternatively, the expectation of life at birth, are the corresponding improvements at the older ages. This is illustrated in Table 1, where the figures for the expectation of life at age 40 are shown side by side with those for age zero. It is at once apparent that the gain is very largely concentrated in the early ages. In other words, the improvement is concentrated in the infant and childhood years and early adult life. This is not saying that there has been no improvement at the older ages, especially when comparison is made with the more remote past. For example, in Sweden, for which, as already mentioned, we have an especially long series, at age 40 there has been an increase from 23.8 years in the late eighteenth century to 32.5 years at the most recent date available, 1931–35. This is an increase of somewhat over one-third, whereas we noted above that the expectation of life at birth had almost doubled in this period. A somewhat similar though less pronounced picture is seen for the extreme dates in the

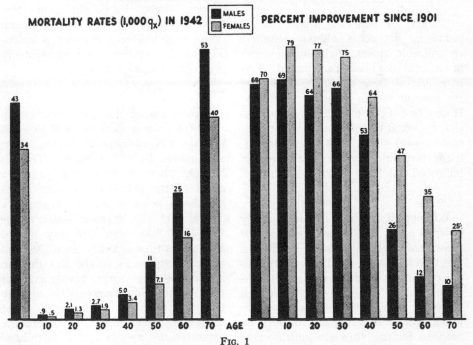

FIG. 1

series for the United States at age 40.

The average length of life, or expectation of life at birth, is the resultant of mortality at successive ages. Such an average gives in a sense a blurred picture of the significant facts, which must be brought to sharp focus by a more detailed scrutiny of the components entering into the resultant. With this in view, Figure 1 has been prepared. It shows for the United States the mortality at every tenth year of life and the per cent change in these figures from 1900–02 to 1942. The comparison is most striking. It is immediately apparent that the most substantial improvements have been at the younger ages, and that they have been greater for females than for males.

But the scrutiny can be carried further than merely an analysis by age. The question forces itself upon us irresistibly, what are the fundamentally underlying causes of these improvements?

RISE IN STANDARD OF LIVING

Changes of such magnitude and rapidity do not come without definitely recognizable causes. Actually a number of circumstances have contributed. Perhaps first of these should be mentioned the general rise in standards of living. It may be difficult to make any quantitative appraisal of this, but it is not difficult to point out at least some outstanding factors which the very broad term of improved standards of living includes.

Housing

Without attempting enumeration by order of merit, first among these may be mentioned better housing conditions. We, who live in the middle of the twentieth century, can hardly realize the fearful conditions that existed even in such places as New York City about eighty years ago, as reported for instance by Stephen Smith,[2] then Commissioner of

[2] *The City That Was* (New York: Frank Allaben, 1911), 211 pp.

the Metropolitan Board of Health of New York. To select only one passage from his report, we read how in filthy surroundings some 18,000 persons were living in cellars within a small area. "In a dark and damp cellar about 18 feet square and 7 feet high lived a family of 7 persons. Within the past year two have died of typhus, two of smallpox, and one has been sent to the hospital with erysipelas."

Great as has been the progress since these dark days, much still remains to be done, and the subject of housing is indeed receiving the close attention of authorities both in the United States and in England. The latter country, of course, has very special problems arising from the extensive war damage. More generally, in the rehabilitation of the European countries, reconstruction of dwellings will be one of the outstanding tasks and the application of modern methods and the modern point of view as to town planning should give opportunity for furthering general health conditions. Even though the actual performance may fall short of the dream house that has been featured occasionally in the popular press, undoubtedly great opportunities do exist.

Food

Second among the great benefits derived from the modern mode of living is the provision of more abundant, better, and more diversified food. This is brought about in part as a secondary effect of the Industrial Revolution, as has been pointed out by Warren S. Thompson.[3] He draws attention to the fact that "the very brilliancy of the achievements of industry since 1750 has tended to blind us to the fact that an almost equally great revolution has taken place simultaneously in agriculture. . . . The net result was that one worker in agriculture came to produce several times as much food as a hand

[3] *Plenty of People* (Lancaster, Pa.: Jaques Cattell Press, 1944), 246 pp.

worker had before 1800." This agricultural revolution not only resulted in obvious direct benefits, but released energy and labor which could now be spent on sanitary and general improvements for the people.

While improvements in agricultural methods resulted in increased harvests and hence more abundant food for home consumption or export, another circumstance has worked towards greater diversification of foods. Not only is our general system of transportation improved beyond recognition over the conditions about the middle of the last century, but, in particular, the distribution of foodstuffs within our own boundaries and from outside has taken on a new aspect with the introduction of refrigerated cargo space on ships, freight cars, auto trucks, and presently airplanes. With our modern knowledge of vitamins and protective foods we realize that this diversification is not a mere luxury but is of importance in preserving the best possible health conditions.

Education and social services

It would be sad if we should not be able to claim that great advantage has come, too, from the better general level of education, leading to a more rational attitude towards personal hygiene, a better understanding of general rules of health, and better co-operation of the individual with medical aid when the requirement arises.

Another major factor, especially - in more recent times, has been the increasing development of social agencies to promote health and welfare. Our Social Security program falls into this category and, as is well known, some other countries have proceeded somewhat further along this line than we ourselves.

Working conditions

A special aspect of social improvements closely bearing on prolongation of life is the movement for the control of working hours and for the introduction of industrial hygiene and safety practices. Not only have the terrible sweatshop practices of twenty-five or thirty years ago come to be duly recognized as nothing less than criminal, but even within the limits of socially approved methods working hours have been reduced to a point in conformity with reasonable comfort and opportunity for leisure. The added leisure hours can today be occupied in perhaps better and at any rate more diversified pursuits through the universal spread of the automobile and other improved recreational facilities.

ADVANCES IN MEDICINE AND PUBLIC HEALTH ADMINISTRATION

In this field, progress has been so wide and deep that only a volume devoted to the history of medicine and sanitary science could cover the subject with any degree of completeness. Here only some of the outstanding achievements can be briefly surveyed. At the same time, we have the advantage that we can appraise quantitatively individual detailed items of progress, since vital statistics in the more advanced countries list mortality not only as an over-all figure but by individual causes of death. By way of example, we shall concentrate our attention mainly on the United States.

Infectious diseases

If we extend our study back to, say, the beginning of the nineteenth century, we are there confronted with very serious epidemics of diseases which in our modern metropolis are practically extinct today, such as yellow fever, cholera, and smallpox. From about the last quarter of the nineteenth century, the more general introduction of systematic sanitary and public health measures begins to show itself clearly in the records, and by the turn of the century the old-time pes-

TABLE 2—AVERAGE ANNUAL CRUDE DEATH RATES PER 100,000 FOR SELECTED CAUSES—DEATH REGISTRATION STATES OF THE UNITED STATES FROM 1900 TO 1942

Cause of Death	1900–04	1905–09	1910–14	1915–19	1920–24	1925–29	1930–34	1935–39	1940	1941	1942
All Causes	1622.3	1529.2	1385.8	1439.0	1198.0	1179.4	1100.1	1100.0	1074.1	1050.4	1035.5
Typhoid fever	26.8	25.0	18.2	12.0	7.4	5.7	4.0	2.2	1.1	.8	.6
Communicable diseases of childhood	65.3	54.1	46.8	37.4	34.0	20.9	14.0	8.4	4.3	5.8	4.2
Measles	10.0	10.1	9.8	9.1	7.2	4.5	3.1	1.7	.5	1.7	1.0
Scarlet fever	11.8	9.4	8.1	3.2	4.0	2.3	2.1	1.4	.5	.3	.3
Whooping cough	10.7	11.4	10.4	10.4	9.0	6.8	4.5	3.1	2.2	2.8	1.9
Diphtheria	32.8	23.2	18.5	14.7	13.8	7.3	4.3	2.2	1.1	1.0	1.0
Influenza and pneumonia	184.4	160.9	142.5	257.0	141.1	131.0	101.9	99.0	70.1	63.9	55.7
Influenza	22.9	18.0	12.2	92.2	35.2	38.3	24.0	21.4	15.3	15.8	8.1
Pneumonia	161.5	142.9	130.3	164.8	105.9	92.7	77.9	77.6	54.8	48.1	47.5
Tuberculosis, all forms	184.8	169.7	147.9	139.5	97.1	80.7	63.5	52.2	45.8	44.5	43.1
Syphilis, all forms	12.9	13.1	15.4	18.1	17.5	16.6	15.5	15.7	14.4	13.3	12.2
Cancer, all forms	67.6	71.9	76.9	80.9	86.8	94.7	101.5	112.9	120.0	120.2	122.1
Diabetes mellitus	12.2	13.9	15.4	16.5	17.0	18.0	21.0	23.8	26.5	25.5	25.4
Cerebral hemorrhage	106.3	100.0	92.8	93.8	93.4	90.3	86.6	87.4	90.9	89.1	90.2
Diseases of the heart	147.7	157.5	157.4	164.1	166.1	199.5	224.0	265.2	291.9	290.2	295.2
Diarrhea and enteritis	115.6	114.3	88.7	69.1	43.2	29.7	19.7	14.2	10.3	10.5	8.8
Appendicitis	9.3	10.3	11.1	11.8	14.0	14.9	14.6	11.9	9.9	8.1	6.3
Nephritis, chronic	84.2	86.3	87.9	91.4	81.4	89.1	82.8	78.0	78.8	72.8	70.2
Accidents, all forms	79.1	86.8	82.6	79.7	71.6	78.5	76.5	77.8	73.4	76.3	71.7
Motor vehicle accidents [a]	—	.8	2.9	8.0	12.8	21.4	26.2	27.8	26.1	30.0	21.2
Infant mortality [b]	—	—	—	96.4	77.1	69.2	60.4	53.2	47.0	45.3	40.4
Maternal mortality [b]	—	—	—	7.1	6.9	6.7	6.3	5.0	3.8	3.2	2.6

Sources: 1900–39, Bureau of the Census, *Vital Statistics Rates in U. S., 1900–1940*, Table 15; 1940–42, Bureau of the Census, *Vital Statistics Special Reports*, Vol. 19, No. 3, and Vol. 20, No. 2.

[a] Excludes automobile collisions with trains and streetcars and motorcycle accidents for 1906–25 inclusive.   [b] Rates per 1,000 live births; data relate to Birth Registration States.

tilences have become practically extinct in a city like New York. But even since then some further spectacular changes have occurred, as may be seen in Table 2. For example, in the period 1900–04, typhoid fever still recorded a death rate of nearly 27 per 100,000 population. Our latest figure for 1943 is only one in 200,000, and we have come to look upon typhoid fever as almost a sign of criminal neglect on the part of the community where it occurs. Again, diphtheria at the beginning of the century was a serious threat to childhood, with a death rate of 33 per 100,000. Today, thanks to the widespread adoption of anti-diphtheria inoculations, both preventive and curative, the death rate from this cause is reduced to less than one per 100,000 and is still showing a downward trend, as indeed it should, until the disease becomes practically extinct.

At the same time, the other typical communicable diseases of childhood— measles, scarlet fever, and whooping cough—have shown marked improvement so that in the aggregate, including diphtheria, their death rate has been reduced from 65 at the beginning of the century to about 4 per 100,000 today. An even more serious threat to children in the first few years of life used to be diarrhea and enteritis, which at the beginning of the present century still claimed 116 victims of all ages per 100,000 population. Today this is reduced to less than 9.

Of the greatest importance is the record for tuberculosis. At the beginning of the century this disease still claimed 185 deaths per 100,000 population. The current death rate is little more than 40. Spectacular advances have recently been made in the fight against pneumonia. At the beginning of the century this caused 161 deaths per 100,000 annually. The figure has recently been reduced to about 50.

The causes of death so far reviewed, those which have shown the most outstanding reductions, all belong to the class of infectious diseases. The mode of transmission of these infections varies considerably, from direct contact in the case of scarlet fever, to transmission by contaminated food and by flies as in the case of diarrhea and enteritis. Equally varied are the very effective means which have been developed in the fight against these diseases, ranging from the control of water and food supply as in the battle against typhoid fever, diarrhea, and enteritis; quarantining and isolation as in the communicable diseases of childhood and tuberculosis; inoculations and serum therapy as in the case of diphtheria and pneumonia; and lastly, the spectacular successes in chemotherapy in the case of pneumonia and the infections generally.

Infant and maternal mortality

Infant and maternal mortality are in a class by themselves. The former, as a whole, has been reduced by more than 50 per cent since 1915–19. But this comparison includes among other things the toll of neonatal conditions largely of congenital character, and not readily amenable to medical control. The spread of prenatal care of the mother has been the approach to the problem here, as also, in large measure, with regard to maternal mortality. In the latter field it has already brought marked benefit. This mortality in the United States until lately was disquietingly high. Currently, it has been reduced to very creditable figures, not much over 2 per 1,000 live births, a decline of fully two-thirds from the figure of 7.1 registered in 1915–19. Latterly, chemotherapy has in this field also brought great benefits in checking the infective hazards of confinement.

Surgery

An entire group of causes of death in

which immeasurable benefits have been derived since the middle of the last century are those amenable to surgical treatment. The contributions of Pasteur and Lister, and those that came after, to antiseptic and aseptic surgery, and of Long and Morton, even before them, to anesthesia, are so well known that mere mention here suffices.

Diseases of advanced age

As for most of the remaining causes listed in Table 2, their death rates clearly confirm the conclusion noted above, namely, that at the higher ages there has not been much reduction in mortality. Diabetes, cancer, and the cardiovascular-renal diseases, conditions typical of the more advanced ages, show either practically no decrease since the beginning of the century, or show an actual increase. Where increases are marked, allowance must be made for the aging of the population, and to some extent for improved diagnosis. The situation is not without its promising possibilities. Research in these fields may well yield the necessary leverage for lowering the death toll, at least in late mid-life.

Insect-borne diseases

We have followed so far mainly the example of the United States as representative of the progressive countries with a temperate climate. Naturally, somewhat different problems exist in backward countries and in countries not blessed with favorable climate. In the latter especially, insect-borne diseases, which with us are largely under control (e.g. malaria and yellow fever) assume a most important role; they may, in fact, render certain regions uninhabitable. It may be recalled that the first attempt to build the Panama Canal was ruined by what at the time was called "adverse climate" but is now known to have been infestation with malarial mosquitoes.

Deficiency diseases and tuberculosis

Other diseases prevalent elsewhere, but of which we are practically free, are certain deficiency diseases, such as beri-beri, although pellagra does still constitute something of a problem for us. The modern development of vitamin physiology has given us very effective weapons in combating this type of disease.

Apart from diseases peculiar to certain parts of the world, but unknown or of very minor importance here, the geographic distribution of the causes of death varies also very greatly. An outstanding example of this is tuberculosis, which in some of the less advanced countries still moves on levels terrifyingly high by our modern standards. An example in point is Chile, which even today registers rates as high as 260 per 100,000, a level maintained over practically two decades. Apparently Chile has not yet reached the point where it has gained control over the disease, for most countries have shown a sharp downward trend over this period.

PROSPECTS FOR IMPROVING LONGEVITY

The progress made by the more advanced countries in decreasing mortality and promoting longevity sets the example for those vast areas containing large populations which still live under primitive conditions. These nations have a long way to go to reach the level attained in the countries of western Europe, North America, and our antipodes. However, even among these more favored peoples the records for longevity are still below what may be considered reasonably possible in the light of modern medicine and public health effort.

From time to time in the past, estimates have been made of the average length of life that could reasonably be expected if the discoveries and techniques in these fields were put to widespread use. These estimates have been expressed in hypothetical life tables, of which the first prepared by one of the authors was presented in 1922.[4] At that time it seemed optimistic to look forward to an average length of life of 64.75 years, the figure then current for the United States being somewhat under 58 years. As things turned out, however, it was later found that the expectations of life at successive ages in this hypothetical table were almost identical with those in a life table based on the actual experience of white females in the population of the United States during the period 1930–39.

The remarkable improvements in mortality had become evident even before this close agreement between the hypothetical table and the actual experience could be observed. Accordingly, to keep pace with the rapid improvements, another hypothetical life table was prepared in 1933. For this the life table for females in New Zealand in 1931 was taken as a guide, the maximum reduction from these observed mortalities being assumed as no more than 15 per cent. The average length of life in this hypothetical table, the second, came to 69.93 years. Shortly thereafter a later life table for females in New Zealand, covering 1935–37, showed again that the hypothetical figures were too conservative, especially at ages under 40 years. This situation called for still another revision of the hypothetical life table. In this, the mortality rates observed for females in New Zealand during 1935–37 were reduced by 20 per cent from ages one to 40. This percentage was tapered off from ages 41 to 49 so that for ages 50 and over the hypothetical rates remained unchanged as in the table constructed in 1933. The mortality rate for

the first year of life was also retained at 25 per 1,000. The average length of life on this new basis came to 70.78 years.

These three hypothetical life tables provide a lesson in optimism.[5] In the first two instances, actual experiences have proved that our forecasts were too conservative. Progress in medicine and sanitary science is so marked that already we are not far from the low mortality rates at the younger ages of the third table. The older ages, however, have not yet reached the low levels that had been hoped for. The situation at this stage of life, however, may not be quite as gloomy as would seem at first sight. We have already noted in the records of the past that there have been appreciable gains in the average length of life at age 40. Our hope for further improvement, particularly at the more advanced ages, arises from the increasingly concentrated study of the diseases of old age, that is, the science of geriatrics. Animal experimentation gives hints of a life longer in years and richer in vitality attainable by proper nutrition. Striking results have also been obtained in recent developments to correct the chemical upsets the aging process seems to induce in the body. The successes of hormone therapy, administered to correct glandular deficiencies, have encouraged further research along these lines.

AMERICAN AND BRITISH FORECASTS

This cheering outlook for the older ages was kept in view when Thompson and Whelpton [6] and the Registrars-General of England and Wales and of Scot-

[4] Louis I. Dublin, "The Possibility of Extending Human Life," delivered before the Harvey Society at the New York Academy of Medicine, Dec. 16, 1922.

[5] Metropolitan Life Insurance Company, "A Lesson in Optimism," *Statistical Bulletin* (New York, Nov. 1941).

[6] National Resources Planning Board, *Estimates of the Future Population of the United States, 1940–2000*, prepared by Warren S. Thompson and P. K. Whelpton (Washington, D. C., 1943), 137 pp.

land [7] prepared their recent estimates of future population. Thompson and Whelpton, after considering the past trends of mortality from specific diseases and the extent of medical progress, were more conservative in their estimates for the older ages than we were. In their so-called "medium" assumptions of future mortality they forecast an improvement in mortality from present levels by about 25 per cent at ages 55 to 59 and by about 15 per cent at ages 60 to 64, at the end of the current century.

The British forecasters took another line of approach. Their premise was that each generation is conditioned, by its environment early in life, to mortality characteristics which it continues to bear thereafter. Thus, a generation starting out with favorable mortality rates in its early years will continue to experience better mortality rates also at later ages, as compared with another generation whose early experience was poorer. In recent periods, successive generations have been showing improving mortality rates in childhood, and the implication is therefore that they will also show improving mortality rates at the later stages of life. Although the hypothesis used by the British group is somewhat different from that used by Thompson and Whelpton, the end result is the same—some improvement in mortality in the years of mid-life and later may reasonably be expected.

The procedure adopted by the British workers presents another interesting development, namely, that we almost certainly outlive our expectation of life as usually computed.[8] To understand this, it must be remembered that this

expectation of life is based upon a cross section of the mortality rates according to age as observed at a particular time or within some relatively short period. Thus, the mortality rates observed for males in England and Wales during the decade 1871–80 led to an expectation of life at birth of 41.4 years. But when the persons born in 1876, the midyear of this period, were followed on the basis of their observed mortality rates as they grew older, it was found that their average length of life was actually 46.3 years. It is seen that the expectation of life, as usually computed, understated the longevity for this generation of males by 4.9 years; the corresponding understatement for females was six years.

This result indicates quite clearly that, with the downward trend in mortality, the expectation of life, as we know it today, is to be regarded as a measure of longevity which errs on the conservative side. That these improvements in longevity which have taken place in the course of a generation are substantial can be seen in still another way. Thus, it was shown that, of the persons now at age 65, about one-third would not now be living if there had been no improvement in mortality since the year of their birth.

BIRTH RATES

From the point of view of the population as a whole, mortality measures only one aspect of national vigor. To maintain the vital balance, not only must the outgo in the form of deaths be controlled but the income by births must be adequate. Actually, the birth rate in most civilized countries has been declining so rapidly for many decades past that, but for the great improvement in the death rate, the demographic situation would have been most serious. Even as it is, a threat exists, especially

[7] "Current Trend of Population in Great Britain" (London: H. M. Stationery Office, 1942), Cmd. 6358.

[8] Louis I. Dublin and Mortimer Spiegelman, "Current Versus Generation Life Tables," *Human Biology,* Vol. 13 (Dec. 1941), p. 439.

for the most advanced of the European countries, though the majority still continue to show an excess of the birth rate over the death rate, that is, a positive natural increase. But, as is now well known, it is not the temporary excess of birth rate over death rate that counts, but the net reproductive rate per generation, which for these countries is well below unity.[9] This situation implies a further decline in the birth rate, associated later with an increase in the death rate, and not many decades hence, with an actual decrease in numbers. Even we in the United States are at best promised an approximately stationary population from about 1980 forward, if we disregard the momentary spurt in the birth rate during the early war years.

[9] Alfred J. Lotka, "Modern Trends in the Birth Rate," *The Annals,* Vol. 188 (Nov. 1936), p. 1.

At the same time, the past downward trend in the birth rate has caused a steady upward movement in the average age of the population, a movement which will inevitably continue for many years to come.

In these critical days of war, with the prospects for the future peace of the world clouded, the seriousness of these population shifts is painfully brought home to us. We have learned that we can no longer think in terms of isolation, geographically or otherwise. Civil and military manpower problems, which in the past we have been inclined to think of as the concern of other nations rather than ourselves, have forced themselves upon our recognition. We shall do well to follow the course of our own demographic indices with concern if we wish to see the position of our country maintained.

RECENT INTERNATIONAL DIFFERENCES AND

TRENDS IN EXPECTATION OF LIFE

By George J. Stolnitz

Fruitful examination of international differences & movements in life expectancy is far more feasible for the years since 1930 than for earlier periods. Documentation of the experience during 1930's is more extensive than for any previous decade, and the recent war and world-wide political disturbances have had remarkably little effect on the scope of the evidence already available for the 1940's. Postwar studies have been published, or reliable recent estimates can be made, for nearly all populations in the West; Finland, Poland, Spain, and Portugal in non-Western Europe; Japan and Ceylon in Asia; and for a hitherto unprecedented number of Latin American areas. The only major populations whose latest life table records antedate 1940 are those of total Germany, Egypt, India, and several Eastern European nations. Although it is impossible to determine recent trends in these areas, their comparative international position can generally be assessed sufficiently well for purposes of global analysis.

The present brief survey is intended (1) to summarize the evidence now available on international differences in life expectancy during the 1930's and 1940's, (2) to review the more salient patterns of change between the two decades, and (3) to point to some future possibilities suggested by recent experience. Throughout, the discussion has been limited to materials relating to expectation of life at the ages 0, 15, and 45. Although widely separated, these ages are adequate for inferring some leading comparative patterns at the successive stages of life.

It should be emphasized that the available data on international life table variations must be interpreted with considerable caution. Despite a proliferation of studies during the better part of a century, knowledge of past and current variations in life expectancy over most of the world remains highly fragmentary. Published information for as many as three of the five decades since 1900 exists for only a handful of populations in Latin America, Africa, Asia, and Eastern Europe. Moreover, the evidence for many populations within these regions is sufficiently unreliable to warrant only rather gross ordinal comparisons. Thus, the risks of dying in the very young ages are likely to be misreported and such errors have greater effect on the accuracy of reported expectation of life at birth than do equal relative errors for later ages. Even among populations with long statistical traditions, the mortality rates found at advanced ages are apt to be subject to substantial error.

It is probably true that among refined vital measures, life expectancy has been the one most widely and accurately documented over time and space. Nevertheless, current efforts to broaden the international scope of life table studies should be increasingly complemented by attempts to evaluate their reliability.

Recent Differences

For summarizing international variations in life expectancy during recent years, as indeed since the earliest periods for which any fairly reliable evidence exists, it is convenient to divide the world's populations into three major groupings. Though heterogeneous in nature, these groupings differ in only minor ways from other commonly used classifications. The first, termed here the "West," comprises the nations of Northwestern and Central Europe, Scandinavia, the Low Countries, the United States, Canada, Australia, New Zealand, the Jews in Israel, and the white populations of the Union of South Africa and Southern Rhodesia. As used below, "non-Western Europe" refers to all other areas on the continent, including Finland, the Baltic states, and perhaps more debatably, Austria and Czechoslovakia. The remaining areas for which life table materials are available in the periods under discussion are grouped under a third major category, "Latin America-Africa-Asia."

In each decade on record before 1940, the lowest expectation of life at birth registered anywhere in the West has, with practically no exception, been close to or above the highest documented for non-Western Europe, and the corresponding comparative pattern has held between the latter bloc and Latin America-Africa-Asia. During the 1930's, the range of male values in the West was 56 to 66, in contrast to the span of 48 to 55 found in non-Western Europe, and one of 35 to 47 in the rest of the world; the corresponding figures for females were 60 to 68, 52 to 61, and 37 to 50.*

Information on life expectancy in the West during the 1930's is very nearly complete, but only ten areas are represented in the above ranges for non-Western Europe and a smaller number, nine, for Latin America-Africa-Asia. As a result, the lower limits of the spans of recorded experience in the last two groups may in good part be a function of the particular areas for which data are available. For example, expectation of life at birth in European Russia in the 1920's was reported as 42 for males and 47 for females, and in India 27 for both sexes. Very probably, average life expectancy during the 1930's in both areas was below the minima indicated above for their respective population groupings.

---

* A life table was taken to refer to the 1930's if the mid-point of its observation period was within the decade. Preference was given to tables very nearly spanning the ten-year period or at least centering closely about 1935. In nearly all instances in which neither selection was possible, life expectancy as of the mid-1930's could be estimated by means of linear interpolation between the measures of successive life tables.

Accordingly, a more indicative measure of inter-group differences is the median. For the three groups of male populations, the median values at birth were 61, 53, and 41 and for females 64, 57, and 44. Almost certainly, the median experience for total non-Western Europe was well below the indicated level, and the upward biases in the available average measures for the rest of the world were even more substantial.

During the 1930's, as in all earlier periods on record, the group differences at age 15 were much smaller than at birth. Nevertheless, the hierarchy of average experience in the three blocs of populations is very clear. The reported medians were 52 for males and 55 for females in the West, 49 and 52 in non-Western Europe, and 42 and 44 in the rest of the world. The ranges of measures for the West and non-Western Europe overlapped to only a minor extent, and the recorded values for Latin America-Africa-Asia were all below the lowest found in either of the other two groups.

At age 45 the differences in recorded average experience decline very markedly, the medians being 26, 25, and 22 for males and 28, 27, and 24 for females. For each sex, the highest measures encountered among the populations in Latin America-Africa-Asia were below the minima in non-Western Europe, but the range of experience in the latter group overlapped substantially with that of the West. Undoubtedly, the comparative picture for this last age is more seriously distorted by inaccuracies in the data. If the common opinion is justified, that the biases were generally upward and more pronounced in the case of the non-Western populations, the above measures probably understate the actual differentials in group averages.

By the end of the interwar period, life expectancy at 0, 15, and 45 in very nearly all of the female populations on record in Latin America-Africa-Asia was below average levels in the West at least a half century earlier. In numerous instances, expectation of life at birth was below the lowest levels documented for the West about 1850. In non-Western Europe, the lags appear to have been appreciably smaller, median levels among the populations on record being remarkably similar to average Western experience three to four decades previously. It is safe to say, however, that the lag in average life expectancy for non-Western Europe as a whole was a good deal larger.

In both non-Western blocs of populations, the lags behind Western experience at all ages intermediate between birth and mid-life were of comparable orders of magnitude.

The comparative picture for the 1940's is obscured to an extent by several factors. First, substantially less information is available for non-Western Europe than for the previous decade, and almost no documentation exists for the major populations of that region. As a result, the inter-group comparisons of major interest are between the West, which was again almost completely documented, and the populations of Latin America-Africa-Asia. Secondly, only limited possibilities exist for minimizing the distorting effects of differences from area to area in the periods of life table observation. For most Western populations with no published data and for Finland, postwar estimates can be made which are sufficiently satisfactory for comparative purposes. On the other hand, three of the six life tables available for non-Western Europe, and six of the eleven tables for Latin America refer to the early part of the decade. Since life expectancy in most of these areas appears to have been increasing during the 1940's, the net effect of variations in observation periods has probably been to overstate the differences between the West and non-West. If so, the biases arising on this score go counter to those arising from incomplete coverage and inaccuracies, noted previously. Finally, in view of the phenomenal rise in life expectancy between 1947 and 1950 in Japan (to be discussed below), it should be noted that the Japanese measures selected for present discussion relate to the earlier year, which is closer to the dates of the remaining life tables. Had the most recent Japanese figures been used instead, several of the upper limits of life expectancy among populations outside of the West and Europe would have been appreciably higher.

Despite these limitations, it is clear that the patterns of international differentials in recent years were similar in most respects to those of the 1930's. Inter-bloc differences in life expectancy at birth were as marked in the 1940's as in the previous decade. The median levels in the West (65 for males and 69 for females) were about 10 person-years above those recorded for non-Western Europe (55 and 59) and about as much more beyond the averages registered in the rest of the world (46 and 48). In order of magnitude these differences are not far from the ones holding for the 1930's—regularities the more remarkable in view of the numerous changes in the scope of the data available for the two non-Western population blocs.

With a range of 60 (Ireland) to nearly 70 (the Netherlands), the lowest male value in the West was above the highest so far in evidence for non-Western Europe (some 57 person-years for Finland and extending to 47 for Spain). Some overlap is found in the ranges of female experience (62 for Ireland to 72 for Norway, and 53 for Portugal to about 65 for Finland and Italy), but all of the measures for non-Western Europe were below the third lowest of the eighteen Western measures. For either sex, the highest life expectancy in the rest of the world (53 for males and 56 for females in Trinidad and Tobago) was close to 7 person-years below the Western minimum. By far the lowest values encountered in Latin America-Africa-Asia were those of Mauritius, 32 and 34.

An interesting recent development has been the overlapping of the recorded ranges of life expectancies at birth among the two non-Western groups. In contrast with the 1930's and earlier decades, when no overlap is found, the six highest male and four highest female measures encountered among the populations in Latin America-Africa-Asia were above the two lowest in non-Western Europe (Spain and Portugal).

Between the 1930's and 1940's, the increase in median life expectancy in the three groups ranged only from 1 to 3 person-years at age 15 and under 2 at 45; as a result, the group differences at these ages during the 1940's are similar to the ones holding for the 1930's. At 15, median expectancy in the West in the past decade was about 4 person-years above the average recorded in non-Western Europe, and the latter about 7 years above the corresponding level in the rest of the world. The analogous gaps at 45 were 1-2 and 3 years, respectively. In each of the last two decades, the differences between the group medians at age 0 were roughly double the ones at 15 and the last about twice the magnitudes at 45.

In recent years at least, international rankings of life expectancy at the successive ages between birth and mid-life have apparently been highly stable. Within each of the above three groups, the ranking from low to high of life expectancy at birth among its component populations was closely similar to the ranking at age 15. The comparative rankings for both sexes at 15 and 45 were only somewhat less similar in the West and non-Western Europe, and for females in Latin America-Africa-Asia; although the correspondence was markedly lower among the male populations of the last bloc, it was nevertheless high.

The evidence on recent sex differentials in life expectancy undoubtedly reflects in part the effects of the war. Nevertheless, it accords in the main with trends which have held rather persistently over much of the world since 1900 or before. By 1950 in a majority of the populations of the West, the excess of female over male life expectancy at 0, 15, and 45, and probably at most intermediate ages, was the highest ever registered. That the same was true for much of the rest of the world as well is strongly suggested by the most recent life table materials for non-Western populations with extended statistical records.

The relatively abundant evidence at hand for the 1940's re-emphasizes the tremendous lag behind Western experience of life expectancy almost throughout Latin América, Africa, and Asia. Despite the often large gains in these regions since the 1930's, average expectation of life from birth through mid-life is today undoubtedly well below median levels in the West before the beginning of the century.

For reasons indicated previously, no firm conclusions on this score can be made for non-Western Europe. The very scanty data at hand show a lag of two to three decades, but the variations from area to area are large and inferences about the region as a whole would be fruitless.

Recent Trends

Life tables for both the 1930's and 1940's are available for somewhat under thirty populations, of which only four are in non-Western Europe, five in Latin America, and only one, Japan, is in Asia. To take account of varying intervals between the periods of observation in the two decades, the changes in life expectancy recorded for each population have been reduced to an average annual basis. In each case the differences between successive life tables have been divided by the number of years between the mid-points of their reference periods. It should be kept in mind that the average annual changes described below are in part a reflection of the particular dates for which life table data exist. In the West, the records for the 1940's are predominantly for postwar years, but about half of the measures for the rest of the world relate to the beginning of the decade. For purposes of interpretation, however, there is probably a large net advantage in the fact that the evidence abstracts almost completely from the war-time experience of the belligerent nations.

Almost without exception, life expectancy at 0, 15, and 45 among

the populations on record rose between the 1930's and 1940's. Undoubtedly, a similar predominance of upward movements also held at intermediate ages. Only the Spanish male population, with respective average
annual declines of .1, .3, and .2 person-years at the above three ages,
suffered a substantial retrogression in life chances. In addition, a trivial
decline was registered for the Australian males at age 45, and somewhat larger decreases were recorded for the Chilean males at 15 and
for both sexes at 45; in the latter country, the changes are almost certainly well within the margins of error in the data. The Spanish male
experience, which relates to the years between the early 1930's and
1940's, reflects the impact of the civil war during the latter part of the
period. The much more favorable trends in all Western areas, composed largely of recent belligerents, attest again the remarkable recuperative powers of industrial societies in the early aftermath of even
major modern wars—at least of the pre-atomic kind.

Recent as well as earlier experience suggests clearly the generalization that the age curve of changes in life expectancy has been predominantly a declining function among the large majority of past and
current populations. Except for the Spanish male population, the universal pattern of change between the 1930's and 1940's was one of declining improvement from one segment of the life cycle to the next. In
every instance of increase at both 0 and 15 the rise at the former age
was larger and the same was true as between the latter age and 45. (As
already implied, the changes at 15 for Australian males and Chilean
males and females were all greater, taking sign into account, than the
ones at 45.)

Moreover, the differences in change from age to age were generally substantial. The median average annual increase for Western
male populations was .35 person-years at age 0, .18 at age 15, and .09
at age 45; for females, the measures were .42, .26, and .15. In Poland
the corresponding recorded changes were .45, .20, and .10 for the former sex and .67, .38, and .21 for the latter. To cite probably the most
reliable measures available outside of the West and Europe, the respective increases in Japan were .28, .10, and .06 and again .38, .22,
and .05.

These patterns of (algebraic) change were far more uniform than
the ones revealed by the corresponding percentage variations. Measured in percentage terms, average annual increases in life expectancy
at birth were less generally above those registered at either 15 or 45.
Thus, the largest gains were at birth among all non-Western populations,
but the experiences of both sexes in Norway, the Netherlands, and Switzerland provide contrary instances in the West. Moreover, as often as
not the percentage changes at 45 exceeded those at 15. It is worth noting that in earlier periods as well as since 1930, international age patterns of percentage changes in life expectancy are much less amenable
to general summary than are algebraic variations.

As the above cited figures suggest, female gains in life expectancy exceeded the improvements among males in the large majority of
instances. In no population with higher male gains did the recorded sex
differential in average annual change reach .05 person-years. Where

the female gains were higher, the differences tended to be larger, though generally under .1 person-years and rarely over .2. Most of the differences above .1 related to non-Western populations.

One of the most notable aspects of the recent trends for the sexes, in view of the special events of the early 1940's, was the very close correspondence between the international rankings of male and female changes. Both over the world as a whole and within each of the three major divisions, the ordinal position of the average annual change for either sex in a given population tended to be a highly reliable predictor of the position for the other. This was true for all three ages examined and probably for intermediate years as well.

In very sharp contrast to the situation holding for levels of life expectancy, there is little basis for distinguishing between recent average trends in the West and non-West. It is true that the highest average annual increases found among non-Western populations at age 0 (close to .6 person-years for both sexes) and for females at 15 and 45 (.45 and .27) exceeded the corresponding Western maxima. On the other hand, about half of the changes registered in the former group were below or close to the lower quartile change in the West, and the increases for French males at 15 and 45 (.44 and .23) were the highest recorded anywhere.

Viewed in terms of comparative percentage variations, the recent experience of the non-Western world stands out much more favorably. Nearly three-quarters of the average annual percentage changes in life expectancy at birth outside the West were above the Western medians and the proportion of similar instances for 0, 15, and 45 combined was well over half. In particular, the highest percentage increases recorded in Latin America at each age and for both sexes were very substantially above the highest encountered in the West.

These contrasting patterns point up the importance of emphasizing the type of measure used to compare trends in what are commonly classified as developed and underdeveloped areas. To an extent, failure to make explicit the distinction between absolute and percentage variations explains the conflicting assertions to be found on whether the gap between Western and non-Western life chances is being narrowed or is likely to become so in the near future. Undoubtedly, the fragmentary evidence as yet available for the underdeveloped areas has also contributed to a lack of accepted generalizations on this score. But perhaps above all, the existing indecision is a result of the historically unprecedented gains which have been achieved recently by very restricted and short-run developmental programs in a number of areas. Several such instances are discussed below.

Some Future Possibilities

In the West, future declines in pre-adult mortality can at best lead to relatively minor gains in life expectancy at birth. Even with no deaths under age 15 during the 1940's, the median rise beyond the levels actually recorded would only have been about 4 person-years for females and 5 for males. With unchanging risks of dying beyond 15, the maximum possible increases resulting from falling female mortality would have ranged from 2-3 years (Australia, the Netherlands, Norway, and Sweden) to about 6 years (Ireland). The same populations would have also been found at the extremes of the corresponding range for males, from 3-4 to nearly 7 years. [See chart on front cover.]

Seen in the perspective of past trends in the West, these magnitudes are decidedly secondary. Among very nearly all Western female populations—Ireland and probably Germany being the only notable exceptions—such maximum gains are less than the ones registered between the 1930's and 1940's. The comparison for males is only somewhat less compelling; recent rises were greater in nearly half of the male populations and no more than a year less in about four-fifths.

Broadly similar conclusions also hold with respect to future declines in Western mortality through mid-life. With zero mortality to age 45 and the experience of the 1940's for the ages beyond, the increases in life expectancy at birth would have been below the actual rises since as recently as the 1920's among the large majority of female populations. In only a few instances would they have been substantially above the corresponding actual changes for males.

The gains implied by either of these extreme contingencies would be relatively minor in comparison with Western uptrends between 1900 and 1950. No evidence as yet in sight suggests the likelihood that the increases recorded since 1900 will be even approximated during the coming half century.

The scanty, if increasing, evidence at hand for non-Western populations permits no generalizations of comparable scope. That sustained social and economic development will in the long run lead to large increases in expectation of life hardly seems open to question. But the experience in a growing number of areas in Latin America, Asia, and Southern Europe suggests that forecasting by analogy with Western experience may seriously understate the prospects for declining mortality among the world's underdeveloped populations.

In Japan, expectation of life at birth rose by 6 years between 1947 and the end of the decade, a pace several times in excess of the highest rates of increase encountered in the whole of recorded Western experience. It is true that Japanese life expectancy during the 1930's was the highest to be found outside of the West and Europe and that Japan in 1947 was undergoing a series of difficult postwar readjustments. By 1947, however, expectation of life was already substantially above prewar levels. More important, the predominant causes of the increases since that year appear to have been the public health and sanitary programs instituted by the Occupation authorities and implemented with very moderate outlays of skills or funds; changes in economic levels of living were only minor factors. In Ceylon, use of DDT in a short and inexpensive campaign against malaria during 1946 had immediate and dramatic effects. Within a year, the crude death rate dropped by 6 per 1,000 and the infant mortality rate by 39. Life tables for the years just before and after 1946 are not available, but unquestionably the average annual increase in expectation of life at birth was very much greater than even the remarkable changes in Japan. Perhaps less spectacular,

but by average Western standards certainly striking, have been the declines in mortality reported in Cyprus, parts of Greece, and Sardinia; in
all of these instances the initiating and major explanatory factors were
relatively simple and quickly implemented public health programs. Although accompanied by far-reaching economic changes, the same causal
elements were also predominant in Puerto Rico, where expectation of
life at birth rose by about 12 years between 1940 and 1950; again the
annual rate of increase was greatly above, generally by several times,
the highest changes recorded by Western populations.

So far as the immediate facts go, the implications of this cumulating experience appear clear enough. Simple and cheap means are
now at hand for effecting spectacular early declines in mortality among
many of the world's underdeveloped populations. The results recently
observed in a growing number of instances have been comparable to
what the West achieved only after decades, often under more favorable
physical and economic circumstances. In other high mortality areas,
the introduction of even moderate medical, public health, and sanitary
controls should have at least a broadly similar initial impact on mortality levels.

Much more conjectural, however, is the extent to which the comparative inertia of broader social and economic forces may dampen
downtrends in mortality at subsequent stages. For example, the skills
currently available for combating malaria are incomparably more simple and efficient than those that have as yet been brought to bear against
tuberculosis and other respiratory diseases.

Viewed in necessarily broad and conjectural terms, recent experience suggests that in the absence of war future uptrends in life expectancy over much of the non-Western world are most nearly likely to
involve two major phases. Their inception and duration might, of course,
vary considerably from area to area. The first phase would be characterized by increases which are explosive by historical standards to date;
such increases would be initially more closely contingent upon domestic
political stability and foreign cooperation than on the processes of social
and economic modernization. In the second phase these more gradual
processes would become the primary determinants. Upward movements
in life expectancy would tend to taper off, with the growing relative importance of causes of death which are more intimately linked with general environmental conditions. Should they actually come to pass, such
trends would contrast sharply with the past century of experience in the
West, where expectation of life at birth rose far less rapidly before 1900
than subsequently.

Increasingly, students of population have been speculating about
the prospects for unprecedentedly sharp declines in fertility in the
world's densely settled underdeveloped areas. In contrast, the implications of similarly novel trends in mortality have been relatively neglected, and the effects of historically novel trends in both major components of population growth have been almost ignored. There are indications, admittedly sketchy and as yet much less persuasive with respect to fertility than mortality, that demographers of the future will
find the last contingency the most relevant for research and policy.

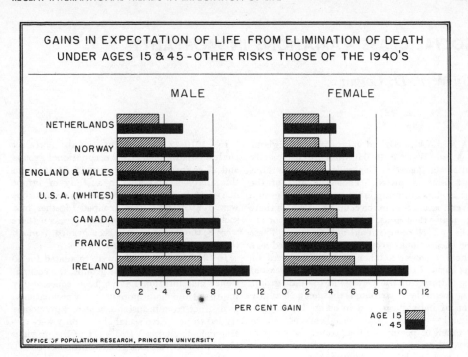

GAINS IN EXPECTATION OF LIFE FROM ELIMINATION OF DEATH
UNDER AGES 15 & 45 - OTHER RISKS THOSE OF THE 1940'S

MALE · FEMALE

NETHERLANDS
NORWAY
ENGLAND & WALES
U. S. A. (WHITES)
CANADA
FRANCE
IRELAND

PER CENT GAIN

AGE 15
" 45

OFFICE OF POPULATION RESEARCH, PRINCETON UNIVERSITY

SOCIAL CLASS VARIATIONS IN MORTALITY

By W. P. D. Logan

AN ANALYSIS of mortality in England and Wales in 1950 in what are customarily called the Registrar General's social classes has just been completed. The basic unit of the social class grouping is the occupational group. Every occupation in the country, of which there are many thousands, is assignable to one or another of 586 occupational unit groups. These 586 occupational groups are each assigned as a whole to one or another of 5 social classes, on the basis of the predominant characteristics of the majority of the persons in the unit group. The social class grouping is thus not a classification of individuals, and in assigning an individual to the appropriate social class no account is taken of personal circumstances other than occupation. Once the occupation of the individual has been established, the social class grading follows automatically.

In the 1951 census, 3.3 percent of the men aged 15 years and over were in social class I (professional occupations), and 15.0 percent were in class II (intermediate occupations); 52.7 percent were in class III (skilled occupations); 16.2 percent were in class IV (partly skilled occupations); and 12.8 percent were in class V (unskilled occupations).

Development of Social Class Studies

In the same way that the social classes are constructed on the basis of an occupational classification, the study of social class mortality variations is a development from the study of mortality in individual occupational groups. It is just over 100 years since the first official study of occupational mortality in England and Wales was undertaken. This was an analysis of deaths from all causes in 1851 in several hundred occupations, related to the populations of these occupations as determined by the 1851 census (1). Similar studies were made of deaths in 1860–61 in relation to the 1861 census, and thereafter, at 10-year intervals, in and around each successive census year, standardized death rates having been introduced to allow for differences in the age structure of different occupations and separate causes of death studied.

In 1910–12, the occupational mortality analysis distinguished 132 occupational groups and 27 causes of death at ages 25–64 (2). In this analysis, and also in a study of infant mortality in 1911 (3), the various occupations were for the first time grouped together into social classes, of which on this occasion there were 8, the first 5 having been graded in much the same way as described above.

In 1921–23 (4), deaths were tabulated for 40 causes in 164 occupational groups, the occupational classification having been considerably improved and made more properly occupational as distinct from industrial, as it had previously tended to be. Five social classes only were distinguished; classes VI to VIII of the previous classification were merged with the others (5).

The last previous occupational mortality analysis was made for the years 1930–32 (6). For men, this was on the same lines as before but with further increase in the detail of causes of death and of occupations. A very important innovation at that time was the study of the mortality of single women classified by their own occupations, and of married women classified by occupation of husband. There are some special difficulties in studying the occupational mortality of single women. For example, many are unoccupied or are only transitorily in employment, and it was because of these difficulties that they had not previously been included. I would not like to claim that their inclusion in 1930–32 has really got us very far.

Analyzing the mortality of married women according to husband's occupation was, however, a great step forward. It has allowed comparison between the mortality of men in particular occupations and of their wives, who generally share the same socioenvironmental circumstances as their husbands but are not usually exposed to the husbands' occupational hazards or disadvantages. It thus became possible in 1930–32 to begin to distinguish between mortality risks that were primarily of occupational origin (though not necessarily due to direct occupational hazards) and those arising rather from the socioeconomic environments in which people in various kinds of occupations tend to live (7).

Limitations of This Method

There are well-recognized limitations in the study of occupational mortality and, to a less extent, of social class mortality, by the method traditionally employed. This method depends on the relating of occupational information obtained at death registration to occupational information derived from the census. These limitations have been discussed in great detail in the various official reports, and I shall only mention two.

One type of error can arise from differences between the occupational description given by an individual himself on the census schedule and that given by a relative when registering the person's death. The individual probably knows best what his occupation really is but may not describe it properly or in sufficient detail on the census schedule, whereas at death registration the registrar is in a position to elicit details, including information about the previous occupation of a retired person, but occasionally the informant may not have sufficient knowledge to provide the information accurately.

A different type of difficulty arises in attempting to interpret the recorded mortality rates; it then becomes necessary to consider the extent to which an apparently high or low mortality rate recorded for an occupation may be due to physically or medically selective recruitment or discharge. An occupation such as the police may recruit only the physically fit, whereas other types of occupations may attract or become the refuge of invalids or persons of poor physique. The recorded mortality rates for such occupations might reflect the type of people engaged therein more than the risks of the occupation itself. Furthermore, the recorded

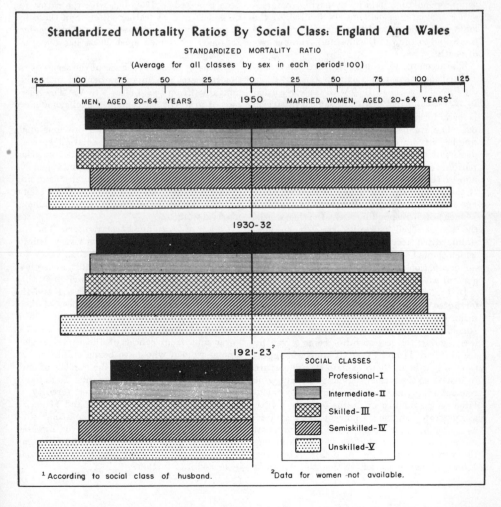

Standardized Mortality Ratios By Social Class: England And Wales

STANDARDIZED MORTALITY RATIO

(Average for all classes by sex in each period= 100)

MEN, AGED 20-64 YEARS · 1950 · MARRIED WOMEN, AGED 20-64 YEARS[1]

1930-32

1921-23[2]

SOCIAL CLASSES
Professional-I
Intermediate-II
Skilled-III
Semiskilled-IV
Unskilled-V

[1] According to social class of husband. [2] Data for women not available.

mortality rate of a dangerous or of a physically onerous occupation may be understated owing to persons in failing health transferring to a less exacting job sometime before they die.

The 1950 Analysis

The latest England and Wales analysis deals with deaths in 1950 (8) related to the 1951 census 1-percent sample results. It constitutes a preliminary and much restricted survey of what we may expect to find in the full analysis which will shortly be commenced and which will cover deaths in the 5 years, 1949–53, probably in greater detail than ever for occupations and for causes of death. But, as this full analysis will not be completed for several years, and as it is now more than 20 years since the last one was made, it seemed desirable to take advantage of the opportunity offered by the 1-percent sample population data by preparing some advance tabulations, deliberately limited to the main social classes, and some major divisions of these, and to a few of the most important causes of death.

The accompanying chart compares the standardized mortality ratios of men aged 20–64 in the 5 social classes in 1950 with those recorded in 1921–23 and 1930–32. The same comparison is made for married women for 1950 with 1930–32. The standardized mortality ratio is the number of deaths of men or the number of deaths of women, classed to a particular occupational or social group, expressed as a percentage of the number that would have occurred if the group had experienced at each separate age the death rates of all groups of men (or women) of corresponding age. In other words, the standardized mortality ratio is an age-standardized occupational mortality index which shows how far the mortality of a particular occupation or social class differs from the general average.

In 1921–23 and 1930–32, there was an uninterrupted upward gradient of mortality from social class I (professional) to social class V (unskilled). In 1950, the gradient was much less regular, the lowest ratios being given by social classes II and IV. All kinds of suggestions might be made to explain this departure in 1950 from the former regular gradient. But remembering that the ratios have been calculated on the number of deaths for only 1 year, as numerator, and on a 1-percent census sample, as denominator, it would be advisable to await more comprehensive figures before exploring the various possibilities in detail. However, I find it difficult to believe that the irregular

trend can have arisen only as a result of random fluctuation in the figures.

The social class mortality gradient for married women has also become less regular in 1950 than it was in 1930–32, the only previous occasion on which this group has been studied. However, only social class II was out of step; the others increased from class I to V.

Individual Causes of Death

Mortality from more than 30 causes of death has been tabulated for 1950, and table 1 shows how the results for a few of these causes compare with earlier findings. Ratios calculated upon less than 50 actual deaths are italicized to indicate that their significance is uncertain.

Respiratory tuberculosis. For men aged 20–64, the steeply rising gradient from social class I to V seen in 1921–23 and again in 1930–32 has been repeated in 1950, but with the ratios for classes II and IV rather lower than those for classes I and III, respectively. The gradient for married women aged 20–64 has remained steep and regular.

Cancer of stomach. Each of the series of ratios indicates a regular gradient of increasing mortality from social class I to V. The steepness of gradient has remained unchanged since 1921–23.

Cancer of lung. In the two previous analyses, the evidence for an association between cancer of lung and social class was somewhat equivocal, but the 1950 figures for men aged 20–64 seems fairly definitely to suggest a rising gradient from social class I to V. There are no signs, however, of a similar gradient among married women.

Cancer of breast and of cervix uteri. The first of these two conditions displays a very definite gradient downward from social class I to V for married women. The second condition displays an opposite tendency, with lower mortality among the married women of class I and the highest mortality in class V. Cancer of these two sites is known to be correlated with childbearing. Mortality from cancer of the breast is lower and from cancer of the cervix higher among women who have borne children than among those who have not, the number of children borne being also important. It is likely therefore that the much higher fertility of classes IV and V over classes I and II goes a long way toward explaining the social class mortality pattern of these two diseases. Whether it is the whole explanation, I cannot at present say; it is something that will have to be looked into further.

Table 1. Standardized mortality ratios by cause and social class for men and married women aged 20–64 years: England and Wales, for specified time periods

Cause of death and year	Men					Married women				
	Social class					Social class				
	I	II	III	IV	V	I	II	III	IV	V
All causes:										
1921–23	82	94	95	101	125	(1)	(1)	(1)	(1)	(1)
1930–32	90	94	97	102	111	81	89	99	103	113
1950	97	86	102	94	118	96	84	101	104	117
Respiratory tuberculosis:										
1921–23	49	81	95	97	137	(1)	(1)	(1)	(1)	(1)
1930–32	61	70	100	104	125	52	67	99	106	132
1950	64	62	103	95	149	43	52	104	107	166
Cancer of stomach:										
1921–23	60	82	100	106	130	(1)	(1)	(1)	(1)	(1)
1930–32 [2]	[3] 59	[3] 84	[3] 98	[3] 108	[3] 124	54	78	104	104	121
1950	57	67	100	114	132	57	72	101	106	138
Cancer of lung:										
1921–23	100	109	97	79	124	(1)	(1)	(1)	(1)	(1)
1930–32	107	95	100	92	114	95	100	108	81	94
1950	80	79	108	89	116	120	94	104	96	91
Cancer of breast:										
1930–32	(4)	(4)	(4)	(4)	(4)	136	116	103	84	82
1950	(4)	(4)	(4)	(4)	(4)	144	100	106	76	97
Cancer of cervix uteri:										
1950	(4)	(4)	(4)	(4)	(4)	61	69	98	109	150
Leukemia:										
1930–32	153	125	96	94	85	167	118	107	76	76
1950	153	101	107	81	88	145	73	110	91	95
Coronary heart disease:										
1930–32	[3] 237	[3] 148	[3] 95	[3] 66	[3] 67	157	126	93	85	88
1950	150	110	104	79	89	92	93	101	100	108
Myocardial degeneration:										
1930–32	[3] 77	[3] 92	[3] 94	[3] 105	[3] 122	54	75	99	110	129
1950	67	82	97	98	137	66	67	98	120	134
Bronchitis:										
1921–23	26	55	94	121	177	(1)	(1)	(1)	(1)	(1)
1930–32	31	57	91	124	156	27	56	99	119	155
1950	33	53	97	103	172	33	48	100	130	152
Diabetes mellitus:										
1921–23	125	145	92	75	66	(1)	(1)	(1)	(1)	(1)
1930–32	122	155	95	82	69	56	89	104	108	106
1950	167	97	97	91	108	86	88	98	109	117

[1] Data not available. [2] Includes esophagus. [3] Ages 35–64 years only. [4] Data not applicable.

NOTE. All social classes=100 in each specified group. Social class of married women grouped according to husband's occupation. Ratios based on less than 50 deaths are italicized. Social class groupings: I—professional, II—intermediate, III—skilled, IV—semiskilled, V—unskilled occupations.

SOURCE: See reference 8.

Leukemia. This is one of the diseases that give a fairly definite downward gradient of mortality from social class I to class V, in both sexes, though many of the ratios shown in table 1 are based on inadequate numbers. Better diagnosis in class I than in V may be the explanation, in the same way that it may be the explanation of the steady increase year by year in the numbers of deaths that are being recorded; on the other hand, it may not.

Coronary heart disease. In 1930–32, mortality from this cause was decidedly higher in social classes I and II than in classes IV and V in both sexes. In 1950, this gradient is still quite evident for men, but for some reason the ratios for women aged 20–64 run in the opposite direction, that is, upward from class I to V

instead of downward. What the explanation is of this sex difference, I have no idea. To account for the male pattern of gradient, the suggestions that have been made from time to time include social class and occupational differences in death certificate terminology, in mental stress, in dietary habits, and in physical activity. My own leaning at present is toward a combination of the last two.

Myocardial degeneration. The mortality ratios for this condition among men aged 20–64 run in the opposite direction to those for coronary disease, that is, they are lowest in social class I and increase to class V; and the gradient for women is the same as for men.

Bronchitis. This disease gives the steepest and most uniform social class mortality gradient of all, with mortality at ages 20–64 roughly 5 times higher in social class V than in class I. Clearly, this is something that has to be taken into account in any studies of geographic variations in the incidence of bronchitis in relation, let us say, to climate or to atmospheric pollution.

Diabetes mellitus. I have included this condition in order to show that the sex difference in the social class mortality gradient observed in 1930–32 has remained as evident in 1950. For men, mortality is highest in social class I and declines toward social class V. In women, the gradient runs in the opposite direction.

Stillbirths and Infant Mortality

The infant mortality rate, as has often been pointed out, is a sensitive index of social conditions, particularly with regard to the postneonatal period, that is, from 4 weeks of age up to 1 year, where, as table 2 shows, the death rate is persistently 4 times higher in social class V than in class I. It is worth noting that in

Table 2. Comparative ratios for stillbirth rates, neonatal (under 4 weeks) and postneonatal (4 weeks to 1 year) mortality rates by social class of father: England and Wales, for specified time periods

Ratio and year	Social class				
	I	II	III	IV	V
Stillbirth:					
1939	67	92	98	104	110
1950	75	87	99	109	117
Neonatal mortality:					
1921	69	83	99	108	109
1930–32	72	90	97	106	108
1950	71	90	97	109	121
Postneonatal mortality:					
1921	33	60	95	117	133
1930–32	35	57	90	111	142
1950	44	54	94	124	168

NOTE: All social classes = 100 in each specified group. Data for legitimate births only. Ratios computed from stillbirth rates per 1,000 live births and stillbirths combined, and from neonatal and postneonatal mortality rates per 1,000 live births. Social class groupings: I—professional, II—intermediate, III—skilled, IV—semiskilled, V—unskilled occupations.

SOURCE: See reference 8.

spite of the tremendous reduction of infant mortality rates during the past 30 years there has been absolutely no narrowing of the difference between the various social classes, that is, no tendency for the gradient to become less steep.

There has likewise been no tendency for the social class differences in stillbirth and neonatal (under 4 weeks) mortality rates to become less

in recent years. The gradient is much less steep for stillbirths and neonatal deaths than for deaths occurring later in the first year of life.

Conclusion

As a postscript to this abridged review of occupational and social class mortality variations in England and Wales, I should like to add a word about the value of this kind of analysis. To tabulate one or several years' death by sex, age, occupation, and cause and to calculate corresponding mortality rates is a big job which could only be justified if the results were really worth having and served a useful purpose whether for administration or for research. On what grounds, then, are these large occupational mortality analyses really justifiable?

Greenwood (9) certainly thought they were justified when he described them as "the most valuable single instrument of sociomedical research our national armory contains."

It cannot be claimed that our occupational mortality studies have revealed many specific industrial hazards that were not already known. The sandblasting risk, for instance, was not discovered by the revelation in the official mortality tables that those who followed this occupation were subject to an exceptionally high mortality. In respect of occupations such as this which have a well-known special hazard, the tabulations have confirmed rather than discovered the hazard. In addition, however, they have allowed comparisons to be made from time to time and between one occupation and another.

Sandblasting, we know, is or was dangerous. Is it, or was it, more dangerous than hotelkeeping? In 1930–32, sandblasting was much more dangerous. The respective standardized mortality ratios were 304 and 155. Coal gas workers and medical practitioners, who also suffer certain occupational risks, had standardized mortality ratios of 115 and 106, but the Anglican clergy, evidently having a less dangerous occupation, had a standardized mortality ratio of 69. We are thus given the opportunity of getting different occupations into perspective so that the relative risk can be appraised as between one occupation and another.

By grouping together occupations that seem to enjoy much the same living standards, we are able to show that "mortality is influenced more by the conditions of life implied by various occupations than by the direct occupational risks entailed" (4). This approach to the study of mortality variations has been greatly advanced by the decision in 1930–32 to take account also of the mortality of married women.

The cynic can of course remark, after it has been shown that a disease is closely correlated with adverse living conditions, there is little more that we can do about it. It is admittedly beyond the ordinary powers of physicians to transfer their patients from social class V to class I and so relieve them of some of their bronchitis, tuberculosis, and myocardial degeneration (although increasing their risk of coronary thrombosis in return). But this is quite the wrong approach. Having discovered that the mortality from a disease is influenced to a significant degree by so-called social conditions, as our next step we should study these conditions in the greatest possible detail to determine precisely by what mechanism the behavior of a disease is different in one group of people from that of another, or in what way one group is receiving an advantage or a disadvantage that the other group does not have. It may even be practicable, with the recognition that the risk from a disease is greater in one group than in another, to take special precautions for the individuals within the vulnerable group and so reduce their risk.

A third contribution that these occupational and social class mortality studies make is the additional information they provide about the natural history of disease—their contribution to epidemiology and to the application of the epidemiological method. The observation that coronary disease kills men in professional and managerial occupations much more than those doing unskilled work, although not revealing the cause or causes of the disease, has at least provided some useful leads. Even if the pursuit of such leads does not in fact prove fruitful, whenever any hypothesis is propounded about

the pathogenesis of a disease, that hypothesis, to be accepted, must adequately account for at least the majority of the already established epidemiological features.

For reasons such as these, I myself have no doubts about the fundamental value of these extensive occupational mortality studies as an instrument of medical research and, despite their various special limitations, I believe that these studies will be needed periodically for a long time to come.

REFERENCES

(1) Great Britain. Registrar General: Annual report, 14th . . . England and Wales, 1851. London, Her Majesty's Stationery Office, 1855.

(2) Great Britain. Registrar General: Decennial supplement, England and Wales, 1911. Part 4. Occupational mortality. London, His Majesty's Stationery Office, 1923.

(3) Great Britain. Registrar General: Annual report, 74th . . . England and Wales, 1911. London, His Majesty's Stationery Office, 1913.

(4) Great Britain. Registrar General: Decennial supplement, England and Wales, 1921. Part 2. Occupational mortality. London, His Majesty's Stationery Office, 1927.

(5) Stevenson, T. H. C.: The vital statistics of wealth and poverty. J. Roy. Stat. Soc. 91: 207–220 (1928).

(6) Great Britain. Registrar General: Decennial supplement, England and Wales, 1931. Part 2a. Occupational mortality. London, Her Majesty's Stationery Office, 1938.

(7) Stocks, P.: The effects of occupation and its accompanying environment on mortality. J. Roy. Stat. Soc. 101: 669–708 (1938).

(8) Great Britain. Registrar General: Decennial supplement, England and Wales, 1951. Part 1. Occupational mortality. London, Her Majesty's Stationery Office, 1954.

(9) Greenwood, M.: Some British pioneers of social medicine. Oxford, Oxford University Press, 1948, p. 79.

Chapter III

FERTILITY, NUPTIALITY, AND REPLACEMENT

Fertility is a more complicated subject than mortality. Each member of a population is exposed to the risk of death throughout life, and must ultimately die once and only once. Hence mortality experience can readily be summarized in the form of mortality rates and life tables using straightforward applications of probability theory. The risk of childbearing, however, applies only to women of a certain age (roughly 15 to 50 years), of whom some have no child, and others have several children. Exposure to risk is a function of marital status, to a considerable degree, and hence a function of the many social influences determining age at marriage and proportions marrying. Furthermore, whereas most people in most times and places have sought actively to minimize their own chances of death, it is only under special conditions that conscious, rational control of fertility is exercised; as a rule the traditional institutional norms surrounding marriage and family life have been observed. But under conditions of controlled fertility not only the number, but also the timing of births may be subject to planning, either indirectly, through the timing of marriage, or directly, through the use of contraception.

Several consequences of these circumstances should be noted.

The "crude birth rate," or number of births occurring in a year per 1,000 of the average population of that year, can be computed on analogy with the crude death rate; it shows the rate at which the population is being augmented by births. But it is even less directly a reflection of fertility than the crude death rate is of mortality.

One can obtain a cross-sectional pattern of "age-specific fertility rates" by dividing the number of children born to women of each age group (usually a five-year age interval) in a given year by the average total number of women in that age group in that year. If this cross-sectional pattern is then viewed hypothetically as the experience of a cohort of women at successive age periods, and it is assumed that none of the cohort dies, it is possible to compute average birth expectancies per woman for the entire reproductive period, or the "total fertility rate." A similar computation, based only on female births, yields the "gross reproduction rate", and if the women are assumed to be subject to a constant schedule of mortality drawn from an appropriate life table, the "net reproduction rate" can be calculated. The latter may be interpreted as the ratio of total daughters to total potential mothers, i.e., as a measure of replacement. If the analysis is carried one step further, and the mean length of a generation is ascertained, the net reproduction rate (which refers to replacement over a period of one generation) can be converted into the annual "intrinsic rate of natural increase," Lotka's invention. The intrinsic rate of natural increase has often been interpreted as the best available single measure of the reproductive potential of a population; but the validity of such an interpretation, as may be seen from its description, is contingent, since the necessary assumptions may not be realized in practice.

The last fifteen years have witnessed rather extreme fluctuations in the birth rate, in reproduction rates, and in other indicators of fertility based on cross-sectional data. As a consequence, demographers have been forced to re-examine the assumptions on which measures of long-run reproductive performance (or potential) are founded, and they have necessarily given increasing attention to the complications surrounding fertility analysis, some of which were mentioned in the first paragraph. As the papers by Stolnitz and Ryder and by Kiser make evident, this re-study of methodological problems, though productive of many new insights about fertility, has yielded results that are uncomfortably indeterminate. It now appears impossible to determine precisely the relation of currently observed natality to the longer run tendencies of population growth. An annual net reproduction rate may show, for example, that the cross-sectional schedule of observed fertility rates is insufficient to replace a population if the rates are maintained indefinitely; yet at the same time it may be that each cohort of women is actually bearing more than enough daughters to replace itself. The annual cross-sectional rate may, then, be reflecting merely the distribution of the births in time; it may not be indicating the ultimate fertility performance of the group of women then of childbearing age at that time.

That fertility is subject to marked fluctuations in the short run is amply demonstrated in the papers of Galbraith and Thomas, Kirk, and Hauser. Dislocations occasioned by war and misfortunes attendant upon depression tend to lower the birth rate; demobilization and prosperity have the opposite effect. Galbraith and Thomas show that these effects on the birth rate operate in part indirectly by way of the marriage rate; but there remain residual effects which are apparently explainable only by shifts in the timing of births within marriage. Whelpton's methods for studying the fertility of successive actual cohorts of women (described in Kiser's paper) make possible some estimate of the extent both of "postponement" of births and of "borrowing on the future," neither of which shifts need necessarily affect greatly the number of births that ultimately occur to a cohort over its entire reproductive history.

Hajnal's analysis of the "marriage boom" shows that recently there has been a decline in the age at which people marry in a number of countries. Such a change undoubtedly helps to explain the post-World War II "baby boom." Its longer run implications for fertility remain obscure. Conceivably the impetus given the birth rate by a drop in the age at marriage would be only temporary, if couples had no larger families than in the past, but merely had them at an earlier age.

Fluctuations and trends in marriage rates and in rates of marital dissolution are of interest not only for their bearing on natality, but also as indicators of changes in family organization. A number of statistical series are analyzed from this standpoint in the paper by Davis.

In view of the short-run fluctuations in natality discussed above, and of the repeatedly observed patterns of differential fertility by social and economic status (described in Kiser's paper), many demographers have concluded that variations in fertility under a "modern" regime are produced largely by variations in the extent to which family size is subjected to control by married couples. Consequently, it has seemed advisable to discover what factors in the experience and orientations of individual couples may lead them to adopt a regime of planned parenthood and condition the number of children they plan to have. The pioneer study in this field is that carried out in 1941 in the city of Indianapolis by a committee of cooperating demographers and social psychologists. The results of the study, summarized by Kiser and Whelpton, document conclusively the role of contraceptive practices in producing socio-economic differentials in fertility in the population studied. The study failed, however, to disclose the extent to which factors of aspiration, interest, motivation, and the like are determinants of the prevalence and the effectiveness of contraception. Whether future studies, employing more refined social-psychological techniques and hypotheses, will be productive of more conclusive findings remains to be seen.

RECENT DISCUSSION OF THE NET

REPRODUCTION RATE

By George J. Stolnitz and Norman B. Ryder

There has recently developed a large literature attesting to mounting dissatisfaction with the traditional net reproduction rate. At least two general levels of criticism have been discernible. Many demographers, focusing on the net reproduction rate in its simple synthetic form, i.e., based on the (male or female) age–specific fertility rates and survivor proportions of a given period, have emphasized the need for refining the technique to control for such factors as nuptiality, marital duration, and parity. A second major area of criticism has been touched off by the volatility of fertility movements in Western countries during the past two decades. The synthetic net reproduction rate has been characterized as likely to be an unreliable barometer of growth potential in societies subject to precipitous short–run fluctuations in marital and childbearing patterns. In such situations, it has been stressed, short–run variations of the synthetic rate, however refined, will tend to be deceptively large in the light of long–run movements of family formation. Accordingly, the proposal has been made that the focus of reproductivity analysis be shifted to the temporal arrangement of the marital and childbearing experience of successive cohorts born or married in the same period.

The Synthetic Net Reproduction Rate

An examination of the literature of recent decades indicates that the synthetic net reproduction rate was variously advocated for several distinct, though closely related purposes. It was frequently pointed out that this rate showed to what extent a population could be considered as replacing itself in the light of the fertility and mortality conditions observed in a given period [37]. Crude birth and death rates were recognized to be largely affected by age composition, in turn the consequence of a long and variable demographic past. The net reproduction rate was alleged to be independent of current age structure and thus a more apt measuring rod of growth potential [36]. The need for a measure performing this "purifying" function was demonstrated by the many documented instances of regions characterized by an excess of births over deaths, yet with net reproduction rates below unity.

The use of the synthetic net rate in a projective context derived support from an independent line of development. In 1911 Sharpe and Lotka demonstrated that a population subject to fixed age-specific fertility and mortality would eventually approach a stable form, i.e., one in which the age composition would remain fixed, the size of the total population changing at a constant "intrinsic" or "true" rate [51]. The synthetic net reproduction rate was a central characteristic of this stable population. The female rate, for example, could be interpreted either as the mean number of daughters a women would bear or the rate at which the total (stable) population would change during a period approximately equal to the mean age at confinement of a single female generation passing through life [12]. Thus the net reproduction rate could be regarded as fulfilling the dual function of measuring individual reproductive behavior and aggregate population change. Its great advantage stemmed from the precision with which it could be interpreted in the seemingly unambiguous case of a (stable) population whose characteristics were completely determined by the demographic behavior of an actual population during a given period [36].

During the 1930's, the synthetic rate also came to be employed widely as an instrument of interspatial or intertemporal comparison. Possibly the adoption of the net rate for this purpose evolved as a natural extension of the use of the life table in the investigation of comparative mortality. Introduction of both techniques can be attributed, in considerable measure, to the attempt to refine comparative analysis by effectively eliminating the influence of age composition.

By 1940 the synthetic net reproduction rate, customarily fe—male, was the single measure most often used in projective and com—parative analyses of reproductivity.

Methodological Background

Much of the recent discussion of the traditional net repro—duction rate is concerned with the validity of observed age—specific female fertility rates for measuring current reproductivity. The issue can be summarized briefly. Any female age—specific rate ob—served during a given period can be regarded as a weighted sum of fertility rates specific for additional demographic categories, such as parity, marital duration, age of husband, or birth interval. It may be considered, for example, equivalent to a weighted sum of female age—parity—specific rates, where the weights consist of the proportions of women in the age group during the period belonging to each parity category. (As used here, the expression "age—parity—specific rate" denotes the ratio of births of a given order to women of cited age during a time interval to the mean number of females of that age and parity equal to the birth order minus one.) This reasoning being general, a female age—specific fertility rate can likewise be shown to be a weighted sum of fertility rates specific for marital duration, age of husband, or birth interval. Since the latter are derivatives of past marital and childbearing patterns and hence dependent upon the prior sex—age composition of the popula—tion, the traditional net reproduction rate is, in fact, a function of the same "adventitious" elements that it was expressly designed to elim—inate.

The foregoing criticism has had direct bearing on the recent appraisal of the usefulness of the traditional net reproduction rate in a projective context. It has long been recognized that the stable age technique, though customarily derived from fertility and mor—tality rates specific for age alone, could, with equal formal facility, be adapted to deal with more refined measures of fertility or mor—tality. Only recently, however, has stress been placed explicitly on the fact that the traditional stable age model would be almost cer—tain to differ from one calculated on the basis of rates specific for additional demographic categories. The latter type of stable age model is clearly a more detailed representation of the long–run implications of the reproductive behavior of a population during a given period. The actual age–parity and mortality history, and hence the parity composition of persons belonging to an actual age group, can be expected to differ from that of a hypothetical cohort assumed to have been subject throughout its previous reproductive history to the age–parity experience of the period under study. The parity composition of hypothetical and actual cohorts being unlike, their respective age–specific fertility rates will, in all probability, differ. Accordingly, both the internal structure and the magnitude of the traditional and the parity–adjusted net reproduction rates will diverge. A fortiori, net rates adjusted not only for parity but also for duration of marriage, age of spouse, and the timing of childbearing between successive parities, may be strikingly different from unadjusted ones. This general methodological consideration underlies recent attempts to refine the synthetic net rate as an instrument for measuring the reproductive potentialities of a population.

The use of synthetic net rates as indices of intertemporal change in reproductive behavior has been a second major focus of recent attention. It has been argued, notably by Hajnal, Vincent, and Woofter, that time series of synthetic net rates, however refined, are likely to possess elements of instability which distort the long–run prospects of family formation and size [19, 56, 66]. The suggestion has been advanced that Western demography has been confronted, during the past two decades, with a relatively new type of situation—one in which short–run fluctuations, probably self–compensatory in the main, may have predominated over a clear–cut secular trend. A measure of a priori and empirical support has been adduced in favor of the view that marital and childbearing patterns in Western regions are becoming more sensitive to temporary states of economic activity and individual security. In consequence, traditional modes of analysis need to be reoriented to cope with the short– and long–run implications of situations in which large–scale cyclical movements in nuptiality and fertility are superimposed on underlying secular trends.

Proposed Refinements of the Synthetic Approach

Since the marriage rate is responsive to changing social, economic, and political conditions, demographers have frequently analyzed changing fertility in conjunction with varying marital behavior [17, 26, 34, 53]. In 1931, Wicksell developed all the essential features of the nuptiality table, and showed how to derive a nuptially controlled net reproduction rate [65]. Since that time these have become accepted methods of studying reproductivity. But the projective implications of the fact that reproduction rates adjusted for nuptiality ordinarily differ from the traditional simple rates, have only recently been examined intensively [19, 20, 56, 57].

As previously indicated, any age–specific rate may be viewed as a weighted sum of fertility rates differentiated with respect to marital status. The simple rate, computed for a given period, is implicitly a function of the existing marital composition. A number of writers have pointed out that this composition is intimately related to past demographic movements, notably changes in the sex–age composition of the population. Two conclusions derive from this fact. The first is that age–specific fertility rates, and consequently simple net reproduction rates, do not effectively remove the influence of past demographic history. Secondly, nuptiality patterns must be explicitly taken into account in analyzing the progress of the age structure of the population from its current to its stable form. Otherwise, the assumption of constant age–specific fertility rates would, in general, imply changes in marital composition, marital fertility, or both—results hardly consonant with an analytical approach predicated on the assumption of "fixed" fertility conditions.

Much attention has been devoted to an analysis of short–run fertility fluctuations as a function of changing distribution of marriages classified by duration. The fertility of marriages of short duration (age being held constant) tends to be higher than that of marriages of long duration [45, 52]. Fluctuations in marriage rates have a twofold effect upon intertemporal changes in fertility. During the period of low marriage rates, there will be a decline in

the proportion of the population recently married, i.e., in the marital groups with the highest duration—specific fertility rates. Consequently, assuming constant duration—specific fertility, age—specific
fertility rates will tend to decline. For analogous reasons, the latter will tend to increase in the aftermath of rising marriage rates.

Hyrenius has extended Wicksell's analysis of the nuptiality
table to take account of the rate of dissolution of marriage in order
to obtain the duration composition of a hypothetical cohort assumed
subject to the age—duration—specific fertility rates observed during a
given period. On the assumption of perpetual maintenance of the
current vital record, this type of analysis may be used to derive the
reproductivity of a hypothetical population whose cross—classification by age, nuptiality, duration, or other categories controlled in
analogous manner, is derived from current demographic conditions.
[See also 2, 7, 10, 15, 28, 49, 64.] It may be added that the assumption is generally implicit that mortality does not vary significantly
within the categories controlled. This seems to call for empirical
investigation.

Varying economic and political conditions affect not only the
formation of potential childbearing unions, but also reproductive
experience within marital unions previously formed. Intra—marital
fertility experience may be more fully investigated by detailing the
birth order of the children and the parity distribution of the population [43, 56]. In 1939, Quensel proposed extending the specification of fertility by age (and the stable structure derived therefrom)
to encompass parity as well [47]. Whelpton has independently demonstrated this technique and applied it to American data [63].

The discussion of parity by these authors is the analogue of
the duration case. A woman cannot become the mother of a third
child unless she has already borne two—just as she cannot be married three years until she has been married two. The observed
fertility rate for any age group may be considered as the weighted
sum of rates specific for individual parities, the weights being the
relative numbers in the actual population classified by number of
children previously born. After a period of widespread postponement of births, the parity distribution of the population will be concentrated in the lower orders. This leaves the population suscep-

tible to a change in age—specific fertility, even though the age—parity—specific rates remain unchanged. In this regard as well, it has been pointed out, age—specific fertility rates are affected by past demographic experience. Furthermore, there is no reason for believing that the current parity composition will be maintained in each age group as the population is moved hypothetically through time. Consequently, the assumption of fixed future age—specific fertility rates is tantamount to assuming variations in age—parity—specific rates.

Whelpton has shown how to build up a female population which will maintain over time a constant set of age—specific fertility rates derived from the age—parity—specific rates of a given period [63]. This represents a further step in the elimination of effects of the past from current demographic measures, and, consequently, the derivation of a fertility regime whose component parts can be prolonged into the future.

War and migration generally affect the male and female components of the population unequally. Such disturbances of sex composition have long been known to diminish nuptiality, and thus fertility [34]. Calculation of reproduction rates on a male rather than on a female base is not uncommon in the literature, particularly in the field of differential fertility [3, 22, 23, 36, 54, 55]. The phenomenon of conflicting male and female reproductive measures for the same population has also been recognized [8, 13, 38, 41, 42, 46]. But only recently, and primarily as the work of Karmel [27, 29—31], have such observations crystallized into a rigorous discussion of the theoretical and practical implications of sex imbalance for traditional measures of reproductivity. [See also 20, 21, 24, 25, 48, 49, 57.]

Karmel's argument runs as follows. In a stable population, the rate of growth per annum of the males must be the same as that of the females. If this were not so, the sex ratio of the population would approach zero or infinity—a patent absurdity. However, the male and the female "intrinsic" rates of natural increase calculated for observed populations will generally be found to be different. The fundamental reason is that, although the numerators (births) of male and female fertility rates will be related for the two sexes by an approximately constant sex ratio at birth [6, 27], the denomina—

tors (numbers of males and females) are the result of past demographic behavior, and thus reflect past mortality and migration differentials between the sexes. If the present population be projected
into stable form on the basis of fixed fertility and mortality (however the latter may be calculated), then the sex distribution will
change from its current form in the transition. Accordingly, the
assumption that age–specific fertility of either sex will remain unchanged implies that changing sex distribution is an insignificant
determinant of fertility. This is clearly unrealistic, particularly
for populations that have recently experienced large–scale wars or
migratory movements. The effects of the sex–age composition of
observed populations have been concealed by the almost exclusive
use of the female net reproduction rate [27]. The sub–replacement
levels of reproductivity indicated on the basis of this rate for many
countries of Western Europe in the last few decades were partly a
function of a sex distribution necessarily temporary under the assumptions of a closed population and fixed fertility and mortality.

The conflict between stable growth rates calculated on a male
or on a female basis cannot be resolved by the use of fertility rates
jointly specific for age of mother and father [31]. There still remains the question of selecting between male and female net joint-
nuptial tables, which are needed to obtain the distribution of the
married population by ages of husband and wife. The difficulty is
that the male and female nuptial tables are almost certain to be inconsistent in the sense that they imply unequal numbers of brides
and bridegrooms in future periods [30, 31]. This is so, since
the male and female nuptial tables derived on the basis of the experience of a given period are dependent on the sex–age structure
of the population, which, in turn, will change as the population ages.
The assumption of fixed future nuptiality on the part of one sex
necessarily involves the assumption of variable nuptiality on the
part of the other [30].

It follows that, when both sexes are explicitly considered,
there is no unique way of selecting a schedule of male and female
age–specific fertility or nuptiality rates as a basis for investigating
stable models implied by the conditions observed in current populations. Although it is formally possible to derive stable models based

on consistent male and female nuptiality or fertility (for a given regime of mortality), further research into the relationship between nuptiality and sex—age distribution is needed to give empirical foundation for the particular set of male and female rates selected for various analytical purposes. [See 24, 49, 57.]

These considerations have important bearing on the use and interpretation of female measures of reproductivity. Hopkin and Hajnal have emphasized the role played by differences in sex composition when fertility differentials between regions or classes in a population are measured by means of the female net reproduction rate [22]. Projections extrapolated on the basis of female fertility rates observed during a period of low ratios of males to females are likely to contain substantial downward bias. Karmel has pointed out that the gross reproduction rate, generally regarded as "a pure measure of fertility," is in fact dependent upon the sex—age composition of the population and, consequently, upon mortality [31].

Real Cohort Reproductivity

The rationale for the use of a synthetic population system in a projective context is that the observed demographic performance of a population during a given period of time may be regarded as representing the experience of birth cohorts aging through time. It has generally been observed, however, that time series of the mortality and fertility behavior of successive real cohorts are relatively more stable than are the synthetic rates calculated for the same period. Derrick, analyzing mortality in 1927 [cited in 18, Ch. 8], and Barclay and Kermack [1], studying fertility change a decade later, have commented along these lines.

More recently Woofter, using American data to estimate generation reproduction rates, has concluded that "...calendar year reproduction rates are of doubtful validity for long—time comparisons to indicate past trends and especially for future estimates." The same author has stressed the importance of measuring the size and the temporal arrangement of the complete fertility experience of successive real cohorts [66]. Hajnal, citing the German experience from 1933 to 1940, has argued that "...long—term prospects of population growth should be discussed in terms of the size of family, which remains stable, and not in terms of fertility rates, whose level this year is no reasonable guide whatever to their level next year" [19]. He has concluded that "...demographic analysis in future must study changes in the number of children born over the whole of their married lives to successive cohorts of marriages and relate yearly fertility rates to the number already born to the marriages in question" [19]. Thus a body of presumptive evidence has been accumulated supporting the view that real cohort analysis is a superior approach to the study of secular population trends, especially for regions not significantly subject to migration. [See also 9, 11, 14, 44, 58, 59.]

Proposals for measuring real cohort reproductivity have been advanced to abstract long–run trends from short–run fluctuations in marriages and intra–marital fertility. A number of writers working along these directions have recognized the difficulties inherent in this approach. The needed data are cumulated relatively slowly and are complete only for age or marital cohorts past the reproductive span. The achievement of statistical comparability over time is difficult. Generation reproduction rates must be adapted to take account of migration movements, comparable to those of the low fertility countries during the last century. The recent literature on sex differentials in reproductivity measurement suggests that real male and female cohorts of the same or slightly differing ages will often yield unlike generation net rates. Real marriage cohorts do not present this problem, if an insignificant degree of remarriage be assumed, because marital reproductivity experience is joint. The study of the latter, however, covers only half of the problem. It must be supplemented by an investigation ot the proportions of each real sex–age group eventually married or remarried in order to bridge the gap between marital reproductivity and population growth. This seems to be an important area for future research.

Conclusion

Until recently the course of population development in Western nations was generally believed to be well charted and understood. This is now a matter of some doubt. It is natural, therefore, that the prevalent state of indecision concerning the nature of past movements should extend to the measures customarily used to describe and interpret them.

The traditional net reproduction rate is not likely to be used as unqualifiedly in the future as it has been in the past. Each of its major properties—its synthetic nature, dependence on female experience, and the use of rates specific for age only—has been called into serious question. In view of the criticism as a whole, the traditional net rate cannot be expected to retain a central analytical position in future demographic research, at least for Western nations.

Since recent discussion has not yet crystallized into a positive confirmation of methods needed in the study of reproductivity, any attempt to particularize probable future development in this area is likely to be premature. The literature of the past few years is, however, broadly suggestive of new directions of methodological emphasis and research interest.

Future research is likely to be more centrally focused on the structure and timing of individual family formation and completion. The shift of emphasis to a micro–demographic point of view is implied by the recent stress on the importance of refining vital statistics measures by the introduction of additional controls. The documentation of the past, current, and prospective empirical significance of such refinements, assessed individually and severally, is urgently needed. Recent demographic developments in Western countries constitute an inviting, and challenging, historical backdrop for this type of investigation.

Events of the past few years have reaffirmed the long recognized need for the development and testing of dynamic models of demographic response to changing social, economic, and psychological climates. Population study has developed no conceptual framework for investigating short–run variations in marital and childbearing patterns. In addition, theoretical consideration of the long–run, as distinguished from the short–run, aspects of population change is likely to be an increasingly important prerequisite to the refinement of future empirical research. The proliferation of emphasis on generation reproductivity is symptomatic of growing research interest in this direction. A promising avenue of future investigation is the analysis of rates pooling the reproductive experience of successive real male and female age or marriage cohorts.

Research in these directions will require substantial extension of theoretical and methodological frontiers. Such advance will undoubtedly enable more efficient exploitation of available empirical data.

SELECTED BIBLIOGRAPHY

1. Barclay, R. S., and Kermack, W. O. "The decline of the birth rate: regularities revealed by an analysis of the rates observed in certain European countries." Proceedings of the Royal Society of Edinburgh 58(1):55–72. 1937–1938.

2. Bourgeois–Pichat, J. "Un nouvel indice de mesure de la fécondité." Population 3(2):293–312. April–June, 1948.

3. Charles, E. "Differential fertility in Canada, 1931." Canadian Journal of Economics and Political Science 9(2):175–218. May, 1943.

4. Charles, E. "Differential fertility in Scotland, 1911–1931, Part II." Transactions of the Royal Society of Edinburgh 59:673–686. 1938–1939.

5. Charles, E. "The nuptiality problem with special reference to Canadian marriage statistics." Canadian Journal of Economics and Political Science 7(3):447–477. Aug., 1941.

6. Ciocco, A. "Variation in the sex ratio at birth in the United States." Human Biology 10(1):36–64. Feb., 1938.

7. Clark, C., and Dyne, R. E. "Applications and extensions of the Karmel formula for reproductivity." Economic Record 22(42): 23–39. June, 1946.

8. Connor, L. R. "Fertility of marriage and population growth." Journal of the Royal Statistical Society 89(3):553–566. May, 1926.

9. Depoid, P. Reproduction Nette en Europe depuis l'Origine des Statistiques de l'Etat Civil. Statistique Générale de la France, Etudes Démographiques No. 1. Paris, 1941. 42 pp.

10. Depoid, P. "Tables d'extinction des mariages et des couples suivant la durée de l'union." Congrès International de la Population 5:51–60. Paris, 1937.

11. Dublin, L. I., and Spiegelman, M. "Current versus generation life tables." Human Biology 13(4):439–458. Dec., 1941.

12. Dublin, L. I., and Lotka, A. J. "On the true rate of natural increase of a population." Journal of the American Statistical Association 20(151): 305–399. Sept., 1925.

13. Fisher, R. A. The Genetical Theory of Natural Selection. Oxford, The Clarendon Press, 1930. Pp. 22–30.

14. Frost, W. H. "The age selection of mortality from tuberculosis in successive decades." Milbank Memorial Fund Quarterly 18(1):61–66. Jan., 1940.

15. Germany. Statistisches Reichsamt. "Der Reproduktionsindex." Pp. 73–77 in: Neue Beiträge zum deutschen Bevölkerungsproblem. Sonderhefte zu Wirtschaft und Statistik, No. 15. Berlin, 1935. 96 pp.

16. Glass, D. V. "Changes in fertility in England and Wales, 1851 to 1931." Chapter IV, pp. 161–212, in: Hogben, L., editor. Political Arithmetic. London, George Allen and Unwin, Ltd., 1938.

17. Glass, D. V. "Economic fluctuations and marriage frequency." Congrès International de la Population 5:13–21. Paris, 1937.

18. Glass, D. V. Population Policies and Movements in Europe. Oxford, The Clarendon Press, 1940. Chapter 8 and Appendix.

19. Hajnal, J. "The analysis of birth statistics in the light of the recent international recovery of the birth–rate." Population Studies 1(2):137–164. Sept., 1947.

20. Hajnal, J. "Aspects of recent trends in marriage in England and Wales." Population Studies 1(1):72–98. June, 1947.

21. Hajnal, J. "Some comments on Mr. Karmel's paper 'The relations between male and female reproduction rates.'" Population Studies 2(3):354–360. Dec., 1948.

22. Hopkin, W. A. B., and Hajnal, J. "Analysis of the births in England and Wales, 1939, by father's occupation." Part I. Population Studies 1(2):187–203. Sept., 1947; Part II. Ibid. 1 (3):275–300. Dec., 1947.

23. Husson, R. "La fécondité bigène de la population française en 1931." Congrès International de la Population 1:220–221. Paris, 1937.

24. Hyrenius, H. "La mesure de la reproduction et de l'accroissement naturel." Population 3(2):271–292. April–June, 1948.

25. Hyrenius, H. "Om beräkningar av nettoreproduktionstal." Ekonomist Tidskrift 47(3):233–244. Sept., 1945.

26. Hyrenius, H. "The relation between birth rates and economic activity in Sweden, 1920–1944." Bulletin of the Oxford University Institute of Statistics 8(1):14–21. Jan., 1946.

27. Karmel, P. H. "An analysis of the sources and magnitudes of inconsistencies between male and female net reproduction rates in actual populations." Population Studies 2(2):240–273. Sept., 1948.

28. Karmel, P. H. "Fertility and marriages — Australia, 1933–1942." Economic Record 20(38):74–80. June, 1944.

29. Karmel, P. H. "A rejoinder to Mr. Hajnal's comments." Population Studies 2(3):361–372. Dec., 1948.

30. Karmel, P. H. "The relations between male and female nuptiality in a stable population." Population Studies 1(4):353–387. March, 1948.

31. Karmel, P. H. "The relations between male and female reproduction rates." Population Studies 1(3):249–274. Dec., 1947.

32. Karpinos, B. D. "Stabilized method of forecasting population."
     Public Health Reports 54(40):1807–1822. Oct. 6, 1939.

33. Kirk, D. "The relation of employment levels to births in Ger-
     many."   Milbank Memorial Fund Quarterly 20(2):126–138. A-
     pril, 1942.

34. Kramm, E. R., and Thomas, D. S. "Rural and urban marriage
     in relation to the sex ratio." Rural Sociology 7(1):33–39. March,
     1942.

35. Kuczynski, R. R. "The analysis of vital statistics: I. Marriage
     statistics." Economica 5 N.S. (18):138–163. May, 1938.

36. Kuczynski, R. R. Fertility and Reproduction. New York, Fal-
     con Press, 1932. Chapters 3 and 5.

37. Kuczynski, R. R. The Measurement of Population Growth. New
     York, Oxford University Press, 1936. 255 pp.

38. Landry, A. "Notes de démographie pure." Congrès Internation-
     al de la Population 1:85–95. Paris, 1937.

39. Lotka, A. J. "Analyse démographique avec application particu-
     lière à l'espèce humaine." Actualités Scientifiques et Indus-
     trielles, 780. Paris, Herman et Cie., 1939. 149 pp.

40. Lotka, A. J. "Modern trends in the birth rate." Annals of the
     American Academy of Political and Social Science 188:1–13.
     Nov., 1936.

41. Lotka, A. J. "Orphanhood in relation to demographic factors."
     Metron 9(2):37–109. Aug. 15, 1931.

42. Lotka, A. J. "The stability of the normal age distribution."
     Proceedings of the National Academy of Science 8(11):339–345.
     Nov., 1922.

43. Lotka, A. J., and Spiegelman, M. "The trend of the birth rate
     by age of mother and order of birth." Journal of the American
     Statistical Association 35(212):595–601. Dec., 1940.

44. Merrell, M. "Time–specific life tables contrasted with observed
     survivorship." Biometrics Bulletin 3(3):129–136. 1947.

45. Müller, J. H. "Human fertility in relation to the age of husband
     and wife at marriage and duration of marriage." Annals of Eu-
     genics 4(3–4):238–278. May, 1931.

46. Myers, R. J. "The validity and significance of male net repro-
     duction rates."   Journal of the American Statistical Associa-
     tion 36(214):275–282. June, 1941.

47. Quensel, C.-E. "Changes in fertility following birth restriction."
     Skandinavisk Aktuarietidskrift 22(3–4):177–199. 1939.

48. Quensel, C.-E. "Några kritiska anmärkningar röranda begrep-
     pet reproduktionstal." Ekonomisk Tidskrift 43(3):227 ff. 1941.

49. Quensel, C.-E. "Population movements in Sweden in recent
     years." Population Studies 1(1):29–43. June, 1947.

50. Sauvy, A. "La reprise de la natalité dans le monde. Ses causes, ses chances de durée." Population 3(2):249–270. April–June, 1948.

51. Sharpe, F., and Lotka, A. J. "A problem in age distribution." Philosophical Magazine 21:435–438. April, 1911.

52. Szulc, S. "L'influence de l'âge des femmes au moment de la conclusion du mariage sur la fertilité et la natalité." Congrès International de la Population 5:133–147. Paris, 1937.

53. Thomas, D. Social Aspects of the Business Cycle. London, G. Routledge and Sons, 1925. 217 pp.

54. Tietze, C. "Differential reproduction in England." Milbank Memorial Fund Quarterly 17(3):288–293. July, 1939.

55. Tietze, C. "The measurement of differential reproduction by paternity rates." Eugenics Review 30(2):101–107. July, 1938.

56. Vincent, P. "Comment déterminer la tendance de la fécondité?" Population 2(3):465–480. July–Sept., 1947.

57. Vincent, P. "De la mesure du taux intrinsèque d'accroissement naturel dans les populations monogames." Population 1(4):699–712. Oct.–Dec., 1946.

58. Whelpton, P. K. "Effect of increased birth rate on future population." American Journal of Public Health 35(4):326–333. April, 1945.

59. Whelpton, P. K. The Fertility of Successive Cohorts of Women in the United States. Washington, D.C., Aug. 8, 1947. 6 pp.

60. Whelpton, P. K. "Is family size increasing?" Vital Statistics—Special Reports 23(16):317–326. Aug. 29, 1947.

61. Whelpton, P. K. "The meaning of the 1947 baby boom." Vital Statistics—Special Reports 33(1):1–10. Oct. 7, 1948.

62. Whelpton, P. K. and Jackson, N. E. "Prolificacy distribution of white wives according to fertility tables for the Registration Area." Human Biology 12(1):35–58. Feb., 1940.

63. Whelpton, P. K. "Reproduction rates adjusted for age, parity, fecundity, and marriage." Journal of the American Statistical Association 41(236):501–516. Dec., 1946.

64. Wicksell, S.D. "The fertility of married women in Sweden according to age and duration of marriage." Congrès International de la Population 5:163–177. Paris, 1937.

65. Wicksell, S.D. "Nuptiality, fertility, and reproductivity." Skandinavisk Aktuarietidskrift 14(3):125–157. 1931.

66. Woofter, T. J. "Completed generation reproduction rates." Human Biology 19(3):133–153. Sept., 1947.

FERTILITY TRENDS AND DIFFERENTIALS
IN THE UNITED STATES

By Clyde V. Kiser

M UCH interest has been aroused over the spectacular increase in the birth rate in this country during the past decade. This paper is concerned mainly with two broad questions: Does the increase in the birth rate connote an actual reversal in the long-time downward trend in average size of completed family or is it simply a temporary phenomenon associated with wartime and postwar conditions? In what manner have the increases in the birth rate varied among different elements of the population and what bearing does this have on the trend of fertility differentials? The data presented in this paper do not permit categorical answers to these questions. Whelpton's materials indicate beyond doubt that much of the increase in the crude birth rate is due to increases in marriages and first births and they make it seem improbable that crude birth rates of the 1947–1950 levels will be maintained very long. On the other hand, they also indicate the strong possibility of at least a slight and temporary reversal of the downward trend in average number of births per woman of completed fertility. This average may easily be somewhat higher for the cohorts of native-white women born during 1910–1914 and 1915–1919 than for those born during 1905–1909. As for differentials, samples drawn by the Census Bureau's Current Population Survey leave little doubt that increases since 1940 in fertility ratios (children under 5 per 1,000 married women of childbearing age) have been proportionately highest among groups previously characterized by lowest fertility. However, the consequent marked narrowing of group differences in fertility ratios since 1940 may have no more duration than a flash-flood increase in number of children under 5.

FERTILITY TRENDS

A brief historical setting is essential for interpretation of recent fertility trends. Like other highly modernized countries, the United States has had a long history of declines in fertility. In fact, this country may provide an exception to the usual tendency for declines in mortality to precede declines in fertility. Whatever that situation may be, there is good evidence that fertility ratios began declining in this country at least by the second decade of the last century. Census data for the 1810–1940 period indicate a decline in the number of children under 5 per 1,000 white females 20–44 years of age with each successive census except one (that of 1860) and that exception may not be real. At all events, the fertility ratio of about 1,358 in 1810 was reduced by approximately one-third by 1850, by about one-half by 1900, and by about two-thirds by 1940, when it was 419.[1] However, a sharp reversal is evident from the preliminary age distributions for the 1950 Census, which yield a fertility ratio of about 561 for whites with no adjustment for underenumeration of children.[2]

In terms of birth rates, Thompson and Whelpton have estimated that in 1800 and 1810 there were approximately 55 births per 1,000 white population, about 43 in 1850, and about 30 in 1900.[3] During the period of the expanding birth registration area, birth rates for whites and nonwhites combined, corrected for underregistration and adjusted to the country as a whole, declined from 29.5 in 1915 to a low point of 18.4 in 1933. During this period the chief interruption of the decline came in 1920 and 1921 following the return of World War I soldiers in 1919. During the remainder of the 'thirties there was a slow and irregular increase to 19.2 in 1938 and 18.8 in 1939.

After 1940, and particularly after 1945, the upward trend of the birth rate was little short of phenomenal. The crude rate (adjusted for underregistration) rose from 19.4 in 1940 to a wartime high of 22.9 in 1943. Then with millions of men overseas, the birth rate declined to 20.7 by 1945. Following demobilization, the birth rate jumped again and in 1947 it reached 27.0, its highest point since 1921. The rate then dropped to 25.4 in 1948 and 25.1 in 1949.[4]

Although the relation of birth rates to marriage rates is by no means simple, the major dips and peaks of the annual birth rate have, with a lag of about one year, tended to follow those of the marriage rate during the past 20 years. This may be due mainly to a close relation of marriages in one year to first births the next year.[5] Owing to the economic depression, the marriages occurring in 1932 dropped to

---

[1] For the complete series of fertility ratios for whites from 1810 to 1940, increased 5 per cent for underenumeration of children, and (for censuses after 1820) standardized for age of women, *see:*

Whelpton, P. K. *et al.*, *Forecasts of the Population of the United States, 1945–1975.* (Bureau of the Census, Washington: Government Printing Office, 1947), p. 16.

[2] U. S. Bureau of the Census: *1950 Census of Population, Preliminary Reports.* General Characteristics of the Population of the United States, April 1, 1950, Series PC-7, No. 1, February 25, 1951, pp. 6–8.

[3] Thompson, Warren S. and Whelpton, P. K., *Population Trends in the United States* (New York: McGraw-Hill Book Company, 1933), p. 263.

[4] National Office of Vital Statistics:

Vital Statistics of the United States, 1948, Part I (Washington: Government Printing Office, 1950), p. xix (Table Y).

Births and Birth Rates in the Entire United States, 1909–1948. *Vital Statistics—Special Reports*, Vol. 33, No. 8 (September 29, 1950), p. 141.

Summary of Natality Statistics, United States, 1949. *Vital Statistics—Special Reports*, Vol. 36, No. 1 (May 14, 1951), p. 4.

[5] A reader of this paper has pointed out (a) that the same factors stimulating marriages may also cause couples already married to have a child, and (b) that on a monthly basis, adjusted for seasonality, there are some wartime and postwar peaks due to second and third child births two to three years after a peak in the marriage rate.

7.9 per 1,000 population, the lowest rate on record for this country. This was followed by an all-time low in the birth rate in 1933. The increases in employment associated with defense preparations in 1940–1941 were accompanied by sharp increases in the marriage and birth rates. Pearl Harbor and our entrance into the war provided an added stimulus and December 1941 brought a sharp rise in the marriage rate. As already noted, the wartime birth rates reached their peak in 1943 in so far as complete years are concerned. On a monthly basis a wartime peak of 24.9 was reached in September and October 1942, nine and ten months after Pearl Harbor. After the war the marriage rate reached 16.4 per 1,000 population in 1946, the highest on record for this country, and this was followed by the postwar peak in the birth rate in 1947. On a monthly basis the postwar peak in the marriage rate came in June, 1946 and that of the birth rate in December, 1946.[6]

Demographers and many others are keenly interested in the significance of the wartime and postwar increases in the birth rate. P. K. Whelpton has studied this problem more intensively than has anyone else in the United States. His first analysis, published in 1945, served at once to point up the important bearing of marriages and first births on increases in fertility during the early 1940's and an important inadequacy of the net reproduction rate. To quote from this article: "With 1942 came the impossible. In a cohort having 1942 age-specific rates for first births, 109 of each 100 women living through the childbearing period would have at least one child."[7] A later article showing trends in the number of births to native-white women during 1920–1947, by order of birth, brings out clearly the fact that the depression dip and the wartime and postwar increases in the births were sharpest for lower orders of birth.[8] Computations based upon births per 1,000 females 15–44, by order of birth, reported by the National Office of Vital Statistics, indicate that the percentage increase from 1940 to 1947 was highest for first births and became successively lower with increasing order of births through the seventh. The increases in this fertility rate were 67 per cent for first births, 59 per cent for second births, 48 per cent for third births, 29 per cent for fourth births, 16 per cent for fifth births, 2 per cent for sixth and seventh combined, and a decrease for births of eighth and higher orders. It should also be noted, however, that the 1947–1949 *decrease* in the birth rate was due mainly to a decrease in first births. There were slight

---

[6] The following recent report from the National Office of Vital Statistics is also of interest: "In April, 1951 the estimated number of live births increased sharply over the figure for April, 1950 (13.1 per cent). This was the greatest rise in the monthly number of births from one year to the next since 1947. It follows by 9–10 months the beginning of the upswing in marriage licenses in the middle of 1950 which was coincident with the outbreak of hostilities in Korea." *Monthly Vital Statistics Bulletin*, Vol. 14, No. 4 (June 20, 1951), p. 1.

[7] Whelpton, P. K., "Effect of Increased Birth Rate on Future Population,' *American Journal of Public Health*, Vol. 35, No. 4 (April, 1945), p. 330.

[8] Whelpton, P. K., "The Meaning of the 1947 Baby Boom," *Vital Statistics—Special Reports*, Vol. 33, No. 1 (October 7, 1948), p. 5.

increases in the rates of second and higher order births from 1947 to 1949.[9]

The most thorough-going analysis of fertility trends in this country is afforded in Whelpton's recently completed study, *Cohort Fertility: Native White Women in the United States*, being published by the Princeton University Press. The writer is indebted to Professor Whelpton for the privilege of examining his manuscript and for permission to give a preview of certain data included and several of the outstanding conclusions.

In scope and detail of data and in potential value to demographers of the future, this latest work of Whelpton stands easily on a par with T. H. C. Stevenson's monumental report on the fertility of British marriages.[10] The manuscript consists of about 400 typed pages, about half of which are fertility tables for cohorts. There are seven chapters of text including about 175 typed pages exclusive of tables. Whelpton emphasizes that the need for making estimates was constantly encountered in preparing the various tables from census and registration data available and that the results must be regarded as approximate rather than as exact. For instance, total births are those adjusted to the total United States up to 1933 and for underregistration throughout the whole period considered. Estimates were needed, particularly in the early years, for distribution of births by order. They were required at various stages for the preparation of the population bases. For these reasons, work tables are presented in detail and there is much discussion in the text and in the Appendices of the methods used and probable nature of bias entailed.

As explained by Whelpton, "Fertility tables for two types of cohorts . . . 'actual' and 'hypothetical' . . . are presented in this monograph. Each actual cohort consists of white women who were born in the United States during a given 12-month period centering on January 1. For example, the native white women born from July 1, 1899 to June 30, 1900, inclusive, constitute the actual cohort of 1900. . . . In tracing the fertility and mortality experience of each actual cohort through its life the assumption is made [as in the case of life tables] that all members of the cohort were born during the first instant of January 1. This means . . . that . . . the women of the 1900 cohort were exactly 15 years old on January 1, 1915, and exactly 47 on January 1, 1947" (Chapter 2).

For purposes of this study, Whelpton also assumes that the childbearing ages are 15–46 inclusive. Owing to inadequacy of birth registration data before 1920, the actual cohorts are restricted to women within any part of this age group from 1920 to 1949 inclusive. This

---

[9] National Office of Vital Statistics, "Births by Age of Mother, Race, and Birth Order, United States, 1949," *Vital Statisics—Special Reports*, Vol. 36, No. 9 (October 15, 1951), p. 140.

[10] *Fertility of Marriage*. Census of England and Wales (1911), Vol. XIII (London: His Majesty's Stationery Office, 1917), 477 pp.

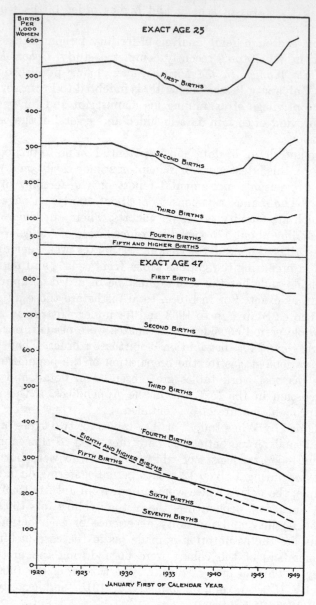

FIGURE 1. Trends since 1920 in numbers of births of specified order occurring prior to ages 25 and 47 per 1,000 native white women surviving to these ages January first of specified calendar year. (Adapted from P. K. Whelpton: *Cohort Fertility: Native White Women in the United States. Tables for Actual Cohorts.* In publication.)

means that the only actual cohorts that could be considered are those of women born during 1874–1934. Most of the discussion relates to women born during 1890–1930.[11]

The first table gives, for each actual cohort in turn, cumulative birth rates,[12] by order of birth, of women surviving to specified single year of age and calendar year. Extracts of these data are charted in Figures 1 and 2. Figure 1 shows trends from 1920 to the beginning of 1949 in the number of children of given order previously born per 1,000 native-white women attaining ages 25 and 47. It should be noted (a) that each of any twins or other multiple births that occur is given a different order on the birth certificate, so no woman is assigned more than one birth of a given order; and (b) that women having, say, four births before age 25 are credited not only with fourth births but also with third, second, and first births. Hence the cumulative rates by order of birth can be interpreted *as proportions of women already having at least* one birth, two births, etc. upon reaching any given age.

As indicated in the top section of Figure 1, the number of first births per 1,000 women surviving to age 25 rose slightly from 526 at the beginning of 1920 to 541 at the beginning of 1928, then declined to 462 by 1936 and remained approximately at this level until 1940. Thereafter the trend was upward, until a wartime peak of 557 was reached at the beginning of 1944. Dropping slightly during the next two years the rate climbed again and reached 616 by January 1, 1949 and 625 by January 1, 1950.

Although the actual magnitudes of yearly changes tend to be smaller, the trend in the number of second births per 1,000 women by age 25 follows essentially the same pattern as that described above. The trend in the rate of third births by age 25 also reflects the decline associated with the economic depression and the rise associated with the war. The rate of fourth births by age 25 declined slowly from 62 per 1,000 at the beginning of 1920 to 33 by 1940 and then rose to 39 by 1949 and 40 per 1,000 at the beginning of 1950.

With the arithmetic scale the top section of Figure 1 points up the fact that the absolute declines following 1928 and the absolute increases following 1940 (in cumulative birth rates prior to age 25) become smaller with increasing order of birth. Experimental plotting

[11] Whelpton's monograph also presents cumulative birth rates and distributions by parity of women in "hypothetical" cohorts of each year from 1920 to 1949 but these will not be discussed here. The assumption is made that "the women composing a hypothetical cohort are born on January 1 of the specified year, and have throughout their lifetime the age-specific death rates which all women, and the age-parity specific birth rates which the fecund women who will marry by age 47, actually have in that year" (Table HA). The cumulative birth rates for the hypothetical cohorts presented in Whelpton's tables can be converted into gross reproduction rates (adjusted for parity, sterility, and spinsterhood) by the application of appropriate sex ratios at birth.

[12] Cumulative birth rates "are the numbers of births prior to specified age and date per 1,000 women surviving to that age and date." (Table A.)

of the data on semilogarithmic paper indicated that (a) the *rate of decline* following 1928 becomes larger with increasing order of birth, and (b) *rate of increase* following 1940 becomes smaller with increasing order of birth after the first. The 1940–1950 percentage increase in proportion of women having second births by age 25 is higher than that of women having first births by this age.

Although the data for ages between 25 and 47 are not charted, the sharpness of the rise in first births after 1940 decreases with age and virtually disappears by age 40. As indicated in the lower section of Figure 1, there has been a virtually constant downward trend since 1920 in the proportion of women having births of any order by the end of the childbearing period. The relative importance of the decline increases with order of birth and reflects the long-time decrease in size of the completed family. The fertility of women reaching the end of the childbearing period during the past decade, of course, is affected little if at all by the conditions of that period.

Whereas Figure 1 presented cumulative fertility rates for successive cohorts reaching two given ages, Figure 2 follows the survivors of three cohorts through successive ages (beginning with age 16) and shows the number of births of given order (first through seventh) per 1,000 women reaching the successive ages shown on the axis. The three cohorts chosen for comparison are those of women born at the beginning of 1905, 1915, and 1925 and thus reaching age 16 at the beginning of 1921, 1931, and 1941, respectively. Since the charted data terminate with the beginning of 1949,[13] they relate to ages 16–44 for the 1905 cohort, 16–34 for the 1915 cohort, and 16–24 for the 1925 cohort.

Among women in the 1905 cohort, there were 476 first births per 1,000 women surviving to age 24 (in 1929), 729 per 1,000 reaching age 34 (in 1939), and 770 per 1,000 reaching age 44 (in 1949). The 1915 cohort, reaching age 16 in 1931, belong to the group in which many marriages and births were postponed because of the depression. The rate of first births was consistently lower for this cohort than for the earlier one throughout ages 17–28. Reaching 26 years of age January 1, 1941, these women apparently were still young enough to participate in the marriage and birth boom of that decade. By age 34, reached in 1949, the rate of first births was 767 per 1,000 survivors, higher than that (729) for women of comparable age in the 1905 cohort. In fact, the rate was virtually as high by age 34 for the 1915 cohort as it was by age 44 for the 1905 cohort.

The number of second births per 1,000 women by age 34 was also higher for the 1915 than for the 1905 cohort, but the differences were in the other direction with respect to third and higher orders of birth by age 34.

[13] The data will be extended to the beginning of 1950 in Whelpton's published monograph.

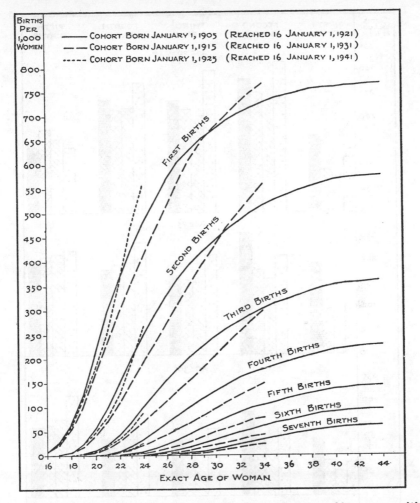

FIGURE 2. Comparison of three actual cohorts of native white women with respect to number of births of specified order occurring prior to given age, per 1,000 women surviving to that age. (Adapted from P. K. Whelpton's data cited under Figure 1.)

The fertility of the women born in 1925 is of special interest, since this group reached age 16 in 1941. The occurrence of first births by age 24 was conspicuously high for this group, 553 per 1,000 survivors as compared with 476 for the cohort of 1905 and 409 for the cohort of 1915. The 1925 cohort also outranked the 1905 cohort in rate of second births by age 24, but it fell between the 1905 and 1915 cohorts with respect to third or higher orders of birth by age 24. Thus the 1925 cohort got off to an auspicious start with respect to proportions marrying and having first and second births by age 24. Only time will reveal

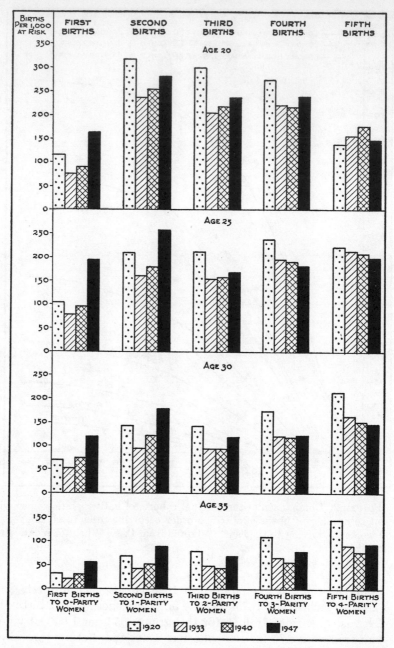

FIGURE 3. Number of births of given order during specified age and calendar year, per 1,000 native white women entering this age and at risk for birth of given order at the beginning of the calendar year. (Adapted from P. K. Whelpton's manuscript cited under Figure 1.)

the fertility behavior of this cohort and other young couples in the future.

The addition of the cumulative birth rates of all orders of birth for a given cohort and age yields the total number of children ever born per 1,000 women surviving to that age. By differencing the cumulative birth rates of successive orders, it is also possible to convert these rates into percentage distributions of women living to a given age by number of children ever born, by that age.[14] The distributions by parity again point up the heavy role of low-order births in the increase in fertility since 1940. For instance, the total number of births prior to age 30 was 1,453 per 1,000 women in 1941 and 1,786 in 1949. At the earlier date, 35.5 per cent of the women 30 years of age were childless as compared with only 21.8 per cent among women 30 years of age in 1949. The proportion of women with only one child by age 30 was approximately the same (24 per cent) in 1941 and 1949. The proportion with two or three children was 30 per cent in 1941 and 42.5 per cent in 1949. The proportion with four or more children by age 30 was 10 per cent in 1941 and 11 per cent in 1949.

In another series of tables, Whelpton presents annual birth probabilities, by age, by parity of women in actual cohorts. The probabilities are the numbers of births of specified order to women during specified calendar year and age, per 1,000 women at risk for such birth order at the beginning of the year. The rates are computed by relating the number of nth births during the year to the number of women having borne $n-1$ children by the beginning of the year. Figure 3 is based upon data of this type for several specific ages and birth orders for the years 1920, 1933, 1940, and 1947. It will be noted that the probability of first births to zero-parity women (e.g., women who have borne no children) was over twice as high in 1947 as in 1933 for each of the four ages considered. However, the probability of fourth births to three-parity women was actually lower in 1947 than in 1933 among women at age 25, about the same for women at age 30, and somewhat higher for women at age 35. Also, the probability of fifth births to four-parity women at ages 25 and 30 appears to have declined rather continuously since 1933. In most cases, birth probabilities in 1933 were much below those of 1920.

The chapter devoted to the postponing, "making up," and "moving ahead" of births by women in various cohorts is of special interest. In order to estimate the magnitude of birth "deficits" accruing from the depression and of subsequent wartime birth " surpluses," Whelpton first computed numbers of births that would be "expected" with stable economic conditions and no major war after 1930 and then

---

[14] For example, if there are 646 first births and 411 second births per 1,000 women by age 30, there are 235 women per 1,000 (or 23.5 per cent) having one birth but no more by that age.

compared the "expected" with the actual numbers. He provides three sets of "expected" births—"high," "medium," and "low."[15]

The results are striking, especially with reference to first births. As Whelpton indicates, the depression of the 1930's, the prosperity of the 1940's, and World War II caused large changes in the timing of first births to native-white women. The development during 1929–1933 of a "deficit" of between 307,000 and 344,000 first births to women aged 15–39 on January 1, 1934, the increase of the "deficit" to between 519,000 and 609,000 by January 1, 1939, and its virtual elimination by January 1, 1944, point to the large-scale postponement of first births from the first two to the third of these five-year periods.

As for more recent years, Whelpton interprets his findings to mean that the 1947–1950 levels of the crude birth rate are temporary rather than permanent. He points out that about 81 per cent of the changes in first-birth rates may result from changes in marriage rates, since the coefficient of correlation between marriage rates and first-birth rates one year later is about 0.90 for the period under consideration. In view of his estimated "deficits" of fourth and higher births (and possibly of third births) on January 1, 1949 he interprets the rise in numbers of births mainly in terms of an advance in the time schedule of marriage and starting of a family.

Regarding trends during the coming decade, Whelpton points out that to have approximately as many births during 1949–53 and 1954–58 as during 1944–48 will require an unusually favorable combination of circumstances. One group of requirements includes the continuation of prosperity and the avoidance of a major war—in short, the maintenance of conditions which encourage early marriage and the starting of families, and adding of children to families already begun. Another group of requirements includes decreases in the proportions of couples wanting and able to be childless or to have only one or two children which are sufficiently large to balance the increases which seem sure to occur in the proportions able to prevent unwanted fifth and subsequent pregnancies. That the 1950's will meet all of these requirements seems doubtful to him.

It is also important to note, however, that Whelpton's projections, under different assumptions, of the cumulative birth rates by order of birth among cohorts reaching or nearing the end of the childbearing period suggest strongly that the total number of children ever born per native-white woman of completed fertility will reach a low point

---

[15] The "high" assumption was that the average annual percentage decline after 1930 would be half as large as that of 1920–1930 and would stop at the end of 1944. "The 'medium' assumption regarding the 'expected' trend of cumulative birth rates since 1930 is that with stable economic conditions and no major war or other catastrophe the cumulative age-order specific birth rates would have the average annual percentage decrease computed from the difference between the 1920 and 1930 rates." The "low" assumption was that the annual percentage decline after 1930 would be one and one-half times as large as it was during the previous decade.

for the cohort of women born during 1905–1909 and will be somewhat higher for the cohorts of 1910–1914 and 1915–1919. Whether this upward trend will continue among the younger cohorts cannot be predicted with assurance.

Although the readers of Whelpton's monograph doubtless will be impressed by the huge amount of work represented in it, many of them probably will regret that it contains no data for cohorts of married women separately. Whelpton's use of cohorts regardless of marital status has the advantage of yielding fertility trends resulting from the combined factors of change in marriage rates and change in fertility of married women. In the absence of a parallel series of data for married women alone, however, he could do little more than resort to indirect and somewhat crude methods for estimating the relative importance of the two factors. To say, for instance, that about 81 per cent of the changes in first births result from changes in marriage rates because a correlation of 0.90 is found between marriage rates and rates of first births a year later, will not completely satisfy persons schooled in the tradition that correlation does not necessarily imply causation. As already stated, factors stimulating marriages may also stimulate married couples to have a child.

The need for separate data for married women is also keenly felt in the discussion regarding trends in average numbers of births to women of completed fertility. The data relating to all women of completed fertility are highly valuable in their own right. However, it is only when such data relate to married women alone that they can be strictly interpreted as trends in the size of completed family.

The above remarks do not mean that the writer attaches higher value to fertility data relating to cohorts of married women than to cohorts of women regardless of marital status. Both types of data are needed for adequate interpretation.[16]

DIFFERENTIAL FERTILITY RATIOS SINCE 1940

In view of the marked increases in births during the past decade, questions arise concerning the incidence of these increases among different elements of the population and the bearing of this on trends in fertility differentials. It should be emphasized at the outset that the data available for study of these questions are far less satisfactory than those considered in the previous section. For well-controlled analyses of recent trends in fertility differentials, we must await 1950 Census materials of the type which will be described later.

The data presented relate mainly to fertility ratios and replacement rates reported in Census Bureau releases during the past few

---

[16] For a study of changing family size among cohorts of married women in Canada, *see* Ryder, Norman B., "The Cohort Approach: Essays in the Measurement of Temporal Variations in Demographic Behavior," Ph.D. Thesis, Department of Economics and Social Institutions, Princeton University, 1951 (unpublished).

years and based upon samples of households included in the Current
Population Survey. The data have various types of limitations. The
samples are too small to maintain through the various analyses adequate breakdowns by such factors as age and rural-urban residence.
Furthermore, it must be remembered that since the fertility ratios
and replacement indices are based upon numbers of children under 5
years of age, they reflect natality conditions only for the preceding
five years. On the basis of the previous discussion there is good reason
for believing that the decade of the 'forties was highly abnormal with
respect to births. Nevertheless, it is of interest to review the Current
Population Survey materials on differential increases in fertility ratios
and reproduction rates since 1940.

In general, the increases in fertility ratios since 1940 have tended to
be proportionately heaviest among groups previously characterized by
lowest fertility and lightest among groups of highest fertility. Thus
the percentage increases have been larger in the Northeast than in the
South, larger among whites than nonwhites, larger among urban than
rural-farm populations, and probably larger in the "upper" than in
the "lower" socio-economic classes. By region, the 1940–1947 increases
in marital fertility ratios[17] were 26 per cent in the Northeast, 25 per
cent in the West, 20 per cent in the North Central States, and only 6
per cent in the South. The increases in the estimated net reproduction
rates extended from 41 and 42 per cent for the Northeast and West to
22 per cent for the South.

By color, the fertility ratios increased 18 per cent for whites and 5
per cent for nonwhites from 1940 to 1947. The increases of the net
reproduction rates were 33 per cent for the whites and 28 per cent for
the nonwhites. In this case the greater proportionate gain in mortality
among nonwhites than whites doubtless helps to account for the small
white-nonwhite difference in increase of the net reproduction rate.

By type of community, the 1940–1947 increases in fertility ratios
were 29 per cent in urban areas, 10 per cent in rural-nonfarm areas,
and only 4 per cent in rural-farm areas. The corresponding percentage
increases in net reproduction rates were 49, 27, and 12. Woofter[18]
has pointed out, however, that higher increases in fertility ratios for
urban than for rural areas may not accurately reflect trends in "indigenous fertility" because the ratios for urban areas may be unduly raised
by recent influxes of migrants from rural areas. However, one would
need to know more about the fertility characteristics of migrants in
order to assess the importance of this factor. There is good evidence

[17] Except those by occupation, the fertility ratios from the Current Population Survey that are
discussed in this paper relate to children under 5 per 1,000 *married* women 15–49 years of age. Those by
color and residence are not standardized for age. The net reproduction rates and indices of replacement
are estimated from children under 5 in relation to all females 15–49 and refer to the five years preceding
1940 and 1947.

[18] Woofter, T. J., Jr., "Trends in Rural and Urban Fertility Rates," *Rural Sociology*, xxiii, No. 1
(March, 1948), pp. 3–9.

that migration tends to select the unmarried and some evidence of selective factors in favor of childless couples and small families. The 1950 Census data should provide information on this point.

Preliminary age distributions from the 1950 Census for the country as a whole afford a more comprehensive basis for comparisons of changes in fertility ratios by color and residence than that afforded by samples from the Current Population Survey. It should be emphasized that fertility ratios based upon final figures from the 1950 Census probably will differ somewhat from those in Table 1. It should also be stated that whereas the previous discussion was concerned with changes in number of children under 5 per 1,000 *married* women 15–49 (with husband present), the fertility ratios in Table 1 are based upon children under 5 in relation to women 15–49 *regardless of marital status*. Hence, the percentage changes given in Table 1 are influenced by changes in proportions married to a much larger extent than those previously considered.

As indicated in Table 1, the percentage increase in the general fertility ratio from 1940 to 1950 probably was somewhat higher for the whites than nonwhites in the country as a whole. This, however, appears to be due entirely to differences by color in type of residence. Within each type of residence considered separately, the provisional figures indicate a slightly higher percentage increase in the fertility ratios for nonwhites than for whites. The percentage increase in general fertility ratios, like that of marital fertility ratios, was highest in urban areas and lowest in rural-farm areas. Among the nonwhites, however, the 1940–1950 increase apparently was about the same in rural nonfarm as in rural farm areas.

To return to the Current Population Survey data by education of the woman, the 1940–1947 percentage increase in fertility ratios was highest (34 per cent) for wives reporting four or more years of college and lowest (12 per cent) for those reporting only 5–6 years in grade school. The slightly higher increase (13 per cent) for the group reporting under five years of grade school was the only exception to a complete direct relation between educational attainment and percentage increase in fertility ratio. A still wider contrast was found with respect to increases in replacement indices which extended from 82 per cent for "college 4+" women to 21 per cent for the "grade school 5–6" group and 29 per cent for the group reporting under five years of school attendance.[19] The much higher increase in the replacement index for "college 4+" women than in the fertility ratio for married women of the same educational level suggests a large increase from 1940 to 1947 in the proportion of "college 4+" women who are married.

[19] U. S. Bureau of the Census: *Current Population Reports—Population Characteristics*, Series P-20, No. 18 (June 30, 1948), pp. 2–15.

TABLE 1

NUMBER OF CHILDREN UNDER FIVE PER 1,000 FEMALES 15–49 YEARS OF AGE
IN 1940 AND 1950 AND PERCENTAGE INCREASE BY RESIDENCE AND COLOR

Residence and Color	Children Under Five Per 1,000 Females 15–49 Years of Age*		Per Cent Increase 1940–1950 (Preliminary)
	1940	1950 (Preliminary)	
Total U.S.	292	423	44.9
White	287	418	45.6
Nonwhite	339	472	39.2
Urban	227	383	68.7
White	227	382	68.3
Nonwhite	224	394	75.9
Rural Nonfarm	359	492	37.0
White	358	489	36.6
Nonwhite	376	520	38.3
Rural Farm	430	526	22.3
White	409	492	20.3
Nonwhite	535	739	38.1

* The 1940 fertility ratios were computed from age data in U. S. Bureau of the Census: *Sixteenth Census of the United States, 1940. Population*, Vol. II. *Characteristics of the Population* (Washington: Government Printing Office), 1943, pp. 22–25.

The 1950 fertility ratios were computed from preliminary age distributions presented in U. S. Bureau of the Census: *1950 Census of Population, Preliminary Reports. General Characteristics of the Population of the United States, April 1, 1950*, Series PC-7, No. 1 (February 25, 1951), pp. 6–8.

The ratios presented above include no adjustment for under-enumeration of children or for the change in definition of "urban" population in 1950. They are not standardized for age. Final figures for 1950 are expected to differ somewhat from the above since the preliminary age distributions are only approximate (given in thousands only).

Despite their higher proportionate increase in children, the groups that were characterized by lowest reproduction rates during 1935–1940 tended still to be so characterized during 1942–1947. It is of interest to note, however, that whereas the net reproduction rate for the total Northeast was only 794 per 1,000 (or about 21 per cent below replacement requirements) during 1935–1940, it was 1,123 (or 12 per cent above replacement requirements) during 1942–1947. Similarly, the net reproduction rate for urban areas (726) was about 27 per cent below replacement requirements during 1935–1940 and 8.5 per cent *above* during 1942–1947.[20] The net reproduction rate for the urban groups was about 19 per cent above replacement requirements for the still later period from April, 1944 to April, 1949.

During 1935–1940 the replacement index for women reporting 1–3 years of high school was 997 per 1,000, or almost precisely unity. Above this educational level, reproduction was under replacement requirements. The deficits were 26 per cent for women completing four years of high school, 33 per cent for those attending college 1–3 years, and 48 per cent for these completing four or more years of

[20] *Ibid.*, p. 5.

college attendance. During 1942–1947 the replacement index was below unity only for the "college 4+" group and it was only about 5 per cent below in this instance.[21]

As a result of the trends described above, the magnitude of class differences in fertility ratios has tended to diminish since 1940. An example of this is apparent in Figure 4 showing number of own children under 5 per 1,000 employed men 20–59 years of age, by major occupational group. Except for the relatively high rates for unskilled laborers, the familiar inverse relation of fertility ratios to occupational class of nonagricultural workers is virtually absent. The ratios were lowest for clerical workers in both 1947 and 1949. The fertility ratio for professional men was almost as high as that for semi-skilled workers in 1947 and almost as high as that for skilled craftsmen in 1949. In both years, however, the usual ranking of highest ratios for the farm laborers and next-highest for farmers and farm managers was maintained.

Figure 5 showing fertility ratios to married women 15–49 years of age, by cash income of the family in 1949 and by educational attainment of the woman in 1940 and 1947, yield the familiar inverse relation of fertility to socio-economic status. The census release presenting the data by income and occupation contained the following statement: "The findings just discussed [by occupation] may appear to be in conflict to some extent with those shown . . . for women by family income, wherein a consistent inverse relation was found between rates of children and economic status. It may be inferred that fertility varies by income within an occupation group in such a manner that when all people of given income are grouped together without regard to occupation, the pattern of inverse association between fertility and income becomes apparent. The failure of the various major occupation groups to show a consistent relation between rates of children and the average income level of a group shows that factors such as the mores and nonpecuniary goals of the group also have an important effect on fertility."[22] The last sentence doubtless is true, but a more elementary though perhaps partial explanation might simply be that whereas the classification by occupation rather automatically tends to separate the urban and rural (or at least the agricultural and nonagricultural) workers, the straight classification by income for the country as a whole does not do this. One might reasonably suppose, particularly since "money income" is used as the basis for classification, that the proportion of rural people in the different income groups would become progressively smaller with increase of income. Likewise, it would seem safe to assume that the lower educa-

[21] *Ibid.*, p. 6.

[22] U. S. Bureau of the Census: *Current Population Reports—Population Characteristics.* Series P-20, No. 27 (February 3), 1950, p. 4.

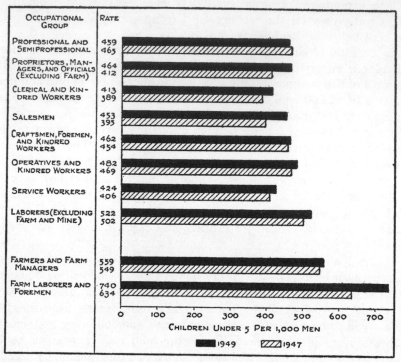

FIGURE 4. Number of own children under 5 per 1,000 men 20–59 years of age, married and wife present, by major occupational group. Rates standardized for age and relate to civilian employed males in the United States, April 1947 and 1949. (Adapted from U. S. Bureau of the Census: *Current Population Reports—Population Characteristics*, Series P-20, No. 27 (February 3, 1950), p. 11.)

tional classes are more heavily weighted with rural people than are the college groups. If this is true, the rural-urban fertility differentials serve to enhance the apparent differentials by income and education in Figure 5.

Limitations of this type are partially removed in Figure 6 showing fertility ratios in 1947 by monthly rent for urban and rural-nonfarm renters separately. For both types of communities, the inverse relation of fertility ratio to monthly rental is clear-cut and consistent. In this instance, however, it seems somewhat unfortunate, particularly for the urban sample, to consolidate rentals of $50 and over. It will be recalled that the 1940 Census data concerning children ever born by monthly rental value of the dwelling unit generally portrayed at least a leveling off, and frequently a reversal, of fertility rates at higher rental-value levels.[23] The decennial census data, of course, permit more detailed

[23] For original data on this point, *see* U. S. Bureau of the Census: *Population. Differential Fertility 1940 and 1910. Women by Number of Children Ever Born* (Washington: Government Printing Office), 1945, pp. 386–400. For a charting of fertility rates computed from these data and relating to average number of children ever born per ever-married native-white woman 45–49 years of age, by region and type of community, *see* Kiser, Clyde V. and Whelpton, P. K., "Social and Psychological Factors Affecting Fertility. IX. Fertility Planning and Fertility Rates by Socio-Economic Status," The Milbank Memorial Fund *Quarterly*, xxvii, No. 2, April, 1949, p. 189 (Reprint p. 360).

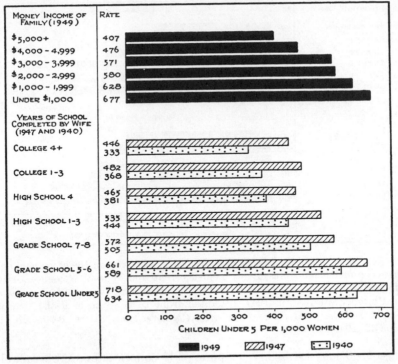

FIGURE 5. Number of children under 5 per 1,000 women 15–49 years of age, married and husband present, by total money income of the family, 1949 (top section), and by years of school completed by the wife, 1947 and 1949 (lower section). Rates standardized for age. (Adapted from U. S. Bureau of the Census: *Current Population Reports—Population Characteristics*, Series P-20, No. 18, June 30, 1948, p. 6 and Series P-20, No. 27 (February 3, 1950), p. 10.)

classifications than do the relatively small samples covered in the Current Population Survey.

Collectively, however, the materials from the Current Population Survey indicate a sharp contraction since 1940 in various types of group differences in fertility ratios. It is difficult to judge the significance of this in terms of general trends in fertility differentials. As already noted, the small size of the samples prevents sufficient subdivision of the data for adequate analysis. Also, various limitations are inherent in the use of fertility ratios for measures of trends in fertility differentials. The preceding section has indicated that the stream of births during the past decade was greatly affected by the "postponing," "making up" and "moving ahead" of marriages and first births. It may well be that the "postponing" and "making up" of marriages and births were more characteristic of the urban than of the rural and of the "upper" than of the "lower" socio-economic classes. If this is true, the sharp narrowing of differentials in fertility ratios

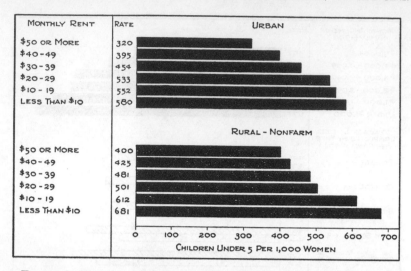

FIGURE 6. Number of children under 5 per 1,000 women 15–49 years of age, married and husband present, by monthly rent and type of residence. Rates standardized for age and relate to renters in urban and rural-nonfarm areas of the United States, April, 1947. (Adapted from U. S. Bureau of the Census: *Current Population Reports—Population Characteristics*, Series P-20, No. 18 (June 30, 1948), p. 17.)

since 1940 may be highly temporary. If cohort data were available, they probably would indicate a considerably less narrowing of differentials since 1940 than that suggested by the fertility ratios.

By way of perspective it is useful to note that whereas any trend toward a contraction of group differences in fertility since 1940 resulted largely from differential *increases* in fertility, in previous years the trend of fertility differentials probably was closely related to the spread of contraception and to the differential *declines* in fertility. If, as seems likely, contraceptive practices originated among the "upper" urban classes and subsequently spread downward in the socio-economic hierarchy and outward to rural areas, the process would yield first a widening and later a narrowing of class differences in fertility.

There is clear evidence of a marked widening of differences in fertility by occupational class in England and Wales during the quarter century preceding 1891.[24] As for later years, Innes' analysis suggests a sharp contraction of differences in birth rates by occupational class from 1921 to 1931.[25] This latter finding is not corroborated by more recent studies made for the Royal Commission on Population but the main report of that body does state that the difference between

[24] *See* T. H. C. Stevenson's analysis in *Fertility of Marriage*, Census of England and Wales (1911), Vol. XIII, Part II (London, His Majesty's Stationery Office), 1917.
[25] Innes, J. W., "Class Birth Rates in England and Wales, 1921–1931," The Milbank Memorial Fund *Quarterly*, xix, No. 1 (January, 1941), pp. 73–75.

average size of family of the manual and non-manual workers "has perhaps been narrowing."[26]

As for the United States, there are at least suggestions of the enlargement of differences in fertility by occupation during 1850–1910.[27] There are also indications of some diminution of class differences in fertility after about 1925. In his study of 1930 Census materials for the East North Central States on number of children under 5 per couple married 5–9 years, Notestein found that exceptions to the inverse relation of fertility ratios to monthly rental value of the home occurred within the highest rental-value groups.[28] The present writer found analogous exceptions by occupation, education, and family income in his analysis of National Health Survey data relating to births during the preceding year.[29] The more comprehensive 1940 Census data on children ever born indicate similar types of exception to the generally inverse relation of fertility to occupational group, education, and, as previously stated, monthly rental value of the home.[30]

The same type of exceptions to an otherwise inverse relation of fertility of socio-economic status was also found for the total group of "relatively fecund" couples in the Indianapolis Study of Social and Psychological Factors Affecting Fertility. When the analysis was restricted to couples having no pregnancies except those that were deliberately planned by stopping contraception in order to conceive, a rather consistently *direct* relation of fertility to income, occupation, education, and rental value of the home was found. Furthermore, as noted in Figure 7, among these same "number and spacing planned" couples, fertility was *directly* associated with rating of each spouse on an "index of economic security," which was based mainly upon the self-ratings of each spouse on a variety of specific items such as confidence in meeting future expenses and frequency of facing the possibility of husband's pay-cut or unemployment.

[26] Royal Commission on Population, *Report* (London: His Majesty's Stationery Office, 1949), p. 152.

[27] Sallume, Xarifa and Notestein, Frank W., "Trends in the Size of Families Completed Prior to 1910 in Various Social Classes," *American Journal of Sociology*, xxxviii, No. 3 (November, 1932), pp. 398–408.

Kiser, Clyde V., "Trends in the Fertility of Social Classes from 1900–1910," *Human Biology*, v, No. 2 (May, 1933), pp. 256–273.

[28] Notestein, Frank W., "Differential Fertility in the East North Central States," The Milbank Memorial Fund *Quarterly*, xvi, No. 2 (April, 1938), pp. 173–191.

[29] Kiser, Clyde V., *Group Differences in Urban Fertility*. (Baltimore: The Williams and Wilkins Company, 1942.)

[30] *See* footnote 23 above, and U. S. Bureau of the Census: *Population. Differential Fertility, 1940 and 1910. Fertility by Duration of Marriage* (Washington: Government Printing Office), 1947, 338 pp.

Note: Caution must be exercised in comparing 1910 and 1940 Census materials on fertility differentials by occupational class on the basis of data avialable. Both sets of published data are based upon samples and there may be differences arising from changes in urbanization and composition of broad occupational classes. However, among native-white married women, whereas the wives of professional men tended rather uniformly to exhibit lowest age-specific fertility rates throughout ages 20–49 in 1910 in both urban and rural-nonfarm areas, the wives of men of the clerical class frequently exhibited lowest rates in 1940. Also, within urban (but not rural-nonfarm) areas, the proportionate excess in the fertility of the unskilled laborers over that of the professional group was higher in 1910 than in 1940 throughout ages 20–49.

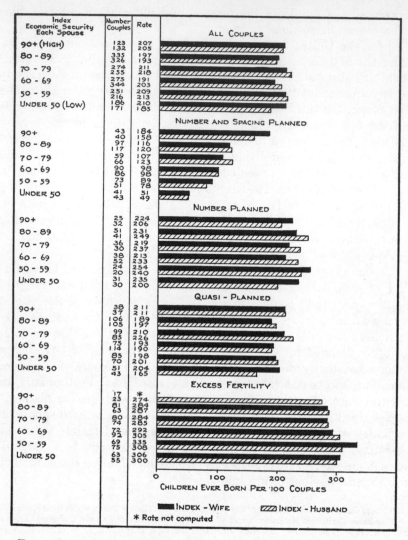

FIGURE 7. Number of children ever born per 100 couples, by fertility-planning status and index of economic security of each spouse. Data relate to 1,444 "relatively fecund" couples in the Indianapolis study. (From The Milbank Memorial Fund *Quarterly*, Vol. xxix, No. 1 (January, 1951), p. 83.)

The 1950 Census secured data on number of children ever born for a $3\frac{1}{3}$ per cent sample of ever-married women in the United States. Like the data collected in the 1940 Census, these materials can be analyzed not only by such factors as age, color, nativity, geographic area, type of residence (urban, rural nonfarm, rural farm), but also by measures of socio-economic status, such as occupational class of the husband and educational attainment of the wife, and by refinements regarding times married, age at marriage, and duration of marriage.

In addition, data on spacing of children have been prepared for a sub-sample of families in which all children ever born were living at home at the time of the 1950 Census. Although budgetary restrictions may prevent the Bureau of the Census from carrying out tabulations on differential fertility as extensive as those contained in the valuable series of special reports entitled *Differential Fertility, 1940 and 1910*, it is hoped that the Bureau will be able to provide a really substantial body of 1950 data on differential fertility in this country. These data would be of enormous help in interpreting the trends of fertility differentials during the past decade. They would also be of value to persons concerned with other aspects of our population problems.

Although the materials presented in the two sections of this paper provide little basis for judging the future trend of either fertility or fertility differentials, they do suggest that people having fertility under control through either delay of marriage or practice of contraception have contributed more than their proportionate share to the increase in births during the past decade. It seems possible that as the knowledge of means of family limitation becomes more widespread, short-run fluctuations in the birth rate may become more common than they have been in the past. Another implication of the spread of knowledge of fertility control is the increasing importance of learning more about attitudes and motivations regarding family size and how these are affected by current economic and social conditions.

BIRTH RATES AND THE INTERWAR

BUSINESS CYCLES

By Virginia L. Galbraith and Dorothy S. Thomas

As YULE remarked in 1906: "It seems a curious fact that while the relations of the marriage-rate to economic factors have comparatively frequently drawn the attention of statistical writers, their effects on the birth-rate do not appear to have been so fully discussed. Yet such a discussion must form the very basis of the theory of population in a modern industrial state."[1] Yule's own analysis of this relationship was one of the first which met the essential statistical requirements of eliminating secular trends and computing correlation coefficients between the deviations from the trends of the series under consideration. Analyzing first the relationship between indexes of business cycles, namely a price index (1865–1896) and an index of unemployment (1870–1895), and marriage rates for England and Wales, he found correlation coefficients of +.795 and −.873 respectively. These results confirmed the results of earlier studies by Hooker[2] and March[3] with similar data and similar methods. Proceeding then to an analysis of the correlation of the marriage rate and the birth rate, for the period 1850–1896, he found a maximum correlation of +.479 with the birth rate lagging two years, and concluded that the oscillations in the birth rate were influenced by economic oscillations not only indirectly through their response to oscillations in the marriage rate, but also directly. Because of defects in the data at his disposal, he confessed himself unable to make a clearcut analysis of the causal nexus. However, by calculating the course of marriage rate deviations and deducing the birth rate deviations for each year "using rough graphically interpolated values for the births per thousand married women,"[4] he estimated that the direct factor possibly accounted for half of the amplitude of the oscillations. In a later paper (1925),[5] he did not carry this type of analysis further, but correlated marriage, birth (with a lag of

[1] G. Udny Yule, "On the Changes in the Marriage- and Birth-Rates in England and Wales During the Past Half Century; with an Inquiry as to Their Probable Causes," *Journal of the Royal Statistical Society*, vol. 69, 1906, p. 122.

[2] R. H. Hooker, "Correlation of the Marriage-Rate with Trade," *Journal of the Royal Statistical Society*, vol. 64, 1901, pp. 485–492.

[3] Lucien March, "Comparaison numérique de courbes statistiques," *Journal de la Société de Statistique de Paris*, vol. 46, 1905, pp. 255–277; 306–311.

[4] Yule, *loc. cit.* (1906), p. 124.

[5] G. Udny Yule, "The Growth of Population and the Factors Which Control It," *Journal of the Royal Statistical Society* vol. 88, 1925, pp. 1–58.

two years) and death rate deviations with a foreign trade series for 1859–1908. The coefficients of correlation were +.78, +.47, and +.18 respectively. He concluded that, in the case of death rates, there was not "definite consonance between the waves. . . . The waves in the marriage-rate, on the other hand . . . show a remarkable consilience with those in trade, and the birth-rate also exhibits, up till about 1895 at least, waves with a lag of two years, or rather more, on the trade waves. . . . It suffices to note that here again it is the 'preventive check' rather than the 'positive check' which appears to be operative."[6]

One of the earliest analyses based on American data was made by Ogburn and Thomas in 1922.[7] Using marriage and birth rates for the period 1870–1920 for six states (Connecticut, Massachusetts, Michigan, New Hampshire, Rhode Island, and Vermont) and a composite index of business cycles for the United States, they found a correlation coefficient of +.87 between business cycles and marriage rates and of +.33 between business cycles and birth rates, when births lagged by one year. They, too, concluded that the latter relationship was partly direct, partly to be attributed to the "fact that marriages are so highly correlated with business conditions."[8] Thomas, in 1925,[9] correlated birth rates in England and Wales with a composite index of British business cycles for the period 1854–1913, after first demonstrating a correlation of +.67 between business cycles and marriage rates. The birth rate correlation amounted to only +.29 with two years' lag, and to +.30 with three years' lag behind business cycles. She, too, emphasized the "preventive check," giving considerable weight, in her interpretations, to the fact that the correlations between marriages and business cycles tended to diminish during the period under consideration, while those between births and business cycles rose steadily to a maximum of +.64 for the subperiod 1895–1913. "It suggests the interesting hypothesis that, whereas a business depression formerly led to 'prudential restraint' through abstention from marriage, it now leads to a more widespread and deliberate use of birth control." In common with the other investigators mentioned, she assumed, without rigorous proof, that "the response of the birth-rate to the business cycle, then, is probably partly direct, through the differential conscious control of births in prosperity and depression, and partly indirect, through a reflection of the fluctuations in the marriage rate."[10]

Other studies have appeared sporadically in the course of the past two decades. In general they have confirmed the tendencies noted by the earlier investigators, but, with one exception, which will be noted

[6] Yule, *loc. cit.* (1925), p. 30.

[7] William F. Ogburn and Dorothy S. Thomas, "The Influence of the Business Cycle on Certain Social Conditions," *Quarterly Publications of the American Statistical Association*, vol. 18, 1922, pp. 324–340.

[8] *Ibid.*, p. 339.

[9] Dorothy S. Thomas, *Social Aspects of the Business Cycle*, London, 1925.

[10] *Ibid.*, pp. 99–100.

in the following paragraph, have added nothing new. They were hampered by the fact that the World War had introduced a major break in the continuity of the time series and that not enough time had passed to give a new series that would be statistically significant. With the onset of a second World War, it is now apparent that the experience of the two decades separating the two wars will, whether long enough for statistical significance or not, make possible the only analysis for some time to come of the "normal" impact of business cycles upon birth rates. This is our justification for the present short-period analysis.

A recent study by Lotka and Spiegelman[11] provided us with data more suitable than any available earlier for such an analysis. These investigators computed maternity frequencies for the white population according to order of birth for the expanding Birth Registration Area of the United States by years from 1920 through 1938. "For this purpose, maternity frequencies have been computed separately for each order of birth within each quinquennial age group of women in the reproductive period. Then the frequencies were summed for all these quinquennial age groups so as to give a total for each order of birth, without regard to the age of the mother."[12] Thus, for the interwar period, "efficient" rates of births on the basis of those exposed to the risk of giving birth are available, whereas earlier studies had to depend on crude rates, the variations in which were partly due to extraneous variations in the base on which they were computed. Furthermore, the Lotka-Spiegelman series, being of the abstract type, are uninfluenced by variations in the proportions of women at different ages *within* the childbearing period. Finally, their organization of the data by order of birth makes possible more clear-cut analysis of the direct response than has been possible previously.

Lotka and Spiegelman did not smooth their series nor did they analyze the cyclical fluctuations. Their primary interest was in the general direction of change in the several orders of birth. They referred, however, to analyses which had been published in the *Statistical Bulletin of the Metropolitan Life Insurance Company* where first differences of birth rates and of marriage rates for New York State were correlated and showed that "almost without exception, an increase in the marriage rate from one year to the next was followed—with a lag of one year—by an increase in the birth rate of first children. When we recall the high correlation that has been found to exist between the marriage rate and economic conditions, it is to be expected that the time series of first births will also be closely correlated with economic conditions." They pointed out further that "the year 1933 marks an important turning

    [11] Alfred J. Lotka and Mortimer Spiegelman, "The Trend of the Birth Rate by Age of Mother and Order of Birth," this JOURNAL, vol. 35, 1940, pp. 595–601.
    [12] *Ibid.*, p. 596.

point" for first births and also, but to a lesser degree, for second births, both of which exhibited a marked upswing as a response to improving economic conditions. They detected no such upswing in births of higher order. They suggested, therefore, that "since . . . the birth rate is being influenced in increasing degree by the maternity frequency of first births, it appears that economic conditions are playing a greater role than in the past in determining the course of our birth rate."[13]

There are, clearly, alternative hypotheses that should be tested in order to determine the role that economic conditions play. On the one hand, it might be inferred that the economic influence is entirely an indirect matter: economic conditions influence the marriage rate, the marriage rate influences the rate of first births, and variations in first births are sufficiently strong to influence the course of variations in total births. It is our contention that an hypothesis of this sort can be tested only if the divergent trends are first eliminated from each order of birth series and deviations from these trends are then correlated with deviations from the trend of an index of economic conditions. If the oscillations of birth orders higher than the first are uncorrelated with business cycles, this hypothesis will (within the limits set by the data and the techniques of analysis) be confirmed. If, however, these oscillations are significantly correlated with business cycles, the evidence may be considered to favor an alternative hypothesis, namely, that there is a direct response of births to business cycles, independent of the correlation of marriage rates with birth rates.

Through the courtesy of Dr. Lotka, the Metropolitan series were made available to us, and it is the purpose of this paper to explore these series with the same techniques used in analyzing the relationship of other series to business cycles. At the same time, in order to bring the Ogburn-Thomas analysis up to date, we have made a similar analysis of births by order and of marriages for a group of northeastern industrial states. We refer to these series subsequently as "Metropolitan series" and "our series."

A brief description of our series follows. *Marriage rates:* From compilations made by Stouffer and Spencer,[14] from scattered published reports of State Bureaus of Vital Statistics, and by correspondence, we were able to obtain the yearly number of marriages from 1919 to 1939 for New York, Connecticut, and Massachusetts; 1919–1938 for New Jersey; 1921–1937 for Pennsylvania; 1919–1937, and 1939 for Rhode Island. These were combined into a single series and rates per 1,000 estimated annual population computed, annual population being estimated by straight line interpolation between the censuses of 1920

[13] *Ibid.*, p. 598.

[14] Samuel A. Stouffer and Lyle M. Spencer, "Marriage and Divorce in Recent Years," *Annals of the American Academy of Political and Social Science*, vol. 188, 1936, pp. 56–59.

Samuel A. Stouffer and Lyle M. Spencer, "Recent Increases in Marriage and Divorce," *American Journal of Sociology*, vol. 44, 1939, pp. 551–554.

and 1930, and between those of 1930 and 1940. *Crude birth rates:* The total number of births for each of the same states was obtained annually from 1919 to 1938 from *Vital Statistics of the United States,* and *Birth, Stillbirth, and Mortality Statistics,* and rates per 1,000 population similarly computed. *Birth rates by order of birth:* First, second, third, fourth, and fifth and subsequent births were obtained from the same source for all these states except Massachusetts, which does not collect data on order of birth. Rates were again computed per 1,000 population.

Our marriage series thus included one more state than our birth order series. Due, however, to the introduction of residence and medical requirements for marriage in several of these states, it was felt that the inclusion of Massachusetts data gave a fairer picture of variations in the marriage rate than if this series had included exactly the same states as used in the birth order series.

As noted, the Metropolitan series consists of maternity frequencies by order of birth. We used their data for first, second, third, and fourth births and combined their data for all orders higher than fourth into a series comparable with our "fifth and subsequent births." Our birth order series have one advantage over the comparable Metropolitan series: they are limited to a group of highly industrialized states and the same states are included throughout the period, whereas the Metropolitan series cover the expanding birth registration area. Since the states admitted to the area during the period under consideration were among the most rural in the nation, the Metropolitan series cannot be considered as economically homogeneous. But the Metropolitan series are far superior to ours in another respect, namely, control of the factors of age and sex in the basic population.

As an index of business cycles, we used the United States Bureau of Labor Statistics adjusted index of factory employment, with the base period at 1923–1925.[15]

Our techniques of analysis may be briefly described as follows: Trends were computed for all series (ours, Metropolitan, and business cycles). Linear trends were found, upon trial, to be unsatisfactory. Second degree parabolas were, therefore, fitted by the least squares method, and were found to cut the cycles satisfactorily. Per cent deviations of data from trends were then correlated as follows: business cycles with marriages; business cycles with each order-of-birth series and with total birth series; marriages with our first-birth series. In all cases, birth series lagged by one year. Both linear and curvilinear (second degree parabolic) regressions were computed, as well as the net regression of first births (our series) on business cycles holding the marriage rate constant. Similarly, both the Pearsonian correlation coeffi-

---

[15] *Monthly Labor Review* and *Federal Reserve Bulletin,* various issues since 1935.

CHART I

RELATIONSHIP BETWEEN BUSINESS CYCLES 1919-1937 AND BIRTHS (ONE YEAR'S LAG) AS SHOWN BY SCATTER DIAGRAMS AND REGRESSIONS, INCLUDING NET REGRESSION OF FIRST BIRTHS, HOLDING MARRIAGE RATES CONSTANT

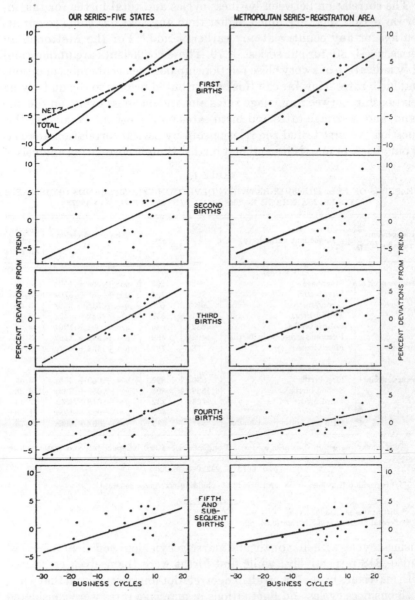

cient (r) and the correlation index (ρ) were computed for each series. The relationships were, in all cases, approximately linear (see Chart I). There was slight second degree curvilinearity in the relationship between business cycles and some of the higher orders of birth. The curvilinearity was, however, so slight and of such doubtful statistical significance, that we accepted the relationship as being linear. Analysis of our series and the Metropolitan order-of-birth series yielded highly consistent results.

The correlation between business cycles and total births for this interwar period was very much higher than any that has come to our attention for any country at any earlier period.[16] For the Metropolitan series, $r = +.80$; for our series, $+.79$. These coefficients are unquestionably indicative of a very close relationship between economic conditions and birth rates. How far can this be attributed merely to the underlying relationship between marriage rates and the business cycle, on the one hand, and marriage rates and birth rates on the other? To answer this question, we first tested the relationship by partial correlation analysis of our series for marriages and first births. Simple correlation analysis of

TABLE I

MEASURES OF RELATIONSHIP BETWEEN DEVIATIONS FROM TRENDS OF BUSINESS CYCLES, MARRIAGE RATES, AND BIRTH RATES, 1919–1937*

Independent variable (x)	Dependent variable (y)	r	ρ**	Linear regression equation	Standard error of estimate
	(Our series)				
Business cycles	Marriages	.848	.868	$y = +.363 + .460x$	3.38
	First births	.793	.795	$y = +.685 + .370x$	3.37
	Second births	.623	.626	$y = -.018 + .238x$	3.54
	Third births	.831	.837	$y = -.052 + .269x$	2.13
	Fourth births	.632	.646	$y = +.061 + .199x$	2.88
	Fifth and subsequent births	.493	.499	$y = +.381 + .158x$	3.30
Marriages	First births	.778	.781	$y = +.458 + .671x$	3.47
	(Metropolitan series)				
Business cycles	First births	.830	.832	$y = -.089 + .308x$	2.44
	Second births	.589	.593	$y = -.056 + .202x$	3.28
	Third births	.723	.732	$y = -.048 + .189x$	2.14
	Fourth births	.571	.595	$y = -.022 + .105x$	1.78
	Fifth and subsequent births	.531	.535	$y = -.007 + .092x$	1.75

Total linear regression, business cycles (x_1) and marriages (x_2) independent, and births (y) dependent.

$$y = .5675 + .222x_1 + .3245x_2$$

Net regression (business cycles and first births, holding marriages constant).

$$y = .7229 + .222x_1$$

* Birth rates lagging one year.
** Second-degree parabolic relationship.

business cycles with first births and marriages yielded coefficients of $+.793$ and $+.848$ respectively; while first births were themselves correlated with marriages by $+.778$. Multiple correlation analysis showed that when both business cycles and fluctuations in marriage rates were considered as independent variables and first births as the dependent variable, the

[16] Correlation coefficients between the total birth series of each of the six states and the business cycle index were also computed. They are: Massachusetts, $+.46$; Rhode Island, $+.58$; Connecticut, $+.79$; New York, $+.68$; New Jersey, $+.77$; Pennsylvania, $+.70$. The damping down of the coefficients for individual states due to random fluctuations, is apparent, since the coefficient for the six states combined was $+.79$.

coefficient was +.818. Taken in conjunction with the simple coefficients of +.793 and +.778 this result leads to the inference that the increase in "explainable" variance attributable to business cycles may be somewhat greater than the comparable increase attributable to marriage fluctuations. That is, when marriage fluctuations are held constant, the partial correlation between business cycles and first births is +.40; whereas where business cycles are held constant, the partial correlation between marriage rates and first births is +.33. Since the differences are of doubtful statistical significance, partial correlation analysis gave rather ambiguous results, and was further unsatisfactory because of the small number of observations and the inherent unreliability of our marriage series.

The question can be approached far more directly by analyzing the correlation with business cycles of orders of birth higher than the first. For it is highly improbable that births of higher order than first are dependent to any extent upon marriages of the year preceding these births. Any observed relationship between business cycles and second, third, fourth, fifth, and subsequent births of the following year may, therefore, be assumed to indicate direct control and release of births in response to economic conditions.

From second through fifth and subsequent births, both our series and the Metropolitan show what might be called a very high to moderately high correlation with business cycles; for second births, +.62 and +.59, for third, +.83 and +.72; for fourth, +.63 and +.57; and even for fifth and subsequent, +.49 and +.53. The regression coefficients are, in all cases, unquestionably significant (see Chart I). The slope is steepest for first births and lessens rather systematically through subsequent orders. On the average, a change of 10 in the per cent deviations of business cycles from their trend is accompanied by the following changes in the same direction in our series: 3.7 per cent in first births; 2.4 per cent for second; 2.7 per cent for third; 2.0 per cent for fourth; and 1.6 per cent for fifth and subsequent. The changes in the Metropolitan series are consistent in pattern, but slightly less in amount, namely: 3.1 per cent, 2.0 per cent, 1.9 per cent, 1.1 per cent, and 0.9 per cent. Thus, although the correlation is marked, there is evidently a diminishing effect from first through subsequent orders. When, however, the net regression (for our series), of first births on business cycles, holding marriage rates constant, is computed, the slope is greatly diminished (from 3.7 per cent per 10 units to 2.2 per cent), becoming, in fact, less than those of second or third births and only slightly greater than that of fourth births. This suggests that the direct restriction of first births during depressions is somewhat less than that of immediately higher orders, a finding that is compatible with the spread of the small family system. The conclusion seems inescapable that, during the past two decades, the preventive check has been extensively in operation. Marriages are

CHART II

RELATIONSHIP BETWEEN BUSINESS CYCLES AND MARRIAGES AND BIRTHS (ONE
YEAR'S LAG) AS SHOWN BY TIME SERIES OF PER CENT DEVIATIONS
FROM TRENDS (IN UNITS OF STANDARD DEVIATIONS)

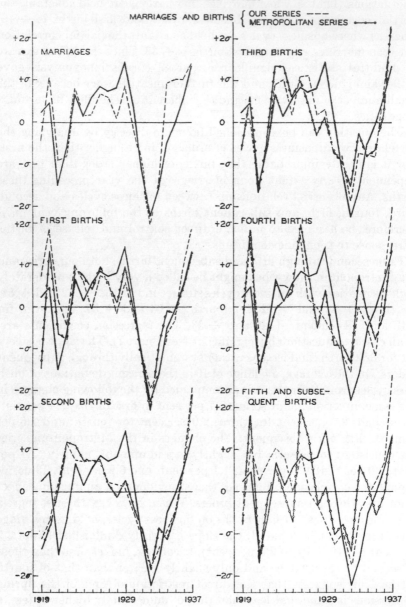

TABLE II

BUSINESS CYCLES INDEX, BIRTH RATES BY ORDER OF BIRTH, FIVE STATES; AND MARRIAGE RATES, SIX STATES

Crude rates per 1,000 population

Year	Business cycle index	Marriages	First births	Second births	Third births	Fourth births	Fifth and subsequent births
1919	106.7	9.8	5.6	5.2	3.7	2.6	6.1
1920	107.1	10.4	6.8	4.9	3.6	2.5	6.0
1921	82.0	8.9	7.1	4.9	3.5	2.6	6.1
1922	90.7	8.7	6.4	5.0	3.2	2.3	5.6
1923	103.8	9.4	6.1	5.1	3.2	2.2	5.5
1924	96.4	8.8	6.5	4.9	3.3	2.2	5.3
1925	99.8	8.6	6.3	4.8	3.2	2.1	5.0
1926	101.7	8.7	6.0	4.7	3.0	2.0	4.6
1927	99.5	8.5	6.2	4.6	3.0	2.0	4.5
1928	99.7	8.1	6.1	4.6	2.9	1.8	4.1
1929	106.0	8.4	5.8	4.3	2.7	1.7	3.8
1930	92.4	7.8	6.0	4.2	2.6	1.6	3.5
1931	78.1	7.3	5.7	4.0	2.4	1.5	3.2
1932	66.3	6.6	5.4	3.8	2.3	1.4	3.0
1933	73.4	7.1	5.1	3.6	2.1	1.3	2.7
1934	85.7	8.3	5.2	3.6	2.1	1.3	2.6
1935	91.3	8.5	5.5	3.6	2.0	1.2	2.4
1936	99.0	8.8	5.5	3.6	2.0	1.1	2.2
1937	108.6	8.8	6.0	3.7	1.9	1.1	2.0
1938	89.7	7.7	6.0	3.7	1.9	1.1	2.0
1939	96.9	8.1	6.3	3.9	1.9	1.1	1.9

Per cent deviations from secular trends*

Year	Business cycle index	Marriages	First births	Second births	Third births	Fourth births	Fifth and subsequent births
1919	2.7	−2.9	4.0	−5.0	.3	−2.3	−2.1
1920	5.5	6.6	10.2	−3.0	.3	−5.7	−3.9
1921	−17.7	−5.9	.9	1.0	−5.6	−2.7	−1.0
1922	−7.3	−5.3	−2.4	5.2	−2.7	1.9	−2.6
1923	7.9	5.1	5.5	3.4	3.4	1.9	−3.9
1924	1.7	1.0	3.4	3.2	3.9	1.5	−3.1
1925	6.7	1.1	−4.2	3.3	4.2	6.4	3.4
1926	10.0	4.3	3.4	3.4	4.3	.6	−.0
1927	8.6	3.8	3.9	.7	.7	−.0	−1.3
1928	9.6	.5	−3.3	.5	−1.2	−1.2	−3.0
1929	17.1	5.5	−1.2	−2.2	−2.8	−2.6	−4.8
1930	−2.4	−1.1	−5.9	−5.0	−3.0	−4.1	−3.8
1931	−13.4	−6.9	−10.8	−7.9	−7.1	−5.8	−6.6
1932	−26.5	−15.5	−8.9	−6.0	−2.9	−1.6	−1.9
1933	−18.9	−9.2	−3.5	−4.0	−3.1	−4.3	−.4
1934	−5.9	5.9	−1.8	−1.9	2.7	1.9	−.9
1935	6.5	6.5	5.3	3.1	8.6	8.9	2.6
1936	6.9	6.6	10.3	11.1			10.5
1937	15.9	9.0					

Constants of Secular Trends

	Period	Origin	a	b	c	Standard deviations of per cent deviations from secular trends
Business cycles	1919–1939	1929	90.50	−.37	+.0965	11.81
Marriages	1919–1939	1928–29	7.96	−.09	+.0126	6.40
First births	1919–1938	1928–29	5.87	−.05	+.0035	5.52
Second births	1919–1938	1928–29	4.31	−.09	+.0009	4.52
Third births	1919–1938	1928–29	2.73	−.10	−.0001	3.83
Fourth births	1919–1938	1928–29	1.75	−.09	+.0010	3.72
Fifth and subsequent births	1919–1938	1928–29	3.98	−.25	+.0009	3.80

* Birth rates lagging by one year.

"controlled" during depressions, and, within marriages, births of all orders are likewise controlled. Since birth rates of higher orders are overweighted with births to the lower income, occupational, and educational classes, it is clear that the birth control movement has penetrated deep into the social structure during the past two decades.

Examination of Chart II throws further light on the nature of the relationships. The depression of the early twenties is clearly reflected in all orders except second and fifth and subsequent; while the depression and subsequent revival of the late thirties leave their marks on all orders. Third and later orders, however, show a sharper revival in 1934 and more of a recession in 1935–36 than the index of employment for 1933 and 1934–35 would lead one to expect. There is, of course, always a possibility that bad trend fitting in one or the other series distorts the relationship. The failure of second births to follow the business cycle index during most of the twenties cannot be readily explained, especially since third and even fourth births responded so well. The lack of correspondence may, of course, be due in part to the aftereffects of the exceptionally high marriage cohorts of 1918. The post-war inflation of marriages would probably have had its primary effect on first births in 1919, which is not included in our series. By 1921–22, these cohorts might well have had a sufficient number of second children to affect this series. That the rhythm extended beyond the second child is, however, highly doubtful.

Table II gives the basic data and the statistical constants for our own series.

THE RELATION OF EMPLOYMENT LEVELS

TO BIRTHS IN GERMANY

By Dudley Kirk

SINCE 1933 Nazi Germany has made an organized effort to raise the German birth rate, and the success of this positive population policy is evidenced by a notable rise in births prior to the present war. The birth rate, which had declined to 14.7 per 1,000 in 1933, had risen to 20.3 in 1939. The latter is not a particularly high birth rate and represents a fertility only slightly above that required for permanent replacement of the population. But because fertility was so low before, the rise is an important one. In absolute terms there were 436,000 more births in the Old Reich in 1939 than in 1933. In the German-speaking areas of the Greater Reich the increase was about 500,000. The comparative magnitude of this increase is suggested by the fact that there were only 612,000 births in France in 1938, 67,000 less than in 1933.

A number of students of population, including Whelpton, Hankins, Glass, and the Taeubers, have appraised the German population effort with some care.[2] All of these writers have pointed to the difficulties of sorting out the effects of specific policies, such as marriage loans, grants to large families, family allowances, suppression of abortions, etc., as over against other factors influencing fertility. It is the purpose of this article to evaluate one of the most important of the "other factors," namely, employment conditions. Also, it is hoped that certain of the conclusions may have more general ap-

[1] From the Office of Population Research, Princeton University, in cooperation with the Milbank Memorial Fund.

[2] Whelpton, P. K.: Why the Large Rise in the German Birth Rate? *American Journal of Sociology*, November, 1935, xli, No. 3, pp. 299-313; Hankins, Frank H.: German Policies for Increasing Births. *American Journal of Sociology*, March, 1937, xlii, No. 5, pp. 630-652; Glass, David V.: POPULATION POLICIES AND MOVEMENTS IN EUROPE. Oxford, 1940, pp. 269-313; Taeuber, Conrad and Irene B.: German Fertility Trends, 1933-39. *American Journal of Sociology*, September, 1940, xlvi, No. 2, pp. 150-164.

plicability regarding the relations between economic conditions and births.

Employment indices, as opposed to other economic data, were selected for a number of reasons. Among the most important is that the condition of employment or unemployment is a fact of immediate and decisive importance in people's lives. As a motivating factor, it is probably far more important than diffuse concern about rising costs of living, annoyance over increased taxes, or even the fear and the fact of wage reductions. These things pale by comparison with the personal and familial calamity of losing one's job without much hope of getting another one.

A conclusive reason for using this index for the purpose at hand is the fact that in Nazi Germany other economic indices of significance to population trends, such as wages, cost of living, etc., remained practically constant, while births rose. On the face of things, these other economic variables could not have been important direct influences on fertility. They would be such only if constancy itself tended to increase the number of births through the economic security that predictability suggests. Under a revolutionary regime that stressed turmoil and change, it would be surprising if this were the case.

In contrast with wage and price changes, changes in employment were enormous. When Hitler became Chancellor in 1933 there were fewer than 12,000,000 employed persons and about 6,000,000 unemployed. At the outbreak of war in 1939 there were about 21,-500,000 employed and about 40,000 unemployed in the same territory; that is, practically all the unemployed were reabsorbed into the economy and about 4,000,000 more were drawn from other sources, including immigration from abroad.

It should be noted in passing that these figures do not relate to the total labor force, but to persons covered by the sickness insurance system, which includes practically all wage employees. This system does not include peasants, many artisans and professional people, entrepreneurs, and persons in the higher income brackets. It does include persons in labor camps, but not members of the armed forces. That is, the increase in the size of the Germany army was over and above the increase in the number employed. For "Folk" Germans employment opportunities in Hitler's Germany were much superior to what they had been in the latter years of the Republic. Also, they were better than in neighboring countries, judging by the fact that there was a net immigration of 500,000 persons between 1933 and 1939. This was in excess of the much more publicized out-migration of refugees. It does not include organized migration of the Baltic and other Eastern Germans to the Reich.[3]

The impact of this reemployment on the economic outlook of the German people must have been very important. A comparable achievement in the United States would have involved the reemployment of perhaps 20,000,000 persons between 1933 and 1939. It is unbelievable that such an increase in employment would have had no effect on fertility.

In order to carry out an organized attack on the problem of the influence of employment on births, a set of *a priori* hypotheses was formulated to be tested by whatever statistical evidence was available. The hypotheses were:

(a) In the short run, changes in the birth rate are closely associated with employment levels. Employment conditions are not an independent cause of long range secular trends in birth rates, but they may be decisive in determining short range fluctuations.

(b) The relationship should have increased as fertility declined in time.

(c) The relationship should be greater in urban and industrial regions and countries than in rural regions and countries.

Considering the first of these, it seems rather evident that the secular trend of the birth rate could not be associated positively with employment conditions, because over any considerable time period, birth rates have declined and employment has not. To check the influence of employment over shorter periods, a series of correlations of employment indices and births by months and by quarters was made, using data from various countries and for various time periods. Experimentation revealed that the highest correlations were achieved where births lagged nine months, or three-quarters, behind employment, depending on the nature of the data. The correlations in Germany were generally high.

Figure 1 presents the monthly fluctuation of employment indices

[3] On the basis of census data for Austria and the Sudetenland, it seems likely that the bulk of the immigrants into Germany between 1933 and 1939 were German-speaking persons from these areas.

Fig. 1. Employment indices and births in Germany, 1930-1939, births lagged nine months.

and births from 1930-1939, with births lagged nine months. The correspondence of the two is clear throughout, though the rise of births much outdistanced the rise in employment in the first years of Nazi control. Over the whole period the correlation was $+.79$ for quarterly data.

A first question obviously arises as to whether the apparent high correlation was merely the result of the chance concatenation of basic trends. The association of employment and births in the early 'thirties might well be a fortuitous relationship arising from the

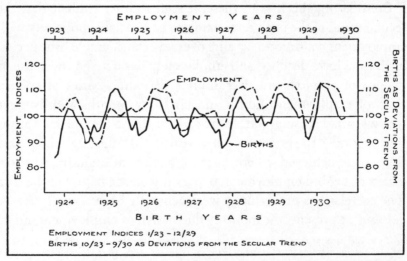

Fig. 2. Employment indices and births in Germany, 1923-1930, births lagged nine months with secular trend removed.

effects of depression conditions on employment and the quite unrelated continuation of the downward secular trend of births. In the
later period the rise of employment and of births might well be the
result of completely independent aspects of Nazi policies. As is well
known the degree of correlation in time series may be greatly mag-
nified by such coincidence in trends.

To test this possibility, reference was made to the relationship
between employment and births in the period from 1923 to 1930.
The correlations in the earlier period were not of a very high order,
but they were statistically significant. However, when the downward secular trend of births was removed, as in Figure 2, the coefficients were found to be quite high. This was especially true of
the period after 1926. The association was weak in the earlier years,
perhaps in part because of the vagaries of inflation and its aftermath, which so disturbed the German economy through 1923 and
1924. The coefficient of correlation in the period 1923-1926 was only
$+.37$, as compared with $+.88$ in the period 1926-1929, and $+.62$
over the entire series.

This chart also affords something of a test of the second hypothesis, namely, that the relationship between employment and births
should have increased as fertility declined in time. The relationship
in the early part of the period was somewhat tenuous, later increasing and rising to a rather impressive association in the latter part.
However, as has been indicated, the early period was much disturbed by inflation and this test is not completely adequate, though
what little evidence there is accords with the hypothesis. The testing of this hypothesis in other countries was generally hampered by
the difficulties of getting coherent employment series for periods
before 1930.

It is apparent in the entire series from 1923-1940 that seasonal
variation of employment and births (lagged nine months) coincide
and that this fact might possibly explain much of the correlation
noted. When seasonal variation in addition to secular trend is removed, as in Figure 3, there is clearly no significant correlation in
the earlier 'twenties. Births reacted at once to the stabilization of
the Reichsmark in November 1923, whereas employment rose
more slowly. When employment did rise, births failed to respond.
Between 1926 and 1930 there was a close correspondence in the
movements of the two variables despite adjustment for seasonal

Fig. 3. Employment indices and births in Germany, 1923-1930, adjusted for seasonal variation, births lagged nine months with secular trend removed.

variation, and the correlation was high, namely +.77. The correlation in this period indicates that the relationship is not a transitory one that might have arisen in the 'thirties owing to a chance association of trends.

The coefficient of correlation in the period from 1930-1939 was somewhat higher for the adjusted data (+.83) than for the uncorrected data presented in Figure 1, indicating that the relationship of the variables was independent of seasonal fluctuation. An-

Fig. 4. Employment indices, marriages, and births in Germany, by quarters, 1930-1939, adjusted for seasonal variation, births lagged nine months.

other factor, however, clearly disturbs the relationship in this period, namely marriages. The correlation coefficient for marriages and births was +.72, indicating a degree of interdependence almost as great as between employment and births. Examination of Figure 4 will reveal that fluctuations of births often appear to be a compromise between changes in employment and in marriages. The great increase in births in 1934 in particular seems to have been as much influenced by marriages as by employment, no doubt as a result of the official policy of encouraging marriages through marriage loans without interest. In the later period the pull of reemployment seems to have been greater. The logic of this explanation is upheld by the fact that the initial rise of births in Germany was mostly a function of first births, whereas in the later period rises in fertility were brought about by increases in the higher orders of parity, especially in second and third births. When marriages were held constant the correlation coefficient between employment and births rose to +.90 for the period 1930-1939.

Surprisingly enough, the number of marriages does not appear to be very closely linked to employment conditions. The coefficient of correlation for the period 1930-1939 was only +.33. However, the decline in marriages contrary to employment trends in 1935 may be explained by the fact that the high marriage rates of late 1933 and 1934 could not be indefinitely maintained, owing to the limited number of marriageable persons available once the marriages postponed from the depression years were consummated.

According to the last of the three hypotheses, the relationship between employment and births should be greater in urban and industrial regions and countries than in rural regions and countries. On *a priori* grounds this should be true (1) because the impact of employment conditions in rural areas is cushioned by the high proportion of peasants and small town merchants and craftsmen, (2) because more rational control of fertility is to be expected in the city than in the country.

Within Germany births in large cities appear to be more responsive to changing employment conditions than in the country as a whole, particularly in periods of declining employment. However, large cities seem to have been more affected by the rapid increase of the marriage rate than the rural areas, and births rose more rapidly in the cities than in the remainder of the country in the first years of the Nazi regime. Employment also rose more rapidly in these areas.

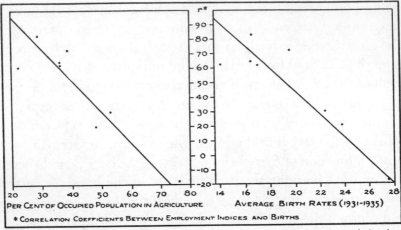

Fig. 5. Relation of r in selected countries[1] to per cent of occupied population in agriculture and to birth rates.

[1] The coefficients of correlation and time periods to which they apply were: Germany +.83 (1930-1939); Czechoslovakia +.72 (1931-1937); France +.64 (1930-1935); Sweden +.62 (1933-1938); United States—A. F. of L. data— +.61 (1935-1939); Hungary +.30 (1933-1940); Italy +.20 (1929-1936); and Poland —.18 (1931-1938). Except for the United States the proportions of the occupied population in agriculture were obtained from the League of Nations. EUROPEAN CONFERENCE ON RURAL LIFE 1939. POPULATION AND AGRICULTURE WITH SPECIAL REFERENCE TO AGRICULTURAL OVER-POPULATION, p. 8. Birth rates were taken from *Population Index*, July, 1941, vii, No. 3, pp. 244-245.

Comparisons between countries reveal that there is a negative relation between the proportion of the occupied population in agriculture and the association between births and employment. In Figure 5, the correlation coefficients between employment and births are plotted against percentage of the working force in agriculture. The countries and time periods were selected on the basis of the availability of the data.[4] Because of the character of the data and the varying time periods used the precise relationships between

[4] The coefficients were computed, as for Germany, with births lagged nine months. Employment indices were taken from various issues of the *International Labour Review* and birth data from official sources of the countries concerned. Great Britain was omitted because its employment series in certain respects is noncomparable with those used. On the basis of the British employment figures as given and without adjustment for secular trend of births, there is a negligible correlation between employment and births. When the secular trend and seasonal variation of births are removed (assuming the years 1924-1931 to represent the true secular trend) the correlation between employment and births from 1924-1938 was +.86.

countries are of little significance. However, the general pattern is clear. Poland, Italy, and Hungary, with relatively high proportions of their populations in agriculture, had low or even negative associations between employment and births. In contrast, the more industrial nations of Western Europe generally had significant correlations between the two variables.

The pattern is equally distinct as regards the level of birth rates, also presented in Figure 5. Countries of high birth rates, notably Poland and Italy, had no significant relation between employment and births. Countries of low birth rates, such as Sweden, France, Germany, and the United States, had a rather close association.

In general the *a priori* hypotheses on the relationship of employment and births were supported by the data. The high degree of covariation in Germany therefore fits into a logical scheme that greatly strengthens the purely statistical evidence. Both logic and statistical evidence bear out the belief that employment must have been an important element in the rise of the German birth rate.

A final series of evidence may serve to strengthen the argument and give some quantitative estimate of the importance of employment conditions. Examination of changes in employment levels and birth rates between 1932-1933 and 1938-1939 suggests that a large increase in births in Germany might well have been anticipated on the basis of reemployment alone. In Figure 6 these changes are presented for those countries demographically comparable[5] to Germany for which data on general employment levels are available. The countries are arranged from left to right in order of the ratio of employment in 1938 to employment in 1932. These columns are paired with similar ratios for birth rates in 1939 as compared with 1933.

Germany experienced the greatest increase in employment and at the same time much the greatest rise in the birth rate. Sweden, and to a lesser extent the United States and Great Britain, also achieved considerable reemployment with some recovery in births. In The Netherlands, where reemployment amounted to only 12 per cent, the birth rate remained about constant, and in France and Austria employment and births both declined in the period.

[5] Though employment series were available for certain Eastern European countries, they were not included. In these predominantly agricultural countries of high fertility, birth rates continued to decline regardless of changes in employment conditions.

In every country except Austria the position of employment in the later year relative to the earlier was better than that of births. This fact tends to confirm the frequently expressed opinion that the checking and even reversal of birth rate declines in the late 'thirties does not represent a true deviation from the downward secular trend but a temporary reaction to improved economic conditions. Among the countries considered a certain increase of employment was necessary to hold the birth rate constant, and barring such increase, birth rates tended to pursue their downward course. In Sweden, for instance, a 32 per cent increase in employment produced a rise of only 12 per cent in the birth rate; in the United States a 23 per cent employment rise brought a birth rate increase of only 4 per cent; and in The Netherlands a 12 per cent rise in employment was not quite sufficient to hold the birth rate at its former level. In France and Austria, where employment conditions worsened, the downward trend of births continued.

In so far as Germany is concerned, it seems certain that on the basis of comparative experience an important rise in the birth rate could have been predicted from reemployment alone. At least a third of the birth increase may be assumed to be a function of reemployment, since in Sweden, with far less

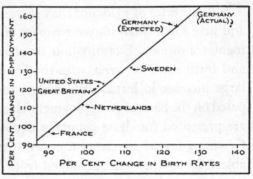

Fig. 7. Changes in birth rates relative to changes in employment indices.

increase in employment, the birth rate rose almost one-third as much as it did in Germany. On the other hand, if the rise in births followed the rise in employment at the same distance as it did in Sweden (*i.e.* 20 per cent), almost all of the rise in German births would have to be assigned to the improved employment situation.

The experience of other countries demonstrates that the latter interpretation is unlikely. There is clear evidence that, at least among the countries considered, successive improvements in employment conditions did not bring about a proportionate rise in births. The spread between changes in employment and in birth

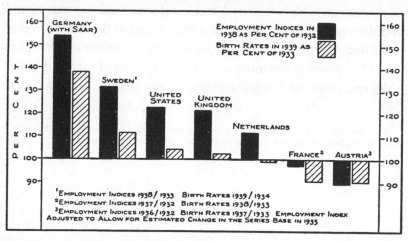

Fig. 6. Changes in employment indices and birth rates.

rates broadened as the employment ratio rose. Thus the spread was only 7 per cent in France, 13 per cent in The Netherlands, 19 per cent in Britain, 18.5 per cent in the United States, and 20 per cent in Sweden.

The graphic presentation of the relationship between changes in employment and birth rates in these five countries (Figure 7) reveals a striking regularity in the diminishing influence of employment on births as the employment ratio goes up. This is indicated by the relatively small deviations of the plotted points from the computed line of regression. With employment changes known, the change in the birth rate in any one of these countries could have been estimated with reasonable accuracy from the experience of the other four. The experience of these typical countries suggests a high degree of predictability in the association between employment and birth rates in Western industrial nations generally.

Assuming that Germany reacted to changing employment conditions as did these other Western countries, a 23 per cent rise in the birth rate could have been expected from reemployment alone.[6] The actual increase was 38 per cent. On this basis almost three-fifths of the actual increase may be explained by reemployment, leaving only two-fifths to be allocated to other changed conditions in the Reich, including all direct population measures.

Most will agree that, behind the Nazi façade of collective expressions that are so objectionable and so dangerous, the Germans are human beings with hopes and fears and with reactions to stimuli not unlike our own. If this is true, a major part of the Nazi successes on the demographic front must have been the result of reemployment, as opposed to the more spectacular appeals of race and "folk" on the one hand, and specific inducements to childbearing on the other.

⁶ This percentage may be obtained by reading the expected increase in the birth rate at the actual employment ratio from the extrapolated line of regression in Figure 7.

THE IMPACT OF WAR ON POPULATION

AND VITAL PHENOMENA

By Philip M. Hauser

The past decade, with its years of depression, has witnessed many population changes, some of them representing the continuation of long-time trends and others reflecting the impact of economic distress on American life. The new decade, begun with war, has already greatly modified many of the population changes of the thirties and will undoubtedly bring even more profound alterations of population patterns in its wake.

The effects of World War II on the population of the United States may be thought of as having three distinct phases: first, the effects which follow preparation for war; second, the effects of full military participation in the war; and, third, the effects of post-war adjustment. Obviously, it is possible at this time to describe factually only the first of these phases. Although the demographic records of World War I and those available to date for belligerents in World War II leave much to be desired,[2] it is possible, on the basis of these records, to describe the pattern of population changes which may be anticipated in the second and third phases of World War II, in the United States, and to point to some of the problems that will be attendant upon them.

[2] Quantitative data on the trends in births, deaths, and migration in the various nations of Europe during the last war are extremely inadequate. This is, in part, inevitable, since invasions and the military and economic exhaustion of total war are likely to be accompanied by the disruption of even the basic statistical services of a country. Comparisons of pre-war and post-war census age distributions, with computations of what "normal" births and deaths would have been, give a measure of the net changes presumably because of the war. Refined analysis, however, is impossible without the continuation of registration services and the meas-

THE EFFECTS OF PREPARATION FOR WAR

In a social and economic sense, American participation in the war antedates December 7, 1941. The defense, lend-lease, and victory programs had already been initiated when Pearl Harbor was attacked. These programs, which successively expanded into a program of full war production, profoundly affected the course of the business cycle and produced one of the nation's most active boom periods. It has been demonstrated that many population phenomena are highly sensitive to the business cycle.[3] It is to be

urement of migratory movements.

It is possible that more adequate statistical records may be kept during this war. Census and registration procedures are better developed in most countries, and professional research personnel are more numerous. In addition, the need for quantitative information on manpower and economic potential is more widely realized. However, as war becomes more acute, many of the types of statistics desired by social scientists are relegated to the category of nonessential information. Neither the English, the French, nor the Italians took their censuses in 1941. The Polish, Greek, and Yugoslav statistical organizations were destroyed. Hence the needs of government agencies and the interests of social scientists in the problems of war and population must be met by increasingly inadequate data. Current information on population in all parts of the world, belligerent and neutral alike, is being systematically covered by various war agencies and by the Census Library Project of the Library of Congress. Citations to much of the published material are made available currently in *Population Index*.

[3] William F. Ogburn and Dorothy S. Thomas, "The Influence of the Business Cycle on Social Factors," *Journal of the American Statistical Association*, XVIII (September, 1922), 324-40; Dorothy S. Thomas, *Social Aspects of the Business Cycle* (New York: E. P. Dutton & Co., 1925); Maurice B. Hexter, *Social Consequences of Business Cycles* (Boston and New York: Houghton Mifflin Co., 1925).

expected, therefore, that the effects of the war on American population phenomena to date, both before and after December 7, 1941, are, to a considerable extent, the effects of the recovery and prosperity phases of the business cycle (see Chart I). Let us turn to an examination of some of them.

Total population growth.—Official estimates are available giving the monthly growth of the population of the United States from April 1, 1940, the date of the Sixteenth Decennial Census, to July 1, 1941.[4] During this fifteen-month period it is estimated that the population of the United States increased by 1,369,481 persons—from a total of 131,669,000 to 133,039,000. This represents an annual increase of 1,095,585 persons, or 0.83 per cent, as compared with an average annual increase of 889,423 persons, or 0.70 per cent, between 1930 and 1940. The more rapid growth of the population of the United States during this fifteen-month period was effected partly as the result of a small immigration, that is, a net immigration of 90,236 persons.[5]

Since the most striking population phenomena of the thirties was the great decline in the rate of national population growth[6] the rapid acceleration of population growth in the new decade, as a concomitant of the war, merits further examination. This can be achieved by an analysis of the components of population growth, namely, the birth rate, the death rate, and net immigration.

The birth rate.—The major factor in the acceleration of the population growth of the nation was the increase in the birth rate. The crude birth rate (births per 1,000 persons), which reached a low of 18.1 in 1933,

increased in 1938 to 19.1, reflecting economic recovery in 1937; dropped in 1939 to 18.7, with the recession in 1938; and rose to 19.3 in 1940 and to 20.4 in 1941[7] (Chart I). The increase in the birth rate from 1940 to 1941 may well be interpreted as a phenomenon attributable largely to the economic recovery stimulated by the war.

The war played a more direct role in the increase of the birth rate, however, as is evidenced by other considerations. The crude birth rate, after elimination of seasonal influences, has been plotted by months for the period 1939–41 in Chart II. It is to be observed that peaks in fertility are reached in April and July, 1941. It is more than a coincidence that these peaks occurred approximately nine months after the introduction in and passage by Congress, respectively, of the Selective Service Act. It seems reasonable to conclude that compulsory conscription necessitated by the war resulted in a sharp increase in the birth rate.

The death rate.—The crude death rate (deaths per 1,000 persons) shows a downward linear trend during the period from 1925 to 1941, with some slight fluctuation. The 1940 and 1941 crude death rates—11.1 and 10.8, respectively—are approximately what is to be expected from the linear trend. It may be concluded, therefore, that at this stage of our participation in the war the death rate has not been visibly affected.[8]

Natural increase.—Since the birth rate has, during the period studied, been relatively sensitive to social, economic, and political changes, while the death rate has remained relatively stable, it is to be expected that the rate of natural increase from 1925 to

---

[4] Department of Commerce, Bureau of the Census, *Population, Series P-3, No. 28* (Washington, D.C., June 11, 1942).

[5] During the intercensal decade, April 1, 1930, to April 1, 1940, there was a net emigration of 46,518 persons from the United States (see Bureau of the Census, *Population, Series P-3, No. 10* [March 15, 1941]).

[6] See Philip M. Hauser, "Population," *American Journal of Sociology,* XLVII (May, 1942), 816–28.

[7] Standardized birth rates for the same period show substantially the same pattern. On the basis of provisional reports the crude birth rate in the first quarter of 1942 was 21.0, as compared with 19.4 in the first quarter of 1941. The rates are adjusted for underregistration of births.

[8] Standardized death rates for the same period show substantially the same pattern. On the basis of provisional reports the crude death rate in the first quarter of 1942 was 11.4, as compared with 11.9 in the first quarter of 1941. The rates are adjusted for underregistration of deaths.

CHART I

ANNUAL INDEX OF INDUSTRIAL PRODUCTION AND SELECTED
POPULATION TRENDS, FOR THE UNITED STATES: 1925 TO 1941

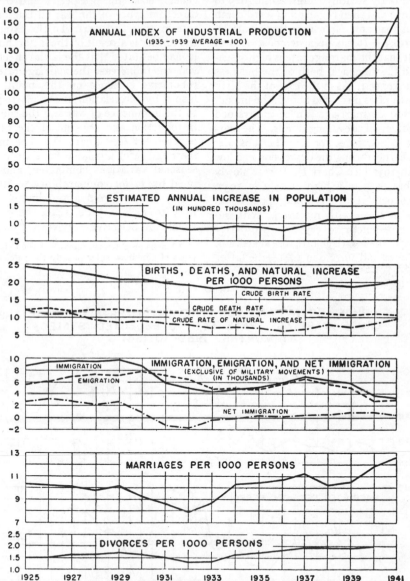

SOURCES OF DATA FOR CHART I

Annual index of industrial production.—"Industrial Production, New or Revised Series," *Survey of Current Business* (Washington: Bureau of Foreign and Domestic Commerce, September, 1941), p. 24.

Annual increase in population.—Estimates based on data supplied by the Division of Vital Statistics, Bureau of the Census.

Crude birth and crude death rates.—Rates for 1925–32 based on revised estimates by W. S. Thompson and P. K. Whelpton. Rates for 1933–41 based on data published in *Special Reports*, Vol. 15, Nos. 35 and 36, Division of Vital Statistics, Bureau of the Census, July, 1942, corrected for underregistration.

Annual immigration and emigration for the United States.—Data supplied by Bureau of Naturalization and Immigration. Net migration figures for January 1, 1930, to July 1, 1941, as published in U.S. Department of Commerce, Bureau of the Census, *Population, Series, P-3*, No. 28, June 11, 1942; figures for July 1, 1941, to January 1, 1942, unpublished. Military movements excluded.

Crude marriage and crude divorce rates.—Rates for 1925 to 1940 based on annual data as published in *Special Reports*, Vol. 15, Nos. 13 and 18, Division of Vital Statistics, Bureau of the Census. Rate for 1941 based on data for sixteen selected states only, as reported to the Division of Vital Statistics.

1941 closely parallels that of the birth rate. The crude rate of natural increase (the crude birth rate minus the crude death rate) declined fairly steadily·from 12.2 in 1925 to 6.3 in 1936 and then began an upward climb to 8.3 in 1940 and 9.6 in 1941 (see Chart I).

Marriage.—It has been demonstrated in the past that the marriage rate is highly sensitive to the influences both of the business cycle and of war. As in the case of the birth and death rates discussed above, the impact of the war on marriage can be understood only in terms of prevailing trends. The marriage rate (marriages per 1,000 persons) declined sharply during the depression to a low of 7.9 in 1932 (see Chart I). It rose slowly after that date to a high of 11.2 in 1937, with economic recovery, and dropped again to 10.2 in 1938, with recession. With renewed economic recovery and prosperity since 1939, the marriage rate rose sharply to 11.9 in 1940 and to 12.6 in 1941—the latter

being the highest rate ever recorded in the United States.[9]

It is difficult to separate the influence of general economic prosperity and the more direct influence of the war on the marriage rate in 1940 and 1941. To the extent that the former is a result of the latter, however, it may be stated that the initial effect of the war was to increase the marriage rate. Corroborative evidence on this point is furnished by·the relation of the marriage rate to·the imminence of war and the coincident introduction and passage of the Selective Service Act (see Chart II). The monthly marriage rate) available for sixteen states, seasonal variations eliminated, and multiplied by 12 for comparability with annual rates) jumped from approximately 9.6 in May to 14.1 in June, 1940, the month in which the Selective Service Act was intro-

[9] Marriages per 1,000 females fifteen to forty-four years of age show substantially the same pattern.

CHART II

THE CRUDE BIRTH RATE FOR THE UNITED STATES AND THE CRUDE MARRIAGE RATE FOR 16 SELECTED STATES, BY MONTHS: 1939 TO 1941

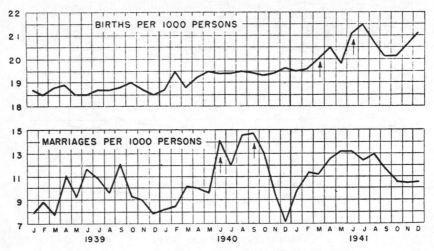

SOURCES OF DATA FOR CHART II

Arrows on chart showing birth rate indicate dates nine months after introduction into and passage by Congress of the Selective Service Act. Arrows on chart showing marriage rate indicate dates of introduction into and passage by Congress of the Selective Service Act.

Based on reports to the Division of Vital Statistics, Bureau of the·Census. Birth rates corrected for underregistration. Marriage rates for the following sixteen selected states only: California, Connecticut, Delaware, District of Columbia, Florida, Iowa, Maryland, Michigan, Mississippi, New Jersey, New York, Oregon, South Dakota, Vermont, Virginia, Wisconsin.

duced in Congress; it dropped to 12.0 in July, and reached a peak of 14.7 in September, 1940, the month in which the Selective Service Act was passed.

Divorce.—The divorce rate is also positively correlated with the business cycle. It is not surprising, therefore, that the divorce rate increased in 1939 and 1940 with the economic prosperity produced by war. The divorce rate (divorces per 1,000 persons), which is plotted for the period 1925–40 in Chart I, dropped to a low of 1.28 in 1932, rose to 1.93 in 1937, dipped to 1.38 in 1938, and then rose to an all-time peak in the United States of 2.00 in 1940 (see Chart I).

Foreign immigration.—The volume of foreign immigration, which reached new lows for the United States in a nonwar period during the thirties, declined sharply after 1937. The quota laws, together with the effects of the international depression, were primarily responsible for the decline in immigration in the first half of the thirties. The increase in immigration from 1933 to 1937 may also be interpreted as essentially a business-cycle phenomenon (Chart I), although, in some measure, it reflects the unsettled international situation which resulted in a flow of refugees from countries of active Axis persecution to the United States. This flow was interrupted in 1937, with *Anschluss*, and dropped abruptly after 1939, with the invasion of Poland.

Emigration from the United States also declined during the early stages of the depression in the thirties and paralleled the increase in immigration from 1933 to 1937. The decline in emigration subsequent to 1937 and the sharp drop after 1939 closely followed the pattern of immigration outlined above.

Net foreign immigration, although it followed the pattern of both immigration and emigration from 1930 to 1937, showed an increase from 1937 to 1940 and a drop after 1940. In the three years 1931–33 there was a net emigration from the United States; from 1934 to 1936 the number of emigrants was approximately the same as the number of immigrants; the years 1937–41 showed a small net immigration—in each case fewer than 100,000 persons.

Internal migration.—The tremendous industrial expansion occasioned by the war has undoubtedly altered the direction and volume of population movement which characterized the thirties. Few nation-wide facts, however, are available on this movement [10] The most important body of data relating to post-censal migration is that compiled by the Work Projects Administration in a series of surveys on defense migration for fifty-one cities conducted in May, September, November, and December of 1941. Each of these studies measures the movement of in-migrants from October, 1940, to the date of the survey. Despite the lack of exact comparability in time interval involved, some general conclusions are possible, and these have been ably stated by Dr. Howard B. Myers, director of research, Work Projects Administration, in his testimony before the House Committee Investigating National Defense Migration.[11] Some of the basic aspects of Dr. Myer's statement are summarized as follows:

1. Since the date of the last census the volume of internal migration has increased rapidly. The increase in population movement is attributable, on the one hand, to the concentration of war contracts resulting in increased demands for labor in a relatively few centers and, on the other hand, to the increased effect of priority regulations and material shortages forcing temporary unemployment of workers engaged in nonwar production.

2. There have been two main types of defense migration: (*a*) a relatively temporary movement of construction workers to new

[10] The sugar-ration registration figures of the Office of Price Administration, if they prove to be satisfactory, may permit the estimation of total population and net migration. For an outline of a method whereby current population statistics might be obtained see Philip M. Hauser, "Proposed Annual Sample Census," *Journal of the American Statistical Association*, XXXVII (March, 1942), 81–88.

[11] See mimeographed statement, "Defense Migration" (Washington: Work Projects Administration [A3898], 1942). For a condensed version of this statement see Howard B. Myers, "Defense Migration and Labor Supply," *Journal of the American Statistical Association*, XXXVII (March, 1942), 69–76.

plant and camp sites and (b) a movement of relatively long duration of both defense and nondefense workers to war-industry centers.

3. The rate of migration (number of in-migrants as a percentage of the 1940 population) varied from 1 per cent in Philadelphia to 26 per cent in San Diego, for the fifty-one cities surveyed. Half of the fifty-one areas had a migration rate of 5 per cent or less, while ten of the fifty-one cities had a migration rate of 10 per cent or more. In three cities the number of in-migrants exceeded 50,000, being 103,000 in Los Angeles, 60,000 in San Diego, and 52,000 in Washington, D.C.

4. It is estimated that approximately 2,250,000 persons, including a million workers, resident in cities of over 25,000 population in October, 1941, had entered these cities after October 1, 1940. The over-all migrant rate for cities over 25,000 population is estimated at 4.3 per cent.

5. The defense in-migrants included relatively small proportions of Negroes, ranging from less than half of 1 per cent in eleven of the fifty-one cities to approximately 20 per cent in Macon, Georgia. Three per cent or less of the migrants were Negroes in half of the surveyed cities. "Even in the South, migration rates for the Negroes are much lower than for whites."[12]

6. Women constituted a relatively small proportion of the in-migrants, ranging from 10 per cent in Johnstown, Pennsylvania, to 45 per cent in the District of Columbia. Half of the cities reported 18 per cent or fewer women among the migrants.

It is possible to obtain at least clues to the important areas of in-migration from a broad national standpoint, through analysis of the distribution of defense and war con-

tracts. Up to January, 1942, the conversion and expansion of existing facilities, as measured by contracts awarded, resulted in great new demands for labor in the Northeast and Pacific Coastal States, in the Great Lakes States, and in the South Atlantic States.[13] New production facilities were provided in considerable quantity in the Gulf Coast region, especially in Texas, the Tennessee Valley, and southern California (areas which were experiencing considerable pre-war industrial growth), and also in western and middle-western areas, away from large metropolitan centers, in which practically no industrial development existed and in which mainly explosive and shell-loading plants were constructed.

Many of the new war-production plants, in keeping with the pre-war trend toward the suburbanization of industry, have been located in outlying areas of metropolitan districts rather than in the large central cities.[14] This policy of plant location may well have accelerated the shift of population from the central cities toward the peripheral areas of metropolitan districts.

The conversion, expansion, or construction of war-production facilities cannot be interpreted as necessarily indicating a large in-migration of workers. The extent to which in-migration actually occurred in the areas in which war-production facilities were concentrated was dependent on the extent to which it was possible to absorb the local labor reserve of unemployed, on the number of workers who became available for war work after conversion of nonwar industries, and on the number of potential workers among persons in the area not normally in the labor force. In general, however, it is probable that a high correlation existed between the allocation of war contracts and in-migration.

Materials for the country as a whole re-

---

[12] Dr. Myers makes the following comment on this phenomenon: "This is understandable, in view of the widespread discrimination against Negroes in war industries. It contrasts sharply with experience in the first World War, however, when a large-scale migration of Negroes to northern industrial centers took place. As the demand for labor increases and present employment restrictions are relaxed, it is probable that Negroes will begin to move in greater numbers."

[13] Edgar M. Hoover, Jr., and Glenn E. McLaughlin, "Strategic Factors in Plant Location," *Harvard Business Review*, XX (winter, 1942), 1933–40; Joyce Campbell and Catherine R. Harris, "Migration and National Defense," *Social Security Bulletin*, IV (September, 1941), 12–19.

[14] Hoover and McLaughlin, *op. cit.*, p. 139.

lating to out-migration are also sketchy. The Bureau of Agricultural Economics has estimated that the net movement from farms to cities increased from approximately 500,000 in 1940 to about a million in 1941.[15] From what is available in the employment figures of the Bureau of Employment Security of the Social Security Board and in the hearings of the House Committee Investigating National Defense Migration,[16] it would seem that there has been a steady stream of workers out from the Mountain States and the Dust Bowl to the Pacific Coast and to other defense production centers. There seems to have been considerable out-migration from Wisconsin and Minnesota. In general, most states in the area ranging from Montana on the north to New Mexico on the south, and Nevada in the west through Missouri in the east, seem to have lost workers to industrial areas of the Middle and Far West.[17]

THE EFFECTS OF FULL MILITARY PARTICIPATION IN THE WAR

The basic pattern of demographic changes resulting from full military participation in war is fairly well charted and, assuming a prolonged war which will require large expeditionary forces, may be predicted for the United States in the present war. In brief, it is to be expected that the pattern of population changes in the United States in the coming months will parallel that which occurred among European belligerents in World War I. It is in order, therefore, to review briefly the effects on population of World War I.

Population changes during World War I. —It is estimated that total military deaths in

World War I numbered 13,055,000 and that civilian deaths indirectly attributable to the war numbered 28,379,000.[18] Thus mortality directly or indirectly attributable to World War I amounted to 41,434,000.[19] Military deaths constituted approximately 3 per cent of the total population of Europe, and civilian deaths indirectly attributable to the war a like percentage.[20]

A better indication of the military mortality rate is obtained by expressing military losses during the war as a percentage of males fifteen to forty-nine years of age before the war.[21] Of the men in this age class, who numbered 108,794,000 in the European countries for which data are available, 11.6 per cent lost their lives in military service. This percentage varied from less than 2 per cent in Ireland and Portugal to more than 15 per cent in Turkey, Russia, Serbia, and Montenegro, reaching a peak of 26.7 per cent in Serbia and Montenegro. In France, 13.2 per cent of the men fifteen to forty-nine years of age were killed in military service; in Germany 12.3 per cent; in England and Wales 6.9 per cent.

The birth rate in all belligerent countries fell sharply as World War I progressed.[22] In France, for example, the birth rate of 18.8 (births per 1,000 of the population) in 1911–

---

[15] These statistics were kindly made available in advance of publication by Dr. Conrad Taeuber, acting head, Division of Farm Population and Rural Welfare (see Human Agricultural Economics, Department of Agriculture, *Farm Population Estimates*).

[16] *National Defense Migration: Hearings before the Select Committee Investigating National Defense Migration, House of Representatives, Seventy-fifth Congress, First Session* (Washington, 1942).

[17] Campbell and Harris, *op. cit.*, p. 18.

[18] Considerably more than a third of the total civilian deaths indirectly attributable to World War I—11,750,000—occurred in British India and in the Indian native states.

[19] L. Hersch, "Demographic Effects of Modern Warfare," in *What Would Be the Character of a New War?* (New York: Random House, Inc., 1933), p. 291.

[20] Most of the civilian deaths during World War I were attributable to disease and famine. These phenomena are not discussed here because of their inapplicability to the situation in the United States.

[21] Walter F. Willcox, "Military Losses in the World War," *Journal of the American Statistical Association*, XXIII, No. 163 (new ser.; September, 1928), 304–5. Based on data given by L. Hersch. These estimates are necessarily based on defective population statistics and on inadequate records of war mortality.

[22] Metropolitan Life Insurance Co., "War and the Birth Rate," *Statistical Bulletin*, XIX (March, 1940), 3–6.

13 dropped to 9.5 in 1916; in Germany the birth rate of 28.0 in 1911–13 had dropped to 13.9 by 1917; and in England and Wales the birth rate, which averaged 24.2 from 1911 to 1913, dropped to 17.7 in 1918. In the United States (Birth Registration Area) the birth rate, which averaged about 25.0 in 1915 and 1916, dropped to 22.2 in 1919. In most of the belligerent countries the birth rates seem to have decreased by approximately 50 per cent at the low point reached during the war and then, largely as a result of remedial measures instituted, slowly to have increased even during the course of hostilities.

The marriage rate also dropped sharply during the war.[23] In France the marriage rate (marriages per 1,000 persons), which was 7.7 for the period 1911–13, dropped to a low of 2.3 in 1915; in Germany the marriage rate of 7.8 in 1911–13 dropped to a low of 4.1 in 1915 and 1916; and in England and Wales the marriage rate dropped from 7.8 in 1911–13 to 6.9 in 1917. In the United States the marriage rate of 10.1 in 1911–13 dropped to 9.7 in 1918.

Despite the large military and civilian mortality and the great decline in the marriage and birth rates, the total population of some of the belligerent countries increased between 1910 and 1920.[24] The population of England and Wales increased by almost 1,500,000 between these dates, while that of the German Empire increased by 1,400,000. The populations of France, Austria, Poland, and Russia showed appreciable decreases, however, between 1910 and 1920. France decreased by about 2,300,000 during this period; Austria, by 240,000; Poland, by 2,700,000; and Russia, which was ravaged by famine and revolution as well as by war, by 13,900,000. The population of the countries of western Europe increased by 6,200,000, or by about 3 per cent, between 1910 and 1920, while the populations of those countries of

eastern Europe for which estimates are available decreased by approximately 16,-600,000 persons, or by 10 per cent. The European population as a whole[25] decreased by at least 10,400,000 persons between 1910 and 1920, or by about 3 per cent.

Although World War I reduced the population of Europe by only 3 per cent, this figure, of course, does not tell the whole story, because the war, particularly through the loss in births which might have occurred had there been no war, greatly decelerated the rate of population growth.

World War I produced another demographic distortion of considerable significance, particularly in its indirect effect on the marriage and the birth rates, namely, the imbalance of the sexes of marriageable age. In 1919, for example, Germany had 2,214,000 more women than men aged twenty to forty-nine years. In 1921 France had a surplus of 1,227,000 women in the same age class, and England and Wales had a surplus of 1,209,000 women.[26] Similar surpluses of women existed in virtually all the belligerent nations after the war.[27] Although some surplus of women is normal in European populations, largely because of the combined influence of previous wars and of out-migration, the great surpluses outlined above are primarily attributable to the military mortality in World War I. Even these figures, however, do not tell the entire story of the imbalance between the sexes, because large numbers of partially or totally disabled men in the post-war populations of Europe were unequal to the task of carrying on normal family life and of providing a livelihood for their dependents.[28]

[23] Metropolitan Life Insurance Co., "Marriage Rate in War Time," Statistical Bulletin, XX (November, 1939), 4–6.

[24] Walter F. Willcox, "Population and the World War: A Preliminary Survey," Journal of the American Statistical Association, XVIII (new ser.; June, 1923), 700–712.

[25] For the estimate for countries containing in 1910 about seven-eighths of total European population see ibid., p. 708. The figures for eastern Europe are less reliable than that for western Europe because of the poor quality of its censuses.

[26] See International Statistical Year Book, 1926–28 (Geneva: League of Nations, 1928), p. 22.

[27] Metropolitan Life Insurance Co., "Post-war Depletion of Ranks of Men at Marrying Ages," Statistical Bulletin, XXI (February, 1940), 3.

[28] Willard Waller, War and the Family (New York: Dryden Press, 1940), p. 23; and E. L. Bogart,

Another important demographic scar is visible in European populations as a result of World War I. The age pyramids of the populations of belligerent nations, particularly those which suffered large mortality, show great deficiencies for both males and females in the age classes representing "war babies." These "hollow classes" have a special significance for future population growth, particularly because the babies of the last war are in the age class which must fight the present one. Future population pyramids of Europe will show particularly large gaps because World War II mortality will reduce even further the relatively small numbers of children the World War I babies would have normally reproduced, and, thus, World War II mortality will make more pronounced the "echo" effect which may be expected to persist for generations.[29]

Pattern of changes to be expected in the United States.—It would be hazardous indeed to attempt to predict actual military or civilian mortality or the specific birth, death, and marriage rates for the United States during the period of active military participation in the war which lies immediately ahead. As a result of changes in the methods of warfare and of the unpredictability of the actual battlefields and the length of the war, any extrapolation based on the experience of World War I, or even of World War II, would probably be greatly misleading.

The general pattern of population changes which may be expected, however, can be described in the light of the experience of the past. It may be expected that, with the increase of the armed forces in the United States and with the increase in the size of our expeditionary forces, the marriage rate will drop precipitately to a point probably well below that ever before recorded for this country. During the course of the war the birth rate will drop to a new low,

as will also the rate of natural increase. The rate of total population growth will, therefore, also decrease appreciably because international migration, except for troop movements, will virtually cease. Internal migration toward war-production centers will undoubtedly continue until the peak in war production is reached, and it may be expected to include larger proportions of Negroes and perhaps of women as labor shortages grow more acute. The flow of workers to centers of war production will increase the urban concentration of population in selected areas. Of course, if intensive aerial warfare is brought to our large cities, counteracting forces tending toward decentralization will be set in motion.

The relatively short period of our participation in World War I resulted in a relatively low military mortality for this country. Although it may reasonably be anticipated that the United States will be involved in a long and difficult war,[30] it would be unwise to attempt to predict actual military mortality. If, however, the United States suffers a loss of as many as half a million men, the war will produce a sex ratio (number of males per 100 females) of less than 100 for the first time in the history of the nation and may create a surplus of women of marriageable age which will affect marriage rates for some time to come.[31] Moreover, if our military efforts are conducted on a large scale, appreciable numbers of partially and totally disabled men may result, who, in varying degree, will be unfit for the fulfilment of normal family and economic responsibility.

The decline in the birth rate during the war will produce the same gaps in the age pyramid for the United States that already characterize the populations of most of the belligerents of World War I. These "hollow

---

Direct and Indirect Consequences of the Great World War (New York: Carnegie Endowment for International Peace, 1919), p. 274.

[29] Horst Mendershausen, *The Economics of War* (New York: Prentice-Hall, Inc., 1940), pp. 262 ff.

[30] See President Roosevelt's Annual Message to Congress, *New York Times*, January 7, 1942. In the President's words, "We must face that fact of a hard war, a long war, a bloody war, a costly war."

[31] In 1940 there were 66,061,592 males and 65,607,683 females in the United States; the sex ratio was 100.7 (see Bureau of the Census, *Population, Series P-10, No. 14* [May 14, 1942]).

classes" will remain visible in the American age structure throughout the life-span of World War II babies and will be reflected in the age structure of the generations to come.

Civilian deaths indirectly attributable to the war will probably be relatively light, particularly if the war is not brought to American shores. However, the possibility of great epidemics like that of influenza in 1918 cannot be entirely discounted, and the possibility of increase in the incidence of disease is, of course, augmented by the great decrease in the medical services which will be available to the civilian population during the war.[32]

EFFECTS OF POST-WAR ADJUSTMENT

The prediction of post-war population changes, although even more hazardous in some respects than the prediction of changes during the war, is also possible in broad pattern. Again the experience of Europe after World War I may be drawn upon.

In France the birth rate rose from its low point of 9.5 in 1916 to a peak of 21.4 in 1920; in Germany, from 13.9 in 1917 to 25.9 in 1920; and in England and Wales, from 17.7 in 1918 to 25.5 in 1920.[33] The marriage rate in France increased from 2.3 in 1915 to 16.0 in 1920—by far the highest marriage rate from 1851 to date; in Germany, from 4.1 in 1916 to 14.5 in 1920; and in England and Wales, from 6.9 in 1917 to 10.1 in 1920.[34]

The birth and marriage rates in the United States after World War I were also visibly affected. The birth rate increased from a low of 22.3 in 1919 (for the Birth Registration Area) to 24.2 in 1921, while the marriage rate increased from a low of 9.7 in 1918 to 12.0 in 1920. With the return of the expeditionary forces and the demobilization of the Army and Navy after the war, it may be anticipated that the birth rate and the marriage rate will show sharp increases. The rate of natural increase will rise considerably, as will also the rate of total population growth.

These increases, however, cannot be expected to be of long duration. There is no reason to expect a reversal of the long-time downward trend in fertility. On the contrary, the war, in the long run, will probably accelerate the downward trend of the birth rate because of military mortality and disability; the emergence of "hollow classes"; the imbalance of the sexes of marriageable age; the effects of war on human motivation in the rearing of offspring; and the acceleration which may be expected in the diffusion of contraceptive methods. Moreover, social, economic, and political disorganization occasioned by war, and the exposure of millions of men to new and intensely stimulating cultural contacts, may be expected to break the "cake of custom" and to depress particularly the high fertility rates of rural areas[35] upon which the nation is, in the long run, dependent for natural increase.

The anticipated surplus of women of marriageable age in the post-war American population will probably result in increased proportions of the married in the male population but decreased proportions of the married among females. Moreover, if we are to judge by the experience of the past, there will be an increase in the divorce rate after the war. The surplus of millions of women in Europe after the last war led to fairly widespread discussions of the advisability of permitting polygamy and giving it legal status.[36] The war will undoubtedly produce a generation containing a relatively high proportion of women who will remain spinsters, and many of whom may constitute a permanent increment to the nation's labor force.

The volume of immigration to the United States after the war will, to a considerable

[32] Total Army and Navy requirements for doctors by December 31, 1942, are set at 42,000, or at approximately 25 per cent of the total number of doctors, by the War Manpower Commission.

[33] Metropolitan Life Insurance Co., "War and the Birth Rate," op. cit., p. 5.

[34] Metropolitan Life Insurance Co., "The Marriage Rate in War Time," op. cit., p. 6.

[35] Bureau of the Census, Population, Series P-5, No. 4 (February 21, 1941).

[36] Metropolitan Life Insurance Co., "Post-war Depletion of Ranks of Men at Marrying Ages," op. cit., p. 3.

extent, depend on international and national political factors and upon the economic role of this nation in the post-war world-economy. The speculative character of these factors makes it unwise to hazard any prediction on this point at this time. The pattern of post-war internal migration is similarly unpredictable, since it will depend largely on the condition of our economy, on whether depression or prosperity prevails. This, in turn, will depend on the success with which we are able to convert war-production facilities to "normal" consumer production; on the extent to which the national economy can absorb the flood of manpower which will be released through demobilization;[37] and on our general position in the world economic order. It is possible that American ingenuity in transforming production for war into production for peace may greatly raise even the pre-war standard of living and may radically alter traditional patterns of urban-rural and regional population distribution.[38] In the absence of wise and effective national policies, however, the post-war period may possibly witness the recession of the migrant worker from a role of respectability and importance to the role of the pariah "Okies" and other destitute depression migrants. It is possible that the control of internal population movements may be a major national problem in the post-war order and may profoundly affect the general welfare of the American people.

Prior to the onset of the war, the returns of the Sixteenth Decennial Census made it clear that the population growth of the United States was decelerating rapidly and corroborated the predictions of population students to the effect that the nation would be faced with a stationary or even a declining population in three or four decades.[39] If the war had not diverted the attention of the nation, it is probable that population phenomena would have had an even more central position in the nation's consciousness. Since the war will undoubtedly accelerate the decline in the rate of population growth, it is likely that population problems will increasingly attract the attention not only of scholars but also of statesmen and of the general public.

It has been pointed out that population growth has been an important ingredient of our national economic development and prosperity.[40] To the extent that this thesis is true, the decrease in the rate of population growth may have far-reaching and serious economic consequences.

SUMMARY

In the interest of an orderly presentation, the materials above have been organized largely with respect to the time sequence of population changes which have occurred or which may be anticipated. These changes are first summarized and then analyzed briefly, with respect to their short-run and long-run implications, in the paragraphs which follow.

The effects of preparation for war on the population of the United States have been largely, but not entirely, the effects of the recovery and prosperity phases of the business cycle. The birth rate and the marriage rate, partly in response to economic prosperity

---

[37] See National Resources Planning Board, *After Defense—What?* (Washington, D.C., 1941) and *After the War—Full Employment* (Washington, D.C., 1942).

[38] The widespread use of "flivver" airplanes after the war, for example, or a revolutionary mechanization of agriculture may profoundly change the present urban-rural, metropolitan-regional, distribution of population.

[39] See estimates of future population by Warren S. Thompson and P. K. Whelpton, of the Scripps Foundation for Research in Population Problems, in National Resources Committee, *The Problems of a Changing Population* (Washington, D.C.: Government Printing Office, 1938), pp. 22 ff.

[40] See Alvin Hansen, "Economic Progress and Declining Population Growth," *American Economic Review*, XXIX (March, 1939), 1–15; W. B. Reddaway, *The Economics of a Declining Population* (New York: Macmillan Co., 1939); Mordecai Ezekiel, "Statistical Investigations of Savings, Consumption and Investment," *American Economic Review*, XXXII (June, 1942), 272–307; Sumner H. Schlichter, "The Conditions of Expansion," *American Economic Review*, XXXII (March, 1942), 1–21; Stuart Chase, *The Road We Are Travelling, 1914–1942* (New York: Twentieth Century Fund, 1942).

and partly as a result of military conscription, have greatly increased—the latter to a new high in the history of the United States. Largely in response to economic prosperity, the divorce rate also reached a new high. Since the death rate was not visibly affected, the high birth rate produced an appreciable rise in the rate of natural increase. The high birth rate and a slight net immigration have been responsible for an acceleration in the rate of population growth of the nation. The volume of migration between the United States and other nations, both immigration and emigration, declined appreciably as a result of unsettled international conditions. The great expansion in industries producing the instruments of war has accelerated the movement of workers into selected urban industrial centers and has created new specialized war-production concentrations of population, drawing in-migrants from urban areas without war-production activities, from villages, and from farms.

Large-scale military participation in the war may be expected to result in great declines in the birth rate, the rate of natural increase, the rate of population growth, and the marriage rate. It may be anticipated that international migration will virtually cease, while internal migration continues along the lines outlined above until a peak in war production is reached. If military mortality is relatively great, it will result in a surplus of women in the population for the first time in the history of the United States. The decline in the birth rate during the war will produce great gaps in the population age pyramid of the nation.

In the post-war period it may be expected that the birth rate, the rate of natural increase, the rate of total population growth, the marriage rate, and the divorce rate will temporarily increase. The volume and character of both international and internal migration will be dependent on a complex of political, social, and economic factors, both national and international, which defy prediction at this time.

The impact of the war on population, arranged in time sequence of events above, may also be considered with respect to its short-run and long-run effect.

In the short run a cyclical movement of vital phenomena is generated in which the birth rate, the rate of natural increase, the rate of population growth, the marriage rate, and the divorce rate successively pass from peak to trough to peak with preparation for, participation in, and cessation of hostilities. During the cyclical movement of these phenomena, mortality, particularly military mortality, may be expected to increase with the progress of actual military conflict and, then, to drop precipitately with the close of the war. This general pattern of demographic changes will probably characterize the impact of war on the populations of all the actively belligerent nations.

The long-run effects of war on population in the United States are those which will result largely from the demographic scars which the war will produce—represented by the surplus of women of marriageable age in the population; the gaps in the age structure of the nation—the "hollow classes"; an appreciable number of disabled men; and the distorted internal distribution of population produced by hurried preparation for war. A surplus of women in the population, if we may judge from the experience of the past, will result in increased proportions of married among men and decreased proportions of married among women. Such a surplus will produce a relatively large number of women who will remain spinsters, many of whom will augment the labor force and further complicate the problem of "full employment" after the war.

The "hollow classes" will tend to persist for generations, since the relatively few war babies of World War II will normally produce relatively few offspring for the subsequent generation, thus tending to perpetuate the original deficit created by World War I. Large numbers of partially or totally disabled men will create problems of adjustment that will have many social, economic, and political ramifications.

The redistribution of population within the nation effected by the war involving great concentrations in specialized war-production centers, both old and new, and possible shifts in the urban-rural and in the regional distribution of the population may also create problems which, depending on the direction and soundness of future national policy, may persist for some time in the future.

In combination, these effects, together with the disturbance of human motivation, the breaking of the "cake of custom," attendant social unrest, the widespread diffusion of contraceptive methods, and the uncertainty of the future will probably accelerate the downward trend of fertility and decelerate the rate of national population growth. The fertility of rural areas upon which, in general, the nation is dependent, in the long run, for natural increase may be especially depressed. To the extent that our national economy has been dependent on population growth for maintenance and expansion, further decline in the rate of national growth may have serious long-run economic implications.

It would be remiss to close this paper on the effects of war on population without at least mention of the effects of population on war. From almost the beginning of recorded history, and certainly from the time of Malthus,[41] it has been clear to population students that differences in the pressure of population on resources have been at least one important factor in the wars of the peoples of the world. The voice of the demographer who has pointed to the fundamental problems in the world-wide distribution of population and resources and to measures designed to deal with these problems has indeed been a voice in the wilderness.[42]

The writers of the Treaty of Versailles did not include a demographer. It may be that the winning of the peace, which in every respect is as important as the winning of the war, will in large measure depend on the recognition and the resolution of the "population problem."

In the troubled days which lie ahead the demographer may be expected to continue to describe the relation of population to war, as well as the relation of war to population, and to point to the many problems arising out of these relationships. It may be expected that population problems will be among the major problems of post-war adjustment. The solution of the problems which the demographer poses, however, will depend entirely on the extent to which they are recognized and dealt with by the general citizenry and their public representatives.

[41] Charles E. Stangeland, *Pre-Malthusian Doctrines of Population* (New York: Columbia University Press, 1904); T. R. Malthus, *An Essay on Population* (New York: E. P. Dutton & Co., Inc., 1933).

[42] E.g., see J. M. Keynes, *The Economic Consequences of the Peace* (London: Macmillan & Co., 1919); Henry Kittredge Norton, "Birth Control or War," *Outlook and Independent*, CLIV, No. 13 (March 26, 1930), 485-87, 515; Raymond Pearl, "War and Overpopulation," *Current History*, XLIII (1936), 589-94; Warren S. Thompson, *Danger Spots in World Population* (New York: Alfred A. Knopf, 1929).

THE MARRIAGE BOOM

By John Hajnal

A sudden rise in marriage rates in recent years has been common to most of Central, Northern, and Western Europe and the English speaking countries overseas. These were the countries in which low fertility in the 1930's gave rise to concern over "depopulation." The recent "baby boom" in these countries has been due in part to the "marriage boom." In other regions also, recent years have witnessed perturbations in marriage rates partly, no doubt, because of the war and events subsequent to it. Owing to the inadequacy of statistics in most countries, it is not possible to determine how far developments in those countries which have experienced rises in the number of marriages are similar to changes in the areas of low birth rates with which this paper is mainly concerned.

For general orientation, crude marriage rates may be used even though they do not accurately reflect changes in the marriage rates of the marriageable population and are likely to be particularly misleading as an index of nuptiality in periods of rapid change. We may begin with a comparison of the general level of the crude marriage rate over the whole period since the middle of the 1930's. In Table 1 the principal European countries for which continuous series are available are ranked by the proportion in which their average marriage rate in the period 1935-1950 exceeded the level of the rate in 1925-1934. It will be seen that broadly it was the countries of Northwest Europe which experienced a "marriage boom" during 1935-1950, whereas the average marriage rate in Southern and Eastern Europe fell below that of 1925-1934. The United States and the populations of European origin in the countries of the British Commonwealth recorded an increase in marriage rates of about the same magnitude as Northwest Europe.

The increase in marriage rates did not follow the same pattern in all countries. The rhythm of economic recovery and the events of the war had, as might be expected, a strong influence on marriage rates. In neutral Sweden there was a gradual rise in the crude marriage rate to a maximum around 1942-1944, followed by an equally gradual decline. The belligerent countries experienced sharper fluctuations. Marriage rates were often low during the war years and there was a sharp post-war peak. The bulk of the "marriage boom" generally occurred later than in Sweden. (See chart.)

One might be tempted to proceed to a more detailed study of the marriage boom by means of marriage rates specific by age and previous marital status. The prospects for such an undertaking, however, are not promising owing to the paucity of marriage data in several countries and the lack of population estimates to serve as bases for rates. Fortunately, however, the proportion of single persons in the population in different age groups provides a means of throwing light on several important aspects of the marriage boom. Proportions single are easily available; indeed, a recent international collection of data on this subject is to be found in the United Nations Demographic Yearbook, 1949-50. Those portions of the following discussion which deal with the technique of studying marriage by means of proportions single are based on a more technical paper to be published in the journal Population Studies [1].

Table 1

Crude Marriage Rates
Annual Averages for 1925-1934 and 1935-1950 *

Country	1925-1934	1935-1950	Per Cent Increase
Europe			
Norway	6.2	[8.4]/a	[35]
Sweden.....................	6.8	9.0	32
Finland	7.1	9.3	31
Austria	7.2	9.2	28
Ireland	4.6	5.4	17
Denmark	8.0	9.2	15
England and Wales	7.8	8.9	14
Netherlands	7.4	8.2	11
Switzerland	7.6	8.0	5
Portugal..................	6.8	7.1	4
Italy	7.2	7.3	1
Hungary	8.8	[8.8]/b	[0]
Czechoslovakia	9.0	[9.0]/c	[0]
Bulgaria	9.6	[9.5]/d	[-1]
Spain	7.0	6.8	-3
France	8.0	7.5	-6
Belgium	8.6	7.7	-10
Greece	7.1	[6.0]/c	[-15]
Non-European Countries			
Canada	6.8	9.2	35
Australia	7.3	9.6	32
New Zealand	7.5	9.6	28
United States	9.5	11.9	25
Union of South Africa			
Europeans	9.2	10.9	18

a/ Excluding 1942.
b/ Excluding 1944 and 1949-1950.
c/ Excluding 1950.
d/ Excluding 1948-1950.

* For sources of all tables, see References, pp. 98-101.

Table 2 shows the striking recent fall in proportions single in a number of countries [2]. Figures are included for those countries about which information could be found for a date since 1945. The recent figures are compared with figures for a date as near as possible to the beginning of the high-marriage period. In general, there was no choice since data on the distribution of the population by marital status are, in most countries, obtained only at censuses. Comparisons between countries have to be made with caution where the dates for which figures are available differ widely. Even where the dates are similar for two countries, the pattern of differences in the timing of the marriage boom needs to be kept in mind. There are also variations in the reliability of the data. In the case of men, some of the recent figures for proportions single may be affected by the exclusion from the data of some or all of the armed forces.

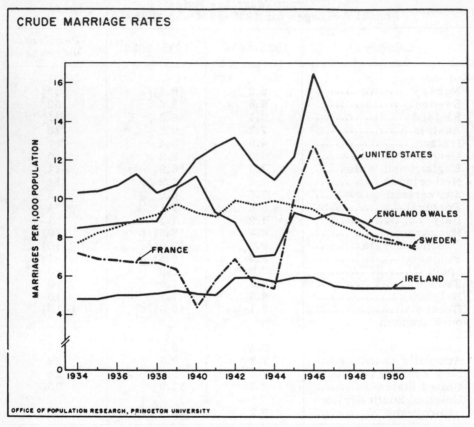

CRUDE MARRIAGE RATES

OFFICE OF POPULATION RESEARCH, PRINCETON UNIVERSITY

The marriage boom is reflected in the proportions single at the younger ages, i.e., the proportion remaining single among groups whose marriages occurred in recent years. At the older ages there has so far been little change, for most of the first marriages of persons now aged over 40 occurred before the marriage boom. The following comments refer to proportions single at the younger ages. There has been a sharp decline in proportions single in Australia, New Zealand, and the United States. In Europe there is a clear decline in the proportions single for women in all countries covered except France; the figures for men fail to show much decline in Ireland and the Netherlands, as well as in France. In the remaining five countries (Denmark, Great Britain, Norway, Sweden, and Switzerland) there were declines in proportions single for both sexes, though the changes were greater for women than for men.

The Recent Changes in Historical and World-wide Perspective

The changes described above must be viewed in relation to past experience. Only then can their magnitude be appreciated. Table 3 shows historical series of proportions single for a number of Western countries. These series are census data, with the exception of the long and careful set of estimates made by Sundbärg for Sweden, which extends back to 1750 [3].

Table 2

Proportions Single at Specified Ages
in Selected Countries at Two Recent Dates

Country	Year	Men			Women		
		20-24	25-29	45-49	20-24	25-29	45-49
Europe							
Denmark	1935	.89	.51	.10	.68	.35	.16
	1945	.85	.44	.10	.59	.26	.16
France	1936	.79	.36	.10/a	.49	.23	.13/a
	1949	.81	.39	.12/a	.54	.22	.11/a
Great Britain	1939	.83	.47	.10	.66	.35	.17
	1951	.77	.35	.10	.53	.22	.15
Ireland	1941	.97	.83	.34	.88	.64	.26
	1946	.95	.80	.33	.83	.57	.26
Netherlands	1930	.90	.49	.11	.75	.38	.15
	1951	.89	.48	.09	.71	.31	.13
Norway	1930	.94	.65	.15	.81	.52	.23
	1946	.90	.59	.16	.73	.40	.22
Sweden	1935	.94	.66	.17	.78	.49	.23
	1945	.87	.52	.17	.64	.30	.21
Switzerland	1941	.94	.62	.14	.80	.45	.20
	1950	.86	.50	.13	.66	.31	.19
Non-European Countries							
Australia	1933	.87	.56	.15	.69	.38	.14
	1947	.76	.38	.14	.52	.21	.13
New Zealand	1936	.90	.56	.14	.72	.38	.14
	1945	.82	.45	.12	.63	.28	.13
United States	1940	.72	.36	.11/b	.47	.23	.09/b
	1951	.52	.20	.08/b	.31	.11	.07/b

a/ Age group 40-49.
b/ Age group 45-54.

The countries included in Table 3 may be divided into three groups: (1) Denmark, Great Britain, the Netherlands, Norway, Sweden, and Switzerland; (2) the United States; (3) France and Ireland. In the

Table 3

Historical Series for Proportions Single
at Specified Ages in Selected Countries

Country	Year	Men			Women		
		20-24	25-29	45-49	20-24	25-29	45-49
Denmark							
	1787	.80/a		.09/b	.64/a		.09/b
	1801	.80/a		.12/b	.63/a		.09/b
	1840	.82/a		.09/b	.70/a		.09/b
	1880	.76/a		.10/b	.64/a		.12/b
	1901	.70/a		.10/b	.59/a		.15/b
	1930	.71/a		.10/b	.55/a		.16/b
	1945	.65/a		.11/b	.43/a		.16/b
France							
	1881	.87	.49	.13	.60	.32	.13
	1901	.90	.48	.11	.58	.30	.12
	1911	.89	.44	.11	.55	.27	.11
	1936	.79	.36	.10/b	.49	.23	.13/b
	1949	.81	.39	.12/b	.54	.22	.11/b
Great Britain							
	1851	.80	.45	.12	.70	.41	.14
	1871	.78	.40	.10	.66	.37	.13
	1911	.86	.50	.13	.76	.44	.17
	1931	.86	.48	.12	.74	.42	.17
	1951	.77	.35	.10	.53	.22	.16
Ireland /c							
	1861	.91	.66	.16	.76	.49	.14
	1891	.96	.78	.20	.86	.59	.17
	1936	.96	.82	.34	.86	.64	.25
	1946	.95	.80	.33	.83	.57	.26
Netherlands							
	1830	.89	.56	.11	.81	.49	.14
	1849	.94	.65	.13	.87	.57	.15
	1879	.90	.54	.13	.78	.43	.14
	1909	.89	.51	.13	.78	.42	.16
	1930	.90	.49	.11	.75	.38	.15
	1951	.89	.48	.09	.71	.31	.13
Norway							
	1801	.73/a		.09/b	.64/a		.15/b
	1875	.76/a		.13/b	.67/a		.17/b
	1910	.73/a		.14/b	.64/a		.22/b
	1930	.80/a		.16/b	.67/a		.23/b
	1946	.75/a		.17/b	.56/a		.22/b
Sweden /d							
	1750	.84	.42	.06	.73	.43	.10
	1800	.87	.50	.07	.78	.48	.12
	1850	.92	.59	.09	.84	.51	.12
	1870	.94	.62	.10	.84	.54	.16
	1910	.93	.62	.15	.80	.51	.22
	1930	.94	.67	.17	.80	.52	.23
	1945	.87	.52	.17	.64	.30	.21

Table 3

Historical Series for Proportions Single
at Specified Ages in Selected Countries (Continued)

Country	Year	Men			Women		
		20-24	25-29	45-49	20-24	25-29	45-49
Switzerland							
	1860	.93	.68	.20	.83	.55	.20
	1880	.90	.59	.18	.77	.44	.20
	1910	.92	.58	.15	.78	.43	.18
	1930	.93	.60	.14	.82	.48	.19
	1950	.86	.50	.13	.66	.31	.19
United States							
	1890	.81	.46	.09/e	.52	.25	.07/e
	1910	.75	.43	.11/e	.48	.25	.09/e
	1930	.71	.37	.11/e	.46	.22	.09/e
	1951	.52	.20	.08/e	.31	.11	.07/e

a/ Age group 20-29.
b/ Age group 40-49.
c/ Figures for 1861 include Northern Ireland. Subsequent years relate to territory of the Republic of Ireland only.
d/ Years 1750-1850: Estimates.
e/ Age group 45-54.

---

first group of countries, the recent proportions single for women at the
lower ages are below any recorded in the last hundred years. In the
Scandinavian countries the data extend back for several decades before
the middle of the nineteenth century; the recent proportions single for
women are well below those observed for that period. Among men the
recent proportions single are also unprecedented in Denmark, Great
Britain, and Switzerland. However, in Norway and the Netherlands they
are slightly above the lowest previously recorded, and according to the
estimates for eighteenth century Sweden, the proportions single for men
at that time were below those of today but rose to the present levels at
the beginning of the nineteenth century.

In the United States the recent proportions single fall below any
recorded since 1890, when data first became available. However, it
seems likely that for several decades before 1890 the proportions single
were above the recent figures. This conclusion is supported by data on
proportions single available for a few states in this period [4].

The present situation is thus largely unprecedented in recent
Western history. It is not only the level of proportions single in the
last few years that deserves special notice. The reduction has taken
place with unparalleled suddenness. No one examining the trend of proportions single up to the early 1930's—or the trend of any other statistical index for marriage—could have predicted the recent changes. Reductions in the proportions single were indeed occurring in some countries before 1930, but they were very slow in comparison with what has
occurred in the last two decades.

The cases of France and Ireland require special discussion. France, so far as data available at present show, has not participated in the recent dramatic change in proportions single[5]. Two points relevant to the interpretation of the contrast between France and the Northwest European countries in group (1) need to be mentioned. In the first place, France experienced a far greater disruption of normal marriage trends during the war since a larger proportion of marriageable men were outside the country. Secondly, in regard to marriage as in other respects, the demographic history of France has differed from the general pattern of Northwest European countries. In France a fairly substantial reduction in proportions single occurred in the first three decades of the century. In the early 1930's the pattern of proportions single in France was outside the range of experience of Northwest Europe and near that of the United States. As a result of the recent changes in the other Northwest European countries, France is no longer conspicuous among them as a country of early marriage.

Table 4

Proportions Single at Specified Ages in Selected Countries /a

Country	Year	Men			Women		
		20-24	25-29	45-49	20-24	25-29	45-49
Germany	1939	.91	.51	.07/b	.64	.31	.15/b
Austria	1939	.89	.60	.10/b	.68	.42	.18/b
Portugal	1940	.85	.48	.09	.69	.40	.18
Spain	1940	.94	.63	.09	.79	.44	.14
Italy	1936	.91	.54	.10	.69	.39	.14
Greece	1928	.83	.52	.07	.56	.26	.04
Czechoslovakia	1930	.88	.43	.06	.62	.30	.10
Hungary	1941	.88	.46	.06	.53	.24	.09
Poland	1931	.83	.41	.04	.61	.30	.07
U.S.S.R.	1926	.51	.18	.03/b	.28	.09	.04/b
Bulgaria	1934	.56	.20	.03	.35	.11	.01
Yugoslavia	1931	.60	.27	.05	.35	.15	.05
Turkey	1935	.49	.24	.03	.18	.06	.03
India	1931	.35	.14	.04	.05	.02	.01
Ceylon	1946	.80	.43	.08	.29	.12	.03
Malaya Malays	1947	.54	.17	.02	.07	.02	.01
Korea	1930	.33	.10	.01	.02	.01	.00
Formosa	1930	.52	.19	.04	.15	.04	.00
Japan	1951	.83	.34	.02	.55	.15	.02

a/ All figures relate to territories as of the dates stated.
b/ Age group 40-49.

The demographic history of Ireland is remarkable in many respects. In the middle of the nineteenth century, the proportions single were similar to those of some other Northwest European countries [6]. After that, a steady increase occurred up to the 1930's. Ireland developed a unique pattern of very late marriage with very large proportions of both men and women remaining single throughout life. The proportions single have been diminishing slightly in the last decade after increasing for a century, but there still seems no radical departure towards levels nearer to those of other countries. In interpreting the proportions single the large volume of emigration from Ireland must be taken into account. Presumably, far fewer of the migrants than of those who stayed at home remained unmarried. The patterns of late marriage and heavy emigration in Ireland are generally interpreted as a reaction to the great famine of the 1840's.

It is instructive to view recent trends in countries of the industrial West in comparison with the rest of the world as well as in relation to their own past experience, although such a comparison faces difficulties arising out of errors and incomparabilities in the data.

The family as an institution is not the same in different cultures, and it is not possible to define "marriage" in a unique way for statistical purposes in all countries. Clearly, the term "married" has a different meaning in a country such as India where child marriage is traditional, from that which it has in a European setting. Moreover, the data on age distribution in many countries are known to be inaccurate, and marital status data are also often suspect. With these reservations in mind, it nevertheless seems worth while briefly to consider the recent Western industrial experience in relation to that of some non-Western countries. Table 4 shows figures for a selection of countries where data are available. Latin America has been omitted because the consensually married persons in that region form a large proportion of the population and their statistical treatment is so uncertain that comparisons become problematical.

Most of Europe has been characterized by very high proportions single in comparison with most other parts of the world. Proportions single are high by world standards not only in the countries discussed so far, but also in the remainder of Central Europe and in Southern Europe (Germany, Austria, Hungary, Poland, Spain, Italy, etc.). However, several Eastern European countries (Bulgaria, Russia, Yugoslavia) depart completely from the general European pattern [7]. In this group of countries, which will here be denoted as the "Eastern European group," the proportions single are much lower. People marry earlier and there are very few left single after age 30. The gap separating the Eastern European group from the remainder of Europe may be characterized in various ways. We may note, for example, that among men aged 20-24 the proportion single in the Eastern European group is below 60 per cent. No country in the remainder of Europe (until very recently) recorded a figure below 75. The Asian countries display a variety of patterns, but the proportions single are, in most cases, far lower even than in Eastern Europe. Ceylon and Japan are striking exceptions. Ceylon may be only an apparent exception since it is believed that at censuses in that country a large number of persons whose marriages have not been registered fail to be reported as married [8]. In Japan the proportions single have increased since 1920, when data first became available, as the following figures show:

	Men				Women		
	20-24	25-29	45-49		20-24	25-29	45-49
1920	.71	.26	.02		.31	.09	.02
1935	.84	.35	.02		.45	.11	.02
1951	.83	.34	.02		.55	.15	.02

Reference to Table 2 shows that the recent changes in Western European countries have been too small to close the gap between them and even the Eastern European countries, not to speak of most of Asia. However, the proportions single in the United States, which before 1940 were slightly below the Western European level, have now come within the Eastern European range.

A recital of statistical facts seems to call for some comment on the social factors underlying the figures. In spite of the huge volume of literature on marriage and the family, little attention has been devoted to the statistics, and little attempt has been made to explain the observed variations in the frequency of marriage and age at marriage. There is no well developed body of thought which could serve as a starting point for an explanation of the recent "marriage boom." One widespread impression—that the special marriage pattern of Western Europe is due to the rise of "urban industrial civilization"—is demonstrably false. It seems to be based largely on the view that marriage used to occur at a very much earlier age in Western Europe. The evidence for this view is literary—for example, Juliet's marriage at the age of 14 has been frequently cited. Whatever the position in the Middle Ages may have been (it has been suggested that the upper classes married much earlier than the mass of the people), such statistical data as exist for the eighteenth and early nineteenth centuries indicate that the marriage pattern in Northwest European countries had not changed substantially between that time and the 1930's. The main evidence is provided by the proportions single. (See Table 3.) The earliest data in all countries fall clearly within the Western European and not the Eastern European pattern. The modern marriage pattern clearly existed before Western Europe became industrialized or urbanized. Moreover, it has not been true within Western experience that agricultural populations marry to a greater extent or earlier than urban populations; in fact, on the whole both nineteenth and twentieth century statistics show the reverse, at least for the male population[9]. A special pattern of marriage (relatively late marriage and high proportions never marrying) has apparently characterized for centuries the civilization which gave rise to modern industrial society.

The Decline in Age at Marriage

By this time, the reader is probably impatient of "changes in the proportions single." "Obviously," he may say, "the age at marriage has declined—would it not be much more interesting to measure the decline?" Unfortunately, the measurement of the age at marriage (and other aspects of marriage) is a more complex problem than is often supposed. There is no simple answer to the question often asked, "What is the age at marriage in the United States today?" and there would be

no simple answer even if all relevant statistical data were available.
A number of methods may be used to measure the age at marriage; they
often differ considerably and their variation over time is by no means
the same. Which method should be used depends, as it generally does
in demography, upon the purpose of the measurement; which method can
be used depends upon the availability of data.

Table 5

Crude Mean Age at Marriage in Selected Countries /a

Country	Men				
	1926-30	1931-35	1936-40	1941-45	1946-49
Denmark	29.3	29.3	29.3	29.4/b	-
England and Wales	29.1	29.0	29.0	28.9	29.7
France	28.7	28.7	29.8	29.5	-
Netherlands	29.1/c	-	29.1	29.4/d	30.3
Norway	29.9	30.2	30.3	30.2/e	30.4
Sweden	30.5	30.6	30.5	30.1	30.0/f
Switzerland	30.7	30.5	31.0	31.2	-
Australia	29.2	29.1	29.2	29.0	28.8/g
New Zealand	29.6	29.8	29.8	-	29.8/h

Country	Women				
	1926-30	1931-35	1936-40	1941-45	1946-49
Denmark	25.6	25.7	25.5	25.6/b	-
England and Wales	26.6	26.4	26.2	25.9	26.5
France	25.3	25.4	26.3	25.8	-
Netherlands	26.3/c	-	26.4	26.5/d	27.2
Norway	26.4	26.7	26.8	26.9/e	27.0
Sweden	26.9	26.9	26.9	26.7	26.8/f
Switzerland	27.2	27.2	27.7	27.6	-
Australia	25.6	25.5	25.7	25.7	25.6/g
New Zealand	26.2	26.1	26.2	-	26.2/h

a/ Mean ages of all marriages (including remarriages) concluded in
years stated.
b/ Excluding 1942 and 1944.
c/ 1910-1919.
d/ Excluding 1944.
e/ Excluding 1942.
f/ 1946-1947 only.
g/ 1946-1948 only.
h/ 1946-1950.

The statistical study of marriage is a neglected field compared with that of births and deaths. The technique of the life table has indeed been applied to marriages; the idea of calculating how many "survive" unmarried at each age is an obvious one, but few "nuptiality tables" have been computed. (The term "nuptiality table" has found even less acceptance than the technique itself.) Demographers have devoted their attention mainly to births and deaths. Sociologists and others concerned with marriage and the family, even when they have used statistics, have generally been unaware of the problems of measurement technique.

Perhaps one reason for the neglect of marriage by demographers has been that, while striking changes were occurring in fertility and mortality, nothing much was happening to marriages apart from obvious year-by-year fluctuations. One much documented conclusion in works of population statistics is that the secular decline of the birth rate was not caused by any drastic change in the frequency of marriage or the age at marriage.

The marriage boom poses an obvious challenge to students of measurement technique. The data on proportions single suggest that, in some sense, a decline in age at marriage is in process. "If today twice as many people are married by age 20 as there were fifteen years ago," one might ask, "doesn't that mean that people are marrying younger?" Yet the crude general mean age at marriage (the mean of the distribution by age of all marriages, including remarriages, occurring in a given period) has shown no consistent declining trend, as Table 5 illustrates. There are no similar data for the United States, but there is no reason to suppose that, if such figures were available, they would show a different result.

The proportions single have, in the past, been employed for the study of marriage mainly because they are often available even when registration data on marriage are deficient. Examples are Brazil, the United States, and the Arab population of Palestine. The United Nations has recently included a paper on this subject in a collection of studies intended to assist in the exploitation of census data in countries where registration statistics are defective [10]. The recent "marriage boom" is an indication that proportions single can be useful also in other circumstances.

The remainder of this paper will be devoted to indicating (1) what kind of indices relating to marriage—and particularly to age at marriage—can be derived most easily from proportions single, and (2) what kind of guess at the decline in the age at marriage results from the application of these techniques. The term "marriage" will denote "first marriage" unless otherwise stated.

The use of proportions single is particularly simple if two conditions are approximately fulfilled. (1) If the incidence of mortality and migration at each age is the same for both the single and the general population, the proportion of persons in an age group who are single is determined only by the frequency of first marriage experienced by the group up to the date of observation. (2) If the rates of first marriage in a community are constant over a period of time, the proportions single provide a very simple means for the study of the rates of marriage of single persons. For, in such a community, a table of proportions single recorded at a census for successive ages may be taken to represent the experience of a cohort passing through life. By observing the progressive reduction in proportions single with increasing age, the rates of first marriage by age may be deduced.

From an age schedule of marriage rates, as from an age schedule of fertility or mortality rates, various measures may be constructed. One way of proceeding is to envisage a hypothetical cohort, in which there are no deaths of persons in the marriageable ages, and which is subject at each age to the marriage rates implied by the proportions single. The distribution of marriages in such a cohort can be computed without using any additional data and the proportion left single at each age is simply the proportion single recorded at the census or survey. When such a calculation is made using marriage rates computed by relating registered marriages to the single population (rather than derived from proportions single), it is called a gross nuptiality table. The underlying conception is obviously closely similar to that of the conventional gross reproduction rate. (Indeed the words "gross" and "net" are clearly applied by analogy to reproductivity.)

The conception described in the last paragraph may be usefully interpreted in another way. For simplicity of language, it is convenient to do this in terms of a particular index. Since we are concerned with measuring the age at marriage, we take the average age [11] at marriage of persons marrying under 50 in a hypothetical cohort such as is described in the last paragraph [12]. This index will, for want of a better term, be called the "singulate mean age at marriage."

If the first of the conditions mentioned above is roughly fulfilled, then the experience of the hypothetical cohort without mortality is roughly the same as that of those members of a real cohort who survive to age 50. The mean age at marriage in the hypothetical cohort is the same as the mean age at marriage of those who survive to age 50 and have married by that age. (This figure will, of course, be slightly higher than that which would be obtained if the marriages of those who died under 50 were taken into account.)

The singulate mean age at marriage fulfills the general purpose of refined indices in demography in "eliminating" the effects of variations in age structure and other perturbations considered irrelevant to the purpose in hand. It depends only on the marriage frequencies implied by the proportions single and does not involve any other element; for example, unlike standardized rates, it involves no arbitrary age distribution. Moreover, it can be computed in a few minutes from data in five-year age groups. Finally, the proportions single are easily available and thus comparisons over time and between countries which would demand great labor if other methods were used, become practicable.

As an index of marriage age some may prefer the mean age at which all marriages (with no upper limit) occur in a cohort subject to mortality as well as to marriage. This index differs from that which has here been termed the singulate mean age at marriage in two respects: the inclusion of marriages over 50, and allowance for mortality. The first factor is usually small; the second is small if mortality is

Table 6

Decline in Age at Marriage in Selected Countries
between Specified Years

Country	Years	Men		Women	
		Marriage Age before Decline/a	Estimated Decline/b	Marriage Age before Decline/a	Estimated Decline/b
United States	1940, 1951	25 1/2	2.0	22 1/2	1.6
France	1936, 1949	26	[0.3]/c	23	[0.4]/c
England and Wales	1935, 1951	27 1/2	1.2	25 1/2	2.1
Netherlands	1930, 1951	27 1/2	0.1	25 1/2	0.5
Denmark	1935, 1945	28	0.6	25	0.9
Australia	1933, 1947	28	1.7	25	1.7
New Zealand	1936, 1945	28	1.1	25 1/2	0.9
Switzerland	1941, 1950	29	1.4	26	1.6
Sweden	1935, 1945	30	1.5	26 1/2	1.7
Ireland	1941, 1946	32 1/2	0.5	28 1/2	0.7

a/ Singulate age at marriage of persons marrying under 50 computed from proportions single at the earlier date.

b/ Estimated minimum decline in years (compared with previous column) indicated by proportions single at second date.

c/ Increase in age at marriage.

---

low. The two factors work in opposite directions, and in countries where mortality is low there is likely to be little difference between the two indices [13].

The second condition mentioned above (fairly constant proportions single over time) was reasonably well fulfilled in most Western countries in the first four decades of the twentieth century. Table 6 shows the singulate mean age at marriage as derived from the data of the 1930's. However, since there were some fluctuations in marriage rates over time, and other disturbances (notably correlation between mortality and migration on the one hand, and marital status on the other) affect the data, the figures are given only to the nearest half year.

The pattern revealed is well known. The United States and Ireland stand out as the extremes of early and late marriage in the Western world. However, if the singulate mean age at marriage is computed from the data of the 1931 census of India, the result is 19 years for men and 12.5 years for women. (See chart on front cover.)

Estimating the decline in age at marriage which is occurring in the Western countries is more complex. In a transition period, one of the conditions of the use of the singulate age at marriage (the condition that proportions single have been constant over a period of time) is clearly violated.

The position may be illustrated by the following figures on proportions single among women in Sweden in 1935 and 1945.

Age Group	Per Cent Single	
	1935	1945
15-19	99	97
20-24	78	64
25-29	49	30
30-34	34	20
35-39	27	19
40-44	24	20
45-49	23	21
50-54	22	21

The figures for 1935 form a steadily diminishing series. They might represent the proportions recorded by a cohort at successive ages. On the other hand, the proportions for 1945 clearly represent a transitional stage. It is inconceivable that either in a single cohort or permanently in a population a larger proportion of people should have been married at 35-39 than at 40-44. It would not make much sense to compute a singulate mean age at marriage from a series of this sort.

The comparison of the two sets of proportions single does, however, permit the inference that, in a significant sense, the age at marriage in Sweden is declining. Consider, for example, the women aged 25-29 in 1945. They were born in the years 1916-1920. Seventy per cent of them had married by the end of 1945. Ten years earlier among women of the same age (i.e., born 1906-1910) only 51 per cent had married. Obviously, a far greater proportion of the later group had married before they were 25. Of course, this group had not completed its marital history by 1945; but it is clearly most unlikely that when that history is complete it will turn out that the mean age at which all their marriages occurred will be higher than the mean age for the earlier group. There simply are not enough women left in the later group to get married at the higher ages and thus raise the mean age at marriage.

Thus, it may be shown that in a number of Western countries the cohorts who are now in their twenties and thirties are marrying earlier than their predecessors. In order to obtain a measure of this decline in the age at marriage, it is obviously necessary to make a guess at the number and age distribution of the future marriages of the cohorts in question. A crude guess can be made using no other materials than the proportions single. Table 6 gives minimum figures for the decline in age at marriage deduced on the basis of the proportions single in Table 2 [14].

The picture of the change in age at marriage obtained in this way differs substantially from that shown by the crude general age at marriage as given in Table 5. The difference is partly attributable to the fact that the singulate mean age at marriage "eliminates" changes in age structure and relates to first marriages only. (In several countries there have recently been sharp fluctuations in the proportion of first marriages to remarriages both for men and women.) In addition, however, in a period of rapidly changing marriage rates, the actual distribution of marriages by age shows special temporary features that arise because the marriages at the older ages are those of cohorts whose earlier marriages took place in accordance with a different pattern. For a discussion of this point as well as for details of the procedures by which Table 6 was computed, the reader must be referred to the more technical study mentioned above [15].

Table 6 shows substantial declines in age at marriage for both sexes in the United States, Australia, and New Zealand and in the following European countries: Denmark, England and Wales, Sweden, and Switzerland. The process of decline had presumably not been completed in the interval of time covered by the data, and the length of the interval is not the same for all the countries. Perhaps the most significant statement is that the age at marriage has been declining in the countries mentioned at an average rate of at least one-tenth of a year per annum for the female population. (In Denmark and in England and Wales the rate of reduction was apparently slightly less for men.) Such a rate of decline cannot go on for long, particularly in a country such as the United States, where by Western standards people already marry young.

Similar argument shows that the proportion of persons who never marry in the course of their lives is likely to diminish in these same countries. The probable diminution is particularly striking among the female population in the Western European countries. In these countries in the past, a far larger proportion of women than of men had remained single. This difference between the sexes seems likely to disappear.

FOOTNOTES

1. Population Studies, Vol. 7, No. 2. Nov., 1953.

2. Sources for Table 2 are given below under References. Some additional materials relating to the recent changes in marital composition may be noted, though they were not suitable for comparison with the figures in Table 2.

(1) After the war Czechoslovakia experienced a reduction of territory and large population transfers. Thus data from the censuses of 1930 and 1947 are not precisely comparable. The proportions single are as follows:

	Men		Women	
	20-24	25-29	20-24	25-29
1930	.88	.43	.62	.30
1947	.85	.46	.54	.23

[Source: United Nations. Demographic Yearbook, 1949-50. New York, 1950. P. 217.]

(2) For Hungary proportions married (but not proportions single)

as obtained from the census of January 1, 1949, have been published in Statisztikai Szemle, Vol. 3, No. 3, p. 203. March, 1951. The comparison between 1941 and 1949 is as follows:

	Men		Women	
	20-24	25-29	20-24	25-29
1941	.12	.53	.47	.735
1949	.24	.58	.52	.725

(3) The problem of Germany is complicated. It would be worth exploring to what extent the "marriage boom" in 1933-1939 was similar to what has occurred elsewhere more recently. Analysis of the postwar picture is rendered difficult by the difference in area between the Federal Republic (for which current data are available) and prewar Germany and by the sharp perturbations in age-sex composition resulting from the two world wars and the aftermath of World War II. In the following table, the figures for 1925 and 1939 relate to the territory of Germany in those years; the data for 1946 and 1950 are for the area of the Federal Republic of Germany. The proportions single are:

	Men		Women	
	20-24	25-29	20-24	25-29
1925	.89	.45	.75	.37
1939	.91	.51	.64	.31
1946	.88	.52	.73	.36
1950	.83	.47	.68	.34

[Source: Myers, Paul F., and Mauldin, W. Parker. Population of the Federal Republic of Germany and West Berlin. U. S. Bureau of the Census, International Population Statistics Reports, Series P-90, No. 1. Washington, 1952. P. 25.]

3. Cross tabulation of age by marital status is available only for the Swedish censuses from 1870 on. Sundbärg based his estimates mainly on the separate classifications by age and by marital status. Citation to Sundbärg's article and other sources for Table 3 are given below under References.

4. See Monahan, Thomas P. The Pattern of Age at Marriage in the United States. Philadelphia, Stephenson Brothers, 1951. Pp. 81 ff.

5. There is also other evidence which suggests that the French marriage pattern has not changed substantially since before the war. After the postwar peak in marriages the age-specific marriage rates had returned in 1949-1950 to a level which was only slightly above that of 1935-1937. [See France. Institut National de la Statistique et des Etudes Economiques. Bulletin Mensuel de Statistique, Nouvelle Série, Supplément, July-Sept., 1951, p. 4; and Gasc, Paul. "Chronique de démographie." Journal de la Société de Statistique de Paris, Vol. 93, Nos. 7-8-9, p. 215. July-Sept., 1952.]

6. From the censuses of Ireland in 1841 and 1851 figures on proportions single are available in the larger age groups:

   1841:   Men   Women

           17-25 26-35 46-55   17-25 26-35 46-55
            .92   .43   .10   .81   .29   .13

   [Source: Report of the Commissioners Appointed to Take
   the Census of Ireland, 1841. Dublin, 1843. Pp. 438-439.]

   1851:   Men   Women

           17-24 25-34 45-54   17-24 25-34 45-54
            .96   .59   .12   .89   .40   .13

   [Source: The Census of Ireland, 1851. Part VI. General
   report. Dublin, 1856. P. xlvi.]

   The data for 1841 fall within the experience of other Northwest
   European countries. Nevertheless, the proportions single are fairly
   high and there is nothing in these figures to indicate that before the
   famine the Irish were remarkable for early marriage. (This view
   has recently been put forward by K. H. Connell in his book The Population of Ireland, 1750-1845. Oxford, Clarendon Press, 1950.)

7. No data appear to be available for Romania since 1889. At that date
   and for the territory of the period, the proportions single in the age
   groups 20-24 and 25-29 were .67 and .21, respectively, for men and
   .20 and .08 for women. [See Institut International de Statistique.
   Annuaire international de statistique. I. Etat de la population (Europe). La Haye, 1916. P. 92.]

8. At the census of 1901, the proportion single in the age group 20-29
   was found to be .48 for men and .18 for women. In 1911 the corresponding figures were .61 and .21. The report on the 1911 census
   expresses the belief that the 1901 data were more complete because
   public opinion at that time attached less significance to the registration of marriages. The proportions single recorded at the censuses
   of 1921 and 1946 were very close to those of 1911. In 1946 for the
   first time, the enumerators were instructed to distinguish in their
   entries between registered and customary marriages. Of those reported as married in the age range 20-29, about one-third were recorded as married by custom. [See Denham, E. B. Ceylon at the
   Census of 1911, Being the Review of the Results of the Census of
   1911. Colombo, 1912. Pp. 323 and 348; and Ranasinha, A. G. Census of Ceylon, 1946. Colombo, 1951. Vol. I, Part 2, p. 102.]

9. Evidence relating to differences in marriage patterns between city
   and country and between those in agriculture and those in other economic activities is scattered through the censuses and vital statistics
   of Western countries. Most of it has never been analyzed. The
   study of the marriage habits of groups to which people often successively belong in the course of their lives is beset with special
   difficulties; for example, there has been a tendency for particularly
   heavy migration of the unmarried to cities. Only a brief indication
   of the type of data available can be given here. Thus, for Switzerland in the last quarter of the eighteenth century the following three
   lines of evidence may be cited:

(1) Proportions single for men were higher in the country than in the city; for women the relationship was reversed. Thus in 1888 among men aged 25-34 living in cities 45 per cent were single; among those of the same age living in rural areas, 48 per cent were single. Among the women the corresponding figures were 44 per cent for the urban and 39 per cent for the rural population. [See Switzerland. Résultats du recensement fédéral du 1er décembre 1900. Vol. IV. Exposé des résultats généraux du recensement. Statistique de la Suisse, 162e Livraison. Berne, 1908. P. 90*.]

(2) Proportions single for men employed in agriculture were above the national average. Thus, at the census of 1900 the following proportions were recorded as single in the specified age groups:

	20-24	25-29	30-39	40-49
Agriculture and related occupations	94	69	37	23
All occupations	90	57	27	16

[Source: Switzerland. Mariages, naissances et décès en Suisse de 1891 à 1900. Première partie. Mariages contractés et mariages dissous. Statistique de la Suisse, 158e Livraison. Berne, 1908. P. 42*.]

(3) Marriage rates (marriages related to the number of single, widowed, and divorced men aged 18 or more) were lower in agricultural than in industrial districts. (The districts were classified on the basis of the percentage of the occupied population employed in agriculture.) The marriage rates (per 1,000) were as follows:

	1871-1890	1891-1900
Industrial districts	59	61
Mixed districts	47	49
Agricultural districts	42	40

These differences were consistent over time for different age groups and within religious and language groups. [Source: Ibid., p. 23* ff.]

Data of this sort, particularly the first two kinds, are available for many countries and periods; the differences usually run in the same direction and are of roughly the same order of magnitude as those quoted for Switzerland. Other types of data have been used in various special studies, such as marriage registration data classified by occupation, census occupation data where questions on age at or duration of marriage had been asked, etc. The following are examples:

Ogle, William. "On Marriage Rates and Marriage Ages with Special Reference to the Growth of Population." Journal of the Royal Statistical Society, Vol. 53, No. 2, p. 274. 1890.

Gasc, Paul. "Chronique de démographie." Journal de la Société de Statistique de Paris, Vol. 93, Nos. 7-8-9, p. 217. 1952.

Stevenson, T. H. C. "The Fertility of Various Social Classes in England and Wales from the Middle of the Nineteenth Century to 1911." Journal of the Royal Statistical Society, Vol. 83, No. 3, pp. 424 ff. 1920.

Notestein, F. W. "Differential Age at Marriage According to Social Class." American Journal of Sociology, Vol. 38, No. 1, pp. 22-49. July, 1931.

Monahan, Thomas P. The Pattern of Age at Marriage in the United States. 1951. Pp. 237-286.

10. United Nations. Department of Social Affairs. Methods of Using Census Statistics for the Calculation of Life Tables and Other Demographic Measures (with Applications to the Population of Brazil). By Giorgio Mortara. Population Studies, No. 7. Lake Success, New York, Nov., 1949.

11. Any other measure of central tendency could, of course, be used in place of the mean. The United States Census Bureau uses the median.

12. It is usual to impose an upper limit, because the fluctuations from age group to age group in the proportions single among very old persons reflect factors which are clearly not connected with marriage frequency. For the quantitative effect of the limitation to age 50, see the next footnote.

13. The orders of magnitude involved may be illustrated by means of gross and net nuptiality tables. Thus, in a net nuptiality table for females in England and Wales, 1930-1932, the mean age at which marriages of all ages occurred was 25.70. In the gross nuptiality table the mean age for all marriages was 25.90; that for marriages under age 50, 25.55. For the United States in 1940, the corresponding figures were 25.54, 25.74, and 25.54 for men and 22.74, 22.81, and 22.71 for women. For Switzerland, 1939-1944, one obtains 28.92, 29.14, and 28.88 for men; 26.02, 26.12, and 26.00 for women. [The nuptiality tables for England and Wales are given by R. R. Kuczynski in "The Analysis of Vital Statistics: I. Marriage Statistics." Economica, Vol. 5 (New Series), No. 18, pp. 144-145. May, 1938. The net nuptiality table for the United States is to be found in Wilson H. Grabill's "Attrition Life Tables for the Single Population." Journal of the American Statistical Association, Vol. 40, No. 231. Sept., 1945. A gross nuptiality table was computed from the marriage probabilities there given. The Swiss tables have been published in: Switzerland. Schweizerische Volkssterbetafeln, 1939/44. Ausscheide- und Überlebensordnungen nach dem Zivilstand. Bern, 1953. Of these sources only Kuczynski uses the terms "gross" and "net" nuptiality tables.]

14. However, two differences between Tables 2 and 6 require mention: England and Wales has been substituted for Great Britain (with a change in the dates) and Norway has been omitted since, at the time when the computations were made, the proportions single for Norway in 1946 were available only in ten-year age groups.

15. Population Studies, Vol. 7, No. 2. Nov., 1953.

REFERENCES

1. Source for Table 1:

   United Nations Statistical Office. Demographic Yearbook, 1952.
   Table 23.

2. Sources for Table 2:

   Most of the data were taken from: United Nations Statistical Office.
   Demographic Yearbook, 1949-1950, Table 6. The following notes
   indicate the other sources used and give some qualification of the
   data. The statistical offices of the Netherlands and Switzerland
   kindly supplied unpublished estimates of population by marital status.

   France
   1936: U. S. National Office of Vital Statistics. Summary of Inter-
       national Vital Statistics, 1937-1944. Washington, Govt. Print-
       ing Office, 1947. Pp. 94-95.
   1949: France. Institut National de la Statistique et des Etudes
       Economiques. "Le mouvement naturel de la population au
       cours de l'année 1949." Bulletin Mensuel de Statistique,
       Nouvelle Série, Supplément, July-Sept., 1951. P. 2.

   Great Britain
   1939: Great Britain. Royal Commission on Population. Papers
       of the Royal Commission on Population. Vol. II. Reports and
       selected papers of the Statistics Committee. London, H. M.
       Stationery Office, 1950. Pp. 201, 204.
   1951: England and Wales, General Register Office, and Scotland,
       General Registry Office. Census 1951: Great Britain. One
       per cent sample tables. Part I. London, H. M. Stationery
       Office, 1952. Table I, 1, p. 2.

   Netherlands
   1951: Estimates of the population by marital status and age were
       supplied by the Netherlands Central Bureau of Statistics.

   Norway
   1946: Norway. Statistisk Sentralbyrå. Statistisk Årbok for Norge,
       70. Årgang, 1951. Oslo, 1951. P. 14.

   Switzerland
   1950: Estimates of total and single population by age were supplied
       by the Swiss Federal Statistical Office. The Statistical Of-
       fice stated that an allowance for migration is included in the
       estimates of total population but not in those of the single
       population. The proportions single derived from these es-
       timates are probably somewhat too low.

   Australia
   Excluding full-blooded aborigines.

   New Zealand
   Excluding Maoris.

   United States
   1951: U. S. Bureau of the Census. "Marital status and household
       characteristics: April 1951." Current Population Reports,

Series P-20, No. 38. April 29, 1952. These data are for
the "civilian population," but about 610,000 members of the
armed forces living off post or with their families on post
are covered; other non-civilians are excluded. The sampling variation (estimated at the 5 per cent level) of some of
the proportions single exceeds 0.01.

3. Sources for Table 3:

Sources for the most recent data are given in notes to Table 2.

Denmark
Westergaard, Harald. "On the Study of Displacements within a
Population." Journal of the American Statistical Association,
Vol. 17, No. 3, p. 386. Dec., 1920.
Denmark. Statistiske Departement. Befolkningsforholdene i Dan-
mark i de 19 Aarhundrede. Statistisk Tabelvaerk, Femte Raekke,
Litra A, No. 5. København. P. 66.
Denmark. Statistiske Departement. Folketaellingen i Kongeriget
Danmark den 5. November 1930. Statistisk Tabelvaerk, Femte
Raekke, Litra A, No. 20. København, 1935. P. 22.

France
France. Statistique Générale de la France. Annuaire statistique
de la France, Septième année, 1884. Paris, 1884. P. 7.
France. Statistique Générale de la France. Résultats statistiques
du recensement général de la population, effectué le 5 mars 1911.
Tome I, 2e partie. Population présente total. P. 23.

Great Britain
Great Britain. Royal Commission on Population. Papers of the
Royal Commission on Population. Vol. II. Reports and selected
papers of the Statistical Committee. London, H. M. Stationery Office, 1950. Pp. 199-205.

Ireland
Ireland. Census of Ireland, 1871. Part III. General report. P. 220.
Ireland. Department of Industry and Commerce. Census of Population, 1936. Vol. V, Part I. Ages, orphanhood and conjugal conditions. Dublin, 1939. Pp. 26-27.

Netherlands
Netherlands. Centraal Bureau voor de Statistiek. Volkstelling 31
December 1930. Part IX. 's Gravenhage, 1934. Pp. 81-85.

Norway
Norway. Departementet for det Indre. Tabeller Vedkommende
Folketaellingerne i Aarene 1801 og 1825. Norges Officielle Sta-
tistik udgiven i aaret 1874; C. No. 1. Christiania, 1874. Table 1.
Norway. Statistiske Centralbyraa. Annuaire statistique de la Nor-
vège, Première année, 1879. Kristiana, 1879. Table 6.
Norway. Statistiske Centralbyraa. Folketaellingen i Norge 1 De-
cember 1910. Femte Hefte. Folkemaengde fordelt efter kjon, al-
der og egteskabelig stilling samt fødesteder. Norges Officielle
Statistik, VI. 8. Kristiana, 1914. Table 4.

Sweden
Sundbärg, Gustav. "Fortsatta Bidrag till en Svensk Befolknings-
statistik för Åren 1750-1900." Statistisk Tidskrift, No. 3, pp. 186-
187. 1906.
Sweden. Statistiska Centralbyrån. Folkräkningen den 31 Decem-

ber 1910. Vol. II. Folkmängdens fördelning efter kön, ålder och civilstand. Stockholm, 1913. P. 47*.
Sweden. Statistiska Centralbyrån. Folkräkningen den 31 December 1930. Vol. II. Stockholm, 1936. P. 50*.

Switzerland
Switzerland. Eidgenössisches Statistisches Amt. Eidgenössische Volkszählung 1. Dezember 1941. Vol. 21, Tabellenteil I. Bern, 1948. Pp. 84-87.

United States
United States. Bureau of the Census. Sixteenth Census of the United States: 1940. Population. Vol. IV. Part I. Washington, Govt. Printing Office, 1943. Table 5, p. 16.

4. Sources for Table 4:

Data were taken from: United Nations Statistical Office. Demographic Yearbook, 1949-1950, Table 6, except for the following countries:
Germany, Austria, and U.S.S.R.
U. S. National Office of Vital Statistics. Summary of International Vital Statistics, 1937-1944. Washington, Govt. Printing Office, 1947. Table 7.

Malaya
Malaya. Federation of Malaya and the Colony of Singapore. A Report on the 1947 Census of Population. By M. V. Del Tufo. London, 1949. Table 20.

Japan
Japan. Bureau of Statistics. Population Census of 1950. Vol. III. Results of ten percent sample tabulation. Part I. Tokyo, 1952.

5. Sources for Table 5:

Data for years up to 1945 have been taken from: Colombo, Bernardo. La Recente Inversione nella Tendenza della Natalità. Padua, 1951. P. 28. For some countries, Colombo computed the mean age at marriage from the distribution of marriages by age groups. Such series have not been continued beyond 1945. For countries where the mean age at marriage is published by the official statistical agency, recent data have been added from the following sources:

England and Wales
England and Wales. Registrar General. Statistical Review of England and Wales for the Year 1949. New Annual Series, No. 29. Tables. Part II. Civil. London, 1951. P. 72.

Netherlands
Netherlands. Centraal Bureau voor de Statistiek. Jaarcijfers voor Nederland, 1947-1950. Utrecht, 1951. P. 21.

Norway
Norway. Statistisk Sentralbyrå. Statistisk Årbok for Norge. 69. Årgang, 1950, p. 24; 70. Årgang, 1951, p. 24.

Sweden
Sweden. Statistiska Centralbyrån. Statistisk Årsbok för Sverige. 37. Årgången, 1950. Stockholm, 1950. P. 63.

Australia
Australia. Commonwealth Bureau of Census and Statistics. Of-

ficial Year Book of the Commonwealth of Australia. No. 38, 1951. Canberra, 1951. P. 591.

New Zealand
New Zealand. Census and Statistics Department. New Zealand Official Year-Book, 1951-1952. Wellington, 1952. P. 74.

6. Source for Table 6:

Data were taken from article to be published in Population Studies, Vol. 7, No. 2. Nov., 1953.

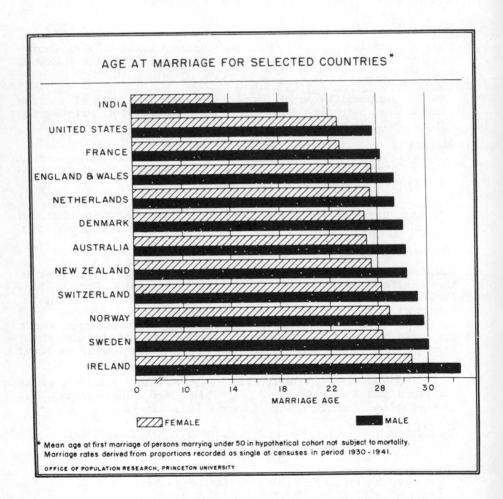

AGE AT MARRIAGE FOR SELECTED COUNTRIES*

* Mean age at first marriage of persons marrying under 50 in hypothetical cohort not subject to mortality.
Marriage rates derived from proportions recorded as single at censuses in period 1930 - 1941.

OFFICE OF POPULATION RESEARCH, PRINCETON UNIVERSITY

STATISTICAL PERSPECTIVE ON MARRIAGE

AND DIVORCE

By Kingsley Davis

IN the Western world, family behavior has become increasingly subject to short-run fluctuations. These fluctuations, recently gaining in speed and amplitude, are integrally related to the economic and political fluctuations which characterize our highly interdependent type of society. Individuals increasingly make their marital and reproductive decisions deliberately, taking into account their personal situation of the moment as they see it. Since the personal outlook of masses of individuals is affected in a similar way by the general economic and political conditions of the moment, the result is that whole populations tend to make the same kind of decision at the same time. Finding conditions bad, they postpone marriage or childbearing. Later, finding conditions good, they decide to marry or, if already married, to have children, thus driving up the marriage and birth rates in some cases by 100 per cent. Superficially, it appears that family behavior has fallen into the zone of what we call fashion; and there is doubtless an element of fashion in the fluctuations, but the causes are deeper than the term implies.

In addition, certain long-run trends have occurred which cut through the fluctuations. One of these is the decline in completed family size (the total number of children that couples have during their lives). Another is the tendency to stop reproduction early in life, thus bunching one's children in a limited period. Added to this is a slight decline during the last few decades in the age at marriage, which enables the mother all the more easily to complete her fertility before age 30. With the extension of the average length of life in modern society (to approximately 70 years for females), couples have a much longer period remaining after their children are born and after the children have left home. The reduced burden of child care and the longer period of life after the burden is over mean that women can enter the labor force in greater abundance. This in turn makes marriage less of a financial commitment for the husband, strengthens the tendency to marry earlier, and gives marriage more of a personal or companionate character. The redefinition of marriage in these terms means, finally, that the breaking of marriage is taken more lightly—so that there has been a rising rate of family dissolution, especially by legal divorce. In fact, death has been displaced as the chief home breaker, its place being taken by divorce and separation.

These changes, some of which are documented in the present paper, have amounted to a revolution in the family institution. They have, however, hardly appeared in most of the world, because most of the world is still in the peasant-agricultural stage of cultural evolution. As the urban-industrial stage continues to diffuse, the new family organization will doubtless diffuse with it.

FLUCTUATIONS IN THE MARRIAGE RATE

The degree to which modern populations compress their weddings into particular periods is truly remarkable. In the United States, for example, the number of marriages per 1,000 population reached an all-time high in 1946, when it was 16.4. This was double the all-time low of 1932, which was 7.9.[2] Later, in 1949, it was already down to 10.7, a drop of 35 per cent from the 1946 peak.[3] In England and Wales the highest recorded rate was reached in 1940, when there were 11.2 marriages per 1,000 population, which was almost 50 per cent higher than the 1932 figure of 7.6 eight years earlier.

The main causes of short-run fluctuations in the marriage rate are the business cycle and war, as Figure 1 shows. When these causes are operating jointly in favor of marriage, the highest rates occur. During the four deep depression years, 1930–33, approximately 800,000 marriages did not occur in the United States which normally would have occurred.[4] After that, conditions began slowly to improve, and the marriage rate

gradually climbed. But, except for 1937, when the marriage rate was 116,000 above normal, the depression was not really over until rearmament got under way in 1940. The great improvement of business conditions, with the threat and execution of the draft coming *at the same time,* not only led many of the postponed marriages to be consummated but also induced many to marry earlier than they would otherwise have done. The result was the most gigantic wave of marriages the country had ever seen. During the ten years 1940–49, there were approximately 3,670,000 more marriages than would have been normally expected.[5] We may naturally expect a marriage rate below normal in the 1950's even if economic conditions are good, because a large portion of the marriageable population has been, so to speak, used up in the matrimonial marathon of the 1940's.

As Figure 1 shows, the experience of the United States fairly well epitomizes the recent marital history of other western nations, with due allowance for special conditions.

THE CONSTANT PROPENSITY TO MARRY

Although the moment of history when people choose to marry now fluctuates markedly, the decision ultimately to marry has remained notably stable. In other words, people may postpone or advance the date of their marriage in accordance with current conditions, but they do not put off marrying forever. In Great Britain, the United States, and New Zealand, for example, where there have been gyrations in the annual marriage rate, the percentage of persons aged 45–54 who are or who have been

---

[2] National Office of Vital Statistics, "Provisional Marriage and Divorce Statistics, 1947," *Vital Statistics—Special Reports,* Vol. 29, No. 4, p. 54. The series runs from 1867 to 1949. The official marriage rate in the United States is an estimate in a double sense. It is based on an estimated midyear population and an estimated number of marriages. The registration of marriages is much poorer and less uniform than the registration of births and deaths. In some states there is a central collection of marriage data, but in others there is no central collection and the data must be obtained from counties. For some counties which do not report, the marriages must be estimated; others send in inaccurate reports. The National Office does the best it can with limited funds, using information on marriage licenses granted, marriages performed, and marriages reported. *Ibid.,* p. 50.

[3] National Office of Vital Statistics, advance release, April 16, 1950, p. 1.

[4] Bureau of the Census, "The Wartime Marriage Surplus," Series PM–1, Nov. 12, 1944, p. 2. Samuel A. Stouffer and Lyle M. Spencer, "Marriage and Divorce in Recent Years," *The Annals of the American Academy of Political and Social Science,* Vol. 188 (Nov. 1936), p. 64.

[5] Bureau of the Census, "The Wartime Marriage Surplus," *loc. cit.* This source, published in 1944, gives the expected normal number of marriages until 1950. The writer has simply made the necessary calculations after 1944 by filling in the actual marriages from later official reports.

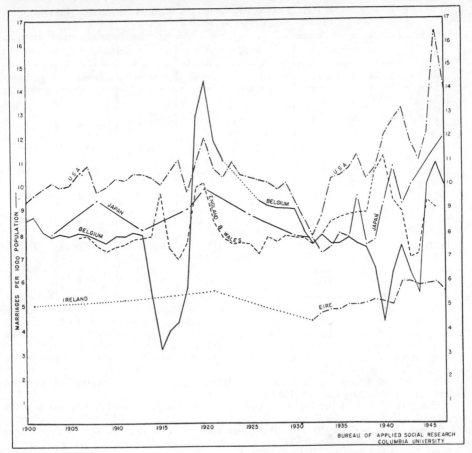

Fig. 1.—Marriages per 1,000 population in selected countries.

married has remained remarkably constant, as Table 1 shows. The only trend observable is a consistent downward trend among females in both Britain and New Zealand, due mainly to an increasingly feminine sex ratio in the relevant ages.[6]

The stability of the proportion who ever marry shows that the changes in the marriage *rate* from one year to another do not represent lifetime decisions to enter or stay permanently out of wedlock, but rather decisions as to the particular time of marriage. This is the

[6] In New Zealand in 1881 no less than 60.4 per cent of the adults were males, whereas in 1945 only 47.8 per cent were males.

real meaning of "postponement" or "borrowing on the future." It follows that a period of low marriage rates is almost sure to be followed by a period of high rates, and a period of high rates by one of low rates.

AGE AT MARRIAGE

Although the fluctuations in current rates do not affect the proportion who ultimately marry, they do affect the age at marriage. In addition, the age at marriage is also affected by other factors, some of a long-run character. As between one country and another, a high age at marriage is generally connected with a low proportion who ever

TABLE 1—PERCENTAGE OF PERSONS AGED 45–54 WHO HAVE EVER MARRIED.
SELECTED COUNTRIES

Approximate Date[a]	Gr. Britain[b]		New Zealand[c]		U. S. A.[d]		India[e]
	Males	Females	Males	Females	Males	Females	Females
1871	89.9	86.9					
1876							
1881	90.0	87 1	92.7	98.7			
1886			91.9	98.6			
1891	89.6	86.8	92.5	98.5	90.9	92.9	99.1
1896			94.1	98.5			
1901	88.5	85.7	94.9	98.4	89.7	92.2	99.0
1906			95.2	97.8			
1911	87.4	83.7	95.2	96.7	88.8	91.4	98.9
1916			92.5	94.9			
1921	87.4	83.2	93.2	94.0	88.0	90.4	98.8
1926			93.6	93.5			
1931	88.6	83.1			88.1	89.1	99.2
1936			94.4	93.6			
1941	90.1	82.9			88.9	91.3	99.0
1946	90.9	83.5	93.3	93.3	90.9	92.1	

[a] Except for the last entry, these are the dates for censuses in British and Commonwealth areas. The United States has its census one year earlier. The figures in the last row for Britain and U. S. A. refer actually to 1947, and represent estimates (as does the figure for 1941 for Britain); whereas the last figure for New Zealand represents a census count in 1945.

[b] Royal Commission on Population, *Report* (London: His Majesty's Stationery Office, 1949, Cmd. 7695), p. 23.

[c] New Zealand, Population Census, 1945, Vol. IV, "Ages and Marital Status" (Wellington: Census and Statistics Department, 1949), p. 38.

[d] Sixteenth Census of the United States: 1940. Population, Vol. IV, *Characteristics by Age*, Part I, "U. S. Summary," p. 16. Census Bureau, Current Population Reports, *Population Characteristics*, Series P-20, No. 10, "Characteristics of Single, Married, Widowed, and Divorced Persons in 1947," pp. 10–11.

[e] Computed from Census of India, Vol. 1, Part 2, for dates cited. In 1941 only a few provinces and states reported statistics; so the figure for this date is based on a sample only. The data for males, though not computed, show almost as high and steady a proportion ever married.

marry. Thus in India, where a high percentage of females 15–19 are married, the proportion who ever marry is extremely high; whereas in Ireland, where almost no females are married at young ages, the proportion who ever marry is extremely low. To see this we have merely to glance at Figure 2, which shows the proportion ever married by age.

The lowest ages at marriage are generally found in peasant-agricultural countries, such as India and China. During the rapid growth phase of urban-industrial nations, the average age

at marriage apparently rises; but later the age at marriage once more turns downward, though not rapidly. In the United States the median age at first marriage has declined steadily since 1890, as Table 2 shows.[7]

The postponement of marriage during the depression decade tended to keep the median age stationary among men and to advance it a third of a year

[7] Bureau of the Census, "Age at First Marriage," Series P–45, No. 7, May 28, 1945, p. 1; and "Characteristics of Single, Married, Widowed, and Divorced Persons in 1947." Series P–20, No. 10, p. 2.

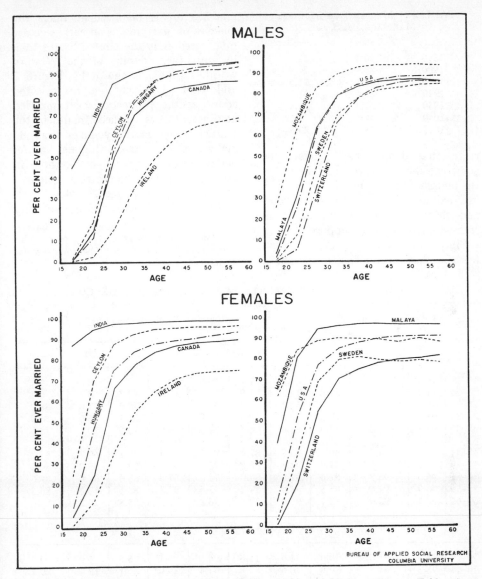

FIG. 2.—Percentage ever married, by age and sex, selected countries. (Source: Table 3.)

among women, but the high marriage rates of the 1940's accelerated the downward trend. Similar phenomena have been noted in Australia, Canada, and Great Britain.[8]

In so far as there has been a trend in advanced countries toward earlier marriage, it can perhaps be attributed to the fact that fertility has been controlled by other means than late mar-

[8] W. D. Borrie, *Population Trends and Policies* (Sydney: Australasian Publishing Co., 1948), p. 68. Enid Charles, *The Changing Size of the Family in Canada* (Ottawa: Dominion Bureau of Statistics, Eighth Census of Canada, 1941, Census Monograph No. 1, 1948), pp. 45–47. Royal Commission, *op. cit.* note *b* under Table 1, p. 47.

TABLE 2—MEDIAN AGE AT FIRST
MARRIAGE, U. S. A.

Year	Male	Female
1890	26.1	22.0
1900	25.9	21.9
1910	25.1	21.6
1920	24.6	21.2
1930	24.3	21.3
1940	24.3	21.6
1947	23.7	20.5

riage, that divorce has generally become easier to procure, that the size of the household has diminished, that more married women are in the labor force, and that the state has taken an increased share in child support.

Since our own country most exemplifies the changes inducing a low age at

marriage, it is no accident that "the chances of marrying at an early age are much greater in the United States than in any other country of the Western world." [9] This is shown by Figure 2 and Table 3, which give for selected countries the proportion ever married at different ages. Indeed, males in the United States marry younger than do males in Ceylon, and both males and females marry younger than do those in Hungary. In 1940 more than a fourth of our young men aged 20–24 were already married, whereas in Ireland only

[9] Metropolitan Life Insurance Co., *Statistical Bulletin,* Vol. 28 (Feb. 1947), p. 8. This source contains data from a few countries not shown here.

TABLE 3—PERCENTAGE EVER MARRIED, BY AGE GROUPS, SELECTED COUNTRIES[a]

Age	India 1931	Mozambique 1940	Malaya[b] 1947	Ceylon 1946	U. S. A. 1940	Hungary 1940	Canada 1941	Sweden 1945	Ireland 1941	Switzerland 1941
				Males						
15–19	45.9	26.4	3.9	1.2	1.7	0.6	0.5	0.2	0.2	—
20–24	64.9	62.4	31.9	19.5	27.8	12.4	16.2	12.7	3.2	6.4
25–29	86.3	83:1	64.9	56.7	64.0	53.7	50.3	48.0	17.0	38.2
30–34	91.4	90.5	79.2	77.6	79.3	78.0	71.0	70.1	35.9	66.9
35–39	94.8	93.8	83.9	87.6	84.7	87.2	78.9	78.2	50.1	78.8
40–44	95.6	94.7	86.7	90.8	87.4	91.9	83.4	82.1	60.2	83.7
45–49	96.4	94.8	87.2	92.5	88.8	93.7	85.8	83.4	65.9	86.2
50–54	96.6	95.2	87.6	92.5	89.0	94.8	87.0	85.0	67.6	87.0
55–59	96.9	94.6	86.5	93.6	89.2	95.6	87.2	85.4	69.2	86.5
60–64	97.1	95.0	88.4	92.9	89.5	96.2	87.3	85.8	70.2	88.0
				Females						
15–19	87.3	61.8	40.0	24.6	11.8	9.6	5.7	3.3	1.0	0.8
20–24	95.3	84.8	80.8	70.6	52.8	47.4	39.0	36.1	12.4	20.2
25–29	98.2	89.1	95.4	88.2	77.2	75.7	67.1	69.7	36.5	55.1
30–34	98.5	90.6	96.8	93.4	85.3	84.3	78.9	80.1	55.5	71.5
35–39	98.9	90.2	97.5	95.7	88.8	88.1	84.1	81.3	65.1	76.2
40–44	99.0	90.0	97.0	96.0	90.5	90.0	87.0	80.0	71.5	78.6
45–49	99.2	88.7	96.7	96.6	91.4	91.4	88.8	79.1	74.0	79.9
50–54	99.2	90.2	96.7	96.4	91.3	92.6	89.7	79.5	74.5	80.9
55–59	99.3	88.4	96.4	96.9	91.3	94.1	90:2	78.4	75.2	81.6
60–64	99.3	89.4	96.7	96.8	90.7	94.4	89.6	78.5	75.6	83.4

    [a] Except where otherwise noted, computed from U. N. *Demographic Yearbook* 1948, pp. 160–201.
    [b] Malayan Census, 1947, Tables 12–18, 20–26.

3 per cent and in Switzerland only 6 per cent of them were. The proportion who ever marry by an advanced age is also high in the United States, although not quite so high as in Ceylon or Hungary.

The United States thus stands in marked contrast to such countries as Sweden, Switzerland, and Ireland, where both the age at marriage and the proportion who remain permanently single are high. In 1941 Ireland was still the least-married country in the world. Only 36 per cent of its women had ever been married prior to age 30, and over a fourth of the women remained unmarried throughout the reproductive span. It is primarily through the postponement of marriage that Ireland has reduced its birth rate, whereas in the United States the birth rate has been brought down by the use of contraception in wedlock.

At the other end of the scale stands India, where almost nine out of every ten girls are married by age 20, and where 98 out of every 100 are married by age 30.[10] Other peasant-agricultural countries, such as Malaya and Mozambique, are in much the same situation. Malaya, because of heavy Chinese and Indian immigration, has a surplus of males; consequently its males marry late, but its women marry earlier than do those in any western country, and the proportion of women who eventually marry is noticeably higher than the proportion of men who do so. Ceylon, which also has a large immigrant population, manifests a late age at marriage for males as compared with other Asiatic areas.

[10] An Indian custom increasing the percentage ever married is the taboo on the remarriage of widows. If a man cannot take a widow to wife when he himself is widowed, he must choose a woman who is not yet married—and in a country where mortality is high, this means that every available woman is taken.

THE WIDESPREAD INCREASE IN DIVORCE

The divorce rate, like the marriage rate, is characterized by fluctuations connected with war and the business cycle, but (as Figure 3 shows) there is an unmistakable tendency for the rate to rise over a long period. In the United States this can be shown in two ways—in the census data on divorced persons and in the registration statistics on divorces as they occur. Table 4 shows that the number of divorced persons per 100 married was 0.54 in 1890 and 2.82 in 1949, representing an increase of 521 per cent; and the average number of divorces per 100 marriages was 5.56 during the 1881–90 decade and

TABLE 4—INDICES OF DIVORCE IN THE UNITED STATES, 1890–1949

Year	Divorced Persons[a] per 100 Married (from *census* data)		Average Divorces[b] per 100 Marriages (from *registration* data)	
	Number	Index	Rate[c]	Index
1890	0.54	100	5.70	100
1900	0.72	132	7.56	133
1910	0.95	176	9.79	172
1920	1.18	217	12.02	211
1930	2.02	373	15.79	277
1940	2.40	443	18.36	322
1947	2.80[d]	517	26.16	459
1948	3.17[d]	586	26.59	467
1949	2.82[d]	521	26.79	470

[a] Sixteenth Census of the United States: 1940. Population, Vol. IV, *Characteristics by Age*, Part I, "U. S. Summary," p. 16.

[b] Computed from National Office of Vital Statistics, Vital Statistics—Special Reports, *National Summaries*, Vol. 29, No. 4 (Sept. 9, 1948), pp. 54–55; and advance release, April 4, 1949.

[c] The rate for each year is the number of divorces occurring in that year per 100 marriages occurring on the average during each of the previous ten years. These rates were then averaged for the decade of which the year in the present table was the last.

[d] U. S. Census Bureau, Current Population Reports, *Characteristics by Age*, Series P-20, Nos. 10, 23, and 26.

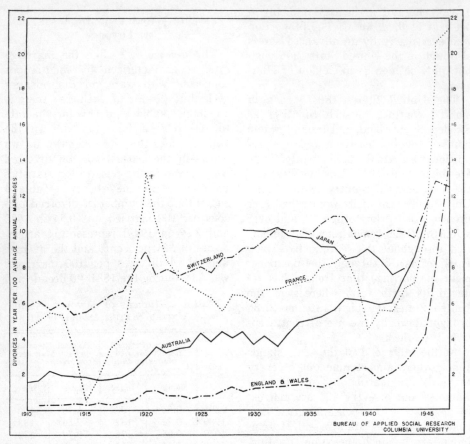

FIG. 3.—Divorces per 100 average annual marriages, selected countries. (The marriages on which the rates are calculated are those occurring each year during the decade preceding the year in which the divorces occurred. Source: Metropolitan Life Insurance Co., *Statistical Bulletin*, Vol. 30 (April 1949), p. 2. Some additional recent rates have been added from official reports.)

25.89 in the 1940–49 decade, representing an increase of 466 per cent. Although the registration of marriage and divorces is inaccurate in the United States,[11] the fact that both sets of data show the same rapid trend (as seen in Figure 4) is proof enough of its existence.[12]

[11] See Samuel C. Newman, "Needs and Future Prospects for Integrating Marriage and Divorce Data with Other Vital Statistics," *American Journal of Public Health*, Vol. 39 (Sept. 1949), pp. 1141–44; and "The Development and Status of Vital Statistics on Marriage and Divorce," National Office of Vital Statistics release, Nov. 22, 1949. Earlier plans to form a marriage registration area and a divorce registration area are discussed by Bernard M. Cohen, "Centralized Collection of Marriage and Divorce Records and Their

Uses," *American Journal of Public Health*, Vol. 31 (Aug. 1941), pp. 824 ff.; and Bureau of the Census, "Tentative Plans for the Collection of Marriage and Divorce Statistics," *Vital Statistics—Special Reports*, Vol. 9 (May 9, 1940), pp. 491–95. The official estimates are occasionally alluded to in articles by Paul H. Jacobson, *op. cit.* note 17 and 20 *infra*.

[12] The fact that the ratio of divorced persons to those married has risen faster than the divorce rate itself may be in part fictitious. It may be that, with the liberalization of attitudes toward divorce, more people are now willing to admit to the census taker that they

The rising rate of divorce characterizes not only the United States but all other countries touched by urban-industrial civilization (Figure 3). It is therefore not merely an "American" phenomenon, but is somehow related to the evolution of the family in western society in general. It is a consequence of the changing structure of the family —lowered fertility, loss of economic functions, absorption of women in the labor force, emphasis on personal gratifi-

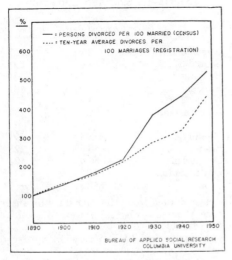

FIG. 4.—Indices of increase in the ratio of persons divorced to those married and in the average annual divorces per 100 marriages during each preceding decade. 1890 = 100. (Source: Table 4.)

cation and "happiness" in marriage. This changing structure is in turn a consequence of the changing social system—the decline of the local community and its social controls, the acceleration of geographical and social mobility, the growth of large industries, cities, and so forth. These developments have all

are divorced, thus producing a spurious increase. This interpretation seems cogent in view of the fact that a rising rate of remarriage would tend to dampen the index based on census data to a greater extent than the index based on registration data.

tended to make people less inclined to continue unions that seem unsatisfactory, and less restrained from getting out of such unions. Divorce laws have gradually become more liberal during the last century, but custom and opinion have changed much more rapidly than the laws, with the result that, regardless of the legal forms, the Western world is in fact achieving divorce by mutual consent.[13]

INTERNATIONAL DIFFERENCES IN DIVORCE

However, neither the divorce rates nor their rates of change have been uniform in all western countries. Some of these countries, such as Italy, Spain, and Ireland, apparently do not permit absolute divorce at all. Others have strict or lenient laws or other traits or changes that influence the probability of divorce.[14] Furthermore, there are great differences in the incidence of divorce as between nonindustrial countries. India, for example, has rather little divorce, whereas Egypt has a rate that has generally exceeded that of the United States.

Such great differences as between countries of the same general type show that the rate of legal divorce depends in part on special conditions. The rates in western countries, for example, are not determined simply by the conditions of urban-industrial civilization. In 1945–47 the American divorce rate was almost six times that of England and Wales, yet the latter area is more urbanized than our country.

It should not be surmised, however, that differences in divorce rates necessarily represent true differences in the

[13] Kingsley Davis, "Divorce," in Morris Fishbein and Ernest W. Burgess (Eds.), *Successful Marriage,* Garden City, N. Y.: Doubleday, 1947.

[14] The striking rise in the rate in England since 1940 is due to the liberalization of divorce laws in that country.

amount of marital dissolution. As we shall see in a moment, a legal divorce is only one way of breaking a marriage, and in the absence of opportunity for divorce, these other ways may play a compensatory role. Unfortunately, the causes of international differences in divorce rates have been little investigated, despite their importance for a sociological understanding of marital dissolution.[15] Yet the generalization can be made that wherever in western countries divorce has been permitted, its incidence has tended to rise during the last century.[16]

Is There a Saturation Point?

How high will the divorce rate eventually go? Did the United States figure of 40 divorces per 100 marriages in 1946 represent a permanent peak? Nobody knows the answers, but certain considerations suggest that the saturation point is at least in sight.

First of all, there is a theoretical limit to the divorce rate. Over an extended period there cannot be more divorces than marriages; in fact, there must always be fewer, because some marriages must necessarily end in death rather than divorce. More to the point is the fact that the rise in the divorce rate has on the whole been greater where the rate was formerly low, and less where it was high. For instance, the percentage rise in the rate per 100 average annual marriages between 1910–12 and 1945–47 is shown in Table 5.

Those countries that began with a divorce rate of less than 3 per 100 aver-

age marriages experienced by and large a fourfold to tenfold increase, while those beginning with more than 3 experienced in general only a twofold increase. This tendency for the rate of increase to be less in countries with an already high incidence of divorce suggests that the trend in divorce can be represented by a typical growth, or logistic, curve; and for some countries

TABLE 5—RISE IN DIVORCE RATE PER 100 AVERAGE ANNUAL MARRIAGES, 1910–12 TO 1945–47, SELECTED COUNTRIES[a]

	Three-Year Average Rate 1910–12	Per Cent Increase by 1945–47
England and Wales	2.2	3,867
Scotland	7.4	691
Belgium	19.4	301[b]
Sweden	19.6	481
Netherlands	23.5	378
New Zealand	24.1	489[b]
Denmark	38.8	391
France	50.6	225
Switzerland	58.6	108
United States	105.6	221
Japan[c]	137.5[d]	−7[e]

[a] Computed from Metropolitan Life Insurance Company, *Statistical Bulletin*, Vol. 30 (April 1949), p. 2.
[b] Average rate 1945–47 based on two years only.
[c] Computed from Ryoichi Ishii, *Population Pressure and Economic Life in Japan* (Chicago: University of Chicago Press, 1937), pp. 97, 100.
[d] Average annual marriages for preceding decade based on 1898, 1903, and 1908 only.
[e] Divorces based on 1946 only.

having a long enough series of data, this is the case.

The significance of such a shape in the trend is that it clearly points to an eventual leveling off of the divorce rate. Whatever the forces in western society that have brought about the remarkable increase in divorce, they will not work indefinitely in the same direction. A new equilibrium is being established involving a divorce rate much higher than the preindustrial one, but not an

---

[15] A brief attempt at comparative analysis was made by the writer in "Children of Divorced Parents: A Sociological and Statistical Analysis," *Law and Contemporary Problems* (Summer, 1944), pp. 700–20.
[16] In its preindustrial state, Japan had a high divorce rate. With the acquisition of western customs, the rate went down prior to World War II, but has tended to rise since then.

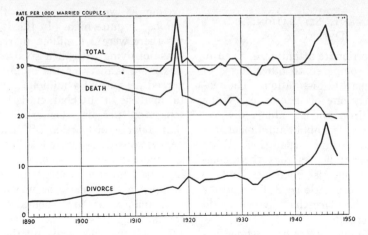

FIG. 5.—Marital dissolutions by death and divorce, United States, 1890–1948. (Source: Metropolitan Life Insurance Company, *Statistical Bulletin*, Vol. 30 (Nov. 1949), p. 2.)

Note—The figures for divorce include annulments, and those for mortality include deaths overseas during World Wars I and II. Rates for 1948 are provisional.

increasing rate. Unless there is a major social revolution—such as the complete removal of child rearing from the family's functions—it seems doubtful that the divorce rate in any country will go far beyond the 1946 peak in the United States.

DIVORCE AND BROKEN HOMES

The rising rate of divorce has not meant, as is commonly assumed, a corresponding rise in the number of broken families. The latter is kept low, in the first place, by the capacity of the decline in mortality to compensate for the increase in divorce, and in the second place, by the tendency of most divorced persons to remarry and thus be absorbed into new families.

If the marriages broken by death are added to those broken by divorce, one finds that in the United States, with the exception of the two world wars, the total rate of marital dissolutions from these two combined causes was downward from 1890 to 1915 and relatively constant thereafter (Figure 5).[17]

[17] Paul H. Jacobson, "Total Marital Dissolutions in the United States," in George F.

Along with the increase of divorce, the rate of remarriage has apparently been rising, at least in the United States. Census data show that in 1940 the proportion of remarried women among those previously widowed or divorced was about one-sixth greater than in 1910. In the age group 25–34, more than three-fifths were remarried according to the 1940 data, as compared with about one-half in 1910.[18] A census survey in 1948, combined with registration data, revealed that approximately 75 per cent of those procuring divorces during the five years from 1943 to 1948 were already remarried in 1948. Of those divorced earlier—between 1934 and 1943 —approximately 86 per cent had remarried by 1948.[19]

Mair (Ed.), *Studies in Population* (Princeton: Princeton University Press, 1949), pp. 3–11. See also "Have Broken Families Increased?" Metropolitan Life Insurance Company, *Statistical Bulletin*, Vol. 30 (Nov. 1949), pp. 1–3.

[18] "The Frequency of Remarriage," Metropolitan Life Insurance Company, *Statistical Bulletin*, Vol. 30 (Jan. 1949), pp. 8–10.

[19] Paul C. Glick, "First Marriages and Remarriages," *American Sociological Review*, Vol. 14 (Dec. 1949), pp. 729–30.

ANNULMENT, SEPARATION, AND DESERTION

Disproportionate attention is given to divorce as compared to other forms of voluntary marital dissolution. The reason is partly one of ignorance. While we know little enough about divorce, we know even less about annulment, desertion, and informal separation. What we do know indicates that their combined frequency is imposing, and in countries having little legal divorce they often take the place that divorce would otherwise occupy.

In the United States as a whole, annulments constitute only a small proportion of legal dissolutions. At their peak in 1946, when almost 22,000 annulments were granted, they represented only 3.5 per cent of the total. But according to Jacobson,

In California and New York, however, they were of much greater importance. Thus in California, annulments constituted somewhat more than one-ninth of all legal marriage dissolutions in 1948. In New York they were an even larger proportion of the total; almost one-quarter of the marital dissolutions in 1940, and since 1946 almost one-third. In at least five counties in New York, the number of annulments now exceeds the number of absolute divorces.

From 1940 to 1948 the annulments in New York State constituted almost one-third of all annulments in the Nation. New York has this high annulment rate because it grants divorce only for adultery but gives annulments for any one of eight different grounds, many of which are ill-defined.[20]

Unfortunately there is hardly any statistical information concerning the number of desertions and informal separations in the United States. Such infor-

mation as we have suggests that the number is quite high. In the 1940 census there were 3.1 million married persons not living with their spouses, which was more than twice the number of divorced persons (1.4 million). By careful analysis of the characteristics of the separated persons, Ogburn concluded that a large proportion of them might be permanently separated. "Separations are more numerous among non-whites, in cities, in the young and old age groups, in the service occupations, and . . . among the low-income groups of the laboring class."[21]

Sample surveys made by the Census Bureau in 1947–49 show that, while the number of married persons and of divorced persons had increased, the number of separated persons had declined slightly. Thus, whereas the separated were 4.5 per cent of all persons ever married in 1940, they were only 3.4 per cent in 1949; and whereas they were more than twice as numerous as the divorced at the earlier date, they were only about a third more numerous in 1949. If accurate, these data suggest that divorces are being obtained by people who would formerly have merely remained separated. Since desertion and separation have been the main bulwark of the poor, this result could be expected with increasing real income and better education.

CONCLUSION

The long-run trends discussed or cited in this article amount to a major revolution in the family structure of industrial society. The combination of in-

[20] Paul H. Jacobson, "Marital Dissolutions in New York State in Relation to their Trend in the United States," Milbank Memorial Fund Quarterly, Vol. 28 (Jan. 1950), pp. 35–37.

[21] William F. Ogburn, "Marital Separations," American Journal of Sociology, Vol. 49 (Jan. 1944), pp. 316–23. See also "Effect of Family Disruption on Fertility," Metropolitan Life Insurance Company, Statistical Bulletin, Vol. 30 (Feb. 1949), pp. 6–8, where it is shown that there were fewer mothers among the separated women than among any other category, including the divorced and twice married.

creasing longevity, a slightly earlier age at marriage, and a tendency to control fertility and bunch reproduction in ages below 30, has freed married women for economic pursuits and led to a new conception of marriage as a personal rather than a community or kinship matter. Marriage, divorce, and reproduction have accordingly become much more responsive to current conditions, almost like the swings of fashion.

Yet behind the fluctuations are abiding regularities, among them a rather constant tendency to enter matrimony ulitmately, to remarry more frequently after divorce, and to have a family of modest size. Although legal divorce has experienced a general rise, it does not bring a commensurate number of broken families. Death has declined as a cause of dissolution, and remarriage has tended to reabsorb the divorced. Also, legal divorce has perhaps taken the place formerly occupied by desertion and informal separation. In any case, the new family structure seems to be integrated with the general character of modern society. Its main features will remain as long as that kind of society lasts, although it is a mistake to think that certain trends, such as a rising divorce rate, will persist indefinitely.

RESUME OF THE INDIANAPOLIS STUDY OF SOCIAL AND
PSYCHOLOGICAL FACTORS AFFECTING FERTILITY

By Clyde V. Kiser and P. K. Whelpton

This paper will describe briefly (1) the purpose, scope and methods of the Indianapolis Study; (2) the outstanding findings from the tests of hypotheses on the relation of given factors to fertility-planning status and size of planned family; and (3) the weaknesses of the study and their implications for future research in this field. The section on findings is restricted to results from the testing of the hypotheses. It includes no discussion of ancillary findings such as those based upon the Household Survey,[2] the analysis of the relative roles of contraception and impairments of fecundity in lowering fertility rates,[3] and effectiveness of specific methods of contraception.[4]

I. Purpose, scope and methods of the study

The purpose, scope and methods of the Indianapolis Study have been described in published articles.[5] Briefly stated, two types of situations, existing during the late thirties, prompted the study. One was the generally low level of birth rates of the period, especially in cities. It was believed that further knowledge of the social and psychological factors affecting fertility would be needed if this country were ever to attempt any form of legislation designed to encourage larger families. The other situation was the existing status of research in differential fertility. Previous studies of data of the census type had indicated the relation of fertility to such factors as region, rural-urban residence, colour, nativity, occupation, education and other measures of socio-economic status. These had been followed by a series of studies which indicated that the observed group differences in fertility had arisen almost altogether from group differences in age at marriage and in prevalence and effectiveness of contraceptive practice rather than from group differences in fecundity—the physiological capacity to reproduce. It was realized, however, that contraception is only the *means* of family limitation, and that the next step might

[2] P. K. Whelpton and Clyde V. Kiser, *Social and Psychological Factors Affecting Fertility*, vol. I, *The Household Survey in Indianapolis*, The Milbank Memorial Fund, New York, 1946, 138 pp.

[3] Whelpton and Kiser, 'The comparative influence on fertility rates of contraception and impairments of fecundity', *Social and Psychological Factors Affecting Fertility*, vol. II, *The Intensive Study—Purpose, Scope, Methods, and Partial Results*, 1950, pp. 303–57.

[4] Data on the prevalence, acceptability and effectiveness of specific methods of contraception used by Indianapolis Study have been presented by C. F. Westoff, L. F. Herrera, and R. K. Whelpton 'The Use, Effectiveness and Acceptability of Methods of Fertility Control'. Social and Psychological Factors Affecting Fertility, vol. xx, *Milbank Memorial Fund Quarterly*, vol. xxxi, no. 3, July, 1953, pp. 291–357.

[5] Whelpton and Kiser, 'Developing the schedules, and choosing the type of couples and the area to be studied' and 'The sampling plan, selection, and the representativeness of couples in the inflated sample', *Social and Psychological Factors Affecting Fertility*, vol. II, pp. 139–207.

well be that of trying to investigate the social and psychological factors affecting resort to contraception and the size of the planned family.

The development of methodology in the field was regarded from the beginning as an important purpose of the study. This, rather than the probability of securing much in the way of definitive results, was emphasized in seeking financial support for the study.

The specific aims and scope of the study developed with the discussion and field experimentation which went on over a period of two years during 1938-40. They were finally set by the decision to try to test twenty-three hypotheses concerning the relation of fertility planning and size of planned family to given social and psychological factors. Altogether, six separate schedules and questionnaires were developed, which provided for upward of 1000 specific items of information, most of them being pertinent to one or more of the twenty-three hypotheses.

The study was conducted in Indianapolis in 1941. Data for testing the hypotheses were obtained from an adjusted sample of 1444 'relatively fecund'[1] couples with the following characteristics: husband and wife native white, both Protestant, both finished at least the eighth grade, married during 1927-9, neither previously married, husband under 40 and wife under 30 at marriage, and residents in a large city most of the time since marriage. Couples with these characteristics were located by means of a preliminary Household Survey of virtually all white households in Indianapolis.

II. SUMMARY OF FINDINGS[2]

A rather arbitrary classification of the twenty-three hypotheses under five categories is shown in Table 1. Under each category the hypotheses are listed in the order in which they will be considered in the report.[3] An effort has been made to indicate in applicable cases (a) the direction (i.e. direct or inverse) of the relationship found between the variable dealt with in the hypothesis and both fertility-planning status and size of the 'number and spacing planned' family,[4] and (b) whether or not the

---

[1] All couples reporting four or more live births were classified as 'relatively fecund' regardless of other circumstances. Couples with three or fewer live births were classified as 'relatively fecund' unless they knew or had good reasons for believing that conception was physiologically impossible during a period of at least 24 or 36 consecutive months since marriage (24 for never-pregnant couples, 36 for others). Failure to conceive when contraception was not practised 'always' or 'usually' during periods of the above durations was considered good reason for such belief. Couples not classified as 'relatively fecund' were considered 'relatively sterile'. There were 533 of these in the adjusted sample and these were not asked to supply the information needed for testing the hypotheses.

[2] This summary is based on analytical work done by twelve people on the various hypotheses. Detailed reports on most of these hypotheses have been published; the titles and authors are cited. The statements made in this article concerning the findings for the other hypotheses must be regarded as tentative. They are based on information obtained from persons who are analysing the data considered and whose names are cited at appropriate places.

[3] For full wording of the hypotheses, see *Social and Psychological Factors Affecting Fertility*, vol. II, pp. 147-9.

[4] The hypotheses relate to size of 'planned families', i.e. the 'number and spacing planned' and the 'number planned' groups combined. However, whereas the data rather frequently yield little in the way of systematic relationship of fertility to the variables considered within the total group of 'planned families' they also indicate rather persistent differences between the 'number and spacing planned' and the 'number planned' groups with respect to patterns of differential fertility. In view

findings support the hypothesis. It should be emphasized that 'support' of the hypothesis does not necessarily mean scientific confirmation, but merely that the direction of the relationship found is or tends to be the same as that hypothesized. The table provides inadequate indication of either the quality of the data or of the strength or consistency of the relationships found. However, a few cases of especially inadequate data are noted, and the term 'partially' supported is used for cases in which the relationship is weak, not complete, or is known to arise almost entirely from the influence of another variable.

Cases of 'no support' of the hypothesis might arise from finding no relationship at all (indicated by 'O' in columns 4 and 5), or a relationship of the direction opposite that hypothesized. The report of 'zero' relationship does not necessarily mean that none really exists, but simply that none was found in this study.

Status and security

The first hypothesis listed is: 'The higher the socio-economic status, the higher the proportion of couples practising contraception effectively and the smaller the planned families.' As expected from previous studies, the first part of this hypothesis is definitely borne out, for the proportion of couples practising contraception effectively[1] tends to increase rather sharply and consistently with rising socio-economic status.[2] The second part of the hypothesis—positing an inverse relation of fertility to socio-economic status among planned families—is not supported. As expected, the familiar inverse relation of fertility to socio-economic status is rather sharply manifested for the total sample of 1444 'relatively fecund' couples. It is also found to some extent within the 'number planned' group considered separately. Within the 'number and spacing planned' group, however, the opposite type of relation is found. The fertility rates for this group are relatively low, but they tend to be directly instead of inversely related to socio-economic status.[3] This direct relation is most sharply manifested when husband's income is used as the measure of socio-economic status, but it is also found rather consistently in classifications by rental value of the home, net worth, occupation, education, and score on Chapin's Social Status Scale.

The 'number and spacing planned' couples are highly homogeneous with respect to success in preventing unwanted pregnancies. The group is composed

of this, and because the 'number and spacing planned' group is by definition more successful in planning fertility than the 'number planned' group, the results given in Column 5 of Table 1 pertain to the 'number and spacing planned' group. The fertility rates are given for the remaining fertility-planning groups in the article cited, and reference is frequently made in the text to the results for the total group of planned families. It is recognized that some further analyses are needed to attempt to ascertain the reasons for the dissimilarity between the 'number and spacing planned' and the 'number planned' groups with respect to internal variations in fertility.

[1] Couples were considered as practising contraception 'effectively' if they were classified either as 'number and spacing of pregnancies planned' or as 'number planned'. See Whelpton and Kiser, 'The planning of fertility', *Social and Psychological Factors Affecting Fertility*, vol. II, pp. 225–31.

[2] Kiser and Whelpton, 'Fertility planning and fertility rates by socio-economic status', *Social and Psychological Factors Affecting Fertility*, vol. II, pp. 381–93.

[3] Because of the contrasting nature of the results for the two sub-groups of 'planned families', little relation of fertility to socio-economic status is found among the consolidated group of 'planned families.' Ibid. pp. 393–412.

Table 1. *Indianapolis Study hypotheses. Classification and results of analyses*†

Class and subject of hypothesis	Hypothesis number see vol. II, pp. 147-9	Published article number	Direction of relation found		Has the hypothesis been supported?	
			Fertility-planning status	Size of completely planned family	Fertility-planning status	Size of completely planned family
(1)	(2)	(3)	(4)	(5)	(6)	(7)
I. Status and security:						
Socio-economic status	3	IX	+	+	Yes	No
Economic insecurity	2	XI	−	−	No	Yes
Economic tension	1	*	−	+	No‡	No‡
II. Community and family background:						
Family and childhood situations	12	*	±‡	±‡	Partially	Partially
Residence and migration history	11	XVI	±	±	Partially	Partially
Doubling-up of families	4	XIII	+	−	No	No
Health of wife and husband	21	XIII	+	−	No§	No§
Health of children	22	XIII	+	−	No§	No§
III. Interest in home and children:						
Liking for children	5	*	O	+	No	Partially
Children wanting brothers and sisters	6	*	DNA	+	DNA	Partially
Parental preferences re sex of children	10	XIV	DNA	±	DNA	Partially
Reasons for second child:						
Belief 'only child' handicapped	8	*	DNA	+	DNA	Partially
Desire to insure against childlessness	9	*	DNA	+	DNA	Partially
IV. Personality characteristics:						
Personal inadequacy	16	XVII	−	−	No	Partially
Feeling children interfere with personal freedom	7	*	−	+	No	No
Ego-centred interest in children	18	XVIII	+	−	Partially	Partially
Fear of pregnancy	23	XIX	+	−	Partially	Partially
Rationality of behaviour:						
Tendency to plan	17	XII	+	−	Partially	Partially
Interest in religion	15	X	−	+	Partially	Partially
Adherence to traditions	14	XV	−	+	Partially	Partially
Conformity to group patterns	13	*	−	+	Partially	Partially
V. Marital adjustment and husband-wife dominance:						
Marital adjustment	20	VII	+	O	Yes	Partially
Husband-wife dominance	19	VII	O	O	No‖	No‖

† Symbols:
* = unpublished data—results preliminary (col. 3).   + = direct relation with hypothesis variable (cols. 4 and 5).
− = inverse relation with hypothesis variable (cols. 4 and 5).   O = no relation with hypothesis variable (cols. 4 and 5).
DNA = does not apply (cols. 4 and 6).
‡ Results believed to be spurious because of selective factors.   § Data on health very inadequate.   ‖ Some results found on reformulated hypothesis.

(*a*) of couples who practised contraception regularly after marriage and had no pregnancies, and (*b*) of couples whose every pregnancy was deliberately planned by stopping contraception in order to conceive. Hence, the factor of differential prevalence and effectiveness of contraceptive practice (the factor underlying the general inverse relation of fertility to socio-economic status) is removed for this group.

The next hypothesis is: 'The greater the feeling of economic insecurity, the higher the proportion of couples practising contraception effectively and the smaller the planned families'. The classifications by feeling of economic security are based mainly upon the multiple-choice replies of wives and husbands to a series of questions about confidence in meeting future expenses, frequency of facing the possibility of husband's pay cut or unemployment, and the like.

The first part of the hypothesis is not borne out by the data. Among the couples studied, the effective practice of contraception is directly associated with economic security rather than with economic insecurity, but this relation virtually disappears when socio-economic status is held constant.[1] The second part of the hypothesis is supported by the data. The size of 'planned families' and particularly the size of 'number and spacing planned' families is directly associated with economic security, or, as the hypothesis states, inversely associated with feeling of economic insecurity.[2] This relationship is maintained, but to a smaller degree, when socio-economic status is held constant.[3]

The hypothesis [1] labelled 'economic tension' was phrased 'The greater the difference between the actual level of living and the standard of living desired, the higher the proportion of couples practising contraception effectively and the smaller the planned families'. Actually the results tend to yield the opposite types of relationship, but there is also good evidence of the existence of selective factors in the measures used.[4]

An effort was made to get at the difference between actual and desired level of living through two types of approach—the quantitative and the qualitative. The quantitative approach was that of comparing what the couples had with what they wanted with respect to three items: income, home and automobile. Thus, certain sections of the schedules provided data on family income, value or rental value of home, and purchase price of the car if a car was owned. Other sections furnished the replies of wives and husbands to such questions as how much income the family would need in order to live in a *satisfactory* manner, how much they would have to pay to buy or rent a house in which they would *like* to live, and how much they would have to pay for the automobile that they would *like* to own. In each case the amount of the desired item was coded as a percentage of the actual.

[1] Kiser and Whelpton, 'The interrelation of fertility, fertility planning, and feeling of economic security' in *Social and Psychological Factors Affecting Fertility*, vol. III, pp. 476–95.

[2] Ibid. pp. 495–537.

[3] There is a particularly strong tendency for voluntary childlessness to be associated with economic insecurity among the 'number and spacing planned' couples. For instance, only 12 % of the couples scoring highest (90 +) on the summary index of economic security were childless, whereas 57 % of the couples scoring lowest (under 60) on this scale were childless. This accounts for much but by no means all of the direct relation of fertility to economic security ratings of the 'number and spacing planned' couples in the Study.

[4] Unpublished data being analysed by Kiser and Whelpton.

The qualitative data were the multiple-choice replies, ranging from 'very much' to 'very little', to questions regarding amount of additional income needed, interest in having a better home, and interest in having a car or better car.

With both types of data the degree of economic tension (i.e. the extent of the difference between actual level of living and standard of living desired) is inversely related to socio-economic status. This is true despite the fact that the quantitative data manifest no tendency for the poorer people to be unrealistic in their statements regarding what they wanted. Nevertheless, the owner of a second-hand car bought for a few hundred dollars could quite reasonably—and frequently did—express a desire for an automobile costing two or three times this amount. This almost always placed them in a higher 'tension' category than, say, the persons who owned a Cadillac that was purchased new. Thus the groups with high economic 'tension' are weighted with couples of low socio-economic status. This probably helps to account for the failure of the data to support the first part of the hypothesis—the higher the degree of economic tension the larger the proportion of couples practising contraception effectively.

It was noted above that within the 'number and spacing planned' group, fertility is directly associated with socio-economic status. Selection of this type should operate toward support of the second part of the hypothesis—the greater the difference between the actual and desired levels of living the smaller the planned family. However, it seems reasonably sure that another type of selection affects the classifications by economic tension, for couples with large families would tend to be the ones stating that they need more income. Since they need room for children they would also tend especially to think in terms of a larger house and hence a more expensive house. Selection of this type probably accounts partly for the observed direct (rather than inverse) relation of 'economic tension', as measured, to size of planned family. Whatever the reason, it is certain that the measures of the difference between actual and desired levels of living which were used in the study were far from adequate. The hypothesis appears important on logical grounds; it is to be hoped that satisfactory measures can be developed for testing it in future studies.

Community and family background

Five hypotheses are listed under the heading 'Community and family background'. The first (Hypothesis 12) is concerned with family and childhood situations, such as 'by whom reared', 'parents' marital history', 'parents' fertility', and 'happiness of parents'. The analysis of this hypothesis has not been completed, but the preliminary results suggest rather marked correlations between some of the situations in question and fertility planning and/or size of planned families. They also suggest, however, that much of the relationship may be due to the influence of socio-economic status.[1] The preliminary conclusions are that many of these same variables should be included in any projected re-study of this problem, and the sample should be larger in order to provide sufficient cases for the cross-classifications which should be made.

[1] Information supplied by J. F. Kantner.

Hypothesis 11, listed next, states that 'the number, size, and location of communities in which couples have lived affect the proportion of couples practising contraception effectively and the size of planned families'. This hypothesis, consisting of several parts, is partially supported. Families are larger for couples reporting continuous residence in Indianapolis since marriage than for in-migrant couples who had always lived in northern and western cities. Couples with some rural residence since marriage are too few to yield a reliable planned-fertility rate, but they appear to be characterized by highest fertility. The data yield no relationship between fertility-planning status or fertility and number of migrations of the couples since marriage or number of migrations of either spouse before marriage. The authors emphasize, however, that the restriction of the Indianapolis Study to couples living in a large city most of the time since marriage severely impairs the value of the data for studies of residence history and migration.[1]

The hypothesis on doubling-up within families is the only one of the twenty-three for which no formal report is planned. The data are inadequate from two standpoints. First, the amount of doubling experience is relatively small, for the field work of the Indianapolis Study was completed before the war-time housing shortages developed. Secondly, whereas other studies have indicated that families living with parents and in-laws tend to be weighted by childless couples and small families, they also suggest that this is largely selective and temporary. Newly married couples frequently start by living with their parents but move out shortly before or after the first child is born.

Although more adequate measures of health of the wife, husband and children would be needed for a rigorous testing of hypotheses 21 and 22, the data that are available fail to support the hypothesis that the poorer the health of the wife, husband or children, the higher is the proportion of couples practising contraception effectively and the smaller are the planned families. In most cases, the opposite types of relationship are found.[2] To some extent the direct relationship observed between health and fertility-planning status can be explained by the fact that each is directly affected by socio-economic status. There is, of course, little doubt that the hypothesis regarding size of planned family holds for certain families with specific types of illness. Doubtless there are many families who refrain from having more children because the wife is tuberculous, diabetic, or has had only Caesarean deliveries in the past. However, this type of relation appears to be lost in a small sample of the general population in which such cases are relatively few. As noted in Table 1, the measures of health are quite inadequate; they are mainly self-appraisals on general health since marriage.

[1] Kantner and Whelpton, 'Fertility rates and fertility planning by character of migration' in *Social and Psychological Factors Affecting Fertility*, vol. III, pp. 705–40.
[2] Herrera and Kiser, 'Fertility in relation to fertility planning and health of wife, husband, and children' in *Social and Psychological Factors Affecting Fertility*, vol. III, pp. 575–620.

Interest in home and children

'Liking for children' is the first of the five hypotheses listed under the heading 'interest in home and children'. The final report on this hypothesis has not been completed, but the preliminary results[1] indicate that the first part of the hypothesis—the stronger the interest in and liking for children, the lower the proportion of couples practising contraception effectively—is not sustained by the data. Instead, the reverse holds true among couples with a small number of children. Among these, the stronger the interest in and liking for children, the *greater* is the proportion of couples practising contraception effectively. For couples with large families, there is no relationship between liking for children and the effectiveness of fertility planning.

The original statement of the hypothesis assumed liking for children as the independent variable, and the extent of fertility planning as the dependent variable. The analysis indicates, however, that liking for children is a *result* of planning behaviour as well as a motivating cause for it, for the proportion of couples who strongly like children is larger among the effective planners of fertility than among the ineffective planners. Thus it is possible that not only does strong interest in children motivate one to plan fertility, but that those who have carefully planned their family are in a social situation more conducive to the development of favourable attitudes toward children than are those who live within an unplanned family. Hence, liking for children may be both an independent and a dependent variable with respect to fertility-planning behaviour.

The second part of Hypothesis 5 states that strong liking for children is accompanied by high fertility among couples who plan their fertility. This is not completely sustained. Those who are greatly interested in children will have *some* children rather than *none*. But those who like children are *not* more apt to have several children than those with lower interest in children.

Hypothesis 6 states that 'the interest of children in, and their desire for, brothers and sisters affects the size of the family', without suggesting the direction of the relationship. The preliminary analysis[2] indicates only very limited support of the hypothesis and the need for more adequate data than those available in order to make a definitive appraisal of its importance.

Hypothesis 10 also lacks specificity regarding direction of relationships, being worded, 'preferences regarding the sex of children affect the size of the family'. When this hypothesis was formulated it was realized that the factor could operate in both directions. It might encourage some couples to 'keep trying' until they have a child of the sex preferred. On the other hand, it might be a deterrent to further fertility among couples having children of the sex preferred. Within their limitations the data suggest the actual existence of both types of relationship (indicated by ± in Column 5 of Table 1), but they also indicate that the factor of sex preference is not a major determinant of family size except among a small

---

[1] The preliminary results on Hypothesis 5 are those found by Lois V. Pratt.
[2] Preliminary analysis by Jeanne E. Clare and Kiser.

proportion of the couples.[1] An important weakness of the data is that the statements regarding sex preference in children are *ex post facto*. The existence and direction of parental preferences regarding sex of children are based mainly upon the replies of wives and husbands to suppositional questions such as 'If you could have only one child, would you rather have: —— a boy; —— a girl; ——don't care?' 'If you could have only two children would you rather have: —— a boy and a girl; —— two boys; —— two girls; —— don't care?' The fertility rates are consistently lowest for couples having sex preferences fulfilled with respect to first child and first two children and highest for those not having sex preferences fulfilled in this manner. The couples replying 'don't care' are in an intermediate position with respect to fertility. It is also apparent, however, that couples with only one child and only two children were most likely to state preferences that were in accord with the actual sexes of the first child or first two children. This would help to account for the fertility differentials observed. Furthermore, the mere fact that the couples tend to state preferences in terms of the actual sex of the children suggests that they rather quickly became satisfied with what the stork brought. However, a small proportion of the couples did appear to bear out the old proverb that the wish for sons is the father of many daughters. In general, the hypothesis on sex preferences is regarded as having been partially supported.

Hypothesis 8 states that 'the belief that an only child is handicapped is an important reason for having a second child', and Hypothesis 9 states that 'the desire to insure against childlessness is an important reason for having a second child'. Most of the data for testing these hypotheses relate exclusively to 550 couples with one child living at the time of conception of the last child. The preliminary analyses suggest that the factor mentioned in Hypothesis 8 is a more important reason for the second child than is the factor mentioned in Hypothesis 9, but that neither is of much consequence.[2]

Personality characteristics

The first hypothesis listed under the 'personality characteristics' category is number 16, which reads: 'The stronger the feeling of personal inadequacy, the higher the proportion of couples practising contraception effectively and the smaller the planned families'. Like economic security, personal adequacy is directly related to both fertility-planning status and size of the planned family.[3] 'It is true, however, that the "number and spacing planned" couples are responsible for...the...direct relation of fertility to adequacy for all "planned families" (i.e. the "number and spacing planned" and "number planned" groups combined...). The relation is very irregular within the "number planned" category alone.'[4]

When socio-economic status is held constant, the direct relation of personal

[1] Clare and Kiser, 'Preferences for children of given sex in relation to fertility' in *Social and Psychological Factors Affecting Fertility*, vol. III, pp. 621–73.
[2] Preliminary analysis by Kiser and Clare.
[3] Charles F. Westoff and Kiser, 'The interrelation of fertility, fertility planning, and feeling of inadequacy' in *Social and Psychological Factors Affecting Fertility*, vol. III, pp. 741–99.
[4] Ibid. p. 783.

adequacy to fertility planning persists only slightly, and the direct relation of adequacy to size of planned family disappears altogether. A classification by jointly considered summary indexes of personal adequacy and economic security yields an interesting result. On the one hand, success in *planning* the size of family seems to be more dependent upon the presence of the emotionally stable, self-confident, well-satisfied personality than the more narrowly circumscribed confidence that accompanies a feeling of economic security. On the other hand, the actual number of children had by couples who effectively plan their family size is related much more to a feeling of economic security than to personal adequacy.

The analysis of Hypothesis 7, 'the stronger the feeling that children interfere with personal freedom, the higher the proportion of couples practising contraception effectively and the smaller the planned families', is still in process. As measures of the strength of the 'feeling' there are self-ratings, the interviewer's rating of each spouse, and a battery of questions on how much more time was wanted for various activities such as attending movies and visiting friends.

It now appears that both parts of the hypothesis are contradicted by the bulk of the data.[1] For couples with children a summary index of 'feeling that children interfere with personal freedom', based on three items, indicates for both husbands and wives that successful planning is associated with less 'feeling'; a summary index based on five items about 'more time wanted' for various activities shows the same association. Childless couples show more 'feeling' than couples with children on the three-item index, due mainly to the extreme ratings given by interviewers who presumably judged these respondents *would* be bothered if they had children. The 'more time wanted' index distributes childless wives much like wives who successfully planned their children, but childless husbands are more numerous in the group that thought they would be considerably bothered by having less time for various activities.[2]

The average number of living children is larger for husbands, for wives, and for the spouses considered as couples, who indicate more 'feeling' and 'much more time wanted'. This relationship holds among both successful and unsuccessful planners, and is unaffected by holding socio-economic status roughly constant.

The above statements are purposely made in the most general terms. The results are clear and consistent when planning success and summary indices of attitudes are dichotomized, but much less consistent when more detailed classifications are used. Considered separately, most of the component attitude items show a low but statistically significant relationship to planning success and number of children, but the direction of the relationship is not consistent, and the net balance contradicts the hypothesis. The most reasonable general interpretation is that the questions asked are tapping attitudes which are more a function of the respondent's current

---

[1] The tentative description of results concerning Hypothesis 7 was supplied by Ruth Riemer.

[2] The 'more time wanted' items are suppositional questions for childless couples, while for couples with children they refer to actual experience, so that direct comparability is lacking. For instance, the childless couples were asked how much they would mind having less time for movies, visiting, etc., *if* they had children. The couples with children were asked how much more time they would have liked for these activities *since their first child was born*.

responsibility for child care than a function of factors which helped to determine the couple's family planning in the past. For deliberately childless couples, the questions may be tapping attitudes more directly relevant to planning status, but all that can be said with assurance is that a fairly large proportion of such couples, and more especially of husbands, 12–15 years after marriage, think that they would be bothered if their personal freedom were to be curtailed by child care.

The meaning of Hypothesis 18, which reads 'the greater the extent to which interest in children is a matter of *personal* satisfaction, the higher the proportion of couples practising contraception effectively and the smaller the planned family', may be clarified by use of the term 'ego-centred interest in children'. Whereas Hypothesis 5 (liking for children) may be described as one relating to 'child-centred interest in children in general', the present one is concerned with 'ego-centred interest in one's own children'. For measures of the latter, there are eight questions (six restricted to parents) on such matters as whether the respondents wanted their children to be independent even if this meant that the children would not always take their advice, the right of parents to expect children to appreciate the sacrifices made for them, and degree of comfort found in thinking how much their children love and need them.

Classifications by replies to some of the questions support the hypothesis. In general, however, the data for couples with children fail to show a consistent relation between 'ego-centred interest in children' (as measured) and fertility-planning status, and provide only very slight support of the suggested inverse relation between this interest and size of planned family. The replies to the two questions that were not restricted to parents suggest that the proportion of couples that are childless may be directly related with the degree of ego-centred interest in children. In general, however, it appears that the specific questions are not good indicators of 'ego-centred interest in children', and hence, that the hypothesis has not been adequately tested.[1]

Fear of pregnancy (Hypothesis 23) appears to be no important deterrent to fertility after the first childbirth. In other words, among 'planned families' the proportion of childless couples increases with fear of pregnancy, but there is little relation of fertility to 'fear' among couples with children. Since the childless couples, by definition, are largely in the 'number and spacing planned' group, they also are responsible for the slight direct relation of fear of pregnancy to fertility-planning status.[2]

In the analyses of three hypotheses—tendency to plan in general (17), religious interest (15) and adherence to traditions (14)—it has been suggested that these variables may be different aspects of a single larger variable called 'rationality of behaviour'. By rationality is meant 'the extent to which behaviour is a result of calculated choice between alternatives rather than the unquestioning acceptance on

[1] Marianne DeGraf Swain and Kiser, 'The interrelation of fertility, fertility planning, and ego-centered interest in children', *The Milbank Memorial Fund Quarterly*, vol. XXXI, no. 1, January 1953, pp. 51–84.
[2] Nathalie Schacter and Kiser, 'Fear of pregnancy and childbirth in relation to fertility-planning status and fertility', *The Milbank Memorial Fund Quarterly*, vol. XXXI, no. 2, April 1953, pp. 166–215.

faith of the traditional behavioural standards of the group to which the individual belongs'. The findings indicate that traditionalism, general planning and religion are each related to fertility variables, but that the relationships are in large measure a joint function of the socio-economic status of the couples interviewed.[1] In general, the findings lend only modest support to the hypotheses. The bearing of the three sets of specific findings on the more general hypothesis of the relationship between rationalism and fertility is inconclusive although suggestive.

The analysis of Hypothesis 13 (conformity to group patterns) is not likely to lead to conclusive results. The distribution of the replies to many questions is so skewed or there is such a concentration in neutral categories as to make refined analysis impossible.[2]

The analysis of the data for Hypothesis 20 concerning marital adjustment yields several points of interest. Among the total group of 'relatively fecund' couples the proportions of couples reporting happy marriage, little disagreement over family matters, and 'little desire to improve the spouse' decrease consistently with number of living children. In other words, for the total sample, marital adjustment appears to be inversely related to fertility. However, this may be the result of the direct relation which is found between marital adjustment and success in preventing unwanted pregnancies. Furthermore, within the 'number and spacing planned' group marital adjustment appears to be positively correlated with success in having *as many children* as wanted. Stated in more general terms, the data suggest that among Indianapolis couples marital adjustment is directly related to successful family planning both with respect to preventing unwanted pregnancies and, among the 'number and spacing planned' couples at least, with respect to success in having as many children as wanted.[3]

Hypothesis 19, which reads: 'That member of the couple who is dominant in general family matters tends also to be dominant in determining whether conception shall be controlled and [in determining] the size of the planned family', could not be tested in the form presented because of the infrequency of cases in which either the wife or husband could be classified as 'dominant in general family matters'. In an attempt to measure 'dominance' the wives and husbands were asked who made the decisions on a variety of things, e.g. who usually decided whether or not the family could afford a new car, which movies to see together, which radio programme to hear, which couples to keep as friends, and which house

---

[1] Ronald Freedman and Whelpton, 'Fertility planning and fertility rates by religious interest and denomination' in *Social and Psychological Factors Affecting Fertility*, vol. II, pp. 417–66; 'The relationship of general planning to fertility planning and fertility rates' in *Social and Psychological Factors Affecting Fertility*, vol. III, pp. 549–74; 'Fertility planning and fertility rates by adherence to traditions' in *Social and Psychological Factors Affecting Fertility*, vol. III, pp. 675–704.

[2] Information received from J. F. Kantner.

[3] Robert B. Reed, 'The interrelationship of marital adjustment, fertility control, and size of family' in *Social and Psychological Factors Affecting Fertility*, vol. II, pp. 259–92. Note: The 'number and spacing planned' couples were considered to have as many pregnancies as wanted if the number of pregnancies (or live births, if live births exceeded pregnancies due to multiple births) experienced was as large as the number given by both wife and husband in reply to the question, 'If you could begin your married life over again and the size of your family could be determined only by your liking for children, how many would you have?'

to rent or buy. Some three-fourths of the wives and husbands reported that these matters were decided on a fifty-fifty basis. Furthermore, among the remaining replies, a rather frequent pattern was that of the husband appearing to be dominant in certain spheres and the wife in others. Thus if the decision as to which house to buy or rent was not made on a fifty-fifty basis it was more likely to be made by the husband than the wife. In contrast, the wife tended to be the one who decided which friends to visit, which movies to attend, which radio programmes to listen to, etc. It is quite possible, of course, that different results would be found for another group or with different criteria of dominance.

A positive finding that emerges from the analysis concerns dominance with respect to contraception and size of family. The data suggest that fertility planning was most successful among couples in which both the wife and husband state that responsibility for contraception was a fifty-fifty proposition, and was least successful among couples in which each spouse said that the other should take the responsibility regarding contraception. When each wished the burden on the other, apparently neither spouse took much responsibility; these are the couples who on the average had the largest number of unwanted pregnancies.[1]

III. Weaknesses of the Indianapolis Study and
Implications for Future Studies

As indicated earlier, one of the main reasons for conducting the Indianapolis Study was to find out how to study more effectively the social and psychological factors affecting fertility planning and family size. It is evident that the Indianapolis Study has several weaknesses, particularly with respect to measures of attitudes and beliefs. There are also reasons for questioning again some of the sampling procedures and the general conceptualization. These topics will be considered briefly, with special reference to their implications for future studies in the field concerned.[2]

The size of the sample has proved too small to permit all the breakdowns needed for adequate analysis or to yield definitive results in many instances; hence it will be highly desirable to secure a larger sample in a future study. To do so, however, will require not only a larger budget, but one or more of the following: (a) location in a larger city, in two or more cities, or in an area at least partly rural, or (b) wider variation in such characteristics as age, age at marriage, duration of marriage, education, or religion. Most changes along such lines will lessen the efficiency of the sample for certain purposes, and partially offset the gain from larger size.

The restriction of the sample to native-white, urban, Protestant couples with at least a grammar school education is a source of at least two types of weaknesses, for it severely narrows the area for possible generalization as to findings, and has the methodological disadvantage of narrowing the internal variations in fertility which

---

[1] Ibid. pp. 292–301.

[2] The 'implications' discussed here are to be regarded only as the tentative ideas of the authors of this report. They are not intended either to reflect the ideas of the full committee or to anticipate the actual nature of any future study that may be planned.

are to be studied. Nevertheless, a lowering of sample restrictions would not substantially increase the number of large families that were planned as to size. It is believed that until further progress has been made in evaluating the effect on fertility planning and family size of psychological factors and of other demographic and social factors than those just mentioned, the advantages of such restrictions probably will continue to outweigh the disadvantages.

It seems rather clear that the scope of the study is too broad; certainly the data for some of the hypotheses are very thin. It would be well for a future study to concentrate on fewer hypotheses and to provide more adequate data on the hypotheses selected. This means not only clearer conceptualization but a more adequate pre-testing of the validity and reliability of the specific questions to be asked. The hypothesis on migration is one which might well be put aside. The sample drawn in Indianapolis proved ill-suited to testing most of this hypothesis. The funds that would be required to obtain an adequate sample in another study may be used to better advantage on other hypotheses.

The Indianapolis Study has pointed up certain pitfalls such as the selective factors inherent in the questions used to measure economic tension—the difference between actual and desired level of living. It is to be hoped that in another project help can be secured from some of the people studying measures of family consumption levels in relation to standards of living. Also, special analyses of study materials have indicated that objective measures of actual social mobility, in both inter-generational and intra-generational contexts, are feasible. They have suggested that, at least within certain limits, these phenomena are systematically related to fertility and are worthy of considerably more attention in a future study.[1]

As in other studies of human behaviour, the difficulties inherent in the interaction of the variables considered constantly confronted the analysts. Thus, certain variables may affect and also be affected by size of family; the two-way relation between fertility and economic security is a case in point. As indicated, various analysts have found cause to question the assumption implicit in the hypotheses that the hypothesis variable is independent and that the fertility planning and size of planned family variables are dependent.

The Indianapolis Study presents a challenge to learn the reasons for the overriding influence of socio-economic status. There is good reason to believe that it is not socio-economic status *per se* but rather the underlying attitudes and psychological characteristics of these classes that account for the fertility behaviour. And yet, whereas characteristic patterns of fertility differentials are found consistently in classifications by socio-economic status, most classifications by psychological characteristics *within socio-economic groups* fail to show such patterns. The chief exception is that concerning economic security. Failure to secure good measures of the psychological characteristics may account for their apparent lack of relation

---

[1] For purposes of their doctoral dissertations at the University of Michigan, J. F. Kantner and Ruth Riemer analysed Indianapolis Study materials on, respectively, inter-generational and intra-generational social mobility in relation to fertility planning and fertility. See also Charles F. Westoff, 'The changing focus of differential fertility research', *The Milbank Memorial Fund Quarterly*, vol. XXXI, no. 1, January 1953, pp. 24–38.

to fertility. It may be that too much reliance was placed on the multiple-choice questionnaire and that there was not enough preliminary testing of these questions for validity and reliability. Improvement should be feasible in another study. It is also possible that further cross-tabulation of the Indianapolis data themselves will provide a clue as to whether given socio-economic classes are characterized by given constellations of psychological characteristics which are related to fertility. At all events, some work on this problem is planned.

It is also possible that there has been too much dependence on what might be called the atomistic approach—on classifying couples by a given characteristic and then by another characteristic and each time attempting to find variations in fertility planning and fertility by the characteristic considered. This approach probably does not take sufficient recognition of the fact that the subjects studied arc human beings whose decisions regarding fertility planning and fertility are made individually on the basis of multiple and complex motivations. Perhaps the classifications by socio-economic status serve also to classify people by these patterns and complexes, but it would certainly be a defeatist attitude to conclude that it is impossible to go much beyond these classifications.

The study has been criticized for not giving some indication that the 'baby boom' would occur later in the 1940's; it has been suggested that another study of social and psychological factors affecting fertility should be planned so as to indicate probable fertility changes during ensuing years. In this connexion it should be remembered that women as old as those in the Indianapolis Study (most of whom were born between 1902 and 1911) have contributed relatively little to the baby boom; it is the women in the cohorts of 1915–34 that have been primarily responsible. This indicates that a study which will forecast a phenomenon like the baby boom cannot have as high requirements for duration of marriage and age of bride as those used in Indianapolis (12–15 years, and less than 30, respectively). If the period of married life is much shorter, however, there will be less basis for determining the actual size of completed families as compared with number of children born to date or total number expected. Using number of births to date will mean focusing the analysis more on the timing of children; using the expected number will involve allowing for the wide differences that frequently are found between anticipated and actual behaviour. One solution may be to broaden the range in duration of marriage and age of bride, but this will necessitate including a correspondingly larger number of couples and will raise costs proportionately.

Since 1945 there has been a strong tendency for women to marry younger and to have at least one or two children earlier than formerly. Whether this will tend to increase the size of completed families, or whether it is largely a matter of timing which forecasts a drop in annual birth rates, remains to be seen. The best way to study the implications of these changes and to evaluate the factors bringing them about may be through a longitudinal study, retrospective as to the recent past and begun at a very early date. It would be expensive, of course, to follow a group of couples through their childbearing period (with visits at six-monthly or yearly intervals), and would require special arrangements to provide continuity of investigators and to minimize the effects of the interviews on the co-operating couples. Such a study probably could be made more feasible by linking it to similar undertakings in other fields, for example, health and marital adjustment, where such research probably will become increasingly frequent. Since problems of fertility may be related to these other problems, perhaps it is not too far-fetched to visualize joint undertakings of this nature.

Finally, it is to be hoped that in future studies there will be even more inter-disciplinary participation in the planning, execution and analysis aspects than was the case in the Indianapolis Study. The panel of people participating should include representatives at least from the fields of sociology, economics, demography, psychology, social psychology, statistics, cultural anthropology, public health and medicine.

Chapter IV

INTERNATIONAL DISTRIBUTION OF
POPULATION AND MIGRATION

Extreme unevenness characterizes the distribution of population, income, resources, and technological attainment over the earth's surface. This has been
confirmed most recently by compilations undertaken by Colin Clark, W. S. Woytinsky, the United Nations, and others. International migration is essentially a
response to this unevenness, an effort to escape its incidence.

Extreme skewness characterizes the distribution of the world's population.
About five-ninths of the world's population are situated within three major concentrations (the Far East, India and Ceylon, and Western and Central Europe)
which embrace about one-sixth of that 38 per cent of the world's area which is
at least moderately populated. The population density of these concentrations
ranges from over 310 to over 500 per square mile. Another 16 per cent of the
world's population are found within a few lesser concentrations that comprise
about 4 per cent of the world's area which is at least moderately populated,
namely, Indochina, Philippines, Indonesia, Northeastern United States, Nigeria,
Egypt, and the coastal regions of North and South America. The population
density of these concentrations ranges from over 160 to nearly 500. Within the
moderately populated eight-tenths of the relatively well inhabited portion of
the world live only three-tenths of its population, and density approximates 41
per square mile; within sparsely populated areas comprising about 27 per cent
of the world's area are found only one-sixtieth of its population. About 35 per
cent of the world's area is uninhabited.

Capacity to make a living, as reflected in reported per capita incomes, is also
distributed very unevenly. Thus in 1949, according to a United Nations study,
the per capita incomes of well over one-half of the world's population were
below $100; only the eight richest countries, with less than one-tenth of the
world's population, enjoyed per capita incomes above $600. Incomes of in excess
of $200 were found only in but one small country in Asia (Israel), in the Union
of South Africa, in two islands lying off the American coast (i.e., Cuba and Puerto
Rico), in three South American countries, in Australia, New Zealand, Canada,
the Soviet Union, and the U.S.A., and in all but four European countries. In
nearly all of the countries in which per capita income is below $200 the actual
and/or the potential rate of natural increase is high. Whence, since a high rate
of natural increase is unfavorable to capital formation and hence to the increase
of per capita income, there exists a tendency for low and high incomes, together
with international income differentials, to perpetuate themselves.

Land and natural resources are very unevenly distributed. Only in Europe
is as much as three-tenths of the land classified as arable; in North America, Asia,
and the USSR the percentage is only 10 to 13. Whereas arable land per capita
exceeds three acres in North America, Oceania, and the Soviet Union, it approximates only an acre in Europe and two-thirds of an acre in Asia; it is appreciably
lower in Africa and Latin America than in North America. While mineral resources
are distributed even more unevenly over the earth's surface than is good land, it
is not possible to express this inequality in a single summary measure. Mineral and
energy consumption are more disparate even than mineral and energy produc-

tion, since some of the high-level consumption nations import considerable quantities. In the United States, for example, mineral consumption per head is above ten times that found in the rest of the non-communist world.

Both productive man-made equipment available per head and the capacity of nations to form assets vary greatly with country, much in the manner that per capita income does. For the wealth of nations tends to approximate 4 to 6 times their national incomes, while populations can readily save 10 to 15 per cent of their incomes and convert these savings into productive assests. In some countries, of course, the rate at which productive assets are formed is much lower, often because gross reproduction and/or the rate of natural increase are so high. In others, when there is duress or strong social pressure to save, the rate may run as high as 20 per cent, in part because the capacity to form capital tends (within limits) to grow faster than income when income growth is accelerated. As a rule, judging from F. C. Mills' finding that in the United States only about one-third as much of gross national product was converted into capital as appears to have been theoretically possible, capital tends to be formed at a lower rate than is theoretically attainable.

Technological attainment, together with access thereto, varies greatly from country to country. Suitable indexes are not available. Woytinsky's data suggest, however, that the technological attainment of perhaps three-fourths of the world's population is quite low while that of little more than a tenth may be described as quite high. International differences in the rate of technological progress have played a major part in increasing many-fold the international income differences which obtained 150 years ago. The importance of technological progress is suggested also by the fact that in the United States improvements in technology have been at least as important as capital formation for the increase of per capita income.

The upshot of what has been said is that the conditions under which individuals and groups live, and the opportunities to which they have access, vary widely. Life as it is lived in certain countries therefore will be preferred to life as it is lived in other countries, at least by some of those who are aware of the differences. Among those with such preferences will be found inhabitants in every country, but above all informed inhabitants of countries in which opportunities are quite inferior. Some of these individuals will find themselves prompted to take steps to reduce the spread between the situations in which they find themselves and the situations they believe to be had abroad or at home in the future.

The spread may be reduced in two ways. It may be reduced, first of all, through the introduction into a country of policies designed to increase the effectiveness with which resources and manpower are used, to step up the rate at which capital is formed, and to accelerate greatly the rate at which the most advanced technology is efficiently employed. The spread may be reduced, secondly, by international migration.

Of the two ways of proceeding, migration is much the less effective. It benefits principally the emigrant; and the emigrants from a country usually form a very small fraction of its population and but a minor fraction of its natural increase. Emigration is not suited to transform a country's economy and remedy the conditions which gave rise to it in the first place; nor is it very likely to bring about a marked decline in its age-specific fertility and rate of natural increase.

The first way of proceeding is much more likely to provide a comparatively satisfactory long-run solution for the population problem in countries therewith afflicted. It tends to give release to a complex of synergistic forces, each reenforcing the other. It tends to bring about modernization of a country's economy, transformation of its culture, and modification of its value structure. It tends to be accompanied by sustained increases in both per capita income and the rate of capital formation. Above all it tends to bring about decline in age-specific fertility and a balance between births and deaths at low natality and mortality levels. This outcome is itself favorable to income growth since it entails a considerable increase in the relative number of persons of productive age and in the ratio of the labor force to the population.

In both the introduction to Chapter V and in several of the papers included therein attention is given to some of the forces making for the concentration of economic activities and hence for the agglomeration of population. Natural circumstances—the distribution of land and of mineral, energy, and other resources—largely determine the location of extractive industries, of manufactures directly linked therewith, and of productive activities having to do with the servicing of those engaged in extractive and related industries. Even when natural circumstances do not dominate industrial location, economies of scale and of agglomeration tend to make for the concentration of various manufacturing and related activities and hence of service and other employments carried on for the benefit of those engaged in these activities. Even the location of employments based upon tourism is dominated by climatic conditions which make for considerable concentration. There are present in modern industrial society, in short, strong centripetal forces making for the concentration of a large fraction of every country's population in a small fraction of its area. Urbanization is but one manifestation of these forces.

While the pressure of these centripetal forces is most evident within the sovereign state, where their impact is not much cushioned by international boundaries, it is present also in the international sphere. For since small states cannot wholly counterbalance these forces, they affect the international as well as the intranational distribution of economic activities and population. They generate a certain amount of international migration, therefore, and they would generate a good deal more if legal and related barriers to international trade and migration were reduced.

It is to be noted that there have been very substantial migrations of population in the past—in the Mediterranean world in ancient times, in Asia and Europe in early centuries of the Christian era, and in Europe when its settlement was extended after the tenth century. These migrations were not essentially transmarine and intercontinental, however. Vast migration of that sort did not begin until several centuries after the opening up of the new world and Oceania. It required for its initiation and continuation a rather unique set of circumstances: a continuing and tremendous demand for population, a continuing supply, sufficient proximity of source and destination, a good transport system, and adequate provision of capital and supplementary goods. The demand was supplied by the vast new lands and resources continuously being opened up for exploitation in the new world and Oceania and requiring many decades for completion of their development. The transfer of population to these lands was facilitated by the fact that most of them were not too far removed from Europe, that sea transport had become effective and continued to become ever more effective, and that Europe was able to spare enough real capital to get self-sustaining development processes under way in a number of these transmarine lands. The population could be supplied because European mortality continued to fall, and sufficiently to offset later declines in natality, with the result that natural increase remained sufficiently high to satisfy both the domestic demand for population occasioned by the spread of the industrial revolution and the demand emanating from the new world. Supply of population was facilitated also by the fact that the industrial revolution did not spread fast enough to provide as much economic opportunity at home as was desired by a steadily expanding European labor force. With the substantial disappearance after 1914 of the favorable conjuncture of circumstances just described, the volume of intercontinental migration greatly declined. It was the absence of such a conjuncture that helped to keep emigration from Asia at low levels.

International flows of capital, people, and goods are interrelated. People and capital being complementary to each other, the movement of one tends to be accompanied or succeeded by that of the other. This complementarity was especially striking before 1914 when the process of settling America and Oceania was in full swing. It has since come to be obscured somewhat by other factors. Although the international distribution of population has played an important direct and indirect role in building up markets, extending international division of labor, and enlarging the volume of international trade, international trade is, within limits, a substitute for international migration. When trade takes place, goods move in which the labor of countries relatively long on labor is incorporated in comparatively large measure. These goods tend to be exchanged for other goods into which labor enters in a relatively lesser degree. It may be said, therefore, that when labor-long countries export labor-oriented goods, their labor is migrating by proxy. Accordingly, when migration is not free but trade is relatively free, labor-oriented goods tend to move from populous countries and ease population pressure therein, provided that international technological differences do not unduly offset inequalities in the international distribution of labor.

In the papers comprising this chapter circumstances giving rise to emigration and immigration are described and some of the economic and other effects of immigration are indicated. Questions of assimilation are treated by Kiser, who shows how a new kind of national culture may be brought into being by the conjuncture of immigrant streams of diverse ethnic and cultural origins.

SOME ECONOMIC ASPECTS OF IMMIGRATION

INTO THE UNITED STATES

By Joseph J. Spengler

> Pleasure or businesse, so, our Soules admit
> For their first mover, and are whirld by it.
> Hence is't, that I am carryed towards the West.
> John Donne

This paper has to do with the economic aspects of American immigration—among them, the capacity of the American economy to absorb immigrants and the probable response of the American economy to variations in the volume of immigration. Accordingly, both a historical and an analytical approach are employed. Part I is given to an historical résumé of the economic dimensions of American immigration. A summary account of the actual effects of immigration upon the American economy is presented in part II. Parts III and IV are devoted to an outline of the implications of economic-demographic theory for the subject under consideration. In part V, conclusions for policy based upon the preceding historical and analytical sections are indicated.

I

HISTORICAL BACKGROUND

The movement of population from Europe to the lands across the sea during the past century and a half is divisible into two parts; a redistribution of population within the Atlantic economy, and a passage of people from Europe to countries situated outside the Atlantic economy.[1] Redistribution of population within the Atlantic economy accounted for the major part of this transoceanic movement, and emigration to the United States dominated this redistributive process. Between 1800 and 1950, about 67 million emigrants crossed the ocean, of whom "approximately 60 million were Europeans, and, of these, some 40 million came to the United States."[2] While many of these migrants returned to Europe, somewhat in excess of

---

[1] See BRINLEY THOMAS, MIGRATION AND ECONOMIC GROWTH cc. 1, 14 (1954).

[2] W. S. AND E. S. WOYTINSKY, WORLD POPULATION AND PRODUCTION 72 (1953). Some 45 million persons emigrated from Europe to North America between 1600 and 1950, of whom some 25 million remained; approximately 20 million, of whom close to 18 million remained, went to Middle and South America; over 5 million went to Oceania and Africa. Negro slaves imported into the Americas numbered nearly 15 million. See *id.* at 69, 72. Asiatic migration has been much less intercontinental than has European. Only about 3 million emigrants left Asia in 1800-1950. Of the 30 million emigrants who left India and Pakistan in 1834-1937, about 24 million returned, while of the approximately 5 million persons of Indian descent living outside India around 1940, about four-fifths resided in Burma,

70 per cent remained, with the ratio of net to gross immigration declining from close to 100 per cent in the 1820's to around 65 per cent in 1900-30.[3]

TABLE I

IMMIGRATION AND POPULATION GROWTH, THE UNITED STATES, 1850-1950 (IN MILLIONS)

| Census Year | Population (reported by Census) | FOREIGN-BORN WHITE POPULATION | | Gross Immigration in Preceding Decade | Net Immigration in Preceding Decade |
		Total	Increase in Preceding Decade		
1850	23.2	2.2	...	1.7	1.42
1860	31.4	4.1	1.9	2.6	2.56
1870	39.8	5.5	1.4	2.3	2.07
1880	50.2	6.6	1.1	2.8	2.58
1890	62.9	9.1	2.5	5.2	4.96
1900	76.0	10.2	1.1	3.7	3.69
1910	92.0	13.3	3.1	8.8	6.24
1920	105.7	13.7	0.4	5.7	2.23
1930	122.8	14.0	0.3	4.1	3.34
1940	131.7	11.4	−2.6	0.5	.07*
1950	150.7	10.2	−1.2	1.0	.88*

SOURCES: Cols. 2-5, U. S. DEP'T OF COMMERCE, STATISTICAL ABSTRACT OF THE UNITED STATES (1954) [hereinafter cited as STATISTICAL ABSTRACT], and HISTORICAL STATISTICS OF THE UNITED STATES, 1789-1945 (1949) [hereinafter cited as HISTORICAL STATISTICS]; Col. 6, W. S. THOMPSON AND P. K. WHELPTON, POPULATION TRENDS IN THE UNITED STATES 303 (1933).
*Based on STATISTICAL ABSTRACT, supra.

Figures presented in Table I suggest the order of magnitude of post-1850 immigration into the United States, by decade, and the ostensible[4] contribution of immigration to population growth. In the period 1800-40, about 800,000 immigrants came to the United States, of whom about 750,000 remained. Thereafter, and until the 1930's, gross immigration usually exceeded 200,000 per year and on six occasions

Malaya, and Ceylon. Of the approximately 8.5 million Chinese living outside China around 1940, only 300-400 thousand lived outside of Asia. Of the approximately 3.5 million Japanese living outside Japan proper in 1940, only about one-fifth were situated outside Asia. Nearly all the Koreans emigrating from Korea remained in Asia. See J. ISAAC, ECONOMICS OF MIGRATION 59-67 (1947); KINGSLEY DAVIS, THE POPULATION OF INDIA AND PAKISTAN c. 13 (1951); United Nations, *International Migrations in the Far East During Recent Times*, 1 POPULATION BULL. 13 (1951), 2 *id.* at 27 (1952).

[3] See 2 WALTER F. WILLCOX, INTERNATIONAL MIGRATIONS 89 (1931). A recent estimate suggests that Willcox underestimated the ratio of net to gross, and that census enumerations somewhat understate the number of foreign-born. See S. KUZNETS AND E. RUBIN, IMMIGRATION AND THE FOREIGN BORN 14-30, 87-94 (1954). *Cf.* cols. 5 and 6 in Table I. The fall in the ratio of net to gross immigration is attributed in considerable measure to the fact that the number of departures is a function of an increasingly large foreign-born population, whereas the number of arrivals is a function of a less rapidly expanding source of migrants.

[4] Benjamin Franklin, F. A. Walker, and others have contended that when immigrants move into an already occupied country, their coming causes the fertility of the population resident in that country to fall and stimulates some members of this population to emigrate. These writers have concluded, therefore, that, in the long run, a net influx *m* of immigrants will increase the population of a given country of immigration by less than *m* if it increases that population at all. Some admit, of course, that the rate at which this population increases will rise at first in consequence of the influx of immigrants, only to decline subsequently. It is not possible to subject the Walker thesis to careful empirical tests. It is arguable, however, that an influx of immigrants may increase, decrease, or not affect at all the longer-run rate of growth of a resident population, with the actual outcome depending on what conditions hold. See THOMPSON AND WHELPTON, *op. cit. supra* Table I, at 302-11; also Spengler, *On the Effects Produced in Immigrant-Receiving Countries by Pre-1939 Immigration*, in INTERNATIONAL MIGRATION (Brinley Thomas ed. to be published 1956).

exceeded 1,000,000 per year, while the average annual volume of net immigration ranged between 140 and 620 thousand. In consequence, the foreign-born white population long increased somewhat more rapidly than the native population, the ratio of foreign-born to the total population rising from .097 in 1850 to a peak of .145 in 1910. Immigration contributed significantly to American population growth, net immigration approximating 8 per cent of the total population in 1838-61 and, thereafter, gradually declining to 2 per cent in 1918-32.[5] Net immigration accounted for about 31 per cent of the increase in population taking place in the period 1840-1910. By 1920, according to one estimate, of the 94.8 million whites living in the United States, 53.5 million represented immigrant stock, with immigrants, children of immigrants, and grandchildren and later generations of immigrants, respectively, numbering 13.7, 19.2, and 20.6 millions.[6] Nonetheless, despite the continuation of a high incremental rate of immigration, the rate of growth of the American population began to decline after the Civil War; it fell from the level of 33-36 per cent per decade obtaining in 1790-1860 to levels of approximately 26 per cent per decade in 1860-90, 21 per cent in 1890-1910, and, thereafter, except for the depression decade 1930-39, 15 per cent.

The decline in gross immigration which set in after it had reached maximum levels in 1900-14 was not attributable entirely to a decline in emigration from Europe. The number of European emigrants declined, it is true, from 11.3 million in 1901-10 to 7.6 and 6.6 millions in the two decades that followed, and then slumped to 1.9 million in 1931-40 and some 1.6 million in 1941-50. This decline, occasioned initially by World War I, was attributable in part to the introduction of quota and other restrictions on immigration, to the recurrence of unfavorable business conditions, and to political circumstances which culminated in World War II and the post-war spread of Communist governments. In the absence of these adverse conditions, emigration from Europe would probably have continued in considerable volume, despite the decline in the rate of natural increase in northern and western Europe. For around 1930, there still existed in southern and eastern Europe a "surplus" agricultural population of perhaps 37 million, and around 1940, it appeared likely that the population of these parts of Europe would increase another 26 million by 1970.[7] Even so, the relative number of European emigrants going to the United States would have declined somewhat, though not nearly so much as it did after the introduction of restrictive measures in the United States, for the economies of Canada, Australia, Brazil, and Argentina had developed sufficiently by the late nineteenth century to attract immigrants in volume. As it was, the percentage immigrants into the United States constituted of all intercontinental migrants declined from about 70 per cent in 1821-90, through about 60 per cent in 1890-1910 and 50

---

[5] See KUZNETS AND RUBIN, op. cit. supra note 3, at 2, 21-26.

[6] See Spengler, *The Merits and Demerits of the National Origins Provisions for Selecting Immigrants,* 10 Sw. POL. & Soc. SCI. Q. 155 (1929). See also THOMPSON AND WHELPTON, op. cit. supra Table I, c. 3.

[7] See W. E. MOORE, ECONOMIC DEMOGRAPHY OF EASTERN AND SOUTHERN EUROPE 56-76 (1945).

per cent in 1911-30, to 20 per cent in 1931-40; it may have amounted to as much as 46 per cent in 1941-50. Most of the European immigrants who did not go to the United States went to British dominions and colonies (principally Australia, New Zealand, Canada, Africa) or to Latin America (principally Brazil and Argentina).[8]

In as much as migrants are prompted to move by the prospect of improving their situations, and since they usually interpret prospects in economic terms, the movement of immigrants into a country is dominated by the conditions surrounding the demand for labor in that country, while the movement of emigrants out of a country is usually dominated by the rate at which the labor force is growing, together with the circumstances governing job opportunities. The conditions surrounding the demand for labor in the United States were attractive in terms of European standards, it will be indicated later, except in periods of transient unemployment. The internal conditions by which the disposition of Europeans to emigrate was chiefly affected were four in number: (1) the movement of relative and absolute natural increase; (2) the movement of surplus labor out of agricultural areas; (3) the progress of industrialization and urbanization; and (4) variations in the rate at which capital was formed in the nonagricultural sector.

(1) Absolute natural increase expanded little in Europe between 1820 and 1914, but it fluctuated considerably, producing fluctuations in the growth of the labor force fifteen or more years later, and in the volume of emigration about twenty-five years later. Moreover, after 1880, the rate of natural increase of the agricultural countries rose relatively to that of the industrial countries, with the result that population pressure in the agricultural countries came to exceed even more than formerly that found in the industrial countries.[9] (2) Throughout the period 1820-1940, an excess of labor was to be found in many rural areas, ready to move in response to the prospect of a slight improvement or under the impact of adversity (e.g., Irish crop failure; depression of European agricultural prices by agricultural expansion abroad); it had to find employment in domestic industry or in lands of immigration. (3) Industrialization and urbanization progressed, spreading eastward and southward, usually very slowly, but sometimes at a rate sufficient to increase employment opportunities for those seeking work in the nonagricultural sector and to produce changes in the social structure. (4) While capital was increasingly to be had in northern and western Europe, not a great deal was formed or otherwise obtainable in southern and eastern Europe, even though the absolute increment in population was growing; whence, additions to the labor force in these

[8] See WOYTINSKY, op. cit. supra note 2, at 76-80. Quota immigrants from Europe aggregated 624 thousand in 1940-50; all immigrants from Europe numbered 746 thousand in 1941-50. See id. at 81, 83. For emigrants from Europe, see id. at 75. Cf. S. N. PROKOPOVICH, L'INDUSTRIALISATION DES PAYS AGRICOLES ET LA STRUCTURE DE L'ÉCONOMIE MONDIALE APRÈS LA GUERRE 126-39 (1946). Because of the pull of the American economy, Canada lost more migrants to the United States than she attracted from abroad in 1861-1901, but thereafter, usually experienced net immigration. See Nathan Keyfitz, The Growth of Canadian Population, POPULATION STUDIES 62 (1950).

[9] See THOMAS, op. cit. supra note 1, at 80-81, 116-18, 156-58, 218-19, 313-14; PROKOPOVICH, op. cit. supra note 8, at 154-56, 308-09; I. SVENNILSON, GROWTH AND STAGNATION IN THE EUROPEAN ECONOMY C, 4 (1954).

parts were under pressure to emigrate. With (3) and (4) was associated a diminution in the physical and the monetary costs of immigration.[10]

The conditions described varied from country to country. They changed, with
the eastward and southward spread of the forces of economic development, in such
manner that, as the disposition to emigrate diminished in the lands facing the
North Atlantic, it increased in the lands lying to the East and the South. Prior to
1850, northwestern Europe was the source of somewhat more than four-fifths of inter-
continental emigration of European origin. As late as 1871-80, it furnished 65.4 per
cent, and central Europe 23.4 per cent, of this emigration. After 1880, and especially
after 1890, the relative number of emigrants from Latin and East-European countries increased, rising from one-fourth of the total in 1881-90 to about one-half in
1891-1930. The fraction contributed by the British Isles, 76.1 per cent in 1821-40, fell
to 53.2 per cent in 1861-80, 25.6 per cent in 1881-1920, and 13 per cent in 1931-38. The
proportion originating in the industrial countries of Europe, comprising nearly all
emigrants before 1840, fell to 81 per cent by 1861-80, and to about 27 per cent by
1901-20; it rose to 43 per cent in 1921-38 as a result of the establishment of selective
quotas in countries of immigration. These changes are reflected in the fact that by
1930, only 39 per cent of the foreign-born population was from Germany and northwestern Europe, whereas, in 1850 and 1890, the corresponding percentages were
90 and 77. In general, emigrants tended to come from economies, which, being agricultural and relatively unprogressive, could not absorb their growing labor force on
terms comparatively satisfactory to workers, rather than from progressive economies
which were providing improved industrial opportunities for those entering the nonagricultural labor force.[11]

The southward and the eastward shifts of the sources of immigration were accompanied by changes in the composition of the immigrant stream and in the
nature of its impact on the American economy. An increasingly large proportion
of the immigrants came from relatively underdeveloped agricultural countries, with
the result that the occupational composition of the immigrants came to be increasingly inferior to that of an American population which was living in one of the
industrially most progressive parts of the world. Many of the "new" immigrants
from predominantly agricultural southern and eastern Europe were comparatively
illiterate and lacking in occupational and industrial skills. Moreover, many of those

---

[10] See THOMAS, op. cit. supra note 1, cc. 3, 10, 12, and 13; D. S. THOMAS, SOCIAL AND ECONOMIC
ASPECTS OF SWEDISH POPULATION MOVEMENTS cc. 2-3 (1941); PROKOPOVICH, op. cit. supra note 8, c. 4;
D. KIRK, EUROPE'S POPULATION IN THE INTERWAR YEARS cc. 4-6, 8 (1946); C. CLARK, CONDITIONS OF
ECONOMIC PROGRESS cc. 9, 11 (2d ed. 1951); H. FEIS, EUROPE, THE WORLD'S BANKER, 1870-1914 passim
(1930); SVENNILSON, op. cit. supra note 9, c. 4.

[11] See WOYTINSKY, op. cit. supra note 2, at 75-76; PROKOPOVICH, op. cit. supra note 8, at 126-27.
The increase in the relative number of migrants of Latin origin accounted in part for the increase in
the relative number of European emigrants who went to Latin America. While emigration from
Europe rose from 1 per 1000 inhabitants in 1846-50 to 2.5 in 1901-05 and 4.3 in 1913, it attained
higher levels in particular countries, e.g., 8.4 in the United Kingdom in 1853-55 and 11.6 in Italy in
1906-10. Net emigration reached 7 per 1000 in Sweden in 1886-90, 6.3 in Italy and 5.5 in Finland in
1901-05. See ISAAC, op. cit. supra note 2, at 64-65.

who possessed craft and occupational skills, finding them not to be ones in great demand, entered new occupations. It became possible to make effective use of this vast influx of unskilled workers because, in the late nineteenth century, American industry became technologically and economically adapted to the utilization of many workers possessing little or no skill, with the result that craft and handicraft skills were diluted and reduced in relative significance.[12]

The absorption of so large and sustained a volume of immigrants into the American economy was greatly assisted, as was that of domestic population growth, by the availability of land for settlement and by the high rate at which capital was formed. Between 1850 and 1935, farm land increased from 294 to 1,055 million acres, and crop land from 113 to 416 million acres, at a rate less rapid than that at which the number of farms or the total population grew, but more rapid than that at which the farm population grew. Investment in agricultural plant progressed about 3 per cent per year in 1870-1920, thereafter to increase only .26 per cent per year; but yields per acre, after having risen relatively little for three to five decades, increased sharply after the middle 1930's.[13] Reproductive tangible wealth grew much more rapidly than population, with real wealth per head increasing 2.5 per cent per year in 1850-1900, when population was growing 2.4 per cent per year, and 1.3 per cent per year in 1900-1950, when population was advancing 1.4 per cent per year.[14] The rapidity with which real wealth per head grew is attributable to the high levels of productivity early achieved in American industry,[15] to the maintenance of a high rate of capital formation, to the fact that the United States was spared the cost of producing a considerable fraction of its population, and to the influx of foreign capital which helped to equip the immigrant population.[16]

The economic absorption, though not necessarily the assimilation, of immigrants

[12] E.g., see THOMAS, op. cit. supra note 1, at 60-63, 148-51, 165-74, 268-72; H. D. ANDERSON AND P. E. DAVIDSON, OCCUPATIONAL TRENDS IN THE UNITED STATES 53-57, 166-67, 572-74 (1940); also Spengler, supra note 4.

[13] HISTORICAL STATISTICS, op. cit. supra Table I, at 29, 95, 121; J. F. DEWHURST, AMERICA'S NEEDS AND RESOURCES 793-99 (1955); A. S. TOSTLEBE, THE GROWTH OF PHYSICAL CAPITAL IN AGRICULTURE, 1870-1930 passim (1954).

[14] See S. KUZNETS AND R. W. GOLDSMITH, INCOME AND WEALTH OF THE UNITED STATES 269 (1952).

[15] See Rothbarth, Causes of the Superior Efficiency of U.S.A. Industry as Compared With British Industry, 46 ECON. J. 383 (1946); Frankel, Anglo-American Productivity Differences: Their Magnitude and Some Causes, 45 AM. ECON. REV. 94 (1955).

[16] Net capital formation approximated 13 per cent of net national product in 1869-1928, according to KUZNETS AND GOLDSMITH, op. cit. supra note 14, at 155. Even so, the rate at which capital was formed was much below the level at which it might have been formed. See F. C. MILLS, PRODUCTIVITY AND ECONOMIC PROGRESS 14 (1952). If, as of 1930, a value of 3-10 thousand dollars is placed on each of the 27.5 million net immigrants into the United States in 1821-1930, the product, $82-275 billion, represents a large fraction of the country's accumulated wealth, $362 billion, in 1929. See de Vita, Der kapitalisierte Wert der 1820-1930 in die Vereinigten Staaten von America Eingewanderten, 52 WELT-WIRTSCHAFTLICHES ARCHIV 31 (1940); KUZNETS AND GOLDSMITH, op. cit. supra note 14, at 198. Even if a lower value is set upon each immigrant, on the ground that the alternative use value of the resources incorporated in personal capital would have been less, the capital value of resources saved would still be large. Between 1880 and 1910, net foreign investment exceeded $800 per foreign worker added to the labor force. This amount exceeded the value of equipment per worker prior to the early 1900's, but was much less than the amount of reproducible capital per member of the labor force. See id. at 78, 155, 197, 204-05, 300-07, 323.

was facilitated by the fact that most of them settled in a small number of states and largely within towns and cities in those states. In 1850, 83.6 per cent of the foreign-born whites lived in the New England, Middle Atlantic, and East North Central States; the corresponding percentage was 72.1, 77.3, and 69.7 in 1900, 1930, and 1950. By 1890, 17 per cent were situated in the West North Central States; but by 1950, this percentage had declined to 8.3, while that reported for the Pacific Coast had risen to 11.6.[17] The geographic concentration of immigrant settlement was accompanied also by industrial concentration, in part because cultural and other disadvantages under which immigrants often labored reduced their access to some employments. Among the industries into which they crowded were mining, quarrying, clothing, textiles, woolen and worsted mills, bakeries, meat packing, car and railroad shops, silk and carpet mills, brass and rolling mills and blast furnaces, breweries, tanneries, hat factories, lime, cement, and gypsum factories, marble and stone yards, rubber factories, piano and organ factories, construction and maintenance.[18] Concentration of immigrants in cities where they and their children had access to educational opportunities facilitated the occupational and industrial progress of persons of immigrant stock.[19]

II

IMMIGRATION AND THE AMERICAN ECONOMY

Immigration into the United States produced a diversity of effects which, in turn, modified the magnitude, the structure, and the behavior of the American economy. Immigration augmented the rate of growth of the net national product, made possible a better combination of productive agents, and until around the turn of the century, probably accelerated the rate at which product per capita increased. Immigration augmented the rate of growth of the net national product, made scribed in part I, in part because the aboriginal population was sparse, in part because the external economic relations of the American economy were good, and in part because the American population, though of heterogeneous origin, shared a developing culture that was suited to give it sufficient socio-economic unity while reinforcing values conducive to material productivity.

Among the specific effects produced by immigration, the following may be noted:

(1) A disproportionately large fraction of the immigrants were of working age; thus, whereas, in 1870-1910, immigration increased the population by about 15 per cent, it swelled the labor force by about 20 per cent.

(2) During the first three-quarters or so of the nineteenth century, many of the immigrants brought with them scarce but useful occupational skills and superior

[17] See THOMPSON AND WHELPTON, *op. cit. supra* Table I, at 247; STATISTICAL ABSTRACT, *op. cit. supra* Table I.

[18] See Eckler and Zlotnick, *Immigration and the Labor Force,* 261 ANNALS 92 (1949); OSCAR HANDLIN, BOSTON'S IMMIGRANTS, 1790-1865 *passim* (1941).

[19] See THOMAS, *op. cit. supra* note 1, c. 9.

industrial methods, together with some relaxation of the customs and horizons by which their efforts had been bound in the countries of provenience.[20]

(3) The mingling of peoples of diverse cultural backgrounds may have given rise to cultural as well as to biological heterosis, thereby augmenting productive power.[21]

(4) The manner in which one ethnic group has succeeded another as a dominant element in the stream of immigration, together with the resulting intensification of social and economic capillarity (see part III), helped to foster the pursuit of material success and to generate that spirit of comparatively unrestricted economic competition which appears to distinguish the American from most other economies.[22]

(5) Immigration fostered homogeneity of tastes and, therewith, the development of a large market for the standardized products of highly mechanized industries; for, no one ethnic group being able to impose its tastes on other groups, each and all adopted the tastes that they found in America and readily acquiesced in the changes technologically minded producers found it economical to make in their products.[23]

(6) The comparative docility of immigrant workers operated, in and after the last quarter of the nineteenth century, if not earlier, to facilitate the introduction of efficient, highly mechanized, mass-production methods.

(7) Heavy and continuing immigration of relatively unskilled workers prevented the real earnings of unskilled labor and of much manufacturing labor of somewhat more skill from rising significantly, when they rose at all, in the period 1890-1914, even though output per man-hour was rising perhaps as much as 44 per cent; and it may account for the fact that real wages rose relatively less in the United States in 1860-1913 than in the United Kingdom and some West-European countries.[24]

(8) Presumably, immigration, by depressing the ratio of wages received to marginal product, somewhat augmented the "surplus" whence most capital comes.[25]

[20] See R. T. BERTHOFF, BRITISH IMMIGRANTS IN INDUSTRIAL AMERICA 1790-1850 passim (1953); M. L. HANSEN, THE IMMIGRANT IN AMERICAN HISTORY passim (1940); Herbert Heaton, The Industrial Immigrant in the United States, 1783-1912, 95 PROC. AM. PHIL. SOC'Y 519 (1951); CLARK, op. cit. supra note 10, at 206-07, 245. "The immigrants developed the physical riches of America: and, in return, the new hope, freedom, and changefulness of their lives developed in them germs of high spirit and initiative," germs latent in most people, but especially in those "who seek new lands." ALFRED MARSHALL, INDUSTRY AND TRADE 143 (1927).

[21] See Snell, Hybrids and History, The Role of Race and Ethnic Crossing in Individual and National Achievements, 26 Q. REV. BIOL. 331 (1951).

[22] The American culture is shot through with ingredients making for productivity. See T. PARSONS, SOCIAL SYSTEM c. 5 (1951); and cf. MARSHAL, op. cit. supra note 20, at 149-50.

[23] The wide separation of the producer from the consumer, as Marshall observed, also served "to suppress those methods of production which depend for their strength largely upon the adaptation of products to the special requirements or tastes of the purchaser." MARSHALL, op. cit. supra note 20, at 146-47.

[24] See PAUL H. DOUGLAS, REAL WAGES IN THE UNITED STATES, 1890-1926 passim (1930); W. COOMBS, THE WAGES OF UNSKILLED LABOR IN THE MANUFACTURING INDUSTRIES IN THE UNITED STATES, 1890-1924, c. 5 (1926); W. S. THOMPSON, POPULATION: A STUDY IN MALTHUSIANISM 39 et seq. (1915); KUZNETS AND GOLDSMITH, op. cit. supra note 14, at 71; Brown and Hopkins, The Course of Wage-Rates in Five Countries, 1860-1913, 2 OXFORD ECON. PAPERS 236 (1950).

[25] Both gross and net capital formation were higher between 1884 and 1904 than before or after this time. KUZNETS AND GOLDSMITH, op. cit.. supra note 14, at 155.

(9) Immigration certainly affected and may have retarded the progress of trade unionism in the United States, thereby insuring its own continuation since organized labor favored the restriction of immigration.[26]

(10) The international mobility of population made possible largely by free migration to America before World War I, together with such economic fluidity as it produced, helped make workable the system of fixed exchange rates in effect in many countries before 1913.[27]

(11) As has been noted, the availability of capital was affected by the volume of immigration. Before 1914, the influx of immigrants, and sometimes the mere prospect of such an influx, stimulated inflows of capital from Europe, then the world's banker. Immigrants brought some capital with them and, as remarked above, by their coming, spared America the cost of producing some 25 million people. Furthermore, immigration, in so far as. it increased the profitability of American industry, stimulated domestic capital formation. On the whole, therefore, immigration may be said to have produced side effects which made for capital formation and, thus, counterbalanced much of the increase in capital requirements occasioned by immigration and the disposition of immigrants to make remittances. It did not, presumably, generate much, if any, inflationary financing of capital formation, or produce much, if any, unemployment. That immigration did, however, absorb a portion of the annual supply of capital is suggested by the increase that took place in the supply of American funds available for foreign investment after quota restrictions had reduced the inflow of immigrants.[28]

(12) Immigration stimulated the growth of net national product per head in at least two ways in addition to those discussed above. (a) So long as the Atlantic economy remained subject to increasing return, the movement of people to under-settled parts of this economy, especially to the United States, stimulated the growth of these parts, and their increased import demands fostered economic development in the lands of immigrant provenience, with the result that the consequently increased import demands of these countries, in turn, stimulated further growth in the immigrant-receiving countries.[29] (b) Because of the magnitude of immigration into the United States before 1914 and its acceleration of the growth of the American population and its economy, this economy was continually outstripping its stock of capital, with the result that investment was less risky than in other countries, even though capital was being formed and introduced at a higher rate than elsewhere. At the same time, labor (or at least many forms of labor) was usually in short

[26] See H. A. MILLIS AND R. E. MONTGOMERY, ORGANIZED LABOR 14-15. 48-49, 88-90, 124, 154-55 (1945); S. PERLMAN, A HISTORY OF TRADE UNIONISM IN THE UNITED STATES 84 et seq., 179-221 (1923); THOMAS, op. cit. supra note 1, at 204-05. The role of immigration in a trade union movement depends, of course, upon the background and industrial and union experience of the immigrant workers. Many of the immigrants to America had had no such experience. In Australia, by contrast, a powerful trade union movement was established early.

[27] See A. P. LERNER, ECONOMICS OF EMPLOYMENT 358 et seq. (1951).

[28] See THOMAS, op. cit. supra note 1, at 199-201. In the 1920's, capital was formed at a lower relative rate than earlier. See KUZNETS AND GOLDSMITH, op. cit. supra note 14, at 155.

[29] See ROYAL COMMISSION ON POPULATION, Report of the Economics Committee, in 3 PAPERS 5 (1950).

supply. There was no substantial opposition, therefore, to the increasing mechanization of American industry and the continual introduction of ever more effective labor-saving machinery. Furthermore, because of the high rate at which the stock of capital was being increased, a considerable fraction of this stock was made up, at all times, of relatively new and highly productive forms.[30] In short, immigration kept the growth process triggered off while it was bringing into being ever more efficient ways of combining productive agents. It stimulated both capital formation and technological change, the two forces which have been responsible for the major part of the increase in output per head experienced in the past 150 years.

Migratory movements are subject to both short-period and long-period fluctuations, which have their origin both in countries of provenience and in countries of destination; and many of the effects consequent upon immigration reflect these variations. In the past, arrivals, departures, and net arrivals have moved together, but net arrivals have varied most; for while arrivals fluctuated with business cycles, departures tended to contract during expansions and to expand during contractions, perhaps because they were less subject than arrivals to legal controls.[31] Waves of arrivals had their origin in the European births cycle and in the impact of innovations in Europe, only to be succeeded by "minor secular upswings in the rate of economic growth."[32] Long "swings in net immigration tended to *follow* those in gross national product per worker, and to precede those" in nonfarm residential construction, which, together with capital expenditures by railroads, made up what Kuznets calls "population-sensitive" capital. Swings in this sector of capital formation were positively correlated with swings in population growth and negatively correlated with swings in other sectors of capital formation, probably because enough savings were not forthcoming in the United States to meet fully the demands for both categories of capital.[33] Thomas found that, as a rule, immigration preceded building activity in the United States, which was inversely associated with building activity in Great Britain, the other main member of the Atlantic economy and a major source of the building-stimulating migrants. He reports also that whereas in 1844-63 immigration preceded the movement of railroad construction, merchandise imports, and fixed-capital investment, it lagged after rail construction from 1869 on, and after the output of coal and pig iron from 1899 on. He infers that immigration was under the dominance of European "push" factors before 1870, only to pass under that of American "pull" factors, among them, the pace of investment, after 1870.[34] While immigration may have prolonged boom periods by continuing to make labor available on satisfactory terms and may, therefore, have

---

[30] J. M. Keynes and E. A. G. Robinson have drawn attention to the importance of point (b). *Cf.* KUZNETS AND GOLDSMITH, *op. cit. supra* note 14, at 86-88, for evidence of the buoyancy with which American entrepreneurs assumed risks.

[31] See KUZNETS AND RUBIN, *op. cit. supra* note 14, at 36-37.

[32] THOMAS, *op. cit. supra* note 1, at 174.

[33] KUZNETS AND RUBIN, *op. cit. supra* note 3, at 27-34. The connections between swings in population and capital are treated by Kuznets in a forthcoming study.

[34] See THOMAS, *op. cit. supra* note 1, cc. 7, 10, and 11.

intensified the severity of the depressions that followed, it is not evident that the ratio of years of prosperity to years of depression was significantly affected.[35]

In the light of what has been said in parts I and II, a strong case can be made for the proposition that until the close of the nineteenth century and possibly until the outbreak of World War I, immigration contributed directly and indirectly to the complex of synergistic forces that were making for the growth of both net national product and the amount produced per head. It is doubtful, however, whether this proposition remained valid after World War I. In the two parts that follow, grounds for this doubt are set forth.

III

Substitutive, Complementary, and Aggregative Effects of Immigration; Social Capillarity[36]

For purposes of analytical and expositive convenience, the economic effects produced by immigration into a country may be divided into two categories: (a) those which are substitutive, complementary, or (if there be such) neutral in character; and (b) those which are describable as aggregative in nature. Effects falling into category (a) are fairly easy to identify and impute, particularly if it is supposed that they are either substitutive or complementary. Effects belonging under (b) are not so easy always to identify, and they usually are very difficult to impute, since they are also producible by agents other than immigration. We shall note later to what extent the two kinds of effects may be added algebraically, and in what measure they may be considered indicative of changes in "economic welfare."

Let us first consider substitutive and complementary effects. Suppose that migrants moving from country A to country B include a relatively large number of workers who fall into four occupational categories, a_1, a_2, a_3, and a_4, and that country B has a very low propensity to import and export. In the event that B's labor force embraces four analogous occupational categories of workers, b_1, b_2, b_3, and b_4, the immigrant workers will be substitutable for native workers in these categories. In consequence (abstracting from income or aggregative effects and proceeding on the assumption that the immigrant workers find employment in their occupational categories), the *relative* rates of remuneration received by native workers in these occupational categories will decline. Simultaneously, the *relative* rates of remuneration received by native workers in other occupational categories than these four will rise, in part because the increase in categories b_1-b_4, which are *complementary* to all or most of categories b_5-b_n, elevates the schedule of demand for (and the value productivity of) workers in the latter group of categories. In general, therefore, the native labor force will at first experience both substitution and

[35] See H. Jerome, Migration and Business Cycles 242 (1926); W. C. Mitchell, Business Cycles 410 (1928).

[36] In this section, the writer has drawn heavily upon the argument presented in Spengler, *supra* note 4.

complementary effects from the immigrant workers, with the substitution effect being overriding in proportion as the relative number of workers enrolled in categories b_1-b_4 was large already prior to the arrival of the immigrants.

Given (other things being equal) a change in the earnings structure consequent upon an influx of immigrants, native workers may respond variously. Those enrolled in occupational categories b_1-b_4, having had their relative and (perhaps) their absolute earnings reduced by the competition of these immigrants, may remove to less peopled part of country B, or even emigrate abroad; or they may attempt to enter occupations b_5-b_n, in which event, members of these occupations will experience substitutive as well as complementary effects; or, if denied these recourses, they may reduce their net reproduction rate, thereby probably diminishing the potential number of recruits available for occupations b_1-b_4 fifteen to twenty years later. In each instance, the savings rates of the affected persons will tend to be reduced. Native workers in occupations to which the activities of the immigrants are complementary will undergo a contrary set of reactions. They will be less inclined to migrate or emigrate, less inclined to change occupation, and disposed to increase both their net reproduction and their savings rates.

If it be assumed that country B has a high propensity to import and export and that its economy is open, as was the American in the nineteenth century, the impact of immigration into B may be largely cushioned. Suppose that individuals engaged in occupations b_1-b_4 produce largely for export markets, the price-elasticity of demand for $B's$ contribution thereto being very high. Then (assuming a sufficiency of land and other complementary imputs, the accession of immigrant workers in categories a_1-a_4 will not greatly depress the relative levels of earnings characteristic of occupations b_1-b_4, since the product of these additional workers can be sold abroad at but slightly reduced prices. Under these circumstances, much of the burden of adjustment will fall upon individuals living abroad who are members of occupations b_1-b_4 and whose situation may temporarily have been improved by the removal of the migrants in question. At the same time, the net aggregate impact experienced by the labor force enrolled in occupations b_5-b_n will not be great, since the returns from the sale abroad of the additional exports must, in effect, be expended abroad. In sum, when (complementary inputs being assumed available) immigrants enter export industries for whose products price-elasticity of demand is great, the effect of their coming is relatively widely diffused, the domestic economy is more easily accommodated to their coming, the wage structure is less affected, and conditions of full-employment-insuring, balanced growth are more speedily approximated.

Let us now consider the aggregative effect of the influx of immigrants into B. There will be an increase in the aggregate amount of income produced in B. In fact, if B is still subject to increasing return, or if the advent of the immigrants sufficiently stimulates capital formation, the introduction of superior methods, and technological progress, and produces others of the salutary effects described in the preceding part, the income of B will increase in greater proportion than the population of B has increased as a result of immigration, and income per head will rise. Under these circumstances, the aggregative effect of immigration would probably swamp its adverse substitution effects after enough time had passed to permit adjustment. Initially, absolute income per worker would rise in many of the occupations to which the economic activities of the immigrant workers were complementary. This rise would be relatively widespread after the composition of $B's$ labor force had become sufficiently adjusted to the influx of immigrant workers. It is not likely, however, that absolute income per worker would rise in occupations b_1-b_4 unless the population of B had been subject to increasing return and a sufficient number of native workers in these occupations had moved into occupations b_5-b_n. The relative level of remuneration obtaining in occupations b_1-b_4 would remain lower than it had been prior to the coming of the immigrants, unless a distribution of workers among occupations substantially similar to that obtaining before the influx of immigrants had been restored.

So long as a significant amount of immigration continues and the occupational composition of the immigrant stream differs from that of the native population, both substitution and complementary effects will be experienced from the foreign-born immigrants. Even if the inflow of immigrants ceases but the occupational composition of their descendants continues to differ from that of the descendants of the native population, elements in the latter will experience substitution or complementary effects of immigrant-stock origin. If, however, immigration ceases, and, in time, the descendants of the immigrants become distributed in the same manner as the natives throughout the occupational structure, the natives will no longer be sensible as formerly of substitution or complementary effects from persons of immigrant stock. When this has become the situation, therefore, the economic status of the natives may be said to be better or worse than it would have been in the absence of immigration accordingly as the amount of equipment and wealth per head, together with the level of technology and related circumstances, is more or less advanced than it would have been in the absence of the influx of the immigrants. The long-run outcome, in short, turns on how powerful the aggregative effect was.

The advent of immigrants is likely to be accompanied, for a time, by an increase in social capillarity. Many, though not all, immigrants into the United States, particularly after 1880, were under occupational, linguistic, personality, intellectual, and other handicaps, some transient and some not entirely removable. But these handicaps did not usually persist beyond the second or third generation. Accordingly, as these handicaps were dissipated, the positions occupied by persons of immigrant stock underwent change.

Let the occupational structure of a country be represented by four categories, A, B, C, and D, into which fall 10, 20, 30, and 40 per cent, respectively, of the gainfully employed. Then, if there arrived 10 units of immigrants culturally and otherwise identical with the natives, the 10 would tend to be distributed among categories *A-D* in the same proportions as the native population, namely, 1, 2, 3, and 4 units, respectively. If, however, the immigrants suffered under handicaps of the sort described above, more than 4, say 8, of the 10 units might have to enter category *D*, and, say, 1 each, into categories *C* and *B*. Then, one of two outcomes would be possible. If the underlying determinants of occupational equilibrium were such as to maintain the proportions which prevailed prior to the arrival of the immigrants, there would be set in motion an upward movement of the native members of the occupational -structure, eventuating, say, as follows: *A*, 11 natives; *B*, 21 natives and 1 immigrant; *C*, 32 natives and 1 immigrant; *D*, 36 natives and 8 immigrants. If, as is probable, equilibrium occupational composition changed, relative expansion would take place in the lower portions of the occupational pyramid, and there would eventuate a distribution such as the following: *A*, 10 natives; *B*, 20 natives and 1 immigrant; *C*, 31 natives and 1 immigrant; *D*, 39 natives and 8 immigrants.

The occupational composition of the children of immigrants would approximate more closely that of the natives than did the occupational composition of the immigrants themselves; and the occupational composition of the grandchildren of the immigrants would approximate that of the natives even more closely than did the occupational composition of the children of the immigrants. The rapidity with which the occupational composition of the immigrant stock approached that of the natives would depend upon how technologically, and, hence, occupationally, dynamic the country of immigration was, upon the extent and the rigidity of artificial and institutional barriers which tend to prevent interoccupational movement that would otherwise take place, and upon the degree to which these barriers impeded the interoccupational movement of persons of immigrant stock even more than that of natives. To illustrate: Earlier we put at .4 the probability that a native would be enrolled in occupational category *D* and at .8 the corresponding probability for the immigrant; yet, all or nearly all of the spread between these two probabilities, being attributable to eliminatable differences between immigrants and natives, would disappear after one or several generations had passed. Then, the descendants of immigrants of a given period would no longer differ significantly from the descendants of natives of that same period.

It is said that immigration tends to make a population more fluid or mobile than it otherwise would be. This result is likely under two conditions: (a) when the occupational (or other) composition of the immigrants differs from that of the labor force of the country of immigration, with the result that a series of substitution effects is generated; and (b) when the coming of the immigrants produces or facilitates fundamental changes in the technological and related determinants of the occupational structure and sets both aggregative and substitutive effects in motion. For in either instance, the relative amount of movement from some to other occupational categories would increase and then remain at "abnormally" high levels until the labor force had become accommodated to the basic occupational structure and a

model approximating that of Cairnes' and Taussig's relatively noncompeting groups
had come into being. Initially, the upward mobility of the native population would
increase in much greater degree than total mobility of the immigrant population.
But, as the immigrants and their children became assimilated and, hence, freed of
transient disabilities, their upward mobility would increase, and natives who no
longer were capable of competing effectively with the upward-moving immigrant
stock would be displaced downwards: When, however, the initial occupational
composition of the immigrants is quite similar to that of the natives, the coming of
the immigrants produces little change in the relative amount of interoccupational
mobility, since little change is required to permit permanent occupational assimilation
of the immigrants.

Substitution and social capillarity are readily illustrated: (a) It has already been
indicated that *relative* earnings fell in industries and occupations into which immigrants entered in relatively large numbers. (b) Many immigrants changed their
employments, and younger ones frequently improved their situations markedly.[37]
(c) After several generations had passed, persons of immigrant stock had virtually
as free access to the upper reaches of the occupational pyramid as had had natives
of some generations standing.[38] (d) That immigrants and Negroes frequently are
substitutively related to one another is suggested by the fact that few immigrants
have settled in the South, that the migration of Negroes to industrial states did
not become great until immigration had fallen off, and that interstate migration of
foreign-born was sometimes inversely correlated with that of native whites and
Negroes. As a rule, however, overriding influences which may be looked upon
as aggregative in character have been dominant, with the result that Negroes, for-
eigners, and native whites have all alike been drawn from their points of origin
to states, cities, and metropolitan centers where industrial opportunities abound
for all.

Aggregative effects are easy to describe and sometimes to identify—a number
of them have been described in part II—but they are seldom easy to assess in
quantitative terms. It is rarely, if ever, possible to separate sharply income increases attributable to an influx of immigrants, particularly when that influx is continuous, from income increases imputable to increases in the stock of capital, to
improvements in technology, or to similar agents. In the preceding part, however,
we inferred that prior to 1900, and possibly prior to 1914, the aggregative effects of
American immigration were sufficiently powerful to swamp most of its substitutive
and complementary effects, and that, given a virtual discontinuance of immigration
and time for all its effects to work out, the aggregative effects probably would have

[37] See Bloch, *Occupations of Immigrants Before and After Coming to the United States* 17 PUBL'NS
AM. STAT. ASS'N 750 (1920-21); P. E. DAVIDSON AND H. D. ANDERSON, OCCUPATIONAL MOBILITY IN AN
AMERICAN COMMUNITY 117-33, 188 (1937).
[38] NATALIE KOGOFF, RECENT TRENDS IN OCCUPATIONAL MOBILITY c. 7 (1953); DAVIDSON AND
ANDERSON, *op. cit. supra* note 37, at 130-33; THOMAS, *op. cit. supra* note 1, c. 9.

swamped the substitution and complementary effects completely. In the next part, we shall inquire whether this conclusion continues to hold.

IV

IMMIGRATION, POPULATION DENSITY, CAPITAL REQUIREMENTS

An influx of immigrants makes itself felt aggregatively, both directly and indirectly. Both sorts of effects were noted in part II. Here, we are concerned with what usually are the two major effects of immigration: its effect upon capital requirements, and its effect upon division of labor and the ratio of population to resources.

When a country's population grows, whether from natural increase or from net immigration, the increment in population must be provided with capital in suitable forms and amounts; otherwise, living conditions and output per worker or per capita will fall. The capital required is of three sorts: (a) industrial capital of the kinds combined with the worker in the employment in which he engages; (b) economic overhead capital, or investment in improvements in transport, building, water supply, utilities, etc., not allowed for under (a), but still essential to an increase in the volume of activity; and (c) social overhead capital, or capital utilized in residential, educational, ecclesiastical, governmental, and other facilities not provided for under (b). It may be possible, when a country is undergoing accelerated development, to skimp on forms of (b) and (c). It is essential, however, that all forms be allowed for when the longer-run impact of immigration is under consideration.

Of the two modes of estimating aggregate wealth or capital requirements, the savings-income method is most satisfactory. In a country like the United States, all wealth together approximates in value to five times the income produced in a year. Suppose now that population increases 1 per cent per year. Then, if 5 per cent of the national income is saved and converted into all the forms of wealth required, the wealth-population ratio will remain constant and, other things being equal, the level of per capita income will continue substantially unchanged. Five per cent, therefore, indicates the order of magnitude of the proportion of national income required to offset a 1 per cent per year rate of population growth. In as much as reported wealth-income ratios vary—in part because of differences in the methods of estimating employed—it may be supposed that the ratio falls within a range of 4:1 to 6:1, and that, therefore, the required saving rate lies between 4 and 6 per cent.

An increase in population of 1 per cent per year is not obtained without cost, even though enough saving is done to offset the increase in question. For, the capital invested in population growth might otherwise have been invested in augmenting the wealth-population ratio and increasing productive power per head. It is probable that the capital required to support a 1 per cent per year rate of population growth might otherwise have been utilized to increase per capita income between .5 and 1 per cent per year. If so, the cost of a 1 per cent per year rate of population growth is the sacrifice of .5-1 per cent per year increase in income per head.[39]

The amount of capital required to equip a given rate of immigration may also be estimated by adding to the amount required, on an average, to set up an immigrant in a job, allowance for other forms of wealth required to meet the housing and other needs of himself and his dependents, and applying the resulting sum to the immigrant stream. This procedure is not very satisfactory, however, since capital invested per worker varies greatly with industry, and since it is not easy to arrive at suitable amounts for the other forms of wealth required. The savings-income method provides the most satisfactory rule of thumb, therefore, for estimating the impact of immigration upon capital requirements and income growth, even though the composition of the immigrant stream usually differs somewhat from that of the resident population.

A country may be considered subject to increasing return when an increase in numbers—that is, in over-all population density—makes possible increase in the division of labor and the undertaking of methods more efficient that would have been possible in the absence of this increase in numbers. So long as the condition of increasing return obtains and increases in population make for increases in per capita income, a population may be said to be below income-optimum in size. Whether a population is below income-optimum size, however, depends, in part, upon the methods of production in use in that population's economy. Thus, the new methods introduced in the nineteenth century increased the magnitude of the income-optimum for many countries in which agriculture still predominated around 1800. Most students would probably agree, nonetheless, that further technological improvements and related changes would be unlikely to increase the magnitude of the income-optimum further in the United States. Immigration may not, therefore, be pointed to as a force giving release to increasing return in the United States, even though it probably would still produce such effect in Canada. Accordingly, an economic case for continued immigration into the United States cannot be made if maximization of per capita income, or of its rate of growth, is the objective sought.

The economic case against the continuation of immigration is strengthened when account is taken of: (a) the fact that the population of the United States is growing from natural increase at a rate of 1.5 per cent per year or more and is likely to continue growing at this rate for several decades or more; and (b) the fact that many of the resources of the United States are either relatively fixed or depletable in quantity. There is not a great deal more land available for putting into continuous cultivation. The limits of the water supply are being reached in some states. An increasing amount of minerals must be obtained from foreign sources, many of them

[39] This argument is developed in Spengler, *The Population Obstacle to Economic Betterment* 41 Am. Econ. Rev. 343 (1951).

uncertain or produced under conditions of increasing cost. In short, at the same time that the American population is growing remarkably, increasing economic entropy is shrinking the resource base of the American economy and perhaps reducing slightly its income-optimum population magnitude under present technological circumstances.

The burden of the argument presented in this part is that the aggregative effects of immigration are no longer likely to be sufficiently powerful to accelerate the rate at which per capita income advances. Accordingly, since the economic case for continuing immigration rests ultimately upon its aggregative effects, because, in the longer run, social capillarity dissolves its substitution and its complementary effects, a case cannot be made unless other sources of aggregative effect described in part II are more powerful than is commonly supposed.[40]

V

POLICY IMPLICATIONS

It is not our purpose to make policy recommendations, since what is to be recommended turns on what objectives are being sought. Moreover, we are not concerned with political arguments for immigration, even though they may, at times, be persuasive. The implications of what has been said for possible courses of action may, however, be indicated.

(1) Continuation of immigration at a net rate of 250,000 per year—it has been running somewhat lower—is not likely to affect the progress of per capita income significantly, provided this rate is not continued indefinitely. This rate—about one-tenth of the incremental rate of natural increase—would serve to increase the population only about .15 or less per cent per year. It would not absorb much capital, and, even though it pressed population beyond the optimum point, it would affect income much as if returns were constant. It is not likely, of course, that immigration at this rate would long give rise to aggregative effects sufficient to increase per capita income above the level at which it otherwise would have been. Yet, as is suggested in (7) below, highly selective immigration can have salutary complementary and aggregative effects.

(2) Immigration at a rate considerably in excess of 250,000 per year would almost certainly operate to reduce the rate at which per capita income was increasing. This outcome is made all the more likely by the fact that European countries are not disposed to have the more skilled members of their labor force depart, and these, in turn, are less disposed to leave than are those in unskilled and semiskilled categories.

(3) It is not possible to translate substitution, complementary, and aggregative effects into acceptable and nonarbitrary welfare terms for the economy as a whole.

[40] No attempt will be made here to translate economic effects into welfare terms, because of the difficulties involved. See Spengler, *Welfare Economics and the Problem of Overpopulation*, 89 SCIENTIA 128, 166 (1954); also H. LEIBENSTEIN, A THEORY OF ECONOMIC-DEMOGRAPHIC DEVELOPMENT c. 9 (1954).

In the individual case, substitution, complementary, and some aggregative effects can be assessed and added. But this cannot be done for the population as a whole, in large part because it is impossible to appraise with precision the aggregative effects associated with immigration. Furthermore, even if these effects could be expressed in income terms, they could not be translated into welfare terms unless suitable as-sumptions were made and accepted. For this reason, it is not easy to formulate an immigration policy designed to maximize something like welfare per head.

(4) It has been suggested that capital in the United States at present is relatively more scarce than labor, although this argument has been subjected to criticism.[41] If this argument be valid, then the capital-cost of immigration is greater than has been assumed.

(5) It is said, by proponents of the view that underemployment equilibrium is typical of the American economy, that immigration, by increasing the level of in-vestment and, hence, the level of activity in this economy, makes for fuller employ-ment and a higher level of per capita income than would otherwise be attained. This argument is not acceptable as a basis for policy, however, since a very small amount of state intervention would produce the same effect, without increasing population density, and since immigrants are not likely at all times to find ready access to jobs in the United States.[42]

(6) Because the American trade union movement is so powerful, and because it exercises so much direct and indirect control over access to job opportunities in the United States, it is much more difficult for the American economy to absorb immigrants today than in the pre-1914 era. Because of trade-union influences, immi-grants might either be denied access to jobs or be compelled to take jobs at wages in excess of marginal productivity, with the result that inflation from the cost side would be stimulated.

(7) If a certain number of immigrants are free to come to the United States and accept employment where it is offered, their coming will be favorable to all those who are engaged in complementary activities and to those who employ the services of immigrant labor, whether as employers or as the purchasers of services. Un-doubtedly, there are many instances in which the resident population would experi-ence little or no adverse substitutive effect and marked complementary and aggre-gative effects from limited and selective immigration. A striking example is labor which immigrates only seasonally; it benefits everyone and injures no one.

(8) It would be impossible for the United States to afford significant relief to overpopulated countries situated within or outside Europe. At most, it could ac-commodate enough immigrants to ease certain disequilibria in European economies. The number of immigrants the United States can absorb, at no marked cost in terms

---

[41] See Leontief, *Domestic Production and Foreign Trade: The American Capital Position Re-examined,* 97 PROC. AM. PHIL. SOC'Y 332 (1953); Valavanis-Vail, *Leontief's Scarce Factor Paradox,* 62 J. POL. ECON. 523 (1954); Ellsworth, *The Structure of American Foreign Trade: A New View Examined,* 36 REV. ECON. & STAT. 279 (1954).

[42] See Spengler, *Population Threatens Prosperity,* 34 HARV. BUS. REV. 85 (1956).

of income, is small, far too small to approximate more than 1 per cent, if that, of the annual natural increment in the population of the overpopulated countries. Moreover, it would cost far more to establish a given number of immigrants industrially in the United States than in their countries of origin. Finally, and of paramount importance, emigration does not tend to bring about natality-reducing changes in the countries of emigration,[43] whereas investment in the industrialization of these countries may produce such effect. In short, a given amount of American investment in the modernization of the backward economies of overpopulated countries can contribute far more to the eventual relief of population pressure than can a similar amount of investment devoted to bringing immigrants to the United States from overpopulated countries and settling them here. There it can transform both the way of life and the mode of production and thereby bring down natality.

[43] Ireland apparently is the only exception. See A. M. CARR-SAUNDERS, WORLD POPULATION 64, 90-92, 114-16 (1936); C. M. ARENSBERG AND S. T. KIMBALL, FAMILY AND COMMUNITY IN IRELAND cc. 6-8 (1940).

OVERSEAS MIGRATION FROM EUROPE

SINCE WORLD WAR II

By Dudley Kirk and Earl Huyck

SINCE World War II there has been a substantial revival of overseas migration from Europe. Much of this is related to war displacements of population. But the publicity attending the more dramatic refugee movements has obscured the resurgence of voluntary "free" migrations such as those that peopled North America, Australasia, and large parts of South America from Europe in the last two centuries.

The passage of eight years since the close of the war offers an opportunity to view this revived mass migration with some perspective on its volume, direction, and pattern. How large was it? Where did it come from and where did it go? Who went and why? What is its significance? What are its future prospects?

It is the purpose of this paper to give summary answers to these questions and to make some comparisons of the postwar movements with the great overseas migrations of the past.

Until recently there was no official or international survey of European migration data for the postwar period. The data are widely scattered in country statistics with greatly varying definitions, coverage, and degrees of accuracy. Migration statistics for Europe are far less complete than census and vital statistics.[1] The summary that follows is drawn from special compilations laboriously made from numerous sources and presented much more fully in a longer publication.[2]

[1] Cf. United Nations Department of Social Affairs, *Problems of Migration Statistics,* New York: UN publication ST/SOA/Series A/5, No. 5, 1949; and United Nations Statistical Office, *International Migration Statistics,* New York: UN publication ST/STAT/Series M/No. 20, 1953.

[2] Dept. of State, Office of Intelligence Research, *Survey of Overseas Emigration from Europe, 1946–51* (Unclassified Intelligence Report 6054, May, 1953), and *Overseas Emigration from Europe During 1952* (Unclassified Intelligence Report 6054S, Aug., 1953). For prewar materials this summary also draws heavily on two earlier studies of migration by Kirk: (1) *Europe's Population in the*

HOW MANY?

Since the war at least 5 million persons have emigrated from Europe, a mass migration exceeding the total population of Switzerland. In the average postwar year about 650,000 emigrants were recorded as leaving Europe for overseas, and the actual figure was undoubtedly larger. "Return" migration amounts to about one-third of this total. The identifiable net outward movement in the period 1946–52 was 3.2 million or about 450,000 per year. This substantial movement represents the highest figures reached since the application of severe restrictive measures by the United States in the early 1920s. In gross volume it is comparable to European emigration from 1880–1900. It has not, however, attained the huge totals registered immediately prior to World War I.

Overseas migration drained off approximately one-eighth of the natural growth of population in Europe since the war, as compared with about one-fifth removed by the maximum movements in the years 1900–1914.

WHERE FROM?

Much of the controversy concerning migration restrictions in the United States and other countries of immigration has revolved around the displacement of "old" migration from Northwest Europe by the "new" migration from Southern and Eastern Europe which came into predominance among overseas emigrants around the turn of the century. Trends in *gross* emigration from the chief regions and countries of origin are shown in Table 1.

The pattern of *gross* emigration resembles that of the 1920s. The United Kingdom, Germany, Italy, Spain and Portugal each recorded a roughly parallel emigration in the two periods, both in numbers and in

Interwar Years, League of Nations, 1946, Chapters 4–7; (2) "European Migrations: Prewar Trends and Future Prospects," *Milbank Memorial Fund Quarterly,* 25 (April, 1947).

percentages of the European total. Gross emigration from Eastern Europe was higher than in the 1920s but much lower than at the turn of the century. The other major difference is the new emigration from the Netherlands, which is chiefly responsible for the rise in the figure for France and the Low Countries.

The pattern of *net* emigration is somewhat different because of the large return migration, particularly to the United Kingdom, to the Netherlands, and to Spain and Portugal. The total net emigration by country of origin and destination is shown

Irish emigration now goes almost wholly to Britain rather than overseas.

WHERE TO?

While the United States has continued to be the leading destination of European migration, it does not hold the commanding position that it did in the days of unrestricted movement, when the U. S. was receiving from a half to two-thirds of all European emigrants. Since the war the U. S. has played host to only about one-third (950,000) of the net movement, while Canada, Australia, and Argentina have each

TABLE 1. GROSS OVERSEAS EMIGRATION FROM EUROPE, 1901–52 (AVERAGE ANNUAL IN THOUSANDS)

Regions of Old Emigration	1901–10	1911–20	1921–30	1931–40	1946–52*
British Isles	195	183	180	32	165
Germany	27	9	56	15	40
Scandinavia	49	20	25	4	12
France, Low Countries, Switzerland	16	12	13	5	63**
Regions of New Emigration					
Italy	362	219	110	26	107
Portugal, Spain	142	171	86	23	74
Eastern Europe ***	447	271	123	34	188
Total	1,238	885	593	139	649
Per cent "old" emigration	23	26	47	40	43
Per cent "new" emigration	77	74	53	60	57

* For a number of individual countries average for the years 1946–51.
** Excluding movement of Algerian workers returning to Algeria from France, estimated to average 53,000 per year in 1946–51, inclusive.
*** Including Austria, Finland. Greece, Yugoslavia, and Soviet Orbit.

in Table 2. The leading countries are the United Kingdom and Italy (over 600,000 each), Poland (460,000), Germany (290,-000), U.S.S.R. (230,000), Spain and Portugal (180,000 each), and Rumania (160,000). Some 300,000 Dutch emigrated overseas since the war but these were largely offset by repatriations and other immigration from Indonesia. France was the only European country of overseas *immigration,* which resulted from the mass migration of North Africans to the metropole.

As in the latter days of unrestricted migration, the leading sources were in Eastern and Southern Europe. Of the eight countries supplying over 100,000 emigrants since the war, six were in these regions. Certain older areas of emigration, such as Ireland and Scandinavia, were notably under-represented.

absorbed well over half a million. Australia in particular has been receiving immigrants at a ratio to population far exceeding that for the United States even at our greatest period of immigration. Immigration to Australia and Canada has been chiefly drawn from among British subjects and other Northwest Europeans on the one hand and displaced persons on the other, with limited numbers from other sources. Argentinian immigration has been almost wholly from Italy and Spain, with less than ten per cent of the total being displaced persons. About half of the U. S. immigrants were displaced persons admitted under special legislation; the remainder follow in the order of magnitude of the quotas, which favor immigrants from Northwest Europe.

The final major country of immigration

is of course Israel, which alone in the postwar period owes its existence as an independent nation to large-scale immigration. The 370,000 Jews from all parts of Europe for whom it provided a refuge have contributed spectacularly in establishing the demographic base for the Jewish state—the new immigrants constituted 43 per cent of the total population at the end of 1951. The days of large-scale "rescue migration" appear to be over, however, for only 23,000 arrived in 1952 as compared with 191,000 in the previous year.

In the receiving country immigrants went primarily to the urban areas. Immigrants into the United States in 1952, for example, went overwhelmingly into the cities—nearly three-fifths into the big cities of 100,000 or over, 27 per cent into other urban areas, and only the small remainder into the rural areas. Over one-half of the 1952 arrivals in Canada went to Ontario, the most industrialized province, one-fifth went to Quebec, and only about one-sixth went westward to the Prairie provinces.

Of the immigrants arriving in Australia from 1947 through 1951 only 18 per cent classified themselves as farm workers, and the flow of immigrants has gone almost exclusively into the cities. Similarly, in Israel only one-fourth of those permanently settled had gone into agriculture. The traditional policy in Latin America of putting immigrants on the land has generally been unsuccessful, and there has been a pronounced drift to the cities in search of better employment even where initial settlement was made on the land.

HOW?

Prior to World War I emigrants left Europe as individuals without governmental assistance. Since World War II, two-fifths of all European emigrants have been moved with governmental or international assistance. The cost of moving displaced persons up to 1951 was entirely borne by the International Refugee Organization (IRO). Its successor, the Intergovernmental Committee for European Emigration (ICEM), is continuing international sponsorship of such movements. Most of the movement to Israel, aside from that financed by the IRO, has received assistance from Jewish agencies of an official or semi-official character. Over half of the migration to Australia has been subsidized by the Commonwealth government under various postwar immigration schemes at an average cost of 2500 dollars per immigrant.

In addition, the United Kingdom and Italy, as major countries of emigration, have assisted their nationals by entering into bilateral agreements with the Dominions in the one case and with Latin American countries in the other. The United Kingdom provides 1,500,000 pounds sterling annually to assist migrants under the Empire Settlement Bill. A substantial minority of Italian emigrants have migrated under "controlled emigration" schemes planned and financially assisted by their government.

Financial aid to migration also was supplemented by special legislation, particularly in the United States. The Displaced Persons Act of 1948 as amended in 1950 and 1951 made available 341,000 additional immigrant visas for entrance into the United States over and above the established quotas for European countries in the postwar period. Through the provisions of the Act certain quotas were technically mortgaged for periods ranging from 3 to more than 300 years. The Refugee Act of 1953 provides for a further 214,000 immigrants in the next three years over and above the quotas for selected countries with special problems of refugees or of population pressure. Such legislation has played a large role in reducing the refugee problem.

Despite the greater element of government control and assistance in the postwar period the self-financed, individual migrant is still the predominant type, whether in the United States or in the overseas countries as a whole. With the liquidation of the most immediate refugee problems individual migration is now a growing part of the total.

WHO WENT?

Almost all of the postwar migrants of Eastern European origin (about one million) were either displaced persons or refugees from Communism—by definition, since countries in the Soviet orbit now generally prohibit emigration except in special circumstances, such as the expulsion of ethnic Germans and of Jews from satellite countries.

TABLE 2A. NET EMIGRATION FROM EUROPE, 1946–52: A. WESTERN AND SOUTHERN EUROPE (IN THOUSANDS)

Area of Immigration	British Isles [1]	Scandinavia [2]	Germany	Netherlands	France	Italy	Portugal	Spain	Greece	Yugoslavia	Other [3]	Total
Area of Emigration												
North America												
Canada	189	11	63	63	17	61	*	1	6	12	47	470
U.S.A.	170	26	180	18	23	66	5	2	17	39	52	598
Latin America												
Argentina	1	*	9	*	2	314	7	141	*	10	5	489
Brazil	2	*	9	2	3	49	95	6	1	1	6	174
Venezuela	*	*	*	*	*	61	7	13	*	2	3	86
Other [4]	1	4	1	20	*	17	2	18	*	2	9	74
Africa												
South Africa	70	*	6	14	1	6	*	*	1	*	4	102
Other [5]	35	1	*	2	−193	−1	59	*	*	*	4	−93
Asia [6]	−65	*	8	−111	3	2	1	*	3	8	6	−145
Oceania												
Australia	225	2	16	40	3	68	*	*	11	24	17	406
New Zealand	47	*	*	9	*	*	*	*	*	1	12	69
Total	675	44	292	57	−141	643	176	181	39	99	165	2,230

General Note. The international migration statistics presented in this table are derived from European, overseas. and international sources, all of which are in varying degrees incomplete, inaccurate, and inconsistent. Since there generally is better recording of arrivals than of departures, this table is in principle based on the statistics of the receiving country, i.e. the country receiving the outward bound migrants from Europe as immigrants and the European country receiving the repatriates. Statistics of the country of emigration combined with those of the International Refugee Organization (IRO) and the Intergovernmental Committee for European Migration (ICEM) have been used where data of the receiving country either are not compiled, are incomplete, or unavailable (notably Argentina, Brazil, Venezuela, Indonesia, India and Pakistan). The cross-tabulation is cast in terms of *identifiable* migrants or those that can be traced with a reasonable degree of certainty. It therefore almost certainly understates the actual volume of movement.

Wherever possible "country of birth" data were employed in the classification; elsewhere, residence ör political nationality. This is inconsistent but unavoidable. Data are generally presented for calendar rather than fiscal years and refer only to "permanent migration" of at least twelve months duration. The time lag in official publications permits using statistics covering only the period 1946–1951 for certain countries (primarily Belgium, Scandinavia and Soviet European Satellites) and in addition some 1952 data used are preliminary.

[1] Including 40,000 from Ireland chiefly to U.S.A.

[2] Including Denmark (17,000), Norway (15,000) and Sweden (12,000); in each case primarily to North America.

[3] Including Austria (35,000), Belgium (30,000), Finland (11,000) and Switzerland (19,000) generally to North America.

[4] Primarily Netherlands to Surinam, Italy to Uruguay and Peru, and Spain to Cuba.

[5] Chiefly: 34,000 British to Southern Rhodesia, Algerian workers to France, and Portuguese to dependencies (notably Angola and Mozambique).

[6] Primarily Israel, but negative balances reflect net movement of 119,000 from Indonesia to the Netherlands and 68,000 from India and Pakistan to the British Isles.

Although motivated by political oppression, this movement was nonetheless in accord with underlying economic and demographic forces. The great displacements of population in Central and Eastern Europe have been successful precisely because they were in accord with population pressures from East to West. Conversely German efforts to colonize the East were unsuccessful essentially because the educated, urbanized German could not compete effectively for the land against the prolific, peasant Slav. Similarly, the displaced persons from the Soviet Union were not Great Russians but chiefly more advanced peoples thrust aside by the Westward push of the Russians—the Baltic

TABLE 2B. NET EMIGRATION FROM EUROPE, 1946–52: B. THE SOVIET EUROPEAN ORBIT (IN THOUSANDS)

Area of Immigration	Bulgaria	Czecho-slovakia	Hungary	Poland	Rumania	U.S.S.R.	Total Soviet Orbit	Total West and South Europe	All Europe
North America									
Canada	1	10	9	77	6	31	134	470	604
U.S.A.	1	28	22	169	14	120	354	598	952
Latin America									
Argentina	*	1	3	13	1	6	24	489	513
Brazil	*	1	2	4	1	1	9	174	183
Venezuela	*	1	2	3	*	4	10	86	96
Other	*	*	1	3	*	4	8	74	82
Africa									
South Africa	*	*	*	*	*	*	*	102	102
Other	*	*	*	*	*	*	*	−93	−93
Asia [6]	38	22	18	121	134	9	342	−145	197
Oceania									
Australia	1	11	13	71	2	55	153	406	559
New Zealand	*	*	*	1	1	1	3	69	72
Total	41	74	70	462	159	231	1037	2230	3267

peoples, the Poles, and the Jews. In this regard the movement paralleled the "Russian" emigration of the early part of the century—actually largely a migration of these same minority peoples from the old Russian Empire.

The free world had another type of migration of European "displaced persons." Whereas much of Eastern Europe was integrated closely into the Soviet security bloc, much of Asia achieved full independence with a displacement of the former colonial administrators. The flow back to the mother countries, particularly from India and Pakistan to the United Kingdom (110,000 strong) and from Indonesia to the Netherlands (230,000), represented the return of long-term administrators, businessmen, their families and associates. The immigration into the Netherlands also included a number of Eurasians whose positions in Indonesia had been jeopardized by native nationalism.

But who were the majority of the European emigrants who were not displaced persons or refugees? They were individuals and families impelled by economic motives in the traditional manner to seek their fortunes

abroad. Few of them sought land, which ceased to be the chief lure to overseas migrants generations ago. The typical postwar migrant was neither a farmer nor did he aspire to become one. He rather sought out and often was assisted by his relatives and friends in New York, Toronto, Sydney, Buenos Aires, or Sao Paulo. Even if he had been a farmer in Italy or Portugal his was an essentially rural-urban migration across the seas. He would indeed be foolish to exchange his status as a poor tenant on an Italian *latifundium,* for example, for an even worse fate as a plantation laborer on a Brazilian *fazenda.* But this in principle is what many in countries of immigration would have him do—to settle empty lands and to do jobs that natives are reluctant to undertake for sound economic reasons.

The immigrant naturally has sought his own kind, where problems of personal adjustment are least. If an Englishman he followed the flag to English-speaking lands overseas. If Italian he will be found first of all in Argentina where Italian is almost as well understood as Spanish. If Portuguese he will be found almost entirely in Brazil and the Portuguese colonies; if Spanish, almost exclusively in Latin America. These "natural" movements still constitute the bulk of overseas migration. It is the cross-cultural refugee movements, involving major changes in language and customs, that have created the acute need for formal intervention by governments and international agencies.

NET POST-WAR OVERSEAS MIGRATION, EUROPE   1946-52 (in thousands)

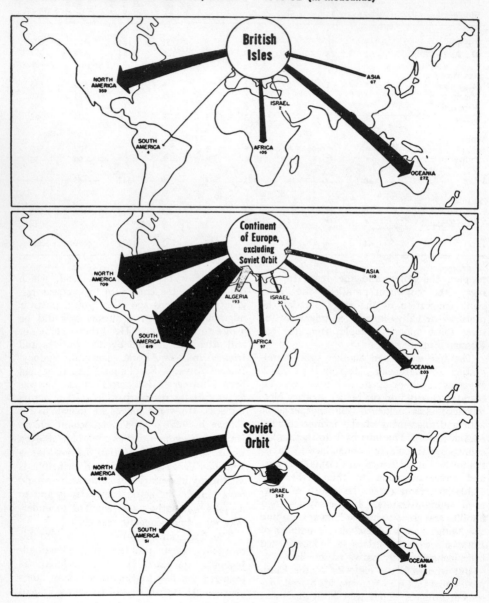

FIGURE 1

WHO?—AGE, SEX AND OCCUPATIONAL COMPOSITION

Demographic differences between immigrants and the total populations of the major immigrant-receiving countries are illustrated in Table 3. Historically it was the young adult, especially the single male, who migrated across the oceans to better his socio-economic status. Younger people of both sexes have continued to form the bulk of migration in the postwar period. In Canada, Australia, and New Zealand, for

States, whose soldiers on foreign occupation duty learned to love the girls they were near and brought them back as brides from Germany, Italy, the United Kingdom, and wherever they were stationed. In the fiscal year 1952 these numbered some 5,800 from Europe. These brides, plus the generally favored position of wives and dependents for admission, explain the fact that females outnumber males in the current immigration into the United States.

Owing to its age composition, overseas

TABLE 3. ILLUSTRATIVE COMPARISONS OF THE AGE-SEX COMPOSITION OF CURRENT IMMIGRATION AND OF TOTAL POPULATIONS IN MAJOR COUNTRIES OF IMMIGRATION

Country		Males per 100 Females	Per Cent in Age Group 20–39
United States	Fiscal 1952 immigration	96	44.2
	1952 population estimate	99	29.4
Canada	1951 immigration	162	56.7
	1951 census	102	30.5
Argentina	1950 immigration *	147	47.6
	1947 census	105	32.5
Israel	5/48–12/51 immigration	103	34.0
	1952 population estimate	104	31.6
Australia	1950 immigration	140	53.3
	1951 population estimate	102	31.0
New Zealand	Fiscal 1951 immigration	110	54.1
	1951 census	101	29.0
Union of South Africa	1949 immigration	100	43.9
	1946 census of Europeans	101	31.8

* Aliens arriving from overseas by 2nd and 3rd class passage; age group 22–40.

example, the proportion of immigrants who were in their twenties and thirties was very much higher than among the total populations. Similarly, migration into Argentina continues to be predominantly composed of young males. But new patterns were also becoming evident. The displaced persons and the uprooted Jews of Europe wanted to be resettled as families. There were virtually as many females as males among the migrants who entered Israel from the founding of the state to the end of 1951, and the age distribution in the large-scale "rescue" type of immigration that took place was little different from that of the total population.

Another modification of the prewar pattern is visible in the case of the United

migration includes a high percentage of workers, and thereby contributes disproportionately to the labor force in countries of immigration. Statistics on occupational status of migrants are not a reliable indicator of what immigrants will do after their arrival, and therefore are of limited usefulness. In reporting their occupation, migrants tend to up-grade their work and to give an occupation they believe to be preferred by the receiving country.

In both its regular quotas and in its refugee legislation the United States has given occupational preference to certain categories of immigrants. Nearly four-fifths of the 79,000 displaced persons entering in the fiscal year 1952 had first preference status, i.e., were farm, household, construction, clothing and garment workers, and others with specialized training and professional qualifications.

Though official policies in overseas countries, especially in Latin America, have favored the immigration of farm workers, they have been unsuccessful both in recruiting such workers and in holding immigrants on the land when they have initially been settled there. Immigrants into less developed countries have generally included larger proportions of skilled workers and of the professional and managerial classes than the native labor force. These migrants have done much to spur local economic development in Latin America. Immigration into South Africa has been almost entirely of the white collar and managerial classes as one might expect in this *apartheid* nation. Postwar immigration into Israel reflects the urban characteristics of its origin; only five per cent were listed as agricultural, while 37 per cent were previously white collar workers, and 44 per cent "craftsmen, production process workers, and laborers." [8]

SIGNIFICANCE OF POSTWAR IMMIGRATION

Overseas emigration historically served Europe in two ways: (1) it afforded a relief from population pressure and an outlet for the discontented and oppressed; (2) it strengthened ties with overseas countries, whether these bonds were political, economic, or cultural.

The revival of emigration in the postwar period has certainly contributed to the solution of European refugee problems. The successful liquidation of the displaced persons problem was possible only through this recourse. While emigration has fallen short of objectives in some overpopulated countries, it is nevertheless contributing significantly to the solution of unemployment and underemployment in Southern Europe. For countries living in postwar austerity, such as Britain, emigration has been alternative to living under a rationed economy.

The great free migrations before World War I were an integral part of the expansion of Europe. They provided the human sinews of European colonization and empire. Where they were not an instrument of European political expansion they promoted trade, capital movements, and cultural ties that enhanced European influence in the world.

European colonization of new lands is no longer a major aspect of European migration unless the Jewish settlement of Israel could be so regarded. The vast majority of emigrants now go to areas already occupied by populations of European race. This is true even in Latin America—at least three-fourths of all European immigrants to this region went to Argentina or to the predominantly European regions of Southern Brazil.

The most important exception, aside from the dubious case of Israel, was the European immigration into Africa south of the Sahara, a net movement of at least 200,000, chiefly of British, Portuguese, and French administrators, entrepreneurs and settlers in their respective territories. The Boer-controlled government of South Africa officially encourages the immigration of Dutch and Germans, but the chief effect of Boer policies has been to greatly reduce immigration from the British Isles and to stimulate a movement of British to Southern Rhodesia. In no case, however, was the migration sufficient to create a European majority even in local areas, or to change materially the minority position of Europeans in every country south of the Sahara.

The huge British emigration, 500,000 of which has gone to members of the Commonwealth, has certainly strengthened the ties that hold together this loose association. But most European emigration is no longer an instrument for European political control.

The countries receiving European immigration have generally profited by this movement, if for no other reason than that they have acquired a number of skilled workers and entrepreneurs without bearing the cost of their education and childhood dependency. The economic problems of assimilation were minimized by the high levels of economic activity prevailing in the postwar period. In the underdeveloped countries, especially of Latin America, even comparatively small numbers of European immigrants are playing a disproportionately large role in the rapid economic development now occurring

---

[8] Norman Lawrence, *Israel: Jewish Population and Immigration*, Washington: International Population Statistics Reports of U. S. Bureau of the Census, Series P-90, No. 2, 1952, p. 54.

in that continent, since they bring skills, work habits, and enterprise not commonly available in the less developed countries. Only in Australia and in Israel has immigration been so large as to create serious economic maladjustments, notably in shortages of housing and other primary facilities.

The chief conflicts created by European immigrants have been social and cultural rather than economic. But the fear of cultural inundation, expressed in widespread immigration restrictions, has certainly far exceeded the fact. Easy cultural accommodation has been facilitated by the fact that individual migration flows preferentially to countries of common language and political allegiance. Aside from immigration restrictions this preference has in fact been much more important than theoretical economic advantages in determining the actual sources, direction and volume of voluntary overseas migration. Obviously economic advantage is necessary to induce voluntary overseas migration. But in the choice of alternative overseas destinations the emigrant will almost always forego theoretical maximum opportunity for the practical advantages of locating among relatives, friends, and countrymen overseas. In fact the impetus to emigration more often comes from such connections than from a simple desire to emigrate without specific opportunities in mind.

Assimilation problems have understandably been most difficult in the case of the displaced persons and political refugees, often precisely because political restrictions and domestic policies made it impossible to send such persons to overseas communities of similar cultural background. While the particular assimilation problems met in the several countries of immigration are of great sociological interest they are too complex for discussion in this summary treatment.[4]

[4] Among the literature on this and related problems are *Cultural Assimilation of Immigrants*, Supplement to *Population Studies: A Journal of Demography*, March 1950, Cambridge: University Press, 1950, 118 pp.; Rudolf Heberle and Dudley S. Hall, *New Americans: A Study of Displaced Persons in Louisiana and Mississippi*, Baton Rouge, La.: Displaced Persons Commission, 1951; Maurice R. Davie and Samuel Koenig, "Adjustment of Refugees to American Life," *Annals of the American Academy of Political and Social Science*, 262 (March, 1949), pp. 159–165.

Assimilation problems have generally proved less than anticipated. They have been least where displaced persons were permitted to make their own adjustment, usually in cities, and greatest when they were restricted in choice of occupation and residence by domestic policies, as for instance in requiring the settlement of displaced persons on the land.

FUTURE PROSPECTS

With the resolution of the displaced persons problem largely through overseas migration, individual migration is again the predominant form. Such migration is now forbidden by Eastern European countries. Aside from a few intrepid individuals who successfully escape through the Iron' Curtain, Eastern Europe is ceasing to be a source of overseas migration and probably will continue to be so, barring a radical change in its political complexion. For this reason potential migration to Israel from Europe has been greatly reduced. The leadership of that country, which is largely of European origin, is concerned about cultural inundation from areas of new Jewish immigration (from Asia and Africa) just as are the "older" European stocks in overseas countries with regard to immigrants of different cultural background.

From the problem of displaced persons, interest in sponsored European emigration has shifted to the problem of German refugees and of population pressure in Southern Europe and the Netherlands. While the German refugees are far more numerous than the displaced persons who were handled by the International Refugee Organization, they have far less impetus to emigrate, since they are now resident in a country of their own nationality. Furthermore, the rapid economic recovery in Western Germany in recent years is providing them employment opportunities. These opportunities are less favorable than are those for natives of Western Germany, but more favorable than they might expect to encounter in many overseas countries.

Most of Western Europe has now passed the demographic stage which brought about the great swarming of Europeans overseas in the 19th and early 20th centuries. Declining birth rates in the 1930s have so reduced the size of cohorts entering the labor force that pressure to seek opportunities abroad has been greatly reduced. In Ireland, in Scandinavia, and even in Germany there is much less pressure to migrate from demographic causes than a generation ago. The lower birth rates now prevailing in Southern Europe assure that pressure from this source will also shortly recede in that region, especially in Italy, where the birth rate is now quite low, lower even than in France, the classic country of depopulation, and much lower than in the United States.

In peace, the major continuing reservoir of "normal" overseas migration in Western Europe is the underemployed rural populations of Southern Italy, Spain, Portugal, Greece, and to a less extent the Netherlands. This reservoir is declining, but its need for an outlet still poses one of Europe's most pressing economic problems. At least for the next ten years it should furnish the basis for continued overseas migration, until such time as further economic development, on the one hand, and demographic trends, on the other, may have resolved the problems of population pressure in these countries as they have in much of Northwest Europe.

CULTURAL PLURALISM

By Clyde V. Kiser

IN a broad or literal sense "cultural pluralism" might mean any type of cultural diversity within a given area, and might be applied to classification by race, ethnic group, religion, rural-urban status, occupation, income,· or general level of living. Because the term has been used more frequently by students of race, immigration, and ethnic problems than by other social scientists, it generally relates to ethnic diversity. This more restricted interpretation is used in the present article, which deals briefly with our ethnic diversity and certain problems of assimilation.

COLONIAL ORIGINS OF ETHNIC DIVERSITY

The origins of our ethnic diversity are to be found in the conditions under which the area now constituting the United States was settled. In the first place, the Indian-white dichotomy began when the first white settlers arrived. The persistence of that dichotomy is a matter of history. It is a history first of attempted extermination, of the whites pushing the Indians westward, and later of establishing the surviving Indians on reservations as wards of the Federal Government.

The importation · of Negro slaves brought another white-colored demarcation early in our population history. First imported as slaves about the time the Pilgrims were settling at Plymouth,[1] the Negroes increased rapidly during the colonial period and were destined to become our largest minority group.

[1] Warren S. Thompson, *Population Problems* (New York: McGraw-Hill Book Co., 1942), p. 128.

The origins of our intra-white ethnic diversity are to be found in the multiple-power attempts at colonization. Although the English became the dominant colonists in early areas of settlement, the Dutch left their stamp on New York, the French on Louisiana, and the Spanish on California and the southwest.

Furthermore, although the settlers of the British colonies were predominantly from the mother country, sizable groups also came from other areas—particularly from northwestern Europe and notably from Germany. In numerous instances small groups of non-English peoples were allowed or even encouraged to come because of political and religious persecution. Some of these afford the best examples we have of the role of noneconomic factors in our early immigration.

It is not possible to determine exactly the net effect of these policies relating to Indians, importation of slaves, and origins of white settlers on the size and ethnic composition of this country's population by the close of the colonial period. Records of colonial censuses carried out about 1770–75 in most of the provinces are available, but these did not enumerate Indians in most instances and simply differentiated the Negroes from the whites with no indication of the ethnic origin of the latter. On the basis of these and other materials, however, Sutherland has concluded:

In the period of 167 years elapsing between the settlement of Jamestown in 1608 and the outbreak of the Revolution, the population of the American colonies grew to 2,507,180, exclusive of Indians . . .

about 533,500 were Negroes, and perhaps 200,000 more were of German or other alien stock; the remainder were British.[2]

According to Sutherland's figures, Negroes constituted about 21 per cent of the total population (exclusive of Indians), and about 90 per cent of the white persons were of British origin. The latter figure corresponds closely to, and is probably based upon, the United States Census Bureau's estimated distribution by ethnic origin of the whites enumerated in the 1790 Census of the United States.

COMPOSITION OF OUR POPULATION IN 1790

In 1790, according to our first census, Negroes comprised 19.3 per cent of the total population enumerated within the United States boundaries of that date. That census did not enumerate Indians and gave no direct information on ethnic stock of the white population. In a special volume published in 1909, however, the Bureau of the Census provided an estimated distribution of the whites in the 1790 Census, according to country of origin, based largely on family names. According to these estimates, 82.1 per cent of the whites enumerated in the United States in 1790 were of English lineage, an additional 7 per cent were of Scottish descent, and 1.9 per cent were Irish. In other words, about 91 per cent of the whites were from, or descendants of people from, the British Isles. Most of the remainder were German or Dutch [3] (see Table 1).

The above figures, however, have not been universally accepted. Many students have stressed the possibilities of

serious pitfalls in the use of family names in this country as a basis for determining national origin. In 1927 the American Council of Learned Societies appointed a committee of experts in historical and genealogical research to study the problem. The report of this committee, which was released in 1932, not only presented a reclassification of the enumerated white population of 1790, but also provided estimates of whites in unenumerated areas.[4] According to this reclassification, persons of English origin formed only about 60 per cent of the whites in continental United States in 1790. Those of English, Scotch, and Irish descent combined accounted for about 78 per cent. In general, however, although this later analysis of the family names in the 1790 Census suggests a wider variety of origins of the original white population, it does not alter the general conclusion that the British constituted the dominant element and that there were few people from southern and eastern Europe at the time of the first census of the United States. Rare also were the Orientals.

SUBSEQUENT INCREASES IN DIVERSITY

The subsequent increase in diversity of the population was due to the great influx of immigrants from varied sources during the nineteenth century and early part of the twentieth. Other papers in this series ably describe the volume and changing character of immigration during that period and discuss the development of our immigration policy.[5]

To summarize very broadly, three

[2] Stella H. Sutherland, *Population Distribution in Colonial America* (New York: Columbia University Press, 1936), p. 271.

[3] U. S. Bureau of the Census, *A Century of Population Growth* (Washington: Government Printing Office, 1909), p. 121.

[4] American Council of Learned Societies: "Report of the Committee on Linguistic and National Stocks in the Population of the United States," *Annual Report of the American Historical Association, 1931,* Vol. I (Washington: Government Printing Office, 1932), p. 124.

[5] See especially the papers by Carl Wittke and Henry Pratt Fairchild.

TABLE 1—Percentage Apportionment of the White Population of the United States in 1790 and 1920, by Country of Origin[a]

Country of Origin	1790		1920
	U. S. Bureau of Census Estimates of 1909[b]	ACLS Comm. Estimates of 1932[c]	Prepared as Bases for Immigration Quotas[d]
Total	100.0	100.0	100.1
Quota countries (for 1920 data)	—	—	94.5
Northwestern and central Europe (approx.)	99.7	92.4	83.0
England	82.1	60.1	
Wales	e	e	41.4
Scotland	7.0	8.1	
North Ireland	1.9	5.9	
Irish Free State		3.6	11.2
Austria	f	f	0.9
Belgium	f	f	0.8
Czechoslovakia	f	f	1.8
Denmark	f	f	0.7
Estonia	f	f	0.1
Finland	f	f	0.4
France	0.6	2.3	1.9
Germany	5.6	8.6	16.3
Hungary	f	f	0.6
Latvia	f	f	0.2
Netherlands	2.5	3.1	2.0
Norway	f	f	1.5
Sweden	f	0.7	2.1
Switzerland	f	f	1.1
Southern and eastern Europe (approx.)	f	0.8	11.2
Greece	f	f	0.2
Italy	f	f	3.6
Lithuania	f	f	0.2
Poland	f	f	4.1
Portugal	f	f	0.3
Rumania	f	f	0.2
Spain	f	0.8	0.2
Turkey	f	f	0.1
U.S.S.R. (Europe and Asia)	f	f	1.8
Yugoslavia	f	f	0.5
All other quota countries (1920)	f	f	0.3
Nonquota countries (1920)	f	f	5.6
Canada and Newfoundland	f	f	4.3
Latin America	f	f	1.3
Other or unknown (1790)	0.3	6.8	—

[a] Throughout this paper the writer has followed the regional classifications of European countries adopted by the Office of Population Research of Princeton University.

[b] See text reference 3.

[c] See text reference 4.

[d] See text reference 8.

[e] Welsh included with "English" in data for 1790.

[f] Included with "other or unknown" if represented at all in 1790.

distinct periods stand out in our immigration history both with respect to origins and policy. Prior to 1882 the immigrants were mainly from northern and western Europe. Attracted by the opportunities for free land, they and their descendants helped to push our frontiers westward and their dispersal facilitated rapid mergence into our culture. It was a period of virtual absence of Federal restrictions against immigration, and during the last thirty years of it many Chinese took advantage of this situation.

The second period, 1882–1923, was characterized by declining immigration from northern and western Europe, and by the ascendancy of migrants from southern and eastern Europe. Just as the British, Irish, and Germans predominated in the earlier movement, the Italians, Russians, and Poles were especially conspicuous in the second period. Besides these peoples, however, hundreds of thousands of immigrants from other southern and eastern European countries helped to swell six annual totals above the million mark during 1905–14. The whole period was one of declining opportunities for free land but of increasing opportunities for industrial employment. Hence, it was the period of urban concentration of immigrants and of the formation of ghettos—Little Italys, Little Hungaries, and Little Russias in New York, Pittsburgh, and other large cities.

With respect to policy, the period witnessed replacement of state control by Federal control. The first Federal restriction of consequence was the Chinese Exclusion Act of 1882, a move instigated by whites on the Pacific Coast. The Alien Contract Labor Law was passed in 1885 and the assumption of complete Federal control of immigration came in 1891 with the establishment of the Office of Superintendent of Immigration. Further modifications of the open-door policy were enacted during the ensuing years of the period, the most important of which was the passage of the literacy tests of 1917. However, except for the Chinese Exclusion Act and the Gentlemen's Agreement with Japan of 1907, these restrictions were leveled at individuals rather than at particular ethnic groups.

The third and last period, that since 1924, is characterized by small numbers of immigrants from any source, by quotas favoring northwestern Europe, by the higher relative importance of immigration from countries of the Western Hemisphere, and by the admission of a fairly sizable body of refugees in recent years.

Owing to our past history of immigration, our population is considerably more heterogeneous than it was in 1790. This is true to some extent for the colored population; it is conspicuously the case for the whites.

Proportionate declines

Negroes easily form our most numerous minority group, white or colored, and Indians, though numbering only about 334,000 in 1940, are the most numerous of our non-Negro colored elements. Negroes have declined in proportionate importance in the total population from about 19 per cent in 1790 to 10 per cent in 1940. This is attributed mainly to the fact that since 1808 (when further importation of slaves was banned) the growth of the Negro population has been limited to natural increase. Accretions through voluntary immigration have been very small.

Likewise, although no figures can be given regarding size of the Indian population in 1790, there is no doubt that until recently Indians have formed a constantly decreasing percentage of our population, despite the accession of new groups with the westward extension of

United States boundaries. As late as two decades ago these peoples could be aptly described as our "vanishing Americans." Furthermore, the heterogeneity of the colored population is increased by the presence of the Japanese, Chinese, and other Asiatics. Although these groups are small in proportion to the total or even to the total colored population, they were scarcely represented at all in 1790.

Several types of census materials are available for studying changes in the ethnic composition of the white population, but each has definite limitations. The central difficulty is the lack of data, or even the virtual impossibility of securing accurate data, on ethnic origin of all native whites of native parentage.[6] Since 1850, however, the census has provided data on country of origin of the foreign-born population, and since 1890 such data have been available for the total "foreign-white stock" (foreign-born whites, plus native whites of foreign or mixed parentage). In addition the Census Bureau has collected data on mother tongue of certain elements of the population since 1910.

ACLS and other estimates

Changes in the ethnic composition of the total white population since 1790 can best be shown by comparing the ACLS estimates for 1790 with those that were made for 1920 as a basis for our present immigration quotas, as is shown by Table 1. The latter work was done by a committee set up by the departments of State, Commerce, and Labor.[7] It should be emphasized that

[6] Probably the two chief reasons for the census omission of this question for native whites of native parentage are (1) the presumption of minor influence of national origin on these people, and (2) the existence of multiple origins due to intermarriage.

[7] For original source see 70th Cong., 2d sess., S. Doc. 259, *Immigration Quotas on the Basis of National Origin*. The distributions in the

the limitations of the data and the nature of the problem itself preclude precise comparisons. Each of the classifications listed in Table 1 was originally submitted with accompanying statements regarding the difficulty of classifying peoples of mixed strains and emphasizing that the distributions should be interpreted simply in terms of the relative importance of the various national origins in the total white population considered.[8]

Whatever the limitations of the data may be, there is no doubt about the decrease in the proportionate importance of English stock in our white population. On the basis of the two estimates mentioned above, 74.1 per cent of our white population was of British and North Irish origin in 1790; the proportion was 41.4 per cent in 1920. On the other hand, "Irish Free State" origins accounted for 3.6 per cent in 1790 and 11.2 per cent in 1920. German origins formed 8.6 per cent in 1790 and 16.3 per cent in 1920. Southern and eastern European origins, scarcely represented in 1790, collectively formed over one-tenth of the white population of the United States in 1920. The two chief origins in this category were Poland (4.1 per cent) and Italy (3.6 per cent).

Country-of-birth data

Next to immigration statistics themselves, the census data on country of

last column of Table 1 were adapted from W. S. Thompson and P. K. Whelpton, *Population Trends in the United States* (New York: McGraw-Hill Book Company, 1933), p. 91.

[8] The chief fault that the ACLS Committee found with the Census Bureau's estimate of the 1790 composition was that it was based simply on a tabulation of reported family names and that no account was taken of changes in names. The persons responsible for the 1920 estimates had the benefit of help from the ACLS; they also had the benefit of census data on country of origin and mother tongue of the foreign-white stock.

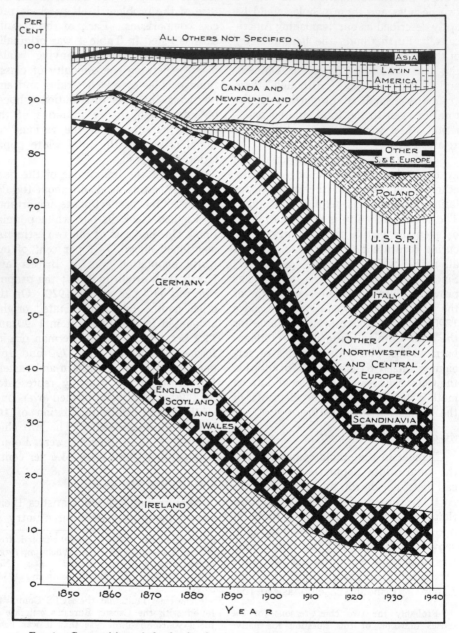

Fig. 1.—Composition of the foreign-born population of the United States by country of birth, 1850–1940. Computed from data in Fourteenth Census of the United States, 1920, *Population*, Vol. II, p. 695 (giving data for 1850–1920), and from Sixteenth Census of the United States, 1940, *Population*, Vol. II, p. 19 (giving data for 1930–40). For purposes of the chart, foreign-born Negroes reported in 1930 and 1940 were assumed to be of Latin American origin, and foreign-born Chinese, Japanese, and other Asiatics were assumed to have been born in Asia.

birth of our foreign-born population are most sensitive to changing origins of our immigrants. Thus, as charted in Figure 1, in 1850 about 43 per cent of our foreign-born population were from Ireland, 26 per cent from Germany, and 17 per cent from England, Scotland, and Wales. Southern and eastern European countries collectively were represented by only one-half of 1 per cent of the foreign-born population. In 1940, on the other hand, natives of Italy outnumbered those of any other country in our foreign-born population and constituted 14 per cent of the total. Those of Germany stood in second place with 11 per cent. Close behind, each group constituting 8–9 per cent of our foreign-born population, were immigrants from Canada, Russia, Poland, Great Britain (England, Scotland, and Wales), and the Scandinavian countries combined. Ireland contributed only about 6 per cent. Collectively, 38 per cent of our foreign-born population of 1940 came from countries of southern and eastern Europe, 46 per cent from northwestern and central Europe, 14 per cent from countries of the Western Hemisphere, and the remainder from other places.

Although the foreign-born whites in 1940 numbered only 11.4 million and constituted only about 9 per cent of our total population, there were about 23.2 million native whites of foreign or mixed parentage. Hence, about 34.6 million, or about 26 per cent of our total population, were classified in the 1940 Census as members of "foreign-white stock." Among the persons of foreign-white stock those of German origin stood in top position numerically with about 15 per cent of the total. In descending order of magnitude these were followed by Italians with 13 per cent, British (including North Irish) with 9 per cent, Russians, Canadians, Poles, each with about 8 per cent, and

Free State Irish with 7 per cent (see reference 14–b).

MOTHER TONGUE

In the 1940 Census "mother tongue" was defined as "the principal language spoken in the home of the person in his earliest childhood; English was reported as the mother tongue only if no foreign language was spoken." On the basis of returns from a 5-per-cent sample of the total population, tabulations have been published regarding mother tongue of the total white population, and these are also given separately for the foreign-born whites, native whites of foreign or mixed parentage, and native whites of native parentage.[9]

Among the total whites English was reported as the mother tongue by 78.6 per cent, German by 4.2 per cent, Italian by 3.2 per cent, Polish by 2.0 per cent, Spanish by 1.6 per cent, Yiddish by 1.5 per cent, and French by 1.2 per cent. No other single foreign mother tongue was reported by as much as 1 per cent of the total white population. The foregoing percentages represent the following total numbers of whites: English mother tongue, 93 million; German, 4.9 million; Italian, 3.8 million; Polish, 2.4 million; Spanish, 1.9 million; Yiddish, 1.75 million; and French, 1.4 million.

As one might expect, the proportion reporting English mother tongue was lowest (22.6 per cent) for foreign-born whites, intermediate (52.6 per cent) for native whites of foreign or mixed parentage, and highest (93.1 per cent) for native whites of native parentage. Within each of these three groups, German was the most frequent foreign mother tongue reported and Italian stood second within the two foreign

[9] U. S. Bureau of the Census, *Mother Tongue of the White Population: 1940. Population*, Series P-15, No. 4 (Washington: Govt. Printing Office, September 28, 1942).

stock groups. Thus, among the foreign born, German was reported by 14.3 per cent, Italian by 14.1 per cent, Yiddish by 8.3 per cent, Polish by 7.2 per cent, Spanish by 3.9 per cent, Swedish by 3.8 per cent, and French and Russian each by 3.2 per cent.[10]

No census prior to that of 1940 collected data on mother tongue of native whites of native parentage. In the 1930 Census, the collection of such data was restricted to persons of foreign birth and the published tabulations to foreign-born whites. In the 1910 and 1920 censuses the published data related to persons of foreign-white stock but, as will be explained later, only those for the foreign-born whites are comparable with the 1940 materials for whites of corresponding nativity. In general, the 1910–40 comparisons for the foreign born point up the shift of linguistic origins from northwestern and central Europe to southern and eastern Europe. For instance, in 1910 German was reported as the mother tongue by 20.7 per cent of the foreign-born whites and Italian by 10.2 per cent. In 1940, as already noted, these two languages were about equally represented; the percentages were 14.3 and 14.1, respectively.

Definitions and interpretations

If properly interpreted, data on mother tongue for groups other than the foreign born are useful as indices of readiness to adopt the English language. The qualification is stated because two instances of what appear to be unwarranted generalizations have been encountered recently by the writer. One of these is the following statement in a census release:

Nearly 53 per cent of the second generation whites [native whites of foreign or mixed parentage] reported English mother tongue in 1940, as compared with only

[10] *Ibid.*, p. 4.

about 30 per cent in 1920 and about 35 per cent in 1910 . . . Since the proportion of immigrants from English-speaking countries has been declining for many decades, it would appear that immigrants of a foreign mother tongue are less inclined than formerly to use it in their homes and thus teach it to their children.[11]

The apparent increase in the percentage reporting English probably was due in large part simply to the change in definition and concept of mother tongue as applied to native whites of foreign or mixed parentage. In the 1910 and 1920 censuses, mother tongue was defined essentially as "the language of customary speech in the homes of the immigrants before immigration." [12] The data related to foreign-born whites and to the parents of native whites of foreign or mixed parentage. Native whites of foreign or mixed parentage were automatically classified according to the mother tongue of their foreign-born parents. They could not be classified as "English mother tongue" unless the foreign-born parent spoke English before coming to this country. In brief, in so far as native whites of foreign or mixed parentage are concerned, the 1940 data relate to principal language spoken in the United States homes of these people themselves; the 1910 and 1920 data relate to the language spoken in the foreign homes of the parents of the persons concerned.

The other instance of what seems to be unwarranted generalization is Smith's statement regarding the greater frequency of German mother tongue than of any other foreign mother tongue among native whites in this country in 1940:

[11] *Ibid.*, p. 2.
[12] Thirteenth Census of the United States, 1910, *Population*, Vol. I (Washington: Govt. Printing Office, 1913), p. 959. Fourteenth Census of the United States, 1920, *Population*, Vol. II (Washington: Govt. Printing Office, 1922), p. 967.

Analysis shows that more than any other group, immigrants speaking the German tongue placed their descendants partially at the mercy of incipient demagogues in the old country by giving the use of German a preference over English in the home. Native-born Americans whose formative years were passed hearing, speaking, and thinking mainly German totaled over 3⅓ millions. Those who received the bulk of their conditioning via the Italian, Polish, Spanish, and French languages follow in the order named.[13]

The above statement is based upon numbers rather than percentages; it relates to the magnitude of numerators without taking into account the size of the denominators. One would like to know how the percentage of native whites of German descent who report German mother tongue compares with, say, the percentage of native whites of Italian descent who report Italian mother tongue. Such percentages are not available for all native whites because of the unknown national origin of the native whites of native parentage. It is possible, however, to derive equivalent comparisons from the 1940 Census data for native whites of foreign or mixed parentage of given national origin.

Figure 2 presents the proportions reporting English mother tongue in 1940 among native whites of foreign or mixed parentage of selected non-English national origins.[14] It will be noted that the proportion reporting English

[13] T. Lynn Smith, *Population Analysis* (New York: McGraw-Hill Book Co., 1948), p. 85.
[14] The numerators and denominators for the computations were secured from the two following census releases, respectively: (a) *Mother Tongue of the Foreign White Stock by Sex, Nativity, and Country of Origin: 1940. Population*, Series P–15, No. 11 (Washington: Govt. Printing Office, March 19, 1943). (b) *Foreign White Stock of the United States by Country of Origin: 1940. Population*, Series P–15, No. 6 (Washington: Govt. Printing Office, Nov. 5, 1942).

was highest (66.1 per cent) for persons of Danish origin and lowest (7.0 per cent) for those of Mexican origin. Approximately one-half (49.7 per cent) of the native whites with one or both parents born in Germany reported English mother tongue. In contrast, only 29.2 per cent of the native whites with one or both parents born in Italy reported English mother tongue. In making comparisons of this type, of course,

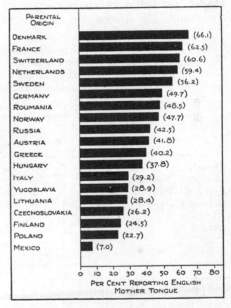

FIG. 2.—The reporting of English as the mother tongue among native whites of foreign or mixed parentage of selected national origins, 1940 (see text reference 14).

one would like to hold constant such factors as age of the person and period of the migration of the parents to this country. Despite the absence of such controls, however, the percentages in Figure 2 probably give a truer indication of differential readiness to adopt the English language than do the simple numerical distributions by mother tongue. It is recognized, of course, that for some purposes numbers are more significant than percentages.

INTERMARRIAGE AMONG FOREIGN-WHITE STOCK

Since amalgamation is commonly regarded as the final step in assimilation, data on intermarriage afford some indication of the extent of amalgamation or, conversely, of the relative amounts of clannishness among the various elements of our foreign-white stock. For some years prior to 1942, the annual reports of the New York State Department of Health carried data on marriages by color and, for whites, by country of

and females of foreign-white stock were represented in 39 per cent of the total. Like census materials, the marriage data considered here afford no indication of the ethnic origin of native whites of native parentage. Also like the census materials, however, they afford distributions by country of origin for each of the three subdivisions of the foreign-white stock, i.e., foreign born, natives of foreign parentage, and natives of mixed parentage. The specific country-of-origin categories shown in Table 2 follow the published data.

TABLE 2—PER CENT OF WHITE FOREIGN-STOCK GROOMS AND BRIDES OF GIVEN NATIVITY AND COUNTRY OF ORIGIN CHOOSING FOREIGN-STOCK MATES OF SAME COUNTRY OF ORIGIN: NEW YORK STATE EXCLUSIVE OF NEW YORK CITY, 1941

Country of Origin	Grooms by Nativity			Brides by Nativity		
	Foreign Born	Natives of Foreign Parentage[a]	Natives of Mixed Parentage[b]	Foreign Born	Natives of Foreign Parentage[a]	Natives of Mixed Parentage[b]
Canada	15.2	13.7	12.5	16.5	15.3	11.2
Denmark, Norway, Sweden[c]	28.9	12.5	6.4	33.7	15.0	8.3
England, Scotland, Wales[c]	17.5	9.3	5.6	18.9	9.1	7.2
Germany, Austria[c]	44.1	19.6	10.4	45.3	22.5	12.8
Hungary	46.8	14.5	8.3	46.7	14.4	15.1
Ireland	40.1	12.1	7.0	37.5	13.8	9.2
Italy	79.7	64.7	52.2	84.2	71.4	56.7
Poland	59.8	54.9	48.7	58.8	51.8	51.8
Russia	45.9	41.0	35.9	55.7	44.2	45.3

[a] National origin determined by country of birth of father.
[b] National origin determined by country of birth of foreign-born parent.
[c] Group considered as a unit.
Source: *Computed from* State of New York, *Sixty-Second Annual Report of the Department of Health* for the year ending December 31, 1941 (Albany, 1942), Vol. 2, pp. 230–35.

birth of grooms and their parents, according to country of birth of brides and their parents. The data for 1941 have been analyzed for brief discussion here. Although the data are restricted to New York State, exclusive of New York City, that area is one in which the foreign-white stock is large in number and widely heterogeneous. Males of foreign-white stock were represented in 42 per cent of the total 61,356 marriages registered in this area in 1941,

Table 2, computed from detailed cross-classifications of grooms and brides by country of origin, simply indicates the extent to which grooms and brides of given national origin chose mates of the same national origin. The percentages are given separately for the three subclasses of foreign-white stock. However, in each case they relate to mates of the same national origin but not necessarily of the same subclass of foreign stock. For instance, 15.2 per cent of the grooms born in Canada chose brides who were classified as being of Canadian origin either on the basis of their birthplace or that of their parents.[15]

"Same national origin" marriages

Several points of interest stand out in the figures. First of all, it will be noted that within each "country of origin" group, the proportion of "same national origin" marriages was highest for the foreign born; it was in intermediate position for the natives of foreign parentage, and lowest for natives of mixed parentage. In the second place, the proportions of "same national origin" marriages tended to be a little lower among males than among females but the differences were slight in all cases, as may be noted by comparing the right and left sections of the table.

Of chief interest, however, are the relatively high proportions of "same national origin" marriages among persons of Italian, Polish, and Russian origin as compared with those of Canadian and northwestern and central European origin. Differences of this type are especially prominent among the natives of foreign or mixed parentage. Even among the foreign born, however, "same national origin" marriages were much more prominent for Italians and Poles than for the other groups. About 80 per cent of the Italian-born grooms and 60 per cent of the Polish-born grooms found wives of the same country of origin. Comparable figures were 40–47 per cent for grooms born in Germany, Hungary, Ireland, and Russia, and 15–29 per cent for those born in Canada,

[15] Though not shown in the table, the 15.2 per cent is the sum of 8.1 per cent marrying Canadian born, 2.4 per cent marrying native brides of foreign parentage (father born in Canada), and 4.7 per cent marrying brides of mixed parentage (foreign-born parent born in Canada).

the Scandinavian countries (considered as a unit), and Great Britain.

The data for the non-foreign-born groups suggest that in-marriages continue into the second generation to a greater degree among those of Italian, Polish, and Russian stock than among the other stocks considered. Thus, among native-white grooms of foreign parentage "same national origin" marriages were reported for 65 per cent of the grooms of Italian parentage, for 55 per cent of the grooms of Polish parentage, and for 41 per cent of the grooms of Russian parentage. These percentages are from two to seven times higher than the comparable figures for other national origins. Likewise, among grooms of mixed parentage the proportions choosing brides of "same national origin" were from three to nine times higher for those of Italian, Polish, and Russian origin than for those of other origins considered.

Several limitations of the data should be pointed out. The factor of age should be taken into account. Age differences by country of origin probably are reduced somewhat by separation of the data into subclasses but probably in each subclass the grooms and brides of Italian, Polish, and Russian origin tend to be younger than those of other origins. A careful analysis of sex ratios of marriageable persons of given age and country of origin would be another prerequisite to definitive conclusions.

Perhaps the most important limitation of the data for purposes of ascertaining relative amounts of clannishness stems from (1) lack of information regarding ethnic origins of native whites of native parentage, and (2) unequal availability of mates of the same national origin from native whites of native parents. Due to the comparative recency of immigration, persons of Italian, Polish, and Russian descent in this country have not yet built up as large a backlog of native whites of native parentage as have the others. To take an illustration, of the native-white grooms of mixed parentage (and foreign-parent Irish), only 7 per cent chose brides of Irish birth or parentage. The original data show that nearly two-thirds chose brides simply classified as native white of native parentage. Probably many of the latter were entirely or mainly of Irish descent.

THE MELTING POT VERSUS CULTURAL PLURALISM

The existence of these ethnic diversities raises the question of assimilation. The rationale for immigration quotas favoring countries of northwestern Europe was the belief that peoples from those areas could be more readily assimilated than others. Whatever may be the validity of that assumption, there is no doubt that the virtual stoppage of immigration itself has tended to mitigate problems of assimilation. Although still concentrated heavily in urban areas of the north, the foreign-born group is aging rapidly. If there are no drastic changes in our immigration laws, the foreign-born whites will continue to decrease in numerical and proportionate importance. The children and grandchildren of the foreign-born whites will probably become less and less distinguishable from the descendants of the early white settlers. In view of common social attitudes, it is not to be expected that a similar assimilation of the colored groups will occur in the foreseeable future.

Public policy regarding the Americanization and assimilation of these various foreign stocks appears to be changing from one based on the concept of the "melting pot" to one based on the newer idea of cultural pluralism. The term "melting pot" was popularized by Israel Zangwill, journalist,

dramatist, and founder of the International Jewish Territorial Organization. Zangwill's play, "The Melting Pot," extolled America as "God's Crucible, the great Melting Pot where all the races of Europe are melting and re-forming!" In the final scene the chief character exclaims:

> There she lies, the great Melting Pot . . . Celt and Latin, Slav and Teuton, Greek and Syrian, black and yellow . . . Yes, East and West, and North and South, the palm and the pine, the pole and the equator, the crescent and the cross—how the great Alchemist melts and fuses them with his purging flame! Here shall they all unite to build the Republic of Man and the Kingdom of God.[16]

The date of the play's first production (1908) was in the midst of the 1905–14 decade of maximum immigration to this country. It was the period of great influxes from southern and eastern Europe and of increase in the variety and size of ghettos in American cities. Some writers had already pointed out the dangers of continued large-scale immigration, others had defended it, and many rank and file Americans were vaguely uneasy and puzzled. The concept of America as a melting pot attained some popularity, especially among proponents of immigration, because it seemed to be an answer to the problem. But whatever may have been the initial popularity and influence of the melting-pot symbol, the outbreak of World War I interrupted large-scale immigration, and by the time the war was over effective sentiment was in favor of severe restrictions.

The philosophy underlying the melting-pot theory, however, carried over into problems of assimilation. These

[16] Israel Zangwill, *The Melting Pot* (New York: The Macmillan Company, 1923, revised edition), pp. 184–85.

did not terminate with the enactment of restrictions against immigration but are still with us and probably will remain with us, although in diminishing degree, for a long time to come.

Various students have emphasized the unfortunate influence of the melting-pot theory on programs of Americanization and public education, although they have not always agreed as to what that theory implied.[17] However varied the criticisms, there has been increasing doubt as to the efficacy of the old melting-pot hypothesis. From the outset the concept was at wide variance with our established policies and practices with reference to Negroes, Indians, and other colored groups. It was also at variance with the tendency for immigrants of given ethnic groups to cluster together and form cultural islands within our cities. In general, it did not square up with the ethnic diversity of our population.

Assimilation a slow process

Furthermore, as various writers have pointed out, the melting-pot hypothesis was based on false assumptions regarding the nature and rapidity of assimilation. The "purging flame" was generally interpreted to be somewhat analogous to the founder's blast which rapidly transformed the raw ore into finished steel. This assumption led to superficial programs of rapid Americanization or, as Fairchild put it, to attempts at "enforced patriotism." Through these devices it was hoped to transform immigrants themselves—not their children or future grandchildren —into Americans and in fairly short

[17] See, for example: H. P. Fairchild, *The Melting-Pot Mistake* (Boston: Little, Brown and Co., 1926), p. 154; and E. George Payne, "Education and Minority Peoples," a chapter in Francis J. Brown and Joseph S. Roucek, *One America* (New York: Prentice-Hall, Inc., 1946), p. 500.

order. We now know that assimilation is a slow process and that even under favorable circumstances several generations may be required for its completion.[18]

The newer concept of cultural pluralism, on the other hand, recognizes the ethnic diversity of our population and takes cognizance of the time element in processes of assimilation. It acknowledges the reality of the white-colored demarcations and of the variety of cultures associated with national origins of our foreign stock. As a philosophy, cultural pluralism denies the assumption that there is one American culture fixed once and for all by our colonial ancestors. It assumes that our culture is variegated and dynamic, and that all immigrant groups have contributed toward its enrichment.

It should not be inferred from the above that the adherents of cultural pluralism favor reinstatement of large-scale immigration to this country. Probably most of them do not. The philosophy of cultural pluralism as interpreted above, however, is believed by many to offer the basis for a more rational approach to problems of all minority groups in this country. Payne states that "through recognizing the fact of cultural pluralism we achieve cultural democracy" and emphasizes the de-

[18] Marshall's recent study of Welsh and Norwegian stocks in a rural community of Wisconsin led him to conclude that these groups had "successfully withstood the erosion of their heritage for nearly 75 years." Although he found that "consciousness of kind is not only corroded by time but by the inability of most groups 'to live unto themselves,'" he thought it fitting to close his paper "with a remark of the late George S. Wehrwein that 'it takes three generations of a family to own a piece of land and four generations to erase their more obvious old world characteristics.'" See Douglas G. Marshall, "Nationality and the Emerging Culture," *Rural Sociology*, Vol. 13 (March 1948), pp. 43, 47.

sirability "of preserving cultural traits, of dignifying qualities and practices different from our own, and of creating a feeling of pride in the folkways, mores, customs, conventions, and social patterns characteristic of the immigrant in his homeland as well as of the Negro and the Indian." [19]

[19] E. George Payne, *op. cit.* note 17 *supra*, p. 501.

Chapter V

INTERNAL DISTRIBUTION AND MIGRATION

The most striking fact about the distribution of population over any substantial portion of the earth's surface is its unevenness, its variation in density from place to place. Even in the absence of other factors, unevenness in population distribution would be produced by the lack of uniformity in climate, soil fertility, resource endowment, and the like, as well as by variation in the length of time that areas have been settled. While the development of efficient transportation networks may counteract some of the localizing force of an uneven distribution of resources, it also permits aggregation of population in urban areas. In industrial countries, by far the most important aspect of population distribution is the concentration of population in cities and towns. How industrial and non-industrial countries differ in respect of urbanization is described in the paper by Davis and Hertz. These differences have come about largely within the last few centuries. Their genesis is described by Eldridge in her account of the process of urbanization. Eldridge's observation that urbanization proceeds by "the multiplication of points of concentration and the increase in size of individual concentrations" is borne out by Stewart's equations describing the "fundamental structure of population" in the United States. Some of the social concomitants of population concentration are suggested by comparisons of cities of different sizes, as in Duncan's paper.

Changes in the pattern of population distribution in a country are produced by internal migration and by variations in the rate of natural increase. The latter factor alone, in a country marked by significant regional and rural-urban differentials in fertility, would produce a considerable change in the pattern of population distribution in the course of a generation. Internal migration often operates to offset changes in the pattern of population distribution arising from differences in fertility; thus cityward migration has offset the impact of high natural increase in rural areas. In terms of the net balance of natural increase and internal migration, units such as states or counties may be classified as areas of "depopulation," if net out-migration exceeds natural increase or if net in-migration is insufficient to compensate for a negative natural increase; as areas of "dispersion," if there is a net out-migration smaller in magnitude than the natural increase; or as areas of "absorption," if there is a net in-migration in addition to natural increase, or larger in magnitude than a negative natural increase. A representative analysis of factors in population redistribution is given in Shryock's paper.

A good deal of research on patterns of internal migration has served to confirm the general validity of several "laws of migration" set forth in two papers under that title by E. G. Ravenstein in 1885 and 1889: (1) The bulk of migration involves moves of only short distances. (2) A city absorbs population by drawing most heavily on its immediate hinterland, with the rate of migration declining progressively as distance from the city increases. Cityward migration can thus be viewed as proceeding step by step from the remote rural districts to large cities (this does not imply that all steps in the series are taken by the same migrants). (3) The pattern of movement out of cities is the inverse of the pattern of absorption. (4) Each main current of migration generates a weaker counter-current. (5) The destinations of long-distance migrants are typically large centers of commerce and industry. (6) In short-distance cityward movement females generally outnumber males. These rules account for the finding of many investigators that the "gross" migration, or the total of movements in and out of an area, is usually much larger than the "net" migration, or balance of the in- and out-movement. Ravenstein rationalized the first and second rules on the following grounds: "Suppose there exists a surplus of labour in one province and a deficiency in another, whilst the intervening provinces are able to find remunerative occupation for all their inhabitants. Will the labourer, in search of work, travel across these intervening provinces, in order to supply the deficiency? I say, no!" This "theory of intervening opportunities" was elaborated and formalized by Stouffer in 1940, and has been subjected to several tests, among them the one reported in Isbell's paper.

The sensitivity of internal migration to economic conditions can be inferred from the fact that urban population growth tends to be more rapid in prosperity than in depression. On the whole, the "pull" of urban employment opportunities is probably a more important cause of year-to-year variations in the rate of cityward migration than is the "push" of rural population pressure. However, the latter factor, population pressure, is shown in Hamilton's paper to be important in explaining area-to-area variation in the rate of rural-urban migration. The paper also sketches the method of estimating net migration which demographers are often forced to employ in the absence of statistics of population movements.

Many research studies have dealt with the question of whether migrants differ in significant ways from non-migrants with respect to social, psychological, or biological characteristics. Nonetheless, information concerning the selectivity of migration remains very incomplete. Dorothy Thomas' comprehensive review of the available evidence on migration differentials, published in 1938, concluded that only one relatively imprecise generalization could be considered securely established, i.e., that migrants are drawn disproportionately from the adolescent and young adult population. It is doubtful that the conclusion of such a review would be greatly different today, despite the accumulation of additional research. Thomas' paper in this volume summarizes some of the better studies of other differentials, and indicates certain reasons why there is a dearth of verified theory in this field. The paper by Lee reviews one of the best-known studies (Klineberg's) of intelligence differentials in migration, and reports a replication of that study. The paper brings out one point which is amply confirmed by other research: To demonstrate selection with respect to a characteristic that is susceptible to environmental modification, one must use a study design that distinguishes between selectivity as such and differences between the migrant and non-migrant populations appearing subsequent to migration. It seems unlikely that research will ever validate simple, highly generalized propositions about migration differentials. Rather, it is to be expected that the degree, and even the direction, of selectivity will vary with the circumstances of the migration, e.g., the stage of the business cycle at which it occurs, the type of community of origin and destination, and the distance spanned in the movement. Unfortunately, demographers ordinarily have not had the means of making extensive studies in which variations in such conditions could be treated comparatively.

THE WORLD DISTRIBUTION OF URBANIZATION

By Kingsley Davis and Hilda Hertz

With reference to the earth as a whole there are three fundamental facts to note about the distribution of urbanization. First, although the modern world is more urbanized than it has been in any previous time, it is still primarily a rural world. Second, the areas manifesting a high degree of urbanization are few in number and highly concentrated. Third, despite the predominantly rural character of the world as a whole and the limited scope of highly urbanized areas, urbanization has (like other traits of modern civilization) spread over the entire globe to some degree. The present chapter gives the evidence for these conclusions and discusses their meaning.

STILL A RURAL WORLD

That the world's population is as yet not a *city* population is shown by our finding, for dates centering around 1950, that the proportion living in cities of 100,000 or more is approximately 13 per cent. Indication that the world's population is not even an *urban* population is shown by the finding that the proportion in places of 20,000 or more is only 21 per cent; and in places of 5,000 or more, about 30 per cent. (See Table 1.) These figures may be inaccurate by varying margins[1], but they give a good enough indication of the small proportion of the world's population living in urban centers.

---

[1] Whenever statistics are given for the entire globe, they are composed in part of estimates. In some cases these are official estimates of the countries concerned; in other cases they are our own estimates. Naturally, our data are better for the larger than for the smaller cities and towns. Thus we are on safer ground when speaking of cities of 100,000 or more inhabitants, and it is for this reason that we frequently rely on this class as an index of urbanization.

TABLE 1

World's urban Places of various Sizes, 1950

urban places by size class	number	population (millions)	per cent of world population
5,000–plus	27,600	717	30
20,000–plus	5,500	502	21
100,000–plus	875	314	13
500,000–plus	133	158	7
1,000,000–plus	49	101	4

The fact that the world is still not an urbanized world agrees with our comparative material on the percentage of gainfully occupied males engaged in agriculture. It appears that 76 per cent of the people and 74 per cent of the area of the earth are found in what may be described as peasant-agricultural countries[2]. The close and significant connection between agriculturalism and urbanism is discussed at length below.

As Table 1 shows, there are only about 50 cities with more than a million inhabitants. These contain something like 100 million inhabitants, or roughly 4 per cent of the world's population, as compared to the 314 million, or 13 per cent, in all cities of 100,000 or more. The extreme concentration of these city people can be gathered by assuming that the average 100,000-plus city occupies an area of about 33 square miles (a figure somewhat below the average for the cities of the United States in that category)[3], which then yields a total of about 30,000 square miles, or 0.06 per cent of the world's habitable area. In other words, the average density in the cities is approximately 10,500 per square mile, which is more than 200 times the average density of the rest of the world's population, according to 1950 data.

THE UNEQUAL DISTRIBUTION OF POPULATION

If the urban population were equally distributed over the world in the same spatial pattern as the total world population, each region would manifest the percentages given in Table 1. But the actual situation is

---

[2] See Kingsley Davis, "Population and the Further Spread of Industrial Society," *Proceedings of the American Philosophical Society*, Vol. 95 (Feb. 1951), pp. 8-9.

[3] The average area of cities of 100,000-plus was computed on the basis of data concerning 301 cities of various sizes above this limit. These were stratified by size class and the average for each size class was weighted by its percentage of all cities in the world. The average area of cities 100,000-plus in the United States in 1940 was 50 square miles.

quite different. The urban population is highly concentrated in particular regions, and these are not always the regions having high concentrations of the general population. The disparity can be seen if we use a
rough continental breakdown of the world's land surface. As Table 2
shows, the major continental areas have highly disproportionate shares
of the urban population. The most urbanized of these areas is Oceania,
with 47 per cent of its population in places of more than 20,000, and 41
per cent in places of 100,000 and over (Table 3). Next is the American
continent north of the Rio Grande, with 42 and 29 per cent in the two
classes of cities. It so happens that both of these regions are sparsely
populated in comparative terms. The United States and Canada, with
only about 1/14 of the world's total population, have 1/7 of the world's
people in cities of 100,000 and over. Europe, with a fifth of the world's
population, has about a fourth of the number in cities of this size, whereas
Asia, with about half the world's population, has a third of the population
in cities of·100,000-plus.

TABLE 2

Share of City and Non-city Population in major World Areas, 1950

	total population		non-city population*		cities 20,000-plus		cities 100,000-plus	
	number in '000	per Cent	number in '000	per cent	number in '000	per cent	number in '000	per cent
World	2,402,354	100.0	1,900,160	100.0	502,194	100.0	313,711	100.0
Asia[1]	1,279,178	53.2	1,109,370	58.4	169,808	33.8	105,575	33.7
Europe[1]	393,499	16.4	255,554	13.4	137,945	27.5	83,066	26.5
N.America[2]	165,534	6.8	95,807	5.0	69,727	13.9	47,809	15.2
U.S.S.R.	193,000	8.1	132,784	7.0	60,216	12.0	35,126	11.2
S.America	111,105	4.6	81,717	4.3	29,388	5.8	20,520	6.5
Africa	197,171	8.2	178,568	9.4	18,603	3.7	10,223	3.2
M.America[3]	50,435	2.1	39,800	2.1	10,635	2.1	6,245	2.0
Oceania	12,432	.5	6,560	.4	5,872	1.2	5,147	1.6

* Not to be confused with "rural" population, this is simply the population living in places smaller
than 20,000.
[1] Without U.S.S.R.
[2] Includes U.S.A. and Canada.
[3] Includes countries of Central America and the islands of the Caribbean.

TABLE 3

Percentage City Population in major World Areas, 1950

	percent of cities 20,000-plus	population in cities 100,000-plus
World	21	13
Oceania	47	41
N. America[1]	42	29
Europe[2]	35	21
U.S.S.R.	31	18
S. America	26	18
M. America[3]	21	12
Asia[2]	13	8
Africa	9	5

[1] Includes U.S.A. and Canada.
[2] Without U.S.S.R.
[3] Includes countries of Central America and the islands of the Caribbean.

However, the continental distribution does not give the full story of the unequal dispersion of urbanization. For instance, Oceania appears to be heavily urbanized because of the predominance in the area of three extremely urbanized countries: Australia (51 per cent in 100,000-plus cities), New Zealand (36 per cent), and Hawaii (50 per cent). The rest of Oceania contains no cities above the 20,000 level. Similarly, Europe is not all equally urbanized. Northwestern and Central Europe have nearly twice the proportion (27 per cent) in 100,000-plus cities that southern and eastern Europe have (14 per cent).

It is plainly necessary to break down the continental figures into their component parts to get a better picture of what may be called the concentration of urban concentration. If we group the most urbanized countries into regions, we find that there are only four major regions of urban settlement in the world—Northwestern Europe, Australasia, U.S.A.-Canada, and Southern South America. Together, these four regions contain 21 per cent of the world's total population but 45 per cent of the world's population in cities of 100,000-plus. The ten most urban countries of the world contain 13 per cent of the world's people but 30 per cent of the inhabitants of large cities.

CONCENTRATION WITHIN COUNTRIES

Urbanization is more concentrated than even the global location of the various countries indicates, for it usually happens that within a given country some parts are much more heavily urbanized than other parts. In the United States, for example, the ten most urban states plus the District of Columbia had in 1940, according to the United States census definition of urban, 62 per cent of the country's urban population but only 47 per cent of the total population and 13 per cent of the area. Even in such an urbanized country as Germany, the regions show remarkable differences in degree of urbanization.   Omitting Hamburg and Bremen as purely urban subdivisions, we find that the political districts of the Western German Republic vary, according to the 1950 census, from 4 per cent to 40 per cent in cities 100,000 and over.   At one extreme Nordrhein-Westfalen, with 21 large cities, is ten times as urban by this index as Rheinland-Pfalz at the other extreme, with one large city[4].

Percentage in the Largest City.   One way of looking at the concentration of urbanization within a particular country is to take the percentage of the total population, or total urban population, in the largest city. Table 4 gives for a selected group of countries and regions the percentage

TABLE 4

Proportion of great City Population residing in largest City, ca. 1950

selected countries by region[1]	per cent in cities 100,000 and over[2] living in largest city
South America and Caribbean	71.2[3]
Uruguay	100.0
Chile	81.1
Cuba	73.5
Argentina	50.4
Australasia	53.7[3]
Hawaii	100.0
Malaya	65.1
New Zealand	44.0
Australia	38.1
Japan	25.3
Europe	49.8[3]
Ireland	100.0
Austria	74.7
Denmark	70.2
Sweden	57.8
Belgium	43.6
Switzerland	40.0
Spain	29.6
Netherlands	26.6
United Kingdom	17.5
North America	24.4[3]
Canada	31.1
U.S.A.	17.8

[1] Regional averages, both unweighted and weighted are for *all* highly urbanized countries of the region with cities 100,000-plus.

[2] 100.0 per cent in this column means that the country listed has one city only in the size category of 100,000 and over.

[3] These regional averages are unweighted.   Corresponding weighted averages obtained by dividing the total number in the largest cities of the highly urbanized countries of the region by the total number in all cities 100,000 and over in these countries are:

South America and Caribbean	61.9
Australasia	30.1
Europe	28.6
North America	18.7

[4] *Berliner Statistik*, Vol. 5, No. 4 (April 1951), p.95.

of the great city population living in the largest city. There is a marked variation. Those having more than 50 per cent in the largest city are extreme cases. In general, the countries of Latin America show distinctly higher concentrations than do their northern neighbours. However, a considerable number of European countries, such as Denmark, Austria, and Ireland, rank high in this respect. Presumably the concentration of a country's urban population in the principal city is proportionate to the number of functions combined in that city. Thus if the national *political* capital is also the centre of *commerce*, the centre of *industry* and the centre of *recreation*, it will have an extremely dominant position. Countries differ especially in the degree to which they combine the central political and economic functions in the same place. Frequently, the political capital is selected because of its equidistant geographical location (as in many states of the United States) rather than because of its economic importance.

Concentration Around the Largest City. Because, for lack of data, we are dealing with cities proper rather than with metropolitan districts, we find that there is a tendency for other large cities to be located *close to* the largest city. In Argentina, for instance, not only does one-third of the large-city population live in Buenos Aires, but also most of the rest of it lives near that city. Similarly, in Japan the bulk of the large-city population lives either in or near Tokyo, with an additional centre of concentration around Kyoto and. Osaka. In 1948 there were four prefectures—Tokyo with 84 per cent of its population in large cities, Konagawa with 61 per cent, Koyote with 58 per cent, and Osaka with 58 per cent which had 16 per cent of the total population of the country but 50 per cent of the large-city population. In short, not only does urbanization represent a concentration of many people in little space, but also is itself highly concentrated within a country or a region.

WHERE THE LARGE CITIES ARE

The distribution of the world's large cities is shown in Table 5. As expected from what has already been said, the majority of them are located in a few major regions and, within these regions, in a few countries. But the table does not tell us as much as our analysis has already told us, because the regional concentration of large cities is determined by two factors: (a) the share of the world's population contained in any given area and (b) the level of urbanization prevailing in the area. Thus Russia, which is only moderately urbanized, contains nevertheless, because of the additional fact of its sheer size, the second-highest number of large cities, exceeded in this respect only by the United States. In contrast, Oceania is the region with the fewest large cities (10 in all) despite the fact that its population, at least in three countries, is very highly urbanized,

Our analysis has tried to exclude the effect of sheer size but to include the effect of the second factor—the level of urbanization— in order to demonstrate to what extent the city population of the earth is not distributed in accordance with the general population.

TABLE 5

Location of the World's large Cities ca. 1900 and 1950

| region and country | number of cities with population of | | | |
| | 1 million-plus | | 100,000-plus | |
	1900	1950	1900	1950
World	10	49	272	875
Europe[1]	5	14	131	262
Asia	1	20	59	311
North America	3	6	39	116
U.S.S.R.	1	2	21	90
South America	—	3	10	37
Africa	—	1	5	32
Central America and Caribbean	—	1	3	17
Oceania	—	2	4	10

[1] European Turkey has been included in Europe.   U.S.S.R. is excluded.

WHY THE UNEQUAL DISTRIBUTION OF URBANIZATION

The causes of the disproportionate distribution of urban people are connected with the factors bringing about the great spurt of urbanization in modern times. It may simply be noted that the achievement of high levels of urbanization had to await the Industrial Revolution. This remarkable transformation had its rise in one part of the world, western Europe, and thence spread to other parts as industrialism spread. With the exception of Japan, the centres of urbanization today are the places where industrialization has gone hand in hand with the expansion of European civilization. In many instances, the spread of this kind of civilization has embraced "new" areas of vast extent and sparse native populations, such as North and South America and Australasia. In a sense, then, the urbanism of Europe was directly transplanted to these new areas, so that they became highly urbanized without acquiring overall dense populations. In other words, the new regions of European expansion overseas were not hampered by the necessity of a slow evolution from densely settled peasant-agriculturalism to modern industrialism. They brought their industrial proclivities with them and consequently built up rapidly an urban society without ever having built up a heavy average density. Thus we find that some of the most urbanized regions of the world are among the most sparsely settled, with a resulting disproportion between the distribution of the urban population and the distribution of the total population of the earth.

Having started the Industrial Revolution, and having become rather densely settled in the process, Europe itself still contains a large number of the world's large cities—about one-fourth of them. Within Europe those countries most intimately connected with the great transition and having the largest populations—Germany, the United Kingdom, Italy, and France—include about two-thirds of the large cities of the region (57, 71, 18, and 22 respectively). Some of the newer areas, though highly urbanized, do not contain many large cities because their populations are not large compared to that of Europe. Thus Oceania includes only 10 large cities, and America north of the Rio Grande only one-seventh of the total. Asia, outside of Japan and the U.S.S.R., has approximately 248 such cities, most of them located in the few large countries that have huge populations—India, Pakistan, and China[5]. Although the 248 cities for Asia, apart from Japan and the Soviet Union, represent almost one-fourth of the total number of large cities in the world, one has to remember that this part of Asia contains half of the world's total population. Peasant Asia is therefore the main area that is deprived of cities in relation to its population, just as the "new" regions of western civilization are the ones that have the greatest share of cities in relation to total numbers. Africa, the least urbanized of all the continents, is deprived of cities to an even greater extent than Asia. Most of the large cities are concentrated at the northern and southern end of the continent. For example, Egypt and the Union of South Africa, each with 7 large cities, together contain about half of all such cities on the continent. But Africa is sparsely settled. Her urbanization in relation to population may be expected to gain more rapidly than that of Asia.

THE URBAN MONOPOLY OF THE TEMPERATE ZONES

Most of the world's cities are located in the temperate zone. In fact, if we divide the world into tropical and temperate regions, we come out with the results shown in Table 6. The distortions of the usual Mercator projection of the world tend to hide from us the fact that the tropics contain a sizable portion of the earth's habitable area and total population. For some reason, however, the forces giving rise to urbanization there are not so strong as those encountered in the temperate regions. Of course, it is true that altitude as well as latitude affects climate, and that therefore some of the cities located within the tropical zone (such as La Paz, Bolivia) do not in fact have a tropical climate. But the truth is

---

[5] The number of cities 100,000 and over in China is a rough estimate. For a detailed discussion of urbanization in China, see *The Pattern of World Urbanization*.

that most of the world's large cities, for better or worse, are located at low altitudes—primarily because of the importance of water transport. Furthermore, there are some cities in the temperate zone which clearly have a tropical climate (e.g. Foochow, Benares, Baghdad, Cairo, and Miami). So, since the two types of error tend to cancel each other, the data of Table 6 should be roughly accurate with respect to the degree of urbanization in the two kinds of climate. And these data show that the temperate areas are, on the average, far more highly urbanized. Although to the inhabitants of the cooler climates there seems something almost incongruous in the idea of a giant city in the tropics (one thinks of steaming Manila or stifling Calcutta as somehow unnatural simply because they are unbearable), but there is no inherent reason why tropical regions cannot become heavily urbanized. Their backwardness in this respect is a function of their backwardness in other respects. The Industrial Revolution arose in the temperate zone and has been spread by people whose cultures were adapted to a cool climate. These peoples have found it easier to exploit tropical regions, to draw away their riches to cooler lands, than to settle in those regions and set up their industrial and urban civilization there. As a consequence, the distribution of large cities according to climate is but another illustration of the unequal dispersion of urbanization in the world.

TABLE 6

Climatic Distribution of World's 100,000-plus Cities ca. 1950

	total population		large cities		population in large cities	
	number (millions)	per cent	number	per cent	number (millions)	per cent
world	2,403	100	877	100	307	100
temperate[1]	1,577	66	713	81	273	89
tropical[1]	826	34	164	19	34	11

[1] Tropical refers to all those countries and their large cities that lie wholly or largely between the Tropic of Cancer and the Tropic of Capricorn. All other countries have been classed as Temperate.

THE WIDESPREAD DIFFUSION OF URBANIZATION

The emphasis just given to the disproportionate distribution of cities, or the customary tendency to view some parts of the globe as agricultural and others as industrial, should not lead us to the false conclusion that there are large regions without urbanization. On the contrary, *some* degree of urbanization is present virtually everywhere. Even when cities of 100,000 or more are used as the index of urbanization, the diffusion over the earth is quite wide. Not only is there no major continent without a city of this size, but also there is no major country without one. Albania, Iceland, Costa Rica, and Saudi Arabia are among the few independent countries without such cities. Although there are still some colonial territories with sizable populations which boast no city of 100,000 or more, it nevertheless can be safely said that all major areas of the world have at least a small proportion of their people living in large cities.

The diffusion of urbanization is even wider, of course, if we take as our measure of urbanization the proportion of the population living in cities and towns of 20,000-plus or 5,000-plus. On the 5,000-plus basis, only such areas as New Guinea and Papua, Muscat and Oman, Portuguese Timor and Portuguese Guiana show no evidence of urbanization.

The explanation of the world-wide, if unequal, diffusion of urbanization is seemingly the fact that industrialism has had an impact nearly everywhere. Though concentrated in certain centres, it has thrown out its influence through a network of commerce—commerce which brings to non-industrial areas the products of industry and exchanges them for the raw material necessary for industry. In many areas, the influence has of course gone much farther. It has extended to political control, to direct operation of primary industries, to control of railways, customs collection, public health, etc. Such extensive contact and control has led to the growth of cities in undeveloped areas—cities which, in a sense, are the foreign gateways to the resources of large rural regions. Thus Singapore, Calcutta, and Bombay; Tientsin, Shanghai, and Hong Kong; Algiers, Casablanca, and Brazzaville-Leopold-ville; Caracas, Trujillo and Kingston —these are the typical urban gateways to the regions of little urbanization. The urban mode of settlement has spread around the globe, albeit thinly in most regions.

NATIONS THAT LIVE IN CITIES

For convenience the 15 most urbanized countries have been placed together in Table 7, arranged according to the proportion of people living in places of 20,000 and over. They are all countries in which this proportion amounts to a third or more. According to the average relation prevailing between the populations in different size-classes of city, if a third of the people live in places of 20,000 and over, more than half of them live in places of 5,000 and over. We may therefore say that all of these countries have a majority of their people urban, This is especially true in view of the fact that, as the reader will recall, we are dealing with cities rather than with metropolitan areas[6].

[6] Most countries supply data only with reference to cities, although some of them come nearer to including all people aggregated in urban districts than do others. In the United States in 1950 the proportion of the population living in cities of 100,000 or more was 29.6 per cent; in standard metropolitan areas of 100,000 or more, 55.1 per cent.

TABLE 7

Proportion in Cities in the 15 most urbanized Countries of the World ca. 1950[1]

countries[2]	year	in cities 20,000 and over per cent	rank	in cities 100,000 and over per cent	rank
United Kingdom	1951	66.8	1	38.2	4
Australia	1947	56.7	2	51.4	1
Netherlands	1950	56.4	3	31.4	8
Hawaii	1950	55.5	4	49.1	2
New Zealand	1945	49.3	5	36.2	6
Argentina	1947	48.2	6	37.2	5
Israel[3]	1950	45.7	7	42.0	3
U.S.A.	1950	42.8	8	29.4	11
Belgium	1950	42.2	9	34.4	7
Germany	1950	41.7	10	27.1	12
Japan	1950	41.7	11	25.6	13
Chile	1950	40.0	12	25.3	15
Denmark	1945	37.7	13	25.6	14
Autstria	1951	36.7	14	29.7	10
Uruguay	1950	36.2	15	32.6	8

[1] The countries included are the 15 most urbanized countries both with respect to cities 20,000-plus and 100,000-plus.

[2] Iceland has been omitted from this list since it has no cities 100,000 and over.

[3] The figures refer to the present territory of the state of Israel, and do not include the remainder of the former mandated territory of Palestine.

It is noteworthy that all 15 of the countries in the list, with the sole exception of Japan, are European in culture. Six of them are in Europe, and three of them—Australia, New Zealand, and the United States—are off-shoots of British colonization. Some of the countries are densely settled—e.g. the United Kingdom with 538 per square mile, the Netherlands with 802, Belgium with 732, and Austria with 216. Others are sparsely settled—e.g. Australia with 3 per square mile, New Zealand with 19, Chile with 20, and the United States with 51. A high degree of urbanization therefore bears no particular relationship to average density.

Australia, one of the newest countries, ranks first with over half in places of 100,000 or more. Despite the importance of wool, wheat, and meat in its economy, it is truely a country where the population lives in cities. But the United Kingdom ranks highest in the percentage of its

people living in places of 20,000 or more. Such countries demonstrate
how urbanized a whole nation can become and show what is possible for
the rest of the world. At the same time they do not necessarily indicate
any limit on how urban certain countries may *ultimately* become.

The presence of Japan among the most urbanized countries of the world
is of interest for two reasons. *First*, Japan stands in marked contrast to
the rest of Asia, particularly to that part of Asia lying nearest to Japan.
Aside from Japan the Middle East is the most urbanized subregion of Asia.
It has, if we include Egypt, approximately 12.4 per cent of its people in
cities of 100,000 or more. In that area Israel is the most urbanized country—indeed the most urbanized country in all of Asia—having approximately 46 per cent of its population in large cities; but its total
population is so small (about 1,390,000 in 1951) that it does not have the
significance of the Japanese case. Also, it is culturally more European
than Oriental, despite the recently heavy Oriental immigration. Outside of the Middle East, Malaya and the Crown Colony of Singapore, if
they are taken together, form the most urbanized unit, with 17 per cent
of the population in large cities[7].

This figure is in marked contrast to Thailand with 6.7 per cent, Indo-china
with 5.2 per cent, Burma with 5.0 per cent, and Indonesia with 7.0 per cent.
Among such Asiatic countries, Japan stands in marked contrast. *Second*,
Japan raises the question of whether an Oriental country more highly
urbanized than most Western nations has any peculiarities in the pattern
of its urbanization. Do its cities differ in any essential respect from those
of the other industrialized nations? Here it is sufficient simply to note
Japan's outstanding position in the Far East.

Our list in Table 7, it will be noted, includes three Latin American
countries in the most highly urbanized category. Indeed, Argentina
holds fourth rank among the world's urbanized areas, resembling Australia in this and many other respects. The fact that Latin America is
ordinarily regarded as an agricultural region causes its degree of urbanization to come as something of a surprise. It should be noted, however,
that the most urbanized countries in Latin America are the three most
southern in South America, where the climate is that of the temperate
zone. Table 8 shows the various subregions of Latin America, where it
is seen that even with Brazil and Paraguay included, the so-called ABC
area has by far the highest average percentage in large cities. It should
be noted, however, that Panama, Cuba, and Puerto Rico all show considerable urbanization— the percentages in large cities being 15.3, 20.0,

---

[7] For an analysis of urbanization in Malaya, see Eunice Cooper, "Urbanization in
Malaya." *Population Studies*, Vol. 5, No. 2 (November 1951), pp. 117-131,

and 16.2 respectively. These particular countries are tied more closely
with the United States economy than are the others in Latin America[8].

It has been mentioned that six of the 15 most urbanized countries of the
world are located in Europe. This continent therefore still keeps its
primacy, but the six European countries in the list are located chiefly
in northwest and central Europe, as Table 9 shows. Like every other
continent, Europe has a highly uneven development with respect to urbanization. The fact is that the most urbanized countries of the world are
spread rather widely around the globe, despite certain areas of concentration.

TABLE 8

Urbanization in the Americas, by Region ca. 1950

region[1]	per cent in cities 100,000 and over
A.B.C. area	23.6
Argentina	37.2
Uruguay	32.6
Chile	25.3
Brazil	13.9
Paraguay	9.0
Western South America	12.7
Venezuela	16.6
Ecuador	15.5
Colombia	13.9
Peru	11.0
Bolivia	8.0
Middle America, incl. Mexico	8.2
Panama	15.3
Mexico	13.5
Nicaragua	10.2
Guatemala	10.2
El Salvador	8.6
Costa Rica	——
Honduras	——

[8] For a detailed discussion of urbanization in Latin America, see Kingsley Davis
and Ana Casis, *Urbanization in Latin America* (New York: Milbank Memorial
Fund, 1946).

TABLE 8—*Contd.*

Caribbean, Major Antilles	13.1
Cuba	20.0
Jamaica	16.3
Puerto Rico	16.2
Haiti	4.6
Dominican Republic	——
North America	26.3
U.S.A.	29.4
Canada	23.2

[1] All regional percentages are unweighted averages, obtained by adding the percentages of the component countries and dividing by the number of countries in the region. The corresponding weighted averages obtained by multiplying the percentage for each country by the population of that country and dividing the accumulated result by the total population of the region are:

A.B.C. Area	18.0
Western South America	13.0
Middle America	12.0
Caribbean, Major Antilles	13.9
North America	28.9

TABLE 9

Urbanization in Europe, by Regions, ca. 1950

regions[1]	per cent in cities[2] 100,000 and over
Northwest and Central Europe	26.6
United Kingdom and Ireland[3]	37.1
West Central Europe[4]	23.7
Northern Europe[5]	18.9
Southern and Eastern Europe	13.6
Southern Europe[6]	16.2
Eastern Europe[7]	11.0

[1] Iceland, Luxembourg, Channel Islands, Isle of Man, and Trieste have been omitted from this table.
[2] Weighted averages.
[3] Countries included: United Kingdom, Ireland.
[4] Countries included: Austria, Belgium, France, Germany, Netherlands, Switzerland, Czechoslovakia.
[5] Countries included: Denmark, Finland, Norway, Sweden.
[6] Countries included: Italy, Portugal, Spain.
[7] Countries included: Albania, Bulgaria, Greece, Hungary, Poland, Romania, Yugoslavia.

Highly versus Lightly Urbanized Countries

Since urbanization is a widely diffused phenomenon, since there are today no major societies without cities, urbanization can be treated as a gradient along which the world's countries and territories are aligned.

In an earlier section, in Table 2, the continental percentages of population in cities 100,000 and over were given. Table 10 organizes the data in terms of *countries*, rather than regions, as the units. This mode of handling the material makes the continental figures less meaningful, because the result depends in part upon the size and number of countries contained in the region. Thus 100 per cent of the population of America north of the Rio Grande lives in highly urbanized countries, simply because, if the demographically insignificant territories of Alaska and Greenland are ignored, this area contains only two countries, both of which are quite urban. In Oceania, about 85 per cent of the people live in highly urbanized countries—Australia, New Zealand, and Hawaii; and in Europe about 77 per cent do so. Table 10 shows once more that the highly urbanized countries contain a greater share of the world's territory than of the world's people.

TABLE 10

Proportion of Area and Population of heavily and lightly urbanized Countries, by Continents, 1950

region	highly urbanized countries			lightly urbanized countries		
	number	population (per Cent)	area (per cent)	nmber	population (per cent.)	area (per cent)
World	44	35	46	99	65	54
U.S.S.R.	1	100	100	—	—	—
North America	2	100	100	—	—	—
Oceania	3	85	94	4	15	6
Europe	18	77	69	9	23	31
South America	5	27	27	7	73	73
Africa	4	18	8	38	82	92
Central America & Caribbean	4	16	5	11	84	96
Asia	7	8	3	30	92	97

THE PROCESS OF URBANIZATION

By Hope Tisdale Eldridge

URBANIZATION is a process of population concentration. It proceeds in two ways: the multiplication of points of concentration and the increase in size of individual concentrations. It may occasionally or in some areas stop or actually recede, but the tendency is inherent in society for it to proceed until it is inhibited by adverse conditions. Whether or not a saturation point, an "urban maturity," followed by stabilization or subsidence of the process, can or will be reached is not known. There is some evidence that points toward such a development, but the contingent and derivative nature of urbanization makes this a difficult question to answer.

The restriction of the definition of urbanization to terms of population concentration may at first seem too limited, but an investigation of the possibilities of broader or different definition will show that this is the only one which does not lead to ambiguity and other forms of intellectual distress. Its concreteness and simplicity further recommend it; it gives us something definite to lay hold of. Logically and etymologically, it is unassailable. The societal point of view demands it, since it comprehends the totality of the process both in time and in space. It eliminates or throws into different categories other processes which, though associated with urbanization, may have opposing effects upon it. The concomitants of urbanization are not to be ignored; they are simply to be distinguished from it.

Consistent with the definition of urbanization, cities may be defined as points of concentration. There is no need at this juncture to fix lower limits to the size and density which qualify a concentration as a city. There is no clear-cut level of concentration at which a city suddenly springs into being. It is convenient from time to time arbitrarily to name certain levels beyond which concentrations are designated as cities. This is necessary in analyzing data and identifying characteristics of various size groups, but it does not alter the validity of the original concept.

In defending the strictness and simplicity of the definitions offered here, it is in order to examine some other definitions and explain why they have been rejected. There are two classes of definition which are deemed unacceptable. The first regards urbanization as a process of radiation whereby ideas and practices spread out from the urban center into surrounding areas. This is an objectionable definition because it makes the city the cause of urbanization rather than the result or the product of urbanization. It does not explain the appearance and growth of cities. It posits the pre-existence of cities. It says, "In the beginning, there were cities." Not that cities do not radiate powerful influences. Indeed they do. But calling this radiation urbanization introduces the element of ambiguity mentioned earlier in this discussion. If the process by which people congregate in cities (and surely it cannot be said that this is *not* urbanization) and the process by which influences go out from the city are both called urbanization, we have a hybrid definition, a definition on two levels, in two senses. It will be necessary always to specify the sense in which it is being used. To use it in both senses at once is to be abstruse. The two types of phenomena are related. They act upon each other. But unless we dissect them apart, we cannot understand the nature of their association.

The second class of definition is more objectionable than the first, and more peculiar. It defines urbanization as the increase in intensity of problems or traits or characteristics that are essentially urban. Again, we have the confusion of cause and effect, the pre-supposition of cities before urbanization, which gives the definition only a strictly contemporary application. The chief objection to it, however, lies in the necessity of admitting its corollary, that as problems are solved, as traits disappear, as characteristics change, deurbanization sets in. This cannot be true unless we are able to discover some problems, traits and characteristics which are so essentially urban that they never diminish or disappear as cities increase, only as they decrease. The one trait which can be demonstrated to have a complete and consistent positive association with urban growth is population concentration. If this is the only trait, it should itself be the definition.

In our time, we observe many urban traits. We must refuse to call their intensification urbanization until we are sure that the growth of cities cannot proceed without their intensification, and also that the traits cannot intensify without a concomitant urban increase.

There is a third class of definition which is partially acceptable. It is the implied definition. Perhaps the best way to understand what is meant by a word is to study how it is used rather than to accept a formal definition. This does not belittle the importance of scientific definition, which is the chief object of the present discussion, but rather emphasizes the importance of making the definition consistent with the use of a word. Some writers do not attempt to define urbanization; they merely use the term with a meaning made obvious by its context. Occasionally, it is defined one way and used another. This is a serious blunder.

In most cases, the implied meaning of urbanization is the one we have chosen, the concentration of population. This is the only meaning it should be given. No wonder at the miracles of modern technology, no bewilderment with the complexity of modern urban life, no impotence before the stubbornness of modern social problems should be allowed to obscure this fact. Any definition of urbanization which calls for a transcendence of cities is a definition of something else, because urbanization must culminate in the city if it is to be the process which makes the city.

Just as long as cities grow in size or multiply in number, urbanization is taking place. It can stop, recede or go on at any point in time or space. There can be urbanization at one time and not at another. There can be urbanization in one area and not in another. There can be rapid urbanization and slow urbanization; there can be de-urbanization. There can be urbanization before there are cities and after there have been cities. Furthermore, there can be absence of urbanization even though there are many cities. As soon as population concentration stops, urbanization stops. How far urbanization can go, we are unable to say, because we do not know what limits of concentration society may be able to tolerate.

Urbanization is a process of becoming. It implies a movement, not necessarily direct or steady or continuous, from a state of non-urbanism toward a state of complete urbanism, or rather from a state of less concentration toward a state of more concentration. It is put in motion by events or conditions which make concentration both possible and desirable. These events are not to be confused with the process itself. The discovery and utilization of electricity, for example, constitute a series of events which have served to stimulate urbanization, but they are not to be identified with urbanization because urbanization is not their sole effect; they also de-urbanize.

For much the same reasons that the definition of urbanization must be restricted, that of cities must also be restricted. Cities have been defined as ways of life, states of mind, collections of traits, types of occupation and the like. Such definitions are bound to get us in trouble sooner or later because none of the attributes named are constants of the city and all of them spill over into other areas. Traits change, occupations change, political organization changes, the economic system changes. The only trait that is constant is that the city is different from what is not the city. The nature of this difference varies. If we say that the city is a collection of traits, we cut ourselves loose from the only solid base on which we can set up definite criteria and neck-deep in a sea of difficulties connected with the isolation of urban traits. It means that whatever we find more of in the city is an urban trait. But what is the city? Why, it is a collection of urban traits. How do we identify these traits? By their high intensity in the city. But what is the city? A collection of traits. And so forth. The only way to break this deadlock is to go back to population concentration. The criterion must be in terms of population. Then we can study traits, relationships, and characteristics to our heart's content.

Of course there are many things about these concentrations which are different. Of course there are ways of behaving, physical aspects, kinds of organization, types of activity which develop in and by virtue of the city. Some are different because they are in the city; some are in the city because they are different. Some are in society, if not in the city, because the city is in society. We call them civilization. Civilization is a pattern, or a groups of patterns, in the matrix of social change which is a concomitant of urbanization but which transcends the city. It is the culture of an urban or citified society. It is not one kind of thing, like urbanization, but many kinds of things, and it has to be studied in parts. There are civilizations, but only one urbanization. With the exercise of a little imagination, we can pick out from the matrix of social change the basic pattern of urbanization and relate it to other patterns.

In a sense, everything that affects population movement affects urbanization one way or the other. Most events of any significance are complex enough to have a bifurcated effect upon it. Because of the intricate interdependence and the almost infinite ramifications of consequences of everything that does happen in a society, we are brought to the conclusion that it is the total effect of social change in all of a society upon population distrbution that determines the course of urbanization. This is one reason why it is so important to lay hold of something definite like population and work backward, forward, and outward from it.

Social change is a name we can give to all the processes by which social organization continually adapts to new conditions, new problems, and new ideas. If we can place a finger upon the mainspring of human action, we shall have it also upon the source of social change. What is the dynamic force which launches man on countless enterprises, scatters him over the earth, and makes society forever different though always the same? It is man's urge to live on, his tireless quest of fulfilled desire. Survival? Yes, but survival on a dozen planes; survival on earth, survival in heaven, survival in his children, survival in the minds of other men, survival in his own conscience, survival in every way that he was born demanding or has learned to value. We need no more than this to account for the immense diversity of human behavior and the persistence of social change.

We posit that social change has existed as long as social life has existed. This may well be as long as man has existed in any significant numbers. Human beings show a disposition to live together. Whether this "consciousness of kind," as Giddings called it, is an inherited urge or an accident of association or a result of necessity does not matter a great deal. The biological peculiarities of human birth and infancy would be enough to establish habits of togetherness, regardless of whether the chromosomes carry genes for such behavior or not. If human beings had not stuck together to some extent, there probably would be none of them now. The fact that they stuck together as much as they did is one reason for there being so many of them now.

This being together in scattered and wandering groups, this original differential density, might be called urbanization of a sort. Certainly, it carried the germ of urbanization. But urbanization is togetherness of a progressive nature, that is, an increasing concentration. Insofar as these groups were increasing in size, as some of them must have done, urbanization was taking place, even though there were as yet no cities in any acceptable sense of the word, not even any villages.

Somewhere along the line, groups began to take up more or less permanent abode. We infer this from the observation that man now pretty generally lives in permanent dwellings. We can guess at the way it happened. A localized means of sustenance was necessary to a permanent abode. Agriculture was the answer. Agriculture developed, not through the operation of some external force inexorably set upon such a course, but because somebody thought of it, or several or many somebodies. Maybe it was thought of because people did not want to wander any more and were casting about for ways and means of settling down. Possibly, someone just stumbled on the idea and then people stopped wandering because they did not like to leave the crops. Perhaps groups were getting too big to wander conveniently and they did not want to separate because they were safer and happier together. All of these things may have happened. However the idea was born, agriculture filled some sort of felt need or it would never have been adopted. Historically, agriculture did not always appear in conjunction with permanent habitation, but except where it did, urbanization would have been stalemated at a relatively low level.

With habitation fixed and agriculture developing, urbanization was moving along. Now that they no longer wandered, groups could grow larger without becoming unwieldly. Concentration tolerance was increased. Death rates may well have decreased at this time. Probably other groups, still wandering, came upon the settled groups, liked the idea, and themselves settled there or elsewhere, if they were not killed off by a militant village population. Thus we see that agriculture, which is now the chief occupation of non-urban dwellers, was one of the earliest steps in the long process of urbanization that could one day make a New York. No doubt, hunting, fishing, and the domestication of animals also played their part in urbanization, but they could not have tied the people to the land so effectively as agriculture did.

But agriculture was to play a further role in the process. The next step that had to be made in order for urbanization to proceed was the releasing of some of the population from the necessity of working on the land. It had to be possible for a part of the population to produce enough to feed all the population. Just how this came about is a matter of conjecture. It probably came about in many ways. But some method or methods of food production and preservation, some technological devices, which allowed one person to produce as much as had been produced before by more than one person, must have been discovered. And from that time to this, it has been improvement in agricultural methods and the increase in per capita agricultural productivity that have created a surplus of population which could leave the land and follow other pursuits. Reduce agriculture to the subsistence level today and our cities will be gone tomorrow.

This freeing of part of the population from the land in no direct way forced the appearance of cities. It merely furnished the personnel which made cities a possibility. In order for cities to appear, there had to be both motivation and means for their development. These were provided by a combination of predisposing conditions. Among them were the survival complex already described, the patent advantages of mutual aid and cooperative enterprise, the safety of concentration, geography, and the general improbability that man would think up only those projects which he could carry out single-handed or in small groups. Consequently, productive activity which required people's living in compact groups began to grow and the groups with it, in the same unplanned expediential manner as characterized agricultural development. When conditions prompted, urbanization proceeded and cities eventually emerged and grew. Not everywhere or all at once, but gradually as need and ideas arose. Each stage of urbanization was pregnant with the possibility of further urbanization, though it did not always and everywhere come to fruition.

Probably there has never been such perfect coordination between people and technics that the expansion of nonagricultural activity and attendant urbanization neatly took up the slack produced by agricultural improvements. Perhaps there never will be. The difficulties of planned

social change are enormous. It has been the tendency, however. One point that should be clear by now is that cities are not creatures of spontaneous generation with a life of their own, but gradual accumulations in the grand concourse of a society, made possible by population surpluses, replenished and nurtured by the society as a whole, and as long as they last, an integral part of that society.

At the beginning of this discussion, it was stated that urbanization is inherent in society. This raises the question of inevitability. There are two ways to look at inevitability. One is to regard it as the inescapable approach of the predestined march of fate. The other is to see it as the simple outgrowth of what has gone before. If we accept the latter, we may say that urbanization was inevitable, inevitable in the limited sense that it was quite natural, inevitable in the way that a man will put on his coat when the wind blows cold.

When you compress the whole of human history into a few pages, as we have just done, history looks much simpler than it was, even though we are dealing with but a single aspect of it. The process of urbanization looks much smoother from where we sit than it was. Actually, for hundreds of thousands of years it had its ups and downs, its advances and retreats. There were interferences like the ice age and other cataclysms of nature, pillage and conquest by predatory peoples, epidemics and scourges, droughts and crop failures, and thousands of things that we know nothing about. Occasionally, there were concatenations of circumstances such that a certain amount of isolation and a certain amount of intergroup contact conspired to produce a local urbanism of impressive proportions. There were Egypt and Greece and Rome, the Mayan urbanization in America, the Chinese urbanization in Asia, and a number of others. Some of them were swallowed up in waves of social change; some of them were only heavily drained.

In our time, urbanization has been so rapid that we can see it happening, but there were other times when it moved so slowly that the trend would have been imperceptible. Now, it occurs on an almost world-wide scale. In the past, it was sporadic and localized. In this country, we have a laboratory in which we can trace the process rather closely from a very early stage, at least so far as this one area and this civilization are concerned.

Two conditions appear to be necessary for urbanization. One is people and the other is technology. Population increase and surplus feed the process; technology gives it form and focus. All three of them, population increase, technology and urbanization, work along together. A population does not necessarily reach a certain density before it begins to urbanize. Technology does not have to wait on population. The whole thing is a spiral arrangement whereby technology produces population surplus and encourages population increase, population surplus and increase encourage further technology, and the upshot is urbanization.

As to population increase, the tendency to multiply up to the limit of the food supply is probably just as characteristic of human beings as of any order of organic life. But Malthusian law could operate freely only under conditions of status quo. Man often circumvents it by exercising his ingenuity to increase the population tolerance of the area he inhabits. Not that this idea is uppermost in his mind. His immediate objective is to achieve life, satisfaction, and security for himself and those in whom he is interested. He naturally seeks the easiest and most effective way to do this. He never consciously takes the hard way. The result is technology. Population increase is bound to give some impulse to this kind of enterprise, but it is not the sole incentive. Technology can develop to some extent without it. It so happens that the net effect of technology has been to permit the increase of both total and concentrated populations, but its specific application is usually in terms of immediate and individual wants and problems, and it often acts to decrease populations. At this very moment, an application of technology is doing a competent job of decreasing populations, both total and concentrated.

Urbanization is so closely bound up with technology that we can say without qualification that technology is the sine qua non of urbanization. The reverse is not true. Technology is not the exclusive property of the city; it operates in every province and pocket of society. It was technology that released potential urban dwellers from the land. Although urbanization could not proceed without it, technology may prove to be the means of deurbanizing our own civilization. This has happened before. If technology has been the

means for population concentration, it has also been the means of population spread, through exploration, trade, and commerce. Commerce, by the way, is a technological complex with unusually bifid urbanizational potentialities. It appears absolutely essential to a high degree of urbanization, but it involves at the same time a dispersal of population which goes beyond anything that unconcentrated society ever dreamed of. It is by the grace of technological achievement that Europeans people the Americas, that Britishers live in India, and that Africans are at home in the Southeast.

Technology is our name for the ways that man has discovered and invented of doing things which he wanted to do but could not do with any already known methods. This includes both the doing of things which had never been done before and the doing of old things by quicker and more effective methods. In these matters, man does not act as a group; society does not function as a unit. The total effect of the execution of a technological idea is not anticipated and provided for. Consequently, many difficulties and contradictions arise. Each technological innovation solves certain problems but creates others. Many of these problems have to do with population distribution.

The close interrelation between urbanization and technology is perhaps one reason why the definition of urbanization has not been clearer. The double-edged effect of technology upon society whereby it both disperses and compacts, both facilitates and frustrates, both preserves life and destroys it, has given rise to every conceivable emotional state and all manner of confusion. The identification of cities with technology has confounded the issue by directing the intensity of every passion from love to loathing upon them both.

But cities are both good and bad, no matter what moral criterion we choose to apply. It is not justifiable even to say they are more one than the other. By the same token, technology is not one instrument in the hands of a clumsy society, but many instruments in the hands of many groups and individuals, which they are using rather cleverly on the whole, looking at it from their viewpoints. It remains to be seen whether our society will acquire a consciousness of common interest and become organized in such a way that the groups who now find themselves technologically disadvantaged will be allowed to participate more fully in what are considered to be the benefits of technology.

To recapitulate, urbanization is a process of population concentration. It comes about through the utilization of technological devices, the result if not the object of which, is to increase the population tolerance of the areas in which they operate. Population increase is an incentive to technological advance and urbanization, but it is not the sole incentive. Both can develop somewhat independently of it, given the indefinite expansibility and diversity of man's desires and his capacity for exercising ingenuity in achieving them. The products of the concentrative process, cities, give to society a cultural character which we call civilization. Different people and different technologies produce different civilizations, but urbanization is one and the same throughout though it varies in rate and scope from time to time and from place to place.

The problem of the urban sociologist is to measure and study the process and its products and attempt to determine as specifically as possible the relationships which obtain between it and other elements in the general flow of social change.

EMPIRICAL MATHEMATICAL RULES

CONCERNING THE DISTRIBUTION AND

EQUILIBRIUM OF POPULATION

By John Q. Stewart

T HERE was a time when scholars did not realize that number had the principal role in the description of the phenomena of physics. The transition from medieval to modern science. was made in celestial mechanics, in three stages. These can be concisely represented by Tycho Brahe's extensive observations of planetary motions, Kepler's faith in mathematics as a means of insight into phenomena, and Newton's progress from Kepler's empirical rules for the solar system to the mechanics of the entire universe.

We are now seeing a similar development in the social studies. Astonishing amounts of significant numerical data have been accumulated by· conscientious social statisticians. Publications of the Bureau of the Census, for example, are comparable in extent and variety with catalogues of stars or tables of spectroscopic wave lengths, even if the numerical precision necessarily is much less. Thus the observational stage is well advanced. A few investigators whose training is not confined to the social fields are beginning to proceed with the condensation of the voluminous sociological data into concise mathematical rules. The final rational interpretation of such empirical rules cannot come until after the rules themselves are established.

The way of progress is obstructed by the opinion, common among authorities on economics, politics, and sociology, that human relationships never will be described in mathematical terms. There may be some truth in this as regards the doings of individual persons. Even the physicist has given up the idea that the behavior of individual particles can be precisely described thus and necessarily contents himself with discussions of averages. But the time to emphasize individual deviations is after the general averages have been established, not before.

Demography, the study of populations, offers an especially favorable field for the study of averages of social behavior. This paper presents four empirical rules relating to populations and their mutual influences. Two of these have been stated by the writer previously, the third has been published by others; new supporting evidence and development of these three are given, and a fourth rule is presented for the first time.

The Rank-Size Rule for Cities

Professor George Kingsley Zipf of Harvard University described with much emphasis in a book published half a dozen years ago[1] the rank-size rule for cities. The original statement was by Auerbach,[2] but Zipf gave it far more attention. The rule applies to certain groups of cities and is

$$R^n S_R = M. \tag{1}$$

Here M and n are constants for the given group, S_R stands for the number of people who live in the Rth city in the group, and R is the rank in the group of that city. The rank is a city's order number in a list that runs consecutively from the largest city in the given group to the smallest one. Thus for cities of the United States in 1940 we have the following ranks, R: New York, 1; Chicago, 2; Philadelphia, 3; .....; Utica, 92; .....; Sharon, Pa., 401; and so on. There were 3464 cities and towns greater in size than 2500; smaller villages are classed by the United States census as "rural."

The rank so defined is necessarily a positive integer. When R is 1, equation 1, whatever the value of n, requires that S is then M; hence the constant M is equal to the size of the largest city in the group. However, since the rule holds only to a statistical approximation and is not rigorous, a better average fit in practice may be obtained by an adjustment of M to a value that is not exactly equal to the size of the largest city. The value of 8,660,000 in 1940 fitted the average run of United States city sizes better than New York's actual size of 7,454,995.

Throughout this paper we must guard, on the one hand, against giving the impression that any one of the empirical rules presented is at all exact and, on the other, against suggesting that the approximations are so rough as to be without profound interest and meaning. If we divide 8,660,000 by 401, the population indicated for Sharon, Pa., comes out 21,600, as compared with its actual 25,622. As another illustration, the population of Indianapolis was 386,972, which, divided into 8,660,000, would correspond to a rank of 22, whereas the actual rank of Indianapolis in 1940 was 20.

If there are C cities of sizes not less than a certain lower limit, S_C—the size of the city of rank C being S_C—equation 1 requires:

$$C^n S_C = M = S_1, \tag{2}$$

---

[1] G. K. Zipf: National Unity and Disunity, Bloomington, Ind., 1941.

[2] Felix Auerbach: Das Gesetz der Bevölkerungskonzentration, *Petermanns Mitt.*, Vol. 59, 1913, pp. 74–76. See also A. J. Lotka: Elements of Physical Biology, Baltimore, 1924, pp. 306–307; the same: The Law of Urban Concentration, *Science*, Vol. 94 (N.S.), 1941, p. 164.

the size of the largest city being S_1 or M. In 1940 there were 3464 cities larger than 2500 population; the product of 3464 x 2500 is the 8,660,000 already mentioned as the adjusted value of M in 1940.

It is obvious that, when we assign a numerical value to any S, a difficulty which will often arise is that the usual census figure is for the "political" city, whose people live within the somewhat arbitrary "city limits."[3] The "physical" city, a single urban concentration that presumably functions as a single whole, may be considerably larger than the political city. This is not a fundamental difficulty, but one of refinement merely; it is worth special study, which can be postponed.

If an arbitrary group of cities is selected—for example, the largest city in one state, the second largest in another, and so on—equation 1 will not be found to hold. It does not hold for the cities of Great Britain, unless they are considered with all other European cities. But it is a fact that when all the cities in the United States larger than 2500 (or than some lower limit greater than 2500) are examined in any one of the 16 censuses 1790–1940, equation 1 holds approximately, and always with n equal to 1, or nearly 1. For each census, M, as expressed in equation 2 with $n = 1$, is found to approximate the size of New York City at that census.[4] Since the number of cities above 2500 increased from 24 in 1790 to 3464 in 1940, this is a very large range of agreement. It at once establishes the rank-size rule as an important empirical relation, with the presumption that it is the result of major underlying demographic tendencies.

Readers whose training has been verbal rather than mathematical may be impatient to be told at once what the underlying reasons are for the rank-size rule and what applications it has to immediately practical problems. These are reasonable inquiries, but their answers can only come in due course, and such readers will be blind to the lessons of physical science if they lose patience and interest when it is confessed that full answers cannot yet be provided.

The total population of a number of cities of consecutive ranks has a formula easily derived from the rank-size rule. The value of n in (1) may be between 0 and 1, 1, or more than 1. Since by definition the largest city has rank 1, it is clear that n must not be negative. Three excellent approximations to the exact sum can be written for these three cases.

Let P_u stand for the total population of the largest R cities. Evidently,

---

[3] J. K. Wright: Certain Changes in Population Distribution in the United States, *Geogr. Rev.*, Vol. 31, 1941, pp. 488–490.

[4] As tabulated in Sixteenth Census of the United States, 1940: Population, Vol. 1, Number of Inhabitants, Table 12 (pp. 32–33), which totals the people who lived in what now are the five boroughs.

since the city of rank 1 is expected to have size M, that of rank 2 has the size $M/2^n$, that of rank 3, $M/3^n$, and so on, if the rank-size rule holds. Hence

$$P_u = M (1 + 1/2^n + 1/3^n + \dots + 1/R^n). \tag{3}$$

For a given value of n, the series in the parentheses can always be summed by direct computation; but when R is in the hundreds or thousands, that is extremely laborious. When R is not too small, direct summation is unnecessary, because the following approximate formulas can be established:

When n is between 0 and 1:

$$P_u = M \left(\frac{R^{1-n}}{1-n} + \frac{1}{2R^n} + K_n \right). \tag{4}$$

When n is 1:

$$P_u = M \left(\log_e R + \frac{1}{2R} + K_1 \right). \tag{5}$$

When n exceeds 1:

$$P_u = M \left(\frac{1}{2R^n} - \frac{1}{(n-1)R^{n-1}} + K_n \right). \tag{6}$$

In each case K_n is a special constant: its value depends only on n and not on R. The term $1/2R^n$ becomes unimportant as R increases. The series in the parentheses of (3) has received much study from mathematicians. Equations 4, 5, and 6 are simplifications of an exact formula, which has the form of an infinite series in descending terms of R.[5]

In order to use these equations for total urban populations, it is necessary to have the proper numerical values of K_n. These are tabulated in Table I, for a practical range of values of n.

We see that P_u, the sum of the populations of the R largest cities, is determined as a function of the size, S_R, of the Rth city, provided n is known. Note that when n exceeds 1, P_u approaches a finite limit, namely MK_n, as R gets larger and larger. When n is 1 or less, P_u grows without limit as R increases—provided the rank-size rule holds all the way.

The best determination from census data of M and n for a particular group of cities is made by the well-known statistical method of "least squares." This is time-consuming, and for the purposes of the present survey adequate solutions have been obtained by trial and error, or by graphing. When logarithms are taken, (1) becomes

$$\log S_R = \log M - n \log R.$$

Consequently, when values of S_R are plotted to a logarithmic scale as ordinates, against corresponding values of R as abscissas, for an actual group

---

[5] See J. W. L. Glaisher: The Constants That Occur in Certain Summations by Bernoulli's Series, *Proc. London Math. Soc.*, Vol. 4, 1871, pp. 48–56.

of cities approximately obeying the rank-size rule, the plotted points scatter somewhat but nevertheless define *a straight line* that slopes downward from left to right. Its negative slope is *n,* and its intersection with the axis of S when R is 1 fixes log M.

TABLE I—VALUES OF K_n (EQUATIONS 4, 5, 6)

n	K_n	n	K_n	n	K_n
0.1	−0.60	1/4	−0.81	10/9	+9.58
0.2	−0.73	1/3	−0.97	9/8	+8.59
0.3	−0.90	1/2	−1.46	8/7	+7.59
0.4	−1.14	2/3	−2.45	7/6	+6.59
0.5	−1.46	5/7	−2.95	6/5	+5.59
0.6	−1.96	3/4	−3.45	5/4	+4.60
0.7	−2.78	10/13	−3.78	4/3	+3.60
0.8	−4.44	4/5	−4.44	3/2	+2.61
0.9	−9.42	5/6	−5.44	7/4	+1.96
1.0	+0.58	6/7	−6.43	2	+1.64

NOTE.—Values not listed by Glaisher (*loc. cit.*) were computed by applying the Euler-Maclaurin formula (cf. E. T. Whittaker and G. Robinson: The Calculus of Observations, London 1924, p. 138). The variation of K_n with n, except near $n = 1$, is regular and smooth, and can be interpolated graphically between the above values. For $n = 3$, $K_n = +1.20$.

Tables II and III present observational confirmation of the applicability of the rank-size rule and its corollaries for cities of the United States over a period of many censuses, and for the 601 cities of the world that in the 1930's were listed as larger than 100,000. The respective values of *n* are 1 and 10/13, but least-square solutions would show some tolerance in each estimate.

United States census data are not complete for the villages. These, unless incorporated, are lumped indistinguishably with their farm neighbors in each minor civil division. Therefore it is not possible to give the lower limit of size, above which the rank-size rule holds. If it held down to individual persons, the rank of the "final community" of one person always would be M; compare equation 2. If we ignore the difficulty of having communities comprised of whole people plus a fractional person, equation 5 would require that the population of all the M communities—i. e. the total population of the United States—should be

$$P_T = M (\log_e M + 0.58). \tag{7}$$

In each census before 1930 substitution of the observed value of M gives too small a value of the total population—much too small in earlier days. Therefore equation 7 is inapplicable. This matter has been discussed by Zipf, in his second chapter, in a speculative way.

When in (7) the value $S_C C$ is substituted for M, and S_C is taken as 2500

TABLE II—THE INVARIANT POPULATION PATTERN OF THE UNITED STATES

C = number of cities of sizes > 2500

U = urban fraction = PU/PT

PU = urban population, which the census reports as the sum of the populations of the cities

PT = total population

M = population of largest city = $2500\ C$

PR = rural population (towns < 2500 and country districts)

Census	C	f(C)	Computed values					Observed values				
			U	log M	log PU	log PR	log PT	U	log M	log PU	log PR	log PT
1790	24	3.76	4.8	4.78	5.35	6.65	6.67	5.1	4.69	5.36	6.57	6.59
1800	33	4.07	5.6	4.92	5.53	6.75	6.78	6.1	4.90	5.51	6.70	6.72
1810	46	4.41	6.6	5.06	5.71	6.85	6.88	7.3	5.08	5.72	6.83	6.86
1820	61	4.69	7.6	5.18	5.85	6.95	6.97	7.2	5.18	5.84	6.95	6.98
1830	90	5.08	9.3	5.35	6.06	7.05	7.09	8.8	5.38	6.05	7.07	7.11
1840	131	5.45	11.2	5.52	6.25	7.15	7.20	10.8	5.59	6.27	7.18	7.23
1850	236	6.04	15.0	5.77	6.55	7.31	7.38	15.3	5.85	6.55	7.29	7.37
1860	392	6.55	19.4	5.99	6.81	7.43	7.52	19.8	6.07	6.79	7.40	7.50
1870	663	7.07	25.2	6.22	7.07	7.54	7.67	25.7	6.17	7.00	7.46	7.59
1880	939	7.42	30.0	6.37	7.24	7.61	7.77	28.2	6.28	7.15	7.56	7.70
1890	1348	7.78	35.9	6.53	7.42	7.67	7.86	35.1	6.40	7.34	7.61	7.80
1900	1737	8.04	40.8	6.64	7.54	7.71	7.93	39.7	6.54	7.48	7.66	7.88
1910	2262	8.30	46.5	6.75	7.67	7.73	8.01	45.7	6.68	7.62	7.70	7.96
1920	2732	8.49	51.1	6.84	7.76	7.75	8.06	51.2	6.75	7.73	7.71	8.03
1930	3165	8.65	55.0	6.90	7.84	7.75	8.10	56.2	6.84	7.84	7.73	8.09
1940	3464	8.73	57.6	6.94	7.88	7.75	8.12	56.5	6.87	7.87	7.76	8.12

TABLE IIIA—LEADING CITIES OF THE WORLD

Rank R	Size S	log M	Rank R	Size S	log M
1	8,655,000	....	52	790,398	7.218
2	7,154,300	7.168	66	662,000	7.221
3	5,875,667	7.136	83	570,622	7.233
4	4,251,000	7.091	104	489,488	7.241
5	3,641,500	7.099	130	386,900	7.213
7	3,489,998	7.193	163	310,118	7.193
10	2,739,800	7.207	204	261,226	7.193
12	1,972,700	7.125	257	211,000	7.177
15	1,666,100	7.126	323	173,573	7.167
18	1,354,100	7.097	406	140,500	7.155
22	1,257,890	7.131	510	116,687	7.228
27	1,148,129	7.160	601	100,000	7.137
34	1,029,700	7.189			
42	910,154	7.207		Average	7.172

NOTE.—A card index of all 601 cities was prepared, each card being marked with the size and corresponding rank of a city. In this illustrative table examples are chosen at random scattered over the whole range of ranks. In the third column values of log M are computed from the assumed formula $M = R^{0.769} S$. These of course scatter somewhat about their average, 7.172—which corresponds to $M = 14,860,000$. London is not nearly big enough to fill rank 1. (The size of New York is from the same compilation as the others and is less than in the 1940 census.)

TABLE IIIb—THE WORLD'S LARGEST CITIES

Rank R	City	Computed size S	Actual size
1	London	14,900,000	8,655,000
2	New York	8,710,000	7,154,300
3	Tokyo	6,380,000	5,875,667
4	Berlin	5,120,000	4,251,000
5	Moscow	4,310,000	3,641,500
6	Chicago	3,750,000	3,397,700
7	Shanghai	3,330,000	3,490,000
8	Osaka	3,010,000	2,990,000
9	Paris	2,740,000	2,830,000
10	Leningrad	2,530,000	2,740,000
48	St. Louis	747,000	830,000
125	Kansas City, Mo.	339,600	412,600
473	Trenton, N.J.	130,000	124,000

NOTE.—From the formula $S = M/R^{0.769}$, with $M = 14,860,000$, values of S are computed for the first ten ranks and certain others. London does not fit the formula. But for New York to move into rank 1 would require an increase of 75% not only in its size but in the size of other American cities, since these are subject also to their own rank-size rule with exponent 1. The sum of the computed populations of the nine cities of ranks 2–10 inclusive is 39,880,000. This compares well with the sum from equation 4, with $n = 0.769$, and $K_n = -3.78$; namely 39,800,000.

(the rural limit), we obtain, if we write P_U for the population of the cities—the total urban population—

$$P_T = P_U + M \log_e 2500.$$

This equation, also, does not apply; the observed relation between urban, rural, and total populations is given in (9) and (10) below.

Applicability of the rank-size rule is not confined to city sizes. With $n = 1/2$ it is Pareto's rule for the size of incomes.[6] Condon found that the rule, with $n = 1$, described the frequency of occurrence of words in written English,[7] and Zipf has found that the rule has further applicability to other word counts.[8] Yule's objection[9] to it has no immediate relevance. Lotka[10] found that the rule, with $n = 2$, described the distribution of scientific papers among different authors.

In physics, the Boltzmann distribution of energies among the molecules of a gas in thermodynamic equilibrium offers a general analogy, but only a general one. It seems that the rank-size rule is one which occurs, or at any rate is closely approximated, in a different type of equilibrium among competing elements, which has not yet been recognized in physics, though it occurs in the above-mentioned widely different sociological cases.

A consideration of what factors produce the hypothetical equilibrium will be aided by a comparison of demographic and social conditions that are expressed in different values of the exponent n. Censuses of Japan 1920–1935 indicate a country in transition, because n increased from about 2/3 to 1 for *shi* above 20,000. This contrasts with the stability of n over 150 years in the United States. Sufficient census data are available also for India 1891–1941. The rank-size rule there for cities above 5000 population has $n = 5/7$ approximately, during this entire period.

The author is not familiar with any study which relates the rank-size rule or the potential of population to existing studies dealing with the location of cities[11] and with the degree of concentration of communities.[12]

---

[6] Zipf, *op. cit.*, Chap. 5.

[7] E. U. Condon: Statistics of Vocabulary, *Science*, Vol. 67 (N.S.), 1928, p. 300.

[8] See list of references in G. K. Zipf: The Repetition of Words: Time, Perspective, and Semantic Balance, *Journ. of General Psychology*, Vol. 32, 1945, pp. 127–148.

[9] G. U. Yule: The Statistical Study of Literary Vocabulary, Cambridge, England, 1944, p. 55.

[10] A. J. Lotka: The Frequency Distribution of Scientific Productivity, *Journ. Washington Acad. of Sci.*, Vol. 16, 1926, pp. 317–323. This paper includes additional interesting references.

[11] See, for example, Edward Ullman: A Theory of Location for Cities, *Amer. Journ. of Sociology*, Vol. 46, 1940–1941, pp. 853–864, which discusses Walter Christaller's factor of centrality. See also E. M. Hoover, Jr.: Location Theory and the Shoe and Leather Industries, Harvard Univ. Press, 1937; Chaps. 1–6; the same: The Location of Economic Activity (In preparation).

[12] References to the work of Albert Demangeon and others are included in the note "The Geography of Rural Settlements," *Geogr. Rev.*, Vol. 24, 1934, pp. 502–504.

The Relation of the Number of United States Cities
and the Urban Fraction

We pass now to a hitherto unpublished empirical relation, which is well established only for one special case. At present writing this new rule is far from having the variety of observational significance that the rank-size rule possesses. As has been said, the United States Bureau of the Census defines a village as "rural" when it has fewer than 2500 people; and of course

TABLE IV—RELATION OF URBAN FRACTION TO NUMBER OF CITIES, UNITED STATES

Year	Number of Cities C	Urban fraction U Observed	Computed	$\log \dfrac{C}{10450U^2}$
1790	24	0.051	0.048	−0.055
1800	33	.061	.056	− .070
1810	46	.073	.066	− .082
1820	61	.072	.076	+ .050
1830	90	.088	.093	+ .045
1840	131	.108	.112	+ .032
1850	236	.153	.150	− .016
1860	392	.198	.194	− .020
1870	663	.257	.252	− .017
1880	939	.282	.300	+ .054
1890	1348	.351	.359	+ .017
1900	1737	.397	.408	+ .023
1910	2262	.457	.465	+ .034
1920	2732	.512	.511	+ .005
1930	3165	.562	.550	− .019
1940	3464	.565	.576	+ .017

NOTE.—Values of U usually are stated in percentages: thus 0.051 corresponds to 5.1 %, etc. The last column shows the close agreement of the formula (10) with the facts. The statistical "probable error" in the logarithm (base 10) is ±0.0277, corresponding to a factor of 1.066.

dwellers in the open country are classed as rural. People who live in all larger towns are "urban." This distinction is made in each of the 16 censuses. As everyone knows, the proportion of city dwellers has been consistently increasing in the United States. The number of cities above 2500, which we shall call C, likewise has increased considerably.

The urban fraction, U, is defined as the fraction of the total population, P_T, that lives in cities above 2500. Thus

$$P_U = UP_T, \tag{8}$$

P_U being the total urban population of the C cities. Letting P_R stand for the rural population, we have

$$P_R = P_T - P_U. \tag{9}$$

Table IV shows that the relations

$$C = 10450\ U^2, \tag{10}$$

$$U = 0.009782\sqrt{C}, \tag{11}$$

hold very well, from census to census, 1790–1940.

If the rank-size rule represents an equilibrium among competing cities, this relation of U to C must mean that there is also an equilibrium between the competing attractions of rural and urban life.

Values of U are also available for India, but the range of change in the

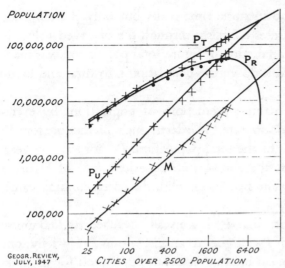

POPULATION

100,000,000

10,000,000

1,000,000

100,000

25   100   400   1600   6400
CITIES OVER 2500 POPULATION

FIG. 1—Structure of the population of the United States (See Table II). Observed values at the 16 censuses are indicated by the crosses and dots; curves or straight lines show the values computed from the observed number of cities, C, of size larger than 2500, as base variable, by equations 12. Up to $C = 10,450$ the extrapolated curves likewise follow these equations. Any one of five quantities — total population, P_T, urban population, P_U, rural population, P_R, population of largest city, M, and number of cities, C, — could be taken as the *single independent variable*. Additional computed curves, and compatible observations, could be given for selected groups of cities; for example, the number and summed populations of those between sizes 10,000 and 25,000.

available censuses is too small to establish equally well relations corresponding to (10) and (11). The evidence is that the exponent of U in the relation corresponding to (10) for India is reduced perhaps to 12/7.

THE FUNDAMENTAL STRUCTURE OF UNITED STATES POPULATION

Figure 1 shows how well the simple equations we have developed describe the rural-urban distribution in every United States census. It graphs data of Table II, with extrapolations to the future. The continuous curves represent computed values of the various components of populations; the x's, crosses, or circles represent the actual populations, census by census. The number, C, of cities larger than 2500 is taken as the base variable. In terms of it the following quantities are computed: S_1 or M, the size of the largest city (New York, people living in the present five boroughs); P_U, the total urban population of the C cities; P_T, the total United States population; and P_R, the rural population.

The applicable equations are brought together here for clarity (cf. equations 2, 5, 11, 8, 9). We take $n = 1$, for the United States, and $S_C = 2500$:

$$\left.\begin{aligned}
M &= S_C\,C; \\
P_U &= S_C\,C\left(\log_e C + \frac{1}{2C} + 0.577\right); \\
U &= 0.009782\sqrt{C}; \\
P_T &= P_U/U; \\
P_R &= P_T - P_U.
\end{aligned}\right\} \tag{12}$$

Note that Figure 1 has no intrinsic time scale, but only the empirical time scale that successive censuses establish, through the observed values of C from decade to decade. A prediction of future total population was made by Pearl,[13] but he did not break down the population into rural and urban components.

Demographers are now making predictions of populations by extrapolating the birth rate and death rate. The latest such prediction for the United States[14] gave estimates of the total population, P_T, for various years until 2000. If we assume that the equilibrium equations (12) of Figure 1 will continue to hold, these values of P_T establish the corresponding values of C, M, P_U, P_R.

Since the equations indicate that P_R has already reached its maximum value, the expected increase in P_T all goes to an increase in P_U. Briefly, one can say that the outlook is for an increase in urban population for the next 20 or 25 years at the rate of 1 per cent a year of the present urban population. The same prediction applies to every United States city, large or small, that holds its present rank among our cities. Of course, some will make relative gains, others will lose rank.

Figure 1 in itself does not mean that the population will increase rather than decrease. However, if P_T ever becomes 260,000,000, the indication is that the rural population will have disappeared—except, doubtless, for a stubborn remnant that has not yet made its resistance evident in the data. If that time ever comes, all the people will be living in 10,400 cities greater than 2500, and the largest city (still New York?) will have a population of 26,000,000.

If populations should still go on increasing after that highly problematical time, an extrapolation of the above treatment suggests that the larger cities

---

[13] Raymond Pearl: Introduction to Medical Biometry and Statistics, 3rd edit., Philadelphia, 1940, Chap. 18.

[14] U. S. Bureau of the Census, Population—Special Reports, Ser. P-46, No. 7, September 15, 1946.

would then begin to eat up the smaller ones, and that finally everyone would live in a single great H. G. Wells city. Its population when that epoch begins works out as 6¼ billions—but these extreme extrapolations had better be regarded as just a little fun with arithmetic.[15]

THE POTENTIAL OF POPULATION

The evident tendency of people to congregate in larger and larger cities represents an attraction of people for people that turns out to have a mathematical as well as a merely verbal resemblance to Newton's law of gravitation. Lagrange in 1773 found that where the attraction of several planets at once was under consideration, a new mathematical coefficient, not used by Newton, simplified the calculations. This coefficient amounted to a measure of the gravitational influence of a planet of mass m at a distance d, and it was as simple as possible, merely m/d.

Later mathematical physicists, Laplace and Poisson, further elaborated the m/d concept in celestial mechanics. Not until 1828 did Green find that similar measures existed of the influence of an electric charge, e, and of a magnet pole, p, at a distance d; namely e/d and p/d respectively. To these quantities the name "potentials" was given—the gravitational potential, the electrostatic potential, the magnetic potential.

In 1939 evidence was uncovered which suggested that the influence of people at a distance could be expressed by a similar coefficient, namely N/d —N being the number of people, and d their distance away.[16] For this coefficient the name "potential of population" was at once suggested, because of the physical analogies.

As examples of "influence" reference may be made to:[17] (1) the drawing power of a college or school on given communities or states (enrollment in seasoned, privately endowed, "national" institutions tends to be proportionate to the population of a state divided by its distance from the campus); (2) attendance at the New York World's Fair in 1940 by states (proportionate to the population of a state divided by its distance from Flushing, Long

---

[15] The last time the author used in print the expression "fun with arithmetic" was in connection with extravagant illustrations of the enormous size of the constitutional energy of matter—illustrations that have been widely reproduced since August 6, 1945, in popular explanations of nuclear fission (The Search for the Source of Stellar Energy, *Journ. Franklin Inst.*, Vol. 204, 1927, p. 464).

[16] I. Q. Stewart: The Gravity of the Princeton Family, *Princeton Alumni Weekly*, Vol. 40, 1940. pp. 409–410; *idem:* An Inverse Distance Variation for Certain Social Influences, *Science*, Vol. 93 (N.S.), 1941, pp. 89–90; *idem:* A Measure of the Influence of Population at a Distance, *Sociometry*, Vol. 5, 1942, pp. 63–71.

[17] Cf. J. Q. Stewart: Coasts, Waves, and Weather for Navigators, Boston, New York, etc., 1945. Chap. 11.

Island); (3) circulation of the *St. Louis Star-Times* by counties (copies sold varied according to county population divided by distance from the city).

In each of these three cases the population-divided-by-distance rule held only to a certain boundary. The colleges and schools examined included Princeton, Yale, Harvard, Massachusetts Institute of Technology, Vassar, Stanford, Exeter, and Lawrenceville—all of them seasoned, privately endowed, "national" institutions. For all the eastern ones there was a systematic tendency for enrollment to include two or three times more students from the Rocky Mountain States and, particularly, from the West Coast States, than the formula indicated. The same tendency applied to attendance at the World's Fair. But Princeton undergraduates included roughly 10 times fewer Canadians and 25 times fewer Mexicans than the formula required. As regards the circulation of the St. Louis newspaper, it was found to be confined to a territory in adjoining states that was rather sharply limited by the Kansas City, Chicago, and Memphis competitions.

Again, the World's Fair "pulled" so strongly at a distance of hundreds of miles that extrapolation close at hand in accordance with the inverse-distance rule was obviously absurd. Likewise, the *Star-Times* sold so many copies at a moderate distance that extrapolation of the rule into the city of St. Louis itself led to the impossible requirement that everyone there ought to have bought several copies apiece. Any college draws at any distance so few students per 100,000 of the population that a similar "saturation" effect does not occur close to the campus. Also, college competition, unlike that of most newspapers, is not of the "all or none" type: Yale draws students who live within a mile of Nassau Hall.

Dr. Kingsley Davis, in a recent discussion,[18] made the interesting and logical general suggestion that the "demographic influence" of population N at a distance d is always N/d, but that its realization in various types of "social influence" is subject to special considerations in individual cases.

Further examples of such "social influences" related to potential of population have been furnished by Professor Zipf. These include such surprising agreements as the expectation of the occurrence of obituaries from specified cities in the *New York Times* and of news items in inside pages of the *Chicago Tribune;*[19] also the number of bus passengers between specified cities; the number of telegrams and of telephone messages interchanged; the number of railroad tickets sold.[20]

---

[18] Kingsley Davis: The Development of the City in Society, First Conference on Long Term Social Trends, Auspices of Social Science Research Council, March 22, 1947.

[19] G. K. Zipf, *Amer. Journ. of Psychol.*, Vol. 59, 1946, pp. 401–421.

[20] Zipf, *Amer. Journ. of Psychol.*, loc. cit.; idem, *Journ. of Psychology*, Vol. 22, 1946, pp. 3–8; etc.

"Energy of Interchange"

In the physical analogies, the potential is the energy in the field (gravitational, electrical, or magnetic) of a unit mass (or charge or pole). The energy of any given mass at a point is the potential at that point multiplied by the said mass. Likewise, we may consider that the "demographic energy" or "interchange" between a population N_1 and a second population N_2 at distance d is N_1 times N_2/d. This demographic energy is the same whether it is computed at the first or the second population, since N_1/d times N_2 equals N_1 times N_2/d.

The data for college undergraduates, when we come to consider them in this way, appear as one example of such "interchange," proportionate to N_1N_2/d, because doubling the size of the student body (without eclectic selection) would be expected ultimately to double the number of students from each state.

It may be asserted with confidence that N_1N_2/d, like potential, is a very important demographic quantity. The evolution of our civilization has been in the direction of increasing it.

Maps of Potential of Population

Density of population is a familiar demographic index—so familiar that we forget its wholly *physical* nature. In order to determine the potential at any point in the United States produced by all the people, it is necessary to start with what amounts to a rather complete survey of the population densities. However, if a very detailed, or "fine-grained," map of potentials is not required, it is enough to have the populations of individual states or larger districts.

On a density map each person—or, more usually, a given number of persons—may be represented by a dot.[21] Such a map shows where people live, but does not show how strongly their influence extends from that place.

Instead of representing a person by a dot, think of each as surrounded by a great sand pile.[22] Suppose that the sand is piled in a ring with a one-mile radius about the individual's residence to some arbitrary height, such as a foot. Then suppose that wider rings are piled, the height decreasing pro-

---

[21] See, for example, the Sixteenth Census of the United States, 1940: Population, Vol. 1, p. 2. For a series of density maps of the United States 1790–1930 see C. O. Paullin: Atlas of the Historical Geography of the United States, edited by J. K. Wright, Carnegie Institution of Washington and American Geographical Society, *Carnegie Instn. Publ. No. 401*, 1932, Plates 76–79.

[22] This description of the "sand-pile citizen" is adapted from Stewart, Coasts, Waves, and Weather, *loc. cit.*

portionally as the radius increases, so that in the two-mile ring the sand is 0.5 foot high and in the 1000-mile ring it is only 0.001 foot high. Then the height of his hypothetical sand pile anywhere in the country symbolizes the person's "demographic influence" there, on the basis of the assumed inverse-distance rule.

Suppose that there is a similarly constructed sand pile around the place of residence of every individual in the country. Then suppose that all this sand is superposed. At any point the total height of the sand will be the sum of all the heights of the sand piles of the individuals at that point. Let a contour map be made of the elevations of the resultant terrain.

Where the influence of people sums up to large values, we have "highlands" and "peaks" of influence. Such points are nearer to more people, and all kinds of sociological activities are expected to be at a high level there. Where few people are near, there are "lowlands" of influence—areas that appeal to hermits.

Every city is a separate peak. Each city peak rises from the general level that holds throughout the rural districts around that particular city. The rural districts immediately surrounding New York City are already at the highest level of all the nonurban regions in the country, and from this high platform the "New York peak" rises to the maximum.

The reader will understand that we are speaking only in general terms and that the computed demographic potential is not always effective as a visible sociological factor. Thus the Ramapo Mountains in New Jersey are only 30 miles from New York City, but the "New York Walk Book"[23] says of conditions there: "Most of the farms of the early settlers have reverted to forest, and of these several occur along the Cannonball Road. None of the houses are left, but apple trees remain to mark their place."

Evidently the summed-up value, at any point in the country, of all the individual sand piles is the total potential of population at that point. The physiographic contour map just described is exactly equivalent to a map of potential of population. Along each contour the potential is constant.

Thus we see that a potential map results when a density map is smoothed in accordance with the inverse-distance formula. The original density map cannot be reconstructed from the potential map. Each type of map has its special advantage and use; the two are supplementary, not mutually exclusive. Each concept is a *physical* one.

Figures 3 to 15 present a number of geographical maps, all of which

---

[23] R. H. Torrey, Frank Place, Jr., and R. L. Dickinson: New York Walk Book, *Amer. Geogr. Soc Outing Ser. No. 2,* 1923, pocket edit., p. 90.

except the one of Europe (Fig. 4) were computed by the writer and his students.[24]

THE CONSTRUCTION OF POTENTIAL MAPS

The general procedure in constructing contours of equipotentials of population may be clarified by consideration of a special case (Fig. 2), in

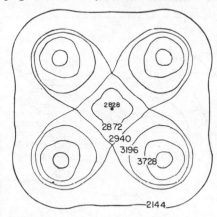

FIG. 2—Equipotentials surrounding four equal charges at the corners of a square. The four equal charges (populations, masses, magnetic poles), if actually concentrated at points would give rise to infinite potentials at these points; but this never happens: each charge always is diffused over a finite space, however small. At a distance (outside the diagram) the equipotentials are nearly circular. The "mountain" rises, with four ridges and four ravines, to the level 2940. Above that it breaks into four peaks, each rising above 3728. A central crater falls to a level of 2828. These values of potential are each proportional to the sum of the four reciprocals of respective distances to the four corners.

which we have a very simple situation on the original density map, namely four equal concentrations. The contours of Figure 2 were constructed as follows: The symmetry of the situation reduces the problem to one of drawing the contours for a single quarter—indeed, for half of this. A number of points over the general area of one octant were selected. For each point the four distances were measured to the four corners of the square and tabulated in four columns. Since the four concentrations were supposed to be equal, summation of the four reciprocals of the distances gave the total potential at each point. (Of course, a constant multiplying factor could have been applied, the same at every point, to allow for any assumed size of the equal concentrations of population at the four corners of the square.)

After such potentials had been determined by measurement and computation for a number of different selected points, the equipotentials shown in the diagram were sketched within the octant by interpolation. In a situation such as this, labor is saved by the shrewd selection of which contours should be drawn first, because often there are certain contours that serve as general controls. Then over the entire area of the square the contours were sketched by symmetry.

In actual demographical cases the population is spread out over wide areas, and it is always necessary to begin with an approximation. The whole

---

[24] See the reference in Stewart, Coasts, Waves, and Weather, loc. cit.

area is divided into a number of districts. On the map of the United States
(Fig. 3) 24 such districts were selected, larger in area in the thinly peopled
West than in the densely settled East. Each district comprised one full state
or more, so that the population could conveniently be taken from census
data. The population of each district was arbitrarily supposed to be concentrated at some chosen point within it. Distances in miles were measured

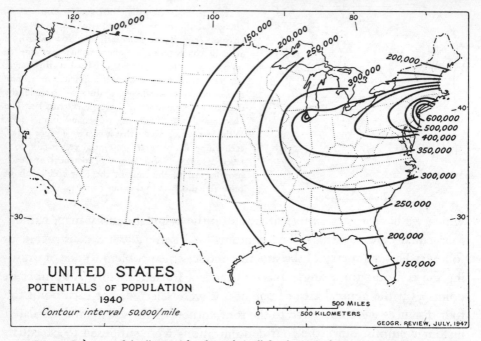

Fig. 3—Contours of the "potentials of population" for the United States, 1940. The potential is a
measure of the propinquity of people. Each individual contributes to the total potential at any place an
amount equal to the reciprocal of his distance away; contours therefore are in units of "persons per mile."
Potential as a sociological influence exerts an effect measurable in many ways. For example, along any
one of these contours of equipotential, the density of rural population tends to a constant value, observed
to be proportional to the square of the potential. The reader is warned again that none of the maps are
precise; in particular the actual contours near large cities differ in that every city presents a separate peak
of potential.

on a United States map between the 24 x 23/2, or 276, pairs of districts.
Each distance was recorded in its appropriate box in a square diagram having
24 rows and 24 columns. The population of each district was recorded at
the head of its column. Also, the name of each district was written alongside
one particular row. Down every column the population of the corresponding
district was divided by the distance between it and the district represented
by each row. The resultant quotient was entered in its appropriate box,
corresponding to row and column, and was the potential produced by one
district (column) at the other (row). When these partial potentials were

summed along a row, the result was the potential at the district (corresponding to the row) that was produced by all the other districts.

To this had to be added the potential of the district "on itself." If there are many districts, each is small enough to make this contribution to the total potential relatively minor, so that precision in its computation is not very important.

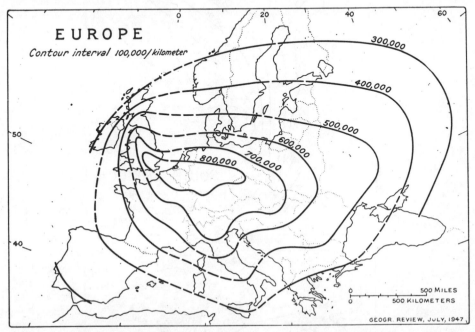

FIG. 4—Potentials of population for Europe in the 1930's. This map is the finest-grained yet computed, with 93 control points, as compared with only 24 for the United States. Consequently relatively minor inflections in the contours are presented with reasonable accuracy. The kilometer is the unit of distance: potentials are in persons per kilometer and must be multiplied by 1.609 to give persons per mile. (Dudley Kirk and Population Research Office.)

The potential of a district on itself can be approximated by one of a number of expedients. Under no circumstances in actual practice is it excessively large. For example, the potential at the center of a disk having uniform density of population can be computed (by integral calculus) as the population divided by half the radius.

Even the potential of a person "on himself" is finite. If we take, for purposes of illustration, a man's average distance from himself as one foot or 1/5000 mile, the potential comes out 5000 persons per mile. This is far less than any potential represented in Figure 3 for the United States. Since potential of population is population divided by distance, it is always expressed in units of people per mile or per kilometer, or in millions of persons

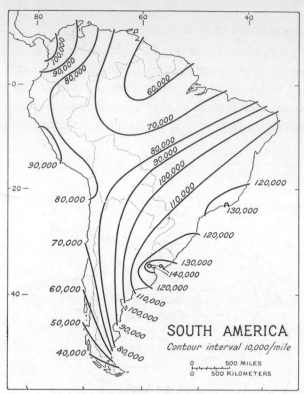

SOUTH AMERICA

Contour interval 10,000/mile

0   500 MILES
0   500 KILOMETERS

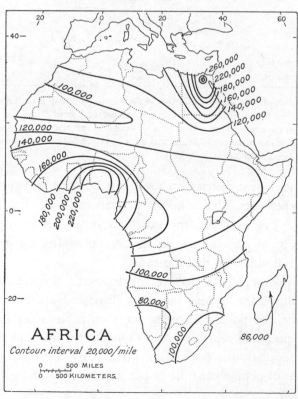

AFRICA

Contour interval 20,000/mile

0   500 MILES
0   500 KILOMETERS

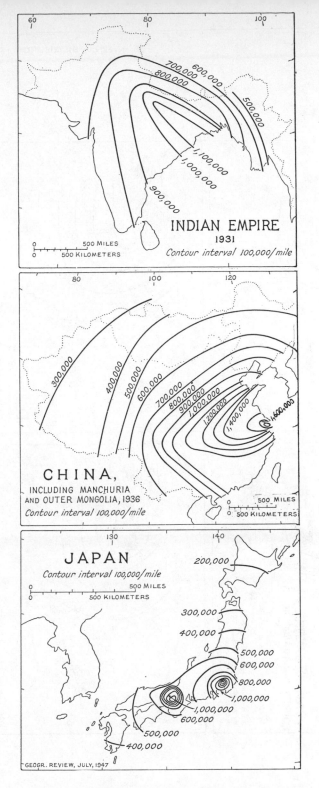

FIGS. 5–9—Population potentials for South America, Africa, India, China, and Japan. Potentials are in persons per mile. The map of India is only a rough approximation. The major peaks of potential in every continent are at salt-water metropolises. The demographic   influence of great river valleys is clearly evident except in the case of the Amazon.

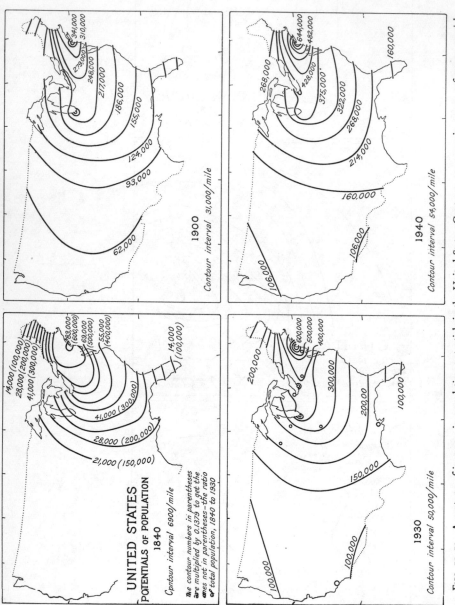

FIGS. 10–13—A century of increases in population potentials in the United States. Contours on successive maps refer to potentials (of persons per mile) which have been selected in proportion to the nation's total population—which increased by a factor of about 7 from 1840 to 1940. If this increase had been uniform in every state and county, successive maps would be identical. Actually contours which in 1840 extended west of Chicago have moved farther west, while those east of Chicago have tended to cluster closer to New York.

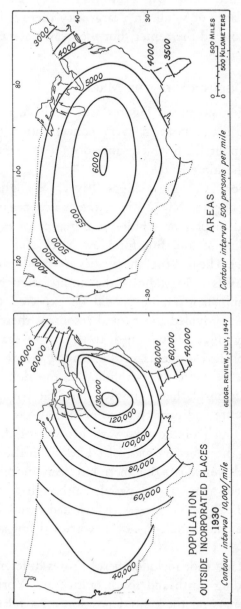

Fig. 14—Potentials for population outside of incorporated places in the United States, 1930. The peak potential is not far from Cincinnati and Louisville.

Fig. 15—Potentials for uniform population density in the United States. If one person lived in each square mile of land area, the total population would be 2,977,128, and the peak potential, about 6000 persons per mile, would be in Kansas. Compare with Figure 3; so much for the illusion that Kansas is the demographical center of the country.

per mile, etc. Density of population is expressed in persons per unit area—square mile or square kilometer.

If a potential map is computed by means of a large number of small districts, such a "fine-grained" map will show that every city constitutes a local peak of potential, large or small. In a large city there is heavy concentration of population toward the center, but the peak potentials do not exceed 2 or 3 millions per mile.

DISCUSSION OF THE MAPS

The maps of population potential, Figures 3 to 9, have two striking features in common. The major peak in every concentration (except for Nigeria) is a seaport metropolis, from which runs a dominant axis or "ridge," descending gradually in the hinterland.

In some cases, namely Calcutta–Ganges River, Shanghai–Yangtze River, Cairo–Nile River, Nigeria–Niger River, the major peaks and their ridges might be explained in part or wholly as a matter of easy internal communication and fertility of soil. But for New York and London the explanation is not so simple. The fact that these cities are the dominant peaks of their great human massifs must indicate the nonisolation of the two continents. An isolated human grouping would be expected to have its major peak near its center, provided the natural resources there permitted it—and certainly not away off at one side, next to the empty sea.

Figures 10 to 13 show developments in the United States since 1840. Even in 1840 New York was already established as the dominant peak, though the axis west of Pittsburgh then ran down the Ohio River. That was the effect of good agriculture and easy river communications.

School children hear much of the westward growth of this country. The growth is evident in the contours west of Chicago: in this little series of maps they have moved westward. But there has been another development, which has involved many more people, although less area—the growing prominence of the New York peak, which had barely been established in 1840. This represents, in effect, not a westward but an eastward migration!

A potential map for 1790 (not included here) shows different contours —long semiellipses extending north and south, with New York City not yet the major peak but enjoying the central position on a relatively high principal "plateau" that extended perhaps from Richmond, Va., to Salem, Mass.[25] It may have been even then a blunder in demography to establish

---

[25] Computations by C. R. Rourke and J. W. Thompson, Princeton undergraduates.

Washington, D. C., instead of New York, as the federal capital. The Ohio River axis of 1840 was, of course, not yet evident; instead there was the line of Cumberland Gap toward Kentucky.

In physics the rate of change of potential with distance in any direction measures the "field intensity" in that direction. The field intensity is the number of people divided by the square of their distance away; it is a directed, or "vector," quantity, while potential is a "scalar" quantity without direction. "Lines of force" define the field and always run at right angles to the contours of equipotential. The sharpening of the New York peak, which presumably is still going on, is one indication that in this respect also the physical analogue carries into demography. Populations tend to shift slowly along the lines of force toward the peaks of potential. Japan's double peak has endured in defiance of this tendency, because the mountains that intervene keep the Tokyo-Yokohama and Kyoto-Osaka concentrations separated, notwithstanding their mutual attraction.

Major routes of communication, such as river valleys, show up on density maps as thickly settled ribbons and therefore of necessity are evident on the potential maps as lines of force, at right angles to the contours of equipotential.[26]

Figures 14 and 15 are additional potential maps. Figure 14 is for one class only of the population, people living outside incorporated places in 1930. The old Ohio River axis is still dominant in this agricultural picture. The peak is far from New York. (A map for the rural farm population ought to be made.)

Figure 15 shows what would result if the whole country were populated with uniform density, one person per square mile. The maximum potential of 6000 persons per mile in Kansas thus applies for a total population of only about 3,000,000. If this were increased to the 132,000,000 of 1940, the level would rise to 260,000 persons per mile, as compared with the actual 650,000 in rural territory near New York City in Figure 3.

Apologies are due to our Canadian friends for the failure of all these

---

[26] Reilly stated a "law of retail gravitation" for trade areas, which described the equilibrium point or "breaking point" between two competing cities; he used population divided by the square of the distance. See W. J. Reilly: Method for the Study of Retail Relationships, *Univ. of Texas Bull. No. 2944*, 1929. Some such rule as his would follow from the concept of potential of population, if a given trade area extended only as far as the farthest-out contours of potential which closed around a city. For a recent study of this phase, see P. D. Converse: A Study of Retail Trade Areas in East Central Illinois, *Univ. of Illinois Bull.*, Vol. 41, No. 7 (Business Studies No. 2), 1943; also his "Retail Trade Areas in Illinois," *ibid.*, Vol. 43, No. 68 (Businesss Studies No. 4), 1946.

An early examination of the distance factor in sociology was made by J. H. S. Bossard: Marriage and the Child, Philadelphia, 1940, Chap. 4.

United States maps to include the potential exerted by the population of Canada. That is not large enough to be of primary importance, even along the frontier, but no doubt it ought to have been included.

The typical major-peak-and-ridge distribution deserves further thought and comment. It is clear that the tendency of the summed coefficients $N_1 N_2 / d$ for a human grouping to tend toward a maximum must be resisted by a counterbalancing tendency, or "demographic force." Otherwise there would be one city at the peak and no ridge or rural lowlands. The student in elementary celestial mechanics is told that a planet's gravitation toward the sun is balanced by the centrifugal force of the planet's orbital motion. The corresponding outward demographic tendency can also be given mathematical expression, but this is reserved for a later paper.

Thus the ridges down from the major peaks seem to be a result of the tendency for people to draw together, while at the same time some of them must keep spread out in order to maintain thorough contact with the soil and the herds, the minerals and the sea.

"Induced" Rural Population

By no means all dwellers in rural areas are occupied directly with rural matters. A large number are there to perform services for the remainder; and many others, who work in cities, live in the country for one reason or another. Acreage that is near many people—and thus at a high potential of population—is likely to be utilized for the residences of commuters, and also of local workers, because such an area offers special opportunities for livelihood. One expects, then, a relationship between potential and the density of rural population. The relation previously announced[27] has been abundantly confirmed:

$$D_R = k\, V_T^2, \tag{13}$$

where V_T is the potential at any point produced by the total population, D_R is the rural density at and near the given point, and k is a constant for the isolated human grouping that is being considered (the United States or Europe).

This equation has been verified for all the censuses of the United States that were studied; namely 1840, 1900, 1930, and 1940. Agreement state by state is relatively more regular in later years.

Equation 13 evidently is equivalent to

$$P_r = k\, V_T^2\, A, \tag{14}$$

---

[27] Stewart, An Inverse Distance Variation; *idem*, Coasts, Waves, and Weather, p. 164.

where P_r is the rural population of a given small area A having potential V_T^2. Summing (14) over the entire United States, or any district thereof, we have

$$P_r = k\ \Sigma V_T^2 A, \tag{15}$$

P_r being the total rural population of the district. This equation permits the easy determination of k from the observed data. Values of V_T are taken

TABLE V—RELATION OF THE DISTRIBUTION OF THE U. S. RURAL POPULATION (1940) TO THE POTENTIAL
OF THE TOTAL POPULATION (EQUATION 15)

State	$V_T^2 A$	P_R		State	$V_T^2 A$	P_R	
		Obs.	Comp.			Obs.	Comp.
N. J.	26×10^{14}	77×10^4	92×10^4	Vt.	8×10^{14}	24×10^4	28×10^4
Conn.	13	55	46	N.H.	8	21	28
R. I.	2	6	7	Wis.	40	146	141
Penna.	90	331	318	Mo.	51	182	181
Del.	4	13	14	Iowa	35	145	123
Mass.	17	46	60	Me.	12	50	42
Md.	18	74	63	Kans.	36	105	127
N. Y.	77	231	272	Minn.	32	140	113
Ohio	62	229	219	Okla.	30	146	106
W.Va.	34	137	120	Nebr.	28	80	99
Ind.	51	154	180	Tex.	84	350	295
Ill.	73	209	257	S.D.	20	48	70
Va.	52	173	183	N.D.	14	51	49
Ky.	48	200	169	—	—	—	—
Mich.	57	180	201	Sums	1022	3603	3603

NOTE.—The over-all ratio 3603/1022, or 3.525, is multiplied into each $V_T^2 A$ to get the computed P_R, which compares well with the observed values. Values of V_T were taken by inspection from Figure 3—a rough average for each state. In the table the states are arranged in decreasing order of the potentials, from 520,000 for N. J. to 140,000 for N.D. In the products $V_T^2 A$ the unit of area is the square mile.

from a potential map for each area A, averaged, by inspection, over the area.

In Table V data for 1940 are given for 28 states east of Colorado, not including nine states of the deep South. The indicated value of k is

$$(351 \pm 45) \times 10^{-12}\ \text{people}^{-1}.$$

The "probable error" of only 13 per cent shows the regularity of the agreement.

But when the rural equilibrium so indicated is extended to the deep South, we have the results of Table VI. Each of the nine states had an excess over the computed rural population. The total excess amounted to 5,600,000. For comparison, the total rural Negro population of these states in 1940 was about 5,000,000. The agreement is doubtless significant.

The equilibrium of Table V holds also for the 11 Rocky Mountain and Pacific Coast States if all are taken together. A deficit of about 2,000,000 rural dwellers below the formula in the eight states of mountain and desert is balanced by an equal surplus in the three Pacific states.

It is worth noting that (13) is the only form of the relation—of rural density to potential of total population—that is independent of absolute space. If the United States were to be doubled in length and breadth while the same people kept on living in the same counties, the existing rural

TABLE VI—"OVERPOPULATION" IN RURAL DISTRICTS OF THE DEEP SOUTH (1940)

State	$V_T{}^2 A$	P_R	
		Obs.	Comp.
N. C.	49×10^{14}	260×10^4	173×10^4
Tenn.	42	189	148
S. C.	22	143	78
Ga.	40	205	141
Ala.	32	198	113
Ark.	33	152	116
Miss.	28	175	99
La.	22	138	78
Fla.	15	85	53
Sums	283	1545	999

NOTE.—The excess of actual observed rural population over that computed is 5,460,000. Values of P_R computed are obtained by multiplying the numbers in the second column by 3.525, according to the equilibrium established in the states of Table V.

equilibrium would not be disturbed, because all potentials would be reduced by a factor of two while all areas would be increased by a factor of four.

The equations hold also for Europe, for censuses in the 1930's corresponding to the potentials of Figure 4. The most conspicuous deviation there is a latitude effect. There are fewer-than-formula rural dwellers in the high northern latitudes of Scandinavia and Russia if the value of k is chosen so as to give the best average fit for all of Europe (that is to say about 150×10^{-12} people^{-1}).

It is thus proved that potential of population, as regards the effect on rural population density, can jump international boundaries as though these were nonexistent. Sociologists point to the relatively small movement of people across certain European frontiers, but physicists know that, although rapid mobility within a system shortens the time required to reach equilibrium, the characteristics of the equilibrium itself may be independent of this time, whether long or short. Equation 14 and its corollary, 15, describe an equilibrium of the rural population, in relation to the total population. Presumably *some* mobility, rather than *large* mobility, is enough to establish this equilibrium everywhere.

At present writing, the four empirical rules, equations 1, 11, 13, and the equation for potential of population, must be considered mutually independent. The equation for potential (or energy) is doubtless the fundamental one, and it is possible that a way will be found to derive one or more of the other three from it.

The rank-size rule for cities presumably expresses an equilibrium that results from urban competition. The rural-density rule, equation 13, as has been said, expresses an equilibrium between the rural population and the total population. The existence of any relation of C to U, such as equation 11, points to a third equilibrium—one between the rural and the urban populations as a whole.

Further applications of the rank-size rule have been worked out and will be published later, including applications that hold for relatively small samples of people; namely those classified by the census as employed in some particular occupation in each of the larger cities of the United States. Still other empirical relations, not touched on at all in this paper, have been found.

There is no longer excuse for anyone to ignore the fact that human beings, on the average and at least in certain circumstances, obey mathematical rules resembling in a general way some of the primitive "laws" of physics. "Social physics" lies within the grasp of scholarship that is unprejudiced and truly modern. When we have found it, people will wonder at the blind opposition its first proponents encountered.

Meanwhile, let "social planners" beware! Water must be pumped to flow uphill, and natural tendencies in human relations cannot be combated and controlled by singing to them. The architect must accept and understand the law of gravity and the limitations of materials. The city or national planner likewise must adapt his studies to natural principles.

OPTIMUM SIZE OF CITIES

By Otis Dudley Duncan

What is the best size for a city?—The question can only be answered intelligently (if, indeed, there is an answer) by assuming a general viewpoint from which criteria of good, better, and best can be derived; working out an explicit set of such criteria; and examining the empirical validity of the criteria.

This procedure will be illustrated here by (1) assuming the viewpoint of the theorist of city planning interested in setting general standards for the planning of cities; (2) abstracting from the literature of city planning theory a list of specific criteria which have been offered therein for determining optimum city-size; and (3) examining each of the criteria on the list from the standpoint of observable relationships between city-size and the empirical variables involved in the criteria. The logical justification for this approach rests on the truism that any criterion of optimum population involves, implicitly or explicitly, two elements: first, the normative element, which places a positive or negative valuation on a particular situation; and second, a factual element which has the force of a statement of empirical relationships between variation in city-size and variation in the situation in question.

Suppose a criterion of optimum city-size is that a city's size should be that which is most favorable to the health of its population. This criterion takes health as a positive value, and ill health a negative one. Beyond this, it implicitly posits some significant correlation between city-size and health; for if there were no such correlation, there would obviously be no "most favorable" size, i.e., no optimum.

The establishing by scientific inquiry of a dependable relationship like that implied by a given criterion may be termed a process of empirical *validation* of the criterion. Normative issues are not involved here:—the value once assumed, validation of a criterion of optimum city-size is a purely empirical procedure, which, to be sure, may be carried out more or less adequately, depending on quality of data, soundness of method, and the like.

Clearly, examining optimum city-size from the viewpoint of the city planning theorist provides only one illustration of the proposed procedure for validating the concept of optimum city-size. It is, however, not a trivial illustration. There is good reason to suppose that the list of criteria furnished by the planning literature includes many criteria which would also be forthcoming under alternative viewpoints. There is the further point that planning standards based on the notion of optimum city-size have historically played an important role in the development of the theory and practice of planning. Some writers on city planning—notably those influenced by Ebenezer Howard [1]—have gone so far as to insist that realistic planning presumes some initial consensus as to the desirable size of the urban units planned for; [2] while others have urged that control of city-size is among the most important means of achieving the ends of city planning. [3] Though these may be extreme positions, they are influential ones, as is instanced by the planning efforts got under way in Britain after World War II. [4] Both enthusiasts for and opponents of such positions would do well to subject to searching scrutiny the underlying concept of optimum city-size. Thought and discussion on this question have been jolted by the recent bold proposals for meeting the threat of atomic war by dispersing the urban population. The idea that cities should be small enough to have a low probability of atomic destruction is, of course, a criterion of optimum size, and the discussion of this idea has raised anew the question of size considerations in city planning. [5]

General population theory discusses optimum population in terms of an economic criterion applicable, abstractly, to a closed economy. [6] This formulation has little application to the present problem, since cities are intrinsically "open" economies. Though some writers have sought to justify city optima on economic grounds, the economist himself has by and large remained neutral on the question of optimum city-size. [7] The general trend of discussion is in line with Firey's view that in this area explicit recognition should be given to a variety of interests, all having just claims as criteria of optimum population, and not all mediated in any obvious manner by purely economic factors. [8] The criteria considered in this paper are those which appear in discussions of optimum city-size in the literature of city

1. Howard's *Garden Cities of To-Morrow* first appeared at the turn of the century; it was reissued in 1946 (London: Faber and Faber, Ltd.).

2. F. J. Osborn, *Transport, Town Development and Territorial Planning of Industry*, No. 20, The New Fabian Research Bureau (London: Victor Gollancz, Ltd., 1934), p. 20.

3. Lewis Mumford, *The Culture of Cities* (New York: Harcourt Brace, 1938), p. 488.

4. Ministry of Town and Country Planning, New Towns Committee, *Final Report*, Cmd. 6876 (London: H. M. Stationery Office, 1946).

5. William F. Ogburn, "Sociology and the Atom," *American Journal of Sociology*, LI (January, 1946), 267-275; Tracy B. Augur, "The Dispersal of Cities as a Defense Measure," *Bulletin of the Atomic Scientists*, IV (May, 1948), 131-134.

6. Manuel Gottlieb, "The Theory of Optimum Population for a Closed Economy," *Journal of Political Economy*, LIII (December, 1945), 289-318.

7. Paul Samuelson, "The Business Cycle and Urban Redevelopment," *The Problem of the Cities and Towns*, ed. Guy Greer (Report of the Conference on Urbanism, Harvard University, March 5-6, 1942).

8. Walter Firey, "The Optimum Rural-Urban Population Balance," *Rural Sociology*, XII (June, 1947), 116-127.

planning and allied disciplines.[9] The classification of these criteria is the writer's and has merit only for reasons of its convenience. It will be obvious that, at least in the aggregate, planners have been hopeful of attaining far-reaching transformations and ameliorations of the urban way of life through control of city-size. The realism of such hopes is closely bound up with the validity of the concept of optimum city-size.

While the data on which this paper is based are to be summarized rather sketchily, most of them are from published sources; and in any case, there is elsewhere available to the specialist a complete and critical exposition of detailed empirical and methodological problems.[10]

EMPIRICAL OBSERVATIONS. 1. *Physical Plan of the City.*—The theorist of optimum city-size frequently demands that cities be small enough to enable ready access to the country-side and a reasonably moderate journey to work. The desirable area of a city is in question here, along with the bearing of area on transportation problems. According to a relationship between population size and area demonstrated for our cities as of 1940,[11] the average city of 10,000 will have a radius of one mile; the city of 100,000 a radius of 2.3 miles; and the city of a half-million 4.1 miles, on the idealized assumption of circular areas. For the average resident, accessibility to the various functional areas of the city varies inversely with its radius. With increasing city-size walking or cycling to work and play rapidly becomes out of the question, and automotive and mass transportation become indispensable. A 1942 survey showed that the average resident of cities over a half-million lived 4.8 miles from work, and required 24 minutes to get to his job. In these cities three-fifths traveled to work by mass transportation media, and three-tenths by auto. In the cities of 5,000–25,000 the median distance to work was but 0.8 of a mile, the journey to work requiring 9 minutes. Fewer than half utilized automotive and mass transportation. Respondents in large cities expressed somewhat more dissatisfaction than those in small cities over

9. The following are representative: National Council of Social Service, *The Size and Social Structure of a Town* (London: George Allen & Unwin, Ltd., 1943); William F. Ogburn, *op. cit.;* F. J. Osborn, *op. cit.; Report of the Royal Commission on the Distribution of the Industrial Population,* Cmd. 6153 (London: H. M. Stationery Office, 1940); Thomas Sharp, *Town Planning,* rev. ed. (Harmondsworth, Middlesex: Penguin Books, 1945); Raymond Unwin, "The Town and the Best Size for Good Social Life," *Town Theory and Practice,* ed. C. B. Purdon (London: Benn Brothers, Ltd., 1921).

10. Otis Dudley Duncan, "An Examination of the Problem of Optimum City-Size," microfilm (Chicago: University of Chicago Libraries, 1949). See also the following compilations of data on differential characteristics of cities by size: Fenton Keyes, "The Correlation of Social Phenomena with Community Size," Ph.D. dissertation, Department of Sociology, Yale University, 1942; *The Municipal Year Book* (Chicago: The International City Managers' Association, annual); William F. Ogburn, *Social Characteristics of Cities* (Chicago: The International City Managers' Association, 1937); U.S. Bureau of the Census, *Cities Supplement, Statistical Abstract of the United States* (Washington: Government Printing Office, 1944).

11. John Q. Stewart, "Suggested Principles of 'Social Physics,'" *Science,* CVI (August 29, 1947), 179-180.

parking facilities and the distance their children had to travel to high schools.[12] Some form of local mass transportation is apparently required in cities over 15,000, since virtually all cities of this size have buses or street cars.[13] The automobile is a much less effective mode of transit in the large city: A fragmentary survey in 1942 indicated that in cities of 25,000-100,000 about four-fifths of vehicular passengers arriving in the central business district travelled by auto, as against only two-fifths in cities over a half-million; the remainder in each case arrived by some means of mass transportation.[14] Families in cities over 100,000 spend more than four times as much for non-automotive transportation as families in smaller cities.[15]

Although the statistical data are not adequate for a thorough cost analysis of transportation, the unequivocal indication is that the advantages of time, expenditure, and convenience all lie with the moderate sized or small city.

2. *Health.*—One of the most frequently mentioned criteria of optimum city-size concerns the environmental and institutional aspects of the city-dweller's health. It can readily be shown that the ratio of physicians to population increases with increasing city-size, at least up to the million mark, with even more marked differences between large and small cities in the ratios of medical specialists to population than holds for general practitioners. Of the eleven numerically most important types of medical specialists, eight are regularly found only in cities over 50,000 population (as indicated by a ratio of one such physician per city).[16] Ninety-five per cent of the cities over 10,000 have general hospitals, as compared to three-fourths the cities of 5,000-10,000 and two-fifths the cities of 2,500-5,000; and the model size of these hospitals varies directly with city-size.[17] Nine-tenths of the births to residents of cities over 10,000 now occur in hospitals, as compared to three-fourths in the case of cities below 10,000; and over half the large city deaths occur in hospital beds as compared to one-third in

12. Melville C. Branch, Jr., *Urban Planning and Public Opinion* (Princeton: Princeton University Bureau of Urban Research, 1942).

13. "Suburbs' Growth Expands Use of Cars," *Automobile Facts*, III (March, 1944), 1, 3.

14. Kendrick Lee, "Local Transportation," *Editorial Research Reports*, I, No. 18 (May 15, 1942), 311-325.

15. National Resources Planning Board, *Family Expenditures in the United States, Statistical Tables and Appendices* (Washington: Government Printing Office, 1941), Tables 1, 196, 198, 200, and 202.

16. R. G. Leland, *Distribution of Physicians in the United States* (Chicago: Bureau of Medical Economics, American Medical Association, rev. ed., 1936).

17. Commission on Hospital Care, *Hospital Care in the United States* (New York: The Commonwealth Fund, 1947), Table 14.

the smaller centers.[18] Health services and facilities are, therefore, clearly more accessible to large city residents than to small.

The actual health status of the populations of different sized cities is perhaps most reliably, though indirectly, shown by mortality statistics. Infant mortality varies inversely with city-size, and in recent years the smallest cities have had rates two-fifths larger than cities over the million mark. The association with city-size is uniform, and the differentials by city-size have increased, rather than diminished, with the nation-wide improvements in infant mortality rates of the past three decades.[19] Likewise, the larger cities experience an advantage with regard to maternal mortality, though here the differences are smaller—perhaps of the order of ten per cent—and have diminished considerably in recent years.[20] For combined sexes in the total white population, the life expectancy at practically all ages was higher in 1940 for residents of cities of 10,000-100,000 than for residents of cities larger or smaller than this. The superior longevity in this city-size group is a function of age, increasing to age 35 and being most marked in the age range 35–65. However, at best these cities experience only a three per cent superiority over larger cities, and a much narrower margin over smaller cities.[21] Further, there are important variations by population subgroups. In the West and the North, life expectancies of both races are higher in the smaller cities, but the reverse is true in the South. In general, the advantage of the smaller cities increases with advancing age, amounting to as much as 5 to 15 per cent at the old ages in the North and West.[22] Among the important causes of death, large cities have the highest death rates from cancer, heart disease, tuberculosis, diabetes, stomach ulcers (white population), and suicide. Small cities have higher rates for pneumonia and influenza, appendicitis, intracranial lesions, nephritis, and hernia and intestinal obstruction.[23] Recalling the higher infant and maternal mortality of the small cities, and the fact that their life expectancies are relatively greater at advanced than at early ages, there is, therefore, some indication that the principal health advantages of the large cities are in regard to the immediate accessibility of superior services for the treatment of acute diseases and childbirth; whereas the populations of these large urban centers are more vulnerable to the long-term, accumulative environmental hazards eventuating

18. U.S. Bureau of the Census, *Vital Statistics—Special Reports*, vol. 22, no. 1, 1945; and vol. 10, no. 51, 1941.

19. U.S. Bureau of the Census, *Vital Statistics of the United States* (Washington: Government Printing Office, annual).

20. *Ibid.*

21. Life tables computed from data in U.S. Bureau of the Census, *Vital Statistics Rates in the United States, 1900–1940* (Washington: Government Printing Office, 1943).

22. U.S. Bureau of the Census, *Vital Statistics—Special Reports*, vol. 23, no. 15, 1947, Table IV.

23. U.S. Bureau of the Census, *Vital Statistics—Special Reports*, vol. 23, no. 1, 1945.

in chronic and psychosomatic disorders. This picture is, of course, much different nowadays from that of a few decades ago before the control of epidemic infectious diseases. Recent advances in public health have presumably benefited the large cities more than the small. It is impossible to make a categorical generalization about the relative advantages of large and small cities with regard to health; but the probability is that the magnitudes of the historical differences in the health of populations in cities of different sizes are diminishing, on the whole.

City-Size:	100,000 and Over	25,000– 100,000	10,000– 25,000	2,500– 10,000
Per cent of cities with psychiatric clinics, 1947	83	25	4	1
Per cent of births occurring in hospitals, 1943	92	88	84	74
Infant deaths per 1,000 births, 1948	29	31	33	36
Life expectancy, 1940:				
—At birth (sexes combined)	64.3	64.0		62.5
—At age 45 (sexes combined)	26.0	26.7		26.6
Age-adjusted death rates per 100,000 population, 1940:				
—From heart and circulatory diseases	354	309		295
—From pneumonia and influenza	64	67		77

3. *Public Safety.*—It is sometimes stated that small cities are safer places in which to live than large cities. This assertion may be checked against the statistics of crime, auto accident deaths, and fire losses.

Most of the 24 offense categories used in *Uniform Crime Reports* show a tendency for crime rates, as measured by crimes known to police, or by persons charged, to increase with city-size. The relationship is not always of a simple character, but in general cities over 50,000 have higher rates than cities under 50,000, though the very largest cities by no means have the highest rates in all or most of these categories.[24] Lacking data to measure directly the cost of crime, it may be observed that per capita expenditures for city police forces increase directly with city-size, differences among city-size groups being of the order of three or four to one, comparing cities over a half million to cities below 10,000.[25] A similar comparison for per capita size of police force gives a ratio of roughly two to one.[26] These ratios of differential effort and expenditure are greater than the ratios of differential incidence in most categories of crime. Therefore, it may

24. Federal Bureau of Investigation, *Uniform Crime Reports* (Washington: Government Printing Office, semiannual).

25. U.S. Bureau of the Census, *City Finances: 1942*, Vol. III; and *Finances of Cities Having Populations Less Than 25,000: 1942* (Washington: Government Printing Office, 1944).

26. *Uniform Crime Reports, op. cit.*

be generalized that the large city not only experiences a greater relative amount of crime, but also pays proportionately more heavily for it.

Statistics of automobile accident death rates are none too reliably compiled, and consequently exhibit certain illogical irregularities over the years. In general, occurrence rates based on population are lower for cities between 10,000 and 50,000 than for larger cities, for the recent years for which data are relatively complete. Occurrence rates based on numbers of registered vehicles give a somewhat clearer picture. Again cities of 10,000-50,000 have the lower rates, with the rates increasing regularly with city-size in the statistics of recent years. Although it is not entirely clear in what size group of cities there is the greatest personal risk of dying in an auto accident, it is obvious that the larger the city, the more lethal an instrument the automobile becomes. And it seems fairly clear that the cities below 50,000 enjoy the greatest safety from auto accidents, by perhaps ten per cent as measured by population based rates, and by a much larger margin in relation to the number of automobiles owned by residents.[27]

City-Size Group	Average Annual Auto Accident Deaths per 100,000 Vehicles, 1942–46	Per Capita Police Expenditure, 1942	Average Annual Criminal Offense Rate per 100,000 Population, 1940–1947		
			Murder	Robbery	Rape
1,000,000 +	68	$6.71	5	73	} 14
500,000 —	54	5.80	} 8	} 74	
250,000 —	50	3.80			
100,000 —	46	3.57	7	56	11
50,000 —	40	3.37	6	40	9
25,000 —	35	2.89	4	29	7
10,000 —	35	2.34	4	23	8
5,000 —	..	2.06	} 4	} 22	} 8
2,500 —	..	1.64			

In regard to fire hazards, the results vary according to the statistical measure chosen. Per capita fire loss, in dollars, shows little systematic association with city-size, except for the possibility that within a given city-size group, there is greater variation in the scale of losses by individual cities among the smaller cities. This would indicate a greater vulnerability of the small city to losses from an occasional large fire.[28] Fire loss expressed as a percentage of total real property value is larger in the cities of 30,000-50,000 than in the cities over 1,000,000, the differences being greater when measured by the size group mean than when measured by the size group median—again indicating a skewing toward extreme values among smaller cities.[29] The annual number of fires per capita is related inversely to city-size, with fires being relatively one-third more frequent in cities 25,000–50,000 than in cities 500,000 and over.[30] On the other hand, the loss per building fire is more than fifty per cent greater in the larger of these two city-size groups.[31]

27. National Safety Council, *Accident Facts*, Annual editions of 1933–1947.
28. *The Municipal Year Book, op. cit.*, editions of 1940 and 1945.
29. Mabel L. Walker, *Municipal Expenditures* (Baltimore: The Johns Hopkins Press, 1930), Table II.
30. *The Municipal Year Book, op. cit.*, annual editions of 1941–1945.
31. *Ibid.*

There are only slight differences by city-size in regard to per capita size of fire departments, but the cities over a half-million spend 15 per cent more for them in relation to their population, than do the cities of 10,000-25,000.[32] While there is no unequivocal measure of fire hazard and of fire-fighting efficiency, the suggestion is that among all sizes of city larger than 25,000 the differences in fire losses are rather due to inherent fire hazards than to differences in the mobilization of resources for fire protection. While the choice among the above quoted indices is somewhat subjective, perhaps a fair case could be made for the greater safety of the small or medium sized city, on the average.

In most persons' minds, no doubt, the preeminent question about a city's public safety nowadays is its potential destruction by the Bomb in a future war. Fortunately, there are no statistics on the relative vulnerability of cities of different sizes to A-bombs; we have to rely on statements of authorities and certain *a priori* considerations. The question is not, of course, one of the destructive power of the Bomb in a direct hit, but rather of the probability of a city's suffering such a hit. It has been argued that the small city is safer, first because it is a smaller target, more difficult to locate and hit directly; second, because it is likely to be a less attractive target; and third, because the potential enemy's A-bomb supply may be limited, thus diminishing the probability of an A-bomb attack on any given small city. From considerations such as these, the National Security Resources Board urges that "further urban concentrations of more than 50,000 people . . . be avoided." [33]

4. *Municipal Efficiency.*—It is a plausible hypothesis that the efficiency with which municipal services can be rendered should increase with increasing city-size to a point of diminishing returns, with an optimum size somewhere between the extremes. However, it is virtually impossible to get data to test this hypothesis. The existing data on municipal expenditures show, in general, a direct relationship between city-size and per capita costs in most of the 14 categories of expenditure: The larger cities spend more for highways, sanitation, public welfare, correction, schools, etc., than small.[34] However, these data reflect the separately varying factors of unit costs, amount, and quality of services. Hence they show little about municipal efficiency. From previously cited data, it may be seen that despite their greater expenditures, the large cities apparently enjoy no better situation than small with regard to crime and traffic control, fire protection, or health. This would argue that either these services are rendered less efficiently in large cities, or—what is more probable—that the initial problems of large cities are intrinsically more difficult. On the other hand, as will

32. *The Municipal Year Book, 1945, op. cit.*
33. *National Security Factors in Industrial Location,* NSRB Doc. 66 (Washington: National Security Resources Board, rev., July 22, 1948), p. 4.
34. *City Finances: 1942, op. cit.; Finances of Cities Having Populations Less Than 25,000: 1942, op. cit.*

appear later, the higher levels of expenditure for schools, libraries, and recreation apparently reflect greater amounts and/or qualities of these services. Whether the increment of service is commensurate with the increment of cost cannot be accurately judged.

In only one area of municipal service can some tentative optimum population be established—the provision of residential electric service. Unit costs decline with increasing city-size up to the million mark, with cities between a half and one million getting electricity the cheapest.[35] Except for this one observation—which can by no means be immediately generalized—optimum city-size from the standpoint of municipal efficiency is still *terra incognita*.

5. *Education and Communications.*—A variety of measures of city school systems may be cited. Larger cities have longer school years—one week longer in cities over 100,000 as compared to those below 10,000. But the difference is smaller in regard to average per pupil school days attended. The average annual salary of teachers increases markedly with city size, quite overshadowing any cost-of-living differentials. Likewise, per pupil expenditures of large city schools exceed those of small city schools, and a greater proportion of the total school budget goes directly into costs of instruction. Large cities are much more frequently able to provide such special services as summer schools and night schools. On the other hand, the pupil/teacher ratio is greater in large cities, though the difference between large and small cities is only of the order of ten per cent.[36]

Facilities for advanced education are considerably limited by city-size. If we somewhat arbitrarily estimate the "population base" for a facility as that city-size at which 50 per cent of cities have the facility, the population base for a college or university is around 100,000, about the same for a junior college, and about 25,000 for a business college.[37] Accredited professional schools in such fields as business, engineering, law, medicine, and social work require larger population bases, of the order of 500,000.[38]

Despite the demonstrably superior educational facilities of large cities, their populations are at but slightly higher levels of educational status than those of small cities. As between cities of 250,000 and over and those below 25,000 superiorities of 0.2-0.3 in median school years completed are typical

35. *Cities Supplement, Statistical Abstract of the United States, op. cit.,* Table 4.
36. U.S. Office of Education, "Statistics of City School Systems 1937–1938," *Biennial Survey of Education in the United States,* Bull. No. 2, 1940 (Washington: Government Printing Office, 1940), Ch. III; and "Statistics of City School Systems 1939–1940 and 1941–1942," *Biennial Surveys of Education in the United States 1938–1940 and 1940–1942* (Washington: Government Printing Office, 1944), Vol. II, Ch. VII.
37. Clarence Stephen Marsh, ed., *American Universities and Colleges* (Washington: American Council on Education, 4th ed., 1940); *Directory of Private Business Schools in the United States* (Washington: War Emergency Council of Private Business Schools, 1943); *Directory of Junior Colleges, 1941* (Washington: American Association of Junior Colleges, 1941).
38. U.S. Office of Education, *Education Directory 1941, Part III, Colleges and Universities,* Bulletin 1941, No. 1 (Washington: Government Printing Office, 1941).

for ages below 18, but the slight observed differences amongst the adult populations are not all in this same direction.[39]

With regard to agencies of public enlightenment other than schools, estimates of population bases have been made as just indicated. For an art museum the population base is 100,000, with a somewhat higher figure for science and historical museums. The population base for a public library is 2,500, for a daily newspaper 5,000, for a radio station 10,000, for an FM station 50,000, and for television 500,000. Current trends suggest a raising of the required population base in the future for newspapers, and a lowering for libraries, FM, and television.[40]

City-Size Group	School Expenditures Per Pupil, 1937–38	Median School Years Completed, Native White Males, 18-44, 1940	Per Cent of Cities with— College or University, 1940	Per Cent of Cities with— Art Museum, 1938	Per Cent of Cities with— AM Radio Station, 1946
250,000 +	} $120	11.0	100	86	100
100,000 —			56	53	89
50,000 —	99*	} 11.2†	43	25	72
10,000 —	85*		19	4	39
2,500 —	75·	11.1†	6	1	5

* The dividing line between these two groups is 30,000, rather than 50,000.
† The dividing line between these two groups is 25,000, rather than 10,000.

A more detailed analysis of libraries shows that they generally meet desirable minimum professional standards only in cities as large as 50,000-75,000.[41] Although libraries in large cities have larger book stocks and spend more money per capita, their service to the population is less as measured by per capita book circulation. For a sample of 103 cities in 1943 there was a negative correlation of −.64 between city-size and per capita circulation. Holding constant percent of population registered as borrowers, book stock in volumes per capita, branch libraries per capita, and per capita expenditures, the correlation remained at −.51.[42] Another writer has demonstrated a negative correlation between city-size and per capita museum attendance.[43] Apparently for those facilities which do not operate by mass distribution, the superior facilities of the large city are purchased at the price of diminished community participation.

39. U.S. Bureau of the Census, *Sixteenth Census of the United States: 1940. Population. Education, Educational Attainment of Children by Rental Value of Home* (Washington: Government Printing Office, 1945), Table III; and *Educational Attainment by Economic Characteristics and Marital Status* (Washington: Government Printing Office, 1947), Table 17.

40. Laurence Vail Coleman, *The Museum in America* (Washington: The American Association of Museums, 1939), Vol. III; *The American Library Directory, 1939* (New York: R. R. Bowker Co., 1939); *Directory, Newspapers and Periodicals, 1946* (Philadelphia: N. W. Ayer & Son, 1946); "Directory of Broadcasting Stations of the United States," *Broadcasting, 1946 Yearbook Number*, pp. 71-190; Jack Alicoate, ed., *The 1947 Radio Annual* (New York: Radio Daily, 1947).

41. Lowell Martin, "The Optimum Size of the Public Library Unit," *Library Extension: Problems and Solutions*, ed. Carleton B. Joeckel (Chicago: University of Chicago Press, 1945), pp. 32-46.

42. Original data taken from "Public Library Statistics," *Bulletin, American Library Association*, XXXVIII (April, 1944), 154-167.

43. Paul Marshall Rea, *The Museum and the Community* (Lancaster: The Science Press, 1932).

6. *Public Recreation.*—An accepted professional standard for park acreage is one acre per 100 population. This standard is attained by one-fifth the cities between 50,000 and 250,000, by practically no city above that size, and by somewhat lesser percentages of the smaller cities. Parks in large cities have a much wider variety of recreation facilities, special use areas and buildings, and spend larger per capita amounts for operation and maintenance. On the other hand, the accessibility of parks, as indicated by the number of parks per capita is much greater in the small cities. In those cities reporting parks there are four for every 10,000 persons in the city of 25,000-50,000 as compared to 1 in the city over 1,000,000.[44] The optimum population for parks, on any equilibrium of these four variables, is clearly in the middle size range of cities.

The population base for zoos (estimated as before) is 100,000;[45] approximately the same figure holds for symphony orchestras.[46] Resident grand opera is found in only three or four of the country's largest cities, and the population base for opera of any sort is apparently above a quarter million.[47] On the other hand, motion picture theaters are found in every city, and even cities as small as 10,000-25,000 have variety and choice of cinematic offerings, with an average of three movies each.[48]

		Per Cent of Cities with—		
City-Size Group	At Least One Park Acre Per 100 Population 1940	Park Expenditure of at Least $1.00 Per Capita, 1940	Zoo, 1940	Symphony Orchestra, 1946
1,000,000 +	0	80	100	100
500,000 —	0	100	100	89
250,000 —	9	58	76	78
100,000 —	20	42	57	55
50,000 —	21	42	32	18
25,000 —	17	27	15	5
10,000 —	15	14	8	0
5,000 —	14	13	2	0
2,500 —	12	7	1	0

7. *Retail Facilities.*—The oft mentioned values of the large city as a shopping center cannot be denied. However, in many standard lines of merchandise this advantage is slight, the real superiority of the large city being in style and specialty trade. It is worth observing that in no more than three of the 65 kinds of retail outlet listed by the census is a population base of over 50,000 apparently required.[49] Another study suggests that for some lines of specialty goods, stores in the largest cities apparently

44. National Recreation Association, *Municipal and County Parks in the United States, 1940* (New York: National Recreation Association, 1942).
45. *Ibid.*
46. "Symphony Orchestras in the United States and Canada," *The International Musician*, XLIV (June, 1946), 7-8.
47. *Pierre Key's Music Year Book, 1938.* (New York: Pierre Key, 1938).
48. *Motion Picture Theatres in the United States: A Statistical Summary, 1948* (New York: Motion Picture Association of America, Inc., 1948).
49. Population base estimated as city-size where number of stores per city is 1.0, by graphic interpolation; U.S. Bureau of the Census, *Sixteenth Census of the United States: 1940. Census of Business: 1939. Retail Trade Analysis by City-Size Groups* (Washington: Government Printing Office, 1942), Table 12C.

have no more "drawing power" for non-resident trade than those in cities of 100,000.[50] The optimum city population for adequate retail outlets, even for specialized trade, may therefore be no higher than 50,000 to 100,000.

8. *Churches and associations.*—Criteria of optimum city-size involving the organized group life are ordinarily not precisely stated. Rather there is usually some general reference to the desirability of a certain degree of variety and diversity of groups, preferably without too much loss of community consensus and cohesion. The following data will doubtless seem somewhat tangential to this formulation.

There are only 20 religious denominations in the United States (1936) which have as many as 1,000 urban local churches. These cover three-fourths of all local churches and nine-tenths of all memberships in urban areas. Perhaps 20 could therefore be regarded as a generous estimate of the minimum desirable number of denominations. From census data on number of denominations per city, it is estimated that 30,000 is the population base for this degree of denominational variety.[51]

There are no comparative statistics on the variety of voluntary associations present in cities of different sizes, and only fragmentary data on certain national organizations. From these, the estimated population bases for certain kinds of organization are as follows: Rotary Club, 5,000; Elks lodge, 10,000; Lions Club, 15,000; Boy Scout Council, 25,000; YMCA, 25,000; YWCA, 25,000.[52] The population base for any two or more of these would be somewhat higher, but in all probability most organizations of these types are well represented in cities no larger than 25,000-50,000.

9. *Family life.*—Advocates of small cities and decentralization often stress the greater strength of the family institution in small cities. Statistical support for this position may be found in the data on marriage and fertility. Of the native white population 18-64, only three-fifths are married in cities over a quarter million as against over two-thirds in cities 2,500-25,000.[53]

In 1940 no city-size group in the urban white population had a fertility level up to the permanent replacement quota. The cities of 2,500-10,000 were reproducing at 15 per cent below replacement, whereas cities over 1,000,000 were 35 per cent below.[54] In previous census periods the persistent inverse association of city-size and effective fertility has also been marked.

50. John Adams Pfanner, Jr., *A Statistical Study of the Drawing Power of Cities for Retail Trade* (Studies in Business Administration, The Journal of Business of The University of Chicago, Vol. X, No. 3, April, 1940).

51. U.S. Bureau of the Census, *Religious Bodies: 1936, Vol. I. Summary and Detailed Tables* (Washington: Government Printing Office, 1941), Table 13.

52. Official Directory 1935–1936 (Chicago: Rotary International, 1935); Keyes, *op. cit.*, p. 162.

53. U.S. Bureau of the Census, *Educational Attainment by Economic Characteristics and Marital Status, op. cit.*, Table 37.

54. Warren S. Thompson, *The Growth of Metropolitan Districts in the United States: 1900–1940* (Washington: Government Printing Office, 1947); and special computations from 1940 Census data.

Another important aspect of family living—housing—has been minutely described by the 1940 census. The principal differentials by city-size are as follows: Home ownership is more frequent in small cities; rentals increase with increasing city-size; and owner-occupied units are less frequently mortgaged in small cities. Thus both ownership and rental are easier propositions in the smaller centers. Dwelling units in large cities are better equipped with regard to private bath, running water, central heating, flush toilet, mechanical refrigeration, and gas or electric cooking. They are also in better repair, being somewhat newer on the average. In small cities a majority of dwelling units are in single family structures, whereas the reverse is true of large cities. However, there is somewhat more room overcrowding in small cities, as measured by the standard of more than one and one-half persons per room.[55] In sum, not all the advantages in regard to good housing lie with any one size group of cities.

	Cities of—			
Housing Characteristics, 1940	250,000 and Over	50,000– 250,000	10,000– 50,000	2,500– 10,000
Home ownership	29%	38%	45%	49%
Average rent, tenant units	$32	$25	$23	$18
Single family units	33%	51%	61%	71%
Room overcrowding	5%	6%	6%	7%
Units needing major repairs	8%	11%	14%	17%
Units without running water	3%	6%	8%	15%

10. *Miscellaneous Psychological and Social Characteristics of Urban Life.*—There remains a residual category of attributes, desirable and undesirable, which are sometimes mentioned as criteria of optimum city-size. Such epithets as provincialism, friendliness, community participation, standardization, anonymity, strain, spontaneity, and the like are perhaps applied with more heat than light in the absence of precise specification and reliable measurement of such urban traits.

One writer claims to find evidence of greater "social contentment" in cities below 25,000 in the fact that survey respondents there voice fewer complaints on certain questions about neighborhood and community characteristics.[56] Another attempt to get at some of the more intangible traits of cities through an analysis of student community reports[57] must be deemed methodologically unsound.

There is but one trait of this miscellany for which some approximate measurements can be made. This is the status of the city as a center of innovation and cultural diffusion. Rose's data indicate a positive correlation between city-size and cultural innovation.[58] Bowers has shown that amateur

55. *Housing—Special Reports,* Series H-44, Nos. 1-7 (Washington: U.S. Bureau of the Census, 1944–1945).

56. Branch, *op. cit.,* p. 31.

57. Walter T. Watson, "Is Community Size an Index of Urbanization?" *The Southwestern Social Science Quarterly,* XVII (September, 1936), 150-160.

58. Edward Rose, "Innovations in American Culture," *Social Forces,* XXVI (March, 1948), 255-272.

radio followed a diffusion cycle from large to small cities.[59] Data assembled for the present study indicate that commercial broadcasting, FM, and television follow a similar pattern. Another kind of measurement is the per capita incidence of persons in certain eminence groups. Inventors, artists, and persons in *Who's Who* are present in greater numbers, relative to population, in large cities than in small.[60]

DISCUSSION. The above summary of a considerable mass of data leads to the following comments: The optimum size of cities is quite different from the standpoint of certain criteria from what it is on the basis of others. It is found that even an apparently unitary criterion—e.g. health—may give conflicting indications of the optimum. There is no immediately obvious way in which these various optima may be objectively equilibrated, compromised, weighted, or balanced to yield an unequivocal figure for *the* optimum population for a city. Any numerical choice of a figure for the optimum population is involved in subjective value preferences and impressionistic weighting systems. Most theorists proposing a size or size range as the optimum adopt this procedure, or the alternative one of confining attention to a few of the many criteria of optimum city-size that have been proposed in the literature. Thus if the preeminent interest is in the planning of cities for safety in atomic war, some population, say 25,000 or 50,000, will be taken as a maximum desirable city-size. Some other interests will be compatible with this choice, e.g. those of physical plan, health, and public safety. Attention to the remaining criteria which indicate larger sizes is then shifted to a consideration of the sacrifices involved in limiting city-size. Data such as those cited in this paper furnish the starting point for such a consideration, assuming the relationship between city-size and urban characteristics to be those of the present time. The degree to which city and national planning could mitigate these sacrifices is a question which is still open, scientifically speaking, though there is no dearth of assertion on the subject.

The problem of optimum city-size originates in the realm of values and, ideally, eventuates in action. Only the middle term of the translation of values into action is open to scientific procedures, for the choice of values and the decision to act are intrinsically beyond the scope of science. Nevertheless, both valuation and action should profit from an occasional summing up of the evidence and its implications. This paper has reported an initial effort of that kind.

59. Raymond V. Bowers, "The Direction of Intra-Societal Diffusion," *American Sociological Review*, II (December, 1937), 826-836.

60. Sample of inventors from U.S. Patent Office, *Index of Patents, 1940* (Washington: Government Printing Office, 1941); sample of artists from *Who's Who In American Art, Vol. III, 1940–1941* (Washington: The American Federation of Arts, 1940); R. D. McKenzie, *The Metropolitan Community* (New York: McGraw-Hill Book Co., Inc., 1933), Table 48.

REDISTRIBUTION OF POPULATION: 1940 to 1950

By Henry S. Shryock, Jr.

T HE forced movements of masses of European and Asian people during and after the last World War challenge our imaginations, but the less spectacular movements inside the United States have been of similar magnitude and have probably resulted in rather more net change in geographic distribution. In contrast to the flight of refugees, the forced transfers of ethnic groups, and the deportation of minorities, American internal migration has consisted of voluntary moves by individuals or families, motivated largely by economic considerations. In the absence of violence, it has also been possible to measure the shifts of our own population considerably more accurately. In this same period, all the components of population change were quite different from what they had been in the depressed 'thirties. All differed relative to the initial population in the various geographic areas. As usual, however, the differing patterns of migration rates and rates of natural-increase tended to work against each other as areas of high fertility and low economic opportunity sent out to areas of low fertility and high economic opportunity many more migrants than they received.

INEQUALITIES OF POPULATION CHANGE

The 19 million increase in the population of the United States between 1940 and 1950 had not been equalled in any previous decade, and yet many areas experienced actual decreases in population. Among the States, the percentage change ranged from +53.3 for California to −4.4 for Oklahoma. Among the more notable effects of this redistribution of population among the States will be the shifts in the House of Representatives. Fourteen seats will be shifted, seven States gaining and nine States losing seats. The geographic center of the House is shifting westward.

Distribution of counties by intercensal change[1]

All counties.—Among the 3103 counties or equivalent areas, almost half lost population [1]. The distribution by percentage change is given in Table 1. It will be noted that in each geographic division there was a wide range of change. Even in the Pacific division, which increased by 49 per cent as a whole, about one-tenth of the counties lost population; and even in the West North Central division, which increased by only

4 per cent as a whole, about one-twentieth gained by 20 per cent or more. The rate of change will not be compared here among the divisions or among the States, but later on a better unit for geographic analysis will be used.

TABLE 1

DISTRIBUTION OF COUNTIES ACCORDING TO PERCENTAGE CHANGE IN POPULATION, BY GEOGRAPHIC DIVISION: 1940 TO 1950

(1950 figures are preliminary)

| Division | Total counties | Per cent of total counties | | | | | | | |
| | | Loss | | | | Gain | | | |
		20 and over	10 but under 20	5 but under 10	0 but under 5	0 but under 5	5 but under 10	10 but under 20	20 and over
United States	3,103	6.1	17.0	13.0	13.5	12.6	9.9	11.8	16.1
New England	67	—	1.5	3.0	9.0	26.9	25.4	25.4	9.0
Middle Atlantic	150	—	3.3	5.3	12.0	16.0	27.3	22.7	13.3
East North Central	436	0.9	7.6	10.8	14.2	17.4	15.4	19.3	14.4
West North Central	620	5.2	27.6	20.0	19.2	10.2	6.0	6.6	5.3
South Atlantic	582	1.9	11.2	11.9	13.7	15.1	11.3	13.7	21.1
East South Central	364	4.4	24.2	17.9	16.2	14.6	6.6	8.0	8.2
West South Central	470	21.3	23.8	10.9	7.4	5.7	6.0	7.7	17.2
Mountain	281	9.3	17.8	11.7	13.2	10.7	6.4	10.0	21.0
Pacific	133	1.5	3.0	3.0	3.0	7.5	6.8	12.8	62.4

Some of the counties with high rates of growth were considerably affected by the new method of enumerating college students. Prior to 1950 students were counted at their parental homes unless they were employed in the college community, were married, or said they had no home except in the college community. In 1950, all college students were supposed to have been enumerated where they were living while attending college. Many students, of course, live in their parental homes so were unaffected by the change. Even under the old procedure, college communities would have had fairly large increases because of the influx of ex-servicemen, who were more likely to be married and independent financially, and because of the expansion of staff and of service industries resulting from increased enrollment. This change in enumerative procedure had most effect upon the percentage change of otherwise relatively small counties that contained a large college or university. For example, Tompkins County, N. Y., the seat of Cornell University, increased by 39.8 per cent; and Centre County, Pennsylvania, where Pennsylvania State College is located, increased by 24.8 per cent. It will never be possible to determine exactly what part of the intercensal changes are due to this factor, but perhaps estimates can be made later.

---

[1] All figures other than those for states are preliminary and exclude 841,769 persons not yet allocated within the states at the time of this writing.

Metropolitan and nonmetropolitan counties

More than half of the population of the United States was living in one of the 168 standard metropolitan areas in 1950 [2]. (So that a classification could be made including all the counties, the standard metropolitan areas in New England, which are defined on a town basis, are approximated here on a county basis; as was also done when the State economic areas were delimited.) While the population in the counties of the standard metropolitan areas was increasing by more than twenty per cent, that in the other counties was increasing by only about six per cent. The concentration of population in metropolitan areas, which slowed down during the depression, was greatly accelerated by the war and the postwar period of prosperity.

Following a technique of analysis recently used by Bogue [3], we may classify the metropolitan counties by the size of the central city in 1940 and the nonmetropolitan counties by the size of the largest urban place in 1940. The results are presented in Table 2. Every size category of metropolitan counties had a higher rate of increase than the national average for all counties. The metropolitan counties with central cities

TABLE 2

CHANGE IN THE POPULATION OF METROPOLITAN AND NONMETROPOLITAN
COUNTIES OF THE UNITED STATES CLASSIFIED BY SIZE OF LARGEST
INCORPORATED PLACE: 1940–1950

Type of county by size of largest place	1950* population	1940 population	Amount of change	Percentage change
Total	149,855,591	131,669,275	18,186,316	13.8
Metropolitan Counties† by size of central city of the Metropolitan Area in 1940:	82,514,342	68,425,343	14,088,000	20.6
1,000,000 and over	29,280,369	24,979,735	4,300,634	17.2
500,000 to 999,999	15,350,352	12,856,068	2,494,284	19.4
250,000 to 499,999	12,272,757	9,700,703	2,572,054	26.5
100,000 to 249,999	14,571,901	11,734,149	2,837,752	24.2
50,000 to 99,999	11,038,963	9,154,688	1,884,275	20.6
Nonmetropolitan Counties by size of largest urban place in 1940:	67,341,249	63,243,932	4,097,317	6.5
25,000 to 49,999	10,307,604	8,482,738	1,824,866	21.5
10,000 to 24,999	16,879,497	14,894,745	1,984,752	13.3
5,000 to 9,999	14,342,943	13,574,508	768,435	5.7
2,500 to 4,999	12,345,053	12,251,584	93,469	0.8
No urban place	13,466,152	14,040,357	−574,205	−4.1

* Preliminary counts of the population of counties as of April 1, 1950 from U. S. Bureau of the Census, Series PC-3, No. 4. Approximately 700,000 individual census reports are excluded from these figures.

† Counties classed as metropolitan in Series PC-3, No. 3 except that counties in metropolitan areas the central city of which was less than 50,000 in 1940 are classed as nonmetropolitan. New England counties classed as metropolitan or nonmetropolitan according to whether in metropolitan or nonmetropolitan State Economic Areas.

of intermediate size experienced somewhat more population growth on the average than did those with either very large or small central cities. Among nonmetropolitan counties, the rate of growth was greater the larger the most populous place in the county. The combined counties without an urban place in 1940 lost population. Only those non-metropolitan counties with an urban place of at least 25,000 in 1940 gained population at above the national average rate. This class compared favorably with the metropolitan counties. Many new standard metropolitan areas were recruited from this class, of course.

State Economic Areas

Figure 1 is a map showing the percentage change from 1940 to 1950 for the 443 state economic areas [4]. State economic areas are groups of counties that are similar with respect to a large number of demographic, social, agricultural, and industrial indices [5]. These areas reveal patterns that are concealed in areas as large as states and are difficult to detect among the mass of detail for the 3103 counties.

Metropolitan Economic Areas. First, we may note on the map the small scattered areas of rapid growth that represent metropolitan state economic areas.[2] Almost all these metropolitan areas increased in population, and many increased by one-third or more. In what follows, gains or losses of 20 per cent or more will be described as "heavy," those of 10 to 19 per cent as "moderate," those of 5 to 9 per cent as "slight," and populations changing by less than 5 per cent will be described as "static."

Along the Atlantic Coast, the rate of increase tends to be greater as we proceed from north to south. Above Delaware Bay, only the Stamford-Norwalk area experienced a heavy increase; and the population of the Fall River-New Bedford area was relatively static. From Wilmington and Baltimore south, all the increases were at least 20 per cent. The Miami, Norfolk-Portsmouth, and Jacksonville areas increased by about 80, 60, and 40 per cent, respectively. All of the five metropolitan state economic areas on the Gulf Coast also had heavy increases, ranging from 23 per cent for New Orleans to 61 per cent for Mobile. On the Pacific Coast, there were even heavier gains, ranging from Portland's 40 per cent to San Diego's 85 per cent. The picture along the Great Lakes is less straight-forward. Erie, Detroit, and Muskegon had heavy gains, but most of the other metropolitan areas had moderate gains; and the Duluth-Superior area had slight change. Some of the port

---

[2] Metropolitan state economic areas are the standard metropolitan areas that had a central city of 50,000 or more and a total population of 100,000 or more, both *prior* to 1950. Where such a standard metropolitan area is in two or more states, each part is a separate state economic area. The standard metropolitan areas in New England, which are made up of towns and cities, are approximated on a county basis to constitute state economic areas.

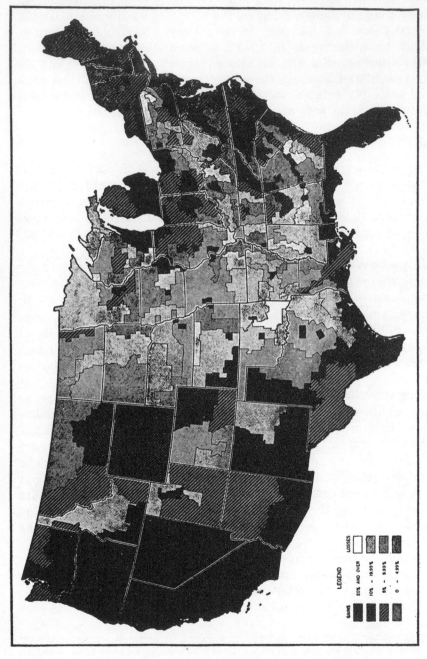

FIGURE 1. Per cent change by State Economic Areas: 1940 to 1950. (Preliminary data.)

areas reached population peaks during the war and afterwards dropped off somewhat as naval and shipbuilding installations were closed.

Looking at the inland metropolitan areas, we find relatively fewer heavy increases. In some broad regions, however, all of the inland metropolitan areas had heavy gains; this trend is true of the Southwest, the Rocky Mountains, and the Central Valley and other inland parts of California. Some of the most rapid growth in the nation occurred here, for example, 77 per cent in the Phoenix area and 74 per cent in the San Bernardino area. In the Southeastern Piedmont, six out of seven metropolitan areas had heavy gains (although the largest was only 35 per cent); and the seventh, Winston-Salem, had a moderate growth.

In the Appalachians as along the Atlantic Coast, the growth of metropolitan areas tended to be greater in the South. The Scranton and Wilkes-Barre–Hazleton areas, in the depressed anthracite region, were the only metropolitan state economic areas in the nation with losses of more than 10 per cent. Furthermore, the Altoona, Johnstown, and Wheeling areas were static, and the Pittsburgh area had only a slight gain. Moderate to heavy gains occurred south of the Mason-Dixon Line, with the Knoxville area (which contains Oak Ridge) increasing by more than one-third.

In the Northeast between the coast and the mountains, there were slight to moderate increases. Inland from the Great Lakes, Midwestern areas were fairly evenly divided between those with moderate and those with heavy increases, with only one below this range. Both the largest and the smallest increases were to be found near the western limit of the Corn Belt—Wichita, which gained by more than half, and Sioux City, which was static. Nearby Wright Field contributed to Dayton's growth of over one-third. Finally, from the Ohio River down into the Deep South but outside the mountains and coastal plain, there were moderate to heavy gains except for the Huntingdon-Ashland area, which had only a slight gain. The Columbus, Ga., and Memphis metropolitan areas increased by about one-third.

In summary, there tended to be heavier growth among the metropolitan areas along the coast and around the Great Lakes than among the inland metropolitan areas. The younger metropolitan areas of the South and West tended to grow more than the maturer areas of the Northeast and Middle West. This latter generalization would be reinforced if we included the areas that first qualified as metropolitan in 1950. Most of these were areas of heavy increase in the South and West.

Nonmetropolitan Economic Areas. A tendency toward more rapid growth along the Atlantic, Pacific, and Gulf Coasts than in the heart of the country was characteristic of nonmetropolitan as well as of metropolitan state economic areas. There were heavy gains in the hinterland coastal areas of California, Oregon, and Texas; Kitsap County, Washington; the delta area at the mouth of the Mississippi River; the Gulf Coast of Mississippi; most of Florida; North Carolina south of Cape Hatteras; the lower Virginia "Peninsula"; southern Maryland; New Jersey; and as far north as Naragansett Bay in Rhode Island. There are important military installations in some of these areas. Areas of moderate increase comprise the northeastern shore of Puget Sound, southwestern Louisiana, the Alabama Gulf Coast, a thinly-settled belt across northern Florida from Gulf to Ocean, the South Carolina Low Country, the Virginia "South Side," southern Delaware, eastern Connecticut, and the coast of New Hampshire. Gains were slight in northwestern Washington, south central Louisiana, Tidewater Virginia from the Potomac to the York, the Eastern Shore of Maryland, and southern Maine. Finally, the North Carolina Tidewater above Hatteras, the Eastern Shore of Virginia, and northeastern Maine were static areas. All the areas in these last two growth classes were highly rural.

Around the Great Lakes, the heavy gains occurred in the industrial area of north central Ohio, in the counties bordering the Detroit metropolitan area, and on Lake Michigan between Muskegon and Gary. Gains were slight to moderate from Green Bay down to the Chicago area, in the other parts of southern Michigan that front on Lake Michigan or Lake Huron, and eastward to include most of the shore of Lake Ontario. The Great Lakes economic areas to the northward were static as to population change except for part of the Upper Peninsula of Michigan that had a moderate loss. Thus nonmetropolitan population increase around the Great Lakes tended to be greatest near the Chicago, Detroit, and Cleveland metropolitan areas and to fall off progressively to the east, west, and north.

The economic areas of Michigan, Wisconsin, and Minnesota around Lake Superior are part of the "Lake States Cut-over Area," which in 1935 was characterized as one of "six rural problem areas" by the Federal Emergency Relief Administration [6]. The state economic areas further inland in the Cut-over also had very little population change.

When we follow the Appalachians through the pertinent nonmetropolitan economic areas down from New York through Alabama, we find none with heavy gains and none with moderate or heavy losses. Two mountainous areas in Pennsylvania, one characterized by anthracite and the other by bituminous coal mining, had slight population losses. Furthermore, a great many areas were static; and, since they were generally areas of high fertility, they must have had substantial outmigration during the decade. The moderate gains begin with the rich Blue Ridge farming area of south central Pennsylvania and include the southwestern coal fields of West Virginia, the Shenandoah Valley, the North Carolina Blue Ridge, the easternmost state economic areas of Tennessee, and small parts of Georgia and Alabama.

Of the predominantly dairying areas that are neither coastal nor mountainous, most were static or had slight gains. A few such areas had moderate gains. One in Illinois had a heavy gain, and one in Minnesota had a moderate loss. These dairying economic areas ranged geographically from Maine to Minnesota and south to the Capital's milkshed in Virginia.

The Corn Belt, which extends from Ohio northwesterly into South Dakota, contained mostly state economic areas with slight losses to slight gains in population. A few had moderate gains, and one area in southern Michigan experienced a heavy increase. The only Corn Belt area with a loss of more than 10 per cent was in northern Kansas.

The major wheat-producing state economic areas are in the Great Plains and in the eastern Columbia River basin. Population trends here were quite variable, ranging from slight losses to heavy gains. Eight of the 19 areas of this type were static. The heavy gains occurred in Washington and Oregon and in the Texas Panhandle. (The growth of the natural gas industry was a factor in the last of these.)

The range livestock region contains state economic areas in both the Great Plains and the Rocky Mountains. Those in the plains ranged from moderate losses to moderate gains, those in the mountains from a slight loss to heavy gains. The heavy gains occurred in New Mexico, Arizona, and Nevada.

Turning east again, we may examine the predominantly tobacco-growing state economic areas. Of the 11 of these, only one is coastal and another mountainous. The heavy gain in southern Maryland is primarily attributable to military installations. Areas in the Piedmont, sand hills, and valleys ranged from static to those with moderate population growth.

The vast Cotton Belt extends from North Carolina to Texas and includes about 60 of the state economic areas. Population in about one-third of these was static. About one-third each had from slight to heavy losses, and from slight to heavy gains. Many of the areas of moderate loss were in the Black Belt, in the heart of the cotton empire.

About half of the general farming areas are in the mountains, and most of the remainder are inland. The few extant areas of self-sufficing agriculture are of this type. The mountainous general farming economic areas were mostly static or had slight population gains. The nonmountainous inland areas were mostly static or had slight population losses.

The state economic areas where fruit and truck crops predominate are mostly coastal. All but one experienced a gain of at least five per cent, and many had heavy gains. The coastal areas of Louisiana and Texas that specialize in rice growing had population gains ranging from slight to heavy.

It may be noted also that the former Dust Bowl has recovered its population losses of the 'thirties. The state economic areas that approximate the areas that had had major wind erosion [6] had a total population of 4,386,000 in 1930, 4,238,000 in 1940, and 4,398,000 in 1950—a decrease of 3.4 per cent from 1930 to 1940, and an increase of 3.8 per cent from 1940 to 1950. Better weather and a sustained demand have brought back prosperity to the wheat farmers and stockmen of these areas, particularly in southwestern Kansas. Also new oil and natural gas fields have been developed in the Texas Panhandle.

This description of population change among nonmetropolitan state economic areas has been made mainly by classifying them as to type of farming and as to topography. A fairly wide range of change was found within each type. Presumably this range would be considerably narrowed if we could cross-classify the state economic areas further by urban-rural residence. Data from the 1950 Census for making this classification were not available at the time of writing.

Suburbanization

The data so far examined have indicated a general trend of concentration of population in metropolitan areas and along the coasts. This process has been going on for some decades, but the prosperous 'forties saw a great acceleration as compared with the depressed 'thirties. Within metropolitan areas, the well-known process of decentralization—from central city to suburbs—has also continued, however.

Let us return to the 168 standard metropolitan areas to examine this process of suburbanization. The preliminary figures show that while the central cities as a group were increasing by 13.0 per cent, the outlying parts of the metropolitan areas were increasing by 34.7 per cent [2]. Nearly half of the population increase of the nation took place in these suburban areas. In only 37 of 168 areas did the outlying parts grow less rapidly than the central city. In some of these exceptions, the central city had annexed part of its suburbs during the decade.

It is true that these relationships are affected by such arbitrary factors as the area of counties and the practices of state legislatures with respect to size of areas to be incorporated as municipalities and with respect to annexations. Nonetheless, the data indicate the extent to which the inhabitants of the economic city have their homes outside the boundaries of the political city and are thus in a large degree independent of its administration. Studies now being made at the Scripps Foundation and elsewhere are showing that, in the period 1935 to 1940, the in-migrants to the suburbs came largely from the central city but in-migrants to the central city came largely from outside the metropolitan area [7].

THE ROLES OF NATURAL INCREASE AND MIGRATION

What were the roles of natural increase and migration in effecting the redistribution of population during the 'forties? Figures 2 and 3 show by states: (1) the excess of births over deaths[8] and (2) net migration, both as a percentage of the 1940 population [8]. Net migration is an estimate derived by subtraction and includes not only interstate migration but also international migration. (The latter amounted to about a million persons net for continental United States.)

All the States had a natural increase. The United States average was 13.7 per cent of the 1940 population. The percentage increase from this cause ranged from eight per cent for New York to 26 per cent for New Mexico. Twenty-six of the States had a net out-migration; but, in all but four of these, the natural increase was large enough to overcome this deficit. Areas of out-migration included: (1) Northern New England; (2) Pennsylvania; (3) the West North Central States plus Wisconsin; (4) The South except for Delaware, Maryland, the District of Columbia, Virginia, Florida, and Texas; (5) Montana, Idaho, and Wyoming. As a percentage of the 1940 State population, Florida, Arizona, Nevada, and the Pacific States had a net migratory gain of at least 20 per cent. California's net migration was more than one-third of its population at the beginning of the decade. Maryland's migratory gain was about 15 per cent; and 6 other States, all east of the Mississippi, gained by 5 to 10 per cent. Fifteen States had a net migration of less than 5 per cent, plus or minus. Ten States had migratory losses of 5 to 10 per cent, and seven had losses of 10 to 15 per cent. The latter were either in the South or in the Great Plains. Finally, Arkansas, Mississippi, North Dakota, and Oklahoma had a net migratory loss of more than 15 per cent.

Net civilian migration by States from April 1, 1940 to November 1, 1943, was estimated by Eldridge on the basis of war ration book registrations [9]. The amount of net migration for this period is compared with the civilian net migration for the whole decade in Figure 4. The differences should represent largely civilian net migration between 1943 and 1950 plus that portion of the civilian changes of State of residence between 1940 and 1950 that was made by persons who had been in the armed forces in 1943. The larger differences should be fairly reliable indicators of what happened after 1943.

---

[8] These are births and deaths occurring to residents of the area regardless of migration status. Thus this figure does not give the change that would have occurred during the decade had the population of the state remained "closed."

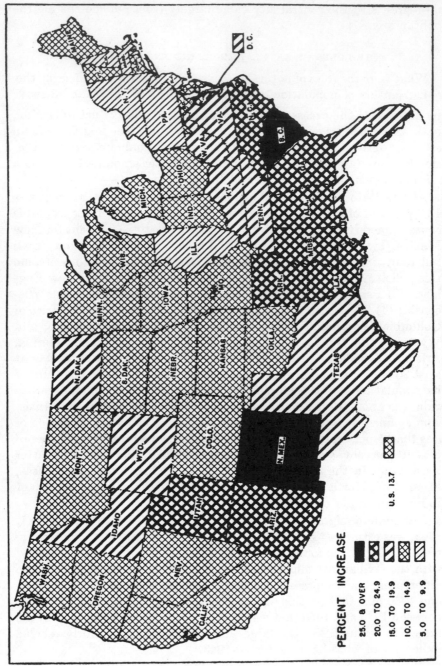

FIGURE 2. Natural increase, 1940 to 1950, as per cent of 1940 population, by States

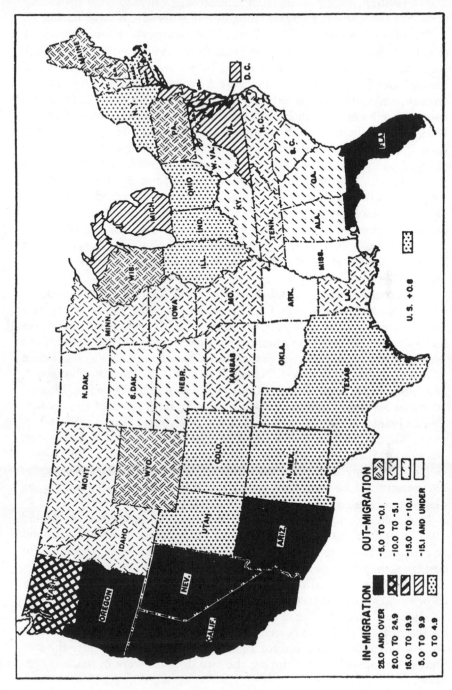

FIGURE 3. Net migration, 1940 to 1950, as per cent of 1940 population, by States

Net civilian immigration from abroad was only 305,000 up to the middle of the war but 1,600,000 for the whole decade. A large part of all immigration has gone to New York. The comparative figures suggest that the following States had net gains from civilian migration in both parts of the decade: Massachusetts, New Jersey, Ohio, Indiana, Illinois, Michigan, Delaware, Florida, Arizona, Nevada, Washington, Oregon, and California. Relatively heavy gains in the 1943–1950 period seem to have occurred in Florida and Oregon. Connecticut and Maryland, which gained through migration up to the middle of the war, had little if any net gain thereafter. Important war plants in these States reduced operations after 1945, creating a considerable reduction in employment that was not fully offset by peacetime production. States where this situation had an even heavier impact were Rhode Island, the District of Columbia, Virginia, and Utah, all of which had smaller civilian migratory gains for the whole decade than for the first half. The large amount of new housing constructed in the Maryland and Virginia suburbs of Washington was an important factor in the postwar exodus from the capital.

Of the states that had had a net loss from civilian migration up to 1943, four had a net gain for the whole decade. These were New Hampshire, New York, Colorado, and New Mexico. About 10 states had a smaller net migratory loss for the period 1940 to 1950 than for the period 1940 to 1943, also suggesting a net gain from migration between 1943 and 1950. These were Maine, Vermont, Wisconsin, Minnesota, Iowa, South Dakota, Texas, Montana, Idaho, and Wyoming. Finally, 16 states evidently had net out-migration in both parts of the decade: Pennsylvania, Missouri, North Dakota, Nebraska, Kansas, West Virginia, North Carolina, South Carolina, Georgia, Kentucky, Tennessee, Alabama, Mississippi, Arkansas, Louisiana, and Oklahoma. Out-migration after the middle of the war seems to have been relatively heavy as compared with the earlier out-migration in the bloc of states comprising Georgia, Alabama, Mississippi, Louisiana, and Tennessee.

It should be emphasized that the statements concerning the period 1943 to 1950 are based on differences of differences and are thus subject to considerable error. The characterizations of Texas and Wyoming, for instance, may well be quite erroneous.

It has been pointed out by Shryock and Eldridge that the number of net migrants by states in a given period has had a high positive correlation with the number in another period, at least up to twenty years earlier or later [10]. The correlation coefficient of the present estimates for 1940 to 1950 with those for 1930 to 1940 is $+0.91$, despite the fact that economic conditions during the two decades were in marked contrast.

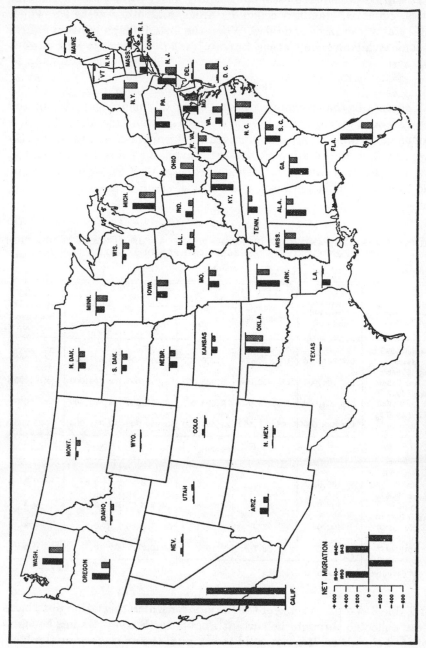

FIGURE 4. Net civilian migration, 1940 to 1950, and 1940 to 1943, by States

It will be possible to estimate net migration from 1940 to 1950 for cities, counties, standard economic areas, and other areas for which vital statistics can be compiled. When the final 1950 population figures become available, the Census Bureau intends to prepare estimates of this sort.

GROSS MIGRATION

The data of the foregoing section do not tell us anything about the total amount of migration, in-migration to a given area, out-migration from a given area, or streams of migration from one area to another. So far, very little information of this sort is available from the new census. For an indication of what happened during the 'forties, we must turn to the Current Population Survey, a national sample survey.

TABLE 3

MIGRATION STATUS AND TYPE OF MIGRATION FOR THE CIVILIAN POPULATION OF THE UNITED STATES: SELECTED PERIODS, 1940 TO 1950

Number

Period	Population 1 year old and over	Non-migrants	Migrants			Persons abroad at beginning of period
			Total	Intrastate	Interstate	
March 1949 to March 1950	146,864,000	138,124,000	8,250,000	4,360,000	3,889,000	491,000
April 1948 to April 1949	144,101,000	135,289,000	8,335,000	3,992,000	4,344,000	476,000
April 1947 to April 1948	141,698,000	132,228,000	9,008,000	4,638,000	4,370,000	462,000
April 1940 to April 1947	122,633,000*	96,565,000	25,469,000	13,081,000	12,388,000	599,000

Per cent

Period	Population 1 year old and over	Non-migrants	Migrants			Persons abroad at beginning of period
			Total	Intrastate	Interstate	
March 1949 to March 1950	100.0	94.0	5.6	3.0	2.6	0.3
April 1948 to April 1949	100.0	93.9	5.8	2.8	3.0	0.3
April 1947 to April 1948	100.0	93.3	6.4	3.3	3.1	0.3
April 1940 to April 1947	100.0	78.7	20.8	10.7	10.1	0.5

* Seven years old and over.

Table 3 compares some of the periods for which migration data have been collected through the current Population Survey. As has been explained elsewhere, it is not valid to compute the average annual migration by dividing the total reported for the period 1940 to 1947 by seven, Nor do we obtain any meaningful figures for the decade by adding the absolute figures for the component periods [11]. It can be safely inferred from the available data, however, that internal migration took place at a higher annual rate during the war and reconversion periods than during the prewar period. There was also some falling off of civilian migration in the last two years of the decade.

Not very much is known as yet about the migration to and from specific parts of the United States. Some information for selected cities and counties is furnished by the Census of Congested Production Areas taken in 1944 and by pretests of the 1950 Census taken between 1947 and 1949. For 1941 to 1945 and 1940 to 1947, the movement to and from each of the four census regions was obtained in the Current Population Survey.

Data on movements to and from farms are available from both the Current Population Survey of the Bureau of the Census and from a national sample survey conducted annually by the Bureau of Agricultural Economics. The latter is chosen for discussion here because it provides an annual series back to 1940. Table 4 is condensed from the latest report. It may be noted that in addition to the well-known movement from farms, hundreds of thousands of persons move *to* farms every year.

TABLE 4

ANNUAL ESTIMATES OF THE FARM POPULATION, NATURAL INCREASE OCCURRING IN THE FARM POPULATION, AND NUMBER OF PERSONS MOVING TO AND FROM FARMS, FOR THE UNITED STATES: 1940 TO 1949

(Population in 000's)

Year	Farm population on January 1	Natural increase	Change through migration						
			Total	Civilian migration			Military migration		
				Total	To farms	From farms	Total	To farms	From farms
1949	27,776								
1948	27,440	479	−143	−123	1,178	−1,301	−20	−79	59
1947	27,550	483	−593	−640	914	−1,554	47	−69	116
1946	26,850	419	281	−266	1,077	−1,343	547	−159	706
1945	25,190	354	1,306	603	1,684	−1,081	703	−191	894
1944	25,521	345	−676	−476	817	−1,293	−200	−300	100
1943	26,659	355	−1,493	−988	994	−1,982	−505	−605	100
1942	29,048	390	−2,779	−1,920	819	−2,739	−859	−859	—
1941	29,988	417	−1,357	−1,146	814	−1,960	−211	−211	—
1940	30,269	400	−681	−606	690	−1,296	−75	−75	—

Source: U. S. Bureau of Agricultural Economics. *Farm population estimates, January, 1949.* June 1949.

It is usually the case that gross migration for an area is much larger than net migration and that short-distance mobility is much larger in

volume than long-distance migration. These generalizations fit what
we know about the 'forties rather well. The most important exceptions
are on the Pacific Coast. The amount of net in-migration for many
areas there was not very much smaller than the amount of gross in-
migration. Furthermore, many migrants to the West Coast came from
hundreds of miles away.

DIFFERENTIALS IN POPULATION REDISTRIBUTION

It is well known that migration is selective of particular population
groups. The Current Population Survey of April 1947, for instance
indicated a disproportionately heavy movement of Negroes from southern farms since 1940. In addition to color, these surveys have related-
migration status to sex, age, marital status, duration of marital status,
family status, educational attainment, employment status, major occupation group, and income. These data are presented in various publications of Census Bureau Series P-20, P-50, and P-60.

From a preliminary sample of the 1950 Census, a few data on migration status are being published for the United States, the 10 largest
states, and the 55 standard metropolitan areas and 36 cities of 250,000
or more in 1940 [12]. Distributions for the United States from this
source may be compared with those from the Current Population Survey: The differences are too large to be explained by the small variation
in dates or by sampling error. There is by now considerable evidence

Residence in 1949	April 1949 to April 1950, 1950 Census	March 1949 to March 1950, C.P.S.
Same house	82.4	80.9
Different house, same county	11.3	13.1
Different county or abroad	6.3	6.0

that the better trained, experienced enumerators of the Current Population Survey obtain a more nearly complete identification of the unemployed and the marginal members of the labor force than do the
decennial census enumerators. It seems likely that they would also get
a more nearly accurate classification by other items defined by answers
to a series of questions, such as migration status, but we have no direct
evidence on this point. Further information on accuracy should be obtained later from the Postenumerative Survey of the 1950 Census and
from other studies.

Among the 46 Standard Metropolitan Areas for which these figures have been published to date, the percentage of those reporting their 1949 residence who were migrants (or immigrants from abroad) ranged from 1 per cent to 16 per cent. This percentage varied roughly with the metropolitan area's rate of population increase during the whole dec-

TABLE 5

PER CENT DISTRIBUTION BY RESIDENCE IN 1949 OF THE POPULATION
1 TO 20 YEARS OLD, BY AGE, FOR THE UNITED STATES: 1950

Residence in 1949	Total 1 to 20 years old	1 to 4 years	5 to 9 years	10 to 13 years	14 to 17 years	18 to 20 years
Total	100.0	100.0	100.0	100.0	100.0	100.0
Same house as in 1950	80.8	77.2	82.5	85.8	86.1	70.5
Different house, same county	11.4	13.8	10.8	9.2	8.4	15.2
Different county, same state	3.3	3.9	2.9	2.2	2.4	5.5
Different state or abroad	3.2	.4.0	2.6	1.8	2.1	6.6
Residence not reported	1.3	1.2	1.2	1.0	1.1	2.3

ade. At the extremes, it was below 3 per cent in Johnstown, Scranton, Wilkes-Barre-Hazleton, and Worcester and above 10 per cent in Denver, Miami, and Washington. For metropolitan areas containing two or more counties, this movement includes migration within the metropolitan area.

For use at the Midcentury White House Conference on Children and Youth, some preliminary sample data on migration from the 1950 Census have been published for the population under 21 years old [13]. Table 5 also is derived from this source. Of the 50,800,000 children and youths 1 to 20 years old, 9,100,000 had lived in a different house year earlier. Of these, 3,300,000 had lived in a different county and are thus classified as migrants. Those coming from a different state or from abroad numbered 1,600,000. The age groups of Table 5 are the most detailed for which census migration data have been presented. They reflect some interesting aspects of the family cycle. Note the decline in mobility from "1 to 4" years to "5 to 9" years and the further decline to "10 to 13." There is little change at "14 to 17" and a sharp rise at "18 to 20." Many families move to the suburbs when the first child is old enough to play outdoors. When children are in high school, families are relatively settled and unlikely to move. Up to about age 18, most children move with their parents. Thereafter they often move on their own to attend college, serve in the armed forces, take jobs, or get married. Presumably the age differentials examined would be even sharper if the data were restricted to first children. Similar variations of migration status with age were observed for the urban, rural-non-farm, and rural-farm populations of the United States and for each region.

THE 1950 PROGRAM OF MIGRATION STATISTICS

Considerably more light should be shed on the ways in which population redistribution has been affected if the Census Bureau's contemplated program in this field can be carried out. The estimates of net migration for the period 1940 to 1950 have already been mentioned. Revised intercensal population estimates as of each year in that decade are being prepared for states and the larger cities and standard metropolitan areas. These should indicate the fluctuations of growth in various parts of the country as they were affected by extraordinary military and economic events.

From the migration questions on the 1950 Population schedule, many facts are potentially available about mobility in the year preceding the enumeration. Migration status will be published for counties, cities of 10,000 or more, and census tracts. The tables showing migration from each state to every other state that were published in 1940 will again be prepared. The new state economic areas will also figure importantly in the reports on internal migration. Other new emphases will be on the short-distance movements from one house to another within the same county and, for the larger streams of migration, on social and economic characteristics cross-classified by age. Outlines of the data to be tabulated may be obtained by writing to the Population and Housing Division, U. S. Bureau of the Census, Washington 25, D. C.

SUMMARY

The record-breaking amount of population growth between 1940 and 1950 was very unevenly distributed over the Nation. World War II and its prosperous aftermath accelerated the concentration of people in metropolitan areas and around our sea coasts, as almost half of the counties lost population. At the same time, the decentralization within metropolitan areas also continued. Differentials in the excess of births over deaths have contributed to population redistribution; but migration, and notably internal migration, has been more important in this respect.

Some of the survey data concerning internal migration that have been collected during the 'forties are summarized in the accompanying tables and maps, along with the first migration statistics from the 1950 Census. Within the next few years, it is hoped that this source will give us a much fuller knowledge of the dynamics of population redistribution.

REFERENCES

[1] U. S. Bureau of the Census. *Preliminary counts.* Series PC-3, No. 4. "Population of Counties: April 1, 1950." November 5, 1950.

[2] U. S. Bureau of the Census. *Preliminary counts.* Series PC-3. No. 3. "Population of Standard Metropolitan Areas: April 1, 1950." November 5, 1950.

[3] Bogue, Donald J. "Changes in Population Distribution since 1940," *American Journal of Sociology*, 56(1): 43–57. July 1950.

[4] U. S. Bureau of the Census. *Preliminary counts.* Series PC-3, No. 7. "Population of State Economic Areas: April 1, 1950." December 27, 1950.

[5] U. S. Bureau of the Census. *State Economic Areas*, by Donald J. Bogue. Government Printing Office, Washington, 1951.

[6] Beck, P. G. and Forster, M. C. *Six rural problem areas.* Federal Emergency Relief Administration, Research Monograph I, Washington, 1935: 137.

[7] See, for example: Thompson, Warren S., and Bogue, Donald J. "Subregional Migration as an Area of Research." *Social Forces*, 27 (4): 395. May 1949.

[8] U. S. Bureau of the Census. *Current population reports. Population estimates.* Series P-25, No. 47. "Provisional Estimates of the Population of Regions, Divisions, and States: July 1, 1940 to 1949." March 9, 1951.

[9] U. S. Bureau of the Census. *Population—Special Reports.* Series P-44, No. 17. "Interstate Migration and Other Population Changes: 1940 to 1943," by Hope Tisdale Eldridge, August 28, 1944.

[10] Shryock, Henry S., Jr., and Eldridge, Hope Tisdale. "Internal Migration in Peace and War." *American Sociological Review*, 12(1): 27–39. February 1947.

[11] Shryock, Henry S., Jr. "Wartime Shifts of the Civilian Population." *Milbank Memorial Fund Quarterly*, 25(3): 270. July 1947.

[12] U. S. Bureau of the Census. *Preliminary counts.* Series PC-7, No. 1 "General Characteristics of the Population of the United States: April 1, 1950." February 25, 1951; . . . Series PC-6, Nos. 1-10. "Characteristics of the Population of [State]." March 20–April 10, 1951; Series PC-5, Nos. 1-55. "Characteristics of the Population of the . . . Standard Metropolitan Area: April 1, 1950." March 28, 1951 to date.

[13] U. S. Bureau of the Census. *Current Population reports. Population characteristics.* Series P-20, No. 32 "Children and Youth: 1950." December 4, 1950.

INTERNAL MIGRATION IN SWEDEN AND

INTERVENING OPPORTUNITIES

By Eleanor Collins Isbell

THE PRESENT ATTEMPT to test Stouffer's theory of intervening opportunities as a generalized expression of the relationship between migration and distance[1] was prompted by the belief that the potential utility of the theory justifies repeated efforts to determine its adequacy and by the availability of Swedish census data which could be employed for the purpose. The results of the current test, like those of the earlier ones by Stouffer and by Bright and Thomas,[2] tend to substantiate the theory despite the crudeness of measurements and the doubtful suitability of the data used as criteria of opportunities.

In Stouffer's words, his theory "assumes that there is no necessary relationship between mobility and distance. . . . It proposes that *the number of persons going a given distance is directly proportional to the number of opportunities at that distance and inversely proportional to the number of intervening opportunities. . . .* The relation between mobility and distance may be said to depend on an auxiliary relationship, which expresses the cumulated (intervening) opportunities as a function of distance."[3] The results of both Stouffer's application of this theory to data on residential mobility in Cleveland and Bright and Thomas' experiment with net interstate

[1] Samuel A. Stouffer, "Intervening Opportunities: A Theory Relating Mobility and Distance," *American Sociological Review*, 1940, 5:845-867.

[2] Margaret L. Bright and Dorothy S. Thomas, "Interstate Migration and Intervening Opportunities," *American Sociological Review*, 1941, 6:773-783.

[3] Stouffer, *op. cit.*, pp. 846-847. The basic formula is $\dfrac{\Delta y}{\Delta s} = \dfrac{a}{x} \times \dfrac{\Delta x}{\Delta s}$, Δy equalling the number of persons migrating from an origin to a circular band of width Δs; x, the number of intervening opportunities; Δx, the number of opportunities within the band of width Δs.

migration data for the United States as of 1930 were "encouraging" in showing conformity between *patterns* of expectation and observation; but Stouffer recognized that many discrepancies were too large to attribute to chance, while Bright and Thomas' application of the chi-square test to Stouffer's and their own results indicated that "a real discrepancy" was involved in both cases. They suggest, however, that the chi-square test may be too sensitive to be applicable.

Bright and Thomas found discrepancies of two sorts, one of which they were able to reduce markedly by increasing the qualitative similarity of "opportunities" (i.e., by eliminating migration to California in their computations) and by holding constant the factor of direction. The other discrepancy, namely, an excess of expected over observed net migrants in the two smallest distance intervals, was attributed (1) to necessary crudeness of measurements which meant that these intervals represented "nearest migration" or " 'opportunities' without 'intervening opportunities' "; and (2) to the fact that Stouffer's formula, "although the theory on which it is based postulates no necessary relationship of migration and distance, . . . does overweight appreciably *absence of distance* in the first interval merely because intervening opportunities are necessarily measured in terms of distance bands."[4]

For further investigation of these possible sources of discrepancy, Swedish census data on intercommunity migration seemed especially suitable. The census of 1930 tabulates all persons migrating from one community to another in Sweden between 1921 and 1930 by county of origin and county of destination of *last migration*,

[4] Bright and Thomas, *op. cit.*, p. 779.

by sex;[5] and for intracounty migrants the tabulation is further broken down into districts (*bygden*) of origin and destination.[6] Applying Stouffer's terminology to the data for males the "opportunities" in each county can be defined as the total number of males settling in the county, including those migrating from one community to another within the county as well as in-migrants from all other counties, between 1921 and 1930. Obviously, some short-term "opportunities" superseded by subsequent migra-

those which primarily involve employment. Only if the ratio of young and old to middle-aged migrants were relatively constant for all distances would the effect of this heterogeneity be minimized. A further limitation of the Swedish data derives from the fact that, although they do not include intracommunity or purely residential moves, some of the short-distance moves between adjoining communities and counties, particularly between cities and their suburbs, in all probability do represent merely resi-

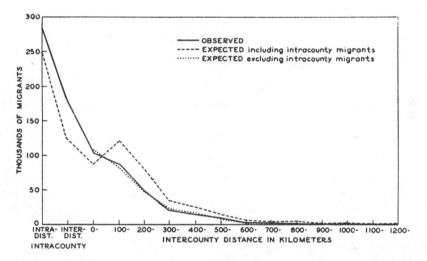

CHART 1. Observed and Expected Male Intercommunity Migrants, Sweden, 1921-30, by Distance of Last Migration

tions are· not included, but the picture is far more nearly complete than that which would be shown by net intercounty migration. A more serious limitation of the data, for our purposes, is the heterogeneity of the opportunities represented by male migrants of all ages. The migrations of young and middle-aged men doubtless do represent opportunities of an economic nature, but the incidental migrations of children as members of family groups and the moves made by older men who have retired reflect very different sorts of opportunities from

[5] *Sveriges Officiella Statistik, Folkräkningen den 31 December 1930*, II, 178-185 (Table 21).
[6] *Ibid.*, pp. 206-227 (Table 24).

dential moves; and this introduces another element of dissimilarity in "opportunities" which will be seen to be a disturbing factor.

With the above definition of opportunities, "intervening opportunities" were, of course, the cumulated number of male migrants settling in all counties between the county of origin and the county of destination. Expected migrants or settlers at given distances were calculated for each county of origin by applying Stouffer's formula to these opportunities, intervening opportunities, and the number of male migrants originating in the county. Only crude approximation of migration distances was possible. The distances between the population centers of each pair of counties as computed in the census of 1920[7] were available;[8] and 100-kilometer intervals were used for computing expected intercounty migrants, preceded by two intervals for intracounty migrants, in general representing less distant moves than those to the nearest

respects the computation procedure was identical with that described by Bright and

kilometer distance group or arbitrarily in a single "nearest" group seemed to improve the agreement of expected and observed migration enough to warrant a preliminary application of Stouffer's formula

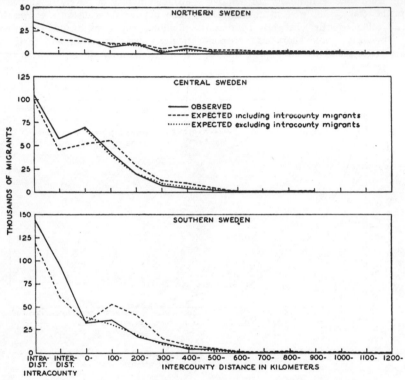

CHART 2. Observed and Expected Male Intercommunity Migrants, 1921-30, by Region of Origin and Distance of Last Migration

counties: (1) intracounty migrants moving within the same district (*bygd*), i.e., on the whole the shortest moves; and (2) migrants between districts in the county.[9] In other

[7] *Sveriges Officiella Statistik, Folkräkningen den 31 December 1920,* II, 92.

[8] Stockholm University, Institute for Social Sciences, *Population Movements and Industrialization, Swedish Counties, 1895-1930,* Stockholm Economic Studies No. 10 (London: P. S. King & Son, 1941), pp. 72-73.

[9] Use of these two nearest classes instead of including all intracounty migrants in the 0-100

on the basis of the smaller geographical unit, the district or *bygd*, so as to estimate "opportunities" for intradistrict movement in each county and avoid the assumption that their number was identical with the actual number of migrants in this category (the only one in which the definition of opportunities is affected by origin of migrants). The procedure was based on the assumption that on a county basis opportunities for intradistrict movement could not be separated from other opportunities in the county, and that opportunities in any district were represented by all moves into the district. Hence preliminary computations of expected migrants from each district to itself, to the rest of the county, and to all other counties at 100-

Thomas,[10] except that counties were substituted for states and total migrants over a period, for net migrants as of a particular date.

When the resultant distributions of expected migrants by distance were compared with those of observed migrants from the

tween the patterns of distribution of observed and expected migrants was again close enough to be termed "encouraging." (See Charts 1 and 2 and Table 1.) Major discrepancies were again found in the first two intervals (representing intracounty or nearest migration), but in contrast with

TABLE 1. MALE INTERCOMMUNITY MIGRANTS IN SWEDEN, 1921–30, BY REGION OF ORIGIN AND DISTANCE OF LAST MIGRATION, COMPARED WITH NUMBERS EXPECTED ACCORDING TO STOUFFER'S THEORY

Thousands of Migrants

Distance (kilometers)	Total Sweden		Northern Sweden (5 Counties)		Central Sweden (9 Counties)		Southern Sweden (11 Counties)	
	Observed	Expected	Observed	Expected	Observed	Expected	Observed	Expected
Intracounty								
Intradistrict	282.6	248.0	34.4	28.8	105.1	99.6	143.1	119.5
Interdistrict	178.9	123.6	26.0	15.4	58.7	46.5	94.1	61.7
Intercounty								
0—	102.6	85.9	—	—	70.1	52.3	32.5	33.6
100—	86.5	120.4	7.9	10.9	42.6	56.2	36.0	53.3
200—	49.0	80.9	11.5	11.5	19.1	28.3	18.4	41.1
300—	20.4	34.4	1.4	5.3	7.3	13.3	11.7	15.8
400—	14.0	26.1	5.6	7.4	4.3	9.1	4.1	9.6
500—	8.4	13.9	1.4	3.6	2.9	4.8	4.1	5.6
600—	2.9	6.6	1.7	3.9	.4	.4	.8	2.2
700—	2.5	3.9	1.5	2.6	.8	.8	.2	.6
800—	1.7	4.1	.9	2.1	.4	.3	.5	1.7
900—	.6	1.1	.3	.6	.1	.2	.2	.3
1000—	.9	1.7	.5	.8	—	—	.4	.8
1100—	.2	.3	.1	.2	—	—	.1	.2
1200—	.4	.7	.2	.3	—	—	.2	.4
Total	751.6	751.6	93.4	93.4	311.7	311.7	346.4	346.4

respective counties (24 counties and the separate administrative area of Stockholm City) and combined to afford comparison for the nation as a whole and for geographic divisions,[11] the correspondence be-

kilometer distance intervals were made, and the expected intradistrict movement summed for the districts in each county to approximate the opportunities which would be taken up by intradistrict moves in the county. Subtracting this sum from the total in-migrants to the county gave an estimate of the remaining opportunities in the county.

[10] Bright and Thomas, *op. cit.*, p. 777.

[11] The divisions used are combinations of those delineated in Dorothy S. Thomas, *Social and Economic Aspects of Swedish Population Movements 1750-1933* (New York: The Macmillan Company, 1941), pp. 203-204. Divisions I, II, and III are combined as Southern Sweden; IV, V, and VIII, as Central Sweden; and VI and VII as Northern Sweden.

Bright and Thomas' results, the observed migrants were greatly in excess of the expected. In the four counties of Malmöhus, Gothenburg and Bohus, Östergötland, and Stockholm, which are the sites of Sweden's four largest cities, this discrepancy was much reduced or reversed in the first interval and very much exaggerated in the second, containing the large cities. (See Table 2. For Stockholm County the latter characteristic appears in the 0-100 km. interval containing Stockholm City.) Several factors may account for this divergence of the pattern of correspondence: first, the data for these counties are not strictly comparable with those for other counties. In the first three, intradistrict migrants are relatively few because the cities of Gothenburg,

TABLE 2. MALE INTERCOMMUNITY MIGRANTS FROM SWEDISH COUNTIES CONTAINING LARGE CITIES AND
REMAINING COUNTIES OF CENTRAL AND SOUTHERN SWEDEN, 1921–30, BY DISTANCE OF LAST
MIGRATION, COMPARED WITH NUMBERS EXPECTED ACCORDING TO STOUFFER'S THEORY

Thousands of Migrants

Distance (kilometers)	Central Sweden							
	Stockholm City		Stockholm Co.		Östergötland Co.		6 Remaining Counties	
	Observed	Expected	Observed	Expected	Observed	Expected	Observed	Expected
Intracounty								
Intradistrict	—	—	15.8	22.5	19.9	19.2	69.5	57.9
Interdistrict	—	—	9.1	10.0	16.7	9.3	33.0	27.2
Intercounty								
0—	19.1	16.9	30.1	11.7	—	—	20.9	23.7
100—	2.6	5.1	1.3	4.9	10.5	15.0	28.2	31.2
200—	3.7	4.3	1.9	4.6	1.8	3.5	11.6	15.8
300—	3.1	2.8	.8	2.5	.7	2.1	2.7	5.9
400—	1.4	1.4	.8	2.4	—	—	2.1	5.3
500—	1.6	1.2	.5	1.5	.3	.6	.6	1.6
600—	—	—	—	—	—	—	.4	.4
700—	.4	.2	.1	.2	.1	.2	.2	.2
800—	—	—	—	—	—	—	.4	.3
900—	—	—	—	—	.1	.2	—	—
1000—	—	—	—	—	—	—	—	—
1100—	—	—	—	—	—	—	—	—
1200—	—	—	—	—	—	—	—	—
Total	31.9	31.9	60.3	60.3	50.1	50.1	169.5	169.5

Distance (kilometers)	Southern Sweden					
	Gothenburg & Bohus Co.		Malmöhus Co.		9 Remaining Counties	
	Observed	Expected	Observed	Expected	Observed	Expected
Intracounty						
Intradistrict	6.7	13.7	28.1	29.2	108.2	76.6
Interdistrict	21.3	9.5	32.3	15.7	40.6	36.5
Intercounty						
0—	4.4	3.8	6.9	5.4	21.2	24.3
100—	2.4	4.6	2.7	5.3	30.9	43.4
200—	2.6	6.3	2.3	8.5	13.4	26.3
300—	3.3	1.9	.8	4.0	7.7	10.0
400—	.7	1.2	.6	3.7	2.8	4.7
500—	—	—	3.6	4.2	.4	1.3
600—	.2	.4	.2	.6	.4	1.2
700—	—	—	—	—	.2	.6
800—	.1	.1	.2	.9	.2	.7
900—	—	—	—	—	.2	.3
1000—	.1	.1	.1	.3	.2	.4
1100—	—	—	—	—	.1	.2
1200—	—	—	.1	.3	.1	.1
Total	41.8	41.8	77.9	77.9	226.7	226.7

Malmö, and Norrköping constitute separate districts for which intradistrict migrants are identical with intracommunity migrants who are not included in the census tabulations; and for Stockholm County intradistrict migration is relatively infrequent compared with the great number of migrants crossing the boundary into Stockholm City. At the same time, as Bright and Thomas

point out, because of the "absence of distance" in the first interval the opportunities in it are relatively overweighted compared with those in the second and higher intervals. Also, the great excess of observed migrants in the intervals containing great cities strongly suggests a qualitative difference in the opportunities in such cities not adequately allowed for in an application of

TABLE 3. MALE INTERCOMMUNITY MIGRANTS IN SWEDEN 1921–30 BY REGION OF ORIGIN AND DISTANCE OF LAST MIGRATION, EXCLUDING MIGRANTS WHOSE LAST MOVE WAS INTRACOUNTY, COMPARED WITH NUMBERS EXPECTED ACCORDING TO STOUFFER'S THEORY

Thousands of Migrants

Distance (kilometers)	Total Sweden		Northern Sweden (5 Counties)		Central Sweden (9 Counties)		Southern Sweden (11 Counties)	
	Observed	Expected	Observed	Expected	Observed	Expected	Observed	Expected
0—	102.6	107.4	—	—	70.1	68.6	32.5	38.9
100—	86.5	81.2	7.9	10.2	42.6	40.2	36.0	30.8
200—	49.0	48.3	11.5	9.5	19.1	19.1	18.4	19.7
300—	20.4	22.1	1.4	2.8	7.3	9.8	11.7	9.5
400—	14.0	15.9	5.6	4.3	4.3	6.1	4.1	5.5
500—	8.4	7.6	1.4	1.9	2.9	3.0	4.1	2.6
600—	2.9	2.6	1.7	1.6	.4	.2	.8	.7
700—	2.5	2.2	1.5	1.4	.8	.7	.2	.2
800—	1.7	1.3	.9	.6	.4	.2	.5	.5
900—	.6	.4	.3	.2	.1	.1	.2	.2
1000—	.9	.6	.5	.3	—	—	.4	.3
1100—	.2	.2	.1	.1	—	—	.1	.1
1200—	.4	.2	.2	.1	—	—	.2	.1
Total	290.1	290.1	33.0	33.0	147.9	147.9	109.2	109.2

Central Sweden

Distance	Stockholm City		Stockholm Co.		Östergötland Co.		6 Remaining Counties	
	Observed	Expected	Observed	Expected	Observed	Expected	Observed	Expected
0—	19.1	18.3	30.1	22.8	—	—	20.9	27.5
100—	2.6	4.0	1.3	3.2	10.5	10.6	28.2	22.3
200—	3.7	3.9	1.9	3.5	1.8	1.7	11.6	9.9
300—	3.1	3.2	.8	2.4	.7	.8	2.7	3.4
400—	1.4	1.4	.8	2.3	—	—	2.1	2.4
500—	1.6	.9	.5	1.0	.3	.2	.6	.9
600—	—	—	—	—	—	—	.4	.2
700—	.4	.2	.1	.2	.1	.1	.2	.1
800—	—	—	—	—	—	—	.4	.2
900—	—	—	—	—	.1	.1	—	—
1000—	—	—	—	—	—	—	—	—
1100—	—	—	—	—	—	—	—	—
1200—	—	—	—	—	—	—	—	—
Total	31.9	31.9	35.4	35.4	13.5	13.5	67.0	67.0

Southern Sweden

	Gothenburg & Bohus Co.		Malmöhus Co.		9 Remaining Counties	
	Observed	Expected	Observed	Expected	Observed	Expected
0—	4.4	5.7	6.9	6.9	21.2	26.3
100—	2.4	2.6	2.7	3.0	30.9	25.3
200—	2.6	2.9	2.3	3.2	13.4	13.6
300—	3.3	1.7	.8	.8	7.7	7.0
400—	.7	.7	.6	1.1	2.8	3.8
500—	—	—	3.6	2.1	.4	.5
600—	.2	.1	.2	.1	.4	.4
700—	—	—	—	—	.2	.2
800—	.1	.1	.2	.2	.2	.3
900—	—	—	—	—	.2	.2
1000—	.1	.1	.1	.1	.2	.2
1100—	—	—	—	—	.1	.÷
1200—	—	—	.1	.1	.1	.1
Total	13.8	13.8	17.6	17.6	77.9	77.9

Stouffer's formula to total migration data.

The fact that most of the counties and the nation as a whole exhibit excesses of observed over expected migrants in the nearest intervals may be attributable to one of the limitations of the data, namely, the inclusion of some purely residential moves which as "opportunities" are distributed over the whole range but as observed migrants are all included in the nearest intervals. On this account the estimates of near-distance migration would always tend to be deficient compared with the observed numbers. This assumption could be tested, of course, by eliminating the majority of such moves from consideration by excluding all migrants whose last move was intracounty from both opportunities and outmigrants in the computation of expected migrants. Calculations were consequently carried through on this basis; and the results seem to confirm our assumption. As can be seen from Charts 1 and 2 and Table 3, the two intervals which now represent the nearest migration distances do not consistently show excesses of observed over expected migrants; there is a striking improvement in the correspondence between the *patterns* of observed and expected intercounty migrants; and the relative differences between the actual and estimated numbers in each distance class are with few

exceptions reduced considerably for the nation as a whole, for the geographic divisions, and for the counties which are sites of large cities. Application of the chi-square test to results of the two series of computations gave values of chi-square shown in the first two rows of Table 4. As Bright and Thomas found, the computed values are so enormous as hardly to justify their calculation; but they are impressively reduced when intracounty moves are omitted. While most of this improvement may perhaps fairly be ascribed to an increased similarity in opportunities due to the exclusion of residential moves, a part of the improvement may be traceable to a resulting reduction in the amount of overlapping between groups in our crude classification of moves by distance.

Although the omission of intracounty moves weakened or eliminated the characteristic excess of observed over expected migrants to nearest distances, the direction of the discrepancy in the first two intervals was not consistently reversed so as to agree with the pattern found by Bright and Thomas. There was, however, a fairly strong tendency toward reversal in the first interval in which two-thirds of the counties and the nation as a whole now showed excesses of expected over observed migrants. For the nation this excess would have been more pronounced were it not for the weight of the discrepancy in the opposite direction in Stockholm County and Stockholm City, where the influence of residential moves was not much diminished by the exclusion of intracounty moves.

With the elimination of intracounty migrants the factor of direction can be held relatively constant. An earlier analysis of direction of intercounty migration based on birth-residence indexes revealed that the main "routes" of net intercounty migration

TABLE 4. CHI-SQUARE VALUES*

Group of migrants	Total Sweden			Northern Sweden			Central Sweden					
							Stockholm City			Stockholm County		
	n	x^2	$P=.05$	n	x^2	$P=.05$	n	x^2	$P=.05$	n	x^2	$P=.05$
All intercommunity	14	73,100	24	13	24,147	22	6	2,094	13	8	≷8,081	16
All intercounty	12	1,648	21	11	2,632	20	6	1,359	13	6	6,631	13
Intercounty north or east	12	1,314†	21	4	47†	9	5	3,274	11	6	3,262	13
Intercounty south or west	12	1,489†	21	11	2,188	20	5	1,613	11	5	789	11
Intercounty north or east excluding migrants to St. City	12	1,470†	21	—	—	—	—	—	—	6	124	13
Intercounty south or west excluding migrants to St. City	12	1,103†	21	11	809	20	—	—	—	—	—	—.

Central Sweden—*Continued*

	Östergötland Co.			6 Remaining Counties			Total (excl. St. City & Co.)		
	n	x^2	$P=.05$	n	x^2	$P=.05$	n	x^2	$P=.05$
All intercommunity	7	9,186	14	10	9,577	18	11	15,423	20
All intercounty	5	57	11	8	4,037	16	9	3,415	17
Intercounty north or east	5	72	11	8	1,322	16	9	1,073	17
Intercounty south or west	2	20	6	5	474	11	5	417	11
Intercounty north or east excluding migrants to St. City	5	77	11	8	1,044	16	9	844	17
Intercounty south or west excluding migrants to St. City	—	—	—	5	324	11	5	339	11

Southern Sweden

	Gothenburg & Bohus Co.			Malmöhus Co.			9 Remaining Counties			Total (11 Counties)		
	n	x^2	$P=.05$	n	x^2	$P=.05$	n	x^2	$P=.05$	n	x^2	$P=.05$
All intercommunity	9	22,652	17	11	29,992	20	14	27,053	24	(not computed)		
All intercounty	7	1,846	14	9	1,590	17	12	2,622	21	12	3,716	21
Intercounty north or east	7	785	14	9	1,590	17	12	1,790	21	12	2,620	21
Intercounty south or west	2	228	6	—	—	—	3	1,087†	8	4	488†	9
Intercounty north or east excluding migrants to St. City	7	544	14	9	485	17	12	1,029	21	12	983	21

* Slide-rule computations. n=number of degrees of freedom.
† In chi-square computations, counties for which observed and expected totals were the same, because only one county was classified in a particular "direction," were omitted.

TABLE 5. MALE INTERCOUNTY MIGRANTS* IN SWEDEN, 1921–30, BY ORIGIN, DIRECTION, AND DISTANCE OF LAST MIGRATION, COMPARED WITH NUMBERS EXPECTED ACCORDING TO STOUFFER'S THEORY

Thousands of Migrants

Distance (kilometers)	Total Sweden		Northern Sweden (5 Counties)		Central Sweden						Southern Sweden (11 Counties)	
					Stockholm City		Stockholm County		7 Remaining Counties			
	Obs.	Exp.	Obs.	Exp.	Obs.	Exp.	Obs.	Exp.	Obs.	Exp.	Obs.	Exp.
To North or East:												
0—	55.1	58.0	—	—	.9	2.6	28.4	24.5	10.8	13.3	15.0	17.6
100—	46.3	46.4	3.1	3.3	.8	.9	.5	1.3	20.4	18.3	21.4	22.6
200—	25.2	25.8	3.9	3.7	1.6	.9	.9	2.3	4.2	3.6	14.6	15.3
300—	12.5	11.2	.2	.3	—	—	.3	1.0	.6	1.0	11.3	8.9
400—	6.8	6.6	.8	.7	1.0	.4	.1	.4	.9	.8	4.1	4.3
500—	4.9	3.6	—	—	.3	.1	.1	.5	.5	.5	4.1	2.5
600—	1.3	1.2	.2	.2	—	—	—	—	.4	.4	.8	.6
700—	1.0	1.1	—	—	.4	.1	.1	.5	.3	.3	.2	.2
800—	.8	.6	—	—	—	—	—	—	.4	.2	.5	.4
900—	.3	.2	—	—	—	—	—	—	.1	.1	.2	.1
1000—	.4	.2	—	—	—	—	—	—	—	—	.4	.2
1100—	.1	.1	—	—	—	—	—	—	—	—	.1	.1
1200—	.2	.1	—	—	—	—	—	—	—	—	.2	.1
Total	155.1	155.1	8.2	8.2	5.0	5.0	30.5	30.5	38.5	38.5	72.9	72.9
To South or West:												
0—	47.5	46.4	—	—	18.1	15.9	1.7	2.2	10.1	10.4	17.5	17.8
100—	40.3	41.5	4.8	6.1	1.8	3.0	.8	1.1	18.3	18.1	14.6	13.2
200—	23.7	23.9	7.6	7.7	2.1	2.6	1.0	.6	9.3	8.1	3.7	4.8
300—	8.0	10.0	1.2	2.4	3.1	3.7	.6	.5	2.7	3.1	.4	.4
400—	7.2	6.6	4.8	3.5	.4	.9	.7	.4	1.3	1.7	.0	.0
500—	3.4	2.9	1.4	1.4	1.3	.8	.3	.1	.4	.6	—	—
600—	1.5	1.4	1.5	1.4	—	—	—	—	—	—	—	—
700—	1.5	1.3	1.5	1.3	—	—	—	—	—	—	—	—
800—	.9	.5	.9	.5	—	—	—	—	—	—	—	—
900—	.3	.1	.3	.1	—	—	—	—	—	—	—	—
1000—	.5	.3	.5	.3	—	—	—	—	—	—	—	—
1100—	.1	.1	.1	.1	—	—	—	—	—	—	—	—
1200—	.2	.1	.2	.1	—	—	—	—	—	—	—	—
Total	135.0	135.0	24.8	24.8	26.9	26.9	4.9	4.9	42.1	42.1	36.3	36.3

* Excluding migrants who made subsequent moves within the county.

up to 1930 had led to Stockholm City and its environs, one route coming from the counties to the south and west, another from the counties to the north.[12] These two routes form a sort of migration axis along which, for our purposes, the counties can be so ranked that migration from any county to all counties preceding it is chiefly southerly or southwesterly in direction, and

[12] Stockholm. University, Institute for Social Sciences, *op. cit.*, pp. 51–60.

migration from any county to those following it is northerly or northeasterly.[13] No new computations were necessary, of course,

[13] The ranking of counties is as follows: 1 Malmöhus, 2 Kristianstad, 3 Blekinge, 4 Kronoberg, 5 Halland, 6 Jönköping, 7 Kalmar, 8 Gotland, 9 Gothenburg and Bohus, 10 Älvsborg, 11 Skaraborg, 12 Östergötland, 13 Värmland, 14 Örebro, 15 Södermanland, 16 Stockholm, 17 Stockholm City, 18 Uppsala, 19 Västmanland, 20 Kopparberg, 21 Gävleborg, 22 Jämtland, 23 Västernorrland, 24 Västerbotten, 25 Norrbotten. The first eleven counties constitute

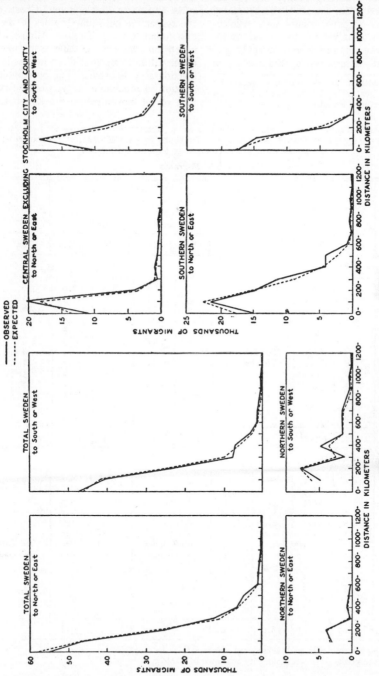

CHART 3. Observed and Expected Male Intercounty Migrants, 1921-30, by Region of
Origin, Direction, and Distance of Last Migration

for the most southerly county nor for the most northerly, but for all others estimated distributions of out-migrants were recalculated for two universes—migration northward or eastward, and migration southward or westward—determined by the position of

Southern Sweden in our delineation of geographic regions; the next nine, Central Sweden; and the last five, Northern Sweden.

the county-of-origin in this array. The results appear in Table 5 and Chart 3, and the respective chi-square values in the third and fourth rows of Table 4. Almost without exception the correspondence between the observed and expected distributions is again considerably improved. The outstanding exception is Stockholm City, where classification of all movement to Stockholm County

TABLE 6. MALE INTERCOUNTY MIGRANTS* IN SWEDEN, 1921–30, EXCLUDING THOSE WHOSE LAST MOVE WAS TO STOCKHOLM CITY, BY ORIGIN, DIRECTION, AND DISTANCE OF LAST MIGRATION, COMPARED WITH NUMBERS EXPECTED ACCORDING TO STOUFFER'S THEORY

Thousands of Migrants

Distance (kilometers)	Total Sweden†		Northern Sweden (5 Counties)		Central Sweden				Southern Sweden (11 Counties)	
					Stockholm County		7 Remaining Counties			
	Obs.	Exp.	Obs.	Exp.	Obs.	Exp.	Obs.	Exp.	Obs.	Exp.
To North or East:										
0—	24.9	27.8			2.6	2.4	6.4	7.9	15.0	14.9
100—	40.9	37.5			.5	.8	15.0	13.3	21.4	19.2
200—	20.3	20.2			.9	.8	2.9	3.0	11.0	11.8
300—	5.2	6.8			.3	.3	.6	1.0	4.0	5.2
400—	5.6	5.4			.1	.1	.9	.8	2.9	3.4
500—	2.0	2.1			.1	.1	.5	.5	1.1	1.4
600—	1.3	1.3	See Table 5		—	—	.4	.4	.8	.8
700—	1.0	.7	(No change)		.1	.1	.3	.3	.2	.2
800—	.8	.6			—	—	.4	.2	.5	.5
900—	.3	.2			—	—	.1	.1	.2	.1
1000—	.4	.3			—	—	—	—	.4	.3
1100—	.1	.1			—	—	—	—	.1	.1
1200—	.2	.1			—	—	—	—	.2	.1
Total	103.1†	103.1†			4.6	4.6	27.4	27.4	57.9	57.9
To South or West:										
0—	44.4	42.1	—	—			7.1	6.1		
100—	37.3	36.9	4.8	4.5			15.3	15.1		
200—	18.6	20.4	5.5	5.6			6.3	6.7		
300—	8.0	9.6	1.2	2.0			2.7	3.1		
400—	4.8	5.2	2.4	2.3			1.3	1.6		
500—	2.8	2.5	.8	1.0			.4	.5		
600—	1.5	1.4	1.5	1.4	See Table 5		—	—	See Table 5	
700—	.7	.8	.7	.9	(No change)		—	—	(No change)	
800—	.9	.6	.9	.6			—	—		
900—	.3	.2	.3	.2			—	—		
1000—	.5	.3	.5	.3			—	—		
1100—	.1	.1	.1	.1			—	—		
1200—	.2	.1	.2	.1			—	—		
Total	120.0†	120.0†	18.9	18.9			33.1	33.1		

* Excluding migrants who made subsequent moves within the county.
† Includes migrants *from* Stockholm City as shown in Table 5.

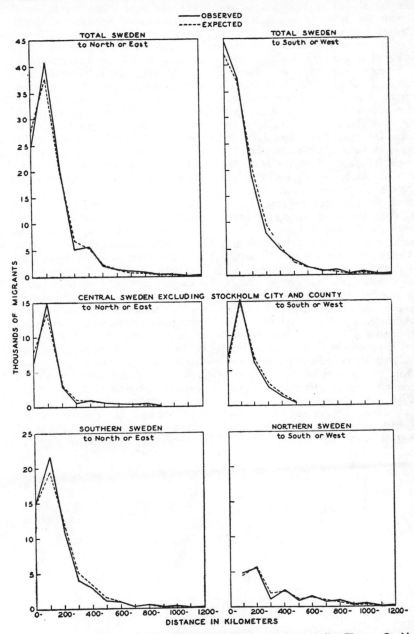

CHART 4. Observed and Expected Male Intercounty Migrants, 1921-30, Excluding Those to Stockholm City, by Region of Origin, Direction, and Distance of Last Migration

as southward grossly violates the facts.

Inspection of this series of curves suggested that the major discrepancies now consisted of excesses of observed over expected migrants to the distance intervals containing large cities, principally Stockholm. Expected migrants were therefore recalculated omitting moves to Stockholm City from both opportunities and out-migrants, and the results were the most satisfactory yet obtained (see Table 6 and Chart 4). The chi-square values (fifth and sixth rows of Table 4) show that the fit of the respective pairs of curves has again improved in nearly every case. That the opportunities in the capital have a distinctive character, attracting migrants regardless of the number of intervening opportunities cannot be doubted.

Something of the kind is presumably true also of the other large cities but inspection of the distributions of migrants from the separate counties does not suggest that excluding migrants to these cities from the calculations would remove the discrepancies in our final results. There are quite consistent excesses of observed over expected migrants in the second distance interval and frequently similar excesses in the first interval, where the opposite might be expected from the nature of the formula. It is possible that these excesses of observed migrants to nearer distances may be explained by Thomas' findings in a study as yet unpublished. With thoroughly adequate Swedish data she has shown that migrants to near destinations have tended to comprise disproportionate numbers of family members; migrants to far destinations, disproportionate numbers of "lone" persons. In our calculations, family members, like residential moves discussed above, are distributed as opportunities over the whole range of distance, but as observed migrants they may tend to be concentrated in the nearer intervals and consequently underestimated there. A desirable next step, if possible, would be to apply Stouffer's formula separately to "lone" migrants and to those who are heads of families, omitting other family members entirely. The hypothesis might account for the distributions of the separate groups of migrants better than for their combined distributions; but if distance *per se* appeared to influence one class more than the other, Stouffer's assumption of no necessary relationship between mobility and distance might need qualification.

The results of this study emphasize the need for testing Stouffer's theory with more homogeneous data than were available, if a conclusive demonstration is to be had. As in Bright and Thomas' study, increasing the similarity of opportunities and of the group of migrants under consideration repeatedly strengthened the evidence supporting the theory, but that evidence is still inconclusive. It is suggested that more convincing tests of the theory will depend upon refinement of definitions of opportunities.

POPULATION PRESSURE AND OTHER FACTORS

AFFECTING NET RURAL-URBAN MIGRATION

By C. Horace Hamilton

THE purpose of this paper is to describe and evaluate the application of several statistical techniques to a study of certain factors affecting net migration from farms. The original data for this paper came from the United States Census reports of 1930 and 1940. Using the well-known survivor-residual method, we have estimated the amount of net migration from the farms of North Carolina counties between 1930 and 1940, by age as well as for the total population above 10 years of age in 1940. By multiple and partial correlation analysis, we have attempted to account for the variation in net migration from farms in terms of population pressure and changes in agricultural production. Although the results obtained in this study are interesting within themselves, our primary emphasis will be on method—particularly on those statistical applications peculiar to this study.

METHODS OF ESTIMATING NET MIGRATION

First, let us review the present status and recent developments in the theory and application of the survivor-residual method of estimating net migration. In its simplest form, this method is based on the following components of population change: births, deaths, in-migration and out-migration. That is to say

$$P_1 - P_0 = B - D + M_i - M_0$$

where P_o and P_1 represent the population of an area at the beginning and end of a time period; B, of course, represents births; D, deaths; M_i, in-migrants; and M_o, out-migrants. This formula, as a means of estimating migration, is written

$$M_i - M_0 = P_1 - P_0 - B + D$$

Thus, the estimate of net migration is a residual—and as a residual it inherits the net error in census enumeration and vital statistics reporting. Fortunately, this net error very likely is a small percentage of net migration.

For the purposes of this discussion, the above formula will be referred to as the *direct vital*

statistics method of estimating net migration. It is suitable particularly for estimating net migration for total populations of areas for which the required census and vital statistics data are available. For instance, this is the method used by Tarver in his analysis of changes in the Arkansas population.[1] Since the final 1950 county census data are already available, similar analyses can easily be made.

The *direct vital statistics* formula may also be used in estimating net migration for age group cohorts. However, the computation is complicated by the fact that deaths are not reported year by year for small areas by single years. Hence, it is necessary to use little gadgets known as "separation factors" as a means of estimating deaths for such age groups as 11–15, 12–16, 13–17, and so on covering a decade of mortality experience for the aging cohort.

If the needed data are available, the direct vital statistics method is the most accurate one to use. It automatically and correctly classifies as migrants only that part of the natural increase which migrated. Other methods do not have this quality unless certain adjustments and assumptions are made.

Although the direct formula is a good one, it cannot be used in estimating net migration among population groups for whom no vital statistics data are available; e.g., the rural-farm, rural-nonfarm, and urban segments of the population. For the purposes of estimating rural-urban migration, the natural increase factor may be allowed for by the use of survival expectancy ratios based on either a suitable life table or on United States Census data by age, sex, and color, or on some combination of these two methods.[2] It is not the purpose of this paper to discuss the whole problem of developing survival expectancy ratios which

---

[1] J. D. Tarver, *Changes in the Arkansas Population.* Arkansas AESB Report Series 21 (December 1950).

[2] C. H. Hamilton, "Use of the Survival Rate Method in Measuring Net Migration," *Journal of the American Statistical Association*, 39 (June 1944), pp. 197–206.

reflect relatively well local mortality experience by residence, age, sex, and color. Although such ratios are not readily available, they have been and can be devised so as to keep residual errors within reasonable limits. Empirical studies are needed to determine the relative error involved in using regional and state survival ratios for estimating net migration by counties.

Recent theoretical discussions have led to some clarification of the use of survival expectancy ratios.[3] For the purpose of this discussion, we shall refer to this method as the *survival rate method*. It may be worked both forward and backward. That is, the forward survival rate method provides an estimate of expected population at the end of a decade, which is the product of a survival expectancy rate and the population at the beginning of the decade. The difference between the *expected* and *actual* populations at the end of the decade is defined as *net migration*, or more accurately as "change in population attributable to migration." The formula for the forward survival rate method is

$P_m = P_1 - rP_0$ where

P_m = estimated net migration

r = the survival expectancy rate, and

P_0 and P_1 = the enumerated populations at the beginning and end of the census period

The reverse of the survival rate method, sometimes called the "revival" rate method, may be expressed as follows:

$$P_m = \frac{P_1}{r} - P_0 = \frac{P_1 - rP_0}{r}$$

Obviously, these two formulas cannot possibly yield the same results. The forward formula, if applied to age groups, yields a smaller estimate of net migration than does the reverse formula because r is less than unity. The discrepancy between these two approaches is easily explained. The forward method, in effect, assumes that all the migration occurs on the last day of the census period, whereas the reverse method assumes that all the migration occurs on the first day of the period. The forward method underestimates net migration by

approximately the difference between deaths of in-migrants and deaths of out-migrants, whereas the reverse method overestimates net migration by approximately the same amount. These statements are based on assumptions that in- and out-migration and mortality are more or less evenly distributed over the census period. Such is rarely the case; but unless some objective evidence is available for making adjustments, one may just as well calculate net migration by the forward survival rate method, and the allowance for deceased migrants by using the following formula:

$$P_m = \frac{1 + r}{2r} [P_1 - rP_0]$$

This formula is a simple average of the results obtained by the forward and reverse survival rate methods.

It should be emphasized here that the forward survival rate method does, without adjustment, provide a reasonably good estimate of "change in the population attributable to migration." For some purposes it may not be necessary to determine the number of migrants who died after migrating. In the study on which this paper is based, we did not consider it necessary to make adjustments for dead migrants.

It may be observed also that a suitable net migration rate may be calculated by taking the ratio of living net migration to the expected living population at the end of the decade. The expected living population at the end of a decade represents the total number of living people who could have migrated from the area. If deceased persons, migrants and non-migrants, were incorporated into this formula, the rate would be no different unless we had some knowledge that the deceased people had migrated at a different rate from that of the surviving population.

Although more discussion of the validity of the survival rate method might be in order, we must move on to the major theme of this paper.[4]

MEASURES OF NET MIGRATION

In this study, we have developed two similar correlation problems based on two measures of net migration. In the first problem we have used

---

[3] Discussions among members of the Social Science Research Committee on Migration Differentials, Dorothy S. Thomas, Chairman.

[4] This subject will be discussed more fully in a forthcoming paper by Jacob S. Siegel and C. Horace Hamilton, Some Considerations in the Use of the Survival Rate Method of Estimating Net Migration, in an early issue of the *Journal of the American Statistical Association*.

as the dependent variable (X_0) the amount of net migration among the population above 10 years of age in 1940; i.e., the surviving population of the total population above zero years of age in 1930. In the second problem, the dependent variable (X_0) was the net migration among the population from 25 to 29 years of age in 1940. This group, on the average 20–24 years of age during the decade, was from 15–19 years of age in 1930.

In neither case did we use rates of migration. We preferred to use the actual amount of net migration because we wanted to express our partial regression coefficients in terms of numbers rather than rates. That is, we wanted to show how many persons migrated per unit of change in certain crop acreages, and so on.

INDEPENDENT VARIABLES

Our unit of enumeration was a county and the sample included the 100 counties of North Carolina. These counties, of course, varied in size from a few thousand up to thirty or more thousand farm population. Since our dependent variables were expressed in numbers instead of rates, it was necessary to hold size of county constant by means of partial correlation. For this purpose, the size of county was expressed as an independent variable (X_2) in terms of the 1930 total rural-farm population for the first problem; and the 1930 rural-farm population from 15 to 19 years of age for the second problem.

A second and most important independent variable in this study is a measure of population pressure (X_1). For this purpose we used the expected increase in the population as of 1940 by age over the corresponding age groups of 1930. These quantities showed how much each county would have increased in population had no migration at all taken place. For instance, the average county's rural-farm population above 10 years of age would have increased about 3,000 people between 1930 and 1940 had there been no migration.

In view of the fact that agricultural opportunities are limited by the amount of land and other factors, this prospective increase in the population did constitute population pressure of an intense sort. Had migration to cities not provided some opportunity for release of this pressure, the level of living of the farm population would have gone down. However, an increasing demand for farm commodities, and consequent increasing farm incomes, makes it possible for more of the surplus farm population to stay on the land. On the other

hand, increasing farm mechanization and agricultural technology operate in the other direction. In any case, the expected increase in a population during a decade provides a simple, pure statistical measure of the amount of pressure being exerted.

It is most important to break this population pressure down by age groups. A big crop of babies, such as we have had since 1945, does not exert

TABLE 1. CORRELATION MATRICES

	1	2	3	4	5
Problem I. No Regional Corrections					
0	−.7514	−.7257	.7453	.0469	−.6559
1		.9761	−.7485	.2878	.8041
2			−.7388	.3087	.7883
3				−.3887	−.8466
4					.3852
Problem I. With Regional Corrections					
0	−.6929	−.6322	.6367	.1850	−.4888
1		.9678	−.6271	.2180	.7361
2			−.6212	.2649	.7245
3				−.3244	−.7283
4					.3188
Problem II. No Regional Corrections					
0	−.9260	−.8457	.7803	−.1524	−.7017
1		.9372	−.7808	.3480	.7833
2			−.7435	.2769	.8165
3				−.3887	−.8466
4					.3852
Problem II. With Regional Corrections					
0	−.9047	−.8183	.7449	−.1026	−.6393
1		.9066	−.6945	.3277	.7186
2			−.6095	.2040	.7465
3				−.3244	−.7283
4					.3188

immediate population pressure. The real pressure will be felt when these babies reach 15 years of age and begin to enter the labor market in large numbers. It was with this thought in mind that we decided to make one of the major purposes of this study, the correlation of population pressure with migration from farms, among young people who were 15 to 19 years of age in 1930 and 25–29 in 1940.

We might add here a note on the method of calculating expected increase in the population. Let

P_0 = the total enumerated rural-farm population of a county in 1930

r = the survival rate

rP_0 = the expected population above 10 years of age in 1940

$_1P_3$ = the enumerated population above 10 years of age in 1930

The expected increase is, therefore,

$$I = rP_0 - {}_1P_3$$

Do not confuse this calculation with the very similar technique of calculating net migration. The computation of net migration does make use of the rP_0 values; but it does not make use of the 1930 population in any other way. As shown earlier, net migration represents the difference between *expected* and *actual* population at the *end* of the census period, 1940 in this study.

The application of this technique to a specific age group, say 15–19 in 1930 to 25–29 in 1940, may be expressed as follows:

P_0 = the enumerated rural-farm population 15–19 years of age in 1930

rP_0 = the expected rural-farm population 25–29 years of age in 1940

P_3 = the enumerated rural-farm population 25–29 years of age in 1930

Expected increase, if no migration should occur, is

$$I = rP_0 - P_3$$

Other independent variables used in this study were:

Change in cotton acres (X_3)

Change in tobacco acres (X_4)

Change in other crop acres (X_5).

These variables were expressed in actual acres of change rather than in percentage change for reasons already indicated. Other independent variables might well be included and some have been tried. However, for the purposes of this paper, it is neither practical nor necessary to treat them here.

TABLE 2. CORRELATION AND REGRESSION COEFFICIENTS

COEFFICIENTS	PROBLEM I		PROBLEM II	
	Corrected	Uncorrected	Corrected	Uncorrected
Multiple and partial correlation coefficients*				
$R^2_{0.12345}$	.7496	.7765	.9054	.9211
$R^2_{0(1345).2}$ ~	.5829	.5278	.7137	.7280
$R^2_{0(345).12}$	.4958	.4876	.4541	.4303
$R^2_{01.2345}$	.1656	.0823	.5616	.5882
Constant factors in multiple regression equations				
$a_{0.12345}$	47	2	−16	−25
Partial regression coefficients and standard errors†				
$b_{01.2345}$	−.9988(.2361)	−.5133	−.7186(.0726)	−.8537
$b_{02.1345}$	.1098(.0724)	.0112	.0265(.0706)	.1676
$b_{03.1245}$	.0999(.0140)	.1046	.0127(.0020)	.0115
$b_{04.1235}$	.1967(.0278)	.2155	.0260(.0039)	.0299
$b_{05.1234}$	.0448(.0172)	.0215	.0056(.0025)	.0052
Standard partial regression coefficient				
$B_{01.2345}$	−.9264	−.5236	−.8801	−1.0736
$B_{02.1345}$	.3446	.0380	.0328	.2129
$B_{03.1245}$	.5669	.6399	.3266	.3011
$B_{04.1235}$	.4073	.3851	.2441	.2283
$B_{05.1234}$	.2265	.1285	.1287	.1325

* All multiple and partial correlation coefficients shown are significant at the 1 percent level by F-test.

† Standard errors of partial regression coefficients are shown in parentheses.

STATISTICAL PROCEDURE

As already indicated, we set up two multiple correlation problems: (1) analysis of net migration among the total rural-farm population of 1930; and (2) a similar analysis for the rural-farm population having an average age of 20–24 years during the decade. In addition to using the usual linear correlation techniques, we used two devices which require some explanation. These are explained below.

1. *Regional analysis.*

The State of North Carolina was subdivided into four regions: Mountain, Piedmont, Coastal Plain, and Tidewater. All correlations were first computed for the State as a whole and then, a set of correlations was run taking deviations from regional rather than from State means. The reason for doing this was to eliminate the disturbing effects of broad regional differences which might obscure some of the relationships under investigation. In Problem II we made all the correlations and calculations on both a State and regional basis. In the case of both problems we show the results for the State as a whole in two parts: (1) without any corrections for regional means and (2) with corrections. State sums of squares and sums of products were computed by means of the following formula:

$$\Sigma x^2 = \Sigma X^2 - \Sigma X_1 \bar{X}_1$$
$$- \Sigma X_2 \bar{X}_2 - \Sigma X_3 \bar{X}_3 - \Sigma X_4 \bar{X}_4$$
$$\Sigma xy = \Sigma XY - \Sigma X_1 \bar{Y}_1$$
$$- \Sigma X_2 \bar{Y}_2 - \Sigma X_3 \bar{Y}_3 - \Sigma X_4 \bar{Y}_4$$

where $x = X - \bar{X}$, $y = Y - \bar{Y}$, and the four subscripts refer to the four regions of the State.

2. *Use of multiple-partial correlation coefficients.*

In order to determine the correlation between the dependent variables and one or more independent variables, and at the same time hold constant one or more other independent variables, we found it necessary to use a formula which is apparently a stranger to most writers of college textbooks in statistics. However, since reputable mathematical statisticians have given their blessings orally to this formula, we felt justified in using it. It is based on the conventional partial correlation formula

$$r^2_{01.2345} = \frac{R^2_{0.12345} - R^2_{0.2345}}{1 - R^2_{0.2345}}$$

which says simply that a partial correlation coefficient squared is the ratio of the variance explained by including a new variable *to* the total variance which remained unexplained before including the new variable. Incidentally, this is also a good definition of a simple coefficient of correlation squared.

TABLE 3. REGIONAL DIFFERENCES PROBLEM II (25–29)

COEFFICIENTS	MOUNTAIN	PIEDMONT	COASTAL PLAIN	TIDEWATER	STATE (CORRECTED)
$R^2_{0.12345}$	.9249	.9415	.9191	.8882	.9054
$R^2_{0(1345).2}$	.5718	.8010	.7687	.4761	.7137
$R^2_{0(345).12}$	.4546	.2095	.7311	.1340	.4541
$R^2_{01.2345}$	.3201	.6288	.3894	.4123	.5616

Constant factors in multiple regression equations

$a_{0.12345}$	0	−4	−47	−15	−16

Partial regression coefficients

$b_{01.2345}$	−.4183	−.8017	−.6335	−.5817	−.7186
$b_{02.1345}$	−.2729	.0589	.0938	−.2379	.0265
$b_{03.1245}$	.0335	.0067	.0164	.0113	.0127
$b_{04.1235}$	.1261	.0128	.0256	.0075	.0260
$b_{05.1234}$	.0183	−.0015	.0053	.0118	.0056

Standard partial regression coefficients

$B_{01..345}$	−.5343	−.8749	−.8629	−.8259	−.8801
$B_{02.1345}$	−.3275	.0552	.1517	−.3455	.0328
$B_{03.1245}$	.3453	.1723	.5379	.1639	.3266
$B_{04.1235}$	.1772	.0529	.4232	.0459	.2441
$B_{05.1234}$	.2915	−.0299	.1502	.3372	.1287

Now the same logic may be used in stating the formula of a multiple-partial coefficient. That is

$$R^2_{0(1345).2} = \frac{R^2_{0.12345} - r^2_{02}}{1 - r^2_{02}}$$

and

$$R^2_{0(345).12} = \frac{R_{0.1234} - R^2_{0.12}}{1 - R^2_{0.12}}$$

Note that any two combinations of independent variables desired may be used. The second term of both numerator and denominator includes only the dependent variable and those independent variables being held constant. The independent variables being correlated with the dependent variable are left out of the number two term of both numerator and denominator. The first term of the numerator of course always includes the entire battery of variables.

Needless to say, the use of the multiple-partial formula adds great flexibility to the handling of any multiple correlation problem.

RESULTS OF THE ANALYSIS

Tables 1, 2, and 3 show the results of the analysis which has been described. Without quoting all figures in detail, we shall try to summarize the most important findings in a few general statements.

1. Migration from farms is highly correlated with population pressure, particularly at the age when farm youth enter the labor market. More than one-half of the variance in net migration by counties can be accounted for by correlation with population pressure even when the changes in crop acreages are held constant. Note in Table 2, Problem 2, that $R^2_{01.2345} = .5616$ for the State as a whole.

2. Correlation of population pressure with migration does not appear to be so important in the case of the total population (10 and up in 1940). The partial correlation coefficient squared (adjusted for regional variation) is only .1656. A large crop of farm babies may constitute pressure on the standard of living, but it is not a pressure which can be relieved by migration. Incidentally, children can be supported more easily on the farm than in the city where food must be bought with cash and where child labor is prohibited.

3. Changes in crop acreages are highly correlated not only with the migration of rural youth but with the migration of the population as a whole. An increase in crop acres for whatever reason attracts population; and a decrease has the opposite effect.

In the case of the total population, as indicated by the regression coefficients—

A decrease of 1,000 cotton acres displaces about 100 farm people of whom 13 are youth (20–24). (Other variables being held constant.)

A decrease of 1,000 tobacco acres displaces about 200 farm people, 26 of whom are youth (20–24).

A decrease of 1,000 "other" crop acres displaces about 45 farm people, about 6 of whom are youth.

Increase in crop acres, of course, has an opposite effect—attracting population.

Between 1930 and 1940, North Carolina tobacco acreage increased 89,525 acres and this increase attracted 17,900 migrants (net) to the farms of the State. The decrease in cotton acres pushed 93,000 farm people off farms; and an increase of 1,000,000 other crop acres attracted about 45,000 people to farms.

Balancing all of these trends against population pressure and the influence of unknown factors, the farms of the State lost about 200,000 by migration alone during the 30's. This migration of 200,000 failed by 100,000 of taking all the population increase from farms. Possibly other resources than crops were available for the support of the extra 100,000. Off-the-farm employment, not included as a variable in this problem, very likely has made it possible for the North Carolina population to continue to expand.

4. Adjustment of correlation coefficients for regional variation has very little effect on the multiple and partial correlation coefficients. A possible exception is the case of $R^2_{01.2345}$ for the total population. Note also the big change in the corresponding regression coefficient, b_{01}.

However, in this connection, it is interesting to study Table 3, showing a comparison between the four regions in the case of youth migration.

By correlation analysis, we were able to account for nearly 80 percent of the variance in net migration in the Piedmont and Coastal Plain areas, but only from 48 to 57 percent in the Tidewater and Mountain areas, respectively.

In the Piedmont and Tidewater areas, population pressure was more highly correlated with net migration than was change in crop acres; but in the Mountains and the Coastal Plain areas, change in crop acres was more important.

SELECTIVE INTERNAL MIGRATION:

SOME IMPLICATIONS FOR MENTAL HYGIENE

By Dorothy Swaine Thomas

ALL population aggregates are heterogeneous: they consist of persons of various age levels; and at the different age levels there are varying proportions of males and females, and of the single, married, divorced and widowed. Each of these classes, in turn, consists of persons more and less well equipped to withstand disease; of more and less mental endowment and performance; upon various rungs of the occupational and social ladder; and in possession of more and less worldly goods. It is recognized that these various classes of a population are not equally good risks from the point of view of mental hygiene: we know that the proportion of maladjustments will be higher for some than for others, even though the class-specific rates of mental breakdowns and their etiological background have not yet been determined precisely.

But not only do we find considerable heterogeneity of population in every community, but marked differences between communities themselves. A community may have a generally low or a generally high plane of living; a stratified or elastic occupational structure; an oversupply of labor, with concomitant low wages and unemployment, or an undersupply of labor, with high wages and full employment; a scarcity of tillable land or other natural resources or an abundance of undeveloped, rich land and unexploited natural resources; a closely-knit familistic organization with a rigid code of behavior, or a diffuse, individualistic organization with a variety of conflicting codes and considerable personal and social freedom; the monotony of a farm-and-fireside way of life, or the varied stimulations of a metropolis. Without any doubt, different types of communities also represent good and bad mental hygiene risks, and the expectation of mental breakdown will vary from one type of community to another, just as it varies from one population class to another within a given community.

Internal migration, producing as it does, continuous shifts of classes of the population from one type of community to another, and even producing changes in type in the communities themselves, is a factor that must be considered by the student of mental hygiene. He will want to know the extent and nature of the selection or sifting of population classes in the process of migration, of their assimilation and adjustments to new environments, and of their effects in modifying the environments of both sending and receiving areas through the withdrawal or introduction of diverse cultural and personal elements. Specifically, he may ask: Are migrants among the better endowed (or the better performers) in the community from which they came or the community which they are entering? If so, are they able to maintain this superiority of performance after settling in the new environment? Finally, in what respects does the introduction of this superior group enrich the environment of the receiving group and deplete that of the sending group? Of course, if the answer to any of these questions is negative rather than positive, the formulation of any following question must be correspondingly modified.

The student of mental hygiene will want to be assured that answers to these questions are not based on pure speculation. There follows, therefore, a brief résumé[1] of the

[1] This résumé is based on a report of the Committee on Migration Differentials of the Social Science Research Council, prepared by the writer, and published in August, 1938, as Bulletin 43, Social Science Research Council, New York, under the title "Research Memorandum on Migration Differentials."

present empirical foundation of knowledge regarding selective internal migration—a foundation in which many gaps will be apparent but which has recently been strengthened by a number of well-controlled studies, directed towards various aspects of these questions, and focused, in the main, on cityward migration from rural areas.

Physical Fitness. The question of the *selection of the physically fit* has been approached indirectly by way of analyses of differential mortality, for, with so few positive criteria of health, and such a paucity of data regarding the incidence of sickness, comparability from one area and one period to another can be achieved only in terms of mortality experience. Migration of the physically fit, then, is to be inferred if the age- and sex-specific mortality experience of migrants is more favorable than that of non-migrants. Methodologically the most satisfactory of the various studies in this field is E. P. Hutchinson's (1936) recent analysis of Stockholm and rural Swedish data on tuberculosis mortality. All residents were classified as born in the community or born elsewhere, hence migrants (by definition, those resident outside the community of birth) could be isolated, to some extent,[2] from non-migrants. Hutchinson used great care in controlling and checking his data; death records for 1921 and 1922 were allocated to place of residence at the time of the 1920 census, thus "removing whatever disturbance was due to post-censal changes of residence" (p. 280) and eliminating deaths of the *de facto* population; and these records were related to the appropriate age and sex classes of the population from the census of 1920, thus assuring strict comparability in the numerator and denominator of the mortality fractions. By confining the analysis to a limited area, errors due to unequal accuracy of diagnosis were eliminated. When standardized for age "the tuberculosis death risk of the Stockholm-born was found to be from 25% to 30% greater than that for the in-migrant (non-native) resident population" (p. 279);

[2] Not wholly, since persons resident in their community of birth may be "return" migrants.

and in rural areas, the observed mortality of the locally born was about 10 per cent greater than that of the migrants. Whether these differentials indicated "a stronger selective process incident in rural-to-urban migration than in the case of rural-to-rural change" (pp. 283–84) can not be determined from this analysis, for, unfortunately, the data were not classified in terms of both origin and destination of the migrants, and it is not known to what extent either the Stockholm or rural migrant group contained persons originating in towns. But even allowing for all the uncertainties inherent in data and methods of analysis, the evidence seems to point to selection of the physically fit in internal migrations, particularly cityward migrations from rural areas. Regarding the strength of this selection and its variation under a variety of conditions, however, little can be said with assurance.

That Hutchinson's findings may have a more general applicability than would be apparent from the limitations imposed by the particular sample considered is suggested by the fact that they confirm the tendencies observed by other investigators for other areas and periods, even though these other investigators were forced to approach the problem even more indirectly than Hutchinson, viz., by comparing the mortality experience of population groups known to have increased and lost by internal migration, without identification of the migrating classes. Hill (1925 and 1936), for example, studied rural and urban aggregates in England, the former known to have lost by migration, the latter to have gained. He demonstrated that the losses and gains had been age-selective of adolescents and sex-selective of females, and that the death rates of female adolescents in urban areas were consistently favorable in comparison with those of all other ages, of males generally, and of rural areas generally. There was, furthermore, a distinct negative correlation between net migration and death rates, age by age, on a regional basis. Finally, comparison of a period of slight net migration with a period of heavy net migration showed a disappearance of the favorable differential when the net migration fell off. A similar study by Dorn (1934), with Ohio data for a year (1930) following two decades of heavy rural-urban migration, known to be age- and sex-selective, led to similar inferences, since urban death rates showed a consistently favorable differential over rural rates for the age classes which were augmented by migrants.

Intelligence Levels. The question of the possible *selective action of internal migration in drawing off the more intelligent strata of the rural population to towns and cities* has been intensely speculative and relatively slightly worked up on the empirical side. One study in this field, however, by Otto Klineberg (1935), may be considered really pathfinding and another, more recent, study, by Gist and Clark (1938), pushes forward the research frontier. Both these studies emphasize the following points strongly : standardized performance or intelligence tests are the most adequate measuring instruments available for such studies, but it is almost universally recognized among scientists that something more than innate intelligence is measured by these tests. In using test results as a basis for inferences about selective migration, therefore, it is of the utmost importance to control environmental factors. It would be misleading, for example, to compare rural aggregates, known to have lost by migration, with urban aggregates known to have gained, for environmental differences (particularly in respect to education and richness of material culture) may always be suspected of being determining factors in observed differences. If this instrument is used, therefore, comparisons must be made in terms of a migrant group in the community of origin *before* migration has taken place and of a control group of non-migrants in the same communities, or between migrants and non-migrants in the community of destination, with careful allowance for varying periods of exposure to the environment of this community. Of these comparisons, the former requires intelligence ratings *prior* to migration, the latter, ratings *subsequent* to migration.

For lack of anything better, Klineberg, who was primarily interested in selective migration of the northward and cityward bound Negro migrants from the South, was forced to use school records in the first type of comparison, since the required ratings are only now becoming available. These, however, were transmuted into a per cent rank order, thus assuring comparability of various groups. Children known to have migrated to the North from Birmingham (1914–24) were slightly below the average of their class; those migrating from Nashville (1921–30) were slightly above average. The results suggest a community differential but are inconclusive with respect to selection. Klineberg found the second type of comparison, which attempts to show the correspondence of changes in "intelligence" (as measured) with time spent in a given cultural environment, much more satisfactory methodologically : standardized intelligence tests were given to more than 3,000 Harlem school children, and age, sex, and grade were controlled. The results of these tests suggested that residence in New York tended to increase the "intelligence" of migrant children, and that the increase "is roughly proportionate to length of residence in the more favorable environment" (p. 119). Thus, Klineberg's various studies tended to show that cityward migration of these groups of Negroes was, on the whole, unselective, in comparison with non-migrants in the community of origin; and that the differential between migrants and non-migrants in the community of destination tended to disappear after a period of residence. That the results can not be taken as conclusive evidence is due partly to sampling limitation; and partly, as Klineberg points out, to the fact that the children were not the originators of the migrations but went passively with their parents.

Gist and Clark's study was based on standardized test scores of about 2,500 high school students in farm and rural non-farm areas in Kansas. The tests were given in 1922–23; migration was determined on the basis of residence in 1935 as compared with residence at the time the tests were given. Those who had migrated to urban areas had an intelligence quotient slightly (but statistically significantly) higher than those who remained in rural areas and the whole distribution of the samples suggests that "the superior persons . . . are tending to migrate more frequently to the cities than those in the inferior or average classes" (p. 57). As was true of Klineberg's study, the results can not be accepted as conclusive, because of sampling limitations of various sorts, one of the more important being that high school students (particularly during the early 1920s) were not the most appropriate sample for testing selective migration as they "had already undergone a selective process in the education system" (p. 57). Thus, the most adequate studies in this field are contradictory: one suggests random selection; the other, selection of the higher grades of intelligence.

Mental Fitness. So far as *selection in terms of mental health or illness* is concerned, we have very little direct knowledge as to the selective operation of migrations. A recent study by Malzberg (1936), however, is suggestive of differentials. He found a decidedly higher rate of first admission to New York State mental hospitals among native whites born in other states than among native whites born in New York State. The "crude" rate of the former was $3\frac{1}{2}$ times that of the latter, despite the probability that a higher proportion of these native whites from other states were of native parentage and that "natives of native parentage have lower 'crude' rates of mental disease than natives of foreign or mixed parentage" (p. 546). The differential is so great that it is impossible that it could disappear entirely (although it would certainly be reduced) if differences in the age structure of the two groups could be allowed for. Malzberg does not interpret the differential in terms of selective migration but attributes it to "more favorable circumstances of life surrounding the indigenous population" (p. 548). In another study (Malzberg, 1936) of Negro migrants (on the same basis), he develops this point of view further, and minimizes selective migration as an "adequate explanation."

He says "It is more probable that it is differences in the modes of life. . . . The migratory group leads a less secure economic existence. Moreover, because of a less stable family relationship the migratory group is more exposed to venereal diseases and to alcoholic addiction. It seems a justifiable conclusion, therefore, that migration is in itself and through its attendant circumstances an important contributory factor in the causation of mental disease" (p. 109).

It will be noted that Malzberg assumes without proof that migrants are socially maladjusted in general, and have less stable family relationship, in particular. There is, as a matter of fact, very little valid evidence on this point. Sociologists, it is true, have long claimed that mobility is associated with social disorganization, but the attempts to verify this hypothesis by statistical analysis have been technically unsatisfactory and inconsistent. Case studies suggest that pathological Wanderlust does exist, but apparently its incidence is not high. So far as criminals are concerned, there is some evidence of an association between delinquency areas and areas of high mobility, but age and other contributing factors have not been adequately controlled.

As has been suggested in several of the studies discussed above, migration is unquestionably age selective: the greater part of most streams of migrants consists of young people "starting out" for themselves, and, naturally, most of them are unmarried at the time of migration.

Familial Adjustment. The *relative success or failure of these young migrants in establishing new family ties* has not been thoroughly investigated. Data from the Swedish census of 1930 do, however, throw some light on this question, for the resident population is classified by age, sex, civil status and migration status, for both rural areas and towns and cities. Migration status, on the nativity basis, is further subclassified crudely in respect to distance between birthplace and residence, *i.e.,* residence in a community in the same region

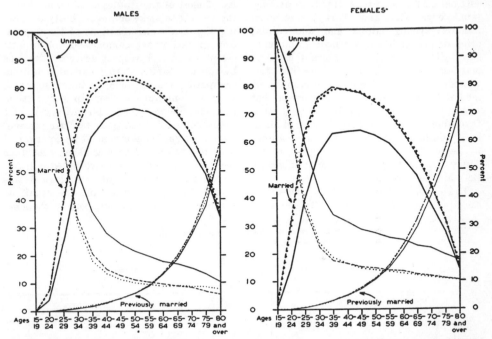

Resident in community of birth ————
Resident in region (not community) of birth — — — —
Resident outside region of birth • • • • • • •

MALES

FEMALES·

CHART. 1. PER CENT MARRIED, PREVIOUSLY MARRIED, UNMARRIED BY AGE GROUPS, RURAL AREAS, SWEDEN, 1930.

as the community of birth, and residence outside the region of birth.[3]   Charts 1 and 2 show the migration differential in terms of marital status and demonstrate clearly that migrants into a community are markedly more successful in achieving marriage than are those residing in the community of birth.   This favorable differential holds consistently for both sexes, age by age, in both rural areas and towns and cities, irrespective of the distance spanned in the migration.   The maximum differential amounts to about 85–100 per cent for migrants aged 20–24 in rural areas, declining, for both sexes to about 20 per cent after 40 years of age.   The favorable differential

[3] Bulletin 43, Social Science Research Council, *op. cit.*, pp. 26–28 for the definitions used in the Swedish census; and pp. 88–90 for the tables on which Charts 1 and 2 are based.

for migrants to towns and cities is somewhat less in the earlier years for both males and females; around 10 per cent for males over 30 years of age, but about 20 per cent for all female "near" migrants and 15–20 per cent for "far" migrants from ages 30–54 and even higher for older ages.   The interpretation of these data can not, however, be entirely in terms of selective migration, for it is probable that a number of migrants leave home in order to marry.   Nevertheless the consistency of the differential for all classes considered suggests strongly that selection is at least one of the factors involved.

SUMMARY AND CONCLUSIONS

The evidence is by no means clear-cut in respect to selective internal migration.   It suggests that migrants, particularly city-ward migrants from rural areas, are somewhat better physical risks than non-migrants (Hutchinson, Hill, Dorn); of average (Klineberg) or slightly better than average intelligence (Gist and Clark); disproportionately young adults and adolescents; often disproportionately females; and more successful than their non-migrant brothers and sisters in establishing marital ties (Swedish census). From the standpoint of mental hygiene, these findings suggest that migrants, by and large, will represent more favorable than unfavorable risks. Yet Malzberg's findings, though inconclusive, can not be neglected: they suggest a greater tendency towards psychoses among migrants than among non-migrants.

The obvious conclusion is that problems of selective migration have not yet been suffi-

ciently worked up on the empirical side to give us really definitive answers to the questions raised at the beginning of this paper. One reason for this is the statistical fallibility of most of the studies considered, due to the neglect to make or impossibility of making significant classifications of the population groups under comparison. Minimum essentials in this respect are classifications by age, sex, family status, marital condition, occupation and income, distance spanned, type of communities of origin and destination, and the phase of the business cycle. Of these factors, at least those referring to economic and family status must be determined both before and after migration. Another reason is the lack of a coordinated culture-historical, economic and sociological approach to the definition of the situations surrounding the migrants, both in the com-

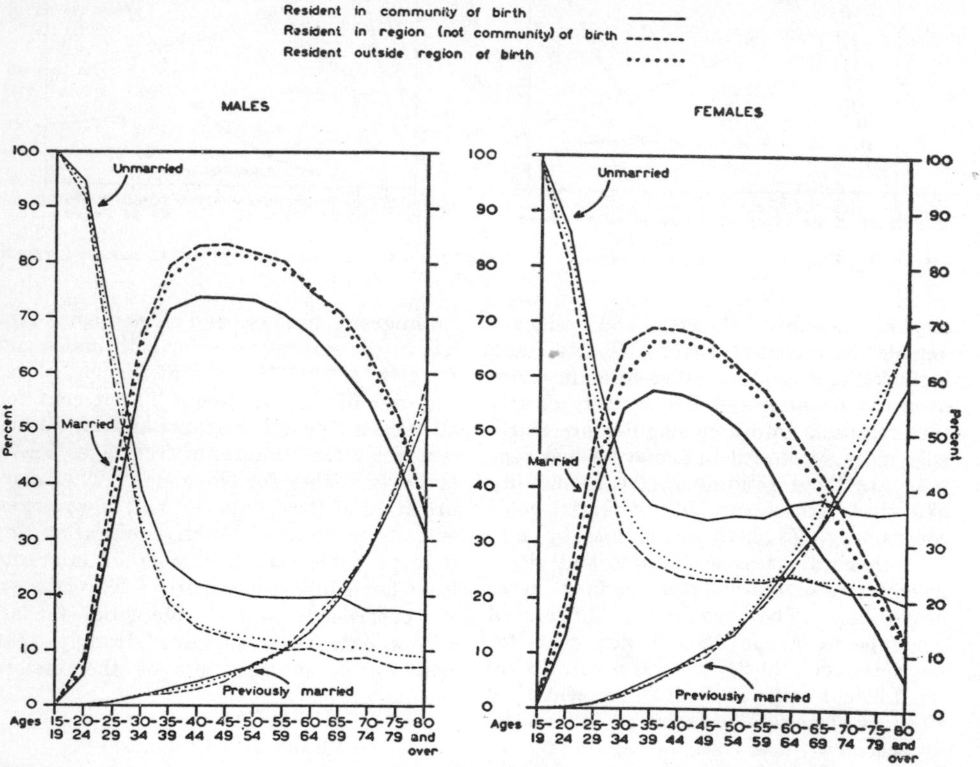

CHART. 2. PER CENT MARRIED, PREVIOUSLY MARRIED, UNMARRIED BY AGE GROUPS, TOWNS AND CITIES, SWEDEN, 1930.

munities of origin and in the communities of destination.

Finally, we can throw little light on the adjustment or assimilation of migrants until we can so organize studies as to observe the migrants' behavior before and after migration, and obtain their "own stories" of the goals they hope to achieve through migration; their stated grievances and dissatisfactions with the situations surrounding them; and the extent of goal-achievement or goal-modification after migration. That this type of approach is not impossible of attainment is suggested not only by the experience of students of immigration (Thomas and Znaniecki, 1927) but also by recent studies of internal migrants. Clyde Kiser (1932), for example, followed up a group of Negro migrants from St. Helena Island to Harlem, in their transition from rural to urban life. His records of the migrants' experiences, based on observation as well as interview, go far towards disclosing motivations, urges, and personal crises which are not apparent in mass statistics. Robert Littmarck (1930), similarly, tracing a group of landless Swedish agricultural migrants through their successive wanderings, suggests the close interdependence of economic and psychological motives: the migrants hope to better their economic condition and to obtain higher wages, but equally urgent is the "need for new horizons" and the escape from the monotony of long hours and hard physical labor. Then, too, the close dependence of the laborer on the employer makes the question of *where* he will be employed almost the only one in which he can exercise choice and maintain independence and self-respect.

The increasing tendency of psychiatrists to emphasize the etiological importance of environmental factors in mental disease and mental health should predispose them to give further attention to the role of internal migration in transplanting selected classes of persons from one environment to another.

REFERENCES CITED

DORN, HAROLD F. 1934. The Effect of Rural-Urban Migration upon Death-Rates. *Population*, 1: 95–114.

GIST, N. P., AND C. D. CLARK. 1938. Intelligence as a Selective Factor in Rural-Urban Migrations. *Am. Jour. Sociol.*, 44: 36–58.

HILL, A. B. 1925. Internal Migration and Its Effects upon the Death-Rates: with Special Reference to the County of Essex. London: Medical Research Council Special Report Series, No. 95.

————. 1936. The Recent Trend in England and Wales of Mortality from Phthisis at Young Adult Ages. *Jour. Roy. Statist. Soc.*, 99: 247–296. Pt. II.

HUTCHINSON, E. P. 1936. Internal Migration and Tuberculosis Mortality in Sweden. *Am. Sociol. Rev.*, 1: 273–285.

KLINEBERG, OTTO. 1935. Negro Intelligence and Selective Migration. New York: Columbia University Press.

KISER, CLYDE V. 1932. Sea Island to City: A Study of St. Helena Islanders in Harlem and Other Urban Centers. New York: Columbia University Studies in History, Economics and Public Law, No. 368.

LITTMARCK, ROBERT. 1930. Mälardalens Nomader (Nomads of the Mälar Valley). Stockholm: Svenska Kyrkans Diakonistyrelses Bokförlag. (For an adaptation in English see Social Science Research Council, Bulletin 43, *op. cit.*, pp. 130–140.)

MALZBERG, BENJAMIN. 1936. Migration and Mental Disease among Negroes in New York State. *Am. Jour. Phys. Anthrop.*, 21: 107–113.

————. 1936. Rates of Mental Disease among Certain Population Groups in New York State. *Jour. Am. Statis. Assoc.*, 31: 545–548.

THOMAS, W. I., AND F. ZNANIECKI. 1927. The Polish Peasant in Europe and America. New York: Knopf.

NEGRO INTELLIGENCE AND SELECTIVE

MIGRATION: A PHILADELPHIA TEST OF

THE KLINEBERG HYPOTHESIS

By Everett S. Lee

Beginning about World War I and swelling to unprecedented proportions during and after World War II, the migration of southern Negroes to northern cities has effected a remarkably rapid redistribution of the Negro population of the United States. Are these migrants more intelligent than those who remained in the South? The Army intelligence tests of World War I showed a definite superiority of the northern over the southern Negro. Was this because of selective migration or can the superior showing of the northern Negro be laid to a more stimulating environment?

The most extensive attempt to answer this question is found in Otto Klineberg's *Negro Intelligence and Selective Migration.*[1] There are two major parts of this work, the first of which is concerned with a direct comparison between the relative marks in the southern schools of Negro children who migrated to the North and those who remained in the South. The school records in Birmingham, Alabama; Nashville, Tennessee; and Charleston, South Carolina were examined and it was found that migrating children did not differ regularly or consistently from their non-migrating classmates in the matter of school marks.

The second method used by Klineberg was to give intelligence and performance tests to southern-born Negro children living in New York and then compare the groups with different lengths of residence in New York. On the Stanford-Binet and National Intelligence Tests the scores of the migrants increased fairly regularly with increasing length of residence in New York and tended, after several years, to approximate those of the New York-born. However, on the Otis Self-Administering Examination and on the different performance tests there was no clear pattern of improvement associated with length of residence in New York. From these results Klineberg concluded:

There seems to the writer to be no reasonable doubt as to the conclusion of this study. As far as the results go, they show quite definitely that the superiority of the northern over the southern Negroes, and the tendency of northern Negroes to approximate the scores of the Whites, are due to factors in the environment, and not to selective migration.[2]

A number of criticisms have been made of this study. Klineberg himself pointed out the inadequacy of school marks as a measure of intelligence and admitted that even though the migrant children from Birmingham, Nashville, and Charleston were not superior to their classmates, their parents, the originators of the northward migration, may very well have been. On the whole, more weight is accorded the second part of the study. Here, one of the major criticisms is that Klineberg's conclusions are based on comparisons made among different groups rather than upon successive tests of the same individuals. Presumably, these groups differed only as to length of residence in New York but it is possible that they may have differed in native ability as well. It has been conjectured that the earlier migrants were superior to the later ones and that there has been less selectivity for intelligence as northward migration increased, a not illogical supposition. Nevertheless, Klineberg's study remains by far the best of its kind.

As is too often the case in the social sciences, there has been no independent repetition of this study, perhaps partly because of the time and expense involved in testing large numbers of children. Fortunately in the Philadelphia public schools there has been a long-continuing and intensive program of intelligence testing, the results of which may be gathered from the cumulative record maintained for each pupil. Thus it is possible to set up in Philadelphia a study which somewhat parallels Klineberg's

---

[1] New York: Columbia University Press, 1935.

[2] Klineberg, *op. cit.*, p. 59.

New York study. Like New York, Philadelphia is of special interest because of the large volume of recent Negro migration from the South.

Following Klineberg, an attempt was made to test the hypothesis that there is a significant improvement in the intelligence test scores of southern-born Negro children as the length of residence in Philadelphia increases. The following conditions were held essential to an adequate test of the hypothesis.

(1) *A repetition of tests on the same individual.* It has been mentioned that the Klineberg study has been criticized because its comparisons are between different groups rather than between successive tests of the same individuals. One of the advantages of the Philadelphia testing program is that the Philadelphia Tests of Verbal and Mental Ability constitute a well correlated series, the different tests of which are given at various times during the pupil's school career and therefore offer an opportunity to determine whether there is a trend in the "IQ's" of the same individuals over a range as great as nine years. This, of course, does not preclude the use of intergroup comparisons, but adds evidence beyond that obtainable from such comparisons alone.

(2) *Tests of specific abilities.* It is conceivable that an increase in score on a general intelligence test may be indicative of improvement in a single ability. For example, an improvement in verbal ability would, in itself, raise the total score on a general intelligence test, even though there was no improvement in other factors. The Chicago Tests of Primary Mental Abilities, used in the Philadelphia schools, break intelligence into six factors, allowing an opportunity to determine whether any improvement in general intelligence is associated with only one or two abilities. To this is added the Minnesota Paper Form Board Test, a test of spatial ability and one of the tests used by Klineberg.

(3) *A control group of non-migrants who do not differ from the southern-born in the matter of pre-school training.* Over a third of the Philadelphia-born children have had pre-school training and some psychologists maintain that this raises the "IQ" for at least the first few years thereafter.[3] It follows, therefore, that kindergarten training alone might serve to differentiate the non-migrants from the south-ern-born children, since very few of the latter have had pre-school training.

For practical reasons it was necessary to select a few schools for intensive study rather than attempt to sample the entire school population. On the basis of available information these schools were chosen from localities which presented widely diverse socio-economic characteristics. Two of the schools were in the heart of the city, one was near the city line, and the others were distributed widely in the intermediate area. One of the schools was a vocational school and another was chosen because a high percentage of its students were the children of foreign-born parents. Two of the schools drew children almost entirely from low rent districts; for the others, the pupils came from areas of higher rents with considerable variation from school to school. A major criterion in the selection of schools was the percentage of Negro students, which varied from a low of 23 to a high of 92. All of the schools were either junior or senior high schools and all of the students considered had attained at least the ninth grade. Nine schools were included in the investigation. The criteria for selection were, of course, arbitrary and no claim can be made that their populations are truly representative of those of the Philadelphia public schools in general.

Within the schools the records of each Negro student who had come to Philadelphia from a state south of the District of Columbia and east of the Mississippi River were included. As a control group a 20 per cent sample of the Philadelphia-born Negro students was selected by taking the record of every fifth Philadelphia-born Negro whose name appeared in alphabetical listings of each class. The control group was designed to be a check against the possibility that an increase in the test scores of migrants on succeeding tests is only a general trend to be found among all students.

The Philadelphia-born students were divided into two groups, those who had attended kindergarten and those who had not. Migrants were divided into five classes, according to the grade in which they entered the Philadelphia school system, and roughly at two-year intervals. Time of entering the Philadelphia schools was taken as the best possible estimate of the time of arrival in Philadelphia even though, in some cases, several months may have elapsed between the time of migration and the time of entering school. Place of last residence before coming to Philadelphia was taken from the school transfer and time and place of birth from the school's record of the birth certificate.

[3] See James L. Mursell, *Psychological Testing*, New York: Longmans, Green and Co., 1949, p. 315 ff.

FINDINGS

The mean scores and standard deviations of the Philadelphia Tests of Mental and Verbal Ability are shown in Table I. These tests form a series of group intelligence tests, somewhat similar to the Otis series, and are given to pupils in grades IA, 2B, 4B, 6B and 9A. They have been standardized on Philadelphia school children, and equal scores on different tests represent equal distances, in terms of standard deviations, from the mean scores of the groups upon which the tests were standardized. The 1A test relies on oral instructions and includes such performance items as drawing the circle, square, triangle, and diamond, but beginning with the 2B test the series becomes increasingly verbal.

All of the individuals included in Table I took every test in the Philadelphia series given after they entered the school system. Because they had missed one or more of these tests, 292 of the 1,234 migrants whose records were examined were excluded from this table along with 326 of the 962 Philadelphia-born. Twelve migrants who had attended kindergarten were also excluded in order not to affect the comparison between the migrants and the Philadelphia-born who had not attended kindergarten. This is, of course, a loss of material, but it has the advantage of making the comparison of the scores of the same individuals on succeeding tests of this series possible.

From Table I, it is immediately apparent that there is a steady improvement in test rating as each of the migrant groups increases its length of residence in Philadelphia. For each of the three groups of migrants entering before grade 5A there is a significant difference between the first rating obtained on the Philadelphia tests and the rating on the last, or 9B test. In other words, the improvement in mean test rating could have been due to chance less than five times in one hundred for each of these three groups of migrants.[4] For the groups enter-

ing in grades 5A—6B we have only two test scores and the difference is not statistically significant. The trend, however, is upward, there being a 2 point increase in mean score. Of far more importance than the tests of significance is the steady improvement of the test rating within each of the migrant groups.

Table I may be used to make intergroup comparisons as well. Reading upwards, instead of from left to right, a comparison can be made between groups with different lengths of attendance in the Philadelphia schools. With only one exception (the group of migrants entering in grades 5A—6B is slightly better than the group which entered in grades 3A—4B) there is a steady improvement in rating associated with early entrance in the Philadelphia school system. On each test where a comparison can be made there is a significant difference between the mean of the migrant group entering in grade 1A and the group which had last entered and was taking its first test of this series.

A still further series of tests can be made. The hypothesis can be set up that there is no significant difference between the scores of the southern-born group entering the school system in grade 1A and the Philadelphia-born who did not attend kindergarten. For tests 1A, 2B, and 4B the hypothesis must be rejected, but on tests 6B and 9A the conclusion is that the groups are samples of the same population. In other words, the difference between the two groups, which was quite large in grade 1A, has narrowed until by grade 6B the difference is no longer significant.

The Chicago Tests of Primary Mental Abilities afford an opportunity to determine whether the improvement noted on the Philadelphia tests of general intelligence can be attributed to improvement in one or two specific abilities. These results are given in Table II, where again there is a striking association between the test score and the length of school attend-

---

[4] In testing the significance of the difference between the mean scores of the same individuals of the two tests, account must be taken of the correlation involved. Therefore, the difference between the two scores for each individual was taken, resulting in a set of N individual differences. If there is no significant difference between the two sets of scores, the mean difference should not be significantly different from zero. The Student t distribution was used to test the significance of the deviation of the mean of the individual differences from zero. In making intergroup comparisons where the factor of correlation is not involved, i.e. when the two groups

are composed of different individuals, the standard error of the difference between mean scores was calculated by the formula:

$$\sigma_{\bar{x}_1 - \bar{x}_2} = \sqrt{\frac{(N_1 + N_2)(\Sigma x_1^2 + \Sigma x_2^2)}{N_1 N_2[(N_1 - 1) + (N_2 - 1)]}}$$

(See Croxton and Cowden: *Applied General Statistics*, p. 330.)

In each case, the t test was preceded by the F test for equality of variances, since equality of variances is a prerequisite for the t test.

ance in Philadelphia. The one exception to the general pattern of improvement is the memory test, the scores of which seem to vary at random from group to group; indeed, the second highest mean score was registered by the group which had last come from the South. On all the other tests there is a significant difference between the means of the migrant group entering in grade 1A and the means of the migrant group entering in grades 7A to 9A. In three out of the six sub-tests, the migrant group entering in grade 1A surpasses the Philadelphia-born non-kindergarten group. Since there is an improvement in every category except that of memory, no single factor can be said to account for the over-all improvement in the intelligence test scores of the migrants.

In Table III are listed the scores on the Minnesota Paper Form Board Test. Contrary to the findings of the Klineberg study, where the results were not clear, there is a definite association between length of attendance in the Philadelphia schools and the scores on the test. The numbers of cases in this study are, however, considerably larger than those of the Klineberg study, which in some of his groups were as low as 23 or 25. This may explain the difference between these results and his.

There are still two major reservations that must be made before accepting the conclusions that there has been a general increase in the ability of the southern-born children to cope with intelligence tests. First, there is the factor of increasing familiarity with the tests and with the testing situation. These alone could account for a rise in the scores of the migrants. However, it would be expected, if this were an important factor, that there would be a similar rise in the scores of the two control groups of Philadelphia-born children. These persons, in general, would have even more familiarity with the tests and with the testing situation, but there is no upward trend in the scores of either of these groups.

TABLE I. MEAN "IQ's" ON PHILADELPHIA TESTS OF MENTAL AND VERBAL ABILITY

Group	N	Grade in which test was taken:				
		1A	2B	4B	6B	9A
Philadelphia-born who attended kindergarten.	212					
Mean		96.7	95.9	97.2	97.5	96.6
σ		14.3	14.8	15.0	13.9	14.2
Philadelphia-born who did not attend kindergarten.	424					
Mean		92.1	93.4	94.7	94.0	93.7
σ		13.8	14.4	14.6	14.1	15.1
Southern-born entering Philadelphia school system in grades:						
1A	182					
Mean		86.5	89.3	91.8	93.3	92.8
σ		13.2	13.3	14.1	14.5	13.6
1B—2B	109					
Mean			86.7	88.6	90.9	90.5
σ			15.2	13.6	14.4	16.1
3A—4B	199					
Mean				86.3	87.2	89.4
σ				15.3	14.8	13.7
5A—6B	221					
Mean					88.2	90.2
σ					15.1	14.7
7A—9A	219					
Mean						87.4
σ						14.3

TABLE II. MEAN SCORES ON CHICAGO TESTS OF PRIMARY MENTAL ABILITIES

Group	N	Number	Verbal	Spatial	Sub-Tests: Word Fluency	Reasoning	Memory
Philadelphia-born who attended kindergarten.	105						
Mean		72.1	45.3	38.2	43.1	31.2	12.3
σ		23.8	20.1	24.6	15.1	13.2	3.8
Philadelphia-born who did not attend kindergarten.	193						
Mean		67.3	40.2	34.2	42.4	29.2	12.0
σ		21.7	19.6	25.4	14.6	13.7	3.9
Southern-born entering system in grades:							
1A	83						
Mean		68.2	34.9	35.3	41.9	27.4	12.4
σ		25.3	21.3	23.7	15.1	14.5	4.1
1B—2B	61						
Mean		64.3	35.6	32.4	40.3	27.9	12.3
σ		24.6	22.2	22.9	13.8	15.1	4.6
3A—4B	74						
Mean		61.6	32.9	28.5	40.8	26.3	12.6
σ		26.1	20.7	21.3	15.4	14.4	5.1
5A—6B	87						
Mean		62.1	30.7	29.7	39.3	25.4	11.9
σ		24.3	21.6	24.5	14.2	15.1	4.2
7A—9A	77						
Mean		59.1	28.8	30.8	34.1	23.2	12.5
σ		25.6	20.8	25.1	15.9	15.6	4.4

TABLE III. MEAN SCORES ON MINNESOTA PAPER FORM BOARD TEST

Group	Mean Score	Standard Deviation	N
Philadelphia-born who attended kindergarten	33.1	14.3	244
Philadelphia-born who did not attend kindergarten	30.3	13.5	468
Southern-born entering system in grade:			
1A	28.8	16.0	209
1B—2B	26.6	13.9	133
3A—4B	23.4	15.4	226
5A—6B	24.8	13.7	249
7A—9A	20.6	14.5	252

Finally, it is conceivable that the persons who missed tests in the Philadelphia series were persons who had done badly on one test and thereafter stayed away from school on the day the tests were given. Or it may be that there is an inverse correlation between test scores and absences from school. Either of these factors, if true, could operate in a way to affect intergroup comparisons, but could not explain away the rise in test ratings of the same individuals over a period of time. To make certain of the effect exercised by the exclusion of these records, however, the means and standard deviations of the Philadelphia series of tests were recomputed using both complete and incomplete records. Intergroup tests of significance were then made. While there were slight changes in the means, the general pattern was undisturbed and the difference between the means of different groups was judged significant or not significant, exactly as before.

CONCLUSION

Klineberg's hypothesis that there is an increase in the intelligence scores of southern Negro migrants to New York with increasing length of residence in New York is, in the main, substantiated by independent evidence in Philadelphia. There is a significant and continuous upward trend in the intelligence test ratings of southern-born Negro children as their length of residence in Philadelphia increases. This increase manifests itself not only on a general intelligence test but also on each of the subtests of the Chicago Tests of Primary Mental Abilities with the single exception of memory. The increase in general score cannot, therefore, be attributed to an increase in any one specific ability. Nor can the increase be laid to increasing familiarity with the tests or the testing situation, or to a general trend to be found among all students since there is no such increase in the scores of Philadelphia-born students. It can further be shown that the migrant children, who entered the first grade in Philadelphia are on the first three tests definitely inferior to the Philadelphia-born on the Philadelphia series of tests, but by the time they have reached the sixth grade there is no significant difference in their test ratings and those of the Philadelphia-born group, who, like them, had not attended kindergarten.

Chapter VI

POPULATION COMPOSITION AND UTILIZATION OF HUMAN RESOURCES

By the composition of a population, in the most general sense, is meant the joint frequency distribution of all measurable characteristics—attributes or variables —of its members. In theory there is no limit to the number of characteristics that may be identified; phrased otherwise, the number of ways in which members of a population can be classified is unlimited. In practice, however, the information available on the composition of any large population (e.g., all persons residing within the territorial limits of a national state) is confined to relatively few population characteristics. First, a population enumeration or registration system assembles information concerning only those characteristics that can be recognized clearly and recorded quite easily and inexpensively; the number of items is further limited by the comparative smallness of governmental appropriations for census purposes. The development of modern methods of representative sampling, however, by markedly reducing the absolute number of returns necessary to characterize a population adequately, has greatly widened the scope of economically obtainable information regarding population composition. Second, heretofore the characteristics on which information has been gathered have been restricted largely to those considered significant from a particular point of view, especially that of the state whose officials conduct a census. That modern censuses describe population composition much more comprehensively than did early ones is largely attributable to a broadening of the concerns of the state with the activities and welfare of its citizenry.

The analysis of population composition is usually focussed on three kinds of characteristics: (1) Those known to be important determinants of demographic processes. The rate of mortality is a function of age. Births occur to only one of the sexes during but a fraction of the life span, and largely, though not exclusively, to married women. Migration is almost universally selective of younger persons. Hence, all but the most superficial treatments of population dynamics must consider the composition of population according to age, sex, and marital status. (2) Characteristics which delineate the basic outlines of the social structure. These include classifications or measures of economic activity, group memberships, civil status, racial or ethnic background, and level of living. Such general headings obviously encompass a variety of specific items, for example: employment status, occupation, industrial classification, religious affiliation, household status, school attendance, membership in the Armed Forces, citizenship, nativity, national origin, income, and home ownership. (3) Measures of the qualifications —abilities or disabilities—of members of the population for performing their social and economic roles. These include, among others, literacy, educational attainment, work experience, physical or mental defects, morbidity, and intellectual capacity.

The study of characteristics in the third group is often designated as the field of "population quality." But apart from the normative considerations which it may entail, the analysis of population quality is but an aspect of the study of population composition—in particular, it involves quantitative considerations, just as do all other aspects of demography, so that there is no logical basis for an opposition between population "quantity" and "quality." The student of population quality is concerned with discovering how changes in the level and distribution of qualifications take place. The logically necessary first step in such a study is often taken for granted: the specification of the roles or functions to be considered, and the determination of the qualifications needed for their effective performance. (It is usually assumed, without demonstration, and perhaps contrary to fact, that the qualifications which make for individual success are necessarily those which must be maximized in an entire population to assure that its functions are performed at the highest level of efficiency.) This step taken, the problem becomes one of discovering the factors affecting the potential ability of the human organism to perform a given kind of function, and the determinants of the degree to which these potentialities are realized. Research in this area is greatly handicapped both by the crudeness of the available measures of realized qualifications, and by lack of knowledge of the role of constitutional factors in potential qualifications, together with the genetic determinants of these constitutional factors. Most students agree that no known system of social and economic organization develops all the potentialities of a population or makes full use of all its qualifications. But again knowledge is inadequate, for there is a lack of definite criteria and specific measures of the effectiveness of human resources utilization, and sociological research has succeeded only in isolating some general and fairly obvious determinants of the ways in which human talents and skills are exercised in a society. The degree to which human resources are wasted probably varies considerably over time and from place to place, but undoubtedly it is high everywhere. The problem comes into prominence especially when certain functions are imperilled by a shortage of qualified personnel.

The distribution of a population among classes or categories may or may not be dominated by a social mechanism that tends to preserve an interclass equilibrium of sorts, or that at least sets limits to the way individual members of a population get distributed among the categories. Consider the distribution of workers among occupations. This distribution is dominated by a social mechanism that is economic in character, at least in a society that is not rigidly stratified. If an occupation becomes comparatively crowded, the relative rate of earnings per year enjoyed by workers in that occupation falls. As a result some workers quit the occupation for others, while most of those entering the labor force for the first time tend to avoid the crowded occupation and enter others instead. It may be said, therefore, that there is a limit to the extent to which any given occupation is likely to become comparatively crowded. The distribution of population between rural and urban occupations is similarly affected.

Not all distributions of population among categories are affected in the manner described, though sometimes, when a distribution deviates greatly from that which is desired, a society may employ its apparatus of state to reduce the degree of deviation. Thus a society's age composition is not subject to equilibration of the sort that affects its occupational composition. If, however, it is believed that there are relatively too many old persons in a population, a society may seek to modify this distribution by encouraging an influx of young immigrants, or by subsidizing the reproduction and rearing of children. By contrast, if a country's comparative supply of some forms of talent or realized ability is short, the wages commanded by persons with these talents will rise, and the shortage will be somewhat reduced. Moreover, the state may intervene to increase the short supply of these forms of ability. Equilibrating tendencies will be less powerful, however, than were those described in the preceding paragraph; and they will be even less powerful in respect of genetic composition. For if a population's genetic composition becomes relatively unfavorable, this condition will elicit a somewhat compensatory response only if the state intervenes to encourage an increase of those elements that are relatively scarce, or if there takes place a relative increase in the wages commanded by realized abilities founded upon those genetic elements or combinations. Even then, because of the complexity of the relationship obtaining between the production of changes in genetic composition and the production of changes in the comparative supply of realized talents or abilities, the compensatory response may turn out to be negligible.

It is not possible in the limited space available to present examples of demographic treatments of all the characteristics mentioned, nor to include a great variety of descriptive data and trend analyses concerning population composition. Instead, the aim of the readings in this chapter is to indicate something of the way in which the demographer deals with the causes of variations and changes in population composition and the implications of these for social change and population adjustment.

The first paper, by Chaddock, brings out clearly the necessity for analytical control of age and sex composition in the study of almost any other population characteristic or population change. The next two papers, those by Lorimer and Notestein, indicate something of the complexity of the problem of determining the reasons for shifts in age composition; in particular, the papers illustrate the way in which constructed models of population systems help to isolate the components of such shifts. The relationships of the vital processes, on the one hand, and several sorts of population characteristics, on the other, with family status are dealt with in Glick's paper. Determinants of the composition of a population according to cultural characteristics are similarly brought out in Mayer's article.

The first five papers, then, form a group of more or less strictly "demographic" analyses. From these, the discussion shifts to questions of the utilization of human resources, as represented in a series of six papers. Here the issue is primarily that of the relation between the characteristics of a population and employment in productive activities. The term "human resources" is seldom, if ever, carefully defined in a technical sense. But the wide usage of the term testifies to a general recognition that wealth and welfare depend not only on the available endowment of nature and the cultural heritage of art and artifact, but also on human capacities and skills, together with their effective mobilization and organization. Many of the problems of human resources utilization are now treated in the specialized field of "manpower," "working force," or "labor force" analysis, some broad aspects of which are outlined in Hauser's paper. Wolfbein and Jaffe investigate the bearing of changes in population composition on the size of the labor force. This problem is treated in Spengler's paper also, but the latter deals more specifically with possible consequences of a shift in age composition within the working force. The two succeeding articles bring out two important socio-cultural factors in the utilization of human resources: in Moore's paper the role of institutional conditions that impede labor mobility and consequently retard industrialization, and in Golden's study the relation between the educational level of the working force and economic development. The problem of the supply of highly trained persons is discussed in Wolfle's paper, wherein it is shown that despite the prolongation of schooling in the United States, there remains a reservoir of persons not receiving the advanced education they are capable of using.

Also relevant to the question of the supply of human ability is the discussion traditionally carried on under the heading of "population quality" and represented by the last five papers in this chapter. These deal largely with human capacities—as distinguished from realized abilities—and the genetic determinants of the distribution of these capacities in a population. In view of the evidence in Wolfle's paper and a considerable body of supporting research that human capacities are underutilized even in an advanced economy, the limits on the supply of ability imposed by the genetic structure of a population may best be viewed as potential rather than immediate. Nevertheless, it is evident that unfavorable genetic shifts could not be counteracted indefinitely by socio-environmental adjustments. The papers of Snyder, Dorn, and Woodward deal in general terms with the problem of population quality, summarizing some of the known principles of population genetics and outlining methodological criteria for effective research on this subject. The last two papers, by Osborn and Duncan, respectively, are given over to critical consideration of hypotheses concerning trends in population composition with respect to intellectual capacity.

In reading the last five papers it is well to keep in mind the distinction between *genetics,* the science which deals with (among other things) the determinants of the distribution of hereditary characters in a population, and *eugenics,* which embraces both a philosophy of quality and a program for improving the quality of populations by modifying the comparative frequency of desirable and/or undesirable hereditary traits. The aspirations of the eugenist have sometimes outrun the scientific achievements of the geneticist, for it has proved difficult, in general, to ascertain (a) what aspects of complex human characteristics are genetically determined, and (b) the mode of inheritance of traits believed to have a genetic basis. In the absence of a fuller knowledge of the laws of human genetics than we now possess, discussion of population quality sometimes tends to become controversial and unduly permeated with personal and professional bias. Presumably, with the improvement of our knowledge of human genetics and of the limitations which surround the application of such knowledge to human populations, the influence of bias will diminish.

AGE AND SEX IN POPULATION ANALYSIS

By Robert E. Chaddock

BIRTH rates, death rates, and migration determine the growth or decline of any population, sometimes characterized as the *movement* of that population, in contrast to its structure. The characteristic groupings which make up the peculiar structure of a population at any particular time or its changing structure over a period are known as its *composition*. Of these groupings none are more important than age and sex.

AGE COMPOSITION AND SOCIAL STUDIES

In social and demographic studies, attention to the age of the population is absolutely essential in order that comparisons may be valid and that apparent differences may be understood. For example, in measuring criminality from statistics of prisoners in penal institutions in 1890, the census authorities reached the conclusion that the tendency toward criminality among the foreign born in the United States was twice as great as among the native-born population. In making this inference, differences in age distribution of the two groups compared were entirely neglected. But prisoners were recruited largely from adults, the proportion of which among a given number of the foreign born was much larger than among the same number of native born. Consequently a grave injustice was done to the foreign group, and when the same data were compared with proper regard for age differences, the conclusion was reversed.[1]

[1] J. R. Commons, *Races and Immigrants in America* (xiii + 242 pp. New York: Macmillan, 1907, first edition), pp. 168–169.

A second illustration is offered, this time from the field of vital statistics. The annual report of the Secretary of War in 1899, replying to criticism concerning the high death rate from disease among our soldiers in the Philippines, compared the annual rate of mortality among the soldiers (17.2 per 1,000) with that which prevailed in the total population of the cities of Washington and Boston. Since the rates were almost identical, it was argued that the soldier rate was not excessive. But soldiers are a selected group both as to age class where death rates are normally very low, and as to physical condition. Therefore deaths among 1,000 soldiers are never comparable with deaths among the same number of the general urban population, which includes children and the old, whose rates are always relatively high.

One more example may be given, from the field of differential fertility. The Massachusetts State census of 1905 used a schedule for females which recorded the number of children born to each living mother in the State, and also the number born to her own mother in the preceding generation. A bulletin was prepared from these records comparing the average number of children born to mothers of two successive generations, in different classes of the population. It was stated that "while the native-born mothers (then living) had an average of 2.77 children, their own mothers (preceding generation) had an average of 6.47." This startling comparison of the native-born mothers of two generations was invalid because many of the mothers living in 1905 had not completed the childbearing period, and their families would continue to grow.

Knowledge of differences in age distribution and their significance is essential for investigators in many fields. Comparisons in respect to productive capacity and consumption requirements can be made only after exact reference to the proportions of the population within the adult ages, 20–64 years, in contrast to the economically dependent portions outside these ages, young and old. The relative burden of maintenance for young and old persons varies in relation to the proportions of the specific populations within the productive ages, in different regions of the United States, in urban and rural districts, and among native and foreign born. For example, the comparative burden of providing educational facilities in any community depends in part upon the ratio of children of school age to the productive population. This ratio is much higher in the rural areas than in cities, especially the large urban centers. Larger families in the country and migration from the young adult group to the city because the labor has not been needed on the farms, have produced this high ratio of children and young persons under 20 years.

The natural increase of any population (excess of births over deaths) is essentially related to the age composition of that particular population. A high ratio of women in the childbearing ages, 15–44, explains in part the high crude birth rate of our foreign born. A relatively high proportion of children under 5 years and of old persons over 65 years in the rural-farm population tends to produce a high general death rate as compared with city populations, which have larger proportions than the country in the middle ages where death rates are low. Therefore the crude general death rates of rural and urban groups are not at all comparable. The proportion of France's population over 50 years of age is almost one half greater than that in the United States, and France's general death rate is much higher than ours (about 16 as compared with about 11 per 1,000).

Migration fundamentally changes

TABLE I—Percentage Age Distribution of Populations, 1930
(U. S., specific classes and geographic units)

Age	U. S. Total	West [a]	South [b]	N. C.	Rural-Farm [c]	Urban 2,500–	Detroit	N. Y. City	Los Angeles	U. S. Foreign Born
Under 20....	38.8	34.4	44.6	49.3	47.3	34.5	35.0	32.9	26.5	4.6
0–4........	9.3	8.2	11.0	12.3	11.1	8.2	9.3	7.7	6.4	0.2
5–19......	29.5	26.2	33.6	37.0	36.2	26.3	25.7	25.2	20.1	4.4
20–44......	38.3	39.8	36.4	34.1	31.0	42.3	48.4	45.9	45.6	46.8
45–64.......	17.5	19.6	14.8	12.9	16.5	18.1	13.8	17.4	21.6	36.1
45–54.....	10.6	12.0	9.3	8.2	9.8	11.2	9.3	11.0	13.3	21.6
55–64.....	6.9	7.6	5.5	4.7	6.7	6.9	4.5	6.4	8.3	14.5
65 and over..	5.4	6.2	4.2	3.7	5.2	5.1	2.8	3.8	6.3	12.5
Total.....	100.0	100.0	100.0	100.0	100.0	100.0	100.0	100.0	100.0	100.0

[a] West is composed of Mountain and Pacific divisions.

[b] South is composed of South Atlantic, East South Central, and West South Central.

[c] The rural nonfarm group (villages) in 1930 had only 40.3 per cent under 20 years, but 6.6 per cent in age group 65 and over.

the age composition of the population from which the migrants come and of that to which they go. Migrants are drawn from the young adult and middle age groups, leaving behind the young and the old. The economic, political, and social consequences of these population movements cannot be interpreted without constant reference to changes in age.

Table I presents some of the striking differences in age distribution which appear in different geographic areas and in specific classes, urban, rural-farm, and foreign born, compared with each other or with the entire population of the United States.

THE SOUTH COMPARED WITH OTHER REGIONS, 1930

The South has a much larger proportion of its people under 20 years of age than any other region of the United States; 44.6 per cent in 1930, contrasted with the lowest percentage in the West, 34.4 per cent (Table I). Today the crude birth rates of the Southern States are among the highest in the country. [2]

From the economic viewpoint, in the most productive age group, 20–44 years, the South has a relatively low proportion, 36.4 per cent, compared with the highest percentage in the West, 39.8 per cent. In the South, in other words, for every 100 persons in the age group 20–44 there are about 122 persons under 20 years, compared with only 87 in the West. These facts suggest that the productive workers in this region carry a relatively much heavier burden for child care and for education than do those of other regions. This unequal burden is an important part of the explanation as to why educational facilities are less adequate in the South than elsewhere, and

[2] Mississippi 24.4 per 1,000, and North Carolina 23.6, the highest in the South, in 1934.

why child labor laws are less stringent and child welfare standards less satisfactory.

On the other hand, the South has the smallest percentage 45 years and over —19.0 per cent in 1930. The lighter economic burden of the aged dependents compensates in part for the heavier cost of youthful persons. However, it is clear that the South, so far as age differences can indicate the situation, has a considerably larger proportion of naturally dependent persons, that is, those under 20 and over 65 years, than any other section of the country.

RURAL AND URBAN POPULATIONS COMPARED, 1930

The more distinctly agricultural a community is, the larger the percentage of children 0–4 years and of youth 5–19 years (Table I). The difference between large cities and the rural districts in this respect has been increasing, owing to the more rapid decline of the birth rate in cities and the migration of young adults from the country after they have been reared and educated. The relative burden of child care and education therefore rests more heavily upon the productive workers of rural communities than upon those of cities. If we should assume a high school education or its equivalent to be desirable for all children, requiring school attendance through the eighteenth year, each 100 persons in the most productive group, 20–44, would have to provide facilities for about 4/5 more children in the country districts than in cities of 500,000 or more.

Certainly it is to the interest of the city to share the burden of care and education of its future citizens, if by doing so the standards of health and training can be raised in the rural communities. Subsidies from state revenues for rural schools and health work are now being given in many states in order to equalize these burdens and to furnish to rural children facilities more nearly like those of the city.

The proportion 20–64 years of age is much greater in urban communities, especially in large cities, than in rural districts, which gives a decided advantage in productive capacity to cities (Table I). In the change from an agricultural to an urbanized industrial economy, cities have strongly attracted the middle age groups, both from the rural areas and from other lands.

Both the rural-farm and the rural-nonfarm (village) populations have relatively high percentages of old people, 65 years and over. Many retire from farms to villages and some return from cities to spend their last years. The comparatively low age-specific death rates of rural areas allow larger proportions to survive to old age in the country.

Table I indicates the wide differences which occur between individual cities in the proportion of persons at the older productive age, 45–64, and at the age 65 and over. Los Angeles has more than twice as large a proportion over 65 years as has Detroit (6.3 per cent and 2.8 per cent respectively in 1930). It is the contrast between a young and growing industrial center and a city which attracts older persons mainly on account of climate. Moreover, for several decades Detroit has been in the unique situation of having a declining percentage of its population over 65 years of age, owing to the rapidly increasing middle age groups.

At present there are only about 10 elders, 65 years and over, in cities of over 500,000, to every 100 persons in the most productive ages, 20–44, contrasted with a ratio of 18 in rural areas. It follows from the facts presented in this section that the productive workers in rural districts are carrying a relatively much heavier *double* burden of maintenance for both young and old dependents than the same group of workers in cities. The rural population should not be expected to support this unequal economic burden alone.

As is well known, the foreign born are concentrated to a great extent in urban industrial centers. They have a very small percentage in the age group under 20 years (4.4 per cent), and a very high proportion in the adult and older age periods (Table I). This influences strongly the age composition described above as characteristic of cities. The foreign born now have over twice as high a proportion over 65 years as the entire country (12.5 per cent in 1930 compared with 5.4 per cent), owing to restriction of immigration and the aging of the foreign born already here. This situation is interesting from the viewpoint of the cost of old age pensions for this class in our population.

CHANGES IN AGE COMPOSITION

Time has worked significant changes in the age composition of the population of the country as a whole and of its various regions and classes. The expectation of life at birth has doubled since the early nineteenth century in the United States, thanks to the control gained over diseases affecting infancy and youth, and over tuberculosis which decimated those in middle life—in short, thanks to postponement of death until the older ages. The rapidly declining birth rate, especially since 1900, has lowered the proportion of young persons at the same time that health measures have prolonged the lives of those born. Immigration, which for many decades contributed millions to the most productive age group, 20–44, has been greatly restricted, and those who continue to come are older at arrival, while those already here are growing older.

The net result of all these changes is a steadily declining proportion under 20 years and a corresponding increase over 45 years of age, with little change in the proportion in the most productive group, 20–44 years.[3] It is in the group 65 and over that the most striking proportional change has been going on and will no doubt continue. The estimate for 1980 suggests that the proportion over 65 years of age may more than double in the next fifty years (5.4 per cent in 1930; 12.1 per cent in 1980). In absolute numbers the change is even more startling. These elders were over tenfold as numerous in the population of 1930 as in that of 1850, although the total numbers had grown little more than fivefold. It is estimated that the number of elders may increase threefold over the present by 1980.

TABLE II—A CENTURY OF POPULATION TRENDS IN THE UNITED STATES, BY AGE GROUPS

Age	1880	1930	1980 [a]
Under 5	13.8	9.3	6.4
5–19	34.3	29.5	20.3
20–44	35.9	38.3	35.4
45–64	12.6	17.5	25.8
65 and over	3.4	5.4	12.1
Total	100.0	100.0	100.0

[a] Estimated by Thompson and Whelpton in *Population Trends in the United States* (X, 415 pp. New York: McGraw-Hill Book Co., 1933), p. 109, "medium" estimate.

With this increase at older ages interesting problems of old age security arise—jobs for older workers, pensions for the aged, and the economic burden of dependency. What will be the effect upon economic productivity and the general standard of living? If we view the broad range of economically productive ages 15–64 years as a whole,

[3] Table II. Estimate also for 1980, made by Thompson and Whelpton.

we find a slightly larger proportion in 1930 than in 1920 within these age limits in the United States, but their total contribution to living standards depends upon employment opportunities at both ends of this range.

Until the 1930 census the largest five-year age group in the total population had always been that of 0–4 years, but in 1930 this group was smaller than the next older five-year group.

CHANGING AGE COMPOSITION AND RATES OF NATURAL INCREASE

An unstable age composition is responsible for the deceptive nature of the crude birth and death rates and of the resultant rates of natural increase in the United States. The usual method of computing natural increase has considered only crude rates current at a specific time in the given population. But the crude birth rate at any time depends upon the proportion of women in the childbearing period. This proportion in our population has been and still is relatively high, owing to heavy immigration in past years of young persons and to the higher birth rates which prevailed in earlier times. For a similar reason the general death rate has been and is deceptively low. The concentration at young adult ages, where mortality is normally low, depresses the general death rate. *The result is a deceptively high rate of natural increase by excess of births.*

This concentration at the young adult ages is disappearing as the age composition shifts to larger proportions at older ages, as indicated in Table II. Now, if we assume that the age-specific birth and death rates current at any specific time continue to operate without change as the new generation comes to maturity, and that no migration disturbs the situation, the changing age distribution will cause the crude birth rate to become lower and the general death rate higher, and the resulting rate of natural increase to be really less than at present appears. This has been characterized as the "true rate of natural increase," as distinguished from the actual excess of births over deaths observed at any given time.[4] It is the expected natural increase after time has been given, during the maturing generation, for the age concentration of persons at the young adult ages to become adjusted into older age classes, while preserving in operation the present birth and death rates at each specific age.

SOME CONSEQUENCES OF AGE TRENDS

Some of the consequences of age changes in the United States are already becoming evident, while others are matters for interesting speculation. Certain of these have been suggested in the course of the foregoing discussion. Some deserve special emphasis here, and none is more interesting than the effect of age changes upon the declining general death rate.

This decline of the general death rate was characteristic of the last century and of the first two decades of the present century. Since 1920, however, its level has remained almost the same. True, it has been abnormally low (11 or 12 per 1,000), because our population has been concentrated at the young adult ages. As the time approaches when births will equal deaths and when the age distribution will be-

[4] Louis I. Dublin and Alfred J. Lotka, "On the True Rate of Natural Increase," *Journal of the American Statistical Association*, Vol. 20 (Sept. 1925), pp. 305–339. This article develops a valid technique for measuring the natural increase which recognizes the situation described above. See also "Modern Trends in the Birth Rate," in this volume.

come stabilized, with larger proportions at older ages in a stationary population, the general death rate must rise, owing to the influence of age. Its decline has already slowed up and the rise will soon begin. It may rise to a level of 15 or 16 per 1,000, as is the situation in France today. This expected rise will occur probably in the face of medical and scientific discoveries and of public health measures, and will be due to the aging of our population.

The actual number of children at certain ages, in the entire country, is now declining. This fact has important economic and social implications. At the census of 1930, the white children at each of the first five years of age were fewer in number than in 1920. These children under 5 years in 1930 have now advanced into the next older age groups and most of them are in school. This means that several of the early grades in the elementary schools of the entire country have begun to decline in actual numbers. When the next census count is made, in 1940, the same condition will doubtless prevail throughout the elementary school grades and in most of the high school classes, as well as at preschool ages.

This decrease in numbers of school age may be compensated by better attendance standards and by extension of the school age. More adequate facilities for the smaller numbers may be provided, and better preparation for living in an increasingly complex environment may result by means of a longer training under more specialized instruction. Certainly one of the important factors in reducing child mortality and improving child care in recent years has been the decreasing size of family and the fewer children to care for. This continuing trend gives an opportunity to catch up in the quality of service in this field.

The fact that persons at older ages are rapidly increasing, both relatively and in actual numbers, has grave economic and social consequences. We have at present in the United States over 6½ millions 65 years of age and over, and it is estimated that this number may be trebled within a half-century. This is a rapidly increasing burden upon the productive workers.

Furthermore, with the prolongation of life and the aging of the foreign born, a rapid increase has been taking place and will continue in the proportion of workers in the later age group, 45–64 years (Table II). This situation makes it impossible to ignore longer the problem of jobs for older workers. The period of youth in our industrial organization is passing, and our economic structure must be adapted to age changes. Institutions and agencies for the care of the aged, the burden of old age pensions, and the costs of dependency will increase rapidly.

How will these conditions affect the general standard of living? The increasing burden of the aged upon the productive workers need not adversely affect the standard of living, because the proportion of persons in the productive ages, 20–64, is not decreasing, and the burden of support for the young dependent group is declining. During the next half-century, age changes need not be unfavorable to an even higher standard of living; but only on condition that expanding wants on the part of a population approaching a stationary condition as to numbers, create jobs to employ the workers; and on condition that our industrial structure can be adapted to employ the ever increasing number of older workers, 45–64 years of age, thus utilizing their productive capacity. Otherwise, an increasing proportion of these older workers may become semi-

dependent and thus increase the total burden of support resting upon the productive workers. This is a present and future problem of employment and involves adjustment of industrial policies to the needs of an aging population—a new challenge to American business management.

SEX COMPOSITION

The relation between the number of males and of females in any population is usually described by the *sex ratio*, which is the number of males to 100 females. When the ratio is over 100 the males are in excess, and when less than 100 the females predominate. This relation is sometimes expressed as per cent male and per cent female in the given population. Like age, sex is a necessary cross classification for many other groupings, since it is essential to the proper interpretation of almost every other phase of population statistics.

TABLE III — SEX RATIOS AND PROPORTIONS MARRIED, 15 YEARS AND OVER, FOR VARIOUS POPULATIONS IN THE UNITED STATES, 1930

Population Group	Sex Ratio, 1930	Males Per Cent Married	Females Per Cent Married
United States–Total.....	102.5	60.0	61.1
Rural–Farm............	111.0	57.9	66.0
Urban.................	98.1	60.5	58.5
Negro.................	97.0	59.8	58.5
New England States....	97.2	58.7	55.8
East North Central.....	104.1	60.8	62.9
South Atlantic.........	99.6	60.6	60.0
West South Central.....	103.3	61.9	64.0
Pacific................	108.7	57.2	62.3
Massachusetts.........	95.1	58.0	53.7
Montana..............	120.0	52.6	65.4
Boston................	96.4	52.1	48.9
Charleston, S. C........	83.8	60.9	50.3
Cleveland.............	103.0	59.4	60.4

The sex ratio varies at any one time by regions of the country and by classes of the population, urban and rural, native and foreign born, white and Negro. When one sex outnumbers the other in any population, the proportion of that sex married is usually less than that of the other. Also the degree of disparity in the proportion married varies roughly with the disparity between the number of each sex in the community. Table III presents the sex ratios in 1930 for various groupings and for the total population of the United States, indicating how the proportions married, male and female, vary in relation to these sex ratios.

The ratio varies also with time. For example, in 1880 the sex ratio of Washington State was 157.7, influenced strongly by the predominance of males in the westward movement. That of Massachusetts was only 92.8, affected by this very movement of males out of New England. By 1930 the ratio for Washington had declined to 112.1, and that for Massachusetts had risen to 95.1. The trend in the entire population of the country has been downward, from 106.0 in 1910, when the predominance of males among the foreign born had a marked influence, to 102.5 in 1930. The trend for the white population is toward equality of the sexes and toward a corresponding equality in proportions of males and of females married. Table IV illustrates these trends.

Westward migration 'of males has left an excess of females in certain eastern states and has caused an excess of males in western states and cities, which is becoming less marked decade by 'decade. The excess of females among Negroes apparently increased in the decade 1920–30 (99.2 in 1920; 97.0 in 1930). The recent Negro movements from the South, as is usual in migrations, have shown an excess of males (101.0 in North, 95.9 in South, in 1930). In cities there is àn excess of females (Table III), indicating that there has been a more rapid movement

TABLE IV—TRENDS IN SEX RATIOS COMPARED WITH PROPORTIONS MARRIED, MALE AND FEMALE, 15 YEARS AND OVER, 1900–1930

Population Unit			1900	1910	1920	1930
U. S. Total...............	Sex ratio		104.4	106.0	104.0	102.5
	% married	M.	54.5	55.8	59.2	60.0
		F.	57.0	58.9	60.6	61.1
West North Central Div.............	Sex ratio		109.7	109.9	106.1	104.2
	% married	M.	53.3	54.1	58.0	59.4
		F.	60.0	60.4	61.4	61.9
Pacific Div................	Sex ratio		128.2	129.5	113.9	108.7
	% married	M.	44.7	46.7	55.0	57.2
		F.	58.1	60.5	62.4	62.3
Washington State..................	Sex ratio		142.2	136.3	118.1	112.1
	% married	M.	43.0	45.7	54.8	56.9
		F.	65.5	64.1	65.7	64.6
Detroit....................	Sex ratio		95.1	106.6	119.1	110.1
	% married	M.		55.8	56.6	60.0
		F.		57.0	65.4	66.1
Seattle...................	Sex ratio		176.7	136.2	113.5	103.7
	% married	M.		42.5	54.6	57.2
		F.		58.7	61.7	59.4

of females than of males from rural districts, and as a consequence a larger proportion of unmarried females.

Disparity of the sexes in numbers is important for social and economic studies. If males are in excess, as in our Western communities, many will not be able to marry; if females predominate, as in our cities and in many European countries because of war and emigration, there will be relatively large proportions of unmarried women. As a result of these disparities, crude death and birth rates are affected; and the growth of the population, and the health, the social morality, and the family life of communities are influenced.[5]

[5] For more extensive presentation of data and their analyses by age and sex, refer to *Population Trends in the United States, op. cit.*, Chap. IV and V.

DYNAMIC ASPECTS OF THE RELATION OF

POPULATION TO ECONOMIC DEVELOPMENT

By Frank Lorimer

1. GENERAL THEORY

Up to some fifteen years ago, economic theories of population were chiefly directed to the formulation of fixed relations between natural resources, population and production. The whole dynamic field of social institutions, technology, and cultural values was introduced into these formulations merely as a limiting constant—"at a given stage of arts," as described by M a l t h u s, or "within a particular population cycle" as specified by P e a r l. This neglect of the social aspects of economic-demographic relations was not very serious when the analysis is limited to societies with relatively static cultures; but such rigid formulations are quite inappropriate to conditions of rapid social change. The role of social structure was emphasized in Marxist analysis, and this was an advance; but the treatment remained dogmatic, and the effect of demographic changes on economic and social processes was ignored.

As a result of contributions by K e y n e s and other modern economists and of simultaneous advances in social theory and demography, studies of the economic aspects of population trends in advanced capitalistic societies now have a quite different character. Such static concepts as "over-population," "under-population," and "optimum population" are recognized as relatively insignificant in comparison with the analysis of inter-relations between changes in population, changes in the composition and characteristics of the labor force, the distribution of income, rates of capital formation, productivity, cultural values, *et cetera.*

Unfortunately, the older static concepts are still commonly over-emphasized in dealing with the problems of technically under-developed countries. This causes confusion, sometimes leading to a fallacious conception of changes in population and changes in production as alternative means of promoting progress, rather than as mutually dependent, interacting processes. This false emphasis also distracts attention from the vitally important analysis of potential relations between changes in population and changes in economic and social institutions.

The significance of relations between population and natural resources should not be minimized. It would be improper to ignore the accidental advantage now enjoyed by nations such as the United States and the Soviet

Union, which occupy great belts of fertile land that were almost uninhabited three hundred years ago and which have large and diverse fuel and mineral resources—in comparison with nations situated where ancient civilizations promoted the gradual accumulation of great populations supported by intensive land utilization. Eventually such differences in demographic situation must be taken into account in the organization of world economic relations.

On the other hand, apparent relations between natural resources, population, and production are powerfully influenced by variations in replaceable capital, techniques, and social structure. There is little doubt that the volume of agricultural production could be doubled in most regions where productivity is low at present by an effective application of knowledge that was already available in the 1930's, but in most of these countries agricultural production has not kept pace with the growth of population during the intervening period, according to estimates by the Food and Agriculture Organization. The potentialities of increased production in industry are even more obvious, but it may be economically and socially impossible to achieve their realization. Social obstacles to economic progress may be as formidable, across decades or even centuries, as mountain barriers. New exploration constantly increases the stock of available natural resources, and the advance of scientific knowledge constantly increases their potential value. Potential production, defined in terms of natural resources and abstract knowledge about techniques, could, in most countries, provide support for a much larger population at a much higher level of living than at present. However, actual advance toward such a hypothetical level of production may require profound changes involving formation of new capital equipment, the acquisition of new skills, advances in general levels of health and education, and changes in social institutions and in social values. Such changes may be dependent in part on changes in population trends, and the modification of population trends may be in part dependent on such social changes. The analysis of these inter-relations is the crux of the most acute population problem of the modern world.

I do not deny the theoretical value of such concepts as "optimum population" and "over-population" or "under-population" (defined with reference to such a hypothetical optimum). It should be recognized, however, that the hypothetical optimum in a particular situation at a particular time might be appreciably changed within a year by a change in social structure or the discovery of some new technique. In any case, the determination that an actual population was above or below the optimum would provide no firm basis for public policy, because rapid transition toward the optimum might have serious adverse effects on economic and social life. I, therefore, propose a *moratorium* on all discussions involving these relatively sterile concepts until more progress has been made in dealing with the dynamic aspects of the interrelation between population and economic and social changes.

The sound determination of public policy waits upon an answer to such questions as the following: How will various possible trends of population affect the rationalization of agriculture, the rate of capital formation, the advancement of educational levels, the structure of social institutions, *et cetera?* And, in turn, how will each of these changes and other possible changes affect future population trends? The provision of adequate answers to such questions is the joint responsibility of economists, sociologists, and demographers.

2. SOME EMPIRICAL OBSERVATIONS

A merely empirical approach to such questions, through observations on various historical situations, can easily be misleading, due to differences in circumstances. This approach may, however, provide some useful suggestions. In this connection, studies of the two nations where advance from a low level to a relatively high level of productivity during the last fifty years has been most rapid, i.e., Japan and the Soviet Union, are particularly interesting. A few major aspects of these transitions can be summarized very briefly. Economic advance in Japan was aided by the extension of imperial control over neighboring countries; it was facilitated in the Soviet Union by the development of new resources in outlying areas. Foreign capital was not available to the Soviet Union and there was relatively small in-movement of foreign capital to Japan; but in both countries governments played an important role in promoting rapid increase of capital equipment while permitting only moderate increases in levels of consumption. There were concomittant advances in agriculture and industry in both countries, along with rapid expansion of provisions for health and education. In both countries the population directly dependent on agriculture remained practically constant, so that the entire increase of population was absorbed in new commercial, industrial, and administrative occupations. Population trends in both countries were modified by declines in human fertility, due in part to the rapid growth of cities and to extensive employment of women in industry. The crude birth rate of Japan was about 35 per thousand in early 1920's (well below that of most predominantly agrarian countries today); it declined to 27 per thousand in 1938. The crude birth rate of the Soviet Union was about 45 per thousand in the middle 1920's; it declined to about 30 per thousand in 1933 and 1934, but recovered about one-half of this decline from 1934 to 1937. The initial rapid decline of fertility in the Soviet Union was due both to profound social changes and to the public provision of unrestricted facilities for abortion. As a result, there were some 13 million fewer children in the Soviet Union in 1940 than there would have been at that time if fertility had remained at the 1926 level. Therefore, during the critical period of initial industrialization the ratio of persons at productive ages to those in the non-productive age classes was raised appreciably, along with a release of the energies of many potential mothers for immediate economic production. And, perhaps equally important, the promotion of education was facilitated by a lowered ratio of children to persons capable of providing instruction.

We have noted a few interesting parallels in transitional processes in Japan and in the Soviet Union, but in many respects there were obvious differences between the developments in these two countries, as well as between the course of events in either of these countries and the earlier more gradual transition in European society. Similarly, economic advance may be achieved in other countries along quite different lines.

These considerations lead to a redefinition of the scientific job to be done. It can be divided into two phases: (1) What universally valid principles can be discovered in inter-relations between demographic changes and economic and social changes? The formulation of such principles can be approached through the logical and mathematical development of related processes under hypothetical conditions. This is a field for abstract analysis. (2) What specific relations between demographic changes and economic and social changes can be expected in particular situations, taking into account our abstract knowledge about economic, social and demographic principles? These empirical problems must be investigated specifically in each situation by social scientists intimately familiar with the cultural context of these problems in that particular situation.

3. Dynamics of Age Structure

The remainder of this paper represents a very limited attempt to contribute to the advancement of knowledge on one aspect of the required analysis on the abstract level. It deals with the dynamics of age structure, specifically in a transitional situation from initially high levels of mortality and of fertility. The present brief exposition is based on material presented in greater detail in the current issue of the *Demographic Bulletin* of the United Nations (Volume 1, Number 1). Treatment of this specific topic is preceded by a brief consideration of some characteristics of stable populations resulting from an indefinite continuance of constant vital rates.

The analysis is carried out for various age classes, in order to permit alternative divisions between major age groups. However the exposition here is chiefly with reference to broad age classes divided at ages 15 and 65 years. The latter limit is selected in definition of the broad central age class because in a majority of all countries for which such information is available a majority of all males aged 60 to 65 years are engaged in gainful production. If the group 15 to 60 years is used as a central age group, rather than 15 to 65 years, the variations are much smaller, though usually in the same direction.

Three levels of mortality, covering a wide range of experience, are represented in the specific death rates used in constructing the stable populations shown in Figure 1. The rates are those of the official life tables for the following populations, with the following expectations of life at birth:

Population	Expectation of life at birth in years	
	Males	Females
New Zealand, 1934-38	65.46	68.45
Japan, 1926-30	44.82	46.54
India, 1921-31	26.91	26.56

It is important to remember that different stationary populations resulting from different sets of constant age-specific death rates are conditioned by different levels of fertility. In fact, within the range of actual observations to date, variations in fertility exercise a far more powerful influence on age structure than variations in mortality. This relation is sometimes ignored, just because hypothetical stationary populations are obtained statistically from age-specific death rates, whereas the required levels of fertility are merely implicit in the assumption (that the population be stationary at a given level of mortality). The same consideration applies to various stable populations at assumed constant rates of increase or decrease.

Figure 1 presents a series of hypothetical stable populations, calculated in accordance with the principles defined by Lotka. It is apparent that, at any given level of mortality, a higher level of fertility (giving a higher rate of natural increase) results in an increase in the proportion of children and a decrease in the proportion of aged persons—as compared with any lower level of fertility. Within the range of variations in mortality treated here, a higher constant level of fertility gives a smaller proportion of persons within the broad central age group, 15 to 65 years— except at very low levels of fertility in combination with low levels of mortality, where this relation is reversed.

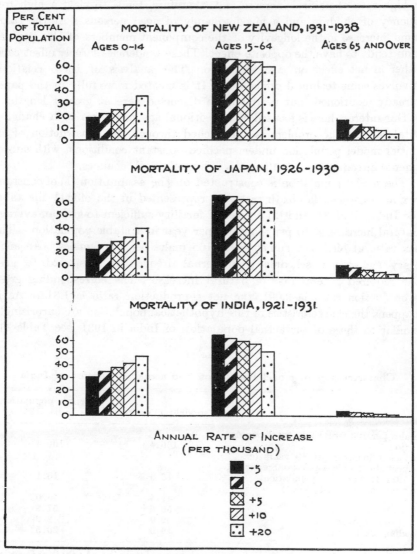

AGE DISTRIBUTIONS OF STABLE POPULATIONS WITH SELECTED SCHEDULES OF MORTALITY AND SELECTED CONSTANT RATES OF INCREASE

Fig. 1

On the other hand, at any given level of fertility differences in levels of mortality have little influence on the distribution of stable populations by broad age classes. Proportions of children, adults at productive ages, and aged persons all remain at about the same values within the range of variations treated in this series. This is due to the operation of two conflicting tendencies. Low mortality at a given level of fertility gives a high rate of natural increase and, therefore, tends to yield a high frequency of children and a low frequency of aged persons. At the same time, increase in the longevity of the component members of this population tends to have the opposite effect. These tendencies largely offset each other in net effect on age structure. The analysis of these relations involves some technical difficulties. It is treated more fully in the paper already mentioned, but need not be discussed here at greater length.

Our interest here is focused on transitional age structures with changing vital rates. The problem is approached through the construction of an initial model population under specified constant conditions, with subsequent introduction of alternative hypothetical changes.

The model population is constructed on the assumption (1) of constant sex and age specific death rates, as represented in the official life table for India, 1921-31, and (2) a level of fertility sufficient to give an average natural increase of 10 per thousand per year in a stable population. The sex ratio at birth is assumed to be 105 males per 100 females. An arbitrary age-specific schedule of maternal frequencies was used to give the required general rate of natural increase. The corresponding gross reproduction ratio is 3.061; the net reproduction ratio is 1.318. As it happens the characteristics of this hypothetical population are surprisingly similar to those of the actual population of India in 1931 (see Table 1).

TABLE I

Characteristics of model Population and actual Population of India

	model population	census population India, 1931
males per 100 females in total population	105.4	106.4
per cent increase per 10 years (expected in stable population; reported, 1921-31, in census population)	16.0	16.1
per cent at specified ages:		
0–14 years	41.4	40.0
15–64 years	56.6	57.8
65 or over	2.0	2.2
median age in years	19.0	20.5

It is arbitrarily assumed that the model population has 1,000,000 females at the beginning of the experiment—giving a total population of about 2,054,000 persons. This population is then projected over a thirty-year period on two alternative hypotheses:

Hypothesis A. Age-specific fertility rates remain constant. Death rates (by five-year age classes) decline (in straight lines) to give, at the end of thirty years, the age-specific death rates of the Japanese life tables, 1926-30.

Hypothesis B. Mortality declines as in Hypothesis A. Fertility rates also decline in straight lines to give the same female net reproduction ratio at the end of the thrity-year period as ,at the start. The required reduction gives fertility rates at the end of the period that are, on the average, slightly less than two-thirds as high as at the start.

In reducing the age-specific fertility rates to give the required general level, it is assumed, in the light of experience in other countries, that the decline is least rapid at ages 25-29 years and most rapid at ages 15-19 years and at ages over 40 years. At the end of the thirty-year period the maternal frequencies, daughters only, per thousand women by five year age classes, are as follows: 21.6, 89.3, 109.5, 89.3, 56.9, 25.5, 3.1. These give 1.976, as a gross reproduction ratio and, in combination with the reduced mortality, the same net reproduction ratio, 1.318, as at the start. The·assumed relative frequencies at the end, like those of the initial population, are arbitrary; their general level is that required by the hypothesis.

The nature of the hypothetical decline in mortality is indicated by a comparison, by particular ages, of death rates in the Japanese life tables, 1926-30, and death rates in the Indian life tables, 1921-31 (see Table II).

TABLE II

Specific Death Rates (Life Table q_x Values):
India 1921-31 ; Japan 1926-30

exact age in years	males			females		
	India 1921-31 A	Japan 1926-30 B	ratio B/A	India 1921-31 A	Japan 1926-30 B	ratio B/A
0	248.7	140.1	.56	232.3	124.1	.53
1	91.8	43.1	.47	86.5	42.1	.49
2	56.4	22.4	.40	50.6	22.7	.45
3	39.2	15.0	.38	34.0	15.6	.46
4	27.4	9.8	.36	23.3	10.6	.45
5	19.3	6.4	.33	16.5	7.1	.43
10	7.9	2.6	.33	8.1	3.0	.37
15	9.8	5.0	.51	11.5	7.3	.63
20	12.7	9.8	.77	17.6	10.6	.60
25	15.3	8.6	.56	21.6	9.6	.44
30	19.3	7.4	.38	25.1	8.9	.35
35	24.1	7.7	.32	29.3	9.3	.32
40	29.4	9.6	.33	34.5	10.1	.29
45	34.9	12.7	.36	39.0	10.2	.26
50	41.0	17.5	.43	43.1	12.6	.29
55	48.1	25.0	.52	47.5	16.9	.36
60	57.9	36.7	.63	54.3	24.2	.45
65	72.7	54.9	.76	66.6	37.1	.56
70	97.6	80.4	.82	88.8	57.7	.65
75	142.7	117.5	.82	130.1	88.9	.68
80	218.0	170.2	.78	206.6	138.5	.67

The effects of these alternative hypotheses on the age structure and other characteristics of the model population over a thirty-year period are shown in Table III. The total population, as would be expected,   increases more

TABLE III

Projections of a model Population, from stable Population with Indian Mortality 1921-31 and with initial increase 1 per cent per annum

Hypothesis A. Specified decline in mortality; fertility constant.
Hypothesis B. Same decline in mortality, with comparable decline in fertility.

	hypo-thesis	time in years						
		0	5	10	15	20	25	30
total population	A	2,054	2,176	2,341	2,552	2,820	3,153	3,569
(thousands)	B	2,054	2,165	2,295	2,446	2,619	2,814	3,034
males per 100	A	105.4	105.3	105.1	104.8	104.4	104.1	103.7
females	B	105.4	105.3	105.1	104.9	104.6	104.2	103.8
median age in	A	19.0	19.0	18.9	18.7	18.5	18.3	18.2
years	B	19.0	19.1	19.4	19.7	20.3	21.0	21.3
age classes (% of total)								
0—14	A	41.4	41.5	41.8	42.3	42.8	43.2	43.5
	B	41.4	41.2	40.7	39.8	38.8	37.6	36.5
15—19	A	10.8	10.7	10.5	10.3	10.3	10.3	10.3
	B	10.8	10.7	10.7	10.8	10.7	10.5	10.3
20—49	A	39.2	39.1	38.8	38.3	37.7	37.0	36.3
	B	39.2	39.3	39.6	40.0	40.6	41.1	41.6
50—59	A	5.1	5.1	5.2	5.3	5.4	5.5	5.7
	B	5.1	5.1	5.3	5.5	5.8	6.2	6.7
60—64	A	1.6	1.6	1.6	1.6	1.7	1.7	1.8
	B	1.6	1.6	1.6	1.7	1.8	1.9	2.1
15—64	A	56.6	56.5	56.1	55.6	55.0	54.5	54.1
	B	56.6	56.7	57.2	58.0	58.8	59.8	60.6
65 or over	A	2.0	2.0	2.1	2.1	2.2	2.3	2.4
	B	2.0	2.1	2.1	2.2	2.4	2.6	2.9
birth rate	A	47.6	47.5	47.1	46.4	45.6	44.9	44.3
(per 1,000)	B	47.6	44.9	42.3	39.7	37.2	34.7	32.5
death rate	A	37.6	34.5	31.0	27.9	24.4	21.6	18.2
(per 1,000)	B	37.6	33.8	29.9	26.6	23.0	20.3	16.9
natural increase	A	10.0	13.0	16.1	18.5	21.2	23.3	26.1
(per 1,000)	B	10.0	11.1	12.4	13.1	14.2	14.4	15.6

rapidly on Hypothesis A (declining mortality, constant fertility) than on Hypothesis B. It may, however, appear surprising that the rate of increase also rises during this period on Hypothesis B, although fertility is reduced so as to keep the net reproduction ratio constant[1]. The

---

[1] This statement needs minor qualification. There is some variation in the net reproduction ratio at intervening intervals, because mortality trends and fertility trends are treated independently. There is precise equality between the ratios only at the beginning and at the end of the period.

moderate rise on Hypothesis B and the more rapid rise on Hypothesis A result chiefly from the conspicuous decline of the death rate. On Hypothesis B, the absolute number of births remains practically constant throughout the series, while the birth rate falls in the growing population.

The rapid decline of the death rate, here indicated, must be attributed in part to the fact that the population is initially "young", with a very small percentage of aged persons, and remains "young" on either hypothesis in spite of marked improvement in mortality. The decline of the death rate is somewhat accelerated on Hypothesis B, due to a decrease in the proportion of infants, whereas the distribution of the adult population with respect to relative numbers of young, middle-aged, and aged persons is not radically changed during this thirty-year period.

The stable population that would eventually result from the age specific death rates and fertility rates in effect on Hypothesis A at the end of the thirty-year period, if these rates then remained fixed indefinitely, has also been computed. The intrinsic rate of natural increase used in this computation is 25 per thousand per year. The intrinsic birth rate of this stable population is 43.78 per thousand; its intrinsic death rate is 18.78. Crude rates similar to these intrinsic rates have been observed in some populations which have experienced rapid decline in mortality while traditionally high fertility remains in effect. The age composition of this stable population would be as follows:

Age class (years)	Per cent of total population
0–14	43.6
15–19	10.5
20–49	35.9
50–59	5.4
60–64	1.8
15–64	53.7
65 or more	2.7

It will be noted that this stable population (corresponding to the final intrinsic vital rates obtained on Hypothesis A, i.e., lower mortality but constant fertility) has both a somewhat larger proportion of children under 15 years and a somewhat larger proportion of aged persons, 65 years or more, than the initial model population. The proportion in the central age group, 15-64 years, is therefore smaller (53.7 per cent as compared with 56.6 per cent).

The stable population that would result from the specific fertility and mortality rates in effect at the end of the period on Hypothesis B is, of course, a stable population with Japanese mortality (1926-30) and natural increase at 10 per thousand per year (shown in Figure 2).

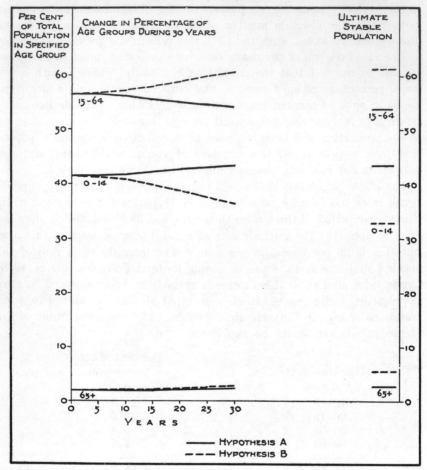

Fig. 2

The most striking result of these experiments with a model population on the conditions described above, is that age structure changes very slightly on Hypothesis A (declining mortality, constant fertility). Improvement in mortality, in accordance with the age-specific changes assumed here, does not in itself tend to increase the proportion of adults in the population, because reduction of very high mortality in the first few years of life tends (like a rise in fertility) to increase the proportion of children. There is a decrease of children and an increase of adults on Hypothesis B, but the changes are less pronounced than might have been expected.

The proportion of children under 15 years rises from 41.4 per cent to 43.5 per cent with declining mortality and constant fertility (Hypothesis

A.)   On Hypothesis B the proportion of children declines over the thirty-year period from 41.4 per cent to 36.5 per cent.   It is then only slightly above the proportion (33 per cent) in a stable population with Japanese mortality (1926-30) with a constant increase of 10 per thousand per year.

The proportion of persons aged 65 years or over rises on either hypothesis, changing during the thirty years from 2.0 per cent to 2.4 per cent (Hypothesis A), or 2.9 per cent (Hypothesis B).   In stable populations resulting from specific rates in effect at the end, if continued indefinitely thereafter, the proportion would remain within this range on Hypothesis A, but on Hypothesis B it would rise to about 5.6 per cent.

The proportion in the central age group, 15-64 years, declines slightly with declining mortality and constant fertility (Hypothesis A) from 56.6 per cent of 54.1 per cent.   It rises gradually with concomitant declines in mortality and fertility (Hypothesis B) from 56.6 per cent to 60.6 per cent.

In conclusion, it is necessary to emphasize the arbitrary character of the assumptions made in this analysis and its limitation to one hypothetical population.   The study suggests that the "inefficient" age structure of a population with high mortality and high fertility is not necessarily improved and may be slightly aggravated by a decline in mortality without a concomitant decline in fertility.

The experiment also shows that the effect of a decline of the general level of mortality, without decline in fertility, in accelerating the rate of population growth, may be reinforced by the persistence of a youthful age structure. Under such conditions a considerable decline of fertility, though modifying the rate of increase that would otherwise result from a decline in mortality, may allow a continuation or even an acceleration of the initial rate of natural increase.   An actual decline in the crude rate of natural increase would require a very rapid decline in fertility.

SOME DEMOGRAPHIC ASPECTS OF AGING

By Frank W. Notestein

VIEWED as a whole the "problem of aging" is no problem at all. It is only the pessimistic way of looking at a great triumph of civilization. The population of the United States, and of the Western world in general, has grown older because it has learned to be efficient in the renewal of its life. Today one thousand births yield about twice as large a fund of life as they produced in Colonial times, and as they produce today among more than one-half of the world's population. We are a relatively old population partly because so many of us have been successful in achieving our goal of individual survival. So, with a perversity that is strictly human, we insist on considering the aggregate result of our individual successes as a "problem."

It is true that much more than the attainment of low death dates is involved in the aging process. Indeed, as we shall see presently, movements of the birth rate are likely to be more important in determining the speed of the aging process than changes in the death rate. The two rates, however, are closely connected. It is at least possible to doubt that death rates would have fallen so low if birth rates had failed to decline. Moreover, it is difficult to imagine that we could have achieved anything like the existing level of material prosperity if modern mortality had been coupled with pre-modern fertility. Such a combination would yield increases of at least 3 per cent per year. This rate of increase doubles a population in twenty-three years, and yields a twentyfold increase in a century. If our population had grown at that rate after 1850, as it did in fact for a century before, we would now have more than 450 million, and by the year 2000 we would have more than 2 billion people in the United States. In the presence of such growth we may doubt the possibility of attaining either prosperity or exceptional health.

To suggest that the aging of the population should be viewed as an asset is, of course, not at all to suggest that there are no problems of economic and social adaptation to be faced. Naturally there are such problems, for the changes in the composition of the population have been rapid and have brought with them changes in the labor force and in the burden of dependency.

Figure 1 shows the trend by decades from 1900 to 1950 for the population in four major groups:

under age 20, 20–44, 45–64, and 65 or more years of age. No special virtue except that of convenience is claimed for this grouping. The group under 20 years may be taken to stand approximately for young dependents although many persons begin to support themselves in their 'teens. We may take 20–44 as the ages from which the younger labor force is drawn, and 45–64 as those furnishing the older labor force. Old age is also arbitrarily defined as above age 65 without any imputation that all persons over that age are unproductive, or that age 65 ought to be the age of retirement.

The left hand panel shows that the largest increases from 1900 to 1950 came in the young working ages, and the next largest in the older working ages. Additions to the working ages were very much larger than additions to the ages of dependency. In spite of the sharp reduction in births in the depression decade, the population under age 20 increased by 17 million after 1900, whereas the population over age 65 grew only 9 million. The right hand panel of figure 1 presents the same data on a logarithmic scale to permit a comparison of rates of increase. It is evident that the increase of the aged, although the smallest in absolute size, was much the most rapid. Indeed, between 1900 and 1950, that over age 65 increased fourfold. It is also evident from the chart that the older workers were increasing at a faster rate than either the younger workers or the population under age 20.

To gain some impression of future trends it is necessary to speculate about the future course of mortality. First of all, it is evident that nothing useful can be said in this context if there is a full-scale global war, except that the "problem of the aged" may be quickly, if unpleasantly, resolved. Apart from this contingency the task of predicting death rates is difficult enough. In the present case there is one saving factor. The purpose of the analysis is to direct attention to the expected rapid increase of the older segments of the population. It will be well, therefore, not to exaggerate this increase; hence to project a conservative future decline in mortality. This bias is a useful one, for most forecasts have been outstripped by the actual course of events.

Figure 2, which relates to white males, sum-

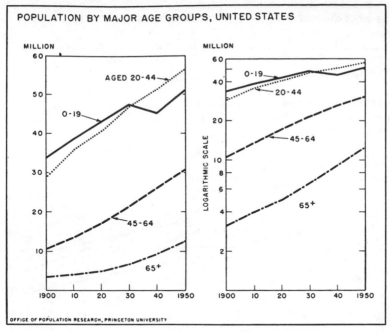

POPULATION BY MAJOR AGE GROUPS, UNITED STATES

OFFICE OF POPULATION RESEARCH, PRINCETON UNIVERSITY

FIG. 1.

marizes the recent trends of death rates for the various age groups. In it the life-table death rates for the three-year period centered on 1930 are connected by straight lines with the corresponding values for 1949, the rates being plotted on a logarithmic scale. It is evident that the intermediate points fall rather close to the lines connecting the values for 1930 and 1949. In other words, during the nineteen years from 1930 to 1949 the death rates for each age group tended to decline at rather constant rates. The decline was most rapid in the youngest ages. It was 3.4 per cent per year for infants, 6.7 per cent between 1 and 5 years, and remained above 3 per cent until age 40. By age 50 the decline had dwindled to less than 1 per cent, and by age 60, to half of 1 per cent. In other words the spectacular reductions in the risk of death took place at ages under 50, and after that age the declines were rather gradual.

The data for white females present much the same picture, except that the death rates were substantially lower and declined more rapidly than those for males. Annual rates of decline exceeded 1 per cent up to age 80. Again straight lines connecting the logarithms of the rates for 1930 and 1949 describe the trend fairly well.

The data for non-whites tell much the same story, except that the death rates were uniformly higher than the corresponding ones for whites, and above age 15 they were falling much more rapidly. Unfortunately the data for non-whites

are much less reliable than those for whites. Above age 65 the life-table values can be given little credence.

It is not the purpose of this paper to enter into a meticulous examination of the prospective changes in mortality. That has already been excellently done by Harold F. Dorn of the National Institutes of Health.[1] He not only studied the trend of death rates from all causes for whites and non-whites, but also studied the annual rate of change from accidents, cancer, cardiovascular-renal diseases, and all other conditions as a group. His forecasts for the year 1970 assume somewhat less rapid future improvement in the younger ages and somewhat more rapid improvement in the older ages than those to be presented here. However, for our purposes the results are effectively the same. For the white population the projected life expectancies to be used here run a bit higher than those derived by Dorn. The largest difference is half a year for the 1970 expectation of life at birth for females. In general, for non-whites the values to be used in this study run below those used by Dorn, but the differences are not important for present purposes.

Our problem is not that of forecasting the future rate of dying. Instead it is that of gaining some insight into the size of the surviving adult popula-

---

[1] Dorn, Harold F., Prospects of further decline in mortality rates, *Human Biology* **24**: 234–261, 1952.

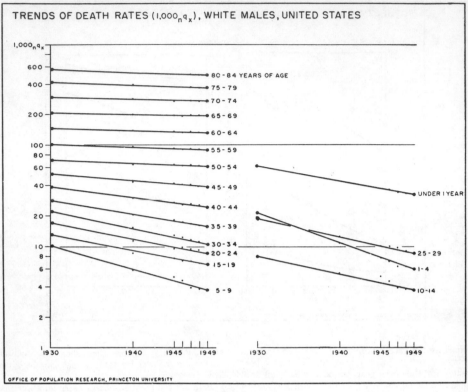

TRENDS OF DEATH RATES ($1,000_n q_x$), WHITE MALES, UNITED STATES

OFFICE OF POPULATION RESEARCH, PRINCETON UNIVERSITY

FIG. 2.

tion. In doing so it will be well to use simple methods that are obviously inadequate in order to emphasize the fact that no one can really forecast future developments. Our results will not show the precise nature of future developments, but the general sort of situation that may be expected from a continuation of past trends.

Accordingly the life tables needed for projecting surviving populations at five-year intervals from 1950 to 1970 have been constructed by assuming a continuation of the average annual per cent decline observed between 1930 and 1949 for each age-sex group of the white and non-white populations. There were two exceptions. It was assumed that the expectation of life at age 85 would remain at the 1949 level of 3.7 years for the white population, and that this value would also hold for non-white males and females, instead of the incredible 8 and 11 years shown by the official life tables. It was further assumed that wherever the values of the non-white tables dropped below those of the corresponding table for the whites, the values of the latter should be substituted. Such cases occurred at ages above 65.

The resulting gains in life expectancy for se-

lected ages are shown in figure 3. The projected expectation of life at birth for white females rises from 71.5 years in 1949 to 76.9 in 1970. White males fare less well. By 1970 their life expectancy at birth is 70.1 years, a figure well below that observed for females in 1949. The growing difference projected between the sexes means only that the difference grew in the base period. The projected values for non-white males at birth in 1970 are well above those for white males in 1949, and the projected values for non-white females in 1970 are higher than those for white males in 1970. At the higher ages the projected increases in the years of life remaining are, of course, substantially smaller. Even so, for age 60 the life expectancies projected for 1970 exceed the 1949 values by between one and two years.

The significance of these changes is shown more clearly by the number of survivors to each age from one thousand births. Figure 4 gives the results for white males and females. It must be understood that here we are not dealing with populations. The figures show only what would be the life history of a class of births if, as it passed through life, it were submitted to the risks of

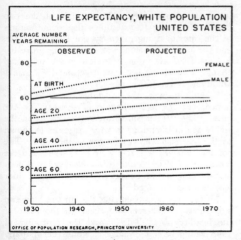

FIG. 3.

death that characterized a particular calendar year. They portray something of the efficiency with which life is maintained by showing, as areas under the curves, the years that a group starting life together would spend in youth, middle life, and old age under various schedules of dying. Obviously the saving of life has been enormous since the beginning of the century. In the 1949 table for both sexes combined more persons reached age 55 than reached age 5 in the table of 1901. In the table projected for ·1970 more survivors complete the entire working span of life than. entered the working ages in the table for 1901. The years lived after age 65 have also increased, but the significant fact is that the additions to the working ages have been very much larger than those to the ages

under 20 and over 65 taken together. Moreover, the life table projected for 1970 implies larger additions between ages 20 and 65 than before and after those ages.

The years gained in the working ages through the improvement in mortality have exceeded those added in the dependent ages but, as figure 5 shows, the ratio of years in dependency to years in the working ages has risen for females and may well continue to rise. For males the ratio has remained almost steady since 1930 and very little rise is projected. Of course this only means that the rise in the ratio of years in old age to years in the working span has been almost cancelled by the fall in the ratio of years spent in youth to years in the working ages. On the strength of such figures one can only conclude that the great economies that result from our growing ability to survive through the working span of life have not been, and in the near future are not likely to be, cancelled by the growing burden of years spent in old age.

Thus far we have dealt with only one part of the problem. We have considered only the implications of changes in mortality as they are reflected in the life patterns of a group of people moving through the life span. But these are not populations. The number of the aged during the next sixty-five years will depend, apart from migration, on death rates during the next sixty-five years. So far as their social-economic impact is concerned, however, the number of the aged is perhaps less important than the proportion of the aged in the population. In populations with low death rates such as our own this proportion of the aged is much more likely to be altered by changes in the birth rate than by changes in the

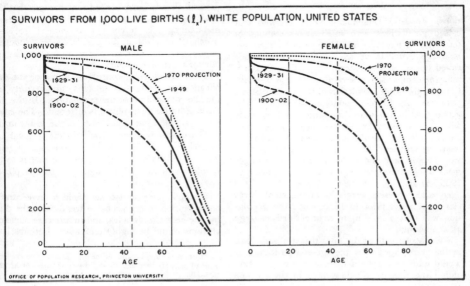

FIG. 4.

death rate. At first glance this proposition may seem surprising, but it is obvious on a moment's reflection.

Imagine a population in which the number of births has increased steadily at 1 per cent per year for a century. The number of births seventy years ago from which the population currently aged 70 survives would be only half as large as the number of births in the current year. The ratio of oldsters to youths depends on the comparative size of the birth classes from which the two groups survive, as well as on the proportions surviving.

The comparative influence on the age composition of changes in fertility and mortality can be vividly illustrated by use of stable age distribu-

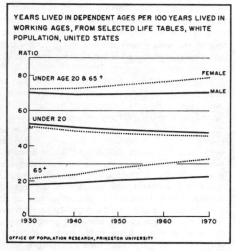

YEARS LIVED IN DEPENDENT AGES PER 100 YEARS LIVED IN WORKING AGES, FROM SELECTED LIFE TABLES, WHITE POPULATION, UNITED STATES

FIG. 5.

tions. In 1925 Dublin and Lotka showed that closed populations with fixed age schedules of fertility and mortality would approach characteristic age distributions as a limit.[2] These they called the stable age distributions. Figure 6 permits the comparison of several stable age distributions for the white population of the United States with the actual white population of 1950. The actual distribution shows the large number under age 10 contributed by the high birth rates of the past decade, the sharp drop in the early adult years from the reduced number of births in the depression decade, and the heavy loading of the ages from 25–44 from the large birth classes prior to 1925. It also shows rather low proportions of the aged who represent survivors of the small birth classes of years prior to 1885, when the population was only a little more than a third as large as at present.

By contrast both of the lines that are very high in the young ages show the age composition that would ultimately arise if there were no migration and if the rates at which women in the various

ages bore children during the year 1948 were to be indefinitely maintained. The higher of the two lines in the young ages assumes also a continuance of the rates of dying given by the 1948 life table, and the lower assumes the rates of dying projected for the 1970 life table. Obviously the projected change in mortality between 1948 and 1970 makes an almost trivial difference.

When, however, the mortality of 1948 is retained, but the age schedule of fertility for the years 1939–1941 is substituted, the change in the stable age distributions is very large, as is shown by the line that is lowest in the young ages. The combination of the fertility of 1939–1941 and the mortality of 1948 would ultimately lead to a population that would be heavily loaded with older workers and the aged.

All this amounts to saying that in the long run a population that renewed itself on the basis of the fertility of 1939–1941 and the mortality of 1948 would be old because it would be virtually stationary. On the other hand, a population having the fertility of the year 1948 would be young because it would be growing by 1.3 per cent per year if its mortality were that of the year 1948 and by 1.4 per cent per year if its mortality were that projected for 1970.

Lest those who think it advantageous to maintain a young population become too enthusiastic about the virtues of a high birth rate, we should hasten to point out that youth is to be maintained in spite of low death rates only at the cost of perpetual growth. The rate of growth that would be generated by a maintenance of 1948 fertility and mortality is a very high one. Indeed a continuation of a 1.3 per cent rate of increase from 1950 onward would give the United States a population of half a billion within the lifetime of persons already born. It may be doubted that the advantages of youth would cancel the liabilities of maintaining such a continuous rate of increase. Much of our youth in the past has been a function of our growing number of births rather than of our unfavorable mortality.

Thus far we have considered some of the implications of changes in mortality and fertility for the age composition of the population. In the immediate future the problem is different. The labor force and the aged dependents of the years up to 1970 are already born. Births in the interval between now and 1970 are chiefly relevant in relation to the load of young dependents that is to be coupled with that of the aged for the people of working age to support.

It would carry us too far afield to give careful consideration to the probable trend of births during the next two decades, and in any case our conclusions would be highly tentative. Perhaps it is

[2] Dublin, Louis I., and Alfred J. Lotka, On the true rate of natural increase, *Jour. Amer. Statis. Assoc.* **20**: 305–339, 1925.

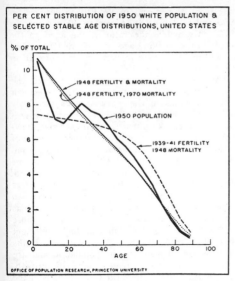

FIG. 6.

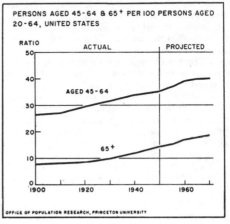

FIG. 8.

sufficient to observe that the number of births may well decline in the next five years. Two principal factors support this expectation. In the first place, the short birth classes of the depression decade are now entering the childbearing ages, so that the number of potential parents is being reduced. In the second place, a considerable part of the recent increase in births has come from a progressive decline in the age at marriage. The number of births should fall off when this decline stops. If an economic recession were to lift the age at marriage, the ensuing decline in the number of births might be quite sharp. Any such decline, however, should not last very long for by the early

1960's the large birth classes of the 1940's will enter the childbearing ages and increase the number of potential parents very rapidly. By 1970 there is a strong probability that the population under age 20 will be considerably larger than it is now. Over the next two decades it is rather unlikely that the increase of the aged will be counterbalanced by any decline in young dependents.

The age structure of the population could also be altered rather quickly by migration, for in the foreseeable future the United States can attract immigrants almost without limit. It seems unlikely, however, that we shall be willing to accept immigration on a scale that will change the fundamentals of our position in the next two or three decades.

Turning then to speculate about the trend of the adult population up to 1970, we may neglect migration and use the somewhat rough and ready procedure of also neglecting both the underenumeration of children and the number of troops overseas in 1950. Such obvious omissions have the advantage of not obscuring the fundamentals of the situation while emphasizing the fact that no precise forecast is intended. Figure 7 gives the total population over age 20 by broad age groups at five-year intervals between 1950 and 1970. It is obtained by using the projected life tables already discussed to move the 1950 census count forward in age and time by five-year steps to 1970. If there is no major migration, and no global war, and if death rates decline during the two decades after 1950 at the same rates they declined during the two decades before 1950, figure 7 shows approximately what will happen.

On these projections the increase in the number of people of working age is about 4 million less between 1950 and 1970 than it was between 1930 and 1950. In the older working ages the population increases about one million more between 1950 and 1970 than it did between 1930 and 1950. It is in the young working ages that growth is

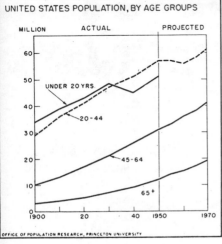

FIG. 7.

most severely cut. Between 1930 and 1950 it increased by 9.7 million, whereas the increase projected for 1950 to 1970 is only 4.7 million. The increase projected for the two decades following 1950 is less than half that which occurred in the two decades prior to 1950. On these assumptions we must expect smaller increases in the number of people of working ages in the near future than in the recent past, and a progressive aging of the labor force.

Meanwhile the increase of the aged during the twenty years following 1950 should be about one million larger than it was during the twenty years before 1950. The estimate is probably conservative because it makes no allowance for possible acceleration in the decline of death rates up to 85 and no allowance at all for improvement after that age. There is every prospect that the aged sector of the population will grow the most rapidly. The projected figure of nearly 19 million persons over age 65 in 1970 is almost three times the number in 1930. That for the population in the older working ages is nearly twice the number in 1930, and that for the population in the younger working ages in 1970 is only about one-third higher than the number in 1930.

As may be seen in figure 8, the proportion of persons in the working ages who are over 45 years rose from 31 per cent in 1930 to 35 per cent in 1950 and is projected to rise to 40 per cent in 1970. Meanwhile the ratio of the aged to the people in the working ages rose from 10 per cent in 1930 to 14 per cent in 1950 and is projected to rise to 18 per cent in 1970.

The trends toward an aging labor force and toward higher ratios of persons in the dependent ages to persons in the working ages are fairly rapid and the magnitudes are of some consequence. Just to keep matters in perspective, however, we should note that from the point of view of economic fundamentals we are only moving from an exceptionally favorable situation toward one that is very favorable indeed as such matters go. Most of the world's population probably suffers the terrible cost of losing before age 20 more than 40 per cent of those born. Any population such as our own that does not lose 40 per cent of those born until after age 65 is making highly efficient use of its human resources. So long as its births are sufficient to maintain the population and are not so numerous as to create a damaging growth, our problems do not lie in the fundamentals of the demographic situation. Instead they are the simpler ones of social-economic adjustment to the fact that we have learned how to avoid the gross waste of premature death.

THE LIFE CYCLE OF THE FAMILY

By Paul C. Glick

WITHIN the life cycle of a given family, a host of demographic and economic changes take place that require continuous readjustments of the habits and values of the family members. Moreover, the secular and cyclical changes in age at marriage, size of completed family, and length of life have greatly affected the patterns of family formation, development, and dissolution. In this paper, some of the implications of these several types of change are analyzed with respect to the family in the United States.[1]

In the discussion which follows, frequent reference is made to both "married couples" and "families." The former is defined by the U. S. Bureau of the Census as a married man and his wife who are living together. A "family" is defined as two or more persons related to each other who are living together; thus, if two married couples live together and are mutually related, they are counted as one family. The source materials include numerous reports of the decennial censuses of population, the Current Population Surveys (sample surveys covering about 25,000 households), and annual vital statistics.[2] In some instances, the

available data are fragmentary; in other instances, they provide only approximations to the information desired. The shortcomings are not sufficiently serious, however, to invalidate the central point of the discussion, namely, that married couples now have many more years of family life remaining after their children have married than did couples of earlier generations.

STAGES OF THE LIFE CYCLE OF THE FAMILY

Marriage. The average young man in the United States in 1950 entered marriage for the first time at about the age of 23 years and his wife at about the age of 20. (See table 1 and figure 1.) Both the groom and the bride in 1950 were more than a year younger, on the average, than the corresponding young persons who were entering their first marriage a decade earlier. This decline stands in contrast with the fact that during the entire 50-year period from 1890 to 1940, the average (median) age at first marriage for grooms had declined only about two years and that for brides only about one-half year, according to the best estimates available.[3]

---

[1] A similar analysis, based largely on data for 1940 and earlier dates, was published by the author as "The Family Cycle" in the *American Sociological Review*, XII: 164-174, April, 1947.

[2] A selected bibliography of census and vital statistics reports used is as follows: U. S. Bureau of the Census, *U. S. Census of Population: 1950*, Vol. II, *Characteristics of the Population*, Part 1, U. S. Summary (tables on marital status and relationship to head of household); Vol. IV, *Special Reports*, Part 2, Chapter D, Marital Status; and Vol. IV, *Special Reports*, Part 1, Chapter A, Employment and Personal Characteristics. U. S. Bureau of the Census, *U. S. Census of Housing: 1950*, Vol. II, *Nonfarm Housing Characteristics*, Chapter 1. U. S. Bureau of the Census, *Current Population Reports*, "Marital Status, Number of Times Married, and Duration of Present Marital Status: April 1948," Series P-20, No. 23; "Marital Status and Household Characteristics: (date)," Series P-20, Nos. 33 (March 1950), 38 (April 1951), and 44 (April 1952); "Fertility of the Population: April 1952," Series P-20, No. 46; "Marital Status, Year of

Marriage, and Household Relationship: April 1953," Series P-20, No. 50; "Household and Family Characteristics: April 1953," Series P-20, No. 53; "Marital Status of Workers: April 1953," Series P-50, No. 50; and "Family Income in the United States: 1952," Series P-60, No. 15. U. S. Bureau of the Census, *Differential Fertility, 1940 and 1910—Fertility for States and Large Cities*. National Office of Vital Statistics, U. S. Public Health Service, Department of Health, Education, and Welfare, *Vital Statistics of the United States*, reports for selected years from 1917 to 1950.

A closely related report was published by the National Office of Vital Statistics shortly after the meeting in 1954 of the World Population Conference; this report is entitled "Demographic Characteristics of Recently Married Persons: United States, April 1953," *Vital Statistics—Special Reports*, Vol. 39, No. 3. It contains the results of a sample survey conducted for the National Office of Vital Statistics by the Bureau of the Census.

[3] Averages are in terms of medians and represent estimates

TABLE 1. MEDIAN AGE OF HUSBAND AND WIFE AT SELECTED STAGES OF THE LIFE CYCLE OF THE FAMILY,
FOR THE UNITED STATES: 1950, 1940, AND 1890

Stage of the life cycle of the family	Median age of husband			Median age of wife		
	1950	1940	1890	1950	1940	1890
A. First marriage	22.8	24.3	26.1	20.1	21.5	22.0
B. Birth of last child	28.8	29.9	36.0	26.1	27.1	31.9
C. Marriage of last child	50.3	52.8	59.4	47.6	50.0	55.3
D. Death of one spouse[1]	64.1	63.6	57.4	61.4	60.9	53.3
E. Death of other spouse[2]	71.6	69.7	66.4	77.2	73.5	67.7

[1] Husband and wife survive jointly from marriage to specified age.
[2] Husband (wife) survives separately from marriage to specified age.

Earlier marriages have become more common during recent years when married women have found it easier to gain employment outside the home. More and more women now work for a period before marriage, continue their employment after marriage until they start the childbearing period, then in a few years return to work outside the home. Women who are in the labor force have received more education, on the average, than those not in the labor force. In the marriage boom of the last decade, greater gains in the proportion married in the United States were made by the more-educated than by the less-educated sections of the population.[4]

An interesting sidelight on the changing age at marriage is an apparent decline in the gap between the median ages of husbands and

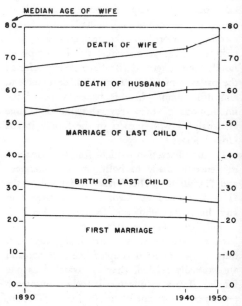

FIGURE 1. STAGES OF THE LIFE CYCLE OF THE FAMILY IN THE UNITED STATES: 1890, 1940, AND 1950.

wives at first marriage. The average husband of recent years is his wife's senior by about three years, whereas his grandfather was likely to have been senior by about four years.[5]

based on marital status and age distributions from decennial census reports for the respective dates. For an explanation of the methodology, see Current Population Reports, Series P-20, No. 38, p. 7. The report, "Demographic Characteristics of Recently Married Persons" (see footnote 2), shows median ages at first marriage for men (23.2) and women (20.4) who married in 1950. These figures are quite close to those shown in table 1 of this paper; both sets of figures are based on census data by single years of age. In Vol. I of the 1950 Vital Statistics of the United States, the median ages at first marriage for grooms (23.9) and brides (21.5) in 19 reporting states were computed from distributions of marriages by 5-year age groups and are therefore somewhat higher. The differences between the various sets of medians may be attributed not only to the use of different age groupings but also in part at least to the use of different types of basic data and in part to the over-representation of highly urbanized states among the 19 reporting.

[4] John Hajnal, "Differential Changes in Marriage Patterns," American Sociological Review, 19: 148-154, April, 1954. Similar findings were reported by Calvin L. Beale in "Some Marriage Trends and Patterns Since 1940," an unpublished paper which was presented at a special meeting of the District of Columbia Sociological Society, May 3, 1952.

[5] The median difference between the ages of husbands and wives in their first marriages in 1948 was 2.8 years. (See Paul C. Glick and Emanuel Landau, "Age as a Factor in Marriage," American Sociological Review, XV: 517-529, August, 1950.) This figure is of approximately the same order of magnitude as the difference (3.3 years) between the median age of husband at first marriage and the median age of wife at first marriage derived from the same census

To simplify the treatment of our subject, we have limited our discussion to first marriages. It is recognized, of course, that many of these marriages become broken within a relatively short time[6]; in such cases, most of the marriage partners are at ages when remarriage rates are relatively high. In 1948, about 13 per cent of the married women living with their husbands had remarried after the dissolution of an earlier marriage; in 1910, the corresponding proportion was probably about seven or eight per cent.[7] Among persons who married since the end of World War II, about one fifth were entering a second or subsequent marriage.[8]

Childbearing. The average mother who was having her first child in 1950 was 22.5 years old, according to vital statistics data on order of birth by single years of age of mother. The difference between the median age at first marriage based on census data and the median age at birth of first child based on vital statistics data, however, provides an unsatisfactory measure of the average interval between marriage and the birth of the first child. Similar data are used here to approximate the average interval between marriage and the birth of the last child only because the relative error is much less in this case. More precise measurement of child-spacing intervals is now being undertaken by the Bureau of the Census in cooperation with the National Office of Vital Statistics, on the basis of data from the 1950 Census of Population and from the Current Population Survey.[9]

For women who had married and had reached the end of their reproductive period (45 to 49 years old) by 1952, the average number of children born per woman was about 2.35. By making use of this fact in conjunction with 1950 statistics on order of birth, it is estimated that approximately half of the women have borne their last child by the time they are 26 years old. Thus, the median length of time between marriage and the birth of the last child is probably close to six years.[10]

Because families have declined so sharply in size, the usual span of the childbearing years has become only about half as long as it was two generations ago. The average mother whose family reached completion in 1890 had borne 5.4 children, with an estimated interval of ten years between marriage and the birth of the last child. She had not given birth to her last child until she was about 32 years old. For 1940, the last of three (3.0) children was born when the mother was about 27 years old.

Women who had never borne a child constituted only about eight per cent of all women who had married and completed their period of fertility by 1890. This percentage approximately doubled by 1940 (15 per cent); it continued to rise by 1952 to 19 per cent for women 45 to 49 years old but there was evi-

data. In the absence of a direct measure of the difference between the ages of spouses in 1890, it is assumed that the difference between the median ages of spouses provides a usable approximation for that date.

[6] Paul H. Jacobson, "Differentials in Divorce by Duration of Marriage and Size of Family," *American Sociological Review*, XV: 236-244, April, 1950.

[7] Paul C. Glick, "First Marriages and Remarriages," *American Sociological Review*, XIV: 726-734, December, 1949.

[8] *Op. cit.*, and *Current Population Reports*, Series P-20, No. 53.

[9] Several studies have provided significant information about child spacing for selected areas within the United States. For example, see P. K. Whelpton and Clyde V. Kiser, "Social and Psychological Factors Affecting Fertility. VI. The Planning of Fertility," *The Milbank Memorial*

Fund Quarterly, XXV: 63-111, January, 1947. See also Harold T. Christensen and Hanna H. Meisner, "Studies in Child Spacing: III—Premarital Pregnancy as a Factor in Divorce," *American Sociological Review*, 18: 641-644, December, 1953.

[10] For each stage of the life cycle of the family, the ages given in table 1 for a given year are based on experience relating to marriages, births, or deaths as near to that year as available nation-wide data permit. The average number of children per ever-married woman 45 to 49 years old in 1952 (2.35) was used as an estimate of the average number of children that women who married in 1950 will have. Women who married in 1950, however, will not be at the end of their childbearing period until about 1975. If they were to bear, say, 2.8 children, on the average, instead of 2.35 as assumed, the estimated median age of mother at birth of the last child (and at the time the last child leaves home) would be increased about one year. As the practice of family limitation becomes more nearly universal, the number and spacing of children may vary more widely with changes in economic conditions. For a valuable analysis of past and probable future changes in size of completed families, see P. K. Whelpton, *Cohort Fertility: Native White Women in the United States* (Princeton, N.J.: Princeton University Press, 1954).

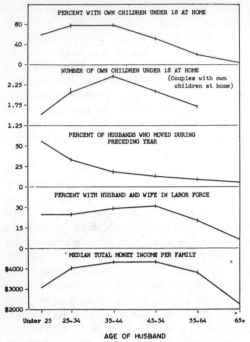

FIGURE 2. CHARACTERISTICS OF MARRIED COUPLES BY AGE OF HUSBAND, FOR THE UNITED STATES: 1952.

dence that it would fall sharply for younger women.

During the next decade or two the average number of children per completed family is likely to rise moderately and the proportion of women who remain childless throughout their reproductive years is certain to decline. Changes in patterns of marriage and childbearing which have developed since about the beginning of World War II will apparently have the effect of reversing, at least temporarily, the 150-year decline in the average size of completed family.

Children leaving home. From the time the last child is born until the first child leaves home, the size of family usually remains stable. Changes in family living during this period are those related to the growth and maturation of the children and the changing economic status of the parents.

If we make some allowance for mortality among the children, and if we assume that the children will marry and leave home at the same age that their parents married, we find that the average woman who married in 1950 will be about 48 years of age when her last child leaves home. By comparison, the average woman of her grandmother's day was about 55, if she lived that long, when her last child got married.

Dissolution of the family. The combined effects of earlier marriages, smaller families, and longer average length of life have produced a remarkable change in the length of time that married couples live together after their children have set up homes of their own. Under conditions existing in 1950, a couple could expect to have about 41 years of married life before either the husband or the wife died; during their last 14 years together, the couple would ordinarily have no unmarried children remaining with them. Thus, the couple would have half as many years of married life with no young children at home as they would have with children at home.

By contrast, conditions existing in 1890 assured only about 31 years of joint survival for the husband and wife; in fact, the chances were 50-50 that one spouse or the other would die at least two years before their youngest child married.

Because men are usually older than their wives at marriage and have higher mortality rates, age for age, wives generally outlive their husbands. The wife can expect to live much longer after her husband's death if she is the survivor than the husband can expect to live after his wife's death if he is the survivor.[11]

---

[11] All estimates of age at death were based on chances of survival from age at marriage. Age at "death of one spouse" is the age to which half of the married couples are expected to survive jointly. Age at "death of other spouse" is the age to which half of the husbands (wives) are expected to live, without regard to the age to which their spouse lives. The difference between age at "death of one spouse" and age at "death of other spouse" is somewhat less than the expected period of widowerhood (widowhood) for the surviving marriage partner who does not remarry; but if age at "death of other spouse" had been calculated with age at "death of one spouse" as the point of departure, the overall

TABLE 2. CHARACTERISTICS OF MARRIED COUPLES BY AGE OF HUSBAND, FOR THE UNITED STATES: 1952

Age of Husband	Per Cent of Couples With No Own Children Under 18 at Home	Own Children Under 18 at Home Per Couple With Children	Per Cent of Husbands Who Moved During the Preceding Year	Per Cent of Couples With Husband and Wife in Labor Force[1]	Median Total Money Income Per Family[2]
All ages	44.8	2.15	20.2	24.5	$3,890
Under 25 years	42.4	1.51	55.8	24.9	$3,069
25 to 34 years	20.9	2.08	32.9	24.9	$4,030
35 to 44 years	20.9	2.46	18.2	29.5	$4,339
45 to 54 years	49.4	2.08	⎰ 10.3	30.9	$4,355
55 to 64 years	79.6	1.71	⎱	20.5	$3,805
65 years and over	96.2	[3]	6.6	6.5	$2,276

[1] Based on 1953 data.
[2] Income in 1952, for families surveyed in 1953.
[3] Fewer than 100 cases in sample.

In this final stage of the family life cycle, the length of time that the remaining marriage partner survives has not changed greatly in the last two generations, but the expected ages during which the lone survivor is in this phase have been advanced several years.

CHANGES IN COMPOSITION AND ECONOMIC CHARACTERISTICS

As the family proceeds through its life cycle, it expands in size with the addition of each child and eventually contracts as the children marry and depart from their parental home. Many variations in this pattern exist, of course. Some families have no children; in others, one or more children remain at home longer than usual, often after marriage; and in still other cases, one or more of the parents or parents-in-law spend their later years with their children. Adjustments in living accommodations are commonly made in order to meet the needs of the family and changes in the economic activity of the family members generally occur as conditions make such changes feasible and advantageous.

These dynamic aspects of family living are traced in this section by studying changes in characteristics of married couples as the age of the husband advances. (See table 2 and figure 2.)

length of the family cycle would have been somewhat elongated. United States life tables for all races in 1890 and 1940, and abridged life tables for whites in 1950, were used.

Family composition. On the basis of data for a recent year (1952), about 45 per cent of the married couples of all ages combined have no sons or daughters under 18 years of age in their homes. About four tenths of the husbands below the age of 25 years have no dependent children, but only 21 per cent of those between 25 and 44 have none in the home. Above the age of 45, the proportion of husbands without young children of their own at home rises sharply and continuously until, among those above the age of 65, nearly all have none living with them.

The number of children in homes with children rises until it reaches two or three, on the average, by the time the husband is 35 to 44 years old, then declines. Thus, the average family group, comprising the husband, wife, and young children, grows from two persons to four or five and then diminishes gradually to the original two parents.

There are seldom any additional relatives living with the couple while the husband is under 40 years of age. From that time until old age approaches, however, there are likely to be one or more adult relatives (usually grown children of their own) in about one half of the homes and one or more other young relatives (usually grandchildren) in about one home out of ten. When a young married couple lives with the husband's or wife's parents, the chances are nearly two out of three that the couple will stay with the wife's parents. This arrangement is most common perhaps largely because the wife is likely to spend more time in the home than her husband, and because close daily contacts between a mother and her daughter are less likely to create tensions than similar contacts between a mother-in-law and her daughter-in-law.

Residential location. About four fifths of the persons who marry change residences at the time of marriage or within the ensuing year. Thereafter, the mobility rate decreases sharply as the number of years married increases. By the time couples have been married 10 to 15 years, only about 20 per cent move to another home in the course of a year's time. By this time, most of the changes of residence required to provide room and a measure of privacy for the various family members have been made. Moreover, the difficulty of moving all of the belongings of the family when it is at its maximum size probably serves as a deterrent to residential changes during this stage of family life. The continued decline, rather than an increase, in mobility during the later years of life perhaps suggests, among other things, that families do not ordinarily move into smaller quarters after their children have left home. Data from the 1950 Census of Housing also suggest that the shifts to smaller homes are relatively few in number during this period of life and that most of them take place after the husband reaches 65 years of age.

Labor force participation. Half of the young men have begun employment by the time they are about 18 years of age, that is, five years before the median age at marriage. Between the ages of 25 and 60, about 85 per cent or more of the men are in the labor force, and close to half of them remain in the labor force until they reach the age of 70.[12]

Although it is characteristic of husbands to be in the labor force from marriage until the age of retirement, at no time does the proportion of wives in the labor force exceed one half. In 1953, one fourth of all women living with their husbands were in the labor force, that is, had a job (or were seeking work) other than their own home housework. In 1940, the corresponding proportion was only 15 per cent. This striking change has taken place despite the fact that the average number of children that married women under 35 years of age have borne has increased by about 20 per cent.

During the first year after marriage about 40 per cent of the wives have jobs away from home. During the second or third year, many drop out of economic activity to have children and the proportion of working wives falls to about 30 per cent. For the period when women have children of preschool age (under 6 years old), only about 15 per cent are labor force participants. After all of the children have reached school age, nearly one third of the wives are in the labor force. Aside from the first couple of years of marriage, this is the period when the wife is most likely to be supplementing the husband's earnings by working outside the home; it is probably also the period when women are most likely to contribute volunteer service to their communities.

Among older couples, whose children have married and left home, it seems probable that fewer wives feel the necessity to remain in the labor force. Furthermore, as the situation exists at present, the average wife who has reached her upper fifties probably lacks the necessary skills, experience, and other qualifications for remunerative employment. Since many more of the younger wives now than formerly have had work experience, it seems reasonable to expect that a larger proportion of those who advance to later middle age in future years will be qualified to contribute to the family income by engaging in work away from home.

In 1952, one third of the families had two earners—usually the husband and the wife. In one tenth of the families, there were three or more earners, usually including the wife and/or young adult children.

[12] See U. S. Bureau of the Census, *U. S. Census of Population: 1950*, Vol. IV, *Special Reports*, Part 1, Chapter A, Employment and Personal Characteristics. Also, see U. S. Department of Labor, Bulletin No. 1001, *Tables of Working Life: Length of Working Life for Men*, on pages 4 and 36 of which are data for 1940 and 1947.

Family income. The median income of families in 1952 was about $3,900.[13] Although family incomes had increased about 50 per cent over the 1944 level, the gain was largely absorbed in higher prices paid to meet the rising cost of living. During this period, the increases have been distributed fairly evenly among families in various stages of the life cycle; recently, however, the older families have shown the largest proportionate gain in income.

For families that are newly formed, there are many demands for household goods to equip the home and, in some cases, to start a business. Furthermore, within a short time the wife is likely to be preoccupied with child rearing and hence unable to help her husband make a living. During this period, while the husband's work experience is still limited, the family income is relatively low. Within about ten years, however, the family income generally has increased about one third. Between the ages of 35 and 54, when the wife may have returned to the labor force and some of the older children who live with their parents may be working, the family income is at its peak, about 40 per cent above the level for newly-formed families. After the family head has passed age 65, the family has only about half the income it had at its peak.

[13] The income figures used here are based on data for all families, in the absence of data for all married couples and in the absence of data for husband-wife families by age of the husband. The median income of husband-wife families in 1952 ($4,061) was about $175 higher than that of all families. The median income of married couples and their unmarried children living at home is probably lower than that of husband-wife families.

Partly as a consequence of declining income in old age and partly as a means of being better cared for at that time, the proportion of married couples who live in the homes of others increases somewhat from a low point of less than three per cent in their late 50's but amounts to only about five per cent for couples above the age of 65 years. Some older couples invite a married son or daughter to move in with them for similar reasons.

Concluding statement. From the foregoing analysis, it is evident that the average family in the United States undergoes many significant changes in the course of its life cycle. At the same time, the pattern of these changes is different in important respects from that which prevailed a generation or two ago.

The effects of most of the changes since 1890 have been cumulative. Trends toward earlier marriage, smaller families, and longer length of life have culminated in the fact that couples now spend one third of their married life with no unmarried children of their own in the home. In 1890, the average married couple did not survive jointly to see their last child get married.

The recent upsurge in the number of births has resulted from increases in the number of women of childbearing age, in the proportion of persons in this age group who have married, and in the average number of children per married couple. The rise in the birth rate since 1940 is less significant for its effect on the current pattern of family development, however, than it is for its implications that more of the young adults are marrying and having a moderate-sized family.

CULTURAL PLURALISM AND LINGUISTIC

EQUILIBRIUM IN SWITZERLAND

By Kurt Mayer

NEXT to its scenic beauty, what fascinates the whole world most about Switzerland is the amazing spectacle of its cultural pluralism which is nevertheless integrated into a stable and harmonious unity. Switzerland is the famous and oftquoted exception to the rule in contemporary Europe that marks of cultural diversity generally serve as rallying points for hate and conflict. No wonder that "the concept of Switzerland as a microcosm, an orderly little world of its own, reflecting the reconciled components of the greater, but disorderly, world around it, has caught the fancy of not a few dispensers of good advice,"[1] and has been held up as a shining example for a sick world to follow.

The phenomenon of Swiss harmony, however, is often only imperfectly understood. Historically the Swiss nation has originated from the desire of a group of heterogeneous communities to preserve their local independence through a system of mutual defense alliances. As a result of this long and often very stormy historical process, the Swiss have finally learned to blend their cultural differences into a national equilibrium. Today they no longer regard their cultural heterogeneity as an obstacle to the perpetuation of national unity and political stability. To a large extent this national equilibrium rests on an underlying balance of demographic factors which is not always perceived. Even the Swiss themselves do not commonly realize how fortunate it is for Swiss harmony that the basic demographic equilibrium has remained practically undisturbed for more than a century. The two most important ingredients of Swiss cultural pluralism are the ethnic-linguistic and the religious structure of the Swiss population.

[1] J. Christopher Herold, *The Swiss Without Halos*, New York: Columbia University Press, 1948, p. 3.

This paper will be concerned only with the former.

Data on the linguistic composition of the Swiss population have been collected since the Census of 1850, but the methods of enumeration have varied somewhat. In 1850 it was attempted to ascertain the linguistic distribution of the population on the basis of the official language spoken in each community, while in the censuses of 1860 and 1870 the language spoken in each household was recorded. Only since the Census of 1880 has each individual been enumerated by the language spoken. The Swiss Census asks for the "usual" or customary language of the individual; only in the case of children who cannot talk is the "mother" tongue recorded. No questions are asked about knowledge of other languages.

TABLE 1. PERCENTAGE DISTRIBUTION OF THE SWISS POPULATION BY LANGUAGE, 1850–1941

Years	German	French	Italian	Romansh	Other
1850	70.2	22.6	5.4	1.8	...
1880	71.3	21.4	5.7	1.4	0.2
1888	71.4	21.8	5.3	1.3	0.2
1900	69.8	22.0	6.7	1.2	0.3
1910	69.1	21.1	8.1	1.1	0.6
1920	70.9	21.2	6.2	1.1	0.6
1930	71.9	20.4	6.0	1.1	0.6
1941	72.6	20.7	5.2	1.1	0.4

Source: *Statistisches Jahrbuch der Schweiz, 1948.*

The national languages of Switzerland are German, French, Italian, and Romansh, all of which are expressly recognized as equal in the Federal Constitution. They are, however quite unequal in importance: the French-, Italian-, and Romansh-speaking' Swiss are outnumbered by the German-speaking Swiss almost three to one. As Table 1 shows, no changes have occurred in the relative position of each of the four national languages since 1850; in fact, the linguistic composition of the population has remained remarkably stable on the whole. From 1850 to 1941 roughly 70 per cent of the Swiss population have always been German-speaking and a little above 20 per cent have been French-speaking. Indeed, the same relation between these two most important languages seems to have obtained even earlier; according to an estimate approximately 22 per cent of the population spoke French, and at least 70 per cent spoke German in 1798.[2]

From 1850 to 1880 only very minor shifts occurred between the language groups; moreover, due to the different methods of enumeration the figures of 1850 and 1880 are not strictly comparable. From 1880 to 1910 somewhat greater changes took place; the proportion of both the German-speaking and the French-speaking decreased somewhat while the Italian-speaking rose from 5.7 to 8.1 per cent. The explanation lies in a strong wave of Italian immigration: whereas only 42,000 Italian citizens resided in Switzerland in 1880, their number had increased to 203,000 by 1910. After the outbreak of the first World War, however, a large proportion of the Italians returned home, and consequently the percentage of Italian-speakers in Switzerland was again reduced. Since 1910 the language distribution has been enumerated separately for Swiss citizens and for alien residents. Table 2 shows that the proportion

TABLE 2. PERCENTAGE DISTRIBUTION OF SWISS CITIZENS AND OF ALIEN RESIDENTS BY LANGUAGE, 1910-1941

Years	German	French	Italian	Romansh	Other
		Swiss Citizens			
1910	72.7	22.1	3.9	1.2	0.1
1920	73.0	21.7	4.0	1.2	0.1
1930	73.7	21.0	4.0	1.2	0.1
1941	73.9	20.9	3.9	1.1	0.2
		Alien Residents			
1910	48.6	15.3	32.1	0.2	3.8
1920	52.3	17.6	25.0	0.2	4.9
1930	53.2	14.7	26.3	0.2	5.6
1941	49.1	18.1	27.7	0.4	4.7

Source: *Statistisches Jahrbuch der Schweiz,* 1948.

of Italian-speaking Swiss has remained practically stable since 1910; the fluctuations of the Italian language are therefore entirely

[2] Wilhelm Bickel, *Bevoelkerungsgeschichte und Bevoelkerungspolitik der Schweiz,* Zurich: Buechergilde, Gutenberg, 1947, p. 140.

attributable to the migrations of Italian citizens.

Not all the shifts in the linguistic struc-

TABLE 3. THE BIRTH RATES OF THE SWISS CANTONS, 1901-10 AND 1941-48

Cantons	Live Births per 1,000 Population	
	1901-10	1941-48
German-Speaking:		
Zurich	24.4	17.4
Berne[a]	29.0	20.6
Lucerne	27.7	21.9
Uri	32.7	25.3
Schwyz	28.6	22.2
Obwalden	28.5	24.6
Nidwalden	29.7	27.0
Glarus	22.6	19.2
Zug	25.8	21.3
Solothurn	30.8	21.2
Basel-Stadt	25.1	15.0
Basel-Land	25.7	18.3
Schaffhausen	24.8	19.8
Appenzell Ausser-Rhoden	26.7	17.2
Appenzell Inner-Rhoden	32.2	19.8
St. Gall	28.0	20.5
Grisons[b]	24.7	21.3
Aargau	27.5	21.0
Thurgau	25.4	19.8
French-Speaking:		
Vaud	24.7	16.5
Neuchatel	24.5	15.2
Geneva	17.9	12.6
Preponderantly French-Speaking:		
Fribourg[c]	33.4	23.2
Valais[d]	30.0	24.7
Italian-Speaking:		
Ticino	29.0	15.9
Switzerland Total	26.9	19.2

[a] In 1941, 83.6 per cent of the population spoke German, while 15.4 per cent spoke French.

[b] In 1941, 54.9 per cent of the population spoke German, 31.3 per cent spoke Romansh, and 12.8 per cent spoke Italian.

[c] In 1941, 66.8 per cent of the population spoke French, 32.4 per cent spoke German.

[d] In 1941, 65.5 per cent of the population spoke French, 33.2 per cent spoke German.

Source: *Statistiches Jahrbuch der Schweiz,* 1948.

ture are due to international migrations, however. Apart from the fluctuations of Italian, it is evident from Tables 1 and 2 that in recent decades the German language has been gaining slightly on the French, not only in the population as a whole, but also among the

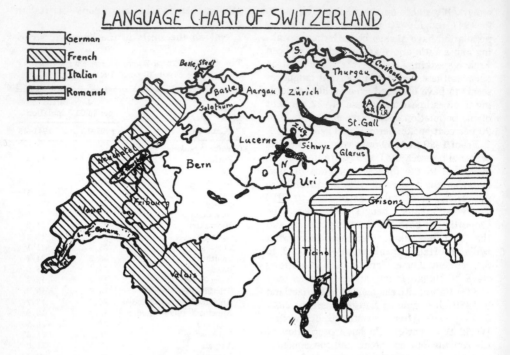

LANGUAGE CHART OF SWITZERLAND

German
French
Italian
Romansh

Swiss citizens themselves. The explanation must be sought in the considerable fertility differentials which exist between the French- and the German-speaking areas of the country. As Table 3 shows, the three wholly French-speaking cantons—Geneva, Neuchatel and Vaud—have had considerably lower birth rates than most of the German-speaking cantons. This difference, which has widened since the turn of the century, has been only partly offset by the relatively high fertility rates of the preponderantly French-speaking but less populous cantons Fribourg and Valais.

These differences in fertility, which are not offset by differential mortality [3] would undoubtedly lead to a greater ascendancy of the German language and to serious threats to the traditional linguistic equilibrium, were it not for the effects of internal migrations. French is spoken in a compact territorial area which comprises the western part of the

[3] The death rate in 1941, corrected for age, was 10.91 for the nineteen German-speaking cantons and 11.53 for the French-speaking cantons, a differential of only 0.62 per 1,000.

country, while German is the language of the central and eastern regions, and Italian is spoken only south of the Alps. (See the accompanying language map.) However, ever since the Constitution of 1848 guaranteed freedom of migration and settlement within the whole country, increasing numbers of persons have moved across the language boundaries. As Table 4 shows, the Census of 1930 enumerated 114,000 German-speaking persons living in French language territory, but only 53,000 French-speaking individuals living in the German language areas. Thus, the French regions of the country have proved much more attractive to German-speaking migrants than the German regions have to the French-speaking Swiss. Now, the migrants tend to become rapidly assimilated to the new language. This is especially the case with their children who can use only the official language of the region in school. As a matter of empirical fact, therefore, migration regularly involves an eventual change of language: the second generation no longer uses the tongue of its parents but the official language of the area as its customary language. The 114,000 German-speaking persons who lived in French language territory in 1930 must therefore be

TABLE 4. POPULATION OF SWITZERLAND BY LANGUAGE AREA AND LANGUAGE SPOKEN, 1930

Language Spoken	Language Areas Numbers in 000's				
	German	French	Italian	Romansh	Total
German	2,791	114	12	6	2,924
French	53	776	1	..	830
Italian	56	28	157	2	243
Romansh	10	1	..	33	44
Other	10	14	1	..	25
Total	2,921	933	171	41	4,066

Source: W.·Ott, "Sprache," in *Die Bevoelkerung der Schweiz*, 1939, p. 20.

considered as a reservoir for the French language.

Assimilation takes place, of course, among the migrants to all the four language zones, but it is especially rapid in French Switzerland where German is taught only quite perfunctorily in the schools, while French is given much more emphasis as a second language in the schools of both German and Italian Switzerland. Although there are unfortunately no statistics available on the subject, it is a well-known fact that French is the second language of a very large number of German-Swiss, especially those connected with commerce and business, while the reverse is not nearly as true.[4] This difference is, of course, a factor in migration: knowing French fairly well, many German-Swiss find it easy to live in French Switzerland, while the French-Swiss find the language difference to be a barrier.[5]

In general, there is a widespread misconception abroad that every Swiss speaks all the national languages and possibly English as well. In fact, most Swiss know only one language well, although it is true that the proportion of those who have a more or less extensive command of other languages than their own is much greater in Switzerland than in most other countries of the world. A knowledge of several langauges is essential in a country so dependent on foreign trade and on foreign tourists, and it is therefore not surprising that a working knowledge of foreign languages is a prerequisite for many jobs in the fields of commerce and finance, transport and communications, and, above all, in the hotel industry.

The facts, then, are that although Switzerland maintains more than one official language, the four national languages are spoken in clearly defined territorial areas. There is no extensive mixture of divergent tongues; the linguistic boundaries are generally clear (even though the French-German line splits some communities right down the middle); and the individual Swiss are no more bilingual or multilingual than are people in other countries, although it is true that a good many of them have a good working knowledge of several languages in addition to their own.

High mountains mark off the boundaries between the Italian-speaking zone and the rest of Switzerland, thus preserving the Italian language area intact; but the dividing line between the French- and German-speaking zones is not marked by any natural boundaries. This is a purely historical line created at the end of the 5th century A.D. by

---

[4] Herold, *op. cit.*, p. 16.

[5] In justification of the French-speaking Swiss it should be noted here that they face a much greater linguistic handicap when they migrate to the German area than do the German-speaking Swiss when they move into French territory. The reason is that German is a written, but not a spoken language in German Switzerland. Official documents, newspapers, and most literary works are written in standard German, but the spoken tongue is a Germanic dialect, or rather, as every canton has its own, a variety of dialects. These dialects are sufficiently alike to be universally understood in all cantons, but sufficiently different from the standard German spoken in Germany to form a real obstacle in familiar intercourse and to

act as a protective device against too much German influence. The Swiss dialects, moreover, are more than a mere vernacular, since they are spoken by all Swiss Germans regardless of class or level of education, while dialects are usually only the tongue of the uneducated. In fact, therefore, the German-Swiss write standard German but usually speak a dialect so different from it that it is not understood in Germany and their children have to learn to write and speak standard German in school as if it were a foreign language. The French-speaking Swiss, therefore, who wishes to settle in German Switzerland must learn practically two difficult languages, a written and a spoken one, which does not make things any easier.

the influx of German-speaking Alemanni into the territory previously occupied by another Germanic tribe, the Burgundians, who had however, become Latinized. The line dividing the settlements of the Latin-speaking Burgundians and those of the Germanic-speaking Alemanni eventually evolved into the language boundary between the French- and the German-speaking zones of Switzerland. In an age where ethnic diversity has become the focal point of raving nationalism, it is rather amusing to note that the ethnic origin of the French- and the German-speaking Swiss seems to have been the same; but it is true, of course, that the linguistic differences maintained over 1,500 years have led to fundamental cultural divergences between the French- and the German-Swiss.

The dividing line between these two major language areas has remained remarkably stable throughout the centuries although numerous minor changes have occurred in time. The line recognizes no cantonal boundaries: the northwest portion of Berne speaks French while the rest of the canton speaks German (.84 per cent); the canton Fribourg is split into a larger French-speaking (67 per cent) and a smaller German-speaking section, and the same is true of the Valais where 66 per cent speak French. (See map.) Such minor changes as have occurred in the 19th and 20th centuries have been in favor of the French zone which has expanded slightly in the canton of Berne and especially in the Valais where a couple of formerly German-speaking communities have acquired French-speaking majorities as the result of migrations and have accordingly switched their official language.[6]

In the fourteen cantons entirely within the German-speaking area, German is the only official language for all legal relations with cantonal authorities; in the three cantons which are completely inside the French zone, French is the only official language, as is Italian in the canton Ticino; but three of the cantons are officially bilingual, and one is tri-lingual. In Berne, Fribourg, and Valais, German and French are both official, although in Berne, German, and in Fribourg, French, enjoy the privilege of being the original language in which the cantonal Constitution and the laws are drafted, and according to which they are, in case of doubt, to be construed. In the Grisons, German, Italian, and Romansh are all three declared to be official languages, but German, spoken by 55 per cent, is given preference over the other two.[7]

Romansh, a peculiar tongue of Latin origin, has been maintained by the descendants of the native Rhaetii in the Grisons canton without interruption from Roman times to the present day. Spoken by only 46,000 people in Switzerland, it is a branch of the Rhaeto-Romanic tongue which is also spoken in parts of the Italian Tyrol and Friuli, and it has an old and extensive literature. The Romansh language area is entirely located in the Grisons canton. (See map.) It is the only one of the Swiss language areas which has been shrinking as a result of encroachment by the German language. This has been largely due to the tourist trade which has brought German-speakers into some originally Romansh communities that have become internationally famous tourist centers, such as St. Moritz, for example. Partly as an effort to stem this adverse tide, Romansh was elevated to the dignity of a fourth national language in 1938 through an amendment to the constitution adopted by a popular vote. Whether this can stop the shrinkage of its language area remains to be seen.

The linguistic equilibrium manifest in the multilingual principle is of fairly recent historical origin. Up to 1798 German was the only official language of the Swiss Confederation, in which all official documents were drafted.[8] The present French-, Italian- and Romansh-speaking cantons were not equal members of the Confederation politically; they were either semi-independent allies or subject provinces of the German-speaking cantons. Only as a result of the influences of the French revolution were these areas admitted to the Confederation as fully equal partners, German, French and Italian were

---

[6] W. Ott, "Sprache," in *Die Bevoelkerung der Schweiz,* Herausgegeben vom Eidgenoessischen Statistischen Amt, Berne, 1939, p. 20.

[7] William E. Rappard, *The Government of Switzerland,* New York: Van Nostrand, 1936, p. 9.

[8] Cf. Rappard, *op. cit.,* pp. 6–8.

declared to be the national languages of Switzerland in the Constitution of 1848, and Romansh was added 90 years later.

As a legal consequence of the multilingual principle it has been recognized that in all official relations with federal authorities, German-, French-, Italian- and Romansh-speaking Swiss have the right to use their own language. However, in order to save the expense of having to translate all laws and official documents, Romansh was not made an official language of the Confederation; and Italian, although an official language of the Confederation, has not claimed an absolute parity of position. Though all federal laws are published in the three official languages—German, French, and Italian—which are all equally authoritative, most of the official documents appear only in German and French. Even Italian-Swiss representatives usually speak French in the Federal Parliament, as do Italian-Swiss lawyers appearing before the Federal Supreme Court, while the Romansh-speaking Swiss use German on those occasions.

On the other hand, no effort whatsoever is made by the German-Swiss, who are in the overwhelming majority numerically, to assert any linguistic dominance. There are no linguistic minorities in Switzerland either in a legal or in an informal sense. On the contrary, since the multilingual principle is considered an integral element of national unity, great care is taken to preserve the integrity of all the national languages and to keep the linguistic equilibrium intact. Thus, by unwritten law, at least two, and often three, of the seven places on the Federal Council, which is the Swiss cabinet, have always been reserved for French- and Italian-speaking confederates, and only four or five members of the Federal Council can be citizens of German-speaking cantons. Similar informal arrangements also prevail in the selection of justices for the Federal Tribunal.

In summary, the linguistic equilibrium which represents one of the foremost stabilizing and integrating influences in the modern Swiss democracy and which is the envy of a strife-torn world, originated at a time before language was made a symbol of rampant nationalism and has been kept on an even keel for more than a century mainly because of a fortunate balancing of demographic factors. It is quite true, however, that this demographic equilibrium has also been consciously reinforced through wise and statesmanlike political measures designed to prevent any upsets and disturbances throughout an era when other countries have permitted language to become a focus of conflict and division.

THE LABOR FORCE AS A FIELD OF INTEREST

FOR THE SOCIOLOGIST

By Philip M. Hauser

By reason of our historical but artificial division of labor, the labor force as a field of research and teaching has been almost exclusively the province of the economist,[1] and more recently of the psychologist. The sociologist, however, has increasingly become interested in the various aspects of the labor force; and in focusing on the labor force, the contemporary sociologist is with considerable delay following the lead of some of the pioneers of sociology —as for example, Spencer and Durkheim.[2]

The "labor force" in current Census and statistical usage consists of all persons "working" or "seeking work" in accordance with a definite conceptual framework and as determined by prescribed methods of measurement and standard census operating procedures. The labor force consists, then, of that part of the total population engaged in, or seeking, "work" —an activity defined in our culture as one contributing to the production of goods or services in exchange for monetary remuneration or its equivalent. As a field for sociological research, the labor force may be narrowly conceived as being restricted to the size, composition and dynamics of "workers" in the population. Or it may be broadly conceived as including also investigation of the various factors, including the cultural and social psychological, which are related to labor force participation; of the various fields of interaction within the labor force including both formal and informal relations among various categories of workers, most prominent of which, perhaps, is that between "labor" and "management"; and of relations between workers and non-workers. The labor force can be conceived both as a dependent and independent variable in relation

to other aspects, cultural and personal, of society. It is in this broader sense that this essay treats the field as an area of research interest to the sociologist.

There are a number of aspects of the labor force which merit the special attention of the sociologist: first, because of the significant way in which·labor force data, broadly conceived, can illuminate other cultural, institutional, and personal phenomena; and second, because of the contribution which the sociologist can make to a better understanding of labor force structure, processes and problems. Some of the more important fields of sociology in which attention to the labor force is particularly called for, and some of the implications of labor force analysis for sociological research are discussed in the materials which follow.

Demography

Sociology has for some years been the major discipline concerned with the field of population. Formal demography, as evidenced by the earlier population literature, was almost exclusively concerned with the size, growth, and components of growth of population—fertility, mortality, and migration; and with selected attributes of the population, particularly age and sex.

Contemporary students of population, however, are directing increasing attention to the labor force, or at least to its size, structure and dynamics, particularly as related to total population and its structure and dynamics.[3] Also of interest to the population student and sociologist have been the problems of concept and measurement involved in the quantification

[1] This essay was prepared at the invitation of an economist, Seymour L. Wolfbein, who served as Chairman of the session on the Labor Force at the annual meeting of the American Sociological Society held in Denver, September 7 to 9, 1950.

[2] See Herbert Spencer, *Principles of Sociology*, Vol. II, Part III, New York: D. Appleton & Co., 1897.

George Simpson, *Durkheim on the Division of Labor in Society*, New York: The Macmillan Co., 1933.

[3] John Durand, *The Labor Force in the U.S., 1890–1960*, New York: Social Science Research Council, 1948.

A. J. Jaffe, and Seymour L. Wolfbein, "Demographic Factors in Labor Force Growth," *American Sociological Review*, II (August 1946), 392–396.

Gladys L. Palmer, *Labor Force Dynamics and Economic Change in a Metropolitan Community,*. Industrial Research Dept., Wharton School of Finance and Commerce, University of Pennsylvania (forthcoming volume).

of labor force data.[4] The close interrelationship between population and labor force size, composition and change obviously call for continuing investigation and analysis and are likely to receive them. Similarly the problems of conceptual framework and measurement are likely to continue to receive close attention, especially by government, labor and business statisticians and economists, as well as sociologists.

Less obvious and calling for more intensive, and qualitative as well as quantitative, investigations are the factors—cultural, institutional and personal, as well as economic—which account for the differences between the structure and dynamics of the total population and of the labor force. For example, the decreasing labor force participation rates of youth and older persons in the United States is only to a minor, if any, extent, a function of the changing age structure of the total population. The trend towards declining proportions of younger and older persons in the labor force is to be accounted for by cultural and institutional changes and by changes in the attitudes and values systems of our people.[5]

Women, the young, and the old, to a considerable extent make up the "marginal" elements of the labor force—marginal in the sense that the proportion of these categories of the population who enter and leave the labor force during the course of a year or the course of a business cycle—quite apart from secular trend—fluctuates greatly. Research into the factors

which account for the high mobility rate of these groups into and out of the labor force would do much to bolster our understanding of labor force activity as well as to illuminate the cultural, institutional and personal effects of such mobility.

Other fertile fields of investigation of labor force phenomena by the sociologist are afforded through the application of demographic interests and techniques to labor force data. For example, the collection and analysis of data on labor force migration, international and internal, is an almost indispensable aspect of studying population migration in general. The coordinated study of the migration of total population and the labor force would undoubtedly do much to provide a better understanding of the factors in both in- and out-migration.[6]

The application of methods of life table construction and analysis to labor force phenomena promises to open up new and interesting avenues of investigation.[7] Not unrelated to the subject of applying life table methods to labor force analysis is the investigation of differential oc-

---

[4] Louis J. Ducoff, and Margaret J. Hagood, *Labor Force Definition and Measurement.* New York: Social Science Research Council, 1947.

P. M. Hauser, "The Labor Force and Gainful Workers—Concept, Measurement and Comparability," *American Journal of Sociology,* 54 (January 1949), 338–355.

A. J. Jaffe, "The Application of Attitude Research Methodology Toward the Problem of Measuring the Size of the Labor Force," *International Journal of Opinion and Attitude Research,* I (December 1947), 45–54.

[5] See forthcoming report of the recent National Conference on Aging held under the aegis of the Federal Security Agency in Washington, D.C., August 12–15, 1950.

For problems relating to youth in the labor force see: John Durand, *op. cit.,* pp. 28 ff.

For problems relating to women see: *ibid.,* pp. 22 ff.

Hazel Kyrk, "Who Works and Why?", *Annals of the American Academy of Political and Social Science,* May, 1947.

Frieda S. Miller, "Women in the Labor Force," *Annals of the American Academy of Political and Social Science,* May, 1947.

[6] Dorothy Thomas, *Research Memorandum on Migration Differentials,* New York: Social Science Research Council, 1938, pp. 126 ff.

Carter Goodrich, *Migration and Planes of Living,* Philadelphia: University of Pennsylvania Press, 1935, pp. 10 ff.

C. W. Thornthwaite *Internal Migration in the U. S.,* Philadelphia: University of Pennsylvania Press, 1934.

Dudley Kirk, *Europe's Population in the Interwar Years,* Princeton: League of Nations, pp. 97 ff.

Eugene M. Kulischer, *Europe on the Move,* New York: Columbia University Press, 1948.

Clark Kerr, "Migration to the Seattle Labor Market Area, 1940–1942," *University of Washington Publications in the Social Sciences,* 2 (August 1942), 129–188.

Department of Commerce, Bureau of the Census, *Current Population Reports,* "Employment Characteristics of Migrants in the U. S., April 1948," Series P-50, No. 10, Washington, D. C., and other publications. See: *List of Publications Issued.*

Donald J. Bogue, "An Exploratory Study of Migration and Labor Mobility, Using Social Security Data," *Scripps Foundation Studies in Population Distribution,* No. 1, June, 1950.

See also publications of the International Labor Organization.

[7] Seymour L. Wolfbein, "The Length of Working Life," *Population Studies,* 3 (December, 1949), 286–294.

U. S. Department of Labor, Bureau of Labor Statistics, *Tables of Working Life,* Washington, D. C.: Government Printing Office, 1950, Bulletin No. 1001.

cupational mortality.[8] This is an area of research badly restricted in many parts of the world, including the United States, by the lack of adequate data—data which in the United States can be made available only through the combined resources of the Bureau of the Census and the National Office of Vital Statistics. Such data, among other things, may in time also permit the construction of exceedingly interesting occupational life tables.

Finally, reference should be made to the importance of using, and the opportunity in the 1950 census data to utilize, an important labor force datum, income, as a control for demographic as well as other forms of sociological research.[9]

HUMAN ECOLOGY

Human ecology as a field of research in sociology has been broadly described as a point of view and a method. Although formal definitions of this field of sociological research differ, such investigations as have been conducted have been primarily concerned with the spatial and distributive aspects of society.[10] It is desirable, however, that research in human ecology should also focus on the functional sub-structures of human societies as affected by the division of labor, technological development and general economic organization. Such research activity, among other things, would be concerned with the "sustenance" relations of the population[11] and with the basic economic structure of communities insofar as they serve as a foundation for the cultural and institutional super-structure.

Although at least one of the founders of human ecology as a field in sociology has stressed the importance of investigating the economic and functional aspects of the community,[12] little has been done in this respect as

yet in the way of empirical research. Aspects of the problem have been attacked by economists,[13] but rarely by sociologists in the context of a sociological research project.

One of the most fruitful ways of getting at the sustenance and functional economic relations within a community and between communities lies in the analysis of the labor force of the community classified by industrial and occupational composition. Such data are available from the decennial population census or can be obtained at relatively low cost from the Bureau of the Census through special tabulations.[14] Yet despite this relatively readily available source of data, the sociologist has done little with it. It is, in fact, an indication of the undeveloped character of the field of human ecology that relatively little attention is devoted to the labor force and its composition in either of the first two sociological textbooks in human ecology which have just appeared.[15]

Analysis of the differences in the occupational and industrial composition of the labor force of various areas within a metropolitan community would certainly illuminate an important aspect of community structure and interrelationships.[16] Such data based on the population census show place of residence of various occupational and industrial groups.

It is to be hoped that the 1950 Census data will provide both occupational and industrial labor force statistics for both the central cities and the surrounding areas of the new standard metropolitan areas.[17] Such tabulations will

---

[8] P. K. Whelpton, *Needed Population Research,* Lancaster: Pennsylvania Science Press Printing Co., 1938, pp. 28 ff.

[9] See also section below on "Human Ecology."

[10] Louis Wirth, "Human Ecology", *American Journal of Sociology,* 50 (May 1945), 483–488.

J. A. Quinn, "Topical Summary of Current Literature on Human Ecology," *American Journal of Sociology,* 46 (September, 1940), 191–226.

[11] R. D. McKenzie, "Demography, Human Geography and Human Ecology," in L. L. Bernard, ed., *The Fields and Methods of Sociology,* New York: Long and Smith, 1934, pp. 58 ff.

[12] R. D. McKenzie, "Ecological Approach to the Study of the Human Community," in Park & Burgess, *The City,* Chicago: University of Chicago Press, 1925, pp. 63–79.

[13] D. B. Creamer, *Is Industry Decentralizing?,* Philadelphia, 1935.

Glenn E. McLaughlin, *Growth of American Manufacturing Areas,* Philadelphia, 1938.

National Resources Committee, *The Structure of the American Economy,* Part 1, Washington, D. C.: Government Printing Office, 1939, pp. 33 ff.

E. M. Hoover, *The Location of Economic Activity,* New York: McGraw-Hill, 1948.

[14] For example, in the 1940 Census see Vol. III, *The Labor Force,* and *Population and Housing— Census Tract Statistics.* Similar data will be available from the 1950 Census.

[15] Amos H. Hawley, *Human Ecology,* New York: The Ronald Press, 1950.

James A. Quinn, *Human Ecology,* New York: Prentice-Hall, 1950.

[16] See, for example, Calvin Schmid, "The Ecology of the American City," *American Sociological Review,* 15 (April 1950), 264–281.

[17] The Census will use a newly defined standard metropolitan area for the 1950 Population Census and other censuses made up of one or more contiguous counties. See Executive Office of the Presi-

greatly increase the usefulness of the labor force data for ecological research. Moreover, the increase in the number of census-tract cities[18] and the increase in the number of tract grids for outlying as well as the central portions of metropolitan areas will greatly enrich research opportunity.

If occupational or industrial data by place of residence can be supplemented by comparable data showing place of work, important new knowledge will be gained on the way in which differences in place of work and place of residence help to structure our metropolitan areas and affect social and institutional organization.[19] Although the resources available to the Bureau of the Census did not permit the collection of data on place of work of the population as well as place of residence, some exploratory studies at least, are possible on the relation of place of residence to place of work.[20]

Richer data are available for the analysis of the functional and sustenance relations between metropolitan areas and between the regions of the United States than for analysis within any given metropolitan area. Research opportunity for such inter-metropolitan area or inter-regional analysis will be greatly enriched if the 1950 Census plans are carried through. Of particular value will be the proposed tabulations for economic areas. The Bureau of the Census

with the cooperation of other agencies has divided the United States into approximately 450 economic areas comprising the new standard metropolitan areas and homogeneous groupings of other counties.[21] Analysis of labor force data, particularly the occupational and industrial composition of the labor force by these new economic areas, and the broader regions into which they can be combined, may provide rich research opportunities for extending empirical ecological research into regional and national analysis.

Another extremely important item in the labor force data to be provided for the first time by the 1950 Census should also greatly enrich research opportunity for the human ecologist. This is the item of individual and family total income which will make available to the research sociologist the best measure of economic level which has yet emanated from the census. The income data will likely be available by census tracts for census-tracted areas, for the new standard metropolitan areas, for the new urbanized areas,[22] and for the new economic areas. The availability of this direct measure of level of living, together with the new area units, permitting a great expansion in the analysis of data for "natural" as distinguished from political areas should open new vistas of analytical opportunity.

THE FAMILY

The study of labor force participation on a family basis would do much to illuminate many aspects of the family as a unit of social organization central to the interest of the sociologist, and also throw light on many puzzling aspects of labor force structure and dynamics.

Various students—mainly economists—have been interested in the problem of changing family labor-force participation and changing volumes of employment and unemployment within families as related to earnings of the primary worker in the family or to swings in the business cycle.[23] But much remains to be

---

dent, Bureau of the Budget, "Standard Metropolitan Area Definition," January, 1949. (mimeographed)

[18] See forthcoming census tract publications of the Bureau of the Census for 1950; also Department of Commerce, Bureau of the Census, "Census Tract Areas, 1950," December 15, 1949.

[19] Kate K. Liepman, *The Journey to Work: Its Significance for Industrial and Community Life,* London: Kegan, Paul, Trench, Tribner & Co., 1944.

[20] In some areas state or local employment service statistics may provide data on place of work by industry reasonably comparable with the population data on place of residence by industry, for at least some industrial groups. This would permit the analysis by local areas within the metropolitan area on the relation between place of work and place of residence and thus provide some approximate answers. Another type of research is afforded by the analysis of residences of employees of large industrial establishments. A study of changes in residential location of long service employees and differences in location among various classes of employees may help to throw light on this general problem. Such exploratory studies are now being conducted by graduate students at the University of Chicago, the former by Leonard Breen, the latter by Helene Conant.

[21] For a description of these areas see Donald J. Bogue, "Economic Areas as a Tool for Research and Planning," *American Sociological Review,* 15 (June 1950), 409–416, and Bureau of the Census and Bureau of Agricultural Economics, "State Economic Areas of the U. S." Series Census–BAE, No. 15.

[22] See Department of Commerce, Bureau of the Census, "Urbanized Areas," November 15, 1949.

[23] Paul Douglas, *Wages and the Family,* Chicago: University of Chicago Press, 1925; *The Theory of Wages,* New York, 1934; Paul Douglas

done before a clear understanding is gained of the way in which the family as a unit plays an important part in determining labor force participation under varying social and economic conditions. Analytical treatment of already available census materials[24] together with current census data and the returns of the 1950 Census will provide one avenue of research opportunity in this respect. More intensive sampling surveys and case studies, however, will come closer to getting at the various factors —cultural, institutional, social psychological and personal—which are determinants in varying labor force participation rates and their interrelationships.

Research such as that described above would throw considerable light on as yet largely unknown phases of labor force changes. Analysis of labor force participation rates, including both employment and unemployment rates and labor force entrance and egress on a family basis, should also help to provide a better understanding of the family as a changing social institution and as a group of interacting personalities. Fertile suggestions and patterns for research endeavor have in some respects already been

outlined.[25] Many of the important areas of sociological research into the family summarized by Burgess and by Cottrell can be explored with labor force participation of family members considered as both a dependent and independent variable in relation to other aspects of family structure and process.[26] The opportunities for research in this matter are in the main still unexploited.

Finally, the availability in the 1950 Census of data on family income should provide an important opportunity for getting at differences in family organization and structure as affected by and as influencing income as well as labor force participation.

SOCIAL STRATIFICATION AND SOCIAL MOBILITY

The study of social stratification, at least in our society, necessarily involves consideration of labor force participation and status. The relative ranking of a person on an economic, honorific, political, or other scale, by whatever criteria, is almost certainly affected by the nature of his employment and its rewards— monetary, psychic, or other. Contemporary theorists of social stratification have explicitly or implicitly recognized the central importance of the person's role in the labor force as a factor in his ranking in the economic, social or political hierarchy. Yet despite the contribution of the theorists[27] in providing frameworks

and Enka Schoenberg, "Studies in the Supply Curve of Labor: The Relation in 1929 Between Average Earnings in American Cities and the Proportions Seeking Employment," *Journal of Political Economy*, 45 (February 1937), 45–79.

Don D. Humphrey, *Family Unemployment*, Works Progress Administration, Washington, D. C.: Government Printing Office, 1940; "Alleged 'Additional Workers' in the Measurement of Unemployment," *Journal of Political Economy*, 48 (June 1940), 412–419.

W. S. Woytinsky, *Three Aspects of Labor Dynamics, Part III*, Washington, D. C.: Social Science Research Council, 1942, pp. 105 ff.

Clarence Long, *The Size of the Labor Force Under Changing Incomes and Employment*, Conference on Research in Income and Wealth, November, 1946 (mimeographed) 76 pp.; *The Labor Force in Wartime America*, New York: National Bureau of Economic Research, March 1944; "The Labor Force and Economic Changes," in Richard A. Lester, and J. Shuster, *Insights into Labor Issues*, New York: Macmillan, 1948, pp. 329–355. *Labor Force, Income and Employment*, National Bureau of Economic Research (forthcoming volume).

[24] See 1940 Population Census Reports: *Families & Employment Status; Family Wage or Salary Income, 1939;* also *The Labor Force: Employment & Family Characteristics of Women.*

[25] See footnote 23, also S. A. Stouffer, and P. Lazarsfeld, *Research Memorandum on the Family in the Depression*, New York: Social Science Research Council, 1937.

Robert C. Angell, *The Family Encounters the Depression*, New York: Scribner & Sons, 1936.

R. A. Cavan, and K. H. Ranck, *The Family and the Depression*, Chicago: University of Chicago Press, 1938.

Mirra Komarovsky, *The Unemployed Man and His Family*, New York: Dryden Press, 1940.

Paul Glick, "The Family Cycle," *American Sociological Review*, 12 (April 1947), 164–174.

[26] E. W. Burgess, "The Family and Sociological Research," *Social Forces*, 26 (October 1947), 1–6.

Leonard S. Cottrell, Jr., "The Present Status and Future Orientation of Research in the Family," *American Sociological Review*, 13 (April 1948), 123–129. See also discussion of this paper by E. W. Burgess, R. S. Cavan, & M. Komarovsky, pp. 129–136.

[27] See, for example, Max Weber in H. H. Gerth, and C. Wright Mills, *From Max Weber's Essays in Sociology*, New York: Oxford University Press, 1945, Chap. 7.

T. H. Marshall, "Social Class," *American Sociological Review*, 9 (January 1934).

Hans Speier, "Social Stratification in the Urban

for the study of social stratification, and the explicit attention some of them have devoted to various aspects of the labor force participation, relatively little empirical research has been conducted by sociologists in this exceedingly important field.

In the various aspects of labor force participation, occupational affiliation has received the major attention as a key to social stratification —both as a direct measure of economic ranking

Community," *American Sociological Review,* 1 (April 1936), 193–202.

Herbert Goldhamer, and Edward A. Shils, "Types of Power and Status," *American Journal of Sociology,* 45 (September 1939), 171–182.

Talcott Parsons, "An Analytical Approach to the Theory of Social Stratification," *American Journal of Sociology,* 45 (May 1940), 841–862.

Kingsley Davis, "A Conceptual Analysis of Stratification," *American Sociological Review,* 7 (June 1942), 309–321.

Emile Benoit-Smullyan, "Status, Status Types, and Status Interrelations," *American Sociological Review,* 9 (April 1944), 151–161.

For a frame of reference and elaborate research program centering largely around aspects of social stratification in which attention has been devoted to labor force status, see the works of W. Lloyd Warner & Associates listed below:

W. Lloyd Warner, and Paul S. Lunt, *The Social Life of a Modern Community,* Yankee City Series, Vol. 1, New Haven: Yale University Press, 1941.

W. Lloyd Warner, and Paul S. Lunt, *The Status Systems of a Modern Community,* Yankee City Series, Vol. II, New Haven: Yale University Press, 1942.

W. Lloyd Warner, and Leo Srole, *The Social Systems of American Ethnic Groups,* Yankee City Series, Vol. III, New Haven: Yale University Press, 1945.

W. Lloyd Warner, and J. O. Low, *The Social System of a Modern Factory,* Yankee City Series, Vol. IV, New Haven: Yale University Press, 1947.

W. Lloyd Warner, Marchia Meeker, and Kenneth Wells, *Social Class in America,* Chicago: Science Research Associates, 1949.

W. Lloyd Warner, and Associates, *Democracy in Jonesville,* New York: Harper & Bros. 1949.

The work of this group has been severely criticized. For example, see the book review by C. Wright Mills, on *The Social Life of a Modern Community,* in the *American Sociological Review,* April 1942; and more recently, H. W. Pfautz, and O. D. Duncan, "Critique of Warner's Work in Stratification," *American Sociological Review,* April, 1950. It is to be emphasized, however, that Warner and his associates, whatever the shortcomings of their research may be, are attacking a central problem in sociology which is suffering badly from lack of attention, and which calls for investigation by sociologists.

—"class"—and as an index of honorific or social ranking—"status." Various writers have pointed to the importance of the occupation of a person as a basic factor in determining his role in the social order.[28]

There is no doubt that the occupation of a person is a fundamental factor in explaining his position and ranking in the economic and social order. A number of sociologists have discussed this problem, and some have used occupational data as a measure or index of rank in the economic and/or social order. A good introduction to relevant literature as well as challenging proposals for further research are contained in recent publications.[29]

Social stratification will unquestionably remain one of the central problems in the study of social organization. As such it will continue to occupy a central place of interest in sociological research. There is ample opportunity and much need for research directed at improving occupational classification schemes for stratification analysis purposes; clarifying the role of occupation as a measure or index of "class" and of "status" respectively; determining the way in which, and the extent to which, occupation alone or in combination with other factors pro-

[28] Louis I. Dublin and Alfred Lotka, *Length of Life,* New York: Ronald Press, 1936, pp. 220.

Alba M. Edwards, *Comparative Occupation Statistics for the U. S., 1870–1940,* Washington, D. C.; Government Printing Office, 1943.

[29] Carlo I. Lastrucci, "The Status and Significance of Occupational Research," *American Sociological Review,* 11 (February 1946), 78–84.

William H. Form, and Delbert C. Miller, "Occupational Career Pattern as a Sociological Instrument," *American Journal of Sociology,* 54 (January 1949), 317–329.

Eldridge Sibley, "Some Demographic Clues to Stratification," *American Sociological Review,* 7 (June 1942) 322–330.

Paul K. Hatt, "Occupation and Social Stratification," *American Journal of Sociology,* 55 (May 1950), 533–543.

For examples of the use of occupational data for stratification purposes see: Alba M. Edwards, "A Social-Economic Grouping of the Gainful Worker in the U. S.," *Journal of the American Statistical Association,* 28 (December 1933), 377–387; *Comparative Occupation Statistics, 1870–1940,* Part III, U. S. Government Printing Office.

George S. Counts, "Social Status of Occupations: A Problem in Vocational Guidance," *School Review,* 33 (1925), 16–27.

Mapheus Smith, "Empirical Scale of Prestige Status of Occupations," *American Sociological Review,* 8 (April 1943), 185–192.

C. W. Hall, "Social Prestige Values of Selected

vides an efficient and effective measure of stratification; and ascertaining the extent to which,
and the mechanisms whereby, the occupation of
the person is, in fact, a determining factor in
fixing a person's way of life.

As one aspect of the study of social stratification, the sociologist is usually interested in the
problem of social mobility. Here, too, consideration of the labor force affiliation of the person,
especially his occupation, points to important
avenues of research. Utilization of labor force
data for the study of social mobility, although
increasing, is still in a relatively elementary
stage. A number of interesting studies are available, however, and in addition to providing important findings, they also point to profitable
further research.[30]

Groups of Occupations," *Psychological Bulletin,*
November, 1938.

Cecil C. North, and Paul K. Hatt, "Jobs &
Occupations—A Popular Evaluation," in *Sociologi-
cal Analysis* by Logan Wilson and William L.
Kolb, New York: Harcourt, Brace & Co., 1949.

Richard Centers, *Psychology of Social Classes,*
Princeton: Princeton University Press, 1949.

Also see forthcoming study by Paul K. Hatt, and
Cecil C. North, reporting in greater detail results
of the NORC study (No. 2044) resulting in an
occupational rating scale to which reference is
made in the citation above.

[30] P. Sorokin, *Social Mobility,* New York:
Harper, 1927.

P. E. Davidson, and H. D. Anderson, *Occupa-
tional Mobility in an American Community,* Palo
Alto: Stanford University Press, 1937; *Occupational
Trends in the U. S.,* Palo Alto: Stanford University
Press, 1940.

John W. McConnell, *The Evolution of Social
Classes,* Washington, D. C.: American Council of
Public Affairs, 1942.

Richard Centers, "Occupational Mobility of
Urban Occupational Strata," *American Sociological
Review,* 13 (April 1948), 197–203; also see W. H.
Form, and Delbert C. Miller, "A Note on Occupa-
tional Mobility of Urban Occupational Strata, by
Richard Centers," and reply by Centers, *loc. cit.,*
13 (October, 1948), 622–625.

W. H. Form, and Delbert C. Miller, "Occupational Career Pattern as a Sociological Instrument,"
American Journal of Sociology, 54 (January 1949),
317–329.

Richard Centers, "Marital Selection and Occupational Strata," *American Journal of Sociology,*
54 (May 1949), 530–535.

Carson McGuire, "Social Stratification and Mobility Patterns," *American Sociological Review,*
15 (April 1949), 195–204.

Natalie Rogoff, *Recent Trends in Occupational
Mobility,* Ph.D: dissertation, University of Chicago,
March 1950 (unpublished).

INDUSTRIAL SOCIOLOGY

Perhaps the most intensive sociological interest in the labor force is at present to be found,
and will undoubtedly increasingly become manifest, in the emergent field of industrial sociology.
An excellent statement of this interest is to be
found in the editorial foreword to a special
issue of the *American Journal of Sociology* devoted to industrial sociology:[31] "By publishing
such an issue the Editors mean to recognize
and to stimulate a growing interest in the study
of institutions of work as forms of social organization which may be compared with others
and be looked upon as a crucial part of the total
organization of modern society and as the arena
in which much of the individual's struggle for
life, for a social self and personality goes on."
This, to be sure, is a broader statement of the
area of industrial sociology than is conceived
by some students of the field who focus on
industrial relations in the sense of labor-management relations;[32] or on the interaction of
the two bureaucracies represented by corporate
enterprise, on the one hand, and unionism on
the other. But whether the field of industrial
sociology be narrowly or broadly conceived, or,
for that matter, whether "industrial sociology"
turns out to be an ephemeral sociological fad,
it is clear that there is a beckoning and significant task for the sociologist in the explanation
of the phenomena on which attention is focused
in this field.

Turning first to the area of industrial relations, it is manifest that the sociologist has
much to learn and much to contribute in the
investigation of the structure and functioning
of the labor force, as well as of management,
from a cultural, institutional and social psychological approach. A critique of present approaches to this area of investigation, as well as

Eleanor H. Bernert, *The Chicago Labor Force,
1910–1940: A Comparative Study of Trends in the
Labor Force and in Occupational and Industrial
Characteristics,* Ph.D. dissertation, University of
Chicago, 1949.

Gladys L. Palmer, and Ann Rattner, *Industrial
and Occupational Trends in National Employment,*
Industrial Research Department, Research Report
No. 11, University of Pennsylvania, September,
1949.

[31] 54 (January, 1949), 28 ff.

[32] Herbert Blumer, "Sociological Theory in Industrial Relations," *American Sociological Review,*
12 (June 1947), 271–278.

Wilbert E. Moore, "Current Issues in Industrial
Sociology," *American Sociological Review,* 12 (December 1947), 651–657.

a general formulation of the complex research problem involved, is contained in the paper by Herbert Blumer cited above (footnote 32). More detailed suggestions for research in this area, together with pertinent warnings about methodological inadequacies and the need for "analytical" rather than "practical" orientation[33] in the field, are contained in Moore's article, also cited above (footnote 32). Moore's suggestions center around types of research needed with respect to the organization of unions, and the consideration of collective bargaining and labor-management relations in general, as "the meeting of two bureaucracies."[34] Moore's cryptic reference to the field of industrial conflict as a "fertile area for the study of social disorganization—and for the analysis of the bases of functional integration in an urban industrial society"[35] may also be regarded as pregnant with sociological research potential.

It is particularly in industrial sociology that the sociologist can be expected to focus on work as a social institution and on the labor force participation of the person as basic research areas and as fundamental "behavior systems as a field for research" in the sense in which Hollingshead stated the problem.[36] Hughes, in following Durkheim's lead had attacked fundamental aspects of the problem earlier.[37] A useful discussion of the broad significance and potentials of labor force research centered on occupation is to be found in the article by Lastrucci.[38]

Finally, opportunities for sociologically oriented research are to be found in the research proposals and activities of a number of economists and other students, particularly those in labor economics and industrial relations.[39]

Conclusion

This essay is neither a comprehensive nor a balanced statement of the sociologists' interest, or of research opportunities, in the labor force.[40] It may, however, be useful in helping to focus attention, as a field for research, on a sector of contemporary life which is becoming increasingly complex, increasingly fraught with problems, and increasingly significant in the political as well as in the economic and social fields. These trends are concomitants of the increasing tempo of technological and social changes, initiated with the "industrial revolution" but still in progress and still producing new situations and new problems for which neither our social heritage nor our contemporary institutions provide ready or easy solutions. As an area in which many of our more difficult and perplexing domestic problems arise, the labor force is one which particularly merits the interest of the research-minded sociologist who is not perturbed or frightened by the fact that the problems are difficult, practical, and involve important conflicts of vested interests.

Valuable and significant as research opportunities of the various formal and quantifiable aspects of labor force structure and dynamics may be, the unique opportunity of the sociologist, both in contributing to a better understanding of labor force phenomena, on the one hand, and to a better understanding of our society, on the other, will lie in comprehensive research and analysis of work as a social institution, of industry and of the labor force as a fundamental sector of the social structure and process, and of labor force participation as a highly important segment of the person's behavior and way of life.

---

[33] See also P. M. Hauser, "Social Science and Social Engineering," *Philosophy of Science*, 16 (July 1949), 209–218.

[34] See also Robert K. Merton, *Social Theory and Social Structure*, Glencoe: Free Press, 1949, pp. 151 ff.

E. W. Bakke, *Mutual Survival*, New York: Harper & Bros., 1947.

[35] *Loc. cit.*, p. 656.

[36] A. B. Hollingshead, "Behavior Systems as a Field for Research," *American Sociological Review*, 48 (December 1939), 816–822.

[37] E. C. Hughes, "Personality Types and the Division of Labor," *American Journal of Sociology*, 33 (March 1928) 754–768.

[38] "The Status and Significance of Occupational Research," *American Sociological Review*, 11 (February 1946), 78–84.

[39] See: *Memorandum on University Research Programs in the Field of Labor, 1950,* Committee on Labor Market Research, New York: Social Science Research Council, 1950; also research planning memoranda published by the Committee on Labor Market Research of the Social Science Research Council, including:

John G. Turnbull, *Labor Management Relations: A Research Planning Memorandum* (Bulletin 61).

Gladys L. Palmer, *Research Planning Memorandum on Labor Mobility* (Pamphlet 2).

Carroll L. Shartle, *Vocational Counseling and Placement in the Community in Relation to Labor Mobility, Tenure and Other Factors* (Pamphlet 5).

Dale Yoder, *Demands for Labor: Opportunities for Research* (Pamphlet 7).

[40] For a fuller discussion of this entire subject see the forthcoming volume on the labor force by A. J. Jaffe and Charles Stewart, to be published by John Wiley & Sons.

DEMOGRAPHIC FACTORS IN

LABOR FORCE GROWTH

By S. L. Wolfbein and A. J. Jaffe

INTRODUCTION

THE PERIOD of time covering the National Defense Program and our active participation in the war witnessed not only a considerable change in the demographic characteristics of our population, but also served to reveal the great flexibility in the labor supply of the United States. Moreover, at no other time was it so important to understand the connection between population characteristics and the labor supply. Thus, the elementary problems of obtaining the manpower needed for the military as well as for producing the goods for winning the war focussed attention on the potential labor supply among women. No analysis of this potential was possible without knowledge and appreciation of the facts relative to the age, marital, and dependency status of the female population and their bearing upon labor market participation.

That these and many other demographic factors are major determinants of both the size and composition of the labor force at any given time is well known. Only a cursory examination of the relevant Census volume for any decade will make apparent the crucial importance of the age and sex composition of the population, the marital and dependency status of women, or the proportion of colored or foreign-born in determining the size and composition of our working population.

In this paper the attempt will be made to assess the relative importance of demographic factors in the changing size and composition of the labor force over a *span of time*. More specifically, how important have

changes in age, sex, marital status, color and nativity been with relation to changes in the rate of labor force participation between 1890 and 1930? Indeed, what has been their importance in comparison with other social and economic factors which also have a bearing upon the size of the labor force? A similar set of questions will be asked for the war period. And finally, an analysis of the results and their bearing upon estimates of future population and labor force growth will be noted.

THE PERIOD 1890 TO 1930[1]

Practically all of the changes in demographic factors during the forty-year period from 1890 to 1930 operated in the direction of decreasing the worker rate. Thus, women have a much smaller worker rate than men: The sex ratio (for the population 15 years

---

[1] The choice of the period 1890 and 1930 for studying the effects of long-term demographic changes was dictated largely by considerations of available data. The 1890 Decennial Census contained very detailed tabulations of the gainfully occupied population by age, sex, marital status, color, nativity, etc.—more detail than in any ensuing Census until 1940. The 1930 Decennial Census, of course, was the latest with comparable gainful worker data. Finally, the forty-year period was sufficiently long to allow for significant changes in the demographic factors under consideration.

of age and over) dropped from 106.0 in 1890 to 102.4 in 1930. Married women are in the labor force in much smaller proportion: The proportion of married women to total went up from 56.8 to 61.1 during the same period. High worker rates are also characteristic of the foreign born white: Their ratio in the total population fell from 23.3 percent to 16.9 percent. The colored population has always had a higher rate of labor market participation than the whites: The proportion of colored, however, has decreased only from 11.0 to 10.7 over the forty-year period. Even the aging of the population served to operate in the same direction among women, since their worker rates begin to fall after the 20-24 age group. Among the men, a large part of the effect of the aging process was a shift within the middle-age group in which worker rates are close to 100 percent anyway.

One demographic factor which undoubtedly operated in the direction of a higher worker rate was the decrease in fertility. Just how important the decreasing birth rate was in freeing women from the home is difficult to determine, although it may have been fairly important. (Data on dependency status are not available for this period.) If a woman has no children, she generally is free to take a job away from the home; if she has even one small child she is tied to the home almost as much as if she had several.[2] The decrease in fertility resulted in large part from a decrease in proportion of women who had large families (4 or more children ever born), and second-

[2] The relationship of labor force participation to number of small children in the family, is known for 1940. Among all women in the United States, married, husband present, aged 18 to 44 years, we find the following labor force participation rates:

Without children under 10 years of age 25.7%
With 1 child under 10 years of age 9.9%
With 2 or more children under 10 years of age 5.9%

(See 16th Census of the U.S., 1940, *Population, The Labor Force, Employment and Family Characteristics of Women*, Table II, p. 3.)

From these data it would appear that labor force participation for married women drops markedly—15.8 percentage points—with the advent of one young child (under 10 years of age), and then drops much less—4 percentage points—with the advent of subsequent young children.

TABLE 1. EFFECT OF DEMOGRAPHIC AND OTHER SOCIO-ECONOMIC CHANGES ON PROPORTION OF POPULATION, 15 YEARS OF AGE AND OVER, GAINFULLY OCCUPIED, 1890 AND 1930, BY SEX AND MARITAL STATUS

	Total	Male	Female		
			Total	Unmarried[a]	Married
1. 1890 gainful worker rates as enumerated (Decennial Census)	54.8	88.7	18.9	37.7	4.6
2. 1930 gainful worker rates as enumerated (Decennial Census)	55.9	86.2	24.8	45.4	11.7
3. 1930 gainful worker rates expected on basis of changing demographic factors[b]	52.6	88.3	16.0	34.9	4.0
4. Influence of demographic factors (line 3 minus line 1)	−2.2	−0.4	−2.9	−2.8	−0.6
5. Influence of other social-economic forces (line 2 minus line 3)	3.3	−2.1	8.8	10.5	7.7
Percentage change 1890 to 1930 due to:					
Changing social-economic factors	+6.0	−2.4	+46.6	+27.8	+167.4
Changing demographic factors	−4.0	−0.5[c]	−15.3	−7.4	−13.0
Both socio-economic and demographic factors	+2.0	−2.9	+31.3	+20.4	+154.4

[a] Includes single, widowed, and divorced.

[b] Estimated by applying 1890 gainful worker rates by age, sex, color, nativity and for females marital status, to the 1930 population similarly classified. 1890 gainful worker rates, classified by the various characteristics from Department of Interior: *Special Census Report of the Population of the United States at the Eleventh Census, 1890*, Washington, D.C. 1896, pp. 21 et. seq., and *Report on Population of the United States at the Eleventh Census, 1890*, Pt. II, Washington, D.C. 1897, Tables 119 and 120. All figures adjusted for under-enumeration of gainful workers in younger age groups, cf. Department of Commerce and Labor, Bureau of the Census, Twelfth Census of U. S., 1900. Report on Occupation, pp. lxvi to lxxiii.

[c] When applying 1930 specific gainful worker rates to the 1890 population classified as in note b, above, a practically identical percentage change was obtained.

arily from an increase in the proportion of childless women.[3]

Table 1 summarizes the expected effects of demographic changes, assuming 1890 specific gainful worker rates had remained unchanged by 1930, and contrasts them with what actually happened between 1890 and 1930. For example, among all women aged 15 years and over the gainful worker rate *increased* by almost one-third, instead of decreasing by several percentage points as might have been expected on the basis of the demographic factors enumerated above. The contrast is especially marked for the married women among whom the gainful worker rate almost tripled between 1890 and 1930 instead of experiencing the small decline indicated on tne basis of the demographic factors. Among the males, these demographic factors should have caused no change in the gainful worker rate between 1890 and 1930; actually, of course, the proportion of males gainfully occupied decreased somewhat.

It is quite clear, then, that the observed changes in the proportion of the population listed as gainful workers in 1890 as compared with 1930 were determined more by various social and economic factors than by the demographic aspects as such.[4] Perhaps most important was the social acceptance of women in employment outside the home—

a reflection of a variety of forces including the growing importance of white-collar jobs, changes in technology and in industrial organization resulting in factory jobs in which women can perform adequately, the transfer of many activities from the home to the commercial sphere (food preparation, laundry, making of clothes, etc.), the changing role of women as evidenced by their gaining the vote and holding public offices, etc. Among males the decrease in worker rates over the 40-year period is essentially a product of later entrance into the labor force (and, conversely, more years of schooling) and earlier retirement.

Reference to Table 1 will indicate the relative importance of these social and economic factors and the demographic forces.[5]

THE WAR PERIOD

For the period 1940 to 1944, consideration was given to the following demographic factors: As for the previous period age, sex, marital condition (for women) were studied. Data on dependency status of women (responsibility for the care of children under 10 years of age) are also available for this period and were used. No consideration was given to changes in color and nativity in which there was negligible change during this period.

Some of the changes which occurred during this four-year period were as great or greater than those which were noted. in the

---

[3] Cf. 16th Census of the United States, 1940. Population, *Differential Fertility, 1940 and 1910,* Women by Number of Children Ever Born, Tables 1 and 4.

[4] It might be argued that the aging of the entire population (all ages) between 1890 and 1930 should have resulted in an increase in the proportion of the total population who were classified as gainful workers. Thus, the median ages were:

	Males	Females
1890	21.2	20.7
1930	26.7	26.2

This aging of the population should have resulted in an increase in the proportion of all males gainful workers from 60.2 to 65.6; for females there should have been a decrease from 13.1 to 12.8 (standardizing on the basis of the 1890 age-sex, specific rates). Actually, the proportion of males gainful workers increased, by 1930, to only 61.3, and females to 17.7. Here again, the importance of the socio-economic factors is emphasized.

[5] An extremely informative analysis not reflected in any of the tables can be made of the effects of increasing longevity, *per se.* As specific mortality rates decrease, the life table population becomes older, increasing the over-all rate of labor market participation. 100,000 white males born in 1900 and subject to the age specific mortality rates of that year would have worked 3 million years by age 65, at 1890 worker rates. If these white males had been subject to mortality rates of 1929-31, they would have worked some 3,700,000 years—24 percent more. In other words, if the only demographic change that had occurred had been in mortality, 24 per cent additional jobs would have had to be found for the increased number of survivors. Should mortality continue to increase to, say, the level of New Zealand females in 1934-38, the additional number of jobs required would increase to almost 40 per cent. The same situation holds for white females.

40-year period previously discussed. The same pattern, however, is clearly evident. Again, the demographic factors operated toward a decreasing labor force rate. The population did not age appreciably; the sex ratio also did not shift significantly, although the proportion of females did increase very slightly. Most important was the high marriage rate and the increasing proportion of women responsible for the care of small children resulting from the higher birth rate.

Table 2 summarizes the effects of these changes and compares them with other social

Responsible were the war-inspired forces ranging from induction into the armed forces of youths before attaining their normal labor force age to the absence of many husbands in the armed forces to provision of nurseries for working mothers to the high level of wages in war industry.

PREDICTING FUTURE LABOR FORCE GROWTH

The major thesis of this paper—that other social and economic forces are much more important than measurable demographic factors in accounting for changes in the pro-

TABLE 2. EFFECT OF DEMOGRAPHIC AND OTHER SOCIO-ECONOMIC CHANGES ON PROPORTION OF POPULATION, 14 YEARS OF AGE AND OVER IN THE LABOR FORCE, 1940 AND 1944, BY SEX AND MARITAL STATUS

| | Total | Male | Female | | |
			Total	Unmarried[a]	Married
1. 1940 Labor force rates as enumerated (Decennial Census)	52.4	79.1	25.8	41.1	13.8
2. 1944 Labor force rates as enumerated (Monthly Report on the Labor Force, Census Bureau, Feb. 1944)	58.7	85.8	31.8	47.1	21.6
3. 1944 Labor force rates expected on basis of changing demographic factors[b]	51.2	79.3	23.3	39.3	12.6
4. Influence of demographic factors (line 3 minus line 1)	− 1.2	+0.2	− 2.5	− 1.8	− 1.2
5. Influence of the social-economic forces (line 2 minus line 3)	7.5	6.5	8.5	7.8	9.0
Percentage change 1940 to 1944 due to:					
Changing socio-economic factors	+14.3	+8.2	+32.9	+19.0	+65.2
Changing demographic factors	− 2.3	+0.3	− 9.7	− 4.4	− 8.7
Both socio-economic and demographic factors	+12.0	+8.5	+23.2	+14.6	+56.5

[a] Includes single, widowed, and divorced.

[b] Estimated by applying 1940 labor force rates by age, sex—and for females—marital status and dependency status to the February 1944 population similarly classified. All data for 1944 from Monthly Report on the labor Force, Bureau of the Census.

and economic forces. Briefly, it may be said that the net effect of these population factors should have been to decrease the proportion of the population 14 years of age and over, in the labor force by about 2 percent. Actually, of course, the labor force increased by 14 percent. Again, the contrast for married women was most marked. Instead of a decrease of almost 10 percent to be expected on the basis of the demographic changes, the labor force rate more than doubled.[6]

———
[6] A detailed analysis of changes in marital and dependency status of women in the labor force between 1940 and 1944 is available in Technical Memorandum #13, Occupational Outlook Division, Bureau of Labor Statistics, May 10, 1944.

portion of the population in the labor force— is significant for the problem of forecasting changes in the size of the labor force.

Demographic factors are only of secondary importance. The age and sex distribution of the population can be estimated for 1980, 1990, or even the year 2000. Similarly, 1940 or 1945 age-sex specific labor market participation rates could be applied to the extrapolated population. But how far off are we likely to be? What are the long-term trends in the non-demographic factors affecting the proportions of women who will be in the labor force at some future date? How are these socio-economic factors determining the ages at which men and women first enter and leave the labor force? What would be the effect of a deep depression? Of a level approaching full employment? Of a considerably higher plane of living? Of wholesale technological change? Of a much shorter work week? Some of these factors will play a pivotal role even in an estimate of the size of the labor force for so close a year as 1950. It would seem, then, that much more fruitful fields of research would center about these non-demographic factors and their effects upon labor market participation.[7]

[7] One of the few pieces of research which resulted in a projected labor force taking into account more than the usual demographic factors was that of Durand and Wood in their "Normal Growth of the Labor Force in the United States." Census release P-44 No. 12, June 12, 1944. Working with actual Census age-sex specific worker rates since 1920, they automatically concerned themselves with the sum total of all factors bearing upon labor market participation, in extrapolating trends to 1950.

During the last half century (or longer) the proportion of women in the labor force has steadily increased. Among men the proportion decreased somewhat up to the time of the beginning of World War II, after which it increased during the war years. What does the future hold? Will this wartime expansion of the male labor force continue for an indefinite period ahead? Will labor force participation among women continue to increase? Only analysis of the basic underlying socio-economic forces can answer these questions.

THE ECONOMIC EFFECTS OF CHANGES

IN AGE COMPOSITION

By Joseph J. Spengler

THE ECONOMIC consequences of a change in age composition may be grouped under four principal heads: (a) those which affect the *ratio* of workers to the total population; (b) those which affect the net output per continuously employed worker; (c) those which temporarily interrupt the continuity of a worker's employment; and (d) those which affect either the manner in which the working population is distributed among occupations, or the fullness of employment.

Upon these four groups of effects depend virtually all changes in per capita income properly imputable to changes in the age composition of a population. There remain additional economic consequences of a change in age composition, but these have to do with the adjusting of an economy to changes in age composition and not with the income-affecting consequences of such changes.

In Section I the basic theory underlying the analysis in this paper is outlined. Effects (a)–(d) are treated in Sections II–V. In Section VI incidental matters are treated.

I. The Basic Theory

Three circumstances operating separately or in combination may produce a change in the age composition of the population of a national state or one of its sub-divisions. (1) An increase in the expectation of life at birth will operate *ceteris paribus* to augment the relative number of persons in the higher age groups; a decrease will reduce the relative number. (2) A decrease in the gross reproduction rate will operate *ceteris paribus* to reduce the relative number of persons in the lower age groups until the age composition of the population has become adjusted to this lower rate; an increase will augment the relative number. (3) Migration will operate *ceteris paribus* to modify the age composition of a population if the age composition of the migrating population differs, in *net* terms, from the initial age composition of the population subject to the influence of migration.

In this paper we examine certain of the economic consequences which tend to accompany an increase in the relative number of persons in the higher age groups and a decrease in the relative number in the lower age groups. For it is principally this kind of change in age composition that has been produced and is being produced in the populations of the United States and of individual American states by past and/or prospective increases in life expectancy and decreases in gross reproduction. The influence of migration upon age composition, together with its economic consequences, will not be

497

separately considered; for while the influences of prospective migration upon age composition may differ from that of changes in mortality and natality, the analysis of these influences does not differ.

The economic effects of a given change in the age composition of a population originate in such changes in the *relative* numerical importance of economically significant attributes and attitudes as are produced by this change in age composition.

Let us suppose a population with individuals in every year of life from under-one to n. Let n, for the sake of concreteness, be assigned a value of 105. Let A denote the per cent of the total population in any particular yearly age group. Let the subscript 0 denote the single year age group under one year of age; 1, the single year age group lying between the 366th and the 730th days of life inclusive; and so on. Then, given that $n = 105$, the age composition of a population may be represented as follows:

$$A_0$$
$$A_1$$
$$\cdots$$
$$\cdots$$
$$A_{105}$$

Should sex composition also be required, the subscripts m and f may be used to denote male and female, respectively: e.g., A_1 becomes A_{m1} and A_{f1}.

A change in age composition modifies the *relative* numerical importance of those economically significant attributes and attitudes which vary, in each individual, with his age. This variation may be continuous from year to year,

or it may be discontinuous, being manifest only in certain years. Let a denote such an attribute or attitude. Its value will vary with age, increasing to a maximum at some age, and thereafter declining. This variation may be expressed in index number terms, with an index of 100 assigned to the maximum value reached at some age, say 40, and with corresponding index numbers assigned to the values associated with other years. Since there are supposedly 105 single years of life the subscripts 0 to 105 may be used to denote the age of the possessor of the attribute or attitude and, therefore, its known index value. The numerical importance of a in a population may then be represented as follows:

$$A_0a_0$$
$$A_1a_1$$
$$\cdots\cdots$$
$$\cdots\cdots$$
$$A_{105}a_{105}$$

The aggregate value S_a in index terms of a for the population as a whole then is $\Sigma A_0a_0 + A_1a_1 + \cdots\cdots + A_{105}a_{105}$. The numerical importance of each other attribute or attitude b, c, d, etc., may be represented in like manner. It is evident that, if there is an increase in those A values with which high a values are associated, the aggregate value s_a for the population will increase; if these same A values diminish, aggregate value s_a will diminish. Like changes in the A values will produce like changes in the aggregate values $s_b, s_c, s_d \cdots\cdots, s_z$.

Not all economic attributes and attitudes $a, b, \cdots\cdots, z$ are of equal economic significance. If all were of equal economic significance and independent one of another, their aggregate numerical importance s in index value terms might be represented as follows, as of any given time, for each yearly age group:

$$S_0 = A_0(a_0 + b_0 + \ldots\ldots\ldots + z_0)$$
$$S_1 = A_1(a_1 + b_1 + \ldots\ldots\ldots + z_1)$$
$$\ldots\ldots\ldots\ldots\ldots\ldots\ldots\ldots\ldots\ldots$$
$$\ldots\ldots\ldots\ldots\ldots\ldots\ldots\ldots\ldots\ldots$$
$$S_{105} = A_{105}(a_{105} + b_{105} + \ldots + z_{105})$$

The aggregate for the whole population then becomes the sum of the values for the individual years

$$\sum_{S_0}^{S_{105}} s.$$

Since attributes and attitudes a, b, ..., z are not of equal economic significance, a corrective coefficient C designed to reduce the index value for each attribute or attitude to comparable index terms must be introduced. Let this corrective coefficient be assigned a value of 1 for the most important attribute or attitude (say a) and appropriate lesser values for less important attributes or attitudes. Then the preceding summary statement may be rewritten as follows:

$$S_0 = A_0(a_0 C_a + b_0 C_b + \ldots + z_0 C_z)$$
$$S_1 = A_1(a_1 C_a + b_1 C_b + \ldots + z_1 C_z)$$
$$\ldots\ldots\ldots\ldots\ldots\ldots\ldots\ldots\ldots\ldots$$
$$\ldots\ldots\ldots\ldots\ldots\ldots\ldots\ldots\ldots\ldots$$
$$S_{105} = A_{105}(a_{105} C_a + b_{105} C_b + \ldots + z_{105} C_z)$$

The aggregate for the whole population is, of course, $\sum_{S_0}^{S_{105}} s.$

The importance, absolute and relative, of an economically signi-ficant attribute or attitude is not constant but variable through time, being dependent upon what may be called the structure S of an economy. That is, $C_a = f(S)$ $C_b = f(S)$, etc.; or, generally, $C = f(S)$. If only one time period is under consideration, or if S continues essentially unchanged between the two time periods being compared, the value of S may be ignored. If, however, the change in age composition between two periods has been accompanied by a change in S, the latter change must be taken into account; for the net economic effect of the change in age composition is then conditioned by the change in S.

It has been implicitly assumed that attributes and attitudes a, b, ...z are conditioned by age alone. Actually, however, each attribute or attitude is function of both age and the cultural or institutional arrangements I in effect in the economy. Thus, if y denotes the age of the possessor of an attribute a, the value of this attribute $v_a = f(y, I)$. Accordingly, given the age of the possessor of attribute a, its value is governed by I; and the effect of a change in the age composition of a population is conditioned by the institutional arrangements I in effect. Moreover, if I changes at the same time that the age composition changes, the economic effect of the change in age composition as such may be accentuated or partly offset by the change in I.

If all the economic attributes and attitudes conditioned by age are independent of one another, their aggregate numerical importance s in index value terms may be represented as follows, as of any given time, for each yearly age group:

$$S_0 = A_0(a_0C_a + b_0C_b + \ldots + z_0C_z)SI$$
$$S_1 = A_1(a_1C_a + b_1C_b + \ldots + z_1C_z)SI$$
$$\cdots\cdots\cdots\cdots\cdots\cdots\cdots\cdots\cdots$$
$$\cdots\cdots\cdots\cdots\cdots\cdots\cdots\cdots\cdots$$
$$S_{105} = A_{105}(a_{105}C_a + b_{105}C_b + \ldots + z_{105}C_z)SI$$

The aggregate for the whole population composing the economy is $\sum\limits_{S_0}^{S_{105}} s$. If the age composition of the population changes between two time periods, while both the structure S of the economy and its institutional arrangements I continue unchanged, the change in s will be the result solely of changes in the values of $A_0, A_1, \ldots, A_{105}$. If, however, S and/or I undergo modification simultaneously with the change in age composition, the change in $\sum\limits_{S_0}^{S_{105}} s$ may be accentuated or reduced.

II. The Worker: Population Ratio

The *relative* number of workers in a population varies with its age composition. This variation is due in part to the fact that persons below and above certain ages are not members of a nation's labor force, that is, of that group of persons who either are employed or are seeking work. Thus in 1940, when the median age of the American population was 29 years, 71 and 58.8 percent, respectively, of this population were in age groups 15–69 and 20–64; in the year 2000, when the median age will approximate 37.4, these two percentages will approximate 72 and 61, respectively.[1] These figures suggest that for each 100 inhabitants there may be slightly more workers in the future than at present.

This supposition must be slightly modified, however; for circumstances associated with variations in age affect the relative number of persons in the age group 15–75 who are qualified to be members of the labor force of a state or nation. In this section and the following section only data relating to males will be used for purposes of demonstration. This restriction is permissible since males comprise about three-fourths of the labor force, since findings for males hold in substance for females, and since many of the circumstances affecting the actual occupational status of females are not connected with age.

Relevant data for all males are given in Table I. In 1930 gainful employment was at a maximum in the age group 25–44 (col. 2). In 1940 membership in the labor force was at a maximum in the age group 25–44; it was lower in higher age groups, decreasing at an increasing

---

[1] For purposes of discussion in this essay use is made of the population forecast based on the assumption of medium fertility and mortality and no net immigration after July 1, 1945. See Special Report of the Bureau of the Census, Series P-46, No. 7, September 15, 1946. Other forecasts will become available in 1948 upon the publication, by the Bureau of the Census, of *Forecasts of the Population of the United States, 1945–1975.* See also John D. Durand's *The Labor Force in the United States,* 1890–1960 (Social Science Research Council, New York, 1948), which appeared after this study was completed.

rate with the height of the age group (col. 3). Should the percentages reported in column 3 persist, the percentage of all males in the labor force will increase somewhat (under 1 per cent by 1960; about 5 per cent by 2000) in consequence of the change in age composition.

Since membership in the labor force does not imply actual employment, account must be taken of such variations in employment as are associated with age. In column 4 of Table I there is reported by age group the percentage of the labor force employed otherwise than on public emergency work,

March 24–30, 1940; it is only slightly lower in the higher age groups than in the peak range, 25–44. On line 2 of Table II the relative number of males "seeking work" in this same week is given by age. The percentage falls from a maximum in age group 15–19 to a minimum in group 35–44, then rises gradually to a secondary peak in the 60–64 group, thereafter declining slightly.[2] In Table II (last line) are given the fractions by which the median earnings for *all* male members of the labor force, irrespective of months worked in 1939, fell below the median earnings of the continuously employed

TABLE I
Per Cent of Males, Gainfully Employed in 1930 or in Labor Force in 1940, and Median Earnings of Males in 1939, by Age*

AGE GROUP	PER CENT OF MALES IN AGE GROUP REPORTED AS		Per cent of labor force employed (excluding public emergency work) in 1940 [b]	MEDIAN EARNINGS OF MALES EMPLOYED FOR 12 MONTHS, IN 1939 [c]		Index to Productivity [d]
	Gainfully employed, 1930 [a]	In labor force, 1940 [b]		Absolute	Relative	
15–19........	[48.0]	[40.0]	[68.9]	[$512]	[33]	14
20–24........	89.9	88.0	79.7	913	58	53
25–34........	97.3	95.2	87.4	1324	83	81
35–44........	97.7	94.7	88.4	1572	100	95
45–54........	96.4	92.1	86.9	1590	101	92
55–59........	93.0	87.8	84.9	1484	94	83
60–64........	86.8	78.9	84.6	1398	88	70
65–74........	68.4	50.8	89.3	1238	78	40
Over 74.......	32.3	17.8	95.4	....	...	..
All ages.......	76.2	79.0	85.2	1354	85	67

* Figures in brackets are estimates.
  [a] Fifteenth Census: 1930, V, p. 115.
  [b] Sixteenth Census: 1940, III, *The Labor Force. Occupation, Industry, Employment and Income*, p. 19. The per cent (e. g., 9.6 in last line) not accounted for are reported as "seeking work."
  [c] *Ibid., Wage or Salary Income in 1939*, p. 106. The figure for the 65–74 group is based upon that reported for the group over 64.
  [d] Obtained by rounding or slightly adjusting percentages in cols. 3 and 6 and multiplying col. 3 by col. 6

2 According to the National Health Survey in 1935–36 the per cent of urban male workers who were unemployed, were, by age: 15–24, 37.4; 25–44, 17.2 45–64, 22.3; 65 and over, 31; all ages, 22.6. Unemployment varied with age in much the same manner among both white and colored male workers, but unemployment rates were much higher among the latter (see Population Series, Bulletin No. D, pp. 6–7).

(i.e., 12 months) males.[3] This fraction, at a maximum in the 15–19 group, falls to a minimum in the 35–44 group, thereafter rising gradually to a secondary peak in the 65–74 group. While this fraction is dominated by the earnings-depressing effect of unemployment, it should also reflect the similar effect of accidents and sickness; yet only in the 65–74 group is there possibly evidence that the latter effect is relatively significant.[4]

The data presented in this section indicate that the prospective changes in age composition will not increase the relative number of nonworkers in the population, and may even slightly increase the relative number of workers; for the increase in the relative number of older nonworkers will be offset by the decrease in the relative number of younger nonworkers. It is not likely, moreover, that prospective changes in age composition will tend to reduce the percentage of the labor force that is regularly employed. It is not likely, therefore, that the worker: population ratio will be adversely affected by prospective changes in age composition.

III. Age and Output Per Continuously Employed Worker

Information respecting the functional relation between age and output per continuously employed worker, while less complete than precise analysis requires,[5] indicates that a worker's output usually is influenced by his age and tends to fall as he moves into higher age groups. This tendency has its origin principally in psychophysiological concomitants of aging.

It is almost impossible to determine the role of age in

TABLE II
Unemployment and Earnings in Male Labor Force, 1939–40

Age Groups	15–19	20–24	25–34	35–44	45–54	55–59	60–64	65–74	All
Per cent seeking work [a]	23	14.4	8	6.8	7.7	9.5	9.7	8.2	9.6
1 — (wage of all ÷ wage of 12 month workers) [b]	.48	.28	.18	.16	.18	.20	.22	.23	.22

[a] See note (b) under Table I.
[b] Computed from pp. 99,106 of census report cited in note (c) under Table I.
[3] For urban male members of the labor force the corresponding fractions were: 15–19, 48; 20–24, 23; 45–64 and "all ages," 17; 35–44, 14; 25–34, 12.
[4] The Spearman rank correlation coefficient between the unemployment and wage data on the last two lines of Table II is 0.923 with a probable error of 0.127. The 65–74 group ranks 5 in per cent seeking work and 3 in depression of earnings below full-time level.
[5] As a rule variations in output per employed worker must be inferred from variations in his earnings; and these may be used to measure the influence of age upon productivity only when: (a) the worker's behavior rates (i.e., speed, energy output, etc.) are governed primarily by himself; (b) earnings accurately reflect performance; and (c) it is possible to isolate variations in earnings attributable to variations in hours worked.

industrial output. However, on the basis of our physiologic knowledge, it seems probable that work output may diminish in older workers.[6]

Old age weakens most abilities, especially those requiring energy and speed, but the drop from age 50 to age 75 is probably only 1 or 2 per cent per year.[7]

This tendency may also be attributable in some part to an increase in the worker's inclination to restrict output as he advances in age.[8]

The functional relation between output and age varies with occupation; for the physiological and psychological responses of workers vary with age, while the physiological and psychological requirements of occupations differ. Thus, the effectiveness of a boxer is usually at a peak in his twenties, whilst that of a craftsman or of a professional man may remain at or near the peak even in his fifties. In general the more the product of a man's occupational behavior involves experience, wisdom, and judgment, the less marked will be the tendency of this product to decline in

consequence of age-induced physiological and psychological deterioration. Furthermore, in so far as older workers, in comparison with younger workers, tend to perform more evenly and to turn out relatively fewer spoiled or substandard products, they will enjoy a comparative advantage in occupations in which evenness of performance and maintenance of quality is important.[9]

Because the functional relation between age and output varies with occupation, the overall effect of an increase in the age composition of a population will be conditioned by its occupational composition. Such an increase is much more likely to have an adverse effect upon aggregate output in an economy dominated by occupations resembling boxing in its demands upon the practitioner than in an economy dominated by crafts and professions. For the sake of simplicity it will here be assumed that the occupational composition is stable through time. In fact, the changes in occupational composition that are taking place appear to be increasing the relative importance of

---

[6] Dr. N. W. Shock, "Older People and Their Potentialities for Gainful Employment," *Journal of Gerontology*, II, 1947, p. 98.

[7] E. L. Thorndike, *Human Nature and the Social Order*, The Macmillan Company, New York, 1940, p. 55. Various aspects of gerontology are treated in E. V. Cowdry, ed., *Problems of Ageing*, Williams and Wilkins, Baltimore, 2d ed., 1942. On social aspects of ageing and bibliography relating thereto see E. W. Burgess et al, *Social Adjustment in Old Age*, a preliminary mimeographed research planning report sponsored by the Social Science Research Council, New York, 1946.

[8] G. F. Bloom and N. Belfer state that "the inclination to restrict output and the age of the union worker are closely correlated." See "Unionism and Real Labor Income, *Southern Economic Journal*, XIV, 1948, p. 293. Dr. Frank T. de Vyner informs the writer that it is his observation from experience that older workers are less likely than younger workers to restrict output.

[9] W. R. Miles, "Psychological Aspects of Ageing," in Cowdry, *op. cit.* See also R. A. McFarland, "The Older Worker in Industry," *Harvard Business Review*, XXI, 1943, pp. 505–520; H. C. Lehman, "The Most Proficient Years at Sports and Games," *Research Quarterly, American Association of Health and Physical Education*, IX, 1938, pp. 3–19; and C. Tibbitts and O. Pollak in Burgess et al, *op. cit.*, pp. 83–85.

those forms of behavior which are more resistant to age-induced deterioration.

Output appears to vary less with the age of a representative individual than from individual to individual of stipulated age.[10] For a given individual's productivity is conditioned by his Biological Age in greater measure than by his Chronologic Age which is but one of the several determinants of an individual's Biologic Age. The productivity of a given individual will usually exceed, or fall short of, the average productivity of his age and occupational group, if his Vitality Index exceeds or falls short of that representative of this group.[11] An individual's Vitality Index is conditioned by his Biologic Age which is governed in part by genetic and other conditions not susceptible of modification, and in part by conditions which are susceptible of some modification through education and improvements in managerial, medical, and psychological approaches to problems associated with ageing. These

modifying circumstances will operate also in other ways to increase the productivity of individuals of given age, and on the balance to diminish interindividual differences in productivity. Presumably, therefore, although interindividual differences in the functional relation between age and output cannot be eliminated, they can be made less pronounced than at present.[12]

The productivity, or the earnings, of continuously employed workers rise to a maximum, remain there for some years, and then decline. Among male agricultural workers productivity is supposedly at the peak in the 18–44 age group, and thereafter declines.[13] Among railway employees there appears to be a tendency, not completely continuous, for efficiency to decline slightly after the early forties.[14] A careful study, based upon the production records of 249 male weavers, spinners, and nonferrous-metal workers, reveals that output per worker per full-time week was at the maximum in the age group 25–55, about 5 per cent below the

---

[10] Miles, op. cit.

[11] Vitality Index = V.I. = $100[1 \div$ (Biologic Age $\div$ Chronologic Age)]. This index which is analogous to Intelligent Quotient, is suggested by Dr. Harry Benjamin's distinction between Chronologic Age, measured in years, and Biological Age, measured in terms of an individual's health and biologic state. See "Biologic Versus Chronologic Age," Journal of Gerontology, II, 1947, pp. 217–228. The term "usually" is used in the text above because an individual's productivity depends not only upon his Biologic Age but also upon other circumstances.

[12] According to Shock (op. cit., p. 100), effective utilization of older workers presupposes "(1) careful and complete job analysis, (2) development of individual tests to assess the physiological age of various organ systems, (3) development of individual tests for performance capacity, and (4) education of the community to realize the necessity for utilizing the work capacities present in older people."

[13] In the State of Washington male workers in 1943 were considered by farmers to have the following work capacity, expressed in terms of an able-bodied man: 10–14, one-third; 15–17, three-fourths; 18–44, one; 45–64, nine-tenths; 65 and older, three-fifths. See Carl F. Reuss, "Effect of Age and Sex on Productive Capacity at Farm Work," State College of Washington Agricultural Experiment Station, V Circular No. 13, July, 1943, p. 2.

[14] Dan H. Mater, "A Statistical Study of the Effect of Seniority Upon Employee Efficiency," Journal of Business, XIV, April, 1941, p. 195. This study is continued in ibid., October, 1941, pp. 384 ff. as "Effects of Seniority Upon the Welfare of the Employee, the Employer and Society."

maximum in the age group 55–64, about 10–15 per cent below the maximum in the age group 65–74, and about 10 per cent below in the age group 15–24.[15] A study of professional incomes in 1941 reveals the following rough maximum earnings age ranges: veterinarians, 35–39; dentists and osteopaths, 35–49; physicians, 35–54; lawyers, 45–59.[16] It is not wide of the truth to say, in general, that the earnings of the vast majority (i.e., over 90 per cent) of continuously employed workers rise to a maximum in the thirties and remain there for 15–25 years; and that the earnings of the high-income minority reach a peak in the forties or early fifties and remain at this level for a shorter period.[17]

Absolute and relative median earnings data presented in columns 5–6 of Table I for continuously[18] employed males in 1939 indicate that the productivity of such workers is at a maximum in the age group 35–54 and thereafter declines about one point per year. In column 7 of Table I there is presented an index of productivity[19] based upon columns 3 and 6. If the productivity index value for each age group is multiplied by the percentage of the male population in the corresponding age group and the products are summated for any year, a comparative measure of output per capita is obtained. If the sum obtained for 1940 is assigned a relative value of 100, the comparative values for 1960,

---

15 D. L. Palmer and J. A. Brownell, "Influence of Age on Employment Opportunities," *Monthly Labor Review*, XLVIII, 1939, pp. 765–780, Tables 6–7. In pre-1939 Germany and Czechoslovakia earnings reached a peak in the early and middle forties; at age 60 they were about 12 per cent below the maximum (*ibid.*, p. 265). Several American studies cited by McFarland (*op. cit.*, p. 515) show little or no decline in productivity with advancing years. A study conducted by the Erwin Cotton Mills Company, Dr. Frank T. de Vyner informs the writer, suggested no inverse relationship between age of worker and output of worker.

16 E. F. Denison, "Incomes in Selected Professions," *Survey of Current Business*, XXIV, 1944, p. 16. Unlike the previous study, this inquiry is based upon reported actual earnings, and not upon the earnings that would have been realized had each professional worker been continuously employed in 1941. For the influence of the number of years in practice upon professional income see M. Friedman and S. Kuznets, *Income from Independent Professional Practice*, National Bureau of Economic Research, New York, 1945, pp. 237 ff.

17 Data presented by Dublin and Lotka and Leven suggest this pattern. See L. I. Dublin and A. J. Lotka, *The Money Value of Man*, The Ronald Press Company, New York, rev. ed., 1946, pp. 65, 182; M. Leven, *The Income Structure of the United States*, The Brookings Institution, Washington, 1938, pp. 51–52, 156. See also Table I and note 19 below.

18 Males who are reported as having worked 12 months in 1939 are here described as continuously employed even though some may have been absent from work at times because of sickness, accidents, etc. The figures in Table I relate to *all* males in the labor force. While the earnings of *urban* continuously employed males were slightly higher than earnings of all continuously employed males, the relative values, by age group, were almost identical for both groups; substantially the same holds for *all* males and *urban* males, irrespective of months worked.

19 This index differs appreciably only from the one suggested by the Palmer-Brownell study (see note 15 above) which implies that, since productivity per worker varies little with age, a change in age composition will exercise little influence upon average per worker output. See Dublin and Lotka, *op. cit.*, p. 182, and W. S. Woytinski's estimate of taxable wages per worker by age in *Earnings and Social Security in the United States*, Social Science Research Council, Washington, 1943, pp. 100, 127.

1980, and 2000 approximate 101, 106, and 107. In short, if the age composition of the American population changes in the future along the lines noted above, and other conditions remain substantially unchanged, *output per capita*, together with the capacity of the population to satisfy its wants, will increase somewhat. While the future age composition may not develop quite along the lines here supposed, it is unlikely that it will develop in such wise as to bring about a decline in *output per capita*.

IV. Age and Continuity, or Regularity of Employment

The annual output of a member of the labor force may tend to fall as he advances in age if (a), though he be regularly employed, his being on the job declines because of an increasing proneness to accidents, sickness or absenteeism, and uneconomic job-changing; or if (b), when he is out of work, the ease with which he can find employment diminishes. The evidence indicates that, on the whole, the worker's being on the job is not greatly affected by his age; and that the difficulties which the older worker encounters in finding employment have their origin chiefly in misinformation respecting his capacities and in institutional arrangements which may readily be corrected. The circumstances falling under (a) and (b), respectively, will be treated in order.

(a) **Respecting proneness to accidents and their cost, the** evidence suggests that at worst the older worker is not significantly more expensive than the younger worker. First, the annual number of days of disability per worker imputable to accidents is less than one, with accidents accounting for slightly less than one-tenth of the days lost by persons aged 15–64.[20] Second, although the data respecting the incidence of accident by age do not all yield the same conclusion regarding incidence, they do indicate that incidence does not increase significantly with age. Among male workers both all occupational injuries and injuries disabling for a week or more in-

[20] In 1935–36 accidents caused 9.8 and 7.9 per cent, respectively, of the days of disability per year suffered by persons aged 15–64 and by persons of all ages. The days of disability per person per year attributed, respectively, to accident and to all causes, were, by age: 15–24, 0.51 and 5.1; 35–64, 0.88 and 9.9; over 64, 1.97 and 35.1. Among the members of families on relief the corresponding rates were higher than in the population as a whole: 15–24, 0.65 and 8; 25–64, 1.49 and 20.7; over 64, 2.49 and 58. Accidental injuries, disabling for one week or more, per 1,000 urban males, by age, were: 15–24, 20.9; 25–44, 22.7; 45–64, 27; over 64, 30.4. This class of accidents was not so important, however, constituting only 2.74 per cent of all accidents; only 22.5 per cent of this class of accidents were occupational in origin, the disability thereby caused per person being only 0.19 day. See The National Health Survey: 1935–36, Sickness and Medical Care Series, Bulletin 3, pp. 1–5, Bulletin 9, pp. 2, 8, 12, Washington, 1938.

creased slightly with age.[21] Other studies indicate that for some groups of workers the injuries sustained by older workers are more severe and, for this reason and because the rapidity of the healing process slows down with age, disable them longer than the injuries of younger workers disable the latter, but that the frequency of accidents is lower among older workers.[22]

Data relating to age and illness among workers indicate that the incidence and the adverse effects of illness increase with age, but not enough to justify discrimination against older workers. Moreover, as Dr. Shock observes, "most problems of sickness or absenteeism among older workers can be solved by adequate programs of medical care."[23] Some studies indicate that older workers fall sick less frequently than younger workers, but remain sick longer per case of illness.[24] A study of railroad employees indicates that the number of days of disability per employee per year attributable to sickness and nonindustrial accidents causing eight or more calendar days of disability rises with age.[25] The incidence of chronic diseases, which, when it does not permanently disable a worker, reduces his attendance at work, rises with age.[26] In 1935–36 the annual number of days of disability per person attributable to diseases and impairments (other than accidents) rose from 4.59 in the 15–24 age group through 9.02 in the 25–64 group to 33.13 in the

[21] The number of male workers per 100 found disabled (on the day of inquiry) by all illnesses and injuries including and excluding occupational injuries, respectively, were, by age: 15–24, 1.33 and 1.16; 25–34, 1.54 and 1.34; 35–44, 2.05 and 1.81; 45–54, 2.63 and 2.37; 55–64, 3.48 and 3.18. Among manual workers the rates were slightly higher than among nonmanual workers, and the occupational rates—measured by the difference between two rates referred to—rose slightly more than among nonmanual workers. See D. E. Hailman, "The Prevalence of Disabling Illness Among Male and Female Workers and Housewives," United States Public Health Bulletin No. 260, 1941, pp. 9, 14. The annual frequency of industrial injuries lasting 7–365 days per 1,000 male workers and the number of days of disability per worker per year caused thereby are, respectively, by age: 16–24, 11.6 and 0.52; 25–34, 11.2 and 0.50; 35–44, 11.9 and 0.63; 45–54, 12.1 and 0.68; 55–64, 13.0 and 0.77. The rates are higher among manual than among nonmanual workers. See Joan Klebba, "Industrial Injuries Among the Urban Population," United States Public Health Reports, LVI, 1941, pp. 2380, 2385. Both studies are based upon the National Health Survey, 1935–36.

[22] M. D. Kossoris, "Relation of Age to Industrial Injuries," Monthly Labor Review, LI, 1940, pp. 789–804; D. K. Brundage, "A Ten Year Record of Absences from Work on Account of Sickness and Accident," Public Health Reports, XLII, 1927, pp. 529–550; and McFarland's summary of relevant studies, op. cit., pp. 515–18.

[23] Op. cit., p. 100.

[24] McFarland, op. cit., p. 518; Brundage, op. cit.

[25] Days of disability per employee per year by age are: under 25, 4.3; 25–34, 6.9; 35–44, 9.8; 45–54, 14.2; 55–64, 27.9; 65 and over, 39.1. See W. M. Gafafer, "Frequency of Sickness and Nonindustrial Accidents Causing Disability Lasting 8 Calendar Days or Longer Among 60,000 White Male Railroad Employees, 1930–34, Inclusive," U. S. Public Health Reports, LIII, 1938, p. 561; also "Disabling Sickness Among Industrial Workers With Particular Reference to Time Changes in Duration," American Journal of Public Health, XXXI, 1941, pp. 443–51. Cp. Klebba, op. cit., note 21, above.

[26] National Health Survey, Sickness and Medical Care Series, Bulletin No. 6, pp. 8–9; also D. E. Hailman, "Health Status of Adults in the Productive Ages," U. S. Public Health Reports, LVI, 1941, pp. 2071–87.

over 64 group.[27] Rates among persons on relief, while higher, were nearly of the same pattern as those prevailing in the nonrelief population. While disability rates among workers are lower than disability rates in the unselected population as a whole, disability rates among employed workers rise with age.[28] Labor turnover is more frequent among younger than among older workers, length of employment tending to increase with age, and occupational mobility being greater among workers under 35 than among those who are older.[29] This greater mobility is economically desirable in so far as it serves to maintain a proper balance among occupations, or to enable individual workers to find jobs in which their respective aptitudes are at a maximum comparative advantage. Beyond this mobility is economically disadvantageous, for it increases the overall cost of training employees, sometimes diminishes the work output of the job-changing workers, and usually operates directly and indirectly to increase the volume of temporary unemployment.

Since the data relating to incidence of illness, accidents, and labor turnover do not indicate the older worker to be generally inferior to the younger worker, albeit he may be inferior in some occupations, objections to the employment of older workers on grounds of supposedly greater proneness to accidents, illness, and absenteeism are based upon misinformation and therefore are discriminatory. Consideration of the available evidence will dispell these objections.

(b) Employers may object to the employment of older workers on the ground that their addition to the payroll will augment the cost of compensation and/or group insurance, or that of pension plans in effect. These objections may be founded upon a misunderstanding of the facts.[30] When these objections are founded upon fact, they can be overcome in several ways. Premiums and/or claims may be adjusted to the age status of the older worker in such wise that the expense entailed by his employment is not appreciably in excess of the average or mode per worker. Or equalization funds covering a large number of representative firms and industries may be established under private or under governmental auspices. Member firms would pay

---

[27] Computed from National Health Survey, Sickness and Medical Care Series, Bulletin No. 9, pp. 2, 8. According to an earlier study, the frequency of illness that caused the loss of one or more days from usual activities was lower in the 40–64 than in the 25–39 age group. It suggests also that the incidence of time-costing illness does not become relatively high until in the sixties. See S. D. Collins, "The Incidence and Causes of Illness at Specific Ages," *Milbank Memorial Fund Quarterly*, XIII, 1935, pp. 330–34.

[28] The number disabled by illness per 1,000 employed male workers, by age in 1935–36, is: 15–24, 11.7; 25–44, 15.5; 45–64, 23.8; 65 and over, 47.2. The rates among the unemployed were much higher, and rose with age. See National Health Survey, Sickness and Medical Care Series, Bulletin No. 7, pp. 3–5. Cp. also the rates from Hailman, given in note 21 above.

[29] McFarland, *op. cit.*, p. 515.

[30] The grounds of discrimination against older workers are summarised and scrutinized in the *Final Report* of the New York State Joint Legislative Committee on Discrimination in Employment of the Middle Aged, Legislative Document No. 80, Albany, 1940.

into these funds on the basis of the number of covered workers on their payrolls and would be reimbursed by the funds for payments made in excess of average premiums, etc., on behalf of older workers. Either of these arrangements, or a combination thereof, will free any particular firm of such increases in expense as are entailed by the employment of older workers and the consequent necessity of paying higher insurance, compensation, and related rates.

Employers sometimes object to employing older workers on the ground that they must be paid higher wages (or salaries) than younger workers. The principle underlying this objection is valid in an economy such as ours in which remuneration supposedly is based upon productivity. This objection does not hold under pure competition when, irrespective of a worker's age, his wage equals in value his *net* product; nor does it hold, even though competition is not pure and the worker is paid less than the market value of his *net* product, so long as the absolute rate of exploitation per worker is independent of his age and/or the employer's aggregate exploitational return is not reduced by the hiring of older workers. This objection will hold, of course, if neither the former nor the latter condition is met; but then it can be removed either by introducing pure competition respecting the payment of labor, or by establishing appropriate rates of worker exploitation.[31] The preceding argument holds whether the employer sells his product under conditions of pure or of imperfect competition. In view of what has been said it is evident that a wage or salary structure can always be so adjusted as to place older and younger workers on a par respecting their comparative desirability as employees. As a rule, therefore, the age of a worker is not sufficient, by itself, to affect his employability appreciably.

V. Occupational Balance and the Level of Employment

In this section consideration is given to the functional relation between age composition, on the one hand, and both (1) occupational balance and (2) the level of employment, on the other.

(1) Aggregate and per capita income are conditioned by the manner in which the working population is distributed among occupations and industries. In general, so long as workers (who are willing to transfer) could produce and earn more in other occupations than in the ones in which they are engaged, the transfer of such workers from the occupations where they earn less to the occupations where they can earn more will increase their real income and that of the economy as a whole. The optimum distribution of workers among occupations and, therefore, the ideal occupational balance, have been attained when it is no longer possible for workers, though they be free to change occupations if they wish, to improve their situa-

---

31 If an employer is compelled to pay workers at rates exceeding their respective net products, he will endeavor to minimize this exploitation of himself and his choice of older, or younger, workers will be governed accordingly.

tions by changing occupation or place of work.

An increase in the relative number of older workers such as is in prospect may operate in one or several of three ways to make more difficult the maintenance of an optimum distribution of workers among occupations and places of employment: (a) by reducing the relative number of young workers entering the laboring force for the first time; (b) by acting, in conjunction with a deceleration of population growth or a decrease in population, to slow down the adjustment of the distribution of workers among occupations to the structure of the general demand for labor; and (c) by affecting apprenticeship, seniority, and related rules respecting conditions of employment in such manner as to restrict access to relatively attractive occupations and to reduce productivity-increasing mobility of labor between occupations and places of employment. Of course, if the wage structure is permitted to reflect the *relative* scarcity or abundance of labor in particular occupations or places of employment, circumstances (a), (b), and (c) are not likely to occasion much difficulty.[32]

(a) Although the relative number of young workers entering the labor force will diminish somewhat, this diminution will not by itself greatly intensify the task of properly distributing workers among occupations. Changes in the ratio of the number of persons aged 20–24 to that of persons aged 25–69 may be used to measure changes in the relative number of young workers just entering the labor force. This ratio, 0.167 in 1940, will fall to something like 0.132, 0.119, and 0.116, respectively, by 1960, 1980, and 2000. That is, the number of entrants per 100 persons in the labor force will fall from about 3.3 in 1940 to slightly under 2.4 after 1980.[33] This number, if kept out of relatively contracting occupations and directed into relatively expanding occupations, should suffice to preserve the desired occupational distribution, since a considerable fraction of those under 30 and already in the labor force are able and willing to change employment if such change is actually or potentially advantageous.

(b) But suppose that the increase in the *relative* number of older workers is accompanied by a fall in the schedule of demand for labor in particular occupations. This decrease in absolute demand might be caused either by a decline in the size of the total population, or by a decline in per capita consumption of the particular kind of labor[34] in question. Such a decrease

---

[32] In England in 1938–45 the response of workers to changes in the wage structure indicated a high degree of labor mobility. See J. L. Nicholson, "Earnings, Hours, and Mobility of Labor," *Bulletin* of the Oxford University Institute of Statistics, VIII, May, 1946, pp. 156–57, 160, 163.

[33] According to the Census of 1940 only 1.5 per cent of the number in the labor force were reported as seeking work for the first time.

[34] Aggregate demand at any particular price is the product of two variables, that is, of individual demand multiplied by the number of individuals in the population. Accordingly, aggregate demand will decline if population declines with per capita demand remaining constant, or if per capita demand declines with population remaining constant, or, in general, when a decline in one of the two variables is not offset by an increase in the other. A decrease in population, or a decrease in the rate of population growth, therefore may be accompanied by a decline in absolute demand for given kinds of labor.

in the demand for a particular kind of labor need not occasion particularized unemployment, even though the demand for the labor in question is inelastic.[35] For the forces of mortality and retirement alone rapidly deplete the number of workers attached to an occupation, and their influence is reenforced by the withdrawal of mobile workers in the younger age groups. Suppose the age composition of the workers attached to an occupation is the same as that of the (1945) white female life table population lying between 15 and 64, workers entering the occupation at 15 and leaving at 65. If no recruits are added to this occupation, mortality and retirement will reduce its membership about two per cent per year —10.7 per cent in five years and 21.3 in ten years. A projection based upon English mortality and fertility in the early 1930's indicates that the rate at which mortality and retirement reduce the number of workers attached to an occupation is about three times that at which a total population decreases when the rate of decrease becomes stable at 1 per cent per year. Transfer out of an occupation of those in the mobile age groups will raise appreciably above 2–3 per cent the annual rate at which an occupational group diminishes.[36]

In a population whose size is declining, whose age composition is not stable, and whose average age is rising, one would expect the demand for labor serving the needs of youth to decline appreciably. The demand for elementary school teachers is a case in point. Suppose this demand to be directly proportional to the number of children of elementary school age and therefore to decline at the same rate as the number of children. Even then mortality and retirement will reduce the number of teachers over 1.5 times as fast as the need for teachers declines.[37] It may be concluded that, in general, a decline in the relative number of workers in the lower age groups will not operate directly to make much more difficult the maintenance of a desired occupational balance even though the total population should decline in number.

(c) Occupational imbalance may be intensified if the increase in the relative number of older workers is accompanied by changes in apprenticeship, seniority and related rules which reduce interoccupational mobility or make more difficult the entry of young workers into attractive occupations. The motive for such changes would be the desire of older workers to make their situations more secure against cyclical and other declines in the

---

[35] The demand for any particular kind of labor usually is inelastic, since the outlay for such labor usually constitutes a small fraction of the cost of the finished goods or service into whose composition it enters.

[36] Of the (1945) white female life table population lying between 15 and 64, 21.3 per cent were in the age group 15–24. In the stable English population referred to above, those aged 15–24 constitute 18.3 per cent of the male population aged 15–64 at a time when the total male population is declining 1 per cent per year. See Joseph J. Spengler, "Population Movements, Employment, and Income," *Southern Economic Journal*, V, 1938, Table II, and study by E. Charles, there referred to.

[37] See Joseph J. Spengler, "Population Trends and the Future Demand for Teachers," *Social Forces*, XIX, 1941, Table III.

demand for their services and against efforts of employers to substitute (for whatever reason) younger for older workers.

As the relative number of older workers increases they will probably seek to strengthen seniority and related rules in their favor, for the number of older workers presumably will increase more rapidly than the number of "choice" jobs. Not all jobs are equally attractive. The aspiration to hold a choice job probably tends within limits to increase with age. Relatively more older than younger workers hold choice jobs.[38] Suppose that in 1940 30 per cent of all jobs were "choice," and that one-half of these jobs were held by workers over 44. Then "choice" jobs would be held by 50 in each 100 workers over 44, and by 21 in each 100 below 45. By 1980, however, given the then age composition and the supposition that 30 per cent of the jobs remain "choice," there can be only 43 "choice" jobs for each 100 workers over 44 provided that the 1940 rate of 21 per 100 holds for workers under 45; and there can be only 18.8 for younger workers if the 1940 rate of 50 per 100 holds for older workers. Whence there may be a conflict in interest between younger and older workers, and the latter may seek to guard their situations by strengthening seniority and related rules.

The tendency of older workers to resort to strengthened seniority rules may be eased somewhat provided that approximately full employment persists and that hourly productivity and earnings are not adversely affected by advancing age, or that the relative number of choice jobs increases.

If apprenticeship, seniority, and related rules are diffused and strengthened for the purpose of guarding and improving the relative status of older workers, the adverse effects of these rules will be intensified, an ideal occupational balance will not be realizable, and eventualy a conflict will be precipitated between the older beneficiaries and the younger victims of these rules. The apprenticeship rules will restrict the access of younger workers to relatively expanding and economically attractive occupations and reduce the mobility of workers between occupations and jobs. Seniority and related rules substitute for efficiency-generation competition and reward according to merit a system of status which makes an individual's success and progress depend almost entirely upon his growing older.[39] These rules make for inefficiency and incorrect job allocation;[40] for increased resistance to technological change and welfare-favoring price and wage policies; and probably for an intensification of casual and related forms of unemployment. In general these rules, unless carefully circumscribed, make for the diminution of output per worker and income per

38 Joseph J. Spengler, "Some Effects of Changes in the Age Composition of the Labor Force," *Southern Economic Journal*, VIII, 1941, pp. 166–67.
   39 See Mater, *op. cit.*, pp. 413–18.
   40 *Ibid.*, pp. 176, 196, 201, 402, 408.

capita.[41] It is socially desirable, therefore, that present apprenticeship, seniority, and related rules be modified when they reduce mobility and access to occupations appreciably; and it is essential that legal or other precautions be taken last, under the impact of an increasing number of older workers, these rules be changed in a manner detrimental to the general welfare.

Careful consideration of rules such as those respecting seniority implies a distinction between the correct pricing of labor and the provision of enough income to satisfy needs. Improperly conceived seniority rules tend to overprice the labor of older workers and at the same time force their employment; they thus violate the principle of correct pricing and disadvantage younger workers and/or consumers. When the principle of payment of individual workers according to need is introduced, it can be properly introduced only in the form of a family wage system which takes due account of the principle of correct pricing. In any event the principle of needs cannot be used to bolster a set of seniority rules favoring older workers, for the average number of consumption units per male family head falls steadily after he passes

the 39th year; at age 60 his need is what it was at age 25.[42]

(2) The economic condition of the older worker is dependent in marked degree upon the fullness of employment. When employment is nearly full, most older workers who are really capable of working can find employment. In 1942–46, for example, when unemployment averaged only 2.9 per cent of the civilian labor force and never exceeded 4.7 per cent, the situation of the older worker improved greatly. The male population 55 and over was supplying 870,000 workers in excess of "normal" in 1945.[43] In 1942–45 the number of recipients of old-age assistance declined 218,000 whereas, given prewar conditions, it would have increased about 150,000.[44] This decrease was attributable in part to the fact that aged workers receiving assistance—something like half of whom were involuntarily unemployed—could find remunerative employment. When, on the contrary, employment becomes less than full, older workers along with other workers lose jobs, and older workers lose them at a higher rate when there is prejudice against older workers. Moreover, having lost their jobs, older workers have more trouble than younger workers

---

41 On the effects of apprenticeship, seniority, and related rules, see Mater, *op. cit.*; S. H. Slichter, *Union Policies and Industrial Management*, Brookings Institution, Washington, 1941, chaps. 2, 4–5; Frederick H. Harbison, "Seniority in Mass-Production Industries," *Journal of Political Economy*, XLVIII, 1940, pp. 851–64, and Reports No. 17 (*The Seniority Principle in Union-Management Relations*, 1939) and No. 63 (*Seniority Policies and Procedures as Developed Through Collective Bargaining*, 1941) of the Industrial Relations Section of Princeton University.

42 The number of consumption units per male family head at certain years of age is: 20–21, 1.05; 25–26, 2.06; 30–31, 3.05; 39–40, 3.75; 44–45, 3.42; 50–51, 2.71; 60–61, 2.04. Figures for all years have been computed by Dublin and Lotka, *op. cit.*, p. 175.

43 H. Wool, "Recent Trends in the Labor Force," *Monthly Labor Review*, LXV, 1947, Table 2, p. 641, also p. 638. The number of workers 65 years of age and over was nearly one-fourth above "normal."

44 *Monthly Labor Review*, LXII, 1936, p. 388.

recovering them. In a considerable measure, therefore, the real solution of the older worker's employment problem is to be found in the maintenance of approximately full employment.

The existence of full employment makes it much easier for the older workers to adjust to technological changes which displace workers and render acquired skills obsolete. Retraining, adult education, and related programs are essential.[45] But such programs are not adequate in themselves. There must always be present the opportunity for effective demand for such rehabilitated labor to be generated and sustained with ease.

Full employment presupposes among other things that the annual outlay in the form of consumption and investment (a large part of which is independent of the current rate of consumption and therefore autonomous) is sufficient to provide employment for a very large fraction (say 94–95 per cent) of the labor force. As a rule this means, since investment usually is the prime mover, that employment is full only when the rate of investment is adequate. Private investment and, in some measure, public investment tend to be high when creative and innovating entrepreneurs are relatively numerous, and the rate of invention and technological change is high. In some degree younger entrepreneurs probably are more disposed than older entrepreneurs to innovate, invest, and stimulate investment. Innovation is less likely,

therefore, when corporations and partnerships include an insufficient number of younger policy makers. This insufficiency is more likely to arise in a population of the age composition of 30–40 years from now than in one of the present age composition; and it will tend to be accentuated if the control of economic affairs, already highly concentrated, is centered in even fewer hands than at present. This insufficiency can be guarded against, however, through the establishment of an appropriate rule of thumb. It might be provided, for example, that of a corporation's board of directors, one-third must be under 45, one-third 45–60, and not over one-third above 60.

It has been said that, because of the changes in age composition in prospect, the ratio of "consuming units" to "producing units" in the population will decrease slightly,[46] and that, consequently, the tendency to unemployment will increase unless the anticipated decline in the propensity to consume is offset by an increase in the propensity to invest. This argument is open to doubt and not borne out by data on the propensity to consume in medium and low income families. Consumption does vary somewhat with age. Yet an increase in the income of medium and low income groups—and this includes the vast majority—tends to be accompanied by a corresponding relative increase in consumption. It is not likely, therefore, that the anticipated small decrease in the

---

[45] Ewan Clague, "Employment Problems of the Older Worker," *Monthly Labor Review*, LXV, 1947, pp. 662–63.

[46] For such an estimate see W. S. Thompson and P. K. Whelpton, *Population Trends in the United States*, New York, 1933, p. 169.

ratio of "consuming" to "producing" units will have a significant effect upon the level of employment.

If the analysis presented in this section is valid, it may be concluded that prospective changes in age composition may make somewhat more difficult the maintenance of full employment and proper occupational balance. Yet, since these difficulties are easily surmounted, there is no need to view the change in age composition with apprehension.

VI. Miscellaneous Effects

The prospective changes in age composition will also be accompanied by miscellaneous effects, of which the following are examples. The prolongation of life beyond the retirement age of 65 makes it necessary for the individual to make income provision for a larger number of unproductive years after retirement. In 1945 the expectation of life at age 65 for white males was 12.4 years; it may increase to something like 14.75.[47] Accordingly, should the latter expectation figure replace the former, about 15 per cent more money must be accumulated to buy a given annual annuity income.[48]

A change in age composition affects the structure of the demand for goods and services, for the disposition to use some goods and services varies with age. For example, if changing age composition is the only factor influencing demand between 1940 and 1960, the consumption of goods and services designed primarily for persons under 15 will drop about 2 points while that of goods and services used chiefly by persons over 64 will increase about 2.5 points. These changes in the structure of demand should occasion no difficulties, however. For the age structure changes slowly and in a quite predictable manner, and data can be amassed on the extent to which the consumption of classes of goods and services is affected by the age factor. Moreover, since the number of persons attached to an occupation will usually be reduced at least as rapidly by mortality and retirement as the demand for their services is reduced by secular forces, unemployment attributable to the overcrowding of an occupation by age changes will be rare; and if it does arise, it can be eliminated through the removal of younger mobile workers from the overcrowded to other relatively undermanned occupations.

It is frequently said that the structure of values is undergoing a fundamental modification, with emphasis upon economic change and progress giving way in considerable measure to emphasis upon what is somewhat incorrectly supposed to be economic security and stability.[49] Those making this

---

[47] Based on hypothetical life table in Dublin and Lotka, *op. cit.*, p. 130. Expectation of life at age 65 in the 1937 standard annuity male table is 14.4.

[48] A 3 per cent interest rate is assumed.

[49] For example, O. H. Taylor suggests that the present age is groping its way "to some new arrangement of its ruling hierarchy of ultimate, human ends or values, in which . . . economic progress will no longer as decisively outrank security in the sense of a good measure of stability of valued patterns of life, as it did in the nineteenth century." See "Economic Theory and the Age We Live In," *Review of Economic Statistics*, XXIX, 1947, p. 105. See also K. Polanyi, *The Great Transition*, Rinehart & Company, New York, 1944.

observation usually fail to distinguish between insecurity which makes for happiness and progress and insecurity which is wholly or predominantly bad in effect,[50] or to indicate whether there is increased demand for both good and bad security. The change in age composition may accentuate this modification of value structure, but it cannot be said to have been one of its major causes. For the system of values held by a people is determined by many factors, of which age composition is merely one, and probably not even an important one.

In Brief

1. In Section I the theoretical basis of the relationship between age composition and collective economic behavior is stated.

2. In Section II it is shown that the relative number of workers in the population is not likely to decline because of prospective changes in age composition.

3. In Section III it is shown that although in many occupations output per worker does tend to fall in the later years of the representative worker's productive life, prospective changes in age composition will not make for a decline in output and income per inhabitant.

4. **In Section IV it is shown that although proneness to accident and sickness increases with age, this increase is not highly significant and is offset in part by a diminution in labor turnover.**

5. **In Section IV it is also shown that discrimination against the older worker may be corrected through the diffusion of correct information respecting his capacities and use, and through the modification of those institutional arrangements which are unwarrantedly disadvantageous to older workers.**

6. In Section V it is shown: (a) that the change in age composition need not make more difficult the maintenance of an optimum distribution of workers among occupations; (b) that precautions must be taken lest apprenticeship, seniority, and related rules established under collective bargaining become prejudicial, in an economy in which the relative number of older workers is increasing, to the true interests of younger workers and to the general welfare.

7. In Section V it is also shown that if something like full employment can be maintained, prospective changes in age composition will have little or no adverse effect upon the economic situation of the older worker.

8. In Section VI miscellaneous effects of the prospective change in age composition are considered, and it is shown, among other things, that

---

[50] On this distinction see J. M. Clark, *Social Control of Business*, 2d ed., McGraw-Hill Book Company, New York, 1939, pp. 61–62.

these effects are not or need not be adverse with respect to the situation of the older worker.

9. Should the current desire at the close of the sixtieth year come to be realized by most workers, the aggregate output of goods and services will be appreciably reduced. Two decades hence the order of magnitude of this reduction will be ten per cent.

10. **It is shown in general, in this report, that, while the increase in the relative number of older workers will precipitate certain new problems or aggravate certain old problems, it is easy to cope with this new situation, and its advent is no cause for apprehension.**

UTILIZATION OF HUMAN RESOURCES

THROUGH INDUSTRIALIZATION

By Wilbert E. Moore

THE industrial system is rampant in the modern world. Its effects spread to the most isolated regions in some form or degree. Its system of communications and organization of world markets, and the political power that its productive system makes possible, have produced an interdependence of all peoples everywhere. The process is by no means complete, nor is its final fruition in any particular form determinate and inevitable. Even the results so far effected are not entirely clear or their implications commonly understood. Yet one elementary fact stands out: the isolated primitive or peasant community has everywhere lost part of its insularity. The true primitive represents a small and diminishing species. The self-sufficient peasant is shaken by forces beyond his control and perhaps even further beyond his understanding.

The impact of the industrial system on primitive and archaic cultures is a crude empirical phenomenon. It makes irrelevant or academic much of the well-meaning debate about interfering in other cultures. The question in most areas of the world is not whether change under external influence ought to be allowed, but rather the form and degree of change, the interests taken into account, and the human as well as material costs of transition.

Ironically, the arguments in behalf of sealing off the effects of new productive organizations and processes, in order to preserve as much as possible of traditional values in the far places of the world, arrive approximately at the same policy as that of the most cynical "exploiter," who seeks to use native labor but to keep native societies otherwise outside the industrial system. If the effective utilization of human resources for the achievement of health, longevity, and heightened levels of material well-being be the goal, then education strictly "adapted" to *native* needs, wage labor as purely supplementary to primitive modes of production, and public health measures that do not change fertility patterns represent serious compromises in the short run and mixtures of doubtful stability in the long run.

In the present paper some general comments about the nature of the industrialization process are followed by a discussion of labor mobility as a particular aspect of this process, with some field research evidence on a few points.

The Case for Industrialization

The most general case for industrialization rests upon the range of goods and services made available for human consumption. As a productive system, it tends to free both supply and demand from traditional restraint, and to entail a dynamic rather than a static relation between man and nature.[2]

The particular case for industrialization of primary relevance here rests upon enhanced opportunities, through specialization, for utilizing special qualities and aptitudes of producers. Human beings both constitute necessary means and determine the ends of productive efforts. As means, or, following the title of this session of the Conference, as resources, human beings may be considered as coming within the general case for optimum utilization. The duality of the human role in this scheme complicates the issue, however. Inherent in the nature of human society are limitations to efficiency in the utilization of human resources for production, for in no society can production be the sole social function and in no human being can it be the sole motive. Within those limits, industrialism is that system of production which most effectively uses differences in aptitude and interest.[3]

---

[2] This abbreviated and therefore dogmatic formulation rests upon the abstract characteristics of the industrial mode of production and neglects many concrete problems and variations in experience. For example, differences in systems of control of production and allocation of products, and the problems of "balanced economies" as opposed to regional specialization are not irrelevant in the concrete instance but cannot be explored here. It may be maintained, however, that given certain characteristics of the industrial system—for example, utilization of advanced technology and of specialization of labor—other characteristics are inherent and in considerable measure independent of particular goals and procedures—for example, a reasonably elaborate system of exchange and of effective incentives to insure labor mobility and the development of skills. It follows that the case here does not assume or depend upon the institutional structure of liberal capitalism.

[3] Again, this formulation is abstracted from a host of concrete issues and problems: for example, the extent to which various categories of human laborers as means (or, in some economic formulations as "costs") of production share in determining the ends of production; the "dilution" of skill that accompanies some forms of specialization and the attendant problems of motivation; the multitudinous human problems of mobility and its accompanying uncertainty.

LABOR AS A FACTOR IN INDUSTRIAL DEVELOPMENT

Usual Approaches to Industrialization Theory. Industrialization may be viewed with partial accuracy as a process involving an increasing range of resources exploited, an increasing amount and type of goods produced, and an increasing efficiency of capital and technique employed. From this point of view the process may be studied as a dynamic relationship among certain elements or "factors," which in their combination presumably determine both the pattern and rate of economic development.

To the extent that social scientists have investigated basic economic transformation as distinct from economic relations within fairly established institutional conditions, attention has been turned primarily to questions of capitalization, organization or enterprise, resources, and markets.[4] It may be fairly said that none of these is irrelevant to the analysis of industrialization, but that even in combination they do not comprise an adequate set of directives for research. The demographer will urge the importance of population, the political scientist will call attention to the direct and indirect effects of governmental forms and policies, the sociologist will insist on the relevance of variable social structures, and economists of various persuasions will press for the inclusion of transportation, technology, and financial organization.

It is neither possible nor necessary here to attempt a complete analytical framework for the study of industrialization. It is, however, possibly useful to suggest a rough classification of factors necessarily included in such a framework, and then proceed to a particular and particularly neglected element in the process.

With some modification and amendment, the recent work of Chang on the theory of industrialization[5] may serve as a guide

[4] *See*, for example, Clark, Colin: THE CONDITIONS OF ECONOMIC PROGRESS. London, Macmillan and Co., 1940; League of Nations, Economic, Financial and Transit Department: INDUSTRIALIZATION AND FOREIGN TRADE. Geneva, 1945; Mandelbaum, K.: THE INDUSTRIALISATION OF BACKWARD AREAS. Institute of Statistics, Monograph No. 2, Oxford, Basil Blackwell, 1945; Sombart, Werner: Capitalism, *in* ENCYCLOPAEDIA OF THE SOCIAL SCIENCES, 3: 195–208; Weber, Max: THE PROTESTANT ETHIC AND THE SPIRIT OF CAPITALISM, *trans. by* Talcott Parsons. London, George Allen and Unwin, 1930.

[5] Chang, Pei-kang: AGRICULTURE AND INDUSTRIALIZATION. Cambridge, Harvard University Press, 1949, especially pp. 77–90. The "factors" suggested here differ from Chang's treatment principally by addition. Chang does not deal with capital accumulation, transportation, and markets, and he treats "social institutions" as given.

to the factors strategic to the study of the industrialization process. These may be classified as (1) generating factors— entrepreneurship, technology, and capital accumulation; (2) conditional factors—resources, population, and social institutions; and (3) connecting factors—transportation and markets.

It should be noted that the classification, and even the terminology, is in some degree arbitrary. "Population" and "social institutions," for example, are in combination capable of interpretations in terms sufficiently broad to include both generating and connecting factors. A more important consideration, however, is the dynamic interdependence of these variables, and particularly of those labelled "conditional." If in the beginning of the process of industrialization they may be regarded as conditions, they are not static. Resources are always relative to the prevailing state of the useful arts. Population in its size, composition, and distribution enters the economic system both as the source of labor supply and the consumer of products; it is moreover subject to changes touched off by economic transition that may either foster or impede further changes toward industrialization. Social institutions similarly may be viewed as both barriers to and sources of change. In the study of complex phenomena, simplification is both necessary and hazardous.

It is with the role of social institutions and their attitudinal counterparts that the present discussion is primarily concerned, not only because the focus is on "the utilization of human resources," but also because the institutional and organizational features of societies have been more often assumed as "given" than they have been directly studied by students of the industrialization process. And among the institutional conditions necessary for successful industrialization—for example, particular forms of control of property, conditions of specialization, organization of exchange, and solutions to the problem of political order—it may be appropriate to emphasize the importance of *mobility* of the factors of production and especially of labor.

Even with regard to the geographical location of industry, it is rare that raw materials, sources of power, and available labor are in handy juxtaposition. Moreover, capital must be transferable out of agriculture, commerce, and traditional handicrafts into manufacturing and related activities, and workers must be moved to new places of employment and, more importantly, to new types of employment. If this latter movement is the central feature of "utilization of human resources through industrialization," it is also a major source of difficulty in the process.

Labor Mobility in Theory and Fact. In the studies and theories of economic development, the problems of labor supply have been largely neglected. This neglect has arisen in part from an exclusively quantitative, demographic approach to manpower or "labor force," in part from a naive view of economic motivation.

It is evident that a supply of labor judged to be numerically adequate for industrial expansion on the basis of apparent unemployment and underemployment in agriculture will not answer the problem of labor supply unless that labor is in the right place, possesses appropriate skills, and can be induced to enter new places and types of employment.

The question of "economic motivation" is central to the appraisal of labor mobility. This question has not often been raised with reference to the transition from non-industrial to industrial employments, even with regard to the older industrial economies. Economic theorists and their sociological critics have alike concentrated on the motivation of the capitalist or industrial enterpriser. Wage theory in economics has been more concerned with the demand-price of labor—that is, labor as a cost of production—than with the supply-price of labor—that is, the determinants of the worker's willingness to offer his services.[6] Yet to the extent that the willingness of primitive or peasant to enter industrial employment cannot simply be taken for granted, it is of theoretical and practical importance to examine the question.

There has been some recent interest in this occupational shift, emphasizing the theoretical importance of wage differentials in effecting the transfer. The ability of industry to outbid the agricultural sector of the economy for labors then rests upon the greater productivity of industrial labor (made possible by higher capitalization and efficiencies of scale and organization, and related to the greater elasticity of demand for manufac-

---

[6] *See* Moore, Wilbert E.: Theoretical Aspects of Industrialization, *Social Research*, 15: 277–303, September, 1948; reprinted as an Occasional Paper of the Institute of World Affairs.

tured products) and subsequently also upon the displacement of farm workers through mechanization.[7] Wage differentials, expressed in the labor market, thus become the effective device for securing geographical mobility, movements within the same general sphere of production and level of skill, and the acquisition of new and higher skills required by the industrial system of division of labor.[8]

The efficacy of wage differentials rests upon clear if often implicit institutional and motivational assumptions. Those assumptions may be briefly stated as a flexible competitive system at least with regard to occupational placement, made effective by a mobile, financially acquisitive orientation of the worker.[9] It is the absence of these conditions that characterizes non-industrial societies, and gives rise to questions of the relevance of their general and particular structural features as they relate to the possibilities of industrial development.

On the basis of a fairly detailed review of available evidence on labor recruitment and utilization for modern forms of economic activity in newly developing areas, the critical importance of institutional and attitudinal variables can be maintained.[10] The nature of that evidence may be summarized here by a bare and consciously alliterative classification of relevant

---

[7] See especially Chang, op. cit., pp. 51–57, 176–194; Ahearn, Daniel J., Jr.: THE WAGES OF FARM AND FACTORY LABORERS, 1914–1944. New York, Columbia University Press, 1945, Chap. VIII, Wages, Production, and Productivity; Schultz, Theodore W.: AGRICULTURE IN AN UNSTABLE ECONOMY. Committee for Economic Development Research Study. New York, McGraw-Hill Book Co., 1945, Chap. IV: Distribution of the Labor Force and Earnings, and Chap. IX: Underemployment and the Attendant Low Earnings in Agriculture.

[8] With regard to the acquisition of skills, even the pure theory of wages requires a recognition of frictions and time-lags occasioned by the necessity of training. For a fuller discussion of these problems, including the "theory of correct occupational distribution," see Moore, Wilbert E.: INDUSTRIAL RELATIONS AND THE SOCIAL ORDER. New York, The Macmillan Co., 1946, Chap. XI: The Sources of Labor Supply.

[9] It should be emphasized that these assumptions are not stated as the requirements for an industrial system of division of labor, but only of the requirements for the validity of the theory of wages as *the* effective incentive to mobility. However, the claim on empirical grounds that wages do not constitute an adequate incentive for the recruitment of industrial workers in non-industrial societies would not destroy the validity of the requirements of wages and occupational competition as features of the *industrial* system. Indeed, it may be asserted that competitive occupational placement is essential to a full development of individual capacities and skills in production (whatever the competitive incentives may be) and that wages or some equivalent means of exchange and distribution are an essential counterpart of specialization of productive activities. In turn, neither of these propositions has any necessary implication for the effect of wage *differentials*.

[10] An abbreviated summary of the comparative materials on industrial labor recruitment has been published. See Moore, Wilbert E.: Primitives and Peasants in Industry, *Social Research*, 15: 44–81, March, 1948; reprinted as an Occasional Paper of the Institute of World Affairs. A fully documented review will comprise a major portion of the final report on the research project.

factors: the bane of barriers, the prevalence of pressures, and peculiarities of positive incentives.

Perhaps the most impressive, if scarcely surprising, set of social factors that impinge on economic development are those that constitute barriers to innovation. Among these are: ignorance, whether of the existence of alternatives or of the skills and techniques to make them effective; the loss of security, usually assured in non-industrial societies through established relationships to means of production (especially land) and established patterns of social obligations (especially through kinship structures); dislike of industrial disciplines, particularly those of time and impersonal authority; and preference for customary standards, including bases of prestige and esteem, and for customary types and levels of consumption. The existence of customary as distinct from expanding standards and aspirations is a remarkably common problem in early stages of industrial development, whether in twentieth century Java or eighteenth century England. It gives rise to absenteeism, turnover, and complaints that the workers are irrational. Similarly, nepotism and other particularistic intrusions (including ethnic distinctions upheld by enterprisers themselves) constitute a pervasive problem in the expansion of Western economic patterns.

Accumulated experience indicates that at the start of the industrialization process workers are, in terms of crude physical analogy, more often pushed than pulled into factory or other wage labor. This is again scarcely surprising in view of the prevalent social barriers to mobility. Among the more common and effective pressures several may be indicated: land shortage and the coercion of hunger, which may be accentuated by particular consequences of the outside impact, such as partial dispossession of native populations, mortality control without fertility limitation, displacement of handicraft products by cheap manufactured goods; direct and indirect manpower allocation by superior power, including direct coercion through various devices ranging from slavery to "industrial draft," and indirect coercion through taxation payable only by wage-earned money. Hunger and force constitute effective stimuli to new activities, but only so long as the hunger or the coercive sanctions last, and only for unskilled, gang labor. Whether the devices used to accomplish the initial change may be withdrawn in favor of more positive incentives, on the principle of the "entering wedge," clearly depends on the whole functional complex of factors surrounding the change.

Even positive incentives, whether or not mediated through wages, have many peculiarities as they are applied in predominantly non-industrial economies. Wages, for example, are functionally dependent upon markets where goods and services are available. Those goods and services are themselves likely to be most effective as incentives if they readily fit traditional patterns of consumption. Moreover, the new opportunities are likely to be sought most eagerly by disaffected and dissident elements in the pre-industrial setting. On the other hand, the idea of free and universal mobility by merit is exceptional and seems to have something of an explosive quality as it penetrates traditional social structures.

It goes without saying that each of these generalizations may be stated as predictive principles "other things being equal," but that in the concrete case other things are notably unequal and that a more empirically relevant analysis must take into account the interdependence of analytically separable factors.

It is for this reason that an attempt was made to increase the precision with which the intersecting variables could be analyzed, through a direct field investigation specifically oriented to hypotheses on labor mobility in newly developing areas.

Some Results in Mexico

Because the reports on the recruitment of labor for modern economic enterprise are replete with explanations after the event and notably lacking in quasi-experimental controls regarding allegedly important factors, it was considered appropriate to undertake one direct field investigation in an attempt to clarify detailed relationships. On the other hand, it is clear that the results of any local field study beg many questions relating to major cultural and organizational differences, which can only be approached on the basis of comparative analysis.

Mexico was selected as the general area for the field study for several reasons: (1) political independence and active governmental programs looking to industrial development; (2) the co-existence of modern manufacturing plants and tribal villages, with a "culture," whether Spanish or Indian, substantially different from that of the older industrial countries; (3)

the practical considerations of proximity and availability of trained field workers native to the country and famılar with local conditions.[11]

The investigation was made in the "Zone" of Atlixco in the State of Puebla, where modern textile plants and Indian villages are in close proximity (Fig. 1.). The "Zone" includes the market and small-manufacturing city of Atlixco itself, a city of 17,000 population and the seat of a municipio of 34,000, and thirty surrounding municipios with a population of over 189,-000. Outside of the immediate area of Atlixco, the region is a predominantly agricultural and trading area, with only five other population centers over 4,000 in population.[12]

The data of the investigation consist of:

(1) Completed schedules based on interviews with adults in two villages, the villages themselves selected in order to provide quasi-experimental controls on the basis of uniformities and differences. These schedules represent interviews with 365 persons in San Baltasar Atlimeyaya (Municipio of Tianguismanalco), which had a population of about 1,200 in 1940, and 227 persons in San Juan Huiluco (Municipio of Huaquechula), which had a population of around 600 at the last census.

(2) Completed schedules based on interviews with 500 workers in the large textile factory at Metepec (Municipio of Atlixco) and 100 workers in the small factory of La Concepción in the city of Atlixco.

(3) Descriptive data incident and supplementary to the systematic interviews, including the historical and ecological setting

[11] The field investigation was carried out by the Museo Nacional de Antropología under the general supervision of its Director, Dr. Daniel F. Rubín de la Borbolla. Sr. Ricardo Pozas Atciniega was primarily responsible for the actual work in the villages and factories; he was assisted for a short time by Sr. Juan de Díos Rosales.

Arrangements for the study were made through personal conferences and correspondence. The local area selected for study was determined after preliminary investigation in three possible areas, which in turn were chosen as meeting the general requirement that "Indian" villages should be located within the potential labor market area of one or more factories. Interview schedules and instructions were prepared by the writer, translated and modified by the Mexican researchers in view of their knowledge of local idiom and problems of investigation, and further modified on the basis of pre-testing incident to the final selection of the area for the study.

We believe that the selection of a "native" area for study in strict accordance with the theoretical problem being investigated, and the conduct of the investigation centering around a uniform interview schedule supplemented by the more common descriptions of social organization are rare but appropriate procedures.

[12] The five are, in order of size, Cholula de Rivadabia, 8,400, famous for its numerous churches built on the sites of destroyed Aztec temples; San Martín Texmelucan, 7,600; Izúcar de Matamoros, 7,000; Huejotzingo, 4,900; Metepec, 4,300, a factory town in the municipio of Atlixco and the locale of part of the field investigation. Population figures are based on the Mexican Census of 1940. See Estados Unidos Mexicanos, 6º CENSO DE POBLACIÓN, 1940, PUEBLA. México, D.F., Secretaría de la Economía Nacional, Dirección General de Estadística, 1947.

Fig. 1. "Zone" of Atlixco, with location of important population centers
and the villages of San Baltasar Atlimeyaya and San Juan Huiluco.

of the region and characteristics of social organization in the villages and the factories.

(4) Data derived from the 1940 Census, which provides a
variety of results by local areas and allows comparisons within
the "Zone" and of the area investigated with the rest of the
country.

Space does not permit detailed description of data collected,
procedures of analysis, or presentation of more than a very few
of the results. With regard to the region as a whole, its "mixed"
social character may be seen from a few comparisons with all
of Mexico. There is in the "Zone" of Atlixco a higher proportion of the gainfully occupied population (excluding unpaid
family workers) engaged in "industry" than in Mexico as a

whole—13 per cent as compared with 11. On the other hand, the proportion of population over 6 years of age that is illiterate is higher in the local region than the national average—61 per cent and 55 per cent respectively—and by a combined index of Indian cultural characteristics the area is decidedly more "backward" than the national average.[13]

The two villages studied intensively provide some interesting comparisons. They have common cultural traditions (essentially Aztec), a common Indian language (Nahuatl or Mexicano), and common dependence on agriculture and related activities, partly self-sufficient, partly oriented to the sale and barter market in Atlixco. Each has benefited from the *ejido* (land reform), although unequally, and they are about the same distance from Atlixco (approximately 15 kilometers) and served by a bus line that goes directly to the village on the two market days each week.

The contrasts are, however, also significant. San Baltasar Atlimeyaya is located on the lower slopes of the famous volcano Popocatapetl, and is reached by a narrow, rough, and mountainous road. San Juan Huiluco on the other hand lies scarcely a kilometer from the Pan-American highway, over which there is frequent bus service from the south to Atlixco. Not only is it thus more closely linked to the city, but it lies in close juxtaposition to the Puebla State Agricultural School at Champusco, which occupies the central portion of the old *hacienda* of that name, in the breaking up of which San Juan Huiluco was a major beneficiary in *ejidal* lands.

The soils of the mountain village are poor, although adequately watered by irrigation. The soils of the village in the lowlands are good, and sub-tropical climate permits a wider variety of products. Agricultural specialization and market orientation are evident. Although detailed census data are not available for the two villages, data for the municipios of which each is a part and of which each may be regarded as representative indicates that land ownership by males gainfully oc-

---

[13] Data on industrial employment and literacy are derived from the RESUMEN GENERAL and PUEBLA volumes of the 1940 Mexican Census, previously cited. The index referred to cannot be explained here, except to note that it is based on language (Indian exclusively, bilingualism, Spanish exclusively) and various degrees of adaptation to European-style clothing, cross-classified. The basic data are derived from the 1940 Census. The same data are used in a somewhat different way in an especially valuable book by Whetten, Nathan L.: RURAL MEXICO. Chicago, University of Chicago Press, 1948, pp. 360–369.

cupied in agriculture is higher in the mountainous area than on the plain. By contrast, 48 per cent of those interviewed in Huiluco were members of the *ejido*, whereas only 21 per cent were beneficiaries of the land reform in San Baltasar.

Literacy in the two villages does not differ markedly, either as shown by the census for their respective municipios (where illiteracy is indicated as approximately 70 per cent) or as shown by the direct field investigation (about 60 per cent of those adults without work experience outside their villages). Both villages have public schools and local units of the *sindicato* (union of farmers and beneficiaries of the land reform). On the other hand, the municipio in which San Baltasar is located is remarkably more "Indian" in character than the municipio including San Juan.[14] This is confirmed by the results of the direct interviews, which showed that Nahuatl was the mother tongue of 96 per cent of those interviewed in Baltasar, whereas Spanish was the primary tongue of 51 per cent of those interviewed in San Juan.

By all these tests and a number of others, San Juan Huiluco, the village in the lowlands near the highway, is somewhere midway between the "folk" culture of San Baltasar Atlimeyaya and the "urban" culture of Atlixco, or, better, Puebla or Mexico City.[15] The small predictive value of such unilinear progressions is shown up sharply in the present investigation. It is from the folk community, the relatively isolated and seemingly homogeneous village, that men go out to seek work, many of them continuing to live in the village but not forming part of it along traditional lines. Their lives are bound up with the factory and its affairs at least as much as with the local village. And, contrary to expectation on the basis of experience in other transitional areas of the world, they generally regard the change as permanent, whether desirable or not.

Of the adult males who live in San Baltasar, some 17 per cent work outside the village, and of these 86 per cent are engaged in factory work. In San Juan, only 3 per cent work outside the village, and none is engaged in factory employment.

---

[14] The respective index values (on the basis of 5.0 indicating complete Indianness) are 3.6 and 2.2. See preceding note.

[15] *See* Redfield, Robert: THE FOLK CULTURE OF YUCATAN. Chicago, University of Chicago Press, 1941, especially his concluding chapter (XII), The Folk Culture and Civilization.

By inference from the divergent characteristics of the villages, it is the pressure of poverty and not the degree of approximation to urban ways of life in general that accounts for the marked difference in results.

This inference is given direct confirmation by the fact that well over half of the replies to an "open-ended" question on reasons for seeking factory work emphasized "necessity" in comparison to a little over a third that indicated a preference for factory labor.

Although in a more detailed report it will be possible to show many relationships for which space is not available here, one somewhat oversimplified conclusion may be emphasized: within the traditional order of non-industrial societies the barriers of labor mobility are so substantial that acute sensitivity to minor differences in financial advantage should not be expected. Industrial wages are likely to be "high" only in relation to serious poverty, as the new worker is typically unskilled and cheap labor gives a competitive advantage to enterprises in newly developing areas. At least in the shorter or longer transitional period, the shortage of land and the loss of markets for handicraft products are likely to be as important in motivating the search for new opportunities as are more positive incentives. Education may facilitate the transition and is of crucial importance in completing the process through providing both the aspirations and the technical means for mobility.[16] Hunger and dissolution of ancient ways are also effective sources of change.

One final and tentative comment may be made. Although the proposition so far defies exact proof or disproof on the basis of available data, all indirect evidence is consistent with the view that the Mexican land reform (the *ejido*) was a "conservative" step in its relation to further economic modernization. The visitor without a sense of Mexican history is likely to be impressed with the stability of the Indian communities, many of which appear to be little changed since the pre-Columbian era. However, the fact is that many of the "primitive" patterns of life were re-established as recently as 15 years

[16] In this regard, in San Baltasar a significantly higher proportion of those with outside work experience were literate than those who had always worked within the village (67 per cent as compared with 40 per cent). Unfortunately, however, the question concerning where the individual had learned to read and write was inadequately worded to distinguish between those who had learned to read in primary school as children and those who had learned to read "in school" as adult factory employees under the adult literacy campaign. Education may have been the result as well as the cause of mobility.

ago, and many more since the Mexican Revolution of 1917–1920. It appears at least plausible that the land reforms have, aside from their aims regarding the incorporation of the Indian into the national life, succeeded in accentuating agricultural underemployment and the isolation of the native village from the forces of modern life, good or bad.

Although Mexico is not commonly considered to be over-crowded, it does have substantial unused human resources. If further industrialization is an effective way of utilizing those resources toward improved standards of health and material welfare, pressures as well as incentives would seem to be neces-sary to effect the transition, and measures designed to alleviate pressures without changing traditional patterns (or even re-creating them) are likely to represent a short-sighted policy.

LITERACY AND SOCIAL CHANGE IN

UNDERDEVELOPED COUNTRIES

By Hilda Hertz Golden

ABSTRACT

In this paper some of the implications for social change of a country's educational status as compared with its industrial status are analyzed. Although the data show that literacy is an excellent index of a country's socio-economic development, they show further that countries may be *more* or *less* literate than their industrial development would suggest. The countries that are most deviant in this respect were isolated by the use of regression equations calculated on data for all of the world's countries. Analysis of other data for the deviant countries suggests some of the factors affecting educational *vis-à-vis* industrial progress. Countries which are more advanced educationally than industrially are shown to be making faster economic than social progress, and vice versa.

Literacy affords an excellent index of the level of socio-economic development of a country, for behind the degree of literacy lies the whole institutional structure of a society. Thus, one indication of the differential spread of industrialism through the world is the sharp contrast in literacy between urban-industrial and peasant-agricultural nations. One way of identifying the·world's underdeveloped countries is by singling out the highly illiterate countries—those, let us say, with more than half of their adult population illiterate.

But literacy is more than an index: Literacy skills function significantly in the economic advance of underdeveloped areas. Though not essential to traditional agriculture and its related crafts, literacy is required for urban-industrial occupations. Hence, literate and educated manpower constitutes a necessary asset in the transition from peasant agriculturalism to urban industrialism.

This paper will deal first with the close association between literacy and industrial development, and then with the implications for economic growth of a country's being more advanced educationally than occupationally, or vice versa.

DEFINITION AND MEASUREMENT

Educators have long debated the question of where, on the continuum of educational achievement, to draw the line dividing literacy from illiteracy; they are still far from a unanimous answer. Fortunately, almost any point would do for present purposes, since all that is needed is an accurate *indicator* of educational achievement, not a final definition of literacy. The dividing line used here is the one drawn by most governments, particularly governments of underdeveloped countries, for purposes of census enumeration—the ability to read and write one's name. On this basis literacy rates can be readily calculated, and these rates correlate highly with other indices of educational achievement.[1]

---

[1] The proportion of the population aged 10 years and over that is literate correlates highly with the proportion of the population aged 5 to 14 years that is enrolled in school. The coefficient of correlation, based on data for a third of the world's countries including about 42 per cent of the world's total population, is .92.

TABLE 1. ILLITERACY IN DEVELOPED AND UNDERDEVELOPED COUNTRIES, 1950*

Geographical division	Percentage of illiterates in the population aged 10 and over		
	All countries	Developed countries	Underdeveloped countries
World.....................	47	6	70
North America[1].................	2	2	**
Europe........................	8	3	20
Oceania	11	1	88
U.S.S.R.[2]	11	11	**
South America.................	42	17	51
Middle America[3]...............	48	20	52
Asia..........................	70	2	75
Africa	88	55	91

*Developed countries are those with less than 50 per cent of their economically active males in agricultural pursuits, including hunting, fishing, and forestry; underdeveloped countries are those with 50 per cent or more of their economically active males in these pursuits.
**No country in this category.
[1] U.S.A., Canada, and Alaska.
[2] The U.S.S.R. is a borderline case but has been classed here among the developed countries, since today its agricultural labor force is probably slightly below 50 per cent.
[3] The Central American republics and the islands of the Caribbean.

The data have been taken mostly from national censuses. Because definitions differ slightly from country to country, census data occasionally have had to be adjusted to conform to one definition and to refer to one date—1950.[2] To achieve world coverage, however, other educational statistics have been converted into estimates of literacy rates whenever census data were lacking.[3] Even though the estimates may be quite rough and the census data not strictly comparable, the information is sufficiently accurate to place all countries, except borderline cases, within broad categories and to provide

[2] For an excellent discussion of the criteria of literacy used in census enumeration, see UNESCO, *Progress of Literacy in Various Countries*, Monograph on Fundamental Education, No. VI (Paris: UNESCO, 1953), *passim*.

[3] Whenever statistics are given here for the entire world, they are composed, in part, of estimates. In some cases these are official estimates prepared by the statistical offices of the countries concerned; mostly they have been calculated by the staff of the Population Division of the Bureau of Applied Social Research, Columbia University.

a basis for exploring the problem in a world-wide context.

THE RELATION OF LITERACY AND INDUSTRIALIZATION

If those countries in which 50 per cent or more of the gainfully occupied males are engaged in agriculture are regarded as underdeveloped,[4] we find, as expected, that the underdeveloped countries are highly illiterate, with the striking exception of those in Europe (Table 1). But even the latter are far more illiterate than the industrial nations. Despite exceptions, then, Table 1 demonstrates the close association between the levels of educational achievement and of industrialization.

The application of correlation analysis to the data provides both a measure of the degree of correspondence of the variables and a regression equation

[4] For a rationale of this division, see K. Davis, "Population and the Further Spread of Industrial Society," *Proceedings of the American Philosophical Society*, Vol. 95 (Feb. 13, 1951), p. 8; and K. Davis and H. Hertz, *The Pattern of World Urbanization* (New York: Macmillan, forthcoming).

through which deviant cases can be isolated. Literacy and industrialization in 1950 correlate closely: the coefficient of correlation is .87 when industrialization is measured by the proportion of gainfully occupied males in nonagricultural pursuits, and .84 when measured by per-capita income.[5] The closeness of these relationships is further substantiated by historical data for individual countries. In England and Wales, for example, the growth of literacy has been closely associated with that of industrialism, as is confirmed here by a coefficient of correlation of .98.

Establishing the close interrelation of the diffusion of literacy and industrialization invites speculation on why it should exist: Literacy is not essential in the training for or the practice of traditional agriculture and its related handicraft occupations. These occupations can be learned through apprenticeship, by watching an experienced person, by attempting to imitate him by trial and error. The knowledge required for such work can be stored in a person's memory; the principles can be transmitted verbally as part of the apprenticeship process. Since neither business documents nor accounts need be kept, and since the work requires no blueprints, reading and writing are not essential to everyday life.

When most parents follow these traditional occupations, they feel no strong incentive to send their children to school or to arrange somehow that the children acquire literacy skills; they view with indifferent skepticism the practical benefits to be derived from literacy and education. They are easily discouraged by lack of funds, by long distances from school, by their need for their children's labor.[6] Therefore, unless local governments or outside agents push a program of formal education with unusual vigor or attempt with great persistence to diffuse literacy skills, their prospects of success are slight.

Besides the agriculturalist's apathy toward formal education and his poverty, lack of government funds is an additional obstacle to the diffusion of literacy, since governments of underdeveloped countries cannot provide adequate educational facilities even when they want to. Many impoverished governments, for example, exempt rural children from school attendance because providing school facilities for them is too costly.[7]

In peasant-agricultural countries, literacy begins to diffuse beyond a few traditional occupations (such as the scribe's) and beyond the confines of a literate élite when the society is starting to change in its occupational structure. Since urban-industrial occupations require reading and writing for their acquisition and practice, literacy appears as a skill that leads the individual out of traditional agriculturalism. Education begins to be regarded as a passport from the hard and primitive life of the subsistence farmer to the haven of nonagricultural employment.[8] When parents are no longer employed in traditional agriculture but instead have become unskilled industrial laborers, occupa-

---

[5] The second coefficient of correlation is based on data for only 70 countries, but these include more than 85 per cent of the world's population. See Statistical Office of the United Nations, *National and Per Capita Incomes, Seventy Countries: 1949* (New York: United Nations, 1950).

[6] Cf. United Nations, Department of Social Affairs, *Preliminary Report on the World Social Situation* (New York: United Nations, 1952), pp. 60-98.

[7] UNESCO, *Basic Facts and Figures* (Paris: UNESCO, 1952), pp. 13-17.

[8] For an illuminating discussion of the role of education in Africa, see Nuffield Foundation and Colonial Office, *African Education: A Study of Educational Policy and Practice in Tropical Africa* (Oxford: The University Press, 1953).

tional training of children requires time and skills beyond the power of parents to provide. Parents thus acquire incentives to send their children to school; they acquire some notion of the usefulness of primary education and are less likely to demand their children's services at an early age. They may view education as a channel of mobility from unskilled to skilled occupations, from agriculture to industry. Furthermore, with increasing industrialization governments become more able to provide educational facilities and to enforce school attendance. In brief, the growth and diffusion of literacy in underdeveloped countries is closely tied to the growth and diffusion of an urban-industrial civilization.

LITERACY AS A FACTOR IN SOCIAL CHANGE

Although all underdeveloped countries show a glaring lack of trained manpower, some are far more deficient in this respect than are others at the same stage. The skills of a population are, within limits, subject to manipulation, and a few peasant-agricultural countries have diverted an unusually large share of their means toward the diffusion of literacy, others only a small share. As a result, educational progress when compared with industrial advance may be retarded or advanced. Singling out the deviant countries by using the regression equations mentioned earlier serves a twofold purpose: An analysis of the deviant countries may indicate the factors that account for the differential support of education, and it may also suggest the role of educational achievement in future economic development.

Among the underdeveloped nations, the following are noteworthy for their deviation: [9]

---

[9] Those listed are the major countries in which the actual rate deviates approximately 20 or more percentage points from the expected rate.

More Literate than Industrial

Bulgaria	Panama
Colombia	Philippines
Costa Rica	Poland
Ecuador	Rumania
Finland	Thailand

Less Literate than Industrial

Egypt	Libya
India	Malaya
Indonesia	Nepal
Iran	Union of South
Iraq	Africa

The information available about these countries suggests that two kinds of factors largely account for the retardation or advance of educational vis-à-vis industrial development. The first set of factors are those determining the relative claim that a nation's goals, such as mass literacy or the support of religion or an army, have upon a nation's wealth; second, there are those determining the cost of achieving widespread literacy and education, such as linguistic diversity or the esoteric nature of the literary language.

In a few countries the literate and educated class has been particularly narrow in its interests and pursuits; its learning has been oriented away from the everyday life of the community and toward traditionalism, abstruse religious scholarship, and magic. Conversely, in a few nations the literate élite has conceived of education as a means to increased national strength or national independence; the intelligentsia have taken an interest in scientific and technological knowledge, and their scholarship has received the stimulus of daily necessity and economic need. In Bulgaria prior to independence, for example, wealthy persons conceived it their duty to open and to maintain schools despite the opposition of the Turkish state; the élite of the Arab areas of the Ottoman Empire showed no such interest.[10]

One result of a great emphasis on traditionalism by a small literate class in a generally illiterate population is the tendency of the written language to diverge from the spoken vernacular. This process may go so far that the written language becomes meaningless to the masses. If the educated class extols the virtues of the "classical" language instead of working toward reducing the vernacular to writing and toward simplifying the script, there is no chance for widespread diffusion of literacy.[11]

In addition, the great diversity of languages and scripts in some of the world's underdeveloped nations compounds the cost of achieving widespread literacy. Africa south of the Sahara is "a vast mosaic of vernacular languages, spoken by groups ranging in size from a few hundreds to several millions of persons," and this is one of the major difficulties encountered in the diffusion of literacy.[12] Furthermore, the controversy over the medium of instruction, so endemic to the efforts to diffuse literacy and education, is an ample tribute to the magnitude of the problem of linguistic diversity.

In brief, the diffusion of literacy and education in a country beyond the comparable point of economic development, or the retardation behind that point, derives from the factors just mentioned—and perhaps others. Next comes the question of the significance of such retardation or advance for future economic development.

The modernization of peasant-agricultural countries is usually conceived of as a moving equilibrium in which no one element can be for very long out of line with the others, because they are functionally interdependent. On this basis we would expect that countries in which educational retardation is considerable and has lasted for some time would now be making relatively greater headway educationally than economically. Conversely, countries in which the advance is considerable and has lasted for some time should now be making relatively greater progress economically than educationally. Despite the paucity of information, it can be shown that this is true for many countries.

Since about 1900, India has exhibited faster educational than economic progress. It has slowly narrowed the gap created by the more rapid economic development of the nineteenth century, although in 1951 the difference had not yet disappeared (Table 2).[13] Again, in nineteenth-century Egypt, economic development, though spasmodic, took place faster than educational change.[14] During the first three decades of this century, both industrial and educational advances were slight. Since about 1930, educational progress has been faster than economic development, despite the fact that during the period of World War II economic change was rapid. Egypt seems to have entered the phase in which for some time educational advance will remain faster than economic development. The examples of Egypt and India suggest that in countries like them educational progress is likely to accelerate.

---

[10] William F. Russell, *Schools in Bulgaria* (New York: Teachers College, Columbia University, 1924), pp. 7-11; Alfred Bonné, *State and Economics in the Middle East* (London: Kegan Paul, Trench, Trubner, 1948), pp. 46-48.

[11] Frank C. Laubach, *The Silent Million Speak* (New York: Friendship Press, 1943), p. 92.

[12] United Nations Department of Social Affairs, *op. cit.*, pp. 76-78.

[13] Kingsley Davis, "Social and Demographic Aspects of Economic Development in India," to be published soon as part of a symposium sponsored by the Social Science Research Council.

[14] Bonné, *op. cit.*, p. 238.

TABLE 2. ACTUAL AND EXPECTED DECLINE
IN ILLITERACY IN SELECTED COUNTRIES

Country and year	Percentage of illiterates in the population aged 10 and over		Difference (Actual percentage minus expected)
	Actual	Expected[1]	
India: [2]			
1911......	93	64	29
1921......	92	65	27
1931......	91	64	27
1941......	85	67	18
1951......	80	61	19
Egypt:			
1907......	93	67	26
1917......	91	62	29
1927......	86	56	30
1937......	85	61	24
1947......	[3]75	51	24
U.S.S.R.:			
1926......	49	80	−31
1939......	19	39	−20
Brazil:			
1940......	57	61	− 4
1950......	52	52	0
U.S.A.:			
1870......	20	37	−17
1910......	7	5	2

[1] By means of the regression equation, the expected percentages were calculated from the percentages of economically active males engaged in agricultural pursuits in each country (see text).
[2] Data on India's agricultural labor force have been taken from Kingsley Davis, "Social and Demographic Aspects of Economic Development in India," to be published soon as part of a symposium sponsored by the Social Science Research Council.
[3] Estimate.

Among the underdeveloped countries that are more literate than industrial, there are none for which we have as adequate information as we have for India and Egypt. Nevertheless, the scanty information that is available corroborates the contention. For example, Brazil, which in 1950 had a level of literacy commensurate with its level of industrialization, achieved this condition after a decade of considerably more rapid economic than educational progress. Similarly, Puerto Rico's rapid economic expansion began when educational advance had caught up with economic development. Today, Puerto Rico is more literate than industrial—

its actual illiteracy rate is 24 per cent, whereas the expected rate is 32 per cent—and it is also making rapid economic progress. Unfortunately, there is little information available on the Balkan countries; but what there is suggests that they are repeating the pattern characteristic of the U.S.S.R. between 1926 and 1939 and of the U.S.A. between 1870 and 1910 (Table 2).

The differential rates of economic advance for the educationally retarded and the educationally advanced countries point to the importance of the dissemination of literacy and education in the transformation of peasant-agricultural nations into urban-industrial nations. In the "bootstrap" operation in which all underdeveloped countries are engaged, training the population for urban-industrial occupations is crucial to the achievement of higher levels of industrialization. Clearly the countries that today are ahead educationally will find it easier to achieve this goal than those that are behind. The latter countries will find their lack of literate and trained manpower a major obstacle to rapid industrialization. Paradoxically, they will need to spend a great share of their wealth, even though they have almost none, for the long-neglected goal of mass education before they can aspire to become modern industrial states.

CONCLUSION

The purpose of this paper has been to show not only that literacy is an index of socio-economic development but also that it functions significantly in the transformation of underdeveloped countries into modern urban-industrial nations. Because literacy and education stand in a mutually dependent relationship with other aspects of modernization, the underdeveloped countries' low levels of literacy indicate the long road that they still have to travel to reach their goals, whether these be high standards of living, high per-capita productivity, or national power.

To reach these goals, underdeveloped countries must choose where to apply most efficiently their limited means and resources. Caught unequipped in a world-wide competition for national power and economic strength, the governments of underdeveloped countries must perforce ponder the interdependence of the elements in the process of modernization. As we have seen, advances in education beyond the point of industrial progress constitute an advantage in this transformation. In choosing among conflicting demands, the governments of underdeveloped countries need to evaluate their present status in a world context along each of the modernization dimensions. If the analysis is accurate, countries behind educationally will gain the most by a judicious application of resources to education; those that are ahead educationally can afford to concentrate their efforts on economic advance.

THE SIZE AND QUALITY OF FUTURE SCHOOL

AND COLLEGE ENROLLMENTS

By Dael Wolfle

This paper can be summarized in a sentence: enrollment has already started to increase in secondary schools and has or soon will in colleges, but the intellectual quality of the students will remain about as it is now.

In studying the supply of boys and girls who have the potentiality for becoming scientists, humanists, professional men and women, or specialists in other fields for which college work provides a normal preparation, my colleagues and I have investigated past enrollment trends, have projected those trends into future years (4), and have studied the intellectual caliber of the students who progress to different educational levels. Those studies led to the summarizing sentence with which this paper began.

Two factors determine the absolute size of school enrollment. One is the number of boys and girls of appropriate age. The other consists of the social forces which determine the percentage of those boys and girls who choose to attend school instead of doing something else. The population of school age increased fairly steadily for many decades and then fell off, following the declining birth rates of the Twenties and Thirties. Around 1940 the number of births started to increase and then went up very sharply after the end of World War II and has continued high ever since. In fact it seems probable that 1952 will see the largest baby crop in our history.

When these wartime and postwar babies grow old enough to attend school, enrollment figures are bound to start climbing. But over and above the larger population of school age youngsters is the longtime trend for larger and larger percentages of them to go to high school and to go to college. At the high school ages the percentage of boys and girls who were actually in high school increased from 32 per cent in 1920 to 73 per cent in 1940. In round numbers, in 1920 one-third of the 14 to 17 year old age group was in high school; in 1930, half were in high school; and in 1940, three-fourths were there. Those twenty years from 1920 to 1940 covered the period of most rapid increase in high school enrollment and set a rate which obviously could not be long maintained. But while the rate must necessarily slow down, we believe that the percentage in high school will continue to increase. As a basis for projecting future enrollments we have assumed that the average annual percentage increase since 1940 might be about a third as great as the rate during the preceding twenty years. When we apply this percentage increase to the increasing number of boys and girls in the 14 through 17 age bracket we project a total secondary school enrollment going up from 6,780,000 last year to about 9,800,000 in 1959-60, and then continuing to climb to around 12,900,000 in 1965-66.

Perhaps these projections are not sufficiently conservative. Perhaps we have reached a point where the percentage of boys and girls who attend high school will no longer increase. Even if that be true—and I do not believe it—the number enrolled in secondary schools will inevitably go up, for the high schools will soon begin to feel the impact of the increased birth rates of the early Forties and after 1960 will feel the much greater impact of the even higher birth rates of the years since World War II came to an end. I think it highly probable that a dozen years from now the nation's secondary schools will have to accommodate close to twice as many pupils as they now enroll.

College enrollment, like high school enrollment, is a function of the total number of young men and women of appropriate ages and the percentage of those young people who go to college. The first factor, the total number in the college age range, will follow the same time pattern as the one already outlined for high school age youngsters. But colleges naturally will not feel the effect until four years after it becomes apparent in high school enrollments. Right now there are fewer 18 year olds than we have had for some years in the past and many fewer than we will have when the war babies and the postwar babies reach the age of 18. On the basis of the population factor alone, therefore, we can expect college enrollments to drop for a few years and then to begin to climb, at first slowly and then more and more rapidly, with the greatest increases commencing about 1965.

Superimposed on the drop of the next few years is the fact that the veterans of World War II who took advantage of the GI bill are now almost through with their college training. These two factors combined predict an immediate drop in college enrollment and a drop in the number of graduates. In 1950, the peak year, 434,000 students received bachelor's and first professional degrees; the number fell to 325,000 in 1952 and will keep on going down until about 1955 when we expect it to reach a low point of around 272,000.

After 1955 the curve will start up again. We think that it will go up more rapidly than the size of the college-age population alone would indicate. For just as more and more children have been going through high school, so more and more are going through college. Expressed as a percentage of the number of people reaching the age of 22 in a year, the number of college graduates has been increasing by about 3 percentage points a decade. We expect this trend to continue for a while longer. There are not yet any signs of its slackening and freshmen enrollments for the past several years indicate an upward trend. This year's freshmen, for example, are about 14 per cent more numerous than last year's. The educational aspirations which a family has for its children are in part determined by the level of the parents' education. As larger and larger numbers of children come from homes in which the parents have been to college, larger and larger numbers of those children will be expected to go to college.

Consequently, in projecting future college classes we have assumed a continually rising percentage of young men and women graduating from college as well as the rising total population of college age. After the low point is reached about 1955, graduating classes will increase in size to approximately 326,000 in 1960, 454,000 in 1965, and 591,000 in 1970. If you do not believe that the percentage graduating from college will go up as rapidly as we have assumed, you may reduce all of these figures by whatever factor seems to be more reasonable. But even if there is no further increase in the percentage graduating from college, the 1970 class will be about as large as the 1950 class when GI graduates were at their peak.

I have been talking about college graduates rather than total college enrollment because our principal interests have led us to concentrate on the number of people finishing college. But rough estimates of total enrollment are presented in Figure 1. The two curves of that figure indicate what secondary school and college administrators have to anticipate. They must provide teachers, books, classrooms, laboratories, sometimes housing, and other facilities for enrollments which will climb very sharply. Fortunately there will be a few years of grace before the secondary schools are deluged, and four more years of grace for the colleges. But in those years the secondary schools, which have not experienced much growth in recent years, must prepare for a tremendous expansion. The colleges, which can easily remember how much their facilities were stretched when the veterans flocked back to the campus a few years ago, have a little longer time in which to get ready. Even so, they must expand their facilities within the next ten or a dozen years or expect to be more severely strained by the normal growth of the following decade than they were by the GI wave at its maximum.

So much for the size of prospective enrollments. We are also interested in the intellectual quality of future students. We have

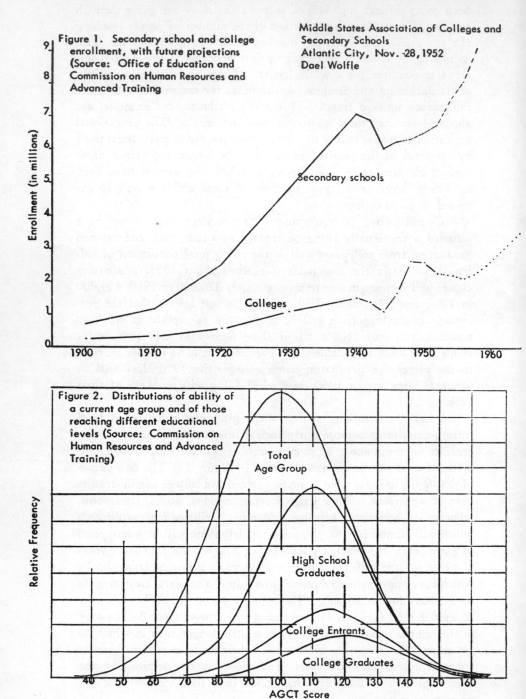

Figure 1. Secondary school and college enrollment, with future projections (Source: Office of Education and Commission on Human Resources and Advanced Training

Middle States Association of Colleges and Secondary Schools
Atlantic City, Nov. 28, 1952
Dael Wolfle

Figure 2. Distributions of ability of a current age group and of those reaching different educational levels (Source: Commission on Human Resources and Advanced Training)

recently completed several studies which fit together to give an up-to-date estimate of the distribution of ability of students who progress to different educational levels. Several of the resulting curves are shown in Figure 2. The curve for the total population is drawn as a normal bell-shaped curve on the baseline used for reporting scores on the Army General Classification Test of World War II. On that scale the average person in an age group, for example all of the people reaching the age of 18 this year, is 100. The standard deviation of the scores for the total population is 20.

The other curves show the successively stricter selection which takes place as one goes up the educational ladder. High school graduates average 110, college entrants 115, and college graduates 121. All four curves are drawn to the same scale so that the size of each indicates the proportion of the total age group which reaches that educational level. Currently 56 per cent finish high school; 20 per cent enter college; and 12 per cent graduate from college.

These curves can be taken as descriptive of the intellectual quality of current student populations for the nation as a whole. It then becomes an interesting problem to try to predict how the larger enrollments of the future will compare with today's students. As a background for such a prediction we can examine several comparisons of current students with those of earlier years. Finch now at the U. of Ill. (3) administered a standard test of academic aptitude to all of the students enrolled in two midwestern high schools. He found both the average scores and the variability of scores to be almost identical with the ones which had been obtained when the same test was administered to all of the students enrolled in the same high schools fifteen years earlier. A much larger percentage of the high school age youngsters were in school at the time of the second testing, but the larger percentage did not result in a lowering of average quality.

Here is another comparison. Some years ago a general intelligence test was given to all of the sixth grade children in a group of Minnesota grade schools. A number of years later Viola Benson (1) tracked down all but a comparatively small number of those former sixth graders to find out how far each had progressed in school. She found—as one would expect—that the brighter the children were the more likely were they to graduate from high school, to enter college, or to graduate from college. When we compared Miss Benson's data with our own more recent studies we found that at all intelligence levels the probability of graduating from high school or of graduating from college had increased, and that the increase was about the same at all intellectual levels.

Here is a slightly different type of comparison. It is generally known that the children of men in professional occupations are more likely to go to college than are the children of farmers, clerks, or laborers. Ralph Berdie (2) recently investigated the post high school plans of pupils who graduated from Minnesota high schools. Among the findings is the fact that pupils bright enough to be included in the top ten per cent of graduating seniors were a little more likely to enter college now than they were in 1938. Moreover the increase in probability of college attendance was approximately the same for the children of professional men as it was for the children of clerks and skilled tradesmen.

These are three examples of studies which suggest that at least during the past two decades the great increases in enrollment have not been accompanied by a lowering of intellectual quality. Whether the same statement could be made if we went back fifty or a hundred years I do not know. I do not even know of any data which would give an anwser over such a long time span.

We can now take up the question of the ability distribution of future students. From Figure 2 it can be seen that at the high school level nearly all of the brighter youngsters already graduate from high school. Further sizeable increases in high school enrollment must of necessity come from the middle and lower ranges of the ability distribution. As such increases occur we will approach a statistical limit, for if every child finished high school the average score of high school graduates would obviously have to be the same as the average score of the entire age group. But that does not necessarily mean a lowering of academic ability. A person's score on a test of academic aptitude is partly a function of the qualities inherited from his parents. But partly it is determined by the kind and amount of previous formal and informal education he has received. If we provide better education to larger numbers of boys and girls they will make higher scores on tests of academic aptitude. We cannot make them into geniuses by giving them good instruction, but we can make them into useful and competent workers in a variety of fields. As the percentage graduating from high school approaches 100, the average score of high school graduates must gradually move down toward the average of the population as a whole. But there is room for a considerably increased enrollment before that limit is reached, and even then better education may make the average high school graduate of 1970 as competent as the average graduate of today.

When we turn to college graduates the picture is different. Where 56 per cent of all 18 year olds graduate from high school, only 12 per cent of all 22 year olds graduate from college. That 12 per cent is spread over the entire upper half of the ability distribution and, in fact, dips down into the lower half. But at no ability level except the very highest is the probability of graduating from college close to unity.   If we take the ability of the average college graduate of today as a point of reference, this seems to be the situation: of high school graduates who are as bright as or brighter than the average college graduate, about 40 per cent earn college degrees, about 20 per cent start to college but do not finish, and about 40 per cent never enter college.   Clearly there is room for a very large expansion of college enrollment without reducing the average ability of college graduates.

In conclusion let me explain that the predictions I have been making should be interpreted as projections of what we believe to be the trends of the past and the present.   It is possible that we have not correctly interpreted those trends.   In that case our projections will gradually get farther and farther out of line with actual events. Moreover, another world war, a generous federal scholarship program, major economic changes, or other factors of comparable influence could alter these forecasts materially.   Many of the precise figures may turn out to be in error.   It would be greatly surprising if they are not.   But the underlying trends seem to be so clear and consistent that they offer guide lines for educational planning: High school enrollment is already increasing and college enrollment will soon turn upward again.   The increases will be fairly small for a few years, but then will gather speed and go up with a rush.   The prospective enrollment increases are not likely to produce a very large lowering of the quality of secondary school students and need not produce any lowering of the quality of college students.

A STATEMENT OF GENERAL PRINCIPLES AND

CONCEPTS OF POPULATION GENETICS

By Laurence H. Snyder

THE first half of the present century has witnessed the extensive development of the principles of genetics. The formulation of these principles was brought about largely through careful laboratory analyses. Only recently has careful attention been given to the study of human genetics. As that study has progressed, it has become apparent that there are important differences between the genetic analysis of human populations and the genetic analysis of laboratory animals.

The laboratory study is *experimental;* that is to say, the matings are controlled in a uniform environment and made according to a definite plan in the mind of the experimenter: a plan designed to test the genetic nature of a trait by specifying the mating so that observable Mendelian ratios may result. Through examination of these ratios, the genetic basis for a trait may be estimated.

Human matings, on the other hand, occur largely at random as far as most gene pairs are concerned, and the number of offspring in a single family is small. It is thus difficult to specify the *genotype* of each individual. Collections of families must therefore be classified largely by *phenotypic* characters. The result is that even the best classified data will contain mixtures of different types of mating.

All the types of mating which the geneticist needs to analyze a trait are probably present in any considerable population of people, but they are largely incapable of being accurately sorted out. Under such circumstances, involving large populations breeding more or less at random, it becomes necessary to invoke certain concepts which need not ordinarily be considered in laboratory analyses. These concepts are the proportions in the population of a gene and its alleles (alternative conditions), and the proportions of the genotypes formed by a gene and its alleles. Thus the genetic analysis must be made, not on the basis of Mendelian ratios, but on the basis of population ratios. In other words, the study of human genetics is largely a study of population genetics.

The concepts of population genetics may be formulated as principles. Some of these principles are germane to this round-table discussion.

1. Classical Mendelian ratios are not to be expected in random samples from a free-breeding population, nor even necessarily among the offspring of a group of families classified together because the parents in any one family are phenotypically identical with the parents in any other family. Classical Mendelian ratios are to be looked for only among the offspring of a large family, or within a collection of families where the parents in any one family are *genotypically* identical with the parents in any other family.

2. Although classical Mendelian ratios are not to be expected among the offspring in a collection of families where the parents are of variable genotypes, even though of identical phenotypes, nevertheless predictable ratios do occur under such situations. These ratios are *population ratios,* in contrast to Mendelian ratios. They are expressed in terms of the proportions in the population of the genes concerned, and they vary as these proportions vary. Thus, where a common Mendelian ratio is, for example, $\frac{3}{4}:\frac{1}{4}$, an equally common and analogous population ratio is $\frac{1+2q}{(1+q)^2}:\frac{q^2}{(1+q)^2}$, where q is the proportion of the recessive gene in the population.

3. A demonstrated correlation between the occurrence of two traits in a randomly breeding population does not necessarily indicate linkage between the genes for these two traits.

4. In a large population, with the effects of mutation, selection and migration negligible or balancing each other, the proportions of the alleles of any set will remain constant from generation to generation. Furthermore, under a system of random mating, the proportions of the genotypes will likewise remain constant. This means that in a large human population, with no appreciable effects of mutation, selection, or migration, the frequency of a hereditary trait will remain constant from generation to generation.

5. The respective proportions of the alleles of a set may, however, be changed by any one of the above phenomena (mutation, selection, and migration), and, particularly in small populations,

by still another process, random drift of gene proportions. Under selection would be included differential fertility.

6. Differential fertility will change the respective proportions of the alleles of any set, and thus presumably the proportions of the traits determined by these genes, provided that

a. The groups having differential fertility differ one from the other in regard to the occurrence of the trait, and

b. The trait concerned is dependent, at least to some appreciable extent, upon genetic factors.

7. Assortative mating in regard to the trait will increase the rate of the effect of differential fertility.

8. Dominant genes can readily be eliminated by complete selection against them, or partially eliminated in proportion to the degree that selection is used (for example, the degree of differential fertility).

9. Recessive genes can never be completely eliminated by differential fertility, even if selection against them is complete. The proportions of such genes can, however, be reduced by differential fertility.

10. Selection against *common* recessive traits is markedly effective at first, less and less so as the genes for the trait become rarer. This effect may be exactly specified. If, under a system of random mating, a recessive trait occurs in 17.2 per cent or more of the population, the trait can be cut to one half of its former frequency or less in a single generation of complete selection against it. Expressed in another way, the half life, under complete adverse selection, of a recessive trait occurring in 17.2 per cent of a randomly breeding population, is one generation. Under similar circumstances, the half life of a recessive trait occurring in four per cent of the population is two generations; that of a recessive trait occurring in two per cent of the population is three generations; and that of a recessive trait occurring in but one per cent of the population is four generations.

As a trait due to a recessive gene becomes rarer, its half life becomes longer.

Differential fertility implies that adverse selection is not complete, hence the half life of a trait in such circumstances becomes correspondingly longer.

The essential things to be established in order to specify the genetic implications of differential fertility are, then, these:

1. Does differential fertility actually exist between certain groups? If so, what is the extent of the differential fertility?

FREQUENCY OF A RECESSIVE TRAIT IN THE POPULATION

Generations of Complete Adverse Selection	.990	.900	.800	.700	.600	.500	.400	.300	.200	.100	.050	.040	.030	.020	.010	.005
0	.990	.900	.800	.700	.600	.500	.400	.300	.200	.100	.050	.040	.030	.020	.010	.005
1	.249	.237	.223	.208	.191	.172	.150+	.125+	.095+	.058	.033	.028	.022	.015+	.008	.004
2	.111	.107	.103	.098	.092	.086	.078	.068	.056	.038	.024	.020	.017	.012	.007	.004
3	.062	.061	.059	.057	.054	.051	.048	.043	.036	.026	.018	.016	.013	.010	.006	.003
4	.040	.039	.038	.037	.036	.034	.032	.029	.026	.019	.014	.012	.010	.008	.005+	.003
5	.028	.027	.027	.026	.025+	.024	.023	.021	.019	.015+	.011	.010	.009	.007	.004	.003
6	.020	.020	.020	.019	.019	.018	.017	.016	.015-	.012	.009	.008	.007	.006	.004	.002
7	.016	.015+	.015+	.015-	.015-	.014	.014	.013	.012	.010	.008	.007	.006	.005+	.003	.002
8	.012	.012	.012	.012	.012	.011	.011	.010	.010	.008	.006	.006	.005+	.004	.003	.002
9	.011	.010	.010	.010	.009	.009	.009	.009	.008	.007	.006	.005+	.005-	.004	.003	.002
10	.008	.008	.008	.008	.008	.008	.007	.007	.007	.006	.005-	.005-	.004	.003	.002	.002
11	.006	.007	.007	.006	.007	.006	.006	.006	.006	.005-	.004	.004	.004	.003	.002	.001
12	.005	.006	.006	.006	.006	.006	.005+	.005-	.005-	.004	.004	.003	.003	.002	.002	
13	.004	.005	.005-	.005-	.005-	.005-	.005-	.005-	.004	.004	.003	.003	.003	.002	.002	
14	.004	.004	.004	.004	.004	.004	.004	.004	.004	.003	.003	.003	.002	.002	.001	
15	.003	.004	.004	.004	.004	.004	.004	.004	.003	.003	.003	.002	.002	.002		
16	.003	.003	.003	.003	.003	.003	.003	.003	.003	.003	.002	.002	.002	.002		
17	.003	.003	.003	.003	.003	.003	.003	.003	.003	.002	.002	.002	.002	.002		
18	.002	.003	.002	.002	.002	.002	.002	.002	.002	.002	.002	.002	.002	.001		
19	.002	.002	.002	.002	.002	.002	.002	.002	.002	.002	.002	.002	.001			
20	.002	.002	.002	.002	.002	.002	.002	.002	.002	.002	.002	.001				
21	.002	.002	.002	.002	.002	.002	.002	.002	.002	.002	.001					
22	.002	.002	.002	.002	.002	.002	.002	.002	.002	.001						
23	.002	.002	.002	.002	.002	.002	.001	.001	.001							
24	.001	.001	.001	.001	.001	.001										
25																

2. Do these groups actually differ in regard to the proportions of a specific trait? If so, what are the respective proportions of the trait in the various groups?

3. Is the trait genetically determined? If so, what is the mode of transmission?

4. Does assortative mating occur in regard to the trait? If so, what is the nature and extent of the assortative mating?

Given the answers to these questions, the geneticist can specify the expected genetic results of differential fertility.

Assume a large population breeding at random, and being in equilibrium for a pair of alleles A and a, where p is the proportion of A and q is the proportion of a. The genotypes in the population will occur in the equilibrium ratio $p^2AA + 2pq\,Aa + q^2aa = 1$. Further assume the instituting of complete selection against the genotype aa. The proportion of aa individuals produced in the next generation will then be $q^2/(1 + q)^2$. These individuals will, of course, be produced entirely from matings of heterozygotes Aa (Snyder 1934).

Table 1 shows the effect of complete selection against the recessive phenotype starting with various proportions in the original generation.

Where selection against the recessive phenotype is not complete, such as in differential fertility, the calculation of the diminishing proportions of recessives is more complex. Haldane (1931) has presented a formula for these calculations as follows:

$$n = 1/k(u_n - u_o - \log_e u_n/u_o)$$

where

n = number of generations required to change the value of u from u_o to u_n;

u = ratio of the frequency of a given dominant gene to its recessive allele;

k = coefficient of selection against the recessive phenotype. If k, for example, is 0.01, the proportion of offspring from dominant and recessive parents, respectively, will be 1:0.99 instead of 1:1.

Haldane's formula may also be written in terms of the more usual gene proportions p and q, as follows (David, personal communication):

$$n = 1/k[1/q_n - 1/q_o + \log_e(p_n/q_n) - \log_e(p_o/q_o)]$$

Selection is extremely slow, but nevertheless effective, even with low values of k. The greater the initial proportion of the recessive phenotype, the more rapidly will selection reduce this proportion in the early generations. The rate of reduction becomes less as the proportion diminishes. With a selection coefficient of 0.01, it would require 1,090 generations to reduce an initial recessive phenotype proportion of 0.9999 to 0.25, but 1,020 generations to reduce it from 0.25 to 0.01.

References

David, P. R.: Unpublished material (personal communication).

Haldane, J. B. S.: THE CAUSES OF EVOLUTION. New York and London, Harper & Bros., 1931.

Snyder, L. H.: A Table to Determine the Proportion of Recessives to be Expected in Various Matings Involving a Unit Character. *Genetics*, 1934, 19: 1-17.

Snyder, L. H.: The Principles of Gene Distribution in Human Populations. *Yale Journal of Biology and Medicine*.

PRESENT KNOWLEDGE CONCERNING THE

EFFECTS OF DIFFERENTIAL FERTILITY

By Harold F. Dorn

IFFERENTIAL rates of reproduction of separate
population groups is not a new phenomenon. Although
accurate statistics permitting measurement of existing
differences in fertility of various groups in the population are
of relatively recent origin, and even now are available only for
a small part of the world's population, nevertheless there is
sufficient historical evidence to support the belief that differential fertility is as old as the human race. Only one example will
be cited here:

About 1650, the population of Europe numbered approximately 100,000,000 and constituted 18 per cent of the estimated total population of the world. In the following three
centuries these people multiplied in number more than seven
times so that by 1933 their descendants had increased to
720,000,000 and their proportion of the total population of the
world had risen from 18 to 35 per cent (1). The people of
Western Europe and North America have passed their peak
of rapid population increase and now are reproducing at a lower
rate than many other large population groups so that they will,
in time, comprise a smaller proportion of the world's population.

Thirty years ago the differential rate of growth of national
population groups was a subject of much discussion. In recent
years however, demographers have devoted more attention to
differential reproduction rates of segments of the population
within national groups, so that today the term differential fertility is usually understood as implying unequal reproduction
rates of social or economic classes of the population.

Differential fertility in this sense probably has become important only in relatively recent times. Many historical accounts exist of the failure of the "upper classes" to reproduce

552

as rapidly as the "lower classes," but the evidence on which these accounts are founded is not clear cut (2). Regardless of their reproduction rates, the "upper classes," until the last century or so, numerically were so small relative to the total population that their fertility had little effect upon either the quantity or quality of the population of which

Table 1. Ratio of the net reproduction rate for specific urban classes to the corresponding rate for the total urban white population, United States, 1935–36.[1]

Class	Ratio
Annual Family Income	
$3,000 and over	.60
$2,000–2,999	.79
$1,500–1,999	.90
$1,000–1,499	1.07
Under $1,000	1.37
Education (Females)	
College	.74
High School	.97
7th or 8th grade	1.23
Less than 7th grade	1.39
Total Population	1.00

[1] From reference 3.

they were a part. Today, however, numerically significant portions of our population are reproducing themselves solely as a result of an age distribution favorable to a large number of births. As the age distribution changes to that which current birth and death rates will support, the excess of births over deaths will change to an excess of deaths over births unless age specific fertility rates are increased. The probable failure of numerically large segments of our population to reproduce themselves means that the physical and mental characteristics of the future population will be determined to an increasing extent by those whose fertility is sufficiently great to provide an excess of births over replacement needs.

Many bases of classification of the population into groups or classes have been used: color, nativity, religion, income, education, occupation, region, and size of community are the more common. The general results of investigations in the United States of the relationship of fertility to groups of the population classified in these ways are well known and are in substantial agreement so that they will be referred to here only briefly.

Table 1 shows the relative rank with respect to net reproduction rates of classes of the urban population when grouped by income and education. Corresponding differences exist when other bases of classification are used. The fertility of Catholics is usually higher than that of Protestants in the same area (4).

Farmers, unskilled laborers, and miners exceed in fertility skilled workers and business and professional people. When population is classified by size of community, fertility rates decline from a high for the rural-farm population to a low for the population residing in large cities (5). No matter what criteria of classification are used some groups of the population are found to contribute a disproportionate number of new recruits to the population of the future. In general, these groups have the lowest income and the least education; they are primarily manual workers and live in areas with the least adequate health, educational, and cultural opportunities and facilities.

What do these differences in fertility portend concerning the characteristics of the future population of the United States? But little progress has been made in assembling scientific evidence from which an answer to this question can be made. In the absence of scientific evidence, opinion and prejudice reign supreme. No general agreement exists among demographers concerning the effects of differential fertility upon the quality of the population.

One reason for the failure of demographers to investigate more thoroughly the effects of differential fertility undoubtedly is the scientific disrepute of many of the statements concerning this subject which have been made by well-meaning but ill-informed eugenists. Contending that those who rise to the top socially and economically have the best genetic and cultural heritage, eugenists claim that the present differential fertility of social and economic classes is dysgenic and that as a result the average ability of the population is being lowered. Perhaps an even more important reason is the fact that human genetics and psychology have not yet accumulated a sufficient body of scientific knowledge about human abilities and their distribution throughout the population to permit a valid determination of the effects of differential fertility.

Neither of these reasons however, is sufficient to excuse the failure of demographers to investigate scientifically the effects of differential fertility. The potential significance of current differences in reproduction rates among social and economic classes for the future population of the nation is great enough to demand the most careful investigation. But before much progress can be made in evaluating the effects of class differentials in fertility it will be necessary to define more specifically the objective.

Firstly, the specific traits which we desire to have perpetuated must be defined. Moreover these must be defined so that valid measures of their presence or absence can be established. Only then can verifiable observations be made of the distribution of these traits among the various social and economic classes of the population. Once traits have been identified and valid measures developed, the relation of these traits to definite types of hereditary behaviour should be investigated in order to ascertain the extent to which they are dependent upon the genetic qualities of the population and the extent to which they arise from the cultural environment. Studies of the change in the proportion of individuals with specific traits between two successive generations would furnish the basis for evaluating the effects of differential fertility upon the quality of the population.

Turning to the evidence which is cited in support of statements concerning the effects of class differentials in fertility it is impossible to find any significant amount of data which meet all the criteria in the preceding paragraph. No general agreement exists concerning the traits which should be preserved in the population. Lack of agreement is not serious however, insofar as investigation of the distribution of traits among social classes is concerned except as it may influence the traits to be investigated.

More progress has been made in the identification, measurement, and determination of the dependence upon genetic factors of physical than of mental traits. Knowledge is accumulating concerning the role of heredity and the mechanism of its action in the development of many physical defects and diseases so that statements concerning the probability of such conditions appearing among offspring can be made with considerable assurance. There is no evidence that biologically undesirable physical defects tend to be disproportionately frequent in certain social and economic classes and, except for some racial extremists, few people believe that differential fertility is causing the physical deterioration of our population. This is not to deny the desirability of discouraging individuals with physical defects, such as Huntington's Chorea, hereditary optic atrophy, and similar conditions whose mode of genetic behaviour is fairly well understood, from procreating children but such action is applicable to individuals and not to entire social or economic classes.

In contrast to our knowledge of physical traits, that concerning mental traits is exceedingly meager. In the eighty years since the publication of Galton's HEREDITARY GENIUS, interest has centered primarily on tests of "intelligence." Even today however, psychologists disagree sharply as to whether intelligence is a single specific mental trait or is a cluster of distinct elements more or less interrelated. Fortunately this disagreement has not prevented continued efforts to improve tests for the measurement of intelligence, to investigate the response of various groups of the population to such tests and to attempt to ascertain the influence of environmental factors upon its development.

Studies of twins and foster children have shown that I.Q. scores can be altered by changes in the environment. Increases of as much as twenty to thirty points have been reported but the average change to be expected is probably in the neighborhood of five to ten points. It is equally clear that heredity places limits upon the possible development of a given individual and that individual differences in I.Q. scores persist in spite of the most enriched environment.

Although a few investigators claim that environmental influences can largely determine an individual's I.Q. score, probably most investigators would agree that genetic factors account for more than 50 per cent. Estimates ranging from 50 to 95 per cent for the relative weight of heredity have been put forth but these depend largely upon the investigator's predilections.

When children are grouped according to father's occupation, arranged in broad social economic classes, the average I.Q. score usually is lowest for children of unskilled laborers and highest for children of professional persons. Some studies have reported a range in average I.Q. score of as much as 20 to 25 points from the lowest to the highest classes. Other investigations show a negative correlation of about 0.2 between I.Q. score and size of family. From these facts some have concluded that the "upper" classes are more intelligent on the average than the "lower" classes so that the effect of differential fertility is to lower the average intelligence of the total population.

Cattell estimated that the average I.Q. is declining at the rate of 3 points per generation (6). Fraser Roberts reported that based upon his studies of the child population of Bath, England, the fall in average I.Q. was about $1\frac{1}{2}$ points per generation (7). In the United States, Lentz calculated that in the urban population the decline in the median score from one generation to another was as much as 4 to 5 points (8). Lorimer and Osborn concluded that the average decline in the median I.Q. score was 0.9 of a point per generation (9).

It should be remembered that these calculations are theoretical and are based upon observations on a single generation. No one has yet reported investigations of I.Q. scores in successive generations which support these claims. The implication exists that intelligence tests measure the most important of all mental traits and that an increase in the average I.Q. score of the population would be desirable. While no one seriously advocates that the quality of the population would be improved by deliberately lowering the average I.Q. score by 25 points, if this were possible, it is not at all clear that raising the average I.Q. score to 130 or 140 would in itself increase the well being of our population.

Certainly there are differences in the ability of an artist, an engineer, a mathematician, an aeroplane pilot, a motor mechanic, a pianist, and a chemist which are not represented by differences in I.Q. scores. Temperament and emotional stability undoubtedly profoundly influence an individual's achievement. Research in the domain of mental traits other than intelligence has made little headway and is no further developed than intelligence testing was forty years ago. Leadership, initiative, ambition, and similar socially desirable characteristics are merely philosophical concepts. Until temperamental, emotional, and volitional traits are defined in such a manner that valid tests can be devised for their measurement, speculation concerning the effect of differential fertility upon their distribution throughout the population, at best, can be but a well informed guess and, at the worst, will be an expression of a preconceived prejudice.

Is the present pattern of differential fertility lowering the average quality of our population? In this form the question is incapable of scientific answer. Not until the general concept, ability, is separated into specific measurable components can the scientific evidence necessary to answer this question be accumulated. As yet, repeatable measurements have been made of only one mental trait, intelligence, and the precise meaning of this trait still is a matter of dispute. Differential fertility of social classes has existed much as it is today for nearly two generations at least. No longitudinal time studies have been reported which support the conclusions drawn by some from cross-sectional time studies that the average I.Q. of our population is decreasing in successive generations.

Even though we do not have sufficient scientific evidence to determine the effects of differential fertility upon the genetic qualities of our population we do have sufficient evidence to be sure that a large proportion of the recruits of the next generation come from the classes of our population which are the least able to provide maximum cultural and health advantages. So long as differential fertility operates in a way that denies opportunity for maximum development of innate ability it acts counter to the professed ideals of our society and as such is a matter of serious concern.

REFERENCES

1. Carr-Saunders, A. M.: WORLD POPULATION. Oxford, Clarendon Press, 1936, pp. 42–45.

2. Rumney, J.: The Problem of Differential Fertility. *Population,* November, 1935, ii, No. 1, pp. 3–23.

3. Karpinos, Bernard D. and Kiser, Clyde V.: The Differential Fertility and Potential Rates of Growth of Various Income and Educational Classes of Urban Populations in the United States. The Milbank Memorial Fund *Quarterly,* October, 1939, xvii, No. 4, pp. 367–391.

4. Whelpton, P. K. and Kiser, Clyde V.: Trends, Determinants and Control in Human Fertility. *The Annals of the American Academy of Political and Social Science,* January, 1945, Vol. 237, pp. 112–122.

5. National Resources Committee: THE PROBLEMS OF A CHANGING POPULATION. Washington, Government Printing Office, 1938.

6. Cattell, R. B.: THE FIGHT FOR OUR NATIONAL INTELLIGENCE. Westminster, P. S. King and Son, Ltd., 1937.

7. Roberts J. A., Fraser: Intelligence and Fertility. *Mental Health,* July, 1940, i, pp. 69–75.

8. Lentz, T. F.: Relation of I. Q. to Size of Family. *Journal of Educational Psychology,* October, 1927, xviii, pp. 486–496.

9. Lorimer, Frank and Osborn, Frederick: DYNAMICS OF POPULATION. New York, The Macmillan Company, 1934, p. 190.

THE FIELD OF POPULATION QUALITY

By Julian L. Woodward

IT IS conventional in the current literature to divide the field of population
sociology into two parts, one in
which primary emphasis is on *numbers*
and individuals are treated as biological
units in enumerations, the other where
the qualities or attributes of these unit-
individuals become the subject of investigation. The two sub-fields overlap since
the division of population into groups for
enumeration is necessarily based on some
classification by attributes and on the
other hand the attention paid to a given
quality trait of individuals will be in
part proportional to the frequency with
which the trait appears in populations.
But while a clear cut line of demarcation
may not be drawn, the differences in
emphasis on quantity or numbers by one
group of students of population and on
quality by another has actually been
sufficiently definite to mark off the two
fields of specialization.

The field of population quality has on
the whole received less attention from
careful scientific investigators and many
of its basic methodological problems
remain unsolved. In spite of this fact
there has been a considerable output of
generalizations and of programs for the
improvement of the quality of succeeding generations of human beings. These
so-called *eugenic* programs have been
widely propagandized and have in some
cases received the official backing of
governments, but the scientific groundwork on which they are supposed to rest
is still in many respects incomplete and
shaky. The field of population quality
as a scientific discipline has suffered from
its too enthusiastic friends. The logic

underlying the eugenic reform programs
needs reexamination, if only to reveal
more clearly the degree to which they rest
on hypotheses and gross approximations
which may eventually prove to be correct and accurate but which are not yet
known to be so.

Of course there have not been lacking
able critics of the eugenics cult[1] and in
recent years their strictures have had the
effect of making eugenists more moderate.
There is now a greater recognition of the
inherent difficulties that stand in the way
of a soundly based program for control
over quality and the measures urged by the
official eugenics societies[2] are neither as
radical nor as hopeful of improvement as
they were fifteen years ago. Changes
have in fact come so rapidly and so recently that it is possible that an effort to
redefine the field of population quality
in the light of these developments may
have some utility. This paper aims to
do this by stating explicitly the basic
assumptions of the eugenist and then
attempting to outline step by step the
chain of reasoning leading from these
assumptions to the eugenics programs of
1939.

I

Quality must of course be defined with
reference to some standard of value or
significance; consequently the problem of
assaying the relative desirability of different types of human beings belongs in its

[1] Among them may be mentioned Pearl, Thompson, Jennings, and Haldane.

[2] Cf. *Practical Eugenics*, a pamphlet issued by the
American Eugenics Society, New York, 1938; and
"Aims and Objects of the [British] Eugenics Society,"
Eugenics Review, 26, pp. 133–135 (July 1934).

broad connotations in the field of social ethics. But while the population sociologist will eventually have to take the mores into account, his basic orientation is naturalistic and transcends the cultural preferences of the people whose quality he assays. He is in the first instance an evolutionary biologist and his criteria of quality arise through an effort to interpret man's current position in the evolutionary order of nature. The criteria apply to hereditary traits and are derived from an attempted long-time view of the developmental history of the species. The population-quality sociologist's (i.e. the eugenist's) problem is to suggest ways in which man's relatively secure position in the organic world of nature may be preserved.

The eugenist starts out, therefore, by viewing man as an organic type whose hereditary characteristics are the result of the same processes as those producing the characteristics of other animals. These processes are essentially summed up in the two terms *mutation*[3] and *natural selection* although other factors such as isolation, population size and (possibly) emergence or an *élan vital* play some part. The possibility of a limited type of La Marckian variation cannot be ruled out also,[4] and there is evidence of a nongerminal form of variation[5] whose rôle in evolution, while probably small, is as

yet unevaluated. Altogether, however, the general view of human evolution as a slow and devious process, dependent on infrequent and "fortuitous" variations for new characters still holds the field.[6] Characters lost through selection are not easily regained, since the frequency of recurrence of any given mutation is very low. It may therefore be maintained that a race needs to conserve its good characters fully as much as it needs to eliminate its bad ones.

Goodness or badness of character can in the naturalistic view be determined only by survival. Quality is measured in terms of fitness to survive and breed descendants, consequently the differential rates of increase or decrease as between two type-forms are the only naturalistic indices of their relative quality.[7] That *homo sapiens* was able to survive as a species even with only a rudimentary culture whereas *homo neandertalensis* was not is an evidence of the superior quality or fitness represented by the former's particular combination of traits. Had man not made great further advances in culture but had instead remained largely cultureless, like the other primates, his continued survival would presumably have depended on the *conservation* of this combination of traits and on modifications to meet changing natural-order conditions. Furthermore any adaptive changes taking place in man's hereditary makeup would under natural-order (pre-cultural) conditions take place at a relatively slow rate.

II

As Hogben points out, ". . . The outstanding biological peculiarity of man is

[3] The term "mutation" is here taken to include such phenomena as the gain or loss of whole chromosomes, the multiplication of sets of chromosomes (polyploidy), and the rearrangement of genes within chromosomes as well as aberrations in single genes (gene mutation).

[4] *Cf.* H. S. Jennings, *Genetic Variations in Relation to Evolution*, Princeton University Press, 1935, for a discussion of the inheritance of environmentally induced characters in unicellular organisms.

[5] The so-called *plasmons*. *Cf.* A. Franklin Shull, *Evolution*, p. 96; Theodosius Dobzkansky, *Genetics and the Origin of Species*, pp. 68–72.

[6] For a description of the modern view of evolution *cf.* Dobzkansky, *op. cit.*, pp. 185–191.

[7] *Cf.* R. A. Fisher, *The Genetical Theory of Natural Selection*, p. 38.

the fact that an infinitude of different behavior patterns is consistent with the same genetic basis."[8] How then does the elaboration of behavior patterns that is implied in human cultural accumulation change the situation with respect to quality? In the first place with the development of culture there came *pari passu* an increase in human population which in terms of the survival criterion may be interpreted as added evidence of the fitness of man's combination of hereditary characteristics. The increased population in turn brought a more rapid rate of evolution[9] and also a greater amount of intra-specific competition and selection. More characters developed that gave men merely an advantage over their fellows without aiding them in the struggle with animal and plant competitors. If there are any instinctive anti-coöperative tendencies in modern man (as, for instance, "pugnacity," "blood lust," "ferocity," "deceitfulness") it is possible that they are the result of this man-to-man struggle for survival. But in the light of our limited knowledge it is hard to be concrete concerning the selective importance of competition of this sort.

However, not all the "benefits" from cultural accumulation were expended in the form of population increase (as they would be among animals). Man early learned to exercise some control over population trends and to create a "surplus of adaptation" that was devoted to raising the plane of living above the subsistence level. In order to explain this new type of evidence of fitness in naturalistic terms it is necessary to extend the survival criterion. An improved plane of living involves more than "mere survival"; it means that a series of biological drives[10] whose place in man's hereditary makeup was originally due to their survival utility have now received more than the minimum amount of satisfaction necessary for species perpetuation. They have become ends in themselves, "subcultural" ends Folsom would call them,[11] and their proximate attainment represents a fuller life for the organism, in turn an index of improved quality still measured in naturalistic terms.

A second important change in the eugenic situation of man is also the outgrowth of his acquisition of culture. A new type of selective influence is introduced as the result of the increasing human *control* over an environment that had hitherto been largely unalterable by man's own agency. In cultural society we may think of two types of selection operating simultaneously on the biological characteristics of populations. The first of these is *natural selection* which is adaptive to the environmental conditions over which man still exercises little or no control, the second is *cultural selection* which is adaptive to man-controlled environmental conditions, both in the biological (fauna and flora) and the physiographic (climate and topography) portions of the environment and especially in culture itself. Cultural selection does not necessarily support natural selection to maintain or improve a quality defined in the naturalistic sense. It may do so but on the other hand culture may set up its own implicit or explicit standards of quality that may be inimical to the long-time naturalistic standards. Furthermore, as

---

[8] Lancelot Hogben, "Some Methodological Aspects of Human Genetics," *The American Naturalist*, 67, p. 259 (May–June 1933).

[9] J. B. S. Haldane, *The Causes of Evolution*, p. 132.

[10] As, for instance, the drive to live as long as possible even beyond the reproductive period, the drive to obtain easier life conditions, the play impulse, etc. No effort is made here to use the term "drive" in any exact sense.

[11] J. K. Folsom, *The Family*, p. 46.

has been often pointed out, cultural selection may be extremely rigorous and modify biological type with relative rapidity; it may therefore overturn within a relatively short period the work of a natural selection operating over many generations.

Cultural selection *may* do these things; the problem is to determine whether and to what extent it *is* doing them. It is one thing to assume that there are certain basic hereditary traits that conduce to survival in a naturalistic order and that are necessary to supply cultural creativeness and adaptibility and quite another to state specifically what these essential traits are. It is still a further problem to discern what is happening with respect to the incidence of these traits now that they are possibly under cultural as well as natural selection. These are obviously difficult problems to solve even in terms of gross approximation yet some answers to them are implied in every real eugenic program. For the primary aim of eugenics must be to protect man's position in nature by conserving the traits that have proved their pre-cultural evolutionary value. A secondary aim is to breed a race that can attain a higher plane of living, with plane of living defined in subcultural terms.

III

In any attempt to describe and enumerate the traits that have unusual eugenic value the unit of investigation will be the *inherited capacity*. A capacity may be defined as a biologically inherited ability to develop a set of powers under optimum environmental conditions. Capacities represent the functional possibilities of certain parts of organic structure which in turn rest upon genic combinations. Most capacities are not simply the result of the action of a single pair of allelomorphs but are instead referable to the complex interaction of a number of gene-pairs. If there are a number of genes whose presence or absence will affect the existence of a given capacity we may have a situation where a particular combination of germinal factors is necessary for the capacity to exist at all and the absence of one factor will eliminate it. This would make the capacity an all-or-none affair. Much more often, however, the presence or absence of a gene will merely influence the *degree* to which the capacity is present.[12] The number of different degrees in which a given capacity can be manifested will depend on the complexity of the genetic basis and can be roughly estimated from the number of genes involved. But we almost never know how many genes *are* involved in any of the eugenically significant capacities,[13] and there are other difficulties[14] which at present make impossible an accurate calculation of the number of discrete steps on most capacity scales.

Ideally the capacities should be defined by identifying the gene combinations that produce them; any other definition makes the capacity only an abstraction. However gene mapping for man has only just been begun[15] and even where mapping is well advanced, as for the banana fly, little is known about the influence of the specific genes or groups of genes on other

[12] A good discussion of the genetics underlying metrical or quantitatively varying characters is to be found in H. S. Jennings, *Genetics*, pp. 223-231.

[13] There are a few defects, or "incapacities," in which it is known that only a single gene-pair is involved.

[14] The genes affecting a particular capacity probably do not act through simple summation of effects but interact with each other in complex ways. *Cf.* Jennings, *op. cit.*, pp. 179-187; J. A. Rasmussen, "A Contribution to the Theory of Quantitative Character Inheritance," *Hereditas*, 18, pp. 245-261 (1933).

[15] *Cf.* Laurence H. Snyder, "Present Trends in the Study of Human Inheritance," *Eugenical News*, 23, pp. 63-64 (July-August 1938).

than purely physical characters. At present, therefore, the problem of arriving even at a catalogue of mutually independent and eugenically significant *physical* capacities (tendencies to develop physical powers like good vision, good digestion, specific disease resistance) cannot be solved by a direct genetic approach. The statement is even more true as regards "temperamental" and "intellectual" capacities. No one knows what sort of gene complexes underlie the so-called mental traits.[16]

The procedure usually followed by eugenists, in default of a better, is a sort of backhanded one. It is to begin with actual observed human behavior and try to work back to the underlying capacities. An attempt is made to segregate behavior into eugenically significant categories (that is into *traits* that are thought to be closely related to race survival and/or to subcultural elements in the standard of living) and then to distill out of each categorized group of behavior fragments its hereditary component. These components are given names as capacities and an effort is made to find out whether they are independent and mutually exclusive hereditary entities. With the limited methodological tools available an attempt is made also to investigate their genetic basis.

A concrete example will serve to illustrate this procedure and to bring out the present flaws in it that have to be covered over with assumptions and hypotheses. Let us suppose that "mechanical ability," the ability to learn mechanical skills and solve mechanical problems, is one of the traits selected for its eugenic

value. Doubtless a tool-fabricating and tool-using ability has always been advantageous to man so that a good eugenic case can be made for any inherited capacities underlying it; the problem is to determine what these are. The first step must be the development of a test for objectively measuring the actual degree of mechanical ability manifested by a subject at a given time.[17] The test must be checked for validity and reliability and in order to provide the best possible foundation for subsequent inferences concerning the rôle of hereditary factors it should be demonstrated that when the test is given to a population sample the results do *not* correlate with those obtained when all other available "special" and "general" ability tests are also tried on the sample group.[18] At present there are not very many ability tests that could be used for such correlations but at least the procedure outlined would yield a sort of negative evidence for the conclusion that mechanical ability as the test tested it was a relatively independent mental faculty, a "unique trait."[19]

The problem for the eugenist, however, is to get from mechanical ability to mechanical capacity. The score which the subject receives on the mechanical ability test will be the result of a certain degree of endowment in one or more inherited capacities which have been to some extent developed by the process of biological maturation and to some extent also by training and experience.

[16] There are a few very doubtful hypotheses concerning the genetics of feeblemindedness, some types of epilepsy, schizophrenia, etc. but they all probably represent gross over-simplifications of the actual genetic situation.

[17] The Stenquist test (J. L. Stenquist, *Mechanical Aptitude Tests*) and the Minnesota test (D. G. Paterson, R. M. Elliott, et al., *Minnesota Mechanical Ability Tests*) are actually available.

[18] The Minnesota test has been shown not to correlate with tests for general intelligence and physical agility. It also does not correlate with height. *Cf.* Paterson, Elliott, et al., *op. cit.*, pp. 245–253.

[19] *Cf.* the discussion of the "theory of unique traits" in *ibid.*, pp. 12–22.

Whether a single, separately inherited capacity is all that is involved or whether mechanical ability (as defined by the test) rests upon a complex of different capacities each inherited in independently varying degrees is an important question for the eugenist but one difficult to answer. If the trait tested is experimentally proved to be an independently varying one, then there is perhaps some presumption that a single, unitary inherited capacity is all that underlies it. However the question brings us into the much battle-scarred field of mental organization' where one-factor theories, multiple-factor theories, theories of specific and group factors are still being debated.[20] If mechanical ability is a composite trait on the side of its hereditary components then the eugenist would want to break it down into more fundamental elements that could be evaluated separately for their eugenic or dysgenic character. At the present time it is clear, however, that neither the state of our theory in relation to mental abilities nor our testing methodology would enable him to achieve this definition of measurable traits in hereditary terms.

There is a second problem that also arises in connection with the transition from mental ability to underlying capacity; this is the familiar one of evaluating the influence of environment on the test score. General intelligence testers have struggled with this problem more even than those working with so-called tests for special ability but no exact solutions have been arrived at; and it is evident that no easy answers are yet available for eugenists. The problem may be approached (1) by attempting to correlate test scores with quantitative indices of possibly significant types of uncontrolled

environmental conditioning,[21] or (2) by a study of the effects of deliberate training on test scores (using an untrained control group). Both methods involve obvious difficulties and do not yield very conclusive results.

To complete this illustrative analysis let us make the presently impossible supposition that the problems discussed in the two preceding paragraphs have been solved and that a mechanical ability test score can be corrected for at least the grosser differentials in environmental conditioning and that when so corrected it does give a good measure of the degree of (a single) mechanical capacity possessed by the subject. Eugenists would then be ready to investigate the genetic basis of the capacity in order to determine the number, location, and dominance or recessiveness of the specific genes involved. In the absence of adequate genealogical records and in view of the difficulties in the way of a conclusive large scale breeding experiment of the type so helpful with *drosophila* recourse would have to be had to highly indirect methods. While some important advances in the methodology of human biometrical genetics have recently been made,[22] the current practical possibility of investigating the genetic basis of a complex graded "mental" character like mechanical capacity is virtually nil.

Mechanical capacity may probably be regarded as sufficiently typical of those capacities of possible eugenic significance to permit of some generalization even on the basis of the single illustration. One

---

[20] For a summary of the different theories now extant *cf.* Anne Anastasi, *Differential Psychology*, pp. 296–305.

[21] This was done for the Minnesota test on a limited scale, with results indicating that the test score differences were innate, *op. cit.*, pp. 254–268.

[22] See the work of Bernstein, Hogben, Wiener, Fisher, Haldane, Burks, Penrose, et al. The most pertinent citation is to L. S. Penrose, "Genetic Linkage in Graded Human Characters," *Annals of Eugenics*, 8, pp. 233–237 (May 1938).

may conclude that we are at present unable with a few doubtful exceptions among the "physical capacities" but almost none among those in either the "temperamental" or the "intellectual" category, to (1) define accurately and measure the manifested abilities that are the result of specific capacities in interaction with environment. We are even less able to (2) define and measure the capacities themselves or to (3) identify the genes that determine how much of a capacity a given subject is to be endowed with.

One might add a fourth "inability" to this list of current gaps in our eugenic technique and knowledge. What a eugenist really needs to know about a particular individual is not what capacities he himself possesses but rather what sort of a contribution he is going to make to the capacity endowments of his offspring. Since the individual may carry recessive genes that do not enter into the determination of his own capacity, but which may be effective when differently paired in his offspring, the problem, especially in view of the complex genetic basis for most capacities, is seen to be an extremely complex one. At present we are able to attack it directly only in the highly special case where the inheritance pattern is a simple Mendelian one and not multi-factorial. And even there it proves extremely difficult to identify the individuals who are carriers of recessive genes for the capacity (or incapacity) in question. An indirect approach via biometry is proving somewhat more fruitful; it is to draw from the population a statistical sample of individuals who manifest a eugenic or dysgenic trait in a significant degree, ascertain the degrees to which the trait appears in their offspring, and calculate the probability of eugenic or dysgenic inheritance from parent to children.

This probability would be compared with that derived from a control sample in which the trait in question was manifested in the parents to a degree not of eugenic significance, and the difference between the two probability coefficients would be an index of the danger in allowing people like those in the first sample group to breed.[23] While this procedure presents grave difficulties, especially in making up the sample group, and is from the genetic point of view highly empirical, it does seem about the only practicable approach for complex multi-factorial characters.[24] If it can be used effectively it will enable eugenists to short-cut the "inabilities" 2, 3, and 4 discussed above.

IV

It is obvious that the gaps in currently available technique and information which have been pointed out in the course of the preceding analysis will actually continue to yawn open for some time to come. That being the case what of practical eugenic procedures for today and tomorrow? Is the degree of uncertainty in currently possible eugenic judgments too great to justify any attempts at interference with custom and social behavior? Or may we proceed cautiously and conservatively to try to achieve a few very limited eugenic aims? These questions must be answered in relation to two different eugenic approaches, each of which has today its group of advocates.

The first approach may be summed up

[23] The method was originally developed by Weinberg and has been improved and modified by Bernstein, Fisher, Haldane, Penrose and others. The literature is too extensive for citation.

[24] The method has been employed chiefly on identifiable physical characters and a few ungraded mental characters like specific psychoses or amaurotic idiocy. The work on the psychoses suffers from uncertain diagnosis (identification).

in the term "eugenics of extreme deviates." Advocates of this approach would say that while we may not be able to form valid judgments about the eugenic quality of individuals in the center of a curve of capacity distribution in a population there are persons at the extremes of the distribution whose eugenic superiority or inferiority is patent. These extreme deviates are held to be proper subjects for investigation and control.

So-called negative or restrictive eugenics aims to eliminate the dysgenic deviates by an artificial selection practiced against their probable parents. Individuals are in general classified as dysgenic parents when it appears extremely likely that they will pass on to offspring tendencies toward serious lack of one or more important capacities. If the offspring are likely[25] to be so handicapped in endowment as to be unable on that account to become independent and self-supporting in any culture a good case can perhaps be made for regarding them as eugenically undesirable. But while restrictive eugenics is the branch of contemporary eugenics that has received greatest public support there are none the less only a very few cacogenic types generally agreed upon as appropriate subjects for control measures. These types are mostly "physical" rather than "mental" defectives whose deficiencies are due to the presence or absence of one or two genes, and whose birth

[25] How likely the offspring's handicap has to be before justifying a eugenic prohibition against his birth is of course a matter of eugenic judgment and zeal for the cause of race purification. Unless the chances of serious defect are high, however, one has to take into account the possibility of compensating virtues in the child's endowment. After all he has a whole "profile" of capacities and he may possess some in considerable degree while being deficient in others. The point is made simply to emphasize the complexity of the problem the eugenist often makes over simple.

rates are low in any event. The more important "mental defective" group involves chiefly incapacities with a complex genetic base, consequently there are many unidentifiable "carriers" of defect-producing genes for every one who indicates his own possession of such genes by actually manifesting the incapacity. It is now clear[26] that an artificial selection operating only against "manifestants" and not as well against "carriers" will have only a minor effect on the genetic makeup of the population as a whole with respect to the capacity in question. One might conclude, then, that the best arguments (and almost the only ones in many cases) in favor of a restrictive eugenic program are at present essentially *euthenic* in nature. When a defective is prevented from having offspring the number of badly reared children is thereby reduced even though there is no great effect on the dysgenic germplasm in the next generation.

Operating at the other end of the curve of distribution of eugenic quality we have *aristogenics*, aimed at increasing the incidence of the eugenically superior. Since there is, however, practically no agreement on criteria for identifying superior individuals aristogenic programs have made little headway. One serious difficulty is the fact that the genius type, whenever he can be defined at all, is usually found to be the offspring of parents who are themselves not of anything approaching the same high capacity rating.

We may term the second major type of approach to eugenic programming *general eugenics* since its distinguishing characteristic is the fact that its measures are applied generally in the whole population and not to some particular segment of it. There are at least three sub-types of

[26] *Cf.* the well known paper of R. A. Fisher in the *Journal of Heredity*, 18, pp. 529–531 (1927).

eugenic approach falling under this main head. The first is termed by Jennings[27] *family eugenics* and it aims at the prevention of close inbreeding in family lines. Incest regulations enforce an outbreeding that tends to distribute defect-producing genes as recessives in heterozygous pairings and also increases the possibility of new and unusually favorable gene combinations. We accept family eugenic measures as a matter of course but it must be remembered that they alone do nothing to improve the total germinal composition of a population, however much they may conceal its dysgenic features. Controlled inbreeding would provide a better basis for an *effective* eugenic policy.

A second form of general eugenics, *group eugenics*, need be mentioned only in passing. It aims at the promotion of increase or decrease of some one population group (race, nationality, religion, social class) on the basis of a doctrine of inherent superiority or inferiority. While doctrines of this sort are pervasive they receive little scientific support.

A third type of general eugenics, the voluntary parenthood program, deserves more consideration than can be here accorded it. By dissemination of birth control information and by family allowances and other subsidies designed to reduce and (relative to income) equalize the *economic* sacrifices involved in parenthood it is proposed to make the strength of the desire for children the most important variable factor in all differential birth rates. This program is supposed to be eugenic in the first instance because it would tend to eliminate a current differential birth rate unfavorable to the upper socio-economic classes who with proper subsidies could marry earlier and have

more children without sacrifice of their relatively high standard of living. These classes are credited with a relatively good native endowment for "cultural-intellectual" development[28] which in turn is held to be a trait having survival value for the race. Voluntary parenthood is also claimed to bring other eugenic benefits. Those couples who would choose to raise the most children would be "above the average not only in physique and health, but in love of children, compatibility of husband and wife, ability to get along with other people, willingness to assume responsibility, and willingness to make sacrifices for the sake of the family."[29] These are all held to be "socially desirable qualities."[30]

Obviously there are some very sweeping assumptions involved in the statements just quoted. While a good *a priori* case may be made for the eugenic importance of the capacities underlying cultural-intellectual development the latter term is difficult to define and its genetic basis is a highly compound one. One may, however, concede that a selection favoring the indicated cultural-intellectual elite would be, in a rough sense at least, eugenic, and selection probably does *not* favor these individuals today. As to the traits supposed to be characteristic of voluntary parents it would first be necessary to formulate some hypothesis concerning the underlying hereditary components in order to bring their appraisal into the field of eugenics. It may be postulated that there are parental "instincts" and temperamental predisposi-

[27] H. S. Jennings, *The Biological Basis of Human Nature*, pp. 231–233.

[28] Frank Lorimer and Frederick Osborn, *Dynamics of Population*, p. 344.

[29] Frederick Osborn, "Development of A Eugenic Philosophy," *American Sociological Review*, 2, p. 391 (April 1937). See also "The Development of Eugenic Policies," *Eugenics Review*, 29, p. 120 (July 1937).

[30] *Ibid.*

tions that are correlated with the desire for parenthood and that are eugenically significant in relation to race perpetuation. It has also been suggested that there are predispositions toward coöperation and sociability involved.[31] It is certainly dangerous at present, however, to rest eugenic claims on theories of innate motives although there may well be genetic factors that promote "compatibility" both within and without the family group.

One other point may be made with respect to the voluntary parenthood plan. Where one is setting up a eugenic program for a whole society and not just the deviates in it, it is important to be sure that the most endangered eugenic traits be made the chief touchstone of quality. One may therefore simply raise the question whether either intelligence (as basic to cultural-intellectual development) or coöperative tendency are in the same danger of deterioration as are such physical characters as the teeth, eyes, feet, nose and sinuses, the female pelvis,[32] and organic resistances to cancer or the allergies. For which general class of traits should primary selection be made?

Of course these objections may appear mere quibbles. The voluntary parenthood program offered as a conservative

[31] Ibid., p. 395.

[32] Cf. E. A. Hooton, Apes, Men and Morons, p. 291.

step in a probably eugenic direction, without prejudice to other steps that may be urged with fuller knowledge, does have certain advantages. In the first place it could be effective in modifying a very powerful (although largely temporary) selection now operating against the socioeconomic elite who, all things considered, probably do have some eugenic advantage over the rest of the population. Second, it could become a convenient and not too greatly resisted adjunct to the inevitable subsidy program that will in time be introduced to arrest the decline in gross population numbers. Third, it would operate without any coercion and would therefore not run counter to our democratic and individualistic tradition. Fourth, it can be strongly defended on euthenic grounds.

Thus, while any eugenic program must seem like amateur meddling with processes we do not yet really understand, the voluntary parenthood program appears at least to be the most reasonable of the long series of eugenicists' proposals. However, there are so many difficulties in the way of setting up a parent-subsidy system that would be really adequate to reduce and equalize parental costs that its immediate future does not appear a very bright one. To damn the program with faint praise is probably the impulse of most sociologists at the moment.

POSSIBLE EFFECTS OF DIFFERENTIAL FERTILITY

ON GENETIC ENDOWMENT

By Frederick Osborn

The people of western Europe and the people of western culture in the new world are moving rapidly through a transitional period in which the old framework of natural selection has been modified and the new framework is not yet established.

Until about a hundred years ago death was the major factor determining which stocks would survive, and this was true for human beings as for all living things. As recently as 1850 in Massachusetts the average years of life remaining to a newborn baby were 38.3 for a boy and 40.5 for a girl.[1] Nearly half of those born were eliminated before they had a chance to reproduce. But today the average length of life is 65.5 years for men and 71 years for women,[2] and over 90 per cent live beyond the middle of their reproductive period. Death no longer provides the major framework for natural selection. Even those deaths which do occur before the time for reproduction, and which are probably even more selective than in the past, select mainly for physical weaknesses. Most deaths occur too early for weaknesses in intelligence or personality to have been contributing causes.

As deaths have declined, differences in births have taken on the major role in the selection of man's higher characteristics. From now on, among European peoples, differences in births will largely determine changes in the genetic basis for personality and intelligence from one generation to another.

Along with the decline in deaths, contraception has been reducing the number of births. But this has been a gradual process. Widely publicised among English-speaking peoples by the Bradley Besant trial in 1877, contraception spread first in England and the United States among the well to do and people in the cities. The immediate effect was to widen the gap in birth rates between the social classes. Among English couples married from 1851-1861, the upper and middle classes had 89 per cent as many children as the average for all classes and agricultural laborers 105 per cent as many. But among couples married 1891-1896, the upper class couples had only 74 per cent of the average, as against 115 per cent for the agricultural laborers.[3]

By 1920, when regional and class differences in the use of contraception were perhaps most extreme, the estimated specific birth rates per thousand native-born white women, age 15 to 44, was 69 for the urban United States, and 128 for the rural United States.[4]

Recently with the continuing spread of birth control, the wide rural-urban and socioeconomic birth differentials appear to be drawing closer together. But we are still in a transitional stage and will be in that stage until contraception is practised effectively by the whole population. Such a final stage has been reached at least approximately by a few people in the United States, and the study of their behavior as regards having children may give us a better idea of what will probably happen in the future, than would any study of groups who use contraception less frequently and less effectively.

One of the first of such studies was that made by Flanagan in 1938-39[5] on psychological factors as they effect variations in births among army aviators; a study which laid some of the groundwork for a larger study made in Indianapolis in 1941, which was to include both social and psychological factors.

The Indianapolis Study was organized during 1938-40 by a group which included psychologists, demographers, and a leading medical statistician. It was based on a preliminary house-to-house canvass and a subsequent intensive study involving personal interviews, and the filling out of carefully prepared and pretested schedules and questionnaires. Twenty-three hypotheses were laid down which it was hoped might be wholly or partially proved or disproved. The analysis of the material bearing on these hypotheses is now nearing completion, with publication in current issues of the *Milbank Memorial Fund Quarterly*. It is material which students of differential fertility will draw on heavily for years to come.[6]

Two types of data were collected in the Indianapolis Study, the first from the Household Survey, covering the 41,594 native white couples, wife under 45 years of age, neither ever divorced, found in the city's 102,877 dwelling units of white families, all of which were visited by the canvassers; this group may be considered typical of the people in any fair-sized American city. The second was from the final Interview Group, covering data for an adjusted and inflated sample of 1,444 "relatively fecund" and 533 "relatively sterile" couples selected on the basis that they were married in 1927, 1928, or 1929 with wife under 30 and husband under 40 at time of marriage, both native white, both Protestant, both having completed eighth grade, and both with at last eight years of residence in a large city since their marriage; this group may be considered typical of the people who practice family limitation in a fair-sized American city; it was further subdivided according to the extent and effectiveness of their practice of contraception.

From these and other studies it is now possible to draw some preliminary generalizations which indicate the contrasts in differential fertility operating in the three different frameworks of (1) Darwinian selection, (2) uneven distribution of contraception, and (3) generally effective contraception. These generalizations are as follows.

I

Among western peoples fertility is more influenced by contraception than by impairment of fecundity.

Contrary to the views frequently expressed in the past, differences in size of family in the United States are chiefly the result of differences in the use of some means of preventing conception. In the Indianapolis Interview Group, fecundity, that is the physical capacity to reproduce, is estimated at 5,265 possible pregnancies, and 4,594 possible births per 1,000 couples during the observed intervals (12 to 15 years) from marriage to interview. This figure for the number of children who would have been born if there had been no use of contraceptives is 27.4 per cent lower than the medium estimate of what the rate would have been if there had been no defects in the reproductive system which reduced the number of conceptions or increased the time required for conception. Taking into account the actual practice of contraception among the couples studied, it appears that defects in the reproductive system lowered fertility 21.3, 18.1, and 13.3 per cent, respectively, under three assumptions of high, medium, and low fecundity. On the other hand, under these same assumptions of high, medium, and low fecundity voluntary control reduced the birth rate by 72.2, 67.2, and 64.4 per cent, respectively. In this selected urban group, there was still an inevitable weeding out of infertile stocks, but there was an even larger weeding out of stocks who under the circumstances intentionally limited their fertility.[7]

II

Age at marriage is an important factor in all types of selection.

Galton, quoting figures obtained for 1871 from the Lying-in-Hospital of St. Georges-in-East, gives the following table.[8]

Age of Mother at Marriage	Average Fertility
15–19	9.12
20–24	7.92
25–29	6.30
30–34	4.60

At the time of this study, contraception was almost unknown, and birth rates were high. Of English wives, married 1861-1871 (age at marriage standardized on upper class American series), over 56 per cent had five or more children.[9]

In the Indianapolis Study, the fertility of the Interview Group (inflated sample), interviewed 12 to 15 years after marriage, and compared to the figures from the 1940 census for cities of 250,000 is shown in Table I:[10]

TABLE I

Fertility Rates by Age and Age at Marriage

Age of Wife		Number of Wives	Children Ever Born per 100 Wives	
At Marriage	At Interview	Indianapolis Interview Groups	1940 Census Cities 250,000	Indianapolis Interview Groups
Under 18	25–29	218	232	205
Under 18	30–34	155	292	243
18–19	30–34	500	219	178
20–21	30–34	381	175	170
20–21	35–39	60	210	140
22–24	30–34	70	137	127
22–24	35–39	381	174	140
25–26	35–39	121	132	125
25–26	40–44	20	162	145
27–29	40–44	62	142	73

The Interview Group in the Indianapolis Study, most of whom used contraception, shows greater variations in size of family by age at marriage than the population at large, a smaller proportion of which used contraception; and both show greater variations than Galton's group, of whom probably very few used contraception.

If, as seems likely, trends in the country as a whole ultimately follow the example set by the group in Indianapolis most of whom practiced contraception, then age at marriage will continue to be an important factor in determining who shall survive.

III

A sense of economic insecurity reduces the size of planned families.

In the United States as in most other countries, there is a direct relationship between socioeconomic status and the use and effectiveness of contraception. Differences in contraceptive practice are quite sufficient to account for the large differences in rates of reproduction between city and country and between different socioeconomic classes. Present differences in contraceptive practice are also sufficient to account for the large differences in rates of reproduction between different countries, which are the despair of our present-day Point Four planners. We assume that the world-wide trend toward an increasing use of contraception will continue, and that a cheap and fully effective contraceptive will probably be developed and generally accepted before present transitory conditions have had any great effect on the distribution of genes. We are therefore particularly interested in the processes of differential fertility among couples who plan the number and spacing of their children, and whose behavior may forecast future trends.

The Indianapolis Study provides a de-tailed analysis of such a group for the first time. The 1,444 "relatively fecund" couples in the "inflated survey group" were used to test the hypothesis: The greater the feeling of economic insecurity, the higher the proportion of couples practicing contraception effectively and the smaller the planned families. The first part of the hypothesis is not born out by the data, but the second part of the hypothesis is supported. The size of "number and spacing planned" families is directly associated with economic security regardless of differences in socioeconomic status.[11]

Six items relating to wives and husbands separately were used to form an index of economic security of the couple. One of them was the interviewer's direct rating, and five were self-ratings of each spouse of questions designed to be indicative of feeling of economic security. Among the "number and spacing planned" families the relation between the index of economic security and number of children was as shown in Table II.[12]

TABLE II

Index of Economic Security	Number of Couples	Children Ever Born Per 100 Couples		Per Cent Childless
		All Couples	Fertile Couples	
90	21	188	213	11.8
80–89	45	107	134	20.0
70–79	58	130	167	21.9
60–69	41	99	145	31.9
Under 60	56	57	135	57.4

The interesting thing about this table is that the association between size of family and economic security is direct rather than reversed as in the previous studies made on groups where there was a less consistent use of contraception. The numbers in this study are too small for basing any final conclusion, especially in the upper group; but the higher proportion of children in the top group corresponds with the change toward an increased fertility at higher economic levels reported in other studies. It appears from the study that there is a positive instead of a negative relationship between a sense of economic security and size of family among people who plan the number and spacing of their children. The picture is all the more striking because there is no evi-

TABLE III

Husband's Average Annual Earnings Since Marriage	Inflated Number of Couples	Number of Couples	Number of Children per 100 Couples
$3,000 and over	55	34	149
$2.000–$2,999	94	68	128
$1,600–$1,999	86	81	91
$1,200–$1,599	123	66	97
Under $1,200	44	88	68

dence that any larger proportion of people planned and spaced their children because of their sense of economic insecurity. In fact fertility-planning status was directly related to feeling of economic security albeit this type of relationship appeared to stem almost entirely from a positive relation of socioeconomic status to both economic security and fertility planning. The couples who planned and spaced their children were definitely not more affected by adverse economic factors than were those who did not plan and space their children.

In a separate study of fertility planning and fertility rates by socioeconomic status,[13] the Indianapolis Study gives further evidence of the reversal of class differentials in fertility among couples who use contraception effectively. Of the 1,444 "relatively fecund couples" in the adjusted sample, about one-quarter successfully planned and spaced the number of their children. Their fertility in relation to the husband's annual average earnings since marriage was as shown in Table III:[14]

It is interesting to note that the fertility rates of this group, all of whom used contraceptives, and used them with unusual effectiveness, are the inverse of the rates for socioeconomic classes in a society like that of the United States today in which some practice contraception and some do not.

So far as we know these are the only broad generalizations which can be supported by any adequate data, on factors affecting fertility among groups of people all of whom are using contraception effectively.

We have suggested three types of social background in which selection may operate; the type envisaged by Darwin in which social organization exerts a minor effect because of the high death rate, and in which fertility is determined by fecundity rather than by social conditions; the transitional type in which, because of the uneven spread of birth control, part of the population is affected by a new and primarily social force, and part is not; and the type which we believe is the type of the future, in which practically all the population are in a position to practice contraception effectively and actually do so, and psychological factors affecting the individual are of major importance in determining who shall have children. The studies we have quoted indicate that in each type of background differential fertility is affected by different factors, or is affected by the same factors in different ways.

The effective use of contraception is spreading rather slowly at the present time. But if there should be discovered a means of deferring conception by some form of inoculation or oral administration of medication or by treating foodstuffs, the situation would probably change overnight. Contraception by such means would seem less related to sex and more like a normal public-health function. People would be in a position to have children only when they wanted them. It would be my guess that there are probably few people in the world who would not choose to be in that position. Under such conditions it is likely that the behavior of the mass of the world's people would approximate that of the "planned number and spacing" group in the Indianapolis Study. If it did, the birth rate would be far below that needed for replacement; though the influence of the depression of the thirties, and the unusually high standards or aspirations of our urban groups might not prevail in other times or places. In any event these studies emphasize the importance of the shift first from physical factors to social factors, then from social factors to psychological factors, which takes place as we move from a background of no contraception, to a period of partial use of contraception and then to a period of full and effective use of contraception.

In the new framework for the operation of selection which we are now envisaging, the possible effects of differential fertility on genetic endowment are limited only by the existing variations in viable human stocks, and by those viable mutations which may take place in the future. To a greater extent than ever in the past, the genetic basis for man's higher qualities of intelligence and personality will for good or evil be sorted out for survival by individual choices as to births.

What would these forecasts mean for the possible future effects of differential fertility on genetic endowment? Our present evidence, insufficient as it is, would point to the following:

Socioeconomic differentials in fertility as we have known them in the past would disappear; or might even be reversed, according to the indications of the Indianapolis Study, and of other studies of small groups using contraception effectively. We do not know what significance this would have for changes in genetic endowment, but there is no reason to believe that it would introduce a dysgenic trend.

There are no equally strong indications for a change in present rural-urban differentials, except that they would probably not be so great. It is easier to raise a large family in the country than in the city, and we may therefore presume that some differentials would remain even if contraception were every-where effective. Since there is no evidence for a different distribution of genes in the country than there is in the city, we would not expect rural-urban differentials to affect genetic endowment.

Under the new conditions which are forecast by present trends, practically all children would be wanted and planned-for children, in contrast to the present when a considerable proportion of children are not wanted. This change would appear certain to raise the level of child care and home environment since parents who want and plan for children are likely to give children better care than parents who do not want them. It would probably also have a slight but continuous effect on genetic endowment; it is difficult to conceive that there are not genetic differences affecting the degree to which people consciously want children and are willing to make sacrifices for them, which would, however, slowly tend toward a new distribution of genes under the conditions of individual choice we are envisaging. It is not unreasonable to hope that a whole complex of socially valuable genes would be involved, for there are some grounds for believing that the conscious desire for children is associated with other socially desirable traits rather than the reverse. But proof of this hypothesis will have to wait on the further findings of the psychologist.

There is very little evidence regarding the effect on fertility of individual differences in the desire to have children. Yet the influence of the desire to have children must so universally affect size of family that one is inclined to consider it more important than age at marriage or economic security, about which we have a good deal of information. There may be, in fact probably are, genetic factors related to the ability to earn a living and to the desire for early marriage, but with respect to both these influences environmental a n d chance factors play so large a part that genetic factors appear secondary. The circumstances of the parents, the customs of the group, the type of occupation, the number of years of education required before developing an earning power, and other similar factors, largely determine age at marriage and economic security during the early years when security makes for fertility.

Economic security and age at marriage would apparently make for a redistribution of genes not directly, but indirectly as the form of any particular society gave them a differential effect. For instance, under conditions as they are today, men and women with scholastic interests and more t h a n average scholastic ability are likely to head toward teaching or research. Their schooling is prolonged, so they average a late age at marriage. Their early years at work are insecure and the pay small in contrast to the demands made on them; as a class they have small families. But the factors of economic security and age at marriage are in the control of society; it would be possible to offer scholarships to married students, and it would be possible to provide greater security for young married teachers, thus modifying present trends or even reversing them.

Social changes which may greatly alter trends in differential fertility are frequently made with quite different purposes in mind. Thus almost all European countries have adopted systems of family or child allowances to provide against the heavy expense of children and to stem a too rapid decline in population. But such measures must reduce the sense of economic insecurity and reduce the pressures in favor of late marriage among large sections of the population. As such measures become more widespread, the distribution of genes will increasingly be determined by couples exercising a freer choice than is possible at present, and under the influence of psychological factors which society itself will have a considerable hand in forming. One of the criteria for a "good" society should then be that it will provide for a distribution of genes which

will tend to make for its own continuation; that is, it will increasingly breed people whose genetic capacities are appropriate to the aspirations of the society to which they belong. The reverse situation probably holds at present.

When society has moved further into the stage of generally effective use of contraception, those physical qualities which hinder survival at the early ages will still be sorted out by differential deaths as in the past. As to defects and physical disabilities which have a genetic base and which develop later in life, it is perhaps reasonable to hope that public health authorities will develop some means of preventing carriers of the more serious defects from reproducing, and that suspected carrier or carriers of mild disabilities will tend to restrict the number of their children under the influence of improved medical advice; while at the same time the science of genetics will be called on increasingly to find means of recognizing carriers.

There are a number of obvious changes which could be made in the present forms of society on the basis of our existing knowledge, which would change the distribution of genes from one generation to another, and in a way which would in the long run help improve the functioning of society. What one might call "mass selection" by measures favoring the fertility of those who had demonstrated their ability to adapt themselves successfully to the forms or needs of their society, and the use of the "progeny test" to provide measures for increasing the fertility of parents whose progeny gave indications of more than average powers of adaptation to their form of society could be made effective on a basis of voluntary choice, and without running counter to other needs of society. The development of such measures will be greatly accelerated as wider use and new discoveries in contraception further reduce the birth rate. If we had a declining population, the public would probably quickly become interested in measures to increase births, qualitatively as well as merely quantitatively.

Meantime the best efforts of the psychologist, the sociologist, and the demographer should be directed at finding out what is going on among that at present small number of people who are practising contraception most effectively and are therefore most representative of the future. Whatever the trends in genetic endowment under present transitional conditions, the future is not without hope. It would be a gloomy prophet who felt that the conscious selection of births marked a backward trend in the progress of the race.

REFERENCES

1. THOMPSON, W. and P. K. WHELPTON, *Population Trends in the United States*, Mc-Graw-Hill, New York, 1933, p. 240.

2. DUBLIN, LOUIS, *The Facts of Life*, Macmillan, New York, 1951, p. 388.

3. LORIMER, FRANK and FREDERICK OSBORN *Dynamics of Population*, Macmillan, New York, p. 79.

4. THOMPSON, W. and P. K. WHELPTON, *op. cit.*, p. 274.

5. FLANAGAN, JOHN, "A Study of Factors Determining Family Size in a Selected Professional group." *Genetic Psychology Monographs*, 1942, 25, 3–99.

6. KISER, CLYDE and P. K. WHELPTON (Editors), *"Social and Psychological Factors Affecting Fertility,"* Milbank Memorial Fund Quarterly, New York, Vol. XXX, No. 3, July 1943; Vol. XXII, No. 1, January 1944; Vol. XXIII, No. 3, July 1945; Vol. XXIII, No. 4, October 1945; Vol. XXIV, No. 1, January 1946; Vol. XXV, No. 1, January 1947 and XXVIII, No. 3, July 1950. This material has also been reprinted in two volumes by the Milbank Memorial Fund.

7. *Ibid.*, pp. 340-341.

8. GALTON, FRANCIS, *Inquiries Into Human Faculty and Its Development*, reprinted by the Eugenics Society, London, 1951, p. 209.

9. LORIMER, FRANK and FREDERICK OSBORN, *op. cit.*, p. 390.

10. *Ibid.*, p. 364

11. KISER, CLYDE and P. K. WHELPTON, *op. cit.*, The Interrelations of Fertility, Fertility Planning, and Feeling of Economic Security, Vol. XXX, No. 1, January 1951, p. 112.

12. *Ibid.*, p. 93.

13. *Ibid.*, pp. 359-415.

14. *Ibid.*, p. 395.

IS THE INTELLIGENCE OF THE GENERAL

POPULATION DECLINING?

By Otis Dudley Duncan

IN his recently published book, *Human Fertility: The Modern Dilemma*, Robert C. Cook calls our attention to an alarming situation:[1]

Competent scholars . . . are agreed that today's differential birth rate makes a decline in intelligence inevitable.

(The 1949 report of the Royal Commission on Population) concluded that the average intelligence quotient of the British people was declining about 2 points every generation. The same pattern exists in the United States, where the experts consider a similar decline to be a "moral certainty." If this trend continues for less than a century, England and America will be well on the way to becoming nations of near half-wits.

Mr. Cook is a competent geneticist and the editor of the *Journal of Heredity*. His book appears with the endorsement of the well-known biologist, Julian Huxley. His statements on this question are buttressed by references to an extensive literature built up by outstanding psychologists and biological scientists. Perhaps it behooves us, as sociologists, to take account of the "gene erosion" which Mr. Cook believes is taking place, and to look into the prospect of the "destruction of modern technological culture" which he fears this loss of ability will entail.

How have "competent scholars"—to use Mr. Cook's phrase—reached this agreement on the "moral certainty" of a decline in intelligence? Two principal types of evidence have been relied on: first, differential fertility according to socio-economic status; second, the inverse correlation of family size and intelligence.

The first mentioned line of argument comes about through the coincidence of two important scientific developments, both of which can be roughly dated from the beginning of this century. On the one hand, since 1900, demographers have been busy building up a body of unequivocal evidence to show that, broadly speaking, in the Western world fertility is inversely related to socio-economic status; that is, the social groups at the top of the stratification pyramid are relatively infertile, whereas those at the base have disproportionately large families. Concurrently psychologists have been devising and perfecting tests of intelligence and applying them freely in an effort to measure the extent of group differences. Almost uniformly they find a *direct* correlation between social status and IQ. Taking them at face value, the juxtaposition of these two relationships naturally leads to fears that the dull are outbreeding the gifted in our population. A classic interpretation of this kind is to be found in the 1934 treatise of Lorimer and Osborn, *Dynamics of Population*.[2] These investigators proceed essentially as follows: Taking a set of typical results giving IQ distributions by occupational classes, they compute two weighted means. The first set of weights is based on the number of births

[1] Robert C. Cook, *Human Fertility: The Modern Dilemma*, New York: William Sloane Associates, 1951, p. 261 and p. 6.

[2] Frank Lorimer and Frederick Osborn, *Dynamics of Population*, New York: The Macmillan Co., 1934, Ch. IX

occurring by occupational class in a current generation; the second set on the number of births projected for the succeeding generation, assuming the persistence of the observed fertility differential by occupation. The difference between the first and second calculations is approximately one IQ point, which is taken by the authors as an estimate of the expected decline in the average intelligence, attributable to differential occupational fertility, over a period of one generation.

The second, and more direct, approach to the problem has been to correlate the measured intelligence of children with the size of the families from which they come. A large number of studies, using a variety of test instruments applied to quite diverse samples, have shown almost without exception a small, but unquestionably significant, negative correlation between number of sibs and intelligence scores of school-age children, with typical coefficients running around —.2 to —.3. Recent mammoth testing projects in Scotland[3] and France[4] have established this relationship as securely as any generalization in the field of differential psychology. With data of this kind it is easy to estimate a figure for the generation decline in average IQ. Suppose tests have been administered to a sample of children all of the same age, say eleven years. The procedure followed embodies the two assumptions that the tested child's IQ may be taken as an estimate of that of the mid-parent, and also as an estimate of the average IQ of his untested siblings. The subjects are classified by family size, that is, the size of the sibships from which they are drawn. A mean IQ is calculated for children in each family size class—only children, two-child families, and so on. With these submeans—which generally show a regular pattern of decrease with increasing family size—one may compute two weighted grand means. The first grand mean, taken to represent the average IQ of the parental generation, uses as weights the number of subjects in the family size class. The second

grand mean takes as weights the number of subjects in a family size class multiplied by the size of family. This second grand mean is, then, regarded as the estimated average intelligence of the entire offspring generation. Given the inverse correlation of intelligence and family size, the second mean is necessarily lower than the first; and the difference is taken to be the measure of decline in average IQ over a generation.[5] Typical estimates of this decline range from two to four IQ points.

It may be noted in passing that the inverse relation between family size and intelligence that appears when a single age group is tested cannot be successfully explained as an artifact produced by a putative correlation between intelligence and order of birth. No such correlation has yet been established. Various studies give conflicting results, and some even suggest an increase in intelligence with birth order.

To the argument that intelligence tests cannot measure a pure hereditary capacity, psychologists have replied that, although environment may account for part of the variance in IQ, heredity must account for at least 50 per cent and probably more of the variance. And even if the estimated decline in IQ were reduced as much as one-half, there would still remain a grave problem of population quality. It may be noted, too, that the negative correlation between IQ and family size is found *within* broad occupation groups, as well as in samples heterogeneous with respect to occupational class.

Despite the unquestioned cogency of the evidence for a negative correlation between fertility and measured intelligence, and in the face of the strong arguments which can be advanced against some of the more obvious objections raised against the thesis, the position taken here is that the hypothesis of declining intelligence need not be accepted—though, admittedly, the problem is one which calls for further research. The arguments against this hypothesis are summarized below, under five heads.

In the first place, the "experts" are by no

[3] Scottish Mental Survey Committee, *The Trend of Scottish Intelligence,* London: University of London Press, 1949.

[4] Institut National D'Etudes Demographiques, *Le Niveau Intellectuel des Enfants d'Age Scolaire,* Cahier No. 13, 1950.

[5] For the most explicit statement of this method of estimating the decline, and its justification, see Betty M. Giles-Bernardelli, "The Decline of Intelligence in New Zealand," *Population Studies,* IV (September, 1950), pp. 200–208.

means as unanimous on the question as they appear in the quotation from Cook. In his plea, Cook has—perhaps out of overenthusiasm for the dire prospect which he envisions—been guilty of some misinterpretation of his sources. The Royal Commission did *not* conclude in its 1949 report "that the average intelligence quotient . . . was declining about 2 points every generation." Rather, its actual conclusion verbatim, is as follows:[6]

We are not in a position to evaluate the expert evidence we have received to the effect that there is inherent in the differential birth rate a tendency towards lowering the average level of intelligence of the nation. This evidence . . . raises very serious issues. There is an urgent need for further research. . . .

One good reason for the Commission's hesitation in making a clear-cut finding is that the statements in evidence they received were conflicting. Strong statements in favor of the hypothesis were made by psychologists Thomson, Burt, and Fraser-Roberts, and supported by the eminent statistician and geneticist, R. A. Fisher. But a most emphatic dissent was registered by the likewise eminent geneticist, J. B. S. Haldane, writing as follows:[7]

I am now in complete disagreement with (Professor Thomson's) conclusion as to the effect of differential fertility. . . . The existing data give no reason to suppose that the level of innate intellectual capacity in our population is falling.

Here again Mr. Cook has been careless in compiling his account of expert opinion, for he overlooks this statement of Haldane's most recent views, and depends on a secondhand quotation from Burt:[8]

Burt points out that even a geneticist who sometimes takes an extremely environmentalist position, J. B. S. Haldane, also concludes that the decline in intelligence in England is "one or

two points per generation in the mean I.Q. of the country."

Outside the ranks of experts available to the Royal Commission the thesis of declining intelligence has perhaps been urged most vehemently by the psychologist Raymond Cattell,[9] while quite firm disagreement has been expressed by L. S. Penrose,[10] a foremost authority on the biology and genetics of mental deficiency. Another prominent geneticist who is unimpressed with the case for the hypothesis is Lancelot Hogben.[11] The point of these citations is not to establish anything one way or another by the method of appeal to authority. But in considering a problem area where they lack the technical skills required—those of human genetics and mental testing—sociologists should be aware of the extent to which those presumably most competent are disagreed among themselves.

A second set of objections to the hypothesis of declining intelligence arises from a consideration of questions which have been raised as to the appropriateness of the fundamental research tool involved—the intelligence test. In 1938, Walter S. Neff, after a thorough review of the literature, found reason to reject the entire body of evidence on socio-economic differentials in innate ability. Supporting his position with citation of a number of studies which showed important environmental effects on IQ, he argued that[12]

. . . the inequality of social and economic opportunity renders suspect one of the major assumptions basic to the construction of the

---

6 *Royal Commission on Population*, Report, Cmd. 7695, London: H. M. Stationery Office, 1949, p. 156. Cook does quote this passage, but only after leaving the impression that the Commission had reached a much more definite conclusion, and in a context which lays emphasis on the last two sentences rather than the first.

7 *Papers of the Royal Commission on Population*, Vol. V, London: H. M. Stationery Office, 1950, pp. 43–44.

8 Cook, *op. cit.*, p. 268.

9 R. B. Cattell, "Is National Intelligence Declining?" *Eugenics Review*, 28 (1936), pp. 181–203.

——, *The Fight for our National Intelligence*, London: P. S. King, 1937.

10 L. S. Penrose, "Genetical Influences on the Intelligence Level of the Population," *The British Journal of Psychology, General Section*, XL (March, 1950), pp. 128–136.

——, "The Supposed Threat of Declining Intelligence," *American Journal of Mental Deficiency*, 53 (July, 1948), pp. 114–118.

11 Lancelot Hogben, *Genetic Principles in Medicine and Social Science*, London: Williams & Norgate, 1931, p. 194.

——, (Ed.) *Political Arithmetic*, New York: Macmillan, 1938, pp. 331–333.

12 Walter S. Neff, "Socio-Economic Status and Intelligence: A Critical Survey," *Psychological Bulletin*, 35 (December, 1938), pp. 727–757.

tests; namely that knowledge and information are a direct function of native ability, and that the former may be used to measure the latter ... these tests cannot be used for measuring the capacity of different social levels within our own society.

This theme has been elaborated more recently by Davis, Havighurst and co-workers.[13] These investigators propose the concept of a "culture-fair" intelligence test. They claim actually to have devised such a test, one which measures intelligence validly, but which does not elicit the mean differences between socio-economic groups ordinarily found with conventional tests.

Should these positions be sustained, there would, of course, no longer be grounds for fearing a decline in intelligence solely on the basis of socio-economic differentials in fertility. However, the negative correlation of intelligence and family size within socio-economic groups might remain. It will be most interesting to see what light the new mental tests will throw on this issue.

Another pertinent question about the conventional mental test is its presumption of a general intellectual factor or capacity. In the whole discussion of declining intelligence, little reference has been made to the contention of some schools of factor analysis that mental ability may be classified into several orthogonal or independent factors. One wonders what correlations each of these factors in turn would show with family size. Presumably not all would necessarily be negative. However, the present situation in factor theory is one of much dispute. Quite recent developments in the statistical theory reported by Guttman[14] appear to give new support to the notion of a general intellectual factor. Certainly the issue should not be prejudged.

While dealing with the major props of the theory of declining intelligence, it might also be pointed out that traditional notions concerning differential fertility itself may stand in need of some revision on the basis

of recent findings. Whelpton and colleagues have reported that although the usual inverse relation between fertility and socio-economic status is found in the Indianapolis survey, when separate study is made of those couples who plan the number and spacing of their children, family size is found to increase directly with income.[15] May this not adumbrate the future diminution, if not disappearance, of socio-economic differentials of the usual sort?

A third weakness in the reasoning supporting the theory of declining intelligence is the dearth of knowledge concerning the actual genetic mechanism involved in the transmission of intellectual capacity. We have to deal in terms of a hypothetical construct twice removed from direct observation. From an operational standpoint, measured intelligence is an *ability* elicited as a function of a particular standardized social situation. By hypothesis, behind this ability lies an organically structured *capacity* which is jointly determinative of observable ability, along with environmental stimuli and constraints. By further hypothesis, the organic structure which carries potential ability, or capacity, is subject to *genetic* determination according to definite but unknown laws of heredity. It is a long leap of logic—if not of imagination—from observed ability to genetic determination, in the absence of secure empirical anchorage points for these constructs and their interrelations.[16]

In a more positive vein, it has been argued by Penrose[17] that the well known correlations in intelligence between mates and relatives and the negative relationship between IQ and family size are entirely compatible with a genetic equilibrium in which the average level of intelligence remains quite constant. Penrose has actually constructed statistical models of such populations in equilibrium which have a certain plausibility, except for the admitted oversimplification as to the mode of inheritance of intelligence. Clearly, though, more com-

[13] Ernest A. Haggard, "Influence of Culture Background on Test Performance," paper presented to the Invitational Conference on Testing Problems, New York, October, 1949.

[14] Louis Guttman, "A New Theory of Factor Analysis," address at the University of Wisconsin, April, 1951.

[15] See Frontispiece, *Population Index,* 13 (July, 1947).

[16] For an excellent elaboration of this viewpoint, see Julian L. Woodward, "The Field of Population Quality," *Social Forces,* 17 (May, 1939), pp. 468–477.

[17] *Op. cit.*

plex assumptions could also well yield the same outcome. The key to Penrose's reconciliation of apparently dysgenic fertility with genetic equilibrium is the assumption of the quasi-lethal nature of extremely low intelligence. This assumption squares with the high death rates and relative sterility of imbeciles and idiots—a fact somewhat neglected by the theorists of declining intelligence.

　　Fourth on the list of qualifications entered,

Consider longevity. There is much evidence for the existence of hereditary dispositions to long or short life spans. And longevity as a biometric character has striking analogues to intelligence in that it is a continuous variable, is probably determined by many genes, and is expressed only through a screen of strong and varied environmental influences. We find the same sort of socioeconomic differential fertility with respect to longevity that has been observed in the case

TABLE 1

Occupational class	Median IQ of Children	Per Cent of Total Births	Reproduction Rate
	(1)	(2)	(3)
Professional	116	3	.76
Business-Clerical	107	18	.85
Skilled	98	15	1.06
Semi-skilled	95	14	1.03
Farmer	91	31	1.32
Unskilled	88	19	1.17

　　Mean, weighted by column (2)　　　　　　=95.7
　　Mean, weighted by product of columns (2) and (3)　=94.6
　　(Source of data: Lorimer and Osborn, *Dynamics of Population*, Fig. 41, and Appendix Q.)

against this theory, and of probably greater consequence than any mentioned yet, is the unacceptability of certain seeming corollaries. Psychologists generally believe that intelligence is positively related to other "desirable" traits—vitality, personality, beauty, etc. But if our IQ genes are "eroding," must we also suppose that dysgenic trends are lowering our capacity for health, reducing the proportion of the physically attractive, and generally debilitating the human organism? Such a conclusion is not generally drawn, but seems to be logically implied.

TABLE 1B

Economic Level	Life Expectancy*	Relative Fertility
I (High)	67.1	.61
II	63.3	.82
III	61.4	.92
IV	58.0	1.12
V (Low)	54.5	1.44

　　Unweighted mean=60.9
　　Weighted mean　=59.6

* (Life expectancies for females in Chicago, 1930, from an unpublished study by Albert J. Mayer.)

of intelligence. Indeed the illustrative computation in Table 1B, modelled after that of Lorimer and Osborn for intelligence, would lead to the expectation that from a genetic standpoint longevity is declining at the rate of one year per generation. (Some simplifying, but not misleading, assumptions are introduced in Table 1; the table is only illustrative.) We know, of course, that length of life has been and is increasing remarkably in the modern period.

　　Or consider Boas' data on the stature of school children in relation to family size, roughly reproduced in Table 2B, along with typical results from an intelligence test survey, Table 2A. On the same logic as was used in producing the specter of a "nation of near half-wits" one could evoke the image of a nation of near-dwarfs (though the rate of deterioration implied would perhaps be slower). Again, the actual trend is the reverse, if anything.

　　The final and most telling blow to the theory of intellectual deterioration is the fact that, not only does no direct evidence exist to confirm the existence of such a trend, but what direct evidence there is shows the opposite movement toward a *rise* in the average level of measured intelligence! The extent to which scientific partisanship can govern response to evidence is nowhere better illustrated than in the temerity of one author who entitles her paper "The Decline of Intelligence in New Zealand" only to confess in passing that her sample scored considerably higher on the IQ test than did the earlier standardization sample taken in the same community.

The three large projects which thus far

The most ambitious resurvey is that of the Scottish Mental Survey Committee[20] which tested the entire year-group of 11-year olds in Scotland in 1947 for comparison with a similar study done in 1932. Some 70,000 subjects were involved. Although this study reiterates the familiar inverse relationship between intelligence and family size, the 1947 mean test score is found to be (the equivalent of) about two IQ points higher than the 1932 mean. The investigators consider carefully

TABLE 2

Number of Children in Family	A Deviation of Average Mental Test Score from Grand Mean[1]	B Deviation of Average Height from Grand Mean of Sample[2]
1	6.0	.21 (cm.)
2	5.5	.10
3	1.7	.05
4	—2.5	0.00
5	—6.6	—.05
6	—9.9	—.06
7	—10.9	—.14
8+	—14.7	—.13

[1] Institut National d'Etudes Demographiques, *Le Niveau Intellectuel des Enfants d'Age Scolaire*, Cahier No. 13, 1950.

[2] Franz Boas, *Race, Language and Culture*, New York, 1940, p. 63, fig. 3.

have been specifically designed to measure the trend of intelligence report the same finding that no decline can be detected, and that, if anything, a rise has taken place. Cattell, who some years ago predicted a decline of one IQ point per decade, reports a positive difference of more than one point in favor of the 1949 group of 10 year olds in Leicester and Devonshire, compared to the previously tested 1936 group.[18]

Collating results from retesting programs in a number of English school districts, Emmett finds that over an average elapsed period of 9.4 years boys' IQ's have changed at the rate of —.09 points per year, girls' at the rate of +.09 points.[19] It is noteworthy that this investigator feels able to rule out the possibility of incentive and test-sophistication effects as working in the direction of an increase.

a number of possible explanations for this unexpected result. Of the various reasons for refusing to credit it at face value, the most appealing to them seems to be the supposition of an increase in test-sophistication.

No evidence of such an increase is offered, nor is any effort made to adduce instances of bona fide test-sophistication effects of this magnitude in comparably heterogeneous populations. In effect, the erstwhile "genetic determinist" has suddenly, but lamely, turned to a grossly environmental explanation of a paradox in his results. The critic will surely ask, if environment is capable of explaining so much at this juncture, might not the explanation of the original, apparently dysgenic, relationship have some nongenetic explanation? Certainly, if the improved nutrition of the children is to be advanced as an explanation of their improved test scores, one would like to see some consideration given the possibility that the lower test scores of children from large families are due to their relative nutritional disadvan-

[18] Raymond B. Cattell, "The Fate of National Intelligence: Test of a Thirteen-Year Prediction," *Eugenics Review*, 42 (October, 1950), pp. 136–148.

[19] W. G. Emmett, "The Trend of Intelligence in Certain Districts of England," *Population Studies*, III (March, 1950), pp. 324–337.

[20] *Op. cit.*

tage compared to children from small families.

Other examples of seeming inconsistency between cross-sectional and longitudinal relationships may be found in the social science literature. Calendar year net reproduction rates for the 1930's showed the United States reproducing below the replacement level, whereas subsequent computations of generation rates have shown that no cohort of women as yet has failed to replace itself. Although cross-sectionally fertility is inverse to income, the birth rate rises with general prosperity.

This paper holds the hypothesis of declining intelligence to be untenable—and the "modern dilemma" in that respect to be most unfortunately misstated. But the assent which sociologists will presumably give to this conclusion does not deny the need for a heroic resolution of the seeming paradox as between apparently dysgenic forces and observed improvements in measured intelligence. Two suggestions are offered as to lines of research which might lead toward clarification. The supposition is that the paradox may inhere (a) in some as yet poorly understood aspect of the relationship between measured intelligence and family size, or (b) in some selective mechanism yet to be discerned. Along the first line, attention might be given the possibility that the inverse correlation of IQ and family size is not just a simple matter of more intelligent parents limiting their families more frequently than duller parents. It might well be that the phenomenon is in part a reflection of differential rates of mental maturation in families of different sizes. Or, in line with the previously mentioned proposal of "culture-fair" intelligence tests, one might suppose that family size is associated with relatively "microscopic" differences in cultural milieux, sufficient to account for some of the observed differences.

As for selection, it is painfully obvious on review of the literature under discussion that there exists not a single well-designed study to get at the association between intelligence and family size from the standpoint of the *parents'* measured intelligence. All the evidence is in terms of children's IQ's as correlated with number of siblings. To remedy this, ideally a cohort of children would be followed from the earliest age at which reliable IQ scores can be determined to the end of the childbearing period, in an effort to discover intelligence differentials in survival, marriage, dissolution of marriage, and fertility. Even a segment of or an approximation to this ideal design would be most welcome in the present state of ignorance. It would contribute far more than would further demonstrations of fertility differentials by intelligence levels, or even efforts to measure IQ trends.

Of course, the sociologist may well share the concern for population quality of the psychologist and the geneticist, but yet feel that the more important problems at the present time lie in the known wastage of available ability, rather than in the hypothetical loss of potential ability. In any case, the concern is well placed, and the research task is challenging.

Chapter VII

SELECTED REGIONAL STUDIES

In the preceding chapters were assembled papers having to do with specific subjects. Even so it has become evident that the demographic history of countries has varied greatly and that they differ widely in respect of their current stages of development and intensity of population pressure. In the present chapter appear a number of studies concerned with the demographic condition and/or the past demographic history of a number of representative countries.

The demographic history of each country may be described, within limits, as unique. For within each country is to be found a conjuncture of values, resources, and technologies out of which have issued what may be described as a demand for population and a disposition to supply population on given conditions. Both the conditions on which population is demanded and those on the basis of which it is supplied undergo change through time. These conditions become reflected in the age structure of the population and thus set limits to the extent to which the rate of population growth and the magnitude of the labor force can be modified in the course of several decades. This has been noted already in Chapter III among others.

For the sake of expositive convenience countries have been variously classified in terms of the stage of demographic development which they have achieved. They have been divided, for example, into: (a) those in which neither mortality nor natality are under effective control and the growth potential is high; (b) those in which natality and mortality, being under effective control, are low and the population is comparatively stationary or possibly even in a state of incipient decline; (c) those in which natality and mortality have been falling, but natality much less rapidly than mortality, with the result that considerable growth will take place before the population becomes transformed into a (b) type; and (d) those which resemble the (b) type in that both mortality and natality are under effective control and comparatively low, but differ from it in that natality, though moderate, significantly exceeds mortality which is very low. The population of India is representative of the (a) type, that of England of the (b) type, that of Japan or Poland of the (c) type, and that of Holland or the United States of the (d) type. In some countries a combination of the (a) and the (c) types may be found, one in which mortality has fallen but natality has been little affected. A five-category scheme was employed in the United Nations study in Chapter I.

Spengler's paper summarizes the demographic history of France, first of the European countries to experience a continuous decline in natality and become illustrative of the (b) type, though now more representative of the (d) type. Colombo's paper reviews the trends prevalent in Italy, a relatively densely populated country; long classifiable as a (c) type but now more nearly a (b) type. The paper on Germany describes the impact of war on a population's age and sex structure and upon its actual and potential growth rates. Eason's paper reveals how the population of the Soviet Union has responded to the developmental plans introduced in that country; it reveals both changes in Russian population policy and the tendency for natality to fall even in a totalitarian society bent upon stimulating population growth.

The papers on Brazil and Puerto Rico describe population types of the sort found in Latin America. The former is representative of a population still in an early stage of evolution, with natality almost typical of type (a) and mortality representative of type (c). The ratio of population to land and other resources is still quite low, however, and hence extreme difficulties of the sort occasioned by high fertility and great population pressure, now present in Egypt and parts of Indonesia, are not yet experienced. In Puerto Rico, on the contrary, the actual and the potential rates of population growth remain high, as in some other Middle American countries, even though the ratio of population to land and the other resources is unfavorable. Considerable relief has been derived from the fact, however, that Puerto Rico, having access to American markets and American capital funds, has been able to develop considerable industry and employment opportunities despite its comparative lack of land and resources.

Badenhorst's paper throws some light upon the population situation in Africa which, as he notes, remains the "dark continent" from a demographic point of view. Issawi's paper treats of the dimensions of the population problem as it exists in that most anciently settled portion of Africa, Egypt, and of the prospects for its solution.

The remaining papers deal with countries of Asia. The two papers on China depict the progress of population in that millenia-old state, the course of whose growth was treated already in Chapter I by Taylor. Taeuber's paper on Japan reveals what happened in the first country of Asia to undergo modernization and industrial development. There population has already nearly trebled since the Meiji Restoration nearly nine decades ago, and it may well increase another third or more if access can be found to food and resources for use in industry. Here we have a unique example of very careful use of all the resources at hand, and yet of but one possibility of escape from a steady increase in the pressure of numbers upon land and resources, namely, a great increase in international trade. The case of Japan is significant indeed in that it signifies that the populations of many other Asian countries will increase 200-300 or more per cent before they become stationary unless natality is reduced much more rapidly than it was reduced in Japan or Western Europe. Van der Kroef's paper depicts what is happening in Indonesia and how population pressure affects the course of economic development in that country. Taeuber's paper on Southeast Asia, viewed as a demographic laboratory, indicates (among other things) how the rate of growth in Ceylon has been augmented by the remarkable decline produced in mortality by modern public health methods. In their paper on Burma, Hauser and Kitagawa treat of the demographic situation of one of the few countries of Asia in which the population-resource ratio remains relatively favorable and there is still opportunity for solution of the population problem.

NOTES ON FRANCE'S RESPONSE TO HER

DECLINING RATE OF DEMOGRAPHIC GROWTH

By Joseph J. Spengler

FOR at least three quarters of a century the Devil of Declining Growth has been present at French council tables, at policy-making conferences, and in the minds of strategically situated decision makers. The Devil has not always been present in the flesh, since that is not the way of devils. But he has always been at the shoulders of the holders of power, and they have usually taken him into account implicitly when not explicitly.

I

The movement of France's population between 1801 and 1936 is susceptible of terse summary. In this interval the French population increased by 52 per cent or 13.7 million, moving from 27.5 to 41.2 million. Of this increase, 77 per cent took place in 1801–1866, and 3.1 million or 23 per cent in 1866–1936. France's population became relatively stationary, therefore, after 1866. Exclusive of Alsace-Lorraine which was ceded to Germany upon the conclusion of the Franco-Prussian War, the population increased only 10 per cent between 1872 and 1911, that of the ceded territory meanwhile growing about 21 per cent. In 1921 after the return of Alsace-Lorraine the French population numbered only 38.8 million or 2 per cent more than in 1866. Although it grew 2.4 million or 6 per cent in 1921–1936, the 1936 population total exceeded by only 3.1 million or 8 per cent that of 1866. In short, in 1866–1936 France's population increased much less rapidly—only 8 per cent—than in 1801–1866 when it grew 38 per cent. While World War II occasioned a smaller population loss than did World War I—about 1.45 instead of 2.85 million—the period 1936–1946 witnessed, according to the census returns, a 2 per cent decline. In 1946 France's population numbered about 40.8 million or only 7 per cent more than in 1866. By mid-1951 the postwar rise in natural increase, supplemented by some immigration, had raised France's population to about 42.2 million or 11 per cent more than in 1866.

France's population growth in 1801–1936—about 14 million—reflects the combined influence of net immigration, the prolongation of life, and the force of reproduction. During this period Landry estimates immigrants, together with their descendants, added about 5.5 million while the prolongation of life accounted for another 16.8 million. From this estimated increase must be subtracted 3.3 million representing the natality and mortality losses occasioned by World War I and an estimated loss of 5.3 million imputable to the decline in reproduction.

Net migration, mortality, and natality behaved somewhat differently in France than elsewhere in Europe in 1801–1936. France was the only European country to experience considerable permanent immigration, most of the others experiencing considerable emigration. Life expectancy and true mortality while more favorable in France than in southern and eastern Europe was somewhat less favorable than in the British Isles, Scandinavia, and several of the smaller West European countries. Prior to the nineteenth century gross reproduction in France may have been as high as 2.65, the level found in East Europe in the late nineteenth century, but by 1800–1820 it had fallen to a level of 2.0. Even so, the French rate was below those obtaining elsewhere, and it remained below until after World War I when gross reproduction in several countries descended below the French level. While the long-run trend was downward in all countries, the French rate fluctuated less than did rates in other countries. Net reproduction declined less and more regularly in France than in other representative countries in 1806–1936, moving from 1.08 in 1806–1820 to 1.01 in 1841–1850 and 1.01–1.04 in 1861–1890 and thereafter declining gradually to .89 in 1936–1939. Even so, net reproduction in France in the 1930's slightly exceeded that recorded in several West European countries.

II

Prior to the nineteenth century France was the demographically dominant power in Europe. Within the confines of France lived about 20 per cent of Europe's population in 1650 and about 15 per cent in 1750. In 1800 the fraction of Europe's population situated in France still approximated 15 per cent, but thereafter it declined appreciably. For Europe's population increased in 1800–1900 at a rate about two and a half times that experienced in France, and, in 1900–1940, at a rate about five times the French rate. By 1850 France's population comprised about 13.5 per cent of Europe's; by 1900, about 9.7 per cent; and by 1939, about 7.9 per cent.

The deterioration in France's relative demographic position was checked only slightly and then but temporarily by the improvement that took place in the age structure during the first fifty or so years of the nineteenth century. This same improvement was subsequently experienced by other countries and then served to accentuate the growth of their populations of productive age relative to that of France.

The movement of population between France and the rest of the world made its relative international demographic position both more and less favorable than it otherwise would have been. For, whereas France sent abroad in 1801–1936 in the neighborhood of 3.1 million emigrants, there came to France from other countries in that same period about 7.1 million immigrants. Accordingly, immigration may be said to have contributed to France's population, as of 1936, about 5.5 million, of which 4 million represent the contribution of net immigration as such and 1.5 million the net natural increase of these net migrants. The migrants who came to France were drawn there largely by anticipation that their economic prospects would be better than in their home countries.

The relative smallness of the number of France's emigrants must have contributed to the weakness of her relative demographic position. For migrants are the principal bearers of the value patterns and tastes peculiar to nations and cultures, while migrants and their descendants, at least so long as they retain esteem for the values and tastes and inhabitants of the mother country, will give it support and may win support for it among other peoples. In the period 1846–1932 about 52 million emigrants left Europe, of whom but 1 per cent were of French origin. For of the 2.8 million French who emigrated from France in 1851–1933, 800,000 remained in Europe while about 34 per cent of those who crossed the sea went to the French colonies. In the 1930's there lived in foreign lands about 540,000 Frenchmen, and, in the French colonies, about 2,322,000 French citizens who made up about 3.3 per cent of the population of these colonies.

III

Let us now see how income, savings, and capital formation behaved in France vis-à-vis other countries and then ascertain if this behavior was affected by population movements. There is little point to examining the movement of aggregates, for aggregate income and savings increased less rapidly in France, falling increasingly below the British and the German levels in the second half of the nineteenth century, because the labor force of France increased less rapidly than that of Britain and Germany. Attention here will be focused, therefore, upon per capita and per worker data.

In the first half of the nineteenth century output per worker in France, while lower than in Britain, apparently was higher than in other European countries for which estimates are given by Clark. After 1870, however, output per worker in Germany rose above that in France. Output per worker rose above the French level in Holland, Denmark, Norway, and perhaps in Belgium during the first decade of the present century, and, after World War II, in Sweden; it was higher in Spain after 1900, if not earlier. Clark's estimates suggest that output per employed worker grew at approximately the same rate in France and Great Britain between the 1830's and the 1860's—about $1\frac{3}{8}$ per cent per year—and at a higher rate in Germany—close to $2\frac{1}{4}$ per cent per year. During the last three or four decades before World War I the rate at which output per employed worker increased declined in all three countries, falling slightly below 1 per cent per year in both England and France and approximating 1 per cent in Germany. This deceleration, reflected also in wage data and experienced even in the United States, though not yet adequately explained, has been attributed in part to the fact that the late nineteenth-century inventions made for new products rather than for reductions in the resource costs of old products. During the period intervening between just before World War I and the best of the interwar years, the annual rate of increase was higher, approximating $1\frac{1}{4}$ per cent in Britain and Germany and $1\frac{3}{4}$ per cent in France. This last figure loses significance, however, since France enjoyed very few years of prosperity during the interwar period.

Output per worker in agriculture, being relatively sensitive to changes in the ratio of agricultural workers to land, remained higher in France than in Britain until around 1911 and higher than in Germany until the interwar period. Clark's figures indicate that output per employed worker in manufacturing in France always lagged behind that reported in Britain and Germany, and (assuming his estimates to be sufficiently reliable) that output per employed worker in manufacturing did not rise above output per male worker in agriculture until the closing third of the nineteenth century. Output per worker in tertiary occupations, always higher than in primary and secondary industries, was higher in Britain and Germany than in France. The growth of per capita output in France, relative to that in Britain and Germany, was slowed down somewhat, since the French labor force was slower than the British and the German in moving out of agriculture into secondary and tertiary employment.

Despite France's reputation as a nation of savers, net saving was less in France than in Britain or Germany throughout most of the period 1860–1930. Between 1871 and 1911 France saved about 10 per cent of her national income; Britain, about 12 to 15 per cent; and Germany, about 15 to 20 per cent. In the 1920's the German rate was close to 10 per cent while the French rate, now slightly above the British, was slightly below the German. As a rule, the German rate, expressed in terms of savings per head, was appreciably higher than the British, and the British appreciably higher than the French. Account must be taken also of the fact that France placed a larger fraction of her investment abroad than did Britain and Germany, the proportion of French savings going abroad rising from about one third in 1850–1870 to over one half by 1911 while the corresponding British and German figures were about one fourth and one tenth. Reproducible capital per person in work was lower in France than in Britain prior to the 1860's and than in Germany by the period immediately preceding World War I.

The comparative lowness of these figures is reflected in the amount of equipment used per worker in France. In the 1920's France ranked ninth among the nations of Europe in the consumption of machinery per capita; in the 1930's it ranked below Germany, the United Kingdom, and several smaller European countries in steel consumption per capita. In 1937 energy consumption per person engaged in agriculture, mining, and manufacturing was not much more than half as high in France as in the United Kingdom. In both 1929 and 1939 France ranked seventh among the countries of Europe in terms of daily output per capita from all major sources of energy.

IV

Population growth may affect, in various and unlike ways, the rate at which equipment per worker increases. First, when a population is growing relatively rapidly, more capital must be formed to provide the same increment in equipment per worker than when it is growing relatively slowly. Second, if, as some economists believe, the relative slowness with which a population grows makes for underinvestment and underemployment, actual national income will fall below potential national income, with the result that capital per head is formed less rapidly than when population is growing more rapidly. Third, saving may be both checked and stimulated. If slowness of population growth makes for a more favorable population-resource ratio, with economies of organization remaining unaffected, per capita income and per capita saving will tend to be higher, *ceteris paribus,* when a population is growing slowly than when it is growing rapidly. This inference is supported by the fact that, other conditions being given, the capacity of individual families to save is inversely related to the number of dependent children in the family. Population growth may, however, affect these other conditions. The relative number of older dependents increases as population growth declines. When a population is relatively sparse and relatively evenly distributed in space, income tends to be distributed more equally than when a population is relatively dense and relatively concentrated in space, with the result that, *ceteris paribus,* saving tends to be less under the former than under the latter conditions. Furthermore, the spread of childlessness in a bourgeois culture may, as Schumpeter suggests, diminish the value attached by a people to making "provision for an indefinite future." Unfortunately, information is lacking respecting most of these supposed effects.

While French employment data are inadequate to reveal the influence, if any, of the decline in the rate of population growth upon employment, France's trade-cycle history does not indicate any significant difference from that of countries whose populations were growing much more rapidly. In France the ratio of years of prosperity to years of depression compared very favorably in 1840–1925 with the corresponding ratios observed in other countries. Furthermore, variations in the length of the trade cycle in France did not differ significantly from variations experienced elsewhere. Presumably, trade-cycle behavior in France reflected the fact that France was somewhat less industrialized than Britain or Germany. French experience lends some support also to Cassel's view that, "if outside labour can no longer be attracted, or only to a slight extent, trade booms cannot occur again with anything like their former intensity." According to this view, outside labor may be drawn from the pool of disguisedly unemployed workers in agriculture or from the stream of immigrants and native-born persons flowing into the labor-force pool for the first time. From none of these sources could labor flow in sufficient volume to give sustained impetus to a boom. Rural natural increase was not very high, while the active agricultural population did not begin to shrink until after 1896 and then only at an average annual rate of about 35,000. Nonrural natural increase was not high. The immigrant population grew slowly, as a rule, and, when economic conditions became adverse, some of its members returned to their homelands, thereby reducing the pool of unemployed workers in France.

Whether the rate at which France's population was growing significantly affected the rate at which capital was formed is not clear. French age composition was not particularly conducive to dissaving. The saving rate may have been relatively low because income was somewhat more evenly distributed in France than in Britain or Germany; in part, perhaps, because of France's population situation, for the slowness with which population grew checked the development of both metropolitan centers and the pressure of numbers upon land and other resources, each of which forms of development may conduce to greater inequality. French savings may have been lower also because produced income per worker was lower in France than in Britain or Germany; yet the German saving rate exceeded the British even though produced income per worker was lower in Germany than in England.

Technical progress apparently contributed less to income growth in France than in Germany and England. In 1893–1913 France's labor force increased about 12 per cent; her produced income, about 26 per cent; and reproducible capital invested in France, about $1\frac{1}{4}$ per cent per year, since about one half her savings was exported. At this time Tinbergen estimates the elasticity of productivity of labor was in the neighborhood of 0.7; that of capital, 0.2; and that of other agents, about 0.1. Application of Tinbergen's coefficients to the increments in France's labor force and capital stock yields a 14 to 17 per cent increase in produced income. The remaining 9 to 12 per cent increase—about $\frac{1}{2}$ per cent per year—may be attributed largely to what Tinbergen calls "technical improvement" or applied invention. Application of Tinbergen's coefficients to data for 1875–1911 and 1853–1911 suggests an even lower rate of technical improvement—about $\frac{1}{3}$ per cent per year. Tinbergen's own studies suggest, however, that technical improvement in a group of countries, of which France was one, increased income about 1 per cent per year.

Population growth may produce a dynamic effect just as do invention and innovation. First, it may make possible economies, such as those arising from greater division of labor, which more than offset the adverse effects of increases in the pressure of numbers upon resources. Second, it may generate a psychic and material milieu that is relatively conducive to salutary change and flexibility; to the exercise of inventiveness, innovation, and effort; to the effective utilization of capital; and, perhaps (in the longer run), even to the formation of capital. While most theorists accept the first proposition, they are not in agreement respecting the magnitude of the income-optimum population for France. Some hold that by the latter part of the nineteenth century France's population was sufficiently large—given her external relations and the state of technology—to exploit division of labor and related sources of economy as fully as was economically justified by the available land and raw materials. Others, among them Sauvy and Létinier, put the optimum for France at 50 to 75 million. Sauvy points out also what writers usually overlook, that when unproductive outlays, such as those for military purposes, are relatively high, a larger population than otherwise would be indicated is required to maximize per capita output and consumption of nonmilitary goods and services. Concerning the validity of the second proposition there is not much that can be said here except that it is very difficult to isolate any dynamic influence exercised by the population variable. Population growth can produce the effects indicated only if there are present in a people's value and culture patterns the necessary facilitating elements. Furthermore, these effects may also result from nondemographic changes. The lowness of the rate of technical improvement reported in the previous paragraph suggests that population growth in France in the period 1850–1911 and perhaps in the past one hundred fifty years has produced little or no dynamic effect under the head of either of the above propositions, for the disclosed rate of technical improvement is so low as to appear imputable entirely to invention and innovation. If this be the case, one might then argue that the present French population may be above the income optimum in size though not necessarily above the military-income optimum.

Cultural factors appear to be much more responsible than purely economic factors for the slowness with which output per worker has progressed. For, while France's resource potential is limited, including only 1.2 per cent of the world's iron and only .4 per cent of the world's energy reserves (exclusive of fissionable materials), the French economy is making inadequate use of the energy and other resources at its disposal. It has been shown that, since energy consumption tends to reflect the use of capital and efficient methods generally, a 1 per cent increase in a nation's energy consumption tends to be accompanied by about a 1/2 per cent increase in output per worker. Yet in 1937 French per capita energy consumption was only one sixth above the over-all European level and below that of at least five leading European countries. Inadequacy in the amount of energy and equipment at the disposal of the French worker is only the immediate cause of the slowness with which produced income progresses. Back of this lie other causes that are more ultimate: the unenterprising character of so much French entrepreneurial behavior; heterogeneity of consumer tastes; hostility to innovation, mechanization, standardization, and selective, cost-reducing competition; unconstructive approaches in the field of labor-management relations; and so on. Not even these factors, however, account for the situation in a manner that is both sufficient and relatively ultimate. For, as Sawyer, Landes, and others have shown, French value patterns, French tastes, the heterogeneous nature of France's cultural heritage, together with the conflicts produced thereby, are acting in combination with other elements in social structure and culture to restrict economic development. These elements, together with France's then political situation, probably played a much larger role than did the slowness of her population growth in diverting savings abroad before 1914. Professor Sauvy's analysis suggests that these elements have also played a part, together with the curtailment of economic competition, in generating an occupational structure not suited to France's economic needs and not sufficiently conducive to the augmentation of real income.

V

Our discussion thus far has had to do principally with the economic reaction of French individuals to a changing demographic situation. Men may also react collectively, in part, because some individual aims can best be pursued collectively, and, in part, because every collectivity as such has ends whose pursuit is variously facilitated by a considerable portion of the population composing it.

Collective reaction to France's population situation has been manifest for nearly a century. Concern was expressed already when deaths temporarily exceeded births in the early 1850's. The alarm many felt at the time the German state was undergoing consolidation became intensified when that country, with a military man power not greatly different from that of France, defeated her. The prescient then foresaw that, given prospective trends, Germany's military man power would steadily outstrip that of France whose status in time would become that of a second-rate power, since victory in historic struggles usually went to growing populous states. Their forecast was borne out, for on the eve of World War I both France's military man power and her income-producing capacity were not quite six tenths that of Germany's. By 1939 the German margin had become appreciably greater.

Two types of action were advocated. On the one hand, measures designed to stimulate natural increase and immigration were proposed and after a time adopted in a slight degree. On the other hand, efforts were made to enlist sources of strength that might make up in part the growing relative deficiency in French military man power and economic strength. Let us consider these types in reverse order.

In this second category fall, besides France's search for allies, her utilization of savings for international political purposes, her post-1870 colonial ventures, and some of her military man-power policies. Exporting one third to one half her annual savings, France, by 1912, had accumulated a foreign investment six times that which foreign investors had placed in France and approximately equal to two fifths of French capital in the form of stocks and one seventh of French wealth. Since three fourths of these loans went to foreign governments, and only 9 per cent flowed into France's colonies, France, unlike England, failed to develop effectively her own overseas territories or to build up permanent markets for her products and permanent sources of raw material. Her failure in this respect, of course, may be, in part, that there were so few French emigrants and bearers of French culture to generate economic situations highly complementary to the French economy. Between 1914 and 1919 about 82 per cent of the net foreign holdings of French investors, as of 1914, were wiped out. By 1938 France had again accumulated considerable foreign holdings only to have much of their value destroyed. While France did not derive outstanding economic gain from pre-1914 foreign investments, she probably enlisted considerable political and military support through them, in particular that of populous and strategically situated Russia, but she acquired this support at the expense of her own and her colonies' development.

France's post-1870 colonial ventures were inspired in part by her supposition that, since her population growth did not permit continental expansion, it might still be possible, despite her slow demographic growth, to develop a colonial empire whose strength would greatly augment her own. French natality would be stimulated, it was believed, by the resulting emigration. Militarily she sought to offset Germany's greater man power by calling into service a much larger fraction of the population eligible for such service. However, the strain occasioned by this method made France anxious to enter into an alliance with populous Russia and prompted some of her military leaders to develop plans for the military and the economic use of her colonial man power in the event of war. Unfortunately, however, French military theory and practice did not develop in a way suited to make economic use of her military man power, with the result that France's losses were relatively heavy in World War I.

The promotion of immigration is considered very important by French population students. Formerly, interest was expressed principally in the size of the immigrant stream. Since the war, however, great stress has been placed upon the age structure of the immigrant population. Because of the impact of war and past variation in natality, the French age structure is uneven, and it will remain uneven for many years even though fertility and mortality become relatively stable. For example, given a continuation of the demographic conditions of 1946–1950 and the resulting slight increase in the population, the percentage of adults in the population, about 54 per cent in 1950, would by 1965 fall nearly to 48 per cent and then, as the population approached stability, settle in the neighborhood of 52 per cent. Other growth patterns yield even greater declines in the relative number of persons of productive age. Whence dissaving by the aged and a decline in productivity are apprehended.

A decline in the relative number of persons of productive age can be met through the deferment of retirement, through the diminution of retirement pay, or through the introduction into a country of enough persons of appropriate age. Prompted in part by fear that the decline in prospect might affect adversely both the family-allowance system and the social-security program, some French students in 1946 put France's immigrant needs at 3 to 5 million, with young adults predominating. Yet not even a minimal estimate of some 100,000 adult immigrants per year has been realized, only 70,000 net of all ages entering France in intercensal 1936–1946 and about a half million since then. Among the circumstances held responsible for the smallness of the immigrant influx are France's failure to enlist and assimilate immigrants effectively, and the fact that East European sources of supply have been cut off.

Opposition on the part of three quarters of the French population to the admission of immigrants prevents the development of an effective, large-scale immigration program. This opposition, which is most pronounced in wage-earning groups and which formerly was fed by the indisposition of immigrants to join trade unions, is based on both fear of immigrant competition and hostility to the cultures of the immigrants; it is not prompted by the Walker immigrant-native-replacement theory which had some currency in nineteenth-century France. The prospective competition of the immigrants is exaggerated, however, for relatively most of them enter less popular employments (for example, mining) and therefore complement rather than compete with most French workers.

Most important of the sets of measures proposed in the nineteenth century to check the downward trend in natural increase was that providing varied economic assistance for families with children. Such measures ran counter to the bourgeois scheme of values and, being based on the principle of need, had to wait for enactment until egalitarian sentiments had become sufficiently strong. For a long time, therefore, the proponents and executors of these measures seemed bent upon trying, though with little success, "to buy babies at bargain prices," since only a small part of the nation's resources was directed to this purpose and since, insomuch as the family-wage system was relied upon, support of family assistance probably came principally out of labor's imputed product.

The family-wage system did not get effectively under way before World War I. Thereafter, despite the temporary opposition of non-Catholic trade unionists, it continued to grow under private auspices until 1932. In that year the state intervened to make membership in a family-wage equalization fund compulsory for employers and thereby to establish the principle of need as a legal determinant of wages and the right to income. In 1939, with the effectuation of the *Code de la Famille,* the fundamental basis of the present system of family aid was completed. For this measure made possible the bringing of the whole population under the family-allowance system, introduced uniform administrative rules, and, by emphasizing pronatalist objectives, effectively distinguished family allowances from ordinary earned income and established a basis for increasing subsidization of the system by the state. In the decade that followed, family assistance was variously augmented while the pronatalist features of the system were strengthened. Even so, the system is still largely financed by employers, though it is now almost universally accepted as a part of the income-distributing mechanism and looked upon as harmonizing the interests of both contemporary groups and successive generations.

The French family-allowance system is not a widow's cruse and is not likely to become one unless output per worker and the aggregate produced income increase greatly. In 1949 the French system, though more generous than the British and the Belgian systems, provided at most only 74 per cent of a child's needs and, in some groups, less than half. Presumably, public expenditure upon youth, which in 1950 approximated 10 per cent of the state budget and nearly 3 per cent of the national income, can be increased. Yet this source is limited, even given effective taxation, since, as of 1950, 71 per cent of the national income would have been required to provide everyone with a "social minimum." Moreover, as the relative number of unproductive aged increases further, more funds will have to be provided for their support, since their resources are limited, and since the needs of an old dependent exceed those of a young dependent. Furthermore, the present shortage of housing and related needs can be overcome only if the comparatively inelastic building industry is sufficiently augmented. Finally, in view of the fact that France already has one of the highest labor-force/population ratios —about 0.5—and that, therefore, the addition of more women workers and the deferment of retirements cannot swell French production significantly, produced income can be greatly increased only if the economy is completely reorganized and modernized.

Despite the difficulties noted, however, natality held up well during the war years and, along with marriages, greatly increased thereafter. In 1946–1950 births were 35 per cent above the 1934–1938 level, and natural increase augmented the population by about 4 per cent. Should the annual number of births remain at 850,000 and life expectancy at birth rise to 70 years, France's population will increase to 61 million even without the assistance of migration, while, if late-1940 net reproduction persists, the population will grow nearly 1 per cent per year. It remains to be seen, however, whether the family-allowance system, together with the social and psychological factors that operated during and after the war, have produced a sufficient change in the French system of values to ensure 850,000 births per year. Public-opinion polls indicate that the average number of children desired per family approximates 2.4, whereas, given current nuptiality and fertility, a standard family of 2.5 to 2.6 children—only about three tenths of the number required two hundred years ago—is needed to replace the population. There is evidence of an increase since 1947 in Malthusian sentiments and in the belief that living standards have fallen. There is evidence also that factors which formerly affected fertility (for example, religiosity; size of community; employment; group social and income differences) are still active.

A nation's rate of population growth is dominated ultimately by two factors: the level and content of the aspirations of its members and the supply of goods and services continually available for the satisfaction of these aspirations. Presumably, a population's elasticity, though less than unity, frequently tends to be positive. This inference is supported by the positive correlation found to obtain between indices of both migration and reproduction and indices of economic activity, and it should be borne out by comparisons of the relative rate of increase in national income with the relative rate of increase in population lagged slightly. Unfortunately, the French income data do not permit a satisfactory determination of French population elasticity in the period 1840–1914. The elasticity, while positive, fluctuated, being highest when income increase was lowest and lowest when income increase was highest. Presumably, therefore, variation in aspirations, short-time insensitivity to variations in real income, and the residual effects of earlier demographic and related events, together with other factors, must have intervened continually in France to offset the population-increasing influence of income growth.

PRELIMINARY ANALYSIS OF RECENT

DEMOGRAPHIC TRENDS IN ITALY

By Bernardo Colombo

The years which preceded World War II produced a wide variety of demographic studies in Italy. The censuses of 1931 and 1936, together with detailed and reliable vital statistics, provided students with material that permitted a thorough analysis of population characteristics and changes and enabled them to elaborate methodological devices which made a substantial contribution to demography.

In recent years the situation has been completely different. Studies of the demographic situation in Italy have been rare and necessarily limited to general description of over-all characteristics. Up-to-date materials for the analysis of demographic developments have been lacking. For various reasons it was not possible immediately after the war to take the census of population which, in accordance with the rule introduced at the 1936 census, should have been taken in 1946. It was only in November, 1951, that the census was finally taken and evidently it will be some time before the detailed results are available.

The publication of vital statistics was interrupted after 1940. In the course of the war Italy was split into two parts and the dividing line between the Allied and the German forces moved northward from time to time. In this period the offices of the Istituto Centrale di Statistica were transferred to North Italy. For some time many of the local registration authorities were unable to send to the central office the data on births, deaths, and marriages which they were currently collecting. A part of this documentation was lost with the destruction of some local offices[a]. Only recently after a long and careful searching and checking of wartime records has the Istituto Centrale di Statistica managed to complete the publication of vital statistics up to 1948. The volume containing data for 1949 is in course of publication.

In two or three years, when the detailed results of the recent census are available and the publication of vital statistics has fully caught up, students of the demographic situation of Italy will have at their disposal a mass of data of great variety and reliability with several historical series of detailed tabulations (e.g., the classification of legitimate births by year of marriage and parity has been available since 1930).

The purpose of this note is to sketch the present demographic situation in Italy so far as the data now available permit. For some aspects (for example, legitimate fertility) it is possible to make a fairly satisfactory analysis; for others (such as nuptiality) it will be necessary to wait for the census materials before a detailed picture can be drawn. This note will necessarily lack balance in the distribution of space between subjects and the discussion will have a preliminary character.

Table 1

Population Growth in Italy: 1901-1952[1]
(De facto population in present area)

Census Date	Total Population (in thousands)	Annual Rate of Increase (per thousand)
February 10, 1901	33,172	6.8[a]
June 10, 1911	35,442	6.4
December 1, 1921	37,143	4.5
April 21, 1931	40,310	8.7
April 21, 1936	42,025[b]	8.4
November 4, 1951	46,738	6.9
February 29, 1952[c]	46,793	

a/ During the period December 31, 1881–February 10, 1901.
b/ Special de facto population, including members of the armed forces and civilians following the armed forces in East Africa, in colonies, and possessions (465 thousand).
c/ Last available estimate.

1/ Source: Annuario Statistico Italiano, 1951, and Bollettino Mensile di Statistica, April 1952.

Population Growth and Natural Increase

The de facto population enumerated at the census of November 4, 1951, was 46.738 million. The difference between this figure and the last estimate published prior to the census (46.672 million for October 31, 1951) is very slight. Meteorological conditions interfered with the taking of the census; in 41 communes in the province of Rovigo and in the commune of Cavarzere in the province of Venezia the census operations had to be interrupted owing to floods. Nevertheless the census was generally carried out with completeness and accuracy. The amount of underenumeration is presumably insignificant.

At the same date the de jure population, which relates to habitual residents including those temporarily absent, was 47.021 million. In a territory of 116,228 square miles, 47 millions correspond to a density of 404 per square mile compared with 285 in February, 1901, within the same boundaries.

In fifty years the population within the present boundaries increased by about 41 per cent. The stages in this increase are shown in Table 1, which gives the de facto population of the present territory at each census since 1901; the table also shows the annual rate of growth in each intercensal period (calculated by the compound interest formula). Heavy emigration and World War I contributed to the maintenance of a relatively low rate of growth in the first two decades. The second world conflict seems not to have had so decisive an influence as the first. The reduction in the number of births was less noticeable and deaths caused by the war were probably less than half of those during the war of 1915-1918. The outward balance of migration in recent years has not assumed significant proportions.

Table 2

Crude Vital Rates in Italy: 1901-1951[a] [1]

Period	Rates per 1,000 Population			Infant Mortality
	Marriages	Births	Deaths	
1900-1905	7.4	32.7	22.0	167
1906-1910	7.9	32.7	21.2	155
1911-1915	6.9	31.5	19.7	140
1916-1920	6.4	23.0	24.4	152
1921-1925	9.0	29.8	17.4	127
1926-1930	7.3	26.8	16.0	119
1931-1935	6.8	23.8	14.1	105
1936-1940	7.6	23.3	13.9	103
1941-1945[a]				
1946-1950	8.6	21.5	10.9	77
1936	7.4	22.4	13.8	100
1937	8.7	22.9	14.3	109
1938	7.5	23.8	14.1	106
1939	7.3	23.6	13.4	97
1940	7.1	23.5	13.6[b]	103
1941	6.1	20.9	13.9[b]	115
1942	6.4	20.5	14.3[b]	112
1943	4.8	19.9	15.2[b]	115
1944	4.8	18.3	15.3[b]	103
1945	6.9	18.3	13.6[b]	103
1946	9.2	23.0	12.1	87
1947	9.7	22.3	11.5	84
1948	8.4	22.0	10.6	72
1949	7.8	20.4	10.5	74
1950	7.7	19.6	9.8	64
1951	6.9	18.1	10.3	67

a/ Data refer to territory as follows: up to 1920, boundaries prior to World War I; 1921-1942, boundaries prior to World War II; beginning 1943, boundaries established by the peace treaty of 1947.

For 1943-1945 it was not possible to obtain data from the localities whose records were destroyed during the war. Therefore, and owing to the boundary changes, no averages for 1941-1945 are shown.

b/ Excluding deaths in military zones of operation and on foreign soil.

1/ Source: See Table 1.

Table 2 presents an over-all picture of the customary crude vital rates since the beginning of the century. Its purpose is to provide a historical background for the more recent period. (The first three series are shown for the entire period of registration on the front cover of this issue of the Index.) These series illustrate the constant decline in the frequencies of births and of deaths—a decline that has been maintained throughout the period apart from the oscillations which can easily be explained by the effect of the two wars. In particular the table brings out the reduction in birth, death, and infant mortality rates between the prewar period and recent years.

Fertility

In Italy the percentage of illegitimate births among all births is very low; since the Second World War it has always been well below four per cent. Thus a study of fertility in the recent past can safely concentrate on legitimate fertility.

Since 1930 the Istituto Centrale di Statistica has published every year a tabulation of legitimate births (including stillbirths) by year of marriage and parity. With such data the births of each parity can be related to the original number of marriages, and it is possible to follow a marriage cohort through the childbearing period. By dividing the births in a year resulting from marriages of a certain duration by the original number of marriages contracted by the relevant cohort one obtains a set of measures of current fertility specific by marriage duration [b]. By adding the rates computed for all marriage durations from the births occurring in a given year one obtains a synthetic measure of the fertility of that year independent of the year-by-year variations in the number of marriages contracted in the past, or, put in another way, unaffected by changes in the mean duration of existing marriages. Such measures of current fertility are approximate because they are based on the initial number of marriages and not on those remaining in the relevant year. The year-by-year variations in these measures are also affected by changes in the rates of dissolution of marriage, by whatever cause, and the migration of married persons. There is, however, no reason to believe that for Italy in the period which is here considered these factors have a significant influence on any conclusions drawn from the data.

These measures of fertility are in effect largely standardized also by age since the mean age at which marriages have been contracted in successive years has remained fairly stable. It is in any case difficult to believe that variations in the age at marriage such as usually occur (of the order of one or two years at most) imply appreciable changes in attitudes regarding fertility.

Table 3 shows for each year from 1930 to 1951 the sum of duration-specific fertility rates obtained as described above. For ease of comparison, indices (taking 1936-1940 as the base period) are also given [c].

The number of births when corrected for fluctuations in the number of marriages was approximately constant in the ten years preceding the war. (The births of 1940 were conceived before Italy's entry into the war.) The slight decline in 1936-1938 can be explained in part by the absence of a limited number of married civilians and members of the armed forces in East Africa and Spain. The five years of World War II witnessed a reduction of about 10 per cent. In contrast the same measures of fertility in other Western countries either remained constant or increased during the war years as a whole. In general, in these countries fertility was very low during the 1930's and the higher fertility during the war years has been interpreted as a making up for the earlier low rates.

The higher fertility in Italy in 1946 can be attributed in part to a making up of postponed births. Presumably the making up was still going on in 1947. Yet it was not sufficient to maintain the corrected fertility rate at its prewar level. Since 1947 there has been a rapid and continuous decline. In 1951 fertility fell to the lowest level yet record-

Table 3

Trends in Net Legitimate Fertility in Italy: 1930-1951

(1930-1942, prewar area; 1943-1951, area
established by the peace treaty of 1947)

Year	Births per 1,000 Original Marriages /a	Index Number (1936-40 = 100)
1930	3,609	111
1931	3,378	104
1932	3,293	101
1933	3,331	102
1934	3,297	101
1935	3,288	101
1936	3,186	98
1937	3,230	99
1938	3,219	99
1939	3,304	102
1940	3,315	102
1941	2,985	92
1942	3,010	93
1943	2,977	92
1944	2,850	88
1945	2,893	89
1946	3,533	109
1947	3,225	99
1948	3,088	95
1949	2,845	88
1950	2,741	84
1951/b	(2,530)	(78)

a/ Sum of over-all durations of legitimate specific fertility rates (stillbirths included) by calendar year of marriage. The rates are calculated on the basis of the original number of marriages in the appropriate cohort, and not on that of marriages surviving to the year of record within the national boundaries.

b/ See text.

---

ed in Italy. If in that year the fertility rates of 1950 for each duration of marriage had been maintained, there would have been 914,430 legitimate births (including stillbirths) or about 885,000 legitimate live births. In fact there were only about 815,500. Applying a corresponding factor to the corrected number of births for 1950 shown in Table 3, we obtain for 1951 a corrected number of births (including stillbirths) of about 2,530 per thousand original marriages. This figure is presented in Table 3 in parentheses. We shall come back later to this measure.

It may be of interest to examine more closely some features of the recent changes in the childbearing habits of Italian marriages. For this purpose Tables 4-6, which are representative of a general trend, have been prepared. Table 4 shows how the distribution of the correct-

Table 4

Distribution by Order of Birth of the Net Number of Births
Shown in Table 3: Italy, 1930, 1940, 1950

(Area as of date)

Birth Order	Number of Births			Per Cent of Total		
	1930	1940	1950	1930	1940	1950
1	872	881	843	24.2	26.6	30.8
2	716	712	650	19.8	21.5	23.7
3	555	519	444	15.4	15.7	16.2
4	422	377	281	11.7	11.4	10.3
5	320	269	175	8.9	8.1	6.4
6+	724	557	348	20.1	16.8	12.7
Total	3,609	3,315	2,741	100.1	100.1	100.1

Table 5

Duration of Marriage at Confinement for the Net Number of Births
Shown in Table 3: Italy, 1930, 1940, 1950

(Area as of date)

Birth Order	Marriage Duration at Confinement (Years)			Ratios		
	1930	1940	1950	1940/30	1950/40	1950/30
1	1.39	1.56	1.58	112	101	114
2	3.93	4.42	4.74	112	107	121
3	6.38	7.05	7.56	111	107	118
4	8.78	9.34	9.83	106	105	112
5	10.92	11.38	12.11	104	106	111

Table 6

Distribution by Marriage Duration of the Net Number of Births
Shown in Table 3: Italy, 1930, 1940, 1950

(Area as of date)

Marriage Duration at Confinement (Years)	Number of Births			Per Cent of Total		
	1930	1940	1950	1930	1940	1950
0-5	1,532	1,418	1,271	42.4	42.8	46.4
5-10	978	895	716	27.1	27.0	26.1
10-15	588	580	416	16.3	17.5	15.2
15-20	352	316	236	9.8	9.5	8.6
20+	159	106	102	4.4	3.2	3.7
Total	3,609	3,315	2,741	100.0	100.0	100.0

Table 7

Trends in Cumulated Net Legitimate Fertility by Marriage Cohorts:
Italy, 1930-1946 /a

Calendar Year of Marriage	Births per 1,000 Original Marriages up to ... Years of Marriage Duration		
	5	10	15

A. Number of births

1930	1,448	2,337	2,894
1931	1,444	2,331	2,864
1932	1,448	2,340	2,879
1933	1,434	2,304	2,827
1934	1,424	2,273	2,776
1935	1,412	2,220	2,732
1936	1,415	2,173	2,678
1937	1,377	2,130	
1938	1,338	2,106	
1939	1,283	2,082	
1940	1,243	2,078	
1941	1,188	2,016	
1942	1,276		
1943	1,349		
1944	1,488		
1945	1,369		
1946	1,333		

B. Index Numbers (1930 = 100)

1930	100	100	100
1931	100	100	99
1932	100	100	99
1933	99	99	98
1934	98	97	96
1935	98	95	94
1936	98	93	93
1937	95	91	
1938	92	90	
1939	89	89	
1940	86	89	
1941	82	86	
1942	88		
1943	93		
1944	103		
1945	95		
1946	92		

a/ For area coverage, see text, page 272.

ed number of births by parity has changed. It must be remembered that this distribution reflects not only the behavior of married couples during the year in question but also the distribution of couples by number of children already born at the beginning of the year. However, there can be no doubt that the decrease between 1930 and 1950 would appear more pronounced for the high orders of births (say fifth and higher) than for births of low order. More detailed calculations show that for married couples surviving after a given duration of marriage and with a given number of children already born fertility has declined.

In 1950 there were fewer births than in 1940, and in 1940 fewer than in 1930. The births of a given parity (at least up to and including fifth births) occurred at increasing intervals after marriage as shown in Table 5. This increase is a clear indication that for lower orders of birth the rate of childbearing for the same fraction of marriage has been reduced.

The distribution of fertility between various periods of marriage has changed in the last ten years (see Table 6). There is now a greater concentration of fertility in the earlier years of marriage as a result of the greater reduction in the number of births of high parity.

By adding up successively the rates relating to a given cohort of marriages and calculated for successive calendar years (and therefore for successive annual classes of marriage duration) one obtains a measure of the cumulated fertility of that cohort since the marriage up to the highest marriage duration whose rate is included in the sum. These cumulated numbers of births are given in Table 7 for the cohorts of 1930-1946 and for marriage durations up to 5, 10, and 15 years. Index numbers are also given; the base used was the number of children to marriages of 1930 since their marriage and up to the given duration. In reading this table it must be kept in mind that the basic yearly rates since 1943 relate to the present territory and the previous ones to the territory within the prewar boundaries. The fertility of population of the lost provinces of Venezia Giulia, which account for almost the total difference, was lower than the national average. Therefore there is some bias in those figures in Table 7 which include the experience of years following 1942; these figures may be somewhat inflated in comparison with the corresponding figures relating to the old boundaries.

In any case, the pattern shown by the indexes of Section B of the table is clear enough and indicates a constant decline in cumulated fertility, at least for the cohorts whose childbearing behavior can be followed for ten or more calendar years. The same trend is apparent in the shortest marriage duration until the cohort of 1941. In looking for an explanation for the higher fertility of the succeeding cohorts during their first five years of marital life one should keep in mind the fact that the cohorts of 1942-1946 included a percentage of young brides (say under 25) notably higher than in 1938-1941. The case of the cohort of 1944 is, in this respect, quite an exceptional one for the recent past.

Mortality

The decline in fertility during the more recent years has been very rapid; so has the decline in mortality, as is shown roughly by the crude rates in Table 2.

During the recent war period, apart from war casualties, Italy, unlike various Western countries, did not show an improvement in mortality rates; in fact, at least in some years, mortality was above the level reached in the prewar period. In contrast, in the more recent years specific mortality rates show a sharp continuing decline. In order to present a fairly complete and synthetic feature of the level now

Table 8

Survivorship Figures from an Abridged Life Table, 1949-1950,
and from the Last Official Table, 1935-1937:
Italy, Female Population /1

(Area as of date)

| Exact Age | Number Surviving to Exact Age x Out of 100,000 Born Alive | |
	1949-1950	1935-1937
0	100,000	100,000
1	93,431	90,379
2	92,206	87,207
5	91,391	85,365
10	90,949	84,391
15	90,595	83,678
20	90,067	82,514
25	89,390	81,034
30	88,611	79,480
35	87,694	77,872
40	86,652	76,107
45	85,293	74,103
50	83,452	71,699
55	80,841	68,534
60	77,077	64,086
65	71,201	57,589

1/ Sources: 1949-1950, computed from unpublished data furnished by
the Istituto Centrale di Statistica; 1935-1937, Tavole di mortalità della
popolazione femminile italiana, 1935-1937. Roma, Istituto Centrale di
Statistica, 1941.

reached in the control of mortality, an abridged life table has been constructed for the most recent period for which data were available. From
unpublished material kindly submitted by the Istituto Centrale di Statistica, the following data were at our disposal: (a) the distribution of the
deaths by age and sex, in annual or quinquennial age groups for 1949 and
1950; (b) the distribution of the population, December 31, 1949, by age
and sex, at least by quinquennial age groups up to the group of 60-65
years of age; after 65 the data were not subdivided. The most recent
official mortality table available is the one relating to females and to
the period 1935-1937. No mortality table was constructed for that period for males. For this reason, and owing to the fact that probably the
female age distribution of the December 31, 1949, de facto population is
more reliable than the contemporary male age distribution, it seemed
advisable to construct the abridged life table for only the female experience.

The method followed for this purpose is the one suggested by
Reed and Merrell [d]. For the age groups 0-1 and 1-2 the generalized
formula was used instead of the tables suggested by these authors, owing to the fact that no adjustment for under-registration was needed in
the case of Italy.

Table 8 shows the l_x column for the official table of 1935-1937 and for the abridged table of 1949-1950. Any comparison between the two different mortality experiences can be only approximate, for various reasons: (a) on December 31, 1949, almost fourteen years had elapsed since the last census; (b) the abridged life table refers to population and deaths recorded within the present boundaries, the official life table of 1935-1937 is for the prewar area; (c) the method by itself can give only approximate but generally satisfactory results. Notwithstanding these elements of uncertainty, the importance of the decline of mortality is striking, as suggested by the fact that the number of survivors at 65 years of age increased by 24 per cent.

Different methods have been used in order to get from the incomplete abridged life table a fairly approximate measure of the expectation of life. The result is that in less than fourteen years the expectation of life at birth for Italian females may have increased by some 8 to 9 years, from the 57.5 years of the 1935-1937 life table to the 65-67 years of the 1949-1950 experience. It is worth while to note that, according to the more recent experience, the control of mortality in Italy appears to have almost reached the level of the most advanced Western countries.

In this connection it may be of interest to point out that, according to the usual characteristics of the control of mortality in Western populations, the order of importance of different causes of mortality has been changing. During the years 1936-1938, for instance, the most important causes of mortality appeared in the following order: diseases of the respiratory system, tuberculosis excluded (2,725 deaths per 1,000,000 persons), of the circulatory system (2,019), of the digestive system (1,730), of the nervous system and sense organs (1,690), infectious and parasitic diseases (1,673), senility (949), cancer and other malignant tumors (898). In 1948 the order was changed to the following: diseases of the circulatory system (2,108), of the respiratory system (1,400), of the nervous system and sense organs (1,389), cancer and other malignant tumors (1,049), infectious and parasitic diseases (1,044), diseases of the digestive system (990), senility (760) [e]. As the figures point out, not only has the order been changed but also the impact of the various diseases. It is perhaps interesting to note that some of the characteristic old evils have been very successfully checked (like typhus, pneumonia and bronchopneumonia, and tuberculosis) or practically eradicated (like malaria). Still some substantial progress, in comparison with other Western countries, has to be made in Italy in controlling infant mortality, particularly the diseases peculiar to the first year of life.

Marriage

Unfortunately a significant analysis of the recent trend in nuptiality of the Italian population is seriously limited because of the lack of data on the marriageable population. The last fifteen years have been peculiar in various respects. During this period the cohorts born during and after World War I have been entering the marriage age. Moreover, the girls of the big baby crop born in the early 'twenties, who were already handicapped by the relatively small number of males born during the late period of World War I, found themselves in a country at war during their most marriageable ages. After World War II these same girls suffered the competition of the younger cohorts.

The lack of equilibrium in the relevant sex ratios and the particular circumstances of the period must have introduced unusual features in the age-sex specific nuptiality rates calculated on the marriageable population as well as they did with the rates calculated on the total population. The consequences of these changes in terms of variations in the proportion married cannot be assessed; neither is it possible to pick up any significant trend in marriage habits. It may be of interest to note that a comparison of the actual number of marriages of the 1940-1948 period with regard to a hypothetical number of marriages calculated on the maintenance of the crude rates of 1938-1939 shows a loss of about 5 per cent with respect to the hypothetical number. This loss was not made up in the following three years, which show a lower nuptiality than in 1938-1939.

In connection with what has been said previously as to the standardization by age in the figures presented in Table 3, it should be noted that the average age at marriage for bachelors and spinsters (who account approximately for 94 and 97 per cent of the total number of marriages of males and females, respectively) has been almost steadily increasing, at least since 1925. In recent years bachelors have married at least one year older on the average than in the late 'thirties; so have the spinsters. However, this mean age is a synthetic measure that does not tell the whole story. The distribution by age also has importance for the resulting marital fertility of the cohort of marriages. In fact, notwithstanding the higher average age at marriage, some cohorts present an unusual percentage of marriages of young people (for instance the cohort of 1944, as previously mentioned) particularly apt to have higher fertility [f].

The figure presented in Table 3 for 1951 of 2,530 legitimate births (including stillbirths), out of a constant number of 1,000 marriages celebrated each year, deserves more careful consideration. In fact, it is so low that it raises some doubt about its being sufficient to ensure replacement. No data are available for the more recent years for a refined computation of a reproduction rate, particularly because of the lack of the necessary data on nuptiality. However, it is possible to have at least a rough idea of the situation in a very simple way. A stock of 2,530 legitimate births corresponds to 1,190 live female births (according to the percentage of stillbirths and to the masculinity of births of 1950). The average age at marriage for females in recent years is slightly over 25.5 years. The percentage of spinsters in the total female population at 70 years of age was above 10 per cent both in 1931 and in 1936 at the date of the censuses. According to the tables constructed by Somogyi [g], which are based on the experience of 1930-1932, a period of presumably low nuptiality owing to the depression, the percentage of spinsters at 70 is above 16 per cent.

According to the abridged life table shown in Table 8, 1,062 girls will reach the age of 25.5 out of 1,190 female live births. At least 10 per cent of these girls probably will never marry; so that 2,530 legitimate births will produce at most 956 new marriages, or 5 per cent, roughly, less than what is needed in order to ensure replacement. It is not probable that such a deficit in legitimate fertility can be filled by illegitimate births, which in Italy are relatively few (slightly more than 3 per cent of the total live births in the most recent years).

It seems unnecessary to state here all the uncertainties inherent in the result that has been reached with regard to the present replacement performance of the Italian population, whatever meaning one may wish to put on the computation of a reproduction rate based on the temporary experience of a very short period. Some remarks, however, may be useful.

The calculated basic figure of 2,530 legitimate births in 1951 not only represents a result of the fertility behavior of the married persons in that year, but it is also affected by such factors as the past fertility, the incidence of mortality, the migratory balance, and the frequency of legal separations experienced in the past by the relevant marriage cohorts still in a position to have children in 1951. Mortality, in this respect, is the most important factor. Certainly, as the abridged life table has clearly shown, marriages celebrated in 1951 will last longer, owing to the reduced mortality, than the marriages of the previous years. They will also have more children during the course of the marital life of the couples than the surviving married persons had in 1951, if the "true" specific rates by marriage duration, calculated on the survivors, are maintained in the future. How many more, it is not easy to determine, because the cohorts on which the rates of 1951 were obtained have been passing through different and changing mortality conditions. It seems, however, that it can be safely assumed that the difference would be only slight, because the group of marriages most important in determining the size of childbearing in a particular year is the group of marriages of very short duration, say under 5 years of marriage duration, which account for almost one half of the adjusted total number of births (see Table 6). It is unlikely that in a short period the survivorship of persons in the reproductive ages has changed greatly. On the other hand, the figure of 10 per cent remaining spinsters throughout life is probably an underestimation of spinsterhood.

A safe conclusion seems to be that in 1951 the Italian population may have reached the critical point in the matter of replacement.

Regional Differentials

The previous discussion refers to the experience of the whole Italian population. The regional variations in recent demographic behavior deserve some comment, too. Italy presents in fact striking differences in the demographic situation among the various geographic subdivisions.

Italy is divided into 19 "regioni" (regions), grouped usually in four major subdivisions: Northern Italy (8 regions), Central Italy (4), Southern Italy (5), Insular Italy (2). The different historical background and socio-economic characteristics of these various parts of the nation need no description here. From the demographic point of view it should be noted, first of all, that the age structure of the population differs markedly from region to region. In Northern Italy, some of the regions, for example, Piemonte and Liguria, showed a typical pentagonal shape in their age pyramids, according to the results of the 1936 census [h]. The case was the same for Toscana, for instance, in Central Italy. At that date, many regions of Southern and Insular Italy presented a markedly triangular shape, for example, Lucania, Calabria, Puglie, and Sardegna. Such differences may have been further accentuated during the last fifteen years.

This difference in age structure should be kept in mind when one studies the figures presented in Table 9. These are the usual crude vital statistics rates relating to the four major geographic subdivisions, within the present boundaries, for the quinquennial periods 1936-1940 and

Table 9

Regional Vital Statistics Rates: Italy, 1936-1950[1]

(Present area)

Geographical Subdivision	Per 1,000 Population					
	1936-40	1946-50	1950	1936-40	1946-50	1950
	Births			Deaths		
Northern Italy	19.9	17.2	15.5	13.0	11.1	10.2
Central Italy	21.3	18.5	16.5	12.3	9.7	8.9
Southern Italy	28.0	27.8	25.5	16.0	11.1	9.4
Insular Italy	27.2	25.4	23.9	14.9	10.8	9.6
	Natural Increase			Infant Deaths[a]		
Northern Italy	6.9	6.1	5.3	88.5	62.3	52.8
Central Italy	9.0	8.7	7.6	77.1	57.7	46.4
Southern Italy	13.8	16.6	16.1	126.7	93.0	79.0
Insular Italy	12.4	14.5	14.3	118.9	83.6	74.0

a/ Per 1,000 live births.

1/ Source: Weighted averages computed from the quinquennial rates 1935-1940 published in Compendio Statistico Italiano, 1949-50, and from yearly rates for 1946-1950 presented in the 1951 issue of the same publication, by the Istituto Centrale di Statistica.

The weights are derived from the regional distribution of the de facto population on December 31, 1950.

1946-1950, and for 1950. The quinquennial averages are not very accurate, because of the lack of-information about the de facto population within the present territory of each region. For averaging the rates of each subdivision and quinquennium the weights used were derived from the distribution of the de facto population at the end of 1950.

However, the difference between the rates of the various zones and the variations in time of the rates of any particular zone are significant enough for preliminary conclusions. One might notice, for instance, that the control of mortality must be on the whole as advanced in Southern and Insular Italy as it is in the Northern and Central parts. This is not the case for infant mortality, with obvious implications for fertility.

The decline in the birth rate since the prewar period is sharper in North and in Central Italy than in the other zones; how much of this difference can be explained in terms of different age and marital distributions of the relevant populations cannot be assessed.

The very much higher natural increase of the Southern and Insular regions will continue in the future to increase Southern and Insular Italy's proportion of the total Italian population. This change will probably be only partially checked by a heavier outward migratory balance from these zones.

Age Composition

Some of the modifications in the age structure of the Italian population deserve brief notice, owing to their obvious sociological as well as economic importance.

The proportion of old people has been continuously increasing: at the end of 1950 there were 1,711,000 males and 1,058,000 females over 55, that is 7.5 and 8.7 per cent, respectively, of the total population. These are not high percentages when compared with those in many other Western populations today. But they are bound to increase pretty sharply in the near future, particularly in the case of females.

A marked increase is shown between 1936 and 1950 both in relative and in absolute numbers, and for both sexes, in the people of productive ages, say between 15 and 65. The increase in the number of people aged 15-65 is higher than the total increase in Italian population since 1936. One might find in this very fact a partial explanation of the heavy mass unemployment and underemployment which has been a deeply felt plague in Italian life since the end of the war.

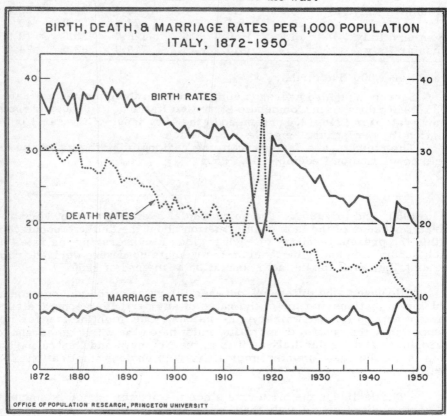

BIRTH, DEATH, & MARRIAGE RATES PER 1,000 POPULATION
ITALY, 1872-1950

BIRTH RATES

DEATH RATES

MARRIAGE RATES

OFFICE OF POPULATION RESEARCH, PRINCETON UNIVERSITY

Migration

The migratory balance has not been a major factor in the demographic growth of Italian population during the recent past. Only a few figures will be considered here. During the period 1946-1951, the outward balance for migrations across the ocean, which account for almost all of the permanent emigration, is slightly above half a million people.

More than fifty per cent of this figure is migration to one nation—Argentina. Other major directions are the United States, Venezuela, Canada, and Brazil. The emigration to Canada is a recent phenomenon, as is the emigration to Australia, owing to the agreement reached between Italy and the two governments for an assisted transfer of 100,000 Italians in a five-year period. The emigration to the United States, after the flow of war brides and of relatives of American citizens, has been, in the last few years, a few thousand above the annual quota of less than six thousand.

FOOTNOTES

[a] A complete list of the missing data is given in an Appendix to Reference 3.

[b] What is called in this paper and in the tables "marriage duration" is in fact not the exact duration of the marriage but the difference between the year of the birth and the year of celebration of the marriage.

[c] It should be noted that in Tables 3-7 the data for 1943 and subsequent years relate to the present territory, whereas figures for years before 1943 refer to the prewar territory. However, it is felt that the effects of this difference in area are not sufficient to invalidate significant comparisons of data before and after 1943. Likewise, it is felt that significant comparisons are possible even though the series are affected by minor inaccuracies due to the lack of data mentioned in Footnote [a] and to the fact that births of unknown parity and marriage duration (or both) had to be arbitrarily distributed; this was done according to the proportional distribution of births of specified parity and year of marriage.

[d] Reed, Lowell J., and Merrell, Margaret. "A short method for constructing an abridged life table." The American Journal of Hygiene, Vol. 30, No. 2, September, 1939.

[e] See also Reference 1. A detailed account of the trend of mortality by cause of death since the beginning of the century is given in the introductory note to Reference 2.

[f] For a discussion on this matter, see the introductory note to Reference 3.

[g] Somogyi, Stefano. Tavole di nuzialità e vedovanza per la popolazione Italiana 1930-1932. Annali di Statistica, Serie VII, Vol. I. Roma, Istituto Centrale di Statistica, 1951.

[h] See: Gradara, Enrico. Il baricentro della piramide delle età per la popolazione del Regno. Compendio Statistico Italiano, 1938. Roma, Istituto Centrale di Statistica.

SELECTED REFERENCES

1. Fazio, Emilio. "Le condizioni demografiche e sanitarie dell'Italia." Rivista Italiana di Demografia e Statistica 3(1-2):182-220. June, 1949.
2. Italy. Istituto Centrale di Statistica. Cause di morte negli anni 1943-1948. Serie III, Vol. I. Roma, 1952. 407 pp.
3. Italy. Istituto Centrale di Statistica. Movimento della popolazione secondo gli atti dello stato civile negli 1943-1948. Serie III, Vol. I. Roma, 1952. 214 pp.
4. Peloso, Mario. La dinamica della fertilità matrimoniale in Italia. Unpublished doctoral thesis, Istituto Universitario di Economia e Commercio, Venice, 1951.
5. Tagliacarne, Guglielmo. "La situation démographique de l'Italie." Population 3(3):467-483. July-September, 1948.

THE DEMOGRAPHY OF WAR: GERMANY

By the Office of Population Research, Princeton University

In three-quarters of a century between 1870 and 1945 Germany engaged in three major wars. The first, limited in scope and intensity, a-chieved its objective of political expansion without undue disturbance of the processes of population replacement and redistribution. The Prussian War Department reported 41 thousand dead among the Germans who crossed the frontiers of France, but only 16 thousand of these died in action. /1 Civilian deaths in Germany increased somewhat in 1871 and 1872, and there was a slight birth deficit in 1871, which left a nick in the smooth regularity of the German age structure that was still discernible in 1939. This was not a population vulnerable to catas-trophe, however, for as late as 1876–1880 the birth rate was 39, the death rate 26, and the rate of natural increase 13. /2

The general symmetry of the age distribution of the German popu-lation in the early twentieth century indicates the demographic well-being of a people characterized by adequate fertility, normal mortal-ity, and limited emigration. (See Figure 1.) The annual number of births reached a maximum of 2.0 million in 1901–1905. A portion of the substantial natural increase of the late nineteenth century was drained off in international migration, /3 but the home population increased from 41 million in 1871 to 65 million in 1910. The number of men in the military ages 20–34 rose from over 4 million in 1871 to 7 million in 1910. By that year the relative numerical equality in military manpower that had existed between France and Germany before the Franco-Prussian War had been replaced by a German numerical supe-riority of over three million men.

World War I

In August of 1914 the confident armies of a virile Germany en-tered the conflict that was to be ended by Christmas, but actually did not end until four years and three months later. The German, Austro-Hungarian, and Russian Empires had disappeared in the war that cost Europe (including Asiatic Russia) some fifty million lives. /4 Ger-many's total population deficit of 5.4 million amounted to 8 per cent of her 1914 population of 67.8 million. There were over 2 million military dead and 737 thousand excess civilian deaths over age one. There was a birth deficit of 3.2 million, for the birth rate, 27.5 in 1913, dropped to 15.2 in 1916 and 13.9 in 1917. /5

During the 'twenties and 'thirties the scars of the German demo-graphic structure were gradually healing. The male cohorts decimated by World War I were advancing in age; by 1940 the age group that had been 20–24 in 1914 was in the upper forties. By 1970 there would have been hardly a scar in the age pyramid to indicate that two million Ger-man men had died in a war over half a century before. In that year, however, there would have been a deep gash among adults aged 50–54, the survivors of the lessened birth cohorts of the years 1915–1918. There would have been a secondary deficit among youths in their twen-ties, for those who were not born during World War I could not con-tribute to future generations.

The Interwar Years

Two decades of peace gave Germany a chance at demographic recovery, but during that period, like other Western powers, she was confronted by a demographic hazard deeper than war, the precipitant decline of fertility. The birth rate increased to 25.9 in 1920 and 25.3
in 1921, then decreased, to reach lows of 15.1 in 1932 and 14.7 in 1933.
Estimates of the imminent decline of the total population flourished.
In 1926 the Statistisches Reichsamt published its first official series. According to these estimates, maintenance of the mortality of
1921-1923 and the fertility of 1924-1925 would have produced continued
population increases through 1975, but a twenty-five per cent decline
in fertility between 1924-1925 and 1954-1955 would have yielded decline in total population soon after 1945. /6 New estimates had to be
issued by 1930 to take account of the continued decline in fertility
below the level assumed in the mid-'twenties. The most publicized projection, which assumed mortality as in the life table of 1924-1926,
age-specific marriage rates for women rising to the 1910 level by 1940,
and fertility falling twenty-five per cent between 1927 and 1955, indicated a declining population by 1960. /7

Germany, once increasing in power potential vis-à-vis her Western neighbors because of her comparatively later industrial and demographic development, now saw herself losing ground relatively to the
more agrarian and still expanding Slavic peoples of the East. Demographic armament appeared imperative to Adolf Hitler and his adjutants
of the Third Reich. Barrages of propaganda, positive inducements to
marriage and childbearing, and the legal prohibition of abortion reinforced economic expansion and a rise in employment as factors conducive to the increase of fertility. New predictions of the Statistisches Reichsamt, published in 1938, pushed the higher fertility of
1936 into the future, assuming decreases in infant mortality and increases in marriages. Austria was included as a part of Greater Germany. On the basis of these assumptions, the total population, 74.9
million in 1938, would approach a maximum of 80.5 million in 1970.
This final prediction by the Statistisches Reichsamt clearly exempli-
fied the military orientation of policy and projections, for this was
an elaborate computation of the population development that would occur if the supply of births in Germany, Austria, and the Sudetenland
were sufficient to maintain the military cohort aged 19 at 755 thousand. /8

The censuses of 1925, 1933, and 1939 mirrored the major political
and demographic events of German history. The population of Germany
within its 1933 area ("Altreich" without the Saar) increased from 57.8
million in 1910 to 62.4 million in 1925, and to 65.4 million in 1933. /9
Children under 15, however, numbered 19.6 million in 1910, 16.1 million in 1925, and 15.8 million in 1933. Children under six had declined 30 per cent in less than a quarter of a century, children 6-14
by 12 per cent. This erosion of the base of the age pyramid was the
cumulative result of the decline in fertility. (See Figure 1.) Above
this eroded base there was a great gash, the children who were not
born during World War I. Youths aged 15-18 were only three-fifths
as numerous in 1933 as they had been twenty-five years before. Wom-
en at the various ages above 30 were some forty per cent more numerous in 1933 than in 1910; in general, the rate of increase became
greater with advancing age. For men, the progression of the age groups

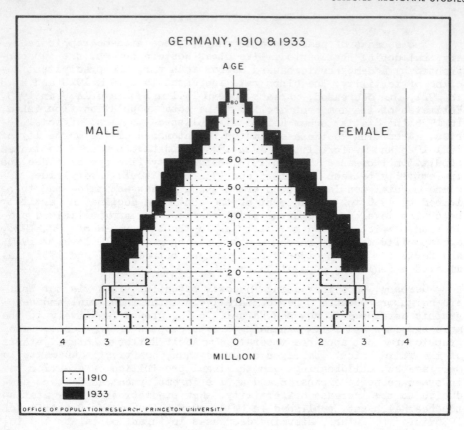

Figure 1

was broken sharply at ages 30-50, for these were the survivors of the men who contributed most heavily to the armies of 1914-1918. Only at ages 50 and above did the age and sex patterns approach the regularity that the entire age structure had had in 1910.

By 1939 figures for "Germany without the Saar" were no longer published. Instead, for purposes of historical comparison there were figures for the "Altreich" (Germany as of 1937), whose 1939 population numbered 69.3 million. Germany's population in her then present boundaries, Greater Germany, was ten million larger, for it included Austria, the Sudeten area, and Memel. Within the 1937 boundaries there had been significant changes in the age structure since 1933, especially the broadening of the base of the age pyramid. The youngest cohort, 0-4, was larger than that aged 5-9 by one million, in fact, larger than any other cohort up to the youths 25-29. The largest age group, however, was that of young adults 30-34.

War and declining fertility were indeed producing in Germany a "Volk ohne Jugend." Compared to the broad base of children in 1910, even the enlarged Hitlerian birth cohort of 1935-1939 appeared inadequate to meet the responsibilities of a militaristic state. As Dudley Kirk's theoretical computations for 1940 so clearly indicate, Germany's approaching decline in military manpower was due primarily to long

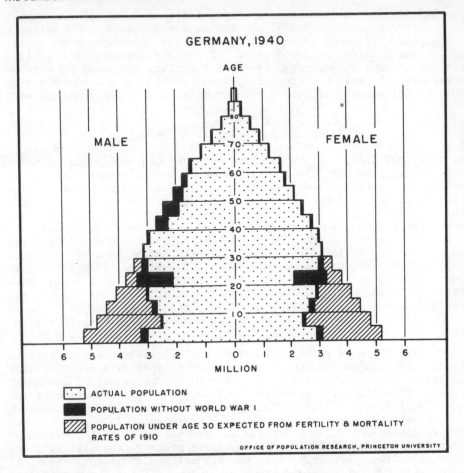

GERMANY, 1940

AGE

MALE

FEMALE

MILLION

[⋅⋅] ACTUAL POPULATION

■ POPULATION WITHOUT WORLD WAR I

▨ POPULATION UNDER AGE 30 EXPECTED FROM FERTILITY & MORTALITY
RATES OF 1910

OFFICE OF POPULATION RESEARCH, PRINCETON UNIVERSITY

Figure 2

continued declines in fertility. (See Figure 2.) The numerically less
important losses of war appeared as irregularities in the age and sex
structure of a population that had little recuperative potential.
Children aged 0-4 in 1940 would have been 494 thousand more numerous
if the birth deficits of World War I had not occurred. They would
have been 4.6 million more numerous if fertility and mortality had remained at the 1910 levels. The comparison for the total population
is also striking. The orderly continuation of the fertility and mortality of the period of the 1910 census would have produced a total
population of 88.7 million in 1940. The dynamics of the period from
1910 to 1940 without war would have produced a population of 75.7 million. The estimated actual population was 69.5 million. Declining
rates of natural increase between 1910 and 1940 cost Germany 13.0 million people; World War I had cost 6.2 million people by 1940. (Both
computations ignore migration.)

The imminent depopulation so feared by prewar Germany was basically a product of the changing balance of births and deaths. It was
accentuated by World War I, not created by it. Both declining fertil-

ity and war act as decelerators of population growth, but the former
is a normal process of social and economic adjustment, the latter a
cataclysmic interlude whose effects are felt throughout the social
and economic structure for decades. A serious demographic situation
existed in prewar Germany, not because fertility declined, but because
a precipitant decline in fertility that carried the net reproduction
rate far below unity coincided with the aftermath of a devastating war.

World War II

By 1939 the effects of economic recovery and population policies
were becoming evident in the enlargement of the base of the deeply
eroded age pyramid. The trend toward biological extinction was beginning to seem less inevitable, although optimism was still limited.
But as summer advanced, the military preparations mounted and the demands for security and "Lebensraum" rose to new heights. Finally the
German armies crossed the frontier of Poland and World War II had begun. This was to be a "Blitzkrieg," a war that would avoid the biological costs commonly associated with international struggles. During the first years of Germany's easy victories, this goal seemed possible of attainment. The decline in natural increase was slight, for
the resources of a conquered continent fed the people of Germany.
Full employment, abundant military furloughs, and the élan of victory
maintained German fertility at little below its 1939 level. /10

Total war on a global scale came in 1941. German armies invaded
Russia with initial success, and a confident Japan attacked the United
States at Pearl Harbor and drove on for the rice regions of Southeast
Asia. German military casualties mounted, while the birth rate of the
home population declined. The murder of Europe's Jewish population
and the ruthless transfer of people and impressment of labor contributed
substantially to the human costs of the war and added to the hatred of
Germany and Germans that was to complicate postwar rehabilitation and
reconstruction. By early 1943 some 2.5 million civilian Germans had
gone out to the occupied countries, while some 6.5 million workers and
prisoners of war were utilized as laborers within Germany. /11 As more
and more of the 2.7 million tons of bombs that were utilized in the
strategic bombing of Germany found their targets, millions of evacu-
ated or fleeing Germans were added to the migratory streams of the
continent. With German defeat millions of people from the East pushed
westward to escape the Soviet armies, while Germans throughout the occupied areas attempted to return to their homeland.

The balance sheet of war cannot yet be drawn. German military
dead are estimated to number some 3.25 million. /12 Over 300 thousand
civilians were killed by air bombardment. /13 Yet losses from increased
civilian mortality and lowered fertility were probably substantially
less than in World War I. The decimated cohorts of adults and the
weakened generations of children were not the only costs of World War
II, however. Throughout the war years Germans had violated the basic
right of free men to choose between movement and stability. In spreading the doctrine of ethnic purity they had emphasized the strategic
dangers of ethnic diversity. In historic retribution, the agreement
of Potsdam stated that "...the transfer to Germany of German populations, or elements thereof, remaining in Poland, Czechoslovakia and
Hungary will have to be undertaken...." The resources of Germany were

cut, the major losses being the restoration of the Saar and Alsace-Lorraine to France and the de facto occupation of the territory east of the Oder-Neisse by Poland. Within this constricted area a Germany which had shouted for "Lebensraum" and ethnic purity was now forced to absorb most of the Germans of the continent.

Migrations

The Allied Control Council was charged with the execution of the Potsdam decision in the four zones. It was estimated that 6.65 million persons would be involved: 3.5 million from Poland, 2.5 million from Czechoslovakia, 500 thousand from Hungary, and 150 thousand from Austria. Kulischer's recent estimates place the number of people who have been transferred as 2.4 million for Czechoslovakia, 2 million for Poland, and 178 thousand for Hungary. In addition, many Germans fled or were expelled before the organized transfers began. According to his estimates there were probably 300 thousand from Czechoslovakia, one million from Old Poland, 4 million from New Poland, 500 thousand from northern East Prussia, annexed by the U.S.S.R., and several hundred thousand from the Balkans. By July 1, 1947, more than 9.5 million German refugees were reported in rump Germany. /14

A brief summary of the published statistics of the American Zone may serve to indicate the changes in demographic composition and social structure that are implicit in these population movements. Between the end of the war and the beginning of 1948, more than 3 million displaced persons had left the Zone, over 2 million Sudeten Germans and Swabians had entered it. There had also been sizable movements within Germany, as people returned to their homes or left their homes to seek employment or food elsewhere. In 1946, one resident in each five in the American Zone reported residence outside the Zone in 1939. Four per cent had lived in Germany west of the Oder-Neisse, 4 per cent in Germany east of the Oder-Neisse, 8 per cent in Czechoslovakia, nearly 4 per cent elsewhere.

Vital Statistics

These mass migrations and the political and economic disorganization of Germany would have made the restoration of vital-statistics registration systems difficult had it not been for the German tradition of reporting and of conforming to governmental requirements. Furthermore, governmental administration had been maintained at the local and the provincial levels. It was not so much the collection of the statistics as their interpretation that presented the difficult problem. The mobility of the population was so great that a numerator of reported vital events for even a relatively brief time span did not correspond to the denominator of an estimated population at a specific time. Moreover, crude rates were inadequate indicators of the reproductive potential in these populations of distorted age structure, surplus women, separated families, and postponed marriages.

Crude vital rates for the Western zones and Berlin have recovered substantially but there is as yet little evidence of that decided increase in fertility that has occurred in many nations. The crude birth rates had reached 16 to 18 per 1,000 total population by the second quarter of 1946. Fragmentary data indicate that they have remained near this level through the first quarter of 1948. Marriage rates appeared to be increasing in late 1947. If this increase was general and was maintained, some increase in births may have occurred. General death rates and infant mortality declined in the early postwar period. By late 1946 and 1947, rates of natural increase of 2 to 7 per 1,000 total population replaced the earlier rates of decrease.

Further indication of the behavior of vital rates is possible from an analysis of the local area data contained in the zonal and German official publications. In most areas the birth deficits of this war did not approach those of World War I, primarily because the decline of fertility had already reduced "normal" fertility to the point where such deep cuts as occurred in World War I were not possible. Urban-rural and regional differentials in levels of fertility and mortality, acute during the late war years, persisted into the years of occupation. The control of mortality maintained by the Germans during the war and the Military Governments during the years of collapse and slow revival is noteworthy. These generalizations may be made somewhat more specific by citations to the vital rates of the city of Berlin, the United States Zone as a whole, and the province of Bavaria.

In Berlin the crude birth rate reached 17.2 in 1941, then declined to 14.7 in 1943, 8.6 in 1944, and 7.6 in 1946. By 1947 it had recovered only to 10 or 11. Crude death rates, 11 to 14 in the prewar period, reached 16.2 in 1944, 24.6 in 1946. Infant mortality stood at 123 per 1,000 live births in 1944, 100 to 125 in 1946. The rate of natural decrease, 7.6 per 1,000 total population in 1944, reached 17.0 in 1946. In the American Zone there was an excess of births over deaths of only 375 thousand in the seven and a half years between the census of 1939 and that of 1946, an annual average of 3.4 per 1,000 per year. There was probably a natural decrease in the Zone as a whole in 1944 and 1945. In Bavaria the birth rate, over 21 in 1939-1941, declined to a low of 14.8 in 1945, when there was a surplus of civilian deaths over births. In 1946, with 7.1 per cent of the population evacuees and 18.1 per cent refugees or expellees, the live birth rate was 18.2, the death rate 13.4, the crude rate of natural increase 4.8. Comparable rates for 1936 had been respectively 20.2, 12.6, and 7.6.

Since no vital statistics are published for the Soviet Zone, it is impossible to estimate the level of births and deaths for Germany as a whole.

Census Enumeration

Materials for the analysis of trends in the number, distribution, and characteristics of the German people are voluminous but on the whole unsatisfactory. Ration registrations and the reports of the employment service furnish continuing inventories, but they are limited in scope and subject to specific and not always systematic biases. An enumeration reported as a "Volkszählung" was taken in the Soviet Zone and Berlin as of December 1, 1945, and a census was taken in the French Zone as of January 26, 1946.

A census of the total population of the American, British, French, and Soviet Zones and Berlin was taken on October 29, 1946. Prisoners of war, displaced persons in centers, and interned civilians were counted by the Occupation authorities, all others by the local German authorities. Fourteen questions were prescribed for the four zones and

Berlin. Zone commanders could add other questions. They also decided upon the form of the card and the method of entry. The fourteen prescribed questions were as follows: 1. - 2. Name; 3. Relationship to head of household; 4. Sex; 5. Day, month, year, and place of birth; 6. Marital status; 7. Citizenship (How secured, when, and country of origin); 8. National origin; 9. Mother tongue; 10. Religious membership; 11. Educational status; 12. Occupation (A. Present occupation or other sources of income, B. Occupational status, C. Place of work); 13. Present residence and legal residence on September 1, 1939; 14. Service in the German armed forces.   There has been no central processing, analysis, or publication of the results of this census. The statistical offices of Military Government in the various zones release data on numbers and distribution for all zones and more detailed data for their respective zones. No information at present available permits assessment of the comparability of presumably identical tabulations.

Many of the fundamental questions as to the present status and potential growth of the German population could not be answered on the basis of the census of October 29, 1946, even in the unlikely event that complete tabulations were published for the four zones and Berlin. The census covered persons within the frontiers of Germany as of the census date, but there were many prisoners of war and missing members of the Wehrmacht whose eventual return might contribute substantially toward balancing the age and sex structure of truncated Germany. In a special registration in the American Zone in early 1947, families reported 822 thousand missing members, of whom only 398 thousand were known to be prisoners of war. /15 Estimates based on the extension of these United States Zone estimates to all Germany indicated 3.2 million absent persons, of whom 1,536 thousand were prisoners of war, 1,652 thousand missing members of the Wehrmacht. To this 3.2 million must be added some 150 to 200 thousand for the area east of the Oder-Neisse. Estimates of the Moscow Conference and later pronouncements indicated 1.8 to 1.9 million prisoners of war in foreign areas. These and other estimates are for differing dates, and none of them can be accepted as definitive for its date of issue.

Furthermore, it should be noted that the censuses of the Soviet Zone in December, 1945, of the French Zone in January, 1946, and of all Germany in October, 1946, are snapshots of an unsettled population recovering from a devastating war whose losses are subject to approximate conjecture, and moving toward a future whose broad outlines are not yet determined. The facts of the present and the problems of the future are suggested rather than measured by the statistics of 1946.

The Germany of October, 1946

The Germany included in the census of 1946 was even more densely settled than that "overcrowded land" for which Hitler demanded "Lebensraum" in the 'thirties.   The 69.3 million Germans resident in 1939 within the area as of 1937 had available to them 470 thousand sq. km. of land; and 60 million Germans resident in 1939 within the area as of 1946 had 357 thousand sq. km. The lost areas constituted 24 per cent of the prewar area, but they had included only 13 per cent of the prewar population. /16 Per capita agricultural acreage was about one-third less than it had been in 1939. /17 Germany had been only eighty per cent self-sufficient in food before the war.   Official American

Table 1

Germany. Area and Population in the Four Zones and
Berlin, Censuses of October 29, 1946, and May 17, 1939*

Zone and Land	Population 1946 (In thousands)	Females per 100 Males	Per Cent Change in Total Population 1939-1946	Persons per Sq. Km.		
				1939	1946	Change
Total	65,911	124.8	10.2	168	185	17
British Zone	22,303	118.7	12.7	203	228	25
Schleswig-Holstein	2,651	118.9	66.7	102	169	67
Hamburg	1,405	115.6	-17.9	2,293	1,882	-411
N. Rhine Westphalia	11,799	119.5	- 1.2	351	347	- 4
Lower Saxony /1	6,448	117.8	42.0	96	136	40
French Zone	5,940	125.6	- 4.3	145	139	- 6
Baden	1,190	129.9	- 3.3	124	120	- 4
Württemberg-Hohenz.	1,129	127.2	4.9	103	108	5
Saarland	883	119.1	4.9	438	459	21
Palatinate of the Rhine, Hesse	1,316	125.9	-10.9	215	191	- 24
Rhineland, Hesse	1,422	124.7	-10.2	116	104	- 12
USSR Zone	17,314	133.7	13.7	141	161	20
Brandenburg	2,516	136.2	5.3	89	93	4
Mecklenburg-Pomerania	2,149	133.2	45.3	63	91	28
Province Saxony	4,162	130.2	21.3	140	170	30
Thuringia	2,943	130.0	20.3	155	187	32
Land Saxony	5,543	137.4	1.1	321	325	4
United States Zone	17,174	120.6	20.5	133	160	27
Bavaria	8,983	120.8	27.7	100	128	28
Württemberg-Baden	3,650	122.1	14.8	202	232	30
Hesse	4,050	119.7	16.4	165	192	27
Bremen /2	492	114.7	-12.7	1,393	1,217	-176
Berlin	/3 3,180	146.4	-26.7	4,908	3,598	-1,310

* Germany. U.S. Zone. Statistical Annex, Issue No. XIII. Report
of the Military Governor, No. 33. March, 1948. Pp. 8-9.

1/ Exclusive of Bremen.
2/ The former enclave of Bremen had a population of 749 thousand, of
whom 346 thousand were males.
3/ The total populations for the sectors were as follows (in '000):
British Sector, 603; French Sector, 422; U.S.S.R. Sector, 1,170;
U.S. Sector, 984. In addition there were 1,143 persons in ship crews.

estimates indicate that the future economy could provide about sixty per cent of the prewar diet if the efficiency of production that existed prior to the war could be restored. /18

The total population within the constricted area numbered 65.9 million, 5 per cent below the total population of the "Altreich" in 1939, but 10 per cent above the 1939 population of the 1946 area. The margin of error in the 1946 figure is difficult to determine. The possibility of incompleteness and inaccuracy in enumeration is high, for conditions were disorganized in many areas. There is also the strong likelihood that illegal migrants from one Occupation zone to another were not reached by census enumerators. More definitive assessment of the completeness and accuracy of the 1946 census will be possible if and when more than simple counts by sex are available for the country as a whole.

The changed distribution of population within Germany is the result of local economic pressures combined with an interplay of political and psychological factors. The movements of the population were generally westward within the country. The percentage increase from 1939 to 1946 was 12.7 for the British Zone, 13.7 for the Soviet Zone, 20.5 for the United States Zone. (See Table 1.) The population of the French Zone decreased 4.3 per cent, that of Berlin 26.7 per cent. Within each zone the movement was from the urban and more densely settled areas to the rural and less densely settled regions. During the war years voluntary migrations and evacuations had dispersed people; during the early postwar years the search for subsistence prevented many Germans from returning to the cities and sent others countryward. The millions of refugees and evacuees were allocated throughout the various areas on the assumption that they could subsist and be absorbed more easily in the less densely settled districts. The effect of these movements on the pattern of population distribution is shown for the American Zone in Table 2. The picture was substantially similar in the British Zone. /19

Sex and Age Structure

An increased density of population within a predominantly industrial country whose technical plants, transportation, and urban buildings have been heavily destroyed by war presents serious problems of subsistence and reconstruction at whatever level of agricultural-industrial production. In Germany these problems have been complicated by the dislocations in sex and age structure that have resulted from the superimposition of the losses of one war on those of a previous war almost exactly a generation earlier.

In 1946 Germany as a whole had 125 women for each hundred men. If the 3.2 million missing members of the Wehrmacht should return, the surplus of women would be reduced to 12.5 per cent. If, as is more probable, only half should return, there would be 118 women for each hundred men. In absolute terms, there were 7.3 million surplus women among the 65.9 million Germans enumerated in October, 1946. The return of all the missing members of the Wehrmacht would leave a surplus of 4.1 million women; the return of half, a surplus of 5.7 million.

The surplus of women varied greatly in the different areas and age groups. (See front cover chart.) It amounted to 18.7 per cent in the British Zone, 20.6 per cent in the United States Zone, 25.6

Table 2

Population Changes in Stadt- und Landkreise
United States Zone, 1939-1946*

Area	Population (In thousands)		Per Cent Change
	1939	1946	
Total	14,258	17,174	20.5
Stadtkreise	5,516	4,972	- 9.9
Major cities	4,344	3,694	-15.0
Other cities	1,172	1,278	9.1
Landkreise	8,742	12;202	39.6
Bavaria	7,038	8,983	27.6
Stadtkreise	2,365	2,314	- 2.2
Major cities	1,652	1,439	-12.9
Other cities	712	875	22.8
Landkreise	4,673	6,669	42.7
Württemberg-Baden	3,179	3,650	14.8
Stadtkreise	1,274	1,096	-13.9
Major cities	1,052	917	-12.8
Other cities	222	179	-19.2
Landkreise	1,905	2,554	34.0
Hesse	3,479	4,050	16.4
Stadtkreise	1,314	1,071	-18.5
Major cities	1,077	847	-21.3
Other cities	238	224	- 5.8
Landkreise	2,165	2,979	37.6
Bremen	563	492	-12.7

* Germany. U. S. Zone. Statistical Annex, Issue No. XIII. Report
of the Military Governor, No. 33. March, 1948. P. 11.

per cent in the French Zone, 33.7 per cent in the Russian Zone, and
46.4 per cent in Berlin. In no area was it distributed equally throughout the life span of the population. The pattern of change is most
apparent in the age distribution by single years of age that has been
published for the British Zone. /20 Boys exceeded girls at all ages
from birth through age 18. The surplus of women began at age 19,
where there were 117 women for each hundred men, then jumped to 156
at age 20, 171 at age 21. There were more than 180 women for each
hundred men aged 22 and 23 in 1946. The relative surplus of women
became less with advancing age, the number of women per hundred men
declining to 150 at age 36, and 111 at age 46. The age cohorts of
1900-1905 were peculiarly fortunate, for their male members were generally too young for service in World War I and relatively old for
active service in World War II. Surpluses of women rose again among
the survivors of the births of the 1890's, for these cohorts had borne
the major military losses of World War I.

This disturbance in the relative numbers of men and women would in itself complicate the smooth functioning of Germany's social and economic system. There is another difficulty, however, in the abnormal relationship of the successive age groups. These demographic barriers to effective social and economic functioning are most apparent in the distortions of the age pyramid for Berlin as of December, 1945. (See Figure 3.) Refugees and evacuees were returning. Transferred peoples, released members of the Wehrmacht, and new streams of refugees added to the difficulties of subsistence, housing, and reconstruction at the same time that they presumably contributed something to the creation of a more balanced labor force.

The costs of successive wars, deflation, and mass migration in a more "normal" situation than that of quadripartite Berlin are evident in the age structure of Württemberg-Baden as determined in the censuses of 1939 and 1946, even though the "sample" of one million returns utilized for the analysis was apparently selected on the basis of date of return and thus was overweighted by the population of the rural areas. /21 If there had been no movement into Württemberg-Baden after 1939 to compensate for the war losses, the male population would have declined one-fourth, the female population one-tenth, below the number expected on the basis of a projection of the prewar situation. There would have been large deficits of males in the ages 0-4 and 19-25. The already decimated birth cohorts of World War I lost half or more of their surviving members in World War II. The migrant population contributed substantially to the increase of the total population, but its age and sex structure was broadly similar to that of the native group. The net result was a total population weighted with children and the aged, and severely limited in the number of males in the productive ages.

It is hazardous to use local or regional populations as a basis for assessing the impact of the war on the population potential of all Germany. The 1946 data available for the French and Soviet Zones and the city of Berlin are not sufficient to make valid estimates of the changing size and structure of the total German population. Hence description that extends beyond city and provincial areas will be limited to the American Zone. It is recognized that the United States Zone itself is neither economically, politically, nor demographically exactly comparable to the other zones. None the less, the broad structure, dynamics, and problems of the postwar German population are similar in all regions. Differences are in magnitude rather than in basic characteristics.

The Population of the American Zone /22

The net effect of the changes between 1939 and 1946 in the American Zone was an increase of 16 per cent in the male population, 33 per cent in the female population. Youths, older workers, and the aged increased in numbers among both men and women. In the age group 14 to 39, however, the number of men decreased approximately 11 per cent, whereas the number of women increased about 28 per cent. /23 The increases that occurred were due primarily to the inclusion of migrant groups. In the absence of war or migration since 1939 the American Zone would have had a native population of 14.5 million; its actual native population was 1.6 million less. Without migration even the

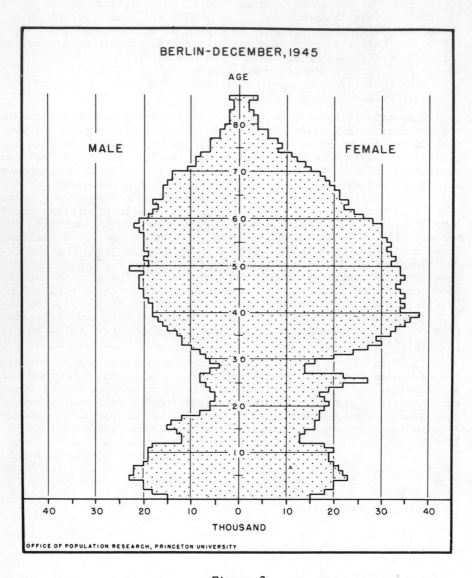

BERLIN-DECEMBER, 1945

OFFICE OF POPULATION RESEARCH, PRINCETON UNIVERSITY

Figure 3

return of all missing members of the Wehrmacht could not have erased a decline of this magnitude.

Migration supplemented the decimated native population of the United States Zone, but it contributed only slightly to the normalization of the age and sex structure. (See Table 3.) Among the German migrants from east of the Oder-Neisse the proportion of children was higher, and the deficits of men less extreme. Migrants from Czechoslovakia and from the British, French, and Berlin areas were similar to natives of the American Zone. Migrants from the Russian Zone included appreciable numbers of men apparently fleeing labor impressment. They alone of all the groups included a surplus of males in the critical ages of 15-19. Their surplus of females at ages 20-29 was small, their surplus of males considerable at ages 30-49. Surpluses of males also appeared among the migrants aged 20-29 from Southeastern Europe. However, these groups with larger proportions of males from the Soviet area of Germany and the Soviet occupied areas of the Southeast were so insignificant numerically that they did little to balance the age and sex structure of the American Zone as a whole.

The Future

Projections were made for the population of the American Zone on the following assumptions: specific mortality remains as in 1932-1934 and specific fertility by marital status as in 1928-1932; the number of potential mothers is limited by the number of married men three years older, and the proportion of men married in each age group remains as in the period before 1933; and, finally, the 570 thousand prisoners of war missing at the time of the census will return by the end of 1949. Under these assumptions the total population, 16.2 million in 1946, /24 will increase to 16.9 million in 1956 and decline slowly to 16.7 million in 1971. The female population will reach its maximum in 1951, but the male population will continue to increase throughout the period as returning migrants and the oncoming normal generations of youth replace the depleted ranks of adults. Surpluses of women in the labor force ages will lessen and eventually disappear.

The normal aging that has characterized the populations of the West will continue in the German population of the American Zone. In the twenty-five years between 1946 and 1971 the total female population will decline 3 per cent, but this will be the net result of a decline of 17 per cent of those under age 15, a decline of 7 per cent at ages 15-64, and an increase of 63 per cent at ages 65 and above.

The recovery of military potential, viewed solely from the demographic standpoint, will be substantial. Males aged 15-34 numbered 1.8 million in 1946. By 1956-1961 they will number over 2.5 million, as the larger birth cohorts of the late 'thirties become adults. By this time, the survivors of the doubly stricken birth cohorts of 1915-1918 will reach middle age and become less important in Germany's military potential. Even in 1971 males aged 15-34 will be 26 per cent more numerous than they were in 1946. The same phenomenon of increasing military manpower appears if the influence of the losses of World War II is eliminated by considering only the age group 15-19, for the boys in this group in 1946 were relatively untouched by the military mortality of the last war. Their number, 606 thousand in 1946, will become 777 thousand in 1956, an increase of 28 per cent that is due

Table 3

Age and Sex Structure of the Population of the U. S. Zone, 1946*
(In thousands)

Area of Origin	Total	Age					
		0–13	14–19	20–29	30–49	50–64	65+
United States Zone	12,918	2,958	1,191	1,581	3,817	2,122	1,249
Number	100.0	22.9	9.2	12.2	29.5	16.4	9.7
Per cent of total	125	95	106	184	142	130	116
Females per 100 males							
Territories East of the Oder-Neisse or Foreign							
Number /1	2,629	602	255	441	780	371	180
Per cent of total	100.0	22.9	9.7	16.8	29.7	14.1	6.8
Females per 100 males	117	95	106	137	123	128	122
Czechoslovakia							
Number	1,345	290	131	193	394	223	114
Per cent of total	100.0	21.6	9.7	14.3	29.3	16.6	8.5
Females per 100 males	127	87	118	180	146	132	115
German Territories East of Oder-Neisse							
Number	697	182	68	127	200	78	42
Per cent of total	100.0	26.1	9.8	18.2	28.7	11.2	6.0
Females per 100 males	117	100	100	131	117	152	133
Southeastern Europe							
Number	300	73	36	44	91	40	16
Per cent of total	100.0	24.3	12.0	14.7	30.3	13.3	5.3
Females per 100 males	97	109	100	69	102	90	129
German Territories West of Oder-Neisse							
Number	678	157	46	143	233	69	30
Per cent of total	100.0	23.2	6.8	21.1	34.4	10.2	4.4
Females per 100 males	119	104	92	147	110	156	150
British and French Zones and Berlin							
Number	492	119	34	92	168	55	24
Per cent of total	100.0	24.2	6.9	18.7	34.1	11.2	4.9
Females per 100 males	128	102	100	171	124	162	140
Soviet Zone							
Number	186	38	12	51	65	14	6
Per cent of total	100.0	20.4	6.5	27.4	34.9	7.5	3.2
Females per 100 males	100	111	71	112	81	133	200

* From pp. 5 and 77–78 of source given in Footnote 24, p. 308 , this issue.

1/Includes 287,000 from "Other foreign countries."

entirely to the fluctuations of the birth rate during the Hitlerian
and the war years. What happens to military potential after 1956 depends on the future of the German birth rate.

Doubtless the future population of the American Zone will deviate
widely from that projected on the basis of the returns of the 1946
census. Not all the absent prisoners of war will return, and other
migrants have and will come in from other regions of Germany and from
German groups not yet transferred. If opportunities are available,
many Germans will leave Germany. Marriage, birth, and death rates are
assumed to reach and remain at the levels characteristic of the middle
of the interwar period. If there is no reasonably adequate solution
to the "German problem" they may do so, but this is unlikely if there
is reconstruction with economic functioning at a level of reasonably
full employment. Furthermore, projections for the American Zone cannot be expanded as the basis of projections for all Germany. None the
less, certain conclusions emerge from analysis of the fragmentary
materials for the various zones, the more detailed materials for the
British and American Zones, and the various attempts to estimate the
future population, of which the official American projection is the
most comprehensive.

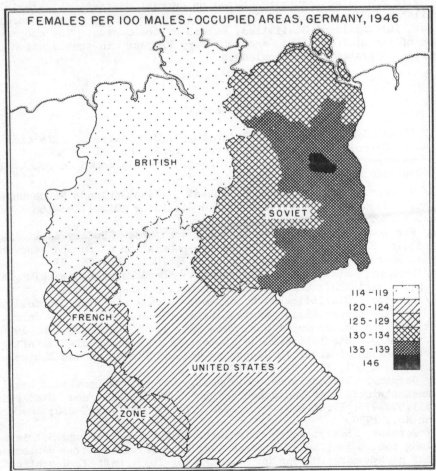

FEMALES PER 100 MALES—OCCUPIED AREAS, GERMANY, 1946

BRITISH

SOVIET

FRENCH

UNITED STATES

ZONE

114-119
120-124
125-129
130-134
135-139
146

Conclusion

World War II did not result in the biological extermination of the German people. The number of the German dead was small in proportion to the total lives lost in Europe and Russia because of German aggression. German military and civilian dead were probably less numerous than the civilians whom the Germans transported to their death in extermination camps. The biological consequences of the war were serious for Germany because the ratio of fatalities to military manpower was high, the effects of this war were superimposed on those of a war a generation earlier that had been even more severe in its demographic impact, and fertility had declined to the point where the resilience of the population was low. It must be emphasized, however, that a united Germany would retain the largest cohesive block of military manpower west of the U.S.S.R. for some time.

The preceding resume is based on current statistical materials available in the Library of Congress and in the Office of the Coordinator, International Statistics, Bureau of the Census. The cooperation of the staff of the Census Library Project in the location of sources is gratefully acknowledged.

Footnotes

1/ Dumas, Samuel, and Vedel-Petersen, K. O. Losses of life caused by war. Oxford at the Clarendon Press, 1923. Pp. 51-53.

2/ Germany. Statistisches Reichsamt. Statistisches Jahrbuch für das Deutsche Reich, 1937. Pp. 11 and 37.

3/ Germany. Statistisches Reichsamt. "Deutschlands Wanderungsbilanz 1933 bis 1939." Wirtschaft und Statistik 20(20):465-468. Second Oct. No., 1940.

4/ War loss estimates of World War I are those of Dudley Kirk. See Notestein, F. W., et al. The future population of Europe and the Soviet Union. Geneva, League of Nations, 1944. Pp. 75, 83.

5/ Germany. Statistisches Reichsamt. "Bevölkerungsentwicklung im Kriege." Wirtschaft und Statistik 22(9):298. Sept., 1942.

6/ Germany. Statistisches Reichsamt. "Richtlinien zur Beurteilung des Bevölkerungsproblems Deutschlands für die nächsten 50 Jahre." Statistik des Deutschen Reichs, Band 316, pp. 37*-50*. Berlin, 1926.

7/ Germany. Statistisches Reichsamt. "Ausblick auf die zukünftige Bevölkerungsentwicklung im Deutschen Reich." Statistik des Deutschen Reichs, Band 401, II. Berlin, 1930.

8/ Germany. Statistisches Reichsamt. "Die voraussichtliche Bevölkerungsentwicklung im Deutschen Reich." Wirtschaft und Statistik 18(23):971-975; First Dec. No., 1938. Ibid. 19(6):247-250; Second March No., 1939.

9/ Germany. Statistisches Reichsamt. Volks-, Berufs- und Betriebszählung vom 12. Juni 1933. Volkszählung. Die Bevölkerung des Deutschen Reichs nach den Ergebnissen der Volkszählung 1933. Heft 2. Geschlecht,

Alter, und Familienstand der Bevölkerung des Deutschen Reichs. Statistik des Deutschen Reichs, Band 451, Heft 2. Berlin, 1936. 177 pp.

10/ "German vital trends in war." Population Index, Vol. 8, No. 4, pp. 255-258. Oct., 1942.

11/ Kulischer, Eugene M. The displacement of population in Europe. Montreal, International Labour Office, 1943. Infold Table opposite p. 170.

12/ Metropolitan Life Insurance Company. "Military deaths in World War II." Statistical Bulletin 27(1):6-8. Jan., 1946.

13/ U. S. Strategic Bombing Survey. Over-all report. European war. Washington, Sept. 30, 1945. P. 95.

14/ Kulischer, Eugene M. Europe on the move: War and population changes, 1917-47. New York, Columbia University Press, 1948. Pp. 282-283, 285-286.

15/ Germany. Württemberg-Baden. Statistisches Landesamt. "Kriegsgefangene und Wehrmachtvermisste." Statistische Monatshefte Württemberg-Baden, June, 1947. Pp. 165-166.

16/ Germany. Bavaria. Statistisches Landesamt. "Die Bedeutung der Gebiete östlich der Oder und Neisse für die Ernährungswirtschaft Deutschland...." Bayern in Zahlen 1(4):75-79. 1947.

17/ Germany. U. S. Zone. Statistical Annex, Issue No. XIII. Report of the Military Governor, No. 33. March, 1948. P. 7.

18/ Ibid. Feb.-March, 1947. P. 5.

19/ Germany. British Zone. Monthly Statistical Bulletin, Vol. 3, No. 4, p. 63. April, 1948.

20/ Ibid., Vol. 3, No. 1, pp. 40-41. Jan., 1948.

21/ Germany. Württemberg-Baden. Statistisches Landesamt. "Die Entwicklung des Altersaufbaus der Bevölkerung des Landes Württemberg-Baden 1939-1946." Statistische Monatshefte Württemberg-Baden, June, 1947. Pp. 158-164.

22/ Unless otherwise specified, the remaining materials are taken from the statistical publications of the Office of Military Government of the United States Zone. Detailed citations are included in the bibliography of this and earlier issues of Population Index.

23/ Data for 1939 are given in: Germany. U. S. Zone. Military Government for Germany. The population of the US Zone of Germany. Part 2. Some results of the census of October 1946 in relation to economic, social and demographic policy. Office of Military Government for Germany, November, 1947. P. 12. Data for 1946 are based on tables in: Germany. U. S. Zone. Statistical Annex, Issue No. XIII. Report of the Military Governor, No. 33. March, 1948. P. 8.

24/ Germany. U. S. Zone. Military Government for Germany. The population of the US Zone of Germany. Part 2. Some results of the census of October 1946 in relation to economic, social and demographic policy. Office of Military Government for Germany, November, 1947. Pp. 27, 88-89. It will be noted that the total population figure of 16.2 million used as the basis for the projections differs from the more complete total of 17.2 million given in Table 1. The 16.2 million excludes Bremen, which was added to the United States Zone after the census, and displaced persons in camp.

POPULATION GROWTH AND ECONOMIC

DEVELOPMENT IN THE U.S.S.R.

By Warren W. Eason

Twenty-five years ago the Soviet Union embarked on a program of rapid industrialization under a series of National Economic Plans. In the intervening years the structure of economic organization has been radically altered and impressive rates of growth have been registered in several sectors.

Sufficient time has passed for relationships between population growth and economic development under Soviet planning to begin to be evident. This paper is an attempt to describe and evaluate some of the most important of these relationships, insofar as it is possible for a nonSoviet scholar to do so, having at his disposal primary data which are far from adequate.

The following aspects of the subject will be treated: the rate of population growth, including birth and death rates; the distribution of the population by urban and rural areas; the distribution by economic sectors; the importance of women in the economy; the problem of skilled manpower and the growth of the educational system.

I. Population Growth and Vital Statistics

On the eve of the First Five-Year Plan (1928), according to official figures reproduced in Table 1, the population of the Soviet Union was increasing at an annual rate of 2.4 percent, the resultant of 42.2 births and 18.2 deaths per thousand population.[1] Comparison in terms of data for pre-Soviet Russia shows that the rate of increase was greater than in the 19th and early 20th centuries, when it varied for the most part between 1.3 and 1.7 percent, because of a fall in the death rate.[2]

In the 12 years between the censuses of 1926 and 1939—including 1927-28, the first and second Five-Year Plans and part of the third—the *average* annual rate of population increase derived geometrically from the census totals was 1.23 percent, or almost half the rate for 1928.[3] This 12-year average is equal to or greater than intercensal rates of increase in many other countries during the thirties,[4] but it is markedly below Soviet (and pre-Soviet) peacetime rates up to 1928.

---

*Compared to the version appearing in the proceedings of the World Population Conference, this paper has certain minor changes, including the addition of data for years prior to 1926 in Tables 1 and 2. The author is indebted to Professor Frank Lorimer for reading an early draft and offering several helpful suggestions. For sources and methods see notes at the end of the paper.

Soviet vital statistics for the prewar plan period do not reveal the full extent of the fall in the rate of increase shown by the census data, because the statistics have not been released for several crucial years (1931-34) and because those which are available embody reporting deficiencies over-stating to some degree the rate of increase at least for the early years. Actually, as will be shown, the fall in the rate of increase seems to have been especially severe during the years for which data are not available (1931-34).

Table 1—Official Vital Statistics: Birth and Death Rates Per Thousand Population and Percentage Rates of Natural Increase, Imperial Russia and the U.S.S.R., 1891-1953

Year	Birth Rate (1)	Death Rate (2)	Percentage of Natural Increase (col. 1—col. 2)/10	
1891-1895	49.0	36.2	1.28	
1896-1900	49.4	32.4	1.70	
1901-1905	47.7	31.0	1.67	
1906-1910	45.2	29.0	1.62	
1911-1913	43.3	26.9	1.64	
1913	43.4	27.9	1.55	
1914	41.0	25.3	1.57	
....				
1920	29.1	38.1	—0.90	
1921	34.1	29.1	0.50	
1922	32.1	33.8	—0.17	
1923	40.5	21.5	1.90	
1924	43.1	22.0	2.11	
1925	44.7	23.2	2.15	
1926	43.6	20.0	2.36	
1927	42.7	21.0	2.19	
1928	42.2	18.2	2.40	
1929	39.8	20.3	1.95	
1930	39.2	20.4	1.88	1.23 (intercensal)
....				
1935	28.6	16.3	1.23	
1936	32.3	18.8	1.35	
1937	38.7	17.9	2.08	
1938	38.3	17.8	2.05	
1939	......	......	......	
1940	......	18.2	......	
....				
1949	......	......	......	
1950	......	......	......	1.49-1.68
1951	......	......	......	
1952	......	......	......	
1953	......	8.9	......	

The annual rate of increase apparently began to fall immediately with the plans. According to Table 1, it reached 1.88 percent in 1930, 20 percent below the rate for 1928, with a lower birth rate and a higher death rate than in 1928. In 1935, the next year for which data are available, the rate was down to 1.23 percent, equal to the 12-year (1926-39) annual average; but by

1937 and 1938 it increased to about 2 percent, approaching the preplan level.

The data thus indicate a downward trend for the first years of the plans and an upward trend to 1937 and 1938 (the latest prewar years for which data are available). However, with the exception of 1935, each of the annual rates is greater than the average annual increase over the 12 years. If the annual data were as reliable as the average from the censuses, the implication would be an absolute population decline over the 1931-34 period as a whole, on an average of 0.02 percent per year. In other words, only if the population declined on the average by 0.02 percent each year, 1931-34, inclusive, could the geometric average of the annual rates of increase for each year, 1927-38, inclusive, equal the geometric annual average from the census totals. As it is, the annual data, at least for the early years of the intercensal period, understate the death rate and, hence, overstate the rate of increase,[5] although probably not in a degree sufficient to account for even a major portion of the difference. The conclusion therefore seems warranted, that the rate of increase in all or at least part of 1931-34, if not negative or zero, was significantly less than the 12-year average.[6]

Changes in the birth rate appear to dominate changes in the rate of population increase during the thirties. By 1930, the number of births per thousand had dropped to 39.2 and by 1935 to 28.6, or 32 percent below the rate for 1928. The rate was probably still lower during 1931-34.[7] The lower birth rate in the first years of the plans may be correlated with the following:

(1) Accelerated industrial development and large-scale migration to urban areas. The concentration of certain of these changes in one or two years seems particularly significant. For example, during the 12 months of 1931 the number of workers and employees (including the overwhelming bulk of the industrial labor force) increased by 6,321,000, an increase in one year equal to that over the preceding four years and over the following seven; while in 1932 and 1933 there was virtually no increase.[8] In 1930-32, net migration to urban areas comprised 9,452,000, or more than half the total net migration from 1927 to 1936.[9]

(2) Rapid transition to collective farming. The possible effect on the birth rate is suggested by the erratic nature of the transition and the fact that it was concentrated in a few years. Between February and March, 1930, the number of collective farms increased from 87,500 to 110,200, and the number of collective farm households from 8 million to 14 million;[10] then, responding to official objections to the speed of collectivization, the respective numbers fell by May to below the February level, remaining there until the end of the year.[11] In 1931, however, collectivization was resumed, and in that one year the number of collective farms increased from 112,800 to 230,400, and the number of collective farm households from 6,577,800 to 15,426,000, or, as a percentage of all households in agriculture, from 26.4 to 62.6 percent.[12] The percentage continued to increase in subsequent years

through the decline in the number of private households in agriculture, but the number of collectivized households did not increase again until 1935.[13] In addition to the pace of the transition, an indication of the disruptive effects on peasant life is seen in the striking losses of livestock between 1928 and 1933.[14]

(3) Liberal administrative regulations regarding marriages and divorces, and the existence of free abortion clinics in Soviet hospitals, starting in 1922.[15] The number of registered abortions increased under this system, although the effect on the birth rate during the twenties was held to be insignificant.[16] In areas for which data are available, a sharp increase in the number of abortions per 100 births by the early thirties was accompanied by a drop in the birth rate. By 1935, the use of artificial abortion was restricted by regulation, and in 1936 the practice was abolished except in certain specific medical cases.[17]

(4) Shift in the population age structure. The probable net effect is not clear. Persons born during World War I and the Civil War, when the birth rate was low, began entering the reproductive age-group (15-49) in the early thirties, tending, other things equal, to reduce the number in this group relative to others and, *ipso facto*, to reduce the crude birth rate. However, as indicated below, the net effect of shifts in age structure *by 1939* was to increase the age group 15-49 relative to others.

After 1935 the birth rate increased rapidly, reaching 38.7 in 1937 and 38.3 in 1938. The difference between the crude rate in 1938 and that in 1926 (43.7) is of an order of magnitude which could be explained by the shift of the population from rural to urban areas, on the assumption of rural and urban birth rates with respect to females of child-bearing ages the same as in 1926.[18]

The crude death rate during the thirties, according to the official statistics (Table 1), appears relatively stable. Compared to 1928 (18.2) it was somewhat higher in 1930 (20.4), somewhat less in 1935 (16.3) and about the same again in 1938 (17.8). In addition to the fact, noted above, that the reported rates understate the true rates, indirect evidence suggests relatively high *age-specific* rates for at least part of 1931-34.[19] The effect on the crude death rate, however, is not necessarily of the same degree, since lower birth rates operate to reduce the number of infant deaths, other things equal, and the latter comprise a large proportion of total deaths.

Higher age-specific death rates can probably be traced in some measure to the rapidity of industrialization and collectivization, discussed above in connection with the birth rate; and in addition, although Soviet sources do not mention it, there is evidence of wide-spread food shortages in 1932-33.[20]

By 1949-51, the next period for which data are available, the rate of population increase was roughly 1.5 to 1.7 percent per year (Table 1)— lower than in 1938 (1.89), but higher than the average for the thirties (1.23). The crude death rate in 1953 was reported as 8.9 per thousand, signifying a marked drop compared to prewar 1938 (17.8). Taken together, the figures show that the birth rate has also fallen, for if we combine the average annual rate of increase for 1949-51 with the death rate for 1953, the result is a crude birth rate of about 24 to 26 per thousand, compared to 38.3 in 1938. This method may result in an understatement of the recent birth rate, because the crude death rate may have been higher in 1951 than in 1953, and the death rate as reported may not be comprehensive.[21] Nevertheless, it seems reasonable to conclude that the crude birth rate in very recent years was less than 30 per thousand.[22]

The reported crude death rate of 8.9 ranks the Soviet Union with the leading countries of the world.[23] An important component of the sharp decline since prewar is the reported fall in infant mortality to less than one-third of the 1940 level.[24] In addition, the lower rate could be expected to reflect the fact that many elderly persons must have died prematurely during World War II, i.e., that the elderly must now be a smaller proportion of the adult population than in 1940. Finally, the rate as reported may reflect an improvement of an order of 15-20 percent in age-specific mortality other than infant mortality.[25]

The decline of the crude birth rate to less than 30 per thousand, together with increasing, steady or only moderately declining rates in most other countries, has reduced the relative position of the Soviet Union.[26] The fall of the rate between 1938 and 1953 may be interpreted in terms of several aspects. First, the continued migration from rural to urban areas, other things equal, and relative to 1926 rural-urban birth differentials,[27] would act to lower the crude birth rate.

On the other hand, the number of females of reproductive ages (15-49) undoubtedly increased not only absolutely but also relative to other groups in the population, an effect which by itself would tend to raise the crude birth rate. The absolute increase in this group was caused by the entry of those born during the twenties, when the birth rate was high. The relative increase reflects in addition the high incidence of mortality among males and the elderly of both sexes during the war, as well as the war-induced birth deficit.

Assuming a net migration of females from rural to urban areas between 1939 and 1950 proportionate to the reported increase in the number of female workers and employees, it can be shown that the effect of the change in the age distribution probably would outweigh that of rural-urban migration,[28] with the result that if only these considerations had been operating, the crude birth rate would have been higher in 1953 than in 1938.

The fact that the rate fell from 38.3 to less than 30 means, therefore, that the average Soviet woman age 15-49, aside from the possible effects of rural-urban migration, is having significantly fewer children now than in 1938.

One factor which may account for this is the increase in the deficit of males relative to females (15-49) from 3 million in 1939 to possibly 7 or 8 million in 1950,[29] although, as Sauvy has illustrated,[30] this could account for only a certain portion of the decline. Furthermore, the deficit as of 1926

(3,372,000), which occurred as a result of World War I and the Civil War (in 1897 there was almost no deficit[31]), did not prevent the birth rate from reaching 43.6 in the same year.

Another factor to explain the lower birth rate may be the larger share of work falling on women, in the city as well as in the country (see below).

Demographic changes during the Five-Year Plans, as seen in the changing rate of population growth and in the pattern of birth and death rates discussed above, modified certain basic relationships within the national economy. First, the absolute size of the population was substantially less under the plans than if preplan rates of population growth had been maintained. According to projections made on the basis of preplan rates, by Novosel'skii and Paevskii,[32] the population in 1939 should have been more than 20 million greater than that reported by the 1939 Census. All age-groups were affected although in different degree, and the result was to reduce more quickly than otherwise the abundance of labor (population) relative to capital, i.e., to increase more quickly than otherwise the ratio of capital to labor. The change in the capital-labor ratio, the overall aim of the Soviet industrialization drive, was therefore hastened in the early stages, albeit fortuitously, by the indicated demographic changes.

Second, the number of adults in the prime working ages (16-59) increased relative to children and elderly persons. Whereas persons age 16-59 were 53.7 percent of the population in 1926,[33] they were 56.0 percent in 1939[34] and probably 59-62 percent in 1950,[35] while if preplan rates had been maintained, the percentage would have fallen.[36] By this shift in age structure, the productive elements in the population increased relative to the nonproductive. This tended to reduce the pressure of consumption on production and, other things equal, enabled a higher rate of investment (nonconsumption) relative to the given population.

Observing that the rate of population increase, the birth rate and the death rate over the Five-Year Plans have fallen significantly compared to the preplan (peacetime) level, it is appropriate to ask whether this trend can be considered "normal" to conditions of Soviet economic development, in the sense that present or lower rates of population growth may reasonably be expected in the future. Or does the trend result from a succession of special circumstances (e.g., transition to industrialization and collectivization, and the effects of World War II) not expected to recur? In the latter case the critical variable, the birth rate, would return to previous levels, and with it the rate of population increase.

As far as the population changes of the thirties are concerned, it would seem reasonable to ascribe a dominant role to unique circumstances, i.e., to the concentration of certain critical developments in the first and second Five-Year Plans. By the Third Five-Year Plan, it will be noticed, when general conditions in industry and agriculture had become relatively stable, the death rate was no greater than preplan and the birth rate was less than preplan by no more than could be accounted for by rural-urban migration.

Using 1928 and 1938 as points to determine a trend, therefore, one could extrapolate a rate of population growth which would change relatively slowly. In the case of the birth rate, this change would be correlated with continued rural-urban migration.

For recent years, however, the degree of fall in the birth rate and in the rate of population growth, compared to 1938, seems too great to be explained entirely by special circumstances (principally the war and its after-effects) and rural-urban migration. This together with the apparent stability of the rate of population increase for recent years (see the sources and methods of Table 1) are reasons for not expecting a sharp upturn in the rate of growth in the near future. By the same token a continued down-ward trend, however gradual, cannot be ruled out.

II. Population Distribution: Urban and Rural Areas

The industrialization program of the Five-Year Plans led to the large-scale migration of the Soviet population from rural to urban areas, as well as to an increase in the number of urban areas. As shown in Table 2, the urban population on the eve of the plans stood at about 28 million, or roughly 18 percent of the total population. It increased rapidly after 1928 and by 1932 was almost 40 million, or 24 percent of the total. The rural population increased from 121 million in 1926 to 127 million in 1932, although the official figures (Table 2) may overstate the rural population between 1931 and 1934 (see the sources and methods of Table 2).

By 1939, the urban population was more than double the number in 1926, part of the increase coming from the areas which were reclassified urban for the 1939 census.

In 1939-40, the Soviet Union acquired territory comprising about 22.5 million persons, of which slightly over 5 million were urban. According to the official figures, which do not allow for the natural increase in the population between 1939 and 1940, the acquired territory acted to lower slightly the urban population as a percentage of the total, from 32.8 in 1939 to 31.6 in 1940.

By 1953, the urban population reached about 80 million. Unfortunately, no official figure for the total (or rural) population has been released since 1939-40, except for the mention of 193 million directly after the war,[37] a figure which, curiously, is identical to the official estimate for 1940. One Soviet source[38] at the end of 1949 refers to the "200 million persons" in the U.S.S.R., but this would seem to indicate an order of magnitude rather than a precise figure, and is identical to a reference at the end of 1940 (see Table 2).

NonSoviet scholars have attempted to estimate the total population from the reported number of election districts[39] and from the number of persons eligible to vote plus school children,[40] but the results are subject to con-siderable margins of error.[41]

Table 2—Official Soviet Figures on the Total, Urban and Rural Population, Imperial Russia and the U.S.S.R., 1897-1940; and Postwar Estimates, Including Official Urban Population, 1950-1953

(Territory is U.S.S.R.: 1897-1939, pre-1939; 1940-1953, post-1939)

Year	Month	Total	Population in Thousands				Percentage Distribution			
			URBAN		RURAL		URBAN		RURAL	
			De Facto	De Jure	De Facto	De Jure	De Facto	De Jure	De Facto	De Jure
1897		103,933	15,826	……	88,107	……	15.2	……	84.8	……
1914	1 Jan	138,199	24,686	……	110,912	……	17.9	……	82.1	……
1920	28 Aug	130,863	20,787	……	110,076	……	15.9	……	84.1	……
1923	15 Mar	133,504	21,563	……	111,941	……	16.2	……	83.8	……
1926	17 Dec	147,028	26,314	24,888	120,714	122,140	17.9	16.9	82.1	83.1
1928	1 Jan	150,450	27,571	……	122,879	……	18.3	……	81.7	……
1929	1 Jan	154,288	29,200	27,630	125,088	126,658	18.9	17.9	81.1	82.1
1930	1 Jan	157,700	30,900	……	126,800	……	19.6	……	80.4	……
1931	1 Jan	160,600	32,000	……	128,600	……	19.9	……	80.1	……
1932	1 Jan	163,692	36,340	……	127,352	……	22.2	……	77.8	……
1933	1 Jan	165,748	……	39,739	……	126,009	……	24.0	……	76.0
1934	1 Jan	168,000	……	41,100	……	126,900	……	24.5	……	75.5
1936	July	……	47,000	……	……	……	……	……	……	……
1937	12 Dec	169,000	……	……	……	……	……	……	……	……
1939	17 Jan	170,467	55,910	……	114,557	……	32.8	……	67.2	……
Annexed Areas		+22,533	+5,090		+17,443		22.6		77.4	
(1940)		193,000	61,000		132,000		31.6		68.4	
1940		200,000								
1950	1 Jan	(190,000-205,000)	69,800		(120,200-135,200)		34-37		63-66	
1953	1 Jan	(200,000-215,000)	80,000		(120,000-135,000)		37-40		60-63	

Within the limits of our knowledge and considering the error in the estimates just cited, it seems reasonable to say only that it was probably between 200 and 215 million in 1953.[42] From this and the reported urban population, the rural population follows as between 120 and 135 million.

A rural population of 135 million in 1953 would represent a 2 percent increase over 1940 (including annexed areas), as against a 5 percent decline between 1926 and 1939 (pre-annexation territory). In other words, the upper estimate of the total population would give a rural population showing little or no change in absolute terms on comparable territory since 1926. A rural population of 120 million in 1953, on the other hand, would represent an 11 percent decline compared to 1940, for an overall decline of about 16 percent on comparable territory since 1926, i.e., an average rate of decline of about 0.5 percent per year.

Soviet economic expansion has thus led to an increase in the urban population from 26 to 80 million in 25 years, or by more than three times, and to an increase in the urban population as a percentage of the total from 17.9 to 37-40 percent. The fact that the rural population over the same period has remained more or less unchanged or declined moderately in absolute terms (within the range of the estimates) points among other things to the overall dynamic character of Soviet population growth since the beginning of the plans. The catastrophic effects of the early thirties and World War II on population growth notwithstanding, Soviet urban expansion has been able to proceed largely by drawing off, so to speak, the net increase in the total population over the whole period. To put it another way, the Soviet Union, for all of its rapid rate of urbanization, and its position as a leading industrial power, still retains the majority of its population (60 percent or more) in rural areas.

The rapid rate of growth of the urban population, as acknowledged by Malenkov,[43] has led to substantial and growing requirements with respect to housing, sanitation, education, etc. In an attempt to meet these requirements in the field of housing, for example, the number of square meters of dwelling space in urban areas has been increased from 163 million in 1928[44] to 258 million in 1941[45] and, as near as can be estimated,[46] to 326 million in 1953, for an overall doubling of dwelling space (not counting construction to replace war losses). The urban population, however, has increased by more than three times, with the result that per capita dwelling space in urban areas has declined, from 5.9 square meters in 1928 to 4.2 in 1941 and 4.1 in 1953.

III. Population Distribution: Agricultural and Nonagricultural Sectors

In 1926, when 82.1 percent of the population was rural, 77.6 percent was in agriculture[47]; and in 1939, when the rural percentage had dropped to 67.2,[48] the percentage in agriculture was 58.[49] The widening of the differential between the two percentages, assuming that no distortion is caused by changes in definition,[50] indicates a relative increase in the nonagricultural rural population.

In 1953, the rural population was 60-63 percent of the total (Table 2). The size of the population (and labor force) in agriculture for the postwar period has not been reported; but if the differential between the rural population and the population in agriculture is assumed roughly the same as indicated above for 1939 (67.2:58), the population in agriculture in 1953 may be estimated as between 52-54 percent of the total, or 104-116 million.

Over the plan period, therefore, the population in agriculture declined from 114 million in 1926 to 99 million in 1939, or by 13 percent; and from an estimated 114 million in 1940[51] (including annexed territory, but excluding the natural increase between 1939 and 1940) to 104-116 million in 1953, or by —9 to +2 percent. The overall decrease in the agricultural population between 1926 and 1953 on comparable territory is thus estimated to be between 11 and 22 percent, for an average rate of decrease of from 0.5 to less than 1 percent per year.

At the same time, the nonagricultural population (by subtraction from the total, for 1953) increased three to four times, comprising in 1953, 46-48 percent of the total, compared to 22.4 percent in 1926.

Available data suggest a slower rate of growth for the total labor force than for the total population, caused by the net effect of changes in the age-sex composition of the population and in the labor force-population ratios for specific age-sex groups.[52] Trends in the distribution of the labor force by economic sectors are obscure because no data have been reported for certain sectors. Much of what can be said, therefore, at least for the postwar period, must be inferred from the reported number of persons working for wages or salaries, the "workers and employees," comprising the bulk of the industrial (and urban) labor force, but even in 1953 less than 40 percent of the total labor force.

The number of workers and employees increased from an average of 11,599,000 in 1928 to 28,610,000 on January 1, 1939, and to an average of 41,250,000 in 1953,[53] for an overall increase of 3.6 times, compared to an increase of 2.9 times for the urban population. The more rapid increase in the number of workers and employees is caused partly by the fact that initial increases in the number to a certain degree consisted of the transfer from a non-hired to a hired status of persons already in the urban labor force, partly from the fact that adults became a larger part of the population after 1928, and partly from a decline in unemployment.

In 1926, workers and employees comprised 11.4 percent of the total number of persons having an occupation plus the unemployed, and in 1939, 32 percent of the estimated total labor force.[54] In 1953, workers and employees were almost certainly less than 40 percent of the total labor force, and within our ability to estimate the size of the total labor force, may have been in percentage terms no greater than in 1939.[55] From the other side of the picture, the non-worker-and-employee labor force as a percentage of the total was the same in 1953 as in 1939 (68 percent) or may have declined somewhat, but in any event has probably not fallen below 60 percent of the total.

Most of the non-workers-and-employees are in agriculture (collective farmers and individual farmers) and most of the agricultural labor force is made up of non-workers-and-employees, the exception being workers and employees on State Farms and Machine-Tractor Stations. The remaining non-workers-and-employees comprise co-op and nonco-op handicraftsmen, the military, and certain elements which are not reported in Soviet sources, notably prison labor.

It is difficult to infer trends in the agricultural labor force since 1939 from those of the non-worker-and-employee labor force, even though agriculture is a major component thereof, because of the nonreported sectors. Another approach would be through the agricultural population, which is estimated (above) in relation to the rural population; but this approach would require an assumption about changes since 1939 in the labor force-population ratio for agriculture, an assumption which would be difficult to make because of the marked changes in the age and sex composition of the population in agriculture.

The absence of postwar data on the labor force in agriculture, as well as the continued policy of not reporting on certain other sectors, thus seriously limits our ability to obtain either a direct or indirect quantitative measure of recent changes in the largest single sector of the national economy.

IV. Women in the Labor Force

The increase in the number of workers and employees gives insight into an aspect of Soviet development which is important from the social as well as the economic point of view, namely, the increasingly vital role of women, a trend which is stressed in the Soviet press. Between 1929 and 1950 (the earliest and the latest date for which employment data by sexes are available), the annual average number of workers and employees increased from 12,168,000 to 37,200,000, or by 25,032,000, and the major share of this increase (54.7 percent) consisted of women. The number of female workers and employees increased by 5.1 times in the 21 years, while the number of male workers and employees increased by 2.3 times. In 1950 almost half of workers and employees were women, compared to 27.2 percent in 1929.[56]

As far as agriculture is concerned, women have always played an important role, in Soviet as well as preSoviet times; for example, in 1926, of 71,736,000 persons with an occupation in agriculture, 35,565,000 or 49.6 percent were women.[57] The percentage of women among those occupied in agriculture apparently increased in the late thirties. On collective farms, comprising more than 90 percent of the total labor force in agriculture, females earning labor-days as a percentage of both sexes increased from

46.2 percent in 1936[58] to 53.2 per cent in 1939[59]; furthermore, women do the major portion of work on the homestead plot of the collective farm household.[60] Considering the number of males lost during the war, the percentage of females among persons occupied in agriculture has probably increased in the postwar period.

Although these two sectors—workers and employees and collective farmers—include most of the labor force and are together probably more than half composed of females at the present time, it cannot be concluded that the total labor force has a majority of females, because the remaining sectors (see above) may have a predominance of males.

V. Skilled Manpower

Soviet economic development was severely handicapped in the early years, not only by the scarcity of skilled personnel but by the fact that manpower from the rural areas came into industry with little or no comprehension of the nature of the work. On-the-job training indoctrinated a whole generation of new proletariat. The fact that the number of workers and employees increased by over 6 million in 1931 alone, after which there was no essential increase for two years and an increase of around 1 million a year until 1940, implies, for much of the period after 1931, emphasis on the more effective utilization of manpower already on the payrolls.

Rapid strides in education are evidenced by the increase in school attendance, although the economy still suffers from a shortage of manpower in many skills. In 1928-29, a total of 12,725,000 students attended all schools, including universities. By the 1934-35 school year, attendance had doubled, and by 1939-40 almost 34 million students were on the rolls.[61] Relative to the population age 7-16, the number of students excluding university increased from 37.7 percent in 1928-29 to 84.5 percent in 1938-39.[62]

Percentagewise the increase during the plans was greatest in secondary schools and universities. Attendance at secondary schools increased by 9 times, at secondary schools for the training of specialists, 5 times, and at universities, 3.5 times.[63] A steady flow of persons into secondary schools for the training of specialists was assured by the creation in 1940 of the State Labor Reserve system, based on the obligatory recruitment of manpower from collective farms.[64]

Total attendance at all schools was higher in 1950-51 (38,247,000) than in 1939-40 (33,994,000),[65] although attendance in secondary schools had dropped in 1947-48 to 31,300,000, compared to 32,056,000 in 1939-40,[66] increasing to 35,108,000 by 1950-51, the latest figure available.[67]

Attendance at universities is now (1953-54) 1,562,000, 80 percent above 1939-40, and at secondary schools for the training of specialists, 1,644,000, 44 percent above prewar.[68]

Recent pronouncements indicate continued emphasis on expanding the number of skilled personnel and improving the quality of technical training.[69]

Sources and Methods of Table 1

Rates for 1891-1930, inclusive, are from Russian and Soviet sources, as shown below. Rates for 1935-1938, inclusive, are in some cases taken directly from Soviet sources. In other cases, since the data are reported only in terms of percentage relationships, for example, the birth rate in one year as a percentage of another year, rates are derived by means of the following equation with respect to a given year:

$$\frac{\overline{P}(b-d)}{1000} = P_1 - P_0$$

Where P stands for the population (P_0 at the beginning of the year, P_1 at the end, and $\overline{P}$ the average of the two), b for the birth rate per thousand population and d for the death rate. The equation is solved for each year in succession, starting with the end of 1938 and working backwards. The population at the end of 1938 is estimated by Lorimer as 170,315,000, from the population of 170,467,000 reported by the census (January 17, 1939) minus an estimated increase for 16 days (*The Population of the Soviet Union: History and Prospects* [Geneva: League of Nations, 1946], p. 134).

To the extent that the reported rates are deficient, as discussed in the text, the derived number of births and deaths and the population at the beginning of each year are in error. However, the rates which are derived should be reasonably consistent with those given. The results differ somewhat from Lorimer (*ibid.*) partly because of data which became available after he wrote, and partly because he applied several percentage changes to the estimated number of births which, on reinterpretation, should be applied to the birth rate.

Rates for 1950 and the postwar years are derived from Soviet sources, as shown below.

1891-1895 to 1911-1913. From TsUNKhU, in B. Smulevich, *Burzhuaznye teorii narodonaseleniia v svete Marksistko-Leninskoi kritiki* (Moscow: 1936), pp. 144-154.

1913. Statisticheskii ezhegodnik Rossii 1915 (Petrograd: 1916), Part II, p. 2.

1914. Materialy shcho do pryrodnogo rukha naselenia Ukrainy 1867-1914 (Kiev-Kharkov: 1924), p. 9; and *Statisticheskii ezhegodnik Rossii 1914 i 1915* (Petrograd: 1915, 1916), pp. 33-57.

1920 to 1922. Estimated on the basis of data for about 55 million of the population. *Sbornik statisticheskikh svedenii 1918-1923* (Moscow: 1924), Part I, pp. 40-42; *Abrégé des données statistiques de l'URSS* (Moscow: 1923), p. 5; and P. Kuvshinnikov, "Estestvennoe dvizhenie naseleniia RSFSR v 1920-1922 gg.," *Vestnik statistiki*, 1925, No. 4-6, pp. 99-133.

1923. Statisticheskii ezhegodnik za 1924 god. (Moscow: 1924), p. 40; *Sbornik . . ., ibid.*, pp. 2-5.

1924 to 1927. Statisticheskii spravochnik SSSR za 1928 god. (Moscow: 1929), p. 74.
1928 to 1930. From TsUNKhU, in Smulevich, *op. cit.*, pp. 144-154.

1935. Birth rate derived, given ratio to 1938 rate, 1/1.337, from *Izvestiia*, June 27, 1939. Death rate from I. Kraval', "Vsesoiuznaia perepis' naseleniia 1937 g.," *Planovoe khoziaistvo*, 1936, No. 12, p. 24. Given the population at the end of the year (beginning of 1936, see below), the above equation gives the number of births as 4,583,000, the number of deaths as 2,612,000 and the population at the beginning of the year as 159,-255,000.

1936. Birth rate derived, given ratio to 1935 rate, 1.128, from *Pravda*, June 27, 1939. Death rate derived from above equation, given the ratio of the number of deaths in 1936 to the number in 1937, 1/.974, from *Pravda*, March 2, 1938, and the population at the end of year (beginning of 1937, see below). The equation gives the number of births as 5,243,000, the number of deaths as 3,045,000 and the population at the beginning of the year as 161,226,000.

1937. Birth rate derived, given ratio to 1936 rate, 1.197, from *Pravda*, June 27, 1939. Percent of natural increase from *Pravda*, January 11, 1939, as quoted in E. M. Kulischer, *Europe on the Move* (New York: Columbia University Press, 1948), p. 80. Given the population at the end of the year (beginning of 1938, see below), the equation gives the number of births as 6,391,000, the number of deaths as 2,956,000 and the population at the beginning of the year as 163,424,000.

1938. Birth rate from *Pravda*, June 27, 1939. Death rate derived from the above equation, given the ratio of the number of births to deaths as '2.157, from S. Sul'kevich, *Naselenie SSSR* (Moscow: 1939), p. 25. Given the population at the end of the year (170,315,000, see above), the equation gives the number of births as 6,457,000, the number of deaths as 3,001,000 and the population at the beginning of the year as 166,-859,000.

Intercensal annual average, 1926-1939. Derived as the average annual geometric rate of increase between the two censuses. See footnote 3.

1940. Death rate derived from the statement in *Pravda,* October 19, 1954, that the death rate in 1953 was 51 percent below the death rate in 1940.

1949 to 1951. Net increase of the population is reported by L. P. Beria, *Pravda,* November 7, 1951, as "for several years . . . more than 3 million," and by G. M. Malenkov, *Pravda,* October 6, 1952, as "for the past 3 years . . . 9,500,000." Reference is taken to be the period 1949-1951, inclusive. Estimating the total population from the beginning of 1949 to the end of 1951 as between 188 and 212 million (see text, below), the average annual percentage increase follows, 1.49-1.68.

1953. Death rate reported by A. I. Mikoyan, *Pravda,* April 27, 1954. See text for a discussion of the postwar birth rate.

Sources and Methods of Table 2

1897. From the census, corrected for boundary changes after World War I. TsUNKhU, *Narodnoe khoziaistvo SSSR, statisticheskii spravochnik 1932* (Moscow: 1932), p. 401.

1914. Estimated in *ibid.*

1920. From the census, in *ibid.*

1923. Urban population from the census; total and rural estimated, in *ibid.*

1926. From the census, *Vsesoiuznaia perepis' . . . op. cit.,* Vol. XVII.

1928. Statisticheskii spravochnik za 1928, op. cit., p. 20.

1929. TsUNKhU, *Sotsialisticheskoe stroitel'stvo SSSR,* 1935 (Moscow: 1935), p. 539; and *Narodnoe khoziaistvo . . . , op. cit.,* p. XXIII. Delineation of urban areas is according to the count of 1931.

1930-31. M. Avdienko, "Sdvigi v strukture proletariata v pervoi piatiletke," *Planovoe khoziaistvo,* 1932, No. 6-7, p. 145. Date of January 1 determined by comparison with population of 162,686,000 for July 1, 1931 given in TsIK, *Sovetskoe stroitel'stvo,* 1932, No. 1, p. 159.

1932. Total population from TsIK, *Sovetskoe stroitel'stvo,* 1932, No. 3, p. 157. Urban as a percentage of total from *Sotsialisticheskoe stroitel'stvo . . . 1935, op. cit.,* p. xxviii.

1933. Sotsialisticheskoe stroitel'stvo . . ., ibid., p. 539. Delineation of urban areas is according to the count of 1931, including changes from 1931 to 1933.

1934. Total population from TsUNKhU, *Sotsialisticheskoe stroitel'stvo SSSR, 1936,* (Moscow: 1936), p. xxx. G. Neiman, "Otmena kartocheck, razvertyvanie tovarooborota i ukreplenie rublia," *Problemy ekonomiki,* 1935, No. 1, p. 50, gives 40,300,000 as the urban population included in the centralized supplying of bread by rationing in 1934, which is inclusive of all except disfranchised persons. The latter may be estimated as roughly 2 per cent of the urban population, and the given total raised accordingly to 41,100,000, on the basis of data for 261 City Soviets of the RSFSR at the time of the local elections to City Soviets in 1931. TsIK, *Pervye itogi vyborov v sovety v 1931 godu* (Moscow: 1931), p. 78.

1935. Data not available.

1936. Only the urban population is available, reported in I. Kraval', *loc. cit.,* p. 32. Figure is reported in discussion of preparations for the 1937 census, and it is known that the urban lists for the census were prepared around the middle of the year (July).

1937. Pravda, December 15, 1937. Total is as of election day, December 12, 1937.

1938. Data not available.

1939. From the census, as reported in *Pravda,* June 2, 1939.

(Annexed Areas) and (1940). Excluding natural increase of population during 1939 and 1940, from speech of Molotov to 7th Session of the 1st Supreme Soviet, as reported in *Izvestiia,* August 2, 1940.

1940. Izvestiia, November 5, 1940.

1950. Total population (as a range) estimated in Eason, *loc. cit.,* Appendix A, pp.

7-20, Table A4, p. 19. Estimation is from data in Soviet sources and by projection based on alternative assumptions regarding birth and death rates, 1940-1950.

Urban population is estimated as 3.4 million per year less than that reported for 1953, on the basis of statement of N. S. Krushchev, *Pravda,* February 3, 1955, that "for the last five years the urban population has increased by approximately 17 million persons." Rural population is by subtraction of urban from total.

1953. Total population estimated as for 1950, above. Urban population reported by G. M. Malenkov, *Pravda,* August 9, 1953.

Footnotes to Text

1. Prewar figures in Table 1 are from prewar sources, as noted in the respective footnotes. Recently what is apparently an official upward revision of the death rate for 1913 and 1927 has appeared. The implications of the revision are discussed below.

2. The birth rate for European Russia (not shown in Table 1) rose from roughly 40 to 50 per thousand during the first half of the 19th century and decreased gradually to 44 per thousand by World War I. The death rate, near 39 per thousand in the 1850's, declined to 29 by 1913 and to 20 by 1926. P. A. Khromov, *Ekonomicheskoe razvitie Rossii v XIX-XX vekakh* (Moscow: 1950), pp. 81 and 239-241. PreSoviet vital statistics (except for 1913 and 1914), reproduced in Table 1, are reported together with those for 1928-1930 in a Soviet source. It therefore probably should be assumed that they are otherwise consistent and have been adjusted for area changes, although not necessarily for reporting deficiencies. The latter as discussed by Lorimer, Ch. IX, is referred to below.

3. The population increased from 147,028,000 on December 17, 1926, to 170,467,000 on January 17, 1939, or by 23,439,000 over the 12.08 years, for an average geometric rate of increase of 1.23 percent per year. The rate as calculated by the United Nations in the *Demographic Yearbook 1948,* p. 97, and the *Demographic Yearbook 1953,* p. 102, is 1.14. This is presumably based on a 13-year period, that is, 1926-39 without taking into account the date within each year on which the respective censuses took place, and therefore understates the average annual rate of growth. The UN rate was inadvertently used in the draft of this paper distributed to the conference. The correct rate is given in *Pravda,* June 27, 1939.

4. The average annual percentage rate of increase between the censuses is greater than that for the United States (1930-40, 0.7), France (1926-31, 0.49; 1931-36, —0.02), Italy (1921-31, 0.87; 1931-36, 0.84), Sweden (1930-35, 0.35; 1935-40, 0.38), England and Wales (1921-31, 0.54), New Zealand (1926-36, 1.13), India in 1921-31 (1.02), Roumania (1930-41, 1.17), Germany (1925-33, 0.55; 1933-39, 0.83), and Canada in 1931-41 (1.04). It is less than that for India in 1931-41 (1.41), Canada in 1921-31 (1.68), Mexico (1930-40, 1.77), Chile (1930-40, 1.60), and Venezuela (1926-36, 1.40; 1936-41, 2.77). *Demographic Yearbook 1953,* pp. 83-102.

5. TsSU, *Smertnost' i prodolzhitel'nost' zhizni naseleniia SSSR, 1926-27. Tablitsy smertnosti* (Moscow: 1930), pp. xi ff., as cited and discussed in Lorimer, *op. cit.,* pp. 113-119. The principal deficiency is due to the underreporting of deaths in rural and scarcely populated areas.

6. The underreporting of deaths is a documented fact (footnote 5), but the degree of underreporting in the USSR as a whole is difficult to estimate. Lorimer's corrections *(op. cit.,* pp. 114-119) raise the crude death rate for 1926-27 by roughly 6 per thousand over that reported for the European part of the Soviet Union (near 20 per thousand, uncorrected). In a recent speech, A. I. Mikoyan reported the death rate for 1913 and 1927 as 30.2 and 22.8, respectively (*Pravda,* April 27, 1954), each of which is higher than rates appearing previously in Soviet sources—28.9 for 1913 (I. Kraval', *loc. cit.,* p. 24) and 21.0 for 1927 (M. Smulevich, cited in Table 1). One possibility is that the higher death rates given by Mikoyan include a correction for underreporting, although a smaller correction than indicated by Lorimer.

Lorimer places greater confidence in the reported crude birth rate for 1926-27 and enters an upward correction of less than 2 per thousand. The net effect of correcting the birth and death rates is to reduce the population increase given for 1926-27 by 4 per thousand. If we reduce each of the given annual rates of increase (1927-30 and 1935-38) by this amount and equate the results to the average annual increase of 1.23, it implies an average annual increase for the years of missing data (1931-34) of 0.8 percent.

On the one hand, this correction may be considered too large, assuming that the reporting of deaths (and births) improved in the late thirties, although the rates per thousand population reported for the middle thirties may be understated to the extent that the total population, on which they are presumably based, was overstated (see Table 2). On the other hand, it has been suggested that the vital statistics of certain special populations were not included in the published rates for the late thirties; but on this question there is no information in Soviet sources.

7. In addition to a lower birth rate inferred from the lower rate of population increase, direct evidence for a lower birth rate in all or part of 1931-34 lies in fragmentary data for certain areas, reproduced in Lorimer (*op. cit.*, pp. 126-130), and also in the fact that between 1938 and 1939 the number of children age 7-10 in school dropped by almost 1 million, reflecting the entry of the class born in 1932 (TsUNKhU, *Kul'turnoe stroitel'-stvo SSSR 1940* [Moscow-Leningrad: 1940], pp. 51-52).

8. TsUNKhU, *Trud v USSR, statisticheskii spravochnik* (Moscow: 1936), p. 10; Ia. Ioffe, *SSSR i kapitalisticheskie strany* (Moscow: 1939), p. 90; *Bol'shaia sovetskaia entsiklopediia* (Moscow: 1947), col. 68; TsUNKhU, *Sotsialisticheskoe stroitel'stvo SSSR, 1933-38* (Moscow-Leningrad: 1939), p. 20; and E. Orlikova "Zhenskii trud v SSSR," *Planovoe khoziaistvo,* 1939, No. 10, p. 113.

9. TsUNKhU, *Sotsialisticheskoe stroitel'stvo SSSR, 1935* (Moscow: 1936), pp. 545-547.

10. *Izvestiia,* March 9, 1930.

11. TsUNKhU, *Kolkhozy vo vtoroi Stalinskoi piatiletke* (Moscow-Leningrad: 1939), p. 1, and *Sotsialisticheskoe pereustroistvo sel'skogo khoziaistva SSSR mezhdu XV i XVI siezdami VKP(b)* (Moscow: 1930), p. 126.

12. A. Karavaeva and V. Iezuntov, "Kolkhoznoe stroitel'tsvo nakanune vtoroi piatiletke," *Sotsialisticheskoe rekonstruktsiia sel'skogo khoziaistva,* 1932, No. 5, p. 8.

13. *Kolkhozy vo vtoroi . . . , op. cit.,* pp. 36 and 40. By January 1, 1935, collectivized households were 77.5 percent of the total ("Pokazateli vypolneniia narodnokhoziaistven-nogo plana za 10 mesiatsev 1935," *Planovoe khoziaistvo,* 1935, No. 10, p. 242).

14. Herds declined by 55 percent in the case of horses, 52 percent for cattle, 65 percent for hogs and 71 percent for sheep and goats. NarKomZem and NarKomSovkhoz, *Sel'skoe khoziaistvo SSSR, ezhegodnik 1935* (Moscow: 1935), pp. 517-519, 527-528 and 523-533; and TsSU, *Statisticheskii spravochnik za 1928* (Moscow: 1929), pp. 158-159.

15. A. Gens, "Iskusstvennyi abort kak sotsial'no-bytovoe iavlenie," *Bol'shaia medit-sinskaia entsiklopediia,* T.I. (Moscow: 1928), cols. 44-48.

16. *Ibid.*

17. For further discussion of this subject, see Lorimer, *op. cit.,* pp. 126-130.

18. W. W. Eason, "Population and Labor Force," in A. Bergson (ed.), *Soviet Economic Growth: Conditions and Perspectives* (Evanston: Row, Peterson, 1953), p. 104.

19. Survival ratios based on given death rates for 1926-27 applied to the population alive in 1926 according to the census, leave a population age 12 and over in 1939 substantially in excess of the number according to the 1939 census (see Lorimer, *op. cit.,* p. 113), and by more than can be accounted for by understatement of the death rate in 1926-27.

20. N. Jasny, *Socialized Agriculture of the USSR: Plans and Performance* (Stanford: Stanford University Press, 1949), pp. 551-555.

21. The suggestion in footnote 6 that the vital statistics of certain special populations were not included in the published rates for the late thirties, may also apply to the postwar period.

22. In a two-year period (1951 to 1953), judging by the experience of other countries in postwar years (*Demographic Yearbook 1953,* pp. 166-175), in the absence of large-scale migration the death rate could not have fallen by more than 2 per thousand, and probably less. This means that only if in addition the death rate as reported is understated by 2 per thousand or more, could the birth rate (derived from the rate of increase in 1951 and the death rate in 1953) as corrected be near 30 per thousand.

23. Among selected countries for which data are complete or virtually complete, the death rate for 1952 is as follows: Italy, 10.0; Spain, 9.7; Canada, 8.6; United States, 9.6;

Venezuela, 10.8; Japan (1951), 10.0; United Kingdom, 11.4; and France, 12.3. *Ibid.* It should be clear from these comparisons that the crude death rate is only the roughest measure of the overall impact of mortality in a country. Conditions of mortality with respect to given age groups unchanged, variation in the age structure of the population can cause wide variation in the crude death rate.

24. M. Kovrigina (Minister of Public Health of the U.S.S.R.), "Nasushchnye nuzhdy sovetskogo zdravookhraneniia," *Pravda,* August 24, 1954.

25. This statement is on the basis of hypothetical calculations made by the present author (*op. cit.,* Appendix A, pp. 7-20, especially p. 20). The nature of the calculations is summarized below in connection with discussion of data in Table 2.

26. The birth rate in Canada in 1952 was 27.4, compared to 20.33-22.2 during the thirties; in the United States, 24.5 compared to 17.2-17.6; in Venezuela, 43.7 compared to 28.2-32.7; France, 19.2 compared to 15.1-17.2. The birth rate in the United Kingdom has remained more or less unchanged, at 15.7 in 1952; while in Spain the rate has declined from 22.0-27.5 in the thirties to 20.8 in 1952; in Italy, from 23.2-24.5 to 17.6; and in Japan, from 29.2-31.8 to 25.4 (1951). *Demographic Yearbook 1953,* pp. 132-141.

27. The number of live births per thousand females age 15-49 in the European USSR in 1926 was 113.3 in urban areas and 176.8 in rural. TsSU, *Estestvennoe dvizhenie naseleniia SSSR v 1926* (Moscow: 1929), pp. 13-14.

28. Eason, *loc. cit.,* p. 104, footnote 9.

29. *Ibid.*

30. A. Sauvy, "Population et doctrine de population en Union sovietique," *Population,* 7e, annee, no. 1 (Jan.-Mar., 1952), pp. 146-147.

31. TsSK, *Pervaia vseobshchaia perepis' naseleniia Rossiskoi imperii, 1897 g.* (St. Petersburg: 1897-1905), Summary Volume.

32. S. A. Novolsel'skii and V. V. Paevskii, *O. svodnykh kharakteristikakh vosproizvodstva i perspektivnykh ischisleniiakh naseleniia* (Leningrad: 1934), p. 16.

33. TsSU, *Vsesoiuznaia perepis' naseleniia 1926 god* (Moscow: 1930), Vol. XVII.

34. Derived from the data of the 1939 Census, reproduced in Eason, *loc. cit.,* p. 103 and Appendix B.

35. Ibid., p. 103 and Appendix A.

36. Novosel'skii and Paevskii; see footnote 32, above.

37. Speech of G. F. Alexandrov, Propaganda Chief of the Communist Party Central Committee, *Pravda,* January 22, 1946.

38. D. Shepilov, "SSSR—znamenosets novoi epokhi," *Kul'tura i zhizn',* November 20, 1949.

39. For example, T. Shabad, *Geography of the USSR: A Regional Survey* (New York: Columbia University Press, 1951), pp. 499 and ff.

40. For example, N. S. Timasheff, "The Postwar Population of the Soviet Union," *American Journal of Sociology,* Vol. LIV, No. 2 (September, 1948), pp. 148-155.

41. For example, in connection with the method based on electoral districts, there is doubt that the changes in the electoral districts follow closely the population changes, especially in the case of districts where the population is declining; and there is also the possibility of error in multiplying each district by the single official population per district (e.g.. 300,000).

42. In estimating the range, known data on the Soviet population are taken into account, within the framework of a population projection from a 1940 base, using alternative assumptions regarding birth and death rates during the war and postwar period. The results are summarized and the method outlined in Eason, *loc. cit.,* pp. 102-105, 116-120, and Appendix A. The estimated total population (as a range) for January 1 of recent years is as follows (in millions):

1949	188—203	1952	197—212
1950	190—205	1953	200—215
1951	193—208		

43. *Pravda,* August 9, 1953.

44. B. B. Veslovski, *Kurs ekonomiki i planirovaniia gorodskogo khoziaistva* (Moscow: 1951), p. 159.

45. A. M. Gol'denberg, *Osnovnye voprosy organizatsii finansov sotsialisticheskogó zhilishchnogo khoziaistva* (Moscow: 1950), p. 22.

46. Estimated on the basis of war losses of 66.2 million square meters, estimated construction and reconstruction of 157.3 million from 1942 through 1953 and a compounded depreciation rate of 0.8 percent annually. A coefficient of 0.67 has been used for 1953 to reduce *obshchaia ploshchad'* (total or "useable" space) to the traditional concept of dwelling space. This adjustment has been applied to public housing only; statistics for private construction evidently still use dwelling space. Data and commentary on housing were furnished by Miss Carolyn Recht of the University of North Carolina.

47. *Vsesoiuznaia perepis' . . ., op. cit.*, T. XXXIV.

48. *Izvestiia*, June 2, 1939.

49. E. S. Varga, "Osnovnaia ekonomicheskaia zadacha SSSR," *Vestnik Akademiia Nauk SSSR*, 1939, No. 6, p. 8.

50. In certain contexts the definition of "agriculture" (*sel'skoe khoziaistvo*) was narrowed during the thirties, by excluding occupations such as fishing. The context of Varga's reference (footnote 49), however, although presumably taken from unpublished portions of the 1939 census, is not known.

51. The rural population of the annexed area is given as 77.4 percent of the total. The population in agriculture is assumed 68 percent of the total, by analogy with the rural-agriculture differential for the USSR in 1939 before annexation.

52. Increasing school attendance lowered the ratio of labor force to population; rural-urban migration of females, under Soviet conditions, also lowered the ratio; the shift in population age structure increased the ratio, and the increase in the male deficit decreased it. For data on these changes see Eason, *op. cit.*, pp. 106-113 and Appendix A.

53. Source for 1928 figure is in footnote 8; for 1939, *Gornyi zhurnal*, 1940, No. 3, p. 4. Figure for 1953 is average of year-end 1952 (41,700,000) and 1953 (43,400,000), with the latter net of 1,400,000 MTS workers heretofore counted with collective farmers. *Pravda*, January 23, 1953 and January 31, 1954.

54. Eason, *loc. cit.*, pp. 108 and 113.

55. *Ibid.*

56. *Ibid.*, Appendix C for a complete listing of sources.

57. *Vsesoiuznaia perepis' naseleniia . . ., op. cit.*, T. XXXIV.

58. E. Orlikova, "Sovetskaia zhenshchina v obshchestvennom proizvodstve," *Problemy ekonomiki*, 1940, No. 7, p. 119.

59. A. P. Teriaeva, *Trud v kolkhozakh vo vremia Otechestvennoi voiny* (Moscow: 1947), p. 13.

60. TsUNKhU, *Proizvoditel'nost' i ispol'zovanie truda v kolkhozakh vo vtoroi piatiletke* (Moscow and Leningrad: 1939), p. 67.

61. *Kul'turnoe stroitel'stvo . . ., op. cit.*, pp. 37 and 102-107.

62. The number of students in 1928-29 (12,548,000) relative to the population age 7-16 from the 1926 census (33,269,000); the number of students in 1938-39 (32,711,000) relative to the population age 7-16 from the 1939 census (38,713,000) as adjusted by Lorimer, *op. cit.*, pp. 143 and 238-239.

63. *Kul'turnoe stroitel'stvo . . ., op. cit.*, pp. 37 and 105-107.

64. M. S. Rozofarov, *Trudovye reservy SSSR* (Moscow: 1950), p. 3.

65. *Pravda*, January 29, 1952, and *Kul'turnoe stroitel'stvo . . ., op. cit.*, p. 37.

66. *Bol'shaia sovetskaia entsiklopediia* (Moscow: 1948), col. 1227, and *Kulturnoe stroitel'stvo . . ., ibid.*

67. *Pravda*, April 17, 1951.

68. *Pravda*, January 31, 1954, including correspondence students for both years.

69. For example, *Izvestiia*, May 19, 1954.

THE DEVELOPMENT AND STRUCTURE OF

BRAZIL'S POPULATION

By Giorgio Mortara

1. INTRODUCTION

An almost insuperable obstacle to the studies on Brazilian demography is the incomplete registration of births and deaths and the negligence of registration officers, who often omit to notify the central statistical service. However, the data collected in the 1940 and 1950 censuses and the information obtained in some areas where registration is adequate have been successfully used to give an adequate picture of the demographic position. The principles and methods of this work have been already explained in international publications[1] and will therefore not be discussed here; only the main results will be given.

2. DEVELOPMENT OF THE POPULATION[2]

According to the 1950 census, the population of Brazil amounted to about 52 millions; on July 1st, 1954, it was estimated at over 57 millions. The population development of Brazil between 1800 and 1953 is compared in Table 1 with that of the population of England and Wales, France and the United States. In the hundred-year period 1850–1950 the population of Brazil increased in the proportion of 1 to 7·2, which is larger than that of the United States (1 to 6·5).

Among the countries of Latin culture, Brazil occupies the first place in regard to population.

In 1850, Brazil had only 7·2 m. inhabitants, in comparison with 36·5 m. in France, 18·4 m. in Italy, 15·3 m. in Spain, 7·5 m. in Mexico and 1·1 m. in Argentina.

[1] See the following studies by the author of the present paper : " The Calculation of Life Tables for Populations Lacking Reliable Birth and Death Statistics, with Application to Brazil ", *Proceedings of the Eighth American Scientific Congress*, Washington, 1943 ; " Quelques possibilités de reconstruction du mouvement de la population à l'aide des recensements démographiques ", *Revue de l'Institut International de Statistique*, 1941 ; " Sur les méthodes appliquées pour la reconstitution du mouvement de la population du Brésil à l'aide des données des recensements ", *Bulletin de l'Institut International de Statistique*, tome XXXII, 2e livraison ; " Methods of Using Census Statistics for the Calculation of Life Tables and Other Demographic Measures, with Application to the Population of Brazil ", United Nations, *Population Studies*, No. 7, 1949 ; " Les méthodes de mesure de la fécondité des populations ou l'enregistrement des naissances est inexistant ou défectueux ", *Proceedings of the World Population Conference*, Rome, 1954.

On the deficiencies of the Brazilian population statistics, see O. L. de Arruda Gomes, " Quelques considérations sur la précision des recensements et des statistiques du mouvement de la population du Brésil ", *Proceedings of the World Population Conference*, Rome, 1954.

[2] The following publications of the Brazilian Institute of Geography and Statistics (I.B.G.E.) may be consulted for more detailed information : *Pesquisas sôbre o desenvolvimento da população do Brasil*, 1951 ; *Pesquisas sôbre as populações urbanas e rurais do Brasil*, 1954 ; " Previsões sôbre o desenvolvimento da população do Brasil ", *Estudos Demográficos*, No. 95, 1954 ; " Censo Demográfico ", *Recenseamento, Geral do Brasil de 1940, Série Nacional*, vol. 11, 1950 ; " Censo Demográfico, Seleção dos principais dados " *Recenseamento Geral do Brasil de 1950*, 1954.

Table 1. *Population growth, 1800 to 1953.*

Year	Mid-year population (Thousands)			
	Brazil	England and Wales	France	United States
1800	3,620*	8,840*	27,130	5,300
1850	7,234*	17,773	35,630	23,260
1860	8,418*	19,903	36,510	31,503
1870	9,797	22,501	38,440	38,655
1880	11,748	25,714	37,450	50,262
1890	14,199	28,764	38,380	63,056
1900	17,984*	32,249	38,900	76,129
1910	22,216	35,792	39,540	92,267
1920	27,404*	37,600*	39,000	106,543
1930	33,568	39,806	41,610	123,091
1940	41,114	41,862	41,000	131,970
1950	51,976	43,830**	41,944	151,677
1953	55,772	44,090	42,800	159,696

* Unofficial figures.
** Estimate not yet revised to accord with latest census.

In 1950, Brazil had 52·0 m. inhabitants, Italy 46·3 m., France 41·9 m., Spain 27·9 m., Mexico 25·7 m. and Argentina 17·2 m. Only in Argentina has the increase in the hundred-year period been relatively greater than in Brazil (1 to 15·6), because of the larger inflow of immigrants.

It must be remarked that immigration has been only a secondary factor in the increase of 44·8 m. between 1850 and 1950. In this period, the net immigration amounted to 3·4 m. and the natural increase (i.e. the excess of births over deaths) to 41·4 m. Of the natural increase, it has been calculated that about 3·4 m. may be regarded as due to immigration and 38·0 m. as independent of it. This enormous natural increase in a high mortality country was made possible by very high natality. In the second half of the 19th century the average birth rate amounted to 47–48 and the average death rate to 31–32 per 1,000 inhabitants ; in the first half of the present century the birth rate fell to 44–45 and the death rate to 24–25 per 1,000. Even to-day the birth rate stands at the level of 42–44 per 1,000 inhabitants, against a death rate of 18–20 per 1,000 ; consequently the rate of natural increase is nearly 24 per 1,000.

Although the present Brazilian birth rate may appear exceptionally high by Western standards, it is normal in Latin America, where Mexico, Venezuela and several minor countries have rates of the same order of magnitude. Even in Europe this level was not unusual a relatively short time ago ; for instance, the average birth rate in Russia in the second half of the 19th century amounted to 50 (against a death rate of 36) per 1,000 inhabitants.

The fall in birth and death rates, which is the dominant characteristic in the demography of many Western countries, has only begun in Brazil. If the rate of natural increase observed between 1940 and 1950 should continue during the next 50 years, this country would have 168 million inhabitants in 2,000.

3. ETHNIC COMPOSITION OF THE POPULATION AND COMPARATIVE INCREASE
OF THE DIFFERENT COLOUR GROUPS[1]

Many different ethnic groups are represented in the population of Brazil, and
some intermixture has taken place.

In the colonial period the influx of Whites from Portugal and other European
countries was followed by the flood of Negroes brought in by the slave traders
from various African regions.

Later, in the mass emigration period, large numbers of immigrants came into
Brazil, not only from Portugal but also from Italy, Spain, several regions of the
former Empires of Germany, Austria-Hungary and Russia, the Levant, and more
recently from Japan.

The relatively small indigenous population was partly destroyed in the struggle
for the country's occupation by the colonists, and partly assimilated and fused
with them. Some independent tribes survive, but their numerical importance
is negligible.

The fusion between white colonists, negro slaves and brown aborigines was
facilitated by the comparatively free sexual *mores* of the colonial period. The
consequent frequency of mixed unions and multiplication of half-breeds fostered
the further development of this fusion after the abolition of slavery in 1888.

Some national groups of white immigrants (above all, the Germans) have been
reluctant to mate with non-white persons, but many others had no such prejudice,
and marriages with light-coloured half-breeds were not uncommon. The
Japanese immigrants are still relatively isolated, mainly because they have only
settled in Brazil relatively recently and are geographically concentrated. Moreover, many differences—ethnic, religious and cultural—separate them from the
local population.

The intermixture of the various ethnic groups has led to such numerous and
complicated groups that it is impossible to achieve a satisfactory ethnic classification of the Brazilians. In the two last censuses, they were classified by colour; in
the 1950 census, 61·79% were declared white, 26·60% brown, 10·98% black
and 0·63% yellow. To avoid misinterpretation, it must be remembered that
in Brazil there is no barrier of prejudice between Whites and Non-whites, as in
the United States, and that in Rio the qualification of " white " is conferred with
a liberality which would be inconceivable in Washington. Therefore, it may be
presumed that an inquiry conducted according to objective criteria would show
a lower proportion of Whites than the census. But it would be extremely difficult
to draw a line separating the darker Whites from light coloured Browns or between
dark Browns and pale Blacks.

However, the gradual " whitening " of the population of Brazil is undeniable,
since in the 1872 census the proportion of Whites was only 38·11%.

There are only slight differences in fertility between the three main colour
groups, but mortality is higher in the brown than in the white group and even

[1] See the following I.B.G.E. publications : *Estudos sôbre a composição da população do Brasil segundo a
côr*, 1950 ; *Pesquisas sôbre os diversos grupos de côr nas populações do Estado de São Paulo e do Distrito Federal*,
1951 ; " Variações aparentes e variações reais, de 1940 a 1950, na composição segundo a côr da população
do Nordeste ", *Estudos Demográficos*, No. 35, 1953.

higher in the black, because of their lower standard of life.   Therefore, the rate of natural increase is higher for the Whites.   Besides, the mass immigration of the last hundred years has directly and indirectly contributed to the growth of the white group, while the black group did not receive free immigrants, after the abolition of slavery.

4.   SEX AND AGE COMPOSITION.[1]

In Brazil, as everywhere, the number of males born exceeds that of females ; but the higher male death rate tends to reduce the proportion of this sex.   In the Brazil-born population, in 1950, there were 987 males per 1,000 females ; but in the foreign-born population the corresponding proportion was 1,273 per 1,000, because of the predominance of males among immigrants ; thus, in the total population the proportion was raised to 993 males per 1,000 females : a situation of approximate equilibrium.

In urban areas, the proportion of males is lower, mainly because of their more unfavourable death rate and because fewer of them move in from the country ; in rural areas, males outnumber females.   In 1950 there were 898 males per 1,000 females in districts officially classed as urban, the corresponding figure in rural districts was 1,041.

The influence of international migration on sex and age composition is now relatively weak ; foreign-born inhabitants constituted only 2·05% of the population in 1950, as against 6·43% in 1900 at the climax of mass immigration.

The sex and age composition of the population according to the last census is given in Table 2.

Table 2.   *Sex and age composition of the population of Brazil* (1st July, 1950)

Age (Years)	Males		Females	
	Number	Per cent. of total population	Number	Per cent. of total population
0– 4	4,235,876	8·17	4,135,004	7·98
5– 9	3,560,850	6·87	3,454,677	6·67
10–14	3,164,704	6·11	3,143,863	6·07
15–19	2,644,531	5·10	2,857,784	5·51
20–29	4,414,772	8·52	4,708,638	9·08
30–39	3,145,715	6·07	3,140,337	6·06
40–49	2,246,107	4·33	2,119,252	4·09
50–59	1,360,580	2·62	1,289,734	2·49
60–69	728,802	1·41	722,666	1·39
70–79	247,755	0·48	297,415	0·57
80 and over	81,432	0·16	127,271	0·25
*All ages**	*25,831,124*	*49·84*	*25,996,641*	*50·16*

* Excluding 53,877 males and 62,755 females of unknown age and 31,597 inhabitants not classified by sex and age.

[1] See E. Alves, " La composition par sexe et âge de la population du Brésil et de ses différentes sections ", *Proceedings of the World Population Conference*, Rome, 1954 ; G. Mortara, " Les erreurs dans les déclarations de l'âge dans les recensements brésiliens de 1940 et de 1950 ", *Bulletin de l'Institut International de Statistique*, vol. XXXIV ; and the following I.B.G.E. publications : " A composição por idade da população do Brasil, segundo o sexo, em 1° de setembro de 1940 ", "A composição por idade da população

The age composition is typical of a population with low immigration, a high death rate, but a higher birth rate and consequently a high rate of natural increase. There is a very high proportion of children and adolescents and a very low proportion of old people. These characteristics are clearly indicated by the data, in spite of many errors in age declarations.

The most frequent types of error are : the concentration of declarations in ages which are multiples of 5 or 2, understatement of age (particularly by middle-aged women) and overstatement of age (particularly by old people). In Table 2, the female age groups of 15–19 and 20–29 years are evidently inflated and those of 40–49 and 50–59 years are strongly deflated as a result of understatement. The " ageing " errors increase the apparent representation of the group 80 and over. The " concentration " errors are partly eliminated in Table 2 by the grouping of ages.

The characteristics of the Brazilian age composition are better brought out by the international comparisons shown in Table 3.

Table 3.   *Population by broad age groups* (per cent. distribution)*

Country	Date of census	Ages (Years)				Total
		0–19	20–39	40–59	60 and over	
Brazil	1950	52·47	29·75	13·53	4·25	100·00
Colombia	1938	52·27	29·61	13·13	4·99	100·00
Peru	1940	51·58	28·53	13·50	6·39	100·00
Venezuela	1941	51·42	30·22	13·98	4·38	100·00
Mexico	1940	51·36	29·67	13·85	5·12	100·00
Russia (European) ...	1899	48·72	28·43	15·93	6·92	100·00
Egypt	1947	48·13	28·97	16·89	6·01	100·00
India	1951	47·90	29·90	16·80	5·40	100·00
Argentina	1947	40·78	32·61	20·05	6·56	100·00
United States	1950	34·28	30·67	22·93	12·12	100·00
Australia	1951	33·62	31·05	22·92	12·41	100·00
France	1950	29·13	27·63	26·59	16·65	100·00
England and Wales ...	1950	28·41	28·75	26·98	15·86	100·00

* According to data published by the United Nations (*Demographic Yearbook*), by the International Statistical Institute (for Russia, *Annuaire international de statistique*, vol. 1, La Haye, 1916) and by O. S. Ventura (for Argentina, in *Tendencias y estructura de la población argentina*, Buenos Aires, 1953).

The age distributions of the populations of Brazil, Colombia, Peru, Venezuela and Mexico have similar characteristics : a high proportion of children and

das Unidades da Federação, segundo o sexo, em 1° de setembro de 1940 ", *Análises de Resultados do Censo Demográfico*, Nos. 273A e 267A, 1946 ; " A composição por sexo e grupos de idade da população do Brasil segundo o censo de 1950 ", " A composição por sexo e grupos de idade das populações urbanas suburbanas e rurais das diversas regiões fisiogràficas do Brasil, segundo o censo de 1950 ", *Estudos Demográficos,* Nos. 79 and 90, 1953.

See also : " A população adulta do Brasil, segundo o estado conjugal por sexo ", *Análises de Resultados do Censo Demográfico*, No. 285A, and O. de Andrade, " Classification de la population du Brésil suivant l'état matrimonial ", *Proceedings of the World Population Conference,* Rome, 1954.

adolescents and a low proportion of old people. This likeness of structure is due to the fact that these countries are in similar stages of demographic development; they are all characterised, although in different degree, by high death rates, very high birth rates, high rates of natural increase and moderate or small foreign immigration. In these countries, the proportion of the 0–19 age group exceeds 50% and that of the 60 years and over group is near to 5%, while in countries with low birth and death rates, as England and Wales or France, the proportion aged 0–19 does not attain 30% and that of old people exceeds 15%.

India and Egypt to-day and Russia half a century ago are other examples of such age distributions. Argentina diverges from the prevalent Latin American pattern, in consequence of lower death and birth rates and larger migratory increase.

The Brazilian age structure is characterised by the high ratio of dependants to the population of working age. If persons of 15–59 years are regarded as of working age, the ratio is 85·58% in Brazil, in comparison with 64·70% in the United States, 62·24% in France, 61·56% in England and Wales and 59·79% in Argentina.

The economic problems arising from this high proportion of infants and old people are partly solved by a large participation of children and old people in productive activities. The number of children under 15 years occupied in agriculture and dairying in 1950 has been estimated at 3·3 million; that of persons of 60 years and over at 0·6 million. Many others were occupied in various other activities outside the home. It is not therefore surprising to find that 56·27% of children aged 10–14 years are illiterate.

This tendency is intensified in the rural population, where the higher birth rate and emigration to the towns contribute to increase the proportion of children and adolescents and to reduce that of adults and old people, while in the urban population the lower birth rate and the strong immigration act in the opposite direction. In 1950 the proportion aged 0–19 years was 56·15% in the rural and 42·22% in the urban population.

The composition of the adult population by marital status does not present any unusual characteristics. In 1950, 42·42% of the men aged 15 and over and 35·71% of the women of similar ages were single. These proportions are relatively high, but it should be noted that many persons living in permanent "consensual" unions, without legal sanction or religious blessing, are included among the single.

The 1940 inquiry on fertility revealed that of 1;531,000 "single" women aged 25 years and over, 541,000 had had altogether 2,446,000 live born children, or an average of 4·5 per head. This high average gives evidence of the permanent character of most consensual unions.

It must be added that about one-quarter of the persons who were returned as "married" in the 1950 census were not legally such, as they had only gone through a religious ceremony of marriage, and had not been through the civil ceremony required by law.

5. ECONOMIC ACTIVITIES[1]

The distribution of the population aged 10 and over by sex and industry is shown in Table 4. It must be remembered that each individual has been classified in the industrial group in which he is employed, and, therefore, not always in the group that includes his occupation. Thus a lorry driver may be classed under agriculture, if he drives a farm truck, under extractive industries if his lorry belongs to a coal mine, under manufacturing if it belongs to a textile factory; a typist in a department store will be in the commercial group, in the army she will be in the defence group, if she works for a lawyer in professional services, etc. Many children who occasionally take part in productive work, especially in the country, were declared as unoccupied, and many women who take an essential part in farmwork were declared as chiefly occupied in domestic activities.

Table 4.   *Population in ages of 10 years and over by sex and industrial group (1st July, 1950).*

Occupational group	Males		Females	
	Number	Per cent.	Number	Per cent.
Agriculture, forestry	9,154,015	50·61	732,900	3·97
Exploitation of natural resources	455,028	2·52	27,988	0·15
Manufacturing industry	1,842,141	10·18	389,057	2·11
Commerce, banking	972,116	5·37	101,805	0·55
Transport and communication ...	668,220	3·69	28,822	0·16
Social services	200,689	1·11	233,626	1·26
Personal services	746,806	4·13	925,973	5·01
Professional services, religion ...	64,631	0·36	14,227	0·08
Public service	220,636	1·22	40,131	0·22
Defence ... ... ∴..	247,528	1·37	4,349	0·02
Domestic and scholastic activities	1,582,206	8·75	14,881,825	80·57
Unoccupied	1,934,259	10·69	1,089,012	5·90
TOTAL[*]	*18,088,275*	*100·00*	*18,469,715*	*100·00*

[*] Excluding some areas, with a total population of 31,597 inhabitants who were not classified by sex, age and activity.

More than half the male population aged 10 and over is occupied in agriculture, dairying and forestry (50·61%). Mining, quarrying, and the exploration of other natural resources, such as fishing, give occupation only to a small fraction of the population (2·52%). Manufacturing claims one-tenth (10·18%); commerce and banking just over one-twentieth (5·37%); transport and communication (3·69%) and personal services[2] (4·13%), lower proportions still.

[1] See G. Mortara, " A distribuição da população do Brasil segundo ramos de atividade ", *Revista Brasileira de Economia,* 1947 ; and the following I.B.G.E. publications : " A população do Brasil, de 10 anos e mais, segundo ramos de atividade principal, por sexo e grupos de idade ", " Análise da distribuição da população de 10 anos e mais, segundo ramos e classes de atividade principal, por sexo ", " Distribuição da população de 10 anos e mais, segundo ramos de atividade principal, por sexo, no Brasil, nas regiões fisiográficas e nas Unidades da Federação ", *Análises de Resultados do Censo Demográfico,* Nos. 366, 390 and 390 bis, 345, 1946/1948 ; " A população economicamente ativa do Brasil, segundo o censo demográfico de 1950 ", " A distribuição da população do Brasil por grandes categorias de atividade, segundo o sexo e a idade ", " A distribuição da população do Brasil por ramos de atividade, segundo o sexo e a idade ", *Estudos Demográficos,* Nos. 97, 98, 99, 1954.

[2] The personal service branch includes paid domestic servants (0·45% in 1940 ; the corresponding proportion in 1950 is still unknown).

Agriculture is predominant throughout Brazil, but there are wide regional variations. In the most advanced State, São Paulo, the proportion of males occupied in agriculture drops to 37·93%, while that in manufacturing rises to 18·54%; the proportions occupied in commerce and banking (7·70%), in transport and communication (5·56%) and in personal services (6·21%) are also above the national average. On the other hand, in the backward State of Ceará, 66·30% of the men aged 10 years and over are occupied in agriculture and only 3·57% in manufacturing.

The proportion engaged in other forms of activities (social services, professional services and religion, public service, defence) is relatively low (4·06%). The proportion who are at school or engaged in domestic activity is 8·75%; if many children were not employed in part-time work, this would be higher. The proportion of unoccupied (mostly children) exceeds one-tenth (10·69%).

In the female population aged 10 years and over, domestic occupations are preponderant (80·57%, including those at school). However, as has been mentioned, the population census understates the number of females engaged in agriculture. In 1940, the agricultural census gave 3,659,000 women engaged in agriculture, as against 1,642,000 classed in the population census as having their principal or supplementary occupation in agriculture, dairying and forestry, and even the figures of the agricultural census must be regarded as minima. The results of the agricultural census of 1950 have not been published, but it may be presumed that the difference between it and the population census will be even greater than in 1940.

After agriculture, to which probably 13–15% of the women aged 10 and over contribute with more or less regular work,[1] the most important group in which women are active is personal service[2] (5·01%). The proportion occupied in manufacture is low (2·11%), but it does not include some home industries (textiles, etc.); commerce and banking and transport and communications employ even fewer. Social services, professional services and religion, public service and defence, together, account for 1·58% of the female population aged 10 and over; the proportion engaged in social service (1·26%) is higher than among men. The proportion of unoccupied (5·90%) is lower among women than among men, because many girls and old women, not otherwise occupied, have some home duties and give this as their occupation.

6. NATALITY[3]

Through direct and indirect information, gathered by the 1940 and 1950 censuses, it was possible to estimate the general birth rate, to calculate fertility

[1] Obviously, if the proportion in agricultural occupations is raised from 4% to 13–15%, the proportion in the domestic and scholastic group must be reduced by the same amount, to 65·5–67·5%.

[2] The personal service branch includes paid domestic servants (3·57% in 1940; the corresponding proportion in 1950 is still unknown).

[3] See G. Mortara, " Conjeturas sôbre os níveis da natalidade e da mortalidade no Brasil " and " A fecundidade da mulher brasileira e a capacidade de reprodução da população do Brasil ", *Revista Brasileira de Estatística,* 1940 and 1941 ; A. V. De Carvalho, " Quelques aspects de la natalité au Brésil ", *Proceedings of the World Population Conference,* Rome, 1954. G. Mortara, *Natality in Brazil and its Economic and Social Factors,* Paris, UNESCO, 1954 ; and the following I.B.G.E. publications : *Estimativas da taxa de*

rates by age of woman, in relation to colour, marital status, duration of reproductive life, order of birth, etc., and to construct fertility tables.

The present birth rate is about 42–44 per 1,000 inhabitants ; the corresponding fertility rate amounts to 170–178 per 1,000 women aged 15–49. In comparison with the fertility rates of the United States (92 in 1950), of France (83 in 1950) and of England and Wales (61 in 1951), the Brazilian rate is very high ; but it may be considered as normal in Latin America : Mexico (182 in 1950) and other countries have rates of the same order ; only in Argentina is the fertility rate low (95 in 1946–48).

The fertility rate is high in all colour groups : a calculation for the 1940–1950 period, based upon the last census, gave rates of 177 live born per 1,000 women aged 15–49 in the total population, 171 in the white group, 196 in the brown, 167 in the black and 200 in the yellow group. The lesser fertility of the white women is probably due, at least in part, to birth control ; that of the black women to their lower chances of being married and to more frequent widowhood at young ages. The higher fertility of the yellow women is due to the more favourable age composition of this group, as a result of recent immigration.

The comparative fertility rates by age, of the three main colour groups, calculated according to the 1940 census, are given in Table 5, and are compared with contemporary rates in England and Wales and in the United States[1] and with rates observed half a century ago in Russia and Hungary.

It may be remarked that the high fertility rates in the 15–19 years age group reflect the frequency of early marriages (or consensual unions). However, they are not exceptionally high, as may be seen from the comparison with post-war rates for these ages in the United States.[2] The relative excess of the Brazilian over the English and American rates grows with age, chiefly in consequence of the limited practice of birth control in Brazil, where recourse to contraceptive practices or voluntary abortion is increasing only in some urban areas.

---

natalidade para o Brasil, as Unidades da Federação e as principais Capitais, 1948 ; *Estudos sôbre a fecundidade e a prolificidade da mulher no Brasil, no conjunto da população e nos diversos grupos de côr*, 1949 ; *A prolificidade da mulher segundo a idade inicial da atividade, no Brasil*, 1949 ; *Estudos sôbre a fecundidade da mulher no Brasil, segundo o estado conjugal*, 1949 ; *Pesquisas sôbre a natalidade no Brasil*, 1ª serie, 1950, 2ª serie, 1953 ; *Estudos sôbre a natalidade e a mortalidade no Brasil*, 1952 ; *Estudos sôbre a natalidade em algumas grandes cidades do Brasil*, 1952 ; " A fecundidade feminina no Estado de São Paulo, segundo os censos de 1940 e de 1950 ", *Estudos Demográficos*, Nos. 92 and 94, 1954.

[1] After the second World War, American and English birth rates rose, while the Brazilian rate remained about at the 1940 level. The birth rates by age groups in 1950 are given below :

Age	Births per 1,000 women	
	England and Wales	United States
15–19	22	79
20–24	126	194
25–29	136	163
30–34	89	101
35–39	48	51
40–44	14	15
45–49	1	1

[2] In 1949 the birth rate in this age group, in the United States, was 82 per 1,000.

Table 5. *Birth rates specific for age of mother (Number of live births per 1,000 women in specified age groups)*

Age of mother (Years)	Brazil, 1940				England and Wales* 1939	United States* 1940	Russia** 1896–97	Hungary** 1900–01
	All women	White women	Brown women	Negro women				
15–19	81	80	88	78	16	49	30	57
20–24	256	254	272	244	94	125	309	259
25–29	308	306	324	302	114	114	334	280
30–34	271	278	270	254	82	77	331	231
35–39	207	212	202	192	47	42	219	161
40–44	127	144	110	84	15	14	130	69
45–49	41	46	34	26	2	1	60	14

* Data from the *Demographic Yearbook* of the United Nations.
** Rates calculated by R. R. Kuczynski (*The Balance of Births and Deaths*, vol. ii, Washington, Brookings Institution, 1931, pp. 154, 163).

For the 1940–1950 period the fertility rate has been calculated as 121 live born children per 1,000 women aged 15–49 years in the urban population, against 202 per 1,000 in the rural population. Most of the difference between the rural and the urban rate is due to the higher proportion of single women and higher average age at marriage, or at the birth of the first child, in the urban population ; birth control is only a secondary factor. However, in the cities of Rio de Janeiro and São Paulo, where this factor is more important, the fertility rate in the same period was much lower (86 and 87 per 1,000) than in the urban population as a whole.

From the data of Table 5 it may be calculated that 100 women surviving to the end of the reproductive period in Brazil would have given birth to 645 children, in comparison with 185 in England and Wales (1939), 211 in the United States (1940)[1], 706 in Russia (1896–1897) and 535 in Hungary (1900–1901). The combination of the fertility table with the life table led to the calculation of Boeckh's coefficient (improperly called " net reproduction rate ") for Brazil. The value of 1.85–1.95 found in 1940 is near to that determined by Kuczynski for Russia in 1896–1897 and about double of the corresponding contemporary values for England and Wales (0·81 in 1939) and the United States (1·02 in 1940).

7. MORTALITY[2]

As has already been mentioned, the present death rate in Brazil is about 18–20 per 1,000 inhabitants. It is high, even by Latin American standards, as rates of

[1] According to the 1950 birth rates, 218 in England and Wales and 302 in the United States.

[2] See G. Mortara, " Retificação da distribuição por idade da população natural do Brasil e cálculo dos óbitos, etc., 1870–1920 ", and " Tábuas de mortalidade e de sobrevivência, 1870–1890 e 1890–1920 ", *Revista Brasileira de Estatística*, 1942 ; " Tábuas brasileiras de mortalidade e sobrevivência ", *Estudos Brasileiros de Demografia*, Rio, Fundação Getúlio Vargas, 1946 ; M. V. Da Rocha, " La mortalité au Brésil ", *Proceedings of the World Population Conference*, Rome, 1954 ; G. Mortara, " A mortalidade da população natural do Brasil ", *Revista Brasileira de Estatística*, 1953 ; and the following I.B.G.E. publications : " Tábuas de mortalidade e sobrevivência brasileiras, Distrito Federal e Município de São Paulo ", *Revista Brasileira de Estatística*, 1945 ; Estudos sôbre a mortalidade nos Municípios de Recife, Salvador, Pôrto Alegre, Belo Horizonte e Belém ", *Revista Brasileira de Estatística*, 1947 ; *Estudos sôbre a natalidade e a mortalidade no Brasil*, 1952 ; *Pesquisas sôbre a mortalidade no Brasil*, 1954 ; " A mortalidade das populações naturais dos Estados de Bahia, Rio Grande do Sul, Rio de Janeiro, Minas Gerais, São Paulo, Pernambuco ", *Estudos Demográficos*, Nos. 64 and 64 bis, 72, 77, 78, 92, 101, 1953 and 1954 ; " Tábuas de sobrevivência para o Município de São Paulo, 1949–1951 ", *Estudos Demográficos*, no. 100, 1954.

the same order are observed only in some minor countries, whereas in Mexico the death rate fluctuated between 15 and 17, and in Argentina stood at about 9 between 1949 and 1952. (It must be remembered, however, that in both countries death registration is probably incomplete.)

Life tables have been calculated for Brazil as a whole, by comparing consecutive censuses, for the periods 1870–1890, 1890–1920 and 1940–1950.[1] Life tables for some States were also calculated, by the same method, for the last period.[2]

The normal method of computing life tables by relating the registered deaths to the numbers at risk, as given by the census could only be applied in some areas where death registration was almost complete. (State of São Paulo, Federal District and some of the larger cities.)

Table 6. *Death rates and expectation of life at birth by sex* (1940–50)

States	Death rate per 1,000 inhabitants			Expectation of life at birth		
	Males	Females	Both sexes	Males	Females	Both sexes
Rio Grande do Sul ...	13·58	11·71	12·64	51·2	59·4	55·2
São Paulo	16·22	14·03	15·13	46·1	53·3	49·8
Pernambuco	23·08	18·84	20·92	39·0	47·8	43·3
Bahia	24·07	20·29	22·15	37·9	44·9	41·4
Minas Gerais	23·86	21·22	22·54	37·6	42·3	39·9
Rio de Janeiro	25·26	22·05	23·63	36·9	42·3	39·5
Brazil	*22·12*	*19·11*	*20·60*	*39·3*	*45·5*	*42·3*

The 1940–1950 Brazilian death rate of 21 is very high in comparison with those of the more advanced countries, where it is of the order of 10 or less. However, it should be remembered that such exceptionally low death rates depend partly upon a very favourable age distribution, which is a transitory consequence of recent demographic evolution.

The expectation of life at birth, which is not subject to this influence, is more convenient for international comparisons. Its value for Brazil, 42–43 years in 1940–1950 and about 45 years to-day, is higher than those of backward countries (e.g. 32 years in India, 1941–1950), but much lower than those of advanced countries (e.g. 70–71 years in Netherlands, 1947–1949, 68–69 in England and Wales, 1949–1950, 68 in the United States, 1948–1950, 65 in France, 1946–1949).

The female death rate in Brazil is lower than the male. This difference, which is almost universal in the countries of Western civilization, is due to social rather than to biological factors.

It may be seen from Table 6 that there are large differences between the death rates of the two more advanced southern States and those of the four other States for which calculations are available. Among the remaining 14 States, there may

[1] For the two former periods, complete life tables for both sexes combined ; for the latter, a summary life table for males and an approximate calculation of the expectation of life for females and for both sexes together. These life tables have been calculated for the Brazilian-born population.

[2] These life tables have been calculated for the population *born* in each State, and not for the *present-in-area* population.

be some with higher mortality than the State of Rio de Janeiro,[1] but it is very improbable that there are any with lower mortality than Rio Grande do Sul.

The characteristics of mortality in Brazil are better seen by the comparison, made in Table 7, between the life tables of the State of São Paulo for 1939–1941 (which may be assumed to represent sufficiently accurately the *present* levels of mortality in Brazil as a whole) and those of England and Wales for 1930–1932.

Table 7. *Life table comparison : State of São Paulo* (1939–1941) *and England and Wales* (1930–32).

Age (Years)	Males		Females	
	São Paulo	England and Wales	São Paulo	England and Wales
	1. Mortality rates per 1,000			
0	168·7	71·9	150·1	54·6
1	69·7	15·3	68·6	13·5
5	4·9	3·4	4·4	3·0
10	2·4	1·5	2·1	1·3
15	2·8	2·0	2·3	1·9
20	5·4	3·2	6·1	2·7
30	7·0	3·4	7·6	3·2
40	10·7	5·6	10·1	4·4
50	18·2	11·3	14·1	8·2
60	35·6	24·2	27·1	17·7
70	75·0	60·4	61·7	44·5
80	159·9	145·0	132·7	118·6
	2. Survivors out of 100,000 born alive			
0	100,000	100,000	100,000	100,000
1	83,133	92,814	84,991	94,545
5	73,927	90,069	75,838	92,024
10	72,628	89,023	74,662	91,082
15	71,760	88,360	73,915	90,420
20	70,453	87,245	72,534	89,383
30	66,322	84,416	67,773	86,792
40	60,961	80,935	62,068	83,690
50	53,199	74,794	55,366	78,958
60	41,368	63,620	45,893	70,204
70	24,635	43,361	30,520	53,144
80	7,745	16,199	11,713	24,869
	3. Expectation of life (Years)			
0	43·79	58·74	46·28	62·88
1	51·57	62·25	53·36	65·48
5	53·86	60·11	55·67	63·24
10	49·78	55·79	51·52	58·87
15	45·35	51·19	47·01	54·28
20	41·14	46·81	42·85	49·88
30	33·38	38·21	35·50	41·22
40	25·85	29·62	28·29	32·55
50	18·85	21·60	21·08	24·18
60	12·71	14·43	14·33	16·50
70	7·82	8·62	8·85	10·02
80	4·55	4·74	5·21	5·46

The expectation of life at birth in the State of São Paulo, is only 43·79 years for males and 46·28 for females, against 58·74 and 62·88 years in England and Wales in 1930–1932 (increased to 66·50 and 71·20 in 1950).

[1] The State of Rio de Janeiro does not include the city of Rio de Janeiro and its suburbs which constitute a separate political unit, the Federal District.

The relative excess of the São Paulo over the English death rates attains its maximum at the earliest ages, but it is still high in adolescence, youth and middle age ; only at old ages does it become lower.

Out of 100,000 live born of each sex, only 71,760 males and 73,915 females survive to age 15 in the State of São Paulo, against 88,360 and 90,420 in England in 1930–1932 (increased to 95,460 and 96,450 in 1950). More than one-quarter of each generation does not live to the beginning of working life.

At 60, only 41,368 males and 45,893 females survive in the State of São Paulo, against 63,620 and 70,204 in England in 1930–1932 (increased to 75,850 and 83,070 in 1950). The proportion of those who survive to the end of working life in Brazil is less than 50%.

The average duration of working life per live born child[1] is therefore much lower in São Paulo (27·29 years for males and 28·17 for females) than in England (37·50 and 41·47 in 1930–1932, increased to 40·67 and 41·68 in 1950). In both populations and in both sexes it equals about 60% of the expectation of life at birth.[2]

For the two metropolitan populations of Rio de Janeiro and the City of São Paulo, life tables have been calculated by relating the numbers of deaths registered from 1949–1951 to the numbers living in 1950. The expectation of life is 54·98 years for males and 60·21 for females in São Paulo City and 49·80 and 55·96 in Rio de Janeiro City, showing a significant improvement over the 1939–1941 period (São Paulo : Males 46·49, Females : 51·63; Rio, Males : 39·75, Females : 45·24).

The high Brazilian death rate is caused chiefly by the high frequency and lethality of infectious or parasitic diseases and diseases of the respiratory and digestive systems. Recent advances in medical science and the progress of public health organization therefore led to substantial reductions. These factors were especially strong in the cities, but their influence is now being extended to the rural areas.

8. TERRITORIAL DISTRIBUTION OF THE POPULATION.[3]

The area of Brazil, nearly 8·5 million sq. km., is divided between 26 " Federation Units ", including 20 States, 5 Federal Territories administered by the central government, and the Federal District, the capital of the Republic, Rio de Janerio. These units may be grouped in 5 regions : North, North-East, East, South and Centre-West.

The distribution of Brazil's area and population by Federation Units and geographical regions is shown in Table 8.

The average density of about 6 inhabitants per sq. km. in 1950 is very low, in comparison not only with those of older countries but also with those of the

---

[1] Ratio of the number of years lived between the ages 15 and 60 and the number of survivors at age 0.

[2] This is a general regularity, as I had occasion to show in my communication to the 27th Session of the International Statistical Institute, " La durée de la vie économiquement active suivant la mortalité ", *Bulletin of the I.S.I.,* vol. xxxiii, part iv.

[3] Area, population and density by municipalities are given in *Anuário Estatístico do Brasil, 1953,* Rio, I.B.G.E., 1953.

United States (19) and Mexico (13). However, the average population density in the whole of South America and in Argentina is of the same order.

The population is very irregularly distributed over the territory, and average densities by themselves are not very useful. A very low density in the North and Centre-West regions contrasts with a relatively high density in the North-East, East and South regions.

Table 8. *Distribution of the* de facto *population by Federation Units and geographical regions* (1st July, 1950).

Federation Unit* — Geographical Region	Population	Area** (sq. km.)	Density of population (per sq. km.)
Guaporé (T)	36,935	254,163	0·15
Acre (T)	114,755	153,170	0·75
Amazonas (S)	514,099	1,595,818	0·32
Rio Branco (T)	18,116	214,316	0·08
Pará (S)	1,123,273	1,188,769	0·94
Amapá (T)	37,477	133,796	0·28
NORTH	*1,844,655*	*3,540,032*	*0·52*
Maranhão (S)	1,583,248	332,239	4·77
Piauí (S)	1,045,696	249,317	4·19
Ceará (S)	2,695,450	153,245	17·59
Rio Grande do Norte (S) ...	967,921	53,048	18·25
Paraíba (S)	1,713,259	56,282	30·44
Pernambuco (S)	3,395,185	97,016	35·00
Alagoas (S)	1,093,137	28,531	38·31
Fernando de Noronha (T) ...	581	26	22·35
NORTH-EAST	*12,494,477*	*969,704*	*12·88*
Sergipe (S)	644,361	21,057	30·60
Bahia (S)	4,834,575	563,281	8·58
Minas Gerais (S)	7,728,104	581,975	13·28
(Serra dos Aimorés)*** ...	160,072	10,137	15·79
Espírito Santo (S)	861,562	40,882	21·07
Rio de Janeiro (S) ...	2,297,194	41,666	55·13
Distrito Federal (FD)	2,377,451	1,171	2,030·27
EAST	*18,903,319*	*1,260,169*	*15·00*
São Paulo (S)	9,141,928	247,223	36·98
Paraná (S)	2,129,327	200,731	10·61
Santa Catarina (S)	1,560,502	93,849	16·63
Rio Grande do Sul (S) ...	4,164,821	267,455	15·57
SOUTH	*16,996,578*	*809,258*	*21·00*
Mato Grosso (S)	522,044	1,262,572	0·41
Goiás (S)	1,214,921	622,463	1·95
CENTRE-WEST	*1,736,965*	*1,885,035*	*0·92*
BRAZIL	*51,975,994*	*8,464,198*	*6·14*

* S =State, T =Federal Territory, FD =Federal District.
** Excluding inland waters.
*** Territory claimed by the States of Minas Gerais and Espírito Santo.

The two former regions together occupy an area of 5,425,000 sq. km., an area larger than that of Europe, excluding the Soviet Union, according to 1938 frontiers. But they have only 3,582,000 inhabitants, against over 400 million in Europe. Thus, they comprise 64·09% of the area, but only 6·89% of the population of Brazil.

The average density is only 0·66 inhabitants per sq. km. ; among the 8 Federation Units of these regions, the maximum density, still very low (1·95), is found in the State of Goiás and the minimum (0·08) in the semi-desert Rio Branco Territory.

The other three regions—North-East, East and South—occupy a total area of 3,039,000 sq. km. and have 48,394,000 inhabitants, i.e. 93·11% of the population live on 35·91% of the area.   The average density is 15·92 inhabitants per sq. km., with large variations in the 18 units   There are zones of low density, as the States of Piauí (with 4·19 inhabitants per sq. km.) and Maranhão (with 4·77), and wide areas in the States of Bahia, Minas Gerais and Paraná ; but there are also zones of relatively high density, as the State of Rio de Janeiro, with 55·13 inhabitants per sq. km., and the States of Alagoas (38·31), São Paulo (36·98) and Pernambuco (35·00).   The exceptionally high density in the Federal District (2,030) is due to the concentration of a very numerous and largely urban population in a small area

The present territorial distribution of the population is very different from that of a century ago

In 1872, at the date of the first Brazilian census, the percentages of the population living in different regions was : North, 3·29% ; North-East 30·60% ; East, 48·40% ; South, 15·53% ; and Centre-West, 2·18%

The corresponding figures in 1950 were : North, 3·55% ; North-East, 24·04% ; East, 36·37% ; South 32·70% ; and Centre-West, 3·34%.

Foreign immigration, internal migration and lower death rates contributed to the larger relative increase of the Southern populations.   Internal migration deprived the North-Eastern populations of a considerable part of their natural increase, while they received only small numbers of foreign immigrants.   The strong internal out-migration from the Eastern States towards other regions largely exceeded foreign immigration and the strong internal in-migration to the Federal District.   Internal migration was the only factor in the more rapid increase of the Northern and Centre-Western populations.

The quotas of the different States in the total populations of Brazil have varied greatly between 1872 and 1950 ; those of the principal Eastern and North-Eastern States declined (Minas Gerais from 20·79% to 14·87%, Bahia 13·64% to 9·30%, Pernambuco 8·32% to 6·53%) ; those of the principal Southern States increased (São Paulo from 8·28% to 17·59%, Rio Grande do Sul 4·42% to 8·01%).

9.   RURAL AND URBAN POPULATION.[1]

Brazil's population is mostly non-urban.   More than two-thirds live in small rural centres or in scattered habitations ; less than one-sixth in cities of more than 100,000 inhabitants ; the proportions living in medium and small cities are also low, as it may be seen from Table 9.

The principal cities are Rio de Janeiro, with 2,377,000 inhabitants in 1950, and São Paulo, with 2,198,000.   These are the populations of the corresponding administrative divisions (i.e., respectively, Federal District and Municipality of

[1] See G. Mortara, " Observações sôbre a discriminação da população urbana no censo de 1940 " Revista Brasileira dos Municípios, 1950, and the I.B.G.E. publication Pesquisas sôbre as populações urbana e rurais do Brasil, 1954.

Table 9. *Distribution of the* de facto *population by classes of urban agglomerations and in rural areas* (1st July, 1950).

Place of Domicile	Number of urban agglomerations	Population	Per cent. of total population
URBAN AGGLOMERATIONS*			
Of more than 500,000 inhabitants ...	3	4,832,458	9·30
Of 100,001 to 500,000 inhabitants ...	8	2,040,777	3·93
Of 50,001 to 100,000 inhabitants ...	22	1,613,409	3·11
Of 10,001 to 50,000 inhabitants ...	187	3,656,858	7·04
Of 5,001 to 10,000 inhabitants ...	258	1,782,267	3·43
Of 2,001 to 5,000 inhabitants ...	692	2,085,588	4·01
RURAL AREAS			
Rural agglomerations and scattered habitations	—	35,933,040	69·18
TOTAL**	*1,170*	*51,944,397*	*100·00*

* Classified according the number of inhabitants in the administrative urban and suburban area (and not in the total area of the municipality or district).
** Excluding 31,597 inhabitants not classified by place of domicile.

São Paulo), but the economic and demographic areas of both these cities contain several satellite towns with hundreds of thousand inhabitants. To-day the population of both metropolitan areas is about 3 millions.

Other important cities are Recife, capital of Pernambuco ; Salvador, capital of Bahia ; Pôrto Alegre, capital of Rio Grande do Sul ; Belo Horizonte, capital of Minas Gerais ; Fortaleza, capital of Ceará ; and Belém, capital of Pará.

10. INTERNAL MIGRATION.[1]

In the absence of statistics of internal migration, the direction and volume of the principal currents may be gauged from census data.

In the last censuses, the Brazilian-born inhabitants were asked to give the Federation Unit of their birth. By combining this information with information on residence at census date, it became possible to construct bi-variate tables of the population by place of birth and place of residence.

Some of these results for 1940 and 1950 are summarised and compared in Table 10. Columns (a) give the number of the Brazilian-born inhabitants present in the specified Federation Unit and born in other Units ; Columns (b) give the number of the Brazilian-born inhabitants born in the specified Unit but present in other Units. The difference between these two, given in Columns (c), represents the balance of the internal migration movements, at census date.[2]

[1] See E. Thimóteo De Barros, " Les migrations intérieures au Brésil ", *Proceedings of the World Population Conference*, Rome, 1954 ; and the following I.B.G.E. publications : *O aproveitamento das apurações do censo demográfico de* 1940 *para a determinação das correntes de migração interior*, 1948 ; *Pesquisas sôbre as populações urbanas e rurais do Brasil*, 1954 ; " Elementos de informação deduzidos do censo demográfico sôbre as migrações interiores ", *Estudos Demográficos*, no. 63, 1953.

[2] The data for the new Federal Territories of Guaporé, Rio Branco and Amapá do not have this significance, because only children born after they were constituted (1943) were regarded as born in these Units, while the other inhabitants born in the same areas were regarded as born in the States (Amazonas, Mato Grosso, Pará) to which these areas belonged at the time of their birth.

The data for the Serra dos Aimorés, a zone contested by the States of Minas Gerais and Espírito Santo, are also fallacious, because many inhabitants of this zone were declared as born in one or in the other of those States.

Table 10.   *Balance of the population exchanges between the Federation's Units (1st September, 1940, and 1st July, 1950).*

Federation Unit*	Brazilian-born inhabitants				Active (−) or passive (−) balance $(c)=(a)-(b)$	
	Born in other Units and present in the specified Unit (a)		Born in the specified Unit and present in other Units (b)			
	1940	1950	1940	1950	1940	1950
Guaporé	—	29,061	—	299	—	+28,762
Acre	22,783	29,309	9,852	13,313	+12,931	+15,996
Amazonas	52,781	49,605	24,289	53,378	+28,492	−3,773
Rio Branco ...	—.	13,844	—	116	—	+13,728
Pará	76,402	71,770	41,017	81,432	+35,385	−9,662
Amapá	—	30,063	—	117	—	+29,946
Maranhão	131,019	161,117	77,194	100,189	+53,825	+60,928
Piauí	66,646	86,330	114,416	144,946	−47,770	−58,616
Ceará	89,618	107,538	205,661	268,486	−116,043	−160,948
Rio Grande do Norte	63,512	77,288	73,521	103,669	−10,009	−26,381
Paraíba	104,183	100,159	158,755	246,780	−54,572	−146,621
Pernambuco ...	131,410	207,310	244,665	311,138	−113,255	−103,828
Alagoas	60,147	66,675	134,920	207,250	−74,773	−140,575
Fernando de Noronha	—	548	—	55	—	+493
Sergipe	33,737	36,170	75,848	107,479	−42,111	−71,309
Bahia	105,888	140,894	339,851	430,217	−233,963	−289,323
Minas Gerais ...	195,792	210,868	829,521	1,367,239	−633,729	−1,156,371
(Serra dos Aimorés)	61,355	118,396	404	—	+60,951	+118,396
Espírito Santo ...	106,070	92,787	67,459	147,854	+38,611	−55,067
Rio de Janeiro ...	202,989	365,756	432,428	504,130	−229,439	−138,374
Distrito Federal ...	633,686	929,846	82,386	142,053	+551,300	+787,793
São Paulo	726,492	1,064,009	231,330	507,248	+495,162	+556,761
Paraná	214,256	661,456	62,658	71,310	+151,598	+590,146
Santa Catarina ...	107,851	151,651	61,451	118,748	+46,400	+32,903
Rio Grande do Sul	38,358	44,435	131,132	205,576	−92,774	−161,141
Mato Grosso ...	70,509	78,070	16,192	36,034	+54,317	+42,036
Goiás	155,480	281,364	36,014	37,263	+119,466	+244,101
Brazil	*3,450,964*	*5,206,319*	*3,450,964*	*5,206,319*	—	—

* See footnotes to table 8.

The main flow of internal migration is directed towards the State of São Paulo, the Federal District and the State of Paraná. The States of Rio de Janeiro, Goiás and some others also received large numbers of migrants from other units. Comparison between the two censuses shows the intensity of the migratory movements in the 1940–1950 period; the relative increase of in-migration was exceptionally high in Paraná.

By far the largest number of migrants come from the State of Minas Gerais; the States of São Paulo, Rio de Janeiro, Bahia, Pernambuco, Ceará and others also supply strong contingents of emigrants.

The largest active balance of migration is found in the Federal District and the States of Paraná and São Paulo; another State with a considerable active balance is Goiás.

The largest passive balance is that of Minas Gerais; Bahia has also a considerable, although much smaller, passive balance.

The main direction of migration is from the North-East and East to the South and Centre-West regions.; a secondary direction is from the North-East to the North region. Large currents flow towards the cities.

The principal factors in internal migration are : the attraction of the cities where industrialization is developing (São Paulo, Rio de Janeiro, etc.), the escape from regions subject to recurrent natural catastrophes (droughts in the North-East, floods in the North, etc.) towards less inhospitable zones, and the abandonment of areas whose resources have been exhausted by careless exploitation (Minas Gerais, Bahia, etc.) for areas not yet exploited (Paraná, São Paulo, Goiás, etc.).

In the ten-year period preceding the 1950 census the population of urban and suburban areas[1] increased by 5,945,000, of which 3,150,000 was due to natural increase, 52,000 to foreign immigration and 2,743,000 to internal migration. The last number also represents the loss of the rural population, which, in spite of a natural increase of 7,600,000, showed a net increase of only 4,917,000 (of which 60,000 was contributed by foreign immigration).

The tendency towards a growing concentration of the population in the urban and suburban areas is evident.

11. *International Migrations.*[2]

The statistics of foreign immigration into Brazil registered about 4,800,000 immigrants in the hundred-year period 1851–1950. It has been estimated that almost three quarters (3,400,000), settled in this country, while the others went back to their countries of origin or emigrated elsewhere.

Most immigrants came from Latin countries ; among the recorded 4,800,000, about 1,540,000 were Italians, 1,480,000 Portuguese, 600,000 Spaniards. Of the smaller contingents, 230,000 Germans and 190,000 Japanese may be mentioned.

The distribution of this immigration by ten-year periods is shown in Table 11.

Table 11. *Foreign immigration into Brazil, 1851 to 1950.*

Years	Immigrants (Thousands)	Years	Immigrants (Thousands)
1851–1860	120	1901–1910	670
1861–1870	95	1911–1920	795
1871–1880	215	1921–1930	835
1881–1890	530	1931–1940	285
1891–1900	1,125	1941–1950	130

In the second half of the 19th century, immigration increased progressively, attaining its maximum in the nineties, when there was a severe economic depression in Europe. Improved economic conditions in that continent led to a

[1] " Urban " and " suburban " areas, according to administrative division, which does not correspond to the criterion applied in Table 9 for the definition of urban population. Explanation of this subject is given in the first paper cited in footnote 1, page 135.

[2] Data on immigration into Brazil are given by I. Ferenczi, *International Migrations*, New York, National Bureau of Economic Research, 1929, for the years 1820–1924, and in *Anuário Estatístico do Brasil, 1953*, Rio, 1953, for the years 1884–1951.

reduction in immigration in the first decade of the present century, and the first world war further interrupted the flow of migration.   Restrictions imposed by the Brazilian government checked the inflow of immigrants after the war, and the grave repercussions of the 1930–1934 crisis on Brazil's economy contributed to restrain it.   The second world war reduced the large current of migration to small dimensions.

In the post-war period immigration shows a marked increase ; in the three years from 1951 to 1953 the number of immigrants amounted to 227,000, of whom, 100,000 came from Portugal, 41,000 from Spain and 40,000 from Italy.

12.   Final Remarks.

The facts in the preceding pages show that Brazil's population is still in an early phase of the typical evolution of Western populations in the last century.

The birth rate is exceptionally high ; its decline has up to now been very slow. The death rate is high, but its downward trend is more marked than that of the birth rate.

Improvidence is the main factor in high natality ; poverty and ignorance are the principal factors of high mortality.   The standard of life is very low for the majority of the population, owing to obsolete techniques, imperfect organisation, low labour productivity and to scarcity of capital, lack of enterprise, deficiency of communications and ineptitude of governmental action.

In consequence the population is characterised by an approximate numerical equilibrium of the sexes, a very high proportion in the infant and adolescent age groups and a very low percentage of old people.   The ratio of dependent to working population is, therefore, high.

Less than one-third of the population live in towns, agriculture and dairying being the predominant activities ; but large internal migration towards the cities tends to increase this proportion, as industrialization progresses.

Other important currents of internal migration are determined by the search for better living conditions in regions where the natural resources are more plentiful or less depleted by wasteful exploitation.

Foreign immigration, which was very scarce in the two decades before 1950, has recently tended to resume some importance as a factor in population growth.

PUERTO RICO: A CROWDED ISLAND

By Kingsley Davis

B Y almost any definition, Puerto Rico is a "crowded island." With approximately 2,285,000 inhabitants in 1952, the island has 668 persons per square mile, a density exceeding that of Japan or the United Kingdom. If continental United States were as densely settled, it would have 1,989 million, instead of 157 million, inhabitants.

But from an economic standpoint, sheer land surface is not important. Some crowded countries such as Belgium and England are prosperous, while some of the less crowded ones such as Costa Rica and New Guinea are not. Is Puerto Rico crowded, then, in relation to its resources? Yes; it has 1,473 persons per square mile of arable land, whereas the mainland has only 220. Furthermore, Puerto Rico depends on its agricultural land for the support of its people more heavily than does the mainland. As of 1940 it had 58.3 per cent of its occupied males in agriculture, as compared with 22.3 in continental United States. The crowded character of its agriculture can be seen from the fact that Puerto Rico has approximately 170 agriculturally employed males per square mile·of arable land, as compared with 9.6 on the mainland. With respect to nonagricultural resources Puerto Rico is even more crowded, because the island has no fossil fuels, a relatively small amount of potential hydroelectric power, and few ores. By any index, Puerto Rico has an exceptionally high ratio of people to resources.

THE GROWTH OF NUMBERS

Puerto Rico's present crowded condition is the result of an extremely rapid population growth. Under the Spanish regime there was a fast increase, but it had begun to taper off toward the end of the nineteenth century. After the United States took over in 1898, the rate of increase again went up, as shown in Table I. It is clear that the

TABLE 1—POPULATION INCREASE

Year	Puerto Rico		United States
	Population (Thousands)	Annual Per Cent Increase	Annual Per Cent Increase
1899	953		
1910	1,118	1.45	1.95
1920	1,300	1.56	1.44
1930	1,544	1.69	1.47
1940	1,869	1.94	0.70
1950	2,211	1.69	1.36

Puerto Rican growth was so fast that the population was doubling itself every forty years. The rate of increase. in fact, was higher on the island after 1910 than it was on the mainland. Such an exceptionally rapid population growth is all the more remarkable when it is realized that Puerto Rico has generally been a country of emigration, whereas the mainland has been a country of immigration. In other words, so great has been the island's natural increase that thousands could leave each year and yet the home population could double itself every four decades. Furthermore, this rapid growth was taking place *after* a high density of settlement had already been reached.

Puerto Rico's rate of natural increase —the excess of births over deaths in relation to population—has risen steadily during the last twenty years. The average annual natural increase per 1,000

671

population is as follows: 1932–36, 19.1; 1937–41, 20.1; 1942–46, 26.1; 1947–51, 28.7. The rate has recently been one of the highest in the world. The average rate for the decade 1942–51 is so high that, if continued without migration, it would double the population in approximately 26 years. This would give the island nearly 9 million inhabitants by the end of the century, nearly 18 million in 75 years, and soon there would literally be standing room only.

Obviously, such a trend could not persist very long. It would be impossible for Puerto Rico's population to grow so fast for more than two or three decades. Even if the rest of the world devoted itself exclusively to the task of maintaining Puerto Ricans, it could not long support such a rapid population increase on the island, for that would become not only economically but also physically impossible.

As a matter of fact, no fixed rate of population growth could be sustained indefinitely. The only difference between a fast and a slow rate in this regard is that the former must cease more quickly. In Puerto Rico, with its already crowded condition, the recent rate of natural increase would yield a population growth impossible to sustain for more than a short time. Anyone who doubts this does not understand the formula for compound interest.

Actually, of course, Puerto Rico's population has not been growing as fast as its natural increase would imply, because its people have been leaving the island for better opportunities in a less crowded land. During the 1940–50 decade, when the natural increase was at its height, there was a net loss of something like 222,000 persons, nearly all of whom came to the mainland. This amounted to more than a third of the natural increase for the decade, and consequently the population did not grow so rapidly between

1940 and 1950 as it did during the previous decade (the decade of the 1930's), when the natural increase was less but emigration was also smaller. Emigration has been Puerto Rico's demographic escape valve. In the future, unless emigration continues on a large scale, the rate of natural increase will inevitably be reduced, either by a drop in fertility or by a rise in mortality.

The reason for Puerto Rico's excessive natural increase is plain. Since 1900 great effort has been made to reduce the death rate, and this effort, as Figure 1 demonstrates, has been remarkably successful. The crude rate of 9.9 per thousand in 1950 and 1951 was only one-third of what it was prior to 1900, and less than half the average rate for the decade 1910–20. The greatest gain in saving lives has been made recently—since 1940. In less than one decade after that date the crude death rate dropped from 18.0 per thousand—a level typical of rates in the United States in the late 1800's—to almost the level that prevails on the continent today. This achievement is the result of modern sanitation; better medical treatment, and a higher level of living.

The five leading causes of death in 1932 all experienced sharp declines. The death rate from diarrhea and enteritis, the leading cause, dropped by two-thirds in only a few years. The rate for tuberculosis and pneumonia, the second and third causes, was cut in half. The most spectacular reduction was in malaria. This disease, the fourth most important cause of death in 1932, was reduced virtually to zero by 1950. Nephritis, the fifth most important cause in 1932, was reduced by 75 per cent by 1948. As a result of the improvements, the average expectation of life at birth rose from 38.5 years in 1919–21 to 55.5 in 1946–48. Thus Puerto Rico has telescoped into a few years the health

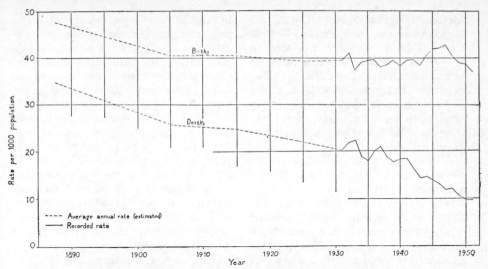

FIG. 1.—Birth and Death Rates in Puerto Rico, 1887–1951.

progress made in advanced countries over several decades.[1]

Fertility, on the other hand, has until now been virtually static. As Figure 1 shows, the crude birth rate has remained almost unchanged for fifty years. A bit depressed in the 1930's, it rose somewhat with the postwar boom in marriages and has declined slightly but steadily since the high point of 42.7 per thousand in 1947. The crude rate of 37.2 in 1951 was the lowest recorded on the island since 1932, the year when birth registration became accurate. This figure, however, was still 53 per cent higher than that for the mainland in the same year. For the whole period from 1932 to 1951 the average crude birth rate on the island was 39.6, or double the average (20.0) for the United States proper.

There are signs that Puerto Rican fertility may soon start declining. The

birth rate is becoming slightly sensitive to economic changes; the groups with the lowest fertility are expanding as a proportion of the total population; and there is a clear desire on the part of Puerto Rican women to reduce their fertility.[2] Yet there seems no likelihood that fertility will decline rapidly enough to reach very soon the low level already reached by mortality. One must therefore anticipate a high rate of natural increase on the island for at least three or four decades, resulting in continued competition between numbers and the level of living.

The rapid growth of population in Puerto Rico, although exceptional from the standpoint of past human history, is quite typical of what has been happening recently in the world. Public health has in the last few years brought

[1] See Jose L. Janer, "Population Growth in Puerto Rico and Its Relation to Time Changes in Vital Statistics," Human Biology, Vol. 17 (Dec. 1945), pp. 267–89. A treatment of mortality will be contained in a book on Puerto Rico's population now in preparation by Jerry W. Combs, Jr., and the writer.

[2] See J. W. Combs, Jr., and Kingsley Davis, "The Pattern of Puerto Rican Fertility" and "Differential Fertility in Puerto Rico," Population Studies, Vol. 4 (March 1951), pp. 364–79, and Vol. 5 (Nov. 1951), pp. 104–16; Paul K. Hatt, Backgrounds of Human Fertility in Puerto Rico (Princeton: Princeton University Press, 1952), Chaps. 2–7. The Combs-Davis articles contain other references.

spectacular declines in mortality to such agrarian regions as Formosa, Ceylon, Cyprus, Malaya, Jamaica, El Salvador, and Mexico, without affecting the birth rate and therefore without avoiding extremely heavy increases in numbers. Not only have the declines in mortality been more rapid in many cases than they were in the industrial nations at an earlier period, but the progress of industrial and social development has not accompanied the decline to the extent that it did earlier.

The orthodox theory has been that the reduction of mortality is a product —and in many cases a late product—of the industrial revolution. But now, because of the international character of science, public health, and public aid, areas which are not noticeably industrializing are nevertheless experiencing a rapid growth in population. This circumstance will make it difficult to maintain the level of living in these areas and hence, in the long run, to maintain the gains in mortality. One fears that more people are being kept alive in order that they may live badly, and that this is necessarily a temporary condition, because the level of living cannot be reduced much without causing mortality to rise again to its former level.

EMIGRATION AS AN ESCAPE VALVE

In two respects, however, Puerto Rico is luckier than most crowded and rapidly growing areas. She has, first, an open door for migration into the world's richest country, and she has, second, a lively program of economic development. Although neither of these advantages can nullify the depressing effect of natural increase on the level of living, they at least temporarily alleviate this effect and strengthen the prospect of an ultimate decline in fertility.

As mentioned above, emigration is taking away a sizable proportion of the natural increase. In recent years this proportion has been increasing. Whereas during the 1930's and during the late war there was little emigration, the movement assumed major proportions from 1944 on. During the eight years 1944 through 1951, approximately 240,000 left. The excess of births over deaths during the same period was 486,000. Thus for a period of eight years emigration from the island (nearly all of it going to the mainland) has taken almost half the natural increase. In the peak year of 1951, which saw some 50,000 leave the island, the emigration was equal to four-fifths of the natural increase.

This way of measuring the effect of emigration, however, is not adequate. The migrants are mostly in the young adult ages. If they had stayed on the island, they would have increased the birth rate and decreased the death rate. Their absence has therefore cut population growth more than the sheer number of migrants indicates. A conservative estimate of how much they have lessened the increase of population can be obtained by assuming that the emigrants would have had the same natural increase as the general population (actually, of course, they would have had a higher natural increase). The result is that if no emigration had occurred, the island would have added during the eight years 1944 through 1951 about 270,000 more to its population than it actually did. In other words, substantially more than a third of the island's theoretical natural increase during the period in question was conveniently lost through emigration.

Had this outward movement not occurred, Puerto Rico's plight would have been even more difficult than it was. Emigration has helped the island not only demographically but economically, because the emigrants earn more than those who stay at home, and they send money back to the island. Furthermore, the net figures do not tell the whole story. It is well known that there is a substantial *seasonal* migration of farm labor to the mainland. In short, the island has been alleviating its demographic impasse, not at home but on the mainland.

ECONOMIC DEVELOPMENT AS A PALLIATIVE

To many observers, Puerto Rico already appeared hopelessly overpopulated in the 1930's. Yet the population continued to grow, as we have seen, and the level of living has risen. During the ten years between 1939–40 and 1949–50 the value of goods and services, in terms of constant prices, rose by 95 per cent. The net income of the island was doubled, and the gross output per man-hour probably increased by 46 per cent, or 4 per cent per year.[3] As a result, the Puerto Ricans were living better in 1950 than they were in 1940, despite the fact that there were 342,000 more of them on the island.

Does this mean that the island was not overpopulated in the 1930's, or that it is not overpopulated now? No. The concept of overpopulation does not imply that no rise in the level of living is possible, but rather that a lesser rise is possible with an increase of numbers. There is every reason to believe that the economic development of Puerto Rico, impressive as it has been, has been retarded and hindered by the growth of numbers, and that the level of living is much lower than it would have been had the population not grown at all. Evidence for this conclusion derives from (*a*) an examination of the manner in which the economic advance has occurred, (*b*) a comparison of per

capita and national income, and (*c*) an assessment of the prospects for holding the gains.

The greatest single factor in stimulating economic improvement on the island was World War II, for it was then that nearly all the gain in output and income took place. During the postwar years there has been a definite leveling off. "Between 1939–40 and 1944–45, the value of goods and services produced on the island increased by 152 per cent. Between 1944–45 and 1949–50, a period of exactly the same length, the increase in output was less than 11 per cent." The expansion in the war years "was due almost entirely to the tremendous expansion of federal government activities in connection with defense and war." The net income from these activities increased by almost 550 per cent, whereas that from all insular sources increased by only 108 per cent.[4] Seen in this light, the recent economic advance in Puerto Rico rests on a largely artificial and temporary basis.

It is true, however, that the insular government has vigorously promoted economic development and that it has had some success. Its developmental activity was made possible by the large budgetary surpluses built up during the war, chiefly from the rum tax. With these surpluses the government originated public enterprises which became a substantial part of the total economy, laid the basis for new private industries, and attracted mainland capital.[5] Private business was also stimulated by the drawing down of assets accumulated by Puerto Ricans during the war in United States bonds, postal savings, and banks.

---

[3] Puerto Rico Planning Board, *Economic Development*, 1940–50, 1951–60 (San Juan, Office of the Governor, 1951), pp. 7–16.

[4] *Ibid.*, p. 18.

[5] See W. Arthur Lewis, "Industrial Development in Puerto Rico," *Caribbean Economic Review*, Vol. 1 (Dec. 1949), pp. 153–76; K. Davis, "Population and Progress in Puerto Rico," *Foreign Affairs*, Vol. 29 (July 1951), pp. 627–31; Puerto Rico Planning Board, *op. cit.*, pp. 20–21 ff.

The result was a continuation of economic development after the war, but at a slower pace.

WARNING SIGNALS

Plainly, despite the advances made after 1940, there are several warning signals ahead.[6]

First, the postwar activity has resulted largely from the drawing down of assets (both public and private) accumulated during the war. As these are used up, Puerto Rico will have to depend more on its own economy to generate capital; but there is evidence that the assets may have been used too heavily to expand consumption and commerce rather than to build industry and capitalize agriculture.

Second, Puerto Rico's terms of trade have remained unfavorable and her trade balance negative. The rise in the level of consumption and in the total number of consumers has forced the importation of food and other consumption items at the expense of machinery and other capital goods. To make up her trade deficit, she has depended heavily on federal government transactions.

Third, Puerto Rico continues to bear a heavy burden of unemployment and underemployment. From 1946 to 1950 inclusive, the unemployed averaged more than 14 per cent of the labor force; the underemployed, 20.6 per cent.

Fourth, the productivity of Puerto Rican agriculture, trade, and manufacturing is still low, partly because of low capitalization and partly because of inexpert management.

Fifth, despite the rise in output and the level of living, the average per capita income is still less than one-fourth that of the United States. Puerto Rico is still a poor country by modern standards.

[6] The facts in this section are drawn from Puerto Rico Planning Board, *op. cit., passim.*

DEPRESSING EFFECT OF POPULATION GROWTH

In most of these warning signs the role of excessive population growth on an already densely settled island can be seen. The most important evidence is the fact that the circumstances causing the insular net income (measured in constant prices) to double between 1939–40 and 1949–50 provided a rise of only 68.6 per cent in per capita income. "In other words, almost a third of the gain was absorbed by the increase in the number of consumers." [7]

Another evidence is found in the inability of even rapid economic advance to employ all Puerto Ricans. Although massive emigration occurred during the period in question, removing at least 115,000 workers from the island, there were still 103,000 unemployed in June 1951. There have been in recent times approximately 16,000 new entrants into the labor force each year; yet the eighty new industries added to the insular economy between 1942 and 1950 had only 13,715 employees in the latter year.

Modern economic advance means the substitution of equipment and inanimate power for human labor. The growth of population in Puerto Rico, by multiplying human labor, is making such substitution difficult. Moreover, the multiplication of human beings in relation to resources causes assets to be spent on direct consumption rather than on income-generating industry. During the decade from 1939–40 to 1949–50, the share of food products in all imports (by value) increased from 27.8 per cent to 31.4 per cent. At the beginning of that decade 46 per cent of all food locally consumed was imported, and by the end of it 54 per cent was imported.

The conclusion seems inescapable that the island is struggling against a strong current. Progress is being made, but it

[7] *Ibid.*, p. 16.

would be much more rapid and secure if, despite emigration, an average of 30,000 to 35,000 were not being added to the population each year. Assuming that the island cannot dump *all* of its natural increase on the mainland, and that it does not wish a rise in mortality, the only way out is a lowering of the birth rate. Otherwise, one cannot help wondering whether the fortunate developments from 1940 to 1952 will prove temporary. The birth rate seems likely to fall in the next thirty years, but not fast enough to prevent rapid population growth. Only if the decline can be hastened deliberately, with continued stimulation of economic development and continued massive emigration, can the level of living keep on rising in the next few decades.

POPULATION DISTRIBUTION AND GROWTH

IN AFRICA

By L. T. Badenhorst

INTRODUCTION

From the demographic point of view Africa remains the 'dark' continent. The majority of the population in this vast area has never been enumerated in an adequate population census. Estimates of population for a large number of African territories are poor. Vital statistics and data on continental and inter-continental movement of population are almost entirely lacking. Small wonder then that the estimated population of Africa increases with every new estimate as more adequate counts and estimates for many African countries become available. Even at the present time the most authoritative estimates[1] of population are no more than rough approximations, while little can be said with confidence about present and past growth rates.

To illustrate the paucity of statistics on the demographic position of Africa, the following may be of interest. According to the United Nations *Demographic Year-book* for 1949[2] areas containing 44% only of the current estimated population of Africa have ever experienced a more or less adequate population census.[3] With the exception of the white population of the Union of South Africa and some few countries on the North African coast, reliable vital statistics do not exist. The *Yearbook* mentioned above also gives information on the types of methods used by the various countries in preparing estimates for three recent years, i.e. 1947, 1948 and 1949. Of those areas for which information was available only five containing 10% of the 1949 population used the relatively reliable method of a census and records of births and deaths, with or without allowance for migration, to arrive at current estimates of population. Seven areas, representing another 10% of the population, prepared estimates by means of mathematical extrapolation of census totals, while two others, representing 2·5% of the total population, applied an estimated rate of population change to a census figure. An additional nine areas, and probably the majority of those for which no information are avilable, use non-censal methods to prepare estimates; these vary from head counts and 'group enumerations' to those based on the number of male taxpayers multiplied by a factor, and some that are hardly more than guesses.

The totals for Africa and the various regions and political subdivisions presented here were derived from the available census figures and the best available official and unofficial estimates for individual countries (see Appendix 1). All official and unofficial estimates were carefully examined to appraise as far as possible their

---

[1] See United Nations *Demographic Yearbook*, 1949, 'World population trends, 1920–49'.

[2] Ibid. Table 1.

[3] The rather lenient criteria set up to qualify a count as a census were: (1) that it covered the majority of the population, (2) that it was obtained by the method of individual enumeration, and (3) that it was effected within the space of less than a year.

completeness and reliability and to correct any apparent errors and inadequacies. An attempt was made to obtain population estimates with a uniform time reference as of the middle of each year. This was found extremely difficult in the case of some countries, especially for earlier years; in these cases approximations for the mid-point of the year in question were obtained by interpolations or extrapolations of population estimates and census data for other years.

SIZE, DENSITY AND GROWTH OF THE AFRICAN POPULATION

The estimates of population in millions and the density of population per square kilometre for each of the years 1920, 1930, 1939 and 1949, together with the average annual percentage increases, are presented in Table 1. The area figures used here were mainly obtained from the data for individual countries shown in the United Nations *Demographic Yearbook*, and relate to land area plus inland waters. The population figures for 1949 were for the greater part taken from this source, but the estimates for the three other years were adjusted where necessary in order to present a reasonably consistent pattern of changes. It should be emphasized that the basis of the estimates in most cases is very weak and the margin of error considerable.

Table 1. *Population estimates and density, Africa, 1920–49*

Year	Mid-year population (millions)	Average annual increase % (since preceding date)	Persons per sq.km.
1920	139	—	4·6
1930	157	1·2	5·2
1939	176	1·3	5·8
1949	198	1·2	6·5

In view of the many reservations with regard to the estimates of the African population, it is evident that no great reliance can be placed on the figures, especially on those for earlier years, and, in particular, on the implied changes in population between the years specified in the table. According to the estimates the population of Africa increased from 139 millions in 1920 to 198 millions in 1949, or by about 59 millions in a generation. This implied increase amounts to an average growth of 1·2% per year over the period 1920–49. The true rate may be considerably lower; nevertheless, there can be little doubt that the population of Africa is increasing very rapidly at the present time. Since 1920 it has certainly been growing at a rate much more rapid than the average of past centuries for this continent. There are indications that while human fertility remains at an extremely high level in most African territories, mortality is gradually being brought under control. If this process continues it is bound to lead to a still more rapid and accelerating rate of population growth in the future.

With an area of approximately 30,252,000 sq.km., Africa is the second largest of the continents. Its area is greater than that of Europe including the whole of the U.S.S.R., and more than ten times that of the combined area of north-west-central and southern Europe. In 1949 Africa, representing 23% of the world's land area, contained only 8% of the world's people. Its population had a density of 7 persons per sq.km., compared with a world average of 18 and a figure many times that in large areas of the world. It would therefore seem as if there is no possibility in the near future of Africa in general having to cope with such problems of sheer numbers in relation to land area as are experienced, for example, in many parts of Asia.

It should be emphasized, however, that the density of population, expressed as the average number of persons per square kilometre of land area, does not take into account important variations in natural resources, topography, climate and economic activity. For example, large parts of the African continent consist of desert area unsuitable for human habitation. In addition, the tropical zone claims a greater proportion of Africa than of any other continent. Fortunately, Africa also has a smaller proportion of low-lying lands than any other continent, and these consist mainly of desert and semi-desert areas rather than unhealthy marshes and rain forest as in the tropical areas of America and Asia. Incidentally, these facts help to explain why European penetration in Africa has remained relatively limited and superficial in spite of its sparse population. Except for small areas in the north and south, with a mediterranean climate and certain high plateaux mostly along the east coast, Africa is a relatively unattractive area for white settlement.

As has been pointed out above, adequate vital statistics for African territories are almost entirely lacking. The majority of countries have no comprehensive systems of vital registration, and in most of the remaining areas such registration as exists is incomplete, so that the official vital statistics understate the birth and death rates. A recent attempt at estimating the current levels of birth and death rates (around 1947) for various regions of the world, including Africa, resulted in a birth rate of 40–$45^\circ/_{\circ\circ}$ and a death rate of 25–$30^\circ/_{\circ\circ}$ population for the whole of the continent.[1] These approximate rates are considered very tentative in view of the fact that adequate birth and death statistics were available for a limited area only and various indirect methods had to be used in order to arrive at average rates for Africa as a whole. A similar attempt at estimating the pre-war birth and death rates of the African population[2] gives the same probable range for the birth rate but a death rate of 30–$35^\circ/_{\circ\circ}$ population.

Africa has begun to experience the kind of population expansion which occurred earlier in Europe and some other parts of the world, with the death rate declining under the impact of social and economic changes, while the birth rate is still kept at a high level by the traditional culture, beliefs and *mores*. How long this period of rapid population growth will continue is uncertain and will depend on the course of political, social and economic events. If the rapid rate of growth experienced during recent years continues to prevail in the immediate future, which is more than likely as a minimum estimate, a population of about 290 millions would result in 1980. That this is a conservative guess is indicated by the results of a recent study of the

[1] United Nations *Demographic Yearbook*, 1949, 'World Population Trends, 1920–49'.
[2] United Nations, *World Population Trends*, 1920–47, ST/SOA/Series A, Population Studies, no. 3, December 1949, p. 10.

population of the Union of South Africa,[1] in which the natural increase rate of the Bantu population was estimated at about $17°/_{oo}$ during the period 1936–46. Census figures for this population indicate that the average growth rate during recent intercensal periods was never lower than 1·5% and often higher than 2·0% per year.

It may safely be stated that births and deaths and not migration have been responsible for the rapid growth of the African population in recent decades. Probably the greatest inter-continental movement of population in the history of Africa was connected with the slave trade of the eighteenth century. The most important inter-continental migration during the last hundred years, as well as at the present time, is that of European settlers to various parts of Africa, particularly South and East Africa. This movement reached a peak of about 75,000 persons per annum during a very brief period immediately following the Second World War, but even this number has been considerably reduced in more recent years. At the present time, people of European stock number about 5 million in the whole of Africa. Some $2\frac{1}{2}$ millions of these live in the Union of South Africa and South-West Africa, another 2 millions in North Africa, and the remaining half million live in various parts of Central Africa, mainly on the east coast.[2]

POLITICAL DIVISION

One of the outstanding characteristics of Africa is its political immaturity. The entire continent, including the islands off the coast, is divided into fifty-one political divisions (see Fig. 1). Of these only four, Egypt, Ethiopia, Liberia and the Union of South Africa, are independent countries. Together they account for about $50\frac{1}{2}$ million people in 1949; the area covered by these countries constitute about 11% of the total area of Africa, while it contains about 25% of the total estimated population (see Table 2).

The rest of Africa is almost entirely divided among a small number of European powers, viz. the United Kingdom, France, Portugal, Spain, Belgium and Italy. The majority of areas with dependent status are non-self-governing territories (colonies, protectorates, etc.), which in varying degrees are administered and controlled by the European governments. At the present time there are no less than thirty-five such territories, about one-half of which are governed by the United Kingdom. In addition to these there are seven Trust Territories under the United Nations trusteeship system, a Condominium (Anglo-Egyptian Sudan), a former Mandated Territory under the League of Nations (South-West Africa), an area under international administration (Tangier), and two areas (Libya and Eritrea) still under United Kingdom military government. Of the latter, Libya is scheduled to become an independent state by 1952, while the final disposition of Eritrea is still under discussion by the United Nations.

The United Nations Trust Territories in Africa, with one exception, represent

---

[1] See L. T. Badenhorst, 'The future growth of the population of South Africa and its probable age distribution', *Population Studies*, vol. IV, no. 1, June 1950.

[2] In 1935 the European population in Africa was estimated at about 4,000,000. See R. R. Kuczynski, *Population Movements*, 1936, p. 95.

pre-World War I German colonies, which were given as mandates, under the League of Nations Covenant, to Britain, France and Belgium. Togoland, on the West African coast between the Gold Coast and Nigeria, was about equally divided between Britain and France; the Cameroons, also on the west coast, went almost entirely to France and the remainder to Britain; Britain also received the greater part of German East Africa, renamed Tanganyika, while the north-west part went

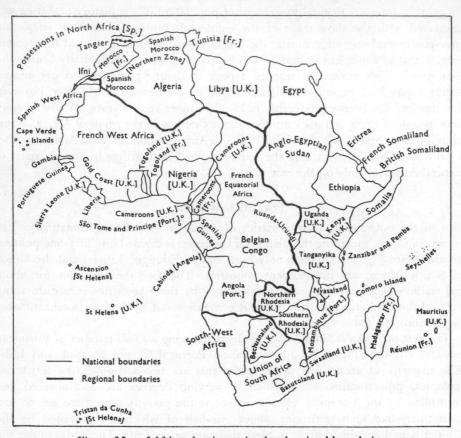

Fig. 1. Map of Africa, showing national and regional boundaries.

to Belgium under the name of Ruanda-Urundi. Under the Charter of the United Nations these former mandated areas became Trust Territories, administered by the same governments. Somaliland, former Italian colony on the north-east African coast, has now also been placed under United Nations trusteeship with Italy as the administering government. Taken together these seven Trust Territories in 1949 constituted about 7% of the land area of the African continent and contained about 18 million people, or about 9% of the total for Africa. In the discussion which follows these areas will be included under the general heading of the administering governments.

The estimated population for the years 1920, 1930, 1939 and 1949, and the area and density of population in 1949 for the main political divisions of Africa according to present political status, are given in Table 2.

Table 2. *Size and density of population, main political divisions, Africa, 1920–49*

Political division	No. of areas 1949	Estimated population (in millions)				Total area in sq.km. ('000)	Persons per sq.km. 1949
		1920	1930	1939	1949		
Independent countries	4	33·6	38·2	43·4	50·5	3,395	15
Areas administered by:							
United Kingdom	21	48·2	53·8	59·4	65·1	7,762	8
France	10	35·4	40·2	44·7	50·5	11,075	5
Portugal	5	7·9	8·5	10·1	11·5	2,059	6
Spain	4	0·8	1·0	1·3	1·6	343	5
Belgium	2	10·7	12·3	14·2	14·9	2,397	6
Italy	1	1·0	1·0	1·0	1·0	513	2
Union of South Africa	1	0·2	0·3	0·3	0·4	823	—
U.K. Military Government	2	1·5	1·7	1·9	2·3	1,884	1
International administration	1	0·1	0·1	0·1	0·2	0·3	—
Total	51	139·4	157·1	176·4	198·0	30,251	7

Although France controls and governs a larger territory in Africa than any other power, the United Kingdom holds by far the greatest number of countries and peoples. These are mostly situated in the eastern part of the continent in a continuous strip of territory from Bechuanaland in the south to the Anglo-Egyptian Sudan in the north. However, some important British possessions in Africa are situated on the west coast, the largest in area and population being Nigeria. This country has the largest population of any one country in Africa (24 millions in 1949) and a density of population nearly four times that of the continent as a whole.

The United Kingdom controls more than one-quarter of the total area of Africa and a third of its people. The density of population for all United Kingdom areas is only slightly higher than that for Africa, but densities vary considerably from country to country. Most densely populated of all are the islands off the east and west coasts; in Mauritius and dependencies as many as 227 persons share a square kilometre, on the average, while density figures for Zanzibar and Pemba and the Seychelles, respectively, are 101 and 86 persons per sq.km. At the other extreme we find Bechuanaland with only two, and the Anglo-Egyptian Sudan with 3 persons per sq.km.

The number of countries and number and proportion of population in specified density categories for the United Kingdom territories are given in Table 3.

The figures in Table 3 do not give a complete picture of the distribution of population in these areas, since averages for entire political units have to be used. Population density naturally varies a great deal within each country according to climatic conditions, topography, mineral deposits, rainfall, soil cultivation, etc. With a few exceptions, however, the most densely populated areas are the coastal regions of North, South, East and North-west Africa.

Table 3. *Distribution of countries, area and population according to density, United Kingdom areas in Africa, 1949*

Persons per sq.km.	No.* of countries	Area in sq.km. ('000)	Population (in millions)	% of population
Less than 5	4	4146	10·0	15·4
5–15	6	2051	16·6	25·5
15–25	5	601	11·6	17·8
25–100	4	960	26·2	40·2
Over 100	2	5	0·7	1·1
Total	21	7763	65·1	100·0

* The areas in the specified density categories are: less than 5: Anglo-Egyptian Sudan, Bechuanaland, Somaliland Protectorate and Northern Rhodesia; 5–15: Cameroons, Kenya, Southern Rhodesia, Swaziland, Tanganyika and Togoland; 15–25: Basutoland, Gold Coast, Nyasaland, St Helena and Uganda; 25–100: Gambia, Nigeria, Seychelles and Sierra Leone; over 100: Mauritius, Zanzibar and Pemba.

France controls more than 11 million sq.km. of African territory, but since much of this is desert or semi-desert the density of population, on the whole, is rather low (5 persons per sq.km. in 1949). French areas in Africa are less scattered than those of the United Kingdom and form one single mass of territory in the north-west part of the continent. On the east coast there are only the small areas of French Somaliland, and the islands of Madagascar and Réunion. Densities vary from 2 persons per sq.km. in French Equatorial Africa (woodland and tropical forests), and four in Algeria and French West Africa (mainly desert), to about 20 persons per sq.km. in Morocco, Tunisia and Togoland. In the Cameroons and on Madagascar and Comora Islands average densities are about the same as for Africa as a whole, but on the small island of Réunion there are about 100 persons per sq.km. of land area.

Table 4 gives the distribution of land and people according to the same density categories as in Table 3.

Table 4. *Distribution of countries, area and population according to density, French areas in Africa, 1949*

Persons per sq.km.	No.* of countries	Area in sq.km. ('000)	Population (in millions)	% of population
Less than 5	4	9412	29·9	59·2
5–15	2	1033	7·3	14·5
15–25	3	627	13·0	25·7
25–100	1	3	0·3	0·6
Total	10	11,075	50·5	100·0

* The areas in the specified density categories are: less than 5: Algeria, Equatorial Africa, Somaliland and West Africa; 5–15: Cameroons and Madagascar and Comora Island; 15–25: Morocco, Togoland and Tunisia; 25–100: Réunion.

Belgium administers two areas in tropical Africa: the large area of the Congo, rich in resources and sparsely populated (6 persons per sq.km.) and the adjacent United Nations Trust Territory of Ruanda-Urundi with a density of more than 70 persons per sq.km. in 1949. Together these constitute 7·9% of the area of Africa and support 7·5% of its population (see Table 2).

Portugal's most important holdings in Africa are Mozambique on the south-east and Angola on the south-west coast. Angola covers nearly twice the area of Mozambique but is less than half as densely populated (4 as against 9 persons per sq.km. in 1949). Other Portuguese possessions in Africa consist of Portuguese Guinea on the north-west coast and the islands of Cape Verde and São Tome and Principe. Like most islands off the African coast, these are densely populated. Together Portuguese areas in Africa cover more than 2 million sq.km., which, in 1949, were the home of 11½ million people.

The only other powers which control African territory are Spain, Italy and the Union of South Africa. Spain holds four small areas in North Africa, viz. Moroccan Protectorate, divided into the widely separated northern and southern zones, possessions in North Africa (Alhucemas, Ceuta, Chafarinas, Melilla and Peñon de Vélez de la Gomera), Spanish West Africa (Ifni, Rio de Oro and Saguia el Hamra) and Spanish Guinea (Rio Muni, adjacent to the French Cameroons, and a number of small islands, chief of which is Fernando Po). The combined population of these areas was 1·6 millions in 1949. Distribution was extremely uneven; for example, the density of population in Spanish West Africa (the Spanish Sahara) and the southern zone of the Moroccan Protectorate is less than 1 person per sq.km., while the small possessions in North Africa, like Ceuta and Melilla, were very densely populated. The northern zone of Morocco has a density of 59 persons per sq.km., while that of Spanish Guinea equals the figure for all African possessions, namely, 6 persons per sq.km.

All that remains of Italy's pre-war African empire is the Trust Territory of Somaliland, a semi-desert area on the coast of North Africa adjacent to Kenya and Ethiopia. With less than a million inhabitants in 1949, this area has a density of barely 2 persons per sq.km.

After the First World War the territory of German West Africa was given under the League of Nations Covenant as a C Mandate to the Union of South Africa to be 'administered under the laws of the mandatory as an integral portion of its territory'. This area was the only C Mandate in Africa, and also the only one for which no trusteeship agreement was negotiated with the United Nations after the last war. Its final disposition is still under discussion by this organization. South-west Africa, as it is now called, consists almost completely of desert and waste land with an irregular and extremely low rainfall. The inhabitants numbered 374,000 in 1949, of whom about one-tenth were of European stock, immigrants from South Africa and Germany. The density of population is less than 1 person per sq.km.

POPULATION DISTRIBUTION AND GROWTH BY REGION

In our present state of knowledge it is difficult to divide Africa into a small number of more or less homogeneous regions with characteristic and significant ethnic, cultural or economic attributes. In addition to the lack of detailed information on characteristics there is the limiting factor arising from the fact that such data usually have as base large political units which are rarely homogeneous from any point of view.

For the purposes of this description we have chosen, rather arbitrarily, four large regions which are somewhat homogeneous with respect to population, climate, topography, nature of contacts with other parts of the world, and which are at the same time easily identifiable geographically. These are North, West Central, East Central and South Africa.

North Africa includes all countries on the North African sea coast from Egypt in the east to French Morocco in the west, including Ifni (part of Spanish West Africa) and the northern zone of the Spanish Moroccan Protectorate. South Africa includes the Union, South-West Africa, Bechuanaland, as well as Basutoland and Swaziland. The central area between these two regions has been subdivided by a line running from north to south along the eastern borders of French Equatorial Africa, Belgian Congo and Angola. All countries to the east of this line, from the Anglo-Egyptian Sudan in the north to the Rhodesias and Mozambique in the south, and including all islands off the east coast, form East Central Africa. All countries to the west of the above line constitute West Central Africa.

The area, density in 1949 and population estimates for each of the years 1920, 1930, 1939 and 1949 are presented, according to the regions described above, in Table 5.

Table 5. *Population, area and density, major regions of Africa, 1920-49*

Area, density and population	Region			
	North Africa	West central Africa	East central Africa	South Africa
Area in sq.km. ('000)	5,561	13,030	8,854	2,806
Persons per sq.km. (1949)	8	6	7	5
Population (in millions):				
1920	27·7	56·5	47·3	7·8
1930	31·7	62·4	53·2	9·7
1939	36·7	68·5	59·7	11·5
1949	43·5	74·4	66·4	13·5

It is evident from Table 5 that there is little difference between the average density of the various regions as defined above. It has been pointed out before, however, that great variations in density occur within each region and even within each political unit. The outstanding example of such uneven distribution is Egypt, where the narrow but extremely fertile Nile Valley is one of the most densely populated areas in the world while the rest of the country is very sparsely populated. A similarly uneven distribution of population prevails in the rest of North Africa. Settlement is mainly concentrated in a narrow coastal zone on the edge of the desert.

The Sahara has always been one of the most effective barriers to communication, movement and cultural contact. As a result North Africa has for centuries been set apart from the rest of Africa. At the same time its geographical location on the Mediterranean sea has made it easily accessible to Europe and the Near East, and the strong influences resulting from this fact are evident to-day in the ethnic, religious and cultural composition of the North African population.

At the other extreme of the African continent European influence has also been strong. People of European stock constitute about one-quarter of the population in South Africa and have played a disproportionate part in the economic and cultural development of that region. The temperate climate of most of this region also forms a contrast to the tropical climate of both East and West Central Africa.

Average population density is lower here than in any of the regions mentioned in Table 5. Again, the distribution of population is uneven. This region includes the larger part of the Kalahari Desert and other desert and semi-desert areas in South-west Africa and Bechuanaland. Rainfall is highest in the east and, except for the south-east and south-west coastal regions, gradually decreases from east to west. Population density, with the important exception of heavy concentration of people in the Witwatersrand gold-mining area, follows the same distribution.

Very little is known about population distribution in the east and west central regions. However, it seems that here, too, the most important concentrations of population are situated in the coastal regions. This is true for the entire east central region and particularly in the case of the northern part of the west central region. In the southern part of the latter region desert and otherwise inhospitable areas sometimes discourage concentration along the coast.

As regards population growth during the last few decades in the regions under discussion, very little can be said with confidence. However, some tentative conclusions may be drawn from the population totals presented in Table 5. First, all four regions show a consistent and rapid growth throughout the period 1920-49. This is entirely in accordance with the known facts about the population factors operating in this area and reasonable deduction on the basis of our knowledge of social and economic conditions prevailing on the continent.

The growth rate over the entire period covered by the table was highest in South Africa; also the region in which the social and economic forces which usually accompany a decline in the death rate have been in operation most effectively and for the longest period of time. But it is a well-established fact that the same forces that are responsible for depressing the death rate—industrialization, urbanization, rising standards of living, improved means of communication, modern sanitation and epidemic control, to mention only a few—may also, in the long run, be responsible for a decline in the birth rate. Although the people of South Africa have a long way to go before they have mortality under control, fertility control has already been effected in a considerable measure. This fact is borne out by the rates of growth implied by the population figures in Table 5. The average rate of growth for this region was 2·2% per year during the period 1920–30, 1·9% during the years 1930–9, and 1·6% only during 1939–49.

The growth rate of the population of North Africa averaged 1·4, 1·6 and 1·7% per year, respectively, for the three periods under discussion. The upward trend is probably significant, and one may venture the conclusion that it is the result of the extraordinarily high death rates being increasingly brought under control, while the high birth rates remain unaffected. For the first time in recent decades the growth rate of North Africa exceeded that of South Africa in the period 1939-49.

The growth rates for West and East Central Africa must be interpreted with extreme caution in view of the tentative nature of the population estimates for countries in these regions. The average annual growth rates implied by the population totals for the years specified were as follows: East Central Africa, 1·2, 1920–30; 1·3, 1930–9; and 1·1, 1939–49. West Central Africa, 1·0, 1920–30; 1·0, 1930–9; and 0·8, 1939–49. Although quite high, the growth rates in these regions were not as high as in the remaining two regions.

APPENDIX 1

Population estimates and area, African countries, 1920–49

Country	Area in sq.km.	Estimated mid-year population ('000)			
		1949	1939	1930	1920
Algeria	2,204,900	8,764	7,590	6,460	5,750
Anglo-Egyptian Sudan	2,505,700	7,558	7,200	6,500	5,700
Angola	1,246,700	4,597	3,900	3,400	3,100
Basutoland	30,343	556	561	537	495
Bechuanaland	712,200	300	275	221	145
Belgian Congo	2,343,930	11,046	10,343	8,764	7,500
Cameroons (U.K.)	88,266	1,000	889	819	650
Cameroons (Fr.)	440,900	3,000	2,633	2,400	2,200
Cape Verde Islands	4,033	139	175	146	160
Egypt	1,000,000	20,045	16,598	14,767	13,222
Eritrea	124,000	1,086	986	900	820
Ethiopia	1,060,000	16,700	15,100	13,500	12,200
French Equatorial Africa	2,510,000	4,347	3,800	3,400	3,100
French Somaliland	21,700	56	45	73	54
French West Africa	4,675,500	16,700	15,200	14,360	12,800
Gambia	10,537	270	291	201	212
Gold Coast	204,089	3,739	3,495	3,100	2,700
Kenya	582,624	5,454	4,753	4,205	3,670
Liberia	111,370	1,648	1,540	1,400·	1,300
Libya	1,759,500	1,174	946	800	685
Madagascar and Comoro	592,200	4,396	4,058	3,759	3,388
Mauritius and dep.	2,094	475	417	403	375
Moroccan Protectorate (Sp.)	45,656	1,172	961	713	556
Morocco (Fr.)	418,645	8,594	7,400	6,200	5,000
Mozambique	771,125	6,251	5,500	4,500	4,200
Nigeria	876,922	24,000	22,400	20,937	19,760
Northern Rhodesia	751,908	1,640	1,494	1,322	953
Nyasaland	122,772	2,314	2,100	1,920	1,750
Portuguese Guinea	36,125	431	450	390	340
Possessions in North Africa (Sp.)	213	159	133	112	84
Réunion	2,511	252	216	196	170
Ruanda-Urundi	53,200	3,865	3,820	3,500	3,200
St Helena and dep.	210	5	5	4	4
São Tome and Principe	964	62	59	54	57
Seychelles	405	35	32	27	24
Sierra Leone	72,323	1,860	1,920	1,746	1,519
Somaliland (It.)	513,000	972	983	1,026	950
Somaliland Protectorate (U.K.)	176,113	500	430	376	325
Southern Rhodesia	389,347	2,022	1,444	1,091	886
South-west Africa	822,876	374	332	283	223
Spanish Guinea	28,051	173	169	154	110
Spanish West Africa	269,150	78	74	70	66
Swaziland	17,364	194	165	139	110
Tanganyika	939,326	7,514	6,519	5,793	5,056
Tangier (Int. Adm.)	349	150	87	70	60
Togoland (U.K.)	33,775	388	381	350	310
Togoland (Fr.)	53,000	982	805	750	670
Tunisia	155,830	3,416	3,000	2,600	2,300
Uganda	243,401	5,050	4,359	3,856	3,365
Union of South Africa	1,223,712	12,112	10,172	8,541	6,842
Zanzibar and Pemba	2,642	268	250	233	207
Total	30,251,501	197,883	176,455	157,068	139,323

POPULATION AND WEALTH IN EGYPT

By Charles Issawi

T HE most powerful factors depressing the standard of living in Egypt during the last thirty years have been the maldistribution of wealth, the population pressure, and the persistent fall in the prices of agricultural products, especially cotton. The first factor will not be dealt with in this article. Suffice it to say that inequality in the distribution of wealth, especially land, has lowered the standard of living both directly—by cutting down the incomes of the poorer classes— and indirectly—by restricting their purchasing power and thus narrowing the market for local industries, a fact which has greatly impeded the progress of industrialization in Egypt. Public opinion is becoming increasingly aware of the necessity of correcting this maldistribution by both an agrarian reform and the steepening of the rate of progressive taxation on large incomes, and important steps have been taken in the latter direction.

GROWTH OF POPULATION

The pressure of Egypt's rapidly growing population on her very exiguous soil has been preoccupying Egyptian economists and sociologists during the last fifteen or twenty years.[2] But the problem is not peculiar to Egypt; it is part of a world-wide phenomenon which can be seen equally well in India or Indonesia today or in Western Europe during the 19th century. Briefly put, the population of these countries is growing, or has grown, because the secular balance between births and deaths has been upset. For in a pre-industrial society the death rate is always high, owing to inadequate nutrition, defective hygiene, the spread of epidemics and the loss in lives resulting

[1] Middle East Section, Department of Economic Affairs, United Nations Secretariat. This article was written before the author joined the United Nations and represents his own personal views—not those of the United Nations.

[2] One of the earliest studies on the subject was Dr. Wendell Cleland's THE POPULATION PROBLEM IN EGYPT. Lancaster, Pennsylvania, The Science Press Printing Company, 1936.

from disorders and wars. In order to compensate for this high wastage, the society favours those customs and institutions that promote a high birth rate, such as stigmatizing celibacy, encouraging marriage at an early age, honoring parenthood and so forth. When as a result of the spreading of industrial civilization, order and security prevail, hygienic conditions improve and more food becomes available, the first effect is a decline in the death rate. The birth rate, however, which is determined mainly by social and religious factors, remains for a long time at its previous high level. It is only when an industrial civilization has prevailed sufficiently long to change the whole customs and outlook of the population that birth rates begin to decline, as they have been doing in Western Europe and North America. Egypt is at present in the first stage, the stage of declining death rates unaccompanied by falling birth rates.

Egypt's population in Pharaonic, Roman, and early Arab times is generally estimated at 6–7 millions. Long centuries of Mameluke misrule, however, combined with the diversion of the trade routes linking Europe with India, caused the population to drop heavily, to perhaps 2,500,000 by the end of the 18th century.

Mohammad Ali Pasha's enlightened and firm rule and the economic expansion that set in under his reign set the population curve on an upward course from which it has not since deviated. More land was brought under cultivation and crop yields increased; hence a larger population could be supported. More particularly, the rapid expansion of cotton cultivation (greatly accelerated by the American Civil War and the consequent stoppage of American exports to England) stimulated the growth of the population, since cotton absorbs much labour, especially child labour.

As a result of these factors, the population doubled in half a century, standing at about 6,800,000 at the time of the British occupation in 1882.

Table 1, based on the census carried out each ten years, shows the increase since that time.

Year	Population	Per Cent Increase During the Decade
1897	9,635,000	—
1907	11,190,000	16.1
1917	12,718,000	13.7
1927	14,178,000	11.5
1937	15,921,000	12.3
1947	19,040,000	19.6

Table 1. Population of Egypt, 1897-1947.

The reported population of 1947 is generally believed to be inflated[3] but it is very unlikely that the true figure is lower than 18,000,000 which would give an increase of about 13 per cent over the decade.

A careful analysis of birth and death rates over the period 1906–1940 was made by Dr. Clyde V. Kiser.[4] The crude birth rates showed no definite trend but fertility ratios (children under 5 per 1,000 women or married women 15–49 years of age) did suggest some decline after 1907. The recorded death rates for Egypt as a whole indicated no decline since 1906. Those restricted to Health Bureau areas (with more adequate registration) were lower after 1920 than during the several years preceding the influenza epidemic of 1918. This remained true despite the upward trends during 1930–1941—increases that may have been due in part to improvements in registration. Infant mortality rates for Health Bureau areas indicated very distinct decreases over the 1906–1941 period. Dr. Kiser's calculations show that, in 1937, the gross reproduction rate for the whole country was 3.11 and the net reproduction rate 1.44. By different methods of extrapolation Dr. Kiser concludes that "it seems reasonable to expect that it [i.e., the Egyptian population in 1970] will be between 18 and 21 million."

[3] When broken down the census returns show an abnormal increase in Alexandria and even more in Cairo. It is probable that many inhabitants of these cities filled their forms wrongly in the hope of getting extra ration cards.

[4] Kiser, Clyde V.: The Demographic Position of Egypt. A chapter in DEMOGRAPHIC STUDIES OF SELECTED AREAS OF RAPID GROWTH. The Milbank Memorial Fund, New York, 1944, pp. 97–122.

These figures may, however, prove to be an underestimate. For the death rate of 26 per thousand, one of the very highest in the world, will probably be brought down by the great efforts which are being exerted to improve hygienic conditions; while the birth rate is likely to remain high.

PRESSURE OF POPULATION

The next question to ask is whether Egypt is in any sense "overpopulated." Put in this form the question hardly admits a scientific answer. Nevertheless it may be safely stated that the population is pressing harder and harder on the very limited resources of the country.

Two facts should be borne in mind. First, Egypt's population has increased sixfold during the last hundred years, from about 3,000,000 to some 18,000,000, a rate of growth probably unparalleled by any purely agricultural country. Second, Egypt is perhaps the most densely populated country in the world.

What then was the increase in resources which accompanied this huge increase in population? No precise indices of production have been computed, but the following figures illustrate the general trend.[5]

In 1830–1840, the cultivated area was about 2,000,000 feddans;[6] in 1944–1945 it was 5,700,000, while the crop area was 9,150,000.[7]

During the same period the yield of wheat rose from about 4 ardeb[8] per feddan to 6 ardeb per feddan, while that of cotton showed a much more spectacular advance from 1–2 cantars[9] per feddan to over 5 cantars.

Finally, cotton exports during that period shot up from about 200,000 cantars per annum to somewhere around 8,000,000 cantars.

[5] *From* Crouchley, A. E.: A Century of Economic Development. *Egypte Contemporaine,* 1939.

[6] A feddan is 4,201 square metres or 1.038 acres.

[7] The difference between the cultivated and crop areas arises from the fact that, over most of the country, more than one crop is grown on each patch of land during the year.

[8] An ardeb is equivalent to 150 kilograms or 330 lbs. approximately.

[9] A cantar is equivalent to 99 pounds or 45 kilograms.

Taking the period as a whole, it is not permissible to say that Egypt's population has outrun her income.

A careful study of the twenty years' period lying between the two world wars, however, can only lead to a pessimistic conclusion.

Table 2. Weighted index of volume of fourteen main crops produced in Egypt. (Average of 1924–1928 = 100).

YEAR	INDEX
1929	111
1930	106
1931	96
1932	102
1933	110
1934	101
1935	113
1936	116
1937	124
1938	112
1939	120
1940	118

VOLUME OF AGRICULTURAL PRODUCTION

First of all it is necessary to examine the increase in the volume of agricultural output, since agriculture is still by far the most important source of Egypt's income and one that absorbs over two thirds of her occupied population. Figures for the fourteen principal crops have been worked out by the present writer[10] on the basis of data compiled by M. Jean Schatz[11] and are shown in Table 2.

These figures show that, with the exception of the depression years, when cotton production was restricted by the Government in an unsuccessful attempt to raise its price, the physical volume of production has steadily risen, by about 20 per cent between 1924–1928 and the outbreak of the war. This increase is due to the extension of perennial irrigation on the one hand and the great improvement in yields on the other. For whereas the cultivated area has shown almost no change since before the first world war the crop area has increased considerably owing to the extension of perennial irrigation, which has enabled the farmer to grow more crops on the same soil. On the other hand the splendid research work carried on in the

[10] Issawi, Charles: Un indice du volume de la production agricole. *Egypte Contemporaine*, 1942.

[11] Schatz, Jean: Mesures pour alleger l'endettement et la crise des cultivateurs. *Egypte Contemporaine*, 1942.

Ministry of Agriculture has resulted in the production of new, longer stapled varieties of cotton with a much higher yield. At the same time the varieties of wheat and maize have been improved and their yields raised.

VALUE OF AGRICULTURAL PRODUCTION

But this increase in *volume* has by no means sufficed to offset the fall in prices, so that the total *value* of the crops has sharply contracted. The main factor responsible for this state of affairs is undoubtedly the catastrophic fall in the world price of cotton. For although Egyptian cotton, because of its high quality, normally stands at a premium over its American, Indian, Russian, and South American competitors, its price is nevertheless bound up with theirs, as was demonstrated only too clearly by the unsuccessful restrictionist measures of the early 1930's.[12]

If Egypt consumed the whole or the bulk of her agricultural production, this fall in value would not have had any significance. But since agricultural products constitute nearly 90 per cent of Egypt's exports the fall in agricultural prices caused the terms of trade to move against her and thus contributed to depress the standard of living.[13]

Table 3 indicates the extent of the fluctuations and fall in the value of the *twelve* principal Egyptian crops.[14] The first column shows the wholesale value of these crops; the second an index adjusted for changes in the cost of living and based on 1939 shows an appreciable drop. The figures show clear cyclical fluctuations: the post-war boom of 1919 is followed by a sharp fall; this in turn leads to an ampler and more solid, though less brilliant, boom in 1923–1928, followed by a very severe slump reaching its trough in 1932; finally there is a slow advance up to 1938, accelerated by the outbreak of war.

[12] The factors determining the price of Egyptian cotton are studied in Charles Issawi: Egypt: An Economic and Social Analysis. Royal Institute of International Affairs, 1947, pp. 66–67.

[13] For the movements in Egypt's terms of trade *see ibid*, pp. 116–117.

[14] These are: cotton, cotton seed, wheat, beans, corn, millet, barley, rice, lentils, fenugreek, onions, and sugar cane.

This decline may have been partly offset by the development of fruit and dairy farming, but both those activities still occupy a very minor place in Egyptian agriculture. Hence it is safe to conclude that the general trend is unmistakably downwards, *in spite of the growth in population.*

Table 3. Value of twelve Egyptian crops, 1917-1939.

Year	Value of Crops (Million Pounds Egyptian[1])	Index Adjusted Value[2] (1939 = 100)
1917	112	146
1918	105	112
1919	193	192
1920	104	88
1921	77	78
1922	91	104
1923	98	122
1924	116	144
1925	102	124
1926	76	94
1927	85	110
1928	89	118
1929	77	102
1930	58	78
1931	49	72
1932	44	70
1933	51	80
1934	59	90
1935	61	94
1936	63	98
1937	63	98
1938	58	88
1939	65	100

[1] An Egyptian pound was worth about $5 before the war and is now worth about $4.
[2] Adjusted for change in cost of living.

GROWTH IN INDUSTRIAL PRODUCTION

In the eighteen twenties and thirties, Mohamed Aly made an ambitious, and largely successful, attempt to set up in Egypt industries catering not only to his army and navy but also for civilian uses. Political factors wrecked his plans, however, and the scarcity of local capital and the hostility of Great Britain to the industrialization of Egypt precluded the renewal of any large-scale attempt at industrializing the country.

In the 1920's, however, when political independence gave the Egyptian government more control of its economic affairs, and even more in the thirties, when tariff protection of Egyptian industries became possible, a brisk industrialization took place. By 1937 it was estimated that about 1,000,000 men, women and children were employed in industry—mainly in transportation, public utilities, oil wells, mining and quarrying, and such light industries as textiles, sugar, cigarettes and, of course, the old industries connected with cotton: ginning, pressing, extraction of cottonseed oil, etc.

The Second World War gave a great stimulus to industry; profits were high and output increased rapidly. Table 4 (taken from the ANNUAIRE STATISTIQUE DE POCHE, or STATISTICAL ABSTRACT, of the Egyptian Government for 1946) shows the volume and gross value of the output of some of the leading industries in 1945.

The figures in Table 4 are quite impressive, but they should not be interpreted to mean that industry has caught up with agriculture as a factor in the national economy, or that it is even within sight of catching up with it. For industrial prices in 1945 were even more inflated than agricultural prices. In that year the value of the twelve main crops was 161,130,000 pounds Egyptian, or over three times that of the main industrial goods. And it should not be forgotten that the *net* income produced by agriculture in Egypt is distinctly higher than that produced by industry.

In other words, the growth of industry in Egypt had, up to the outbreak of the Second World War at any rate, *probably not* sufficed to offset the decline in the value of agricultural products due to the fall in their prices.

Table 4. Quantity and value of main industrial goods produced in Egypt in 1945.

	QUANTITY (Thousands of Tons)	VALUE (in Thousands of Pounds Egyptian)
Cotton Piece Goods	37	24,261
Mineral Oils	981	6,092
Cement	444	2,024
Refined Sugar	148	8,477
Cottonseed Oil	74	4,107
Beer	38	3,151
Cottonseed Cakes	297	2,017
Phosphates	349	a

a Value not given in government report.

Consumption

Some confirmation of the preceding statement may be found in the trends of consumption. Table 5 shows indices of consumption of certain staple articles from 1920 to 1939. The figures for tobacco, coffee and tea are taken from official figures; those for sugar and cereals have been computed from figures of production, imports and exports, and can be regarded as reasonably accurate. Textile consumption is not so easy to determine, since the exact production of local handlooms cannot be determined for the years under study. It is probable that the figures given in Table 5 *overstate the decline,* but not to any very great extent. Similarly figures for meat consumption cannot be relied upon too closely, but there is no reason to believe that those shown above distort the trend.

A glance at the table will show that all the consumption figures except tea and sugar show a downward trend. It only remains to add that these figures show *total* consumption and not *per capita* consumption. In view of the increase in population, per capita figures would have registered a much sharper decline.

Table 5. Indices of consumption of specified staple articles in Egypt, 1920–1938. (Average volume of 1920–1937 = 100).

Year	Tobacco	Coffee	Tea	Sugar	Meat	Textiles	Cereals
1920	126	99	39	50	80	—	96
1921	114	107	36	50	97	—	94
1925	111	89	87	106	107	116	105
1926	110	108	76	114	107	88	103
1929	113	109	117	148	102	105	105
1930	103	111	109	130	101	92	104
1931	88	86	138	111	105	79	106
1932	81	86	148	86	101	94	116
1933	77	98	124	99	101	105	89
1934	81	76	145	106	97	101	90
1935	83	91	121	114	94	105	97
1936	86	92	137	117	94	102	97
1937	86	90	143	124	94	107	95
1938	—	—	139	124	97	95	99
1939	—	—	125	—	—	—	101

Moreover, there are good reasons to believe that the same volume of agricultural production could be produced with a rural population of 1,500,000 families, instead of the present figure of over 2,000,000.[15] In view of this evidence, it seems safe to say that, in Egypt, population is pressing harder and harder on the means of subsistence. The present writer would go even further, and affirm categorically that if ever the word "overpopulated" could be applied to a country, that country is Egypt.

SOCIAL AND POLITICAL EFECTS OF POPULATION PRESSURE

The direct economic effect of the population pressure has been to lower the standard of living. Its indirect social and political effects also deserve mention.

With a density of three inhabitants per acre of cultivated land, or about 2,000 per square mile, Egypt is one of the most thickly populated regions in the whole world. This has, in the absence of large-scale industry, created a land hunger which has forced up land values and rents to very high levels indeed. As a result the landowning class is the wealthiest in the country and has played a dominant part in its politics.

Conversely, the poverty of the rural population has limited the expansion of industry and so prevented the emergence of a powerful industrial middle class. It required the stimulus of recent war conditions to develop industry to the point where a new industrialist class could measure itself against the landlords and begin significantly to determine policy.

Another social class whose development has been held up by the pressure of population is the urban working class. For, so far, all attempts to raise the level of this class have been defeated by the large-scale influx from the countryside to the towns, an influx which has naturally depressed wages and increased unemployment.

Finally, it may be said that the population pressure and consequent economic distress have produced a general uneasiness in political life. On one issue it is perhaps possible to be more definite. Egypt's desire to reduce British influence in the Sudan is largely motivated by reasons of national security and by the desire to secure the water supply of the Upper Nile which

[15] *See* Cleland, Wendell: A Population Plan for Egypt in DEMOGRAPHIC STUDIES OF SELECTED AREAS OF RAPID GROWTH. Milbank Memorial Fund, 1946, and Issawi, Charles: *op.cit.* pp. 201–202.

is literally vital to her. It may, partly, be motivated by the hope of sending Egyptian colonists to certain sparsely populated parts of the Sudan, thus reducing the pressure at home. There are, of course, other factors, such as the ethnic, linguistic, and religious ties between Egypt and the Sudan.

COTTON PROSPECTS

Having described the present situation, it becomes necessary to examine the possibilities of ameliorating it. And since Egypt's income is still predominantly derived from agriculture, the prospects of agriculture must first be surveyed.

Although the combined value of the wheat and maize crops was up to 1939 about equal to that of the cotton crop, and is today somewhat greater, cotton is still the most important Egyptian crop, accounting as it does for about 80 per cent of the country's exports. The reduction in Egypt's income between the two World Wars was mainly due to the catastrophic fall in cotton prices, both absolutely and in relation to the prices of Egypt's imported goods. Hence, a reversal of the past trend of cotton prices would mean prosperity for Egypt, while their persistence in a downward direction, or even their stabilization at their present level, would spell poverty.

Cotton prices have risen considerably during the war, from about $10 per cantar for Ashmuni Fully Good Fair in May, 1939, to $37 per cantar in May, 1947, and $65 in May, 1948. This high level of prices may be expected to last for a few years, but there is every reason to fear that after that the price of cotton will once more decline, both absolutely and relative to other goods. For one thing, the war has stimulated production in many places and notably in South America. For another, the production of rayon, nylon, and other fibres which compete with long-staple Egyptian cotton has enormously increased and their costs of production have been considerably reduced. Hence, unless such a high level of production is maintained all over the world as to absorb all fibres, it is unlikely that cotton will enjoy an expanding market and boom prices. Egypt must therefore look for other means of ameliorating its standard of living.

EXPANSION OF CULTIVATED AREA

One partial solution would be to expand the cultivated area by reclaiming new tracts of land. Unfortunately narrow limits to such a process have been set by the configuration of the Nile Valley. The banks of the river rise so steeply that the cost of raising water to all but the immediately adjacent spots is prohibitive. Moreover, any vast extension of cultivated area would require a water supply which the Nile cannot at present provide and which would necessitate irrigation works in Egypt, the Sudan, and Abyssinia—such as dams on Lake Tana and the clearing of the Sudd swamps in the Southern Sudan—estimated to cost hundreds of millions of dollars. Even so, experts believe that the upper limit for cultivation in Egypt is about 7,100,000 feddan as compared with the present figure of 5,700,000.

A certain amount of cultivation has recently been carried on in the Mediterranean fringe of the Western desert. The region undoubtedly offers some possibilities, and much would be learned from American methods of "dry farming" and from the experience of the Italians in Cyrenaica. But the contribution of the Western desert towards solving Egypt's population problem cannot be very great.

Fruit and Dairy Farming

But if the cultivated area cannot be greatly extended, there is no reason why the value of the agricultural production should not be considerably increased by the introduction of new crops, or the extension of others which are at present grown on only a small scale but which are highly profitable. Among these are soya beans, jute, flax, and, above all, fruit and vegetables. Egypt's marvellous weather should make of her the fruit garden of Europe when Europe shall have sufficiently recovered to become once more a great market for such goods. Similarly, dairy products might be developed on a large scale, since Egypt's milk is particularly rich in fats.

Birth Control

Faced with a rapidly expanding population and a much less rapidly expanding income, many Egyptians, as well as some foreign students of Egyptian affairs, have recommended birth control as a means of lightening the population pressure.

Of course birth control involves issues which go well beyond the economic field. Religious and moral, as well as political and social, considerations must be taken into account, and although the Rector of al Azhar, the 1000-year-old Moslem University in Cairo, has issued a declaration permitting the use of contraceptives, it is still to be seen whether the body of religiously minded Moslems will follow his lead. At present, the prevailing social attitudes and customs all favour early marriages and the rearing of large families. Moreover, in an agricultural economy, children become economic assets at an early age since they can be put to work in the cotton, and other, fields.[16]

Some measure of birth control is probably necessary in Egypt, but it must not be looked upon as a short-term, or even medium-term, solution of the population problem. For one thing it takes birth control methods a long time to get diffused, especially in a predominantly rural population like that of Egypt, living at a relatively low economic and cultural level; birth control flourishes mostly in an urban environment offering people many distractions outside their homes. Again it takes at least a generation for birth control to affect appreciably the size of the population. Hence one cannot expect a reduction in the size of the Egyptian population due to birth control for at least another fifty years or so.

EMIGRATION

In the meantime two partial solutions present themselves: emigration and industrialization.

One of the most permanent traits of the Egyptians, throughout the six or seven millenia of their history, has been their reluctance to leave their country. In contrast to the Lebanese, Palestinians, and Southern Arabians (all of whom have a longer commercial tradition and live near the sea), the Egyptians have not emigrated much and the Egyptian communities abroad are few and far between. It will take considerable economic distress to overcome this reluctance, but the process might be considerably eased if the government sponsored and guided the movement, transplanting whole village communities rather than isolated individuals or families. This transfer, naturally, involves considerable expense, and international aid might be required.

The next question that arises is that of the *place* to which Egyptians could migrate. In the past, there was a small movement to Palestine, but that country is today suffering from severe congestion. The natural growth of the Arab population —which has about doubled in thirty years—as well as the in-

[16] For a more detailed account *see* Cleland, *op.cit.*

flux of Jewish immigrants have combined to produce a heavy population pressure.

The same is true of Lebanon, whose population has also doubled in thirty years, and whose density of population is very high. The Arabian Peninsula has always been, of course, a center of emigration, not immigration.

North Syria offers certain possibilities in spite of the rapid growth in the Syrian population, while Iraq could absorb a very large number of immigrants. Moreover, conditions of climate and soil in those two regions are quite similar to those of Egypt, as are the language, customs, and religion of the inhabitants. The Sudan too, if properly developed, might serve as in important outlet for the surplus Egyptian population.

All this of course requires a considerable measure of understanding between the countries concerned, and while there is no doubt that the Arab countries are drawing closer and closer together, it would be premature to affirm that they are at present prepared to take in each other's excess populations.

INDUSTRIALIZATION

There remains, finally, industrialization. As was pointed out above, industry has greatly developed in Egypt during the last fifteen years, especially during the war years. Many of the prerequisite conditions of industrialization are present in Egypt while others are lacking. Thus there are quite a number of minerals, notably cement, manganese, and phosphates. Large deposits of very high grade iron ore have been discovered near Aswan and will doubtless be exploited as soon as cheap hydro-electric power is available. Agricultural raw materials are abundant, such as cotton, leather, sugar cane, fruits, and vegetables, etc. Cheap power can be obtained either from Egypt's expanding oil wells—which at present more than cover domestic requirements of most kinds—or from electricity generated by the falls of the Aswan dam. The Aswan dam hydro-electric scheme, planned to produce a considerable electric power, is now being put into execution, after having been held up by internal and external political difficulties for about a quarter of a century.

Capital is now available in large quantities, since profits were considerable during the war years and large reserves have been built up. Finally, there is no longer any lack of skilled workers, though Egypt still does need the services of foreign technicians.

It is not however sufficient to be able to produce: a country must also be able to dispose of its goods if it is to set up a large industry. There is little doubt that the main obstacle encountered by Egyptian industry is the narrowness of its market. This is due mainly to the poverty of the rural population, who normally should form the main consumers of Egyptian products. This poverty is aggravated by the maldistribution of land and income alluded to at the beginning of this article which restricts the purchasing power of the masses while it allows the richer classes to spend their money on foreign-made goods.

Nor can Egypt hope, for a long time to come, to compensate for the narrowness of her internal market by building up a large export trade, for the competition of the older industrial centres is likely to prove overwhelming. Egyptian industry must market its goods at home and the fact that the present maldistribution of wealth is holding up industrial development has reinforced the urge towards more progressive taxation and an agrarian reform.

Such, then, is Egypt's population problem. The different suggestions indicated above may constitute a solution of that problem, but it is certain that their execution will tax to its utmost limits the energy and intelligence of those responsible for the country's destiny. Egypt is facing a very difficult situation, and she needs all the sympathy and help of the outside world in dealing with it.

NOTES ON THE RATE OF GROWTH

OF THE CHINESE POPULATION *

By A. J. Jaffe

HE population of China today is officially estimated by the Chinese Government as some 450 millions (11, p. 6). Various estimates have been made of the probable historical growth of the population and these have been summarized by Chen (3, p. 5) in the following table:

YEAR	ESTIMATED POPULATION (in thousands)
A. D. 2	59 500
742-56	52 900
1098-1100	43 000
1573-1620	60 600
1933-	400 000

Whether the above really represents the approximately true rate of growth of the Chinese population is difficult to say. We can only be sure that the population sometime in the past—say at the beginning of the Christian Era—must have been considerably smaller than it is at present. Chen makes the point that changes in the size of the population have probably been cyclical, or at least have fluctuated. In favorable years there may have been considerable increases; with the advent of famine, flood, or epidemic diseases, the death rate might have been increased to the point where any population gains of previous years were nullified. Indeed, the figures presented above represent what he calls the peak points of various cycles. "From the beginning of the Christian Era down to the present, 5 cycles have been found in Chinese population, each reaching the highest point as shown in . . . [the table above]."

With reference to present times he believes that the peak of the fifth cycle has perhaps been reached and that actual population decline

* The views expressed here are those of the author and do not necessarily reflect any opinions held by the U. S. Bureau of the Census. The author wishes to thank Mr. Henry J. Dubester of the Census-Library Project of the Library of Congress for his extensive bibliographical assistance.

may be setting in. For the last century or so he thinks that China's population increase has been negligible (see also reference 13).

Chen feels that the fifth cycle should not really be compared with the preceding four cycles. During the earlier periods there was no evidence of a trend in population growth, but simply the cycles around a horizontal line. He says (3, p. 5) :

> "By nature of the population data, the four cycles should be separated from the fifth one, chiefly because the former purported to include only portions of the nation's population and the latter its total. The linking-together of the two series of cycles, as is usually done by the scholars in China and abroad, causes confusion. The very fact that the peaks of the first four cycles fluctuated within a narrow range between 43,000,000 and 60,000,000 in a period longer than sixteen hundred years indicates that, in the past, China's population moved only in a zig-zag fashion, mainly in relation to peace and order; whereas, beginning with the fifth cycle, a different course of events may be shown, since the figures purport to include the total population of the country."

However, he offers no suggestions as to the facts which lead to this remarkable increase of perhaps five-fold during the last 300 years.

DATA AVAILABLE FOR STUDY OF THE PRESENT POPULATION

Altogether twelve "censuses" which have been taken in various parts of China, during the last fifteen years, were found by the writer.[1] These have all been small enumerations and the populations covered range from 20,000 to a maximum of 600,000 persons. Some of these have been complete enumerations of designated areas, and some have been sample studies. Unquestionably they are of variable reliability.

For all of these twelve enumerations the age distributions for both sexes combined are available; for seven of them the distributions by age and sex are available.

Vital statistics were obtained from the volume, *An Experiment in the Registration of Vital Statistics in China* (6), and from the volume by Chen (3).

AGE DISTRIBUTION

In Fig. 1 is presented the age distributions of the various populations in the following intervals: 0 to 14 years, 15 to 34 years, 35 to 54 years, and 55 years of age and over. Instead of drawing a line to represent

---

[1] Although demographic data are available for the Chinese population living in Formosa, it was felt that the experiences of this group are not necessarily similar to those of the peoples living in China proper. The main difference, of course, stems from the fact that Formosa had a politically stable government under the Japanese; this factor of the degree of political stability unquestionably has an important bearing on the demographic problems of the Chinese living in China.

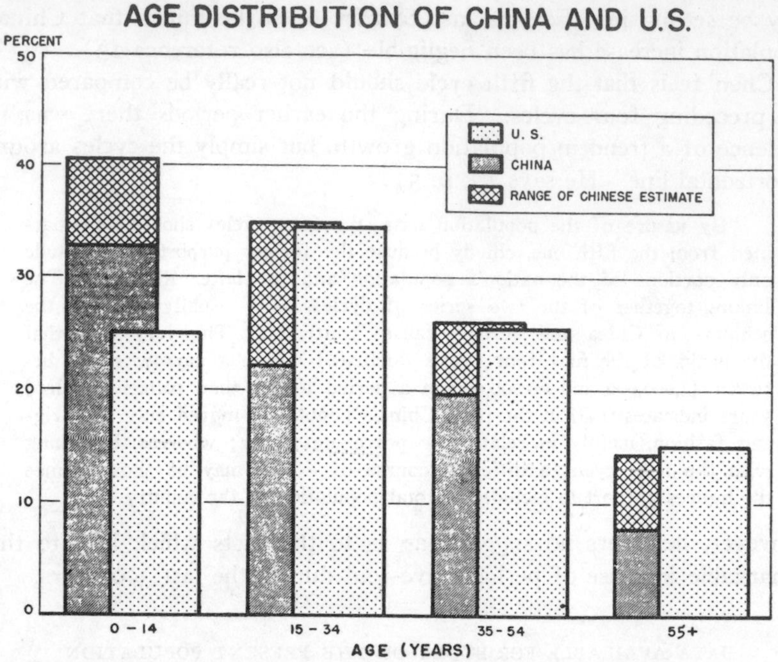

AGE DISTRIBUTION OF CHINA AND U.S.

Fig. 1. Percentage Age Distribution of China and the United States

the percentage for a specific age group, a band has been drawn showing the upper and lower limits as obtained from the different censuses.
Comparison of this distribution with that for the United States leaves
no doubt but that the Chinese population is younger than that of the
United States. No Chinese enumeration produced as low a figure for
the percentage under age 15 as exists in the United States, nor as
high a figure as that of the United States for the population 55 years
of age and over. In the two intermediate age groups the percentages
registered in the United States age distribution are the maximum
reached by any Chinese enumeration (see also Table 1).

This high proportion of young people, of course, suggests a high
birth rate, and accordingly, let us examine the available vital statistics.

PRESENT BIRTH AND DEATH RATES

Various studies have been made of the vital statistics of the nation.
As early as 1902 the International Settlement at Shanghai began an
attempt to collect death statistics. Since then numerous other compilations have been made including the excellent one jointly conducted
by the Scripps Foundation for Research in Population Problems, and
Nanking University.

Chen, in reviewing the reported crude birth rates, lists 17 rates
"as being relatively more reliable." The range of these rates was from

TABLE 1

Percentage age distribution, China

		UNDER 15 YEARS	15 TO 34 YEARS	35 TO 54 YEARS	55 YEARS AND OVER	TOTAL
Kiang Ying	(1932)	40.2	31.2	19.8	8.8	100.0
Chu Yung	(1933)	40.7	31.1	20.6	7.6	100.0
Kiang Ning	(1933)	38.8	30.5	21.7	9.0	100.0
Ting Hsien	(1934)	33.3	30.2	23.9	12.6	100.0
Chang Lu	(1935)	32.7	34.7	23.0	9.6	100.0
Lan Hsi	(1936)	36.3	32.8	21.3	9.6	100.0
Cheng Kung	(1938)	34.8	28.4	24.9	11.9	100.0
Szechwan	(1942)	37.8	22.0	25.9	14.3	100.0
Kunming Lake Region	(1942)	33.7	33.3	23.7	9.3	100.0
North China	(1930)	33.7	32.2	23.2	10.9	100.0
South China	(1930)	36.5	34.2	21.0	8.3	100.0
Nanking	(1939)	34.5	27.8	25.1	12.6	100.0
United States	(1940)	25.0	34.4	25.7	14.9	100.0

Sources: Chen (3), Appendix Table 7, for all but the last three areas of China. Data for North and South China from Chiao (4). Data for Nanking from Bates (1).

a low of 12.2 for Shanghai in 1932 to a high of 58.4 in Yen Shan, Hopei, 1923. On the basis of these various reported rates, Chen (3, p. 29) estimates a national birth rate for China of 38 per 1,000 population.

In the opinion of the writer a rate of 38 is probably too low. As far as can be learned from studying the various age distributions available, 38 would appear to be a minimum rather than average figure. The crude birth rates as estimated from these age data range from a low of about 36 to a high of perhaps over 50.[2]

With regard to deaths, Chen reports rates for 17 areas which are "comparatively more reasonable." These range from a low of 13 per 1,000 population in Tsing Yuan, Shansi in 1926-1928, to a high of 37.1 in Yen Shan, Hopei in 1923. On the basis of these, Chen (3, p. 32) estimated the national death rate as 33 (1934).

---

[2] The minimum crude birth rate as estimated from the age distribution for Chang Lu in Hopei is 26 per 1,000 population. Chen, in commenting on the census of Chang Lu, suggests that this enumeration may have been rather deficient. "This census seems to have been taken on the basis of the *de jure* population, but its definition was not strictly adhered to; hence there was a good deal of confusion regarding the total population of the *hsien*." The next lowest birth rate was observed in Ting Hsien, in Hopei province, a birth rate of 36 per 1,000 population (see Table 2).

TABLE 2
Estimated vital rates, China*

		ASSUMING MORTALITY SCHEDULES OF:		
		CHINESE LIFE TABLE	INDIAN LIFE TABLE 1921-30	INDIAN LIFE TABLE 1901-10
Gross reproduction rates				
Hsiao Chi, Kiangyin	(21,864)	2.78	2.97	3.20
North China		2.35	2.52	2.72
South China		2.40	2.57	2.77
Szechwan				
Penghsien Hsien	(368,868)	3.46	3.71	4.00
Shwanglin Hsien	(152,458)	3.19	3.41	3.68
Chungning Hsien	(94,331)	3.14	3.36	3.63
Ting Hsien		2.58	2.76	2.97
Nanking		1.93	2.07	2.22
Cheng Kung		2.67	2.86	3.08
Net reproduction rates				
Hsiao Chi, Kiangyin		1.34	1.28	1.19
North China		1.14	1.09	1.01
South China		1.16	1.11	1.03
Szechwan				
Penghsien Hsien		1.68	1.60	1.49
Shwanglin Hsien		1.54	1.47	1.37
Chungning Hsien		1.52	1.45	1.35
Ting Hsien		1.25	1.19	1.10
Nanking		.94	.89	.83
Cheng Kung		1.29	1.24	1.15
Crude birth rates (as estimated from the age composition)				
Nanking	(7,161)	28	30	33
North China	(28,740)	37	40	43
South China	(36,644)	37	40	43
Szechwan	(619,471)	39	42	45
Ting Hsien	(439,259)	36	39	42
Kiang Ying	(21,864)	45	48	52
Chu Yung	(279,455)	44	47	51
King Ning	(562,063)	39	42	45
Chang Lu	(227,801)	26	28	30
Lan Hsi	(276,468)	40	43	46
Cheng Kung	(71,223)	38	41	44
Kunming Lake Region	(507,216)	38	41	44

Sources: Hsiao Chi, Chiao, Thompson, and Chen (6) ; North and South
China, Chiao (4) ; Szechwan, *Statistical Abstract of the Republic
of China,* 1945 (11) ; Ting Hsien, Lee (8) ; Nanking, Bates (1) ;
all other areas, Chen (3).

* See footnote next page.

How accurate these estimates are is difficult to say. The one thought which appears pertinent is that most likely both the birth and death rates reported above refer to relatively peaceful time periods. During the periods of catastrophe—flood, famine, disease, war—the death rate obviously would increase considerably, and the birth rate would probably fall. Hence, the death rate, if calculated over a long period of time so as to include the proper proportion of droughts, floods, and epidemics, would undoubtedly be higher than the average of 33 estimated by Chen. Incidentally it is claimed that China has had an average of 49 droughts somewhere within its boundaries every 100 years, and an average of 48 floods every 100 years. In addition, epidemics may break out on an average of every 5 years. Thus, it would appear that some catastrophe hits some part of the country every year on the average (3, p. 37).

The crude rate of natural increase, according to Chen's calculations, should thus be some 5 per 1,000 population per year—in relatively peaceful times.

GROSS AND NET REPRODUCTION RATES

Obviously any figure purporting to represent all of China is an estimate whose degree of reliability is probably open to serious question. Accordingly, the attempt was made here to analyze the various available age distributions in an effort to determine the likely range within which the "true" figure for China may lie. Since the number of births of necessity must be estimated from the reported number of young children, two methodological questions are immediately raised: (a) what, if any, is the degree of underenumeration of these children, and (b) what survivorship rates should be used in converting the reported number of children into numbers of live births.

For the moment let us table the first question and discuss the latter. In attempting to convert the reported numbers under 5 years of age into numbers of live births, three life table values were used: (a) that for China as reported by Seifert (10), (b) India, 1921-1930, and (c) India, 1901-1910. The female life expectancies as shown by these three life tables are respectively 34.63, 26.56, and 23.31.

As mentioned previously, distributions by age and sex were available for seven areas in China; one of these presented data for its three

---

* None of these rates have been corrected for the probable underreporting of children under 5 years of age. Further, information was not available bearing on the point as to whether the concept of age as utilized in these Chinese enumerations was similar to that used in the western world. Since some of the age distributions designated an age of "under 1 year" it is assumed that the concept of age for census purposes, was intended to be similar to that in the western world.

component counties, making a total of nine age and sex distributions actually available.

If it is assumed that the Chinese life table with a life expectancy of about 35 years is applicable, then the computed net reproduction rates range from a low of 1.14 in the sample of localities in North China to a high of 1.68 in Penghsien. Use of the Indian life table of 1921-30, with a life expectancy of about 27 years, produces a range from 1.09 to 1.60, and the earlier Indian life table, from 1.01 to 1.49. In other words, the minimum net reproduction rate is unity. The only exception is the city of Nanking which seems to have a rate of below unity.

Turning to the gross reproduction rate, a range from a low of 2.35 to a maximum of 4.00 is noted, again depending in part on the life tables used in converting the number of children under 5 years of age into the number of live births (see Table 2).

Census enumerations all over the world have invariably failed to include all the children under 5 years of age. Accordingly, it appears likely that the reported numbers of children in these various Chinese censuses also are below the true number. Both the gross and net reproduction rates, should be increased—perhaps by as much as 10 per cent. With such a correction the minimum observed net reproduction rate then becomes around 1.10.

In summary then, the following can be noted:

(a) Given reasonably normal and peaceful conditions—i.e., with a death rate of between 30 and 40 per 1,000 population—the Chinese population perhaps will grow at the rate of at least 10 per cent per generation.

(b) What the actual rate of growth has been in the past has been largely determined by the death rate. Presumably population changes have fluctuated widely and have been cyclical rather than following any particular trend.

(c) The birth rate is actually so high that any diminution in the death rate would immediately mean a vast population increase. For example, if the minimum observed gross reproduction rate of 2.35 is converted into a net reproduction rate on the basis of a life table having an expectancy of 41 years, (such as is found among the non-white population in the Union of South Africa—1935 to 1937), a net rate of 1.32 is obtained; in other words the population would increase by one-third in a generation.

CONCLUSIONS

The factors repeatedly found to be associated with high fertility throughout the world, are also found in China—namely, an agricultural population, very poor, and highly illiterate. One factor in the Chinese scene which is not so universally found, is the high proportion of the adult population which is married. Data from five censuses reveal a minimum of 70 per cent of the females (15 years of age and over) married, to a maximum of 93 per cent. Even the minimum figure is well above that for the United States. Similarly, larger proportions of the adult males are married. In addition, age at marriage—particularly for the girls—is generally younger in China than in the United States.

Is it possible for the Chinese population to increase? At present there appears to be between ½ and ¾ acre of cultivated land per person as compared with 3 acres per person in the United States. These figures in themselves reveal the "pressure on the land." In addition, China, unlike the United States, has neither great manufacturing industries nor widespread commercial activities to help support the masses. Some Chinese economists think that the amount of cultivated land and agricultural production eventually can be materially increased.[3] If the people should remain satisfied with their present plane of living, then the population can increase in the same proportion as agricultural production; if the population is kept at its present level, then the plane of living can increase as more land is brought under cultivation, and productivity increased.

In the past the attitudes of the people toward population growth apparently were expressed by the following statement (3, p. 72) attributed to Confucius, "To die without offspring is one of the three gravest unfilial acts." Even the thought of limiting population growth was not to be condoned.[4]

---

[3] That increases in the amount of cultivated land and agricultural productivity are possible is suggested by the progress already claimed. The National Conservation Commission, through its establishment of irrigation works, claims to have extended already "the land area for cultivation." In addition it is claimed (11, p. 12) that "since the government started to enforce the policy of promoting agricultural production, area and production of crops have had steady increase in . . . 15 provinces."

Buck suggests that "a well organized program administered by properly qualified technical experts, with international experience and knowledge in the subject matter of each problem will enable China rapidly to improve her agriculture, to raise the standard of living of her farmers, and to enhance the well being of the nation as a whole." A series of 16 points are suggested to implement this program (2, pp. 21-22).

[4] This is not to say that voluntary means of population control have never been practiced in China. Infanticide, abortion, and eunuchism, apparently were, in the past, and perhaps now, are being practiced to some extent. In addition, various contraceptive recipes have been utilized, although it is not known to what extent nor how effectively. Modern birth control methods have begun to make their appearance in China, as witnessed by the opening of clinics in Shanghai and Peiping, and the sale of contraceptives in the modern drug stores. (See Norman E. Himes, *Medical History of Contraception*, The Williams and Wilkins Co., Baltimore, 1936, pp. 105-113).

Today, by contrast, there is a Committee for the Study of Population Policies which has deviated considerably in its thinking from the time honored customs of the past. With reference to the quantity of population this committee concluded (3, p. 76):

"Facing poverty, ignorance, and the low living standards of the masses, the country should not and cannot encourage unconditional and universal increase of population. Increase should occur only where the individuals, as parents, are physically fit and mentally sound, where the families are able to give the children proper care and training, and where the social surroundings are favorable. The parents, after careful consideration of the interest of the family and of the community, may decide for themselves as to the proper number of children they should bring up. In addition, the number of children may also vary with the skill and income of the parents, as well as with the folkways and social wealth of the community. Thus viewed, some individuals may have children, others not; some communities may have population increase, others not. A differential rate of increase will, therefore, have to be worked out between individuals, classes, and communities in the interests of all the parties concerned."

Perhaps the attitudes of the masses are slowly changing in the direction of lowered birth rates and lessened desire for population increase. Such changed attitudes accompanied by political stability, land reform measures, and the growth of manufacturing activity will permit China to realize her potentialities.

REFERENCES

1. BATES, M. S. The Nanking Population, Employment, Earnings, and Expenditures. (Survey conducted on behalf of the Nanking International Relief Committee, Winter-Spring, 1939.)

2. BUCK, J. L. Land Utilization in China. University of Chicago Press, *Chicago*, 1937.

3. CHEN, TA. Population in Modern China. University of Chicago Press, *Chicago*, 1946.

4. CHIAO, C. M. Rural population and vital statistics for selected areas of China, 1929-31. *Chinese Economic Journal*, Vol. XIV, Nos. 3 and 4. (Survey of 22 localities in 11 provinces.)

5. ————. A study of the Chinese population. *Milbank Memorial Fund Quarterly Bulletin*, Vol. 11, pp. 325 ff., 1933. Vol. 12, pp. 85-96, and 171-183, 1934.

6. ————, W. S. THOMPSON and D. T. CHEN. An Experiment in the Registration of Vital Statistics in China (*Oxford, Ohio:* Scripps Foundation for Research in Population Problems, 1938.)

7. LEE, FRANKLIN C. H. An analysis of Chinese rural population. *Chinese Social and Political Science Review*, Vol. 19, pp. 22 ff., 1935-36. (House-to-house census in Ting Hsien Experiment Area by the Social Survey Department of the Chinese National Association of the Mass Education Movement: 1930.)

8. ————. Problems of technique as revealed in population census of Ting Hsien. *Social Science Quarterly* (Tsing Hua University), Vol. II, No. 3, April, 1937. (Available at Orientalia, Library of Congress.) (In Chinese.)

9. NOTESTEIN, FRANK W. and CHI-MING CHIAO. "Population," Chapter XIII, in J. L. BUCK, Land Utilization in China.

10. SEIFERT, HARRY E. Life tables for Chinese farmers. *Milbank Memorial Fund Quarterly*, Vol. 13, No. 3. pp. 223-236, July, 1935.

11. STATISTICAL ABSTRACT OF THE REPUBLIC OF CHINA, 1945. Directorate of Statistics, National Government, *Chungking, China.*

12. THOMPSON, WARREN S. Population prospects for China and Southeastern Asia. *Annals,* Vol. 237, pp. 72-79, Jan. 1945.

13. WILLCOX, WALTER F. The Population of China and Its Modern Increase. *Studies in American Demography,* Cornell University Press, *Ithaca, N. Y.,* 1940.

THE POPULATION OF COMMUNIST

CHINA: 1953

By the United States Bureau of the Census

(Population and related statistics shown in this report for the China mainland are from the 1953 Chinese Communist census, as released by the Communist New China News Agency, or are derived from official statements on the general election recently held by the Chinese Communists. In bringing these figures together and issuing them at this time, the Bureau of the Census takes no position as to their accuracy. Only summary figures have been available so far, and the data issued are insufficient to make any of the usual tests which are necessary to appraise such reports.)

Total population. -- The population of the China mainland has been announced by the Chinese Communists as 582,603,417 on June 30, 1953. Even if the population of China were considerably short of this number, China would be by far the most populous country in the world. This population of China is about 1.6 times that of India, which, as the second most populous country in the world, has more than 360 million persons. It is 2.8 times that of the Soviet Union, which has about 210 million persons, and 3.6 times that of the United States, which has roughly 160 million persons. China, according to the figure announced, has somewhat more than one-fifth of the world's population, currently estimated at about 2-1/2 billion.

Estimates of the population of China have varied considerably. The Chinese Communist regime, prior to the release of the 1953 census data, generally cited the population of China as 475 or 500 million. In 1947, the Chinese Nationalist Government announced the population of China as 456 million, including 6.3 million persons on Taiwan. This population figure, which was described as taken from a "relatively accurate, official census," was actually an estimate of the population and did not include the population in a number of areas in which the Chinese Nationalists has lost control in the civil strife with the Chinese Communists. In the People's Handbook for 1952 the estimated population (including Taiwan) is given as 486.6 million, or about 100 million less than the 1953 figure of the Chinese Communists. If the figure of 582.6 million for 1953 is correct, estimates for earlier periods obviously require a major upward revision.

The census.-- The Chinese Communists claim a remarkably high degree of accuracy for their census. A sample check of nearly 53 million persons--about 9 per cent of the population--reportedly showed that duplications in the census were at a rate of only 1.39

per 1,000 persons and that omissions were at a rate of only 2.55 per 1,000 persons. This check covered only that part--574.2 million out of 582.6 million--of the population "directly surveyed." In some areas the Chinese Communists found it impractical to take a census but relied instead upon reports from local governments. As already indicated, the population counted in this manner was relatively small--8.4 million of the total of 582.6 million.

The meaning of "directly surveyed" is not completely clear. The census regulations required that the head of each household report to a local station established to investigate and register the population for purposes of both the census and the general election. A house-to-house survey was provided for "wherever necessary." These procedures would seem to indicate that the population "directly surveyed" was counted principally by heads of households reporting to the offices established by the census and election officials.

Population growth. -- The population of China is currently increasing at a rate of 2 percent a year, according to the Chinese Communists. This rate of natural increase is based on birth and death rates which derive from a reported survey of over 30 million persons. This survey reportedly showed births at a rate of 37 per 1,000 population, and deaths at a rate of 17 per 1,000 population. The Chinese Communists have not revealed the nature of the survey from which these vital rates were derived. Considering the enormous task that would be involved in actually interviewing several million households on this point, as would be necessary in a survey of 30,000,000 persons, it seems likely that these vital rates derive from a sampling of census returns or of registration statistics, the accuracy of which are highly suspect.

Age distribution. -- Age information thus far released from the 1953 census by the Chinese Communists permits showing the distribution of the population of the China mainland among only three broad age groups. China, as the following table on age distribution reveals, had much larger proportions of its population in the younger ages than the United States had at the same date:

Age (at last birthday)	Mainland China, 1953	United States, 1953
Total.	100.0	100.0
Under 4 years	15.6	8.7
4 to 17 years	25.5	23.9
18 years and over............	58.9	67.4

Sex composition. -- The 1953 census reports that on the China mainland there were more men than women, men outnumbering women by 107.5 to 100. This situation contrasts sharply with that

in the United States, where there were only 98.9 males per 100
females. The sex ratio cited for China derives from the population "directly surveyed." Of 574.2 million persons, 297.6 million
were males and 276.6 million were females. On a percentage
basis, males constituted 51.8 percent of the total and females,
48.2 percent. Similar information is not available for administrative divisions within China.

Ethnic composition.-- The Chinese Communists describe
China as a "unified, multi-national state" in which "all national-
ities are equal." The major national group is the Han race, the
members of which, according to the census, comprise about 94
percent of the population on the China mainland. The 6 percent
of the population--about 35 million--designated as "national
minorities" is distributed among many groups. Census data have
been released for the 10 largest groups--those of one million or
more population--but not for other minority groups. The number
of other groups is probably around 50, according to notices in the
Chinese Communist press, and these comprise 6.7 million persons.
The Chinese Communists have not listed the criteria used in the
census in the determination of national minorities. Some authorities question whether any considerable number of distinct national
minorities can be distinguished in China today. The distribution
of national minorities on June 30, 1953, was reported as follows:

National minority	Number	National minority	Number
Total ...	35,320,360	Miao	2,511,339
		Manchu	2,418,931
Chuang	6,611,455	Mongolian	1,462,956
Uigur	3,640,125	Puyi	1,247,883
Hui	3,559,350	Korean........	1,120,405
Yi	3,254,269	Other	6,718,025
Tibetan	2,775,622		

Rural-urban distribution.-- The population of the China mainland, classified as rural by the Chinese Communists, numbered
505,346,135 on June 30, 1953. The Chinese Communists have not
released a definition of rural--or of urban--population.

Urban population in China reportedly totals 77,257,282. Thus,
though the absolute size of the urban population is large, it constitutes only 13.3 per cent of the total. The three largest cities in
China, the census reports, are Shanghai, 6,204,417; Peiping,
2,768,149; and Tientsin, 2,693,831. The Chinese Communists
have not released population totals for other major cities, but
information available from releases on the election of deputies to
the recent National People's Congress and from other sources makes
it possible to estimate the population of 21 other cities of 500,000
or more population as of June 30, 1953:

City	Population[1]	City	Population[1]
Total	31,666,000	Sian	800,000
		Chang-ch'un	800,000
Shanghai	6,204,000	Cheng-tu.........	800,000
Peiping......	2,768,000	Tsinan	700,000
Tientsin.....	2,694,000	Tangshan........	700,000
Mukden	2,300,000	T'ai-yüan	700,000
Canton	1,600,000	Fu-shun.........	700,000
Chungking...	1,600,000	Hang-chow	700,000
Wuhan......	1,400,000	An-shan.........	600,000
Harbin	1,200,000	Pen-ch'i.........	500,000
Port-Arthur --		K'un-ming	500,000
Dairen.....	1,200,000	Chang-sha.......	500,000
Nanking.....	1,200,000	Wusih..........	500,000
Tsingtao	1,000,000		

[1]Figures for Shanghai, Peiping, and Tientsin are from the 1953 census, rounded to the nearest thousand; figures for all other cities have been estimated by the Bureau of the Census.

A detailed note on the method of estimating the population of the cities listed in the above table will be found in the last section of this report.

Distribution by province.-- The distribution of population among the major administrative divisions is shown in the table below. Provinces have been listed according to the Chinese Communist grouping by regions, though the Chinese Communists are moving away from regional administration, as is evidenced by the abolition. recently of the Northeast, Northwest, North China and Central-South regional administrations. The boundaries of a number of provinces are known to have been altered by the Communists. In the Northeast, for example, the boundaries of five provinces were redrawn, the changes resulting in the consolidation of the five provinces into three. The exact boundaries of provinces are not known.

Method of estimating population of cities of 500,000 or more. --Estimates of the population of An-shan, Fu-shun, Mukden, Pen-ch'i, Port-Arthur--Diaren, Chang-ch'un, and Harbin in the Northeast provinces (Manchuria) and of Canton, Chungking, Sian, and Wuhan are based directly on the reported number of deputies elected by each city to the National People's Congress at the rate of one deputy for each 100,000 population. If the Chinese Communists followed their announced procedure, the estimates for each of the foregoing 11 cities should not vary by not more than 50,000 from the census figure. The method of estimating the population of cities on the basis of the number of elected deputies was applied in the instance of Shanghai, Peiping, and Tientsin and was found to yield estimates fairly close to the reported census figures

POPULATION OF COMMUNIST CHINA, BY MAJOR ADMINISTRATIVE AREAS: JUNE 30, 1953

Area	Population	Area	Population
Total	[1] 582,603,417		
PROVINCES		**PROVINCES -- Con.**	
		Central-South, total ...	176,334,987
		Honan	44,214,594
Northeast, total...	46,893,351	Hunan	33,226,954
Heilungkiang ...	11,897,309	Hupeh	27,789,693
Jehol	5,160,822	Kiangsi	16,772,865
Kirin	11,290,073	Kwangsi	19,560,822
Liaoning	18,545,147	Kwangtung	34,770,059
North, total	50,299,129	Southwest, total ...	98,195,110
Hopei	35,984,644	Kweichow	15,037,310
Shansi	14,314,485	Sikang	3,381,064
		Szechwan	62,303,999
Northwest, total ...	35,359,525	Yunnan	17,472,737
Kansu	12,928,102		
Shensi	15,881,281	**INDEPENDENT CITIES**	
Sinkiang	4,873,608		
Tsinghai	1,676,534	Peiping	2,768,149
		Shanghai	6,204,417
East, total	156,480,845	Tientsin.......	2,693,831
Anhwei	30,343,637		
Chekiang	22,865,747	**OTHER AREAS**	
Fukien	13,142,721		
Kiangsu	41,252,192	Inner Mongolian Autonomous Region .	6,100,104
Shangtung	48,876,548	Tibet and Changtu Area ...	1,273,969

[1]The Chinese Communists claim a total population of 601,938,035, but this total includes 7,591,298 persons on Formosa, which is held by the Government of the Republic of China, and 11,743,320 Chinese living throughout the world, principally in the countries of Southeast Asia.

for these three cities. This result suggests the validity of the method followed, but there is no way of ascertaining the accuracy of the estimates for other cities.

Estimates of population for Cheng-tu, Tangshan, T'ai-yuan, Tsingtao, Tsinan, Nanking, Wusib, Hang-chow, Chang-sha, and K'un-ming are based primarily on information as to the number of deputies elected to the National People's Congress. The number of deputies elected by each of these 10 cities was on the same basis as that for the 11 cities listed above -- that is, one deputy for each 100,000 population. The number of deputies elected by each of the 10 cities just named was not reported separately, however, but was included with the number of deputies reported for the respective provinces in which the cities are located. Each city is known, however, to have elected not less than 5 deputies because these cities had special representation by virtue of the fact that they are industrial cities of 500,000 or more population. Given the total number of deputies reported for each province and the population of each province, it was possible, in a number of instances, to reconstruct the probable distribution of deputies between the industrial city and the rest of the province, using the total population of the privince as a check. To illustrate, a total of 24 deputies was reported for Shansi Province. This province, in which the industrial city of T'ai-yüan is located, has a total population of 14.3 million, according to the 1953 census. If T'ai-yüan had no more than 500,000 population, it would have had but 5 deputies and the rest of the province would have had 19 deputies. Provinces, excluding the industrial cities, elected deputies to the National People's Congress on the basis of one deputy for each 800,000 persons. Thus, in the example cited, the distribution of 24 deputies on the basis of 5 to the city and 19 to the privince would indicate a total population for city and province of 15.7 million (5 times 100,000 plus 19 times 800,000) instead of the 14.3 million population reported. If, however, the distribution of deputies was 7 and 17, then a population of 14.3 million, as reported by the census, is indicated, and thereby suggests that this was the likely distribution and that the population of T'ai-yüan was of the order of 700,000. A slightly different procedure was used for estimating the population of Nanking, Tsingtao, Tsinan, and Wusih. In the instance of K'un-ming, reportedly an industrial city of at least 500,000 population, a special problem was encountered. The population of Yunnan Province, including K'un-ming, was reported by the census as 17.5 million. This figure far exceeds the imputed population--based on deputy data-- of 10.9 million. Inasmuch as the imputed and reported populations could not be reconciled, a minimum figure of 500,000 has been assigned to K'un-ming.

POPULATION INCREASE AND MANPOWER

UTILIZATION IN IMPERIAL JAPAN

By Irene B. Taeuber

T HREE centuries ago the population problems of Asian lands were relatively simple. Asia then included only one-third the number of people who now secure a limited subsistence from its crowded rice lands, its dry plains and its eroded hills. As elements of the culture of the West expanded eastward, the stability and order of centralized governments and controlled economies replaced the civil strife and the hazardous inefficiencies of self-sufficient groupings. Export crops were introduced, subsistence increased and the force of epidemics limited. Mortality declined, but as the life in the peasant villages proceeded in the routine of the centuries the number of children born was not decreased proportionately. The population increase thus generated was long accepted as evidence of the beneficent influence of imported governments and technologies in the East.

As numbers became super-abundant, governments sought solutions through extending irrigation projects, improving agricultural techniques and redistributing people. There was a general lack of awareness of the elementary fact that population cannot increase indefinitely within a finite area, no matter how expansible the resources. It was more comfortable to evade than to wrestle with the fundemental contradictions of an expanding technological culture whose ultimate welfare problems increased in approximate ratio to its economic efficiency and its humanitarianism. Yet analysis of the historical developments in area after area reveals these contradictions. Order, economic development and medical technologies permitted the decline of death rates, while ancient ways of living and thinking among the peasants insured that birth rates remain at or near the levels that had been essential to biological and cultural survival in earlier centuries.

Technical assistance and economic development for the countries of Asia are today discussed as international responsibilities. Their justification is phrased in terms of political, economic, and humanitarian goals that together constitute a rational good for both recipient and donor nations. There are critical differences between this contemporary movement and those that preceded it under imperial auspices, but the basic similarities are sufficient to raise serious questions concerning the demographic consequences. Many students of the East, and probably most demographers, suspect that the major consequence of socially unplanned economic action may be the maintenance of additional people within an all-pervasive poverty. Other students, more immersed in scientific and technical pursuits, see today's potentialities for human subsistence so expansible as to make the problem of man's numbers in the foreseeable future one requiring only minor adjustments. Hence it becomes essential to search within the experience of the past, and particularly that of Asia, for experience that will permit analysis of the demographic consequences of economic development. The classic historical experiment is Imperial Japan, for here industrialization proceeded within an Eastern culture that remained sovereign at the same time that it extended its area of political hegemony and economic utilization to include other Asian peoples.

GENERAL PARALLELS—JAPAN AND THE WEST

The processes of population increase, distribution, and manpower utilization in an industrializing Japan were similar to those that occurred earlier in the countries of the West. In premodern Japan some thirty million people secured a precarious subsistence from the limited land. Deficiencies in the quantity and quality of the food available for local consumption combined with the general ignorance of medical and sanitary practices to make peasant and urban dwellers alike vulnerable to the disorganization and the physical destruction of typhoon, flood, and fire. Famine and epidemic were so common as to be noted in the chronicles only when they became devastating forces of extinction over wide regions. People and culture survived only because the attitudes, the values, and the taboos of family, community and state were compulsive forces channel-

ing the lives of women into early marriage and frequent childbearing.[2]

The opening to the West, and particularly the power-oriented
state that followed the Meiji Restoration, brought an expanded
and more intensive agriculture and an accelerating industrialization that provided employment opportunities for the youth
of the countryside and moved a once-peasant people cityward.
Mortality declined even during the early decades of modernization. Fertility changed more slowly, for the resistances of an
ancient and integrated rural culture were buttressed by the
resources of a state whose preeminent goal involved the creation
of political and economic power within an oligarchic social
structure. The forces generated by the industrialization process
were more compulsive than those that had evolved in the agrarian world of the past, though, for even the conservative forces
of a society continuous for millenia could not achieve that seg-
mentation of culture and personality implicit in the co-existence
of a changing economy and a stable social system. It was impossible to base the industrialization essential to power on an
illiterate peasantry. And a former peasantry, educated, concentrated in cities, subject to the pressures of a pecuniary economy and exposed to the potentialities of that economy for material advancement and psychological liberation, could but
question if it did not evade the obligation of abundant parenthood.

The first three quarters of a century of controlled modernization produced appreciable declines in death and birth rates.
By the 'thirties fertility was falling more rapidly than mortality. Mechanical projection was tempting and many "predictions" were made. Although they varied in the complexity of
their mathematics, all assumed continued declines in fertility
and mortality, without explicit consideration of the social and

[2] This is not to deny the existence of abortion and infanticide as folk techniques
of population control in premodern Japan. The critical question is not their existence
but the extent of their practise throughout the population and the magnitude of
their impact on the number of live births allowed to survive the process of birth and
hence become subject to the very high rates of mortality that existed in the Japan of
that period. The analysis of the hazards implicit in day-to-day living and the recorded losses from famines, epidemics, and the cataclysms of nature indicate that
death rates must have fluctuated irregularly on a very high level. Hence the existence of a relatively unchanging total population in the eighteenth and early
nineteenth centuries would have necessitated a birth rate that, for the country as
a whole and over substantial periods of time, equalled the death rate. The fact that
Japan's population was not declining precipitantly throughout the last century and
a quarter of the feudal period means that the contemporary reports of the frequency
of infanticide must be gross exaggeration if applied to the country as a whole.

economic developments required for the achievement and support of the numbers forecast. The majority of these estimates indicated that the population would increase to some 90 millions by 1960 and reach a maximum of perhaps 100 to 115 millions near or after the end of the century. Eventually the people of an industrialized Japan, as those of an industrialized West, would cease to increase. Moreover, as contrasted with the West, the period of transition would be shortened and the multiplier would be less. Japan would take only a quarter of a century to approach the new stability of low birth and death rates, and population increase would be only three or four-fold. This, it should be noted, is the optimistic picture of the decade before World War II.

If we examine the transformations in the geographical distribution and the internal structure of the population, the situation in Japan is again comparable to that in the West. The proportion of the population that was rural declined with relative consistency from 1872 to 1940; the *number* of people in the rural areas changed little between 1872 and 1930, and declined thereafter. Cities and non-agricultural employment absorbed their own natural increase and the major portion of that of the rural areas beyond maintenance requirements. Youth left agriculture and the rural areas, adjusted early to the relatively greater economic opportunities and the freer social atmosphere of the cities, founded their own families at considerably later ages than would have occurred in the ancestral villages, and limited the numbers of their children to correspond more nearly to the realities of a pecuniary economy. Declining fertility and hence the solution to the problems of growth created by modernization appeared to inhere in urbanization, itself an essential correlate of industrialization. Residential and occupational movement away from the peasant village and its agrarian activities was the overt manifestation of the cultural and psychological transformation that signalized the "Westernization" of the Japanese and their escape from the economic difficulties of increasing numbers.

Japanese experience demonstrates that the population growth which accompanies industralization is time-limited in the East as in the West. It is essential to note, however, that in Japan, a unique combination of political, economic, and social factors facilitated industrialization, urbanization, declining mortality, and declining fertility. Even under these particular circumstances, generally more favorable than those that now exist elsewhere in Asia, the modernization process involved a population increase of more than two and one-half times within its first century. The sheer magnitude of the numbers involved is significant if Japan is regarded as a laboratory experiment in what might happen elsewhere—and the problem of how Japan utilized those increasing numbers is just as relevant a part of her demographic history as is the description of how changing fertility and mortality generated the numbers.

There is a further barrier to the generalization of Japanese experience as a basis for assessing probable occurrences in other modernizing Asian areas, and it is a formidable one. Japan achieved her economic-demographic transition through the intermediation of an imperial system that utilized the products of other regions of Asia without contributing proportionately to the modernization of the subject peoples. The process of capital formation itself involved the assertion of the supremacy of the state over the welfare of the individuals. Thus, whether considered in relation to the people of Japan or to those of the conquered areas, the "success" of Japan's solution to the demographic problems of modernization is not a sufficient answer to the question of its relevance to planning for the future in other areas. Democratic peoples might hesitate to offer or to accept economic assistance if the demographic hazards of the future could be averted only by political, economic, and welfare actions inconsistent with the democratic process. Hence it becomes essential to examine the demographic development of modern Japan in somewhat more detail, with emphasis on the magnitude of the population expansion, its relationship to economic expansion and the urbanization process, and the interconnections of demographic and economic transformations as manifest in changing patterns of manpower utilization with political expansionism and war.

DEMOGRAPHIC EXPANSION

The people of Japan numbered 30 million in the middle of the nineteenth century, 35 million at the time of the Meiji Restoration. In 1920 there were 56 million people. In 1940 there were 73 million. (Table 1). Increase of this order of magnitude is difficult to comprehend. The increase of 17 million in two

AREA	1920	1925	1930	1935	1940[e]
	POPULATION (IN THOUSANDS)				
The Empire	77,729	84,279	91,421	98,934	105,226
Japan Proper	55,963	59,737	64,450	69,254	73,114
Outlying Areas	21,766	24,542	26,971	29,680	32,112
Korea[a]	17,264	19,523	21,058	22,899	24,326
Taiwan	3,655	3,993	4,593	5,212	5,872
Karafuto	106	204	295	332	415
Kwantung[b]	688	766	956	1,134	1,367
South Seas[c]	52	56	70	103	131
	AMOUNT OF INCREASE				
The Empire		6,550	7,142	7,513	6,292
Japan Proper		3,774	4,713	4,804	3,860
Outlying Areas		2,776[d]	2,429	2,709	2,432
Korea[a]		2,259[d]	1,535	1,841	1,427
Taiwan		338	599	620	660
Karafuto		98	91	37	83
Kwantung[b]		78	190	178	233
South Seas[c]		4	13	33	29
	PER CENT INCREASE				
The Empire		8.4	8.5	8.2	6.4
Japan Proper		6.7	7.9	7.5	5.6
Outlying Areas		11.3[d]	9.0	9.1	7.6
Korea[a]		13.1[d]	7.9	8.7	6.2
Taiwan		9.2	15.0	13.5	12.7
Karafuto		92.4	44.9	12.5	25.0
Kwantung[b]		11.8	24.8	18.7	20.6
South Seas[c]		7.8	23.7	47.3	27.9

Table 1. Demographic expansion of the Japanese Empire, 1920–1940.[*]
(Total population of each area.)

[*] Kōjima, Reikichi. *Waga kuni saikin no fuken oyobi toshi jinkō, Shōwa jugō-nen Kokusei chōsa no kekka ni yoru.* (The population of the prefectures and cities of Japan in most recent times.) Toshi mondai pamfuretto (Municipal Problems Pamphlet), No. 41. Tokyo, 1941. 35 pp. Translation by Edwin G. Beal, Jr., in *Far Eastern Quarterly* 3(4) : 313–362. Aug. 1944.

[a] A "special survey" rather than a census was taken in Korea in 1920.

[b] The Kwantung Leased Territory alone is included in this compilation. The South Manchuria Railway Zone, formerly a part of the Empire, was attached to Manchoukuo in 1937.

[c] Nanyō-guntō, the South Sea Islands received as a mandate from the League of Nations.

[d] Since the special survey taken in Korea in 1920 was probably an undercount, the increase between 1920 and 1925 may be over-estimated for Korea and hence for the Outlying Areas and the Empire as a whole.

[e] The censuses of 1920–1935, inclusive, were *de facto* enumerations of the populations of the various areas. In 1940 the enumeration of the general civilian population was *de facto*, but members of the armed forces and persons attached thereto wherever they might be, whether within or outside the Empire, were allocated to the place of enumeration of their nearest of kin.

decades was greater than the population of the Philippine Islands in 1939, as great as that of Korea in 1920. It would have peopled an empty Japan with 115 persons per square mile. Each year there were three-quarters of a million additional claimants to the products of the Japanese economy.

In Japan, as elsewhere in Monsoon Asia, population increase occurred among a people already densely settled on the land suitable for utilization with existing techniques. In 1920, the number of persons per square mile of total area was 380; in 1940, it was 500. These are crude figures, for Japan is a land of mountains and turbulent rivers, where only one acre in each six is cultivable. If we make our assumption of equal distribution somewhat more realistic and allocate the people to the land that was cultivated or regarded as available for cultivation, we secure density figures that are startling. In 1920, in this country still predominantly peasant, there were almost 2,500 people per square mile of cultivable land. If the 17 million people who were added to the Japanese population between 1920 and 1940 had been equally distributed over the cultivable land, there would have been 740 additional persons on each square mile. By October 1, 1940, the hypothetical allocation of equal areas of cultivable land to each person would yield 3,200 persons for each square mile of such land.

Citation of rates of population increase, density figures, or other population statistics for Japan Proper as measures of the demographic transformation of the Japanese people ignore the essential characteristic of that transformation, its integral relationships with political and economic expansionism within and outside the Home Islands. In the late nineteenth century the island of Hokkaido was occupied in a northward thrust that carried the Japanese up through the southern part of Saghalien Island. Expansionism turned southward and the Ryu-ku Islands were added to Japan Proper, Taiwan to the Empire. In the early twentieth century the drive to economic and political advance focused landward. The Kwantung Leased Territory, the South Manchuria Railway Zone and Korea were added to the Empire. The South Sea Islands, which Imperial Germany had once held, were acquired after World War I as a mandate from the League of Nations and added to the Empire in fact if not in legal right.

Japanese moved outward to the islands of the Pacific, across the narrow waters to northeastern Asia, and eventually southward below the Great Wall. (Table 2). In 1920 there were 726 thousand Japanese in the colonial areas outside Japan Proper, including the military; in 1940, there were 1.7 million, excluding the military. This was internal redistribution in a sense, for it was movement under the Japanese flag. Expansion beyond the area of Japanese sovereignty but within the area of political hegemony increased sharply during the 'thirties. In 1920 some 580 thousand were beyond the jurisdiction of Japan, at least in theory. In 1940, the number abroad had increased to 1.9 million, of whom 820 thousand were in "Manchoukuo," 365 thousand in occupied North China. This redistribution and expansion of the Japanese reflected a complex adjustment of social and economic pressures at home, economic opportunities abroad. The main concentrations remained in Japan Proper, though, for here lived 99 per cent of the world's Japanese in 1920, 97.5 per cent in 1940.

The relevance of population increase to economic and political transformation cannot be assessed easily from the statistical data on the maze of movements and counter-movements that produced the internal redistribution and the external expansion portrayed in the preceding tables. It can be deduced in hypothetical form, though, if we assume that on October 1, 1920, all Empire nationals and aliens are expelled from Japan and the Home Islands are sealed as they had been throughout the centuries of Tokugawa control. Within this stable and isolated universe births and deaths occur at the age-specific rates that characterized the actual population of Japan from 1920 to 1940. Let us now limit the analysis to men, and assume that each man enters the labor force at age 15 and remains in it continuously until death or retirement at age 65. Furthermore, there is no expansion of economic opportunities, and no job is vacated except by the death or retirement of its holder. Japan's population problem thus becomes by definition the increase of her manpower between the ages of 15 and 65, for adjustment techniques, whether economic, political, or demographic, are ruled out by definition. Under these assumptions there would have been 180 Japanese entering labor force ages for each 100 vacancies created by death or retirement. One hundred of these

Table 2. Demographic expansion of the ethnic Japanese, 1920–1940.*

AREA	NUMBER OF ETHNIC JAPANESE (IN THOUSANDS)			PER CENT INCREASE IN ETHNIC JAPANESE		
	1920	1930	1940	1920–1930	1930–1940	1920–1940
The World	57,191	65,766	75,372	15.0	14.6	31.8
The Empire[a]	56,611	65,149	73,500	15.1	12.8	29.8
Japan Proper[b]	55,885	63,972	71,810	14.5	12.2	28.5
Outlying Areas[a]	726	1,177	1,690	62.1	43.6	132.8
Korea	377	527	708	39.9	34.3	87.8
Taiwan	164	228	312	39.0	36.8	90.2
Karafuto	103	284	395	176.3	38.8	283.7
Kwantung	79	118	198	50.0	68.1	152.0
South Seas	3	20	77	476.8	292.3	2163.0
Foreign Countries[c]	580	617	1,872	6.3	203.4	222.5

* *1920*: Nihon. Naikaku tōkei-kyoku. (Cabinet Bureau of Statistics): *Taishō kunen Kokusei chōsa ki-jutsu-hen.* (Descriptive summary of the 1920 census.) Appendix. Tokyo, 1933. *1930. Ibid.: Shōwa gonen Kokusei chōsa saishū hōkoku sho.* (Final report of the 1930 census.) Tokyo, 1938. *1940.* Japan. Cabinet Bureau of Statistics: *Census of 1940. Selected tables.* Microfilm copy, Library of Congress, Washington, D. C. Table 1. The number of Japanese in foreign countries in 1940 is based on a compilation from Japanese sources, modified where census or registration data permitted more accurate estimation.

[a] Excluding the South Manchuria Railway Zone, which became part of "Manchoukuo" in 1937 and hence technically outside the Empire.

[b] Ethnic Japanese only, i.e., excluding natives of the Empire and aliens.

[c] Including the South Manchuria Railway Zone, which had a Japanese population of 81 thousand in 1920 and 107 thousand in 1930.

180 potential entrants would be utilized; eighty would find no place within this completely occupied and stationary economy. In other words, 45 per cent of the annual increment to the number of men in the productive ages would be surplus. Given the validity of the assumptions underlying the computations, this would be the measure of Japan's demographic difficulties.

Before considering the actual relationships between numbers, economic development, and politico-economic factors in Japan, let us transfer Japanese rates of demographic expansion by direct analogy to some regions of potential modernization and assess the magnitude of the numerical increase that would occur if their demographic developments should perchance follow those of Japan. Instead of a China or an India where numbers quickly become fantastic, let us consider Indonesia, for here the Outer Islands and their resources may permit an orthodox pattern of economic-demographic modernization for crowded Java. If Indonesia should follow the path of Japan, today's 76 million people would become 140 millions by the second decade of the twenty-first century. Java's own population would be little beyond its present 50 millions, perhaps less, for the necessary food for the increasing people would be produced on lands now utilized only by the inefficient techniques of the native peoples of the Outer Islands. The major portion of the hypothetical increase of some 65 million people would have been absorbed in the new industrial developments, perhaps located in the Outer Islands. Great cities with millions of inhabitants would have replaced the Balipapans of today. Perhaps this is a possible picture, perhaps not. In any event, the internal migration of the maturing youth of Java's over-crowded areas to developing industrial centers in the Outer Islands is implicit in the plans of Indonesia's leaders who are cognizant of the demographic dilemma that underlies their economic development plans.

This planning for the year 2025 would not be terminal, though, for a further fifty per cent increase would lie ahead. Indonesia's ultimate population would go beyond 200 million, the Philippines under comparable assumptions beyond 60 millions.

Economic Transformation

The economic transformation of Japan in the seventy-five years of its history as an expanding imperial power was a movement away from agricultural self-sufficiency toward an industrial and a commercial economy dependent on the world market alike for the purchase of its raw materials and the sale of its finished products. At the beginning of the 'twenties Japan's industry was predominantly textile, cocoons and silks tying the agricultural and the industrial segments of the economy together in dependence on the vagaries of taste and the fluctuating purchasing power of American women. The 'twenties were a period of expansion in the traditional pattern. The major exports were textiles and those cheap products of the small shop and sweated labor that had come to stigmatize the label, "Made in Japan." The depression of the late 'twenties and the early 'thirties shattered the world's demand for Japan's silk and cotton textiles. Poverty spread in ever-widening circles from the employees in the textile mills to the small farmers who supplemented agricultural production with the cultivation of mulberry trees and the raising of cocoons. The depreciation of the yen, increasing efficiency in organization, and controlled sales restored Japanese products to the world markets, but only at the heavy price of depressed wages at home and increased accusations of "dumping" abroad. World trends toward economic autarchy, controlled trade, managed currencies, and the political manipulation of economic relationships seemed to threaten the economy of a nation that required trade to survive.

Awesome predictions of the fate awaiting the multiplying Japanese again proved false. By the end of the 'thirties Japan's strengthened and diversified economy indicated progress toward mature industrialization. The index of industrial productions, with a base of 100 in 1930–1934, reached beyond 200 in 1941. The production of the metal and the chemical industries had trebled, while the manufacturing of machinery had increased six-fold.[3]

The immediate demographic consequence of the economic transformation of the interwar decades was the urbanization of the population structure, for the city-ward movement of the peasant was an essential aspect of the process of capital formation, industrialization, and political expansion. The villages and the smaller towns became producers of children, exporters of youth, and havens for the aged. The maturing youth moved toward the cities and non-agricultural employment in such numbers as to create an urbanization seldom paralleled in the history of the West. (Table 3).

Between 1920 and 1940 the population of the cities (*shi*) increased from 10.1 to 27.6 millions, while that of the rural areas (*gun*) changed only from 45.9 to 45.5 millions. Fewer than five million people lived in cities of 500,000 and over in 1920; 14.4 million lived in such cities in 1940. In relative terms, the population living in communes of 10,000 or less declined three per cent during this twenty-year period, while that in cities of 100,000 and over more than trebled.

---

[3] Economic progress was a by-product of military expansion and preparedness for further expansion. The response of Japan's statesmen and military leaders to a constricting outer world and cumulating internal friction was an outward surge that carried the Kwantung armies into Manchuria and established a Manchu emperor on a puppet throne. The decade of heavy capital investment thus initiated resulted in the establishment of an economic and military bastion from which the Soviet Union could be held while China below the Great Wall was invaded. In Taiwan, Korea, and Karafuto there was forced industrialization somewhat comparable to that of Japan's early post-Restoration period, and here too it was oriented toward heavy industry and military preparedness.

The urbanward movement was predominantly from the rural area to the large city or the great metropolitan center. In 1920 over two-thirds of the total population lived in communes of less than 10 thousand population. Only half lived in such communes in 1940. In 1920 one in each twelve or so persons lived in a city of 100,000 or more. In 1940, one in each five lived in such a city. All the provinces of Japan contributed substantial portions of their natural increase to the great metropolitan cities of Tokyo, Yokohama, Nagoya, Osaka, Kyoto, and Kobe. In fact, for the interwar decades as a whole the net migratory gain of the seven metropolitan provinces (Tokyo, Kanagawa, Aichi, Osaka, Kyoto, Hyogo, and Fukuoka) was greater than the net migratory loss of the remaining forty provinces of Japan, for these provinces attracted not only Japan's own provincials but also the immigrants of Empire.

Table 3. The urbanization of the population structure of Japan Proper, 1920–1947:[*]

YEAR	POPULATION BY SIZE OF COMMUNES[a] (IN THOUSANDS)					
	Total	Under 10,000	10,000–50,000	50,000–100,000	100,000–500,000	500,000 +
Prewar Area						
1 October 1920	55,963	37,927	9,177	2,105	2,128	4,626
1 October 1925	59,737	37,884	9,667	3,445	2,538	6,203
1 October 1930	64,450	38,158	10,409	4,402	3,876	7,605
1 October 1935	69,254	37,502	10,549	3,685	4,873	12,645
1 October 1940	73,114	36,627	11,338	3,858	6,907	14,384
Postwar Area						
1 October 1940	72,540	35,998	11,457	3,792	6,907	14,384
1 November 1945	71,996	39,460	16,126	5,397	5,045	5,969
26 April 1946	73,114	38,482	15,630	5,537	6,389	7,076
1 October 1947	78,098	38,690	16,474	6,148	7,778	9,009

[*] *1920–1940, prewar area.* Compiled from the appropriate volumes of the respective censuses of Japan. *1940–1947, postwar area.* SCAP, Economic and Scientific Section, Research and Programs Division: Distribution of population of Japan by *shi, machi,* and *mura* in selected size groups 1940, 1945, 1946, 1947. *Japanese Economic Statistics, Bulletin, Section III. Population, Labor, Food, and Prices.* Bulletin No. 34, June, 1949. Also Ueda Masau: Some recent tendencies in urban and rural population. Tables. *The Third General Meeting of the Population Association of Japan, Data Paper.* 13 November, 1949.

[a] Commune is used as a general term to include *shi* (cities), *machi* (towns), and *mura* (villages). English equivalents are approximate only. Area classifications are as of the census date.

The Utilization of Increasing Manpower

The economic force that underlay urbanization was industrialization, including under that broad term the expansion of manufacturing industry and the facilities and services necessarily associated with it, as well as the increasing efficiency of primary production that accompanies advances in techniques and facilities for production and distribution. The human aspect of this industrialization was the changing industrial allocation of the labor force. Agriculture, forestry, and fishing declined in relative importance, while manufacturing, commerce, transportation, and communication increased. (Table 4.) The maintenance of a relatively unchanging population in agriculture was accompanied by a rapid increase in both the numbers and the proportions of the people who secured their livelihood from sources other than agriculture. In 1920, agriculture absorbed slightly more than half those reporting themselves as gainfully occupied, whether employed or not; in 1930, it absorbed slightly less than half; in 1940, it absorbed only 43 per cent. This is an under-statement of the extent of the economic transformation, though, for it is distorted by the numbers of women who are reported as gainfully occupied in agriculture. If men alone are considered, the proportion gainfully occupied in agriculture was 46.3 in 1920, 41.2 in 1930, and 33.5 in 1940.

A more incisive picture of the way in which Japan utilized the increasing numbers of people generated by the modernization process is given if attention is focused on the utilization of the increments rather than on the more traditional pattern of the changing proportions within the civilian labor force. If we consider only the increase in the population physically present within Japan Proper, we find that the number of persons aged 10 and above increased 13.5 millions between 1920 and 1940. This figure is complicated in derivation, however, for it represents the balance of the natural increase of the Japanese in Japan Proper, the losses of the Japanese through emigration from Japan, and the gains of Empire Nationals, primarily Koreans, through immigration.

By 1940 over one million Japanese men aged 10 and above had been lost to Japan through the civilian migration that occurred between 1920 and 1940. This removed 14 per cent of the potential increase of 7.7 million men in labor force ages.

Table 4. Economic utilization of the population of Japan Proper, industrial classification of the gainfully occupied, 1920, 1930, and 1940.*

STATUS	TOTAL POPULATION			MALES			FEMALES		
	1920	1930	1940	1920	1930	1940	1920	1930	1940
	NUMBER (IN THOUSANDS)								
TOTAL	55,963	64,450	73,114	28,044	32,390	36,566	27,919	32,060	36,548
Armed Forces	250	243	.1,694	250	243	1,694			
Civilian Population	55,713	64,207	71,420	27,794	32,147	34,872	27,919	32,060	36,548
Unoccupied	28,702	34,830	38,937	11,057	13,360	15,142	17,645	21,470	23,795
Occupied[b]	27,011	29,377	32,483	16,737	18,787	19,730	10,274	10,590	12,753
Agriculture & Forestry	14,128	14,131	13,842	7,750	7,735	6,619	6,378	6,396	7,223
Fishing	558	568	543	517	515	476	41	53	67
Mining	425	316	598	328	271	529	97	45	69
Manufacturing & Construction	5,300	5,876	8,132	3,716	4,428	6,178	1,584	1,448	1,954
Commerce	3,188	4,906	4,882	2,158	3,406	3,006	1,030	1,500	1,876
Transportation & Communication	1,037	945	1,364	975	907	1,214	62	38	150
Government & Professional	1,192	1,762	2,195	884	1,369	1,515	308	393	680
Domestic Service	655	802	709	71	92	39	584	710	670
Miscellaneous	528	71	218	338	64	154	190	7	64
	PER CENT OF GAINFULLY OCCUPIED								
TOTAL	100.0	100.0	100.0	100.0	100.0	100.0	100.0	100.0	100.0
Agriculture & Forestry	52.3	48.1	42.6	46.3	41.2	33.5	62.1	60.4	56.6
Fishing	2.1	1.9	1.7	3.1	2.7	2.4	0.4	0.5	0.5
Mining	1.6	1.1	1.8	2.0	1.5	2.7	0.9	0.4	0.5
Manufacturing & Construction	19.6	20.0	25.0	22.0	23.6	31.3	15.4	13.7	15.3
Commerce	11.8	16.7	15.0	12.9	18.1	15.2	10.0	14.2	14.7
Transportation & Communication	3.8	3.2	4.2	5.8	4.8	6.2	0.6	0.3	1.2
Government & Professional	4.4	6.0	6.8	5.3	7.3	7.7	3.0	3.7	5.3
Domestic Service	2.4	2.7	2.2	0.4	0.5	0.2	5.7	6.7	5.3
Miscellaneous	2.0	0.3	0.7	2.0	0.3	0.8	1.9	0.1	0.5

* 1920. Nihon. Naikaku tōkei-kyoku (Cabinet Bureau of Statistics): Taishō kunen Kokusei chōsa hōkoku. (Reports of the 1920 census). Zenkoku no bu. (Section on all Japan.) Shokugyō. (Occupations) Tokyo, 1929. Reallocations to produce as much comparability as possible with the later classifications of occupied and unoccupied. 1930. Ibid.: Shōwa gonen Kokusei chōsa hōkoku. (Reports of the 1930 census.) Shokugyō oyobi sangyō. (Occupations and industries.) Tokyo, 1935. 1940. United States Strategic Bombing Survey, Manpower, Food, and Civilian Supplies Division: The Japanese Wartime Standard of Living and Utilization of Manpower. Washington, 1947. Table PP, p. 124.

a The armed forces in 1920 and 1930 included only those present in Japan Proper who could not be allocated to another category of the occupational (1920) or industrial (1930) classification. In 1940 the armed forces were reported by their closest civilian relative and include armed forces and persons attached thereto, wherever stationed.

b The unemployed are included, classified according to the industry of the usual employment.

The impact of these migrations on the labor market was greater than this overall figure would indicate, for migration removed one-fourth of the total increase in the number of men in their twenties, one-fifth of the number in their thirties. This was removal for civilian utilization. If we add to the 1.0 million civilian migrants the 1.4 million men removed from the potential increase in the civilian labor pool through absorption into the armed services, we discover that only two-thirds of the increase in adult manpower was available for civilian utilization within Japan Proper. The number of men aged 20 to 24 available for such utilization in 1940 was actually less than it had been in 1920. The real problem of Japan became the inadequacy rather than the increase of manpower—and in the twenty years under consideration more than half a million Korean men aged 10 or over moved in to fill the jobs vacated by the Japanese who had either moved upward occupationally in Japan Proper and the Empire or had been absorbed into the armed forces.

This is a simplified summary of the changing pattern of manpower utilization, civilian and military, within Japan Proper and within the Empire. It may suffice to indicate the complexity of the economic problems presented by rapid and continuing increase in the population in the productive ages. Moreover, it reveals the inadequacy of numerical increase considered apart from an economic and cultural context as a measure of either the nature or the magnitude of the economic and political problems or the relative success of the factors tending toward their resolution. Within Japan Proper there were increasing numbers of persons in the productive ages, but military expansion, the development of the heavy industries and direct war production, all necessary concomitants of imperial expansion, provided employment opportunities for large numbers. There were other factors, for at the same time that the safety valves of emigration and militarism operated to remove persons from the civilian labor market, increased public school education and diffusing retirement practices lessened labor force participation among the young and the old. With these dual drain-offs of potential workers plus the existence of the rural areas as subsistence security for the urban unemployed, Japan solved her problems of increasing manpower.

WAR AND ITS AFTERMATH

Solutions achieved through militarism are necessarily transitory, for the process creates a dynamism that forces its own continuation. For Japan, the end occurred much more speedily than for the British Empire whose history the Japanese imagined themselves to be repeating. The 'twenties were a decade of peace and accumulating population pressure, the 'thirties a decade of war, preparedness for further war, and manpower deficiencies. If the pattern of the past had continued, the 'forties would have been a period of reorganization and economic development preparatory to another politico-economic expansion of the type that had characterized Japanese history from the acquisition of Taiwan to the creation of Manchoukuo. But the pattern broke. The premature challenge of the West was followed by military defeat, the restoration of the Tokugawa boundaries, and the liquidation of Empire.

The Empire vanished, but the people who were the product of industrialization and imperial expansion survived in major part. The four million natural increase of the war years far surpassed the 1.7 million military dead. Almost six million of the emissaries of Empire, civilian and military, were returned to the constricted frontiers of a Japan with levelled cities, ruined industries and vanished markets. The Japan of 1947 with its limited economy included 78.6 million people, 3.5 million more Japanese than lived in all the East in 1940.

This is not the end of the tale. Threatening epidemics were conquered, food supplies restored, and the death rate forced downward. A baby boom contributed further to the increasing population. By January 1, 1949, there were 81 million people in the four main islands of Japan Proper, over ten million more than there had been when this was the heartland of an economic development whose nexus of trade penetrated the East and beyond, the center of a military organization that included 100 millions in the Empire, 40 millions in puppet Manchoukuo, and uncounted millions in the occupied areas of China.

Rapid increase in the numbers of adult men and women will continue for decades in the future. If deaths remain at the level of 1948 and there is no movement to or from Japan except the repatriation of some five to six hundred thousand persons between 1947 and 1953, the number of men in the productive ages between 15 and 60 will increase from some 22 millions in 1947 to some 31 millions in 1967, an increase of over 40 per cent in twenty years. This increase in the coming decades is larger both absolutely and relatively than that which occurred in the twenty years between 1920 and 1940.

THE BROADER RELEVANCE

The heritage which almost a century of economic development left to a Japan whose economic and political system was shattered while her people remained largely intact is considered in another paper in this series. Here we shall attempt a tentative generalization of the relevance of the Japanese experience for other densely settled areas in process of or contemplating comprehensive industrialization.

Japan constitutes one case study in the demographic correlates of modernization of a predominantly industrial type, albeit a peculiarly significant one. Japan's historic culture was Eastern. Her industrial and urban transformation was thus divorced from a base in the non-material culture of the West except in so far as specific elements were deliberately selected for imitation or diffused through more informal mechanisms. Japan was shrouded in the quiescent seclusion of the Tokugawa baku-fu when Europe awakened in the Renaissance and the Reformation. She had no Protestant ethic whose interconnections with the evolution of capitalism could be debated, no church whose familial pronouncements implemented the Pauline philosophy. Yet here within the East the demographic correlates of industrialization were roughly comparable to those in the West.

The population growth that accompanies indigenous and comprehensive industrial development and the slowing of that growth through a progressive limitation of child-bearing are alike products of the changes in ways of living and thinking that are precondition and product of industrialization. The relations of culture and demography proceed through the intermediation of the economic process itself. Political stability, a disciplined labor force and rapid capital accumulation are necessary aspects of substantial industrialization. Cultural factors exert a major influence on the extent and the speed of the economic transformation, for there are cultural preconditions to indigenous economic transformations and cultural limitations to imposed transformations. As industrialization extends over time and expands over wider segments of a nation, the demographic transition of declining mortality and declining fertility becomes a necessary consequence of the accompanying economic pressures and cultural stimuli. But industrialization regarded as economic, political, or social process is in turn modified by the changing dynamics of population. The relationships are complex; the particular constellation of factors that produced the population growth of Imperial Japan will not be duplicated in detail elsewhere. The fundamental fact, though, is that experience within the East corroborates the hypothesis deducible from Western experience: substantial increase in the size of the total population is a correlate of industrialization, but the social and psychological transformations implicit in industrialization result eventually in a lessened rate of reproduction and a slowing growth. Given the technologies and the basic values of the twentieth century, both population growth and the ultimate slowing of that growth are predictable consequences of the industrial and urban transformation of agrarian cultures.

The demographic consequences of industrialization constitute a powerful propulsion toward further industrialization. Phrased in negative terms, industrialization is not a reversible process. To break the dynamism of the economic transformation in midstream is to leave the already cumulated people without the means of procuring the subsistence essential to the maintenance of life. The alternatives in this situation are few. Aggressive action may be attempted, but with a broken economy this is unlikely; if attempted it can only intensify the ultimate problem through defeat. If the political unit has already made the outward thrust and been defeated there may be external subsidy, but this is temporary solution. Hence the most probable consequence of the cessation of expansionism in a situation of continued population increase is a sharp deterioration of living levels. If the industrialization is actually reversed after its long continuation has generated really high densities on limited land, the consequence in the absence of subsidy or flight must be the death of that portion of the people who are "surplus" in the drastically altered resources-cultural-technology matrix.

Japanese demographic evolution paralleled that of the West in earlier decades, with differences explainable in terms of resources, history, technology, and culture. Will Japanese experience then predict within similarly broad limits that which is to occur in other densely settled Eastern areas? This, the critical question for those determining political and economic policy for other under-developed areas, cannot be answered from population analysis alone. To assume complete parallelism between Japan and an industrializing mainland would be unrealistic. But to ignore the possibility that there may be similar integral relations between economic development, population growth, expansionism, and conflict would be politically hazardous.

POPULATION PRESSURE AND ECONOMIC

DEVELOPMENT IN INDONESIA

By Justus M. van der Kroef

I

THE GRAVEST SOCIAL AND ECONOMIC PROBLEM facing the young Indonesian Republic today is the uneven distribution of her people. In the vast Malay Archipelago, areas with some of the highest population density figures in the world alternate with areas where the shortage of people and unattractive living conditions militate against a sound economic development. Overpopulation in Indonesia exists today primarily on the island of Java and in some areas on the islands of Sumatra and Sulawesi (Celebes). Underpopulation, however, is a distinct characteristic of most of Kalimantan (Borneo), the Lesser Sunda islands, the Moluccas and West Irian (New Guinea). An appreciation of the respective density in various parts of Indonesia may be obtained from the following table:[1]

Areas	Total Population (thousands)	Density Per Sq. Km.
Java and Madura (Indonesians)	40,891	361.1
Other islands of Indonesia (Indonesians)	18,246	10.7
Indonesia as a whole	60,727	31.9
Cheribon Valley (West-Java)	2,888	656.9
Serayu valley and south Central Java	1,494	679.3
Adikarta (Jogjakarta, Central Java)	101	826.5
Ploembon (Cheribon)	112	1074.8
Adiwerna (Tegal, Centʒal Java)	152	1637.9

Together with the Nile Valley, the most densely populated areas in the world are the Adiwerna district in Central Java and certain sections of West Java. Especially, the growth of the indigenous population of Java and Madura in the past century or so has been enormous, as the following table indicates:[2]

[1] A. Jonkers, "Het bevolkingsvraagstuk van Java en de landbouwkolonisatie," *Indonesie*, 1 (1947), p. 28. Figures are based on the results of the latest (1930) census for Indonesia. See also *Verspreiding der Inheemse bevolking, Uitgave Centraal Kantoor voor de Statistiek*, Bulletin No. 7, Batavia, 1935, pp. 12–5, which shows the persistence of regional population densities in Java since the turn of the century.

[2] Jonkers, p. 38. See also A. M. Scheltema, "De groei van Java's bevolking", *Koloniale Studien*, 6 (1926), p. 857. The 1940 estimate is derived from the Netherlands Indies Government publication *Pocket edition of the Statistical Abstract of the Netherlands Indies 1940*, published by the Central Bureau of Statistics, Batavia, 1940, p. 6. This estimate is probably too conservative for it excludes Europeans, Chinese,

Year	Total Population (thousands)	Yearly Percentage of Increase During Previous Period.
1815	4,499	
1845	9,374	2.48
1860	12,514	1.94
1870	16,233	2.64
1880	19,540	1.87
1885	21,190	1.83
1890	23,609	2.19
1895	25,370	1.45
1900	28,396	2.27
1905	29,978	1.10
1920	34,428	0.93
1930	40,891	1.79
1940*	47,456	1.93
1950*	50,400	0.96

* Figures are estimated; no census has been held since 1930.

In the islands beyond Java, which contain many untapped resources for economic development, the distribution of the population is generally also uneven. Islands like Bali and Lombok have a density of 170.9 per square kilometer, but the west coast of Sumatra has only 38.7 and the Moluccas and Southeastern Kalimantan (Borneo) have figures that are even below the general density figure for islands other than Java: 1.8 and 3.5 respectively. It should be noted that even on such a small island as Bali the distribution varies greatly from place to place. The district of Gianjar in South Bali has a density of 453, while Djembrana on North Bali has only 56.5 and the northwestern part of Bali is largely uninhabited altogether. Java presents the same picture. Next to the dangerously overpopulated areas as Adikarta and Ploembon, sections can be found where the density is less than 50 (Lebak in Western Java, for example). The surplus of births in Java is alarmingly great. The population increases annually with from 1.25 to 1.5 per cent or on an average of 600,000 persons.[3] Generally, the Javanese marries early; with his seventeenth birthday the man is regarded as an adult, the woman with her

---

Arabs and others, who were not classified as "native" by colonial law. If they are included the 1940 estimate is 48,416,000. This estimate is in keeping with another government estimate in its publication 100 pages Indonesian economics Batavia, 1948, p. 13 where the 1940 population is placed at 48,000,000. The 1950 estimate is that of H. de Meel, "Demographic dilemma in Indonesia", Pacific Affairs, 24 (1951), p. 272. De Meel has also estimated that Java's population in 1942 was 50,100,000; in 1945 50,-000,000; in 1948 49,300,000 and in 1950 50,400,000. According to de Meel the population of the Indonesian islands beyond Java increased steadily in the same period: in 1930 18,700,000; in 1942 25,400,000; in 1946 26,500,000; in 1948 28,500,000 and in 1951 30,600,000. According to a recent estimate of the Indonesian government, however, in Economisch-Statistische Berichten van Indonesie, July, 1952, pp. 119–25, Java's total population increased from 50,000,000 in 1948 to 52,000,000 by the middle of 1952. These figures should be compared with those of the Statistical Office of the United Nations' Monthly Bulletin of Statistics, April, 1953, p. 3, according to which the total population of Indonesia was 73,500,000 in 1948 and 76,500,000 in 1951. Figures for Java alone are not available.

[3] W. Ph. Coolhaas, Insulinde, Mensch en Maatschappij Deventer, 1947, pp. 29–31; 100 pages Indonesian economics, p. 13; Pocket edition of the Statistical Abstract, p. 6.

fourteenth birthday. The rate of increase of the population beyond Java is not known but may be regarded as rapid. The danger in such an increase becomes particularly clear if one considers the fact that the overwhelmingly greater part of the Indonesian population makes its living from agriculture (approximately 75 per cent).[4] The amount of land suitable for agriculture cultivation is relatively limited and the density of the population in terms of the available arable land is the staggering figure of 557 per square kilometer. Put another way, this means that less than half an acre is available to the individual Indonesian peasant.[5]

The reason for this phenomenal population increase, especially in Java, has generally been sought in the fortunate interaction of soil and climate and especially in the benificent results of modern Dutch colonial policy. It has been pointed out that Java's population remained largely stationary during the eighteenth century and in 1800 was estimated at approximately 4,000,000 persons.[6] The nineteenth century saw the beginning of modern hygienic and medical services for the benefit of the Indonesian and as a result the population began to increase. The peace and security which the colonial regime brought and which made an end to the internecine wars in Indonesia has similarly been regarded as facilitating the growth of the population. Without attempting to minimize the obvious validity of this view,[7] it needs to be emphasized, however, that the population of Indonesia has continued to increase over the past ten years as well, notwithstanding the complete collapse of the colonial regime, the destruction of hospitals and the near cessation of hygienic service, the demographic dislocation caused by the Japanese occupation (when thousands of Indonesians marched away in the Japanese labor battalion to find a miserable end), the ravages of the revolutionary period and the accompanying collapse of all order and security, and finally notwithstanding the increasingly high infant mortality rate, especially in certain cities like Makassar on Sulawesi.[8]

[4] *Verslag van de Commissie tot bestudeering van Staatsrechtelijke hervormingen ingesteld bij Gouvernmentsbesluit van 14 September 1940, no. lx/KAB*, Batavia, 1940, vol. 1, p. 17.

[5] Coolhaas, p. 33. E. de Vries, *Problemen van de Javaanse Landbouwer* Wageningen, 1947, p. 5, arrives at different figures. Relating the number of peasant landowners to the total cultivated area, he found that the average amount of land available per peasant was 2.125 acre; in some areas in Java it was as low as from 0.247 to 0.454 acres. In the less densely populated outer islands landholdings were similarly small (1.647 to 2.471 acres) per peasant-owner.

[6] Scheltema, p. 857.

[7] Contrast however J. H. Boeke, *The Structure of Netherlands Indian Economy*, New York, 1942, p. 163: ". . . medical aid has not been able to reduce the death rate among the masses of Java to any great extent, mortality in this island having fluctuated around 1.9 per cent annually . . . for the last twenty years". The *Pocket Edition of the Statistical Abstract* (*op. cit.*) indicates in table 27 the following mortality rate in Java and Madura (Indonesians only) per 1000 inhabitants: 1930, 18.1; 1931, 17.4; 1933, 16.5; 1934, 18.1; 1935, 18.2; 1936, 17.7; 1937, 18.8; 1938, 18.4 and 1939, 18.9. These figures seem to support Boeke's view.

[8] On the infant mortality rate in Makassar see R. Soemitro, "Zuigelingensterfte te Makassar", *Medisch Maandblad*, 3 (1950), p. 81.

Nor does the view that population increase was largely the result of the beneficial effects of colonial rule account for the uneven distribution of the population, especially in Java. If the colonial period brought peace and security more or less uniformly over the Indonesian islands, then it might be supposed that the density would become relatively even over the entire country, barring of course the effect of localized calamities of nature. But this is not the case. Finally it should be pointed out that local overpopulation is apparently not a phenomenon of recent times, but appears, for example, to have existed in Java very early in the nineteenth century. The supposition that it existed even earlier is not unwarranted. In 1802 the colonial official Nederburgh reported that "Java was overcrowded with unemployed," and this at a time when Java could not have had a population larger than 4 million. In 1816 Engelhard, a former director of the province of Java's North East Coast, remarked that in his time the rice fields were cultivated on rotation, because the "population far exceeded the cultivation" of a given village or district. In the well known report of the Commissioner-General Du Bus in 1827, the Javanese village is characterized in general by an excess of *boedjangs* or *menoempangs, i.e.* persons who are not employed on the fields, because of a shortage of land. Du Bus also emphasized the local density in certain areas, which he regarded very early as a threat to the island's future welfare. All this would seem to justify Boeke's pronouncement that the "the Javanese village society has been familiar for centuries and centuries with an enormous population density and a population surplus; both these characteristics have nothing whatever to do with the total population figures."[9]

Local density must rather be accounted for by relating it to the prevailing method of cultivation in the village society of Java and perhaps also of other areas in Indonesia. Wherever the permanent irrigated rice cultivation (*sawah*) exists, a high population density may be expected. Under *sawah* cultivation a close connection exists between the village population and the arable land necessary to support it. In the *sawah* village, the lands lie like a wreath around the inhabited compound.

Traditional village production has a subsistence basis and is not performed to make maximum profits. The amount of land in use by the village, is therefore small, little land is cultivated beyond subsistence requirements, while the cultivation becomes more and more intensive as the population increases and holdings become smaller. The village allots land to the individual family, on the basis of what the manpower of a family as a unit is able to cultivate; the amount of this land is therefore small and directly related to the family's needs. Intensive cultivation of

[9] This and the above citations in J. H. Boeke, *Ontwikkelingsgang en Toekomst van Bevolkings-en Ondernemingslandbouw in Nederlandsch-Indie,* Leyden, 1948, pp. 7, 57.

a limited amount of land on the basis of a subsistence economy results therefore in population concentration in the village.

The local population density is nothing else but the total number of people, in relation to the cultivated area necessary to support them. From this follows that the local density does not need to have any immediate relationship to the total population of the island, of the country or of some other geographic unit at a given time. The density is a feature of the structure of village economy in Java, under which production increases can only be expected if cash demands are made or a surplus population comes into existence, necessitating smaller holdings in the community. This theory also accounts for the relative lower density of the population beyond Java. For on the islands beyond Java, the unirrigated, shifting cultivation (*ladang*) is generally the rule, not the *sawah* production. In general the Indonesian peasant prefers the *ladang* cultivation because it is less cumbersome and requires less care. ' But it requires considerably more land than the *sawah* production, and only if an increase in population reduces the available land or if the soil becomes too exhausted will the peasant undertake permanent irrigated production.[10]

II

To cope with the dangerous economic effects of this population pressure several schemes have been devised in the course of time, most of which, curiously enough, have rarely concerned themselves with an alteration of the structure of agricultural production. Many officials of the colonial and the present national government as well as some scholars have based their hopes on emigration as a solution of the problem.

Professor Pelzer has even gone so far as to maintain that emigration from Java to less densely populated islands "will . . . be able to take care of the population increase . . . for many decades," and that emigration rather than industrialization will provide the necessary relief.[11] This supposition is altogether erroneous. In a given area the daughter

---

[10] *Ibid.*, pp. 5–6, 16. G. J. Vink ("Bedrijfseconomie van den bevolkingslandbouw," pp. 281–2 in C. J. van Hall and C. Van de Koppel, eds., *De Landbouw in den Indischen Archipel* The Hague, 1946, vol. 1) supports Boeke's contention that the sawah cultivation is the result of necessity, caused by a growing population; where sawah cultivation prevails the population density is high. The sawah cultivation, and its attendant culture patterns, became deeply ingrained into Javanese society over time. Its population density—according to Carr-Saunders—is related to these indigenous culture patterns. The penetration of Western estate enterprise opened the opportunity to the Javanese to maintain a traditional standard of living and the prevailing cultural level and *yet* increase the size of his family since work on the estates provided him with an extra cash income. Hence, according to Wertheim, the growth of the population appeared to occur chiefly in the area of Western sugar planatations, which "by providing increased opportunity for employment, increased in turn the means of livelihood" (W. F. Wertheim, *Effects of Western Civilization on Indonesian Society*, New York, 1950, p. 4). For a defense of Carr-Saunders' theory as applied to Indonesian society see H. Th. Fischer, *Kinderaantal en Kinderleven in Indonesie*, The Hague, 1950, pp. 32–3.

[11] Karl J. Pelzer, *Pioneer, Settlement in the Asiatic Tropics, Studies in Land Utilization and Agricultural Colonization in Southeastern Asia*, New York, American Geographical Society, 1945, p. 239.

villages formed by an excess population resemble in economic methods and structure the mother village and the simple and uniform process of production undergoes no change, but is gradually extended over an ever-widening area. The result is that the population does not become more dense at any given point, but spreads itself with equal density over a larger area. "Agriculture faithfully reproduces exactly the same traditional features in the recently cleared corners of Java as it presents in the parts of the islands that have been longest under cultivation. Java is filling up, and when it is full to the brim, this static expansion will continue . . . to the adjacent islands by means of colonization."[12] The very evidence which Pelzer presents does not support his supposition, for he has noted how "through all the discussion of agricultural colonization in the Indies runs the thought that the ultimate aim should be to create villages and communities in the Outer Islands that would be exact duplicates of those in Java, where the people would . . . have the same type of economy".[13] Colonies of Javanese emigrants in southern Sumatra do indeed exhibit the same structure of production as that in Java itself; the population of the colonies begins with a high degree of density, and within a generation it may become so dense that continued colonization and emigration becomes advisable.

Emigration from Java to other Indonesian islands cannot even be regarded as a temporary solution, relieving population pressures for at least "decades." The Central Bureau of Statistics of the Netherlands Indies Government has estimated[14] that if the population increase of Java continues at the present rate for the next five decades, the island would have 116 million souls in the year 2000. If, however, 20,000 families would annually emigrate, each family composed of a man and wife between the ages of 15 and 24, plus a child under five years of age, then the total population would rise only to 74 million. With an emigration of 120,000 childless couples annually for the next half century, the population of Java might be expected to remain more or less stationary at 51 million in that period.

It is perhaps questionable whether there would indeed be such a steady, uniform population increase in Java in the next half century, but the bureau's estimate is not without value. It is clear that the enormous costs involved and the difficulties in the selection of suitable settlement areas alone would make a colonization of the magnitude indicated almost

---

[12] Boeke, *The Structure of Netherlands Indian Economy*, pp. 162–3.

[13] Pelzer, *op. cit.*, p. 320. Compare G. B. van der Leeden, *Het aspect van landbouwkolonisatie in het bevolkingsprobleem van Java*, Dissertation, Leyden, The Hague, 1952, p. 122: "The present form of colonization (i.e. before the war) will give the tani (peasant) a surprisingly increased degree of welfare. *However, in as much as one strives for a social milieu similar to that which he left behind in Java*, this welfare level must fall after a few years." (My italics). Van der Leeden points out that immigrant colonists received far too small a plot of land in their new environment. Thus the local density, as in Java, tended to be augmented.

[14] Cited by Coolhaas, p. 70.

prohibitive, and yet this is the minimum relief that emigration can bring. Even if it were possible to succeed in transplanting 120,000 childless families annually for the next half century, Java, in the year 2000, would still be in the condition of severe overpopulation in which it finds itself in today! And who would suggest that, given Indonesia's economic position today, industry in Java would have taken such a flight in fifty years that it would completely alter the agrarian basis of production?

It should also be noted that such limited emigration as existed before the Second World War was only belatedly successful. The early settlements of Javanese emigrants near Gedong Tatäan in the Lampong districts of Southern Sumatra, which were begun thanks to the tireless efforts of the official Heyting in the period 1905–1907, were at first a fiasco. After 23 years only 24,300 persons, spread over two colonies, resided in the resettlement area; many more emigrants had come over, but had decided to return. Fraudulent financial supervision and the expense of maintenance and clearing of the land, which had cost the government close to 575 guilders per family, did not make colonization seem worth-while. Other colonies in southeastern Kalimantan and Sulawesi had to be abandoned in the first decade of the twentieth century.

Not until the middle of the fourth decade did Javanese emigration to Sumatra become something of a success. By that time much experience had been gained in the selection of emigrants, the method of settlement, and the expenditures required in transportation and medical supervision. In 1932 the population of Gedong Tatäan increased by 27 per cent and a third colonization area, Soekadana, not far from Gedong Tatäan, was opened by the government. By June 1938, this area had already acquired a population of 26,250. Thanks to continued government help and an active propaganda campaign, many emigrants continued to settle in southern Sumatra. In 1936, 13,152 persons migrated there; in 1937, 19,719; in 1938, 32,259; in 1939, 45,339; in 1949, 50,622; and in the first three months of 1941, 47,095.[15] The use of veteran emigrants as propagandists on behalf of further emigration from Java convinced many thousands of Javanese of the advantages of going to "Tanah Sabrang," the land on the other side.[16]

The present government of the Indonesian Republic has continued to voice the need for further emigration, and in January 1951 reported that it would encourage emigration to such islands as Sulawesi and Kalimantan; 10,000 families were scheduled to migrate in January 1951 from densely populated areas in central Java to south Sumatra and central Sulawesi. Under a government-sponsored plan, each family would be

[15] Data based on A. Jonkers, *Welvaartszorg in Indonesie, een geschiedenis en een perspectief*, The Hague, 1948, pp. 143–8 and Centraal Kantoor voor de Statistiek, *Mededeeling no. 20*, Batavia, 1939.

[16] See the methods of government propaganda in C. C. Maassen, *De Javaansche Landbouwkolonisatie in de Buitengewesten*, 2nd. ed., The Hague, 1937.

given five acres of land, a portion of which was to be used for the cultivation of certain export crops.[17] This policy of granting land and holding eventual ownership of it in view follows the established pattern of emigrant colonization in the colonial period. But the great difficulty, as has been pointed out, is that the emigrant colony reverts inevitably to the traditional form of production, relates its cultivation to the existing population and within a decade or so exhibits the same degree of localized density and overpopulation that characterizes the average village in Java.

This repetition of the established method of production and the resulting density is facilitated by the strong communal tradition which the peasant entertains with respect to the village in which he resides. Forms of mutual assistance, lending and borrowing and simple credit devices involving rice and tools, are duplicated; a strong cohesive element develops in the community, with a sense of the essential interdependence of the members in the village.[18] What is needed, however, is a spirit of rationalized individualism in production, not a communal pattern. But despite repeated government encouragement the emancipation of the producer from communal traditions has still a long way to go.

Migration within the island of Java, or from Java to other Indonesian islands, has apparently existed on a voluntary basis for a long time. Thousands of persons in Indonesia now living outside Java are estimated to be of Javanese descent and periodic food shortages, crop failures or natural calamities caused considerable migration within Java all during the nineteenth century.[19] Hence emigration itself is not unfamiliar to Javanese tradition; the great difficulty is rather how to break through the communal ties which keep the peasant in his village, ties which are often so strong that only the direst necessity can sometimes loosen them. Only when western concepts of production and a more rational appreciation of the relationship between food and population increase gains ground can emigration be expected to have a more permanent value.[20] This, how-

[17] *Report on Indonesia*, vol. 11 (Jan. 16, 1951), no. 17, p. 10; vol. 11 (June 25, 1952), no. 25, p. 6. According to a recent government declaration the government expects to move no fewer than 600,000 from Java to colonization areas in Sumatra, Kalimantan (Borneo), Sulawesi (Celebes) and the Lesser Sunda islands by 1956, either to work on the land or in various industrial enterprises. Each peasant family is to receive the same fatally small plot of land as in Java, namely 2 hectares, of which one and three quarters is for farming, the rest for housing and gardening.

[18] This sense of interdependence was undoubtedly encouraged even further by the fact that under the colonization program new immigrants, who could not immediately occupy their new land and houses, resided for some time with older, established colonists who paid them part of their crop in return for their labor in the field.

[19] See for example *Volkstelling 1930*, Batavia, 1935, vol. IV, pp. 33, 182–3. For Indonesian population groups living outside their traditional home environment see also the *Pocket edition of the Statistical Abstract*, p. 9.

[20] The need for thoroughly scientific western methods of cultivation in the emigrant colonies seems doubly pressing, because those areas are by far less fertile than Java and inaccessibility and unfavorable climate require transportation and medical facilities beyond those needed in Java or in southern Sumatra. *Cf.* J. H. Friedericy, "Indonesian Problems", *Annals of the American Academy of Political and Social Science*, July, 1950, p. 137.

ever, cannot occur until the Indonesian government appropriates far greater sums for social emancipation than it is now able to do. Until then traditional patterns of production will persist and localized over-population will remain.

III

ANOTHER ASPECT of the population problem concerns the dangerously rapid growth of the towns. Traditionally Indonesian towns did not contain more than a fraction of the total population, but especially since the Second World War and the establishment of national independence the rate of increase of the urban population has been swift. In cities like Djakarta, Surabaya, Medan and Macassar the problem may be said to be acute and adequate housing and hygienic facilities have not been able to keep pace with this abnormal growth. The result has been slums, a high mortality rate and latent social disturbances.

According to the census of 1920, 6.63 per cent of the population of Java lived in cities, in 1930 8.7 per cent lived in 102 communities of a "more or less urban character." More than half of the urban population lived in cities of over 100,000 inhabitants and the urban population of Java increased at an even more rapid rate than the population of the island as a whole. The larger the city, the quicker its growth. In 1930 Djakarta had a population of 533,000, today estimates place the population close to a million and a half. In Djakarta alone the housing shortage has become so acute that special suburbs have had to be constructed, which are filling up at a rapid rate. Djokjakarta and Surabaya, which in 1930 had a population of 137,000 and 342,000 respectively, now are believed to have close to a million inhabitants.[21]

Since the revolution the urban population has increased due to the growth of the bureaucracy, and the inadequate conditions of security in the country. On the islands beyond Java there were in 1930 only five cities with a population over 50,000 (Palembang, Mascassar, Medan, Bandjermassin, Padang).[22] Today most of these have doubled, while towns on Bali like Den Pasar and Amboyna in Eastern Indonesia have increased by almost 60 per cent in the last decade.

The severe economic dislocation and social difficulties that this urban growth presents have focused attention of national leaders on the need for a rapid industrialization. The development of Indonesian industry beyond the handicraft and household level largely occurred in the fourth decade of the present century and was interrupted by the Japanese occupation and the revolution. The total industrial plant of Indonesia is

[21] Above data are based on W. F. Wertheim, "De Stad in Indonesie," *Indonesie*, vol. V (1951), p. 36 and *Toelichting op de Stadsvormingsordonnantie stadsgemeenten Java*, Batavia, 1938, p. 20 ff.

[22] *Pocket Edition of the Statistical Abstract of the Netherlands Indies 1940*, p. 13.

exceedingly small and billions will be required to bring it to such a state of development that it will help to obviate the economic effects of the population problem.[23] While this is not the place to discuss Indonesia's industrial potential and conditions for its growth, a number of factors need to be pointed out, which make it clear that industrialization as an answer to the population problem now is—and for a long time to come will be—unsatisfactory.

The first factor is the almost inescapable fact that where industrialization has penetrated into Indonesian economy in a given area, the population of that area seems to have responded largely by increasing very rapidly, so that labor remains cheap and indeed becomes so cheap that manual labor is less expensive than machine labor and plants may de-machinize themselves. Wages remain low, and the expected increase in consumption does not take place. Investment of capital does not yield the expected results for the population, as the studies of Burger[24] and Boeke have shown. In fact experience in Indonesia seems to indicate that "Western welfare policy in the shape of capital investment and the promotion of modern industry cannot raise the general standard. of living, not even that of the directly affected groups of small people."[25]

There is every reason to believe that industrialization will result for a long time to come only in an enormous population increase and that that which is regarded as a source of relief will merely aggravate the problem. Secondly there is the factor of demand and the consumption pattern of the Indonesian masses. Even before the outbreak of the Second World War, it became evident that industrial development on its existing limited basis could hardly be expected to expand very much, because the point of consumption saturation was very easily reached,[26] while the quality of industrial goods was such that they could only in rare instances be utilized for large scale export purposes.

Long before the revolution, Indonesia's basic industrial problem was the low level of demand, [27] and while it cannot be disputed that greater sections of the population have in the course of time become more "consumption conscious," their consumption pattern hardly merits comparison with the West or finds a basis in the Western theory of unlimited wants

[23] One expert, J. D. N. Versluys, (*Aspecten van Indonesie's industrialisatie en haar financiering* Groningen, Djakarta, 1949) has estimated that in order to give industrial employment to just *one fourth* of those who annually seek work as a result of Java's increasing population an investment of about 350 million guilders ($100 million) per annum is necessary.

[24] D. H. Burger, *Vergelijking van den economische toestand der districten Tajoe en Djakeman, Regentschap Pati, afdeeling Rembang,* Economische Beschrijvingen vol. IV, Weltevreden, n.d.

[25] J. H. Boeke, "Agrarian reforms in the Far East," *American Journal of Sociology,* 57 (1952), p. 319.

[26] G. H. C. Hart, *Toward Economic Democracy in the Netherlands Indies,* New York, 1942, p. 96.

[27] J. S. Furnivall, *Netherlands India, a Study of Plural Economy,* New York, 1944, pp. 332–3, 372.

of consumption. The subsistence level of production, a basic factor in agrarian overpopulation, also operates in the industrial sphere and deters an overwhelming majority of Indonesians from producing and demanding' beyond that which a local or existing market makes available.

A final factor is the question of capital formation. It is still generally true that the existing village economy exhibits enmity toward the formation of capital[28] and that the principle of thrift as the basis of the formation of capital, making due allowance for the reservations of Keynes, only very sporadically operates in the Indonesian peasant economy. It is therefore evident that the impulse in the formation of capital investment will have to come from abroad and requests to this effect have been made by numerous government officials.

Many obstacles, however, are placed in the way of foreign investment. There is first of all the fact that the government seems to favor a collectivist economic policy and that internal security is still lacking to such a degree that investments from abroad run too great a risk. And secondly the popular aversion to foreign investment is still considerable; it stems from the popular idea that foreign investment is almost synonymous with colonial domination. This condition, for example, has greatly deterred a felicitous economic relationship between the Netherlands and Indonesia since the revolution, while it has also been reflected in the hesitation to accept aid from other sources, including the United States.[29]

Another solution of Indonesia's overpopulation problem has been sought in various forms of birth control. It has already been pointed out that traditionally the Javanese and many other ethnic groups in Indonesia marry early and that large families are frequently regarded as an economic asset. It is evident, however, that birth control in traditional Indonesian society is an impossibility until education and westernization have sufficiently affected the village masses. A recent observer has pointed out, that birth control, quite apart from ritualistic forms of infanticide, is not unknown on the islands beyond Java and that certain methods of abortion, even on Java, are sufficiently widespread to invalidate the thesis that these concepts of population restriction are incompatible with indigenous mentality.[30] Without attempting to invalidate this suggestion, it needs to be pointed out that between these traditional

[28] Cf. J. H. Boeke, Dorp en Desa, Leyden, 1934, p. 32 and N. J. Feldmann, De Overheidsmiddelen van Indonesie in verband met de dualistische economie, Leyden, 1949, p. 144.

[29] Justus M. van der Kroef, "Foreign Aid and Social Tradition in Indonesia", Far Eastern Survey, 20 (1951), p. 184.

[30] H. Fischer, pp. 25–30. Fischer especially attacks Boeke's thesis that there is no rationalized, economically oriented concept of birth control or population limitation among the Indonesians. He also shows that traditionally abortions are practised—and apparently accepted—in Javanese society by indigenous priestesses (dukuns). Elsewhere in Indonesia, abortion and infanticide do not meet with the legal recrimination of the group or of the village, the offender undergoes only slight punishment. See N. W. Lesquillier, Het adatdelictenrecht in de magische wereldbeschouwing, Dissertation, Leyden, 1934, pp. 113–5.

indigenous concepts of birth control, and the modern and specifically western concepts, based primarily on economic motivations and the result of widely different cultural factors, there may be a vast distinction. To make birth control effective a change in mentality will have to take place and new cultural values will have to become dominant.

In the colonial period birth control propaganda by the government was practically nil, not in the least because of the controversial religious and moral issues involved. Today, despite the nominal Islamic character of Indonesian society, chances that intensive birth control instruction will receive the support of the government have improved. The ruling oligarchy of Indonesian intellectuals at the helm of the national republic is essentially secular in outlook (despite Muslim or even Christian affiliation) and has generally no hesitation in applying a rationalized and western concept of population control to the mass of untutored Indonesians. It is not likely however that a widespread, active birth control campaign on the village level will soon be initiated if only because of the cost; such a campaign would require also a far greater degree of administrative control than the central government is now able to effectuate.

IV

OF VITAL IMPORTANCE to the solution of the Indonesian population problem is the degree to which the new State will make its adjustment to western concepts of production, a more rationalized concept of family life, a new and higher standard of living and attain internal security and stability. In this connection a number of recent suggestions and proposals may perhaps be noted.

The Dutch population expert, H. de Meel,[31] has indicated how since the end of the Second World War positive Malthusian checks on population growth, especially in Java, have become effective, with the collapse of order and security in the interior and the inadequate diet of the greater part of the population. De Meel supports his contention with his estimate of the population during the decade 1940–1950, which according to him shows the population to be stationary and even declining (cf. note 2 supra).

His view is open to question, however. In the first place no specific population figures for that period are available. Secondly, it is a fact that since 1948 order and security have returned in increasing degree to Java and to the islands beyond Java even earlier. And finally his belief that the inadequate diet and the resulting malnutrition is a check on population growth is altogether erroneous. Contrary to popular belief malnutrition may cause overpopulation rather than be a result of it. Though starvation reduces the sex drive, persistent malnutrition actually acts as a sexual stimulus. For example protein deficiencies lead to cirrhosis and

[31] "Demographic dilemma in Indonesia", Pacific Affairs, 24 (1951), p. 274 ff.

degeneration of the liver, which in turn cause the release of increased amounts of estrogen with a resulting increase in reproductive capacity and fertility. Japan showed an unprecedented increase of births over deaths (5,100,000) in the period 1945–1949, when the daily individual ration was still almost a thousand calories short of the required minimum. The evidence cited above by Josue de Castro, of the United Nations' Food and Agriculture Organization, points to the fact that at least one Malthusian check requires reconsideration.[32] A continuation of inadequate diet in Java, as might be expected, might well lead to an even increased growth of population.

At the end of the late war, the famed Indonesian scholar Professor J. H. Boeke of Leyden, suggested a possible solution to Java's population problem.[33] Boeke was exceedingly pessimistic that either industry, emigration or birth control, or a combination of all these factors, would yield the expected relief. To him, the population problem was imbedded in the very conflict between the village economy and the dynamics of western enterprise. Boeke proposed therefore to reconstruct the village upon an even stronger communal basis, to put the clock back as it were, lock out the influence of western culture and western enterprise and promulgate in the village sphere an anti-materialistic philosophy of "plain living and high thinking", which would eliminate material needs, make poverty a spiritual asset and eliminate all modernizing influences.

It is to be feared that the realization of this suggestion is almost certainly an impossibility. In the first place it runs counter to the ideology of the political élite in Indonesia today, which would have to be responsible for its promulgation. The westernized intellectuals in the central government welcome the modernization of their country, the rapid introduction of western technology and western organizational methods in production, while they exhibit a vast impatience with the tradition-bound village sphere. Secondly, in the colonial period western economic life penetrated—and has continued to penetrate—in many areas to such an extent that it is almost impossible to undo its influence. It would mean for example, that the Indonesian would have to learn to do without many commodities and services to which he has in the course of decades become accustomed; the painfully created demand pattern would have to be destroyed, and like its creation, this could only occur through pressure and hardship. Finally and most importantly, Boeke's solution is really no solution, because it does not allow for population increases. A growing population and a continued creation of daughter villages— along the very lines that Boeke has suggested—would only result in that

[32] *The Geography of Hunger*, New York, 1952. Mr. de Castro's experiments on the causal relationship between protein deficiencies and an increased sex drive were performed on rats and not on humans, while other aspects of his theory have recently come in for severe criticism by other population experts like Kingsley Davis.

[33] In his *The Interests of the Voiceless Far East*, Leyden, 1948, chap. XI.

the total arable land would be ultimately exhausted and the population problem would return in even greater might. Since the village economy would be restored—with its subsistence consumption pattern—the excess population could certainly not find work in industry—in fact industry would be specifically excluded from the economy of "plain living." Thus Boeke's plan is impossible, it is a flight from reality, not a meeting of it.

While Boeke's plan has found very few supporters, it is also a fact that his critics in their plans for economic reform are often unrealistic. The belief, for example, of a planner like A. Thorenaar that the population problem need not arouse undue concern, because with adequate planning and with the proper preparation of the peasantry in leaving their land and finding employment elsewhere Indonesia would be able to support "even more persons than at present," is in its generalized context open to the most serious reservations. So is his contention that a maximum mechanization of the micro-agricultural enterprise of the peasant will bring about greater welfare.[34] For the oversupplied labor market mechanization merely means increased unemployment.

And what is one to say of a plan like that of Jonkers,[35] who believes that it will be possible to increase the caloric content of the Indonesian's diet to the level reached by 1939, which he suggests is based on an increase in the cash income of the peasant family three times that of the income per family in 1939, by 1964? Within 15 years the greater part of the population increase in the period 1949–1964, which for Java will be some 12 million alone, will have to find industrial employment, according to Jonkers. In other words by 1964, when Java's population will have swollen to about 60 million people, more than 24 million people will have to be employed in areas of enterprise other than agriculture.

Given the demonstrable relationship between population increase and industrial development, the absurdity of Jonkers' views soon becomes apparent, not to speak of the problem of increased purchasing power per family which he posits as indispensable to his plan. Even if a total increase in purchasing power would be possible of attainment, Jonkers appears to have given no thought to such questions as the payment of interest on the enormous amount of capital from abroad required to establish the industrial plant which he envisages.[36]

Other "planners," like the Indonesian vice-president Mohammad Hatta, who also criticized Boeke's suggestions, appear to place their trust not in industrialization so much, but rather in transmigration and agricultural cooperatives and collectives.[37] As to the former, the preceding pages

[34] A. Thorenaar, *Overvloed in Insulinde*, Amsterdam, 1946, p. 13 ff.

[35] Jonkers, *Welvaartszorg in Indonesie*, pp. 222, 228 ff.

[36] A. H. Ballendux, *Bijdrage tot de kennis van de credietverlening aan de "Indonesische Middenstand"*, Dissertation, Leyden, The Hague, 1951, p. 24. Pp. 17–24 contain a vigorous criticism of the plans of Thorenaar, Jonkers and others, and a defense of Boeke's theories.

[37] Mohammad Hatta, *Beberapa fasal ekonomi*, Djakarta, 1950, vol. 1, chap. 7.

have already pointed out the dangers inherent in past and present coloniza-tion plans. The village of colonizers faces the same problems of dy-namization of production that confronts the village in Java itself. Con-solidation of land, incentives to bring crop surpluses to market, improve-ments in transportation, as well as mechanization in its proper proportions, improvements of seed and implements will all have to be brought about in the colony of transmigrants. Mere "cooperation," a mere consolidation of communal bonds or emphasis on collective cultivation and landholding patterns is by no means the solution.

The problem is to bring the cooperative agricultural enterprise actively in touch with the market economy, to make its participants desirous to produce and sell more and to widen the range of their wants. This in-volves a cultural revolution, not a change in the structure of the economy alone. In the words of a leading agricultural expert:[38] "The emancipation and dynamization of the desa (i.e. Javanese village) is primarily a mental process, which from an economic point of view means a more active participation in economic life." The results of the revolutionary period makes such a required change in mental outlook less impossible than before.[39]

The basis of any meaningful solution to the population problem would have to be an alteration in the structure of agricultural production. The communal basis of village economy would have to be ended and in its place would have to come a complete integration of the village into western estate enterprise. Estate production, on a national and not a colonial basis would, as Boeke himself has suggested,[40] be the lever with which the standard of living of the village community would be raised. The excess population could find in estate agriculture, with its thoroughly scientific technique, its highly integrated organization and its international orientation, not only an enduring and diversified source of employment but also a channel of western acculturation. As the demand pattern be-comes more extensive and less restricted in scope, the yield of estate ex-plant rests. The village production itself should be intensified but its products should be exclusively staple crops (rice, corn), and not export products (coffee, sugar, tea) which can be produced better on the estates. From the start wage and price control would be essential and government must direct its fiscal policy toward mastery over and not just the mere penetration of money and exchange market economy in the village sphere.[41]

[38] G. H. van der Kolff, "De dessa en haar welvaart", p. 96 in G. H. van der Kolff, ed., Sticusa Jaarboek 1950, Amsterdam, 1950.

[39] Th. A. Fruin, Dari Ekonomi Pendjadjahan kearah Ekonomi Kebangsaan, Djakarta, 1949, p. 9. See Ballendux, p. 18.

[40] Ontwikkelingsgang en Toekomst van Bevolkings-en Ondernemingslandbouw in Nederslands-Indie, pp. 102–3.

[41] Th. A. Fruin, Het Economische Aspect van het Indonesische Vraagstuk, Amsterdam, 1947, pp. 85–9.

Propaganda, popular credit and agricultural services would be the spearheads in an increased production of staple crops and a stabilization of peasant economy. It is clear that such an alteration of village economy and the adoption or imposition of new culture patterns will be accompanied by a major social and cultural revolution, the earliest signs of which are already evident, but the consequences of which can hardly be gauged as yet. There is however no question that this revolution must be accomplished within the foreseeable future if population pressure will not become so great as to force a continuous political crisis in Indonesia.

POPULATION GROWTH IN SOUTHEAST ASIA

By Irene B. Taeuber

Southeast Asia is a laboratory for the analysis of the interrelations between population, culture, resources, and technologies. Here there are vast diversities in indigenous cultures, cultural interpenetrations, religions, economic organizations, and political forms. Studies of the island microcosms could reduce to basic factors and processes the problem of economic poverty and population increase that characterizes the billion and a half people who live between the Atlantic littoral of North Africa and the islands that fringe the Pacific coast of Asia. Moreover, in Southeast Asia as a whole and in most of its component parts the relations between people and resources are such as to permit the analysis of prospects and possibilities without the spectre of approaching tragedy that haunts so much of the research on population in densely settled agricultural areas.

We know little of the demography of the premodern world of Southeast Asia. The records suggest, however, that diversities in levels of fertility and mortality may have been far greater in former times, that the penetration of the culture of the West may have tended to create uniformities where before there were substantial diversities. Certainly the initial reactions to the West were complex. In many areas the diseases, the guns, and the dislocations of the West brought depopulation or even extinction; in others the transplantation of people led to ethnic intermixture or replacement even during the period when high mortality appeared to be dooming all the island peoples. In other areas, on the contrary, the introduction to the West produced few immediate effects on population outside the centers of occupation.

Gradually as colonialism spread throughout the East a pattern began to emerge, and it was one of population increase. This increase was neither planned nor anticipated, for few administrators even of the late colonial period had read the writings of a Scotch parson named Malthus. The growth of the indigenous peoples was a natural consequence of an imposed political order oriented toward the export markets. The establishment of order reduced direct mortality and lessened the frequency of decimations by disease and famine. The technical guidance and the capital investments of the colonial administrations led to increased and regularized food supplies, while roads and railroads permitted the movement of food and medicine to critical areas. Sanitary cordons, police controls, and vaccinations lessened and then eliminated the pandemics. The episodic catastrophes disappeared, infant mortality dropped, and general mortality declined somewhat. Growth was inevitable if fertility remained at or near the levels that had previously permitted the survival of the people. But the natural dynamics of colonialism which lowered mortality perpetuated if they did not create high fertility. Colonial policy did not favor the industrialization, urbanization, and advancing education that were associated historically with declining fertility among Western peoples. The colonial peoples remained predominantly in villages—and in the villages there were few basic changes in ways of living, social institutions, familial values, or religious sanctions. In so far as the partial diffusion of the Western economy and society influenced the fertility of the East it tended toward increase rather than decrease.

What happened to populations during the colonial era may be history today, but it is history whose heritage is the fundamental fact in assessing the population problems and the population prospects among Asia's peoples. Growth began early in the colonial period, slow and intermittent in most areas, but it became more regular and more rapid over the centuries. Recent estimates of the Population Division of the United Nations may serve to illustrate both the fact and the magnitude of the problem. The population of Asia excluding Asiatic Russia was about 250 million in 1750, 857 million in 1900, 1.3 billion in 1950. If the estimated rates of increase for the years 1946-1948 should continue to 1980, the population would be 1.8 billion. In other words, continuation of rates of increase of the general order of those now occurring would add half a billion to Asia's population within thirty years. Since half a billion is a figure difficult to visualize, I may add that the present population of Pakistan, India, and Indonesia is now about half a billion.

To proceed on the assumption that Asia's population will reach 1.8 billion in the year 1980 and estimate the resources requirements and economic developments for a population of this size would add little to our knowledge and contribute nothing to the solution of our problems. There is little basis for assuming that the Asia of a generation hence will constitute a unit within which there is an interchange of people and a cooperative use of resources. More fundamentally, however, the growth of population within the next generation will represent the combined influence of the size and momentum of present population and the changes in fertility and mortality that are the human responses to changing political, economic, and social conditions. And today there are basic forces that may make the centuries of colonialism prelude to the status of the present but not prediction of the developments of the future.

In Southeast Asia today new governments are responsible to the people for freedom from hunger and needless death, education for children, advance toward the good life, however variously that good life be defined. In the individual nations the aspirations among people and the concepts of the welfare functions of government approach those in the industrial nations of the West, while per capita food production and family income remain considerably below even the severely inadequate levels of the prewar years. In many areas the secular requirements for increases in material levels of living are in scarcely concealed conflict with the cultural forces of the traditional societies; reactions against rationality are widespread. Social changes that would influence marriage, family, and fertility become at once more possible and more difficult.

Into this transitional world of the East have come new advances of Western science whose implications for the future of Eastern populations are even deeper than the political problems of the moment. The advances most eagerly accepted and most effectively adopted are medical in the broad sense—products and procedures that permit the limitation of death without basic changes in economy or society. The most notable are, of course, DDT and the antibiotics. Ceylon's experience may be cited, both because of the startling magnitude of the changes and because the quantitative documentation in censuses and vital statistics is incontrovertible.

In Ceylon, malaria was a severe hazard both to health and to economic development. The northern part of the Island that once supported a dense agricultural population was almost deserted, the great reservoirs of the early Sinhalese kings lost in the jungles. And peasants densely settled on the cultivated land outside the estates of the center and south could produce only a portion of the food requirements of the Island's population. Reclamation projects were tried, but the hazards of the mosquito were so great that it was difficult to find settlers who would receive grants of the newly irrigated land. During the War the armies present in Ceylon demonstrated the procedures for malaria control. After the War there was a comprehensive Island-wide organization for the use of DDT as a contact spray. The death rate dropped almost forty per cent between 1946 and 1947; by 1951 it had dropped to 11.6 per 1,000 total population. By 1952 the expectation of life at birth for males was almost 58 years. The precipitant decline in mortality was not accompanied by any measurable changes in fertility; crude birth rates remained over 40. The increase between the censuses of 1946 and 1953 was almost 21 per cent. And by 1952 the rate of natural increase exceeded three per cent per year.

In the past, the decline in mortality was one aspect of social and economic changes that involved increased production and a wider distribution of social facilities. Today the decline in mortality is occurring with few changes in social life, education levels, nutritive standards, food resources, or industrial facilities. At least in the short run the connection between society, economy, and mortality that has existed throughout human history is broken. But there is no change in the association between village life, the familistic ideal, and human reproduction. Ancient birth rates and modern death rates coexist. The altered dimensions of the population problems of the so-called under-developed areas are obvious.

There is a prevalent opinion that the problems of population increase are merely the frictional difficulties of economic modernization, that fertility declines naturally with industrialization and urbanization. If rounded industrial growth had been developing from the sixteenth century onward, today's vast populations might be approaching demographic balance, with high levels of income and of education, low death rates, and low birth rates. A small portion of the people might be producing the food for that great majority who lived in urbanized areas and labored in nonagricultural pursuits. But the centuries of colonialism occurred; populations have multiplied many-fold; the rural people predominate; and fertility is very high. And manifold evidence from within Asia itself indicates that the high fertility and the consequent high rates of population increase will persist as long as the conditions and the values of the peasant society persist. Fragmented urbanization will result in a reduction of the fertility of that portion of the people who live in cities but only really comprehensive urbanization could lead to substantial reductions in national fertility.

Unless we assume that industrialization and urbanization proceed until Asia's multiplying billions become more urbanized than the Japanese we cannot look for automatic solutions to the problems of population increase through the growth of cities and the development of industries considered apart from changes in the rural areas themselves. But here we have another prevalent view to the effect that improvements within rural society itself lead naturally to declining fertility. The experience within many types of situations in many parts of Asia suggests that this hope of automatic solution to population problems is also likely to prove illusory. Increases in levels of living within the peasant society, whether secured in the original place of residence or in a new settlement, involve no necessary reductions in average size of family. The Japanese in Hokkaido, the Koreans in Manchuria, the Filipinos in Mindanao, the Indonesians in the Outer Islands, the Ceylonese in the newly irrigated areas, all took with them the family institutions and values of the subcultures from which they came. In so far as there was an effect on fertility in was toward an increase, for the pioneer area was favorable to early marriage and abundant child-bearing. The frontiers relieved population pressure in the areas of origin for brief periods of time, but soon the new areas themselves were settled densely with peoples whose fertility remained that of the peasant society. The problems of population density and population increase remained as they had been except that the areas of occupation were larger, the population more numerous, and the lands and other resources for future utilization more meager.

The fact that population growth is not likely to slow quickly as by-product of industrialization and rural improvements does not justify the assumption that fertility will remain at its present levels until the cataclysms of old become again the regulators of man's numbers. The new social forces are deep. Statesmen and students in the individual countries perceive the problem of growth if they do not see solutions to it that are consistent with their ways of living, their ethical systems, and their religious beliefs. That other countries will soon join Japan and India in the search for direct solutions is quite probable. In the meantime the student from another culture can only suggest the preeminent importance of research on population as a basis for evaluating the demographic consequences of social and economic policies now being implemented and for assessing the need for more direct policies.

Political, cultural, and economic developments that occurred without reference to the population factor left the new nations of Asia with the population problems they now have. Continued emphasis on economic development and public health in the new situation of quickened rates of increase may only intensify the population problems of future generations. The neglect of incisive research on fertility in all its demographic, social, and economic interrelationships may be tragic not alone for the advancement of knowledge but for the social advance, the economic well-being, and even the survival of more than half the world's people. Here in the demographic laboratory of Southeast Asia population research would seem to merit high priority.

DEMOGRAPHIC GLIMPSES INTO BURMA, 1952

By *Philip M. Hauser and Evelyn M. Kitagawa*

AFTER about 125 years of colonialism as part of the British Empire, Burma became a completely independent country in 1948. Slightly smaller than Texas, she had an estimated population of 18.9 million in 1952.[1]

Geographically isolated by ranges of hills and mountains on the strategic peninsula of Southeastern Asia, the Burmese population is predominantly of Mongolian stock with an Indo-Buddhist culture. Burma is characterized by a great diversity of racial and ethnic groups and a wide range of economic and social organization, varying from that of nomadic hill tribes to sophisticated urbanites in the great metropolitan center of Rangoon. Like most of Southeastern Asia, colonialism has left Burma with a pluralistic society and with relatively large exogenous population groups, Indians—including both Hindu and Muslim—and Chinese.

Burma has yet to experience the impact of the demographic revolution. Her fertility and mortality, while not precisely known, are both high and conform with the expected pattern in an essentially pre-industrial culture.[2] The Government of the Union of Burma is committed to a policy of induced economic and social development and lays great emphasis on improving the health and decreasing the death rate of the population. Unlike most of her Asiatic neighbors, Burma is resource rich, especially in respect to food, and under favorable circumstances could achieve a high level of living for her peoples. She has requested and received technical assistance for economic and social development from the United Nations and the Specialized Agencies, from the unilateral programs of the United States, and under the Colombo Plan; and in addition she has undertaken development programs on her own initiative with the assistance of expert personnel which she has employed directly from abroad. Although a number of her development

---

[1] United Nations, STATISTICAL YEARBOOK, 1953, New York, 1954, p. 26.
[2] Prior to the war from 1937 to 1939 Burma had reported crude birth rates above 32.0, crude death rates above 23.0 and infant mortality rates above 200 (United Nations, DEMOGRAPHIC YEARBOOK, 1948, New York, 1949).

programs are expressly aimed at the improvement of health and the reduction of mortality, she has as yet taken no official position or action in respect to the control of fertility.

The Union Government is actively engaged in national planning and has created a Ministry of National Planning and an Economic and Social Board chairmaned by the Prime Minister, as agencies to spearhead social and economic development. As an important adjunct of national planning, a Central Statistical and Economics Department, and a Census Office have been established. The latter is now engaged in the conduct of the first Censuses of post-war independent Burma. Pre-test Census operations conducted in 1952 indicated the Census taking in Burma could be as comprehensive and as reliable as in the more advanced nations.[3] The Censuses as a result of internal disorder are being conducted in a series of stages, year by year, as conditions permit.[4] The tabular results of each stage of the Census and eventually of the combined stages[5] will not be available for some time. Preliminary sample tabulations, however, are available from the pre-test Census data collected in 1952.[6] The data were tabulated primarily to provide a basis for finalizing the pre-test Census schedules, rather than to obtain substantive statistics. They, nevertheless, provide some glimpses into the population structure and dynamics of some cities and towns in Burma. While Burma is predominantly rural, only 10 per cent of the population having been residents in cities and towns of 5,000 or more in 1931,[7] it is likely that with the exception of Rangoon, and possibly two or three other relatively large cities, urban-rural differences will be small. The following data are presented, in comparison with statistics for the United States to provide some basis for their interpretation, more to demonstrate the potentialities of the Census of

[3] Hauser, Philip M.: Research Potentialities in Burma, *Population Index*, 19 (4): 260–272, October 1953; and Hauser, Philip M.: DEVELOPMENT OF STATISTICS IN BURMA, 1951–52, United Nations Technical Assistance Program, New York, 1953, pp. 8–10 and pp. 26–31.

[4] The first stage of the Censuses of Population, including the Labor Force, Housing, Cottage Industry, and Industry, was conducted in February, 1953, and included some 250 cities and towns. The second stage of the Census was scheduled for field canvass in February, 1954, and was to include, in addition to accessible towns not previously covered, some approximately 2,300 village tracts, primarily rural in character, but mainly adjacent to cities and towns.

[5] Provision was made in the Census plan for "multi-stage" operations in which complete enumeration of second and subsequent stages would be combined with sample surveys of areas covered in previous stages so as to permit the compilation of sub-area and national totals.

[6] Preliminary manuscript tables were brought back to the United States by the senior author. They are presented in this paper with the permission of the Commissioner of the Census, U Kyaw Khine.

[7] United Nations, DEMOGRAPHIC YEARBOOK, 1952, New York, 1953, p. 176.

Population in Burma, now in process, than to provide information about Burma at this time. The data for the United States used for comparison are at some points not exactly comparable but, it is felt, are close enough to indicate the direction and general magnitude of, if not the precise, differences.

The statistics are based on preliminary sample tabulations of pre-test Census and sample Census data. Pre-test Census operations were conducted in four towns[8] in which the entire population was completely enumerated on a short schedule and more detailed information obtained on a sample basis. The sample comprised 20 per cent of the households systematically selected from the complete list of households enumerated in the Census canvass. The preliminary sample data tabulated for the four towns included 1,552 persons in households systematically selected from the 20 per cent sample.

In addition to the pre-test Census operations conducted in the four towns, a sample Census was conducted in twenty-eight towns[9] partly to obtain badly needed information for the Union Government, and partly to help train personnel and develop procedures for the forthcoming Census operations. Varying sample ratios were used, depending on the population of each town, to obtain a sample of about 2,500 structures in each town. In each case the sample consisted of households in structures systematically selected from a complete list of structures compiled for the coming Census operation. The predominant proportion of all structures were single family dwelling units. The smaller structures were sampled and the larger structures were completely enumerated as a separate sub-universe. The preliminary sample tabulation for the twenty-eight towns included 2,845 persons in a properly weighted household sample of the sample Census returns.

This paper is based primarily on the four-town sample because the schedule used in the pre-test Census operations included a series of fertility questions.[10] Some reference is made, however, to the

[8] Bassein with a population of 83,600 in 1952, Minbu with 9,800, Bhamo with 8,900 and Kyaukpyu with 7,000.

[9] The twenty-eight cities and towns included, in order of size, were: Mandalay, Moulmein, Henzada, Prome, Akyab, Thaton, Tavoy, Myingyan, Toungoo, Mergui, Pakokku, Monywa, Maubin, Myaungmya, Pyapon, Meiktila, Shwebo, Sagaing, Yamethin, Magwe, Thayetmyo, Kyaukse, Tharrawaddy, Katha, Thanatpin, Sandoway, Mohnyin, Mawleik. The total population of these places was estimated from the sample at about 885,000 in March, 1952. The coefficient of variation of the estimated total population for each town was less than 3 per cent.

[10] See Hauser, Philip M.: Research Potentialities in Burma, loc. cit., p. 268.

twenty-eight-town sample, and the data on marital status are based entirely on it.[11]

On the whole, the preliminary sample tabulations are statistically adequate for the analysis undertaken in this paper. For example, the reported percentage of persons 65 years old and over, in the four-town sample, namely 2.8 per cent, is subject to a sampling error of 0.4. Thus the chances are two out of three that the results which would have been obtained from a complete enumeration would have been from 2.4 to 3.2. The number of children ever born to each 1,000 women 10 years old and over ever married, 3,216, is subject to a sampling error of 150; and the number of children ever born per 1,000 women 49 years and older, 5,493, is subject to a sampling error of 380. Thus, the chances are two out of three that a complete census would have produced a figure of children ever born to women ever married between 3,066 and 3,366; and a figure of children ever born to women of completed fertility between 5,113 and 5,873. A table of sampling errors is presented below to provide a basis for the interpretation of most of the figures presented in the tables.[12]

In addition to providing the Union Government with a factual basis for planning purposes, the Burmese Census statistics will provide a demographic benchmark against which to measure the population changes which will occur as the result of Burma's efforts to achieve higher economic levels and to advance the welfare of her people.

General Characteristics

The four towns in Burma included in the sample were inhabited predominantly by an indigenous Buddhist population. About 82 per cent of the inhabitants were Buddhists, primarily Burman, about 8 per cent were Muslim, and the remaining 10 per cent primarily Hindu, Christian, and Animist.

About 35 per cent of the population fifteen years and older, was illiterate in Burmese and about 85 per cent did not read or write any language other than Burmese. Over two-thirds of the persons 5 years of age and over, had no formal schooling in Burmese, and an additional one-fifth had less than 5 years of such schooling.

[11] The question on marital status in the four-town sample, was included on the short schedule used for the complete Census canvass and was not tabulated at the time of the senior author's departure from Burma.

[12] The sampling error reported below is computed on the assumption of simple random sampling. The errors are therefore over-stated because the sample was systematically selected from complete lists of households with complete geographic stratification. The sampling errors, of course, do not include any indication of errors in response or biases of non-reporting.

Standard error of estimated percentages (range of 2 chances out of 3).

Estimated Percentage	Size of Base							
	1,552	1,250	1,000	750	500	250	100	50
2 or 98	.36	.40	.45	.51	.62	.88	1.41	1.97
5 or 95	.56	.62	.69	.79	.97	1.38	2.19	3.08
10 or 90	.76	.85	.95	1.10	1.34	1.90	3.00	4.24
25 or 75	1.10	1.22	1.38	1.58	1.95	2.74	4.36	6.16
50	1.26	1.41	1.58	1.82	2.24	3.16	5.00	7.07

It should be noted that many of the United States data are also based on samples and subject to sampling error. The relatively large size of the United States samples, however, makes the sampling error of United States data negligible. The United States reports to which reference is made contain information about the variances of the United States data.

About 91 per cent of the population had no formal schooling in English and an additional 2 per cent had less than 5 years of English education.

The level of living of the inhabitants of these towns, as was to be expected in the circumstances in Burma, was very low. The median income of persons 10 years of age and older with income, was 376 kyats (formerly rupees) per year—about $75. Seventy-nine per cent had an income of less than 1,000 kyats, or about $200 per year. Of the persons in the labor force almost half were either own-account workers (38.7 per cent) or unpaid family workers (8.6 per cent). The own-account workers were predominantly small entrepreneurs, engaged in cottage industry or in marginal retail sales enterprises. About 85 per cent of the residential structures were made of bamboo or thatched walls and the median value of the dwelling unit was a little over 200 kyats, or about $40. Less than 1 per cent of the dwelling units had running water, and less than an additional 7 per cent had access to water inside their "compound" (grounds). Less than 3 per cent of the dwelling units had electricity, and less than 1 per cent inside toilet facilities. The modal area of the dwelling unit was about 350 square feet.

In general, then, the population covered by the pre-test Census, a preliminary Census tabulation of which is reported on in this paper, was an indigenous Burmese population characterized by high illiteracy, and a low level of living. The data on general population characteristics and on fertility should therefore help to illuminate various aspects of the structure and dynamics of a pre-industrial, albeit urban, population.

Age and Sex Structure. The population of the four-town sample was a very young population and, as was to be expected, considerably younger than the population of the United States. The

Age	Total	Male	Female
Total			
Number	1,552	763	789
Per Cent	100.0	100.0	100.0
0– 4 Years	11.9	13.4	10.4
5– 9	9.0	8.4	9.6
10–14	9.5	9.2	9.8
15–19	13.4	12.3	14.4
20–24	11.0	9.0	12.8
25–34	15.0	15.0	15.1
35–44	13.1	13.6	12.7
45–54	9.4	10.4	8.5
55–64	4.9	5.9	3.9
65 Years and Over	2.8	2.8	2.8
Median Age	22.9	23.8	22.3

Table 1.   Population by age and sex: Four-town sample, Burma, 1952.

median age of the total population was 22.9 years, that of males 23.8 years, and that of females 22.3 years. Corresponding data for the United States in 1950 were, respectively, 30.2 years, 29.9 years, and 30.5 years. The age and sex structure of the Burmese sample populaton are shown in Table 1. The summary data for the United States are shown in Table 9.[13]

Persons under 15 years of age constituted only 30 per cent of the total population, as contrasted with an average of about 40 per cent in the less developed regions of the world.[14] The twenty-eight-town sample had a somewhat larger proportion of children under 15, 34 per cent,[15] but this, also, was below that estimated for most of the less developed areas of the world. In 1931 the Census of Burma reported 37.4 per cent of the population under 15 years of age.[16]

The relatively small proportion of younger persons in the four-town sample may be partly attributable to the fact that the data are for an urban population. The age structure, however, undoubtedly reflects the effects of differential in-migration to the towns as a

[13] To conserve space, the data for the United States are presented only in summary statistical form, in Table 9.

[14] WORLD POPULATION TRENDS, 1920–1947, United Nations, Department of Social Affairs, New York, December 1949, p. 15. This difference was called to the attention of the writers by Dr. John D. Durand, in discussions at the Annual Conference of the Milbank Memorial Fund, 1953, at which a preliminary version of this paper was presented.

[15] The median age of the twenty-eight-town sample was also somewhat lower than that of the four-town sample, 22.2 as compared with 22.9 years. The median age of males was 22.7 years, that of females 21.7 years.

[16] United Nations, op. cit., p. 124.

result of the unsettled conditions in the Burmese countryside, especially during the post-war period.[17]

Persons 65 years and older made up only 2.8 per cent of the population. In consequence of this and the smaller than expected proportion of persons under 15 the ratio of persons of dependent age to persons of productive age in the Burmese towns sampled was relatively low. There were 49.5 persons under 15 and 65 and older for each 100 persons 15 to 64 years old. This proportion of "dependents" was somewhat greater than that in the United States in 1940 (46.8), but below that in the United States in 1950 (53.9). There were 45.4 young persons of dependent age, that is under 15, per 100 persons 15 to 64 years old in the Burmese towns, as compared with 36.7 in the United States in 1940 and 41.4 in 1950. There were only 4.1 older dependents, that is persons 65 and over, per 100 persons 15 to 64 in the Burmese towns, as contrasted with with 10.1 in the United States in 1940 and 12.5 in 1950.

Thus, as was to be expected, the population of the Burmese towns contained a much smaller proportion of older persons than did the United States. Furthermore, despite the relatively small proportion of younger persons for such an area, the Burmese sample contained a larger proportion of younger persons than did the United States in either 1940 or 1950. The difference in the proportion of younger persons in the Burmese sample and in the United States, however, was smaller than expected.

The four-town sample of Burma contained more females than males, the sex ratio being 96.7.[18]

Marital Status. Of the twenty-eight-town sample population 14 years and over, 59.1 per cent were married. This crude proportion of marriage was about the same as that of the United States in 1940 (59.6 for both sexes combined) and considerably below that of the United States in 1951 (68.1) after the post-war marriage boom (*see* Table 2 and Table 9).

The proportion of males 14 years and older married in Burma was greater than that of males in the United States in 1940, 61.6

---

[17] The population of the four-town sample cannot be considered as representative of Burma or even of urban Burma. The fertility data which are presented may be affected to some extent by the age structure of the sample population. This would be particularly true of the fertility ratios. The data on children ever born, however, are less likely to be distorted by the age structure directly, but may be influenced by the differential characteristics of in-migrants —particularly of the refugees from the battle-scarred rural areas.

[18] The sex ratio of the twenty-eight-town sample was 99.2; that of Burma in 1931 as reported by the Census, over 104, United Nations, *op cit.*, p. 124.

as compared with 59.7 per cent; but it was well below that of American males in 1951, 69.9 per cent. The proportion of Burmese females married was below that of American females in both 1940 and 1951, being 56.7 per cent as compared with 59.5 and 66.5 per cent, respectively. Although the proportion of females married in both the Burmese sample and in the United States was below that of males, the difference between the sexes was greater among the Burmese. (See Table 9.)

The differences in crude proportions married are influenced, of course, by differences in the age structures of the population. The age-specific data indicate that Burmese males in 1952 had higher proportions of married than American males at age groupings 14 to 44 years in 1940, and Burmese women a higher proportion married than American women 14–24 years of age in 1940. Burmese males above age 54, and Burmese females above age 34 have lower proportions married than American males and females, respectively, in 1940. By 1951, however, as a result of the post-war boom

Table 2. Marital status of population 14 years old and over by age and sex: twenty-eight-town sample, Burma, 1952.

SEX AND AGE	TOTAL		NEVER MARRIED	MARRIED	WIDOWED	SEPARATED OR RENOUNCED[a]
	Number	Per Cent				
Males						
Total 14 Years and Older	963[b]	100.0	27.3	61.6	4.7	6.4
14–24[c]	321	100.0	65.3	23.7	0.9	10.1
25–34	252	100.0	14.3	77.7	2.8	5.2
35–44	194	100.0	5.3	87.9	2.6	4.2
45–54	127	100.0	3.1	82.8	10.2	3.9
55–64	47	100.0	8.5	70.2	17.0	4.3
65 Years and Older	21	100.0	—	52.3	42.9	4.8
Females						
Total 14 Years and Older	972[d]	100.0	25.0	56.7	15.5	2.8
14–24[c]	359	100.0	47.2	48.0	2.8	2.0
25–34	209	100.0	13.0	77.9	5.3	3.8
35–44	180	100.0	14.5	69.3	13.4	2.8
45–54	126	100.0	10.3	52.4	33.3	4.0
55–64	59	100.0	8.5	32.2	55.9	3.4
65 Years and Older	39	100.0	5.3	15.8	78.9	—

a Separated are shown as equivalent of divorced because marriage and divorce in Burma are by mutual consent. "Renounced" refers to the dissolution of marriage which occurs when the male enters the Buddhist priesthood; it may therefore be considered as divorced.

b Includes one man for whom age not reported. Percentage distributions based on totals excluding ten men of unknown marital status.

c Age tabulations include age groups 10–14 and 15–24 years in the twenty-eight-town sample. Estimates for age 14 only were obtained for all males and females by assuming one-fifth of the 10–14 age group were 14 years old; the five renounced, one widowed and two married persons 10–14 years old were assumed to be 14 years old; and the number of single persons 14 years old was obtained by subtracting the estimated number of 14 year olds in all other marital status categories from the estimated total number of 14 year olds. These estimates for 14 year olds were added to persons 15–24 years old.

d Percentage distributions based on totals excluding four women of unknown marital status.

in the marriage rate, United States age-specific proportions married exceeded the Burmese in all but the youngest age class for women, and all but ages 14–24 and 35–44 for men. The markedly lower proportions of Burmese married in the older age groups of both men and women is attributable to the much earlier incidence of mortality of spouses in the Burmese sample, as evidenced by the data on widowed.

When age structure of the population is controlled through standardization, the difference between the proportion married in the Burmese sample and the United States is decreased. For males, standardization produces a higher proportion married in the Burmese sample than in the United States in 1940 and, in consequence, a higher proportion also for both sexes combined. Using the Burmese sample age structure as a standard, the proportion married of both sexes combined, 14 years and older, was 59.1 in Burma, as compared with 56.1 in 1940, and 63.8 in 1951, in the United States. For males, the proportions married were 60.3 in Burma, and 54.1 and 62.0 in the United States in 1940 and in 1951, respectively. For females, the comparative proportions were 57.9 in the Burmese sample, and 58.2 and 65.3 in the United States in 1940 and 1951. (See Table 9.)

Some glimpse of marital stability in the Burmese sample is afforded by the data on "separated or renounced" which may be considered as approximating the "divorced" and "separated" in the United States. Because of cultural differences this comparison is hazardous, but it provides at least a rough indication of marriage stability in the diverse cultures in one of which marriage is controlled primarily through the mores and in the other through law as well as the mores. In Burma marriage and divorce are both by mutual consent without benefit either of civil or ecclesiastical officiation or record. The Burmese category "separated" is the equivalent of "divorced" in the United States. Burmese marriages may also be dissolved when the married male enters the Buddhist priesthood at which time the marriage is "renounced." The greatest incidence of "renounced" marriages seem to occur in the early and late stages of marriage—that is among males under 25 and 65 and older. In the United States the dissolution of marriage is perhaps better indicated by the combination of the categories "divorced" and "separated" than by the "divorced" alone.

In the Burmese sample, 6.4 per cent of all males 14 years of age and over were reported as either "separated or renounced." These categories are combined in Table 2 because of small sample numbers but actually among the males 5.1 per cent represented the category "renounced" and only 1.3 per cent were "separated." In the United States in 1950, 2.0 per cent of the males 14 years and older were "divorced" and 1.6 per cent "separated," making a total of 3.6 per cent whose marriages were effectively dissolved. An additional 1.9 per cent of the American males reported their wife "absent" at the time of the Census enumeration. It is possible that some proportion of these "absent" spouses may also represent marriages effectively dissolved, although it is also possible that some proportion of the "separated" as well as the "absent" category may be reunited.

Among the Burmese females 14 years and older, 2.8 per cent were "separated" or "renounced" of whom only about one-fifth were "renounced." Among American women, 2.4 per cent were reported "divorced" and an additional 2.0 per cent "separated," making a total in these two categories of 4.4 per cent. An additional 1.5 per cent reported their husbands "absent."[19]

Table 3. Age at first marriage for women of all ages and for women 49 years old and over ever married: Four-town sample, Burma, 1952.

Age at First Marriage	Women of All Ages	Women 49 Years and Older
Total		
Number	371	83
Per cent	100.0	100.0
10–14 Years	7.8	6.0
15–19	65.8	67.5
20–24	20.2	15.7
25–29	6.2	10.8
Median Age	18.2	18.3

In general, then, although marriage and divorce for the Buddhist population in Burma are by mutual consent and controlled entirely through the informal operation of the mores, the available data and firsthand observation of the culture would indicate that marriage in Burma is probably not too different in stability than marriage in the United States.[20]

The four-town sample included inquiries permitting the tabulation of the number and proportion of women ever married. These data are consistent with those presented above for the twenty-eight-town sample. Of the women 20 years and older in the Burmese sample, 74.8 per cent were ever married, as compared with 83.0 per cent in the United States in 1940, and 88.2 per cent in 1950 (Table 9).

[19] U. S. Bureau of the Census. UNTED STATES CENSUS OF POPULATION: 1950, Vol. II CHARACTERISTICS OF THE POPULATION, Part I, United States Summary, G.P.O., Washington, D. C., 1953, p. 182.

[20] Because of the approximate nature of the comparison the data have not been standardized.

Age	Total	Duration of Marriage									Average Duration of Marriage in Years
		0–4 Years	5–9 Years	10–14 Years	15–19 Years	20–24 Years	25–29 Years	30–34 Years	35–39 Years	40 Years and Over	
Total	368[a]	76	71	58	34	44	33	25	12	15	16.1
15–19 Years	36	29	7	—	—	—	—	—	—	—	3.5
20–29	108	38	48	22	—	—	—	—	—	—	6.6
30–39	85	6	12	28	20	19	—	—	—	—	14.5
40–49	71	1	2	5	13	19	19	10	2	—	23.3
50–59	44	—	1	3	—	3	11	13	8	5	31.0
60 Years and Over	21	—	—	—	1	3	3	2	2	10	36.7

[a] Includes three women for whom age and/or duration of marriage were not reported.

Table 4.   Duration of marriage of women 15 years old and over ever married, by age of women: Four-town sample, Burma, 1952.

Age at Marriage, Duration of Marriage, and Age at Birth of First Child. Women in the four-town Burmese sample married earlier, had a longer duration of marriage when the data are standardized for age, and had their first child at an earlier age than women in the United States.

Median age at first marriage of the Burmese women ever married was 18.2 years, as compared with 21.2 years for women in the United States in 1940. Women ever married of completed fertility, those 49 years old and over in the Burmese sample, had about the same median age at first marriage as did all women ever married. (*See* Tables 3 and 9.)

Average duration of marriage of all women ever married in the Burmese sample was below that of American women, 16.1 years, as contrasted with 17.5 years for American women in 1940. This difference, however, was reversed when age was held constant through standardization (*see* Tables 4 and 9). Standardized for age, using the age distribution of the Burmese sample as a standard, average duration of marriage of American women was 15.6 years, as compared with 16.1 years for the Burmese women. This difference would probably have been greater if the data were available by smaller age intervals, because women in the United States tended to be older than the Burmese

Table 5. Age at birth of first child for women ever married with one or more children ever born: Four-town sample, Burma, 1952.

AGE AT BIRTH OF FIRST CHILD	NUMBER OF WOMEN
Total	
Number	288[a]
Per Cent	100.0
10–14 Years	2.1
15–19	46.2
20–24	38.1
25–29	10.1
30–34	3.1
35 Years and Over	0.3
Median Age	20.2

[a] Includes two women for whom age at birth of first child was not reported.

women within the broad age groupings.

Women in the Burmese sample were younger than women in the United States, both in 1940 and 1950, at the birth of their first child. Median age at birth of first child for the Burmese females was 20.2 years, as compared with 23.0 years for American women in 1940 and 22.8 years in 1950 (Tables 5 and 9).

EFFECTIVE FERTILITY RATIO

The use of the effective fertility ratio for the comparative analysis of fertility of populations subject to great differences in mortality is always hazardous. This is illustrated by comparison of the effective fertility ratios in the Burmese sample and in the United States.

In the Burmese sample there were 424 children under 5 years old per 1,000 won.en 15 to 44 years of age. The comparable figure for the United States in 1940 was well below this level, 329, but the effective fertility ratio for the United States in 1950 was appreciably above the Burmese figure, namely 473 (*see* Table 9). The difference between the effective fertility ratio of the United States in 1950 and the Burmese sample in 1952, cannot be interpreted, however, as indicating greater fertility in the United States. Despite the peak in the post-war birth rate of the United States, reflected in the 1950 fertility ratio, the difference, although it is in part attributable to the greater sensitivity of the American birth rate to swings of the business cycle, is probably accounted for in large measure by differences in child mortality. This conclusion tends to be supported by the data on children ever born. Moreover, the relatively small proportion of young persons under 15 years old in the Burmese sample, to which reference has been made above, may also tend to distort the effective fertility ratio as a measurement of fertility.

CHILDREN EVER BORN

All Women Ever Married. The number of children ever born to the sample of Burmese women 10 years and older ever married was considerably greater than the number ever born to comparable women in the United States, both in 1940 and 1952. In the Burmese sample, 3,216 children were born per 1,000 women ever married. This figure is about 33 per cent greater than the American figure of 2,422 in 1940, and 39 per cent greater than the American figure of 2,321 in 1952 (*see* Tables 6 and 9). If the comparison is restricted to mothers—that is to women ever married who bore one or more children—the number of children ever born per 1,000 Burmese mothers was 4,142, a figure about 32 per cent above the 1940 figure of 3,145, and about 44 per cent above the 1952 figure of 2,877 in the United States.

Women Ever Married of Completed Fertility. Fertility comparisons based on children ever born to all women ever married are distorted by differences in the age composition of the female population and differences in the spacing and concentration of births. Despite small sample numbers, therefore, the data on children ever born were also tabulated for women ever married of completed fertility who were married only once (*see* Tables 6 and 9).

In the Burmese sample, there were 5,493 children ever born per 1,000 women of completed fertility. In the United States, in 1940, the comparable figure was 3,315 and in 1952, 2,937. If the comparison is restricted to mothers only, the comparable figures are 6,113 for the Burmese women, and 3,910 for women in the United States in 1940, and 3,542 in 1952.

The differences between the Burmese and American women are greater for women of completed fertility[21] than for mothers of this age group. For all women ever married 50 years of age and older, the number of children ever born to Burmese women was about 66 per cent greater than the United States figure in 1940 and 87 per

---

[21] The preliminary sample tabulations for Burma were actually for women 49 years old and over. Burmans report as their age their year of life rather than age at last birthday. In consequence, a one-column sort on a two-column field for age, based on age as reported, resulted in age 49 rather than age 50 being used for women of completed fertility. Other age classifications were run on both punched card columns to obtain age groups to match United States age-reporting. It should be noted that the reporting of age in Burma tended to be greatly concentrated on the years ending in 0 and 5 and especially in 0. More detailed tabulations are needed completely to evaluate the effect of this phenomenon which seems to exceed similar tendencies in the United States and other Western Censuses.

Table 6. Children ever born to women ever married, for women 10 years old and over and women 49 years old and over: Four-town sample, Burma, 1952, and United States, 1940.

Children Ever Born	Women 10 Years and Older[a]			Women 49 Years and Older[b]			Cumulative Percentage of Children, United States 1940[c]	
	Number of Women	Aggregate No. of Children Ever Born	Cumulative Percentage of Children	Number of Women	Aggregate No. of Children Ever Born	Cumulative Percentage of Children	Women 15–74 Yrs. Old	Women 50–74 Yrs. Old
Total	371	1,193		69	379			
0	83	—	100.0	7	—	100.0	100.0	100.0
1	64	64	94.6	2	2	99.5	91.5	95.9
2	31	62	89.4	5	10	96.8	76.0	86.2
3	46	138	77.9	5	15	92.9	60.8	73.8
4	33	132	66.8	6	24	86.5	47.5	60.9
5	29	145	54.7	10	50	73.4	36.5	48.9
6	23	138	43.1	4	24	67.0	27.5	38.4
7	19	133	31.9	11	77	46.7	20.4	29.8
8	19	152	19.2	6	48	34.0	14.4	21.8
9	16	144	7.1	6	54	19.8	10.0	15.6
10 or More	8	85		7	75			
Children Ever Born per 1,000 Women		3,216			5,493			
Children Ever Born per 1,000 Mothers		4,142			6,113			

a Women ever married, including sixty-four women married more than once and one of unknown number of times married.
b Includes women 49 years and older married only once. Excludes thirteen women married more than once and one unknown.
c Source: 1940 Census of Population, Differential Fertility 1940 and 1910, Fertility by States and Large Cities, p. 2 and Women by Number of Children Ever Born, p. 3. See Table 9 for selected comparable 1952 per cents.

cent greater than in 1952. For mothers only, the Burmese figure was about 56 per cent greater in 1940 and 73 per cent greater in 1952. This pattern of differences reflects the greater childlessness among women in the United States than among women in Burma. Among Burmese women ever married of completed fertility, 10.1 per cent were childless, whereas in the United States in 1940 this per cent was 15.2 and in 1950, 17.1.

Age at Marriage. Although the sample of women married only once and of completed fertility was quite small, it was possible to analyze the number of children by two broad age groups of the women classified by age at marriage, namely, women married under age 20 and at age 20 and over.

The number of children ever born was greater among women of completed fertility for women who married under age 20 than for those who married at older ages. In the Burmese sample, the number of children ever born per 1,000 women of this category who were married under age 20, was 5,980, as contrasted with 4,111 for women married at age 20 and over (*see* Table 7). The fertility of women married at younger ages exceeded that for women married at older ages by about 45 per cent.

In the United States in 1940, children ever born per 1,000 women 50 years of age and older who were married under age 20, was 4,781, as contrasted with 2,769 for the women married at older ages, a difference of over 70 per cent.[22] Thus, earlier marriage in the United States increased fertility relatively more than earlier marriage in Burma. The fertility of the Burmese women married under age 20 was only 25 per cent greater than the fertility of American women married under age 20, whereas the fertility of Burmese women married at older ages was almost 50 per cent greater than that of corresponding women in the United States.

The number of children ever born to mothers of completed fertility also was considerably greater for the women who married at the younger ages. For these women in the Burmese sample who married under age 20, the number of children ever born was 6,354 per 1,000 women—a figure 20 per cent above that of women married at age 20 or older, 5,286. For each 1,000 comparable mothers in the United States who married under age 20, the number of children ever born was 5,053—a figure almost 50 per cent above

22 United States data by age at marriage are for native white women 50 to 74 years old married once, husband present, *see* Table 9.

Table 7. Children ever born to women married only once, for women 49 years old and over by age at marriage: Four-town sample, Burma, 1952.

Children Ever Born	Number of Women			Aggregate Number of Children Ever Born			Cumulative Percentage Children Ever Born		
	Total	Married under 20 Yrs. of Age	Married 20 Yrs. Old and Over	Total	Married under 20 Yrs. of Age	Married 20 Yrs. Old and Over	Total	Married under 20 Yrs. of Age	Married 20 Yrs. Old and Over
Total	69	51	18	379	305	74[a]			
0	7	3	4	—	—	—			
1	2	2	—	2	2	—	100.0	100.0	100.0[a]
2	5	2	3	10	4	6	99.5	99.3	100.0
3	5	3	2	15	9	6	96.8	98.0	91.9
4	6	5	1	24	20	4	92.9	95.1	83.8
5	10	7	3	50	35	15	86.5	88.5	78.4
6	4	4	—	24	24	—	73.4	77.0	58.1
7	11	9	2	77	63	14	67.0	69.2	58.1
8	6	5	1	48	40	8	46.7	48.5	39.2
9	6	6	—	54	54	—	34.0	35.4	28.4
10 or More	7	5	2	75	54	21	19.8	17.7	28.4
Children Ever Born per 1,000 Women				5,493	5,980	4,111			
Children Ever Born per 1,000 Mothers				6,113	6,354	5,286			

[a] Small sample numbers make individual cell entries subject to large sampling error.

the 3,411 children ever born to mothers in the United States who married at older ages. These data on completed fertility better indicate the relatively greater effect of earlier marriage on fertility in the United States than in the Burmese sample. The Burmese fertility rate for mothers of completed fertility married under age 20 was only 26 per cent above the United States level for comparable women, whereas that for Burmese mothers married at older ages, was 55 per cent above the United States level.

Frequency Distribution. A frequency distribution of children ever born to the Burmese women is shown for women ever married and for women of completed fertility in Table 6. Similar data are shown for women of completed fertility by the two classes of age at marriage in Table 7. These data make it possible to analyze the proportion of all children ever born to each category of women by number of children ever born. Some comparative data have been calculated for the United States for 1940 which are also shown in Table 6.

Of the total number of children ever born to women ever married who bore one or more children, 66.8 per cent of the Burmese children, as compared with 47.5 per cent of the American children, were born to mothers with five or more children. In contrast, only 7.1 per cent of the Burmese children ever born, as compared with 10.0 per cent of the American children, were born to women with ten or more children. These data cannot be interpreted, however, as showing real differences in the proportions of children ever born by number ever born, because of the differences in the age structures and fertility spacing patterns of the Burmese and American women ever married.

Age structures, to some extent, and fertility spacing patterns are controlled when an analysis of the type made above is made for women of completed fertility. About 86 per cent of the children ever born to Burmese mothers of completed fertility, as compared with 61 per cent of those born to comparable American women in 1940, were born to mothers with five or more children ever born. Moreover, 19.8 per cent of the Burmese children ever born, as compared with 15.6 per cent of the American children, were born to mothers with ten or more children ever born in 1940. The difference between the Burmese and American distribution of children ever born is greater when the 1952 data are used for the United States. In 1952 about 53 per cent of the American children ever born were born to mothers of completed fertility with five or more

Table 8. Mothers married only once, by number of children ever born classified by number of children now living: Four-town sample, Burma, 1952.

Children Ever Born	Total	Children Alive on Census Date										Aggregate Children		Average Number Alive	Per Cent Children Living
		0	1	2	3	4	5	6	7	8	9	Born Alive	Living		
Total	288ᵃ	27	88	46	52	32	24	10	3	2	2	1,190	699	2.4ᵇ	58.7
1	63	12	51	—	—	—	—	—	—	—	—	63	51	.8	81.0
2	30	2	15	13	—	—	—	—	—	—	—	60	41	1.4	68.3
3	46	5	9	12	20	—	—	—	—	—	—	138	93	2.0	67.4
4	33	4	5	9	10	5	—	—	—	—	—	132	73	2.2	55.3
5	29	2	4	5	9	6	3	—	—	—	—	145	80	2.8	55.2
6	23	1	1	4	3	7	4	3	—	—	—	138	84	3.7	60.9
7	19	—	1	1	4	5	3	4	1	—	—	133	81	4.3	60.9
8	19	1	—	2	3	6	4	1	—	2	—	152	79	4.2	52.0
9	16	—	2	—	1	2	8	1	1	—	1	144	75	4.7	52.1
10 or More	8	—	—	—	2	1	2	1	1	—	1	85	42	5.2	49.4

ᵃ Includes two mothers—one with one child ever born, the other with two children ever born—for whom number of children alive on census date was not reported.

ᵇ To be compared with average number of children ever born to 286 women, namely, 4.1.

Table 9.   Summary of preliminary data for four-town sample, Burma, 1952, and comparable United States data, 1940 and 1950.

ITEM	BURMA MARCH 1952	UNITED STATES* 1950	UNITED STATES* 1940
1. Median Age—Total Population	22.9	30.2	29.0
a. Male	23.8	29.9	29.1
b. Female	22.3	30.5	29.0
2. Per Cent of Population Under 15 Years Old—Total	30.4	26.9	25.0
a. Male	31.0	27.6	25.3
b. Female	29.8	26.1	24.7
3. Per Cent of Population 65 and Older—Total	2.8	8.2	6.9
a. Male	2.8	7.7	6.7
b. Female	2.8	8.6	7.0
4. Dependency Ratios			
a. Persons Under 15 and 65 and Older Per 100 Persons 15–64	49.5	53.9	46.8
b. Persons Under 15 Per 100 Persons 15–64	45.4	41.4	36.7
c. Persons 65 and Older Per 100 Persons 15–64	4.1	12.5	10.1
5. Per Cent of Persons 14 and Older Married[a]			
a. Crude Per Cent: (1) Total	59.1	68.1[b]	59.6
(2) Male	61.6	69.9[b]	59.7
(3) Female	56.7	66.5[b]	59.5
b. Standardized for Age[c]: (1) Total	59.1	63.8[b]	56.1
(2) Male	60.3	62.0[b]	54.1
(3) Female	57.9	65.3[b]	58.2
6. Women Ever Married			
a. Per Cent of Women 20 and Older Ever Married	74.8	88.2	83.0
b. Median Age at Marriage	18.2		21.2[d]
c. Median Age at Birth of First Child	20.2	22.8	23.0
d. Average Duration of Marriage for Women 15 and Older Ever Married			
(1) Crude	16.1		17.5[d]
(2) Standardized for Age[e]	16.1		15.6[d]
7. Effective Fertility Ratio—Children Under 5 Per 1,000 Women 15–44	424	473	329
8. Children Ever Born Per 1,000 Women 10 and Older			
a. Ever Married	3,216	2,321[f]	2,422[g]
b. Ever Married Who Were Mother	4,142	2,877[f]	3,145[g]
9. Children Ever Born Per 1,000 Women			
a. 50 Years and Older Married Once[h]	5,493	2,937[i]	3,315[j]
(1) Married Under Age 20	5,980		4,781[k]
(2) Married at Age 20 and Older	4,111		2,769[k]
b. 50 Years and Older Married Once Who Were Mothers[h]	6,113	3,542[i]	3,910[j]
(1) Married Under Age 20	6,354		5,053[k]
(2) Married at Age 20 and Older	5,286		3,411[k]
10. Per Cent of Women 50 Years and Older and Married Once Who Are Childless[h]	10.1	17.1[i]	15.2[j]
11. Per Cent of All Children Ever Born, Born to			
(a) Women 10 and Older Ever Married			
(1) With 5 or More Children Ever Born	66.8		47.5[g]
(2) With 10 or More Children Ever Born	7.1		10.0[g]
(b) Women 50 Years and Older Married Once[h]			
(1) With 5 or More Children Ever Born	86.5	53.4[i]	60.9[j]
(2) With 10 or More Children Ever Born	19.8	13.1[i]	15.6[j]

Table 9.   (Continued)

a Data for Burma are from 28-town sample (see text).
b Based on 1951 data; see Sources of U.S. Data below.
c Age structure of total population in 4-town Burma sample used as standard.
d Refers to native white women 15–74 years old, married once, husband present.
e Age structure of Burma women ever married used as standard.
f Based on 1952 data for women 15 and older ever married.
g Refers to women 15–74 years old ever married.
h Rates for Burma refer to women 49 and older (see footnote 21, text).
i Based on 1952 data for women ever married rather than for women married once.
j Refers to women 50–74 years old ever married.
k Refers to native white women 50–74 years old married once and husband present.
While these rates indicate the size of fertility differentials by age at marriage, items
9a(1) and 9a(2) are not directly comparable with 9a total; similarly, 9b(1) and
9b(2) are not directly comparable with 9b total. In fact 9a and 9b totals for native
white women 50–74 years old married once and husband present are 3,274 and 3,875
respectively, as compared with 3,315 and 3,910 for all women 50–74 years old ever
married.

* Sources of U.S. Data.
   Item 1.   1950 Census of Population, Vol. II, 1–93.
   Item 2.   Same as Item 1.
   Item 3.   Same as Item 1.
   Item 4.   Same as Item 1.
   Item 5.   Current Population Reports, Population Characteristics, Series P-20
             No. 38 (April, 1952), p. 10.
   Item 6a. 1940 Census of Population. Vol. II, 1–179.
   Item 6b. 1940 Census of Population. Differential Fertility 1940 and 1910, Women
             by Number of Children Ever Born, p. 37.
   Item 6c. National Office of Vital Statistics, Vital Statistics—Special Reports,
             Vol. 37, No. 13 (November, 1953).
   Item 6d. 1940 Census of Population. Differential Fertility 1940 and 1910, Fer-
             tility by Duration of Marriage, p. 7.
   Item 7.   1940 Census of Population. Vol. II, 1–93.
   Item 8.   Current Population Reports, Population Characteristics, Series P-20,
             No. 46 (December, 1953), p. 11.
   Item 9a & 9b. Same as Item 8.
   Item 9a(1), 9a(2), 9b(1), 9b(2). Same as Item 6b, pp. 27 and 49.
   Item 10. Current Population Reports, Population Characteristics, Series P-20
             No. 46 (December, 1953), p. 11.
   Item 11. 1940—Table 6; 1952—same as Item 3 and 1940 Census of Population,
             Differential Fertility 1940 and 1910, Fertility for States and Large
             Cities, p. 2. Since 1952 data were grouped for women with 5 and 6
             children, 7 to 9 children, and 10 or more children, the aggregate
             number of children ever born was obtained by applying the average
             number of children ever born to women with 5 and 6 children, to
             women with 7 to 9 children, and to women with 10 or more children
             in 1940; and the total number children born to mothers with 5 or
             more children by this procedure was adjusted to add to the known
             total (the adjustment involved a shortage of 174,000 children in a
             total of 26,128,000 children born to mothers with 5 or more children).
             The proportion of children ever born to mothers with 5 or more
             children was not affected by this adjustment, but the proportion born
             to mothers with 10 or more children may be slightly affected.

children, and about 13 per cent to mothers with ten or more children (see Table 9).

Thus, if the data for Burma for 1952 are compared with the data
for the United States for 1952, the proportion of all children ever
born, born to mothers of completed fertility with five or more children, is about 62 per cent greater for Burma than for the United
States; and the proportion of Burmese children ever born to mothers
with ten or more children is about 51 per cent greater than the proportion of comparable American children.

The fact that the difference between Burmese and American concentrations of children ever born to mothers with ten or more chil-

dren is not greater may seem surprising. But it is to be remembered that women of completed fertility in 1952 in the United States, as well as in Burma, were born prior to 1903, some well back into the 19th Century. To the extent that fertility has declined more rapidly in the United States than in Burma during the past half century and more, the data on completed fertilities in the two countries tend to obscure the great differences in current fertility. On the other hand, the post-war increase in birth rates in the United States is, in the main, obscured by the data on children ever born to women of completed fertility.[23]

Living Children. Since the schedule contained an inquiry on the number of children alive on the Census date, as well as on the number of children ever born, it was possible to cross-tabulate the responses to these questions. Unfortunately, a preliminary sample tabulation of this type was not made for women of completed fertility.

Of the average of 4.1 children ever born to mothers of all ages in the Burmese sample, 2.4, or about 59 per cent, were alive on the Census date (*see* Table 8). The percentage of the children ever born who were alive on the Census date varied from 81 per cent of the children born to mothers with one child ever born to 49 per cent of the children born to mothers with ten or more children ever born. The data are difficult to interpret without additional controls such as would be provided by a similar tabulation for women of completed fertility only, or by controlling age of mother, socio-economic status and similar factors. In general, the smaller the number of children ever born, the larger was the percentage alive. For example, mothers who bore five or more children produced 67 per cent of all the children ever born, but had only 63 per cent of the children alive. This finding, however, probably merely reflects the greater age, and therefore the greater mortality, of the children born to mothers with larger numbers of children ever born.

These data are presented primarily to indicate a type of analysis that may be highly significant if tabulations with adequate controls of the kind suggested above were obtained, and if comparable data were available for a number of populations.

[23] The number of children ever born to American women was greater in 1952 than in 1940 for women ever married up to age 35. Above age 35 the number of children ever born was smaller in 1952 than in 1940, and enough smaller so that the average number of children born to women of completed fertility was smaller in 1952 than in 1940. *See Current Population Reports, Population Characteristics,* Series P-20, No. 46 (December, 1953), p. 11.

SUMMARY AND CONCLUDING OBSERVATIONS

Preliminary sample tabulations of returns from pre-test Census operations in Burma for March 1952, designed primarily to finalize the Census schedule, provided a basis for some glimpses into the structure and dynamics of a population of some cities and towns in Burma. The pre-test Census schedules included a battery of inquiries relating to fertility, as well as a broad range of other questions comparable in scope to those of the 1950 Census of Population in the United States. The preliminary Burmese sample tabulations therefore, provide data generally not available for a relatively underdeveloped area which can be compared with the data for more developed countries. To provide a better basis for the interpretation of the Burmese sample data, comparisons have been made with the statistics for the United States.

The population covered in the pre-test Census operations in the four towns was predominantly indigenous Burman and Buddhist. The population had relatively little formal education and a low level of living. The comparison of the population characteristics of this sample in Burma, with those of the United States, provide a contrast between almost the extremes in demographic phenomena.

The Burmese sample population was considerably younger than the population of the United States, with larger proportions of persons under 15 years old and considerably smaller proportions of persons 65 years and over. Smaller proportions of the Burmese sample than of the United States population 14 years and older were married, when the comparison was made with 1951 data for the United States.[24] The differences in proportion married were greater for females than for males, and a considerable part of the differences were attributable to differences in age structure. When age was controlled through standardization, the differences between the Burmese sample and the United States in proportion married, were much smaller. In general, age-specific marriage proportions were greater for Burmese men and women only in the youngest age group, 14–24 years. The lower proportions married in the Burmese population 14 years and older, are attributable to the lower proportions married above age 24. The lower proportions married among older persons of both sexes in Burma, and especially among

---

[24] By 1951, of course, proportions married in the United States reflected the high post-war marriage rates. When compared with 1940 data for the United States, the proportion of Burman men married was higher than that for the United States in 1940, but the proportion of Burman women married was lower than in the United States in 1940.

females, were accounted for mainly by the greater incidence of mortality of spouses.

Stability of marriage in Burma is probably not too different from that in the United States, despite the fact that marriage and divorce in Burma, under Buddhist mores, were by mutual consent without benefit of civil or ecclesiastical ceremony or record.

A smaller proportion of the Burmese women 20 years and older, than of the American women either in 1940 or 1950, were ever married. Women in the Burmese sample, however, married earlier than American women. The median age at first marriage of the Burmese women in 1952 was lower than that of United States women in 1940. Crude average duration of marriage was greater for the American than for the Burmese women. But when age was controlled by standardization, average duration of marriage was greater for the Burmese than for the American women. The Burmese women bore their first child at an earlier age than American women did either in 1940 or in 1950.

The effective fertility ratio (children under 5 per 1,000 women 15 to 44 years old) of the Burmese women in 1952, was greater than that of American women in 1940, but smaller than that in the United States in 1950. This ratio is not a satisfactory measurement of fertility differences, however, because of the great differences between the countries in infant and child mortality.

The number of children ever born was considerably greater for the Burmese than for American women. Burmese women ever married had an average of 3.2 children, as compared with an average of 2.4 for women in the United States in 1940, and 2.3 in 1952. Burmese women ever married who were mothers had an average of 4.1 children, as compared with averages in the United States of 3.1 in 1940 and 2.9 in 1952.

The best comparison of the fertility in the Burmese sample population and in the United States, however, is given by the number of children ever born to women of completed fertility. The Burmese women of completed fertility bore an average of 5.5 children, compared with an average in the United States of 3.3 in 1940 and 2.9 in 1952. The Burmese woman of completed fertility who bore one or more children bore an average of 6.1 children, as compared with an average in the United States of 3.9 in 1940 and 3.5 in 1952. The difference in fertility between Burmese and American women ever married is greater than the difference between Burmese and American mothers. This is the result of the greater childlessness of

American women. Whereas only 10 per cent of the Burmese women of completed fertility were childless, over 15 per cent of comparable United States women were childless in 1940 and over 17 per cent in 1952.

Earlier age at marriage resulted in greater fertility than marriage at older ages. The Burmese women of completed fertility who married under age 20 had a greater number of children ever born than those married at age 20 or older, the former averaging 6.0 children, the latter 4.1. For Burmese mothers of completed fertility, the average number of children ever born to women who married under age 20 was 6.4, whereas that for mothers married at age 20 or older was 5.3. Similar patterns of higher fertility obtained among women in the United States who married under age 20 as compared with those who married at older ages. Earlier marriage, however, made a greater relative difference in the fertility of the women in the United States than in that of the Burmese women.

Of the aggregate number of children ever born to Burmese mothers of completed fertility, 87 per cent were born to mothers who bore five or more children, and about one-fifth to mothers who bore ten or more children. In contrast, in the United States in 1952, children born to mothers of completed fertility who bore five or more children, was only 53 per cent of all the children ever born, and to mothers of ten or more children, 13 per cent.

Of the children ever born to all Burmese women ever married, about 59 per cent were living at the time of the Census. There was some tendency for women with the larger number of children ever born to have a smaller proportion living, but this finding is hard to interpret without more tabulation controls than were possible in the preliminary tabulations.

These data are presented more to show the potentialities of the information being collected in the Census of Burma, than to provide a demographic report on Burma at this time. It is to be hoped that final tabulations of these data, and statistics for all of the parts of Burma canvassed in the first and second stages of the Census of Burma, will soon become available to provide more representative, comprehensive and definitive findings.

Bibliography

The bibliography that follows is intended to facilitate the student's supplementing the reading he has done in this volume. Titles reprinted in the present volume have not been included. The titles are limited to those in the English language and—except for items relating to subjects treated in Chapter VII—to articles in periodicals and symposia. For titles in other languages the student may consult such sources of bibliography as *Population Index, Population,* and the *Economic Journal.*

The following abbreviations are used in referring to journals cited frequently:

AAAG: Annals of the American Association of Geographers
AAAPSS: Annals of the American Academy of Political and Social Science
AJS: American Journal of Sociology
ASR: American Sociological Review
BISI: Bulletin of the International Statistical Institute
BWHO: Bulletin of the World Health Organization
CJEPS: Canadian Journal of Economics and Political Science
EG: Economic Geography
EHR: Economic History Review
EN: Eugenical News
EQ: Eugenics Quarterly
ER: Economic Record
FA: Foreign Affairs
GJ: Geographical Journal
GR: Geographical Review
HB: Human Biology
ILR: International Labour Review
JASA: Journal of the American Statistical Association

JEH: Journal of Economic History
JFE: Journal of Farm Economics
JPE: Journal of Political Economy
JRSS: Journal of the Royal Statistical Society
LE: Land Economics
MLR: Monthly Labor Review
MMFQ: Milbank Memorial Fund Quarterly
MSESS: The Manchester School of Economic and Social Studies
PAPS: Proceedings of the American Philosophical Society
PB: Population Bulletin (United Nations)
POQ: Public Opinion Quarterly
PS: Population Studies
RS: Rural Sociology
SAJE: South African Journal of Economics
SF: Social Forces
SM: Scientific Monthly
SSR: Sociology and Social Research

I. Past and Prospective Growth and Distribution of World Population

Australia, Queensland Bureau of Industry, "The Density of World Farm Population," *Economic News,* 16 (October-December 1947) 1-8.

Bainbridge, T. H., "Cumberland Population Movements, 1871-81," *GJ,* 108 (July-September 1946) 80-85.

Bennett, Merrill K., "Population, Food and Economic Progress," *Rice Institute Pamphlet,* 39 (July 1952) 1-67.

Buckatzsch, E. J., "The Constancy of Local Populations and Migration in England before 1800," *PS,* 5 (July 1951) 62-69.

Connell, K. H., "Land and Population in Ireland, 1780-1845," *EHR,* 9 (No. 3, 1950) 278-289.

Davis, J. S., "Our Amazing Population Upsurge," *JFE*, 31 (November 1949) 765-778.

Davis, J. S., "Fifty Million More Americans," *FA*, 28 (April 1950) 412-426.

Davis, J. S., "Our Amazing Population Upsurge," *JFE*, 31 (November 1949) 765-778.

Davis, Kingsley, "The World Demographic Transition," *AAAP55*, 237 (January 1945), I-II.

Fawcett, C. B., "The Numbers and Distribution of Mankind," *SM*, 64 (May 1947) 389-396.

Geddes, Arthur, "Variability in Change of Population in the United States and Canada, 1900-1951," *GR*, 44 (January 1954) 88-100.

Gille, H., "The Demographic History of the Northern European Countries in the Eighteenth Century," *PS*, 3 (June 1949) 3-65.

Grebenik, E., "The Quantitative Aspect of the British Population Problem—A Survey," *Review of Economic Studies*, 10 (Winter, 1942-43) 43-52.

Habakkuk, H. J., "English Population in the Eighteenth Century," *EHR*, 6 (December 1953) 117-133.

Hagood, Margaret Jarman, and Siegel, Jacob S., "Population Projections For Sales Forecasting," *JASA*, 47 (September 1952) 524-540.

Hajnal, J., "The Prospects for Population Forecasts," *JASA*, 50 (June 1955) 309-322.

Hauser, P. M., "World Population Trends," *SSR*, 39 (November-December 1954) 73-80.

Heckscher, E. F., "Swedish Population Trends Before the Industrial Revolution," *EHR*, 2 (No. 3, 1950) 266-277.

Helleiner, K. F., "Population Movement and Agrarian Depression in the Latter Middle Ages," *CJEPS*, 15 (August 1949) 368-77.

Kirk, D., "Population Changes and the Postwar World," *ASR*, 9 (February 1944) 28-35.

McKeown, T., and Brown, R. G., "Medical Evidence Related to English Population Changes in the Eighteenth Century," *PS*, 9 (November 1955) 119-141.

Notestein, Frank W., "Population—The Long View," in *Food for the World*, Theodore W. Schultz, ed. (Chicago: University of Chicago Press, 1945).

Packer, D. R. G., "Victorian Population Data, 1851-61," *Historical Studies, Australia and New Zealand* (May 1953) 307-323.

Pearl, R., and Gould, S. A., "World Population Growth," *HB*, 8 (September 1936) 399-419.

Postan, M. M., "Some Economic Evidence of Declining Population in the Middle Ages," *EHR*, 2 (No. 3, 1950) 221-246.

Rajalakshman, D. V., "Studies in War-Time Demography," *Indian Journal of Economics*, 30 (April 1950) 311-334.

Rich, E. E., "The Population of Elizabethan England," *EHR*, 2 (No. 3, 1950) 247-265.

Russell, J. C., "Late Medieval Population Patterns," *Speculum*, 20 (April 1945) 157-171.

Shryock, Henry S., Jr., "Forecasts of Population in the United States," *PS*, 3 (March 1950) 406-412.

Shryock, Henry S., "Accuracy of Population Projections for the United States," *Estadística*, 12 (December 1954) 587-598.

Smith, C. T., "The Movement of Population in England and Wales in 1851 and 1861," *GJ*, 117 (June 1951) 200-210.

Smith, R. S., "Fourteenth-Century Population Records of Caledonia," *Speculum*, 19 (October 1944) 494-501.

Shulvass, Moses A., "The Jewish Population in Renaissance Italy," *Jewish Social Studies*, 13 (January 1951) 3-24.

United Nations, "The Past and Future Growth of World Population: A Long-Range View," *PB*, No. 1 (December 1951) 1-12.

United Nations, *World Population Trends, 1920-1947* (Population Studies, No. 3, December 1949).

Warriner, Doreen, "Some Controversial Issues in the History of Agrarian Europe," *The Slavonic and East European Review*, 32 (December 1953) 168-186.

Wickens, C. H., "Australian Population: Its Nature and Growth," *ER*, 1 (1925) 1-16.

II. Mortality

Boulding, K., "An Application of Population Analysis to the Automobile Population of the United States," *Kyklos*, 8 (No. 2, 1955) 109-124.

Buckatzsch, E. J., "The Influence of Social Conditions on Mortality Rates," *PS*, 1 (December 1947) 229-248.

Caffin, S. W., "Infantile Mortality Rates," *PS*, 6 (July 1952) 106-108.

Chandrasekhar, S., "Some Observations on Infant Mortality in India: 1901-1951," *Eugenics Review*, 46 (January 1955) 213-225.

Cook, S. F., "Survivorship in Aboriginal Population," *HB*, 19 (May 1947) 83-89.

Daric, Jean, "Mortality, Occupation, and Socio-Economic Status," *Vital Statistics —Special Reports*, Vol. 33, No. 10 (Washington: National Office of Vital Statistics, September 21, 1951) 175-186.

Deevey, Edward S., "The Probability of Death," *Scientific American*, 182 (April 1950) 58-60.

Derksen, J. B. D., "The Calculation of Mortality-Rates in the Construction of Life Tables: A Mathematical Statistical Study," *PS*, 1 (March 1948) 457-470.

Dorn, Harold F., "The Effect of Public Health Developments Upon Population Growth," *Annals of the New York Academy of Sciences*, 54 (May 2, 1952) 742-749.

Dorn, Harold F., "Prospects of Further Decline in Mortality Rates," *HB*, 24 (December 1952) 235-261.

Douglas, J. W. B., "Social Class Differences in Health and Survival During the First Two Years of Life; the Results of a National Survey," *PS*, 5 (July 1951) 35-38.

Duffy, John, "Eighteenth-Century Carolina Health Conditions," *Journal of Southern History*, 18 (August 1952) 289-302.

Elderton, Sir William P., "The Mortality of Adult Males Since the Middle of the Eighteenth Century as Shown by the Experience of Life Insurance Companies," *JRSS*, 106 (Part I, 1943) 1-20.

Grabill, Wilson H., "Attrition Life Tables for the Single Population," *JASA*, 40 (September 1945) 364-375.

Hart, Hornell, and Hertz, Hilda, "The Expectation of Life as an Index of Social Progress," *ASR*, 9 (December 1944) 609-621.

Keith-Lucas, B., "Some Influences Affecting the Development of Sanitary Legislation in England," *EHR*, 6 (April 1954) 290-296.

Kendall, David G., "An Artificial Realization of a Simple 'Birth-and-Death' Process," *JRSS*, Supplement, 12 (No. 1, 1950) 116-119.

Keyfitz, N., "Calculation of Life Tables for Population of Countries and Regions," *Estadística*, 4 (March 1946) 70-78.

Lessof, E., "Mortality in New Zealand and England and Wales," *PS*, 3 (June 1949) 76-99.

Logan, W. P. D., "Mortality in England and Wales from 1848 to 1947," *PS*, 4 (September 1940) 132-178.

Logan, W. P. D., "The Measurement of Infant Mortality," *PB*, No. 3 (October 1953) 30-55.

Martin, W. J., "A Comparison of the Trends of Male and Female Mortality," *JRSS*, 114 (Part III, 1951) 287-298.

Mayer, Albert J., and Hauser, Philip M., "Class Differentials in Expectation of Life at Birth," *Revue de L'Institut International de Statistique*, 18 (Nos. 3-4, 1950) 197-200.

Molyneaux, Lambert, Gilliam, Sara K., and Florant, L. C., "Differences in Virginia Death Rates by Color, Sex, Age and Rural or Urban Residence," *ASR*, 12 (October 1947) 525-535.

Moriyama, Iwao M., "Recent Mortality Trends in Areas of Low Mortality," *Public Health Reports*, 69 (October 1954) 963-969.

Moriyama, Iwao M., "Recent Mortality Trends and Differentials," *JASA*, 46 (June 1951) 213-219.

Pascua, M., "Evolution of Mortality in Europe during the Twentieth Century," *Epidemiological and Vital Statistics Report*, 2 (April 1949) 64-80, and 3 (February-March 1950) 30-78.

Peller, S., "Mortality, Past and Future," *PS*, 1 (March 1948) 405-456.

Pollitzer, R., "Cholera Studies. I. History of the Disease," *BWHO*, 10 (No. 3, 1954) 421-461.

Preas, Sally, "Length of Life of Parents and Offspring in a Rural Community," *MMFQ*, 23 (April 1945) 180-196.

Rhodes, E. C., "Secular Changes in Death Rates," *JRSS*, 104 (Part I, 1941) 15-42.

Roberts, G. W., "A Life Table for a West Indian Slave Population," *PS*, 5 (March 1952) 238-243.

Roberts, G. W., "A Note on Mortality in Jamaica," *PS*, 4 (June 1950) 64-85.

Sadie, J. L., "Differential Mortality in South Africa," *SAJE*, 19 (December 1951) 361-369.

Sarkar, N. K., "A Note on Abridged Life Tables for Ceylon, 1900-1947," *PS*, 4 (March 1951) 439-443.

Smith, T. C., and Friffin, F. L., Jr., "Work-life Expectancy as a Measure of Damages," *Transactions of the Society of Actuaries*, 4 (November 1952) 585-620.

Spiegelman, Mortimer, "The Longevity of Jews in Canada, 1940-1942," *PS*, 2 (December 1948) 292-304.

Stolnitz, G. J., "A Century of International Mortality Trends: I," *PS*, 9 (July 1955) 24-55.

Swaroop, S., and Grab, B., "Snakebite Mortality in the World," *BWHO*, 10 (No. 1, 1954) 35-76.

Tietze, Christopher, "Life Tables for Social Classes in England," *MMFQ*, 21 (April 1943) 182-187.

Unsigned, "Deaths Among Military Personnel," *Statistical Bulletin, Metropolitan Life Insurance Company*, 34 (March 1953) 1-4.

Valaoras, Vasilios G., "Refined Rates for Infant and Childhood Mortality," *PS*, 4 (December 1950) 253-266.

Walker, Harry, "The 'Elas' Life Income Mortality Table," *Transactions of the Society of Actuaries*, 6 (April 1954) 85-98.

Wiehl, Dorothy G., "Mortality and Socio-Environmental Factors," *MMFQ*, 26 (October 1948) 335-365.

Wolfbein, Seymour L., "The Length of Working Life," *PS*, 3 (December 1949) 286-294.

Wolfbein, Seymour L., "Measurement of Work-Life Expectancy," *MLR*, 71 (August 1950) 193-195.

Wolfbein, Seymour L., "The Length of Working Life," *PS*, 3 (December 1949) 286-294.

Wolfbein, Seymour L., "The Changing Length of Working Life," *Proceedings of the Seventh Annual Meeting of the Industrial Relations Research Association*, 7 (1954) 1-10.

Wool, Harold, "Trends in Pattern of Working Life, 1900 to 1975," *MLR*, 71 (October 1950) 438-442.

Yerushalmy, J., "A Mortality Index for Use in Place of the Age-Adjusted Death Rate," *American Journal of Public Health*, 41 (August 1951) 907-922.

III. Fertility, Nuptiality and Replacement

Anderson, W. A., "The Spacing of Births in the Families of University Graduates," *AJS*, 53 (July 1947) 23-33.

Asdell, S. A., "The Fertility of the Only Child," *Fertility and Sterility*, 2 (July-August 1951) 312-318.

Baltzell, E. Digby, "Social Mobility and Fertility Within an Elite Group," *MMFQ*, 31 (October 1953) 411-420.

Banks, J. A., and Banks, O., "The Bradlaugh-Besant Trial and the English Newspapers," *PS*, 8 (July 1954) 22-34.

Bash, W. H., "Differential Fertility in Madison County, New York, 1865," *MMFQ*, 33 (April 1955) 161-186.

Beale, Calvin L., "Increased Divorce Rates Among Separated Persons as a Factor in Divorce Since 1940," *SF*, 20 (October 1950) 72-74.

Berent, Jerzy, "Fertility and Social Mobility," *PS*, 5 (March 1952) 244-260.

Berent, Jerzy, "Relationship Between Family Sizes of Two Successive Generations," *MMFQ*, 31 (January 1953) 39-50.

Beveridge, W., "The Fall of Fertility Among European Races," *Economica*, 5 (March 1925) 10-27.

Borgatta, Edgar F., and Westoff, Charles F., "Social and Psychological Factors Affecting Fertility, XXV. The Prediction of Total Fertility," *MMFQ*, 32 (October 1954) 383-419.

Brass, W., "The Derivation of Fertility and Reproduction Rates from Restricted Data on Reproductive Histories," *PS*, 7 (November 1953) 137-166.

Brass, W., "The Estimation of Fertility Rates from Ratios of Total to First Births," *PS*, 8 (July 1954) 74-87.

Brink, T. van den, "Leveling of Differential Trends in the Netherlands," *EQ*, 1 (December 1954) 230-234.

Brink, T. van den, "Birth Rate Trends and Changes in Marital Fertility in the Netherlands after 1937," *PS*, 4 (December 1950) 314-332.

Bruns, G. R., "War-time Fertility and the Future Population of Australia," *ER*, 19 (December 1943) 185-202.

Caffin, S. W., "Completed Families," *ER*, 27 (June 1951) 77-80.

Chambliss, Rollin, "The Geographic Factor in the Human Sex Ratio at Birth," *SF*, 28 (December 1949) 190-195.

Charles, Enid, "The Nuptiality Problem with Special Reference to Canadian Marriage Statistics," *CJEPS*, 7 (August 1941) 447-477.

Charles, Enid, "Differential Fertility in Canada, 1931," *CJEPS*, 9 (May 1943) 175-218.

Christensen, Harold T., "Rural-Urban Differences in the Spacing of the First Birth from Marriage: A Repeat Study," *RS*, 18 (March 1953) 60.

Clark, Colin, "Age at Marriage and Marital Fertility," *PS*, 2 (March 1949) 413-426.

Clark, Colin, "Regional Differences in Reproductivity in England and Wales," *PS*, 5 (July 1951) 59-61.

Clark, Colin and Dyne, R. E., "Applications and Extensions of the Karmel Formula for Reproductivity," *ER*, 22 (June 1946) 23-39.

Cox, P. R., "Studies in Recent Marriage and Fertility Data of England and Wales," *PS*, 5 (November 1951) 132-152.

Cox, P. R., "Reproductivity in Great Britain: A New Standard of Assessment," *Journal of Institute of Actuaries*, 79 (Part III, No. 353, 1953) 239-273.

Croog, Sydney H., "Premarital Pregnancies in Scandinavia and Finland," *AJS*, 57 (January 1952) 358-365.

Davis, Kingsley, "Human Fertility in India," *AJS*, 52 (November 1946) 243-254.

Dinkel, Robert M., "Occupation and Fertility in the United States," *ASR*, 17 (April 1952) 178-183.

Duncan, Otis Dudley, "Fertility of the Village Population in Pennsylvania, 1940," *SF*, 28 (March 1950) 304-309.

Eaton, Joseph W., and Mayer, Albert J. "The Social Biology of Very High Fertility Among the Hutterites; the Demography of a Unique Population," *HB*, 25 (September 1953) 206-264.

Freedman, R., and Sharp, H., "Correlates of Values about Ideal Family Size in the Detroit Metropolitan Area," *PS*, 8 (July 1954) 34-45.

Freedman, R., Goldberg, D., and Sharp, H., " 'Ideals' about Family Size in the Detroit Metropolitan Area: 1954," *MMFQ*, 33 (April 1955) 187-197.

Freemantle, Anne, "Planned Parenthood," *Catholic World*, 175 (April 1952) 12-18.

Gini, Corrado, "Real and Apparent Exceptions to the Uniformity of a Lower Natural Increase of the Upper Classes," *RS*, 1 (September 1936) 257-280.

Glass, D. V., "Changes in Fertility in England and Wales, 1851 to 1931," in *Political Arithmetic*, ed. by Lancelot Hogben (London, 1938) 161-212.

Glick, Paul C., "The Family Cycle," *ASR*, 12 (April 1947) 164-174.

Glick, Paul C., "First Marriages and Remarriages," *ASR*, 14 (December 1949) 726-734.

Glick, Paul C., and Landau, Emanuel, "Age as a Factor in Marriage," *ASR*, 15 (August 1950) 517-529.

Grabill, W. H., "Effect of the War on the Birth Rate and Postwar Fertility Prospects," *AJS*, 50 (September 1944) 107-111.

Gutman, Robert, "College Men and the Birth Rate—25 Years After," *Journal of Public Health*, 41 (November 1951) 56-64.

Hagood, Margaret J., and Eaton, Mary A., "An Examination of Regional Differentials in Fertility by Analysis of Variance and Covariance," *SF*, 17 (May 1939) 495-502.

Hagood, Margaret J., "Changing Fertility Differentials Among Farm-Operator Families in Relation to Economic Size of Farm," *RS*, 13 (December 1948) 363-373.

Hajnal, John, "Some Comments on Mr. Karmel's Paper. "The Relations Between Male and Female Reproduction Rates'," *PS*, 2, (December 1948) 354-360.

Hajnal, John, "Age at Marriage and Proportions Marrying," *PS*, 7 (November 1953) 111-136.

Hajnal, John, "Analysis of Changes in the Marriage Pattern by Economic Groups," *ASR*, 19 (June 1954) 295-302.

Hajnal, John, "Differential Changes in Marriage Patterns," *ASR*, 19 (April 1954) 148-154.

Hajnal, John, "Aspects of Recent Trends in Marriage in England and Wales," *PS*, 1 (June 1947) 72-98.

Hajnal, John, "The Analysis of Birth Statistics in the Light of the Recent International Recovery of the Birth-Rate," *PS*, 1 (September 1947) 137-164.

Hajnal, John, "The Estimation of Total Family Size of Occupation Groups from the Distribution of Births by Order and Duration of Marriage," *PS*, 2 (December 1948) 305-317.

Harmsen, Hans, "Notes on Abortion and Birth Control in Germany," *PS*, 3 (March 1950) 402-05.

Hill, George W., and Tarver, James D., "Indigenous Fertility in the Farm Population of Wisconsin, 1848-1948," *RS*, 16 (December 1951) 359-362.

Hill, George W., and Marshall, D. G., "Reproduction and Replacement of Farm Population and Agricultural Policy," *JFE*, 29 (May 1947) 457-474.

Hopkin, W. A. B., and Hajnal, J., "Analysis of the Births in England and Wales, 1939, by Father's Occupation," *PS*, 1 (September and December 1947) 187-203, 275-300.

Hubback, Judith, "The Fertility of Graduate Women," *Eugenics Review*, 47 (July 1955) 107-113.

Hyrenius, Hannes, "Reproduction and Replacement," *PS*, 4 (March 1951) 421-431.

Jacobson, Paul H., "Total Marital Dissolutions in the United States: Relative Importance of Mortality and Divorce," in *Studies in Population*, ed. by George F. Mair (Princeton: Princeton Univ. Press, 1949).

Jacobson, Paul H., "The Trend of the Birth Rate Among Persons on Different Economic Levels, City of New York, 1929-1942," *MMFQ*, 23 (April 1944) 131-147.

Jacobson, Paul H., "Marital Dissolutions in New York State in Relation to Their Trend in the United States," *MMFQ*, 28 (January 1950) 25-42.

Jaffe, A. J., "Religious Differentials in the Net Reproduction Rate," *JASA*, 34 (June 1939) 335-342.

Jaffe, A. J., "Urbanization and Fertility," *AJS*, 48 (July 1942) 48-60.

Joint Committee of the Royal College of Obstetricians and Gynaecologists and the Population Investigation Committee, "A Survey of Childbearing in Britain," *PS*, 1 (June 1947) 99-136.

Kantner, John F., and Kiser, Clyde V., "The Interrelation of Fertility, Fertility Planning, and Intergenerational Social Mobility," *MMFQ*, 32 (January 1954) 69-103.

Karmel P. H., "An Analysis of the Sources and Magnitudes of Inconsistencies Between Male and Female Net Reproduction Rates in Actual Populations," *PS*, 2 (September 1948) 240-273.

Karmel, P. H., "A Rejoinder to Mr. Hajnal's Comments," *PS*, 2 (December 1948) 361-372.

Karmel, P. H., "A Note on P. K. Whelpton's Calculation of Parity Adjusted Reproduction Rates," *JASA*, 45 (March 1950) 119-124.

Karmel, P. H., "The Relations Between Male and Female Reproduction Rates," *PS*, 11 (December 1947) 249-274.

Karmel, P. H., "The Relations Between Male and Female Nuptiality in a Stable Population," *PS*, 1 (March 1948) 353-387.

Kephart, William M., "The Duration of Marriage," *ASR*, 22 (October 1953) 24-31.

Keyfitz, Nathan, "Differential Fertility in Ontario, Application of Factorial Design to Demographic Problem," *PS*, 1 (November 1952) 123-134.

Keyfitz, Nathan, "A Factorial Arrangement of Comparisons of Family Size," *AJS*, 58 (March 1953) 470-480.

Kiser, Clyde V., and Whelpton, P. K., "Progress Report on the Study of Social and Psychological Factors Affecting Fertility," *ASR*, 12 (April 1947) 175-186.

Kiser, Clyde V., "Exploration of Possibilities for New Studies of Factors Affecting Size of Family," *MMFQ*, 31 (October 1953) 436-480.

Kiser, C. V., "The Indianapolis Fertility Study—An Example of Planned Observational Research," *POQ*, 17 (Winter 1953-54) 496-510.

Kitagawa, Evelyn M., "Differential Fertility in Chicago, 1922-40," *AJS*, 58 (March 1953) 481-492.

Koya, Yoshio, "A Study of Induced Abortion in Japan and Its Significance," *MMFQ*, 32 (July 1954) 282-293.

Lee, Everett S., and Lee, Anne S., "The Differential Fertility of the American Negro," *ASR*, 17 (August 1952) 437-447.

Leslie, P. H., "On the Distribution in Time of the Births in Successive Generations," *JRSS*, 91 (Part I, 1948) 44-53.

Levin, S. M., "Malthus' Conception of the Checks," *HB*, 10 (May 1938) 214-234.

Lotka, Alfred J., "Evaluation of Some Methods of Measuring Net Fertility with Special Regard to Recent Developments," in *International Statistical Conferences, Proceedings*, Vol. III, Part B (Calcutta: Eka Press, n.d.) 715-730.

Martin, C. J., "Note on the Use of Statistics of Total Fertility to Provide Estimates of Crude Birth Rates," *PS*, 8 (July 1954) 88-91.

Mayer, A., and Kloprodt, C., "Fertility Differentials in Detroit, 1920-1950," *PS*, 9 (November 1955) 148-158.

Moberg, Sven, "Marital Status and Family Size Among Matriculated Persons in Sweden," *PS*, 4 (June 1950) 115-131.

Monahan, Thomas P., "The Changing Probability of Divorce," *ASR*, 5 (August 1940) 536-545.

Monahan, Thomas P., "One Hundred Years of Marriages in Massachusetts," *AJS*, 56 (May 1951) 534-545.

Myers, Robert J., "Effect of the War on the Sex Ratio at Birth," *ASR*, 12 (February 1947) 40-43.

Myers, Robert J., "The Effect of Age of Mother and Birth Order on Sex Ratio at Birth," *MMFQ*, 32 (July 1954) 275-281.

Nag, A. C., "A Study on the Fertility Rates in the Middle Class Population in India," *BISI*, 33 (No. 4, 1954), 83-92.

Quensel, Carl-Erik, "Population Movements in Sweden in Recent Years," *PS*, 1 (June 1947) 29-43.

Ramholt, Per, "Nuptiality, Fertility and Reproduction in Norway," *PS*, 7 (July 1953) 46-61.

Rowntree, Griselda, "Early Childhood in Broken Families," *PS*, 8 (March 1955) 247-263.

Sabagh, Georges, "The Fertility of the French-Canadian Women During the Seventeenth Century," *AJS*, 47 (March 1942) 680-689.

Sabagh, George, and Thomas, Dorothy S., "Changing Patterns of Fertility and Survival Among the Japanese Americans on the Pacific Coast," *ASR*, 10 (October 1945) 651-658.

Sarkar, B. N., "Graduation of Birth Rates," *BISI*, 33 (No. 4, 1954) 93-104.

Shaul, J. R. H., "Derivation of Total Fertility, Gross and Net Reproduction Rates from Census Statistics of Marriage Fertility," *JRSS*, 109 (Part III, 1946) 278-283.

Sinha, J. N., "Fertility and Age at Marriage," *BISI*, 33 (No. 4, 1954) 113-126.

Spiegelman, Mortimer, "The Reproductivity of Jews in Canada, 1940-1942," *PS*, 4 (December 1950) 299-313.

Stouffer, Samuel A., "Trends in the Fertility of Catholics and non-Catholics," *AJS*, 41 (September 1935) 143-166.

Taback, Matthew, "Family Studies in the Eastern Health District, Family Structure and Its Changing Pattern," *MMFQ*, 32 (October 1954) 343-382.

Thompson, Warren S., "Differentials in Fertility and Levels of Living in the Rural Population of the United States," *ASR*, 13 (October 1948) 516-534.

Tietze, Christopher, "Differential Reproduction in the United States: Paternity Rates for Occupational Classes among the Urban White Population," *AJS*, 49 (November 1943) 242-247.

Tietze, Christopher, and Lewit, Sarah, "Recent Changes in the Fertility of Congregational Ministers," *EQ*, 1 (June 1954) 32-38.

Tietze, C., and Lauriat, P., "Age at Marriage and Educational Attainment in the United States," *PS*, 9 (November 1955) 159-66.

Vance, Rupert B., "The Regional Approach to the Study of High Fertility," *MMFQ*, 19 (October 1941) 356-374.

Vandiver, Joseph S., "The Reproductive Pattern of the Rural Negroes of the Yazoo-Mississippi Delta," *SF*, 29 (October 1950) 78-84.

Vincent, Paul E., "French Demography in the Eighteenth Century," *PS*, 1 (June 1947) 44-71.

Westoff, Charles F., "Differential Fertility in the United States: 1900 to 1952," *ASR*, 19 (October 1954) 549-561.

Whelpton, P. K., "Comments on Mr. Karmel's Note," *JASA*, 45 (March 1950) 125-135.

Whelpton, P. K., "Reproduction Rates Adjusted for Age, Parity, Fecundity, and Marriage," *JASA*, 41 (December 1946) 501-516.

Whelpton, P. K., "Cohort Analysis of Fertility," *ASR*, 14 (December 1949) 735-749.

Whelpton, P. K., "Future Fertility of American Women," *EQ*, 1 (March 1954) 4-15.

Woofter, T. J., "Generation Reproduction Rates," *Vital Statistics—Special Reports*, Vol. 33, No. 4 (Washington: National Office of Vital Statistics, January 30, 1950) 65-68.

Woofter, T. J., "Factors Sustaining the Birth Rate," *ASR*, 14 (June 1949) 357-366.

Woofter, T. J., "The Relation of the Net Reproduction Rate to Other Fertility Measures," *JASA*, 44 (December 1949) 501-517.

Woofter, T. J., Jr., "Replacement Rates in the Productive Ages," *MMFQ*, 15 (October 1937) 348-354.

Woofter, T. J., Jr., "Trends in Rural and Urban Fertility Rates," *RS*, 13 (March 1948) 3-9.

IV. International Distribution of Population and Migration

Angus, H. F., "The Future of Immigration into Canada," *CJEPS*, 12 (August 1946) 379-386.

Banton, Michael, "Recent Migration from West Africa and the West Indies to the United Kingdom," *PS*, 7 (July 1953) 2-13.

Barth, Fredrik, "The Southern Mongoloid Migration," *Man*, 72 (January 1952) 5-8.

Bauer, P. T., and Yamey, B. S., "Economic Aspects of Immigration Policy in Nigeria and the Gold Coast," *SAJE*, 22 (June 1954) 223-232.

Bernardelli, H., "New Zealand and Asiatic Migration," *PS*, 6 (July 1952) 39-54.

Blackton, Charles S., "Australia's Immigration Problem," *Far Eastern Survey*, 22 (November 1953) 163-168.

Brigden, J. B., "The Limits of Australian Immigration," *ER*, 1 (1925) 145-147.

Broom, Leonard, and Shevky, Eshref, "Mexicans in the United States, A Problem in Social Differentiation," *SSR*, 36 (January-February 1952) 150-158.

Brunner, Edmund deS., "Immigration to the United States, 1935-40," *ASR*, 13 (February 1948) 95-96.

Bulbring, Maud, "Post-War Refugees in Great Britain," *PS*, 8 (November 1954) 99-112.

Carr-Saunders, A. M., "Migration Policies and the Economic Crisis," *FA*, 12 (July 1934) 664-676.

Carter, Hugh, ed., *Reappraising Our Immigration Policy*, *AAAPSS*, 262 (March 1949).

Chandrasekhar, S., "Indian Immigration in America," *Far Eastern Survey*, 13 (July 26, 1944) 138-143.

Clements, R. V., "Trade Unions and Emigration, 1840-80," *PS*, 9 (November 1955) 167-180.

Condliffe, J. B., "Population Movements and International Trade," *Index*, 11 (1936), Part I, 122-129; Part II, 138-146.

Corbett, D. C., "Immigration and Economic Development," *CJEPS*, 17 (August 1951) 360-368.

Davie, Maurice R., "Recent Refugee Immigration from Europe," *MMFQ*, 25 (April 1947) 189-202.

Eisenstadt, S. N., "Analysis of Patterns of Immigration and Absorption of Immigrants," *PS*, 7 (November 1953) 167-180.

Eisenstadt, S. N., "Communication Processes Among Immigrants in Israel," *POQ*, 16 (Spring 1952) 42-58.

Erickson, Charlotte, "The Encouragement of Emigration by British Trade Unions, 1850-1900," *PS*, 3 (December 1949) 248-273.

Fairchild, H. P., "Immigration and the Population Problem," *AAAPSS*, 150 (March 1930) 7-12.

Fairchild, H. P., "The Immigration Law of 1924," *Quarterly Journal of Economics*, 38 (August 1924) 653-665.

Garces, V. G., "Immigration and Indian Policy in Latin American Countries," *ILR*, 69 (January 1954) 18-30.

Giusti Del Giardino, J., "International Emigration Problem," Banco di Roma, *Review of Economic Conditions in Italy*, 6 (May 1952) 179-195.

Glass, D. V., ed., *Cultural Assimilation of Immigrants*, Supplement to *PS*, 3 (March 1950).

Goodrich, Carter, "Possibilities and Limits of International Control of Migration," *MMFQ*, 25 (April 1947) 153-160.

Glinstra, R. J. P. van, and Maden, F. H. van der, "Emigration from the Netherlands," *ILR*, 67 (May 1953) 453-74.

Handlin, Oscar, "International Migration and the Acquisition of New Skills," in Hoselitz, B., *The Progress of Underdeveloped Areas* (Chicago: University of Chicago Press, 1952).

Harman, Zena, "The Assimilation of Immigrants into Israel," *Middle East Journal*, 5 (Summer 1951) 303-318.

Heald, Morrell, "Business Attitudes Toward European Immigration 1880-1900," *JEH*, 13 (Summer 1953) 291-304.

Heaton, Herbert, "The Industrial Immigrant in the United States, 1783-1812," *PAPS*, 95 (October 1951) 519-527.

Higham, John, "Origins of Immigration Restriction, 1882-1897; A Social Analysis," *Mississippi Valley Historical Review*, 39 (June 1952) 77-88.

Hutchinson, E. P., "The Present Status of Our Immigration Laws and Policies," *MMFQ*, 25 (April 1947) 161-173.

Irie, Toragi, "History of Japanese Migration to Peru," (Translated in part by William Himel), *Hispanic American Historical Review*, 31 (August and November 1951) 437-452; 648-664.

Issac, Julius, "European Migration Potential and Prospects," *PS*, 2 (March 1949) 379-412.

Issac, Julius, "International Migration and European Population Trends," *ILR*, 66 (September 1952) 185-206.

Johnson, Hildegard B., "The Location of German Immigrants in the Middle West," *AAAG*, 41 (March 1951) 1-41.

Kirk, Dudley, "European Migrations: Postwar Trends and Future Prospects," *MMFQ*, 25 (April 1947) 128-152.

Koenig, Samuel, "Immigration and Culture Conflicts in Israel," *SF*, 31 (December 1952) 144-148.

Kuznets, Simon, and Rubin, Ernest, *Immigration and the Foreign Born*, National Bureau of Economic Research, Occasional Paper 46, New York, 1954.

Lasker, B., "Post-war Migration Problems: The Far East," *SF*, 22 (December 1943) 130-136.

Lovett, Robert M., "Migration in United States Literature," *Chicago Jewish Forum*, 9 (Spring 1951) 174-179.

Lowenthal, David, "Colonial Experiments in French Guiana, 1760-1800," *Hispanic American Historical Review*, 32 (February 1952) 22-43.

MacMahon, E. C., "The Attitude of Immigration Countries," *AAAPSS*, 150 (July 1930) 13-24.

Madgwick, R. B., "Immigration," *ER*, 12 (June 1936) 71-82.

Martin, C. J., "A Demographic Study of an Immigrant Community: The Indian Population of British East Africa," *PS*, 6 (March 1953) 233-247.

Maunder, W. F., "The New Jamaican Emigration," *Social and Economic Studies*, 4 (March 1955) 38-63.

Meadows, Paul, "The Right to Migrate," *Social Science*, 29 (January 1952) 23-26.

Mears, E. G., "Financial Aspects of American Immigration," *Economic Journal*, 33 (September 1923) 332-342.

Meenan, James, "Some Features of Irish Emigration," *ILR*, 69 (February 1954) 126-139.

Moore, Wilbert E., "Economic Limits of International Resettlement," *ASR*, 10 (April 1945) 274-281.

Mulgan, Alan, "New Zealand Today and Yesterday: What the Immigrant Finds," *The Geographical Magazine*, 26 (June 1953) 106-118.

Murphy, H. B. M., "The Assimilation of Refugee Immigrants in Australia," *PS*, 5 (March 1952) 179-206.

Murphy, H. B. M., "The Resettlement of Jewish Refugees in Israel, With Special Reference to Those Known as Displaced Persons," *PS*, 5 (November 1951) 153-174.

Oblath, A., "Italian Regulation of Emigration," *ILR*, 56 (October 1947) 408-425.

Phelan, V. C., "Organization of Migration into Canada," *ILR*, 65 (March 1952) 321-347.

Price, Paul H., "Demographic Aspects of the Polish Migration to Brazil," *Inter-American Economic Affairs*, 5 (Spring 1952) 46-58.

Rife, David C., and Paddock, Elton F., "The Myth of the Melting Pot; Genetic Variability and Racial Intermixture," *EQ*, (December 1954) 248-251.

Roach, James R., "Australia's Immigration Program," *Far Eastern Survey*, 21 (June 18, 1952) 102-107.

Roberts, G. W., "Immigration of Africans into the British Caribbean," *PS*, 7 (March 1954) 235-262.

Robertson, C. J., "Geographical Planning of International Migration: A Note on a Franco-Italian Project," *PS*, 4 (December 1950) 345-353.

Rubin, E., "Immigration and Population Trends in the United States, 1900-1940," *American Journal of Economics and Sociology*, 6 (April 1947) 345-362.

Schwartz, C. P., Jr., "American Immigration Policy," *Columbia Law Review*, 55 (March 1955) 311-341.

Scoville, Warren C., "The Huguenots and the Diffusion of Technology," *JPE*, 60 (August and October 1952) 294-311, 392-411.

Shepperson, Wilbur S., "Industrial Emigration in Early Victorian Britain," *JEH*, 13 (Spring 1953) 179-192.

Spengler, J. J., "The Merits and Demerits of the National Origins Provisions for Selecting Immigrants," *Southwestern Political and Social Science Quarterly*, 10 (September 1929) 149-170.

Stadulis, Elizabeth, "The Resettlement of Displaced Persons in the United Kingdom," *PS*, 5 (March 1953) 207-237.

Taeuber, I. B., "Population Displacement in Europe," *AAAPSS*, 234 (July 1944) 1-12.

Tait, D. C., "International Aspects of Migration," *Journal of the Royal Institute of International Affairs*, 6 (January 1927) 25-46.

Tait, D. C., "The International Organization of Migration," *ILR*, 21 (February 1930) 202-216.

Taylor, P. S., "Some Aspects of Mexican Immigration," *JPE*, 38 (October 1930) 609-615.

Thistlethwaite, F., "Atlantic Partnership," *EHR*, 7 (August 1954) 1-17.

Thomas, Brinley, "Migration and the Rhythm of Economic Growth, 1830-1913," *MSESS*, 19 (September 1951) 215-271.

Thompson, Warren S., "The Demographic and Economic Implications of Larger Immigration," *MMFQ*, 25 (April 1947) 174-188.

Timlin, M. F., "Economic Theory and Immigration Policy," *CJEPS*, 16 (August 1950) 375-382.

United Nations, "International Migration in the Far East During Recent Times—The Countries of Emigration," *PB*, No. 1 (December 1951) 13-30 and "The Countries of Immigration," No. 2 (October 1952) 27-58.

Waldeck, C., "The Great New Migration," *FA*, 15 (April 1937) 537-546.

Watson, W., "British and Foreign Immigrant Miners in Fife," *MSESS*, 20 (May 1952) 203-211.

Wood, G. L., "The Immigration Problem in Australia," *ER*, 2 (1926) 229-239.

Tokutaro, "Origin of the Japanese Race," *Contemporary Japan*, 21 (1-3, 1952) 90-107.

Younge, E. R., "Population Movements and the Assimilation of Alien Groups in Canada," *CJEPS*, 10 (August 1944) 372-80.

Zubrzycki, J., "Emigration From Poland in the Nineteenth and Twentieth Centuries," *PS*, 6 (March 1953) 248-272.

V. Internal Distribution and Migration

Alexander, John W., and Zahorchak, George A., "Population-Density Maps of the United States: Techniques and Patterns," *GR*, 33 (July 1943) 457-466.

Allen, G. R., "The 'Courbe des Populations': A Further Analysis," *Bulletin of the Oxford University Institute of Statistics*, 16 (May-June 1954) 179-189.

Anderson, T. R., "Intermetropolitan Migration: A Comparison of the Hypotheses of Zipf and Stouffer," *ASR*, 20 (June 1955) 287-291.

Beegle, J. Allan, "Characteristics of Michigan's Fringe Population," *RS*, 12 (September 1947) 254-263.

Bogue, Donald J., "Changes in Population Distribution Since 1940," *AJS*, 56 (July 1950) 43-57.

Bogue, D. J., "Urbanism in the United States, 1950," *AJS*, 60 (March 1955) 471-486.

Bogue, D. J., and Thompson, W. S., "Migration and Distance," *ASR*, 14 (April 1949) 236-244.

Bogue, D. J., "The Geography of Recent Population Trends in the United States," *AAAG*, 44 (June 1954) 124-134.

Bowley, A. L., "Rural Population in England and Wales, 1911 and 1931," *Economica*, 13 (May 1946) 97-118.

Breese, Gerald, "Demography and Urban Areal Studies," *SM*, 73 (July 1951) 44-46.

Brewster, John M., "Farm Technological Advance and Total Population Growth," *JFE*, 27 (August 1945) 509-525.

Bright, Margaret L., and Thomas, Dorothy S., "Interstate Migration and Intervening Opportunities," *ASR*, 6 (December 1941) 773-783.

Brunner, Edmund deS., "Internal Migration in the United States, 1935-40," *RS*, 13 (March 1948) 9-22.

Brunner, Edmund deS., "Village Growth 1940-50," *RS*, 16 (June 1951) 111-118.

Brunner, Edmund deS., "The Small Village: 1940-50," *RS*, 17 (June 1952) 127-131.

Brush, John E., "The Hierarchy of Central Places in Southwestern Wisconsin," *GR*, 43 (July 1953) 380-402.

Buckatzsch, E. J., "Places of Origin of a Group of Immigrants into Sheffield, 1624-1799," *EHR*, 2 (No. 3, 1950) 303-306.

Cairncross, A. K., "Internal Migration in Victorian England," *MSESS*, 18 (January 1949) 67-87.

Cairncross, A. K., "Trends in Internal Migration, 1841-1911," in *Transactions of the Manchester Statistical Society*, 105th Session 1938-1939 (Manchester, 1939) 21-29.

Clark, Colin, "The Distribution of Labour Between Industries and Between Locations," *LE*, 26 (May 1950) 136-144.

Clark, C., "Urban Population Densities," *JRSS*, 114 (Part IV, 1951) 490-496.

Clark, C., "The Economic Functions of a City in Relation to Its Size, *Econometrica*, 13 (April 1945) 97-113.

Cooper, Eunice, "Urbanization in Malaya," *PS*, 5 (November 1951) 117-131.

Darby, H. C., "The Movement of Population to and from Cambridge-Shire Between 1851 and 1861," *GJ*, 101 (March 1943) 118-124.

Davis, K., "The Origin and Growth of Urbanization in the World," *AJS*, 60 (March 1955) 429-437.

Dodge, Stanley D., "The Depopulation of Maine from 1840 to 1940," *AAAG*, 33 (March 1943) 86-87.

Dorn, Harold F., "Migration and the Growth of Cities," *SF*, 16 (March 1938) 328-337.

Ducoff, Louis J., "Migratory Farm Workers: A Problem in Migration Analysis," *RS*, 16 (September 1951) 217-224.

Duncan, O. D., and Duncan, Beverly, "Residential Distribution and Occupational Stratification," *AJS*, 60 (March 1955) 493-503.

Duncan, O. D., and Duncan, Beverly, "A Methodological Analysis of Segregation Indexes," *ASR*, 20 (April 1955) 210-217.

Dyer, Donald R., "The Place of Origin of Florida's Population," *AAAG*, 43 (September 1952) 283-294.

Firey, Walter, "The Optimum Rural-Urban Population Balance," *RS*, 12 (June 1947) 116-127.

Foley, Donald L., "The Daily Movement of Population into Central Business Districts," *ASR*, 17 (October 1952) 538-543.

Foley, Donald L., "Urban Daytime Population: A Field for Demographic-Eco-
    logical Analysis," *SF*, 32 (May 1954) 323-330.
Folger, John, "Some Aspects of Migration in the Tennessee Valley," *ASR*, 18
    (June 1953) 253-260.
Folger, John and Rowan, John, "Migration and Marital Status in Ten South-
    eastern Cities," *SF*, 32 (December 1953) 178-185.
Freedman, Ronald, and Hawley, Amos H., "Unemployment and Migration in the
    Depression (1930-1935)," *JASA*, 44 (June 1949) 260-272.
Freedman, Ronald, "Health Differentials for Rural-Urban Migration," *ASR*, 12
    (October 1947) 536-541.
Freedman, Ronald, "Distribution of the Migrant Population in Chicago, *ASR*,
    13 (June 1948) 304-309.
Freedman, Ronald and Hawley, Amos H., "Education and Occupation of Migrants
    in the Depression," *AJS*, 56 (September 1950) 161-166.
Geddes, A., "The Population of India. Variability of Change as a Regional Dem-
    ographic Index," *GR*, 32 (October 1942) 562-573.
Gilbert, E. W., "English Conurbations in the 1951 Census," *GJ*, 118 (March
    1952) 64-68.
Gillespie, Sarah C., and Rothschild, G. W., "Migration and the Distributive
    Trades," *The Review of Economic Studies*, 13 (No. 2, 1945-46) 81-83.
Gist, Noel P., "Developing Patterns of Urban Decentralization," *SF*, 30 (March
    1952) 257-267.
Gist, Noel P., "The New Urban Fringe," *SSR*, 36 (May-June 1952) 297-302.
Gross, Edward, "The Role of Density as a Factor in Metropolitan Growth in the
    United States of America," *PS*, 8 (November 1954) 113-120.
Hamilton, C. Horace, and Henderson, F. M., "Use of the Survival Rate Method
    in Measuring Net Migration," *JASA*, 39 (June 1944) 197-206.
Hauser, Philip M., "How Declining Urban Growth Affects City Activities," *Pub-
    lic Management*, 22 (December 1940) 355-358.
Hauser, Philip M., and Eldridge, Hope T., "Projection of Urban Growth and
    Migration to Cities in the United States," *MMFQ*, 25 (July 1947) 293-307.
Hays, Marion, "Regional Differences in Jobs, Income, and Migration, 1929-49,"
    MLR, 71 (October 1950) 433-437.
Heberle, Rudolf, "The Causes of Rural-Urban Migration: A Survey of German
    Theories," *AJS*, 43 (May 1938) 933-950.
Hirsch, G. P., "Migration From the Land in England and Wales, 1871-1950,"
    Farm Economics (Oxford), 6 (April 1951) 270-280.
Hitt, Homer L., "The Role of Migration in Population Change Among the Aged,"
    ASR, 19 (April 1954) 194-200.
Hoffman, L. A., "India: Main Population Concentrations," *GJ*, 111 (July 1948)
    89-100.
Hutchinson, E. P., and Rubin, Ernest, "Estimating the Resident Alien Population
    of the United States," *JASA*, 42 (September 1947) 385-400.
Iklé, Fred C., "Sociological Relationship of Traffic to Population and Distance,"
    Traffic Quarterly, 8 (April 1954) 123-136.
Jaffe, A. J., and Wolfbein, S. L., "Internal Migration and Full Employment in
    the United States," *JASA*, 40 (September 1945) 351-363.
Jaffe, A. J., "Population Trends and City Growth," *AAAPSS*, 242 (November
    1945) 18-24.
Jones, J. D. Rheinallt, "The Effects of Urbanization in South and Central Africa,"
    African Affairs, 52 (January 1953) 37-44.
King, Herbert W. H., "The Canberra-Queanbeyan Symbiosis, A Study of Urban
    Mutualism," *GR*, 44 (January 1954) 101-118.

Kish, Leslie, "Differentiation in Metropolitan Areas," *ASR*, 19 (August 1954) 388-398.

Klove, Robert C., "The Definition of Standard Metropolitan Areas," *EG*, 28 (April 1952) 95-104.

Landis, Paul H., "Rural-Urban Migration and the Marriage Rate—An Hypothesis," *ASR*, 11 (April 1946) 155-158.

Lasker, Gabriel W., "Environmental Growth Factors and Selective Migration," *HB*, 24 (December 1952) 262-289.

Lewis, Oscar, "Urbanization Without Breakdown: A Case Study," *SM*, 75 (July 1952) 31-41.

Lillibridge, Robert M., "Urban Size: An Assessment," *LE*, 28 (November 1952) 341-352.

McCormick, T. C., "An Approach to the Measurement of Farm Population Pressure in Wisconsin," *JASA*, 38 (June 1943) 165-177.

McEntire, Davis, "Characteristics of California's Migrant Population," in *Proceedings* of the Institute of Economics and Finance, Occidental College Bulletin (Los Angeles, 1948) 20-41.

Mather, Eugene, "A Linear-Distance Map of Farm Population in the United States," *AAAG*, 34 (September 1944) 173-180.

Menzler, F. A. A., "An Estimate of the Day-time Population of London," *Journal of the Town Planning Institute*, 38 (March 1952) 116-120.

Morse, Richard M., "São Paulo in the Nineteenth Century: Economic Roots of the Metropolis," *Inter-American Economic Affairs*, 5 (Winter 1951) 3-39.

Neale, E. P., "The Size of Towns," *ER*, 28 (May 1952) 81-88.

Pihlblad, C. T., and Gregory, C. L., "Selection Aspects of Migration Among Missouri High School Graduates," *ASR*, 19 (June 1954) 314-324.

Prais, S. J., "The Formal Theory of Social Mobility," *PS*, 9 (July 1955) 72-81.

Price, Daniel O., "Distance and Direction as Vectors of Internal Migration, 1935-1940," *SF*, 27 (October 1948) 48-53.

Price, Daniel O., "Nonwhite Migrants To and From Selected Cities," *AJS*, 54 (November 1948) 196-201.

Price, Daniel O., "Some Socio-Economic Factors in Internal Migration," *SF*, 29 (May 1951) 409-415.

Price, Daniel O., "Estimates of Net Migration in the United States, 1870-1940," *ASR*, 18 (February 1953) 35-39.

Raza, Moonis, "Urbanization in Prehistoric India," *The Geographer*, 4 (May 1951) 15-29.

Reid, Ira de A., "Special Problems of Negro Migration During the War," *MMFQ*, 25 (July 1947) 284-292.

Roterus, Victor, "Effects of Population Growth and Non-Growth on the Well-Being of Cities," *ASR*, 11 (February 1946) 90-97.

Rumney, George B., "Settlements on the Canadian Shield," *Canadian Geographical Journal*, 43 (September 1951) 117-127.

Schmid, Calvin F., and Griswold, Manzer J., "Migration Within the State of Washington: 1935-40," *ASR*, 17 (June 1952) 312-326.

Schmitt, Robert C., "Fringe Growth and Tax Rates," *National Tax Journal*, 4 (December 1951) 370-371.

Schmitt, Robert C., "Demography and City Planning," *SF*, 30 (March 1952) 300-304.

Schmitt, Robert C., "Differential Migration and City Population Estimates," *SSR*, 37 (May-June 1953) 327-328.

Schnore, L. F., and Varley, D. W., "Some Concomitants of Metropolitan Size," *ASR*, 20 (August 1955) 408-414.

Scudder, R., and Anderson, C. A., "Migration and Vertical Occupational Mobility," *ASR*, 19 (June 1954) 329-334.

Sheldon, Henry D., "Changes in the Rural Population, 1940 to 1950," *RS*, 17 (June 1952) 118-126.

Shryock, Henry S., Jr., "Wartime Shifts of the Civilian Population," *MMFQ*, 25 (July 1947) 269-283.

Shryock, Henry S., Jr., "Internal Migration and the War," *JASA*, 38 (March 1943) 16-30.

Shryock, Henry S., Jr., and Eldridge, Hope T., "Internal Migration in Peace and War," *ASR*, 12 (February 1947) 27-39.

Siegel, J. S., and Hamilton, C. H., "Some Considerations in the Use of the Residual Method of Estimating Net Migration," *JASA*, 47 (September 1952) 475-500.

Simon, Herbert A., "On a Class of Skew Distribution Functions," *Biometrika*, 42 (December 1955) 425-440.

Simon, Herbert A., "Effects of Increased Productivity Upon the Ratio of Urban to Rural Population," *Econometrica*, 15 (January 1947) 31-42.

Smith, T. Lynn, "The Migration of the Aged," in *Growing With the Years*, (Albany: New York State Joint Legislative Committee on Problems of Aging, 1954) 69-80.

Stewart, J. Q., "Demographic Gravitation: Evidence and Applications," *Sociometry*, 11 (February-May 1948) 31-58.

Stouffer, Samuel A., "Intervening Opportunities: A Theory Relating Mobility and Distance," *ASR*, 5 (December 1940) 845-867.

Strodtbeck, Fred L., "Equal Opportunity Intervals: A Contribution to the Method of Intervening Opportunity Analysis," *ASR*, 14 (August 1949) 490-497.

Taeuber, Conrad, "Recent Trends of Rural-Urban Migration in the United States," *MMFQ*, 25 (April 1947) 203-213.

Taeuber, Conrad, "Migration and Rural Population Adjustment," *RS*, 5 (December 1940) 399-410.

Thomas, Dorothy Swaine, "Internal Migrations in Sweden: A Note on Their Extensiveness as Compared with Net Migration Gain or Loss," *AJS*, 42 (November 1936) 345-357.

Thomas, Dorothy S., "Selective Migration," *MMFQ*, 16 (October 1938) 403-407.

Thompson, Warren S., and Bogue, Donald J., "Subregional Migration as an Area of Research," *SF*, 27 (May 1949) 392-400.

Trewartha, Glenn T., "Chinese Cities: Numbers and Distribution," *AAAG*, 41 (December 1951) 331-347.

Trewartha, Glenn T., "Chinese Cities: Origins and Functions," *AAAG*, 42 (March 1952) 69-93.

Truesdell, Leon E., "Problems Involved in the Classification of Population as Farm and Nonfarm," *RS*, 12 (December 1947) 419-423.

Ullman, Edward L., "Amenities as a Factor in Regional Growth," *GR*, 44 (January 1954) 119-132.

Valien, Preston, "Internal Migration and Racial Composition of the Southern Population," *ASR*, 13 (June 1948) 294-298.

Vance, Rupert B., "The Ecology of Our Aging Population," *SF*, 32 (May 1954) 330-335.

Watson, James W., "Rural Depopulation in Southwestern Ontario," *AAAG*, 37 (September 1947) 147-154.

Watson, John E., "Traveling Time to Work: Some Notes From the New Zealand Census of 1945," *SF*, 30 (March 1952) 283-292.

Wendel, Bertil, "A Migration Schema: Theories and Observations," Lund University, Department of Geography, Lund Studies in Geography, Series B, Human Geography, No. 9, Lund, 1953.

Whitney, Vincent Heath, "Rural-Urban People," *AJS*, 54 (July 1948) 48-54.

Wilkinson, Thomas O., "The Pattern of Korean Urban Growth," *RS*, 19 (March 1954) 32-38.

Zipf, G. K., "The P_1P_2/D Hypothesis: On the Intercity Movement of Persons," *ASR*, 11 (December 1946) 677-686.

VI. Population Composition and Utilization of Human Resources

Adcock, Cyril J., "The Decline of Intelligence: A Methodological Note," *PS*, 5 (November 1951) 175-178.

Allen, Gordon, M.D., "Perspectives in Population Eugenics," *EQ*, 2 (June 1955) 90-97.

Anastasi, Anne, "Tested Intelligence and Family Size: Methodological and Interpretive Problems," *EQ*, 1 (September 1954) 155-160.

Anderson, C. Arnold, *et al.*, "Intelligence and Occupational Mobility," *JPE*, 60 (June 1952) 218-239.

Badenhorst, L. T., "The Future Growth of the Population of South Africa and its Probable Age Distribution," *PS*, 4 (June 1950) 3-46.

Bancroft, Gertrude, "Older Persons in the Labor Force," *AAAPSS*, 279 (January 1952) 52-61.

Barclay, G., and Maxwell, James, "The Intelligence of Twins. A Comparative Study of Eleven-Year Old Twins. II, *PS*, 4 (December 1950) 333-344.

Bauer, P. T., and Yamey, B. S., "Economic Progress and Occupational Distribution," *Economic Journal*, 61 (December 1951) 741-755.

Blackburn, Julian, "Family Size, Intelligence Score and Social Class," *PS*, 1 (September 1947) 165-176.

Blacker, Charles P., "Promising Families: Elite and Moiety Eugenics," *Eugenics Review*, 46 (April 1954) 21-27.

Bosanquet, Barbara S., "The Quality of the Rural Population," *Eugenics Review*, 42 (July 1950) 75-92.

Brown, S. P., "Analysis of a Hypothetical Stationary Population by Family Units —A Note on Some Experimental Calculations," *PS*, 4 (March 1951) 380-394.

Burns, R. K., "Economic Aspects of Aging and Retirement," *AJS*, 59 (January 1954) 384-391.

Burt, Cyril, "Family Size, Intelligence and Social Class," *PS*, 1 (September 1947) 177-186.

Carson, Daniel, "Occupational Mobility and Occupational Outlook," *Southern Economic Journal*, 14 (April 1948) 411-419.

Coale, Ansley J., "The Population of the United States in 1950 Classified by Age, Sex, and Color—A Revision of the Census Figures," *JASA*, 50 (March 1955) 16-54.

Dice, Lee R., "Heredity and Population Betterment," *SM*, 75 (November 1952) 273-279.

Dorfman, R., *et al.*, "Economic Implications of an Aging Population," *American Economic Review, Proceedings*, 44 (May 1954) 634-679.

Dorn, Harold F., "A Graphic Representation of the Age and Sex Distribution of the Population of the United States," *American Journal of Hygiene*, 31 (May 1940) 99-108.

Durand, John D., "Population Structure as a Factor in Manpower and Dependency Problems of Underdeveloped Countries," *PB*, No. 3 (October 1953) 1-16.

Eldridge, Hope Tisdale, and Siegel, Jacob S., "The Changing Sex Ratio in the United States," *AJS*, 52 (November 1946) 224-234.

Emmett, W. G., "The Intelligence of Urban and Rural Children," *PS*, 7 (March 1954) 207-221.

Emmett, W. G., "The Trend of Intelligence in Certain Districts of England, *PS*, 3 (March 1950) 324-337.

Fauman, S. Joseph, "Occupational Selection Among Detroit Jews," *Jewish Social Studies*, 14 (January 1952) 17-50.

Foote, N. N., and Hatt, P. K., "Social Mobility and Economic Advancement," *American Economic Review*, Supplement, 43 (May 1953) 364-378.

Fox, Horland, "Utilization of Older Manpower," *Harvard Business Review*, 29 (November 1951) 40-54.

Frumkin, Grzegorz, "Pre-War and Post-War Trends in Manpower of European Countries," *PS*, 4 (September 1950) 209-240.

Giles-Bernardelli, Betty M., "The Decline of Intelligence in New Zealand," *PS*, 4 (September 1950) 200-208.

Glass, Bentley, "The Dynamics of Racial Inter-Mixture—An Analysis Based on the American Negro," *American Journal of Human Genetics*, 5 (March 1953) 1-20.

Glick, Paul C., "Types of Families: An Analysis of Census Data," *ASR*, 6 (December 1941) 830-838.

Glick, Paul C., "Family Trends in the United States, 1890 to 1940," *ASR*, 7 (August 1942) 505-514.

Glick, Paul C., "The Family Cycle," *ASR*, 12 (April 1947) 164-174.

Glick, Paul C., "Family Life and Full Employment," *AJS*, 54 (May 1949) 520-529.

Hauser, Philip M., "Changes in the Labor-Force Participation of the Older Worker," *AJS*, 59 (January 1954) 312-323.

Hauser, Philip M., "Facing the Implications of an Aging Population," *Social Service Review*, 27 (June 1953) 162-176.

Hauser, Philip M., "The Labor Force and Gainful Workers—Concept, Measurement, and Comparability," *AJS*, 54 (January 1949) 338-355.

Hauser, P. M., and Pearl, R. B., "Who Are the Unemployed?" *JASA*, 45 (December 1950) 479-500.

Hopkin, W. A. B., "The Economics of an Aging Population," *Lloyds Bank Review*, 27 (January 1953) 25-36.

Hyrenius, Hannes, "Summary Indices of the Age Distribution of a Population," *PS*, 2 (March 1949) 454-460.

Keyfitz, N., and Robinson, H. L., "The Canadian Sample for Labour Force and Other Population Data," *PS*, 2 (March 1949) 427-443.

Kirk, Dudley, "Dynamics of Human Populations," *EQ*, 2 (March 1955) 18-25.

Kirk, R. L., *et.al.*, "Differential Fertility Between Women of Blood Groups O and A," *British Journal of Preventive and Social Medicine*, 7 (January 1953) 1-8.

Kiser, Clyde V., and Schacter, Nathalie L., "Demographic Characteristics of Women in 'Who's Who'," *MMFQ*, 27 (October 1949) 392-433.

Lamontagne, M., and Falardeau, J. C., "The Life Cycle of French-Canadian Urban Families," *CJEPS*, 13 (May 1947) 233-247.

Lasker, Gabriel W., "The Question of Physical Selection of Mexican Migrants to the United States of America," *HB*, 26 (February 1954) 52-58.

Lehman, Harvey C., "Average Age at Time of Achievement vs. Longevity," *American Journal of Psychology*, 64 (October 1951) 534-547.

Lehman, Harvey C., "Men's Creative Production Rate at Different Ages and in Different Countries," *SM*, 78 (May 1954) 321-326.

Lorimer, Frank, "General Eugenics," *EN*, 32 (March 1947) 1-7.

Lorimer, Frank, "Trends in Capacity for Intelligence," *EN*, 37 (June 1952) 17-24.

McArthur, N., and Penrose, L. S., "World Frequencies of the O, A, and B Blood-Group Genes," *Annals of Eugenics*, 15 (March 1951) 302-305.

McCandless, Boyd, "Environment and Intelligence," *American Journal of Mental Deficiency*, 56 (April 1952) 674-691.

Mautz, W. H., and Durand, John D., "Population and War Labor Supply," *JASA*, 38 (March 1943) 31-43.

Mehrotra, S. N., and Maxwell, J., "The Intelligence of Twins. A Comparative Study of Eleven-Year-Old Twins," *PS*, 3 (December 1949) 295-302.

Nachtsheim, Hans, "Frequency and Distribution of Pathologic Genes in Human Population," *EQ*, 2 (March 1955) 7-17.

Nag, A. C., "Variation of Sex-Ratio Under Different Conditions," *BISI*, 33 (No. 4, 1954) 75-82.

Neel, James V., "The Study of Human Mutation Rates," *The American Naturalist*, 86 (May-June 1952) 129-144.

Nelson, Lowry, "Speaking of Tongues," *AJS*, 54 (November 1948) 202-210.

Nisbet, John, "Family Environment and Intelligence," *Eugenics Review*, 45 (April 1953) 31-40.

Osborn, Frederick, "Effect of Birth Control on the Intelligence and Character of Succeeding Generations," *EQ*, 1 (June 1954) 27-31.

Osborn, Frederick, "Selective Processes in the Differential Fertility of Family Stocks," *American Naturalist*, 86 (July-August 1952) 203-211.

Osborn, Frederick, "The Eugenic Hypothesis, Part I. Positive Eugenics," *EN*, 36 (June 1951) 19-21.

Osborn, Frederick, "The Eugenic Hypothesis, Part II. Negative Eugenics," *EN*, 37 (March 1952) 6-9.

Osborn, Frederick, "New Trends in Human Evolution," *PAPS*, 97 (April 30, 1953) 143-146.

Paish, F. W., and Peacock, A. T., "Economics of Dependence (1952-82)," *Economica*, 21 (November 1954) 279-299.

Papavassiliou, I. Th., "Intelligence and Family Size," *PS*, 7 (March 1954) 222-226.

Perrott, G. S. J., and Holland, D. F., "Population Trends and Problems of Public Health," *MMFQ*, 18 (October 1940) 359-392.

Rosenthal, E., "Trends of the Jewish Population in Germany, 1910-39," *Jewish Social Studies*, 6 (1944) 233-274.

Rucker, Allen W., "Economic Challenge of Longevity," *Harvard Business Review*, 32 (November-December 1954) 94-102.

Sanghvi, L. D., "Genetic Diversity in the People of Western India," *EQ*, 1 (December 1954) 235-239.

Sauvy, A., "Social and Economic Consequences of the Aging of Western European Populations," *PS*, 2 (June 1948) 115-124.

Scientific American (Symposium, Special Issue), "The Human Resources of the United States," Vol. 185, No. 3, September 1951.

Shryock, Henry S., Jr., "1940 Census Data on Number of Years of School Completed," *MMFQ*, 20 (October 1942) 367-388.

Shryock, Henry S., Jr., "The Changing Age Profile of the Population," in *The Aged and Society*, ed. by M. Derber (Champaign, Ill.: Industrial Relations Research Association, 1950) 2-23.

Silcock, H., "Estimating by Sample the Size and Age-Sex Structure of a Population," *PS*, 6 (July 1952) 55-68.

Sjörgren, Torsten, "Distribution of Genes Affecting Characteristics of the Population," *EQ*, 1 (December 1954) 225-229.

Snyder, L. H., "The Effects of Selection and Domestication on Man," *Journal of the National Cancer Institute*, 15 (1954) 759-769.

Sogge, Tillman M., "Industrial Classes in the United States 1870 to 1950," *JASA*, 49 (June 1954) 251-253.

Solomon, Benjamin, "The Growth of the White-Collar Work Force," *The Journal of Business*, 27 (October 1954) 268-275.

Spengler, J. J., "Some Effects of Changes in the Age Composition of the Labor Force," *Southern Economic Journal*, 8 (October 1941) 147-175.

Stecher, Robert N., M. D., "Heredity of Joint Diseases," *EQ*, 1 (March 1954) 16-20.

Sutter, Jean, and Tabah, Leon, "The Break-up of Isolates" *EQ*, 1 (September 1954) 148-154.

Taeuber, Conrad, "Utilization of Human Resources in Agriculture," *MMFQ*, 28 (January 1950) 68-83.

Taeuber, Irene B., and Eldridge, Hope T., "Some Demographic Aspects of the Changing Role of Women," *AAAPSS*, 251 (May 1947) 24-34.

Thomas, Dorothy S., "Some Social Aspects of Japanese-American Demography," *PAPS*, 94 (October 19, 1950) 459-480.

Ullmann, Charles A., "A Note on Predicting Manpower Resources from Health and Educational Data," *MMFQ*, 32 (January 1954) 65-68.

Unsigned, "Educational Level Continues to Rise," *Statistical Bulletin, Metropolitan Life Insurance Company*, 34 (March 1953) 9-10.

Valaoras, V. G., "Some Effects of Famine on the Population of Greece," *MMFQ*, 24 (July 1946) 215-234.

Vance, Rupert B., and Danilevski, Nadia, "Population and the Pattern of Unemployment, 1930-1937," *MMFQ*, 18 (January 1940) 27-43.

Vance, Rupert B., "The Ecology of our Aging Population," *SF*, 32 (May 1954) 330-335.

Vernon, Philip E., "Recent Investigations of Intelligence and its Measurement," *Eugenics Review*, 43 (October 1951) 125-137.

Vernon, Philip E., "Use of Intelligence Tests in Population Studies," *EQ*, 1 (December 1954) 221-224.

Visher, Stephen S., "Some Influences Affecting the Production of Leaders," *EN*, 35 (December 1950) 57-61.

Visher, Stephen S., "Sources of Great Men," *EQ*, 3 (June 1955) 103-109.

Wallace, Bruce, "Genetic Studies of Population," *EQ*, 1 (June 1954) 10-15.

Wolfle, Dael, "Differential Fertility and the Intelligence of New Generations," *Science*, 119 (May 14, 1954) 675-676.

Woofter, T. J., Jr., "A Method of Analysis of Family Composition and Income," *JASA*, 39 (December 1944) 488-496.

Wright, Sewall, "The Genetical Structure of Populations," *Annals of Eugenics*, 15 (March 1951) 323-354.

Yerushalmy, J., "The Age-Sex Composition of the Population Resulting from Natality and Mortality Conditions," *MMFQ*, 21 (January 1943) 37-63.

VII. Selected Regional Studies

Backer, Julie E., "Population Statistics and Population Registration in Norway. Part 1. The Vital Statistics of Norway: An Historical Review," *PS*, 1 (September 1947) 212-226; Part 2, 2 (December 1948) 318-338.

Badenhorst, L. T., "Territorial Differentials in Fertility in the Union of South Africa—1911-1936," *PS*, 6 (November 1952) 135-162.

Barclay, George W., *Colonial Development and Population in Taiwan*, Princeton University Press, Princeton, 1954.

Barclay, George W., "China's Population Problem: A Closer View," *Pacific Affairs*, 23 (June 1950) 184-192.

Bohannan, Paul, "The Migration and Expansion of the Tiv," *Africa*, 24 (January 1954) 2-16.

Bonne, Alfred, "Land and Population in the Middle East," *Middle East Journal*, 5 (Winter 1951) 39-56.

Bonne, Alfred, "Population Growth and Economic Development," *Scripta Hierosolymitona* 3 (1955) 1-19.

Borrie, W. D., *Population Trends and Policies*, Sydney, 1948.

Borrie, W. D., *Immigration: Australia's Problems and Prospects*, Sydney, 1949.

Borrie, W. D., "Aspects of Australian Demography," *Pacific Affairs*, 20 (March 1947) 42-52.

Bower, Francis, "The Population of Soviet Russia," *Contemporary Review*, No. 1032 (December 1951) 337-343.

Bunce, Arthur, "Economic and Cultural Bases of Family Size in Korea," in Milbank Memorial Fund, *Approaches to Problems of High Fertility in Agrarian Societies*, (New York 1952) 18-28.

Calvert, G. M., *The Future Population of New Zealand: A Statistical Analysis*, Wellington, 1946.

Campbell, Eila M. J., "Land and Population Problems in Fiji," *GJ*, 118 (December 1952) 476-482.

Chandrasekhar, S., "The Population Problems of India and Pakistan," *Eugenics Review*, 41 (July 1949) 70-80.

Chang Chih-yi, "Land Utilization and Settlement Possibilities in Sinkiang," *GR*, 39 (January 1949) 57-75.

Chang, C., "China's Population Problem—A Chinese View," *Pacific Affairs*, 22 (December 1949) 339-356.

Chen, Ta, "The Need of Population Research in China," *PS*, 1 (March 1948) 342-352.

Chen, T., "Population in Modern China," *AJS*, 42 (July 1946, Part 2) 1-126.

Charles, Enid, "Population Problems in the British Overseas Dominions," *AAAPSS*, 237 (January 1945) 80-93.

Charles, Enid, "Post-War Demographic Problems in Britain," *ASR*, 11 (October 1946) 578-590.

Chiang, Chih-Ang, "Using the *Pao* as the Primary Sampling Unit. Some Notes and Reflections on the Possibilities of a Census of China by Sampling," *PS*, 2 (March 1949) 444-453.

Chiao, C. M., Thompson, W. S., and Chen, D. T., *An Experiment in the Registration of Vital Statistics in China* (Oxford, Ohio: Scripps Foundation for Research in Population Problems, 1938).

Clarke, John I., "The Population of Tunisia; An Example of Contact Between Modern Civilization and the Moslem World," *EG*, 28 (October 1952) 364-371.

Cleland, W. W., "A Population Plan for Egypt," in *Demographic Studies of Selected Areas of Rapid Growth*, (New York: Milbank Memorial Fund, 1944) 123-137.

Combs, Jerry W., Jr., and Davis, Kingsley, "Differential Fertility in Puerto Rico," *PS*, 5 (November 1951) 104-116.

Combs, J. W., Jr., and Davis, Kingsley, "The Pattern of Puerto Rican Fertility," *PS*, 4 (March 1951) 364-379.

Coolidge, Susannah, "Note on the Fertility of a Number of Women of the Ancient Near East," *HB*, 25 (September 1953) 203-205.

Dajani, Sami W., "The Enumeration of the Beersheba Bedouins in May 1946," *PS*, 1 (December 1947) 301-307.

Dandekar, V. M., and Dandekar, Kumudini, *Survey of Fertility and Mortality in Poona District*, Gokhale Institute of Politics and Economics, Publication No. 27, Poona 4.

Davis, Kingsley, *The Population of India and Pakistan*, Princeton, 1951.

Davis, Kingsley, "Institutional Patterns Favoring High Fertility in Underdeveloped Areas," *EQ*, 6 (March 1955) 33-39.

Davis, Kingsley, "Puerto Rico's Population Problem: Research and Policy," *MMFQ*, 26 (July 1948) 300-308.

Davis, Kingsley, and Casis, Ana, "Urbanization in Latin America," *MMFQ*, 24 (April and July 1946) 186-207, 292-314.

Davis, Kingsley, "Future Migration into Latin America," *MMFQ*, 25 (January 1947) 44-62.

Davis, Kingsley, "Demographic Fact and Policy in India," *MMFQ*, 22 (July 1944) 256-278.

Dore, R. P., "Japanese Rural Fertility; Some Social and Economic Factors," *PS*, 7 (July 1953) 62-88.

Elath, Eliahu, "Population Problems in Israel," *Journal of the Royal Central Asian Society*, 40 (January 1953) 22-36.

El-Badry, M. A., "Some Demographic Measurements for Egypt Based on the Stability of Census Age Distributions," *MMFQ*, 33 (July 1955) 268-305.

Ford, Clellan S., "Control of Conception in Cross-Cultural Perspective," *Annals of the New York Academy of Sciences*, 54 (May 2, 1952) 763-768.

Gabriel, K. R., "The Fertility of the Jews in Palestine. A Review of Research," *PS*, 6 (March 1953) 273-305.

Ghosh, D., *Pressure of Population and Economic Efficiency in India*, Indian Council of World Affairs, New Delhi, 1946.

Glass, D. V., and Grebenik, E., *The Trend and Pattern of Fertility in Great Britain*, Paper of the Royal Commission on Population, Vol. VI, Part I, Report, London, HMSO, 1954.

Goodrich, C., and others, *Migration and Economic Opportunity*, Philadelphia 1936.

Gordon, M. K., "Russia's Growing Population," *AAAPSS*, 237 (January 1945) 57-63.

Grove, A. T., "Soil Erosion and Population Problems in South-East Nigeria," *GJ*, 117 (September 1951) 291-304.

Hansen, M. L., *The Atlantic Migration 1607-1860*, Cambridge (Mass.), 1940.

Hansen, M. L., *Emigration from Continental Europe 1815-1860 with Special Reference to the United States*, Thesis, Harvard University, Cambridge (Mass.), 1924.

Harding, R. D., "A Note on Some Vital Statistics of a Primitive Peasant Community in Sierra Leone," *PS*, 2 (December 1948) 373-376.

Hatt, P. K., *Backgrounds of Human Fertility in Puerto Rico*, Princeton, 1952.

Hawley, Amos H., "Rural Fertility in Central Luzon," *ASR*, 20 (February 1955) 21-27.

Helleiner, K. F., "Population Movement and Agrarian Depression in the Later Middle Ages," *CJEPS*, 15 (August 1949) 368-377.

Ho, Franklin L., "The Land Problem of China," *AAAPSS*, 276 (July 1951) 6-11.

Hobbalah, Mahmound, "Marriage, Divorce and Inheritance in Islamic Law," *George Washington University Law Review*, 22 (October 1953) 24-31.

Houghton, D. Hobart, "Population Structure of a Ciskei Native Reserve, Analysis of the Population of a Sample of 285 Native Homesteads in Kliskama Holk District," *SAJE*, 17 (September 1949) 341-348.

Hubback, E. M., *The Population of Britain*, London, 1947.

Hunt, Edward E., *et.al.*, "The Depopulation of Yap," *HB*, 26 (February 1954) 21-51.

Huntsman, A. G., "Population versus Resources," *Queen's Quarterly*, 59 (Summer 1952) 149-161.

Hurd, W. B., *Racial Origins and Nativity of the Canadian People*, Canada, Dominion Bureau of Statistics, Seventh Census of Canada, 1931, Census Monograph No. 4, Ottawa, 1937.

Hutchinson, E. P., *Current Problems of Immigration Policy*, New York, 1949.

Innes, J. W., *Class Fertility Trends in England and Wales 1876-1934*. Princeton, 1938.

Isaac, Julius, and Van den Beld, C. A., *The Effect of European Migration on the Economy of Sending and Receiving Countries*, An Interim Report (The Hague: Research Group for European Migration Problems, 1953).

Ishii, R., *Population Pressure and Economic Life in Japan*, Chicago, 1937.

Issawi, Charles, and Dabezies, Carlos, "Population Movements and Population Pressure in Jordan, Lebanon, and Syria," *MMFQ*, 29 (October 1951) 385-401.

Janer, J. L., "Population Growth in Puerto Rico and Its Relations to Time Changes in Vital Statistics, *HB*, 17 (December 1945) 267-313.

Japan, Population Problems Research Council, *The Population of Japan*, Population Series No. 1, the Mainichi Press, Tokyo, 1950.

Jurkat, Ernest, "Prospects for Population Growth in the Near East, *MMFQ*, 22 (July 1944) 300-317.

Keyfitz, Nathan, "The Growth of Canadian Population," *PS*, 4 (June 1950) 47-63.

Keyes, Fenton, "Urbanism and Population Distribution in China, *AJS*, 56 (May 1951) 519-527.

Kirk, Dudley, "Population and Population Trends in Modern France," in Earle, Edward, M., ed. *Modern France; Problems of the Third and Fourth Republics*, (Princeton: Princeton University Press, 1951) 313-333.

Kirk, Dudley, *Europe's Population in the Interwar Years*, League of Nations, Geneva, 1946.

Kiser, Clyde V., "The Demographic Position of Egypt," *MMFQ*, 22 (October 1944) 383-408.

Kooijman, S., "Population Study of the Marind-Anim," *South Pacific Commission Quarterly Bulletin*, 5 (January 1955) 21-23.

Kosambi, D. D., and Raghavachari, S., "Seasonal Variation in the Indian Death Rate," *Annals of Human Genetics*, 19 (November 1954) 100-119.

Koya, Yoshio, "A Study of Induced Abortion in Japan and Its Significance," *MMFQ*, 32 (July 1954) 282-293.

Kuczynski, R. R., *A Demographic Survey of the British Colonial Empire*, Oxford University Press, New York, 1949.

Kulischer, E. M., *The Displacement of Population in Europe*, International Labour Office, Montreal, 1943.

Kulischer, E. M., *Europe on the Move: War and Population Changes, 1917-47*, New York, 1948.

Kulischer, Eugene M., "Recent Migration in the Soviet Union," *ASR*, 9 (June 1944) 223-228.

Lawrence, Norman, *Israel: Jewish Population and Immigration*, International Population Statistics Reports, Series P-90, No. 2, U. S. Bureau of the Census, U. S. Government Printing Office, Washington, 1952.

League of Nations, *Population and Agriculture with Special Reference to Agricultural Over-Population*, European Conference on Rural Life, 1939, Monograph No. 3, Geneva, 1939.

Lee Shu-ching, "Pattern of Land Utilization and Possible Expansion of Cultivated Land in China," *Journal of Land and Public Utility Economics,* 23
(May 1947) 142-152.

Lewis, W. Arthur, "Issues in Land Settlement Policy," *Caribbean Economic Review,* 3 (October 1951) 58-92.

Lewis-Faning, E., *Report on an Inquiry Into Family Limitation and Its Influence
on Human Fertility During the Past Fifty Years,* United Kingdom, Royal
Commission on Population, Papers, Vol. 1, London, 1949.

Loftus, P. J., "Features of the Demography of Palestine," *PS,* 2 (June 1948)
92-114.

Lorimer, Frank, "Recent Population Trends in the Soviet Union," *ASR,* 9 (June
1944) 219-222.

Lorimer, Frank, *The Population of the Soviet Union: History and Prospects,*
League of Nations, Geneva, 1946.

Lorimer, Frank, *et al., Culture and Human Fertility,* UNESCO, Paris, 1954.

McCleary, G. F., "Australia's Population Problem," *MMFQ,* 20 (January 1942)
23-34.

Maquet, Jacques J., "The Modern Evolution of African Populations in the Belgian Congo," *Africa,* 19 (October 1949) 265-272.

Martin, C. J., "Some Estimates of the General Age Distribution, Fertility and
Rate of Natural Increase of the African Population of British East Africa,"
PS, 7 (November 1953) 181-199.

Mashayekhi, Mohammad B., *et. al.,* "Some Demographic Aspects of a Rural Area
In Iran," *MMFQ,* 31 (April 1953) 149-165.

Mauldin, W. Parker, and Akers, Donald S., *The Population of Poland,* U. S.
Bureau of the Census, International Population Statistics Reports, Series P-90,
No. 4 (Washington: Government Printing Office, 1954).

Mayer, Kurt B., *The Population of Switzerland,* Columbia University Press, New
York, 1952.

Mehta, F., "Economic Implications of Demographic Growth In India, *Economia
Internazionale* 8 (November 1955) 810-827.

Meel, H. de, "Demographic Dilemma in Indonesia," *Pacific Affairs,* 24 (September 1951) 266-283.

Meggers, Betty J., "A Pre-Columbian Colonization of the Amazon," *Archaeology,*
4 (June 1951) 110-114.

Milbank Memorial Fund, *Approaches to Problems of High Fertility in Agrarian
Societies,* New York, 1952.

Milbank Memorial Fund, *The Interrelations of Demographic, Economic and Social
Problems in Selected Underdeveloped Areas,* New York, 1954.

Moore, W. E., *Economic Demography of Eastern and Southern Europe,* League
of Nations, Geneva, 1945.

Moore, W. E., *Industrialization and Labor: Social Aspects of Economic Development,* The Institute of World Affairs, New School for Social Research, Ithaca
and New York, 1951.

Moore, Wilbert E., "Agricultural Population and Rural Economy in Eastern and
Southern Europe," *MMFQ,* 22 (July 1944) 279-299.

Moore, Wilbert E., "The Migration of Native Laborers in South Africa," *MMFQ,*
24 (October 1946) 401-419.

Muhsam, H. V., "Fertility and Reproduction of the Beduin," *PS.,* 4 (March 1951)
354-363.

Mukerjee, R., *The Political Economy of Population,* Bombay, 1943.

Murphey, Rhoads, "The Decline of North Africa Since the Roman Occupation:
Climatic or Human?" *AAAG,* 41 (June 1951) 116-132.

Myers, Paul F., and Campbell, Arthur A., *The Population of Yugoslavia,* U. S. Bureau of the Census, International Population Statistics Reports, Series P-90, No. 5 (Washington: Government Printing Office, 1954).

Myers, Paul F., and Mauldin, W. Parker, *Population of the Federal Republic of Germany and West Berlin,* U. S. Bureau of the Census, International Population Statistics Reports, Series P-90, No. 1 (Washington: Government Printing Office, 1952).

Myrdal, A., *Nation and Family,* London, 1945.

Myrdal, G., *Population: A Problem for Democracy,* Cambridge (Mass.), 1940.

National Bureau of Economic Research, *International Migrations* (Willcox, W. F., ed.), Vol. I, New York, 1929.

Notestein, F. W., Taeuber, I. B., Kirk D., Coale, A. J., and Kiser, L. K., *The Future Population of Europe and the Soviet Union,* League of Nations, Geneva, 1944.

Notestein, Frank W., "Summary of the Demographic Background of Problems of Undeveloped Areas," *MMFQ,* 26 (July 1948) 249-255.

Notestein, Frank W., and Jurkat, Ernest, "Population Problems of Palestine," *MMFQ,* 23 (October 1945) 307-352.

Pearson, F. A., and Harper, F. A., *The World's Hunger,* New York, 1945.

Pelzel, John C., "Some Social Factors Bearing Upon Japanese Population," *ASR,* 15 (February 1950) 20-25.

Pelzer, Karl J., "Resettlement in Malaya," *Yale Review,* 41 (Spring 1952) 391-404.

Penrose, E. F., *Population Theories and Their Application, With Special Reference to Japan,* Stanford (Calif.), 1934.

Percival, D. A., "Some Features of a Peasant Population in the Middle East," *PS,* 3 (September 1949) 192-204.

Perloff, H. S., *Puerto Rico's Economic Future,* Chicago, 1950.

Price, Paul H., and Marcondes, J. V. Freitas, "A Demographic Analysis of the Population of the State of São Paulo, Brazil," *SF,* 27 (May 1949) 381-391.

Qureshi, D. M., "Population Growth and Food Grains Production in West Pakistan," *Pakistan Economic Journal,* 2 (June 1951).

Reddaway, W. B., *The Economics of a Declining Population,* New York and London, 1939.

Raza, Moonis, "Is India Over-Populated?" *The Geographer,* 3 (December 1950) 36-40.

Roberts, G. W., "Some Aspects of Mating and Fertility in the West Indies," *PS,* 8 (March 1955) 199-227.

Russell, J. C., *British Medieval Population,* Albuquerque (N.M.), 1948.

Russell, Sir John, *World Population and World Food Supplies,* George Allen and Unwin Ltd., London, 1954.

Rottenberg, Simon, "The Problem of 'Over-Population'. in Puerto Rico," *Caribbean Quarterly,* 2 (No. 4, 1952) 50-54.

Ryan, Bryce, "Institutional Factors in Sinhalese Fertility," *MMFQ,* 30 (October 1952) 359-381.

Ryder, Norman B., "Components of Canadian Population Growth," *Population Index,* 20 (April 1954) 71-80.

Sarkar, N. K., "An Estimate of the Future Population of Ceylon," *The Ceylon Economist,* 1 (November 1950) 167-168.

Schechtman, Joseph B., *European Population Transfers, 1939-1945,* New York, 1946.

Schechtman, Joseph B., "Postwar Population Transfers in Europe: A Study," *The Review of Politics,* 15 (April 1953) 151-178.

Senrio, C., *Puerto Rican Emigration*, Social Science Research Center, University of Puerto Rico, Rio Piedras, 1947.

Shaul, J. R. H., and Myburgh, C. A. L., "Provisional Results of the Sample Survey of the African Population of Southern Rhodesia, 1948," *PS*, 3 (December 1949) 274-285.

Shaul, J R. H., and Myburgh, C. A. L., "Vital Statistics of the African Population of Southern Rhodesia in 1948," *PS*, 4 (March 1951) 432-438.

Singh, B., *Population and Food Planning in India*, Bombay, 1947.

Skaug, A., *Memorandum on Fluctuations in Migration from Norway Since 1900, Compared with Other Countries, and Causes of these Fluctuations*, International Institute of Intellectual Cooperation, Norwegian Memorandum No. 1, Paris, 1937.

Skinner, G. William, "A Study in Miniature of Chinese Population," *PS*, 5 (November 1951) 91-103.

Smith, T. E., *Population Growth in Malaya*, London, 1952.

Sofer, Cyril, and Ross, Rhona, "Some Characteristics of an East African European Population," *British Journal of Sociology*, 2 (December 1951) 315-327.

Sovani, N. V., *The Population Problem in India; A Regional Approach*, Poona, 1942.

Sovani, N. V., "Population Planning in India," *Indian Journal of Economics*, 27 (January 1947) 299-316.

Spengler, J. J., "Economic Factors in the Development of Densely Populated Areas," *PAPS*, 95 (February 1951) 20-53.

Spengler, J. J., *France Faces Depopulation*, Durham (N.C.), 1938.

Stamp, L. D. *Land for Tomorrow: The Underdeveloped World*, Bloomington (Ind.), 1952.

Steiner, Jesse F., "Japan's Post-War Population Problems," *SF*, 31 (March 1953) 245-249.

Steiner, Jesse F., "Population Trends in Japan," *ASR*, 9 (February 1944) 36-40.

Stone, Kirk H., "Populating Alaska: The United States Phase," *GR*, 42 (July 1952) 384-404.

Stycos, J. Mayone, "Family and Fertility in Puerto Rico," *ASR*, 17 (October 1952) 572-580.

Stycos, J. Mayone, "The Pattern of Birth Control in Puerto Rico," *EQ*, 1 (September 1954) 176-181.

Taeuber, Irene B., "Population Growth and Economic Development in Japan," *JEH*, 11 (Fall 1951) 417-428.

Taeuber, Irene B., "Migration and the Population Potential of Monsoon Asia," *MMFQ*, 25 (January 1947) 21-43.

Taeuber, Irene B., and Notestein, Frank W., "The Changing Fertility of the Japanese," *PS*, 1 (June 1947) 2-28.

Taeuber, Irene B., "British Guiana: Some Demographic Aspects of Economic Development," *Population Index*, 18 (January 1952) 3-19.

Taeuber, Irene B., "Ceylon as a Demographic Laboratory: Preface to Analysis," *Population Index*, 15 (October 1949) 293-304.

Taeuber, Irene B., and Beal, Edwin G., "The Dynamics of Population in Japan," *MMFQ*, 22 (July 1944) 222-255.

Taeuber, Irene B., "Family, Migration, and Industrialization in Japan," *ASR*, 16 (April 1951) 149-157.

Taft, Donald R., and Robbins, Richard, *International Migrations*, The Ronald Press Company, New York, 1955.

Taylor, Milton C., "Neo-Malthusianism in Puerto Rico," *Review of Social Economy*, 10 (March 1952) 42-54.

Taylor, George, "The Taiping Rebellion, its Economic Background and Social Theory," *The Chinese Social and Political Science Review*, 16 (January 1933) 545-614.

Thomas, Brinley, *Migration and Economic Growth*, Cambridge University Press, London, 1954.

Thomas, D. S., *Social and Economic Aspects of Swedish Population Movements, 1750-1933*, New York, 1941.

Thompson, W. S., *Danger Spots in World Population*, New York, 1929.

Thompson, W. S., *Population and Peace in the Pacific*, Chicago, 1946.

Thompson, Warren S., "The Demographic Revolution in the United States," *AAAPSS*, 262 (March 1949) 62-69.

Thompson, Warren S., "The Need for a Population Policy in Japan," *ASR*, 15 (February 1950) 25-33.

Thompson, Warren S., "Future Adjustments of Population to Resources in Japan," *MMFQ*, 28 (April 1950) 191-202.

Timasheff, N. S., "The Postwar Population of the Soviet Union," *AJS*, 54 (September 1948) 148-155.

Timlin, M. F., *Does Canada Need More People?* Toronto, 1951.

Treadgold, Donald D., "Russian Expansion in the Light of Turner's Study of the American Frontier," *Agricultural History*, 26 (October 1952) 147-152.

Trewartha, Glenn T., and Zelinsky, Wilbur, "The Population Geography of Belgian Africa," *AAAG*, 44 (June 1954) 163-193.

Trewartha, Glenn T., and Zelinsky, Wilbur, "Population Patterns in Tropical Africa," *AAAG*, 44 (June 1954) 135-162.

Tietze, Christopher, "Human Fertility in Puerto Rico," *AJS*, 53 (July 1947) 34-40.

United Nations, *The Population of Western Samoa*, New York, 1948.

United Nations, *The Population of Tanganyika* (by I. B. Taeuber), Document No. ST/SOA/Series A, Population Studies No. 2, New York, 1949.

United Nations, *Preliminary Report on the World Social Situation*, Document No. E/CN.5/267.Rev. 1., New York, 1952.

United States, National Resources Committee, *The Problems of a Changing Population*, Washington, 1938.

Van der Kroef, Justus M., "The Indonesian Minority in Surinam," *ASR*, 16 (October 1951) 672-679.

Whelpton, P. K., "The Outlook for the Control of Human Fertility in Japan," *ASR*, 15 (February 1950) 34-42.

Whelpton, P. K., "A History of Population Growth in the United States," *SM*, 67 (October 1948) 277-288.

Whelpton, P. K., *Cohort Fertility: Native-White Women in the United States*, Princeton, 1954.

Wise, M. J., "Population Pressure and National Resources: Some Observations Upon the Italian Population Problem," *EG*, 30 (April 1954) 144-156.

Woytinsky, W. S. and E. S., *World Population and Production*, The Twentieth Century Fund, New York, 1953.

Wynne, Waller, *The Population of Czechoslovakia*, International Population Statistics Reports, Series P-90, No. 3, U. S. Bureau of the Census, U. S. Government Printing Office, Washington: 1953.

Zimmermann, E. W., *World Resources and Industries*, New York, 1951.

Supplement: Evaluation of Population Data

Bancroft, Gertrude, "Special Uses of the Current Population Survey Mechanism," *Estadística*, 12 (June 1954) 198-206.

Benjamin, B., "Quality of Response in Census Taking," *PS*, 8 (March 1955) 288-293.

Bogue, Donald J., "A Technique for Making Extensive Population Estimates," *JASA*, 45 (June 1950) 149-163.

Carter, Hugh, "Improving National Marriage and Divorce Statistics," *JASA*, 48 (September 1953) 453-461.

Durand, John D., "Adequacy of Existing Census Statistics for Basic Demographic Research," *PS*, 4 (September 1950) 179-199.

Eldridge, Hope Tisdale, "Needed Population Data for Agricultural and Rural Analysis," *RS*, 14 (March 1949) 63-68.

Glass, D. V., "A Note on the Under-Registration of Births in Britain in the Nineteenth Century," *PS*, 5 (July 1951) 70-90.

Goldthorpe, J. E., "Attitudes to the Census and Vital Registration in East Africa," *PS*, 6 (November 1952) 163-171.

Hagood, Margaret Jarman, "New Research Resources for Rural Sociologists in the 1950 Census," *RS*, 16 (March 1951) 63-66.

Hansen, Morris H., Hurwitz, William N., and Pritzker, Leon, "The Accuracy of Census Results," *ASR*, 18 (August 1953) 416-423.

Harvie, C. H., "A Sampling Census in the Sudan," *PS*, 4 (September 1950) 241-252.

Hauser, Philip M., "Some Aspects of Methodological Research in the 1950 Census," *POQ*, 14 (Spring 1950) 5-13.

Hauser, P. M., "The Use of Sampling for Vital Registration and Vital Statistics," *BWHO*, 11 (1954) 5-24.

Jessen, Raymond J., *et. al.*, "On a Population Sample for Greece," *JASA*, 42 September 1947) 357-384.

Kuczynski, R. R., "Demography—Science and Administration," *Eugenics Review*, 37 (April 1945) 12-22.

Linder, Forrest E., "A Case Study of the International Collection of Demographic Statistics," *MMFQ*, 27 (April 1949) 154-178.

Marshall, J. T., "Canada's National Vital Statistics Index," *PS*, 1 (September 1947) 204-211.

Martin, C. J., "The East African Population Census, 1948, Planning and Enumeration," *PS*, 3 (December 1949) 303-320.

Myers, R. J., "Underenumeration in the Census as Indicated by Selective Service Data," *ASR*, 13 (June 1948) 320-325.

Ofstad, Kare, "Population Statistics and Population Registration in Norway, Part 3, Population Censuses," *PS*, 3 (June 1949) 66-75.

Price, Daniel O., "A Check on Underenumeration in the 1940 Census," *ASR*, 12 (February 1947) 44-49.

Schmitt, Robert C., and Crosetti, Albert H., "Accuracy of the Ratio Method for Forecasting City Population," *LE*, 27 (November 1951) 346-348.

Schneider, J. R. L., "Note on the Accuracy of Local Population Estimates," *PS*, 8 (November 1954) 148-150.

Sekar, C. Chandra, and Deming, W. Edwards, "On a Method of Estimating Birth and Death Rates and the Extent of Registration," *JASA*, 44 (March 1949) 101-115.

Seng, You Poh, "Practical Problems in Sampling for Social and Demographic Inquiries in Underdeveloped Countries," *PS*, 3 (September 1949) 170-191.

Shapiro, S., "Development of Birth Registration and Birth Statistics in the United States," *PS*, 4 (June 1950) 86-111.

Shapiro, S., "Recent Testing of Birth Registration Completeness in the United States," *PS*, 8 (July 1954) 3-21.

Shryock, Henry S., Jr., and Lawrence, Norman, "The Current Status of State and Local Population Estimates in the Census Bureau," *JASA*, 44 (June 1949) 157-173.

Shryock, Henry S., Jr., "Opportunities for Social Research in the 1950 U. S. Census of Population," *ASR*, 15 (June 1950) 417-423.

Siegel, Jacob S., *et al.*, "Accuracy of Postcensal Estimates of Population for States and Cities," *ASR*, 19 (August 1954) 440-446.

Siegel, Jacob S., "Forecasting the Population of Small Areas," *LE*, 29 (February 1953) 72-88.

Silcock, H., "Precision in Population Estimates," *PS*, 8 (November 1954) 140-147.

Szulc, Stefan, "The Sample Census of Population in Poland, 1949," *PS*, 4 (June 1950) 112-114.

Voight, Robert B., and Kriesberg, Martin, "Some Principles of Processing Census and Survey Data," *JASA*, 47 (June 1952) 222-231.

Whelpton, P. K., and Badenhorst, L. T., "Population Statistics in Relation to the Development of Under-developed Areas," *Journal of Social Research*, 3 (No. 1, 1952) 5-13.

White, Helen R., "Empirical Study of the Accuracy of Selected Methods of Projecting State Populations," *JASA*, 49 (September 1954) 480-498.

List of Contributors

L. T. Badenhorst is Senior Lecturer in Sociology, University of the Witwatersrand, Johannesburg, So. Africa; served as a Social Affairs Officer and specialist in demography with the United Nations, 1948-51. A number of his papers on demography have to do with the fertility, growth, and distribution of the population of Africa and its parts.

Robert E. Chaddock (1879-1940) was Professor of Statistics and Sociology at Columbia University. He wrote *Principles and Methods of Statistics* (1925) and many studies in demography.

Bernardo Colombo is a member of the faculty specializing in statistics at the Instituto Universitario di Venezia, Italy. Among his publications are papers dealing with demographic measurement, statistical theory, demographic trends, and statistics.

Kingsley Davis, Professor of Sociology, University of California, is author of *The Population of India and Pakistan* (1951), *Human Society* (1950), and numerous shorter sociological and demographic studies; he edited the symposium, *World Population in Transition* (1945).

Harold F. Dorn, Chief, Office of Biometry, U. S. National Institutes of Health, is a specialist on mortality statistics, and has written, as well, numerous papers on population growth and other demographic subjects.

Louis I. Dublin, Consultant on Health and Welfare, Institute of Life Insurance, was formerly Statistician and Vice-President, Metropolitan Life Insurance Company; he is senior author of such studies as *The Money Value of a Man* (1930 and 1946), *Length of Life* (1936 and 1949), and *The Facts of Life from Birth to Death* (1951).

Otis Dudley Duncan is Assistant Professor of Sociology and Associate Director, Population Research and Training Center, University of Chicago, and is co-author of *Social Characteristics of Urban and Rural Communities, 1950* (1956) and other studies in population and human ecology.

Warren W. Eason is Assistant Professor of Economics at Princeton University. He has specialized in the study of the economy of the Soviet Union and has published a number of papers on the growth of population and the development of the labor force in the U.S.S.R.

Hope Tisdale Eldridge is author of several studies on migration and urbanization and recently completed for the International Union for the Scientific Study of Population a report, *Population Policies: A Survey of Recent Developments* (1954).

Virginia L. Galbraith is Assistant Professor of Economics and Sociology at Mount Holyoke College. Her major teaching and research interests lie in the field of economics.

Stuart Garfinkle is a member of the staff of the Division of Manpower and Employment Statistics in the Bureau of Labor Statistics, U. S. Department of Labor. He and others have been carrying on pioneer work in the application of life table methods to labor force problems.

Paul C. Glick is Chief, Social Statistics Branch, Population and Housing Division,

U. S. Bureau of the Census, and in that capacity has supervised the preparation of census reports on characteristics of families and marital status; he has also published numerous analytical studies dealing with marriage, families, and housing.

Hilda Hertz Golden, formerly Research Associate at the Bureau of Applied Social Research, Columbia University, is co-author of *Patterns of World Urbanization* (1956).

John Hajnal is Lecturer in Medical Statistics at the University of Manchester, England. Previously he served on the staff of the Royal Commission on Population, with the Population Division of the United Nations, and with the Office of Population Research. Many of his papers have to do with the measurement of fertility and the factors affecting fertility behavior.

C. Horace Hamilton, Professor of Rural Sociology, North Carolina State College, is author of *Rural-Urban Migration in North Carolina, 1920-30* (1934) and co-author of *Hospital Care in the United States,* and among other demographic studies, has published methodological contributions on the measurement of migration.

Philip M. Hauser is Professor of Sociology and Director, Population Research and Training Center, University of Chicago; he was formerly Acting Director and Deputy Director of the U. S. Bureau of the Census. He is author of *Workers on Relief in the United States, March 1935* (1938) and co-editor of *Government Statistics for Business Use* (1946 and 1955), and has published many demographic studies, particularly in the field of labor force analysis.

Earl E. Huyck is a Research Analyst associated with the Federal Government. He has done a great deal of research on population growth and differential fertility in Ceylon.

Eleanor Collins Isbell is a member of the staff of the Social Science Research Council. Her major research interest has been internal migration and mobility. She is co-author of *Population Movements and Industrialization, Swedish Counties, 1895-1930* (1941); and of *Research Memorandum on Migration Differentials* (1938).

Charles P. Issawi is Associate Professor of Near and Middle East Economics at Columbia University. His research interests in demographic and economic problems are focused upon the Near and the Middle East. Among his publications dealing with this area are *Egypt: An Economic and Social Analysis.*

A. J. Jaffe is Director, Manpower and Population Program, Bureau of Applied Social Research, Columbia University. Among his many contributions to demography is the *Handbook of Statistical Methods for Demographers* (1951); in the field of labor force analysis, aside from shorter studies, he is co-author of *Manpower Resources and Utilization* (1951) and *Occupational Mobility in the United States* (1954).

Dudley Kirk is Demographic Director, The Population Council (New York). He is author of *Europe's Population in the Interwar Years* (1946) and other studies in international demography, migration, and fertility.

Clyde V. Kiser is a member of the Technical Staff, Milbank Memorial Fund, and has written extensively on human fertility, notably the monograph, *Group Differences in Urban Fertility* (1952) and the series of studies, *Social and Psychological Factors Affecting Fertility,* of which he is co-author and co-editor.

Evelyn M. Kitagawa is Assistant Professor of Sociology and Research Associate in the Population Research and Training Center, University of Chicago. She is co-author of *Suburbanization of Manufacturing Activity within Standard*

Metropolitan Areas (1955) and has written papers and monographs on labor mobility and differential fertility.

Everett S. Lee, Assistant Professor of Sociology, University of Pennsylvania, has engaged in extensive studies of population redistribution and is co-author of *Net Intercensal Migration, 1870-1940* (1953), and *Migration and Mental Disease* (1956).

W. P. D. Logan, M. D., is medical statistician of the General Register Office of England and Wales and author of studies in public health and mortality.

Frank Lorimer is Professor of Sociology, The American University, and Administrative Director, International Union for the Scientific Study of Population. He is author or senior author of *Dynamics of Population* (1934), *Foundations of American Population Policy* (1940), *The Population of the Soviet Union* (1946), and numerous other demographic studies.

Alfred J. Lotka (1880-1949), acknowledged as the "father of mathematical demography," retired as Assistant Statistician of the Metropolitan Life Insurance Company in 1947. His many contributions to population analysis were summarized in *Théorie analytique des associations biologiques* (1934 and 1939) and *Elements of Physical Biology* (1925). He was also co-author of *Length of Life* (1936 and 1949) and *The Money Value of a Man* (1930 and 1946), and a prolific contributor to demography and mathematical statistics.

Kurt Mayer, Professor of Sociology, Brown University, is author of *The Population of Switzerland* (1952), *Class and Society* (1955), and other studies in social organization and social stratification.

Margaret Merrell, Associate Professor of Biostatistics, Johns Hopkins University, is co-author of a well-known technique of life table construction and has made numerous research contributions in biometrics.

The *Metropolitan Life Insurance Company* publishes the monthly *Statistical Bulletin*, an authoritative source of current data on population changes and mortality.

Wilbert E. Moore is Professor of Sociology and Research Associate of the Office of Population Research, Princeton University; among his studies in demography and labor force analysis are *Economic Demography of Eastern and Southern Europe* (1945), *Industrial Relations and the Social Order* (1946 and 1951), and *Industrialization and Labor* (1951).

Giorgio Mortara is Technical Advisor to the National Council of Statistics, Brazil. He is the author of many studies dealing with population movements in Italy and Brazil, public health, demographic methods, the behavior of mortality and natality, and problems of migration.

Frank W. Notestein is Professor of Demography and Director, Office of Population Research, Princeton University; he is co-editor of the quarterly journal, *Population Index*, and co-author of *Controlled Fertility* (1940) and *The Future Population of Europe and the Soviet Union* (1944).

The *Office of Population Research*, Princeton University, publishes the quarterly bibliography of population literature, *Population Index*, now (1956) in its 22nd volume, and has sponsored many well-known researches in population, especially in the field of international demography.

Frederick Osborn is Executive Vice-President, The Population Council (New York); his extensive writings on questions of population quality include *Preface to Eugenics* (1940 and 1951) and *Dynamics of Population* (co-author, 1934).

The *Population Division, United Nations,* is responsible for the annual compilation of international population statistics, *Demographic Yearbook;* its staff has also prepared a number of methodological and monographic studies in population.

Josiah Cox Russell is Professor of History at the University of New Mexico. He has published many papers dealing with the impact of demographic change upon the course of history and with the demographic past of man in parts of Europe. Notable among his many interesting studies is *British Medieval Population* (1948).

Norman B. Ryder is Demographer, Scripps Foundation for Research in Population Problems; a specialist on problems of fertility measurement, he has published several papers on cohort analysis and fertility trends.

Henry S. Shryock, Jr., is Assistant Chief, Population and Housing Division, U. S. Bureau of the Census; he has written numerous methodological studies of problems of population estimates and projections in addition to his contributions on internal migration and population redistribution.

Laurence H. Snyder, Dean of the Graduate School, University of Oklahoma, is a well-known geneticist and author of such studies as *Blood Grouping in Relation to Clinical and Legal Medicine* (1929) and *The Principles of Heredity* (1935; 4th ed., 1951).

Joseph J. Spengler is Professor of Economics at Duke University. He has published books and papers dealing with differential fertility, migration, the economic aspects of population change, and the history of population theory.

John Q. Stewart, Associate Professor of Astronomical Physics, Princeton University, is a leader in the movement to develop physical models for demographic phenomena and has published a number of empirical studies in social physics.

George J. Stolnitz, Assistant Professor of Sociology and Research Associate, Office of Population Research, Princeton University, is author of several methodological and empirical studies of mortality and population growth.

Irene B. Taeuber, Research Associate, Office of Population Research, Princeton University, is a specialist in the population problems of Japan and the Far East; among her other studies are *General Censuses and Current Vital.Statistics in the Americas* (1943) and *The Population of Tanganyika* (1949).

K. W. Taylor is Deputy Minister of Finance in the Department of Finance of the Dominion Government, Ottawa, Canada. His research interests have lain in the field of price policy and finance as well as in that of population.

Dorothy Swaine Thomas, Professor of Sociology, University of Pennsylvania, is known for her work on the Japanese-American evacuation in World War II, and for such demographic studies as *Social Aspects of the Business Cycle* (1925), *Social and Economic Aspects of Swedish Population Movements, 1750-1933* (1941) and *Research Memorandum on Migration Differentials* (1938).

The *United States Bureau of the Census,* in addition to its decennial censuses and current surveys of population, maintains a staff of experts on international demography, who have prepared a number of monographic studies of population in various foreign countries.

Abbott Payson Usher is Professor Emeritus of Economic History at Harvard University. In a number of his historical works he has devoted particular attention to population factors and to technological, resource, and other factors by which the growth of numbers and power is conditioned. Among his works are *A History of Mechanical Inventions* (1954) and (with others) *An Economic History of Europe since 1750* (1937).

Justus M. van der Kroef was formerly a member of the Department of Foreign Studies at Michigan State College. His major field of interest at present is Indonesia about whose economic and demographic problems he has written a number of papers and books, including *Indonesia in the Modern World* (1955) and *Indonesian Social Evolution, Some Psychological Considerations* (forthcoming).

P. K. Whelpton is Director of the Scripps Foundation for Research in Population Problems; among his numerous demographic studies are *Needed Population Research* (1938) and *Cohort Fertility: Native White Women in the United States* (1954); he is also co-author and co-editor of the series of studies on *Social and Psychological Factors Affecting Fertility.*

S. L. Wolfbein is Chief of the Division of Manpower and Employment, U. S. Bureau of Labor Statistics, and author of numerous research studies in labor force analysis.

Dael Wolfle is Administrative Secretary of the American Association for the Advancement of Science and was Director of the Commission on Human Resources and Advanced Training, whose report, *America's Resources of Specialized Talent,* appeared in 1954.

Julian L. Woodward (1900-1952) was Professor of Sociology at Cornell University for several years, and, at the time of his death, was a Research Executive with the Elmo Roper survey organization; he wrote numerous studies in the field of public opinion analysis, and was co-author of *Introductory Sociology* (1940).

BOOKS PUBLISHED BY

The Free Press

Lord Acton, *Essays on Freedom and Power* — $6.00

Franz Alexander, M.D. and Hugo Staub, *The Criminal, The Judge, and the Public*, revised and enlarged ed. — 4.00

Aristides, *To Rome* — 1.00

Aristotle, *Constitution of the Athenians* — OP

Raymond Aron, *German Sociology* — 4.00

Mikhail Bakunin, *The Political Philosophy of Bakunin* — 6.00

Edward C. Banfield, *Government Project* — 3.50

Bernard Barber, *Science and the Social Order* — 4.50

Salo Baron, Ernest Nagel and Koppel S. Pinson, eds., *Freedom and Reason: Studies in Philosophy and Jewish Culture in Memory of Morris Raphael Cohen* — 5.00

Karl Bednarik, *The Young Worker of Today* — 3.00

Reinhard Bendix and Seymour M. Lipset, eds., *Class, Status and Power: A Reader in Social Stratification* — 7.50

Bernard Berelson, *Content Analysis in Communications Research* — 4.00

Bernard Berelson and Morris Janowitz, eds., *Reader in Public Opinion and Communication*, revised and enlarged ed. — 6.00

Bruno Bettelheim, *Love Is Not Enough: The Treatment of Emotionally Disturbed Children* — 4.50

Bruno Bettelheim, *Symbolic Wounds: Puberty Rites and the Envious Male* — 5.00

Bruno Bettelheim, *Truants from Life: The Rehabilitation of Emotionally Disturbed Children* — 6.00

Robert Blood, *Anticipating Your Marriage* — 5.00

Eugene Burdick and Arthur J. Brodbeck, eds., *American Voting Behavior* — 6.00

Herbert Butterfield and others, *The History of Science* — OP

Richard Christie and Marie Jahoda, eds., *Studies in the Scope and Method of "The Authoritarian Personality"* — 4.50

Albert Cohen, *Delinquent Boys* — 3.50

Morris R. Cohen, *American Thought: A Critical Sketch* — 5.00

Morris R. Cohen, *A Dreamer's Journey: An Autobiography* — 4.50

Morris R. Cohen, *King Saul's Daughter* — 3.00

Morris R. Cohen, *Reason and Law* — 4.00

Morris R. Cohen, *Reason and Nature*, revised ed. — 6.00

Morris R. Cohen, *Reflections of a Wondering Jew* — 2.75

Commission on Educational Reconstruction, *Organizing the Teaching Profession* — 4.50

Charles Horton Cooley, *The Two Major Works of Charles H. Cooley: Human Nature and the Social Order and Social Organization*, 2 vols. bound in one — 7.50

Lewis Coser, *The Functions of Social Conflict* — 3.50

Donald R. Cressey, *Other People's Money: The Social Psychology of Embezzlement* — 3.00

Herbert Dinerstein and Leon Gouré, *Two Studies in Soviet Controls: Communism and the Russian Peasant* and *Moscow in Crisis* — 4.50

Emile Durkheim, *The Division of Labor in Society* — 5.00

Emil Durkheim, *Education and Sociology* — 3.50

Emile Durkheim, *Elementary Forms of the Religious Life* — 5.00

Emile Durkheim, *Rules of the Sociological Method* — 3.00

Emile Durkheim, *Sociology and Philosophy* — 3.00

Emile Durkheim, *Suicide: A Study in Sociology* — 5.00

Joseph Eaton and Albert J. Mayer,
Man's Capacity to Reproduce 2.00

Joseph Eaton and Robert J.
Weil, M.D., *Culture and Mental
Disorders* 4.00

Abraham Edel, *Ethical Judgment:
The Use of Science in Ethics* 5.00

Paul Edwards, *The Logic of Moral
Discourse* 4.00

S. N. Eisenstadt, *The Absorption of
Immigrants* 6.00

S. N. Eisenstadt, *From Generation
to Generation: Age Groups and
Social Structure* 6.00

Heinz Eulau, Samuel Eldersveld
and Morris Janowitz, eds.,
*Political Behavior: A Reader in
Theory and Research* 7.50

E. E. Evans-Pritchard,
Social Anthropology 3.00

E. E. Evans-Pritchard and others,
*The Institutions of Primitive
Society* 3.00

E. K. Francis, *In Search of Utopia* 6.50

E. Franklin Frazier,
Black Bourgeoisie 4.00

Georges Friedmann, *Industrial
Society: The Emergence of the
Human Problems of Automation* 6.00

Lawrence Fuchs, *The Political
Behavior of American Jews* 4.00

Harlan W. Gilmore, *Transportation
and the Growth of Cities* 3.00

D. V. Glass, ed., *Social Mobility
in Britain* OP

Max Gluckman, *Custom and
Conflict in Africa* 3.50

Max Gluckman, *The Judicial
Process Among the Barotse of
Northern Rhodesia* 6.75

Herbert Goldhamer and Andrew
Marshall, *Psychosis and
Civilization: Two Studies in the
Frequency of Mental Disease* 4.00

Walter Goldschmidt, *As You Sow* 3.50

Joseph Goldstein, *The Government
of a British Trade Union* 5.00

William J. Goode, *After Divorce* 6.00

William J. Goode, *Religion Among
the Primitives* 5.00

Alvin Gouldner, *Patterns of
Industrial Bureaucracy* 4.50

Charles M. Hardin, *The Politics of
Agriculture: Soil Conservation
and the Struggle for Power in
Rural America* 4.00

Charles Hartshorne, *Reality as
Social Process* 4.00

Paul K. Hatt and Albert J. Reiss,
Jr., eds., *Reader in Urban
Sociology*, revised ed. 6.50

Amos Hawley, *The Changing Shape
of Metropolitan America* 4.00

Frederick A. von Hayek,
The Counter-Revolution of Science 4.00

Andrew F. Henry and James
Short, Jr., *Suicide and Homicide* 4.00

Roger Hilsman, *Strategic
Intelligence and National
Decisions* 4.00

George Homans and David
Schneider, *Marriage, Authority
and Final Causes* 2.00

Everett C. Hughes and Helen M.
Hughes, *Where Peoples Meet:
Racial and Ethnic Frontiers* 3.50

W. H. Hutt, *The Theory of
Collective Bargaining* 3.00

Herbert Hyman, *Survey Design and
Analysis* 7.50

Morris Janowitz, *The Community
Press in an Urban Setting* 3.50

Elihu Katz and Paul Lazarsfeld,
*Personal Influence: The Part
Played by People in the Flow of
of Mass Communications* 6.00

Patricia Kendall, *Conflict and Mood:
Factors Affecting the Stability of
Response* 3.50

William Kroger, M.D. and
S. Charles Freed, M.D.,
Psychosomatic Gynecology 8.00

Harold D. Lasswell, *Political
Writngs of Harold D. Lasswell:
Psychopathology and Politics;
Politics—Who Gets What, When,
How; Democratic Character,*
3 vols. bound in one 5.00

Harold D. Lasswell, Charles E.
Merriam and T. V. Smith,
A Study of Power, 3 vols. bound
in one 6.00

Paul Lazarsfeld and Morris
Rosenberg, eds., *The Language
of Social Research: A Reader in
the Methodology of the Social
Sciences* 7.50

Paul Lazarsfeld, ed., *Mathematical
Thinking in the Social Sciences* 10.00

Nathan Leites, *A Study of
Bolshevism* 6.50

Nathan Leites and Elsa Bernaut,
*Ritual of Liquidation:
Communists on Trial* 6.50

Seymour M. Lipset, Martin Trow
and James Coleman, *Union
Democracy: The Internal Politics
of the International Typographical
Union* 7.50

Charles Loomis and others,
*Turrialba: Social Systems and
the Introduction of Change* 3.00

W. J. H. Sprott, *Science and Social Action*   3.50

Chalmers Stacey and Manfred DeMartino, eds., *Counseling and Psychotherapy with the Mentally Retarded: A Book of Readings*   7.50

Alfred Stanton and Stewart Perry, eds., *Personality and Political Crisis*   3.75

George Stern, Morris Stein and Benjamin Bloom, *Methods in Personality Assessment*   6.00

Eric Strauss, *Sir William Petty: Portrait of a Genuis*   5.00

Leo Strauss, *On Tyranny*   2.50

Leo Strauss, *Persecution and the Art of Writing*   4.00

Adolf Sturmthal, *Unity and Diversity in European Labor*   3.75

Sol Tax and others, *Heritage of Conquest: The Ethnology of Middle America*   5.00

Dinko Tomasic, *The Impact of Russian Culture on Soviet Communism*   4.50

Ernst Troeltsch, *The Social Teachings of the Christian Churches*, 2 vols.   OP

Jacob Viner, *International Economics*   5.00

Jacob Viner, *International Trade and Economic Development*   2.75

W. Allen Wallis and Harry V. Roberts, *Statistics: A New Approach*   6.00

Max Weber, *Ancient Judaism*   6.00

Max Weber, *General Economic History*   4.50

Max Weber, *The Methodology of the Social Sciences*   3.50

Max Weber, *The Religion of China*   4.50

Henry N. Wieman, *The Directive in History*   2.50

Harold Wilensky, *Intellectuals in Labor Unions*   6.00

W. M. Williams, *Gosforth: The Sociology of an English Village*   5.00

Martha Wolfenstein, *Children's Humor: A Psychological Analysis*   3.75

Martha Wolfenstein and Nathan Leites, *Movies: A Psychological Study*   4.00